# COMPLETE
## PRICE GUIDE TO
# WATCHES
**BY**
## COOKSEY SHUGART & RICHARD E. GILBERT
*EDITED BY MARTHA SHUGART*

**Important Notice**. All of the information, including valuations, in this book has been compiled from the most reliable sources, and every effort has been made to eliminate errors and questionable data. Nevertheless, the possibility of error, in a work of such immense scope, always exists. The publisher or authors will not be held responsible for losses which may occur in the purchase, sale, or other transaction of items, because of information contained herein. Readers who feel they have discovered errors are invited to write and inform us, so they may be corrected in subsequent editions.

The **Complete Price Guide To Watches** is published independently and is not associated with any watch manufacturer.

This book endeavors to be a **Guide** or helpful manual and offers a wealth of material and information to be used as a tool not as a absolute document. The Complete Price Guides To Watches is like some *watches*, the worst may be better than none at all, but at best cannot be expected to be 100% accurate.

Published by: **COOKSEY SHUGART PUBLICATIONS**
**P. O. BOX 3147**
**CLEVELAND, TN. 37320-3147**
**TEL. OR FAX ( 423 ) 479 – 4813**

Distributed by: **COLLECTOR BOOKS**
**P. O. BOX 3009**
**5801 KENTUCKY DAM ROAD**
**PADUCAH, KY. 42001**

**ISBN 0 – 89145 – 708 – 9**
SIXTEENTH EDITION: JAN., 1996

*European Distributor:* **BUSHWOOD BOOKS**
84 Bushwood Road, Kew Gardens, Surrey TW9 3BQ ( U. K.)

10 9 8 7 6 5 4 3 2 1
**Manufactured in the United States of America**

2

COOKSEY SHUGART

RICHARD E. GILBERT

## ABOUT THE AUTHORS

The Complete Price Guide To WATCHES, published by Shugart Publications, and co-authored by Cooksey Shugart and Richard E. Gilbert. Mr. Gilbert holds both Bachelor's and Master's degrees in Science. Richard Gilbert is the owner of Ashland a multi-million dollar international mail order business, he has an impeccable reputation for honesty and integrity, and has been sought after for years by other dealers as a guide to establishing prices.

Both authors have been active watch buyers since the early 1960's. The authors have been Horologists and members of the National Association of Watch and Clock Collectors since the early 1970's. Both have searched for fine timepieces all over the world and are the foremost experts in the field of antique pocket and wrist watches. Both have enjoyed broadening their knowledge in horology while traveling in Europe.

The co-authors travel extensively to auctions throughout the United States and Europe, to regional and national conventions, meets and shows, and keep an up-to-date pulse of the watch market. They continually expand their horological reference library and their extensive selection of watch photographs. Because of the unique knowledge of the market these two co-authors possess, this volume should be considered one of the most authoritative watch references on the market today. Each edition contains updated and revised information and prices, and has become the accepted standard reference work of the watch market. "We see this book as an extension of the information we have been gathering for years and take great pride in sharing it with other collectors who have a deep and abiding interest in watches," the authors stated.

Mr. Shugart resides in Cleveland, Tennessee, and Mr. Gilbert lives in Sarasota, Florida.

# TABLE OF CONTENTS

**4**

## ACKNOWLEDGMENTS

I am especially appreciative of **Bob Overstreet**, author of The Overstreet Comic Book Price Guide, for his encouragement.

To my wife **Martha,** for her complete understanding and assistance in compiling this book.

To best friend **TOM ENGLE** whose help is invaluable a very special thanks.

A very special thanks to Henry B. Fried.

To the NAWCC Museum, Hamilton Watch Co., and Bowman Technical School, for allowing us to photograph their watches.

To Christie's, Vivian Swift, Osvaldo Patrizzi and Joseph Auction for photographs of watches. And to the following people whose help was invaluable and will be long remembered: Frank Irick, John Cubbins, Harold Harris, Paul Gibson, Robert L. Ravel, M.D., William C. Heilman Jr., M.D., Thomas McEntyre, Paul Morgan, Bill Selover, Oscar Laube, Ed Kieft, Charles Wallace, Bob Walters, Jack Warren, Howard Schroeder, Edward M. McGinnis, James Gardner, Paul Zuercher, Irving E. Roth, Don Bass, Stephen Polednak, Dick Stacy, Ernest J. Lewis, Herbert McDonald, David Steger, Fred Favour, Ralph Warner, Estus Harris, Charles Cleves, Tom McIntyre, Ralph Ferone, Arnold C. Varey, Jeffrey Ollswang, Tom Rohr, Leon Beard, Glenn Smith, Kenneth Vergin, Thomas Rumpf, Frank Diggs, Tom Thacker, Bob Lavoie, Norman Howard, Constantin Tanasecu, Rod Minter, Ernest Luffman, John Amneus, Lawrence D. Harnden, Mike Kirkpatrick, Clint B. Geller, Art W. Rontree, and a special thanks to Peter Kushnir, Dr. J. Mauss, Robert D. Gruen, Jeff Hess, Col. R. A. Mulholland, Dick Ziebell, Jack Warren, Ron Starnes, Dick Flaute, Ralph Vinge, Edward Fletcher, Richard Walker, Alex Wolanguk, Carl Goetz, Miles Sandler, Dave Mycko, Martin & Patrick Cullen, Benjy Rook, Phillip Welsh, Paul Craft, Fred Fox, Fred Andrus, Ellis Gifford, Steve Berger, Bruce Ellison, Lawrence D. Harnden, Geoff White, Bob & Pat Wingate, David Searles, Ray R. Tyulty Jr., Don Levison, Robert M. Toborowsky M.D., Dr. John R. Dimar, Jonathan Snellenburg, Paul A. Duggan, Gregory A. Hill, Bernie Kraus, Veron Willams, Fred Hansen.

\* \* \*

Send only corrections, additions, deletions and comments to
**COOKSEY SHUGART**, P. O. BOX 3147, CLEVELAND, TN. 37320-3147.
*When corresponding, please send a* ✉️*self-addressed, stamped envelope.*

Special Consultants:

**JIM WOLF**

Dan Crawley

Norman Howard

# INTRODUCTION

**This book is dedicated to all watch collectors who we hope will find it an enjoyable and valuable reference to carry on buying trips or to trace the lost history of that priceless family heirloom.**

*The origin of this book began when I was given a pocket watch that had been in our family for many years. After receiving the prized heirloom I wanted to know its complete history, and thus the search began. Because of the lack of a comprehensive reference on American pocket watches the venture took me through volume after volume. Over the course of ten years many hours were accumulated in running down the history of this one watch. The research sparked my interest in the pocket watch field and pointed to the need for a book such as this one. We hope it will provide the information that you are looking for.*

*— The Authors*

Watches are unique collectibles and since the beginning of civilization man has held a fascination for time. When man scooped up a handful of sand and created the hourglass, portable timepieces have been in demand for the wealthy and poor alike. Man has sought constantly to improve his time-measuring instruments and has made them with the finest metals and jewels. The pocket watch, in particular, became an ornamentation and a source of pride, and this accounts for its value among families for generation after generation.

The watch has become precious and sentimental to so many because it is one of the true personal companions of the individual night and day. Mahatma Gandhi, the father of India and one of the rare people in history who was able to renounce worldly possessions, was obsessed with the proper use of his time. Each minute, he held, was to be used in the service of his fellow man. His own days were ordered by one of his few personal possessions, a sixteen-year-old, eight-shilling Ingersoll pocket watch that was always tied to his waist with a piece of string.

Another factor that has made watches unique collectibles is the intricate artisanship with which they are put together. Many of the watches of yesteryear, which were assembled with extreme accuracy and fine workmanship, continue to be reliable timepieces today. They stand out as unique because that type of watch is no longer hand made. In today's world of mass production, the watch with individual craftsmanship containing precious jewels and metals can rarely be found—and, if found, it is rarely affordable.

The well-made watch is a tribute to man's skills, artisanship and craftsmanship at their finest level. That is why the watch holds a special place in the collectible field.

In America, there are about 80,000 avid watch collectors. About 5 million people own two or more watches, and an untold number possess at least one of these precious heirlooms.

6

**The Complete Price Guide to Watches** does not attempt to establish or fix values or selling prices in the watch trade market. It does, however, reflect the trends of buying and selling in the collector market. Prices listed in this volume are based on data collected and analyzed from dealers and shops all over the country. These prices should serve the collector as a **guide** only. The price you pay for any watch will be determined by the value it has to you. The intrinsic value of any particular watch can be measured only by you, the collector, and a fair price can be derived only after mutual agreement between both the buyer and the seller.

Keep in mind the fair market **values** as outlined in this price guide and buying wisely, but don't hesitate, as the better and scarce pieces are quickly sold.

It is our hope that this volume can help make your watch collecting venture both pleasurable and profitable.

Information contained herein may not necessarily apply to every situation. Data is still being found, which may alter statements made in this book. These changes, however, will be reflected in future editions.

Hopefully, everyone interested in horology will research the watch and add to his library on the subject.

## COLLECTAMANIA
### Hobby — Business — Pastime — Entertainment

Just name it. More than likely someone will want to buy or sell it: books, coins, stamps, bottles, beer cans, gold, glassware, baseball cards, guns, clocks, watches, comics, art, cars, and the list goes on and on.

Most Americans seem to be caught up in collectamania . More and more Americans are spending hour after hour searching through antique shops, auctions, flea markets and yard sales for those rare treasures of delight that have been lying tucked away for generations just waiting to be found.

This sudden boom in the field of collecting may have been influenced by fears of inflation or disenchantment with other types of investments. But more people are coming into the field because they gain some degree of nostalgic satisfaction from these new tangible ties with yesteryear. Collecting provides great fun and excitement. The tales of collecting and the resultant "fabulous finds" could fill volumes and inspire even the non-collector to embark upon a treasure hunt.

Collecting for the primary purpose of investment may prove to have many pitfalls for the amateur. The lack of sufficient knowledge is the main cause of disappointment. The inability to spot fakes or flawed merchandise can turn excitement into disappointment. And, in many fields, high-class forgers are at work, doing good and faithful reproductions in large quantities that can sometimes fool even the experts the first time they see them.

Collecting for fun and profit can be just that if you observe a fair amount of caution. Always remember, amidst your enthusiasm, that an object may not be what it would first appear. Next are a few guidelines that may be helpful to you.

# FOCUS - LEARN - CONDITION - TRUST

**"LOOK UNDER THE HOOD"**

1. **Make up your mind** and **FOCUS** on what you want to collect and concentrate in this area. Your field of collecting should be one that you have a genuine liking for, and it helps if you can use the objects. It may also help to narrow your field even further, for instance, in collecting watches, to choose only one company or one type or style and have a method of collecting.

2. **Gain all the knowledge you can** and **LEARN** all about the objects you collect. The more knowledge you have the more successful you will be in finding valuable, quality pieces. Amassing the knowledge required to be a good collector is easier if you have narrowed your scope of interest. Otherwise, it may take years to become an "expert." Don't try to learn everything there is to know about a variety of fields. This will end in frustration and disappointment. Specialize and **learn** fair market **values**.

3. **Buy the best CONDITION you can afford**, assuming the prices are fair. The advanced collector may want only mint articles; but the novice collector may be willing to accept something far less than mint condition due to caution and economics. Collectible items in better condition continue to rise in value at a steady rate.

4. **Deal with reputable dealers** whom you can **TRUST**. Talk with the dealer; get to know the seller; get a business card; know where you can contact the dealer if you have problems, or if you want the dealer to help you find something else you may be looking for.

**FAIR MARKET PRICE**: Fair price may be defined as a fair **reasonable** range of prices usually paid for a watch or a watch of **good value** as used in this book ( *at the RETAIL LEVEL* ). This market level includes a particular time frame, desirability, condition and quality. A guide to fair purchase prices is subject to sales and transaction between a large number of buyers and sellers who are informed, up to date on all normal market influences ( while keeping in mind the difference between compulsiveness and acceptable buying ), and buy and sell on a large scale from coast to coast. A willing buyer and a willing seller acting carefully and judiciously in their own best interest while, doing business in a normal and fair manner and preferable with payment immediately.

Keep in mind the fair market **values** as outlined in this price guide and buying wisely, but don't *hesitate*, as the better and scarce watches are *quickly* sold.

# HOW TO USE THIS BOOK

The Complete Price Guide to Watches is a simple reference, with clear and carefully selected information. The first part of the book is devoted to history, general information, and a how-to section. The second part of the guide consists mainly of a listing of watch manufacturers, identification guides, and prices. This is a unique book because it is designed to be taken along as a handy pocket reference for identifying and pricing watches. With the aid of this book, the collector should be able to make on-the-spot judgments as to identification, age, quality, and value. This complete guide and a pocket magnifying glass will be all you need to take on your buying trips.

Watch collecting is fast growing as a hobby and business. Many people collect for the enjoyment and profit. The popularity of watches continues to rise because watches are a part of history. The American railroad brought about the greatest watch of that time, the railroad pocket watch. Since that time America has produced some of the best quality pocket watches that money could buy. The gold-filled cases made in America have never been surpassed in quality or price in the foreign market. With the quality of movement and cases being made with guaranteed high standards as well as beauty, the American pocket watch became very desirable. Because they are no longer being made in the U. S. A., pocket watches continue to rise in value.

The watch is collected for its beauty, quality in movement and case, and the value of metal content. Solid gold and platinum are the top of the line; silver is also very desirable. (Consider that some watches in the early 1900's sold between $700 and $1,000. This is equal to or greater than the price of a good car of the same period.)

As with limited edition prints, a watch of supreme excellence is also limited and will increase in value. There is universal appeal and excitement in owning a piece of history, and your heirloom is just that. At one time pocket watches were a status symbol. Everyone competed for beauty and quality in the movement and case. Solid gold cases were adorned with elaborate engraving's, diamonds, and other precious jewels. The movements were beautiful and of high quality. Manufacturers went to great lengths to provide movements that were both accurate and lovely. Fancy damaskeening on the back plates of nickel with gold lettering, 26 jewels in gold settings, and a solid gold train (gears) were features of some of the more elaborate timepieces. The jewels were red rubies, or diamond-end stones, or sapphires for the pallet stones. There were gold timing screws, and more. The faces were made by the best artisans of the day. Hand-painted, jewel-studded, with fancy hands and double-sunk dials made of enamel and precious metals.

# HOW TO DETERMINE MANUFACTURER

When identifying a watch, look on the face or dial for the name of the company and then refer to the alphabetical list of watch companies in this book. If the face or dial does not reveal the company name you will have to seek information from the movement's back plate. The company name or the town where it was manufactured will likely be inscribed there. The name engraved on the back plate is referred to as the "signature." After locating the place of manufacture, see what companies manufactured in that town. This may require reading the histories of several companies to find the exact one. Use the process of elimination to narrow the list. Note: Some of the hard-to-identify watches are extremely collectible and valuable. Therefore, it is important to learn to identify them.

In order to establish the true manufacturer of the movement, one must study the construction, taking note of the shape, location, plate layout (is it full or 3/4), shape of the balance cock and the regulator, location of jewels, location of screws, etc. Compare and match your watch movement with every photograph or drawing from each watch company in this volume until the manufacturer is located.

# HOW TO DETERMINE AGE

After establishing the name of the manufacturer, you may be interested in the age of the watch ( where production tables are listed ). This information can be obtained by using the serial number inscribed on the back movement plate and referring to the production table. It is often difficult to establish the exact age, but this method will put you within a two or three-year period of the date of the manufacture.

To establish the age of a pre-1850 watch there are many points to be considered. The dial, hands, pillars, balance cock and pendant, for example, contain important clues in determining the age of your watch. However, no one part alone should be considered sufficient evidence to draw a definite conclusion as to age. The watch as a whole must be considered. For example, an English-made silver-cased watch will have a hallmark inside the case. It is quite simple to refer to the London Hallmark Table for hallmarks after 1697. The hallmark will reveal the age of the case only. This does not fix the age of the movement. Many movements are housed in cases made years before or after the movement was produced.

The case that houses the movement is not necessarily a good clue to the origin of the movement. It was a common practice for manufacturers to ship the movements to the jewelers and watchmakers uncased. The customer then married the movement and case. That explains why an expensive movement can be found in a cheaper case or vice versa.

If the "manufacturer's" name and location are no help, the inscription could possibly be that of a jeweler and his location. Then it becomes obvious there is no quick and easy way to identify some American made watches. However, the following steps may be helpful. Some watches can be identified by comparing the models of each company until the correct model is found. Start by sizing the watch and then comparing the varied plate shapes and styles. The cock or bridge for the balance may also be a clue. The general arrangement of the movement as to jeweling, whether it is an open face or hunting case, and style of regulators may help to find the correct identification of the manufacturer of the movement.

Numbers on a watch case should not be considered as clues to the age of the movement because cases were both American and foreign made, and many of the good watches were re-cased through the years.

## APPRAISING WATCHES

Watch collecting is still young when compared to fields of the standard collectibles: coins and stamps. The watch collecting field is growing but information is still scarce, fragmented, and sometimes unreliable. To be knowledgeable in any field, one must spend the time required to study it.

The value of any collectible is determined first by demand. Without demand there is no market. In the watch trade, the law of supply and demand is also true. The supply of the American watches has stopped and the demand among collectors continues to rise. There are many factors that make a watch desired or in demand. Only time and study will tell a collector just which pieces are most collectible. After the collector or investor finds out what is desirable, then a value must be placed on it before it is sold. If it is priced too high, the watch will not sell; but, on the other hand, if it is priced too low, it will be hard to replace at the selling price. The dealer must arrive at a fair market price that will move the watch. As with limited edition prints, a watch of supreme excellence is also limited and will increase in value. There is universal appeal and excitement in owning a piece of history, and your heirloom is just that. At one time pocket watches were a status symbol. Everyone competed for beauty and quality in the movement and case. Solid gold cases were adorned with elaborate engraving's, diamonds, and other precious jewels.

The movements were beautiful and of high quality. Manufacturers went to great lengths to provide movements that were both accurate and lovely. Fancy damaskeening on the back plates of nickel with gold lettering, 26 jewels in gold settings, and a solid gold train (gears) were features of some of the more elaborate timepieces. The jewels were red rubies, or diamond-end stones, or sapphires for the pallet stones. There were gold timing screws, and more. The faces were made by the best artisans of the day. Hand-painted, jewel-studded, with fancy hands and double-sunk dials made of enamel and precious metals.

There are no two watches alike. This makes the appraising more difficult and often-times arbitrary. But there are certain guidelines one can follow to arrive at a fair market price. When watches were manufactured, most companies sold the movements to a jeweler, and the buyer had a choice of dials and cases. Some high-grade movements were placed in a low-grade case and vice versa. Some had hand-painted multi-colored dials; some were plain. The list of contrasts goes on. Conditions of watches will vary greatly, and this is a big factor in the value. The best movement in the best original case will bring the top price for any type of watch.

Prices are constantly changing in the watch field. Gold and silver markets affect the price of the cases. Scarcity and age also affect the value. These prices will fluctuate regularly.

## APPRAISING GUIDELINES

Demand, supply, condition, and value must be the prime factors in appraising an old watch.

Demand is the most important element. Demand can be determined by the number of buyers for the particular item. A simple but true axiom is that value is determined by the price someone is willing to pay.

In order to obtain a better knowledge in appraising and judging watches, the following guidelines are most useful. Consider all these factors before placing a value on the watch. (There is no rank or priority to the considerations listed.)

1. **Demand:** Is it high or low?
2. **Availability:** How rare or scarce is the watch?
   How many of the total production remain?
3. **Condition** of both the case and movement (very important).
4. Low serial numbers: The first one made would be more
   valuable than later models.
5. Historical value.
6. Age.
7. Value of **metal** content, style or type of case, beauty and eye appeal.

8. Is it in its **original** case? (very important).
9. Is it an early handmade watch?
10. Complications: Repeaters, for example.
11. Type of **escapement**.
12. Size, number of jewels, type of plates (3/4, full and bridge), type of balance, type of winding (key-wind, lever-set, etc.), number of adjustments, gold jeweled settings, damaskeening, gold train.
13. What grade of condition is it? Pristine, Mint, Extra Fine, Average, Fair, or Scrap?
14. Identification ability.
15. Future potential as an investment.
16. Quality (high or low grade), or low cost production watches (dollar watch).
17. How much will this watch scrap for?

## GRADING WATCHES

*Pricing in this book is based on the following grading system:*

**PRISTINE MINT (G-10):** _NEW OLD STOCK_. Absolutely factory new; sealed in factory box with wax paper still intact & all tags & papers etc.

**MINT PLUS (G-9):** Still in factory box _"BUT LOOKS UNUSED"_.

**MINT (G-8):** Same as factory new but with very little use; no faint scratches; is original in every way crystal, hands, dial, case, movement; used briefly and stored away; may be in box.

**NEAR MINT (G-7):** Completely original in every way; faint marks may be seen with a loop only; expertly repaired; movement may have been cleaned and oiled.

**EXTRA FINE (G-6):** May or may not be in factory box; looks as though watch was used very little; crystal may have been replaced; original case, hands, dial, and movement. If watch has been repaired, all original replacement parts have been used. Faint case scratches are evident but hard to detect with the eye. No dents and no hairline on dial are detectable.

**FINE (G-5):** May have new hands and new crystal, but original case, dial and movement; faint hairline in dial; no large scratches on case; slight stain on movement; movement must be sharp with only minor scratches.

**AVERAGE (G-4):** Original case, dial and movement; movement may have had a part replaced, but part was near to original; no brass showing through on gold-filled case; no rust or chips in dial; may have hairlines in dial that are hard to see. All marks are hard to detect, but may be seen without a loop.

**FAIR (G-3):** Hairlines in dial and small chips; slight amount of brass can be seen through worn spots on gold-filled case; rust marks in movement; a small dent in case; wear in case, dial, and movement; well used; may not have original dial or case.

**POOR (G-2):** Watch not working; needs new dial; case well worn, with many dents; hands may be gone; replacement crystal may be needed.

**SCRAP (G-1):** Movement not working; bad dial; rusty movement; brass showing badly; may not have case; some parts not original; no crystal or hands. Good for parts only.

🕐 Pricing in this Guide are for **COMPLETE** watches in **MINT**= (G-8), **EX. FINE**= (G-6), & **AVERAGE**= (G-4) condition.
*Below is an example of how the price is affected by the different grades of the same watch:*

### Hamilton 992B

| | |
|---|---|
| G-10 | $450 |
| G-9 | $425 |
| **G-8** | **$400** |
| G-7 | $355 |
| **G-6** | **$335** |
| G-5 | $310 |
| **G-4** | **$300** |
| G-3 | $175 |
| G-2 | $85 |
| G-1 | $45 |

The value of a watch can only be assessed after the watch has been carefully inspected and graded. It may be difficult to evaluate a watch honestly and objectively, especially in the rare or scarce models.

If the watch has any defects, such as a small scratch on it, it can not be Pristine. It is important to realize that older watches in grades of Extra Fine or above are extremely rare and may never be found.

Watches listed in this book are priced at the collectable retail level, as **COMPLETE** watches having an original 14k gold-filled case and Key Wind with silver, an original white enamel single sunk dial, and with the entire original movement in good working order with no repairs needed.

Keep in mind the fair market **values** as outlined in this price guide and buying wisely, but don't *hesitate*, as the better and scarce watches are *quickly* sold.

## COLLECTING ON A LIMITED BUDGET

Most collectors are always looking for that sleeper, which is out there waiting to be found. One story goes that the collector went into a pawn shop and asked the owner if he had any gold pocket watches for sale. The pawn broker replied, ''No, but I have a 23J silver cased pocket watch at a good price.'' Even though the pocket watch was in a cheaper case, the collector decided to further explore the movement. When he opened the back to look at the movement, there he saw engraved on the plates 24J Bunn Special and knew immediately he wanted to buy the pocket watch. The movement was running, and looked to be in first grade shape. The collector asked the price. The broker said he has been trying to get rid of the pocket watch, but had no luck and if he wanted it, he would sell it for $35. The collector took the pocket watch and replaced the bent-up silver case for a gold-filled J. Boss case, and sold it a month later for $400. He had a total of $100 invested when he sold it, netting a cool $300 profit.

Most collectors want a pocket watch that is in mint or near-mint condition and original in every way. But consider the railroad pocket watches such as the Bunn Special in a cheaper case. The railroad man was compelled to buy a watch with a quality movement, even though he may have only been able to afford a cheap case. The railroad man had to have a pocket watch that met certain standards set by the railroad company. A watch should always be judged on quality and performance and not just on its appearance. The American railroad pocket watch was unsurpassed in reliability. It was durable and accurate for its time, and that accounts for its continuing value today.

If you are a limited-budget collector, you would be well advised not to go beyond your means. But watch collecting can still be an interesting, adventurous, and profitable hobby. If you are to be successful in quadrupling your purchases that you believe to be sleepers, you must first be a hard worker, have perseverance and let shrewdness and skill of knowledge take the place of money. A good starting place is to get a working knowledge of how a pocket watch works. Learn the basic skills such as cleaning, mainspring and staff replacement. One does not have to be a watchmaker, but should learn the names of parts and what they do. If a watch that you are considering buying does not work, you should know how and what it takes to get it in good running order or pass it by. Stay away from pocket watches that do not wind and set. Also avoid ''odd'' movements that you hope to be able to find a case for.

Old watches with broken or missing parts are expensive and all but impossible to have repaired. Some parts must be made by hand. The odd and low-cost production watches are fun to get but hard to repair. Start out on the more common basic-jeweled lever pocket watches. The older the watch, the harder it is to get parts. Buy an inexpensive pocket watch movement that runs and play with it. Get the one that is newer and for which parts can be bought; and get a book on watch repairing.

You will need to know the history and **demand** of a watch. Know what collectors are looking for in your area. If you cannot find a buyer, then, of course, someone else's stock has become yours.

## JOIN THE NAWCC®

The authors of this book Mr. Cooksey Shugart and Mr. Richard E. Gilbert recommend you join the NAWCC ® today.

The National Association of Watch and Clock Collectors ( NAWCC ® ) is a non-profit, scientific and educational corporation founded in 1943 and now serving the horological needs and interests of over 35,000 members ( professional horologists and amateurs ) in the United States and 40 others countries. Help to its members is only a telephone call away.

A WEALTH OF INFORMATION IN PUBLICATIONS FOR MEMBERS.

A **PUBLICATION** sent to you each month.

The **NAWCC ® Mart Sent to you every odd - month**
The **NAWCC ® Bulletin Sent to you every even - month**

The **Bulletin** sent to you every even - month is a absorbing, abundantly illustrated articles on historic, artistic and technical aspects of timekeeping, answers by experts to your questions in the "Answer Box" , concise reviews of horological books, members' opinions and comments in "VOX TEMPORIS", research findings and request, slide programs available to Chapters, news and announcements of Chapter, Regional and National activities.

The **Mart** sent to you every odd - month. An informal medium of exchange in which, for a nominal fee, you can list any horological item you may wish to buy, sell or trade... an absorbing and entertaining way to find items to fill out your collection or dispose of pieces you no-longer want.

TO JOIN THE NAWCC ® Call or Send for a FREE copy of their brochure with additional information on the NAWCC ®, membership and benefits.

**NAWCC, INC.**
**514 Poplar Street**
**Columbia, PA   17512**
**( 717) 684-8261**

Recommended by member COOKSEY SHUGART membership number - 23,843.

Also see AD in the ADVERTISING SECTION of this book.

# THAT GREAT AMERICAN
# RAILROAD POCKET WATCH

It was the late nineteenth century in America. The automobile had not yet been discovered. The personal Kodak camera was still not on the market. Women wore long dresses, and the rub board was still the most common way to wash clothes. Few homes had electricity, and certainly the radio had not yet invaded their lives. Benjamin Harrison was president. To be sure, those days of yesteryear were not quite as nostalgically simple as most reminiscing would have them be. They were slower, yes, because it took longer to get things done and longer to get from one place to another. The U.S. mail was the chief form of communication linking this country together, as America was inching toward the Twentieth Century.

The tremendous impact of the railroad on the country during this era should

not be under estimated. Most of the progress since the 1830s had chugged along on the back of the black giant locomotives that belched steam and fire, up and down the countryside. In fact, the trains brought much life and hope to the people all across the country, delivering their goods and food, bringing people from one city to another, carrying the U.S. mail, and bringing the democratic process to the people by enabling candidates for the U.S. Presidency to meet and talk with people in every state.

Truly the train station held memories for most everyone and had a link with every family.

In 1891, the country had just eased into the period that historians would later term the "Gay Nineties." It was on April 19 of that year that events occurred near Cleveland, Ohio, that clearly pointed out that the nation's chief form of transportation was running on timepieces that were not reliable. The time had come for strict standards and guide lines for accurate pocket watches to be used by the railroad men and the railroad industry with precision in time keeping.

From the ashes of this smoldering Ohio disaster rose the phoenix in the form of the great American railroad pocket watch, a watch unrivaled in quality and reliability.

That April morning the fast mail train, known as No. 4, was going East. On the same track an accommodation train was going West. It was near Elyria, about 25 miles from Cleveland, Ohio, that the engineer and conductor of the accommodation train were given written orders to let the fast mail train pass them at Kipton, a small station west of Oberlin.

As the accommodation train was leaving the station at Elyria, the telegraph operator ran to the platform and verbally cautioned the engineer and conductor, "Be careful, No. 4 is on time." The conductor replied, "Go to thunder. I know my business."

The train left Elyria on time according to the engineer's watch. What was not known was that the engineer's watch had stopped for four minutes and then started up again. Had the conductor looked at his own watch, the impending disaster could have been avoided.

The two trains met their destiny at Kipton; the accommodation train was under full brakes, but the fast mail was full speed ahead. Both engineers were killed as well as nine other people. The railroad companies (Lake Shore Railroad and Michigan Southern Railway) sustained great losses in property as did the U.S. Post Office.

Following this disaster, a commission was appointed to come up with standards for timepieces that would be accepted and adopted by all railroads. The commission learned that, up to the time of the Kipton crash, conductors on freight trains were depending on cheap alarm clocks. The railroading industry had grown, fast new trains were now in service, and the same lines were used by several different railways. Very often, in only a short space of time, two trains would cover the same track. The industry now had to demand precision in its time keeping.

By 1893 the General Railroad Timepiece Standards were adopted, and any watch being used in rail service by railroaders responsible for schedules was required to meet the following specifications:

*Be open faced, size 18 or 16, have a minimum of 17 jewels, adjusted to at least five positions, keep time accurately to within a gain or loss of only 30 seconds a week, adjusted to temperatures of 34 to 100 degrees Fahrenheit, have a double roller, steel escape wheel, lever set, micrometric regulator, winding stem at 12 o'clock, grade on back plate, use plain Arabic numbers printed bold and black on a white dial, and have bold black hands.*

*Some also wanted a Breguet hairspring, adjusted to isochronism and 30 degrees Fahrenheit with a minimum of 19 jewels.*

The railroad man was compelled to buy a timepiece more accurate than many scientific instruments of precision used in laboratories. The American pocket watch industry was compelled to produce just such an instrument which it did. The railroad watch was a phenomenal timekeeper and durable in long life and service. It had the most minute adjustments, no small feat because watchmaking was rendered far more difficult than clock making, due to the fact that a clock is always in one position and powered by a constant force-it's weights,while watches must be accurate in several positions with a variable power source.

The 1893 railroad pocket watch standards were adopted by almost every railroad line. While each company had its individual standards, most all of them included the basic recommendations of the commission.

The key figure in developing the railroad watch standards was Webb C. Ball of Cleveland, Ohio, the general time inspector for over 125,000 miles of railroad in the U.S., Mexico, and Canada. Ball was authorized by railroad officials to establish the timepiece inspection system. After Ball presented his guidelines, most American manufacturers set out to meet those standards and a list of the different manufacturers producing watches of the grade that would pass inspection, was soon available.

According to the regulations, if a watch fell behind or gained 30 seconds in 7 to 14 days, it must be sent in for adjustment or repair. Small cards were given to the engineers and conductors the railroad timekeepers and a complete record of the watch's performance was written in ink. All repairs and adjustments were conducted by experienced and approved watchmakers; inspections were conducted by authorized inspectors.

Because this system was adopted universally and adhered to, and because American watch manufacturers produced a superior railroad watch, the traveling public was assured of increased safety and indeed the number of railroad accidents occurring as a result of faulty timepieces was minimized.

Prior to the 1891 collision, some railroad companies had already initiated standards and were issuing lists of those watches approved for railroad use. Included were the Waltham 18s, 1883 model, Crescent Street Grade, and the B.W. Raymond, 18s, both in open and hunter cases with lever set or pendant set.

By the mid 1890s hunter cases were being turned down as well as pendant set. Watches meeting approval then included Waltham, 18s, 1892 model; Elgin, 7th model; and Hamilton, 17j, open face, lever set.

Hamilton Grade 992, 16 size, 21 jewels, nickel 3/4 plate movement, lever set only, gold jewel settings, gold center wheel, steel escape wheel, micrometric regulator, compensating balance. Adjusted to temperature, isochronism and 5 positions.

By 1900 the double roller sapphire pallets and steel escape wheels with a minimum of five positions were required.

The early Ball Watch Co. movements, made by Howard, used initials of railroad labor organizations such as "B. of L.E. Standard" and "B. of L.F. Standard." Ball also used the trademark "999" and "Official Railroad Standard." Some watches may turn up that are marked as "loaners." These were issued by the railroad inspectors when a watch had to be kept for repairs.

By 1920 the 18 size watch had lost popularity with the railroad men and by 1950 most railroad companies were turning them down all together.

In 1936 duty on Swiss watches were lowered by 50 percent, and by 1950 the Swiss imports had reached a level of five million a year.

In 1969 the last American railroad pocket watch was sold by Hamilton Watch Co.

# RAILROAD GRADE WATCH ADJUSTMENTS

The railroad watch, as well as other fine timepieces, had to compensate for several factors in order to be reliable and accurate at all times. These compensations, called adjustments, were for heat and cold, isochronism, and five to six different positions. These adjustments were perfected only after experimentation and a great deal of careful hand labor on each individual movement.

All railroad grade watches were adjusted to a closer rate to compensate for heat and cold. The compensation balance has screws in the rim of the balance wheel which can be regulated by the watchmaker. The movement was tested in an ice box and in an oven, and if it did not keep the same time in both temperature extremes, as well as under average conditions, the screws in the balance wheel was shifted or adjusted until accuracy was achieved.

The isochronism adjustment maintained accuracy of the watch both when the mainspring was fully wound up and when it was nearly run down. This was achieved by selecting a hairspring of exact proportions to cause the balance wheel to give the same length of arc of rotation regardless of the amount of the mainspring that had been spent.

Railroad watches were adjusted to be accurate whether they were laying on their face or back, or being carried on their edges with pendants up or down, or with the three up or the nine up. These adjustments were accomplished by having the jewels, in which the balance pivots rest, of proper thickness in proportion to the diameter of the pivot and, at the same time, equal to the surface on the end of the pivot which rests on the cap jewel. To be fully adjusted for positions, the balance wheel and the pallet and escape wheel must be perfectly poised. Perfect poise is achieved when the pivots can be supported on two knife-edged surfaces, perfectly smooth and polished and when the wheel is placed in any edge, it will remain exactly as it is placed. If it is not perfectly poised, the heaviest part of the wheel will always turn to the point immediately under the lines of support.

Example: Of a Bunn 16 size, 17-19 jewels, nickel 3/4 plate movement, lever set, gold jewel settings, gold center wheel, double roller, steel escape wheel, micrometric regulator, compensating balance. Adjusted to temperature, isochronism and 5 positions, artistically damaskeened.

🕐 NOTE: Railroad grade watches had a compensation balance made of brass and steel. Brass was used on the outside rim and steel on the inside. Brass is twice as sensitive to temperature changes and twice as thick as the steel balance (one-piece is welded to the steel balance wheel) and after finishing, the rim is cut at one end near the arm of the balance and at the same spot 180 across. In higher temperature, the dominant brass would "grow" longer but welded to the steel rim, it would curve inward, thus, in effect, placing the mass of the balance closer to the center of the balance wheel. This would cause the balance to go faster. However, the steel hairspring in rising temperature would also grow longer but more important would also lose some of its resilience. This would cause the watch to lose time. The balance, remember under the same condition, in effect became smaller and this action by the balance compensated for the loss of the hairspring's elasticity and lengthening. In cold temperatures, the opposite effect took place. This is why the balance is called a "compensation" balance. (It compensates for the temperature errors in the hairspring.)

The micrometric regulator or the patent regulator is a device used on all railroad grade and higher grade watches for the purpose of assisting in the finer manipulation of the regulator. It is arranged so that the regulator can be moved the shortest possible distance without fear of moving it too far. There is always a fine graduated index attached which makes it possible to determine just how much the regulator has been moved.

E. Howard Watch Co. Railroad Chronometer, Series 11, 16 size, 21 jewels, expressly designed for the railroad trade.

The hairspring used on the so-called ordinary and medium-grade watches is known as the flat hairspring. The Breguet hairspring was an improvement over the flat hairspring and was used on railroad and high-grade watches. The inside coil of any hairspring is attached to a collet on the balance staff and the end of the outside coil of the hairspring is attached to a stud which is held firmly by a screw in the balance wheel bridge. Two small regulator pins are fastened to the regulator. These pins clasp the outer side of the hairspring a short distance from the hairspring stud. If the regulator index is moved toward the ''S,'' the regulator pins will move, allowing the hairspring to lengthen and the balance wheel to make a longer arc of rotation. This causes the watch to run slower because it requires a longer time for the wheel to perform the longer arc.

## 𝔅𝔲𝔫𝔫 𝔖𝔭𝔢𝔠𝔦𝔞𝔩

18 Size, 21 Jewels, Adjusted 6 Positions

21 ruby and sapphire jewels; gold settings; adjusted to temperature, SIX positions and isochronism; compensating balance; gold screws including timing screws; double roller; steel escape wheel; Breguet hairspring, patent micrometric screw regulator, safety screw center pinion, beautifully damaskeened with black enamel lettering, double sunk dial.

When the regulator is moved toward the "F" these regulator pins are moved from the stud which shortens the hairspring and makes shorter arcs of the balance wheel, thus causing the movement to run faster. Sometimes, after a heavy jolt, the coil next to the outside one will catch between these regulator pins and this will shorten the length of the hairspring just one round, causing a gaining rate of one hour per day. When this occurs, the hairspring can be easily released and will resume its former rate.

The Breguet <u>overcoil</u> hairspring, which is used on railroad grade movements, prevented the hairspring from catching on the regulator pins and protected against any lateral or side motion of the balance wheel ensuring equal expansion of the outside coil.

Railroad grade watches also used the patent or safety pinion which was developed to protect the train of gears from damage in the event of breakage of the mainspring. These pinions unscrewed in event of mainspring breakage, allowing the force to be harmlessly spent by the spinning barrel.

Some earlier railroad grade watches had non-magnetic movements. This was achieved by the use of non-magnetic metals for the balance wheel, hairspring, roller table and pallet. Two of the metals used were iridium and palladium, both very expensive.

**Rockford** Grades 805-Hunting case & 905-Open Face case, 18 size, 21 ruby jewels in gold settings, beautifully damaskeened, nickel plates, gold lettering, adjusted to temperature, isochronism and 5 positions, Breguet hair spring, double roller, steel escape wheel, sapphire pallets, micrometric regulator, compensating balance in recess.

**Ball Watch Co.** Motto: "Carry a Ball and Time Them All." This case is an example of Ball's patented Stirrup Bow. With the simple easy to read dial, this watch was a favorite among railroad men.

## RAILROAD WATCH DIALS

Railroad watch dials are distinguished by their simplicity. A true railroad watch dial contained no fancy lettering or beautiful backgrounds. The watches were designed to be functional and in order to achieve that, the dials contained bold black Arabic numbers against a white background. This facilitated ease of reading the time under even the most adverse conditions.

True railroad watches had the winding stem at the 12 o'clock position. The so-called "side winder," that winds at the 3 o'clock position, was not approved for railroad use. (The side winder is a watch movement designed for a hunter case but one that has been placed in an open-faced case.)

One railroad watch dial design was patented by a Mr. Ferguson. On this dial, the five minute numbers were much larger than the hour numbers which were on the inside. This dial never became very popular.

About 1910 the Montgomery dials began to appear. The distinguishing feature of the Montgomery dial is that each minute is numbered around the hour chapter. The five-minute divisions were in red, and the true Montgomery dial has the number "6" inside the minute register. These dials were favored by the railroad men.

The so-called Canadian dial had a 24-hour division inside the hour chapter.

The double-time hands are also found on some railroad grade watches. One hour hand was in blue or black and the other was in red or gold, one hour apart, to compensate for passing from one time zone to another.

Rockfork Watch Co., Enamel **Railroad** double sunk dial, with two hour hands for a second time zone the hour hand at 2 O'clock is **BLUE**, the hour hand at 3 O'clock is **RED or GOLD**.

This style Illinois railroad watch cases were fitted with movements, rerated and timed in their specially designed case at the factory as complete watches in a gold filled case with screw back & hinged bezel. Note: Montgomery dial.

## RAILROAD WATCH CASES

Open face cases were the only ones approved for railroad use. Railroad men sought a case that was tough and durable; one that would provide a dust-free environment for the movement.

The swing-out case offered the best protection against dust, but the screw-on back and bezel were the most popular open-face cases.

The lever-set was a must for railroad-approved watches and some of the case manufacturers patented their own styles of cases, most with a heavy bow. One example is the Stirrup Bow by the Ball Watch Co. Hamilton used a bar above the crown to prevent the stem from being pulled out. Glass was most commonly used for the crystal because it was not as likely to scratch.

# RAILROAD GRADE OR
# RAILROAD APPROVED WATCHES

Note: Not all railroad GRADE watches were railroad APPROVED, to be approved each railroad line or company made a list of watch grades that they would approve for example, Southern Railway, Lake Shore Railroad & Santa Fe Railway System etc. Not all watches listed here are railroad approved, even though all are railroad grade.

**BALL**
All official R.R. standard with 19, 21, & 23J, hci5p, 18 &16S, open face.

**COLUMBUS WATCH CO.**
Columbus King, 21, 23, 25J; Railway King, 17-25J; Time King, 21-25J, 18S; Ruby Model, 16S.

**ELGIN**
1. "Pennsylvania Railroad Co." on dial, 18S, 15J & 17J, KW-KS, first model "B. W. Raymond."
2. "No. 349," 18S, seventh model, 17-21J.
3. Veritas, B. W. Raymond, or Father Time, 18S, 21-23J.
4. Grades 162, 270, 280, or 342 marked on back plate, 16S, 17-21J.
5. Veritas, Father Time, or Paillard Non-Magnetic, 16S, 19-23J.
6. 571, 21J or 572, 16S, 19J., also All wind indicator models.

**HAMILTON**
1. 18S= Grade 946= 23J, & 940, 942= 21J, & 944= 19J, & 924, 926, 934, 936, 938, 948 = 17J.
2. 16S = Grades 950, 950B, 950E= 23J, & 992, 992B, 992E, 954, 960, 970, 994, 990= 21J.
3. 16S = Grade 996= 19J & 972, 968, 964= 17J.

**HAMPDEN**
1. Sp. Railway, 17J, 21J, 23J; New Railway, 23J & 17J; No. Am. RR22J.,
   Wm. McKinley, 21J; John Hancock, 21J & 23J; John C. Duber, 21J, 18S
2. 105, 21J; 104, 23J; John C. Duber, 21J; Wm. McKinley, 17, 21, & 23J;
   New Railway, 21J; Railway, 19J; Special Railway, 23J, 16S.

**E. HOWARD & CO.**
1. All Howard models marked "Adjusted" or deer symbol.
2. Split plate models, 18S or N size; 16S or L size.

**HOWARD WATCH CO.**
All 16S with 19, 21, & 23J.

**ILLINOIS**
1. Bunn 15J marked "Adjusted," & Stuart, 15J marked"Adjusted," 18S.
2. Benjamin Franklin,17-26J; Bunn 17-21, 24J; Bunn Special,21-26J; Chesapeake & Ohio Sp.,24J;
   Interstate Chronometer, 23J;Lafayette, 24J; A. Lincoln, 21J; Paillard W. Co., 17-24J;
   Trainsmen, 23J; Pennsylvania Special 17-26J; The Railroader & Railroad King, 18S.
3. Benjamin Franklin,17-25J; Bunn,17-19J; Bunn Special,21-23J; Diamond Ruby Sapphire,21-23J;
   Interstate Chronometer,23J; Lafayette,23J; A.Lincoln,21J; Paillard Non-MagneticW.Co.,17-21J;
   Pennsylvania Special, 17, 21, & 23J; Santa Fe Special, 21J; Sangamo, 21-26J;
   Sangamo Special, 19-23J; grades 161, 161A=21J;163, 163A=23J & 187, and 189, 17J, 16S.

**PEORIA WATCH CO.**
15 & 17J with a patented regulator, 18S.

**ROCKFORD**
1. All 21 or more jewels, 16-18S, All and wind indicators.
2. Grades 900, 905, 910, 912, 918, 945, 200, 205, 18S.
3. Winnebago, 17-21J, 505, 515, 525, 535, 545, 555, 16S.

**SETH THOMAS**
Maiden Lane, 21-28J; Henry Molineux, 20J; 260 Model, 18S.

**SOUTH BEND**
1. Studebaker 329, Grade Nos. 323, and 327, 17-21J, 18S.
2. Studebaker 229, Grade Nos. 223, 227, 293, 295, 299, 17-21J, Polaris,21J; 16S.

**UNITED STATES WATCH CO., MARION**
United States, 19J, gold train.

**U. S. WATCH CO., WALTHAM**
The President, 17J, 18S.

**WALTHAM**
1. 1857 KW with Pennsylvania R.R. on dial, Appleton Tracy & Co. on movement.
2. Crescent Street, 17-23J; 1883 & 1892 Models; Appleton Tracy & Co., 1892 Model; Railroader,
   1892 Model; Pennsylvania Railroad; Special RR, Special RR King, Vanguard, 17 -23J, 1892
   Model; Grade 845, All wind indicators 18S.
3. American Watch Co., 17-21J, 1872 Models; American Watch Co., All wind indicators,
   17-23J, Bridge Models; Crescent Street, 17-21J, 1899 & 1908 Models;
   Premier Maximus; Railroader; Riverside Maximus, 21-23J; Vanguard, 19-23J; 645 16S.

American Waltham Watch Co., Vanguard , 16 size, 19-23 jewels, winding indicator which alerts user to how far up or down the mainspring is wound. This watch was made to promote new sales in the railway industry.

Hamilton Watch Co., This was a favorite railroad style case by Hamilton model NO. 2 supplied in 10K or 14K gold filled. Note the Railroad style dial with red marginal figures as well as the bar-over-crown with "Hamilton Railroad" on crown.

## CANADIAN PACIFIC SERVICE
## RAILROAD APPROVED WATCHES 1899

**WALTHAM**
Vanguard, 18-16S, 19-21-23 jewels
Crescent St., 18S, 19J; 18-16S, 21J
Appleton-Tracy 17J; also No. 845, 21J
Riverside 16S, 19J; Riverside Maximus, 16S, 23J; and 16S, No. 645, 21J
C. P. R. 18-16S, 17J; also C. T. S. 18-16S, 17J
**ELGIN**
Veritas, 18-16S, 21-23J
B. W. R. 18-16S, 17-19-21J
Father Time 18-16S, 21J
Grade 349, 18S, 21J
**HAMILTON**
18S, 946, 23J; 940-942, 21J; 944, 19J; 936-938, 17J
16S, 950, 23J; 960-990-992, 21J; 952, 19J; 972, 17J
**SOUTH BEND**
18S, 327-329, 21J; 323, 17J
16S, 227-229, 21J; 223, 17J
**BALL**
All Balls 18S, 16S, 17-19-21-23J
**ILLINOIS**
Bunn Special, 18-16S, 21-23J; also Bunn 18-16S, 17-19J A. Lincoln, 18-16S, 21J
Sangamo Special, 16S, 19-21-23J
**SETH THOMAS**
Maiden Lane, 18S, 25J; No. 260, 21J; No. 382, 17J
**E. HOWARD WATCH CO.**
16S Series, 0-23J, 5-19J, 2-17J, 10-21J; also No. 1, 21J
**ROCKFORD**
18S, Grade 918-905, 21J; Winnebago, 17J; also Grade 900, 24J
16S, Grades 545, 525, 515, 505, 21J; 655 W.I., 21J; and Grade 405, 17J
**LONGINES**
18S, Express Monarch, 17-19-21-23J
16S, Express Monarch, 17-19-21-23J
**BRANDT-OMEGA**
18S, D.D.R., 23J; C.C.C.R., 23J; C.D.R., 19J; C.C.R., 19J

**Double Hour Time Zone Hands,** used on railroad watches and were reversible in RED & BLUE.

# AMERICAN RAILROAD APPROVED WATCHES 1930

The following requirements for railroad approved watches are outlined by Mr. R. D. Montgomery, General Watch Inspector of the Santa Fe Railway System:

"The regulation watch designated as of 1930 to be standard is described as follows:"

"16 size, American, lever-setting, 19 jewels or more, open face, winding at "12", double-roller escapement, steel escape wheel, adjusted to 5 positions, temperature and isochronism, which will rate within a variation not exceeding 6 seconds in 72 hour tests, pendant up, dial up and dial down, and be regulated to run within a variation not exceeding 30 seconds per week."

"The following listed makes and grades meet the requirements and comprise a complete list of watches acceptable. Watches bearing the name of jewelers or other names not standard trade marks or trade numbers will not be accepted:"

**AMERICAN WALTHAM W. CO.**
(16 Size)
23J Premier Maximus
23J Riverside Maximus
23J Vanguard
    6 position
    winding indicator
23J Vanguard
    6 position
21J Crescent Street
21J No. 645
19J Vanguard
19J Riverside

**BALL WATCH CO.**
(16 Size)
23J Official R.R. Standard
21J Official R.R. Standard
19J Official R.R. Standard

**ELGIN WATCH CO.**
(16 Size)
23J Veritas
21J Veritas
21J B. W. Raymond
21J Father Time
21J No. 270

**HAMILTON WATCH CO.**
(16 Size)
23J No. 950
21J No. 990
21J No. 992
19J No. 952
19J No. 996

**HAMPDEN WATCH CO.**
(16 Size)
23J Special Railway
21J New Railway
19J Railway

**HOWARD WATCH CO.**
(16 Size)
All 23J
All 21J
All 19J

**ILLINOIS WATCH CO.**
(16 Size)
23J Sangamo Special
23J Sangamo
23J Bunn Special
21J Bunn Special
21J Sangamo
21J A. Lincoln
19J Bunn

**SOUTH BEND WATCH CO.**
(16 Size)
21J No. 227
21J No. 229
21J No. 295
19J No. 293

## APPROVED POCKET WATCHES IN
## CP RAIL SERVICE AS OF FEBRUARY 1, 1957

**WALTHAM (16 SIZE)**
23J Vanguard S. # 29, 634, 001 and up

**ELGIN (16 Size)**
21J B.W.R.
21J No. 571

**HAMILTON (16 SIZE)**
23J No. 950B
21J No. 992B

**BALL W. Co.(16 Size)**
21J (Hamilton) No. 992C
21J No. 435C

**ZENITH (16 Size)**
21J Extra RR 56

## APPROVED WRIST WATCHES IN
## CP RAIL SERVICE

**CYMA**
17J RR 2852 M
25J RR 2872 A

**GIRARD PERREGAUX**
17J CP 307H.F.

**LONGINES**
17J RR 280

**UNIVERSAL**
19J RR 1205

**ZENITH**
18J RR 120 T

FERGUSON Patented Railroad Dial : Patent number on back. Valued at ; BALL = $350 to $550 and A.W.W.Co., Elgin, Hamilton, Illinois, etc., = $200 to 350 for MINT dials.

ELGIN WATCH CO., Montgomery Railroad Dial with red marginal numbers at 5, 10, 15, 20, 25, 30, 35, 40, 45, 50, 55, & 60. Valued at $75 to $135.

APPROVED WRIST WATCHES IN
CP RAIL SERVICE 1965
BATTERY POWERED

**BULOVA ACCUTRON**
17J 214
17J 218 Calendar

**RODANIA**
13J RR 2780 Calendar

**WITTNAUER**
13J RR 12 WT Calendar

APPROVED WRIST WATCHES SEMI-MECHANICAL
QUARTZ ANALOG BATTERY POWERED
IN CP RAIL SERVICE AS OF 1978

**CYMA**
7J Calendar RR 9361 Q
6J Calendar RR 960 Q

**BULOVA**
7J Calendar RR 9362 Q
6J Calendar RR 960.111Q

**RODANIA**
6J Calendar 9952.111RR
7J Calendar RR 9361 Q

**ROTARY**
7J Calendar RR 9366 Q

**WYLER**
7J Calendar RR 9361 Q

**WITTNAUER**
7J Calendar RR 2 Q 115 C

# ADJUSTMENTS

There are **nine** basic adjustments for watch movements. They are:

heat 1

cold 1

isochronism 1

positions 6

TOTAL 9

THE SIX POSITION ADJUSTMENTS ARE:

Stem
UP

Stem
Down

This position adjust-
ment not required on
railroad watches.

Stem Left

Stem Right

Dial Up

Dial Down

⊕ A watch marked as **5 positions** is <u>equivalent</u> to one marked *eight adjustments* (the most common found on RR watches) and will be listed in this book as: **"Adj.5P"** ( adjusted to heat,cold, isochronism and 5 positions). A watch marked as **nine adjustments** is <u>equivalent</u> to one marked *6 positions* & listed as **"Adj.6P"** (adjusted to heat,cold, isochronism and <u>6 positions</u>). A watch that is marked as *ADJUSTED* only is adjusted to isochronism & in poise in all temperatures & is listed as **"Adj."**

⊕ Not all railroad GRADE watches were railroad **APPROVED**, to be approved each railroad line or company made a list of watch grades that they would **approve** for example, Southern Railway, Lake Shore Railroad & Santa Fe Railway System etc.

The total number of pocket watches made for the railroad industry was small in comparison to the total pocket watches produced. Generally, watches defined as "Railroad Watches" fall into five categories:

1. **Railroad Approved-** Grades and Models approved by the railway companies.
2. **Railroad Grade-**Those advertised as being able to pass railroad inspection.
3. **Pre-Commission Watches-**Those used by the railroads before 1893.
4. **Company Watches-**Those with a railroad logo or company name on the dial.
5. **Train Watches-**Those with a locomotive painted on the dial or inscribed on the case.

\*      \*      \*      \*      \*

1. Not all railroad employees were required to purchase or use approved watches, just the employees that were responsible for schedules. But many employees did buy the approved watches because they were the standard in reliability.

2. These were used primarily by those railroaders who were not required to submit their watches for inspection.

3. There were many watches made for railroad use prior to 1893. Some of the key wind ones, especially, are good quality and highly collectible.

4. Some manufacturers inscribed terms such as railroader, special railroad, dispatcher, etc. on the back plates of the movements.

## COLONIAL WATCHMAKERS

( PRE—1850 )

Early American watchmakers came from Europe; little is known about them, and few of their watches exist today. Their hand-fabricated watches were made largely from imported parts. It was common practice for a watchmaker to use rough castings made by several craftsmen. These were referred to as "movements in the gray." The watchmaker finished these parts and assembled them to make a complete watch. He would then engrave his name on the finished timepiece.

Some of the early American watchmakers designed the cases or other parts, but most imported what they needed. The so called early **COLONIAL** watchmakers showed little originality as designers and we can only guess how many watches were really made in America.

These early hand-made watches are almost non-existent; therefore, only the name of the watchmaker will be listed. This compilation comes from old ads in newspapers and journals and other sources. It is not considered to be complete.

Because of the rarity and condition of these early watches, prices may vary widely from $400 to $2,000.

George Bowen, Boston Mass., engraved on movement "Chronometer Maker", KW KS, Spring Detent., Ca. 1850.

Davis Watson & Co. Boston, Fusee with right angle escapement lever, serial No. 8028 Ca. 1850.

Example of watch paper placed inside a pair-cased watch by a watch maker. This was a form of advertisement placed in the watch after repair was made.

Ephraim Clark, 18 size, non-jeweled, made between 1780-1790; a good example of a colonial watch. These early watches usually included chain driven fusees, verge type escapements, hand pierced balance cock, key wind & set; note the circular shaped regulator above the balance Cock.

Effingham Clark, New York, on dial & movement, the inner with Roman hour chapter and a sweep second outer dial, diamond stone, serial No. 720, Ca. 1815.

E. EMBREE, NEW YORK engraved on movement, serial # 790, chain driven fusee, silver pair cased watch, ca. early 1800's.

30

**B. F. S. Patten, Bangor, Maine,** LEFT & RIGHT; left a 48mm, 6 jewels, <u>Cylinder</u> escapement bar style Ebauche movement which may have been manufactured by Japy Freres with branches in France, Switzerland & England. Right; showing the movement cover that reads four holes jeweled but 6 jewels exits, Ca.1855 to 1865.("Continental Watch" )

**GREENLEUF & OAKES, Hartford,** Ca. 1805, Greenleuf & Oakes formed a partnership in 1804, verge, pierced cock.

**MARQUAND & CO. , New York,** Ca. 1850s, gold case, right angle lever escapement, fusee, gold dial.

**J. H. MULFORD, Albany, N. Y.,** produced watches from about 1835 to 1875, the two watch movements ( A & B ) are illustrated, A is about size 18, KWKS, gold jewel settings, compensated balance with gold screws. Movement B is 3 arm balance, diamond end stone. Note the J. H. Mulford patented verge style escapement patented # 2465, dated Feb. 21, 1842. illustrated to the far right.

Adams, Nathan (Boston, MA, 1800)
Adams, William (Boston, MA, 1810)
Alden, & Eldridge (Bristol, Conn., 1820 )
Aldrich, Jacob (Wilmington, DE, 1802)
Alrichs, Jonas (Wilmington, DE, 1880 )
Allebach, Jacob (Phila., PA, 1825-1840)
Amant, Fester (Phila., PA, 1793 )
Atherton, Nathan (Phila., PA, 1825)
Atkins & Allen (Bristol, Ct., 1820 )
Atkinson, James (Boston, MA, 1745)
Austin, Isaac (Phila., PA, 1785 )
Backhouse, John (Lancaster, PA, 1725)
Bagnall, Benjamin (Phila., PA, 1750)
Bailey, John (Boston, MA, 1810)
Bailey & Kitchen:(Phila,PA, 1832-46) name
changed to Bailey, Banks & Biddle
Bailey, William (Phila., PA, 1820)
Baker, Benjamin (Phila., PA, 1825)
Banks, Joseph (Phila., PA, 1790)
Banstein, John (Phila.,PA, 1790 )
Barnes, Timothy (Litchfield, Conn. 1790)
Barnhill, Robert (Phila., PA, 1775)
Barrow, Samuel (Phila., PA, 1771)
Barry, Standish (Baltimore, MD, 1785)
Basset, John F. (Phila., PA, 1798)
Batterson, James (New York 1705-30 )
Bayley, Simeon C., (Phila., PA 1795 )
Beard, Duncan (Appoquinemonk, Del.1765)
Belk, William ( Phila., PA 1796 )
Belknap, William (Boston, MA, 1815)
Bell, William (Phila., PA, 1805)
Benedict, S. W. (New York, NY, 1835)
Bigger & Clarke (Baltimore, MD, 1783)
Billion, C. (Phila., PA, 1775-1800)
Billow, Charles & Co. ( Phila., PA 1796 )
Bingham & Bricerly (Phila., PA, 1778-1799)
Birge, Mallory & Co. (Bristol, Conn. 1830 )
Birge, Peck & Co. ( Bristol, Conn. 1830 )
Birnie, Laurence (Phila., PA, 1774)
Blundy, Charles (Charleston, SC, 1750)
Blunt & Nichols (New York, NY, 1850)
Boardman, Chauncey (Bristol, Conn.1815 )
Boardman, & Dunbar (Bristol, Conn. 1811)
Boardman, & Wells (Bristol, Conn. 1815 )
Bode, William ( Phila., Pa 1796 )
Bogardus, Evarardus (New York, 1698 )
Bond, William (Boston,MA, 1800-1810)
Bonnaud (Phila., PA, 1799)
Bower, Michael (Phila., PA, 1790-1800)
Bowman, Joseph (Lancaster, PA, 1821-44)
Boyd & Richards (Phila., PA, 1808)
Boyter, Daniel (Lancaster, PA, 1805)
Brands & Matthey (Phila., PA, 1799)
Brandt, Aime (Phila., PA, 1820)
Brant, Brown & Lewis (Phila., PA, 1795)
Brazier, Amable (Phila., PA, 1795)
Brearley, James (Phila., PA, 1790-1800)
Brewer, William (Phila., PA, 1785-1791)
Brewster &Ingraham(Bristol,CT,1827-39)
Brown, Garven (Boston, MA, 1767)
Brown, John (Lancaster, PA, 1840)
Brown, Samuel (New York, 1820-1850)
Brownell, A. P. (New Bedford, MA.1840-60)
Burkelow, Samuel (Phila., PA, 1791-1799)
Burnop, Daniei ( E. Windsor, Conn., 1793 )
Bush, George (Easton, PA, 1790-1800)

Campbell, Charles (Phila., PA, 1796)
Campbell, William (Carlisle, PA, 1765)
Canby, Charles (Wilmington, Del., 1825 )
Capper, Michael (Phila., PA, 1799)
Carey, James (Brunswick, ME, 1830)
Carrell, John (Phila., PA, 1791-1793)
Carter, Jacob (Phila., PA, 1805)
Carter, Thomas (Phila., PA, 1823)
Carver, Jacob (Phila., PA, 1790)
Carvill, James (New York, NY, 1803)
Chandlee, John(Wilmington,DE,1795-1810)
Chaudron, Co., (Phila., PA, 1799- 1815 )
Chauncey & Joseph Ives (Bristol, CT, 1825)
Cheney, Martin (Windsor, VT, 1800)
Chick, M. M. (Concord, NH, 1845)
Clark,Benjamin(Wilmington,DE,1737-1750)
Clark, Charles ( Phila., PA 1810 )
Clark, Ephraim (Phila., PA, 1780-1800)
Clark, John (New York, NY, 1770-1790)
Clark, John (Phila., PA, 1799)
Clark, Thomas (Boston, MA, 1764)
Claudon,John-George (Charleston SC,1773)
Cook, William (Boston, MA, 1810)
Crow, George (Wilmington, DE, 1740-1770)
Crow, John (Wilmington, DE, 1770-1798)
Crow, Thomas (Wilmington, DE, 1770-98)
Currier & Trott (Boston, MA, 1800)
Curtis, Solomon (Phila., PA, 1793-1795)
Dakin, James (Boston, MA, 1795)
Davis, Samuel (Boston, MA, 1820)
Davis,Watson & Co.(Boston, 1840-1850)
Delaplaine, James K.(New York, 1786-1800)
DeVacht, Joseph & Frances
    (Gallipolis, OH,    1792)
Dix, Joseph (Phila., PA, 1770)
Downes, Anson (Bristol, CT, 1830)
Downes, Arthur (Charleston, SC, 1765)
Downes, Ephriam (Bristol, CT, 1830)
Droz, Hannah (Phila., PA, 1840)
Droz, Humbert (Phila., PA, 1793-1799)
Duffield, Edward W. (Whiteland, PA, 1775)
Dunheim, Andrew (New York, NY, 1775)
Dupuy, John (Phila., PA, 1770)
Dupuy, Odran (Phila., PA, 1735)
Dutch, Stephen, Jr. (Boston, MA.1800-10)
Eberman, George (Lancaster, PA, 1800)
Eberman, John (Lancaster, PA, 1780-1820)
Ellicott, Joseph (Buckingham, PA, 1763)
Elsworth, David (Baltimore, MD.1780-1800)
Embree, Effingham (New York, NY, 1785)
Evans, David (Baltimore, MD, 1770-1773)
Fales, James (New Bedford, MA.1810-20)
Ferris, Tiba (Wilmington, DE, 1812-1850)
Fessler, John (Phila., PA, 1785-1820)
Feton, J. (Phila., PA, 1825-1840)
Filber, John (Lancaster, PA, 1810-1825)
Fister, Amon (Phila., PA, 1794)
Fix, Joseph (Reading, PA, 1820-1840)
Fowell, J & N (Boston, MA, 1800-1810)
Frances, Basil & Alexander Vuille
    Baltimore, MD, 1766)
Galbraith, Patrick (Phila., PA, 1795)
Gibbons, Thomas (Phila., PA, 1750)
Goodfellow, William (Phila., PA,1793-1795)
Goodfellow & Son, William (Phila., PA,
    1796-1799)

Gooding, Henry (Boston, MA, 1810-1820)
Green, John (Phila., PA, 1794)
Griffen, Henry ( New York, 1790 )
Groppengeiser, J. L. (Phila., PA, 1840)
Grotz, Issac (Easton, PA, 1810-1835)
Hall, Jonas (Boston, MA, 1848-1858)
Harland, Theodore (Norwich, CT,1750-90)
Harland, Thomas ( New York, 1805 )
Harland, Thomas (Norwich, CT, 1802)
Harrison, James (Shrewbury, MA, 1805)
Hawxhurst, Nath. (New York, NY, 1784)
Heilig, Jacob (Phila., PA, 1770-1824)
Heilig, John (Germantown, PA, 1824-1830)
Hepton, Frederick (Phila., PA, 1785)
Heron, Isaac (New York, NY, 1770-1780)
Hill, D. (Reading, PA 1830 )
Hodgson, William (Phila., PA, 1785)
Hoff, John (Lancaster, PA, 1800)
Hoffner, Henry (Phila., PA, 1791)
Howard, Thomas (Phila., PA, 1789-1791)
Howe, Jubal (Shrewbury, MA, 1800)
Huguenail, Charles (Phila., PA, 1799)
Hunt, Hiram (Robbinston, ME, 1800)
Hutchins, Abel (Concord, MA, 1785-1818)
Hutchins, Levi (Concord, MA, 1785-1815)
Hyde, John E. (New York, NY, 1805)
Hyde & Goodrich (New Orleans, LA, 1850)
Ingersoll, Daniel B. (Boston, MA, 1800-10)
Ingold, Pierre Frederick (NY, NY,1845-50)
Ives, Chauncy & Joseph (Bristol, CT, 1825)
Jacob, Charles & Claude (Annapolis,MD, Ca.1775)
Jackson, Joseph H. (Phila., PA, 1802-1810)
Jessop, Jonathan (Park Town, PA, 1790)
Jeunit, Joseph (Meadville, PA, 1763)
Johnson, David (Boston, MA, 1690)
Johnson, John (Charleston, SC, 1763)
Jones, George (Wilmington, DE, 1815-35)
Jones, Low & Ball (Boston, MA, 1830)
Keith, William (Shrewbury, MA, 1810)
Kennedy, Patrick (Phila., PA, 1795-1799)
Kincaid, Thomas (Christiana Bridge, DE, Ca. 1175)
Kirkwood, John (Charleston, SC, 1761)
Kumble, Wm. ( New York- 1776 )
Launy, David F. (Boston & N. Y., 1800)
Leavenworth, Mark (Waterbury, CT, 1820)
Leavenworth, Wm. (Waterbury, CT, 1810)
Leslie & Co., Baltimore, MD, 1795)
Leslie & Price (Phila., PA, 1793-1799)
Leslie, Robert (Baltimore, MD, 1788-1791)
Levely, George (Phila., PA, 1774)
Levi, Michael & Issac (Baltimore,MD,1785)
Limeburner, John (Phila., PA, 1790)
Lind, John (Phila., PA, 1791-1799)
Lowens, David (Phila., PA, 1785)
Ludwig, John (Phila., PA, 1791)
Lufkins & Johnson (Boston, MA, 1800-10)
Lukins, Isaac (Phila., PA, 1825)
Macdowell, Robert (Phila., PA, 1798)
MacFarlane, John (Boston, MA, 1800-1810)
Mahve, Matthew (Phila., PA, 1761)
Manross, Elisha (Bristol, CT, 1827)
Martin, Patrick (Phila., PA, 1830)
Mathey, Louis (Phia., PA, 1800)
Maunroe & Whitney (Concord,MA,1800's )
Maus, Frederick (Phila., PA, 1785- 1793)
Maynard, George(New York,NY,1702-1730)

McCabe, John (Baltimore, MD, 1774)
McDowell, James (Phila., PA, 1795)
McGraw, Donald (Annapolis, MD, 1767)
Mends, James (Phila., PA, 1795)
Merriman, Titus (Bristol, CT, 1830)
Merry, Charles F. (Phila., PA, 1799)
Meters, John(Fredricktown, MD,1795-1825)
Miller, Abraham (Easton, PA, 1810-1830)
Mitchell & Atkins (Bristol, CT, 1830)
Mitchell, Henry (N. Y., NY, 1787-1800)
Mohler, Jacob (Baltimore, MD, 1773)
Moir, J & W (Waterbury, CT, 1790)
Montandon, Julien (Shrewbury, CT, 1812)
Moollinger, Henry (Phila., PA, 1794)
Morgan, Thomas (Phila. & Balti., 1774-93)
Moris, William (Grafton, MA, 1765-1775)
Mulford, J. H. (Albany, NY, 1845)
Mulliken, Nathaniel (Boston, MA, 1765)
Munroe & Whitney (Concord, MA, 1820)
Narney, Joseph (Charleston, SC, 1753)
Neiser, Augustine (Phila., PA, 1739-1780)
Nicholls, George (New York, NY, 1728-50)
Nicollette, Mary (Phila., PA, 1793-1799)
O'Hara, Charles (Phila., PA, 1799)
Oliver, Griffith (Phila., PA, 1785-1793)
Ormsby, James (Baltimore, MD, 1771)
Palmer, John (Phila., PA, 1795)
Palmer, John Peter (Phila., PA, 1795)
Park, Seth (Parktown, PA, 1790)
Parke, Solomon (Phila., PA, 1791-1795)
Parke, Solomon & Co. (Phila., PA, 1799)
Parker, James (Cambridge, OH, 1790)
Parker, Thomas (Phila., PA, 1783)
Parry, John J. (Phila., PA, 1795-1800)
Patton, Abraham (Phila., PA, 1799)
Patton, David (Phila., PA, 1800)
Payne, Lawrence (New York, NY,1732-55)
Pearman, W. (Richmond, VA, 1834)
Perkins, Thomas (Phila., PA. 1785-1800)
Perry, Marvin (New York, NY, 1770-1780)
Perry, Thomas (New York, NY, 1750-1775)
Phillips, Joseph (New York, NY, 1713-35)
Pierret, Mathew (Phila., PA, 1795)
Pope, Joseph (Boston, MA, 1790)
Price, Philip (Phila., PA, 1825)
Proctor, Cardan (New York, NY.1747-75)
Proctor, William (New York,NY.1737-1760)
Proud, R. (Newport, RI, 1775)
Potter, J.O.&J.R. (Providence,R.I.1849)
Purse, Thomas (Baltimore, MD, 1805)
Quimby, Phineas & William (Belfast, ME, Ca. 1825)
Reily, John (Phila., PA, 1785-1795)
Rich, John (Bristol, CT, 1800)
Richardson, Francis (Phila., PA, 1736)
Ritchie, George (Phila., PA, 1785-1790)
Roberts, John (Phila., PA, 1799)
Roberts, S & E (Trenton, NJ, 1830)
Rode, William (Phila., PA, 1785)
Rodger, James (New York, NY, 1822-1878)
Rodgers,Samuel (Plymouth,MA,1800's)
Russell, George (Phila., PA, 1840)
Saxton & Lukens (Phila., PA, 1828)
Schriner, Martin (Lancaster, P.A.1790-1830)
Schriner, M & P (Lancaster, PA, 1830-40)
Seddinger, Margaret (Phila., PA, 1846)
Severberg, Christian (NY, NY, 1755-1775)
Sherman, Robert(Wilmington, DE.1760-70)

Sibley, O. E. (New York, NY, 1820)
Simpson, Saml. ( Clarksville,Tenn - 1855 )
Smith, J. L. (Middletown, CT, 1830)
Smith & Goodrich (Bristol, CT, 1827-1840)
Soloman, Henry (Boston, MA, 1820)
Souza, Sammuel (Phila., PA, 1820)
Sprogell, John (Phila., PA, 1791)
Spurck, Peter (Phila., PA, 1795-1799)
Stanton, Job (New York, NY, 1810)
Stein, Abraham (Phila., PA, 1799)
Stever & Bryant (Wigville, CT, 1830)
Stillas, John (Phila., PA, 1785-1793)
Stinnett, John (Phila., PA, 1769)
Stokel, John (New York, NY, 1820-1840)
Store, Marmaduke (Phila., PA, 1742)
Strech, Thomas (Phila., PA, 1782)
Syderman, Philip (Phila., PA, 1785)
Taf, John James (Phila., PA, 1794)
Taylor, Samuel (Phila, PA, 1799)
Tonchure, Francis (Baltimore, MD, 1805)
Townsend, Charles (Phila., PA, 1799)

Townsend, David (Boston, MA, 1800)
Trott, Andrew (Boston, MA, 1800-1810)
Turrell, Samuel (Boston, MA, 1790)
Voight, Henry (Phila., PA, 1775-1793)
Voight, Sebastian (Phila., PA, 1775-1799)
Voight, Thomas (Henry's son) (Phila., PA, 1811-1835)
Vuille, Alexander (Baltimore, MD, 1766)
Warner, George T. (New York, NY, 1795)
Watson, Davis (Boston, 1840-50)
Weller, Francis (Phila., PA, 1780)
Wells, George & Co. (Boston, MA, 1825)
Wells, J.S. (Boston, MA, 1800)
Wetherell, Nathan (Phila., PA, 1830-1840)
Wheaton, Caleb (Providence, RI, 1800)
White, Sebastian (Phila., PA, 1795)
Whittaker, William (NY, NY, 1731-1755)
Wood, John (Phila., PA, 1770-1793)
Wright, John (New York, NY, 1712-1735)
Zahm, G.M. (Lancaster, PA, 1865)

**J.O.& J.R. Potter,** Providence R.I. Fusee with right angle lever escapement, serial No. 8591, Ca. 1850's

**Louis Mathey, Philadelphia** engraved on movement, about 18 size, very thin movement, **Virgule** escapement, key wind & set from back, Ca.1795-1805.

**H. Mitchell,** New York, 18 size, verge chain driven fusee; note the regulator below hand-pierced cock, Ca. 1790.

## AMERICAN MOVEMENT SIZES
### LANCASHIRE GAUGE

| Size | Inches | Inches | mm | Lignes | Size | Inches | Inches | mm | Lignes |
|------|--------|--------|-----|--------|------|--------|--------|-----|--------|
| 18/0 | 18/30 | .600 | 15.24 | 6 3/4 | 2 | 1 7/30 | 1.233 | 31.32 | 13 7/8 |
| 17/0 | 19/30 | .633 | 16.08 | 7 1/8 | 3 | 1 8/30 | 1.266 | 32.16 | 14 1/4 |
| 16/0 | 20/30 | .666 | 16.92 | 7 1/2 | 4 | 1 9/30 | 1.300 | 33.02 | 14 7/8 |
| 15/0 | 21/30 | .700 | 17.78 | 7 7/8 | 5 | 1 10/30 | 1.333 | 33.86 | 15 1/8 |
| 14/0 | 22/30 | .733 | 18.62 | 8 1/4 | 6 | 1 11/30 | 1.366 | 34.70 | 15 3/8 |
| 13/0 | 23/30 | .766 | 19.46 | 8 5/8 | 7 | 1 12/30 | 1.400 | 35.56 | 15 3/4 |
| 12/0 | 24/30 | .800 | 20.32 | 9 1/8 | 8 | 1 13/30 | 1.433 | 36.40 | 16 1/8 |
| 11/0 | 25/30 | .833 | 21.16 | 9 3/8 | 9 | 1 14/30 | 1.466 | 37.24 | 16 1/2 |
| 10/0 | 26/30 | .866 | 22.00 | 9 3/4 | 10 | 1 15/30 | 1.500 | 38.10 | 16 7/8 |
| 9/0 | 27/30 | .900 | 22.86 | 10 1/8 | 11 | 1 16/30 | 1.533 | 38.94 | 17 1/4 |
| 8/0 | 28/30 | .933 | 23.70 | 10 1/2 | 12 | 1 17/30 | 1.566 | 39.78 | 17 5/8 |
| 7/0 | 29/30 | .966 | 24.54 | 10 7/8 | 13 | 1 18/30 | 1.600 | 40.64 | 18 1/8 |
| 6/0 | 1 | 1.000 | 25.40 | 11 1/4 | 14 | 1 19/30 | 1.633 | 41.48 | 18 3/8 |
| 5/0 | 1 1/30 | 1.033 | 26.24 | 11 5/8 | 15 | 1 20/30 | 1.666 | 42.32 | 18 3/4 |
| 4/0 | 1 2/30 | 1.066 | 27.08 | 12 1/8 | 16 | 1 21/30 | 1.700 | 43.18 | 19 1/8 |
| 3/0 | 1 3/30 | 1.100 | 27.94 | 12 3/8 | 17 | 1 22/30 | 1.733 | 44.02 | 19 1/2 |
| 2/0 | 1 4/30 | 1.133 | 28.78 | 12 3/4 | 18 | 1 23/30 | 1.766 | 44.86 | 19 7/8 |
| 0 | 1 5/30 | 1.166 | 29.62 | 13 1/8 | 19 | 1 24/30 | 1.800 | 45.72 | 20 1/4 |
| 1 | 1 6/30 | 1.200 | 30.48 | 13 1/2 | 20 | 1 25/30 | 1.833 | 46.56 | 20 3/4 |

### SWISS MOVEMENT SIZES
**Lignes With Their Equivalents in Millimeters and Decimal Parts of an Inch**

| Lignes | Inches Decimals | Millimeters |
|--------|-----------------|-------------|
| 7 | .622 | 15.79 |
| 8 | .710 | 18.05 |
| 9 | .799 | 20.30 |
| 10 | .888 | 22.56 |
| 11 | .977 | 24.81 |
| 12 | 1.066 | 27.07 |
| 13 | 1.154 | 29.32 |
| 14 | 1.243 | 31.58 |
| 15 | 1.332 | 33.84 |
| 16 | 1.421 | 36.09 |
| 17 | 1.510 | 38.35 |
| 18 | 1.599 | 40.60 |
| 19 | 1.687 | 42.86 |
| 20 | 1.776 | 45.11 |
| 21 | 1.865 | 47.37 |
| 22 | 1.954 | 49.63 |

### GAUGES FOR MEASURING YOUR WATCH SIZE

The size of a watch is determined by measuring the outside diameter of the dial side of the lower pillar plate. The gauges below may be placed across the face of your watch to calculate its approximate size.

AMER. MOVEMENT SIZES

SWISS MOVEMENT SIZES
LIGNES

# SOLID GOLD MARKS

⏱ The term Karat is a word of definition in regards to the quality of gold, one 24th part (of pure gold). For example: Pure or fine gold is 24 karats; 18 Karat (abbreviated 18 K)consist of 18 parts of pure gold and mixed with 6 parts of other metal. The term Carat is a unit of weight for gemstones, 200 milligrams equal 1 Carat.

# GOLD-FILLED CASES

The first patent for gold-filled cases was given to J. Boss on <u>May 3, 1859.</u> Gold-filled cases are far more common than solid gold cases. Only about 5 percent of the cases were solid gold. In making the gold-filled case, the following process was used: two bars of gold, 12'' long, 2'' wide, and 1/2 '' thick were placed on either side of a bar of base metal. The bar of base metal was 3/4'' thick and the same length and width as the gold bars. These three bars were soldered together under pressure at high temperature. The bars were sent through rolling mills under tremendous pressure; this rolling was repeated until the desired thickness was reached. The new sandwich-type gold was now in a sheet. Discs were punched out of the sheet and pressed in a die to form a dish-shaped cover. Finally the lip, or ridge, was added. The bezel, snap, and dust caps were added in the finishing room. Gold-filled cases are usually 10k or 14k gold. The cases were marked ten-year, fifteen-year, twenty-year, twenty-five-year, or thirty-year. The number of years indicated the duration of guarantee that the gold on the case would not wear through to the base metal. The higher the number of years indicates that more gold used and that a higher original price was paid.

In 1924 the government prohibited any further use of the guarantee terms of 5, 10, 15, 20, 25, or 30 years. After that, manufacturers marked their cases 10k or 14k Gold-Filled and 10k Rolled Gold Plate. Anytime you see the terms ''5, 10, 15, 20, 25 and 30-year,'' this immediately identifies the case as being gold-filled. The word ''guaranteed'' on the case also denotes gold-filled.

## Rolled Gold

Rolled gold involved rolling gold into a micro thinness and, under extreme pressure, bonding it to each sheet of base metal. Rolled gold carried a five-year guarantee. The thickness of the gold sheet varied and had a direct bearing on value, as did the richness of the engraving.

## Gold Gilding

Brass plates, wheels and cases are often gilded with gold. To do this, the parts are hung by a copper wire in a vessel or porous cell of a galvanic battery filled with a solution of ferro-cyanide of potassium, carbonate of soda, chloride of gold, and distilled water. An electric current deposits the gold evenly over the surface in about a six-minute period. One ounce of gold is enough for heavy gilding of six hundred watches. After gilding, the plates are polished with a soft buff using powdered rouge mixed with water and alcohol. The older method is fire-gilt which uses a gold and mercury solution. The metal is subjected to a high temperature so the mercury will evaporate and leave the gold plating. This is a very dangerous method, however, due to the harmful mercury vapor.

**JAS. BOSS Railroad Model** 10K Gold Filled cases sold for $14.00 in 1927

# GOLD-FILLED MARKS

The following gold-filled and rolled gold plate marks are not complete, but if you have any doubt that the case is solid gold, **pay** only the *gold-filled* price.

**Important Notice.** All of the information, including valuations, in this book has been compiled from the most reliable sources, and every effort has been made to eliminate errors and questionable data. Nevertheless, the possibility of error, in a work of such immense scope, always exists. The publisher or authors will not be held responsible for losses which may occur in the purchase, sale, or other transaction of items, because of information contained herein. Readers who feel they have discovered errors are invited to write and inform us, so they may be corrected in subsequent editions.

# GOLD FILLED MARKS

☆ 10K ROLLED GOLD PLATE

**BEE HIVE**

*(14K. Filled.)*

*(Jas. Boss 10K. Filled. 20 Years.)*

**CROWN 14K. FILLED**
*(25 Years.)*

*(Keystone Extra, Substitute for All-Gold Case.)*

**CROWN 10K. FILLED**
*(20 Years.)*

*(Rolled Gold.)*

*(Jas. Boss 14K. Filled. 25 Years.)*

**EMPRESS**
*(Gold Filled, 10 Years.)*

**FORTUNE**
*(Gold Filled, 20 Years.)*

*(14K. Filled.)*

**V.**

**XV.**
*(15 Years.)*

**THE BELL 14K.**
*(25 Years.)*

**XX.**

*(10 Years.)*

*(25 Years.)*

**PREMIER**
*(Gold Filled, 25 Years.)*

**CASHIER**
*(Gold Filled, 25 Years.)*

**THE COMET**
*(10 Years.)*

**WARRANTED**
**(N.A.W.Co)**
**20 YEARS**
*(10K. Gold Filled.)*

**(5 Years.)**

**(20 Years.)**

# SILVER CASE MARKS

**A.W.W.CO.**
**WALTHAM.**
**STERLING.**

**A.W. CO.**
**STERLING**

**A.W.W. CO.**
**COIN.**

**STERLING**

*(Discontinued.)*

*(Discontinued.)*

**NEWPORT**
**COIN**
*(Coin Silver with Albata Cap)*
*(Discontinued.)*

**DUEBER**
**COIN**
*(Coin Silver with Silver Cap)*
*(Discontinued.)*

**CHAMPION**
**COIN.**

**STAR W.C.CO**

**STERLING**
**925/1000**
**FINE**
*(Coin Silver, with Silver Caps, Gold Joints and Crowns.)*

**N.A.W.Co**
**STERLING**
*(Sterling Silver.)*

*Sterling Silver*

---

**NICKEL SILVER** is 66% Copper, 24% Zinc, and 10% Nickel ( also known as **Silveroid** etc. )

## SILVER CASE MARKS

*(Sterling Silver.)*

STERLING
SILVER
UNITED STATES
ASSAY
925./1000
FINE.

ILLINOIS
W.C.CO.
ELGIN
STERLING

## HUNTING CASES

A hunting case is identified by a cover over the face ( concealed dial ) of the watch. The case is opened by pressing the stem or the crown of the watch. The hunter style watch was used for protection of the watch and carried by men of status and used as a dress watch.

## HOW TO HANDLE A HUNTING CASE WATCH

Hold the watch in your right hand with the bow or swing ring between the index finger and thumb. Press on the pendant-crown with the right thumb to release the cover exposing the face.

When closing, do not **SNAP** the cover. Press the crown to move the catch in, close the cover, then release the crown. This will prevent wear to the soft gold on the rim and catch.

**Above:** Example of a hunting case

**Right:** Example of a swing-out case

## SWING-OUT MOVEMENT

On some pocket watches the movement swings out from the front. On these type watches the movement can be swung out by unscrewing the crystal and pulling the stem out to **release** the movement. **SEE EXAMPLE ABOVE.**

**Engine -turned**

**Demi-Hunting case**

Example of a 14 Karat gold **BOXED HINGED** case, selling for $94 in 1890.

**Below:** Example of a reversible case to either hunting or open face.

**Left:** Example of a screw bezel and screw back case.

**Note:** The screw on bezel was invented by E. C. Fitch in 1886.

## MOVEMENT IDENTIFICATION

**1.** Grade Number. **2.** Nickel Motor Barrel Bridge. **3.** Center Wheel (2nd Wheel). **4.** Winding Wheel with Jewel Setting. **5.** First Barrel Wheel. **6.** Winding Click. **7.** Case Screw. **8.** Pendant Crown. **9.** Pendant Bow or Swing Ring. **10.** Crown Wheel with Screw. **11** Damaskeening-horizontal pattern. **12.** Number of Jewels. **13.** Center Wheel Jewel with Setting. **14.** Adjusted to Heat, Cold, Isochronism & 5 Positions. **15.** Patented Regulator with Index & Spring. **16.** Balance End Stones (Diamonds, Rubys, & Sapphires were used). **17.** Balance Screws. **18.** Compensating Balance Wheel. **19.** Hairspring. **20.** Escapement Bridge. **21.** Escapement Wheel Jewel with Setting (Diamonds, Rubys, & Sapphires were used). **22.** Escapement Wheel. **23.** Fourth Wheel Jewel with Setting. **24.** Third Wheel. **25.** Fourth Wheel. **26.** Fourth Wheel Bridge. **27.** Third Wheel Jewel with Setting. **28.** Center & Third Wheel Bridge. **29.** Bridge Screw. **30.** Manufacturers Name & Location. **31.** Jewel Setting Screw.

# NOMENCLATURE
# OF
# WATCH PARTS

Ratchet Wheel

Crown or Main Wheel

Click Spring

Setting Cam

Bevel Pinion

Crown or Main
Screw Washer

Winding Arbor

Winding and
Setting Clutch

Setting Spring

Setting
Lever

Click

Setting
Spring Cam

Winding Sleeve

Clutch Lever

# NOMENCLATURE
# OF
# WATCH PARTS

Barrel

Center Wheel

Third Wheel

Fourth Wheel

Escape Wheel

Minute Wheel

Hour Wheel

Center Staff

Center Pinion

Center Arbor Washer

Third Pinion

Fourth Pinion

Escape Pinion

Cannon Pinion

Balance Staff

Pallet Fork and Arbor

Combination Roller

Barrel Arbor

Regulator

Balance Wheel

BRASS    STEEL

EFFECT OF HEAT    EFFECT OF COLD

MEAN TIME SCREWS

Overcoil Hairspring

# CASE PRICES

Case prices are for complete cases with bezel, crystal, stem, crown and bow. Hunting case style watches must have workable lift spring.

## SILVEROID CASES

| Size and Style | Avg | Ex-Fn | Mint |
|---|---|---|---|
| 18S, OF, SW | $15 | $20 | $30 |
| 18S, OF, KW | 35 | 40 | 50 |
| 18S, HC, SW | 40 | 50 | 65 |
| 18S, HC, KW | 50 | 60 | 80 |
| 16S, OF | 20 | 25 | 30 |
| 16S, HC | 40 | 45 | 50 |
| 12S, OF | 10 | 15 | 20 |
| 12S, HC | 40 | 45 | 50 |
| 6S-0S, OF | 10 | 15 | 20 |
| 6S-0S, HC | 35 | 40 | 50 |

## COIN-SILVER CASES

| Size and Style | Avg | Ex-Fn | Mint |
|---|---|---|---|
| 18S, OF, SW | $50 | $60 | $75 |
| 18S, OF, KW | 60 | 70 | 85 |
| 18S, HC, SW | 70 | 80 | 95 |
| 18S, HC, KW | 80 | 95 | 120 |
| 16S, OF | 40 | 50 | 65 |
| 16S, HC | 50 | 60 | 75 |
| 12S, OF | 20 | 25 | 35 |
| 12S, HC | 35 | 45 | 60 |
| 6S & 0S, OF | 15 | 20 | 25 |
| 6S & 0S, HC | 30 | 40 | 50 |

## GOLD-FILLED CASES

| Size and Style | Avg | Ex-Fn | Mint |
|---|---|---|---|
| 18S, OF, Plain | $55 | $65 | $85 |
| 18S, OF, Fancy or RR or Ex-Heavy | 75 | 85 | 120 |
| 18S, HC, Plain | 75 | 85 | 150 |
| 18S, HC, BOX & Fancy or Ex-Heavy | 150 | 175 | 225 |
| 18S, HC, MULTI-COLOR BOX & Fancy | 350 | 400 | 500 |
| 16S, OF, Plain | 50 | 60 | 75 |
| 16S, OF, Fancy or RR or Ex-Heavy | 70 | 85 | 120 |
| 16S, HC, Plain | 75 | 90 | 130 |
| 16S, HC, BOX & Fancy or Ex-Heavy | 200 | 250 | 300 |
| 16S, HC, MULTI-COLOR BOX & Fancy | 250 | 300 | 400 |
| 12S, OF, Plain | 20 | 30 | 40 |
| 12S, OF, Fancy or Ex-Heavy | 25 | 35 | 45 |
| 12S, HC, Plain | 35 | 45 | 60 |
| 12S, HC, Fancy or Ex-Heavy | 50 | 60 | 75 |
| 6S & 0S, OF, Plain | 15 | 20 | 30 |
| 6S & 0S, OF, Fancy or Ex-Heavy | 20 | 30 | 40 |
| 6S & 0S, HC, Plain | 25 | 30 | 45 |
| 6S & 0S, HC, BOX or Ex-Heavy | 65 | 80 | 125 |
| 6S & 0S, HC, MULTI-color BOX | 125 | 150 | 200 |

🕐 Note: Plain enamel single sunk dial bring $15 to $30.

## 14K SOLID GOLD CASES

| Size and Style | Avg | Ex-Fn | Mint |
|---|---|---|---|
| 18S, OF, Plain | $300 | $350 | $425 |
| 18S, OF, Fancy or RR or Ex-Heavy | 350 | 375 | 450 |
| 18S, HC, Plain | 375 | 425 | 475 |
| 18S, HC, Fancy or Ex-Heavy | 400 | 450 | 575 |
| 18S, HC, BOX & Fancy | 575 | 800 | 1,000 |
| 16S, OF, Plain | 250 | 275 | 350 |
| 16S, OF, Fancy or RR or Ex-Heavy | 300 | 325 | 375 |
| 16S, HC, Plain | 350 | 375 | 400 |
| 16S, HC, Fancy or Ex-Heavy | 375 | 400 | 450 |
| 16S, HC, BOX & Fancy | 425 | 550 | 750 |
| 12S, OF, Plain | 150 | 160 | 175 |
| 12S, OF, Fancy or Ex-Heavy | 200 | 235 | 285 |
| 12S, HC, Plain | 225 | 255 | 300 |
| 12S, HC, Fancy or Ex-Heavy | 265 | 285 | 325 |
| 6S & 0S, OF, | 125 | 155 | 185 |
| 6S & 0S, HC, Plain | 155 | 185 | 225 |
| 6S & 0S, HC, BOX or Heavy | 200 | 225 | 300 |

## 18K SOLID GOLD CASES

| Size and Style | Avg | Ex-Fn | Mint |
|---|---|---|---|
| 18S, OF, Plain | $500 | $550 | $625 |
| 18S, OF, Fancy or RR or Ex-Heavy | 550 | 600 | 725 |
| 18S, HC, Plain | 650 | 700 | 800 |
| 18S, HC, Fancy or Ex-Heavy | 750 | 800 | 1,000 |
| 18S, HC, BOX & Fancy | 1,000 | 1,200 | 1,500 |
| 16S, OF, Plain | 400 | 450 | 500 |
| 16S, OF, Fancy or RR or Ex-Heavy | 450 | 500 | 625 |
| 16S, HC, Plain | 500 | 600 | 725 |
| 16S, HC, Fancy or Ex-Heavy | 550 | 650 | 825 |
| 16S, HC, BOX & Fancy | 650 | 725 | 900 |
| 12S, OF, Plain | 250 | 275 | 335 |
| 12S, OF, Fancy or Ex-Heavy | 275 | 300 | 335 |
| 12S, HC, Plain | 350 | 375 | 425 |
| 12S, HC, Fancy or Ex-Heavy | 400 | 450 | 500 |
| 6S & 0S, OF, | 155 | 185 | 225 |
| 6S & 0S, HC, Plain | 200 | 250 | 300 |
| 6S & 0S, HC, BOX or Heavy | 300 | 365 | 450 |

## 14K MULTI–COLOR SOLID GOLD CASES

| Size and Style | Avg | Ex-Fn | Mint |
|---|---|---|---|
| 18S, OF, Plain | $650 | $700 | $800 |
| 18S, OF, BOX or Ex-Heavy | 1,000 | 1,200 | 1,500 |
| 18S, HC, Plain | 850 | 900 | 950 |
| 18S, HC, BOX | 1,500 | 2,000 | 2,500 |
| 18S, HC, BOX & Fancy or Ex-Heavy | 2,000 | 3,000 | 4,000 |
| 16S, OF, Plain | 500 | 650 | 700 |
| 16S, OF, BOX or Ex-Heavy | 650 | 700 | 750 |
| 16S, HC, Plain | 700 | 800 | 900 |
| 16S, HC, BOX | 800 | 900 | 1,100 |
| 16S, HC, BOX & Fancy or Ex-Heavy | 900 | 1,200 | 1,500 |
| 6S & 0S, OF, | 300 | 350 | 400 |
| 6S & 0S, HC, Plain | 400 | 450 | 500 |
| 6S & 0S, HC, BOX & Fancy or Ex-Heavy | 450 | 500 | 575 |

46

## INSPECTING OPEN-FACED WATCHES

For watches with a screw-on front and back, as in railroad models, hold the watch in the left hand and, with the right hand, turn the bezel counter clockwise. While removing the bezel, hold onto the stem and swing ring in order not to drop the watch. Lay the bezel down, check the dial for cracks and crazing, nicks, chips, etc. Look for lever and check to see that it will allow hands to be set. After close examination, **replace** the bezel and turn the watch over. Again, while holding the stem between the left thumb and index finger, remove the back cover. If it is a screw-on back cover, turn it counter clockwise. If it is a snap on cover, look for the lip on the back and use a pocket knife to pry the back off.

**Left**: Example of **OPEN FACE** case.   **Right**: Example of **DAMASKEENING**

## DAMASKEENING

A special American factory terminology used in all their advertisements or a American *IDIOM* or expression. Damaskeening (pronounced dam-a-skeening) is the process of applying ornate designs on metal by inlaying gold or by etching. Damaskeening on watch plates became popular in the late 1870s. This kind of beauty and quality in the movement was a direct result of the competition in the watch industry. Illinois, Waltham, Rockford, and Seth Thomas competed fiercely for beauty. Some damaskeening was in two colors of metal such as copper and nickel. The process may derive its name from Damascus, a city in Syria, most famous for its metal work. Damascening is a type of steel that was made with designs of wavy or variegated lines etched or inlaid on their swords.

⊕ **Damaskeening** is a special American terminology or a American idiom. In European terminology the word *Fausse Cotes* or *Geneva Stripes* is used.

# DISPLAY CASE WATCHES

Display case watches were used by salesmen and in jewelry stores to show the customer the movement. Both front and back had a glass crystal. These are not rare, but they are nice to have in a collection to show off a watch movement.

DISPLAY CASE with a bezel & glass crystal to view movement.

# WATCH CASE PRODUCTION

Before the Civil War, watchmaking was being done on a very small scale, and most of the companies in business were making their own movements as well as their own cases. After the War, tradesmen set up shops specializing exclusively in cases, while other artisans were making the movements. The case factories, because of mass production, could supply watch manufacturers with cases more economically than the manufacturers could produce their own.

A patent granted to James Boss on May 3, 1859, were not the first gold-filled cases made from sandwich-type sheets of metal, but Boss did invent a new process that proved to be very successful, resulting in a more durable case that he sold with a 20-year money-back guarantee.

...Gold
... Base Metal
... Gold

The illustrations at left is a sandwiched type gold-filled case.

# GOLD CASE WEIGHTS BY SIZE

| Size & Style of Case | Ex. Heavy | Heavy | Medium | Light | Ex. Light |
|---|---|---|---|---|---|
| | | **Pennyweights (DWT)** | | | |
| 18 size Hunting Case | 60 to 65 | 50 to 55 | 45 to 50 | 40 to 45 | 35 |
| 16 size Hunting Case | 55 to 60 | 45 to 50 | 40 to 45 | 35 to 40 | 32 |
| 18 size Open Face Case | | 40 to 45 | 38 | 35 | |
| 16 size Open Face Case | | 40 | 36 | 30 | |
| 12 size Open Face Case (Thin) | | | | | 14 |
| 6 size Hunting Case | 24 | 22 | 20 | 18 | |
| 0 size Hunting Case | | | | | 14 to 16 |

An 18 size movement with a full plate weighs 50 DWT; a 16 size movement with a ¾ plate weighs 35 DWT. These weights do not include the case.

TROY WEIGHT = 24 grains=1dwt., 1 Grain= 0.0648 grams, 20dwt = 1 OZ., 12oz = 1 LB.
NOTE: Gold & Silver Standards Vary from Country to Country. U.S.A. Coin Gold =.900 or 21 3/5K, Silver Coin=.900.
Gold Standards: 24K=1,000%or 1.0, 23K=.958 1/3, 22K=.916 2/3, 21K=.875, 20K=.833 1/3, 19K=.791 2/3, 18K=.750, 17K=.708 1/3, 16K=.666 2/3, 15K=.625, 14K=.583 1/3, 13K=.541 2/3, 12K=.500, 11=.458 1/3, 10K=.416 2/3, 9K= .375. 8K=.333 1/3, 7K=.291 2/3, 6K=.250, 5K=.208 1/3, 4K=.166 2/3, 3K=.125, 2K=.83 1/3, 1K=.41 2/3.

# CARE OF WATCHES

To some people a watch is just a device that keeps time. They do not know the history of its development nor how it operates. They have no appreciation for improvements made over the years. That the watch is a true miracle of mechanical genius and skill, is seldom more than a fleeting thought. The average person will know it must be wound to run, that it has a mainspring and possibly a hairspring. Some even realize there are wheels and gears and, by some strange method, these work in harmony to keep time. If for some reason the watch should stop, the owner will merely take it to a watch repair shop and await the verdict on damage and cost.

To be a good collector one must have some knowledge of the components of a watch and how they work and the history of the development of the watch. To buy a watch on blind faith is indeed risky, but many collectors do it every day because they have limited knowledge.

How does a watch measure time and perform so well? Within the case one can find the fulcrum, lever, gear, bearing, axle, wheel, screw, and the spring which overcomes nature's law of gravity. All these parts harmonize to provide an accurate reading minute by minute. A good collector will be able to identify all of them.

After acquiring a watch, you will want to take good care of it. A watch should be cleaned inside and out. Dirt will wear it out much faster, and gummy oil will restrict it and keep it from running all together. After the watch has been cleaned it should be stored in a dry place. Rust is the No. 1 enemy. A watch is a delicate instrument but, if it is given proper care, it will provide many years of quality service. A pocket watch should be wound at regular intervals about once every 24 hours, early each morning so the mainspring has its full power to withstand the abuse of daily use. Do not carry a watch in the same pocket with articles that will scratch or tarnish the case. A fully wound watch can withstand a jar easier than a watch that has been allowed to run down. Always wind a watch and leave it running when you ship it. If you are one who enjoys carrying a watch be sure to have it cleaned at least once every two years.

# EXAMINATION AND INSPECTION OF A WATCH BEFORE PURCHASING

The examination and inspection of a watch before purchasing is of paramount importance. This is by no means a simple task for there are many steps involved in a complete inspection.

The first thing you should do is to listen to a watch and see how it sounds. Many times the trained ear can pick up problems in the escapement and balance. The discriminating buyer will know that sounds cannot be relied on entirely because each watch sounds different, but the sound test is worthwhile and is comparable to the doctor putting the stethoscope to a patient's heart as his first source of data.

Check the bow to see if it is securely fastened to the case and look at the case to see if correction is necessary at the joints. The case should close firmly at both the back and front. (Should the case close too firmly, rub the rim with beeswax which will ease the condition and prolong the life of the rim.)

Take note of the dents, scratches, wear and other evidences of mis-use. Does the watch have a generally good appearance? Check the bezel for proper fit and the crystal to see if it is free of chips.

Remove the bezel and check the dial for chips and hairline cracks. Look for stains and discoloration; and check to see if the dial is loose. It is important to note that a simple dial with only a single sunk dial is by nature a stronger unit due to the fact that a double sunk dial is constructed of three separate pieces.

If it is a stem-winder, try winding and setting. Problems in this area can be hard to correct. Parts are hard to locate and may possibly have to be handmade. If it is a lever set, pull the lever out to see if it sets properly into gear. Also check to see that the hands have proper clearance.

Now that the external parts have been inspected, open the case to view the movement. Check to see that the screws hold the movement in place securely. Note any repair marks and any missing screws. Make a visual check for rust and discoloration, dust, dirt and general appearance. If the movement needs cleaning and oiling, this should be deducted from the price of the watch, as well as any repair that will have to be made.

Note the quality of the movement. Does it have raised gold jewel settings or a gold train (center wheel or all gears)? Are the jewels set in or pressed in? Does it have gold screws in the balance wheel? Sapphire pallets? Diamond end stones? Jeweled motor barrel? How many adjustments does it have? Does it have overall beauty and eye appeal?

Examine the balance for truth. First look directly down upon the balance to detect error truth in the roundness. Then look at it from the side to detect error in the flat swing or rotation. It should be smooth in appearance.

Examine the hairspring in the same manner to detect errors in truth. When a spring is true in the round, there will be no appearance of jumping when it is viewed from the upper side. The coils will appear to uniformly dilate and contract in perfect rhythm when the balance is in motion. Check the exposed portion of the train wheels for burred, bent, or broken teeth. Inspect pinions and pivots for wear. If a watch has complicated features such as a repeater, push the slides, plungers, and buttons to see that they are in good working order.

After the movement and case have been examined to your satisfaction and all the errors and faults are found, talk to the owner as to the history and his personal thoughts about the watch. Is the movement in the original case? Is the dial the original one? Just what has been replaced?

Has the watch been cleaned? Does it need any repairs? If so, can the seller recommend anyone to repair the watch?

Finally, see if the seller makes any type of guarantee, and get an address and phone number. It may be valuable if problems arise, or if you want to buy another watch in the future.

# HOW A WATCH WORKS

There are five basic components of a watch:
1. The mainspring, and its winding mechanism, which provides power.
2. The train which consists of gears, wheels & pinions that turn the hands.
3. The escapement consisting of the escape wheel and balance that regulates or controls.
4. The dial and hands that tell the time & setting mechanism.
5. The housing consisting of the case and plates that protect.

A watch is a machine with a power source that drives the escapement through a train of gears, and it has a subsidiary train to drive a hand. The motion of the balance serves the watch the same as a pendulum serves a clock. The balance wheel and roller oscillate in each direction moving the fork and lever by means of a roller jewel or pin. As the lever moves back and forth it allows the escape wheel to unlock at even intervals (about 1/5 sec.) and causes the train of gears to move in one direction under the power of the mainspring. Thus, the mainspring is allowed to be let down or unwind one pulse at a time.

## WATCH MOVEMENT PARTS

Mechanical watches are small engines powered by a spring, which keeps the balance in motion. The **uniformity** of this motion relies on the balance and escapement; the **durability** rests on the quality of material and construction of the complete movement.

## TRAIN OF A ELGIN MOVEMENT
## & EACH PART NAMED

| | |
|---|---|
| 1 Main Wheel. | 26 Fork. |
| 2 Main Wheel Washer. | 27 Pallet. |
| 3 Main Screw. | 28 Pallet Stones. |
| 4 Ratchet Wheel. | 29 Roller Jewel Pin. |
| 5 Ratchet Wheel Washer. | 30 Safety Roller. |
| 6 Jewel Setting. | 31 Table Roller. |
| 7 Barrel Arbor. | 32 Banking Screws. |
| 8 Barrel Arbor Hub. | 33 Breg. Hair Spring. |
| 9 Barrel Hub Screw. | 34 Hair Spring Stud. |
| 10 Barrel Hub. | 35 Hair Spring Collet. |
| 11 Barrel. | 36 Balance Staff. |
| 12 Main Spring Hooked. | 37 Regulator. |
| 13 Main Spring. | 38 Balance. |
| 14 Recoiling Click. | 39 Index. |
| 15 Click Screw. | 40 Reg. Adj. Nut. |
| 16 First Wheel. | 41 Hour Hand. |
| 17 Center Wheel. | 42 Minute Hand. |
| 18 Center Pinion. | 43 Minute Wheel. |
| 19 Third Pinion. | 44 Hour Wheel. |
| 20 Third Wheel. | 45 Setting Wheel. |
| 21 Fourth Wheel. | 46 Winding Arbor. |
| 22 Fourth Pinion. | 47 Wind. & Set. Clutch. |
| 23 Escape Pinion | 48 Bevel Pinion. |
| 24 Escape Wheel. | **49 Pendant Bar.** |
| 25 Second Hand. | |

First Wheel 78 Teeth, 1 Rev. in 6 Hours, 30 Minutes.

Center Pinion 12 Teeth, 1 Rev. in 1 Hour.

Center Wheel 80 Teeth, 1 Rev. in 1 Hour.

3rd Pinion 10 Teeth, 1 Rev. in 7½ Minutes.

3rd Wheel 75 Teeth, 1 Rev. in 7½ Minutes.

4th Pinion 10 Teeth, 1 Rev. in 1 Minute.

4th Wheel 80 Teeth, 1 Rev. in 1 Minute.

Escape Pinion 8 Teeth, 1 Rev. in 6 Seconds.

Escape Wheel 15 Teeth, 1 Rev. in 6 Seconds.

Balance Vibrates 30 times in 6 Seconds.

300 times in 1 Minute.

18,000 times in 1 Hour.

432,000 times in 1 Day.

157,680,000 times in 1 Year.

Power unit for modern watch showing the various parts.

Early style watch with a stackfreed (tear shaped cam). Note the balance is dumbell shaped.

# THE MAINSPRING

Watches were developed from the early portable clocks. The coiled spring or mainspring provided the drive power. The first coiled springs were applied to clocks about 1450. For the small portable watch, coiled springs were first used about 1470. The power from a mainspring is not consistent and this irregular power was disastrous to the first watches.

The Germans' answer to irregular power was a device called a stackfreed. Another apparatus employed was the fusee. The fusee proved to be the best choice. At first catgut was used between the spring barrel and fusee. By around 1660 the catgut was replaced by a chain. Today, the fusee is still used in naval chronometers. One drawback to the fusee is the amount of space it takes up in the watch. Generally, the simplest devices are best.

The mainspring is made of a piece of hardened and tempered steel about 20 inches long and coiled in a closed barrel between the upper and lower plates of the movement. It is matched in degree of strength, width, and thickness most suitable for the watch's need or design. It is subject to differing conditions of temperature and tensions (the wound-up position having the greatest tension). The lack of uniformity in the mainspring affects the time keeping qualities of a watch.

The power assembly in a watch consists of the mainspring, mainspring barrel, arbor, and cap. The mainspring furnishes the power to run the watch. It is coiled around the arbor and is contained in the mainspring barrel, which is cylindrical and has a gear on it which serves as the first wheel of the train. The arbor is a cylindrical shaft with a hook for the mainspring in the center of the body. The cap is a flat disk which snaps into a recess in the barrel. A hook on the inside of the mainspring barrel is for attaching the mainspring to the barrel.

The mainspring is made of a long thin strip of steel, hardened to give the desired resiliency. Mainsprings vary in size but are similar in design; they have a hook on the outer end to attach to the mainspring barrel, and a hole in the inner end to fasten to the mainspring barrel arbor.

**Mainspring Bridles** showing a few different designs.

By turning the crown clockwise, the barrel arbor is rotated and the mainspring is wound around it. The mainspring barrel arbor is held stationary after winding by means of the ratchet wheel and click. As the mainspring uncoils, it causes the mainspring barrel to revolve. The barrel is meshed with the pinion on the center wheel, and as it revolves it sets the train wheels in motion. Pocket and wrist watches, in most cases, will run up to 40 hours on one winding.

**Jeweled Motor Barrel Unit:** 1. Barrel top jewel screw. 2. Barrel top jewel and setting. 3. Ratchet wheel. 4. Barrel bridge. 5. Barrel hub. 6. Barrel head. 7. Mainspring (in barrel). 8. Barrel. 9. Barrel arbor (riveted to barrel). 10. Barrel lower jewel and setting. 11. Pillar plate.

CLICKS

A **click** acts on the teeth of the ratchet wheel, so that the barrel-arbor can turn in one direction only, that of the winding. The click is made to mesh constantly with the ratchet teeth by the click spring. In older watches a device known as **stop-work** which restricted the two extremes of the mainspring was used. A modern watch uses the **click-work** which prevents the mainspring from being *over wound* by a certain amount of recoil.

Curb pins adjusted
to vary the length
of hairspring

Fig. 1

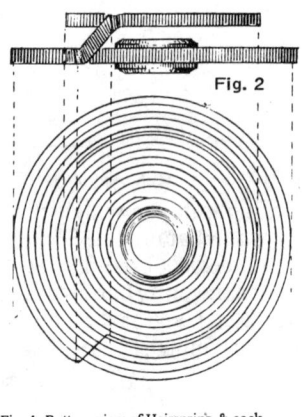

Fig. 2

Fig. 1. Bottom view of Hairspring & cock
Fig. 2. Aside and top view of hairspring

## THE HAIRSPRING

The hairspring is the brain of the watch and is kept in motion by the mainspring. The hairspring is the most delicate tension spring made. It is a piece of flat wire about 12 inches long, 1/100th of an inch wide, 0.05mm or 0.0019685 inches thick, and weighs only about 1/9,000th of a pound. Thousands of these hairsprings can be made from one pound of steel. The hairspring controls the action of the balance wheel. The hairspring steel is drawn through the diamond surfaces to a third the size of a human hair. There are two kinds of hairsprings in the watches of later times, the flat one and the Breguet. The Breguet (named for its French inventor) is an overcoil given to the spring.

There are two methods for overcoil, the oldest is the way the spring is bent by hand; and with the other method the overcoil is bent or completed in a form at one end and at the same time is hardened and tempered in the form. The hairspring contracts and expands 432,000 times a day.

A modern style (Am. Waltham) regulator. Note the triangular shaped hairspring stud which is located on the balance bridge between the screw and curb pin.

# REGULATORS
## Identification

Overcoil concentric to travel of regulator pins
Regulator pins
Curve of Hairspring overcoil
Hairspring stud
Hairspring stud screw
Regulator
Balance Cock

E. Howard & Co.

South Bend

Waltham

Breguet

Swiss

Ball Hamilton 18s

Ball Elgin 18s

Ball Hamilton 16s

Ball Illinois 16s

Ball Waltham 16s

Hampden

Marion

E.Howard & Co.

J.P. Stevens

F R S

Agassiz

Waltham

Petek Philippe

swiss- 2 piece

Fasoldt

Hampden

U.S. Waltham

U.S. Waltham

Waltham

# REGULATORS
## Identification

Fredonia & Peoria

J. Jurgensen

Keystone

Keystone

Waltham

Otay

U.S. Waltham

Elgin

Illinois

Elgin COCK

Improved Swiss

Rockford

Thomas Tompion
1638-1700

Columbus

Hamilton

English & American 1800-1850

Undersprung

Nathaniel Barrow 1750

Grossman Glasshutte

Elevation of a **GEAR-TRAIN**

(a.) barrel, (b.) center wheel ( carries Minute hand ), (c.) third wheel, (d.) fourth wheel ( carries seconds hand ), (e.) escape wheel **8 day watches** use a *intermediate* ( 8 day wheel ) placed between the barrel and the center wheel.

# THE TRAIN

The time train consists of the mainspring barrel, center wheel and pinion, third wheel and pinion, fourth wheel and pinion, and escape wheel which is part of the escapement. The function of the time train is to reduce the power of the mainspring and extend its time to 36 hours or more. The mainspring supplies energy in small units to the escapement, and the escapement delays the power from being spent too quickly.

The long center wheel arbor projects through the pillar plate and above the dial to receive the cannon pinion and hour wheel. The cannon pinion receives the minute hand and the hour wheel the hour hand. As the mainspring drives the barrel, the center wheel is rotated once each hour.

Alignment of chain driven fusee with train. **Fusee** at right and main-spring barrel at left. Note chain between fusee and main-spring barrel.

Actual alignment of **Train Unit**

58

The second or center wheel of the watch turns once every hour. It is the second largest wheel in the watch, and the arbor or post of the center wheel carries the minute hand. The center wheel pinion is in mesh with the mainspring barrel (pinions follow and the wheel supplies the power). The center wheel is in mesh with the third wheel pinion (the third wheel makes eight turns to each turn of the center wheel). The third wheel is in mesh with the fourth wheel pinion, and the fourth wheel pinion is in mesh with the escape wheel pinion. The fourth wheel post carries the second hand and is in a 1:60 ratio to the center wheel (the center wheel turns once every hour and the fourth wheel turns 60 turns every hour). The escape wheel has 15 teeth (shaped like a flat foot) and works with two pallets on the lever. The two pallet jewels lock and unlock the escape wheel at intervals (1/5 sec.) allowing the train of gears to move in one direction under the influence of the mainspring. The lever (quick train) vibrates 18,000 times to one turn of the center wheel (every hour). The hour hand works from a motion train. The mainspring barrel generally makes about five turns every 36 hours.

## SOLID GOLD TRAIN

Some watches have a gold train instead of brass wheels. These watches are more desirable. To identify gold wheels within the train, look at a Hamilton 992; the center wheel is made of gold and the other wheels are made of brass. Why a gold train? Gold is soft, but it has a smooth surface and it molds easily. Therefore, the wheels have less friction. These wheels do not move fast, and a smooth action is more important than a hard metal. Gold does not tarnish or rust and is non-magnetic. The arbors and pinions in these watches will be steel. Many watches have some gold in them, and the collector should learn to distinguish it.

Balance Wheel

Pallet

Verge

Pallet

Contrate Wheel

Crown or Escape Wheel

ABOVE: **Verge Escapement**

## TYPES OF ESCAPEMENTS

The verge escapement is the earliest form of escapement. It was first used in clocks as far back as the early 1300s. The verge escapement consists of a crown escape wheel, a verge which has two flags called pallets, and a balance. Early German watches had a balance shaped like a dumbbell, called a "foliot." Later most other watches used a balance shaped like a wheel. The crude weights of the foliot could be adjusted closer to or farther from the center of the balance for better time keeping. Another design from that period was the circular balance. The circular balance was used by Christian Huygens in 1675 when he introduced the hairspring. This remarkable invention was used from that time onward.

The verge escapement was used by Luther Goddard in America as well as most of the Colonial watchmakers.

Movement of the common chain driven fusee & verge escapement.

**A**- is the **barrel** containing the mainspring. **B** - is the **fusee**, to which the key is applied in winding, and which is connected with the barrel by the chain **b**. **C**- is the **fusee-wheel**, called also the **first** or **great wheel**, which turns with the fusee, and works into the pinion **D**, called the **center-wheel pinion**. This pinion, with the **center-wheel**, or **second wheel**, **E**, turns once in an hour. The center-wheel E works into the **third-wheel** pinion **F**; and on the same arbor is **G**, the **third wheel**, which drives the **fourth** or **contrate-wheel pinion H**, and along with it the **contrate wheel I**. The teeth of this wheel are placed at right angles to its plane, and act in the pinion **K**, called the **balance-wheel pinion**, **L** being the **balance-wheel**, **escape-wheel**, or **crown-wheel**. The escape-wheel acts on the two **pallets**, **m** and **n**, attached to the **verge**, or arbor, of the balance **M**, which regulates the movement.

ABOVE: **Cylinder Escapement**

About 1725 the cylinder escapement was invented by George Graham, an Englishman. His cylinder escapement was a great improvement over the verge. Even so, the cylinder escapement was not popular until Abraham Louis Breguet adopted the idea in the late 1700s.

**Cylinder Escapement**

**Duplex Escapement**

Balance Wheel

Impulse Pin

Short Impulse Tooth

Long Tooth

Escape Wheel

Illustrating and American form of the
**Duplex Escapement** as first employed
by the Waterbury Watch Co.

Impulse Pin

Long Tooth

Escape Wheel

Short Impulse Tooth

61

**VIRGULE ESCAPEMENT**

**CYLINDER ESCAPEMENT**

**PIVOTED DETENT**

Escape wheel teeth: A,B,C

Spring detent

Passing spring

Locking pallet

Escape wheel
Pallet #2
Pallet #1

Staff

**SPRING DETENT** ( chronometer escapement )

The duplex escapement is accredited generally to Pierre LeRoy, a Frenchman, around 1750, but was never popular in France. This type of escapement was favored in England up to the mid 1850s. The New England Watch Co. of Waterbury, Conn., used the duplex from 1898 until 1910. The Waterbury Watch Company used it from 1880 to 1898.

The roller and lever action escapement was invented by Thomas Mudge in 1750.

Rack and pinion lever escapement. 1. Balance wheel pinion. 2. Rack. 3. Lever. 4. Ratchet escape wheel.

Right Angle Lever or Detached Escapement which was used in earlier American made watches. P = *pallet*.

The rack and pinion lever escapement was invented by Hautefeuille in 1722. The famous Breguet used the detached lever escapement early in the 1800s. By 1830 the English watchmakers had established the superiority of the lever escapement. In France and Switzerland the teeth of the lever escapement wheel were boot-shaped to provide a wider impulse plane. In England, pointed or ratchet teeth were preferred, and the right-angle lever was preferred over the straight line lever, also referred to as the Swiss lever. Pitkins and Custer both used the lever escapements. The right-angle lever was used in the Warren & Samuel Curtis as well as early Elgin, Newark, Tremont, New York, early Hampden, early Illinois, and Cornell watches. The American factories settled on a Swiss style escapement (straight line lever and club tooth escape wheel) by the 1870s.

## Purpose of Escape Wheel

If a movement consisted only of the mainspring and a train of wheels, and the mainspring were wound up, the train would run at full speed resulting in the power being spent in a few moments. For this reason, the escapement has been arranged to check it. The duty of the escapement is to allow each tooth of the escape wheel to pass at a regulated interval. The escapement is of no service alone and, therefore, must have some other arrangement to measure and regulate these intervals. This is accomplished by the balance assembly.

The escape wheel is in most cases made of steel and is staked on a pinion and arbor. It is the last wheel of the train and connects the train with the escapement. It is constructed so that the pallet jewels move in and out between its teeth, allowing but one tooth to escape at a time, turnstile fashion. The teeth are club-foot-shaped because of the addition of impulse face to the end of the teeth.

The pallet jewels are set at an angle to make their inside corners reach over three teeth and two spaces of the escape wheel. The outside corners of the jewels will reach over two teeth and three spaces of the escape wheel with a small amount of clearance. At the opposite end of the pallet, directly under the center of the fork slot, is a steel or brass pin called the guard pin. The fork is the connecting link to the balance assembly.

## BALANCE AND HAIRSPRING

The rotation of the balance wheel is controlled by the hairspring. The inner end of the hairspring is pinned to the collet, and the collet is held friction-tight

**EXAMPLE OF FLAT HAIRSPRING**

**EXAMPLE OF BREGUET OR OVERCOIL HAIRSPRING**

64

on the staff above the balance wheel. The outer end of the hairspring is pinned to a stud which is held stationary on the balance cock by the stud screw. The roller jewel is cemented in the large roller assembly, which is mounted on the staff directly under the balance wheel. Under the first roller is a smaller one which acts as a safety roller. This is necessary because of the crescent cut out in the roller table which allows the guard pin of the escapement assembly to pass through.

The balance wheel rotates clockwise and counterclockwise on its axis by means of the impulse it receives from the escapement. The motion of the balance wheel is constant due to the coiling and uncoiling of the hairspring. The impulse, transmitted to the roller jewel by the swinging of the pallet fork to the left, causes the balance to rotate in a counterclockwise direction. The position of the fork allows the roller jewel to move out of the slot of the fork freely and in the same direction. The fork continues on until it reaches the banking pin. Meanwhile the balance continues in the same direction until the tension of the hairspring overcomes the momentum of the balance wheel. When this occurs the balance returns to its original position, which causes the roller jewel to again enter the slot of the fork.

**Modern or Swiss Lever Escapement**

A. Lever
B. Entrance pallet
C. Exit pallet
D. Fork
E. Banking pins
F. Fork slot
G. Horns
H. Impulse roller jewel
K. Safety finger
L. Notch of small plate M
M. Safety roller
N. Roller table
P. Impulse plane of the teeth of the wheel
R. Escape wheel

**Pallet and Escape Tooth Action**. The momentum that has been built up during the return of the balance, causes the roller pin to impart an impulse on the inside of the fork slot. This impulse is great enough to push the fork away from its position against the banking pin. As the fork is pushed away, it causes the pallet stone to slide on the toe of the escape wheel tooth. When the pallet stone has slid down to its edge, it frees the escape wheel tooth, thereby unlocking the escape wheel. The escape wheel, being impelled by the force of the mainspring, starts to rotate. As the escape wheel turns, the tooth glides along the impulse face of the pallet jewel, forcing it to move out of the way. The moving pallet carries the fork with it and imparts the impulse to the roller jewel. The right pallet stone intercepts a tooth of the escape wheel to lock it, as the fork moves toward the banking pin. Having a short "run" left to the banking pin, the pressure of the escape wheel tooth against the locking face of the pallet jewel draws the stone deeper into the escape wheel and, therefore, causes the fork to complete its run and holds it against the banking pin. Meanwhile the balance continues in a clockwise direction until the tension of the hairspring overcomes the momentum of the balance and returns it to its original position.

**Rate of Escape Tooth Release**. Through the motion of the escapement, the mainspring keeps the balance vibrating, and the balance regulates the train. The escape wheel has 15 teeth and is allowed to revolve 10 turns per minute. Thus, 150 teeth glide over each pallet stone in 1 minute. The gliding of the escape wheel teeth over the impulse faces of the pallet stones will cause the balance to vibrate 300 vibrations or beats per minute. These vibrations will continue until the force of the mainspring is spent.

## SCREWS

Screws used in watches are very small and precise. These screws measure 254 threads to the inch and 47,000 of them can be put into a thimble. The screws were hardened and tempered and polished to a cold hard brilliance. By looking at these screws through a magnifying glass one can see the uniformity.

## EQUIDISTANT ESCAPEMENT

The term Equidistant Escapement is a form of lever escapement. The locking of each pallet takes place at the same distance from the pallet arbor. A similar form of escapement is the circular pallet with the circular form of escapement. The impulses are given at equal distance from the center line. The Swiss preferred the equidistant while the Americans preferred the circular. There is little difference in performance between these two types of escapement.

Equidistant form of Escapement

Circular form of Escapement

TRAIN BRIDGE

ESCAPE BRIDGE

PALLET BRIDGE

WATCH — TRAIN SIDE

BALANCE COCK

PILLAR PLATE

BARREL BRIDGE

The plates and bridges which hold all the parts in proper relation to each other.

# THE PLATES

The movement of a watch has two plates and the works are sandwiched in between. The plates are called the top plate and the pillar plate. The top plate fully covers the movement. The 3/4 plate watch and the balance cock are flush and about 1/4 of a full plate is cut out to allow for the balance, thus the 3/4 plate. The bridge style watch has two or three fingers to hold the wheels in place and together are called a bridge. The term bridge (horologically) is one that is anchored at both ends. A cock is a wheel support that is attached at one end only. English balance cock for verge watches and lever watches have but one screw. French and Dutch verge watches have their balance bridges secured at both ends. The metal is generally brass, but on better grade watches, nickel is used. The full plate is held apart by four pillars. In older watches the pillars were very fancy, and the plates were pinned, not screwed, together. The plates can be gilded or engraved when using brass. Some of the nickel plates have damaskeening. There are a few watches with plates made of gold. The plates are also used to hold the jewels, settings, etc. Over 30 holes are drilled in each plate for pillars, pivots, and screws.

The pinion is the smaller of the two wheels that exist on the shaft or arbor. They are small steel gears and usually have six teeth called leaves. Steel is used wherever there is great strain, but where there is much friction, steel and brass are used together; one gear of brass, and a pinion of steel. After the leaves have been cut, the pinions are hardened, tempered, and polished.

LEFT = PILLAR PLATE          RIGHT = TOP PLATE -( 3/4 plate )

### THE FUSEE WAS INVENTED IN 1525
1. MAINSPRING BARREL     2. FUSEE CHAIN     3. FUSEE WHEEL

## THE FUSEE

A mainspring gives less and less power as it lets down. To equalize the power a fusee was first used. Fusee leverage increases as the main spring lets down. A fusee is smaller at the top for a full mainspring. When the chain is at the bottom, the mainspring is almost spent, and the fusee has more leverage. Leonardo da Vinci is said to have invented the fusee.

When the mainspring is fully wound, it also pulls the hardest. At that time the chain is at the small end of the fusee. As the spring grows weaker, the chain descends to the larger part of the fusee. In shifting the tension, it equalizes the power.

On the American watch, the fusee was abandoned for the most part in 1850 and an adjustment is used on the hairspring and balance wheel to equalize the power through the 24 hours. When a watch is first wound the mainspring has no more power than it does when it is nearly run down. With or without the fusee, the number of parts in a watch are about the same: close to 300.

The above is a HAMILTON MODEL 21 **FUSEE** used in a Ships **Chronometer**.

1. Illustration of pivot before 1700. 2. Pivot used in early 1700s. 3. Pivot used in late 1700s to present

## JEWELS AND PIVOTS

Before 1700, holes were drilled only part way into the plates and the pivot rested directly on the bottom of the hole, as in Illustration No. 1. The shoulder of the pivot was above the plate, however, reducing part of the function, as in Illustration No. 1A.

In the early 1700s, a French watchmaker, Sully, improved the pivot friction as seen in Illustration No. 2B. Illustration No. 3 shows a later improvement. Perfected by Julien Le Roy.

N.F. de Duiller of Geneva, in conjunction with Peter and Jacob Debaufre, French immigrants living in London, developed a method of piercing jewels. This method was patented in 1704; however, it was not until around 1800 that holed jewels started to appear in watch movements and then only in high grade watches.

In the mid-1800s experiments were already being made for artificial rubies. In 1891 Fremy solved the problem and by the early 1900s the reconstructed ruby was popular.

A WASHINGTON WATCH CO. WATCH UNDER A MAGNIFYING GLASS

# SHOCK ABSORBERS

When a watch is dropped or subjected to a hard shock, the balance and pivots usually suffer the most.

A shock-resisting device was invented by Breguet in 1789; he called it a parachute. This device was a spring steel arm supporting the endstone. The parachute gives a cushioning effect to the balance staff.

The American pocket watch industry tried to find a device to protect pocket watch pivots, but it was the Swiss who perfected the devices for wristwatches around 1930.

**Above:** Incabloc 1st used about 1933.
**Left:** Parachute 1st used about 1800.
**Below:** Illustrates shock absorbing system. Note end stone and spring in raised position giving a cushioning effect to the balance staff.

Above: Incabloc spring, cap-jewel, hole jewel, bearing block & balance-staff.

Friction **CENTER JEWEL**

**RUBY**

**ROLLER JEWEL**

**BALANCE HOLE JEWEL**

**CURVED**

**FLAT**

Friction **CAP JEWEL**

**RUBY**

Friction **PLATE JEWEL**

**RUBY**

Receiving pallet stone    Discharging pallet stone

**TYPES OF JEWELS.** Watch jewels are of four distinct types, each type having a particular function.

(1) **HOLE JEWELS.** Hole jewels are used to form the bearing surface for wheel arbors and balance staff pivots.

(2) **CAP JEWELS.** Cap jewels (also called end stones) are flat jewels. They are positioned at the ends of wheel staffs, outside the hole jewels, and limit the end thrust of the staff.

(3) **ROLLER JEWELS.** The roller jewel (pin) is positioned on the roller table to receive the impulse for the balance from the fork.

(4) **PALLET JEWELS.** The pallet jewels (stones) are the angular shaped jewels positioned in the pallet to engage the teeth of the escape wheel.

### JEWEL COUNT

Jewels are used as bearings to reduce metal-to-metal contacts which produce friction and wear. They improve the performance and accuracy of the watch, and materially prolong its usefulness. The materials used for making watch jewels are diamonds, sapphires, rubies, and garnets. The diamond is the hardest but is seldom used except for cap jewels. The sapphire is the next in hardness and is the most commonly used because of its fine texture. Garnets are softer than sapphires and rubies.

**Number and Location of Jewels.** Most watches have either 7, 9, 11, 15, 17, 19, 21, or 23 jewels. The location of the jewels varies somewhat in different makes and grades, but the general practice is as follows:

**7-JEWEL WATCHES.** Seven-jewel watches have: one hole jewel at each end of the balance staff; one cap jewel at each end of the balance staff; one roller jewel; and two pallet jewels.

**9-JEWEL WATCHES.** These have the seven jewels mentioned in 7-jewel watches, with the addition of a hole jewel at each end of the escape wheel.

**11-JEWEL WATCHES.** In these, seven are used in the escapement as in 7-jewel watches. In addition, the four top pivots (the third wheel, the fourth wheel, the escape wheel, and the pallet) are jeweled.

**15-JEWEL WATCHES.** These watches have the nine jewels found in 9-jewel watches, with the addition of the following: one hole jewel at each end of the pallet staff; one hole jewel at each end of the fourth wheel staff; and one hole jewel at each end of the third-wheel staff.

**17-JEWEL WATCHES.** The 15 jewels in 15-jewel watches are used with the addition of one hole jewel located at each end of the center wheel staff.

Two views showing upper and lower jewel locations in the plates and bridges.

**19-JEWEL WATCHES**. In these watches, the jewels are distributed as in the 17-jewel watch, with the addition of one for each pivot of the **barrel & mainspring**.

**21-JEWEL WATCHES**. The jewels in these are distributed as in the 17-jeweled grade, with the addition of two cap jewels (**USUALLY** placed on the pallet arbor and escape wheel ) or 2 jewels for the barrel & mainspring.

| | | | |
|---|---|---|---|
| Center Wheel — 2 | Center Wheel— 2 | Center Wheel— 2 | Center Wheel— 2 |
| Third Wheel — 2 | Third Wheel — 2 | Third Wheel — 2 | Third Wheel — 2 |
| Fourth Wheel — 2 | Fourth Wheel— 2 | Fourth Wheel— 2 | Fourth Wheel— 2 |
| Escape Wheel— 2 | Escape Wheel—2 | Escape Wheel—2+2 | Escape Wheel— 2+2 |
| Pallet & Arbor— 4 | **Barrel Arbor** — 2 | Pallet & Arbor— 4+2 | **Barrel Arbor** — 2 |
| Balance Staff — 4 | Pallet & Arbor— 4 | Balance Staff — 4 | Pallet & Arbor— 4+2 |
| Roller jewel — 1 | Balance Staff — 4 | Roller jewel — 1 | Balance Staff — 4 |
| TOTAL — 17J | Roller jewel — 1 | TOTAL—21J | Roller jewel — 1 |
| | TOTAL — 19J | | TOTAL— 23J |

**23-JEWEL WATCHES**. The jewels are distributed as in the 21-jewel watch, with the addition of one for each pivot of the **barrel & mainspring**.

**24J., 25J., and 26 JEWEL WATCHES**. In all of these watches, the additional jewels were distributed as cap jewels. These were not very functional but were offered as **prestige** movements for the person who wanted more. **In many cases, these jewel arrangements varied according to manufacturer. All jeweled watches may <u>NOT</u> fit these descriptions.**

Location of jewels in balance

# WINDING AND SETTING

The simplest, but not the most practical method for winding up the mainspring of a pocket watch was to wind the barrel staff by means of a key, but then it is necessary to open up the watch case. And the key method of winding proved unpopular, as oftentimes the key became lost.

WINDING & SETTING PARTS

| | | | |
|---|---|---|---|
| 1. Ratchet Wheel | 6. Stem and Crown | 10. Clutch Lever | 14. Hour Wheel |
| 2. Crown Wheel | 7. Winding Pinion | 11. Clutch Lever Spring | 15. Minute Wheel |
| 3. Crown Wheel Center | 8. Clutch Wheel | 12. Setting Wheel | 16. Dial Washer |
| 4. Click | 9. Setting Lever | 13. Yoke | 17. Cannon Pinion |
| 5. Click Spring | | | |

WINDING MECHANISM. a-Winding and setting clutch. p-Winding pinion. b-Barrel. r-Ratchet wheel. c-Crown or main wheel. t- Winding arbor.

The modern principle of the winding of the mainspring and hand setting by pulling on the crown, dates back to 1842. We owe this combination to Adrian Philippe, associate of Patek, of Geneva.

The winding and setting mechanism consists of the stem, crown, winding pinion, clutch wheel, setting wheel, setting lever, clutch lever, clutch spring, crown wheel, and ratchet wheel. When the stem is pushed in, the clutch lever throws the clutch wheel to winding position. Then, when the stem is turned clockwise, it causes the winding pinion to turn the crown and ratchet wheels. The ratchet wheel is fitted on the square of the mainspring arbor and is held in place with a screw. When the stem and crown are turned, the ratchet wheel turns and revolves the arbor which winds the mainspring, thereby giving motive power to the train. Pulling the stem and crown outward pushes the setting lever against the clutch lever, engaging the clutch wheel with the setting wheel. The setting wheel is in constant mesh with the minute wheel; therefore, turning the stem and crown permits setting the hands to any desired time.

**SETTING MECHANISM.** Clutch a. meshes with m. and the minute works wheel b. The minute works wheel meshes with the cannon pinion h. The hour cannon d. bears the hour hand H. C. center wheel M. Minute hand.

The dial train consists of the cannon pinion, minute, and hour wheels. The cannon pinion is a hollow steel pinion which is mounted on the center wheel arbor. A stud which is secured in the pillar plate holds the minute wheel in mesh with the cannon pinion. A small pinion is attached to the minute wheel which is meshed with the hour wheel.

The center arbor revolves once per hour. A hand affixed to the cannon pinion on the center arbor would travel around the dial once per hour. This hand is used to denote minutes. The hour wheel has a pipe that allows the hour wheel to telescope over the cannon pinion. The hour wheel meshes with the minute wheel pinion. This completes the train of the cannon pinion, minute wheel, and hour wheel. The ratio between the cannon pinion and the hour wheel is 12 to 1; therefore, the hand affixed to the hour wheel is to denote the hours. With this arrangement, time is recorded and read.

A—PINION
B—CLUTCH WHEEL
C—SETTING WHEEL
D—MINUTE WHEEL
E—CANNON PINION
F—HOUR WHEEL
G—CLUTCH LEVER
H—SETTING SPRING
J—SETTING SPRING CAM

# AUTOMATIC WINDING.

The self-winding watch uses the movements of the body in order to wind up the mainspring slowly and nearly continuously. The first pocket self-winding watches were executed by a watchmaker from Le Locle, Abraham-Louis Perrelet, around 1770. They were improved soon after by Abraham-Louis Breguet. In the case of the pocket watch, the movements causing the winding of the watch were essentially the result of walking. This system of winding was never widely adopted. The watch was a fancy model and not a really useful one. Herman von der Heydt was the only maker in America to work with the self-winding pocket watch. However, inventors always kept the idea of the self-winding watch in mind.

Early self wind pocket watch by Breguet.

ETERNA-MATIC AUTOMATIC WINDING MECHANISM. 1–Oscillating weight. 2–Oscillating gear. 3–Upper wheel of auxiliary pawl-wheel. 4–Lower wheel of auxiliary pawl-wheel. 5–Pawl-wheel with pinion. 6–Lower wheel of pawl-wheel with pinion. 7–Transmission-wheel with pinion. 8–Crown-wheel yoke. 9–Winding pinion. 10–Crown-wheel. 11–Ratchet-wheel. 12–Barrel. 13–Driving runner for ratchet-wheel. 14–Winding stem. 15–Winding button.

In 1923, the British firm Harwood took up once again the solution of the problem of automatic winding, for wrist watches. This was the spark which rapidly resulted in research to improve and simplify this type of mechanism. A company was formed in London to manufacture Harwood's watch, and before long over 500 jewelers in the United Kingdom were selling his automatic watch. A second company was formed in France, and a third in the United States. The business flourished about two and one-half years. Then, in 1931, these companies were liquidated.

Illustration of Self Winding mechanism used by Harwood. NOTE: The 2 BUFFER springs used on earlier movements.

This 1931 wrist watch made by Perpetual Self-Winding Watch Co. of America originally sold for $29.75.

# THE BALANCE ARC OF VIBRATION

If the watch is to function with any degree of satisfaction, the proper arc of motion of a balance must be no less than 225 degrees in a single vibration direction. Wind up the watch, stop the balance; upon releasing the balance, carefully observe the extent of the swing or vibration. After 30 seconds it should have reached its maximum. If it takes longer, the full power of the mainspring is not being communicated strongly enough. With the watch fully wound, the balance should vibrate between 225 degrees and 315 degrees in a single vibration direction.

# JUDGING QUALITY

Judging the quality of a watch need not be difficult. While observing a watch movement there are two major determining factors to keep in mind. (1.) The quality or precious material. (2.) The amount of workmanship and time it takes to produce the parts for the movement . The precious materials such as 18k or 14k gold, diamond or rubies, gold jewel settings or brass jewel settings. The amount of labor may be measured by the finished parts of the movement such as polishing, chamfered parts (removing sharp edges), and bluing of screws. The collector must learn to compare watches from the same time period because changes were made to improve the time keeping. To assist you the partial list below may be helpful in judging the quality of a watch.

LARGE CROWN for EASY WINDING
EXTRA HEAVY PENDANT
SAFTEY RECOILING CLICK
CONCAVED AND POLISHED
WINDING WHEELS
SAFETY CENTER PINION
JEWELED MOTOR BARREL
19 TO 23 SELECTED RUBY AND
SAPPHIRE JEWELS
GOLD TRAIN WHEELS
BREGUET OVER COILED HAIRSPRING

NON PULL-OUT BOW
DUST PROOF CASE
RAISED SOLID GOLD JEWEL SETTINGS
9 ADJUSTMENTS = 6 POSITIONS - 1 HEAT
1 COLD AND 1 ISOCHRONISM
POSITIVE MICROMETRIC REGULATOR
SPRING TEMPERED COMPENSATING
BALANCE WITH SOLID GOLD SCREWS
DOUBLE ROLLER & ENTIRE
ESCAPEMENT IS CAP JEWELED
STEEL ESCAPE WHEEL

**Escapement:** detent, lever or cylinder; gold, steel or brass escape wheel. *Balance wheel;* number of platinum, gold or brass screws, expansion cut, 1/2 cut or uncut. In older movements gold or brass balance wheel. *Balance cock;* diamond or ruby end stone, amount of engraving or hand pierced workmanship. *Regulator;* free sprung, precision or simple. *Hair spring;* helical, elinvar, overcoil or flat. *Adjustments;* Isochronism, temperature, 6 to 3 positions, adjusted or unadjusted.

**The train of gears:** Highly polished, gold or brass gear; chamfered above & below, rounded, beveled or flat spokes. Wolf tooth gearing.

**Finish to the plates:** Engraved, carved, skeletonized, damaskeened is it lavished or conservative finished, highly finished or polished, nickel, brass, gold inlaid, gilt or frosted plates. Hardening of various parts.

**Screws:** Highly finished or polished, chamfered or beveled, oval or flat heads, blued or plain, also chamfered screw holes.

**Jewels and settings:** Number of jewels; diamond, sapphire, ruby, other semi-precious jewels as garnet, aquamarine. Raised gold jewel settings held by screws, flush gold jewel settings held by screws, composition settings or jewels pressed directly into plates.

**Dials:** *Enamel;* enamel on gold or copper, harden or glass; triple, double single or unsunk. *Metal dial;* gold or silver, hand carved or engraved, etched or plated; applied, raised, inlaid or hand painted numbers.

**Cases:** Platinum or white gold, 18k or 14k gold & heavy or light weight, raised applied ornamentation, engraved or engine turned, diamonds or semi-precious jewels, porcelain, enamel or painted, gold or brass inter-dust cover, gold or brass bow, and silver or silveroid cases. Cases made of composition material that look like gold such as "Pinchbeck gold". ( Alloy of copper & zinc that is made to look like gold, but is not. )

**Metals used in watches:** Bell metal or bronze, Beryllium white colored alloyed with iron, cobalt, copper, etc.; Bi-metallic (brass fused to steel), Brass, Carbon steel, Chromium, Chrome steel, Copper; Elinvar, German metal, gilding metal, Glucinum, Gold, Gold-filled, Gunmetal, Invar, Iron, Nickel, Palladium, Platinum, Pinchbeck, Silver, Silveroid, Silver plated, Stainless steel, Steel, Tin, White gold, and Zinc.

## OFFER VERSUS APPRAISALS

When you want to sell your watches you need a offer, not an appraisal. An offer is the actual price someone will pay for your item at a given point in time. The price will be determined by several factors: quality, size, age, metal content, style, grade, rarity and the collectability at that time. Timing may be very critical in determining the price.

Jewelers and most appraisers use the insurance replacement cost, (an estimate of the retail replacement price). This type of appraisal is fine for contemporary watches and jewelry, but not for collectable watches and antique jewelry items. The "FAIR MARKET" value is a more realistic estimate of price. If done by an appraiser with "current market" knowledge, then a FAIR MARKET appraisal will be the correct evaluation of the dollar level at that *time* for your items.

Selling your watches may be a new experience. The task requires experience in the sale of watches. There is a market for watches, but as in any area of sales, knowledge of your BUYER is important. Collectors may not advertise that they are willing buyers; Collectors may not have enough ready cash at the time. Sending watches to a prospective buyer is a judgment call-- is the buyer trustworthy? Will it be worth the time involved? As a seller, you must guarantee the watch to work, offer return privileges, and refunds. The task of selling requires a knowledge of repair, shipping, the cost of advertising, time to market the watch, and someone standing by to talk to the collector. This is a short list and almost imperative that the seller be in the business of selling watches to be successful at selling. The collector may pay a higher price than a dealer, but the collectors are hard to find and may not have the ready cash at that time.

Selling to dealers may be more pleasant. Dealers will have a qualified staff, including buyers and seller, ready to respond to ads, as well as, a cash reserve for purchases. When dealing with an established business, that can provide you with good references and has a trustworthy record. Each customer is handled in a professional manner by a competent staff member. A dealer understands that selling maybe a new experience and will take you through the process one step at a time. Summation: Considering the cost, time and attempting to find a willing collector, you may be ahead to sell your watches to a qualified dealer.

When selling your watches to collectors or dealers it may involve sending the watch from one place to another. To receive the best price it will be vital to see the watches before a offer is made, this is a common practice in the watch market. Suggestions for mailing your package to the buyer. Make a detailed list of the items you are sending. Keep a copy and send a copy also list your name, address and daytime phone number. The jewelry industry sends millions of dollars worth of jewelry by REGISTERED MAIL. The Post Office Service has close control of the registered mail. Each person who handles the package must sign for it and be responsible for it's safety. Your package will be kept in a secure area much like a bank vault. Your package may be insured up to $25,000.00. Your package must also be able to withstand the shipping stress. Before sealing the box make sure to leave a inch of padded space between your watch and the sides, bottom and top of the box. Cushion these spaces with newspaper, tissue, cotton, bubble or foam padding. Seal the box securely then wrap the outside with gummed PAPER tape that can be written on.

When your package arrives at the dealer the mail staff will open and inspect your package, and log each item. One of the experts in charge will examine each item and call as soon as possible with the offer. If you accept the offer a check will be delivered to you. If the offer is turned down the items will be returned.

BRISTOL WATCH CO., KW & KS, serial # 3056. (SWISS FAKE)

"The Nassau" on dial and on movement "Hartford, adjusted, jewels, heat & cold. "(SWISS FAKE)

# COTTAGE INDUSTRY WATCHMAKING IN COLONIAL AMERICA

The cottage industry (pre-1700s to 1800s) consisted of organized, skilled craftsmen having separate divisions for the purpose of producing watches. The movements were handmade using manpowered tools. The parts generally were not given a final finish. The cottage industries were in most countries including France, England, Switzerland, Germany, and others, but not in America. Each skilled parts maker specialized in a specific part of the watch. There were fusee makers, wheel makers, plate and cock makers, spring makers, case makers and enamelers, to name a few. In the cottage industry each maker became an expert in his field. Expenses and overhead were less because fewer tools and less labor were required. Because all components were produced separately, a larger volume of watches resulted.

The enterprising colonial watchmaker in America would order all the parts and assemble them to complete a finished movement. This finisher, or watchmaker, would detail the parts, such as filing them to fit, polishing and gilding the parts, fitting the movement to a case, installing a dial, and adjusting the movement to perform. The finisher would then engrave his name and town of manufacture to the movement or dial. The finisher determined the time keeping quality of the completed watch, thus gaining a good reputation for some watchmakers.

Most watchmakers used this system during this period; even, to some extent, Abraham L. Breguet. A colonial watchmaker or finisher could produce about 50 watches a year. There were few colonial watchmakers because only the wealthy could afford such a prized possession as a watch. Most colonial watchmakers struggled financially, and supplemented their businesses with repair work on European-made watches. Since most of them understood the verge escapement, and imported this type of part from England to produce watches, many colonial watches have the verge escapement. Few colonial watches survive today.

Side-view of 17th Century single-hand movement with fusee and catgut line to barrel. This three-wheel movement normally ran from 15 to 16 hours between windings. Also note the balance has no hairspring.

# EBAUCHES

The stamping out of plates and bridges began with Frederic Japy of Beaucort, France, around 1770. At first, ebauches consisted of two plates with barrel and train bridges, the cock and fusee, pillars, and the clicks and assembly screws. The ebauches were stamped-out or rough movements. Japy invented machinery a common laborer could operate, including a circular saw to cut brass sheets into strips, a machine for cutting teeth in a wheel, a machine for making pillars, a press for the balance, and more. These machines were semi-automatic and hard to keep in alignment or register. But, with the aid of these new machines the principal parts of the movement could be produced in a short period of time with some precision. However, the parts of watches at this time were not interchangeable. These movements in the rough or ''gray'' were purchased by finishers. The finisher was responsible for fitting and polishing all parts and seeing to the freedom and depth of these wheels and working parts. He had to drill the holes to fit the dial and hands. The plates, cock and wheel, after being fitted and polished, were gilded. After the parts were gilded, the movement would be reassembled, regulated for good time keeping, and placed in a case. The finisher had to be a master watchmaker.

In England, during the 1800s, Lancashire became the center of the movement trade. One of the better known English ebauche makers was Joseph Preston & Sons of Prescot. The movements were stamped J. P. Some Swiss ebauches would imitate or stylize the movement for the country in which they were to be sold, making it even harder to identify the origin.

As the watch industry progressed, the transformation of the ebauche to a more completed movement occurred. Automation eventually made possible the watch with interchangeable parts, standard sizing, and precision movements that did not need retouching. This automation began about 1850 (in America) with such talented mechanics as Pierre Fredric Ingold, the Pitkins Brothers, A. L. Dennison, G. A. Leschot with Vacheron and Constantin, Patek, Philippe, and Frederic Japy of Beaucount. The pioneers in the 1850s who set the standards for modern watchmaking included the American Pitkin Brothers, Dennison, Howard, and Jacob Custer. By 1880 most other countries had begun to follow the lead of America in the manufacture of the complete pocket watch with interchangeable parts.

In Switzerland there are four major categories of watch producers : **1. Complete, 2. Ebauche, 3.Parts or Specialized & 4. Finishers**. *Complete* watch producers manufacture entirely on their own premises as Le Coultre. *Ebauche* produce rough movements or movements in the gray called ebauche or blank movements such as ETA in Grenchen. These are made in the valley of Joux and Val-de-Ruz regions, in and around the towns of Granges, Grenchen, La Chaux-de-Fonds, Le Locle and Solothurn, in the Bernese Jura, the valley of St. Imier, Val-de-Travers, at Preseux, in the Ticino, and elsewhere. *Specialized or Parts* are made more or less all over the Swiss regions. Balances more so in Valley of Sagne and at Les Ponts. Lever assortments as the escape wheel, fork, & roller in Jour Valley,at Bienne, in Bernese Jura and especially, at Le Locle. Hairsprings are made at La Chaux-de-Fonds, Geneva, Bienne and St. Imier. Mainspring, dial, hands, cases, jewels, pendent, bow , crowns, crystals, screws, pins, generally speaking are made throughout Switzerland. *Finishers* buy blank movements parts cases etc. and finish the watch as a complete watch with their own name engraved on the watch as *Tiffany & Co., Ball W. Co.* and Etc..

Five typical Ebauches. Three with bar movements, one with a three -quarter plate, one with a half plate. Four with lever escapements, one with a cylinder escapement. The age ranges from 1860 to 1890.

# Ebauches   S.A.

Ebauches S.A. with its main office in Neuchatel, Switzerland, at one time the following 17 affiliated firms were part of Ebauche S.A. and in the year of 1968 they had produced ABOUT- 40,000, 000 WATCHES.

**AS** — A. Schild S.A., Grenchen

**H** — Fabrique d'Horlogerie de Fontainemelon, fontainemelon

**ETA** — Eta S.A., Fabrique d'Ebauches, Grenchen

**L** — Fabrique d'Horlogerie de Fontainemelon, Succursale du Landeron, Le Landeron

**A** — A. Michel S.A., Grenchen

**F** — Felsa S.A., Grenchen

**AV** — Fabriques d'Ebauches Bernoises S.A., Etablissement Aurore, Villeret

**Venus** — Fabrique d'Ebauches Venus S.A., Moutier

**U** — Fabrique d'Ebauches Unitas S.A., Tramelan

**FEF** — Fabrique d'Ebauches de Fleurier S.A., Fleurier

**P** — Fabrique d' Ebauches de Peseux S.A., Peseux

**A** — Fabriques d'Ebauches Reunies Arogno S.A., Arogno

**EB** — Fabriques d'Ebauches de bettlach, Bettlach

**C** — Fabrique d'Ebauches de Chezard S.A., Chezard

**D** — Derby S.A., La Chaux-de-Fonds

**T** — Nouvelle Fabrique S.A., Tavannes

**R** — Valjoux S.A., Les Bioux

**FRENCH EBAUCHE**

Examples of four ebauches: **Upper left:** Example of a Chinese duplex. **Lower left:** An ebauche circa 1900-1930. **Upper right:** A three-finger bridge movement, circa 1890-1910. **Lower right:** Bridge movement, circa 1885-1900.

# WORM GEAR ESCAPEMENT

This oddity was advertised as, "The Watch With a Worm in It," Robert J. Clay of Jersey City was given a patent on October 16, 1886. Mr. Clay said, "The principal object of my invention is to provide a watch movement which is very simple and has but few parts." The worm gear or continuous screw was by no means simple. Mr. Clay and William Hanson of Brooklyn revamped the original worm gear and obtained another patent on January 18, 1887.

The first watch containing a worm gear escapement reached the market in 1887. However, the New York Standard Watch Co. soon converted to a more conventional lever escapement. About 12,000 watches with the worm gear were made, but few survived.

**Enlarged worm gear escapement.** Note endless screw was referred to by the New York Watch Co. as "a watch with a worm in it."

Movement with top plate removed.

# DIAL MAKING

Watch dials were basically hand produced. The base is copper and the coating is generally enamel. In the process the copper plate is covered with a fine white enamel, spread with a knife to a thickness of 3/100ths of an inch. It is then allowed to dry at which time it is placed on a plate and inserted into a red hot furnace. The dial is turned frequently with a pair of long tongs. The copper would melt if it were not coated with the enamel. After the dial has been in the furnace for one minute it is removed and the resulting enamel is soft. The dial is now baked onto the copper plate or "set." The surface is rough after cooling, and it is sanded smooth with sandstone and emery, then baked again. The dial is now ready for the painter, who draws six lines across the dial using a lead pencil. Then, with a pencil of black enamel, he traces the numbers, finishing the ends to make them symmetrical. Then the minute marks are made. Lastly, the name of the watch company is painted onto the dial. The dial is glazed and fired again, then polished. The dial artist used a magnifying glass and a fine camel hair brush to paint the dials and produced about one dozen per hour.

SINGLE SUNK = SECONDS DIAL

Minute Hand
Hour Hand      Second Hand

ABOVE: Single sunk dial .

CENTER DIAL

SECONDS DIAL

Minute Hand
Hour Hand      Second Hand

ABOVE: Side view showing different levels of a double sunk dial.

ABOVE: **DOUBLE SUNK DIAL**.Top view of a Double sunk dial. Single sunk is one level below the hour ring. Double sunk is two levels below the hour ring.

Note: Some single sunk dial have inner marked circle made to look like double sunk dial.

## FIRST DIALS

Thomas Gold was the first to make enamel dials in America in about 1838 in New York City. Thomas had a partner from 1846-51 named Thomas Reeves of Brooklyn.

# CRAZING

The word "craze" means a minute crack in the glaze of the enamel. This is not a crack in the dial because the dial has a backing of copper. Crazing does little damage to the structure of the enamel, even though it may go all the way through to the copper.

# ENAMEL

Enamel may be transparent or colored. Enamel acts as a protective surface on the metals. It is resistant to acid, corrosion, and weather. Enamel is made of feldspar, quartz, silica, borax, lead, and mineral oxides. These materials are ground into a fine powder and then fired at a temperature of about 1500 degrees Fahrenheit. The heat melts the enamel powder and unites it with the surface of the metal.

# PIN LEVER ESCAPEMENT (DOLLAR WATCHES)

The pin lever escapement is sometimes erroneously referred to as "Roskopf escapement" and watches with pin lever escapements are sometimes referred to as "Roskopf watches."

The original Roskopf watch, which was publicly exhibited at the Paris Exposition in 1867, was a rugged "poor man's watch." The chief Roskopf patent, decreases the number of wheels by creating a large barrel whose diameter encroached upon the center of the watch. The loose cannon pinion and hour wheel were driven by a friction-clutch minute wheel mounted to the barrel cover and enmeshing with the loose cannon pinion and hour wheel. The cannon pinion rode loosely on a steel pin threaded to the center of the main plate. The true term, "Roskopf" applies to the barrel with its clutch fitted minute wheel driving the dial train and the Roskopf watch was made in La Chaux-de-Fonds, Switzerland.

⊕NOTE: Some fakes use the name **"Rosskopf."**

# LOW COST PRODUCTION WATCHES
## (DOLLAR WATCHES)

Jason R. Hopkins hoped to produce a watch that would sell for no more than 50 cents as early as the 1870s. He had a plan for which he received a patent (No. 161513) on July 20, 1875. It was a noble idea even though it was never fully realized. In 1876, Mr. Hopkins met a Mr. Fowle who bought an interest in the Hopkins watch. The movement was developed by the Auburndale Watch Co., and the Auburndale Rotary Watch was marketed in 1877. It cost $10, and 1,000 were made. The 20 size had two jewels and was open-face, pendant wind, lever set, and detent escapement. The 18 size had no jewels and was open-face.

In December, 1878, D. A. A. Buck introduced a new watch, at a record low price of $3.50, under the name of Benedict and Burnham Manufacturing Co. It was a rotary watch, open-face, with a skeleton dial which was covered with paper and celluloid. The movement turned around in the case, once every hour, and carried the minute hand with it. There were 58 parts and all of them were interchangeable. They had no jewels but did have a duplex style escapement. The teeth on the brass escape wheel were alternately long and short, and the short teeth were bent down to give the impulse. The main spring was about nine feet long and laid on a plate on the bed of the case. The click was also fastened to the case. The extremely long mainspring took 140 half turns of the stem to be fully wound. It came to be known as the "long wind" Waterbury and was the source of many jokes, "Here, wind my Waterbury for awhile; when you get tired, I'll finish winding it."

"Trail Blazer" by E. Ingraham Co. TOP view is the original Box, bottom. LEFT is Fob "Wings Over The Pole". RIGHT: Watch has original green crystal. Note: engraving on the back of watch is same scene as depicted on box.

**Above:** Example of a Waterbury longwind showing the nine foot long spring.

**Left:** Face illustration of a Waterbury Longwind. The movement can be seen through open skeleton area around edge or face.

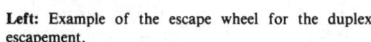

**Right:** Example of a two wheel train rather than the standard four wheel train.

**Left:** Example of the escape wheel for the duplex escapement.

In 1892 R. H. Ingersoll ordered 1,000 watches produced at a cost of 85 cents each. He offered the watch for sale in his mail-order catalog for $1 each and advertised it as, ''The Watch that Made the Dollar Famous.'' These watches were thick, sturdy and noisy and were wound from the back like a clock. The wages in 1892 were about 8 cents per hour, so it took some 13 hours of work to buy a Dollar Watch.

The E. N. Welch Manufacturing Co. was the next low cost production watch manufacturer. Then came the New York City Watch Co., who in 1895, produced a watch with a unique pendant crank to wind the movement. In 1899 came the Western Clock Mfg. Co., which later became the Westclox Corporation.

Also, among the low cost production watches were the ''comic character'' watches. They have become prime collectibles in recent years.

About 70 percent of the watches sold in the U. S. were Dollar type. These watches were characterized by the pin lever, non-jeweled (for the most part), and with a face of paper or other inexpensive material. These watches were difficult to repair and the repairs cost more than the price of a new one. Thus they were thrown away, and today it is hard to find one in good condition.

## DOLLAR WATCH CHARACTERISTICS:

**1.** Sold at a price that almost everyone could afford.

**2.** Used pin lever or duplex escapement.

**3.** Stamped or pressed out parts; also used fewer parts overall.

**4.** Were non-jeweled (except for a few) but rugged and practical.

**5.** Dial made of paper or other inexpensive material.

**6.** Case and movement were sold as one unit.

## PERSONALIZED & CUSTOM WATCHES

It was common practice for some watch manufacturers to personalize watches for **distributors**, jobbers, jewelry firms, and individuals. This was done either by engraving the movement or painting on the dial. Probably the Ball Watch Co. did more of this than any other distributor.

Each manufacturer used its own serial number system even though there may have been a variety of names on the movements and/or dials. Knowledge of this will aid the collector in identifying watches as well as determining age.

In order to establish the true manufacturer of the movement, one must study the construction, taking note of the shape, location, plate layout (is it full or 3/4), shape of the balance cock and the regulator, location of jewels, location of screws, etc. Compare and match your watch movement with every photograph or drawing from each watch company in this volume until the manufacturer is located. The best place to start is at the Hamilton and Illinois sections because these two companies made most of the personalized watches.

"Remington Watch Co."-marked on movement and case, made by N.Y. Standard Watch Co., NOTE: The CROWN wheel and RATCHET without a CLICK, these visible wheels are for show only, 16 size, 11 jewels.

"E.F. Randolph"-marked on movement, made by Illinois Watch Co., 23j, hunting, model No. 4.

16 size, No. 390, made by New York Standard Watch Co. Same model as above.

Model 4, 16 size, made by Illinois Watch Co. Same model as above.

Personalized watch movement by ILLINOIS, engraved on movement & on dial B.A. BELL Chattanooga, Tenn., 18 size, adjusted, 15 jewels, OF.

MODEL 4, 18 size, open face, fine train, this matches the watch on the LEFT

Personalized watch movement by ROCKFORD. Engraved on movement. "W.G. Gane, Special Railway, 17j, Adj, serial No. 344551." To identify, see the Identification of Movement section of all watch companies, noting plate design & screw locations to determine that it is a ROCKFORD Model No. 8.

Personalized watch movement by HAMILTON. Engraved on movement, "Mayer, Chattanooga, Tenn., Adjusted, 21 jewels, serial No. 254507." To identify, see the Identification of Movement section of all watch companies, noting plate design & screw locations to determine that it is an 18 size, open face HAMILTON model. Then by using the serial number, the grade can be determined.

Model 8, 18 size, Rockford, full plate, hunting, lever set. This illustration from the identification section matches the model above.

Grade 936, 18 size, Hamilton, open face. This matches the model above.

The basic **model** will have the key mechanical features and construction. The *decoration,* damaskeening and jewel count determine the __grade.__ Basic models will have such things as, size, hunting or open face, key or stem wind, lever or stem set, and basic layout deign. The 18 size may be Transition models and note the location of the cock to the barrel bridge. The 16 size consider the winding parts may not be seen or they could be exposed (crown & ratchet wheel).

Example: Washington Watch Co. 16 size, 17 jewel, Senate grade. Illinois Watch Co. made a custom watch for ( Montgomery Ward ) using the name Washington Watch Co. and altered the appearance of the movement how ever the basic model was not significantly changed. The mechanical function remain the same to allow the parts to fit the altered model.

**Washington Watch Co.** , SENATE, 16 size, 17J, Adj. 3P, HC, polished jewel settings, damaskeen finish, double sunk enamel dial, pendent set, serial # 2457094.

ALTERED drawing of Illinois W. Co., this matches the watch to the left. NOTE: The extra screw & cut out . This also is the same model as below ( MODEL # 6)

BASIC Illinois Watch Co. **MODEL** 6 as shown in the Illinois W. Co. section this drawing is NOT altered.

After the correct manufacturer has been determined, the serial number can be used to determine the age. Taking the age, grade, size, and manufacturer into consideration, the approximate value can be determined by comparing similar watches from the parent company. If a jeweler's name and location are on the watch, this particular watch will command a higher price in that area.

The custom or personalize watches are really just variations of a type or style of a grade and may show the serial number production dates. The production run may have called for 1,000 movements of a basic model and grade that may contain 700 with the Watch Co. name on movement and 300 of the custom or personalize watches with customers name on the watch. Therefore it difficult to determine how many of this type of custom made watches were produced. Usually the differences between the custom and basic grades can be seen with out a tare down of the movement. Unfortunately it may require a disassembling of the watch and you may want to have a watchmaker to help to make positive identification.

Compare and match the following list which may aid you in the identification of your watches: first determine SIZE, then hunting or open face model, key or lever or pendent set, location of balance cock to winding barrel, location of jewels, location of screws, full, 3/4, 1/2, plate or bridge model. **Grade** differences may include: number of jewels (7-23J.), unadjusted - Adjusted to 3-5 positions, style of regulator & click, (some regulators and click were patented ), style of decoration as damaskeening, *no name* or grade name. The grade without a name were the generic type or style of grade. Generic, nameless, Personalized Jobber Watches or unmarked grades for watch movements are listed under the Company name or initials of the Company, etc. by size, jewel count and description.

**"TEST"** your skill and try to find the basic models below. The **answer** is at bottom of the next page good luck.

(A): ON MOVEMENT: J. P. STEVENS & BRO. 15 jewels, ON DIAL J.P. STEVENS & BRO. ATLANTA, GA. the size is 18 Size, hunting case model,

( B ): ON DIAL *EAGLE* , ON movement illustration of a *EAGLE* and serial number 512929, hunting case model , and 18 size.

⊕ Generic, nameless, Personalized Jobber Watches or unmarked grades for watch movements are listed under the Company name or initials of the Company, etc. by size, jewel count and description.

# FAKE 23 JEWEL WATCHES

MARKED: 23 jewels adjusted, Trainsman Special Chicago U.S.A. on movement, watch has fake 23 jewels and is not adjusted also Trainsman which implies it is a railroad watch. This is a Seth Thomas Model 13, 18 size, HC.

MARKED: 23 jewels adjusted, Locomotive Special Chicago U.S.A. on movement, watch has fake 23 jewels and is not adjusted also Locomotive which implies it is a railroad watch. This is a Trenton M # 6, 18 size, OF.

# SWISS IMPORTED FAKES

Before 1871 a flood of pocket watches were made with names strikingly similar to many well-known American watches. These were made in foreign countries as well as in America and looked and sounded like high quality watches. But they were fakes, inferior in quality.

These key-wind imitations of American pocket watches are a fascinating and inexpensive watch type that would make a good collection. The watches closely resembled the ones they were intended to emulate. Names such as "Hampton Watch Company" might fool the casual buyer into thinking he had purchased a watch from Hampden. "Rockville Watch Co." could easily be mistaken for the American Rockford Watch Co. Initials were also used such as H. W. Co., R. W. Co., and W. W. Co., making it even harder to determine the true identity.

In 1871 Congress passed a law requiring all watches to be marked with the country of origin. The Swiss tried to get around this by printing "Swiss" so small on the movement that it was almost impossible to see. Also the word "Swiss" was printed on the top of the scroll or on a highly engraved area of the movement, making it difficult to spot.

By 1885 these Swiss imitations were of better quality and resembled even more closely what was popular in America. But the Swiss fakes did not succeed, and by 1900 they were no longer being sold here.

( Answer to basic watches )

(A) = Aurora new model and  (B) = Seth Thomas model # 7.

Example of a Swiss imported fake. Note misspelled signature "P.S. Barrett." The authentic American Waltham watch is spelled "P.S. Bartlett."

Example of a NEW HAVEN WATCH CO. imported Swiss fake. Marked on movement New Haven Watch Co. New Haven Conn. Serial # 778883.

# HOW TO IDENTIFY A SWISS FAKE

1. At first they were keywind and keyset; then they became stem wind, full plate, about 18 size, large jewels on the plate side, and used Roman numerals.

2. Most had American-sounding names so close to the original that it looks merely like a misspelling.

3. The material was often crudely finished with very light gilding.

4. The dial used two feet; American watches used three.

5. The balance wheel was made to look like a compensated balance, but it did not have the cut in the balance wheel.

6. The large flat capped jewels were blue in color.

These characteristics are not present with all imported fakes. Some or none of these factors may be present. The later the date, the more closely the fake resembled the American watch.

Will the **true** E. Howard watch please step forward?
Left: E. Howard & Co. Boston serial # 12557 Right: Brooklyn Watch Co. New York serial # 6423.

CONDENSED PRICE LIST
# High Grade Movements.
MANUFACTURED BY THE
## HAMPDEN WATCH COMPANY.

*1898 AD*

*1906 AD*

### 18 Size Movements.  O. F. and Htg.

| | | | | |
|---|---|---|---|---|
| Special Railway | 23 | Jewels, Nickel Adj. | | $35.00 |
| New Railway | 23 | " | " | " | 28.00 |
| John Hancock | 21 | " | " | " | 23.00 |
| Special Railway | 17 | " | " | " | 30.00 |
| New Railway | 17 | " | " | " | 20.00 |
| Anchor | 17 | " | " | " | 16.00 |
| No. 48 or 68 | 17 | " | " | " | 16 00 |
| John C. Dueber Special | 17 | " | " | " | 15.00 |
| No. 47 or 67 | 17 | " | " | " | 15.00 |
| John C. Dueber | 17 | " | " | " | 12.00 |
| No. 43 or 63 | 17 | " | " | " | 12.00 |
| No. 80 or 81 | 17 | " | " | " | 10.00 |
| No. 49 or 69 | 17 | " | Gilt | " | 9.50 |
| Dueber | 17 | " | Nickel | | 8.00 |
| The Dueber Watch Co. | 15 | " | " | | 6.50 |
| No. 45 or 65 | 11 | " | " | | 5.00 |
| No. 46 or 66 | 11 | " | Gilt, | | 4.75 |
| Champion | 7 | " | " | | 3.00 |

John C. Dueber, No. 43 and 63, damaskeened in two colors when specially ordered.

### 18 Size

No. 800 Hunting }
No. 900 Open Face }  **$60.00**

24 extra fine ruby and sapphire jewels in gold settings, sapphire jewel pin, double roller escapement, steel escape wheel, sapphire exposed pallets, compensating balance in recess, adjusted to temperature, isochronism and five positions, mean time screws, Breguet hair spring, patent micrometric regulator, safety pinion, poised pallet and fork, handsomely damaskeened nickel plates, gold lettering, champfered steel parts, double sunk glass, enamel dial with red marginal figures, Roman or Arabic, elegantly finished throughout.  Certificate of rating furnished upon application.

*1926 AD*

*1926 AD*

## BUNN SPECIAL
### 9 Adjustments   21 Jewels
### $45.00

SUGGESTED PRICES:  Complete in any plain screw—
10K Filled Case, $55.00     14K Filled Case, $65.00
Fancy Cases and Fancy Dials Proportionately More.

21 ruby and sapphire jewels; gold settings; adjusted to SIX positions, heat, cold and isochronism; compensating balance; gold screws including timing screws; double roller; steel escape wheel; Breguet hairspring; patent micrometric screw regulator; safety screw center pinion; beautifully damaskeened with black enamel lettering; double sunk dial.

## THE 60 HOUR 6 POSITION
## BUNN SPECIAL
### 23 Jewels, $58.00  ·꞉·  21 Jewels, $50.00
### 9 ADJUSTMENTS
SUGGESTED PRICES:  Complete in any plain screw cases:
23J., 10K Filled Case, $65.00     14K Filled Case, $72.50
21J., 10K Filled Case, $57.50     14K Filled Case, $65.00
Special or Fancy Cases and Fancy Dials Proportionately More.

Ruby and sapphire jewels; raised gold settings; adjusted to SIX positions, heat, cold and isochronism; spring tempered compensating balance with gold screws including timing screws; double roller; steel escape wheel; gold train wheels; safety screw center pinion; Illinois superior motor barrel; patent micrometric screw regulator; recoiling safety click; concaved and polished winding wheels; double sunk dial.
The 23 jewel grade contains the Illinois Superior Jeweled Motor Barrel and two jewels in which barrel staff pivots operate.

---

## No. 89
### 17 Jewels, Adjusted to Temperature
### $22.50

SUGGESTED PRICES:  Complete in any plain screw—
10K Filled Case, $32.50     14K Filled Case, $40.00
Fancy Cases and Fancy Dials Proportionately More.

17 jewels; polished settings; adjusted to temperature; compensating balance with timing screws; Breguet hairspring; patent regulator; safety screw center pinion; polished steel work; damaskeened in attractive pattern; double sunk dial.

## THE 60 HOUR
## BUNN
### 8 Adjustments   19 Jewels
### $43.50

SUGGESTED PRICES:  Complete in any plain screw—
10K Filled Case, $50.00     14K Filled Case, $57.50
Fancy Cases and Fancy Dials Proportionately More.

19 ruby and sapphire jewels; raised gold settings; adjusted to five positions, heat, cold and isochronism; special quality hardened and tempered compensating balance with gold screws, including mean time screws; gold train wheels; double roller; steel escape wheel; Breguet hairspring; safety screw center pinion; Illinois superior mainspring; patent micrometric screw regulator; recoiling click; Illinois superior jeweled motor barrel; concaved and polished winding wheels; double sunk dial.

# MARKET REPORT
## 1995

The **Pocket Watch** Market continued to hold its strength and showed further increases in 1995. High-grade railroad watches were extremely hard to find and brought top dollar when they surfaced. All American railroad watches held their values. High-grade European repeaters and complicated timepieces also showed strong increases.

Good material is very difficult to find, and the numbers of collectors entering the marketplace have given to the pocket watch field as we have never seen before. The future will likely continue along the same lines which were evident in 1995. Better American railroad watches, mint condition watches, pocket watches, watches of all styles, and unique timepieces will be more difficult to locate. This is, again, due to the fact that the bulk of the better material is in the hands of private collectors. The general public and secondary markets vendors ( jewelry, coin, pawn shops) no longer have inventories of desirable pocket watches.

The **Wrist Watch** market on the other hand only strengthened slightly in 1995. Many areas in the market were still soft, especially gold rectangular wrist watches, standard name brands, and watches which still have a contemporary look. For example, 1965 - 1975 gold bracelet wrist watches are very slow to sell. Strong areas continue to be Patek Philippe vintage timepieces, early Rolex, and certain Rolex sport models, especially older Milgauss examples and early Explorer I models.

Lower-end high-grade wrist watches stayed at generally lower levels and were slow to sell. Some increases were shown in the LeCoultre, Breitling, Omega, and Movado watches, especially technical pieces such as high-quality chronographs.

The wrist watch market will most likely continue in this manner, and there are many **good values** in less sought after types.

**Character watches** continued on a level and solid basis. Interesting early material and <u>original boxed</u> items are almost non-existent on the second-hand market. The early vintage pieces in this area of collecting will continue to be strong. The Swatch market was lackluster and has lost the majority of its influence as 1995 elapsed. The early enthusiasm for this new and volatile market has waned and its strength for the future is still questionable.

# AMERICAN LISTINGS
## Pricing At Collectable Fair Market Value At Retail Level
### (As Complete Watches With Case & Movement)

Watches listed in this book are priced at the collectable fair market **value** at the retail level (What a collector may expect to pay for a watch from a watch dealer) and as **complete** watches, having an original 14k gold-filled case with an original white enamel single sunk dial. The entire original movement is in good working order with no repairs needed, unless otherwise noted. Watches listed as 14k and 18k are solid gold cases. Coin or silveroid-type and stainless steel cases will be listed as such. Keywind and keyset watches are listed as having original coin silver cases. Dollar-type watches or low cost production watches are listed as having a base metal type case and a composition dial. Wrist watches are priced as having original gold-filled case with the movement being all original and in good working order, and the wrist watch band being made of leather except where bracelet is described.

Many of the watch manufacturers were commissioned to put jewelers' or jobbers' names on their movements in place of their own. Due to this practice, the true manufacturers of these movements are difficult to identify. These watch models are listed under the original manufacturer and can be identified by comparison with the model sections under each manufacturer. See ''Personalized Watches'' for more detailed information.

These watch manufacturers which personalize watches for jobbers or jewelry firms, with exclusive private signed or marked movements must first be found by using a illustration and matched to the manufacture shown in this book. After you identify the movement now the value can be determined. The valuable collectable watches are listed under the signed or marked movement. Other exclusive private signed or marked movements will have equivalent value are only slightly higher value and should be compared to Generic or Nameless movements. Railroad signed or marked (dials & movements) are usually more collectable & higher in value .

The prices shown were averaged from dealers' lists just prior to publication and are an indication of the collectable retail level or what collectors will pay. Prices are provided in three categories: average condition, extra fine, and mint condition, and are shown in whole dollar amounts only. The values listed are a guide for the *collectable* retail level and are provided for your information only. **Dealers** will not necessarily pay **full retail price**. Prices listed are for watches with original cases and dials.

**Important Notice.** All of the information, including valuations, in this book has been compiled from the most reliable sources, and every effort has been made to eliminate errors and questionable data. Nevertheless, the possibility of error, in a work of such immense scope, always exists. The publisher or authors will not be held responsible for losses which may occur in the purchase, sale, or other transaction of items, because of information contained herein. Readers who feel they have discovered errors are invited to write and inform us, so they may be corrected in subsequent editions.

☉ Descriptions and serial number ranges listed for early watches cannot be considered 100 percent accurate due to the manner in which records were kept by these companies.

**INFORMATION NEEDED—** We are interested in any facts and information you might have that should possibly be considered for future editions. Documented facts are needed, so please send photo or sources of information. Send to: Cooksey Shugart, P. O. BOX 3147, Cleveland, Tennessee 37320-3147. *(WHEN CORRESPONDING, PLEASE INCLUDE A ⊟ SELF-ADDRESSED, STAMPED ENVELOPE.)*

## ABBREVIATIONS USED IN
## THE COMPLETE PRICE GUIDE TO WATCHES

🕐—IMPORTANT NOTE.
★★★★★—only **ONE to FIVE** known to exist (proto type models etc.)
★★★★—**Extremely Rare**; less than 25 to 50 known to exist.
★★★—**Rare**; less than 100 to 200 known to exist.
★★ —**Scarce**; less than 500 known to exist.
★ —**Uncommon**; less than 2,500 known to exist.
ADJ —Adjusted (to temperature, heat and cold, also isochronism)
BASE—Base metal used in cases; e.g., silveroid
BB —Bubble Back ( Rolex style case )
BRG—Bridge plate design movement
Ca. — Circa ( about or approximate date)
Cal. —Calendar also Calibre ( model)
C&B — Case and Band
Chrono.—Chronograph
COIN—Coin silver
DES—Diamond end stones
DMK—Damaskeened
DSD—Double sunk dial
DR—Double roller
DWT—Penny weight: 1/20 Troy ounce
ETP—Estimated total production
ESCAPE.—Escapement
EX—Extra nice; far above average
FULL—Full plate design movement
    3/4—3/4 plate design movement
    F brg—One finger bridge design and a 3/4 plate (see Illinois 16s M#5)
    2F brg—Two finger bridge design
    3F brg—Three finger bridge design.
GF—Gold filled
GJS—Gold jewel settings
G#—Grade number
GT—Gold train (gold gears)
GCW—Gold center wheel
GRO—Good running order
HC—Hunter case
id. — identification
(illo.) —Illustration of watches
J—jewel (as 21J)
K—Karat (as 14k solid gold—not gold filled)
K(w) —WHITE GOLD as 14K(w) = 14 karat white gold
KS—Key set
KW—Key wind
KW/SW— (Key wind/stem wind) transition
LS—Lever set

MCC—Multi-color case
MCD—Multi-color dial
M#—Model number
mm —Millemeter (over all case size )
Mvt.— Only Dial and movement; no case
NI—Nickel plates or frames
OF—Open face
P—as  Adj.5P = Adjusted to  5 positions, 3 positions or 4 positions etc.
PORC—Porcelain (porc. dial )
PS—Pendant set
PW — Pocket Watch
RF# —Reference Factory  number
Reg.—Register on a chronograph
REP.—Repeater
RGJS—Raised gold jewel setting
RGP—Rolled gold plate
RR—Railroad
S—Size
SBB—Screw back and bezel
SRC—Swing ring case
SS—Stainless steel
SSD—Single Sunk Dial
S W—Stem wind
S#—Serial number
TEMP—Temperature
TP—Total production
2T—Two-tone
W/ = WITH
WGF—White gold filled
W.I. also W. Ind. —Wind indicator (up and down indicator)
W W—Wrist watch
YGF—Yellow gold filled

**Generic, Nameless or Unmarked grades** for watch movements are listed under the Company name or initials of the Company, etc. by size, jewel count and
description.

# ABBOTT'S STEM WIND

**Henry Abbott** first patented his stem wind attachment on June 30, 1876. The complete Abbott's stem wind mechanism is arranged in such a way as to convert key wind to stem wind. He also made a repeater-type slide mechanism for winding. On January 18, 1881, he received a patent for an improved stem wind attachment. On the new model the watch could be wound with the crown. Abbott sold over 50,000 of these stem-wind attachments, and many of them were placed on Waltham, Elgin, and Illinois watches.

**Abbott Stem Wind Attachment. LEFT:** normal view of an Illinois watch movement with 'hidden' Abbott Stem Wind Attachment (pat. Jan., 18th, 1881). **RIGHT:** Same watch with dial removed exposing the Abbott Stem Wind Attachment. Serial number 52045. Add $100 to $250 to value of watch with this attachment.

## ABBOTT WATCH CO.
### (MADE BY HOWARD WATCH CO.) 1908 - 1912

Abbott Sure Time Watches were made by the E. Howard Watch Co.(Keystone), and are similar to Howard Watch Co. 1905 model. These watches sold for $8.75 and had 17 jewels. Some of the open face watches are actually hunting case models without the second bits register.

| Description | Avg | Ex-Fn | Mint |
|---|---|---|---|
| Abbott Sure Time, 16S, 17J, OF, GF Case | $150 | $225 | $300 |
| Abbott Sure Time, 16S, 17J, HC, GF Case | 200 | 275 | 350 |
| Abbott Sure Time, 16S, 17J, 14K, HC | 450 | 550 | 700 |

**Abbott Watch Co.,** 16 size, 17 jewels, gold jeweled settings, hunting case. Note similarity to the Howard Watch Co. model 1905. Serial number 993932.

**Abbott Watch Co.,** 16 size, 17 jewels, gold jeweled settings, open face. Note similarity to the Howard Watch Co. series 9.

100

# ADAMS AND PERRY WATCH MANUFACTURING CO.

### Lancaster, Pennsylvania

### 1874 - 1877

This company, like so many others, did not have sufficient capital to stay in business for long. The first year was spent in setting up and becoming incorporated. The building was completed in mid-1875, and watches were being produced by September. The first watches were limited to three grades, and the escapement and balance were bought from other sources. By December 1875, the company was short of money and, by the spring of 1876, they had standardized their movements to 18 size. The first movement went on sale (very few watches were sold from this factory name) April 7, 1876. The next year the company remained idle. In August 1877, the company was sold to the Lancaster Watch Company, after making only about 800 to 1,000 watches. In 1892 Hamilton acquired the assets.

| Description | | Avg | Ex-Fn | Mint |
|---|---|---|---|---|
| 20S, 20J, GJS, PS, KW, 18K original | ★★★ | $2,200 | $2,700 | $3,300 |
| 18S, 20J, GJS, PS | ★★★ | 1,000 | 1,500 | 2,200 |
| 18S, 17J, GJS, PS | ★★ | 700 | 1,200 | 1,600 |
| 18S, 17J, GJS, PS, Coin, Original | ★★ | 900 | 1,400 | 2,000 |

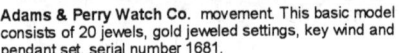

Adams & Perry Watch Co. movement. This basic model consists of 20 jewels, gold jeweled settings, key wind and pendant set, serial number 1681.

J. H. ALLISON movement 16 jewels, gold train and escape wheel with a pivoted detent, key wind and key set, serial number 19.

# J. H. ALLISON

### Detroit, Michigan

### 1853 - 1890

The first watch J. H. Allison made was in 1853; it was a chronometer with full plate and a fusee with chain drive. The balance had time screws and sliding weights. In 1864, he made a 3/4 plate chronometer with gold wheels. He also damaskeened the nickel movement. He produced only about 25 watches, of which 20 were chronometers. By 1883 he was making 3/4 plate movements with a stem wind of his own design. Allison made most of his own parts and designed his own tools. He also altered some key wind watches to stem wind. Allison died in 1890.

| Description | | Avg | Ex-Fn | Mint |
|---|---|---|---|---|
| Full Plate & 3\4 Plate, GT, NI, DMK | ★★★★★ | $6,500 | $8,000 | $10,000 |
| Detent Chronometer Escapement, 16J, KW/KS, GT | ★★★★★ | 10,000 | 12,000 | 14,000 |

# AMERICAN REPEATING WATCH CO.

### Elizabeth, New Jersey
### 1885 - 1892

Around 1675, a repeating mechanism was attached to a clock for the first time. The first repeating watch was made about 1687 by Thomas Tompion or Daniel Quare. Five-minute, quarter-hour and half-hour repeaters were popular by 1730. The minute repeater became common about 1830.

Fred Terstegen applied for a patent on August 21, 1882, for a repeating attachment that would work with any American key-wind or stem-wind watch. He was granted three patents: No. 311,270 on January 27, 1885; No. 421,844 on February 18, 1890; and No. 436,162 in September 1890. Waltham was the only watch company to fabricate repeating watches in America. It is not known how many repeaters were made, but it is estimated to be about **500** to **1,000.**

## 18 SIZE, with 5 MIN. REPEATER ATTACHMENT

| Name — Description | | Avg | Ex-Fn | Mint |
|---|---|---|---|---|
| HOWARD, w/ 5 min. repeater attachment, COIN | ★ ★ | $3,500 | $3,800 | $4,250 |
| GOLD CASE | ★ ★ | 5,000 | 5,500 | 6,250 |
| Keystone, or Lancaster, w/ 5 min. rep. attachment, COIN | ★ ★ | 2,500 | 2,700 | 3,000 |
| GOLD CASE | ★ ★ | 3,500 | 3,700 | 4,000 |
| SETH THOMAS, w/ 5 min. repeater attachment, COIN | ★ ★ | 3,000 | 3,500 | 4,250 |
| GOLD CASE | ★ ★ | 4,000 | 4,300 | 4,800 |

American Repeating Attachment. Illustration at LEFT shows Terstegen's patented repeating attachment only. Illustration at RIGHT shows attachment as normally found on movement. The two outside circles on left illustration are wire gongs. The hammer can be seen at upper LEFT Illustration in the shape of a boot.

🕐 Watches listed in this book are priced at the **collectable fair market value** at the RETAIL level, as complete watches having an original 14k gold filled case, KEY WIND with silver, an original white enamel single sunk dial, and with the entire original movement in good working order with no repairs needed, **unless otherwise noted.**

🕐 Some grades are not included. Their values can be determined by comparing with **similar** age, size, metal content, style, models and grades listed.

## 16 SIZE, with 5 MIN. REPEATER ATTACHMENT

| Name — Description | | Avg | Ex-Fn | Mint |
|---|---|---|---|---|
| COLUMBUS, w/ 5 min. rep. attachment, GF or COIN | ★★ | $2,200 | $2,500 | $3,000 |
| GOLD CASE | ★★ | 4,000 | 4,200 | 4,500 |
| ELGIN, w/ 5 min. rep. attachment, GF or COIN | ★★ | 1,800 | 2,000 | 2,500 |
| GOLD CASE | ★★ | 3,500 | 3,700 | 4,200 |
| HAMPDEN, w/ 5 min. rep. attachment, GF or COIN | ★★ | 1,800 | 2,000 | 2,500 |
| GOLD CASE | ★★ | 3,000 | 3,300 | 3,800 |
| HOWARD, w/ 5 min. rep. attachment, GF or COIN | ★★ | 2,500 | 3,000 | 3,500 |
| GOLD CASE | ★★ | 4,500 | 4,700 | 5,000 |
| ILLINOIS, w/ 5 min. rep. attachment, GF or COIN | ★★ | 2,200 | 2,500 | 2,900 |
| GOLD CASE | ★★ | 3,500 | 3,800 | 4,250 |
| Non-magnetic (Paillard),w/ 5 min. rep. attachment, gold-filled | ★★ | 2,000 | 2,200 | 2,600 |
| GOLD CASE | ★★ | 3,000 | 3,500 | 4,000 |
| WALTHAM, w/ 5 min. rep. attachment, GF or COIN | ★★ | 1,800 | 2,000 | 2,500 |
| GOLD CASE | ★★ | 3,500 | 3,700 | 4,200 |

🕐 Watches listed in this book are priced at the **collectable fair market value** at the RETAIL level, as complete watches having an original 14k gold filled case, KEY WIND with silver, an original white enamel single sunk dial, and with the entire original movement in good working order with no repairs needed, unless otherwise noted.

🕐 Some grades are not included. Their values can be determined by comparing with **similar** age, size, metal content, style, models and grades listed.

# THE AMERICAN WALTHAM WATCH CO.
## 1851 - 1957

To trace the roots of the Waltham family one must start with the year 1850 in Roxbury, Massachusetts, No. 34 Water Street. That fall David Davis, a Mr. Dennison, and Mr. Howard together formed a watch company. Howard and Dennison had a dream of producing watches with interchangeable parts that were less expensive and did not result in less quality.

*Aaron L. Dennison.*

*Edward Howard.*

Howard served an apprenticeship to Aaron Willard Jr. in about 1829. Several years later, in 1842, Howard formed a clock and balance scale manufacturing company with Davis. Howard and Dennison combined their ideas and, with financing provided by Samuel Curtis, the first of their watches was made in 1850. But they had problems. They were trying out ideas such as using jewels, making dials, and producing steel with mirror finishes. This required all new machinery and resulted in a great financial burden. They discovered, too, that although all watches were produced on the same machines and of the same style, each watch was individual with its own set of errors to be corrected. This they had not anticipated. It took months to adjust the watches to the point they were any better than any other timepieces on the market.

Example of a Warren model, about 18 size, 15 jewels, engraved on the movement *Warren NO 44 BOSTON,* plain dial, under sprung, steel balance, right angle lever, escape wheel has pointed teeth, key wind & key set from front, Ca.1853. Note: This movement was made to fit an English size case and will not fit a standard 18 size American case.

But Howard had perfected and patented many automatic watchmaking machines that produced precision watch parts. In 1851 the factory building was completed and the name American Horology Company was chosen. It was not until late 1852 that the first watches were completed bearing the signature "The Warren Mfg. Co.," after a famed Revolutionary War hero. The first 17 watches were not placed on the market but went to officials of the company. Watches numbered 18 through 110 were marked "Warren Boston;" the next 800 were marked "Samuel Curtis;" a few were marked "Fellows & Schell" and sold for $40.

The name was changed to the Boston Watch Company in September 1853, and a factory was built in Waltham, Massachusetts, in October 1854. The movements that were produced here carried serial numbers 1,001 to 5,000 and were marked "Dennison, Howard & Davis," "C. T. Parker," and "P. S. Bartlett." Boston Watch Company failed in 1857 and was sold at a sheriff's auction to Royal E. Robbins. In May 1857, it was reorganized as the Appleton, Tracy & Co., and the watches produced carried serial numbers 5,001 to 14,000, model 1857. The first movements were marked Appleton, Tracy & Co. The C. T. Parker was introduced as model 1857 and sold for $12.00, 399 of these models were made. Also 598 chronodrometers were produced and in January 1858 the P. S. Bartlett watch was made.

Engraved on movement *SAMUEL CURTIS ROXBURY. NO 112,* 18 size, 15 jewels, under sprung, steel balance, Ca. 1853. This movement was made to fit in the typical English size case.

Engraved on movement "*C.T. PARKER WALTHAM MASS. NO 1099"* , 7 jewels, under sprung, steel balance, Ca. November 1857. Note: Balance cock not engraved.

In January 1859, the Waltham Improvement Co. and the Appleton, Tracy & Co. merged to form the American Watch Company. In 1860, as Lincoln was elected president and the country was in Civil War, the American Watch Co. was faced with serious problems. The next year, business came to a standstill. There seemed to be little hope of finding a market for watches, and bankruptcy again seemed close at hand. At this point it was decided to cut expenditures to the lowest possible figure and keep the factory in operation.

American horology owes much to members of the Waltham Watch group such as Bacon, Church, Dennison, Fogg, Howard Marsh, Webster, and Woerd, who contributed much to its development and success. In early 1861, the name "J. Watson" appeared on model 1857 (first run: Nos. 23,601 to 24,300 total production 1,200).

The next model 1857 was the "R. E. Robbins" of which 2,800 were made. The William Ellery, marked "Wm. Ellery," (model 1857) was then introduced with the first serial number of 46,201. It was key wind and key set and had 7 to 15 jewels.

A size 10 woman's watch was made in July of 1861 with first serial numbers of 44,201. It was marked "Appleton, Tracy & Co." gold balance, key wind and key set, 3/4 plate, 13 to 15 jewels. Some were marked "P. S. Bartlett" and a 15 jewel was marked "Appleton, Tracy & Co." A special model, 10 size, serial numbers of 45,801 to 46,200, is extremely rare. The first stem wind, beginning with serial number 410,698, was produced in 1868. By 1880 all watches were quick train. The last key wind was serial No. 22,577,000, about 1919, 18 size, 1883 model, 7J, sterling, produced for export.

## WALTHAM ESTIMATED SERIAL NUMBERS AND PRODUCTION DATES

| DATE — SERIAL NO. | DATE — SERIAL NO. | DATE — SERIAL NO. |
|---|---|---|
| 1852 – 50 | 1888 – 3,800,000 | 1924 – 24,550,000 |
| 1853 – 400 | 1889 – 4,200,000 | 1925 – 24,800,000 |
| 1854 – 1,000 | 1890 – 4,700,000 | 1926 – 25,200,000 |
| 1855 – 2,500 | 1891 – 5,200,000 | 1927 – 26,100,000 |
| 1856 – 4,000 | 1892 – 5,800,000 | 1928 – 26,400,000 |
| 1857 – 6,000 | 1893 – 6,300,000 | 1929 – 26,900,000 |
| 1858 – 10,000 | 1894 – 6,700,000 | 1930 – 27,100,000 |
| 1859 – 15,000 | 1895 – 7,100,000 | 1931 – 27,300,000 |
| 1860 – 20,000 | 1896 – 7,450,000 | 1932 – 27,550,000 |
| 1861 – 30,000 | 1897 – 8,100,000 | 1933 – 27,750,000 |
| 1862 – 45,000 | 1898 – 8,400,000 | 1934 – 28,100,000 |
| 1863 – 65,000 | 1899 – 9,000,000 | 1935 – 28,600,000 |
| 1864 – 110,000 | 1900 – 9,500,000 | 1936 – 29,100,000 |
| 1865 – 180,000 | 1901 – 10,200,000 | 1937 – 29,400,000 |
| 1866 – 260,000 | 1902 – 11,100,000 | 1938 – 29,750,000 |
| 1867 – 330,000 | 1903 – 12,100,000 | 1939 – 30,050,000 |
| 1868 – 410,000 | 1904 – 13,500,000 | 1940 – 30,250,000 |
| 1869 – 460,000 | 1905 – 14,300,000 | 1941 – 30,750,000 |
| 1870 – 500,000 | 1906 – 14,700,000 | 1942 – 31,050,000 |
| 1871 – 540,000 | 1907 – 15,500,000 | 1943 – 31,400,000 |
| 1872 – 590,000 | 1908 – 16,400,000 | 1944 – 31,700,000 |
| 1873 – 680,000 | 1909 – 17,600,000 | 1945 – 32,100,000 |
| 1874 – 730,000 | 1910 – 17,900,000 | 1946 – 32,350,000 |
| 1875 – 810,000 | 1911 – 18,100,000 | 1947 – 32,750,000 |
| 1876 – 910,000 | 1912 – 18,200,000 | 1948 – 33,100,000 |
| 1877 – 1,000,000 | 1913 – 18,900,000 | 1949 – 33,500,000 |
| 1878 – 1,150,000 | 1914 – 19,500,000 | 1950 – 33,560,000 |
| 1879 – 1,350,000 | 1915 – 20,000,000 | 1951 – 33,600,000 |
| 1880 – 1,500,000 | 1916 – 20,500,000 | 1952 – 33,700,000 |
| 1881 – 1,670,000 | 1917 – 20,900,000 | 1953 – 33,800,000 |
| 1882 – 1,835,000 | 1918 – 21,800,000 | 1954 – 34,100,000 |
| 1883 – 2,000,000 | 1919 – 22,500,000 | 1955 – 34,450,000 |
| 1884 – 2,350,000 | 1920 – 23,400,000 | 1956 – 34,700,000 |
| 1885 – 2,650,000 | 1921 – 23,900,000 | 1957 – 35,000,000 |
| 1886 – 3,000,000 | 1922 – 24,100,000 | |
| 1887 – 3,400,000 | 1923 – 24,300,000 | |

🕐 The above list is provided for determining the **APPROXIMATE** age of your watch. Match serial number with date. Watches were not necessarily *SOLD* and *DELIVERED* in the exact order of manufactured or production dates.

C. V. WOERD.
Compensation-Balance.
No. 203,976.          Patented May 21, 1878.

HOWARD, DAVIS & DENNISON: 20 Size, 15 Jewels, 8 day, two mainsprings and gilt movement. The first 17 were made for the officials of the company, Ca. 1852.

Woerd's patented compensating balance the above illustration is a copy of the blue print of Mr. Woerd's patented SAW TOOTH BALANCE. The Saw Tooth Balance may be found on some 16 size 1872 models. (**VERY RARE**)

🕐 Generic, nameless or unmarked grades for watch movements are listed under the Company name or initials of the Company, etc. by size, jewel count and description.

## 20 SIZE
## MODEL 1862,-20-KW
### T. P. 3,500

| Grade or Name–Description | | Avg | Ex -Fn | Mint |
|---|---|---|---|---|
| American Watch Co., 19J, KW, 18K, HC, all original | ★★ | $3,800 | $4,500 | $6,000 |
| American Watch Co., 15 to19J, KW, KS,3/4, vibrating hair-spring stud, silver case | ★★ | 1,400 | 2,000 | 2,500 |
| American Watch Co., 15 to 19J, KW, KS, 3/4, vibrating hair-spring stud, 18K HC, all original | ★★ | 3,500 | 4,000 | 5,500 |
| American Watch Co., 15 & 17J,3/4, KW, ADJ | ★ | 500 | 650 | 900 |
| American Watch Co., 19J,3/4, KW, ADJ | ★★ | 2,200 | 2,600 | 3,200 |
| American Watch Co., 19J,3/4, KW, ADJ, with Maltese cross stopwork, all original silver case | ★★ | 2,800 | 3,200 | 4,000 |
| American W. Co., 15J,3/4, KW | ★ | 400 | 550 | 800 |
| American W. Co., 7-11J,3/4, KW | ★ | 300 | 400 | 550 |
| American W. Co., 19J,3/4W, Stratons Pat. Barrel | ★★ | 2,000 | 2,500 | 3,500 |
| American W. Co., Nashua S# under dial, (below 51,000) | ★★★ | 4,000 | 5,000 | 6,000 |
| American W. Co., Woerd's Pat., Cam Reg. | ★★★ | 2,200 | 2,500 | 3,300 |
| Am'n W. Co., 15J, KW,3/4, coin case | ★ | 300 | 375 | 450 |
| Am'n W. Co., 15J, KW,3/4, Mvt. only | | 150 | 200 | 275 |
| Appleton, Tracy & Co., 15J,3/4, KW, with Maltese cross stopwork, all original | ★ | 500 | 650 | 900 |
| Appleton, Tracy & Co., 15 & 17J,3/4,KW gold balance | ★ | 450 | 550 | 700 |
| Appleton, Tracy & Co., 15 & 17J,3/4, KW | | 250 | 400 | 550 |
| Appleton, Tracy & Co., 15 & 17J,3/4, KW, vibrating hair spring stud, silver case | ★★ | 1,000 | 1,200 | 1,600 |
| Appleton, Tracy & Co., 15 & 17J,3/4, KW, vibrating hair spring stud, 18K HC | ★★★ | 2,800 | 3,200 | 3,600 |
| Appleton Tracy & Co., 15J, KW, Vibrating hairspring stud Straton barrel, Foggs Pat. | ★★ | 800 | 1,000 | 1,200 |
| Appleton Tracy & Co., 15J, KW,3/4, Mvt. only | | 125 | 150 | 225 |
| Appleton Tracy & Co., 19J, KW,3/4 | ★★ | 500 | 600 | 800 |
| Howard, Davis & Dennison, S#1-17, 8 day, Ca.1852 | ★★★★★ | 30,000 | 40,000 | 58,000 |

🕐 Generic, nameless or unmarked grades for watch movements are listed under the Company name or initials of the Company, etc. by size, jewel count and description.

**American Watch Co.**, Model 1862, 20 size, 17 jewels, gold balance and escape wheel, gold jeweled settings, key wind, key set from back, serial number 80111.

**Appleton Tracy & Co.**, Model 20KW, 20 size, 15 jewels, serial number 125004. Note vibrating hairspring stud.

AMERICAN WATCH CO., Model 18KW, 18 size, 15 jewels, serial number 36369. Reversible center pinion, patented Nov. 30th, 1858.

Model 1857, 18 size, 15-16 jewels, "Chronodrometer" on dial, "Appleton Tracy & Co." or "P.S. Bartlett, key wind & set, 1/4 jump seconds, S.# 14,752 . Listed under "**Appleton Tracy & Co. Chronodrometer**", Ist serial # 13,701.

## 18 SIZE
## MODELS 1857, 18KW =1859, 1870, 1877, 1879, 1883, 1892

| Grade or Name – Description | Avg | Ex-Fn | Mint |
|---|---|---|---|
| American Watch Co., 17J,3/4, KW, M#18, KW ......... ★ ★ ★ | $1,400 | $1,700 | $2,200 |
| American Watch Co., 19J, M#1859, 3/4............... ★ ★ ★ ★ | 2,800 | 3,400 | 4,200 |
| American Watch Co., 19J, M#1888, HC, silver ......... ★ ★ | 800 | 1,000 | 1,400 |
| American Watch Co.,15-16-17J, M#1883 ........................ | 75 | 100 | 150 |
| American Watch Co., 21J, M#1883, Special, ADJ, GJS ...... ★ ★ ★ | 400 | 525 | 700 |
| American Watch Co., 15J, M#1859,3/4, Pat. Nov. 30, 1858, Reversible center pinion, original silver case ............... ★ ★ ★ | 3,000 | 3,300 | 4,000 |
| American Watch Co., 17J, M#1859,3/4, KW, Fitts Pat. Reversible center pinion, Originial 18K case .......... ★ ★ ★ ★ | 4,000 | 4,800 | 6,000 |
| American Watch Co., 15J, M#1870, KW ........................ | 200 | 250 | 350 |

🕐 Generic, nameless or unmarked grades for watch movements are listed under the Company name or initials of the Company, etc. by size, jewel count and description.

| | Avg | Ex-Fn | Mint |
|---|---|---|---|
| AMn. Watch Co., 15J, M#1857, KW, KS ........................ | $75 | $100 | $175 |
| AMn. Watch Co., 17J, M#1857, KW, KS ........................ ★ | 200 | 250 | 350 |
| AMn. Watch Co., 14K, HC, heavy box hinged, multi-color (4 colors) ........................ | 2,200 | 2,400 | 3,200 |
| AMn. Watch Co., 11J, thin model, KW, 3/4 plate ............. ★ | 175 | 275 | 500 |
| AMn. Watch Co., 15 & 17J, M#1870, KW, ADJ ............. | 150 | 200 | 300 |
| AMn. Watch Co., 17J, M#1892 ........................ | 85 | 100 | 150 |
| AMn. Watch Co., 21J, M#1892 ........................ | 200 | 225 | 275 |
| AMn. Watch Co., 7J, M#1877 ........................ | 75 | 100 | 125 |
| AMn. Watch Co., 11J, M#1877 ........................ | 75 | 100 | 125 |
| AMn. Watch Co., 7J, M#1883, SW/ KW ........................ | 75 | 100 | 125 |
| AMn. Watch Co., 11-13J, M#1883, SW/ KW ........................ | 75 | 100 | 125 |
| AMn. Watch Co., 15J, M#1883, SW/ KW ........................ | 80 | 100 | 150 |
| AMn. Watch Co., 15J, M#1857, SW ........................ ★ | 200 | 300 | 450 |
| Appleton, Tracy & Co., 7-11J, KW, M#1857 ........................ | 125 | 150 | 200 |
| Appleton, Tracy & Co., 11J, thin model, KW,3/4 .............. ★ | 250 | 350 | 450 |
| Appleton, Tracy & Co., 15J, M#1857, SW ........................ | 100 | 125 | 175 |

🕐 Some watch manufacturers personalize watches for jobbers or jewelry firms, with exclusive private signed or marked movements. The valuable collectable watches are listed under the signed or marked movement. Other exclusive private signed or marked movements will have equivalent value are only slightly higher value and should be compared to Generic or Nameless movements. Railroad signed or marked (dials & movements) are usually more collectable & higher in value.

| Grade or Name–Description | Avg | Ex-Fn | Mint |
|---|---|---|---|
| Appleton, Tracy & Co., 15J, M#1859, 3/4, reverse pinion, Pat. Nov. 30, 1858, orig. silver case ............ ★★★ | $1,200 | $1,450 | $1,800 |
| Appleton, Tracy & Co., 11-15-16-17J, KW, 3/4 ...................★ | 250 | 325 | 450 |
| Appleton, Tracy & Co., 16J, M#1857, **Ist run** (5,001-5,100) Am. W. Co. (Eagle) silver HC .................... ★★ | 600 | 675 | 800 |
| Appleton, Tracy & Co., 15J, M#1857, KW, 18K HC ...................... | 600 | 700 | 1,000 |
| Appleton, Tracy & Co., 16J, M#1857, KW ................................ | 200 | 225 | 375 |
| Appleton, Tracy & Co., 15J, 3/4, KW, with vibrating hairspring stud, Stratton's Pat., coin case ........................ ★★★ | 1,400 | 1,600 | 2,000 |
| Appleton, Tracy & Co., 15J, 3/4, KW, with vibrating hairspring stud, orig. 18K case ................................. ★★★ | 2,000 | 2,400 | 2,800 |
| Appleton, Tracy & Co., Sporting, (Chronodrometer), M#1857, 16J, KW, KS, orig. case, with stop feature ...................... ★★ | 1,500 | 1,900 | 2,500 |
| Appleton, Tracy & Co., 15J, KW, Fitts Pat., pinion................. ★★ | 400 | 475 | 600 |
| Appleton, Tracy & Co., 15J, 3/4, KW.................................★ | 150 | 200 | 285 |
| Appleton, Tracy & Co., 15J, M#1857, SW ............................ | 100 | 125 | 175 |
| Appleton, Tracy & Co., 11-15J, M#s 1877, 1879, SW ................... | 65 | 75 | 100 |
| Appleton, Tracy & Co., 15J, M#1877, KW ............................ | 70 | 85 | 120 |
| Appleton, Tracy & Co., 15J, M#s 1877-1879, SW, OF ................. | 65 | 75 | 100 |
| Appleton, Tracy & Co., 15J, M#s 1877-1879, SW, HC ................. | 85 | 100 | 150 |
| Appleton, Tracy & Co., 15J, M#1883, SW, OF ....................... | 65 | 75 | 95 |
| Appleton, Tracy & Co., 15J, M#1883, SW, HC ....................... | 85 | 100 | 150 |
| Appleton, Tracy & Co., 15J, M#1892, SW, OF ....................... | 70 | 85 | 100 |
| Appleton, Tracy & Co., 17J, m#1863, LS .........................★ | 150 | 200 | 295 |
| Appleton, Tracy & Co., 17J, M#1892, SW, Premiere ................. | 75 | 100 | 150 |
| Appleton, Tracy & Co., 17J, M#1892, SW, OF ....................... | 70 | 95 | 125 |
| Appleton, Tracy & Co., 17J, M#1883, SW, 2 tone mvt. Lehigh Valley Railroad ................................★ | 500 | 650 | 800 |
| Appleton, Tracy & Co., 17J, M#1883, SW, HC........................... | 85 | 100 | 150 |
| Appleton, Tracy & Co., 17J, M#1883, OF ........................... | 70 | 80 | 100 |
| Appleton, Tracy & Co., 17J, M#1892, SW, HC ....................... | 85 | 100 | 150 |
| Appleton, Tracy & Co., 19J, M#1892, SW, OF ....................... | 150 | 175 | 200 |
| Appleton, Tracy & Co., 19J, M#1892, SW, HC ....................... | 175 | 200 | 250 |
| Appleton, Tracy & Co., 21J, M#1892, SW, OF ....................... | 200 | 250 | 300 |
| Appleton, Tracy & Co., 21J, M#1892, SW, HC ....................... | 300 | 325 | 400 |

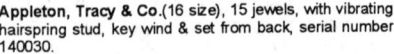

**Appleton, Tracy & Co.** (16 size), 15 jewels, with vibrating hairspring stud, key wind & set from back, serial number 140030.

**P. S. Bartlett,** Model 18KW or 1859, 18 size, 11 jewels, key wind & set from back, serial number 41597.

🕐 Generic, nameless or unmarked grades for watch movements are listed under the Company name or initials of the Company, etc. by size, jewel count and description.

| Grade or Name – Description | Avg | Ex-Fn | Mint |
|---|---|---|---|
| A. W. W. Co., 7-9J, M#1883, KW, OF | $75 | $85 | $100 |
| A. W. W. Co., 7-9J, M#1883, SW, OF | 65 | 75 | 85 |
| A. W. W. Co., 11-13J, LS, HC | 75 | 100 | 150 |
| A. W. W. Co., 11-13J, M#1879, OF | 60 | 65 | 80 |
| A. W. W. Co., 11-13J, M#1883, SW, OF | 60 | 65 | 80 |
| A. W. W. Co., 15J, OF | 65 | 70 | 90 |
| A. W. W. Co., 15J, HC | 75 | 100 | 150 |
| A. W. W. Co., 15J, 14K multi-color boxcase HC | 2,000 | 2,300 | 2,750 |
| A. W. W. Co., 15J, M#1879, OF | 65 | 75 | 90 |
| A. W. W. Co., 15J, M#1883, OF | 65 | 70 | 85 |
| A. W. W. Co., 16J, OF or HC | 75 | 100 | 150 |
| A. W. W. Co., 17J, M#1857, gold bal. wheel, GJS, ★ | 250 | 325 | 450 |
| A. W. W. Co., 17J, "for R.R. Service" on dial ★ | 200 | 295 | 350 |
| A. W. W. Co., 17J, M#1883, OF | 70 | 75 | 90 |
| A. W. W. Co., 17J, M#1892, LS, OF | 80 | 90 | 135 |
| A. W. W. Co., 17J, M#1892, PS, OF | 70 | 80 | 125 |
| A. W. W. Co., 17J, M#1892, HC | 75 | 100 | 150 |
| A. W. W. Co., 19J, M#1892 | 100 | 120 | 150 |
| A. W. W. Co., 21J, M#1892 | 200 | 225 | 250 |
| A. W. W. Co., 23J, M#1892 | 250 | 275 | 325 |

P.S. Bartlett, 18 size, 15 jewels, Model 1857, Engraved on back "4 PR. Jewels." Serial number 13446.

Canadian Railway Time Service, Model 1892, 18 size, 17 jewels, serial number 22,017,534.

| Grade or Name – Description | Avg | Ex-Fn | Mint |
|---|---|---|---|
| P. S. Bartlett, 7J, M#1857, KW, 1st Run (1,401-1,500 ★★ | | | |
| Am.W. Co. (Eagle) silver HC | $700 | $800 | $950 |
| P. S. Bartlett, 15J, M#1857, KW, 2nd Run (1,551-1,650) | | | |
| Am.W. Co. (Eagle) silver HC ★★ | 600 | 700 | 850 |
| P. S. Bartlett, 11J, M#1857, KW, 2nd-3rd Run | 300 | 375 | 500 |
| P. S. Bartlett, 15J, M#1857, KW, 2nd-3rd Run | 325 | 450 | 585 |
| P. S. Bartlett, 11J, LS, HC, 14K | 550 | 650 | 850 |
| P. S. Bartlett, 15J, M#1857, KW, below S#8,000 | 200 | 250 | 400 |
| P. S. Bartlett, 11J, M#1879, KW | 65 | 75 | 125 |
| P. S. Bartlett, 11J, M#1857, KW, Eagle inside case lid | 125 | 150 | 175 |
| P. S. Bartlett, 15J, M#1879, KW | 75 | 100 | 150 |

| Grade or Name – Description | Avg | Ex-Fn | Mint |
|---|---|---|---|
| P. S. Bartlett, 15J, M#1879, SW | $65 | $75 | $80 |
| P. S. Bartlett, 11-15J, M#1870, SW | 75 | 85 | 100 |
| P. S. Bartlett, 11-15J, M#1877, KW | 100 | 125 | 175 |
| P. S. Bartlett, 11J, M#1883, SW | 60 | 70 | 100 |
| P. S. Bartlett, 15J, M#1883, KW | 75 | 100 | 150 |
| P. S. Bartlett, 17J, M#1883, SW | 55 | 70 | 100 |
| P. S. Bartlett, 15J, M#1883, SW | 65 | 75 | 100 |
| P. S. Bartlett, 11J, M#1859, 3/4, thin model, KS from back | 275 | 350 | 450 |
| P. S. Bartlett, 11J, M#1859, 3/4, Pat. Nov. 30, 1858 | 400 | 500 | 625 |
| P. S. Bartlett, 15J, **pinned plates**, M#1857, KW ★ | 700 | 800 | 1,000 |
| P. S. Bartlett, 15J, M#1892, SW | 70 | 75 | 100 |
| P. S. Bartlett, 17J, M#1892, SW, OF, LS | 75 | 85 | 110 |
| P. S. Bartlett, 17J, M#1892, SW, HC | 125 | 145 | 175 |
| P. S. Bartlett, 17J, M#1892, OF, PS | 75 | 80 | 110 |
| P. S. Bartlett, 17J, M#1892, SW, 2-Tone | 85 | 95 | 120 |
| P. S. Bartlett, 19J, M#1892, SW | 150 | 175 | 200 |
| P. S. Bartlett, 21J, M#1892, SW | 200 | 225 | 265 |
| P. S. Bartlett, 21J, M#1892, SW, 2-Tone | 250 | 275 | 325 |
| Broadway, 7J, M#1857, KW, HC | 85 | 100 | 150 |
| Broadway, 11J, M#1857, KW, HC | 100 | 125 | 150 |
| Broadway, 7-11J, M#1877, KW, SW, NI, HC | 100 | 125 | 150 |
| Broadway, 7J, M#1883, KW, HC | 100 | 125 | 150 |
| Broadway, 11J, M#1883, KW, HC | 100 | 125 | 150 |
| Broadway, 11J, M#1883, SW, HC | 100 | 125 | 150 |
| Canadian Railway Time Service, 17J, M#1883-1892, Adj.5P | 325 | 375 | 435 |
| Central Park, 15J, M#1857, KW | 150 | 175 | 225 |
| Champion, 15J, M#1877, OF | 50 | 75 | 100 |
| Crescent Park, 15J, M#1857 | 150 | 175 | 225 |
| Crescent Street, 15J, M#1870, KW | 150 | 185 | 225 |
| Crescent Street, 15J, M#1870, **pin or nail set** | 160 | 195 | 250 |
| Crescent Street, 17J, M#1870, KW ★ | 200 | 225 | 300 |

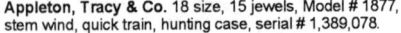

**Appleton, Tracy & Co.** 18 size, 15 jewels, Model # 1877, stem wind, quick train, hunting case, serial # 1,389,078.

**Crescent Street,** Model 1870, 18 size, 15 J., Key wind & set from back, serial number 552,526.

🕐 Watches listed in this book are priced at the collectable retail level, as **complete** watches having an original 14k gold-filled case and Key Wind with silver, an original white enamel single sunk dial, and with the entire original movement in good working order with no repairs needed.

🕐 Some watch manufacturers personalize watches for jobbers or jewelry firms, with exclusive private signed or marked movements. The valuable collectable watches are listed under the signed or marked movement. Other exclusive private signed or marked movements will have equivalent value are only slightly higher value and should be compared to Generic or Nameless movements. Railroad signed or marked (dials & movements) are usually more collectable & higher in value.

| Grade or Name–Description | Avg | Ex-Fn | Mint |
|---|---|---|---|
| Crescent Street, 15J, M#1870, SW | $125 | $150 | $200 |
| Crescent Street, 15J, M#1883, SW, non-magnetic, OF | 100 | 145 | 200 |
| Crescent Street, 15J, M#1883, SW, non-magnetic, HC | 100 | 125 | 175 |
| Crescent Street, 15J, M#1883, SW, 2-Tone | 100 | 125 | 175 |
| Crescent Street, 17J, M#1883, SW, OF | 85 | 100 | 150 |
| Crescent Street, 17J, M#1883, SW, HC | 100 | 125 | 175 |
| Crescent Street, 19J, M#1883 ★ | 250 | 285 | 335 |
| Crescent Street, 17J, M#1892, SW, GJS | 100 | 125 | 175 |
| Crescent Street, 17J, M#1892, SW, OF | 85 | 100 | 135 |
| Crescent Street, 17J, M#1892, SW, HC | 100 | 125 | 175 |
| Crescent Street, 19J, M#1892, SW, Adj.5P, GJS ,OF | 150 | 175 | 200 |
| Crescent Street, 19J, M#1892, SW, Adj.5P, GJS ,HC | 200 | 225 | 265 |
| Crescent Street, 21J, M#1892, SW, Adj.5P, GJS, OF | 200 | 235 | 300 |
| Crescent Street, 21J, M#1892, SW, Adj.5P, GJS, HC | 275 | 300 | 365 |
| Crescent Street, 21J, M#1892, Wind Indicator | 900 | 1,100 | 1,500 |
| Samuel Curtis, 11-15J, M#1857, KW, S# less than200, original 17S silver case ★ ★ | 3,000 | 3,500 | 4,000 |
| Samuel Curtis, 11-15J, M#1857, KW, S# less than 400, original 17S silver case ★ ★ | 2,500 | 3,000 | 3,800 |
| Samuel Curtis, 11-15J, M#1857, KW, S# less than 600, original 17S silver case ★ ★ | 2,300 | 2,700 | 3,500 |
| Samuel Curtis, 11-15J, M#1857, KW, S# less than 1,000, original 17S silver case ★ | 2,000 | 2,500 | 3,200 |
| (Samuel Curtis not in original silver case, deduct $800 to $1,000 from value) | | | |
| Dennison, Howard, Davis, 7J, M#1857, KW, W/original case | 600 | 700 | 800 |
| Dennison, Howard, Davis, 11-13J, M#1857, KW, W/original case | 700 | 850 | 900 |
| Dennison, Howard, Davis, 15J, M#1857, KW, W/original case | 900 | 1,100 | 1,300 |
| Dennison, Howard, Davis, 15J, M#1857, KW, 1st. run (1,002-1,100) W/original case Am.W. Co. (Eagle)silver HC ★ ★ | 1,200 | 1,400 | 1,800 |
| Dennison, Howard, Davis, 15J, M#1857, KW, S# less than 2,000, W/original case Am.W. Co. (Eagle)silver HC ★ | 900 | 1,000 | 1,200 |

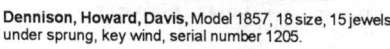

Dennison, Howard, Davis, Model 1857, 18 size, 15 jewels, under sprung, key wind, serial number 1205.

Howard & Rice, Model 1857, 18 size, 15 jewels, under sprung, serial number 6003.

🕐 Watches listed in this book are priced at the collectable retail level, as **complete** watches having an original 14k gold-filled case and Key Wind with silver, an original white enamel single sunk dial, and with the entire original movement in good working order with no repairs needed.

🕐 Some watch manufacturers personalize watches for jobbers or jewelry firms, with exclusive private signed or marked movements. The valuable collectable watches are listed under the signed or marked movement. Other exclusive private signed or marked movements will have equivalent value are only slightly higher value and should be compared to Generic or Nameless movements. Railroad signed or marked (dials & movements) are usually more collectable & higher in value.

| Grade or Name –Description | Avg | Ex-Fn | Mint |
|---|---|---|---|
| Denver & Rio Grande, 21J, M#1892, GJS, Adj.3P ........................ | $950 | $1,200 | $1,500 |
| Dominion Railway, 15J, M#1883, OF, SW, train on dial .............. | 700 | 900 | 1,200 |
| Wm. Ellery, 7-11J, M#1857, Boston, Mass. all original silver HC case with Am. Watch Co.& eagle, serial # below 46,600 ........ ★ ★ | 350 | 450 | 600 |
| Wm. Ellery, 7-11J, M#1857, Boston, Mass. ..................................... | 85 | 100 | 150 |
| Wm. Ellery, 7-11J, M#KW, 3/4 .......................................................... | 150 | 175 | 250 |
| Wm. Ellery, 15J, KW, 3/4 ............................................................★ | 320 | 375 | 450 |
| Wm. Ellery, 7-11J, M#18KW, KW-KS from back, 18K, HC ........ | 1,000 | 1,200 | 1,500 |
| Wm. Ellery, 7J, M#1857, KW, KS from back ............................... | 175 | 200 | 275 |
| Wm. Ellery, 15J, M#1857, SW ...............................................★ | 200 | 300 | 450 |
| Wm. Ellery, 7-15J, M#1877, M#1879, KW ................................... | 85 | 100 | 150 |
| Wm. Ellery, 11-15J, M#1877 & 1879, SW ................................... | 75 | 100 | 150 |
| Wm. Ellery, 7-13J, M#1883 ............................................................. | 65 | 75 | 100 |
| Excelsior, M#1857, KW ..................................................................... | 80 | 95 | 140 |
| Export, 7-11J, M#1877 ...................................................................... | 65 | 75 | 120 |
| Export, 7-11J, M#1883, KW .............................................................. | 75 | 100 | 150 |
| Favorite, 15J, M#1877 ...................................................................... | 75 | 100 | 150 |
| Fellows & Schell, 15J, KW, KS .............................................★ ★ ★ | 1,500 | 1,700 | 2,000 |
| Franklin, 7J, M#1877, SW.................................................................. | 125 | 145 | 200 |
| Home Watch Co., 7-15J, M#1857-1883, KW ................................ | 75 | 95 | 125 |
| Home Watch Co., 7J, M#1877, KW .............................................. | 75 | 95 | 125 |
| Home Watch Co., 7-11J, M#1879, SW........................................... | 75 | 95 | 125 |
| Howard & Rice, 15J, M#1857, KW, KS (serial numbers range from 6000 to 6500)...............................................................★ ★ | 1,200 | 1,400 | 1,700 |
| E. Howard & Co., Boston (on dial & mvt.), English style escape wheel, upright pallets, 15J, M#1857, KW, KS, S#s about 6,400 to 6,500 .........................................★ ★ ★ ★ | 2,500 | 2,800 | 3,500 |
| Martyn Square, 7-15J, M#1857-1877-1879, KW, SW (exported) .. | 120 | 150 | 200 |
| Mermod, Jaccard & KingParagon Timekeeper, 23J, M#1892, Vanguard, LS, GJS, HC .......................................................... | 400 | 450 | 500 |

**Pennsylvania Special,** Model 1892, 18 size, 21 jewels, serial number 14,000,015.

**Waltham Standard,** Grade 1892, 18 size, 19 jewels, Adj5P, open face, note engine & coal car engraved on movement, serial number 10,099,625.

🕐 Some watch manufacturers personalize watches for jobbers or jewelry firms, with exclusive private signed or marked movements. The valuable collectable watches are listed under the signed or marked movement. Other exclusive private signed or marked movements will have equivalent value are only slightly higher value and should be compared to Generic or Nameless movements. Railroad signed or marked (dials & movements) are usually more collectable & higher in value.

| Grade or Name –Description | Avg | Ex-Fn | Mint |
|---|---|---|---|
| Non-Magnetic, 15J, SW, LS, NI | $100 | $125 | $175 |
| Non-Magnetic, 17J, M#1892, SW, LS | 150 | 175 | 250 |
| Paragon, 15J, M#1883, HC | 100 | 125 | 175 |
| C. T. Parker, 7-11J, M#1857, KW, silver HC | 400 | 550 | 800 |
| Chas. T. Parker, 11-15J, M#1857, KW, HC | 350 | 450 | 600 |
| C. T. Parker, 7-11J, M#1857, KW, Am.W. Co. (Eagle)silver HC serial # below 1,200 ★★ | 1,200 | 1,400 | 1,800 |
| C. T. Parker, 7-11J, M#1857, KW, 18K, HC serial # below 1,400 ★★ | 1,800 | 2,000 | 2,500 |
| Pennsylvania R.R. on dial, Appleton, Tracy & Co. on Mvt., KW, KS, M# 1859 ★★ | 2,500 | 2,900 | 3,600 |
| Pennsylvania Special, 21J, M#1892, HC ★★★ | 1,400 | 1,600 | 2,000 |
| Pennsylvania Special, 21J, M#1892, OF ★★★ | 1,200 | 1,400 | 1,800 |
| Pennsylvania Special, 21J, M#1892, HC GOLD DAMASKEENED ★★★★ | 10,000 | 12,000 | 15,000 |
| Pennsylvania Special, 23J, M#1892, OF ★★★ | 2,000 | 2,200 | 2,600 |
| Pioneer, 7J, M#1883 | 60 | 75 | 100 |
| Premier, 17J, M#1892, LS, OF | 125 | 145 | 175 |
| Railroad, 17J, M#1892, LS | 275 | 350 | 425 |
| Railroad, 21J, M#1892, LS | 350 | 450 | 600 |
| Railroader, 17J, M#1892, LS, Adj, GJS, OF ★★ | 500 | 600 | 800 |
| Railroad King, 15J, M#1883, LS | 200 | 250 | 350 |
| Railroad King, 15J, M#1883, 2-Tone | 250 | 300 | 400 |
| Railroad King, 17J, Special, M#1883, LS | 300 | 350 | 450 |
| Railroad Standard, 19J, G#1892, OF ★ | 500 | 600 | 800 |
| (Railroad Watches with R.R. names on dial and movement as follows: ) | | | |
| Canadian Pacific R.R., 17J, M#1883 | 300 | 350 | 425 |
| Canadian Pacific R.R., 17J, M#1892-1908 | 350 | 450 | 575 |
| Canadian Pacific R.R., 21J, M#1892 | 400 | 500 | 625 |
| Santa Fe Route, 17J, M#1883 | 425 | 500 | 625 |
| Santa Fe Route, 17J, M#1892 ★ | 525 | 650 | 800 |
| Conklins Railroad Special, 21J, G#1892 | 500 | 550 | 625 |
| Rio Grande Western, 17J, G#1892, OF ★ | 850 | 900 | 1,000 |
| Riverside, 7J, M#1857 | 100 | 125 | 175 |
| Riverside, 17J, M#1892 ★ | 300 | 350 | 450 |
| Roadmaster, 17J, M#1892, LS ★ | 350 | 400 | 475 |
| R. E. Robbins, 11-15J, M#1857, KW S# (25,101-25,200) ★ | 600 | 700 | 800 |
| R. E. Robbins, 13-15J, M#1877, KW | 200 | 250 | 350 |
| R. E. Robbins, 13J, M#1883 | 100 | 125 | 175 |

Sidereal, model #1892, 17j, 24 hour dial used by astrono-mers.

Vanguard, Model 1892, 18 size, 23 jewels, diamond end stone, gold jewel settings, exposed winding gears, serial number 10,533,465.

| Grade or Name – Description | Avg | Ex-Fn | Mint |
|---|---|---|---|
| Royal, 17J, M#1892, OF ................................................. | $75 | $95 | $125 |
| Royal, 17J, M#1892, HC ................................................. | 125 | 145 | 200 |
| Sidereal, M#1892, 19J, OF .............................. ★★★ | 1,200 | 1,500 | 2,000 |
| M#1892, 17J, Astronomical Sidereal ................... ★★★ | 1,000 | 1,300 | 1,800 |
| Sol, 7-11J, M#1883, OF ................................................. | 65 | 80 | 100 |
| Sol, 17J, OF, PS ............................................................ | 75 | 95 | 125 |
| Special Railroad, 17J, M#1883, LS, OF ..................... | 300 | 345 | 450 |
| Special R. R. King, 15J, M#1883 ................................. | 350 | 400 | 550 |
| Special R. R. King, 17J, M#1883, HC ......................... | 450 | 500 | 650 |
| Sterling, 7J, M#1857, KW, Silver ............................... | 95 | 110 | 150 |
| Sterling, 7-11J, M#1877, M#1879 ............................... | 65 | 75 | 100 |
| Sterling, 7-11J, M#1883, KW ..................................... | 65 | 75 | 110 |
| Sterling, 11-15J, M#1883, SW ..................................... | 65 | 75 | 100 |
| Tourist, 11J, M#1877 ................................................... | 65 | 75 | 100 |
| Tourist, 7J, M#1877 ..................................................... | 65 | 75 | 100 |
| Tracy, Baker & Co., 15J, 18K original A.W.W. Co. case ........................................................... ★★★★ | 4,900 | 5,500 | 6,300 |
| Vanguard, 17J, M#1892, GJS, HC .................... ★★★ | 400 | 500 | 650 |
| Vanguard, 17J, M#1892, LS, Adj.5P, DR, GJS, OF ............... ★★ | 300 | 400 | 550 |
| Vanguard, 17J, M#1892, Wind Indicator, Adj.5P, DR, GJS ......... | 800 | 1,000 | 1,200 |
| Vanguard, 19J, M#1892, LS, Adj.5P, Diamond end stones ........... | 175 | 200 | 250 |
| Vanguard, 19J, M#1892, LS, Adj.5P, DR, GJS, OF ................. | 175 | 200 | 250 |
| Vanguard, 19J, M#1892, Wind Indicator, LS, Adj.5P, DR, GJS..... | 1,000 | 1,200 | 1,400 |
| Vanguard, 19J, M#1892, Adj.5P, GJS, HC .................... ★ | 300 | 350 | 465 |
| Vanguard, 21J, M#1892, Adj.5P, PS ............................. | 200 | 250 | 310 |
| Vanguard, 21J, M#1892, HC, GJS, Adj.5P ................... | 325 | 350 | 400 |
| Vanguard, 21J, M#1892, LS, Adj.5P, DR, GJS, OF ..... | 200 | 235 | 275 |
| Vanguard, 21J, M#1892, LS, Adj.5P, Diamond end stone ............. | 225 | 265 | 300 |
| Vanguard, 21J, M#1892, WI, LS, Adj.5P, DR, GJS ..... ★ | 1,200 | 1,400 | 1,600 |
| Vanguard, 23J, M#1892, LS, Adj.5P, DR, GJS, OF ..... | 300 | 350 | 400 |
| Vanguard, 23J, M#1892, LS, Adj.5P, DR, GJS, HC ................... ★ | 375 | 450 | 500 |
| Vanguard, 23J, M#1892, LS, Adj.5P, DR, GJS, Diamond end stone ......................................................... | 300 | 375 | 450 |
| Vanguard, 23J, M#1892, PS, Adj.5P, DR, GJS, OF ..... | 300 | 350 | 400 |
| Vanguard, 23J, M#1892, Wind Indicator, LS, Adj.5P, DR,GJS. ................................................................. ★ | 1,300 | 1,600 | 1,900 |
| Waltham Standard,17J, Adj., G#1892, OF ...................... | 150 | 175 | 210 |
| Waltham Standard,19J, Adj., G#1892, (locomotive ),OF ............ ★ | 250 | 300 | 375 |

American Waltham Watch Co., Model 1883, 18 size, 15 jewels, serial number 3,093,425

Grade 845, Model 1892, 18 size, 21 jewels, railroad grade, Adj.5P, serial number 15,097,475

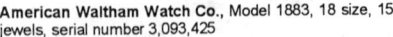

🕐 Watches listed in this book are priced at the collectable retail level, as **complete** watches having an original 14k gold-filled case and Key Wind with silver, an original white enamel single sunk dial, and with the entire original movement in good working order with no repairs needed.

J. WATSON, Boston Mass engraved on movement, 18 size, 11 jewels, hunting case, key wind key set, serial number 28,635, Ca. April 1863.

| Grade or Name – Description | Avg | Ex-Fn | Mint |
|---|---|---|---|
| Warren, 15J, M#1857, KW, KS, S#18-29, original 17S silver case.......................................................... ★ ★ ★ ★ ★ | $20,000 | $24,000 | $30,000 |
| Warren, 15J, M#1857, KW, KS, S#30-60, original 17S silver case................................................................ ★ ★ ★ ★ | 15,000 | 18,000 | 22,000 |
| Warren, 15J, M#1857, KW, KS, S#61-90, original 17S silver case................................................................ ★ ★ ★ ★ | 12,000 | 14,000 | 18,000 |
| Warren, 15J, M#1857, KW, KS, S#91-110, original 17S silver case................................................................... ★ ★ ★ | 9,000 | 12,000 | 16,000 |
| (Warren not in original silver case, deduct $1,000 to $2,500) | | | |
| George Washington, M#1857, KW.................................. | 275 | 350 | 450 |
| J. Watson, 7J, M#1857, KW, "Boston" S# (28,201-28,270)........ ★ | 500 | 700 | 1,000 |
| J. Watson, 7-11J, M#1857, KW, "London"S# (23,700-23,800). ★ | 500 | 700 | 1,000 |
| 45, 19J, GJS, 2-Tone, HC............................................ ★ ★ | 500 | 600 | 800 |
| 454, 21J, GT, 3/4, | 200 | 250 | 325 |
| 845, 21J, M#1892, OF................................................. | 200 | 225 | 265 |
| 845, 21J, M#1892, HC................................................. | 250 | 300 | 350 |
| 820, 825, M#1883..................................................... | 75 | 85 | 100 |
| 836, 17J, DR, Adj.4P, LS, OF....................................... | 75 | 95 | 125 |

American Watch Co., Model 16KW or Model 1868, 16 size, key wind and set from back, Gold Train, serial number 501,561.

American Watch Co., Model 1888, 16 size, 19 jewels, gold jewel settings, gold train, high grade movement, serial number 5,000,297.

🕐 Some watch manufacturers personalize watches for jobbers or jewelry firms, with exclusive private signed or marked movements. The valuable collectable watches are listed under the signed or marked movement. Other exclusive private signed or marked movements will have equivalent value are only slightly higher value and should be compared to Generic or Nameless movements. Railroad signed or marked (dials & movements) are usually more collectable & higher in value.

## 16 SIZE
### MODELS 16KW =1860, 1868, 1872, 1888,
### 1899, 1908, BRIDGE MODEL

| Grade or Name – Description | Avg | Ex-Fn | Mint |
|---|---|---|---|
| AMn. Watch Co., 7-15J, M#1872, KW KS, | | | |
|    sweep sec. with a slide stop button ★★ | $500 | $600 | $750 |
| AMn. Watch Co., 7-11J, M#1888, 3/4, SW | 60 | 70 | 100 |
| AMn. Watch Co., 7-11J, M#1888-1899 | 60 | 70 | 100 |
| AMn. Watch Co., 11J, M#16KW or 1868, KW & KS from back, | | | |
|    original silver case ★★ | 400 | 450 | 575 |
| AMn. Watch Co., 11J, M#1868, 3/4, KW | 175 | 200 | 250 |
| AMn. Watch Co., 13J, M#1888-1899 | 60 | 70 | 100 |
| AMn. Watch Co., 15-17J, M#1868, 3/4, KW | 200 | 225 | 275 |
| AMn. Watch Co., 15J, M#1868-1872, 3/4, SW | 100 | 125 | 175 |
| AMn. Watch Co., 15J, M#16KW, KW & KS from back ★★ | 400 | 450 | 575 |
| AMn. Watch Co., 15-16J, M#1888-1899, HC | 100 | 125 | 175 |
| AMn. Watch Co., 15J, M#1888-1899, SW, HC | 100 | 125 | 175 |
| AMn. Watch Co., 15J, M#1888-1899, SW, | 60 | 70 | 100 |
| AMn. Watch Co., 16-17J, M#1872, 3/4, SW | 150 | 175 | 225 |
| AMn. Watch Co., 17J, M#1888-1899 | 75 | 100 | 125 |
| AMn. Watch Co., 19J, M#1872, 3/4, SW ★★★ | 600 | 775 | 1,000 |
| AMn. Watch Co., 19J, M#1899 | 125 | 150 | 185 |

🕐 Generic, nameless or unmarked grades for watch movements are listed under the Company name or initials of the Company, etc. by size, jewel count and description.

American Watch Co., Model 1888, 16 size, 21 jewels, gold train, note tadpole regulator.

American Watch Co., Bridge Model, 16 size, 23 jewels gold train, Adj.5P.

| Grade or Name –Description | Avg | Ex-Fn | Mint |
|---|---|---|---|
| American Watch Co., 19J Maltese cross stopwork, gilt mvt. | | | |
|    all original 1860 Model, 18K ★★ | $1,500 | $1,800 | $2,200 |
| American Watch Co., 17-19J, 3/4, KW & KS from back, | | | |
|    vibrating hairspring stud, 1860 Model, 18K ★★★ | 1,200 | 1,500 | 1,900 |
| American Watch Co., 19J, 3/4 , KW & KS from back, nickel mvt. | | | |
|    1860 Model, original case, 18K ★★★ | 2,500 | 2,800 | 3,500 |
| American Watch Co., 15J, M#1868, 3/4, KW, Silver ★★★ | 300 | 350 | 475 |
| American Watch Co., 17J, M#1872,3/4,SW,HC,14K ★ | 900 | 1,100 | 1,250 |
| American Watch Co., 17J, M#1868, 3/4, KW, ADJ, Silver ★★ | 400 | 425 | 550 |
| American Watch Co., 17J, M#1899, Adj.5P, ★ | 250 | 275 | 325 |
| American Watch Co., 18J, M#1868, SW, nickel mvt. | 450 | 500 | 600 |
| American Watch Co., 19J, M#1868, SW, nickel mvt. | | | |
|    Silver case ★★★ | 1,500 | 1,800 | 2,400 |
| American Watch Co., 19J, M#1888, SW, nickel mvt. ★ | 400 | 450 | 550 |
| American Watch Co., 19J, M#1899, SW, nickel mvt. ★ | 550 | 600 | 700 |

| Grade or Name — Description | Avg | Ex-Fn | Mint |
|---|---|---|---|
| American Watch Co., 19J, M#1872, 3/4, SW ..................... ★★★ | $600 | $700 | $900 |
| American Watch Co., 19-21J, M#1868-1872, 3/4, GJS, "Woerd's pat. compensating bal.", **With sawtooth bal.**, all original . ★★★ | 2,000 | 2,500 | 3,200 |
| American Watch Co., 19-21J, M#1868-1872, 3/4, GJS, "Woerd's pat. compensating balalance" on movt. **without sawtooth bal.** .... | 1,200 | 1,350 | 1,550 |
| American Watch Co., 19-21J, M#1872, 3/4, SW .................... ★★ | 1,200 | 1,350 | 1,550 |
| American Watch Co., 19-21J, M#1872, 3/4, SW, 18k......... ★★★ | 1,500 | 1,800 | 2,200 |
| American Watch Co., 19J, M#1888, 14K ................................. ★★ | 700 | 850 | 1,050 |
| American Watch Co., 19J, M#1888 ............................................... ★ | 300 | 400 | 550 |
| American Watch Co., 21J, M#1888, NI, 3/4 ........................... ★★ | 400 | 500 | 700 |
| American Watch Co., 23J, M# 1899, Adj.5P, GT, GJS .................. | 600 | 675 | 800 |
| American Watch Co., 23J, BRG, Adj.5P, GT, GJS, 14K original case ................................................................ ★★★ | 1,300 | 1,800 | 2,200 |
| American Watch Co., 23J, BRG, Adj.5P, GT, GJS, 18K original case ................................................................ ★★★ | 1,500 | 1,900 | 2,400 |
| American Watch Co., 23J, BRG, Adj.5P, GT, GJS ..................... ★ | 900 | 1,200 | 1,600 |
| American Watch Co., 21J, BRG, Adj.5P, GT, GJS ..................... ★ | 600 | 650 | 750 |
| American Watch Co., 19J, BRG, Adj.5P, GT, GJS ..................... ★ | 450 | 495 | 550 |
| American Watch Co., 17J, BRG, Adj.5P, GT, GJS ..................... ★ | 300 | 335 | 450 |
| Appleton, Tracy & Co., 15J, M#1860, 3/4, KW & KS from back, all original silver case ............................................ | 500 | 575 | 700 |
| Appleton, Tracy & Co., 15J, M#1868, 3/4, KW ............................. | 300 | 350 | 450 |
| Appleton, Tracy & Co., 15J, KW, with vibrating hairspring stud, all original, silver case ........................... ★★ | 700 | 850 | 1,200 |
| Appleton, Tracy & Co., 15J, 3/4, KW, with vibrating hairspring stud, 18K, original case.................................... ★★ | 1,200 | 1,500 | 2,200 |

🕒 Generic, nameless or unmarked grades for watch movements are listed under the Company name or initials of the Company, etc. by size, jewel count and description.

| | | | |
|---|---|---|---|
| A. W. Co., 7J, M#1872, SW, HC...................................................... | 100 | 125 | 175 |
| A. W. W. Co., 7J, SW, M#1888........................................................ | 55 | 60 | 80 |
| A. W. Co., 7J, SW, DMK................................................................. | 55 | 60 | 80 |
| A. W. Co., 9J, SW, ........................................................................... | 55 | 60 | 80 |
| A. W. W. Co., 11-13J, SW ............................................................... | 55 | 60 | 80 |
| A. W. Co., 11J, M#1899, SW........................................................... | 55 | 60 | 80 |
| A. W. Co., 11-15J, M#1872, SW, HC............................................. | 100 | 125 | 175 |
| A. W. W. Co., 13J, M#1888-99, OF ............................................... | 55 | 60 | 80 |

Woerd's pat. **compensating balance** the above illustration is a copy of the blue print of Mr. Woerd's patented **Saw Tooth Balance.** This bal. **must** be in watch for top prices.

**Crescent Street**, Model 16–S ( CENTER SECONDS ), 16 size, movement, 22J, Adj6p, lever set, Wind indicator.

🕐 Generic, nameless or unmarked grades for watch movements are listed under the Company name or initials of the Company, etc. by size, jewel count and description.

| Grade or Name—Descripion | Avg | Ex-Fn | Mint |
|---|---|---|---|
| A. W. W. Co., 15J, M#1899, OF | $60 | $65 | $85 |
| A. W. W. Co., 15J, M#1888, SW, HC | 75 | 85 | 100 |
| A. W. W. Co., 16J, M#1888, SW, OF | 65 | 70 | 100 |
| A. W. W. Co., 16J, M#1899, SW, DMK, HC | 65 | 80 | 125 |
| A. W. W. Co., 17J, M#1872, SW, DMK, GJS, DES, HC ★ | 200 | 300 | 450 |
| A. W. W. Co., 17J, SW, OF | 75 | 85 | 100 |
| A.W.W.Co., 19J, Adj.5P, LS, OF | 150 | 175 | 200 |
| A.W.W.Co., 19J, Adj.5P, LS, HC | 175 | 200 | 250 |
| A.W.W.Co., 21J, Adj.5P, PS, OF | 200 | 225 | 250 |
| A.W.W.Co., 21J, Adj.5P, PS, HC | 225 | 250 | 300 |
| A.W.W.Co., 23J, Adj.5P, PS, OF | 225 | 250 | 300 |
| A.W.W.Co., 23J, Adj.5P, PS, HC | 250 | 275 | 325 |
| P. S. Bartlett, 17J, M#1899, OF | 65 | 75 | 90 |
| P. S. Bartlett, 17J, M#1899, HC | 100 | 125 | 175 |
| P. S. Bartlett, 17J, M#1908, OF | 60 | 75 | 100 |
| Bond St., 7J, M#1888 | 50 | 55 | 65 |
| Bond St., 11J, M#1888 | 55 | 75 | 100 |
| Bond St., 15J, M#1888 | 55 | 75 | 100 |
| Bond St., 7J, M#1899 | 50 | 55 | 65 |
| Canadian Railway Time Service, M#1908 ★ | 275 | 350 | · 450 |
| Crescent St., 19J, M#1899, Adj.5P, LS, OF | 150 | 175 | 210 |
| Crescent St., 19J, M#1899, Adj.5P, PS, OF | 150 | 175 | 210 |
| Crescent St., 19J, M#1899, Adj.5P, LS, HC | 175 | 200 | 250 |
| Crescent St., 19J, M#1899, Adj.5P, PS, HC | 175 | 200 | 250 |
| Crescent St., 21J, M#1899, Adj.5P, PS, OF | 200 | 225 | 265 |
| Crescent St., 21J, M#1899, Adj.5P, LS, OF | 200 | 225 | 265 |
| Crescent St., 21J, M#1899, Adj.5P, PS, HC | 250 | 275 | 300 |
| Crescent St., 19J, M#1908, Adj.5P, LS, OF | 150 | 175 | 210 |
| Crescent St., 19J, M#1908, Adj.5P, PS, OF | 150 | 175 | 200 |
| Crescent St., 21J, M#1908, Adj.5P, LS, OF | 200 | 225 | 265 |
| Crescent St., 21J, M#1908, Adj.5P, PS, OF | 200 | 225 | 265 |
| Crescent St., 21J, M#1908, Adj.6P, LS, OF | 200 | 225 | 275 |
| Crescent St., 21J, M#1908, Adj.5P, PS, HC | 275 | 325 | 400 |
| Crescent St., 21J, M#1908, Adj.5P, LS, **Wind Indicator** | 550 | 625 | 725 |
| Crescent St., 21J, M#1912, Adj.5P, LS, **Wind Indicator** | 550 | 625 | 725 |
| Crescent St., 22J, M#16–S, Adj.6P, **DECK WATCH** | | | |
| LS, center sec., **Wind Indicator** ★★★★ | 700 | 800 | 1,000 |
| Chronometro Superior, 21J, M#1899, LS, OF | 300 | 375 | 500 |
| Chronometro Victoria, 21J, M#1899, HC | 350 | 425 | 550 |
| Chronometro Victoria, 15J, M#1899, PS, OF | 100 | 125 | 150 |
| Diamond Express, 17J, M#1888, PS, OF, **Diamond End Stones** ★ | 400 | 465 | 550 |
| Electric Railway, 17J, OF, LS, Adj.3P | 150 | 175 | 225 |
| Equity, 7-11J, PS, OF, 16 1/2 Size | 50 | 55 | 65 |
| Equity, 7-11J, PS, HC, 16 1/2 Size | 50 | 55 | 75 |
| Equity, 15-17J, PS, OF, 16 1/2 Size | 55 | 65 | 75 |
| Equity, 15-17J, PS, HC, 16 1/2 Size | 70 | 75 | 90 |
| Gaint, 7-11J, PS, OF, 16 1/2 Size | 50 | 55 | 65 |
| Gaint, 7-11J, PS, HC, 16 1/2 Size | 50 | 55 | 75 |
| Hillside, 7J, M#1868, ADJ | 100 | 125 | 175 |
| Hillside, 7J, M#1868-1872, sweep sec. & STOP ★★ | 450 | 600 | 850 |
| Marquis, 15J, M#1899, LS | 65 | 75 | 100 |
| Marquis, 15J, M#1908, LS | 65 | 75 | 100 |
| Non-Magnetic, 15J, NI, HC | 135 | 155 | 185 |
| Park Road, 16J, M#1872, PS | 100 | 145 | 200 |

Premier Maximus, "Premier" on movement. "Maximus" on dial, 16 size, 23 jewels (two diamond end stones), open face, pendant set, serial number 17,000,014.

American Waltham Watch Co., 5 minute repeater, 16 size, 16 jewels, 3/4 plate, grade 1888, adj, 2 gongs, ca. 1900.

| Grade or Name — Description | Avg | Ex-Fn | Mint |
|---|---|---|---|
| Park Road, 11-13-15-16J, M#1872, PS | $90 | $110 | $135 |
| Premier, 9J, M#1908, PS, OF | 55 | 60 | 70 |
| Premier, 11J, M#1908 | 55 | 60 | 75 |
| Premier, 15J, M#1908, LS, OF | 70 | 85 | 100 |
| Premier, 17J, M#1908, PS, OF | 75 | 90 | 105 |
| Premier, 17J, M#1908, PS, OF, Silveroid | 55 | 60 | 75 |
| Premier, 21J, M#1908, | 175 | 200 | 235 |
| Premier, 22J, M#1908, LS, Adj.6P, **Stainless steel case**, OF | 175 | 200 | 235 |
| Premier, 23J, M#1908, LS, OF | 225 | 250 | 285 |
| Premier Maximus, 23J, M#1908, GT, gold case, LS,GJS, Adj.6P, WI, DR, 18K Maximus case,box & papers ★★ | 8,000 | 9,000 | 10,000 |
| Premier Maximus, 23J, M#1908, GT, gold case, LS, GJS,Adj.6P, WI, DR, 18K Maximus case, no box ★★ | 6,000 | 7,000 | 8,000 |
| Premier Maximus, 23J, M#1908, GT, gold case, LS,GJS, Adj.6P, WI, DR, 18K Maximus case, sterling box and papers, extra crystal & mainspring ★★ | 9,000 | 10,000 | 11,000 |
| Premier Maximus, 23J, M#1908, GT, YGF recased | 2,000 | 2,400 | 3,000 |
| Railroader, 17J, M#1888, LS, NI ★★ | 450 | 475 | 550 |
| Railroad King, 17J, 2-Tone ★ | 325 | 375 | 425 |
| Railroad Watches with R. R. names on dial and movement, such as Canadian Pacific RR, Santa Fe Route, etc., M#s 1888, 1899, 1908 ★ | 425 | 475 | 650 |
| Repeater, 16J, M#1872, original coin case, 5 min. ★★ | 2,000 | 2,500 | 3,000 |
| Repeater, 16J, M#1888, 5 Min., 14K ★★ | 3,300 | 3,750 | 4,250 |
| Repeater, 16J, M#1872, 5 min., 18K ★★★ | 3,750 | 4,500 | 5,500 |
| Repeater, 16J, M#1872, 5 min., chronograph with register, 18K ★★★★ | 4,000 | 5,000 | 6,500 |
| Repeater, 1 min. moon phase, M#1872, Perpetual Cal., 18K case, all original ★★★★ | 30,000 | 35,000 | 45,000 |

🕐 Watches listed in this book are priced at the collectable retail level, as **complete** watches having an original 14k gold-filled case and *Key Wind* with silver, an original white enamel single sunk dial, and with the entire original movement in good working order with no repairs needed.

🕐 Some watch manufacturers personalize watches for jobbers or jewelry firms, with exclusive private signed or marked movements. The valuable collectable watches are listed under the signed or marked movement. Other exclusive private signed or marked movements will have equivalent value are only slightly higher value and should be compared to Generic or Nameless movements. Railroad signed or marked (dials & movements) are usually more collectable & higher in value.

| Grade or Name — Description | Avg | Ex-Fn | Mint |
|---|---|---|---|
| Riverside, 15J, M#1872, PS, NI, OF | $75 | $95 | $125 |
| Riverside, 15J, M#1872, PS, gilted, OF | 75 | 95 | 125 |
| Riverside, 16-17J, M#1888, NI, OF, 14K | 400 | 475 | 600 |
| Riverside, 16-17J, M#1888, NI, OF | 75 | 95 | 125 |
| Riverside, 17J, M#1888, gilded, OF | 75 | 95 | 125 |
| Riverside, 15J, M#1888, gilded, OF | 75 | 95 | 125 |
| Riverside, 17J, M#1888, checker goldtone DMK, raised gold jewel settings, OF | 150 | 175 | 225 |
| Riverside, 17J, M#1899, LS, DR, OF | 75 | 95 | 125 |
| Riverside, 17J, M#1899, LS, DR, HC | 100 | 125 | 165 |
| Riverside, 19J, M#1899, LS, DR, OF | 150 | 175 | 210 |
| Riverside, 19J, M#1908, Adj.5P, LS, DR | 175 | 200 | 235 |
| Riverside, 19J, M#1908, Adj.5P, PS, DR, HC ★ | 180 | 200 | 265 |
| Riverside, 21J, M#1888-1899-1908, LS, DR, OF | 200 | 225 | 285 |
| Riverside, 21J, M#1888-1899-1908, LS, DR, HC | 225 | 250 | 300 |
| Riverside Maximus, 21J, M#1888, LS, ADJ, GJS, GT, DR, HC, GF ★★ | 600 | 700 | 850 |
| Riverside Maximus, 21J, M#1888, LS, ADJ, GJS, GT, DR, HC, 14K ★★ | 1,000 | 1,100 | 1,250 |
| Riverside Maximus, 21J, M#1899, PS, Adj.5P, GJS, GT, DR | 375 | 450 | 600 |
| Riverside Maximus, 21J, M#1899, LS, Adj.5P, GJS, GT, DR | 400 | 500 | 650 |
| Riverside Maximus, 23J, M#1899, LS, Adj.5P, GJS, GT, DR | 400 | 500 | 650 |
| Riverside Maximus, 23J, M#1908, PS, Adj.5P, GJS, GT, DR | 400 | 500 | 650 |
| Riverside Maximus, 23J, M#1908, LS, Adj.5P, GJS, GT, DR | 400 | 500 | 650 |
| Riverside Maximus, 23J, M#1908, PS, Adj.5P, GJS, GT, DR, HC, GF ★ | 600 | 700 | 850 |
| Riverside Maximus, 23J, M#1908, PS, Adj.5P, GJS, GT, DR, 14K, HC ★ | 1,050 | 1,200 | 1,350 |
| Riverside Maximus, 21J, M#1888, LS, GT, Diamond end stones, OF ★★ | 550 | 675 | 750 |

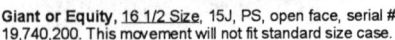

**Giant or Equity,** 16 1/2 Size, 15J, PS, open face, serial # 19,740,200. This movement will not fit standard size case.

**Vanguard,** Model 1908, 16 size, 23 jewels, diamond end stone, gold jewel settings, exposed winding gears, serial number 11,012,533.

🕐 Some grades are not included. Their values can be determined by comparing with similar age, size, metal content, style, models and grades listed.

Stone Mountain, 16 size, 17 jewels, crystal plates, Model 1872, gold train, gold jeweled settings, Adj5p, serial # 20.

Vanguard, 16 size, 23 jewels, Adj6p, note pressed-in jewels rather than gold jewel settings. c. 1945.

| Grade or Name — Description | Avg | Ex-Fn | Mint |
|---|---|---|---|
| Riverside Maximus, 21J, M#1899,LS,GT,Diamond end stone, OF ..........................................................................★ | $450 | $500 | $625 |
| Riverside Maximus, 21J, M#1899, LS, GT, Diamond end stone, HC .........................................................................★ | 600 | 650 | 750 |
| Riverside Maximus, 23J, M#1908, Adj.5P, **Wind Indicator** .. ★ ★ | 3,000 | 3,500 | 4,000 |
| Roadmaster, 17J, M#1899, LS, OF GJS ....................................★ | 200 | 245 | 350 |
| Royal, 15J, M#1872, PS, OF ........................................................ | 70 | 90 | 120 |
| Royal, 17J, M#1888, PS, OF ........................................................ | 75 | 95 | 125 |
| Royal, 17J, M#1888, PS, HC ....................................................... | 100 | 120 | 150 |
| Royal, 17J, M#1899, Adj.3P, OF ............................................... | 65 | 85 | 110 |
| Royal, 17J, M#1899-1908, Adj.5P, OF ..................................... | 70 | 90 | 125 |
| Royal, 17J, M#1899-1908, Adj.5P,HC ....................................... | 80 | 95 | 165 |
| Royal Special, 17J, M#1888 ....................................................... | 100 | 125 | 175 |
| Sol, 7J, M#1888 ........................................................................... | 50 | 65 | 85 |
| Sol, 7J, M#1908 ........................................................................... | 50 | 65 | 85 |
| Stone Mountain, 17J, M#1872, GT, Crystal plates .......... ★ ★ ★ ★ | 7,000 | 9,000 | 15,000 |
| **SWISS** made, 17-25J, ................................................................ | 40 | 50 | 65 |
| Traveler, 7J, M#1888, 1899, 1908 & 16 1/2 size( Equity)............... | 40 | 50 | 65 |
| Tennyson,15J, M#1888, OF........................................................ | 100 | 135 | 175 |
| Vanguard, 19J, M#1899, PS, LS, Adj.5P, GJS, DR, OF ................. | 150 | 175 | 210 |
| Vanguard, 19J, M#1899, PS, LS, Adj.5P, GJS, DR, HC .............. | 200 | 225 | 260 |
| Vanguard, 21J, M#1899, Adj.5P, OF ......................................... | 200 | 225 | 275 |
| Vanguard, 23J, M#1899, Adj.5P, HC ......................................... | 325 | 350 | 380 |
| Vanguard, 23J, M#1899, Adj.6P, OF.......................................... | 200 | 235 | 300 |
| Vanguard, 23J, M#1899, LS, Adj.5P, GJS, DR, OF ...................... | 225 | 265 | 325 |
| Vanguard, 23J, M#1899, PS, Adj.5P, GJS, DR, OF ...................... | 200 | 250 | 310 |
| Vanguard, 23J, M#1899, PS, **Wind Indicator,** Adj.5P, GJS, DR★ | 600 | 650 | 725 |
| Vanguard, 19J, M#1908, LS & PS, Adj.5P, GJS, DR ..................... | 150 | 175 | 210 |

🕐 Watches listed in this book are priced at the collectable retail level, as **complete** watches having an original 14k gold-filled case and *Key Wind* with silver, an original white enamel single sunk dial, and with the entire original movement in good working order with no repairs needed.

| Grade or Name — Description | Avg | Ex-Fn | Mint |
|---|---|---|---|
| Vanguard, 21J, M#1908, Adj.5P, GJS, DR, Diamond end stone .... | $200 | $225 | $275 |
| Vanguard, 21J, M#1908, Adj.5P, GJS, DR, PS, LS, OF ................ | 200 | 225 | 275 |
| Vanguard, 21J, M#1908, Adj.5P, GJS, DR, PS, LS, HC ............... | 300 | 350 | 425 |
| Vanguard, 23J, M#1908, LS, Adj.5P, GJS, DR, OF ..................... | 250 | 300 | 350 |
| Vanguard, 23J, M#1908, LS, Adj.5P, GJS, DR, HC ...................... | 325 | 375 | 425 |
| Vanguard, 23J, M#1908, PS, Adj.5P, GJS, DR ........................... | 250 | 300 | 350 |
| Vanguard, 23J, M#1908, Adj.5P, **Wind Indicator**, GJS, DR ....... | 600 | 650 | 700 |
| Vanguard, 23J, M#1908, Adj.5P, GJS , Diamond end stone ......... | 250 | 300 | 350 |
| Vanguard, 23J, M#1908, Adj.5P, GJS, HC .................................. | 300 | 350 | 425 |
| Vanguard, 23J, OF, LS or PS, 14K ........................................... | 600 | 650 | 700 |
| Vanguard, 23J, M#1908, Adj.6P, **Wind Indicator**, GJS, DR ....... | 600 | 650 | 700 |
| Vanguard, 23J, M#1908, Adj.6P, **Wind Ind.**, **Lossier**, GJS,DR .... | 625 | 675 | 750 |
| Vanguard, 23J, M#1912, Press Jewels ..................................... | 250 | 300 | 350 |
| Vanguard, 23J, M#1912, PS, military (case), **Wind Indicator** ..... | 600 | 675 | 750 |
| Vanguard, 24J, also marked 9J., center sec., 10 made ............ ★★ | 700 | 800 | 950 |
| George Washington, 11J, M#1857 ................................................★ | 225 | 295 | 375 |
| Weems, 21J, Navigation watch, **Wind Indicator** ................ ★★★ | 650 | 785 | 950 |
| M#1888, G #s 650, 640 ......................................................... | 60 | 70 | 85 |
| M#1899, G #s 615, 618, 620, 625, 628, ................................. | 60 | 70 | 85 |
| M#1908, G #s 611, 613, 614, 618, 621, 623, | | | |
| 628, 630, 641, 642 ..................................................... | 60 | 70 | 85 |
| G#637-640=3 pos., G#636=4pos., G#1617=2 pos., ALL=17J....... | 60 | 70 | 85 |
| G#610=7-11J., un Adjusted & 620=15J ............................................ | 55 | 60 | 75 |
| G#625-630-635=17J., Adj., OF................................................... | 60 | 70 | 85 |
| G#645, 21J, GCW, OF, LS ........................................................ | 200 | 225 | 265 |
| G#645, 21J, GCW, OF, LS, wind indicator.................................... | 500 | 550 | 650 |
| G#645, 19J, OF, LS ................................................................. | 100 | 125 | 165 |
| G#665, 19J, GJS, BRG, HC ...............................................★★ | 600 | 695 | 800 |
| G#16-A, 22J, Adj.3P, 24 hr. dial ............................................. | 200 | 250 | 285 |
| G#16-A, & G#1024, 17J, Adj.5P .............................................. | 100 | 110 | 135 |
| G#1621, 21J, Adj.5P ............................................................. | 200 | 225 | 265 |
| G#1622, 22J, Adj.5P ............................................................. | 200 | 225 | 265 |
| G#1623, 23J, Adj.5P ............................................................. | 275 | 300 | 350 |

**Weems** Navigation watch, 21j, Weems pat. seconds dial, pusher for seconds scale setting, ca. 1942.

**Riverside Maximus**, Model 1899, 16 size, 23 jewels, gold train, raised gold jewel settings, diamond end stone, adsusted to 5 positions, hunting case, serial # 12,509,200.

## 14 SIZE
### MODELS 14KW FULL PLATE , 1874,
### 1884, 1895, 1897, COLONIAL-A

| Grade or Name — Description | Avg | Ex-Fn | Mint |
|---|---|---|---|
| Adams Street, 7J, M#14KW, full plate, KW, Coin .......................... | $100 | $125 | $175 |
| Adams Street, 11J, M#14KW, full plate, KW, Coin ....................... | 100 | 125 | 175 |
| Adams Street, 15J, M#14KW, full plate, KW ................................ | 100 | 125 | 175 |

🕐 Generic, nameless or unmarked grades for watch movements are listed under the Company name or initials of the Company, etc. by size, jewel count and description.

| | | | |
|---|---|---|---|
| A. W. Co., 7-11J, M#14KW, full plate, KW ..................................... | 50 | 70 | 100 |
| A. W. W. Co., 7-11J, M#1874, SW, LS, HC ................................... | 75 | 95 | 125 |
| A. W. Co., 7-11J, M#s FP, 1884, & 1895 ..................................... | 40 | 50 | 65 |
| A. W. Co., 13J, M#1884 ................................................................ | 40 | 50 | 65 |
| A. W. Co., 15-16J, M#1874, SW ................................................... | 50 | 60 | 80 |
| A. W. Co., 17J, SW , OF................................................................. | 55 | 70 | 85 |
| A.W.Co., 19J, GJS, GCW .............................................................. | 100 | 120 | 150 |
| Am. Watch Co., 7-11J, KW, ........................................................... | 60 | 75 | 90 |
| Am. Watch Co., 13J, M#1874-84, SW .......................................... | 65 | 75 | 95 |
| Am. Watch Co., 15J, M#1874-84, ................................................ | 70 | 80 | 100 |
| Am. Watch Co., 16J, M#1874, SW ................................................ | 70 | 80 | 100 |
| Am. Watch Co., 7-11J, M#14KW, Full Plate, KW ......................... | 60 | 75 | 95 |
| Am. Watch Co., 16J, M#1884, SW ................................................ | 55 | 75 | 95 |
| Am. Watch Co., 15J, M#1897, SW ................................................ | 40 | 60 | 90 |
| Bond St., 7-11J, M#1895, SW ....................................................... | 40 | 55 | 75 |
| Bond St., 9-11J, M#1884, KW ....................................................... | 75 | 95 | 125 |
| Bond St., 7J, M#1884, SW, PS ..................................................... | 50 | 60 | 90 |
| Beacon, 15J, M#1897, SW ........................................................... | 50 | 60 | 90 |
| Chronograph, 13J, 1874, 14K, OF, **Am. W. Co. case** .................... | 600 | 750 | 1,000 |
| Chronograph, 13J, 1884, 14K, HC, **Am. W. Co. case** .................... | 700 | 900 | 1,100 |
| Chronograph, 13J, 1884, 18K, HC, **Am. W. Co. case** ................ ★ | 1,000 | 1,200 | 1,400 |
| Chronograph, 13J, 1874, 14K, OF, W/ register, **Am. W. Co. case** | 750 | 950 | 1,150 |
| Chronograph, 13J, 1874, 14K, HC, W/ register, **Am. W. Co. case** | 850 | 950 | 1,350 |
| Chronograph, 13J, 1874, 18K, HC, W/ register, **Am. W. Co. case** ★ | 1,200 | 1,350 | 1,600 |

**Chronograph**, Model 1874, split-second, 14 size. Note two split second hands on dial.

**Hillside**, 14 size, 13 jewels, M#1874, stem wind, hunting case, Woerds Pat., serial number 1,696,188, 18K.

🕐 This book endeavours to be a GUIDE or helpful manual and offers a wealth of material to be used as a tool not as a absolute document. Price Guides are like watches the worst may be better than none at all, but at best cannot be expected to be 100% accurate.

| Grade or Name — Description | Avg | Ex-Fn | Mint |
|---|---|---|---|
| Chronograph, 13J, M#1874, SILVER HC, *Am. W. Co. case* ........ | $250 | $325 | $375 |
| Chronograph, 13J, M#1874-1884 , OF.......................................... | 175 | 225 | 300 |
| Chronograph, 13J, M#1874-1884, HC......................................... | 200 | 250 | 350 |
| Chronograph, 15J, M#1874-1884 , OF.......................................... | 185 | 250 | 335 |
| Chronograph, 15J, M#1874-1884, HC ......................................... | 200 | 275 | 375 |
| Chronograph, 17J, M#1874-1884 , OF.......................................... | 195 | 270 | 365 |
| Chronograph, 17J, M#1874-1884, HC.......................................... | 250 | 300 | 400 |
| Chronograph, 17J, split second, Am. W. Co. case .............. ★★★ | 350 | 425 | 600 |
| Chronograph, 15J, split sec., 14K, HC .......................... ★★★ | 1,200 | 1,400 | 1,600 |
| Chronograph, 15J, split second, **min. register**, 14K Am. W. Co. HC ........................................................ ★★★ | 1,400 | 1,600 | 2,000 |
| Chronograph, 16J, double dial, M#1874, 18K, Am. W. Co. case ... | 2,000 | 2,500 | 3,500 |
| Chronometro Victoria, 15J, M#1897, ....................................... ★★ | 100 | 135 | 175 |
| Church St., 7J, M#1884, ..................................................... | 80 | 100 | 125 |
| Crescent Garden, 7-11J, M#14KW, KW ..................................... | 60 | 75 | 100 |
| Crescent Garden, 7J, Full Plate, KW ....................................... | 80 | 100 | 130 |
| Wm. Ellery, 7J, M#1874, SW .................................................. | 50 | 60 | 75 |
| Gentleman, 7J, M#1884, SW .................................................. | 65 | 75 | 100 |
| Hillside, 7-15J, M#1874, SW .................................................. | 50 | 60 | 85 |
| Hillside, 7-11J, M#FP, SW .................................................... | 50 | 60 | 85 |
| Hillside, 7-13J, M#1884, KW ................................................. | 50 | 60 | 85 |
| Hillside, 9-11J, M#1884, KW ................................................. | 50 | 60 | 85 |
| Hillside, 15J, M#1884, SW .................................................... | 65 | 75 | 100 |
| Hillside, 16J, M#1874, (calendar date only on outside chapter) SW, GJS, OF,(calendar sets from back with lever)... ★★★★ | 500 | 600 | 750 |
| Maximus, 21J, Colonial A ..................................................... | 145 | 185 | 275 |
| Maximus, 21J, Colonial A, 14K .............................................. | 300 | 400 | 575 |
| Night Clock, 7J, M#1884, KW ................................................ | 80 | 100 | 150 |
| Repeater (5 min.), 16J, M#1884, SW, LS, 14K ........................... ★ | 3,500 | 4,000 | 5,000 |
| Repeater (5 min.), 16J, M#1884, SW, LS, 18K ........................... ★ | 3,800 | 4,800 | 6,300 |

**Chronograph**, M# 1884-double dial, 14 size, 15 jewels, hunting case.

**Chronograph**, Model 1884-Split Second, 14 size, 15 jewels, open face, gold escape wheel, gold train, serial number 303,094.

🕐 Watches listed in this book are priced at the collectable retail level, as **complete** watches having an original 14k gold-filled case and Key Wind with silver, an original white enamel single sunk dial, and with the entire original movement in good working order with no repairs needed.

🕐 Some watch manufacturers personalize watches for jobbers or jewelry firms, with exclusive private signed or marked movements. The valuable collectable watches are listed under the signed or marked movement. Other exclusive private signed or marked movements will have equivalent value are only slightly higher value and should be compared to Generic or Nameless movements. Railroad signed or marked (dials & movements) are usually more collectable & higher in value.

**Five Minute Repeater**, Model 1884, 14 size, 13-15 jewels, hunting case, slide activated, serial number 2,809,551.

| Grade or Name — Description | Avg | Ex-Fn | Mint |
|---|---|---|---|
| Repeater (5 min.), 16J, M#1884, split second chronograph, 18K case | $5,000 | $6,000 | $7,500 |
| Repeater (5 min.), 16J, M#1884, SW, LS, chronograph, with register, 14K Am. W. Co. case | 3,500 | 4,000 | 5,000 |
| Repeater (5 min.), 16J, M#1884, SW, LS, chronograph, with register, 18K Am. W. Co. case | 4,000 | 5,000 | 6,500 |
| Repeater (5 min.), 16J, M#1884, SW, LS, original Coin | 2,000 | 2,500 | 3,000 |
| Repeater (5 Min.), 18K, HC ★★ | 3,000 | 4,000 | 5,500 |
| Repeater (1 Min.), perpetual calendar, moon ph., 18K ★★★ | 30,000 | 37,000 | 50,000 |
| Riverside, 11-15J, M#s 1874, HC ★ | 150 | 175 | 250 |
| Riverside, 15J, M#1884, OF | 65 | 80 | 100 |
| Riverside, 19-21J, Colonial A, OF ★★ | 150 | 175 | 250 |
| Royal, 11-13-15J, M#s 1874, 1884 | 45 | 55 | 70 |
| Seaside, 7-11J, M#1884, SW | 45 | 55 | 70 |
| Special, 7J, M#1895, HC | 75 | 95 | 125 |
| Sterling, 7J, M#1884 | 45 | 55 | 70 |
| Waltham, Mass., 7J, Full Plate, KW | 75 | 95 | 125 |

## 12 SIZE

### MODELS KW, 1894, BRIDGE, COLONIAL SERIES

| Grade or Name — Description | Avg | Ex-Fn | Mint |
|---|---|---|---|
| A. W. W. Co., 7J, M#1894, 14K, OF | $200 | $225 | $275 |
| A. W. W. Co., 11J, M#1894, also Colonial model | 40 | 45 | 60 |
| A. W. W. Co., 15J, M#1894, also Colonial model | 40 | 45 | 60 |
| A. W. W. Co., 15J, M#1894, Colonial, 14K, HC | 250 | 275 | 350 |
| A. W. W. Co., 17J, M#1894, also Colonial model | 40 | 45 | 60 |
| A. W. W. Co., 17J, M#1894, also Colonial, 14K OF | 200 | 225 | 275 |
| A. W. W. Co., 19J, OF | 45 | 50 | 60 |
| A. W. W. Co., 21J, OF | 50 | 60 | 75 |
| A. W. W. Co., 23J, OF | 60 | 70 | 85 |
| P. S. Bartlett, 19J, M#1894, 14K, HC | 300 | 335 | 400 |
| P. S. Bartlett, 19J, M#1894 | 50 | 60 | 75 |
| Bond St., 7-13J, M#1894 | 40 | 50 | 60 |
| Bridge Model, 19J, GJS, Adj.5P, GT | 100 | 135 | 200 |
| Bridge Model, 19J, GJS, Adj.5P, GT, 18K, HC ★★★ | 500 | 550 | 575 |
| Bridge Model, 21J, GJS, Adj.5P, GT, OF | 150 | 175 | 250 |
| Bridge Model, 21J, GJS, Adj.5P, GT, HC, 14K ★★ | 600 | 700 | 850 |
| Bridge Model, 23J, GJS, Adj.5P, GT | 200 | 250 | 310 |

Actual size illustration of a cushion style shaped watch depicting thinness with emphasis on style and beauty. This watch was popular in the 1930s.

| Grade or Name — Description | Avg | Ex-Fn | Mint |
|---|---|---|---|
| Duke, 7-15J, M#1894 ............................................. | $60 | $80 | $90 |
| Digital Hour & Second Window, 17J ...................... | 75 | 100 | 125 |
| Elite, 17J, OF .......................................................... | 50 | 65 | 85 |
| Ensign, 7J, OF ........................................................ | 50 | 65 | 85 |
| Equity, 7J,adj. ........................................................ | 50 | 60 | 70 |
| Martyn Square, 7-11J, M#KW ............................... | 100 | 125 | 175 |
| Maximus, 21J, GJS, GT ......................................... | 225 | 275 | 350 |
| Premier, 17-19J, M#1894 ...................................... | 65 | 80 | 100 |
| Premier, 21J, M#1894 ........................................... | 75 | 100 | 250 |
| Riverside, 17-19J, M#1894, Colonial ................... | 60 | 70 | 80 |
| Riverside, 19-21J, M#1894, Colonial ................... | 80 | 90 | 100 |

A.W.W.Co., Model 1894, 12 size, 7-11 jewels, open face, serial number 7,565,004.

Riverside, Colonial series, 12 size, 19 jewels, open face or hunting, Adj5p, double roller.

| Grade or Name – Description | Avg | Ex-Fn | Mint |
|---|---|---|---|
| Riverside, 19-21J, M#1894, Colonial, 14K, HC ............ | $350 | $400 | $450 |
| Riverside Maximus, 21J, M#1894, Colonial, GT, GJS, 14K .......... | 400 | 475 | 575 |
| Riverside Maximus, 21J, M#1894, Colonial, GT, GJS................... | 250 | 285 | 325 |
| Riverside Maximus, 23J, M#1894, Colonial, GT, GJS................ ★ | 265 | 325 | 375 |
| Riverside Maximus, 23J, M#1894, Colonial, GT, GJS, 14K ....... ★ | 425 | 475 | 575 |
| Royal, 17J, OF, PS ................................................................... | 45 | 55 | 65 |
| Royal, 19J, OF, PS ................................................................... | 55 | 60 | 75 |
| Secometer, 17J, (revolving seconds dial only) OF ...................... | 75 | 85 | 100 |

## THE OPERA WATCH
10-12 size case & a 6/0 size Jewel Series movement

| Grade or Name – Description | Avg | Ex-Fn | Mint |
|---|---|---|---|
| 12-6/0 size, 17-19J, Adj, 18K **gold case** | $500 | $600 | $750 |
| 12-6/0 size, 17-19J, Adj, 14K **gold case** | 300 | 350 | 400 |
| 12-6/0 size, 17-19J, Adj, **Platinum case** | 550 | 650 | 800 |
| 12-6/0 size, 17-19J, Adj, **gold filled case** | 135 | 150 | 200 |

A unique designed Gents dress watch about 10-12 size case with a **fancy framed** 6/0 movement (Jewel Series).

## 10 SIZE
### MODEL KW, 1861, 1874

| Grade or Name – Description | Avg | Ex-Fn | Mint |
|---|---|---|---|
| Am. W. Co., 7-15J, M#1874-1878, KW, 14K | $200 | $250 | $350 |
| A. W. Co., 7-11J, SW , OF | 45 | 50 | 65 |
| A. W. Co.,15-17J, SW , OF | 55 | 60 | 70 |
| A. W. Co., 19-21J, SW , OF | 65 | 70 | 85 |
| American Watch Co., 11-15J, M#1874, 14K, HC | 275 | 325 | 425 |
| Appleton, Tracy & Co., 15J, M#1861 or 1874, 14K | 200 | 250 | 350 |
| Appleton, Tracy & Co., 15J, M#1861, 18K multi-color box case ★ ★ | 650 | 750 | 900 |
| P. S. Bartlett, 7-11J, M#1861, KW, 14K | 275 | 300 | 375 |
| P. S. Bartlett, 13J, M#KW, gold balance, 1st S# 45,801, last 46,200, 14K, Pat. Nov. 3, 1858 ★ ★ | 300 | 375 | 525 |
| P. S. Bartlett, 13J, M#KW, gold balance, 1st S#45,801, last 46,200, 18K | 600 | 750 | 850 |
| P. S. Bartlett, 13J, M#1861, KW, 14K | 200 | 250 | 300 |

**Appleton Tracy & Co.**, Model 10KW, 10 size, 7-15 jewels, key wind and set from back, serial number 370,411.

**Am. W. Co.**, Model 1873, 8 size, 15 jewels, serial number 691,001.

NOTE: These watches (excluding Colonial) are usually found with solid gold cases, and are therefore priced accordingly. Without cases, these watches have very little value due to the fact that the cases are difficult to find. Many of the cases came in octagon, decagon, hexagon, cushion and triad shapes.

| Grade or Name – Description | Avg | Ex-Fn | Mint |
|---|---|---|---|
| Colonial A , 21J,OF | $60 | $75 | $90 |
| Crescent Garden, 7J, M#1861, KW, 14K | 200 | 250 | 300 |
| Wm. Ellery, 7,11,15J, M#1861, KW, 14K | 200 | 250 | 300 |
| Home W. Co., 7J, M#1874, KW, 14K | 200 | 250 | 300 |
| Martyn Square, 7-11J, M#1861, 14K | 200 | 250 | 350 |
| Maximus "A", 21J, 14K ★★ | 400 | 475 | 600 |
| Maximus "A", 23J, 14K ★★ | 425 | 500 | 600 |
| Riverside, 19–21J, Adj.5P, GF | 80 | 100 | 125 |
| Riverside Maximus, 19-21J, Adj.5P, GJS, GF | 125 | 200 | 275 |
| Riverside Maximus, 19-21J, Adj.5P, GJS, 18K | 450 | 525 | 625 |
| Riverside Maximus, 23J, Adj.5P, GJS, GF | 200 | 250 | 375 |
| Royal, 15J, Adj.5P, GF | 55 | 65 | 80 |

## 8 SIZE
### MODEL 1873

NOTE: Collectors usually want solid gold cases in small watches.

| Grade or Name – Description | Avg | Ex-Fn | Mint |
|---|---|---|---|
| Am. W. Co., 15-17J, M#1873, 14K, Multi-Color Box Hinged case | $500 | $700 | $900 |
| Am. W. Co., 15-16J, M#1873 | 65 | 75 | 85 |
| P. S. Bartlett, 15-16J, M#1873 | 40 | 50 | 60 |
| Wm. Ellery, 7-11J, M#1873 | 40 | 50 | 60 |
| Wm. Ellery, 7J, 14K, HC | 200 | 275 | 350 |
| Riverside, 7-11J, M#1873, 18K, HC | 325 | 400 | 600 |
| Riverside, 7-11J, M#1873 | 65 | 75 | 85 |
| Royal, 7-16J, M#1873 | 40 | 50 | 60 |
| Victoria, 11-15J, tu-tone movement, 18k HC ★ | 325 | 400 | 600 |

VICTORIA, 8 size 1873 model, 11-15 jewels, tu-tone high grade movement, HC, S# 871256

6 size Ladies movement this basic model came in the following grades: J=7 jewels, gilt; Y=7 jewels, nickel; N=15 jewels, gilded or nickel; X=15 jewels, nickel, gold jewel settings; K=16 jewels nickel, raised gold settings; RIVERSIDE=17 jewels, nickel, raised gold settings.

## 6 SIZE
### MODEL 1873, 1889 , 1890

| Grade or Name – Description | Avg | Ex-Fn | Mint |
|---|---|---|---|
| A,B,C,D,E,F,G,H,J,K | $65 | $70 | $85 |
| A,B,C,D,E,F,G,H,J,K, 14K, HC | 200 | 275 | 325 |
| A. W. W. Co., 19J, 18K, HC | 325 | 400 | 475 |
| A. W. W. Co., 19J, 14K, Multi-Color gold case | 450 | 600 | 800 |
| A. W. W. Co., 7J, M#1873 | 40 | 45 | 55 |

| Grade or Name – Description | Avg | Ex-Fn | Mint |
|---|---|---|---|
| A. W. W. Co., 15J, multi-color GF, HC | $175 | $200 | $275 |
| A. W. W. Co., 15J, 2 tone mvt., HC | 75 | 100 | 150 |
| A. W. W. Co., 11J, HC, LS | 75 | 100 | 150 |
| Am. W. Co., 7-11J, M#1889 -1890 | 40 | 45 | 55 |
| American W. Co., 7J, KW & KS from back, 10K, HC | 175 | 225 | 275 |
| Wm. Ellery, 7J, M#1873 | 50 | 60 | 80 |
| Lady Waltham, 16J, M#1873, Demi, HC, 14K | 275 | 300 | 350 |
| Lady Waltham, 16J, M#1873, 18K | 300 | 325 | 375 |
| Riverside Maximus, 19J, GT, Adj., DR, HC | 225 | 250 | 300 |
| Riverside, 15-17J, PS | 50 | 75 | 100 |
| Seaside, 7-15J, M#1873 | 60 | 75 | 85 |
| Royal, 16J, HC | 75 | 90 | 115 |

American Watch Co., Model 1889, 6 size 7 jewels, serial number 4,700,246.

Stone Movement or Crystal Plate movement, size 4, 16 jewels, gold train, open face, serial number 28.

## 4 SIZE

| Grade or Name – Description | Avg | Ex-Fn | Mint |
|---|---|---|---|
| Stone Movement or crystal movement, 4 size, crystal, 16 ruby jewels in gold settings, gold train, exposed pallets, compensation balance adjusted to temperature, isochronism, positions, Breguet hairspring, and crystal top plate, 14K case ★ ★ ★ ★ | $4,000 | $5,000 | $6,000 |

🕐 Watches listed in this book are priced at the collectable retail level, as **complete** watches having an original 14k gold-filled case and *Key Wind* with silver, an original white enamel single sunk dial, and with the entire original movement in good working order with no repairs needed.

## 1 SIZE & 0 SIZE
### MODELS 1882, 1891, 1900, 1907

| Grade or Name – Description | Avg | Ex-Fn | Mint |
|---|---|---|---|
| A.W.Co., 7-16J, OF | $50 | $60 | $75 |
| A.W.Co., 7-16J, HC | 70 | 85 | 125 |
| A.W.Co., 7-15J, multi-color 14K HC | 350 | 475 | 600 |
| A. W. Co., 7J, 14K, HC | 175 | 250 | 350 |
| American Watch Co., 15J, SW, OF &HC | 85 | 100 | 165 |

🕐 Generic, nameless or unmarked grades for watch movements are listed under the Company name or initials of the Company, etc. by size, jewel count and description.

Lady Waltham, Model 1900, 0 size, 16 jewels, open face or hunting, adjusted, stem wind, pendant set.

A.W. Co., Model 1891, 0 size, 7 jewels, stem wind, originally sold for $13.00.

| Grade or Name – Description | Avg | Ex-Fn | Mint |
|---|---|---|---|
| American Watch Co., 15J, S.W., 14K, HC | $175 | $275 | $350 |
| P. S. Bartlett, 11J, M#1891, OF, 14K | 125 | 150 | 175 |
| P. S. Bartlett, 16J, 14K, HC | 175 | 275 | 350 |
| Lady Waltham, 15J, SW, 14K, HC | 175 | 275 | 350 |
| Lady Waltham, 15-16J, SW, HC | 100 | 125 | 175 |
| Maximus, 19J, SW, HC | 125 | 150 | 200 |
| Riverside, 15J,16J,17J, SW, HC | 100 | 125 | 175 |
| Riverside, 15J,16J,17J, SW, HC, 14K | 175 | 275 | 350 |
| Riverside Maximus, 21J, GT, multi-color gold HC, 14K ......★★ | 600 | 750 | 850 |
| Riverside Maximus, 21J, GT | 175 | 200 | 250 |
| Riverside Maximus, 19J, SW, HC | 150 | 175 | 250 |
| Riverside Maximus, 19J, HC, 14K ......★ | 275 | 350 | 475 |
| Royal, 16J, SW, HC | 75 | 100 | 125 |
| Seaside, 15J, SW, HC, 14K | 175 | 275 | 350 |
| Seaside, 11J, SW, OF, multi-color dial, no chips | 125 | 175 | 200 |
| Seaside, 11J, SW, HC | 75 | 100 | 125 |
| Seaside, 7J, HC | 65 | 75 | 100 |
| Seaside, 7J, HC, 14K | 175 | 275 | 350 |
| Special, 11J, M#1891, OF, 14K | 125 | 175 | 200 |

Riverside, Jewel Series, 6/0 size, 17 ruby jewels, raised gold settings, gold center wheel.

Ruby, Jewel Series, 6/0 size, 15 jewels, adjusted to temperature, open face or hunting.

### JEWEL SERIES or 6/0 SIZE

| Grade or Name – Description | Avg | Ex -Fn | Mint |
|---|---|---|---|
| Diamond, 15J, Jewel Series HC, 14K | $200 | $250 | $300 |
| Patrician, 15J, pin set, GJS, OF, 18K ......★ | 300 | 350 | 425 |
| Riverside, 17J, Jewel Series HC, 14K | 200 | 250 | 300 |
| Ruby, 15J, Jewel Series, OF, 14K | 150 | 200 | 250 |
| Sapphire, 15J, Jewel Series, OF, 14K | 150 | 200 | 250 |

**RF # 1A**
gold filled : $90 - $100 - $120

**RF # 2B**
gold filled : $95- $110 - $130

**RF # 3C**
gold plate: $70 - $80 - $95

**RF # 4D**
gold filled : $100 - $115 - $120

**RF # 5E**
gold filled : $110 - $120 - $135

**RF # 6F**
gold filled : $90 - $100 - $120

MONTGOMERY DIAL

**RF # 7G**
**LOCOMOTIVE** model
gold filled : $110 - $120 - $135

1A, 2B, = Gold Filled White or Yellow
3C = Yellow Gold Rolled Plate
4D, 5E, 6F, 7G = Yellow Gold Filled.

🕐 NOTE: Factory Advertised as a complete watch and were fitted with cases of exclusive and unusual design with special heavy bow & movement timed and rated at the factory. The factory also sold _uncased_ movements to **JOBBERS** such as Jewelry stores & they cased the movement in a case styles the **CUSTOMER requested.** All the factory advertised complete watches came with the dial **SHOWN or CHOICE** of other **Railroad** dials.

## AMERICAN WALTHAM WATCH CO.
## IDENTIFICATION OF MOVEMENTS
## BY MODEL NUMBER

**How to Identify Your Watch:** Compare the movement of your watch with the illustrations in this section. Upon matching the movement exactly, the model number and size can be determined. When comparing, note the location of the balance, jewels, screws, gears and type of back plate (Full, ¾, Bridge) which will be clues to identifying the movement you have. Having determined the size and model number, you can now find your watch in the main price listing by name or number (which is engraved on the movement).

20 size, 1862 or KW 20 model. Note vibrating hairspring stud. 1st serial number 50,001

18 size, key wind model 1st serial number 28,821

Model 1857, KW, KS. 1st serial number 1,001

Model 1870, KW, KS from back 1st serial number 500,001

**Model 1877, 18 size**

**Model 1879, 18 size**

**Model 1883, hunting**
**1st serial number 2,354,001**

**Model 1883, open face**

**Model 1892, open face**

**Model 1892, hunting.**
**1st serial number 6,026,001**

**16½ size, Equity open face**

**Model 1868 or Model 16KW,
16 size**

**Model 1872, 16 size open face**

**Model 1872, 16 size hunting case**

**Model 1888, 16 size, hunting**

**Bridge Model, 16 size**

**Model 1899 or Model 1908,
16 size, open face**

**Model 1899 or Model 1908,
16 size, hunting**

**Model 1899 or Model 1908,
16 size, open face**

**Model 16-A, 16 size**

**Model 1622, Deck Watch
16 size, sweep second**

**Model 1874 & 1884, 14 size**

**Model 1874, 14 size, hunting**

**Model 1884, 14 size, open face**

**5 Minute Repeater, 14 size**

**14 SIZE FULL PLATE KW KS
1 st. SERIAL # 909,001**

**Model 1874, 14 size**

**Model 1884, 14 size**

**Model 1895, 14 size,
open face**

**Model 1897, 14 size**

**Colonial A Model, 14 size**

**Colonial Series, 14 size**

**Model 1924, The Colonial**

**Model 1894, 12 size**

Model 1894, 12 size

Model 10KW, 10 size

Colonial A, 10 size

Model 1873, 8 size

Model 1873, 8&6 size

Model 1889, 6 size

Model 1890, 6 size

Model 1890, 6 size

Stone Mtn, 4 size

Model 1882, 1 size

Model 1891, 0 size

Model 1900, 0 size          Model 1907, 0 size          Jewel Series

Model 1900, 0/3 size,       Model 1907, 0/3 size,       Model 1898 & 1912,
open face                   hunting                     0/6 size, hunting

Model 1898 & 1912,          10½ ligne                   10 ligne
0/6 size, open face

🕐 Generic, nameless or unmarked grades for watch movements are listed under the Company name or initials of the Company, etc. by size, jewel count and description.

🕐 Some grades are not included. Their values can be determined by comparing with similar age, size, metal content, style, models and grades listed.

🕐 Watches listed in this book are priced at the collectable retail level, as complete watches having an original 14k gold-filled case and Key Wind with silver, an original white enamel single sunk dial, and with the entire original movement in good working order with no repairs needed.

🕐 This book endeavours to be a GUIDE or helpful manual and offers a wealth of material to be used as a tool not as a absolute document. Price Guides are like watches the worst may be better than none at all, but at best cannot be expected to be 100% accurate.

🕐 Characteristics of watches differ for the same age of both case and movement, because these features vary it may not be accurate to date a watch by one single influence. Example: the second hand was not commonly found on watches before 1750, but common about 1800. The first second hand appeared in 1665 and another in 1690. Therefore statements are broad rather than accurate.

140

# ANSONIA CLOCK CO.

### Brooklyn, New York
### 1896 - 1929

The Ansonia Watch Co. was owned by the Ansonia Clock Company in Ansonia, Connecticut. Ansonia started making clocks in about 1850 and began manufacturing watches in 1896. They produced about 10,000,000 dollar- type watches. The company was sold to a Russian investor in 1930. "Patented April 17, 1888," is on the back plate of some Ansonia watches.

Ansonia Watch Company. Example of a basic movement, 16 size, stem wind.

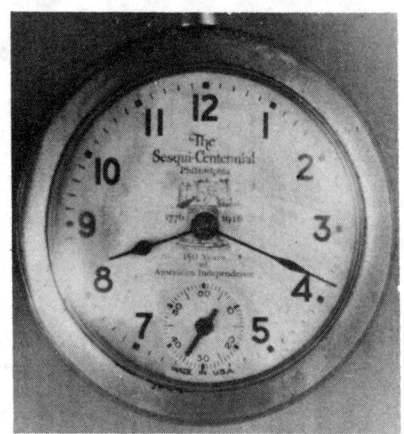

Ansonia Watch Co., Sesqui-Centennial model.

| Grade or Name–Description | Avg | Ex-Fn | Mint |
|---|---|---|---|
| Ansonia watch with a White Dial in Nickel case | $40 | $50 | $70 |
| Ansonia watch with a Radium Dial in Nickel case | 50 | 60 | 85 |
| Ansonia watch with a Black Dial in Nickel case | 40 | 50 | 70 |
| Ascot | 40 | 50 | 70 |
| Bonnie Laddie Shoes | 60 | 95 | 120 |
| Dispatch | 30 | 40 | 60 |
| Faultless | 40 | 50 | 70 |
| Guide | 40 | 50 | 70 |
| Lenox | 35 | 40 | 50 |
| Mentor | 35 | 45 | 55 |
| Piccadilly | 45 | 60 | 75 |
| Rural | 40 | 50 | 70 |
| Sesqui-Centennial | 250 | 275 | 350 |
| Superior | 45 | 60 | 75 |
| Tutor | 45 | 60 | 75 |

Some grades are not included. Their values can be determined by comparing with similar age, size, metal content, style, models and grades listed.

# APPLETON WATCH CO.

## (REMINGTON WATCH CO.)

### Appleton, Wisconsin

### 1901 - 1903

In 1901, O. E. Bell bought the machinery of the defunct Cheshire Watch Company and moved it to Appleton, Wisconsin, where he had organized the Remington Watch Company. The first watches were shipped from the factory in February 1902; production ceased in mid-1903 and the contents were sold off before the end of that year. Most movements made by this firm were modified Cheshire movements and were marked "Appleton Watch Company." Advertisements for the firm in 1903 stated that they made 16 and 18 size movements with 11, 15, or 17 jewels. Serial numbers range from 90,000 to 104,950. During the two years they were in business, the company produced about 2,000 to 3,000 watches.

Appleton Watch Co., 18 size, 7 jewels, "The Appleton Watch Co." on dial. Engraved on movement "Appleton Watch Co., Appleton, Wis." Note that the stem is attached to movement. Serial number 93,106.

| Description | | Avg | Ex-Fn | Mint |
|---|---|---|---|---|
| 18S, 7J, OF, NI, 3/4, DMK, SW, PS, stem attached | ★★★ | $450 | $500 | $600 |
| 18S, 7J, OF, NI, 3/4, DMK, SW, PS, Coin, OF | ★★★ | 400 | 500 | 600 |
| 18S, 15J, NI, LS, SW, 3/4, M#2 | ★★★★ | 500 | 600 | 700 |
| 16S, 7-11J, 3/4, stem attached | ★★★ | 450 | 550 | 750 |

Note: With **ORIGINAL** APPLETON cases add $150 to $250 more. This case is difficult to find.

# AUBURNDALE WATCH CO.

### Auburndale, Massachusetts

### 1876 - 1883

This company was the first to attempt an inexpensive watch. Jason R. Hopkins was issued two patents in 1875 covering the "rotary design." The rotary design eliminated the need of adjusting to various positions, resulting in a less expensive watch. The company was formed about 1876, and the first watches were known as the "Auburndale Rotary." In 1876, equipment was purchased from the Marion Watch Co., and the first rotary designed watches were placed on the market for $10 in 1877. Auburndale produced about 6,000 watches before closing in 1883.

Auburndale Timer, 18 size, 7 jewels, stem wind, 10 minute, second jump timer.

Auburndale 10 min. Timer, 1/4 beat jump seconds, sweep second hand, stop & fly back, back wind.

| Grade or Name – Description | Avg | Ex-Fn | Mint |
|---|---|---|---|
| Auburndale Rotary, 20S, 2J, LS, SW, NI case, detent ...... ★★★★ | $1,900 | $2,500 | $3,200 |
| Auburndale Rotary, 18S, 2J, SW, LS, NI case, lever ........... ★★★ | 1,200 | 1,800 | 2,500 |
| Bentley, 18S, 7J, LS, NI case, SW, 3/4.................................... ★★ | 600 | 800 | 1,100 |
| Lincoln, 18S, 7J, LS, NI case, KW, 3/4.................................... ★★ | 600 | 800 | 1,100 |
| Auburndale Timer, 18S, 5-7J, SW, NI case, 10 min. timer, 1/4 sec. jump second........................ | 300 | 375 | 425 |
| Auburndale Timer, 18S, 5-7J, SW, NI case, 10 min. timer, 1/4 sec. jump seconds, with a 24 hour dial .........................★ | 400 | 500 | 600 |
| Auburndale Timer, 18S, 5-7J, KW, NI case, 10 min. timer, 1/4 sec. jump seconds, with split seconds........................ ★★ | 550 | 750 | 950 |
| Auburndale Timer,18S, marked "207", gold balance, OF .............. | 325 | 375 | 425 |

Bentley, 18 size, 7 jewels, 3/4 plate, stem wind, serial number 2.

Auburndale Rotary, 18 size, 2 jewels, stem wind, lever set, serial number 448.

# AURORA WATCH CO.

## Aurora, Illinois

### 1883 - 1892

Aurora Watch Co. was organized in mid-1883 with the goal of getting one jeweler in every town to handle Aurora watches. The first movements were 18S, full plate, and were first sold in the fall of 1884. There were several watches marked No. 1. The total production was about 215,000; over 200,000 were 18 Size, and some were 6 size ladies' watches. For the most part Aurora produced medium to low grade; and at one time made about 150 movements per day. The Hamilton Watch Co. purchased the company on June 19, 1890.

## AURORA WATCH CO.
## Estimated Serial Nos. and Production Dates

| | |
|---|---|
| 1884 – 10,001 | 1888 – 200,000 |
| 1885 – 60,000 | 1889 – 215,000 |
| 1886 – 101,000 | 1891 – 230,901 |
| 1887 – 160,000 | |

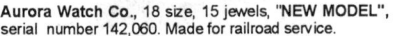

Aurora Watch Co., 18 size, 15 jewels, "NEW MODEL", serial number 142,060. Made for railroad service.

Aurora Watch Co., 18 size, 15 jewels, Adj, engraved on movement "Made expressly R.J.A.," **5th pinion** serial number 73,529.

| Description | Avg | Ex-Fn | Mint |
|---|---|---|---|
| 18S, 7J, KW, KS, Gilded, OF | $150 | $180 | $230 |
| 18S, 7J, KW, KS, Gilded, HC | 175 | 200 | 250 |
| 18S, 7J, 5th pinion, Gilded, LS, SW, OF | 135 | 160 | 195 |
| 18S, 7J, LS, SW, Gilded, new model, HC | 200 | 250 | 325 |
| 18S, 11J, KW, KS, Gilded, HC | 175 | 200 | 250 |
| 18S, 11J, KW, KS, Gilded, OF | 150 | 180 | 230 |
| 18S, 11J, 5th pinion, LS, SW, Gilded, new model, OF | 145 | 175 | 225 |
| 18S, 11J, 5th pinion, LS, SW, NI, GJS, OF | 160 | 200 | 250 |
| 18S, 11J, 5th pinion, LS, SW, NI, GJS, new model, OF | 150 | 180 | 230 |
| 18S, 11J, LS, SW, Gilded, made expressly for the guild, HC | 225 | 275 | 325 |
| 18S, 11J, 5th pinion, LS, SW, NI, made expressly for the guild, OF | 225 | 275 | 325 |
| 18S, 15J, KW, KS, NI, GJS, DMK, OF or HC ★ | 225 | 275 | 350 |
| 18S, 15J, 5th pinion, LS, SW, Gilded, OF | 200 | 250 | 325 |
| 18S, 15J, 5th pinion, LS, SW, NI, GJS, DMK, ADT, OF | 225 | 275 | 350 |
| 18S, 15J, 5th pinion, LS, SW, NI, GJS, DMK, ADJ, new model, OF | 300 | 350 | 400 |
| 18S, 15J, LS, SW, NI, GJS, DMK, ADJ, new model, HC | 300 | 350 | 400 |
| 18S, 15J, LS, SW, NI, GJS, ADJ, 2 Tone DMK, checkerboard or snowflake HC | 325 | 375 | 425 |
| 18S, 15J, LS, SW, NI, GJS, ADJ, 2 Tone DMK, checkerboard or snowflake, 5th pinion, OF ★ | 400 | 550 | 750 |

| Size and Description | Avg | Ex-Fn | Mint |
|---|---|---|---|
| 18S, 15J, LS, SW, NI, GJS, DMK, ADJ, Railroad Time Service or Caufield Watch, new model, HC ....................★ | $400 | $550 | $675 |
| 18S, marked 15 Ruby Jewels but has 17J, 5th pinion, LS, SW, NI, GJS, 2 Tone, ADJ, OF .....................................★★ | 600 | 700 | 900 |
| 18S, marked 15 Ruby Jewels, only 15J, LS, SW, NI, GJS, 2 Tone DMK, ADJ, HC............................................... | 400 | 500 | 600 |
| 18S, marked 15 Ruby Jewels, only 15J, LS, SW, NI, GJS, ADJ, 2 Tone DMK, OF .........................................★ | 450 | 525 | 600 |
| 18S, 15J, Chronometer, LS, SW, NI, DMK, ADJ, new model HC ................................................★★ | 400 | 500 | 625 |
| 18S, 15J, Chronometer, LS, SW, NI, GJS, DMK, ADJ, HC ........★ | 375 | 450 | 525 |
| 18S, 15J, LS, Gilded, "Eclipse, Chicago", new model, HC........... | 275 | 300 | 385 |
| 18S, 15J, LS, SW, NI, DMK, made expressly for the guild, HC..... | 250 | 300 | 375 |
| 18S, 15J, 5th pinion, LS, SW, Gilded, made expressly for the guild, OF ................................................ | 300 | 350 | 400 |
| 18S, 15J, LS, SW, Gilded, made expressly for the "RJA" (Retails Jeweler's Assoc.), HC............................................... | 400 | 500 | 600 |

| Size and Description | Avg | Ex-Fn | Mint |
|---|---|---|---|
| 6S, 11-15J, LS, SW, Gilded, 3/4, HC ............................................... | $125 | $150 | $200 |
| 6S, 11-15J, LS, SW, NI, GJS, DMK, 3/4, HC................................. | 150 | 175 | 225 |
| 6S, 11-15J, LS, SW, 3/4 plate, 14K, HC......................................... | 250 | 300 | 400 |

# BALL WATCH CO.

### Cleveland, Ohio
### 1879 - 1969

The Ball Watch Company did not manufacture watches but did help formulate the specifications of watches used for railroad service. Webb C. Ball of Cleveland, Ohio, was the general time inspector for over 125,000 miles of railroad in the U. S., Mexico, and Canada. In 1891 there was a collision between the Lake Shore and Michigan Southern Railways at Kipton, Ohio. The collision was reported to have occurred because an engineer's watch had stopped, for about four minutes, then started running again. The railroad officials commissioned Ball to establish the timepiece inspection system. Ball knew that the key to safe operations of the railroad was the manufacturing of sturdy, precision timepieces. He also knew they must be able to withstand hard use and still be accurate. Before this time, each railroad company had its own rules and standards. After Ball presented his guidelines, most American manufacturers set out to meet these standards and soon a list was made of the manufacturers that produced watches of the grade that would pass inspection. Each railroad employee had a card that he carried showing the record of how his watch performed on inspection. Ball was also instrumental in the formation of the Horological Institute of America.

🕐 NOTE: BALL WATCHES ARE PRICED AS HAVING A ORIGINAL BALL DIAL.

## ESTIMATED SERIAL NUMBERS AND PRODUCTION DATES
## FOR RAILROAD GRADE WATCHES

| (Hamilton) Date – Serial # | (Waltham) Date – Serial # | (Elgin) |
|---|---|---|
| 1895 - 13,000 | 1900 - 060,700 | 1904-1906 |
| 1897 - 20,500 | 1905 - 202,000 | S # range: |
| 1900 - 42,000 | 1910 - 216,000 | 11,853,000 - 12,282,000 |
| 1902 - 170,000 | 1915 - 250,000 | |
| 1905 - 462,000 | 1920 - 260,000 | (E. Howard & C0.) |
| 1910 - 600,000 | 1925 - 270,000 | 1893-1895 |
| 1915 - 603,000 | | S # range: |
| 1920 - 610,000 | | 226,000 - 308,000 |
| 1925 - 620,000 | | |
| 1930 - 637,000 | (Illinois) | |
| 1935 - 641,000 | Date – Serial # | (Hampden) |
| 1938 - 647,000 | 1929 - 800,000 | 1890-1892 |
| 1939 - 650,000 | 1930 - 801,000 | S # range: |
| 1940 - 651,000 | 1931 - 803,000 | 626,750 - 657,960 - |
| 1941 - 652,000 | 1932 - 804,000 | 759,720 |
| 1942 - 654,000 | | |

The above list is provided for determining the **APPROXIMATE** age of your watch. Match serial number with date. Watches were not necessarily sold in the exact order of manufactured date.

## BALL — AURORA
### 18 SIZE

| Description | | Avg | Ex-Fn | Mint |
|---|---|---|---|---|
| 15-17J, OF, marked Ball | ★★ | $1,500 | $1,750 | $2,000 |
| 15-17J, HC, marked Ball | ★★★ | 1,600 | 1,900 | 2,200 |

Ball-Elgin, Grade 333, 18 size, 17 jewels, rare hunting case model, serial number 11,958,002.

Ball-Elgin, Grade 333, 18 size, 17 jewels, open face model, serial number 11,856,801.

## BALL — ELGIN
### 18 SIZE G. F. CASES

| Description | | Avg | Ex-Fn | Mint |
|---|---|---|---|---|
| 16J, G#327, Commercial Standard, OF, LS | ★ | $275 | $350 | $475 |
| 17J, G#328, Commercial Standard, HC, LS | ★ | 300 | 375 | 500 |

| Description | | Avg | Ex-Fn | Mint |
|---|---|---|---|---|
| 17J, G#328, Coin, HC, LS | ★ | $250 | $325 | $450 |
| 17J, G#329, NI, Adj.5P, LS, HC | ★ | 1,200 | 1,500 | 1,800 |
| 21J, G#330, LS, Official RR std., HC | ★ ★ ★ ★ | 2,000 | 2,500 | 3,000 |
| 16J, G#331, NI, OF, Adj.5P, PS, Commercial Std. | ★ ★ | 375 | 425 | 550 |
| 16J, G#331, NI, HC, Adj.5P, PS, Commercial Std | ★ ★ | 400 | 500 | 600 |
| 17J, G#331, NI, OF, Adj.5P, PS | | 200 | 275 | 350 |
| 17J, G#332, Commercial Std, OF, PS | ★ | 300 | 350 | 400 |
| 17J, G#333, NI, OF, Adj.5P, LS | | 200 | 265 | 325 |
| 17J, G#333, NI, HC, Adj.5P, LS | ★ ★ ★ | 1,300 | 1,600 | 1,900 |
| 21J, G#333, NI, OF, Adj.5P, LS | | 325 | 350 | 400 |
| 21J, G#334, NI, OF, Adj.5P, LS | | 375 | 450 | 500 |

🕐 Note: 18 Size Ball watches in hunting cases are scarce.

## BALL — HAMILTON
### 18 SIZE G. F. CASES

| Description | | Avg | Ex-Fn | Mint |
|---|---|---|---|---|
| 17J, M#936,Superior Grade,early run | ★ ★ ★ | $1,500 | $2,000 | $3,000 |
| 17J, M#938,NI, OF, DR, | ★ ★ | 575 | 625 | 750 |
| 17J, M#-937-939, Official RR std, LS, Adj., HC | ★ ★ | 2,000 | 2,500 | 3,200 |
| 17J, M#999, Commercial Standard | | 300 | 400 | 500 |
| 17J, Off. Ball marked jewelers name on dial & mvt., OF | ★ | 350 | 450 | 575 |
| 17J, M#999, NI, Official RR std, OF, Adj.5P, LS, Coin | | 250 | 300 | 365 |
| 17J, M#999, Official RR std, NI, OF, Adj.5P, LS | | 250 | 300 | 365 |
| 17J, M#999, "A" model adj. | ★ | 350 | 400 | 500 |
| 17J, M#999, NI, OF, Adj.5P, marked "Loaner" on case | | 250 | 300 | 365 |
| 19J, M#999, Official RR std, NI, OF, Adj.5P, LS | | 325 | 375 | 435 |
| 21J, M#999, Official RR std, NI, OF, Adj.5P, LS | | 350 | 400 | 465 |
| 23J, M#999, NI, OF, Adj.5P, LS, Gold Filled Case | | 4,000 | 5,000 | 6,000 |
| 23J, M#999, NI, OF, Adj.5P, LS ,14K case | ★ ★ ★ | 6,000 | 7,500 | 10,000 |
| 23J, M#999, NI, HC, Adj.5P, LS,14K case | ★ ★ ★ ★ | 7,000 | 9,000 | 12,000 |
| Ball & Co., 17J, SR, Coin | | 450 | 600 | 800 |
| Brotherhood of Locomotive Engineers, 17J, OF | | 400 | 500 | 675 |
| Brotherhood of Locomotive Engineers, 19J, OF | | 500 | 600 | 775 |

BALL-HAMILTON, Grade 999, 18 size, 17 jewels, serial number 458,623

BALL-HAMILTON, Grade 999, 18 size, 17 jewels, marked "Railroad Watch Co." serial number 20,793.

Ball Watch Co., Brotherhood of RR trainmen, 18 size, 17J, movement made by Hamilton, serial number 13,020.

Ball Watch Co. (Hamilton). Grade 999, 18 size, 21 J., sun ray damaskeening, serial number 548,157, c.1906.

| Description | Avg | Ex-Fn | Mint |
|---|---|---|---|
| Brotherhood of Locomotive Engineers, 21J, OF | $600 | $700 | $875 |
| Brotherhood of Locomotive Firemen, 17J, OF | 400 | 500 | 675 |
| Brotherhood of Locomotive Firemen, 19J, OF | 500 | 600 | 775 |
| Brotherhood of Locomotive Firemen, 21J, OF | 600 | 700 | 875 |
| Brotherhood of Railroad Trainsmen, 17J, OF | 400 | 500 | 675 |
| Brotherhood of Railroad Trainsmen, 19J, OF | 500 | 600 | 775 |
| Brotherhood of Railroad Trainsmen, 21J, OF | 600 | 700 | 875 |
| Order of Railroad Conductors, 17J, OF | 400 | 500 | 650 |
| Order of Railroad Conductors, 19J, OF | 500 | 600 | 750 |
| Order of Railroad Conductors, 21J, OF | 600 | 700 | 850 |
| Order of Railroad Telegraphers, 17J, OF | 400 | 500 | 650 |
| Order of Railroad Telegraphers, 19J, OF | 500 | 600 | 750 |
| Order of Railroad Telegraphers, 21J, OF | 600 | 700 | 850 |
| Ball Standard **marked** Railroad Watch Co., 16J, OF, LS ....... ★★ | 900 | 1,200 | 1,750 |
| Ball Standard **marked** Railroad Watch Co., 17J, OF, LS ....... ★★ | 1,000 | 1,300 | 1,850 |
| Private Label or Jewelers name, 17J, Adj., OF | 375 | 425 | 500 |

BALL WATCH Co. ( OFFICIAL R.R. STANDARD ) Dial, NOTE: **20th Century bow**, W/ snap back.

BALL WATCH Co. DIAL (Order of Railroad Conductors ), 18 size.

## BALL–DeLONG ESCAPEMENT
### 16 SIZE

| Description | Avg | Ex-Fn | Mint |
|---|---|---|---|
| 21J, 14K OF Case .......................................... ★★★★★ | $2,000 | $2,500 | $3,000 |

Ball-Hamilton, Model 998 Elinvar, 16 size, 23 jewels, with center bridge.

BALL W. CO.(HAMILTON),16 size, 21jewels, official RR standard, ADJ.5p, serial no.611429

## BALL — HAMILTON
### 16 SIZE G. F. CASES

| Description | Avg | Ex-Fn | Mint |
|---|---|---|---|
| 16J, M#976, 977, NI, OF, LS............................................. | $200 | $250 | $300 |
| 17J, M#974, NI, OF, LS .................................................. | 150 | 200 | 265 |
| 17J, Official RR Standard, OF ...................................... | 175 | 225 | 285 |
| 19J, Official RR Standard, OF ...................................... | 225 | 275 | 335 |
| 19J, M#999, NI, Off. RR Stan., OF, LS.......................... | 225 | 275 | 335 |
| 21J, M#999, NI, Off. RR Stan., OF, LS.......................... | 325 | 350 | 400 |
| 21J, M#999B-marked, Off. RR Stan., OF, marked-Adj.6P ....... ★ | 350 | 375 | 425 |
| 21J, M#999, Off. RR Stan., Coin case........................... | 325 | 350 | 400 |
| 21J, M#999 , Off. RR Stan., marked Loaner, coin case........... ★★ | 350 | 400 | 450 |
| 21J, M#992B, NI, marked 992B & Off RR Stan. Adj.6P ..... ★★★ | 600 | 750 | 1,000 |
| 23J, M#999B, Off. RR Stan., NI, OF, LS, Adj.6P .......................... | 600 | 700 | 750 |
| 23J, M#998 marked-Elinvar, Off. RR Stan., Adj.5P ..................... | 700 | 750 | 850 |
| 23J, M#999, NI, Off. RR Stan., OF, LS.......................... | 600 | 675 | 750 |
| Brotherhood of Locomotive Engineers, OF..................................... | 600 | 675 | 750 |
| Brotherhood of Locomotive Firemen, OF ........................................ | 600 | 675 | 750 |
| Brotherhood of Railroad Trainmen, OF ......................................... | 600 | 675 | 750 |
| Order of Railroad Conductors, OF................................................. | 600 | 675 | 750 |
| 17-19J, Brotherhood or Order, HUNTING CASE .................... ★★ | 800 | 900 | 1,000 |
| Private Label or Jewelers name, 21J, Adj., OF.............................. | 250 | 275 | 310 |

## BALL — HAMPDEN
### 18 SIZE

| Description | Avg | Ex-Fn | Mint |
|---|---|---|---|
| 15-17J, LS, SW, HC, marked Superior Grade .................. ★★★ | $1,250 | $1,400 | $1,850 |
| 15-17J, LS, SW, OF, marked Superior Grade ........................ ★★ | 1,000 | 1,200 | 1,600 |
| 15-17J, LS, SW, OF................................................................★ | 275 | 325 | 400 |
| 15-17J, LS, SW, HC .............................................................. ★★★ | 400 | 500 | 650 |

Ball-Hampden, 18 size, 17 jewels, serial number 759,728.

BALL & CO. (E. HOWARD & CO.), Series VIII, 18 size, 17 jewels. Order of Railway Conductors, serial number 307,488. c.1900.

## BALL — E. HOWARD & CO.
### 18 SIZE

| Description | | Avg | Ex-Fn | Mint |
|---|---|---|---|---|
| 17J, 3/4, HC, PS, GJS, 18K, VII, orig. gold HC | ★★★ | $4,000 | $5,000 | $6,500 |
| 17J, 3/4, OF, PS, GJS, 14K, VIII, orig. gold OF case | ★★ | 2,500 | 3,000 | 5,000 |
| 17J, 3/4, OF, PS, GJS, 14K, VIII, Brotherhood of Locomotive Engineers | ★★★ | 3,000 | 4,000 | 6,000 |

BALL W. Co. (E. HOWARD WATCH CO.), 16 size, 21J. (KEYSTONE). This watch believed to be one-of-a-kind prototype, serial number 982,201.

Ball Watch Co., Illinois Model, 16 size, 23 jewels. Note: The CORRECT HANDS FOR BALL ILLINOIS WATCH.

⊕ Some grades are not included. Their values can be determined by comparing with similar age, size, metal content, style, models and grades listed.

⊕ BALL Watches are priced as having a ORIGINAL BALL DIAL & CASE.

## BALL — E. HOWARD WATCH CO.
### 16 SIZE

| Description | Avg | Ex-Fn | Mint |
|---|---|---|---|
| 17J, OF, GJS ................................................................. | $2,000 | $2,500 | $3,500 |
| 21J, KEYSTONE, Adj, GJS, OF ...................... ★★★★★ | 2,500 | 3,000 | 4,000 |

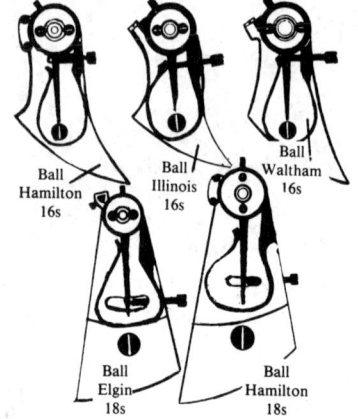

Ball Watch Co., Illinois Model, 16 size, 23 jewels. To identify, note back plates that circle around balance wheel, serial number B801,758.

BALL regulator identification, note: styles and location of hairspring stud.

## BALL — ILLINOIS
### 18 & 16 SIZE

| Description | Avg | Ex-Fn | Mint |
|---|---|---|---|
| 18 size, 11-15J. or (Garland model), OF............................................ | $175 | $195 | $225 |
| 16 size, 23J, 3/4, LS, Off. RR Stan., OF, GJS ...................... ★★ | 1,100 | 1,250 | 1,500 |
| 16 size, 23J, 3/4, Off. RR Stan., OF, GJS, marked 60 hr... ★★★★ | 1,500 | 1,700 | 2,000 |

Top Left: Ball-Hamilton, 16 size, 23 jewels. **Bottom left: Ball-Illinois**, 16 size, 23 jewels. **Above: Ball Waltham**, 16 size, 23 jewels. These three movements are similar in appearance. To identify, note where the hair spring stud attaches to the balance bridge, which is slightly different on each movement.

### BALL — SETH THOMAS
#### 18 SIZE

| Description | Avg | Ex-Fn | Mint |
|---|---|---|---|
| 17J, M#3, LS, OF,3/4, GJS ...................★★★★ | $2,200 | $2,800 | $3,500 |

### BALL — WALTHAM
#### 18 SIZE

| Description | Avg | Ex-Fn | Mint |
|---|---|---|---|
| 1892, 15J, OF, LS, SW, marked Webb C. Ball, Cleveland......★★ | $1,300 | $1,500 | $2,000 |

### BALL — WALTHAM
#### 16 SIZE

| Description | Avg | Ex-Fn | Mint |
|---|---|---|---|
| 15J, Commercial Std.,3/4,HC, GCW .......................★★ | $325 | $400 | $550 |
| 15-16J, Commercial std., OF................................ | 125 | 150 | 175 |
| 16J, Commercial std., HC................................... | 175 | 200 | 250 |
| 17-19J, Commercial std., OF .............................. | 100 | 150 | 175 |
| 17-19J, Commercial std., HC .............................. | 175 | 200 | 250 |
| 17J, LS, 3/4, Adj.5P, Multi-color case, GF, OF ............... | 250 | 300 | 400 |
| 17J, LS, 3/4, Adj.5P, Off. RR Stan., OF..................... | 150 | 200 | 275 |
| 17J,Official RR std., HC................................★★ | 800 | 1,000 | 1,300 |
| 19J,Official RR std., LS, GCW,GJS, OF..................... | 225 | 250 | 300 |
| 19J,Official RR std., LS, GCW,GJS, HC .................... | 350 | 450 | 575 |

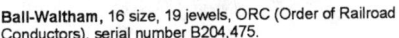

Ball-Waltham, 16 size, 19 jewels, ORC (Order of Railroad Conductors), serial number B204,475.

BALL–WALTHAM, 23 jewels, Official Railroad Standard, lever set, Adjusted to 5 positions, serial# B060,915.

| Description | Avg | Ex-Fn | Mint |
|---|---|---|---|
| 19J, BLF&E ............................................... | $500 | $600 | $725 |
| 19J, Off. RR Stan., GJS, HC ......................★★ | 900 | 1,100 | 1,400 |
| 19J, OF, LS, Off. RR Stan., 14K........................ | 575 | 650 | 750 |
| 19J, OF, LS, Off. RR Stan., stirrup style case ............... | 250 | 300 | 350 |
| 19J, OF, LS, Off. RR Stan., Coin........................ | 225 | 275 | 335 |
| 19J, OF, LS, 3/4, Adj.5P, Off. RR Stan., ................ | 225 | 265 | 325 |
| 19J, OF, LS, 3/4, Adj.5P, Off. RR Stan., Wind Indicator ....★★ | 3,000 | 3,500 | 4,250 |

⊕ Some grades are not included. Their values can be determined by comparing with similar age, size, metal content, style, models and grades listed.

| Description | Avg | Ex-Fn | Mint |
|---|---|---|---|
| 21J,Official RR std., LS, GCW,GJS, OF | $325 | $350 | $400 |
| 21J, OF, LS, 3/4, Adj.5P, Off. RR Stan., | 325 | 350 | 400 |
| 21J, LS, OF, Adj.5P, Off. RR Stan., marked Loaner | 325 | 350 | 400 |
| 17J, Brotherhood, marked ORC, BOFLE & *other etc. dials*, OF | 350 | 400 | 475 |
| 19J, Brotherhood, marked ORC, BOFLE & *other etc. dials*, OF | 400 | 500 | 625 |
| 17-19J, Brotherhood, marked ORC, BOFLE & *other etc. dials*,HC | 600 | 700 | 900 |
| 21J, Brotherhood, marked ORC, BOFLE & *other etc. dials*, OF | 500 | 600 | 750 |
| 23J, LS, OF, Adj.5P, NI, GJS, Off. RR Stand., only one known to exist, **Ex. rare** ★★★★★ | 4,000 | 6,000 | 8,500 |

 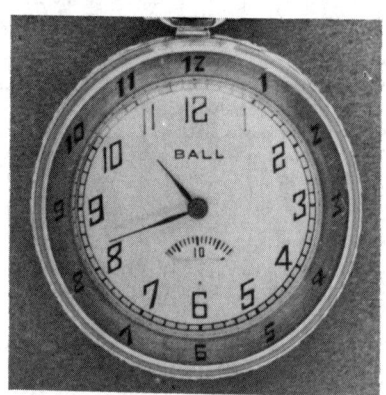

**Ball Watch Co. by Waltham,** 12 size, 19 jewels, open face, digital seconds

## 12 SIZE
### (Not Railroad Grade)

| Description | Avg | Ex-Fn | Mint |
|---|---|---|---|
| 19J, Illinois, OF, PS | $135 | $175 | $250 |
| 19J, Illinois, HC, PS | 200 | 300 | 450 |
| 15J, Waltham,Commercial Standard, OF, PS, | 150 | 200 | 250 |
| 16J, Waltham,Commercial Standard, OF, PS, | 160 | 210 | 260 |
| 17J, Waltham, Commercial Standard, OF, PS, | 150 | 160 | 180 |
| 19J, Waltham, OF, PS, rotating digital sec | 200 | 250 | 300 |

## 0 SIZE
### (Not Railroad Grade)

| Description | Avg | Ex-Fn | Mint |
|---|---|---|---|
| 17-19J, Waltham, OF, PS | $225 | $275 | $375 |
| 19J, HC, PS, "Queen" in Ball case | 350 | 400 | 550 |

## FOR CANADA R.R. SERVICE

| Description | Avg | Ex-Fn | Mint |
|---|---|---|---|
| 16S,3/4,LS,OF,GJS | $500 | $600 | $750 |

## RAILROAD INSPECTOR'S OR JEWELRY CO. NAME
## ON DIAL AND MOVEMENT

| Description | Avg | Ex-Fn | Mint |
|---|---|---|---|
| 18S, 17J, Adj.5P, OF | $700 | $850 | $1,000 |

Ball-Audemars Piguet & Co., 14 size, 31 jewels, minute repeater, open face, serial number 4,220.

Ball-Vacheron & Constantin, 43mm, 18 jewels, hunting; note wolf-teeth winding.

## BALL — SWISS
### 16 SIZE

| Description | Avg | Ex-Fn | Mint |
|---|---|---|---|
| 17J, "Garland" | $100 | $125 | $175 |
| 21J, Time Ball Special,OF | 60 | 75 | 100 |
| 21J, M#435-B, OF, LS, Adj.6P, Ball case, stirrup bow | 200 | 225 | 275 |
| 21J, M#435-C, OF, LS, Adj.6P, Ball case, stirrup bow | 200 | 225 | 275 |
| 21J, M#477-B, Adj.6P (BXC-Record Watch Co.) | 200 | 225 | 250 |
| 40mm Audemar Piguet, min. repeater, jeweled thru hammers, 18K, OF, triple signed Webb C. Ball | 6,000 | 7,500 | 9,500 |
| 43mm Vacheron & Constantin, 18J, HC, 18K | 1,000 | 1,200 | 1,400 |

🕐 A 1902 advertisement for Ball Watch Company read, "We do not sell movements or cases separately.

🕐 200,000 railroad watches, plus 150,000 non-railroad grade watches, were made and sold by the Ball Watch Co., totaling approximately 350,000.

NO. 333
NO. 999

999 STANDARD

OFFICIAL RR STANDARD

OFFICIAL TIME SERVICE STANDARD

STANDARD    B OF RT

B OF LE

Railway Queen

O OF RC

The B. of L. E. Standard Watch.
The B. of L. F. Standard Watch.
The B. of R. T. Standard Watch.
The O. of R. C. Standard Watch.
The Official R. R. Standard Watch.
The O. of R. T. Standard Watch.

SAFETY FIRST

B OF LF

TRADE MARKS REGISTERED IN U. S. PATENT OFFICE

**CATALOG CASE # 106**
gold filled case $125 - $150 - $185

**CATALOG CASE # 110**
gold filled case $150 - $175 - $225

"BOX CAR" Dial
dial found on Hamilton & Illinois made Ball

**CATALOG CASE # 114**
gold filled case $150 - $175- $200

**CATALOG CASE # 118**
gold filled case $175 - $200 - $250

🕐 NOTE: A 1902 advertisement for Ball Watch Company read, ''We do not sell movements or cases separately. BALL Advertised as a **COMPLETE** watch with a choice of BALL dials and was fitted with a certain matched, timed and rated movement and sold in the BALL designed case style as a **COMPLETE** watch. **ALL THE ABOVE CASES ARE GOLD FILLED.**

CATALOG CASE # 122
gold filled case $175 - $200 - $225

CATALOG CASE # 126
gold filled case $125 - $150 - $175

CONVENTIONAL Dial
dial found on Waltham made Ball

CATALOG CASE # 130
gold filled case $150 - $175 - $200

CATALOG CASE # 134
gold filled case $175 - $200 - $225

🕐 NOTE: A 1902 advertisement for Ball Watch Company read, "We do not sell movements or cases separately. BALL Advertised as a **COMPLETE** watch with a choice of BALL dials and was fitted with a certain matched, timed and rated movement and sold in the BALL designed case style as a **COMPLETE** watch. <u>**ALL THE ABOVE CASES ARE GOLD FILLED.**</u>

# BANNATYNE WATCH CO.
## 1905 - 1911

Mr. Bannatyne had previously worked for Ansonia, in charge of watch production. Bannatyne made non-jeweled watches that sold for about $1.50. Ingraham bought this company in 1912.

## ESTIMATED SERIAL NUMBERS AND PRODUCTION DATES

| Date | Serial No. | Date | Serial No. | Date | Serial No. |
|------|-----------|------|-----------|------|-----------|
| 1906 | 40,000 | 1908 | 140,000 | 1910 | 250,000 |

| Description | | Avg | Ex-Fn | Mint |
|-------------|---|-----|-------|------|
| 18S, OF, SW, NI case.................................................. ★ ★ | | $300 | $375 | $500 |

Bannatyne Watch Co. (left), Ingraham Watch Co. (right). Note similarity of movements. Both patented Aug. 27th, 1907 & Sept. 3rd, 1907.

# BENEDICT & BURNHAM MFG. CO.
## Waterbury, Connecticut
## 1878 - 1880

This name will be found on the dial of the first 1,000 "long wind" Waterbury watches made in 1878. These watches had skeleton type movements with open dials that made the works visible. They contained 58 parts and were attractive. The company was reorganized in March 1880 as the Waterbury Watch Co. and in 1886 became the New England Watch Co.

🕐 Watches listed in this book are priced at the collectable retail level, as **complete** watches having an original 14k gold-filled case & *KEY WIND* with silver case, an original white enamel single sunk dial, and with the entire original movement in good working order with no repairs needed.

Benedict & Burnham Mfg. Co. dial & movement, 18 size, long wind, skeletonized dial.

| Description | | Avg | Ex-Fn | Mint |
|---|---|---|---|---|
| 18S, duplex escapement, movement rotates as time advances | | | | |
| long wind,Nickel OF case ................................................ ★★★★ | | $800 | $1,000 | $1,250 |

# BOWMAN WATCH CO.

### Lancaster, Pennsylvania
### 1877 - 1882

In March 1879, Ezra F. Bowman, a native of Lancaster, Pa., opened a retail jewelry and watch business. He employed William H. Todd to supervise his watch manufacturing. Todd had previously been employed by the Elgin and Lancaster Watch companies. Bowman made a 17S, 3/4 plate, fully-jeweled movement. The escape wheel was a star tooth design, fully capped, similar to those made by Charles Frodsham, an English watch maker. They were stem wind with dials made by another company. Enough parts were made and bought for 300 watches, but only about 50 watches were completed and sold. Those performed very well. The company was sold to J. P. Stevens of Atlanta,Ga.

| Description | | Avg | Ex-Fn | Mint |
|---|---|---|---|---|
| 18S, 17J, Hamilton 928, OF, marked E. F. Bowman ............... ★★ | | $300 | $400 | $550 |
| 17S, 19-21J, 3/4, GJS, NI, LS, SW .................................... ★★★★ | | 9,000 | 11,000 | 16,000 |
| 16S, 21J, Hamilton 960, OF, marked E. F. Bowman ............... ★★ | | 350 | 450 | 600 |

Bowman Watch Co., 16-18 size, 17 jewels, 3/4 plate, gold jewel settings, lever set, stem wind. Note free sprung balance. Serial number 17, c.1880.

# CALIFORNIA WATCH CO.

## Berkeley, California

### 1876 - 1877

The Cornell Watch Co. was reorganized in early 1876 as the California Watch Co. The new company bought machinery to make watch cases of gold and silver. In a short time the company was in bad financial trouble and even paid its employees with watches. The business closed in the summer of 1876. Albert Troller bought the unfinished watches that were left. In about four months, he found a buyer in San Francisco. The factory was then closed and sold to the Independent Watch Co. Only about 5,000 watches were made by the California Watch Company. Serial numbers range from 25,115 to 30,174. Inscribed on the movements is "Berkeley."

| Description | | Avg | Ex-Fn | Mint |
|---|---|---|---|---|
| 18S, 15J, FULL, KW, KS, "Berkeley" | ★ ★ | $1,300 | $1,600 | $2,000 |
| 18S, 11-15J, FULL, KW, KS or SW | ★ | 1,000 | 1,200 | 1,600 |

California Watch Co., 18 size, 15 jewels, full plate.

California Watch Co., 18 size, 7 jewels, full plate, serial number 29,029.

# CHESHIRE WATCH CO.

## Cheshire, Connecticut

### 1883 - 1890

In October 1883, the Cheshire Watch Company was formed by George J. Capewell with D. A. A. Buck (designer of the long-wind Waterbury) as superintendent. Their first movement was 18S, 3/4 gilt plate, stem wind, stem set, with the pendant attached to the movement. It fit into a nickel case which was also made at the Cheshire factory. The first watches were completed in April 1885. A new 18S nickel movement with a second hand was made to fit standard size American cases, and was introduced in 1887. By that date production was at about 200 watches per day.

NOTE: George J. Capewell inventor of the Capewell horse shoe nail.

Serial numbers range from 201 to 89,650. All Cheshire watches were sold through L. W. Sweet, general selling agent, in New York City. The factory closed in 1890, going into receivership. The receiver had 3,000 movements finished in 1892. In 1901 O. E. Bell bought the machinery and had it shipped to Appleton, Wisconsin, where he had formed the Remington Watch Company. The watches produced by Remington are marked "Appleton Watch Co." on the movements.

Cheshire Watch Co., 18-20 size, 4 jewels, model number 1. Note stem attached and will not fit standard size case, serial number **201**.

| Description | Avg | Ex-Fn | Mint |
|---|---|---|---|
| 20S, 4-7J, FULL, OF, SW, NI case, stem attached, 1st model, closed top plate .......................................... ★ ★ ★ | $450 | $550 | $700 |
| 18S, 4-7J, 3/4, SW, OF, NI case, stem attached, 2nd model ........ ★ | 300 | 350 | 450 |
| 18S, 4-7J, HC/ OF fits standard case, 3rd model........................... ★ | 250 | 300 | 375 |
| 18S, 11J, HC/ OF, standard case, 3rd model ................................. ★ | 275 | 325 | 400 |
| 18S, 15J, HC/ OF, NI, ADJ, standard case, 3rd model ................ ★ | 300 | 350 | 450 |
| 18S, 21J, HC / OF, SW, Coin, standard case, 3rd model .......... ★ ★ | 400 | 450 | 550 |
| 6S, 3/4, HC/ OF, SW, NI case...................................................... ★ | 200 | 275 | 350 |

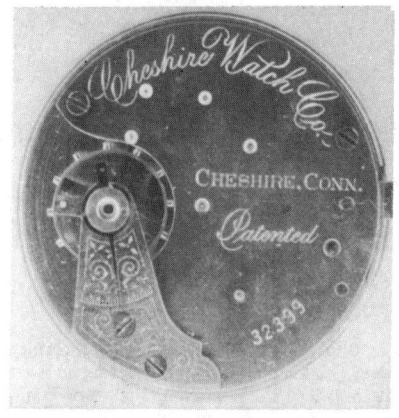

Cheshire Watch Co., 18 size, 4-7 jewels. This model number 2 was manufactured with the stem attached and requires a special case.

Cheshire Watch Co., 18 size, 4-7 jewels. This model fits standard 18 size cases. Model number 3.

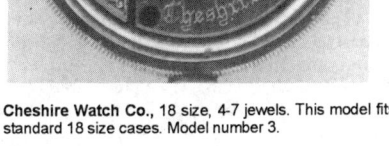 1st & 2nd model Cheshire movements will not fit standard 18 size cases.

160

# CHICAGO WATCH CO.

### Chicago, Illinois
### 1895 - 1903

The Chicago Watch Company's watches were 18 size, 7-15J & 12 size were made by other manufacturer Companies and sold by Chicago Watch Co.

| Description | Avg | Ex-Fn | Mint |
|---|---|---|---|
| 18S, 7J, OF | $100 | $145 | $200 |
| 18S, 7-11J, HC or OF, Swiss | 50 | 60 | 75 |
| 18S, 11J, KW | 325 | 375 | 450 |
| 18S, 15J, OF, SW | 175 | 200 | 300 |
| Columbus, 18S, 15J, SW, NI, OF ★ | 200 | 250 | 325 |
| Columbus, 18S, 15J, SW, NI, HC ★★ | 275 | 300 | 350 |
| Illinois, 18S, 11J, SW, NI ★★ | 200 | 250 | 325 |
| Waltham, 18S, 15J ★★ | 200 | 250 | 325 |
| 12S, 15J, OF | 100 | 145 | 200 |
| 12S, 15J, YGF, HC | 200 | 250 | 325 |

Chicago Watch Co., 18 size, 15 jewels, Hunting case, made by COLUMBUS Watch Co., nickel movement, lever set, serial # 209,145.

Columbia Watch Co., 0 size, 4 jewels, stem wind, open face and hunting, duplex escapement, the escape wheel teeth were milled to give better quality than the Waterbury movements.

# COLUMBIA WATCH CO.

### Waltham, Massachusetts
### 1896 - 1899

The Columbia Watch Company was organized in 1896 by Edward A. Locke, formerly General Manager of the Waterbury Watch Company. The firm began manufacturing an 0-size, 4-jewel gilt movement with duplex escapement in 1897. These movements were marked "Columbia Watch Co., Waltham, Mass." The firm also made movements marked "Hollers Watch Co., Brooklyn, NY," as well as nickeled movements marked "Cambridge Watch Co., New York."

Locke turned the business over to his son-in-law, Renton Whidden, in 1898, and the firm changed to an 0-size, 7- jewel nickel movement with lever escapement called the Suffolk. The firm name was not changed until early 1901.

| Description | Avg | Ex-Fn | Mint |
|---|---|---|---|
| 0S, 4J, SW, OF, HC, Duplex, gilded | $50 | $60 | $75 |
| 0S, 7J, SW, OF, lever escapement | 60 | 75 | 85 |

# COLUMBUS WATCH CO.

### Columbus, Ohio
### 1874 - 1903

Dietrich Gruen, born in Osthofen, Germany in 1847, started a business as the Columbus Watch Co. on Dec. 22 of 1874 in Columbus, Ohio. At the age of 27, he received a U.S. patent for an improved safety pinion. The new company finished movements made from Madretsch, Switzerland, a suburb of Beil. The imported movements were made in a variety of sizes and were in nickel or gilt. The early watches usually had the initials C.W.CO. intertwined in script on the dial. The serial numbers generally ran up to around 20,000's a few examples are in the 70,000's.

D. Gruen and W.J. Savage decided in late 1882 to manufacture watches locally. By August of 1883 the first movements were being produced with a train consisting of 72 teeth on the barrel, 72 on the center wheel, 11 on the center pinion, 60 on the third wheel with a pinion of 9, 70 on the fourth wheel with a pinion of 9 with a 7 leaf escape pinion. The new manufacture primarily made 18 size movements but also pioneered the 16 size watch while reducing the size and thickness. Several new innovations were used into the design including a completely covered main spring barrel, a new micrometric regulator and the ability to change the main spring without removing the balance cock. By 1884 they were making their own dials, but no cases were ever manufactured.

The company went into receivership in 1894 with new management. That same year Frederick Gruen started again as D. Gruen & Son. They had PAUL ASSMANN to produce 18 size & 16 size movements with 18 & 21 jewels with the escapement designed by Moritz Grossman of Glasshute. Soon after this time movements were obtained from Switzerland and the new Gruen veri-thin movement was developed. In 1898 this company moved to Cincinnati.

From 1894 through February 14, 1903 the Columbus Watch Co. produced watches both under the Columbus Watch Co. and the New Columbus Watch Co. name. The re-organized company produced the same models, but switched primarily to named grades such as Time King, Columbus King, etc. The higher grade watches were assigned a special block of serial numbers from 500,000 to 506,000 . In keeping with the industry several models with 25 jewels were produced in this block of serial numbers.

In 1903 the Columbus Watch Co. was sold to the Studebakers and the South Bend Watch Co. started. The machinery, unfinished movements, parts and approximately 3/4 of the 150 employees moved to South Bend, Indiana. Some marked Columbus Watch Co. movements were finished by the South Bend W. Co. Examples exist of dials made in the South Bend style and movements marked Columbus Watch Co.

COLUMBUS WATCH CO., 19 Lignes or about 14-16 size, 16 jewels, gold jewel settings, marked Gruen's Pat. pinion, OPEN FACE model, serial # 5,387. ( Swiss contract )

COLUMBUS WATCH CO., 19 Lignes or about 14-16 size, 15 jewels, engraved on movement *"N.B. Jeter Butter Mo. Pat. Pinion"*, hunting case, serial # 13,011.

## COLUMBUS
### ESTIMATED SERIAL NUMBERS AND PRODUCTION DATES

| DATE— SERIAL NO. | DATE— SERIAL NO. | |
|---|---|---|
| 1875– 1,000 | 1888 – 97,000 | |
| 1876– 3,000 | 1889 – 119,000 | |
| 1877– 6,000 | 1890 – 141,000 | |
| 1878– 9,000 | 1891 – 163,000 | SPECIAL BLOCK |
| 1879– 12,000 | 1892 – 185,000 | OF SERIAL NOS. |
| 1880– 15,000 | 1893 – 207,000 | DATE— SERIAL NO. |
| 1881– 18,000 | 1894 – 229,000 | 1894 – 500,001 |
| 1882– 21,000 | 1895 – 251,000 | 1896 – 501,500 |
| 1883 – 25,000 | 1896 – 273,000 | 1898 – 503,000 |
| 1884 – 30,000 | 1897 – 295,000 | 1900 – 504,500 |
| 1885 – 40,000 | 1898 – 317,000 | 1902 – 506,000 |
| 1886 – 53,000 | 1899 – 339,000 | |
| 1887 – 75,000 | 1900 – 361,000 | |
| | 1901 – 383,000 | |

The above list is provided for determining the **APPROXIMATE** age of your watch. Match serial number with date. Watches were not necessarily *SOLD* and *DELIVERED* in the exact order of manufactured or production dates.

## SWISS, 3/4 PLATE, & MADE FROM 1874–1883

Most marked COL. WATCH CO. with single sunk dials and may be SW/KW Transitional, serial # up to 20,000.

| Grade or Name — Description | Avg | Ex-Fn | Mint |
|---|---|---|---|
| 18S, 7J, pressed J., nickel or gilded, OF | $90 | $120 | $145 |
| 18S, 7J, pressed J., nickel or gilded, HC | 125 | 150 | 175 |
| 18S, 11J, pressed J., nickel or gilded, OF | 100 | 125 | 150 |
| 18S, 11J, pressed J., nickel or gilded, HC | 125 | 150 | 175 |
| 18S, 15J, GJS or pressed J., nickel, Adj., OF/HC | 200 | 225 | 275 |
| 18S, 16J, raised GJS, 2 tone or nickel, Adj., OF/HC | 225 | 275 | 325 |
| 16S, 11J, pressed J., nickel, OF/HC | 175 | 200 | 250 |
| 16S, 15J, pressed J. or GJS, Adj., nickel, OF/HC | 225 | 250 | 275 |
| 16S, 16J, raised GJS, Adj., nickel, OF/HC | 250 | 300 | 325 |
| 14S, 16J, GJS, nickel, Adj., OF/HC | 175 | 200 | 250 |
| 9S, 15J, GJS or pressed J., nickel, Adj., OF/HC | 150 | 175 | 200 |
| 8S, 11J, pressed J., nickel, OF/HC | 125 | 150 | 175 |
| 8S, 15J, pressed J., nickel, OF/HC | 150 | 175 | 200 |

NOTE: These Odd size movements are difficult to case.

COLUMBUS WATCH CO., 19 Lignes or about 16 size, 15 jewels, exposed winding wheels, marked Gruen Patent, OPEN FACE model, serial # 1,661. ( Swiss contract )

COLUMBUS WATCH CO., about 14 size, 16 jewels, gold jewel settings, nickel plates, marked Gruen's pat. pinion, HUNTING CASE model. ( Swiss contract )

## 18 SIZE-KW, FULL PLATE, MODEL # 1 & TRANSITIONAL
Serial # up to 100,000, balance cock set flush to barrel bridge and may have pinned dial.
Marked Col. Watch Co., Ohio Columbus Watch Co.

| Grade or Name — Description | Avg | Ex-Fn | Mint |
|---|---|---|---|
| 11-13J, KW / KS, gilded, OF/HC | $300 | $350 | $375 |
| 13J, KW / KS, nickel,(marked 13 jewels), OF/HC.★★ | 575 | 675 | 750 |
| 15J, KW / KS, gilded, Adj., OF/HC | 350 | 400 | 425 |
| 16J, KW / KS, gilded, OF/HC.★ | 400 | 450 | 500 |
| 11-13J, SW/ KW, gilded or nickel, OF/HC | 175 | 200 | 225 |
| 15J, SW/ KW, gilded or nickel, GJS, OF/HC | 200 | 225 | 250 |
| 16J, SW/ KW, gilded or nickel, GJS, OF/HC | 225 | 250 | 275 |

COLUMBUS WATCH CO., 18 size, marked 13 jewels, pressed jewels, key wind key set, nickel plates, marked on movement Col. Watch Co. Columbus Ohio Pat. pinion, on dial "OHIO COLUMBUS WATCH CO.", serial #40,198.

COLUMBUS WATCH CO., 18 size, 15 jewels, key wind key set, hunting case, on movement "Columbus Watch Co. Columbus, Ohio Pat. Pinion", serial # 66,577.

## 18 SIZE, FULL PLATE, PRE-1894
Marked "Columbus Watch Co. Columbus, Ohio", all marked Safety Pinion

| Grade or Name — Description | Avg | Ex-Fn | Mint |
|---|---|---|---|
| 7J, G#90, pressed J., OF | $75 | $85 | $100 |
| 7J, G#20, pressed J., HC | 85 | 100 | 125 |
| 11J, G#92, pressed J., nickel, OF | 90 | 110 | 125 |
| 11J, G#22, pressed J., nickel, HC | 100 | 125 | 150 |
| 15J, G#64 / G#93, gilded, OF | 90 | 110 | 125 |
| 15J, G#24 / G#32, gilded, HC | 100 | 125 | 150 |
| 15J, G#63 / G#94, nickel, Adj., OF | 90 | 100 | 125 |
| 15J, G#23 / G#33, nickel, Adj., HC | 125 | 150 | 175 |
| 15J, G#95, nickel, Adj., D.S. dial, OF | 100 | 125 | 150 |
| 15J, G#34, nickel, Adj., D.S. dial, HC | 125 | 150 | 175 |
| 16J, G#97, GJS, nickel, Adj., D.S. dial, OF | 150 | 175 | 200 |
| 16J, G#27, GJS, nickel, Adj., D.S. dial, HC | 175 | 200 | 225 |
| 16J, G#98, raised GJS, 2 tone nickel, Adj., D.S. dial, OF | 150 | 175 | 200 |
| 16J, G#28, raised GJS, 2 tone nickel, Adj., D.S. dial, HC | 175 | 200 | 225 |
| 16J, G#99, raised GJS, 2 tone nickel, Adj., D.S. dial, OF | 200 | 225 | 275 |
| 16J, G#18, raised GJS, 2 tone nickel, Adj., D.S. dial, HC | 225 | 250 | 300 |

## 18 SIZE-FULL PLATE, POST-1894

Some Marked "New Columbus Watch Co. Columbus Ohio"

| Grade or Name — Description | Avg | Ex-Fn | Mint |
|---|---|---|---|
| 7J, G#10, pressed J., gilded, OF | $75 | $85 | $100 |
| 7J, G#9, pressed J., gilded, HC | 125 | 150 | 175 |
| 11J, G#8, nickel, OF | 80 | 95 | 125 |
| 11J, G#7, nickel, HC | 125 | 150 | 175 |
| 16J, G#6, nickel, OF | 100 | 125 | 150 |
| 16J, G#5, nickel, HC | 125 | 150 | 175 |
| 16J, G#4, GJS, 2 tone nickel, Adj., D.S. dial, OF | 150 | 175 | 200 |
| 16J, G#3, GJS, 2 tone nickel, Adj., D.S. dial, HC | 175 | 200 | 225 |
| 17J, G#204, GJS, 2 tone nickel, Adj., D.S. dial, OF | 150 | 175 | 200 |
| 17J, G#203, GJS, 2 tone nickel, Adj., D.S. dial, HC | 175 | 200 | 225 |
| 17J, G#2, raised GJS, 2 tone nickel, Adj., D.S. dial, OF | 200 | 250 | 300 |
| 17J, G#1, raised GJS, 2 tone nickel, Adj., D.S. dial, HC | 225 | 275 | 325 |

COLUMBUS WATCH CO., with a "Choo Choo" Railway King double sunk dial.

COLUMBUS WATCH CO., Railway King, 18 size, 17 jewels, 2 tone, serial # 313,005.

## 18 SIZE FULL PLATE, NAMED GRADES

Marked Names, Double Sunk Dials

| Grade or Name — Description | Avg | Ex-Fn | Mint |
|---|---|---|---|
| Am. Watch Club, 15J, 2 tone, Adj., D.S. dial, OF/HC | $250 | $300 | $350 |
| Burlington Route C.B. & QR.R., 15J, nickel, Adj., D.S. dial, OF | 650 | 700 | 800 |
| Champion, 15J, Nickel, Adj., D.S.dial, OF | 125 | 150 | 185 |
| Champion, 15J, Nickel, Adj., D.S.dial, HC | 150 | 175 | 200 |
| Champion, 15J, gilded, Adj., D.S.dial, OF | 100 | 125 | 150 |
| Champion, 15J, gilded, Adj., D.S.dial, HC | 125 | 150 | 175 |
| Champion, 16J, Nickel, Adj., D.S.dial, OF | 150 | 175 | 200 |
| Champion, 16J, Nickel, Adj., D.S.dial, HC | 175 | 200 | 225 |
| * Chicago W. Co. ( see listing under Chicago W. Co. HEADING) | | | |
| Columbus King, 17J, raised GJS, nickel, Adj., D.S. dial, OF | 275 | 300 | 350 |
| Columbus King, 17J, raised GJS, nickel, Adj., D.S. dial, HC | 300 | 350 | 400 |

🕐 Watches listed in this book are priced at the collectable retail level, as **complete** watches having an original 14k gold-filled case & *KEY WIND* with silver case, an original white enamel single sunk dial, and with the entire original movement in good working order with no repairs needed.

| Grade or Name — Description | Avg | Ex-Fn | Mint |
|---|---|---|---|
| Columbus King, 17J, raised GJS, nickel, Adj., choo choo D.S. dial, OF | $425 | $475 | $525 |
| Columbus King, 17J, raised GJS, nickel, Adj., Angled choo choo D.S. dial, OF | 475 | 525 | 600 |
| Columbus King, 21J, raised GJS, nickel, Adj., D.S. dial, OF | 375 | 425 | 475 |
| Columbus King, 21J, raised GJS, nickel, Adj., D.S. dial, HC | 400 | 450 | 500 |
| Columbus King, 23J, raised GJS, nickel, Adj., D.S. dial, OF ...... ★ | 900 | 1,000 | 1,300 |
| Columbus King, 23J, raised GJS, nickel, Adj., D.S. dial, HC ..... ★ | 900 | 1,000 | 1,300 |
| Columbus King, 25J, raised GJS, nickel, Adj., D.S. dial, OF ............ ★★★★ | 3,500 | 4,000 | 4,500 |
| Columbus King, 25J, raised GJS, nickel, Adj., D.S. dial, HC ............ ★★★★ | 3,000 | 3,250 | 3,750 |
| F.C. & P.R.R., 17J, GJS, nickel, Adj., D.S. dial, OF ............ ★ | 500 | 600 | 700 |
| Jackson Park, 15J, 2 tone, Adj., D.S. dial, OF ............ ★ | 325 | 425 | 500 |
| Jay Gould the Railroad King, 15J, nickel,Adj., D.S. dial, OF ..... ★ | 500 | 625 | 750 |
| New York Susquehanna &Western R.R.,16J, GJS, SW/KW, gold flash, D.S. dial, OF ............ ★★ | 900 | 1,000 | 1,200 |
| Non-magnetic, 16J, raised GJS, 2 tone, Adj., OF/HC | 300 | 400 | 500 |
| North Star, 11J, gilded, OF | 100 | 125 | 150 |
| North Star, 11J, gilded, HC | 125 | 150 | 175 |
| North Star, 11J, nickel, OF | 90 | 120 | 150 |
| North Star, 11J, nickel, HC | 125 | 150 | 175 |
| North Star, 15J, nickel, OF | 100 | 125 | 150 |
| North Star, 15J, nickel, HC | 150 | 175 | 200 |
| The President, 17J, GJS, Adj, 2 tone, D.S. dial, OF | 475 | 550 | 575 |
| Railroad Regulator, 15J, GJS, nickel, Adj., D.S. dial, OF ............ ★ | 450 | 550 | 600 |
| Railroad Regulator, 16J, GJS, nickel, Adj., D.S. dial, OF ............ ★ | 450 | 500 | 600 |
| Railway, 17J, GJS, 2 tone, Adj., D.S. dial, OF ............ ★ | 400 | 475 | 525 |

**Columbus King,** 18 size, 25 jewels, open face serial number 503,094. Note two screws between balance cock & barrel bridge.

**Railway King,** 18 size, 23 jewels, adjusted, stem wind, hunting case, serial number 503,315. Note one screw between balance cock & barrel bridge.

🕐 Watches listed in this book are priced at the collectable retail level, as **complete** watches having an original 14k gold-filled case & *KEY WIND* with silver case, an original white enamel single sunk dial, and with the entire original movement in good working order with no repairs needed.

| Grade or Name — Description | Avg | Ex-Fn | Mint |
|---|---|---|---|
| Railway King, 16J, GJS, 2 tone nickel, Adj., D.S. dial, HC ........... | $300 | $325 | $375 |
| Railway King, 16J, GJS, 2 tone nickel, Adj., D.S. dial, OF............ | 275 | 300 | 350 |
| Railway King, 16J, GJS, 2 tone nickel, Adj., (black red blue) choo chooD.S. dial, HC ................................. | 375 | 400 | 450 |
| Railway King, 16J, GJS, 2 tone nickel, Adj., (black red blue) choo chooD.S. dial, OF................................ | 350 | 375 | 400 |
| Railway King, 16J, GJS, 2 tone nickel, Adj., Angled choo choo dial, HC ...................................................... | 475 | 550 | 600 |
| Railway King, 16J, GJS, 2 tone nickel, Adj., Angled choo choo dial, OF...................................................... | 425 | 500 | 575 |
| Railway King, 17J, raised GJS, nickel, Adj., D.S. dial, OF ............ | 300 | 350 | 400 |
| Railway King, 17J, raised GJS, nickel, Adj., D.S. dial, HC............ | 350 | 375 | 450 |
| Railway King, 21J, raised GJS, nickel, Adj., D.S. dial, OF............ | 400 | 450 | 500 |
| Railway King, 21J, raised GJS, nickel, Adj., D.S. dial, HC............ | 450 | 500 | 550 |
| Railway King, 23J, raised GJS, nickel, Adj., Railway King D.S. dial, OF ........................ ★★★ | 1,200 | 1,300 | 1,500 |
| Railway King, 23J, raised GJS, nickel, Adj., Railway King D.S. dial, OF .................................................... ★ | 1,100 | 1,250 | 1,500 |
| Railway King, 25J, raised GJS, nickel, Adj., Railway King D.S. dial, OF ...................................... ★★★★ | 2,500 | 2,800 | 3,250 |
| Railway King, 25J, raised GJS, nickel, Adj., Railway King D.S. dial, HC ...................................... ★★★★ | 3,000 | 3,500 | 4,500 |
| Railway King Special, 17J, GJS, nickel, Adj., D.S. dial, OF.......... | 325 | 375 | 450 |
| Railway Monarch, 17J, GJS, nickel, Adj., D.S. dial, OF .............★ | 300 | 375 | 475 |
| Railway Time Service, 17J, GJS, nickel, Adj., D.S. dial, OF .......★ | 375 | 450 | 500 |
| The Regent, 15J, D.S. dial, OF........................................................... | 225 | 250 | 300 |
| R.W.K. Special, 15J, GJS, Adj., 2 tone, D.S. dial, OF.................... | 250 | 300 | 350 |
| R.W.K. Special, 15J, GJS, Adj., 2 tone, D.S. dial, HC ................., | 275 | 325 | 375 |
| R.W.K. Special, 16J, GJS, Adj., 2 tone, D.S. dial, OF.................... | 250 | 285 | 325 |
| R.W.K. Special, 16J, GJS, Adj., 2 tone, D.S. dial, HC .................. | 275 | 300 | 350 |
| Springfield Mo.W. Club, 16J, GJS, nickel, Adj., D.S. dial, HC ...... | 275 | 350 | 400 |
| Special, 17J, GJS, nickel, D.S. dial, OF............................................. | 200 | 250 | 300 |
| **J.P. Stevens & Co.** ( see listing under J.P. Stevens & Co. **HEADING**) | | | |
| The New Menlo Park, 15J, HC .......................................................... | 100 | 120 | 150 |
| The Star, 11J, nickel, OF/HC ............................................................ | 175 | 200 | 250 |
| Time King, 21J, raised GJS, 2 tone nickel, Adj., D.S. dial, OF...... | 425 | 475 | 550 |
| Time King, 21J, raised GJS, 2 tone nickel, Adj., D.S. dial, HC ...... | 450 | 500 | 600 |
| U.S. Army, 15J, nickel, HC................................................................ | 250 | 285 | 325 |

## 18 Size, 21 Jewels.

# NEW COLUMBUS TIME KING.

Nickel, 21 Genuine Ruby Jewels, set in red, Solid Gold Raised Settings, Escapement Cap Jeweled, Adjusted to temperature, Positions and Isochronism, Breguet Hair Spring, Patent Center Pinion, Patent Regulator, Polished Dust Band and Stem Wind, Beveled Steel Work, Pearled Plates; fine, white, cut and beveled edge, hard enameled, double sunk, Red marginal figured Roman or Arabic Dial; handsomely damaskeened in Gold on Nickel ............................. $25 00

Hunting and Open Face.

1895 AD

## 16 SIZE, 3/4 Plate

Marked "New Columbus Watch Co. Columbus Ohio"

| Grade or Name — Description | Avg | Ex-Fn | Mint |
|---|---|---|---|
| 7J, G#80 / G#20, gilded, OF | $80 | $100 | $120 |
| 7J, G#40 / G#19, gilded, HC | 100 | 125 | 150 |
| 11J, G#81, gilded, OF | 85 | 100 | 125 |
| 11J, G#41, gilded, HC | 100 | 125 | 150 |
| 11J, G#83 / G#18, nickel, OF | 85 | 100 | 125 |
| 11J, G#43 / G#17, nickel, HC | 100 | 125 | 150 |
| 15J, G#84, Adj., gilded, OF | 100 | 125 | 150 |
| 15J, G#44, Adj., gilded, HC | 125 | 150 | 175 |
| 15J, G#86, GJS, Adj., nickel, D.S. dial, OF | 100 | 125 | 150 |
| 15J, G#46, GJS, Adj., nickel, D.S. dial, HC | 125 | 150 | 175 |
| 16J, G#87 / G#316, GJS, Adj., nickel, D.S. dial, OF | 125 | 150 | 175 |
| 16J, G#47 / G#315, GJS, Adj., nickel, D.S. dial, HC | 150 | 175 | 200 |
| 16J, G#14, GJS, Adj., 2 tone nickel, D.S. dial, OF | 175 | 200 | 225 |
| 16J, G#13, GJS, Adj., 2 tone nickel, D.S. dial, HC | 200 | 225 | 275 |
| 16J, G#88, raised GJS, Adj., 2 tone nickel, D.S. dial, OF | 150 | 185 | 225 |
| 16J, G#48, raised GJS, Adj., 2 tone nickel, D.S. dial, HC | 175 | 225 | 275 |
| 17J, G#12, raised GJS, Adj., 2 tone nickel, D.S. dial, OF | 150 | 175 | 225 |
| 17J, G#11, raised GJS, Adj., 2 tone nickel, D.S. dial, HC | 175 | 200 | 250 |
| Ruby, 21J, raised GJS, Adj., 2 tone nickel, D.S. dial, HC ★ | 625 | 675 | 800 |
| Ruby, 21J, raised GJS, Adj., 2 tone nickel, D.S. dial, OF ★★ | 575 | 650 | 750 |

NEW Columbus Watch Co., 16 size, 16 jewels, gold train, 2-tone, serial number 341,339.

Columbus Watch Co., Ruby Model, 16 size, 21 jewels, three quarter plate, gold jewel settings, gold train, Adj.6p.

🕐 Some grades are not included. Their values can be determined by comparing with similar age, size, metal content, style, models and grades listed.

🕐 This book endeavours to be a GUIDE or helpful manual and offers a wealth of material to be used as a tool not as a absolute document. Price Guides are like watches the worst may be better than none at all, but at best cannot be expected to be 100% accurate.

🕐 Characteristics of watches differ for the same age of both case and movement, because these features vary it may not be accurate to date a watch by one single influence. Example: the second hand was not commonly found on watches before 1750, but common about 1800. The first second hand appeared in 1665 and another in 1690. Therefore statements are broad rather than accurate.

### 6 SIZE

| Grade or Name — Description | Avg | Ex-Fn | Mint |
|---|---|---|---|
| 7J, G#102, gilded, OF | $75 | $85 | $100 |
| 7J, G#102, gilded, HC | 85 | 100 | 125 |
| 11J, G#101 / G#51 / G#53, nickel or gilded, HC | 85 | 100 | 125 |
| 13J, G#103, nickel, HC | 100 | 125 | 150 |
| 15J, G#104 / G#55, GJS, nickel, D.S. dial, HC | 100 | 130 | 175 |
| 16J, G#57, raised GJS, nickel, D.S. dial, OF/HC | 125 | 150 | 200 |
| 16J, G#100, raised GJS, 2 tone, D.S. dial, (marked 16J.), OF | 225 | 275 | 325 |
| 16J, G#100, raised GJS, 2 tone, D.S. dial, (marked 16J.), HC | 175 | 200 | 250 |

Columbus Watch Co., 8-10 size, 13 jewels, 3/4 plate, stem wind, serial number 13,372. For price see 2nd page of Columbus W. Co. under Swiss, 3/4 plate (1874-1883).

New Columbus Watch Co. Example of a basic model for 6 size, 3/4 plate, 7-16 jewels, gilded and nickel.

### 4 SIZE

| Grade or Name — Description | Avg | Ex-Fn | Mint |
|---|---|---|---|
| 11J, nickel or gilded, OF/HC ★ | $150 | $200 | $250 |
| 15J, nickel or gilded, OF/HC ★ | 175 | 225 | 300 |

🕐 Watches listed in this book are priced at the collectable retail level, as **complete** watches having an original 14k gold-filled case & *KEY WIND* with silver case, an original white enamel single sunk dial, and with the entire original movement in good working order with no repairs needed.

# CORNELL WATCH CO.

Chicago, Illinois
1870 - 1874
San Francisco, California
1875 - 1876

The Cornell Watch Co. bought the Newark Watch Co. and greatly improved the movements being produced. In the fall of 1874, the company moved to San Francisco, Calif., with about 60 of its employees. The movements made in California were virtually the same as those made in Chicago. The company wanted to employ Chinese who would work cheaper, but the skilled employees refused to go along and went on strike. The company stayed alive until 1875 and was sold to the California Watch Co. in January 1876. But death came a few months later.

**The Chronology of the Development of Cornell Watch Co.**
Newark Watch Co. 1864-1870; S#s 6901-12,000.
Cornell Watch Co., Chicago, Ill. 1870-1874; S#s 12,001 to 25,000.
Cornell Watch Co., San Francisco, Calif. 1874-Jan. 1876; S# s 25,001 to 35,000.
California Watch Co., Jan. 1876-mid 1876.

Cornell Watch Co., J.C. Adams, 18 size, 11 jewels, key wind & set, made in Chicago, Ill, serial number 13,647.

Cornell Watch Co., 18 size, 15 jewels, key wind & set, marked "John Evans," serial number 16,868.

## 18 SIZE

| Grade or Name — Description | | Avg | Ex-Fn | Mint |
|---|---|---|---|---|
| J. C. Adams, 11J, KW | ★ | $400 | $500 | $650 |
| C. T. Bowen, FULL, KW | ★ | 350 | 450 | 600 |
| C. M. Cady, 15J, SW | ★ | 400 | 500 | 650 |
| Cornell, 7J, San Francisco on mvt., KW | ★ | 900 | 1,100 | 1,400 |
| Cornell, 11J, KW | ★ | 300 | 400 | 550 |
| Cornell, 11J, San Francisco on mvt., KW | ★ | 900 | 1,100 | 1,400 |
| Cornell, 15J, KW | ★ | 350 | 450 | 600 |
| Cornell W. Co., 15J, San Francisco on mvt., KW | ★ | 1,100 | 1,300 | 1,600 |

| Grade or Name — Description | | Avg | Ex-Fn | Mint |
|---|---|---|---|---|
| Cornell W. Co., 15J, San Francisco on mvt., SW | ★★ | $1,200 | $1,400 | $1,800 |
| Paul Cornell, 19J, GJS, HCI5P, SW | ★★★ | 1,500 | 1,800 | 2,500 |
| John Evans, 15J, KW | ★ | 350 | 450 | 600 |
| Excelsior, 15J, FULL, KW, KS | ★ | 300 | 400 | 550 |
| H. N. Hibbard, 11J, KW, ADJ | ★ | 400 | 500 | 650 |
| C.L. Kidder, 7J, KWKS, OF | ★ | 300 | 350 | 400 |
| George F. Root, 15J, KW | ★ | 550 | 700 | 900 |
| George Waite, 7J, (Hyde Park), KW | ★★ | 400 | 550 | 650 |
| E. J. Williams, 7J, KW | ★ | 350 | 450 | 600 |
| Ladies Stemwind | ★ | 150 | 200 | 300 |
| Eugene Smith, 17J | ★ | 350 | 450 | 600 |

## JACOB D. CUSTER

### Norristown, Pennsylvania

### 1840 - 1845

At the age of 19, Jacob Custer repaired his father's watch. He was then asked to repair all the watches within his community. Custer was basically self-taught and had very little formal education and little training in clocks and watches. He made all the parts except the hairspring and fusee chains. The watches were about 14 size, and only 12 to 15 watches were made. The 14S fusee watches had lever escapement, 3/4 plate and were sold in his own gold cases. He made a few chronometers, one with a helical spring.

J.D. Custer, 14-16 size, engraved on movement "J.D. Custer, Norristown, Pa. Patented Feb. 4, 1843.

| Description | | Avg | Ex-Fn | Mint |
|---|---|---|---|---|
| 14S, OF, engraved on mvt. *J. D. Custer, Patented Feb. 4, 1843* | | | | |
| very RARE watch | ★★★★ | $8,500 | $12,000 | $18,000 |

# DUDLEY WATCH CO.
## Lancaster, Pennsylvania
## 1920 - 1925

William Wallace Dudley became interested in watches and horology at the age of 13 and became an apprentice making ship chronometers in Canada. When he moved to America, he worked for the South Bend and Illinois Watch companies and the Trenton Watch Co. before going to Hamilton Watch Co. in Lancaster. He left Hamilton at age 69 to start his own watch company. In 1922 his first watches were produced; they were 14S, 19J, and used many Waltham Model 1894 – 1897, 14 size parts, including the train and escapement. The plates and winding mechanism were made at the Dudley plant. Dials and hands were made to Dudley's specifications in Switzerland. At first jewels were obtained from a manufacturer in Lancaster, but by 1925 they were Swiss supplied. The cases came from Wadsworth Keystone and the Star Watch Case Co. Dudley also made a 12S, 19J watch. By 1924, the company was heavily in debt, and on February 20, 1925, a petition for bankruptcy was filed. The Masonic Watch was his most unusual watch.

| DUDLEY WATCHES | | | | TOTAL PRODUCTION |
|---|---|---|---|---|
| Dudley Watch Co. | 1920-1925 | Model No. 1 | = S# | 500—1,900 = 1,400 |
| P. W. Baker Co. | 1925-1935 | Model No. 2 | = S# | 2,001—4,800 = 1,800 |
| XL Watch Co., N.Y. | 1935-1976 | Model No. 3 | = S# | 4,801—6,500 = 1,500 |
| | | | **Total** | **4,800** |

Model No. 1, 14S, 19J, OF, can be distinguished by the "Holy Bible" engraved on the winding arbor plate, and a gilded pallet bridge matching the plates.

Model No. 2, 12S, 19J, used the 910 and 912 Hamilton wheels and escapement, has a flat silver-colored Bible.

Model No. 3, 12S, can be distinguished by the silver Bible which was riveted in place and was more three-dimensional. The 3rd wheel bridge was rounded off at one end.

**Dudley Watch Co.**, Model 1, 14 size, 19J., open face, Masonic form plates, flip back, serial # 1232, Ca. 1924.

**Dudley Watch Co.**, Model 2, 14 size, 19J., open face, with original paper. The watch also came with a keystone shaped box, Ca 1927.

## 12 SIZE - 14 SIZE
## "MASONS" MODEL

| Grade or Name — Description | Avg | Ex-Fn | Mint |
|---|---|---|---|
| 14S, Dudley, 19J, 14K, flip open back, Serial #1 (made 5 experimental models with Serial #1) ......................★ | $5,000 | $7,000 | $10,000 |
| 14S, M#1, 19J, OF, 14K, flip open back .......................★ | 3,000 | 3,400 | 3,800 |
| 14S, M#1, 19J, OF, 14K, flip open back, w/box & papers .........★ | 3,500 | 4,000 | 4,500 |
| 12S, M#2, 19J, OF, flip open back, GF ........................★ | 2,000 | 2,200 | 2,400 |
| 12S, M#2, 19J, OF, 14K, flip open back case ...........................★ | 2,200 | 2,400 | 2,600 |
| 12S, M#2, 19J, OF, 14K display case ...........................★ | 2,000 | 2,200 | 2,400 |
| 12S, M#3, 19J, OF, display case, GF ...........................★ | 2,000 | 2,200 | 2,400 |
| 12S, M#3, 19J, OF, 14K flip open case .......................★ | 2,200 | 2,400 | 2,600 |

Dudley Watch Co., Model 2, 12 size, 19 jewels, open face, serial number 2,420.

Dudley Watch Co., Model 3, 12 size, 19 jewels, open face. NOTE: 3rd wheel bridge is rounded off at one end.

# ELGIN WATCH CO.
## (NATIONAL WATCH CO.)
### Elgin, Illinois
### 1864 - 1964

This was the largest watch company in terms of production; in fact, Elgin produced half of the total number of pocket watches (dollar-type not included). Some of the organizers came from Waltham Watch Co., including P. S. Bartlett, D. G. Currier, Otis Hoyt, Charles H. Mason and others. The idea of beginning a large watch company for the mid-West was discussed by J. C. Adams, Bartlett and Blake. After a trip to Waltham, Adams went back to Chicago and approached Benjamin W. Raymond, a former mayor of Chicago, to put up the necessary capital to get the company started. Adams and Raymond succeeded in getting others to pledge their financial support also. The National Watch Co. (Elgin) was formed in August 1864. The factory site was in Elgin, Illinois, where the city had donated 35 acres of land. The factory was completed in 1866, & the 1st. movement was a B. W. Raymond, 18 size, full plate design.

### Elgin Movements

| | 1st App. | 1st S# | | 1st. App. | 1st. S# |
|---|---|---|---|---|---|
| 18S B. W. Raymond | April 1867 | 101 | 10S Lady Elgin | Jan. 1869 | 40,001 |
| 18S H. Z. Culver | July 1867 | 1,001 | 10S Frances Rubie | Aug. 1870 | 50,001 |
| 18S J. T. Ryerson | Oct. 1867 | 5,001 | 10S Gail Borden | Sept. 1871 | 185,001 |
| 18S H. H. Taylor | Nov. 1867 | 25,001 | 10S Dexter Street | Dec. 1871 | 201,001 |
| 18S G. M. Wheeler | Nov. 1867 | 6,001 | First Stem Wind | June 1873 | |
| 18S Matt Laflin | Jan. 1868 | 9,001 | 1st Nickel Movement | Aug.15, 1879 | |
| 18S Father Time | No date | 2,300,001 | Convertible | Fall 1878 | |
| 18S Veritas | No date | 8,400,001 | | | |

The first watch a **B.W. Raymond** was sold April 1, 1867, selling for about $115.00, and was a 18 size, KW and quick train serial # 101. This **First** Pocket Watch, Serial No. 101, **was once again sold for $12,000.00** in 1988 at a SELL in NEW YORK. The first stem wind model was an H. Z. Culver with serial No. 155,001, lever set and quick train. In 1874, the name was changed to the Elgin National Watch Co., and they produced watches into the 1950s. The first **WRIST WATCH** made by Elgin was sold in 1910.

Some Serial Nos. have the first two numbers replace by a letter; i.e., 49,582,000 would be F 482,000.

| | |
|---|---|
| X= 38 & 39 | F= 49 |
| C,E,T & Y= 42 | S= 50 |
| L= 43 | R= 51 |
| U= 44 | P= 52 |
| J= 45 | K= 53 |
| V= 46 | |
| H= 47 | |
| N= 48 | |

🕐 If the letters do not match the list above; the movement was produced after 1954.

## ELGIN ESTIMATED SERIAL NUMBERS
## AND PRODUCTION DATES

| DATE – SERIAL # | DATE–SERIAL # | DATE–SERIAL # |
|---|---|---|
| 1867 ⎯ 10,000 | 1897 – 7,000,000 Oct.28th | 1927 – 30,050,000 |
| 1868 ⎯ 25,001-Nov.20th | 1898 – 7,494,001 May 14th | 1928 – 31,599,001-Jan.11 |
| 1869 ⎯ 40,001-May 20th | 1899 – 8,000,000 Jan.18th | 1929 – 32,000,000 |
| 1870 ⎯ 50,001-Aug.24th | 1900 – 9,000,000 Nov.14th | 1930 – 32,599,001-July |
| 1871 – 185,001-Sep. 8th | 1901 – 9,300,000 | 1931 – 33,000,000 |
| 1871 – 201,001-Dec.20th | 1902 – 9,600,000 | 1932 – 33,700,000 |
| 1873 – 300,000 | 1903 – 10,000,000 May 15th | 1933 – 34,558,001-July 24th |
| 1874 – 400,001-Aug.28th | 1904 – 11,000,000 April 4th | 1934 – 35,000,000 |
| 1875 – 400,000 | 1905 – 12,000,000 Oct.6th | 1935 – 35,650,000 |
| 1876 – 450,000 | 1906 – 12,500,000 | 1936 – 36,200,000 |
| 1877 – 500,000 | 1907 – 13,000,000 April 4th | 1937 – 36,978,001-July 24th |
| 1878 – 550,000 | 1908 – 13,500,000 | 1938 – 37,900,000 |
| 1879 – 625,001-Feb.8th | 1909 – 14,000,000 Feb.9th | 1939 – 38,200,000 |
| 1880 – 750,000 | 1910 – 15,000,000 April 2nd | 1940 – 39,100,000 |
| 1881 – 900,000 | 1911 – 16,000,000 July 11th | 1941 – 40,200,000 |
| 1882 – 1,000,000- March,9th | 1912 – 17,000,000 Nov.6th | 1942 – 41,100,000 |
| 1883 – 1,250,000 | 1913 – 17,339,001- Apr.14th | 1943 – 42,200,000 |
| 1884 – 1,500,000 | 1914 – 18,000,000 | 1944 – 42,600,000 |
| 1885 – 1,855,001-May 28th | 1915 – 18,587,001-Feb.11th | 1945 – 43,200,000 |
| 1886 – 2,000,000- Aug. 4th | 1916 – 19,000,000 | 1946 – 44,000,000 |
| 1887 – 2,500,000 | 1917 – 20,031,001-June 27th | 1947 – 45,000,000 |
| 1888 – 3,000,000 June 20th | 1918 – 21,000,000 | 1948 – 46,000,000 |
| 1889 – 3,500,000 | 1919 – 22,000,000 | 1949 – 47,000,000 |
| 1890 – 4,000,000 Aug.16th | 1920 – 23,000,000 | 1950 – 48,000,000 |
| 1891 – 4,449,001-Mar.26th | 1921 – 24,321,001-July 6th | 1951 – 49,500,000 |
| 1892 – 4,600,000 | 1922 – 25,100,000 | 1952 – 52,000,000 |
| 1893 – 5,000,000 July 1st | 1923 – 26,050,000 | 1953 – 53,500,000 |
| 1894 – 5,500,000 | 1924 – 27,000,000 | 1954 -- 54,000,000 |
| 1895 – 6,000,000 Nov.26th | 1925 – 28,421,001-July 14th | 1955 -- 54,500,000 |
| 1896 – 6,500,000 | 1926 – 29,100,000 | 1956 – 55,000,000 |

🕐 The above list is provided for determining the **APPROXIMATE** age of your watch. Match serial number with date. Watches were not necessarily *SOLD* and *DELIVERED* in the exact order of manufactured or production dates.

*It required several months for raw material to emerge as a finished movement. All the while the factory is producing all sizes, models and grades. The numbering system was basically "consecutive", due to demand a batch of movements could be side tracked, thus allowing a different size and model to move ahead to meet this demand. Therefore, the dates some movements were sold and delivered to the trade, may not be "consecutive".*

🕐 Generic, nameless or unmarked grades for watch movements are listed under the Company name or initials of the Company, etc. by size, jewel count and description.

Some collectors seek out low serial numbers and will usually pay a premium for them. The lower the number, the more desirable the watch. The table shown below lists the first serial number of each size watch made by Elgin.

| Size | 1st Serial Nos. | Size | 1st Serial Nos. |
|------|-----------------|------|-----------------|
| 18 | 101 | 10 | 40,001 |
| 17 | 356,001 | 6 | 570,001 |
| 16 | 600,001 | 0 | 2,889,001 |
| 14 | 351,001 | | |

B.W. Raymond, 18 size, 15 jewels, model # 1, key wind & set, 1st. run in April of 1867, **serial number 105.**

Father Time, 18 size, 21 jewels, model #8 with wind indicator, free sprung model, serial number 22,888,020

## 18 SIZE

| Grade or Name — Description | Avg | Ex-Fn | Mint |
|----------------------------|-----|-------|------|
| Advance, 11J, gilded, KW, HC, FULL | $75 | $95 | $125 |
| Atlas Watch Co., 7J, HC, LS, FULL | 75 | 95 | 125 |
| California Watch, 15J, gilded, HC, KW, KS, FULL | 145 | 200 | 250 |
| Chief, 7J, gilded, KW, FULL, HC | 75 | 95 | 125 |
| Convertible, 7J, G#98 | 125 | 175 | 225 |
| H. Z. Culver, 15J, gilded, KW, KS, FULL, HC, ADJ, low S# | 200 | 250 | 325 |
| H. Z. Culver, 15J, gilded, KW, KS, FULL, HC, ADJ | 125 | 145 | 200 |
| H. Z. Culver, 15J, KW, KS, 14K, HC | 700 | 785 | 900 |
| H. Z. Culver, 15J, gilded, KW, KS, FULL, HC | 125 | 150 | 200 |
| H. Z. Culver, 15J, gilded, SW, FULL, HC | 75 | 95 | 125 |
| H. Z. Culver, 15J, gilded, KW, FULL, LS, HC | 95 | 120 | 150 |

⊕ Generic, nameless or unmarked grades for watch movements are listed under the Company name or initials of the Company, etc. by size, jewel count and description.

| Grade or Name — Description | Avg | Ex-Fn | Mint |
|----------------------------|-----|-------|------|
| Elgin W. Co., 7J, OF, SW | $65 | $75 | $100 |
| Elgin W. Co., 7J, KW, gilded, HC | 75 | 95 | 125 |
| Elgin W. Co., 11J, KW, LS | 55 | 75 | 100 |
| Elgin W. Co., 11J, LS, SW, HC, 9K-10K | 325 | 375 | 475 |
| Elgin W. Co., 11J, LS, SW, HC, Silveroid | 50 | 60 | 75 |
| Elgin W. Co., 11J, LS, , SW, OF | 55 | 70 | 100 |
| Elgin W. Co., 13J, SW, PS/LS, Silveroid | 50 | 60 | 75 |
| Elgin W. Co., 13J, SW, PS/LS | 60 | 75 | 100 |

⊕ Watches listed in this book are priced at the collectable retail level, as **complete** watches having an original 14k gold-filled case and *Key Wind* with silver, an original white enamel single sunk dial, and with the entire original movement in good working order with no repairs needed.

Elgin W. Co., engraved on movement California Watch, 18 size, 15 jewels, gilded, key wind & set, serial # 200,700.

Convertible, 18 size, 21 jewels, converts to either hunting or open face.

| Grade or Name — Description | Avg | Ex-Fn | Mint |
|---|---|---|---|
| Elgin W. Co., 15J, KW, LS, HC | $100 | $135 | $175 |
| Elgin W. Co., 15J, SW, LS, OF | 65 | 75 | 100 |
| Elgin W. Co., 15-17J, SW, LS, **box–hinge YGF, HC** | 250 | 275 | 350 |
| Elgin W. Co., 15-17J, SW, LS, **box–hinge 14K, HC** | 1,000 | 1,200 | 1,600 |
| Elgin W. Co., 15-17, SW, LS, **Multi-color box YGF, HC** | 400 | 500 | 600 |
| Elgin W. Co., 15-17J, SW, **14K case, OF** | 400 | 500 | 600 |
| Elgin W. Co., 15-17J, SW, **14K case, HC** | 550 | 700 | 900 |
| Elgin W. Co., 15-17J, SW, **18K case, HC** | 650 | 750 | 1,000 |
| Elgin W. Co., 15-17J, SW, **Multi-color, 14K, HC** | 1,800 | 2,000 | 2,500 |
| Elgin W. Co., 15-17J, SW, LS, **COIN** Silver 6 oz, OF | 175 | 200 | 250 |
| Elgin W. Co., 15-17J, SW, LS, **COIN Silver"** , OF | 75 | 100 | 135 |
| Elgin W. Co., 15J, SW, LS, HC | 95 | 125 | 165 |
| Elgin W. Co., 15J, KW, **hidden key, COIN silver case** | 145 | 175 | 200 |
| Elgin W. Co., 17J, SW, LS, **Silveroid** | 60 | 75 | 95 |
| Elgin W. Co., 17J, SW, LS or PS, OF | 75 | 100 | 135 |
| Elgin W. Co., 21J, SW, LS or PS, OF | 200 | 225 | 250 |
| Elgin W. Co., 21J, SW, LS, box case, GF,OF | 300 | 350 | 400 |
| Elgin W. Co., 21J, LS; HC, 14K | 700 | 800 | 900 |
| Elgin W. Co., 21J, SW, LS, Silveroid | 200 | 225 | 250 |
| Elgin W. Co., 21J, SW, LS, HC | 300 | 325 | 375 |
| Elgin W. Co., 23J, SW, LS, OF | 325 | 375 | 425 |

Example of the *nameless* or unmarked *grades* for watch movements which are listed under the Company **name or initials** of the Company, (Elgin W. Co.) etc. by size, jewel count & description.

🕐 Generic, nameless or unmarked grades for watch movements are listed under the Company name or initials of the Company, etc. by size, jewel count and description.

**Pennsylvania Railroad Co. on dial. B.W. Raymond** on movement. One of the first railroad watches commissioned by Penn. RR Co., 18 size, 15 jewels, key wind and set, serial number 123,245, CA. 1874.

| Grade or Name — Description | Avg | Ex-Fn | Mint |
|---|---|---|---|
| Elgin W. Co., 21J, **Wind Indicator**.................................... | $800 | $1,000 | $1,200 |
| Elgin W. Co., 21J, **Wind Indicator, free sprung** ........................... | 1,000 | 1,200 | 1,400 |
| Charles Fargo, 7J, gilded, KW, HC............................................ | 150 | 170 | 200 |
| J. V. Farwell, 11J, gilded, KW, HC ........................................★ | 250 | 300 | 375 |
| Father Time, 17J, NI, KW, FULL, HC .........................................★ | 250 | 350 | 450 |
| Father Time, 17J, NI, FULL, OF ............................................ | 100 | 125 | 175 |
| Father Time, 17J, SW, OF, Silveroid........................................ | 75 | 100 | 150 |
| Father Time, 17J, SW, HC .................................................. | 125 | 150 | 200 |
| Father Time, **20J,** NI, SW, FULL, HC ........................................★ | 300 | 375 | 450 |
| Father Time, 21J, NI, SW, FULL, GJS, OF .................................... | 225 | 250 | 285 |
| Father Time, 21J, NI, SW, 3/4, GJS, DMK, HC .............................. | 300 | 350 | 400 |
| Father Time, 21J, NI, SW, 3/4, GJS, OF .................................... | 225 | 250 | 275 |
| Father Time, 21J, GJT, HCI5P, Diamond end stone, OF................ | 225 | 275 | 310 |
| Father Time, 21J, NI, SW, 3/4, OF, GJS, **wind indicator** ............. | 1,000 | 1,200 | 1,500 |
| Father Time, 21J, SW, 3/4, GJS, **wind indicator, HC** ................... | 1,400 | 1,600 | 1,850 |
| Father Time, G#367, 21J, NI, SW, 3/4, OF, GJS, military style, **wind indicator**, free sprung, **602 sterling case** ...................... | 1,200 | 1,400 | 1,700 |
| Father Time, G#367, 21J, NI, SW, 3/4, OF, GJS, military style, **wind indicator**, free sprung, **35 size with gimbals & Box** ... | 1,000 | 1,200 | 1,400 |
| **85 size,** Model# 600, 14J, **free sprung,** helical hair spring, dent escapement , **wind indicator**, Gimbals & Box............................ | 1,100 | 1,250 | 1,500 |
| W. H. Ferry, 15J, gilded, KW, HC........................................... | 125 | 145 | 175 |
| W. H. Ferry, 11J, gilded, KW, HC........................................... | 125 | 145 | 175 |
| Mat Laflin, 7J, gilded, KW, HC............................................. | 125 | 145 | 175 |
| National W. Co., 7J, KW, KS................................................ | 75 | 95 | 125 |
| National W. Co., 11J, KW, KS .............................................. | 75 | 95 | 125 |
| National W. Co., 15J, KW, KS .............................................. | 85 | 100 | 135 |
| M. D. Ogden, 15J, KW, HC.................................................. | 125 | 145 | 175 |
| M. D. Ogden, 11J, gilded, KW, HC.......................................... | 125 | 145 | 175 |
| Overland, 17J, NI, KW, HC ................................................ | 150 | 170 | 200 |
| Overland, 17J, NI, SW, HC................................................. | 100 | 125 | 175 |
| Pennsylvania Railroad Co. on dial, B. W. Raymond on mvt., 15J, KW, KS (1st RR watches) ....................................★★★ | 900 | 1,200 | 1,500 |
| Railway Timer, 15J, FULL, HC...............................................★ | 300 | 375 | 500 |

🕐 Generic, nameless or unmarked grades for watch movements are listed under the Company name or initials of the Company, etc. by size, jewel count and description.

🕐 Watches listed in this book are priced at the collectable retail level, as **complete** watches having an original 14k gold-filled case and *Key Wind* with silver, an original white enamel single sunk dial, and with the entire original movement in good working order with no repairs needed.

**B.W. Raymond**, 18 size, 23 jewels, wind indicator. Note small winding indicator gear next to crown wheel.

**H.H. Taylor**, 18 size, 15 jewels, key wind & set, serial number 288,797.

| Grade or Name — Description | Avg | Ex-Fn | Mint |
|---|---|---|---|
| B. W. Raymond, 15-17J, KW, low S# under 200 | $600 | $750 | $1,000 |
| B. W. Raymond, 15-17J, KW, low S# under 1000 | 300 | 400 | 550 |
| B. W. Raymond, 15J, gilded, KW, FULL, HC | 125 | 145 | 175 |
| B. W. Raymond, 17J, gilded, KW, FULL, HC | 125 | 145 | 175 |
| B. W. Raymond, 15J, SW, HC | 75 | 95 | 125 |
| B. W. Raymond, 17J, all G#s, NI, FULL, OF | 55 | 75 | 100 |
| B. W. Raymond, 17J, Silveroid | 40 | 60 | 85 |
| B. W. Raymond, 17J, NI, FULL, HC | 100 | 125 | 175 |
| B. W. Raymond, 15J, box case, 14K | 900 | 1,200 | 1,400 |
| B. W. Raymond, 17J, gilded, NI, SW, FULL, ADJ | 75 | 95 | 125 |
| B. W. Raymond, 19J, NI, 3/4, SW, OF, GJS, G#240, GT | 175 | 200 | 225 |
| B. W. Raymond, 19J, 3/4, SW, GJS, **Wind Indicator**, DMK | 700 | 800 | 950 |
| B. W. Raymond, 19J, 3/4, GJS, GT, Diamond end stone | 125 | 150 | 200 |
| B. W. Raymond, 21J, 3/4, GJS, GT, Diamond end stone, OF | 225 | 250 | 300 |
| B. W. Raymond, 21J, SW, Silveroid | 175 | 200 | 230 |
| B. W. Raymond, 21J, SW, GJS, GT, Diamond end stone, HC | 300 | 350 | 400 |
| B. W. Raymond, 21J, NI, 3/4, SW, GJS, G#389 & 390, GT, OF | 200 | 250 | 310 |
| B. W. Raymond, 21J, NI, 3/4, SW, GJS, **Wind Indicator**, DMK | 950 | 1,100 | 1,250 |
| J. T. Ryerson, 7J, gilded, FULL, KW, HC | 100 | 120 | 150 |
| Solar W. Co., 15J, Multi-color dial | 125 | 145 | 175 |
| Standard, 17J, OF, LS | 100 | 120 | 150 |
| Sundial, 7J, SW, PS | 55 | 60 | 75 |
| H. H. Taylor, 15J, gilded, FULL, KW, HC | 100 | 125 | 175 |
| H. H. Taylor, 15J, NI, FULL, KW, HC, DMK | 100 | 125 | 175 |
| H. H. Taylor, 15J, NI, FULL, SW, HC, DMK, quick train | 100 | 125 | 175 |
| H. H. Taylor, 15J, SW, Silveroid | 75 | 95 | 125 |
| H. H. Taylor, 15J, SW, slow train | 75 | 95 | 125 |

🕐 Some watch manufacturers personalize watches for jobbers or jewelry firms, with exclusive private signed or marked movements. The valuable collectable watches are listed under the signed or marked movement. Other exclusive private signed or marked movements will have equivalent value are only slightly higher value and should be compared to Generic or Nameless movements. Railroad signed or marked (dials & movements) are usually more collectable & higher in value.

🕐: Generic, nameless or unmarked grades for watch movements are listed under the Company name or initials of the Company, etc. by size, jewel count and description.

🕐 Some grades are not included. Their values can be determined by comparing with **similar** age, size, metal content, style, models and grades listed.

**Veritas,** 18 size, 23 jewels, solid gold train, gold jewel settings, diamond end stone, serial number 9,542,678.

**G.M. Wheeler,** Grade 369, 18 size, 17 jewels, open face, gold jewel settings, serial number 14,788,315.

| Grade or Name — Description | Avg | Ex-Fn | Mint |
|---|---|---|---|
| Veritas, 21J, 3/4, NI, GJS, DMK, GT, OF | $225 | $250 | $300 |
| Veritas, 21J, 3/4, GJS, GT, Diamond end stones | 250 | 275 | 325 |
| Veritas, 21J, SW, PS, GJS, GT, HC | 300 | 350 | 400 |
| Veritas, 21J, SW, LS, GJS, GT, HC | 300 | 350 | 400 |
| Veritas, 21J, 3/4, GJS, GT, Diamond end stones, HC | 300 | 350 | 425 |
| Veritas, 21J, 3/4, NI, GJS, **Wind Indicator,** DMK,OF | 1,300 | 1,400 | 1,500 |
| Veritas, 21J, 3/4, NI, GJS, **Wind Indicator,** DMK ,HC ★ | 1,500 | 1,750 | 2,000 |
| Veritas, 23J, 3/4, NI, GJS, OF, DMK, GT | 350 | 400 | 450 |
| Veritas, 23J, 3/4, NI, GJS, OF, DMK, GT, Diamond end stone | 350 | 400 | 475 |
| Veritas, 23J, 3/4, **Wind Indicator,** GJS, DMK, GT, **OF, 14K** | 1,700 | 1,900 | 2,400 |
| Veritas, 23J, G#214, 3/4, NI, GJS, **Wind Indicator,** DMK, OF | 1,300 | 1,400 | 1,500 |
| Veritas, 23J, **G#214,** SW, OF | 300 | 350 | 425 |
| Veritas, 23J, 3/4, SW, NI, GJS, GT, LS, HC ★★ | 450 | 500 | 650 |
| Veritas, 23J, SW, **OF, 14K** | 700 | 750 | 850 |
| G. M. Wheeler, 11J, gilded, KW, HC | 75 | 100 | 150 |
| G. M. Wheeler, 13-15J, gilded, FULL, KW | 75 | 100 | 150 |
| G. M. Wheeler, 15J, NI, FULL, KW, DMK, HC | 100 | 125 | 175 |
| G. M. Wheeler, 15J, SW, NI, FULL, DMK, OF | 55 | 75 | 100 |
| G. M. Wheeler, 17J, KW, NI, FULL, DMK, OF | 100 | 125 | 175 |
| G. M. Wheeler, 17J, SW, NI, FULL, DMK, OF | 55 | 75 | 125 |

## MOVEMENTS WITH NO NAME

| Grade or Name — Description | Avg | Ex-Fn | Mint |
|---|---|---|---|
| No. 5 & No. 17, 7J, gilded, FULL, HC | $60 | $75 | $95 |
| No. 23 & No. 18, 11J, gilded, FULL, HC | 65 | 85 | 110 |
| No. 69, 15J, M#1, KW, quick train, HC | 70 | 95 | 125 |
| No. 150, 21J, full plate, GJS, LS | 175 | 200 | 260 |
| No. 274, 21J., marked **274,** GT, Adj.5p, diamond end stone | 200 | 250 | 325 |
| No. 316, 15J, NI, FULL, HC, DMK | 75 | 100 | 150 |
| No. 317, 15J, NI, FULL, ADJ, OF, DMK | 75 | 100 | 150 |

⊕: Generic, nameless or unmarked grades for watch movements are listed under the Company name or initials of the Company, etc. by size, jewel count and description.

⊕ Watches listed in this book are priced at the collectable retail level, as **complete** watches having an original 14k gold-filled case and *Key Wind* with silver, an original white enamel single sunk dial, and with the entire original movement in good working order with no repairs needed.

🕐 Generic, nameless or unmarked grades for watch movements are listed under the Company name or initials of the Company, etc. by size, jewel count and description.

| Grade or Name — Description | Avg | Ex-Fn | Mint |
|---|---|---|---|
| No. 316 & No. 317, 15J, Silveroid | $50 | $60 | $75 |
| No. 326, 15J, OF | 60 | 70 | 85 |
| No. 327, 15J, HC | 75 | 95 | 150 |
| No. 335, 17J, HC | 75 | 95 | 150 |
| No. 336, 17J, NI, FULL, OF, DMK | 55 | 75 | 150 |
| No. 345, 19J, GJS, 2-Tone, HC ★ | 600 | 700 | 900 |
| No. 348, 21J, NI, FULL, GJS, DMK, HC | 200 | 225 | 250 |
| No. 349, 21J, , LS, OF | 175 | 195 | 225 |
| No. 378, 19J, NI, FULL, HC, DMK | 100 | 125 | 175 |
| No. 379, 19J, OF | 100 | 125 | 175 |

Elgin Watch Co., **Leader**, 17 size, 11 jewels, key wind & set, made for English market, serial number 418,220.

Elgin Watch Co., 17 size, 7 jewels, key wind & set, serial number 199,076. Made for Kennedy & Co.

### 17 SIZE

| Grade or Name — Description | Avg | Ex-Fn | Mint |
|---|---|---|---|
| Avery, 7J, gilded, KW, FULL, HC | $75 | $100 | $150 |
| Inter-Ocean, 7J, KWKS, HC | 85 | 110 | 160 |
| Leader, 7J, gilded, KW, FULL, HC | 75 | 100 | 150 |
| Leader, 11J, gilded, KW, FULL, HC, | 75 | 100 | 150 |
| Sunshine, 15J, KW, KS from back | 100 | 125 | 175 |
| The Age, 7J, gilded, KW, FULL, HC | 125 | 175 | 225 |
| M#11, 14, 15, 51, 59, 7J, gilded, KW, FULL, HC | 100 | 125 | 175 |
| 17 Size, KW, Silveroid | 75 | 95 | 125 |

### 16 SIZE

| Grade or Name — Description | Avg | Ex-Fn | Mint |
|---|---|---|---|
| Blind Man's Watch, 9-17J, HC | $100 | $125 | $175 |
| Convertible Model, 11J, BRG, OF | 75 | 95 | 125 |
| Convertible Model, 13J, BRG, OF | 75 | 95 | 125 |
| Convertible Model, 15J, BRG, ADJ, 14K, HC | 600 | 650 | 700 |
| Convertible Model, 15J, ADJ, DMK, GJS, 3F BRG, HC | 150 | 175 | 225 |
| Convertible Model, 15J, 3/4, ADJ, DMK, GJS | 100 | 125 | 175 |

🕐 Some watch manufacturers personalize watches for jobbers or jewelry firms, with exclusive private signed or marked movements. The valuable collectable watches are listed under the signed or marked movement. Other exclusive private signed or marked movements will have equivalent value are only slightly higher value and should be compared to Generic or Nameless movements. Railroad signed or marked (dials & movements) are usually more collectable & higher in value.

Elgin Watch Co., 16 size, 21 jewels, converts to open face or hunting case, serial number 607,061.

Elgin W. Co., 16 size, 21 jewels, three-fingered bridge model, adjusted, gold jewel settings, gold train, serial number 6,469,814.

| Grade or Name — Description | Avg | Ex-Fn | Mint |
|---|---|---|---|
| Convertible Model, 15J, Silveroid | $75 | $100 | $125 |
| Convertible Model, 15J, 3F BRG, OF | 100 | 125 | 150 |
| Convertible Model, 21J, 3F BRG | 900 | 1,100 | 1,450 |
| Convertible Model, 21J, G#72, 3/4, ADJ, GJS, **14K** ★★ | 1,200 | 1,450 | 1,800 |
| Convertible Model, 21J, G#91, 3F BRG, **14K** ★★ | 1,500 | 1,900 | 2,400 |
| Doctors Watch, 15J, 4th Model, NI, GT, sweep second hand, **GF case** | 250 | 300 | 350 |
| Doctors Watch, 15J, 4th Model, gilded, sweep second hand, **coin silver case** | 300 | 350 | 400 |
| Doctors Watch, 15J, 4th Model, sweep second hand, **14K, OF** | 600 | 725 | 900 |

Elgin Watch Co., 16 size, Multi- Color Gold hunting case, the locomotive has a diamond in the lantern, the case has white, yellow, rose flowers & green leaf designs, Ca.1880.

Doctors Watch, 16 size, 15 jewels, fourth model, gold jewel settings, gold train, sweep second hand, serial number 926,458.

⊕ Generic, nameless or unmarked grades for watch movements are listed under the Company name or initials of the Company, etc. by size, jewel count and description.

| Grade or Name — Description | Avg | Ex-Fn | Mint |
|---|---|---|---|
| Elgin W. Co., 7-9J, OF | $50 | $75 | $125 |
| Elgin W. Co., 7-9J, HC | 75 | 100 | 150 |
| Elgin W. Co., 11J, OF | 50 | 75 | 125 |
| Elgin W. Co., 11J, HC | 75 | 100 | 150 |
| Elgin W. Co., 13J, OF | 50 | 75 | 125 |
| Elgin W. Co., 13J, OF, Silveroid | 40 | 50 | 70 |
| Elgin W. Co., 13J, HC | 75 | 100 | 150 |
| Elgin W. Co., 15J, HC | 75 | 100 | 150 |
| Elgin W. Co., 15-16J, OF | 50 | 75 | 125 |
| Elgin W. Co., 15J, OF **14K case** | 285 | 325 | 400 |
| Elgin W. Co., 15J, HC, **14K** | 450 | 550 | 600 |
| Elgin W. Co., 15J, **multi-color gold +diamond**, HC, 14K | 2,500 | 3,000 | 3,500 |
| Elgin W. Co., 17J, OF | 50 | 75 | 125 |
| Elgin W. Co., 17J, **14K, HC** | 450 | 550 | 600 |
| Elgin W. Co., 17J, G#280, 9th model, ADJ5P | 100 | 125 | 175 |
| Elgin W. Co., 17J, HC | 100 | 125 | 175 |
| Elgin W. Co., 19J, OF, LS | 100 | 125 | 175 |
| Elgin W. Co., 21J, HC | 275 | 350 | 375 |
| Elgin W. Co., 21J, OF, **Silveroid** | 175 | 195 | 225 |
| Elgin W. Co., 21J, OF | 200 | 225 | 260 |
| Elgin W. Co., 23J, OF | 300 | 350 | 425 |
| Elgin W. Co., 17J, LS, **multi-color HC, GF** | 250 | 300 | 400 |
| Elgin W. Co., 17J, **multi-color HC, 14K** | 1,000 | 1,200 | 1,600 |
| 3F Bridge Model, 15J, NI, DMK | 50 | 75 | 125 |
| 3F Bridge Model, 17J, Adj.3P, NI, DMK, GJS | 50 | 75 | 125 |
| 3F Bridge Model, 17J, Adj.5P, NI, DMK, GJS, GT | 75 | 100 | 150 |
| 3F Bridge Model, 21J, Adj.5P, NI, DMK, GJS, GT | 275 | 325 | 375 |
| Father Time, 17J, 3/4, NI, OF, GJS, DR, DMK | 100 | 125 | 175 |
| Father Time, 21J, 3/4, NI, HC, GJS, DR, DMK | 200 | 225 | 300 |
| Father Time, 21J, 3/4, NI, OF, GJS, DR, **Wind Indicator** | 650 | 750 | 850 |
| Father Time, 21J, **Silveroid** | 185 | 200 | 250 |
| Father Time, 21J, NI, GJS, DR, OF | 200 | 235 | 275 |

ELGIN W. Co., CHRONOGRAPH, 16 size, 16 jewels, model # 4, lever set.

Father Time, 16 size, 21 jewels, gold train; Note model 19 up and down wind indicator movement does show the differential wheel as does the 18 size, S# 18,106,465.

Lord Elgin, 16 size, 21 jewels, gold train, raised gold jewel settings, 3 finger bridge, serial number 10,249,819.

B.W. Raymond, 16 size, 19 jewels, gold jewel settings, Grade 350, serial number 17,822,991.

| Grade or Name — Description | Avg | Ex-Fn | Mint |
|---|---|---|---|
| Lord Elgin, 21J, GJS, DR, Adj.5P, 3F BRG, **14K, OF** ............ ★ ★ | $1,200 | $1,500 | $2,000 |
| Lord Elgin, 23J, GJS, DR, Adj.5P, 3/4, **14K, OF** ..................... ★ ★ | 1,300 | 1,500 | 2,000 |
| Lord Elgin, 23J, GJS, DR, Adj.5P, 3/4, Gold filled OF ................... | 750 | 850 | 950 |
| B. W. Raymond, 17J, 3/4, GJS, 14K, OF ....................................... | 475 | 525 | 650 |
| B. W. Raymond, 17J, 3/4, GJS, SW, HC....................................... | 200 | 275 | 350 |
| B. W. Raymond, 17J, 3F BRG ............................................. ★ ★ | 400 | 500 | 650 |
| B. W. Raymond, 17J, LS, NI, **Wind Indicator** ........................... ★ | 550 | 600 | 675 |
| B. W. Raymond, 17J, GJS, SW, ALL G#s, OF.............................. | 150 | 195 | 250 |
| B. W. Raymond, 17J, 3/4, GJS, DR, Adj.5P, DMK......................... | 175 | 225 | 275 |
| B. W. Raymond, 19J, 3/4, GJS, DR, Adj.5P, DMK, OF................. | 150 | 175 | 225 |
| B. W. Raymond, 19J, OF, 14K, 30 DWT ..................................... | 500 | 550 | 600 |
| B. W. Raymond, 19J, 3/4, GJS, DR, HCI5P, DMK, **Wind Indicator** | 650 | 700 | 800 |
| B. W. Raymond, 19J, M#8, G# 372, 455, Adj.5P, OF .................... | 150 | 175 | 210 |
| B. W. Raymond, 19J, GJS, G#371, 401,Adj.5P, HC...................... | 175 | 200 | 250 |
| B. W. Raymond, 21J, 14K, OF ................................................ | 525 | 575 | 635 |
| B. W. Raymond, 21J, G#389, 390, 391, 472, 478, 506, | | | |
| G#571, 581, 590, 3/4, Adj.5P, OF ........................................ | 225 | 250 | 285 |
| B. W. Raymond, 21J, 3/4, GJS, DR, Adj.5P, HC........................... | 300 | 325 | 375 |
| B. W. Raymond, 21J, 3/4, GJS, DR, Adj.5P, DMK, OF................. | 200 | 225 | 265 |
| B. W. Raymond, 21J, 3/4, GJS, DR, Adj.5P, DMK,**Wind Indicator** | 700 | 800 | 900 |
| B. W. Raymond, 22J, WWII Model, sweep second hand .............. | 250 | 285 | 300 |
| B. W. Raymond, 23J, 3/4, GJS, DR, Adj.5P, G#376, 494, 540 ...... | 375 | 400 | 475 |
| B. W. Raymond, 23J, 3/4, GJS, DR, Adj.5P, DMK, **Wind Indicator** | 750 | 800 | 950 |
| B. W. Raymond, 23J, 3/4, GJS, DR, Adj.5P, DMK,**Wind Indicator** | | | |
| military style ......................................................................... | 700 | 775 | 850 |

🕐 Watches listed in this book are priced at the collectable retail level, as **complete** watches having an original 14k gold-filled case and *Key Wind* with silver, an original white enamel single sunk dial, and with the entire original movement in good working order with no repairs needed.

🕐 Some watch manufacturers personalize watches for jobbers or jewelry firms, with exclusive private signed or marked movements. The valuable collectable watches are listed under the signed or marked movement. Other exclusive private signed or marked movements will have equivalent value are only slightly higher value and should be compared to Generic or Nameless movements. Railroad signed or marked (dials & movements) are usually more collectable & higher in value.

**Veritas,** 16 size, 23 jewels, solid gold train, gold jeweled settings, Adj5p, serial number 16,678,681.

**Grade 340,** 16 size, 17 jewels, three-fingered bridge model, open face.

| Grade or Name — Description | Avg | Ex-Fn | Mint |
|---|---|---|---|
| Veritas, 21J, GJS, DR, Adj.5P, DMK, 3/4, **Wind Indicator** ........ | $700 | $850 | $900 |
| Veritas, 19J, G#3401, GJS, Adj. 5P., HC .......................... ★ | 300 | 375 | 465 |
| Veritas, 21J, 3F brg, GJS................................................ ★ | 275 | 350 | 400 |
| Veritas, 21J, GJS, DR, Adj.5P, DMK, 3/4, HC..................... | 300 | 375 | 465 |
| Veritas, 21J, GJS, SW, Grade 360 .................................. ★ | 375 | 400 | 475 |
| Veritas, 21J, GJS, SW, Adj.5P, OF, Grade 270..................... | 225 | 275 | 335 |
| Veritas, 23J, GJS, Adj.5P, 14K, OF.................................. | 575 | 675 | 800 |
| Veritas, 23J, GJS, Adj.5P, HC...................................... | 350 | 425 | 500 |
| Veritas, 23J, GJS, DR, Adj.5P, 3/4, OF, G# 375, 376, 453 .......... | 375 | 425 | 500 |
| Veritas, 23J, GJS, DR, Adj.5P, DMK, 3/4, Diamond end stone, Grade 350 ............................................ ★ | 375 | 425 | 525 |
| Veritas, 23J, GJS, DR, Adj.5P, DMK, 3/4, **Wind Indicator** ........ | 800 | 900 | 1,000 |
| G. M. Wheeler, 17J, DR, Adj.3P, DMK, 3/4..................... | 75 | 95 | 125 |
| G. M. Wheeler, 17J, 3F BRG........................................ | 75 | 95 | 125 |
| G. M. Wheeler, 17J, HC, 14K...................................... | 450 | 475 | 525 |
| WWII Model, 17J, OF.............................................. | 100 | 125 | 175 |
| WWII Model, 21J, OF.............................................. | 175 | 200 | 250 |
| M#13, 9J, HC...................................................... | 75 | 85 | 100 |
| M#48, 13J, HC.................................................... | 75 | 100 | 150 |

*(Add $50 to $75 to hunting case models listed as open face)*

## MODELS WITH NO NAMES

| Grade or Name — Description | Avg | Ex-Fn | Mint |
|---|---|---|---|
| Grade #72, 21J, ADJ, 3/4, HC.......................................... ★ | $450 | $600 | $800 |
| Grade #91, 21J, 3F BRG .......................................... ★ ★ | 450 | 550 | 700 |
| Grade #145, 19J, GJS, BRG, HC .............................. ★ ★ | 650 | 750 | 900 |
| Grade #155, 17J, GT, GJS, HC .................................... | 100 | 120 | 150 |
| Grade #156, 21J, 3/4, NI, DR, DMK, GT, GJS, HC .............. ★ | 375 | 425 | 500 |
| Grade #156, 21J, 3/4, NI, DR, DMK, GT, GJS, HC, **14K** .......... ★ | 550 | 600 | 700 |
| Grade #162, 21J, SW, PS, NI, GJS, GT, OF ...................... ★ | 300 | 365 | 425 |
| Grade #270, 21J, 3F BRG, GJS, marked mvt. ...................... | 275 | 325 | 375 |
| Grade #280, 17J, marked on mvt. .................................. | 125 | 150 | 200 |
| Grade #290 & #291, 7J, OF, 3/4, NI, DMK ...................... | 50 | 75 | 90 |

🕐 Generic, nameless or unmarked grades for watch movements are listed under the Company name or initials of the Company, etc. by size, jewel count and description.

🕐 Watches listed in this book are priced at the collectable retail level, as complete watches having an original 14k gold-filled case and Key Wind with silver, an original white enamel single sunk dial, and with the entire original movement in good working order with no repairs needed.

| Grade or Name — Description | Avg | Ex-Fn | Mint |
|---|---|---|---|
| Grade #291, 7J, 3/4, HC, 14K | $400 | $450 | $550 |
| Grade #312 & #313, 15J, 3/4, NI, DR, DMK, OF | 50 | 65 | 90 |
| Grade # 340, 17J, 3 finger bridge, OF | 75 | 100 | 135 |
| Grade #372, 19J, M#15, LS, OF, Adj.5P | 250 | 300 | 375 |
| Grade #374, 21J, M#15, LS, OF, Adj.5P | 275 | 325 | 400 |
| Grade #381 & #382, 17J, 3/4, NI, DR, DMK, OF | 65 | 85 | 125 |
| Grade #571, 21J, Adj.5P, OF | 200 | 225 | 265 |
| Grade #540, 23J, Adj.5P, OF | 200 | 250 | 310 |
| Grade #572, 19J, Adj.5P, OF | 125 | 150 | 185 |
| Grade #573, 17J, Adj.5P, OF | 90 | 110 | 125 |
| Grade #575, 15J, Adj.3P, OF | 60 | 85 | 100 |
| Grade #581, 21J, Adj.5P, center sec, hacking, Army, OF | 125 | 150 | 195 |

### 14 SIZE

| Grade or Name — Description | Avg | Ex-Fn | Mint |
|---|---|---|---|
| Lord Elgin, 17J, SS, OF | $200 | $225 | $275 |
| 7J, M#1, gilded, KW, 14K, HC | 300 | 350 | 400 |
| 7J, M#1, gilded, KW, YGF, HC | 75 | 100 | 150 |
| 11J, M#1, gilded, KW, YGF, HC | 75 | 100 | 150 |
| 11J, M#1, gilded, KW, YGF, OF | 50 | 60 | 85 |
| 13J, M#1, gilded, KW, OF | 50 | 60 | 85 |
| 15J, M#1, gilded, KW, OF | 50 | 60 | 85 |
| 7J, M#2, SW, OF | 50 | 60 | 85 |
| 15J, M#2, SW, OF | 60 | 75 | 100 |
| 15J, M#2, SW, 14K, HC | 275 | 325 | 375 |
| 15J, M#1, grade # 46, KW, 3/4, HC | 75 | 95 | 125 |

### 12 SIZE

| Grade or Name — Description | | Avg | Ex -Fn | Mint |
|---|---|---|---|---|
| Eight Day, 21J, 8-Day Wind Indicator, BRG ............ ★★★★★ | | $2,000 | $2,500 | $3,000 |

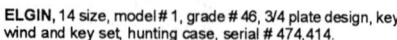

ELGIN, 14 size, model# 1, grade # 46, 3/4 plate design, key wind and key set, hunting case, serial # 474,414.

ELGIN EIGHT DAY, 12 size, 21 jewels, wind indicator, bridge movement, open face, serial number 12,345,678.

**ELGIN W. Co.**, dial signed "U.S. Calendar Watch Co.", 12     **ELGIN W. Co.**, 12 size with Masonic dial, Ca. 1930.
size, hand for date of month & day of week,

🕐 Generic, nameless or unmarked grades for watch movements are listed under the Company name or initials of the Company, etc. by size, jewel count and description.

| Grade or Name — Description | Avg | Ex-Fn | Mint |
|---|---|---|---|
| Elgin W. Co. #30, 7J, gilded, KW, OF | $45 | $55 | $85 |
| Elgin W. Co. #189, 19J, HC | 75 | 100 | 150 |
| Elgin W. Co. #190-194, 23J, GJS, Adj.5P, NI, DMK, GT, OF | 125 | 150 | 200 |
| Elgin W. Co. #190-194, 23J, GJS, Adj.5P, NI, DMK, GT, HC | 150 | 175 | 225 |
| Elgin W. Co. #236 & #237, 21J, GJS, Adj.5P, NI, DMK, GT, OF | 75 | 95 | 150 |
| Elgin W. Co. #236 & #237, 21J, GJS, Adj.5P, NI, DMK, GT, HC | 100 | 125 | 175 |
| Elgin W. Co. #301 & #302, 7J, HC | 50 | 60 | 85 |
| Elgin W. Co. #314 & #315, 15J, HC | 50 | 60 | 85 |
| Elgin W. Co. #383 & #384, 17J, HC | 60 | 70 | 95 |
| Elgin W. Co., 15J, 14K, Multi-color | 500 | 600 | 750 |
| Elgin W. Co., 15J, OF, GF | 50 | 60 | 75 |
| Elgin W. Co., 15J, HC, 14K | 300 | 350 | 425 |
| Elgin W. Co., 17J, OF, 14K | 275 | 300 | 350 |
| Elgin W. Co., 19J, HC, gold filled | 90 | 130 | 150 |
| Elgin W. Co., 19J, HC, 14K | 325 | 375 | 450 |
| Elgin W. Co., 19J, 14K, OF | 275 | 300 | 350 |
| Elete, 17J, GJS, Adj,4P, OF | 50 | 60 | 75 |
| C. H. Hulburd, 19J, thin BRG model (12 /14 size) 18K case ..... ★ | 800 | 1,000 | 1,200 |
| C. H. Hulburd, 19J, thin BRG model (12 /14 size) Platinum... ★ | 1,000 | 1,200 | 1,400 |
| Lord Elgin, 23J, GJS, DR, Adj.5P, DMK, NI, HC | 225 | 250 | 325 |
| Lord Elgin, 17J, | 75 | 95 | 150 |
| Lord Elgin, 19J, HC | 75 | 95 | 150 |
| Lord Elgin, 21J, 14K, OF | 275 | 300 | 375 |
| Lord Elgin, 21J, HC | 175 | 200 | 250 |

🕐 Watches listed in this book are priced at the collectable retail level, as **complete** watches having an original 14k gold-filled case and *Key Wind* with silver, an original white enamel single sunk dial, and with the entire original movement in good working order with no repairs needed.

**Lord Elgin,** 12 size, 23 jewels, gold jewel settings, Adj.5p, originally sold for $110.00.

**G.M. Wheeler,** 12 size, 17 jewels, Adj3p, originally sold for $27.00.

| Grade or Name — Description | Avg | Ex-Fn | Mint |
|---|---|---|---|
| Pierce Arrow, 17J, OF | $125 | $150 | $185 |
| B. W. Raymond, 19J, HC, GJS, Adj.5P, DR, DMK, NI | 100 | 135 | 175 |
| G. M. Wheeler, 17J, DR, Adj.5P, DMK, NI, OF | 40 | 60 | 75 |
| G. M. Wheeler, 17J, DR, Adj.5P, DMK, NI, HC | 65 | 90 | 110 |
| 193, 19J, DR, GJS, Adj.5P, DMK, NI, OF | 185 | 200 | 230 |

**Frances Rubie,** Grade 23, 10 size, 15 jewels, key wind & set.

**Gail Borden,** Grade 22, 10 size, 11 jewels, key wind & set, serial number 947,696.

## 10 SIZE
### (HC)

| Grade or Name — Description | Avg | Ex-Fn | Mint |
|---|---|---|---|
| Dexter St., 7J, KW, HC, 14K | $200 | $275 | $325 |
| Dexter St., 7J, KW, HC, 18K | 250 | 325 | 375 |
| Dexter St., 7J, gilded, KW, HC, gold filled | 50 | 75 | 125 |
| Frances Rubie, 15J, gilded, KW, HC, 14K ★ | 550 | 600 | 700 |
| Frances Rubie, 15J, KW, HC, 18K ★ ★ | 600 | 650 | 750 |

🕐 Watches listed in this book are priced at the collectable retail level, as **complete** watches having an original 14k gold-filled case and *Key Wind* with silver, an original white enamel single sunk dial, and with the entire original movement in good working order with no repairs needed.

| Grade or Name — Description | Avg | Ex-Fn | Mint |
|---|---|---|---|
| Gail Borden, 11J, gilded, KW, HC, 14K | $200 | $275 | $325 |
| Gail Borden, 11J, KW, HC, gold filled | 50 | 75 | 125 |
| Gail Borden, 11J, KW, HC, 18K | 250 | 300 | 375 |
| Lady Elgin, 15J, gilded, KW, HC, 14K | 200 | 250 | 325 |
| Lady Elgin, 15J, KW, HC, 18K | 250 | 300 | 375 |
| Grade # 21 or 28, 7J, gilded, KW, HC, gold filled | 50 | 75 | 125 |
| Elgin, multi-color case, gold filled, HC | 200 | 225 | 275 |
| Elgin, 15J, Silveroid, HC | 30 | 40 | 50 |
| Elgin, 15J, YGF, HC | 50 | 75 | 125 |

Elgin W. Co., Grade 121, 6 size, 15 jewels, hunting, serial number 4,500,445.

Elgin W. Co., Grade 67, 6 size, 11 jewels, serial number 1,149,615.

## 6 SIZE
### (HC Only)

| Grade or Name — Description | Avg | Ex-Fn | Mint |
|---|---|---|---|
| Atlas, 7J, HC | $50 | $75 | $125 |
| Elgin W. Co. #168, 16J, HC | 50 | 75 | 125 |
| Elgin W. Co. #286, 7J, HC, DMK, NI | 50 | 75 | 125 |
| Elgin W. Co. #295, 15J, HC, DMK, NI | 50 | 75 | 125 |
| Elgin W. Co., 7J, HC, 14K | 175 | 225 | 300 |
| Elgin W. Co., 15J, SW, HC, Enamel case, 18K | 800 | 1,000 | 1,300 |
| Elgin W. Co., 15J, YGF, HC | 50 | 75 | 125 |
| Elgin W. Co., 15J, HC, 14K | 175 | 225 | 300 |
| Elgin W. Co., 15J, HC, 10K | 150 | 175 | 225 |
| Elgin W. Co., 15J, HC, 18K | 250 | 325 | 375 |
| Elgin W. Co., 15J, HC, GF multi-color case | 200 | 225 | 275 |
| Elgin W. Co., 11J, HC, 14K | 175 | 225 | 300 |
| Elgin W. Co., 15J, demi-HC | 75 | 100 | 150 |
| Elgin W. Co., 15J, 14K, Multi-color HC | 450 | 500 | 650 |

🕐: Generic, nameless or unmarked grades for watch movements are listed under the Company name or initials of the Company, etc. by size, jewel count and description.

Elgin W. Co., 6 size, 15 jewels

Elgin W. Co., Grade 201-HC, 205-OF, 0 size, 19 jewels, gold train.

Elgin W. Co., Grade 200-HC, 204-OF, 0 size, 17 jewels, gold jewel settings.

## 0 SIZE

| Grade or Name — Description | Avg | Ex-Fn | Mint |
|---|---|---|---|
| Atlas W. Co., 7J, HC | $75 | $100 | $150 |
| Elgin W. Co., 7J, NI, DR, DMK, OF | 35 | 40 | 50 |
| Elgin W. Co., 15J, NI, DR, DMK, OF | 40 | 45 | 55 |
| Elgin W. Co., 15J, NI, DR, DMK, HC | 75 | 100 | 150 |
| Elgin W. Co., 17J, NI, DR, DMK, ADJ, OF | 55 | 60 | 80 |
| Elgin W. Co., 19J, NI, DR, DMK, GJS, ADJ, OF | 55 | 75 | 95 |
| Elgin W. Co., 15J, OF, 14K | 135 | 175 | 225 |
| Elgin W. Co., 15J, HC, 14K | 175 | 225 | 300 |
| Elgin W. Co., 15J, HC, multi-color GF | 175 | 200 | 250 |
| Elgin W. Co., 15J, OF, multi-color dial | 100 | 125 | 175 |
| Elgin W. Co., 15J, HC, 10K | 150 | 175 | 225 |
| Elgin W. Co., 15J, 14K, Multi-color case | 400 | 450 | 525 |
| Elgin W. Co., 15J, 14K, Multi-color case + diamond | 500 | 550 | 625 |
| Frances Rubie, 19J, HC ........................★ | 200 | 225 | 300 |

Lady Elgin, 5/0 size, 17 jewels, gold jewel settings, originally sold for $42.50.

Lady Raymond, 5/0 size, 15 jewels, originally sold for $24.20.

## 3/0 and 5/0 SIZE
## (HC ONLY)

| Grade or Name — Description | Avg | Ex-Fn | Mint |
|---|---|---|---|
| Lady Elgin, 15J, PS, HC | $75 | $100 | $150 |
| Lady Elgin, 15J, 14K, HC | 200 | 225 | 275 |
| Lady Raymond, 15J, PS, HC | 75 | 100 | 150 |
| Elgin W. Co., 7J, HC | 75 | 100 | 150 |

🕐: Generic, nameless or unmarked grades for watch movements are listed under the Company name or initials of the Company, etc. by size, jewel count and description.

STYLE NO. 40
gold filled : $90 - $100 - $120

STYLE NO. 39
gold filled : $95- $110 - $120

STYLE NO. 38
gold filled : $95- $110 - $120

STYLE NO. 19
gold filled : $90 - $100 - $125

STYLE NO. 18
CHROME: $25 - $35 - $45

STYLE NO. 25
gold filled : $95- $110 - $130

STYLE NO. 26
gold filled : $90 - $100 - $120

ANTIQUE BOW
gold filled : $95- $110 - $130

RIGID BOW
gold filled : $100- $122 - $140

GOLD FILLED CASES = 40, 39, 38, 19, 25, 26, and some came with a **solid gold** bow.
CHROME CASES = 18 and ANTIQUE BOW & RIGID BOW= 20 year gold filled case

🕐 NOTE: Factory Advertised as a **complete** watch and was fitted with a certain matched, timed and rated movement and sold in the factory designed case style as a **complete** watch. The factory also sold _uncased_ movements to **JOBBERS** such as Jewelry stores & they cased the movement in a case styles the **CUSTOMER requested**. All the factory advertised **complete** watches came with a enamel dial **SHOWN or CHOICE** of other **Railroad** dials.

## ELGIN NATIONAL WATCH CO.
## IDENTIFICATION OF MOVEMENTS
## BY MODEL NUMBER

**How to Identify Your Watch:** Compare the movement of your watch with the illustrations in this section. Upon matching the movement exactly, the model number and size can be determined. While comparing, note the location of the balance, jewels, screws, gears and type of back plate (Full, ¾, Bridge) which will be clues in identifying the movement you have. Having determined the size and model number, you can now find your watch in the main price listing by name or number (which is engraved on the movement).

**Model 1,** 18 size, full plate, hunting, key wind & set, first serial number 101, Apr., 1867.

**Model 2-4,** 18 size, full plate, hunting, lever set, first serial number 155,001, June, 1873.

**Model 5,** 18 size, full plate, open face, pendant set, first serial number, 2,110,001, Grade 43, Dec., 1885.

**Model 6,** 18 size, three-quarter plate, hunting, open face, pendant set.

**Model 7**, 18 size, full plate, open face, lever set, first serial number 6,563,821, Grade 265, Apr., 1897.

**Model 8**, 18 size, three-quarter plate, open face, lever set, first serial number 8,400,001, Grade 214, Dec., 1900.

**Model 8**, 18 size, three-quarter plate, open face, lever set with winding indicator.

**Model 9**, 18 size, three-quarter plate, hunting, lever set, first serial number 9,625,001, Grade 274, May, 1904.

**Model 9**, 18 size, three-quarter plate, hunting, lever set with winding indicator.

**Model 1**, 17 size, full plate, hunting, key wind and set.

**Model 2**, 17 size, full plate, hunting, lever set.

**Model 1**, 16 size, three-quarter plate, hunting & open face, lever set.

**Model 2**, 16 size, three-quarter plate, bridge, hunting & open face, lever set.

**Model 3**, 16 size, three-quarter plate, hunting, lever set, first serial number 625,001, Grade 1, Feb., 1879.

**Model 4**, 16 size, three-quarter plate, sweep second, hunting & open face, lever set.

**Model 5**, 16 size, three-quarter plate, open face, pendant set.

**Model 5**, 16 size, three-quarter plate, open face, pendant set, first serial number 2,811,001, Grade 105, Oct., 1887.

**Model 6**, 16 size, three-quarter plate, hunting, pendant set, first serial number 6,458,001, Grade 151, Aug., 1895.

**Model 6**, 16 size, three-quarter plate, bridge, hunting, pendant set, first serial number 6,463,001, Grade 156, May, 1896.

**Model 7**, 16 size, three-quarter plate, open face, pendant set, first serial number 6,464,001. Grade 157, Sept., 1895.

**Model 7**, 16 size, three-quarter plate, bridge, open face, pendant set, first serial number 6,469,001, Grade 162, Apr., 1896.

**Model 8**, 16 size, three-quarter plate, bridge, hunting, lever set, serial number 12,283,001, Grade 341, Jan., 1907.

**Model 9,** 16 size, three-quarter plate, bridge, open face, lever set, first serial number 9,250,001, Grade 270, July, 1902.

**Model 13,** 16 size, three-quarter plate, open face, lever set, first serial number 12,717,001, Grade 350, June, 1908.

**Model 14,** 16 size, three-quarter plate, hunting, lever set.

**Model 15,** 16 size, three-quarter plate, open face, lever set.

**Model 17,** 16 size, three-quarter plate, hunting, lever set.

**Model 19,** 16 size, three-quarter plate, open face, lever set with winding indicator.

**Model 20,** 16 size, three-quarter plate, open face, Grades 571, 572, 573, 574, 575, 616.

**Model 1,** 14 size, three-quarter plate, hunting, key wind and set.

**Model 2**, 14 size, three-quarter plate, open face, pendant set.

**Model 1**, 12 size, three-quarter plate, hunting, key wind and set.

**Model 2**, 12 size, three-quarter plate, hunting, pendant set, first serial #7,410,001, Grade 188, Dec., 1897.

**Model 2**, 12 size, three-quarter plate, spread to 16 size, hunting, pendant set.

**Model 3**, 12 size, three-quarter plate, open face, pendant set, serial number 7,423,001, Grade 192, May 1898.

**Model 3**, 12 size, three-quarter plate, spread to 16 size, open face, pendant set.

**Model 4**, 12 size, three-quarter plate, open face, pendant set, serial number 16,311,001, Grade 392, July, 1912.

**Model 1**, 10 size, three-quarter plate, style 1, hunting, key wind and set.

**Model 2**, 10 size, three-quarter plate, hunting, key wind and set.

**Model 3**, 10 size, three-quarter plate, hunting.

**Model 4**, 10 size, three-quarter plate, hunting.

**Model 5 & 6**, 10 size, three-quarter plate.

**Model 1**, 6 size, three-quarter plate, hunting.

**Model 1**, 6 size, three-quarter plate, hunting.

**Model 2**, 6 size, three-quarter plate, hunting.

**Model 1**, 0 size, three-quarter plate, hunting.

**Model 2**, 0 size, three-quarter plate, hunting.

**Model 2**, 0 size, three-quarter plate, hunting.

**Model 3**, 0 size, three-quarter plate, open face.

**Model 3**, 0 size, three-quarter plate, open face.

**Model 2**, 3-0 size, three-quarter plate, hunting.

**Charles Fasoldt's** double escape wheel with odd shaped lever.

**Charles Fasoldt,** 18-20 size, 16 jewels, key wind & set, bar movement; note patented regulator, series II.

## CHARLES FASOLDT WATCH CO.
### Rome, New York    1849 - 1861
### Albany, New York    1861 - 1878

Charles Fasoldt came to the United States in 1848. One of his first watches, Serial No. 27, was for General Armstrong and was an eight-day movement. At about that same time, he made several large regulators and a few pocket chronometers. He displayed some of his work at fairs in Utica and Syracuse and received four First-Class Premiums and two diplomas. In 1850, he patented a micrometric regulator (generally called the Howard Regulator because Howard bought the patent). He also patented a chronometer escapement in 1859-1865, a watch regulator in 1864, and a hairspring stud in 1877. He was also known for his tower clocks, for which he received many awards and medals. He made about 500 watches in Albany and about 50 watches in Rome.

**Charles Fasoldt,** 18-20 size, 16 jewels, stem wind, key set, bar movement, series III.

**Charles Fasoldt,** 18-20 size, 16 jewels, stem wind, key set, bar movement, series III.

| Year | Model | Style | Serial # Range |
|------|-------|-------|----------------|
| 1855 - 1864 | Series I | KW, ½ plate | 5- 40 |
| 1865 - 1868 | Series II | KW, Bar | 41-330 |
| 1868 - 1878 | Series III | SW, Bar | 331-540 |

| Grade or Name — Description | | Avg | Ex-Fn | Mint |
|-----------------------------|---|-----|-------|------|
| 18 - 20 SIZE, 22J, chronograph,dual mainsprings & dual train, GJS, KW or SW, 18K case | ★★★★ | $10,000 | $12,000 | $16,000 |
| 18 - 20 SIZE, 16J, GJS, KW, KS, 18K case | ★★★ | 8,000 | 10,000 | 14,000 |
| 10 - 12 SIZE, 16J, GJS, KW & SW, KS, 14K | | 3,500 | 4,000 | 5,000 |
| Otto H. Fasoldt, 18S, 15J, SW, Swiss made or American | | 175 | 200 | 250 |

# FITCHBURG WATCH CO.

### Fitchburg, Massachusetts

### 1875 - 1878

In 1875, S. Sawyer decided to manufacture watches. He hired personnel from the U. S. Watch Company to build the machinery, but by 1878 the company had failed. It is not known how many, if any, watches were made. The equipment was sold to Cornell and other watch companies.

# E. H. FLINT

### Cincinnati, Ohio

### 1877 - 1879

The Flint watch was patented September 18, 1877, and about 100 watches were made. The serial number is found under the dial.

| Grade or Name — Description | | Avg | Ex-Fn | Mint |
|-----------------------------|---|-----|-------|------|
| 18 Size, 4–7J, KW, Full Plate, OF, Coin | ★★★ | $2,000 | $2,500 | $3,500 |
| 18 Size, 4–7J, KW, Full Plate, 14K, HC | ★★★ | 4,000 | 4,500 | 5,500 |

**E.H. Flint** dial and movement, 18 size, 4-7 jewels, open face, key wind & set, "Lancaster Pa." on dial, "Patented Sept. 18th, 1877" on movement.

Fredonia Watch Co., 18 size, 15 jewels, signature on movement "Cyrus N. Gibbs, Mass.," key wind & set, serial number 4403.

Fredonia Watch Co., 18 size, 15 jewels, adjusted, serial number 8,368. NOTE: FREDONIA Regulator disc will have teeth all around the disc.

# FREDONIA WATCH CO.

## Fredonia, New York
### 1881 - 1885

This company sold the finished movements acquired from the Independent Watch Co. These movements had been made by other companies. The Fredonia Watch Company was sold to the Peoria Watch Co. in 1885, after having produced approximately 20,000 watches.

### Chronology of the Development of Fredonia:

Independent Watch Co.  1875 –1881
Fredonia Watch Co.     1881 –1885
Peoria Watch Co.       1885 –1889

Fredonia Watch Co., with a reversible case; changes to either hunting or open face.

| Grade or Name — Description | Avg | Ex-Fn | Mint |
|---|---|---|---|
| 18S, 7J, SW, OF | $150 | $200 | $300 |
| 18S, 7J, SW, HC | 175 | 225 | 325 |
| 18S, 9J, SW, OF | 200 | 250 | 325 |
| 18S, 9J, SW, HC | 175 | 225 | 325 |
| 18S, 11J, SW, OF | 200 | 250 | 325 |
| 18S, 11J, KW, KS, HC, Coin | 175 | 225 | 325 |
| 18S, 15J, SW, Multi-color, 14K, HC | 1,600 | 1,800 | 2,200 |
| 18S, KW, Reversible case | 500 | 550 | 600 |
| 18S, 15J, SW, LS, **Gilt,** OF | 175 | 200 | 300 |
| 18S, 15J, straight line escapement, NI, marked **Adjusted** | 300 | 350 | 450 |
| 18S, 15J, HC, low serial number | 300 | 350 | 450 |
| 18S, 15J, personalized mvt. | 250 | 275 | 375 |
| 18S, 15J, KW, HC, marked Lakeshore W. Co. | 250 | 300 | 400 |
| 18S, Mark Twain, 11J, KW, KS ★★ | 500 | 650 | 800 |

# FREEPORT WATCH CO.

## Freeport, Illinois

### 1874 - 1875

Probably less than 20 watches made by Freeport have survived. Their machinery was purchased from Mozart Co., and a Mr. Hoyt was engaged as superintendent. The building erected was destroyed by fire on Oct. 21, 1875. A safe taken from the ruins contained 300 completed movements which were said to be ruined.

| Grade or Name — Description | Avg | Ex-Fn | Mint |
|---|---|---|---|
| 18S, 19J, KW, SW, gold train, raised gold jewel settings 18K case ★★★★ | $6,000 | $7,000 | $8,000 |
| 18S, 15J, KW, KS, gold train, friction jewels 18K case ★★★★ | $5,500 | $6,000 | $7,000 |
| **Geo. P. Rose**, Dubuque, Iowa, 18S, 15J, KW, KS, gold train, friction jewels, 18K case ★★★★ | $5,500 | $6,000 | $7,000 |

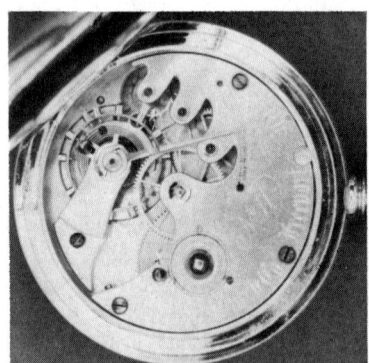

Freeport Watch Co., Example of a basic movement, 18 size, 15 jewels, key wind & set, pressed jewels, gold train, high grade movement, serial number 11.

# SMITH D. FRENCH

### Wabash, Indiana
### 1866 - 1878

On August 21, 1866, Mr. French was issued a patent for an improved escapement for watches. The escape wheel has triangular shaped pins and the lever has two hook-shaped pallets. The pin wheel escapement was probably first used by Robert Robin, about 1795, for pocket watches. Antoine Tavan also used this style escape wheel around 1800. Mr. French's improved pin wheel and hook shaped lever (about 70 total production) can be seen through a cutout in the plates of his watches.

Illustration from the patent office, patent number 57,310, patented Aug. 21, 1866. Note pin wheel escapement with adjustable hook shaped lever.

| Grade or Name — Description | | Avg | Ex-Fn | Mint |
|---|---|---|---|---|
| 18S, 15J, 3/4, KW, KS, gilt, pin wheel escapement, Silver case | ★★★★ | $4,000 | $5,500 | $6,000 |
| 18S, 15J, 3/4, KW, KS, gilt, pin wheel escapement, 18K case | ★★★★★ | 5,000 | 6,500 | 8,000 |

**S.D. French,** about 18 size, 15 jewels, gilt 3/4 movement, key wind & set, with pin wheel escapement, engraved on movement "S.D. French, Wabash Ind., Aug. 21. 1866, No. 24."

**L. Goddard,** 55mm, 7 jewels, full plate movement with solid cock, chain driven fusee, flat steel balance, serial number 235, ca. 1809-1817.

# LUTHER GODDARD

### Shrewsbury, Massachusetts
### 1809 - 1825

The first significant attempt to produce watches in America was made by Luther Goddard. William H. Keith, who became president of Waltham Watch Co. (1861 -1866) and was once apprenticed to Goddard, said that the hands, dials, round and dovetail brass, steel wire, mainsprings and hairsprings, balance, verge, chains, and pinions were all imported. The plates, wheels, and brass parts were cast at the Goddard shop, however. He also made the cases for his movements which were of the usual style open faced, double case-and somewhat in advance of the prevalent style of thick bull's eye watches of the day. About 600 watches were made which were of good quality and more expensive than the imported type. The first watch was produced about 1812 and was sold to the father of ex-governor Lincoln of Worcester, Massachusetts. In 1820 his watches sold for about $60.00.

Goddard built a shop one story high with a hip roof about 18' square; it had a lean-to at the back for casting. The building was for making clocks, but a need for watches developed and Goddard made watches there. He earned the distinction of establishing the first watch factory in America.

His movements were marked as follows: L. GODDARD, L.GODDARD & CO., LUTHER GODDARD & SON, P. GODDARD, L. & P. GODDARD, D.P. GODDARD & CO., D. & P. GODDARD.

Frank A. Knowlton purchased the company and operated it until 1933.

### Chronology of the Development of Luther Goddard:

| | |
|---|---|
| Luther Goddard, L. Goddard, L. Goddard & Son ..... | 1809-1825 |
| L. Goddard & Son ..................................................... | 1817-1825 |
| P.& D. Goddard ......................................................... | 1825-1842 |
| D. Goddard & Son ..................................................... | 1842-1850 |
| Luther D. Goddard ..................................................... | 1850-1857 |
| Goddard & Co. ........................................................... | 1857-1860 |
| D. Goddard & Co., & Benj'n Goddard .................. | 1860-1872 |

D. **Goddard,** 18-20, 15 jewels," Worcester, Mass."on movement, key wind & set, solid balance, under sprung, serial number 8.

L. **Goddard & Co.,**16-18 size, pair case, open face-thick bulls-eye type, and of high quality for the time.

**NOTE: Watches listed below are with original silver cases.**

| Grade or Name — Description | Avg | Ex-Fn | Mint |
|---|---|---|---|
| Benj'n Goddard............................................................................ | $1,000 | $1,200 | $1,500 |
| Luther Goddard, S#1-35 with eagle on balance bridge ...... ★★★★ | 5,000 | 6,000 | 7,500 |
| Luther Goddard without eagle on cock...................................... ★★ | 2,500 | 3,000 | 3,500 |
| Luther Goddard,L.Goddard, Luther Goddard & Son ................... ★ | 2,000 | 3,200 | 4,200 |
| L. Goddard & Co., D. Goddard & Son ....................................... ★ | 1,200 | 1,400 | 1,700 |
| Luther D. Goddard, Goddard & Co., D. Goddard & Co. ............. ★ | 1,000 | 1,200 | 1,500 |
| P. Goddard, with eagle on cock................................................. ★ | 1,000 | 1,200 | 1,500 |
| P & D Goddard, 7J., (Worcester), fusee, KWKS, OF.................... | 800 | 900 | 1,200 |

L. Goddard & Son. Example of basic movement, about 18 size, open face, pair case; most of the parts are made in America but resemble the English style CA.1815.

L. Goddard & Son, about 18 size, pair case, verge escapement, engraved on movement "L. Goddard & Son, Shrewsbury," serial number 460.

## JONAS G. HALL
### Montpelier, Vermont 1850 - 1870
### Millwood Park, Roxbury, Vermont 1870 - 1890

Jonas G. Hall was born in 1822 in Calais, Vermont. He opened a shop in Montpelier where he sold watches, jewelry, silverware, and fancy goods. While at this location, he produced more than 60 full plate, lever style watches. Hall, later established a business in Roxbury, where he manufactured watch staking tools and other watchmaking tools. At Roxbury, he made at least one watch which was a three-quarter plate model. He also produced a few chronometers, about 20-size with a fusee and detent escapement and a wind indicator on the dial.

Hall was employed by the American Waltham Watch Co. for a short time and helped design the first lady's model. He also worked for Tremont Watch Co., E. Howard & Co., and the United States Watch Co. of Marion, New Jersey.

| Style or Name–Description | | Avg | Ex-Fn | Mint |
|---|---|---|---|---|
| 18S, 15J, Full plate, KW KS | ★ ★ ★ | $1,500 | $2,000 | $2,800 |
| 18S, 15J, 3/4 plate, gilded, KW KS | ★ ★ ★ | 2,500 | 3,000 | 3,600 |
| 20S, 15J, Detent Chronometer, KW KS | ★ ★ ★ ★ | 4,000 | 5,000 | 7,500 |

J.G. Hall, 18 size, 15 jewels, full plate, key wind & set, engraved on movement "J.G. Hall, Montpelier, VT.," serial number 25, ca. 1857.

J.G. Hall, 18 size, 15 jewels, 3/4 plate, key wind and set, engraved on movement "J.G. Hall, Millwood Park, Roxbury, VT," no serial number, ca. 1880.

# HAMILTON WATCH CO.

**Lancaster, Pennsylvania**
**December 14, 1892 - Present**

Hamilton's roots go back to the Adams & Perry Watch Manufacturing Co. On Sept. 26, 1874, E. F. Bowman made a model watch, and the first movement was produced on April 7, 1876. It was larger than an 18S, or about a 19S. The movement had a snap on dial and the patented stem-setting arrangement. They decided to start making the watches a standard size of 18, and no more than 1,000 of the large-size watches were made. Work had commenced on Sept. 1, 1877, at the Lancaster Watch Co. The watches were designed to sell at a cheaper price than normal. It had a one-piece top 3/4 plate and a pillar plate that was fully ruby-jeweled (4 1/2 pairs). It had a gilt or nickel movement and a new stem-wind device designed by Mosely & Todd. By mid-1878, the Lancaster Watch Co. had made 150 movements. Four grades of watches were produced: Keystone, Fulton, Franklin, and Melrose. In September 1879 the company had manufactured 334 movements. In 1880 some 1,250 movements had been made. In mid-1882, about 17,000 movements had been assembled. All totaled, about 20,000 movements were made.

THE

*Hamilton Watch*

940

THE
RAIL ROAD TIMEKEEPER
OF AMERICA.

*LANCASTER, PA.*

Grade **936**, 18 size, 17 jewels, serial number 1. c. 1893.      Grade **936**, 18 size, 17 jewels, serial number 2, c. 1893.

The first Hamilton movement to be sold was No. 15 to W. C. Davis on January 31, 1893. The No. 1 movement was finished on April 25, 1896, and was never sold. The No. 2 was finished on April 25, 1893, and was shipped to Smythe & Ashe of Rochester, N. Y. Nos. 1 & 2 are at the N.A.W.C.C. museum.

### Chronology of the Development of Hamilton:

Adams & Perry Watch Co.................Sept. 1874-May 1876
Lancaster, Pa., Watch Co. .....................Aug. 1877-Oct. 1887
Lancaster, Pa., Watch Co. ....................Nov. 1877-May 1879
Lancaster Watch Co. ...................................May 1883-1886
Keystone Standard Watch Co................................1886-1890
Hamilton Watch Co. ..............................Dec. 14, 1892-1969

In 1893 the first watch was produced by Hamilton. The watches became very popular with railroad men and by 1923 some 53 percent of Hamilton's production were railroad watches. The 940 model watch was discontinued in 1910. Most Hamilton watches are fitted with a 42-hour mainspring.

Grade **937**, 18 size, 17 jewels, hunting case. Note serial      Hamilton Watch Co., 18 size, 7 jewels, serial number 2934.
number 1047. **Hunting case models began with 1001.**

The 950B was introduced in 1940 and by this time a total of about 25,000 grade (950) had been sold. The 992 watch sold for about $60.00 in 1929, the price remained the same $60.00 untill 1940.

The Elinvar hairspring was patented in 1931 and used in all movements thereafter. On October 15, 1940, Hamilton introduced the 992B which were fitted with the Elinvar hairspring. Elinvar and Invar are trade names and are the same 36 percent nickel steel. Although the Hamilton Watch Co. is still in business today making modern type watches, they last produced American made watches in about 1969.

## HAMILTON ESTIMATED SERIAL NUMBERS
## AND PRODUCTION DATES

| Date–Serial No. | Date–Serial No. | Date–Serial No. | Date–Serial No. |
|---|---|---|---|
| 1893 —1-2,000 | 1906 — 590,000 | 1919—1,700,000 | 1932—2,500,000 |
| 1894 — 5,000 | 1907 — 756,000 | 1920—1,790,000 | 1933—2,600,000 |
| 1895 — 11,500 | 1908 — 921,000 | 1921—1,860,000 | 1934—2,700,000 |
| 1896 — 16,000 | 1909—1,087,000 | 1922—1,900,000 | 1935—2,800,000 |
| 1897 — 27,000 | 1910—1,150,500 | 1923—1,950,000 | 1936—2,900,000 |
| 1898 — 50,000 | 1911—1,290,500 | 1924—2,000,000 | 1937—3,000,000 |
| 1899 — 74,000 | 1912—1,331,000 | 1925—2,100,000 | 1938—3,200,000 |
| 1900—104,000 | 1913—1,370,000 | 1926—2,200,000 | 1939—3,400,000 |
| 1901—143,000 | 1914—1,410,500 | 1927—2,250,000 | 1940—3,600,000 |
| 1902—196,000 | 1915—1,450,500 | 1928—2,300,000 | 1941—3,800,000 |
| 1903—260,000 | 1916—1,517,000 | 1929—2,350,000 | 1942—4,025,000 |
| 1904—340,000 | 1917—1,580,000 | 1930—2,400,000 | |
| 1905—425,000 | 1918—1,650,000 | 1931—2,450,000 | |

The above list is provided for determining the <u>APPROXIMATE</u> age of your watch. Match serial number with date. Watches were not necessarily **SOLD** in the exact order of manufactured date.

Some serial numbers have the first numbers replaced by a (date) letter such as A, B, C, E, F, G, H, J, L, M, N, R, S, T, V, W, X, Y, CY, HW. These letters were used from late 30's to about late 50's. The date letter "2B + Ser.#" found on 950B **= 1940 to 1942,** the date letter "C + Ser.#" found on 992B = **1940 to 1952,** the date letter "S + Ser.#" found on 950B = **1943 to 1952** and HA = SWISS.

992B with first letter of C + serial no.
1940=C001
1941=C75000
1942=C160000
1943=C185000
1944=C200000
1945=C220000
1946=C235000
1947=C255000
1948=C275000
1949=C290000
1950=C300000
1951=C310000

950B with first letter of 2B + serial no.
1940=2B001
1941=2B400
1942=2B800
950B with first letter of S + serial no.
1943=S001
1944=S1500
1945=S2900
1946=S4000
1947=S4500
1948=S6500
1949=S7500
1950=S8900
1951=S10000

**NOTE:** *It required several months for raw material to emerge as a finished movement. All the while the factory is producing all sizes, models and grades. The numbering system was basically* **"consecutive",** *due to demand a batch of movements could be side tracked, thus allowing a different size and model to move ahead to meet this demand. Therefore, the dates some movements were* **sold** *and delivered to the trade, the serial numbers may not be* **"consecutive".**

### The Hamilton Masterpiece

The adjoining illustration shows the Hamilton Masterpiece. The dial is sterling silver with raised gold numbers and solid gold hands. This watch sold for $685.00 in 1930. All 922 **MP** Models included the following: 12 size, 23 jewels, were adjusted to heat, cold, isochronism, and five positions, with a motor barrel, solid gold train, steel escape wheel, double roller, sapphire pallets and a micrometric regulator.

# HAMILTON SERIAL NUMBERS AND GRADES

To help determine the size and grade of your watch, the following serial number list is provided. Serial numbers 30,001 through 32,000, which are omitted from the list, were not listed by Hamilton. To identify your watch, simply look up its serial number which will identify the grade. After determining the grade, your watch can be easily located in the pricing section.

| Serial | Grade | Serial | Grade | Serial | Grade | Serial | Grade |
|---|---|---|---|---|---|---|---|
| 1-20 | 936 | 27001-28000 | 929 | 56801-900 | 974 | 73001-200 | 975 |
| 21-30 | 932 | 28001-29000 | 999 | 56901-57000 | 976 | 73201-300 | 973 |
| 31-60 | 936 | 29001-800 | 927 | 57001-300 | 977 | 73301-74000 | 977 |
| 61-400 | 932 | 29801-30000 | 935 | 57301-500 | 975 | 74001-400 | 974 |
| 401-1000 | 936 | 32001-300 | 926 | 57501-600 | 973 | 74401-600 | 972 |
| 1001-20 | 937 | 32301-700 | 930 | 57601-800 | 975 | 74601-75000 | 976 |
| 1021-30 | 933 | 32701-33000 | 934 | 57801-58000 | 977 | 75001-76799 | HWW* |
| 1031-60 | 937 | 33001-500 | 931 | 58001-100 | 972 | 76002-76800 | HWW* |
| 1061-1100 | 933 | 33501-800 | 927 | 58101-200 | 974 | 77001-100 | 969 |
| 1101-300 | 937 | 33801-34000 | 935 | 58201-300 | 972 | 77101-300 | 973 |
| 1301-600 | 933 | 34001-500 | 928 | 58301-400 | 966 | 77301-500 | 975 |
| 1601-2000 | 937 | 34501-700 | 930 | 58401-500 | 976 | 77501-600 | 971 |
| 2001-3000 | 7J | 34701-800 | 926 | 58501-600 | 972 | 77601-700 | 973 |
| 3001-100 | 931 | 34801-35000 | 934 | 58601-800 | 974 | 77701-900 | 975 |
| 3101-500 | 935 | 35001-800 | 931 | 58801-59000 | 976 | 77901-78000 | 977 |
| 3501-600 | 931 | 35801-36000 | 935 | 59001-300 | 973 | 78001-500 | 970 |
| 3601-900 | 935 | 36001-37000 | 928 | 59301-500 | 967 | 78501-700 | 972 |
| 3901-4000 | 931 | 37001-38000 | 929 | 59501-700 | 975 | 78701-900 | 974 |
| 4001-300 | 930 | 38001-500 | 926 | 59701-60000 | 977 | 78901-79000 | 976 |
| 4301-5100 | 934 | 38501-600 | 930 | 60001-500 | 976 | 79001-100 | 973 |
| 5101-400 | 926 | 38601-900 | 934 | 60501-700 | 974 | 79101-300 | 975 |
| 5401-600 | 934 | 38901-39000 | 926 | 60701-61000 | 976 | 79301-700 | 977 |
| 5601-6000 | 930 | 39001-200 | 931 | 61001-200 | 975 | 79701-900 | 975 |
| 6001-600 | 936 | 39201-500 | 935 | 61201-500 | 977 | 79901-80000 | 973 |
| 6601-700 | 938 | 39501-700 | 927 | 61501-600 | 973 | 80001-200 | 972 |
| 6701-800 | 936 | 39701-900 | 935 | 61601-800 | 975 | 80201-400 | 974 |
| 6801-7000 | 932 | 39901-40000 | 931 | 61801-62000 | 977 | 80401-600 | 970 |
| 7001-10 | 17J | 40001-200 | 930 | 62001-100 | 972 | 80601-700 | 972 |
| 7011-600 | 937 | 40201-500 | 934 | 62101-300 | 974 | 80701-900 | 974 |
| 7601-700 | 939 | 40501-41000 | 926 | 62301-500 | 976 | 80901-81000 | 976 |
| 7701-800 | 937 | 41001-500 | 929 | 62501-700 | 974 | 81001-300 | 961 |
| 7801-8000 | 933 | 41501-42000 | 927 | 62701-900 | 972 | 81301-500 | 965 |
| 8001-700 | 936 | 42001-43000 | 999 | 62901-63000 | 974 | 81501-82000 | 961 |
| 8701-800 | 938 | 43001-300 | 941 | 63001-500 | 977 | 82001-300 | 972 |
| 8801-9000 | 936 | 43301-500 | 943 | 63501-600 | 975 | 82301-500 | 974 |
| 9001-300 | 937 | 43501-700 | 937 | 63601-800 | 977 | 82501-600 | 970 |
| 9301-600 | 939 | 43701-900 | 941 | 63801-900 | 975 | 82601-700 | 972 |
| 9601-800 | 937 | 43901-44000 | 943 | 63901-64000 | 973 | 82701-800 | 974 |
| 9801-900 | 933 | 44001-02 | 21J | 64001-100 | 976 | 82801-900 | 968 |
| 9901-10000 | 939 | 44003-400 | 938 | 64101-200 | 938 | 82901-83000 | 976 |
| 10001-200 | 938 | 44401-500 | 942 | 64201-300 | 974 | 83001-400 | 977 |
| 10201-400 | 936 | 44501-45000 | 936 | 64301-400 | 972 | 83401-500 | 971 |
| 10401-50 | 932 | 45001-46000 | 929 | 64601-700 | 976 | 83501-700 | 975 |
| 10451-500 | 936 | 46001-500 | 926 | 64701-900 | 974 | 83701-800 | 973 |
| 10501-700 | 938 | 46501-800 | 934 | 64901-65000 | 976 | 83801-900 | 975 |
| 10701-900 | 936 | 46801-47000 | 930 | 65001-200 | 973 | 83901-84000 | 969 |
| 10901-11000 | 938 | 47001-500 | 927 | 65201-300 | 977 | 84001-400 | 974 |
| 11001-12000 | 936 | 47501-700 | 935 | 65301-400 | 975 | 84401-500 | 970 |
| 12001-200 | 939 | 47701-48000 | 931 | 65401-500 | 973 | 84501-700 | 972 |
| 12201-13000 | 937 | 48001-05 | 942 | 65501-700 | 977 | 84701-800 | 968 |
| 13001-400 | 999 | 48006-300 | 940 | 65701-900 | 975 | 84801-85000 | 976 |
| 13401-14000 | 938 | 48301-500 | 942 | 65901-66000 | 977 | 85001-200 | 937 |
| 14001-15000 | 999 | 48501-900 | 940 | 66001-200 | 976 | 85201-900 | 941 |
| 15001-300 | 939 | 48901-49000 | 942 | 66201-300 | 974 | 85901-86000 | 943 |
| 15301-15401 | 21J | 49001-400 | 927 | 66301-500 | 972 | 86001-87000 | 928 |
| 15302-700 | 937 | 49401-900 | 925 | 66501-600 | 976 | 87001-88000 | 929 |
| 15701-16000 | 939 | 49901-50 | 11J | 66601-700 | 974 | 88001-500 | 926 |
| 16001-100 | 931 | 50071-500 | 962 | 66701-800 | 972 | 88501-89000 | 930 |
| 16101-200 | 930 | 50501-750 | 960 | 66801-67000 | 074 | 89001-500 | 941 |
| 16201-300 | 927 | 50751-50850 | 964 | 67001-100 | 977 | 89501-90000 | 937 |
| 16301-400 | 931 | 50851-51000 | 960 | 67101-300 | 975 | 90001-100 | 926 |
| 16401-600 | 927 | 51001-51300 | 16s | 67301-600 | 973 | 90101-950 | 999 |
| 16601-17000 | 931 | 51301-400 | 963 | 67601-800 | 975 | 91001-92000 | 925 |
| 17001-500 | 929 | 51401-650 | 961 | 67801-68000 | 977 | 92001-200 | 940 |
| 17501-18000 | 931 | 51651-720 | 965 | 68001-800 | 960 | 92201-93000 | 936 |
| 18001-200 | 928 | 51751-52000 | 961 | 68801-69000 | 964 | 93001-94000 | 927 |
| 18201-300 | 926 | 52001-300 | 16s | 69001-100 | 977 | 94001-003 | 934 |
| 18301-500 | 928 | 52301-500 | 976 | 69101-200 | 975 | 94004-95000 | 928 |
| 18501-19500 | 930 | 52501-700 | 974 | 69201-400 | 973 | 95001-96000 | 923 |
| 19501-700 | 926 | 52701-800 | 966 | 69401-600 | 975 | 96001-100 | 942 |
| 19701-20000 | 930 | 52801-53000 | 976 | 69601-70000 | 977 | 96101-700 | 940 |
| 20001-300 | 934 | 53001-53070 | 16s | 70001-200 | 976 | 96701-97000 | 936 |
| 20301-500 | 926 | 53071-53500 | 977 | 70201-400 | 970 | 97001-900 | 929 |
| 20501-21000 | 999 | 53501-900 | 975 | 70401-600 | 968 | 97901-98000 | 927 |
| 21001-300 | 935 | 53901-54000 | 967 | 70601-900 | 972 | 98001-99000 | 924 |
| 21301-500 | 927 | 54001-200 | 972 | 70901-71000 | 974 | 99001-100000 | 925 |
| 21501-800 | 935 | 54201-300 | 974 | 71001-200 | 975 | 100001-101000 | 924 |
| 21801-22500 | 927 | 54301-500 | 976 | 71201-500 | 971 | 101001-102000 | 925 |
| 22501-800 | 931 | 54501-700 | 974 | 71501-700 | 975 | 102001-103000 | 922 |
| 22801-23000 | 935 | 54701-800 | 968 | 71701-90 | 973 | 103001-104000 | 927 |
| 23001-200 | 928 | 54801-55000 | 976 | 71791-800 | 969 | 104001-105000 | 940 |
| 23201-500 | 7J | 55001-300 | 973 | 71801-900 | 977 | 105001-500 | 925 |
| 24001-500 | 926 | 55301-600 | 977 | 71901-72000 | 975 | 105501-106000 | 927 |
| 24501-25000 | 934 | 55601-700 | 969 | 72001-100 | 974 | 106001-107000 | 940 |
| 25001-100 | 11J | 55701-800 | 977 | 72101-300 | 976 | 107001-400 | 941 |
| 25101-400 | 927 | 55801-56000 | 975 | 72301-600 | 974 | 107401-500 | 943 |
| 25401-800 | 931 | 56001-300 | 974 | 72601-700 | 968 | 107501-800 | 941 |
| 25801-26000 | 935 | 56301-500 | 976 | 72701-900 | 976 | 107801-108000 | 943 |
| 26001-500 | 930 | 56501-600 | 966 | 72901-73000 | 972 | 108001-200 | 928 |
| 26501-27000 | 928 | 56601-800 | 972 | | | | |

| Serial | Grade | Serial | Grade | Serial | Grade | Serial | Grade |
|---|---|---|---|---|---|---|---|
| 108201-109000 | 926 | 186001-187000 | 942 | 275202-460 | HWW* | 322001-323000 | 974 |
| 109001-500 | 927 | 187001-188000 | 927 | 275462-500 | HWW* | 323001-700 | 975 |
| 109501-110000 | 925 | 188001-189000 | 024 | 276001-277000 | 940 | 323701-324000 | 973 |
| 110001-900 | 940 | 189001-190000 | 925 | 277001-278000 | 941 | 324001-325000 | 960 |
| 110901-111000 | 942 | 190001-191000 | 926 | 278001-279000 | 940 | 325001-100 | 965 |
| 111001-500 | 937 | 191001-192000 | 927 | 279001-280000 | 925 | 325101-326000 | 961 |
| 111501-112000 | 941 | 192001-193000 | 924 | 280001-281000 | 936 | 326001-327000 | 974 |
| 112001-200 | 928 | 193001-194000 | 925 | 281001-282000 | 927 | 327001-300 | 971 |
| 112201-113000 | 926 | 194001-195000 | 926 | 282001-283000 | 926 | 327301-500 | 975 |
| 113001-114000 | 925 | 195001-500 | 935 | 283001-284000 | 925 | 327501-328000 | 975 |
| 114001-003 | 940 | 195501-196000 | 927 | 284001-500 | 934 | 328001-300 | 992 |
| 114004-115000 | 936 | 196001-197000 | 926 | 284501-900 | 924 | 328301-500 | 990 |
| 115001-116000 | 927 | 197001-198000 | 937 | 284901-285000 | 999 | 328501-329000 | 992 |
| 116001-117000 | 940 | 198001-199000 | 936 | 285001-286000 | 925 | 329001-330000 | 975 |
| 117001-118000 | 925 | 199001-200000 | 925 | 286001-287000 | 940 | 330001-100 | 992 |
| 118001-119000 | 999 | 200001-201000 | 926 | 287001-288000 | 927 | 330101-500 | 990 |
| 119001-120000 | 925 | 201001-202000 | 925 | 288001-289000 | 940 | 330501-331000 | 992 |
| 120001-121000 | 924 | 202001-500 | 926 | 289001-290000 | 927 | 331001-200 | 973 |
| 121001-500 | 941 | 202501-203000 | 934 | 290001-800 | 936 | 331201-400 | 975 |
| 121501-122000 | 943 | 203001-204000 | 927 | 290801-291000 | 938 | 331401-500 | 969 |
| 122001-300 | 940 | 204001-100 | 934 | 291001-292000 | 925 | 331501-700 | 971 |
| 122301-400 | 942 | 204101-500 | 926 | 292001-500 | 940 | 331701-800 | 973 |
| 122401-123000 | 940 | 204501-205000 | 934 | 292501-293000 | 942 | 331801-332000 | 975 |
| 123001-124000 | 941 | 205001-206000 | 941 | 293001-294000 | 925 | 332001-200 | 992 |
| 124001-100 | 942 | 206001-207000 | 940 | 294001-295000 | 926 | 332201-800 | 972 |
| 124101-800 | 940 | 207001-208000 | 927 | 295001-296000 | 927 | 332801-333000 | 974 |
| 124801-125000 | 942 | 208001-900 | 999 | 296001-297000 | 940 | 333001-500 | 975 |
| 125001-126000 | 927 | 208901-209000 | 940 | 297001-298000 | 927 | 333501-700 | 971 |
| 126001-127000 | 924 | 209001-210000 | 925 | 298001-299000 | 940 | 333701-900 | 973 |
| 127001-128000 | 941 | 210001-211000 | 940 | 299001-300000 | 925 | 333901-334000 | 975 |
| 128001-129000 | 936 | 211001-212000 | 927 | 300001-300 | 940 | 334001-200 | 972 |
| 129001-130000 | 925 | 212001-213000 | 940 | 300301-600 | 970 | 334201-800 | 992 |
| 130001-500 | 924 | 213001-500 | 941 | 300601-900 | 974 | 334801-335000 | 990 |
| 130501-131000 | 926 | 213501-600 | 937 | 300901-301000 | 968 | 335001-600 | 975 |
| 131001-132000 | 925 | 213601-214000 | 925 | 301001-400 | 975 | 335601-800 | 971 |
| 132001-100 | 926 | 214001-215000 | 924 | 301401-500 | 971 | 335801-900 | 973 |
| 132101-200 | 934 | 215001-216000 | 927 | 301501-302000 | 973 | 335901-336000 | 975 |
| 132201-500 | 926 | 216001-217000 | 940 | 302001-100 | 990 | 336001-200 | 972 |
| 132501-133000 | 924 | 217001-218000 | 927 | 302101-200 | 992 | 336201-337000 | 974 |
| 133001-134000 | 937 | 218001-219000 | 940 | 302201-300 | 990 | 337001-338000 | 975 |
| 134001-135000 | 924 | 219001-220000 | 925 | 302301-900 | 992 | 338001-200 | 974 |
| 135001-136000 | 925 | 220001-221000 | 924 | 302901-303000 | 990 | 338201-900 | 992 |
| 136001-137000 | 926 | 221001-222000 | 927 | 303001-100 | 973 | 338901-339000 | 990 |
| 137001-100 | 11J | 222001-223000 | 926 | 303101-300 | 971 | 339001-300 | 971 |
| 137101-138000 | 927 | 223001-02 | 927 | 303301-900 | 975 | 339301-500 | 973 |
| 138001-139000 | 940 | 223003-04 | 941 | 303801-304000 | 973 | 339501-340000 | 975 |
| 139001-140000 | 937 | 223005 | 937 | 304001-100 | 970 | 340001-200 | 974 |
| 140001-300 | 938 | 223006-224000 | 927 | 304101-400 | 972 | 340201-300 | 972 |
| 140301-141000 | 942 | 224001-225000 | 924 | 304401-305000 | 974 | 340301-600 | 970 |
| 141001-142000 | 941 | 225001-226000 | 927 | 305001-100 | 973 | 340601-341000 | 974 |
| 142001-143000 | 940 | 226001-227000 | 940 | 305101-200 | 971 | 341001-200 | 973 |
| 143001-100 | 927 | 227001-228000 | 925 | 305201-900 | 969 | 341201-342000 | 975 |
| 143101-144000 | 925 | 228001-229000 | 924 | 305301-900 | 975 | 342001-300 | 990 |
| 144001-145000 | 924 | 229001-230000 | 925 | 305901-306000 | 973 | 342301-343000 | 992 |
| 145001-146000 | 925 | 230001-500 | 926 | 306001-400 | 972 | 343001-344000 | 975 |
| 146001-400 | 934 | 230501-231000 | 924 | 306401-307000 | 974 | 344001-200 | 970 |
| 146401-147000 | 924 | 231001-565 | 937 | 307001-100 | 975 | 344201-400 | 972 |
| 147001-148000 | 927 | 231566-232000 | 927 | 307101-300 | 971 | 344401-345000 | 974 |
| 148001-149000 | 940 | 232001-233000 | 940 | 307301-400 | 975 | 345001-346000 | 975 |
| 149001-150000 | 925 | 233001-234000 | 941 | 307401-500 | 973 | 346001-300 | 992 |
| 150001-151000 | 924 | 234001-235000 | 940 | 307501-600 | 975 | 346301-347000 | 974 |
| 151001-400 | 927 | 235001-236000 | 941 | 307601-700 | 971 | 347001-180 | 993 |
| 151401-500 | 935 | 236001-237000 | 936 | 307701-900 | 975 | 347181-200 | 991 |
| 151501-152000 | 927 | 237001-238000 | 941 | 307901-308000 | 969 | 347201-300 | 975 |
| 152001-153000 | 936 | 238001-239000 | 926 | 308001-700 | 990 | 347301-400 | 973 |
| 153001-154000 | 941 | 239001-500 | 943 | 308701-309000 | 992 | 347401-700 | 993 |
| 154001-155000 | 936 | 239501-240000 | 941 | 309001-100 | 971 | 347701-900 | 991 |
| 155001-156000 | 927 | 240001-241000 | 940 | 309101-400 | 973 | 347901-348000 | 973 |
| 156001-157000 | 940 | 241001-242000 | 941 | 309401-310000 | 975 | 348001-200 | 970 |
| 157001-158000 | 925 | 242001-243000 | 940 | 310001-400 | 970 | 348201-800 | 974 |
| 158001-159000 | 940 | 243001-244000 | 927 | 310401-311000 | 974 | 348801-349000 | 972 |
| 159001-160000 | 941 | 244001-245000 | 936 | 311001-700 | 975 | 349001-350000 | 975 |
| 160001-161000 | 940 | 245001-246000 | 925 | 311701-312000 | 973 | 350001-300 | 990 |
| 161001-162000 | 941 | 246001-247000 | 940 | 312001-200 | 970 | 350301-400 | 974 |
| 162001-163000 | 926 | 247001-248000 | 927 | 312201-500 | 972 | 350401-600 | 990 |
| 163001-164000 | 943 | 248001-249000 | 940 | 312501-600 | 968 | 350601-351000 | 992 |
| 164001-165000 | 940 | 249001-250000 | 927 | 312601-313000 | 974 | 351001-352000 | 975 |
| 165001-166000 | 925 | 250001-251000 | 926 | 313001-100 | 973 | 352001-100 | 968 |
| 166001-167000 | 924 | 251001-252000 | 927 | 313101-400 | 971 | 352101-353000 | 974 |
| 167001-168000 | 927 | 252001-253000 | 924 | 313401-600 | 969 | 353001-354000 | 975 |
| 168001-169000 | 940 | 253001-254000 | 925 | 313601-314000 | 975 | 354001-400 | 992 |
| 169001-400 | 935 | 254001-255000 | 940 | 314001-600 | 974 | 354401-355000 | 975 |
| 169401-170000 | 927 | 255001-256000 | 925 | 314601-900 | 972 | 355001-800 | 975 |
| 170001-171000 | 999 | 256001-257000 | 926 | 314901-315000 | 970 | 355801-900 | 973 |
| 171001-172000 | 925 | 257001-258000 | 941 | 315001-100 | 971 | 355901-356000 | 993 |
| 172001-100 | 934 | 258001-259000 | 924 | 315101-400 | 973 | 356001-500 | 990 |
| 172101-173000 | 926 | 259001-260000 | 941 | 315401-316000 | 975 | 356501-357000 | 974 |
| 173001-174000 | 940 | 260001-261000 | 940 | 316001-200 | 992 | 357001-358000 | 975 |
| 174001-175000 | 924 | 261001-262000 | 927 | 316201-300 | 972 | 358001-359000 | 974 |
| 175002-176000 | HWW* | 262001-263000 | 926 | 316301-500 | 992 | 359001-360000 | 975 |
| 175001-699 | HWW* | 263001-264000 | 925 | 316501-317000 | 972 | 360001-550 | 960 |
| 176001-177000 | 940 | 264001-265000 | 940 | 317001-600 | 960 | 360801-361000 | 993 |
| 177001-178000 | 927 | 265001-266000 | 940 | 317601-700 | 969 | 361001-100 | 993 |
| 178001-179000 | 942 | 266001-267000 | 940 | 317701-318000 | 973 | 361101-300 | 991 |
| 179001-500 | 935 | 267001-268000 | 925 | 318001-100 | 972 | 361301-400 | 993 |
| 179501-180000 | 927 | 268001-269000 | 940 | 318101-900 | 974 | 361401-700 | 975 |
| 180001-181000 | 940 | 269001-270000 | 927 | 318901-319000 | 970 | 361701-20 | 973 |
| 181001-182000 | 941 | 270001-271000 | 940 | 319001-100 | 971 | 361721-362000 | 975 |
| 182001-300 | 926 | 271001-272000 | 925 | 319101-320000 | 975 | 362001-900 | 974 |
| 182301-400 | 934 | 272001-273000 | 926 | 320001-300 | 972 | 362901-363000 | 990 |
| 182401-183000 | 926 | 273001-274000 | 941 | 320301-400 | 968 | 363001-364000 | 975 |
| 183001-184000 | 941 | 274001-275000 | 924 | 320401-321000 | 974 | 364001-365000 | 974 |
| 184001-185000 | 940 | 275002-100 | HWW* | 321001-200 | 973 | 365001-100 | 975 |
| 185001-186000 | 925 | 275102-200 | HWW* | 321201-322000 | 975 | 365101-300 | 973 |

| Serial Range | Grade | Serial Range | Grade | Serial Range | Grade | Serial Range | Grade |
|---|---|---|---|---|---|---|---|
| 365301-366000 | 975 | 441001-442000 | 940 | 568001-569000 | 936 | 667001-668000 | 941 |
| 366001-367000 | 974 | 442001-400 | 946 | 569001-571000 | 924 | 668001-669000 | 926 |
| 367001-500 | 975 | 442401-500 | 942 | 571001-576000 | 940 | 669001-670000 | 999 |
| 367501-368000 | 993 | 442501-443000 | 946 | 576001-200 | 942 | 670001-100 | 937 |
| 368001-369000 | 974 | 443001-444000 | 926 | 576201-578000 | 940 | 670101-500 | 925 |
| 369001-370000 | 992 | 444001-445000 | 924 | 578001-580000 | 924 | 670501-673000 | 925 |
| 370001-100 | 990 | 445001-446000 | 927 | 580001-582000 | 926 | 673001-675000 | 926 |
| 370101-400 | 992 | 446001-447000 | 924 | 582001-584000 | 925 | 675001-677000 | 940 |
| 370401-500 | 974 | 447001-448000 | 925 | 584001-585000 | 927 | 677001-678000 | 924 |
| 370501-800 | 990 | 448001-449000 | 926 | 585001-587000 | 999 | 678001-679200 | 927 |
| 370801-371400 | 992 | 449001-450000 | 924 | 587001-592000 | 940 | 679201-680000 | 926 |
| 371401-500 | 972 | 450001-451000 | 926 | 592001-593000 | 926 | 680001-685000 | 924 |
| 371501-373500 | 974 | 451001-452000 | 925 | 593001-594000 | 924 | 685001-687000 | 940 |
| 373501-700 | 990 | 452001-453000 | 940 | 594001-601000 | 940 | 687001-688000 | 925 |
| 373701-374000 | 992 | 453001-454000 | 924 | B600001-601000 | 999 Ball | 688001-689000 | 946 |
| 374001-200 | 974 | 454001-456000 | 940 | 601001-601800 | 926 | 689001-694000 | 940 |
| 374201-700 | 990 | 456001-457000 | 999 | B601001-601800 | 999 Ball | 694001-696000 | 924 |
| 374701-375000 | 974 | 457001-458000 | 940 | 601801-602000 | 934 | 696001-697000 | 941 |
| 375001-100 | 993 | 458001-459000 | 999 | B601801-602000 | 999 Ball | 697001-700000 | 924 |
| 375101-500 | 991 | 459001-110 | 946 | 602001-603000 | 926 | 700001-702000 | 974 |
| 375501-376000 | 975 | 459111-118 | 942 | B602001-603000 | 999 Ball | 702001-703800 | 992 |
| 376001-200 | 972 | 459119-200 | 946 | 603001-604000 | 926 | 703801-704000 | 990 |
| 376201-500 | 974 | 459201-700 | 942 | B603001-604000 | 999 Ball | 704001-400 | 992 |
| 376501-377000 | 992 | 459701-460000 | 946 | 604001-605000 | 926 | 704401-705000 | 990 |
| 377001-200 | 973 | 460001-461900 | 940 | B604001-605000 | 999 Ball | 705001-700 | 972 |
| 377201-378000 | 975 | 461901-462000 | 940 | 605001-606000 | 925 | 705701-706000 | 974 |
| 378001-379000 | 974 | 462001-463000 | 999 | B605001-606000 | 999 Ball | 706001-707000 | 990 |
| 379001-380800 | 992 | 463001-500 | 940 | 606001-607000 | 925 | 707001-800 | 972 |
| 380801-381000 | 990 | 463501-464000 | 940 | B606001-607000 | 999 Ball | 707801-708000 | 990 |
| 381001-382000 | 992 | 464001-466000 | 926 | 607001-608000 | 925 | 708001-709500 | 975 |
| 382001-100 | 990 | 466001-467000 | 924 | B607001-608000 | 999 Ball | 709501-710000 | 973 |
| 382101-383000 | 974 | 467001-468000 | 926 | 608001-613000 | 924 | 710001-800 | 993 |
| 383001-300 | 992 | 468001-469000 | 940 | B608001-613000 | 999 Ball | 710801-711000 | 991 |
| 383301-700 | 990 | 469001-470000 | 924 | 613001-614000 | 925 | 711001-300 | 973 |
| 383701-384000 | 972 | 470001-471000 | 926 | B613001-614000 | 999 Ball | 711301-712000 | 975 |
| 384001-700 | 974 | 471001-472000 | 946 | 614001-616500 | 924 | 712001-600 | 993 |
| 384701-900 | 972 | 472001-473000 | 924 | B614001-616500 | 999 Ball | 712601-713000 | 991 |
| 384901-385000 | 974 | 473001-474000 | 940 | 616501-617000 | 934 | 713001-714900 | 975 |
| 385001-600 | 972 | 474001-475000 | 924 | B616501-617000 | 999 Ball | 714901-715000 | 991 |
| 385601-800 | 974 | 475001-476000 | 940 | 617001-619000 | 926 | 715001-716000 | 993 |
| 385801-386000 | 990 | 476001-477000 | 924 | B617001-619000 | 999 Ball | 716001-100 | 972 |
| 386001-800 | 974 | 477001-478000 | 940 | 619001-620000 | 927 | 716101-717000 | 974 |
| 386801-900 | 992 | 478001-479000 | 926 | B619001-620000 | 999 Ball | 717001-200 | 991 |
| 386901-387000 | 972 | 479001-480000 | 944 | 620001-622700 | 940 | 717201-718000 | 975L |
| 387001-100 | 990 | 480001-481000 | 926 | B620001-622700 | 999 Ball | 718001-721500 | 974 |
| 387101-900 | 992 | 481001-482000 | 927 | 622701-623000 | 942 | 721501-722000 | 992 |
| 387901-388000 | 972 | 482001-483000 | 924 | B622701-623000 | 999 Ball | 722001-724000 | 974 |
| 388001-400 | 990 | 483001-484000 | 926 | 623001-624000 | 941 | 724001-725000 | 972 |
| 388401-389000 | 992 | 484001-485000 | 940 | B623001-624000 | 999 Ball | 725001-726000 | 974 |
| 389001-391000 | 974 | 485001-486000 | 925 | 624001-625000 | 936 | 726001-727000 | 992 |
| 391001-300 | 972 | 486001-487000 | 999 | B624001-625000 | 999 Ball | 727001-728000 | 974 |
| 391301-392000 | 974 | 487001-488000 | 924 | 625001-626000 | 925 | 728001-729000 | 992 |
| 392001-800 | 992 | 488001-489000 | 999 | B625001-626000 | 999 Ball | 729001-730000 | 975 |
| 392801-393000 | 990 | 489001-492000 | 924 | 626001-627000 | 926 | 730001-731000 | 992 |
| 393001-400 | 975 | 492001-493000 | 940 | B626001-627000 | 999 Ball | 731001-732000 | 975 |
| 393401-600 | 973 | 493001-494000 | 946 | 627001-628000 | 924 | 732001-734000 | 992 |
| 393601-394000 | 993 | 494001-495000 | 944 | B627001-628000 | 999 Ball | 734001-735000 | 975 |
| 394001-200 | 972 | 495001-496000 | 940 | 628001-630800 | 925 | 735001-736000 | 974 |
| 394201-395000 | 974 | 496001-497000 | 925 | B628001-630800 | 999 Ball | 736001-738000 | 975 |
| 395001-100 | 993 | 497001-498000 | 999 | 631001-636000 | 940 | 738001-739000 | 974 |
| 395101-900 | 991 | 498001-499000 | 936 | B631001-636000 | 999 Ball | 739001-740000 | 975 |
| 395901-396000 | 993 | 499001-501000 | 940 | 636001-637000 | 941 | 740001-100 | 974 |
| 396001-397000 | 992 | 501001-900 | 926 | B636001-637000 | 999 Ball | 740101-200 | 972 |
| 397001-200 | 990 | 501901-502000 | 934 | 637001-638000 | 936 | 740201-900 | 974 |
| 397201-398000 | 992 | 502001-503000 | 926 | B637001-638000 | 999 Ball | 740901-741000 | 975 |
| 398001-200 | 972 | 503001-504000 | 999 | 638001-639000 | 926 | 741001-742000 | 992 |
| 398201-399000 | 992 | 504001-507000 | 940 | B638001-639000 | 999 Ball | 742001-743000 | 974 |
| 399001-600 | 993 | 507001-508000 | 999 | 639001-640000 | 925 | 743001-300 | 975 |
| 399601-400000 | 975 | 508001-509900 | 940 | B639001-640000 | 999 Ball | 743301-400 | 993 |
| 400001-401000 | 924 | 509901-510000 | 942 | 640001-642000 | 924 | 743401-744000 | 975 |
| 401001-402000 | 940 | 510001-511500 | 940 | B640001-644400 | 999 Ball | 744001-500 | 974 |
| 402001-404000 | 924 | 511501-700 | 942 | 644401-645000 | 940 | 744501-745000 | 992 |
| 404001-405000 | 926 | 511701-517000 | 940 | 645001-645500 | 927 | 745001-747000 | 975 |
| 405001-406000 | 924 | 517001-519000 | 924 | B645001-645500 | 999 Ball | 747001-700 | 972 |
| 406001-407000 | 940 | 519001-521000 | 925 | 645501-646000 | 925 | 747701-748000 | 972 |
| 407001-408000 | 926 | 521001-523000 | 944 | B645501-646000 | 999 Ball | 748001-749500 | 992 |
| 408001-416000 | 940 | 523001-524000 | 946 | 646001-647000 | 926 | 749501-750000 | 974 |
| 416001-417000 | 926 | 524001-531000 | 940 | B646001-647000 | 999 Ball | 750001-100 | 961 |
| 417001-418000 | 940 | 531001-532000 | 926 | 647001-648000 | 940 | 750101-200 | 961 |
| 418001-419000 | 926 | 532001-10 | 934 | B647001-648000 | 999 Ball | 750201-700 | 950 |
| 419001-420000 | 941 | 532011-533000 | 926 | 648001-649000 | 940 | 750701-751000 | 952 |
| 420001-421000 | 940 | 533001-535500 | 999 | B648001-649000 | 998 Ball | 751001-752000 | 960 |
| 421001-422000 | 926 | 535501-536000 | 940 | B649001-650000 | 998 Ball | 752001-500 | 952 |
| 422001-423000 | 924 | 536001-537000 | 936 | B650001-651000 | 999 Ball | 752501-753000 | 950 |
| 423001-425000 | 926 | 537001-538000 | 924 | 651001-652000 | 940 | 753001-500 | 952 |
| 425001-426000 | 924 | 538001-543000 | 940 | B651001-652000 | 998 Ball | 753501-754000 | 950 |
| 426001-500 | 936 | 543001-544000 | 927 | 652001-652700 | 924 | 754001-100 | 960 |
| 426501-427000 | 944 | 544001-200 | 934 | B652001-652700 | 998 Ball | 754101-500 | 960 |
| 427001-428000 | 924 | 544201-545000 | 926 | 652701-652800 | 924 | 754501-755000 | 960 |
| 428001-429000 | 926 | 545001-546000 | 925 | 652801-652900 | 927 | 755001-400 | 992 |
| 429001-430000 | 925 | 546001-547000 | 924 | 652901-653000 | 937 | 755401-500 | 974 |
| 430001-431000 | 924 | 547001-548000 | 926 | 653001-655000 | 940 | 755501-700 | 972 |
| 431001-432000 | 925 | 548001-549000 | 999 | B653001-655000 | 999 Ball | 755701-900 | 974 |
| 432001-433000 | 940 | 549001-551000 | 946 | 655001-655200 | 924 | 755901-756000 | 972 |
| 433001-434000 | 924 | 551001-553000 | 944 | B655001-655200 | 999 Ball | 756001-757000 | 975 |
| 434001-500 | 940 | 553001-555000 | 940 | 655201-656000 | 924 | 757001-300 | 975 |
| 434501-600 | 942 | 555001-556000 | 936 | 656001-657000 | 926 | 757301-500 | 993 |
| 434601-435000 | 946 | 556001-558000 | 924 | 657001-659000 | 927 | 757501-758000 | 975 |
| 435001-436000 | 924 | 558001-560000 | 925 | 659001-660000 | 925 | 758001-100 | 972 |
| 436001-438500 | 940 | 560001-561000 | 999 | 660001-661000 | 927 | 758101-759000 | 992 |
| 438501-800 | 946 | 561001-562000 | 926 | 661001-662000 | 924 | 759001-760000 | 975 |
| 438801-900 | 942 | 562001-564000 | 924 | 662001-664000 | 940 | 760001-400 | 992 |
| 438901-440000 | 946 | 564001-565000 | 926 | 664001-666000 | 924 | 760401-600 | 972 |
| 440001-441000 | 924 | 565001-568000 | 940 | 666001-667000 | 940 | 760601-800 | 974 |
|  |  |  |  |  |  | 760801-761000 | 992 |

| Serial | Code | Serial | Code | Serial | Code | Serial | Code |
|---|---|---|---|---|---|---|---|
| 761001-400 | 975 | 826001-500 | 975L | 898001-899100 | 992 | 1051001-200 | 975 |
| 761401-600 | 993 | 826501-827000 | 993 | 899101-500 | 978 | 1051201-1052000 | 993 |
| 761601-762000 | 975 | 827001-828000 | 975P | 899501-900000 | 974 | 1052001-500 | 972P |
| 762001-200 | 992 | 828001-829000 | 974L | 900001-902000 | 940 | 1052501-900 | 954 |
| 762201-300 | 972 | 829001-830000 | 974P | 902001-904000 | 926 | 1052901-1053000 | 974 |
| 762301-763000 | 974 | 830001-500 | 990L | 904001-906000 | 924 | 1053001-1054000 | 992 |
| 763001-300 | 993 | 830501-831000 | 992L | 906001-914000 | 940 | 1054001-1056000 | 974 |
| 763301-600 | 973 | 831001-100 | 954P | 914001-916000 | 926 | 1056001-1057000 | 975 |
| 763601-764000 | 975 | 831101-200 | 972P | 916001-917000 | 927 | 1057001-1061300 | 992 |
| 764001-300 | 992 | 831201-500 | 954P | 917001-919000 | 925 | 1061301-1062300 | 972 |
| 764301-400 | 972 | 831501-832000 | 974P | 919001-921000 | 940 | 1062301-1066000 | 992 |
| 764401-765000 | 974 | 832001-400 | 974L | 921001-923000 | 924 | 1066001-1068000 | 974 |
| 765001-300 | 992 | 832401-833000 | 992L | 923001-500 | 999 | 1068001-1069000 | 975 |
| 765301-767000 | 974 | 833001-834000 | 990L | 923501-924000 | 925 | 1069001-1070000 | 974 |
| 767001-600 | 992 | 834001-600 | 974P | 924001-926000 | 940 | 1070001-1071000 | 992L |
| 767601-800 | 972 | 834601-800 | 974L | 926001-100 | 927 | 1071001-1073000 | 975P |
| 767801-768000 | 974 | 834801-835000 | 974P | 927001-929000 | 926 | 1073001-1075000 | 992 |
| 768001-769000 | 975 | 835001-600 | 992L | 929001-933000 | 924 | 1075001-1076200 | 974L |
| 769001-700 | 992 | 835601-800 | 990L | 933001-935000 | 925 | 1076201-700 | 972L |
| 769701-770000 | 972 | 835801-836000 | 974L | 935001-937000 | 926 | 1076701-1077000 | 978L |
| 770001-100 | 974 | 836001-500 | 974P | 937001-939000 | 940 | 1077001-1079000 | 974P |
| 770101-771200 | 992 | 836501-900 | 954P | 939001-941000 | 924 | 1079001-1080000 | 992L |
| 771201-400 | 972 | 836901-837000 | 974P | 941001-944000 | 940 | 1080001-100 | 952L |
| 771401-772000 | 974 | 837001-838000 | 975P | 944001-949000 | 926 | 1080101-200 | 960L |
| 772001-773000 | 975 | 838001-839000 | 975L | 949001-952000 | 925 | 1080201-400 | 994L |
| 773001-800 | 992 | 839001-400 | 974L | 952001-958000 | 924 | 1080401-1081000 | 950L |
| 773801-774000 | 972 | 839401-700 | 992L | 958001-960000 | 926 | 1081001-1082000 | 978L |
| 774001-775000 | 975 | 839701-840000 | 990L | 960001-968000 | 940 | 1082001-400 | 993L |
| 775001-500 | 952 | 840001-400 | 952L | 968001-970000 | 926 | 1082401-1083000 | 973L |
| 775501-776000 | 950 | 840401-900 | 950L | 970001-971700 | 924 | 1083001-1084000 | 990L |
| 776001-300 | 973 | 840901-841000 | 952L | 971701-972000 | 948 | 1084001-1085000 | 992L |
| 776301-700 | 993 | 841001-842000 | 975P | 972001-973000 | 924 | 1085001-1086000 | 992L |
| 776701-777000 | 975 | 842001-843000 | 974L | 973001-974000 | 936 | 1086001-1088000 | 974P |
| 777001-300 | 972 | 843001-844000 | 974P | 974001-975400 | 924 | 1088001-1091000 | 992L |
| 777301-778300 | 974 | 844001-200 | 993 | 975401-25 Spec. | 926 | 1091001-200 | 978L |
| 778301-600 | 992 | 844201-845000 | 975 | 975426-976000 | 924 | 1091201-1092000 | 974L |
| 778601-900 | 972 | 845001-200 | 992 | 976001-979000 | 940 | 1092001-1093000 | 992L |
| 778901-779300 | 974 | 845201-400 | 972 | 979001-100 | 942 | 1093001-1095000 | 974P |
| 779301-780100 | 992 | 845401-700 | 954 | 979101-981000 | 940 | 1095001-1096000 | 992P |
| 780101-300 | 972 | 845701-846000 | 972 | 981001-982000 | 948 | 1096001-400 | 974L |
| 780301-781300 | 992 | 846001-500 | 952 | 982001-984000 | 924 | 1096401-1097000 | 974P |
| 781301-400 | 972 | 846501-847000 | 950 | 984001-986000 | 940 | 1097001-1098000 | 992L |
| 781401-500 | 974 | 847001-200 | 972 | 986001-987000 | 946 | 1098001-400 | 975P |
| 781501-782000 | 992 | 847201-849000 | 974 | 987001-988000 | 936 | 1098401-1099000 | 975L |
| 782001-783000 | 975 | 849001-850000 | 975 | 988001-992000 | 940 | 1099001-600 | 993L |
| 783001-600 | 992 | 850001-300 | 992 | 992001-996000 | 924 | 1099601-1100000 | 975P |
| 783601-784000 | 974 | 850301-800 | 990 | 996001-999998 | 940 | 1100001-1104000 | 992L |
| 784001-785000 | 992 | 850801-851000 | 972 | 999999-1000000 | 947 | 1104001-1105000 | 974P |
| 785001-500 | 952 | 851001-400 | 993 | 1000001-1000300 | 972 | 1105001-1106000 | 992L |
| 785501-786000 | 950 | 851401-852000 | 975 | 1000301-1003000 | 992 | 1106001-500 | 978L |
| 786001-787000 | 992 | 852001-853000 | 992 | 1003001-1004000 | 974 | 1106501-1107000 | 972L |
| 787001-400 | 974 | 853001-854000 | 974 | 1004001-900 | 992 | 1107001-1109000 | 992L |
| 787401-788000 | 972 | 854001-600 | 950 | 1004901-1007100 | 974 | 1109001-1111000 | 972L |
| 788001-791300 | 992 | 854601-900 | 952 | 1007101-1008300 | 992 | 1111001-1112000 | 974L |
| 791301-792600 | 974 | 854901-855100 | 960L | 1008301-1009500 | 974 | 1112001-1113000 | 974P |
| 792601-900 | 972 | 855101-856000 | 950L | 1009501-1010700 | 992 | 1113001-1116000 | 992L |
| 792901-793700 | 992 | 856001-857840 | 975 | 1010701-1011200 | 972 | 1116001-900 | 974P |
| 793701-900 | 990 | 857841-858000 | 975L | 1011201-1012700 | 974 | 1116901-1117000 | 974L |
| 793901-794000 | 992 | 858001-500 | 974 | 1012701-1013000 | 992 | 1117001-1119000 | 992L |
| 794001-200 | 972 | 858501-859000 | 972 | 1013001-1015000 | 978 | 1119001-1120000 | 978L |
| 794201-795000 | 974 | 859001-860000 | 974 | 1015001-300 | 974 | 1120001-1122000 | 992L |
| 795001-796400 | 992 | 860001-862300 | 992 | 1015301-1016000 | 992 | 1122001-1123000 | 974P |
| 796401-800 | 972 | 862301-400 | 954 | 1016001-300 | 975 | 1123001-500 | 972P |
| 796801-797200 | 974 | 862401-500 | 972 | 1016301-600 | 973 | 1123501-1125000 | 974P |
| 797201-500 | 954 | 862501-600 | 954 | 1016601-1018000 | 993 | 1125001-1127000 | 992L |
| 797501-798000 | 974 | 862601-800 | 972 | 1018001-1020000 | 992 | 1127001-1128000 | 972L |
| 798001-500 | 990 | 862801-863000 | 974 | 1020001-1022600 | 950 | 1128001-1129000 | 974L |
| 798501-800 | 972 | 863001-864000 | 992 | 1022601-1023000 | 952 | 1129001-1130500 | 974P |
| 798801-799000 | 974 | 864001-865000 | 975 | 1023001-700 | 992 | 1130501-1131000 | 956P |
| 799001-200 | 954 | 865001-866000 | 992 | 1023701-1024500 | 974 | 1131001-1132000 | 992L |
| 799201-600 | 992 | 866001-600 | 974 | 1024501-600 | 974 | 1132001-1133000 | 990L |
| 799601-800000 | 954 | 866601-700 | 954 | 1024601-1025000 | 972 | 1133001-1134000 | 978L |
| 800001-802000 | 974 | 866701-867000 | 972 | 1025001-1027000 | 975 | 1134001-1135000 | 972L |
| 802001-200 | 954 | 867001-868000 | 975 | 1027001-400 | 993 | 1135001-1137000 | 992L |
| 802001-2 | 972 | 868001-869000 | 992 | 1027401-1029600 | 975 | 1137001-1138000 | 956P |
| 802203-300 | 954 | 869001-870000 | 975 | 1029601-1030000 | 973 | 1138001-1139000 | 956P |
| 802301-500 | 972 | 870001-872000 | 992 | 1030001-1032000 | 992 | 1139001-1140000 | 972L |
| 802501-803700 | 974 | 872001-200 | 993 | 1032001-1033000 | 974 | 1140001-1141000 | 972L |
| 803701-804200 | 954 | 872201-874000 | 975 | 1033001-200 | 972 | 1141001-1142000 | 956P |
| 804201-806000 | 974 | 874001-800 | 974 | 1033201-800 | 954 | 1142001-500 | 974P |
| 806001-807000 | 975 | 874801-875000 | 975 | 1033801-1035300 | 974 | 1142501-1145000 | 974L |
| 807001-500 | 993 | 875001-300 | 952 | 1035301-600 | 972 | 1145001-1146000 | 975P |
| 807501-808800 | 975 | 875301-876000 | 975 | 1035601-1036000 | 974 | 1146001-500 | 956P |
| 808801-809000 | 993 | 876001-600 | 993 | 1036001-300 | 972 | 1146501-1149000 | 974P |
| 809001-500 | 974 | 876601-877000 | 975 | 1036301-800 | 954 | 1149001-1150000 | 974L |
| 809501-600 | 972 | 877001-400 | 992 | 1036801-1037000 | 992L | 1150001-600 | 950L |
| 809601-810000 | 974 | 877401-700 | 975 | 1037001-1038000 | 974 | 1150601-1151800 | 952L |
| 810001-300 | 990 | 877701-878000 | 993 | 1038001-1039000 | 992 | 1151801-1152000 | 952P |
| 810301-812000 | 974 | 878001-879400 | 975 | 1039001-200 | 972 | 1152001-900 | 950P |
| 812001-700 | 992 | 879401-880000 | 992 | 1039201-500 | 978 | 1152901-1153200 | 952P |
| 812701-813000 | 974 | 880001-600 | 992 | 1039501-1040300 | 974 | 1153201-300 | |
| 813001-814000 | 974P | 880601-882400 | 974 | 1040301-1041000 | 992 | 1153301-500 | 994P |
| 814001-800 | 974L | 882401-883400 | 992 | 1041001-1042000 | 974 | 1153501-800 | 994L |
| 814801-815900 | 992 | 883401-884100 | 974 | 1042001-700 | 992 | 1153801-1154000 | 960L |
| 815901-816000 | 974L | 884101-885300 | 992 | 1042701-1043000 | 972 | 1154001-500 | 950L |
| 816001-817000 | 974P | 885301-886000 | 974 | 1043001-700 | 978 | 1154501-1155000 | 950P |
| 817001-819000 | 974L | 886001-600 | 992 | 1043701-1044000 | 992 | 1155001-200 | 994P |
| 819001-820000 | 974P | 886601-887000 | 974 | 1044001-1045000 | 974 | 1155201-500 | 994L |
| 820001-821500 | 974L | 887001-300 | 975 | 1045001-1046000 | 992 | 1155501-1158000 | 996L |
| 821501-822000 | 990L | 887301-890300 | 992 | 1046001-1047000 | 975 | 1158001-1160000 | 974P |
| 822001-700 | 992L | 890301-891000 | 974 | 1047001-1048000 | 974L | 1160001-1162000 | 992L |
| 822701-823000 | 974L | 891001-600 | 992 | 1048001-1049000 | 992 | 1162001-500 | 993L |
| 823001-824000 | 974P | 891601-892200 | 978 | 1049001-500 | 990 | 1162501-1164000 | 992L |
| 824001-826000 | 975P | 892201-896200 | 992 | 1049501-1051000 | 992 | 1164001-1166000 | 974P |
| | | 896201-897800 | 974 | | | | |
| | | 897801-898000 | 972 | | | | |

| Serial Numbers | Grade |
|---|---|
| 1166001-1167000 | 974L |
| 1167001-1168000 | 956P |
| 1168001-1169000 | 975P |
| 1169001-1170000 | 974P |
| 1170001-1174000 | 956P |
| 1174001-1176000 | 974P |
| 1176001-1177000 | 992L |
| 1177001-1178000 | 956P |
| 1178001-1179000 | 974P |
| 1179001-1181000 | 996L |
| 1181001-1182000 | 992L |
| 1182001-1183000 | 996L |
| 1183001-1184400 | 974P |
| 1184401-1185400 | 956P |
| 1185401-1186000 | 974P |
| 1186001-1187000 | 992L |
| 1187001-1188000 | 996L |
| 1188001-1189000 | 992L |
| 1189001-1190000 | 974P |
| 1190001-1192000 | 996L |
| 1192001-1193000 | 975P |
| 1193001-1194000 | 974P |
| 1194001-1195000 | 956P |
| 1195001-1196000 | 974P |
| 1196001-1199000 | 992L |
| 1199001-1201000 | 974P |
| 1201001-1202000 | 975P |
| 1202001-1203000 | 992L |
| 1203001-1204000 | 974P |
| 1204001-500 | 956P |
| 1204501-1206000 | 974P |
| 1206001-1207000 | 992L |
| 1207001-1210000 | 974P |
| 1210001-1212000 | 992L |
| 1212001-1213000 | 974P |
| 1213001-500 | 996L |
| 1213501-1214000 | 992L |
| 1214001-1214600 | 993L |
| 1214601-1215000 | 975P |
| 1215001-1216000 | 974L |
| 1216001-1219000 | 992L |
| 1219001-1220000 | 974P |
| 1220001-1221000 | 992L |
| 1221001-1223500 | 974P |
| 1223501-1224000 | 956P |
| 1224001-1227000 | 992L |
| 1227001-1228000 | 972L |
| 1228001-700 | 992L |
| 1228701-1229000 | 990L |
| 1229001-500 | 956P |
| 1229501-1230000 | 974P |
| 1230001-1231000 | 974L |
| 1231001-1232000 | 992L |
| 1232001-1233000 | 974P |
| 1233001-1236000 | 992L |
| 1236001-500 | 974P |
| 1236501-1237000 | 956P |
| 1237001-500 | 996L |
| 1237501-1238000 | 992L |
| 1238001-1239000 | 956P |
| 1239001-1241000 | 992L |
| 1241001-1242000 | 975P |
| 1242001-400 | 974L |
| 1242401-1243000 | 972L |
| 1243001-500 | 996L |
| 1243501-1244000 | 992L |
| 1244001-1245000 | 974P |
| 1245001-1246000 | 992L |
| 1246001-300 | 974P |
| 1246301-800 | 956P |
| 1246801-1247000 | 974L |
| 1247001-1248000 | 992L |
| 1248001-1249700 | 974P |
| 1249701-1250000 | 956P |
| 1250001-1252000 | 983 |
| 1252001-1253000 | 985 |
| 1253001-1257000 | 983 |
| 1257001-900 | 985 |
| 1260001-970 | Chro.* |
| 1260971-1265000 | |
| 1265001-1266000 | 956P |
| 1266001-1267000 | 974P |
| 1267001-1268200 | 978L |
| 1268201-1269000 | 978L |
| 1269001-600 | 992L |
| 1269601-1270000 | 992L |
| 1270001-1271700 | 956P |
| 1271701-1272000 | 974P |
| 1272001-1274000 | 996L |
| 1274001-500 | 993L |
| 1274501-700 | 992L |
| 1274701-1275000 | 992L |
| 1275001-1276000 | 972L |
| 1276001-1277000 | 974L |
| 1277001-1278000 | 992L |
| 1278001-1279000 | 975P |
| 1279001-1280000 | 974P |
| 1280001-1281000 | 992L |
| 1281001-800 | 974P |
| 1281801-1282000 | 956P |
| 1282001-1284000 | 996L |
| 1284001-1285000 | 992L |
| 1285001-1286000 | 956P |
| 1286001-1288000 | 978L |
| 1288001-500 | 993L |
| 1288501-1289100 | 992L |
| 1289101-700 | 990L |
| 1289701-1290000 | 992L |
| 1290001-1291500 | 974P |
| 1291501-1292000 | 992P |
| 1292001-1297000 | 992L |
| 1297001-1298000 | 974P |
| 1298001-1299000 | 992L |
| 1299001-1300000 | 975P |
| 1300001-1301000 | 974P |
| 1301001-1302000 | 974L |
| 1302001-500 | 992L |
| 1302501-1303000 | 990L |
| 1303001-500 | 972L |
| 1303501-1304000 | 972P |
| 1304001-1305000 | 978L |
| 1305001-1306000 | 956P |
| 1306001-1307000 | 974P |
| 1307001-1308500 | 992L |
| 1308501-1309000 | 993L |
| 1309001-1310000 | 974L |
| 1310001-1311000 | 972L |
| 1311001-1312000 | 992L |
| 1312001-800 | 974P |
| 1312801-1313000 | 956P |
| 1313001-1317000 | 992L |
| 1317001-1318000 | 956P |
| 1318001-1321000 | 992L |
| 1321001-300 | 990L |
| 1321301-1322000 | 992L |
| 1322001-700 | 974L |
| 1322701-1323000 | 972L |
| 1323001-1324000 | 992L |
| 1324001-1325000 | 996L |
| 1325001-1326500 | 975P |
| 1326501-1327000 | 993L |
| 1327001-300 | 956P |
| 1327301-1329000 | 974P |
| 1329001-1330000 | 992L |
| 1330001-1331300 | 974L |
| 1331301-800 | 972L |
| 1331801-1332000 | 978L |
| 1332001-1334000 | 992L |
| 1334001-400 | 974P |
| 1334401-1335000 | 956P |
| 1335001-300 | 978L |
| 1335301-1336000 | 972L |
| 1336001-1337000 | 992L |
| 1337001-1338200 | 996L |
| 1338201-1339000 | 996L |
| 1339001-1340000 | 956P |
| 1340001-1341000 | 992L |
| 1341001-300 | 972L |
| 1341301-500 | 974L |
| 1341501-1342000 | 978L |
| 1342001-1343000 | 992L |
| 1343001-400 | 956P |
| 1343401-1344000 | 974P |
| 1344001-1345000 | 992L |
| 1345001-600 | 974L |
| 1345601-1346000 | 972L |
| 1346001-1348000 | 975P |
| 1348001-1349000 | 974P |
| 1349001-1350000 | 992L |
| 1350001-600 | 972L |
| 1350601-1351000 | 974L |
| 1351001-1352000 | 993L |
| 1352001-1352300 | 974L |
| 1352301-800 | 978L |
| 1352801-1353000 | 974L |
| 1353001-500 | 972P |
| 1353501-1354200 | 956P |
| 1354201-700 | 992P |
| 1354701-1355000 | 974P |
| 1355001-1356000 | 992L |
| 1356001-1357000 | 974P |
| 1357001-1359500 | 992L |
| 1359801-1361000 | 996L |
| 1361001-1362000 | 992L |
| 1362001-600 | 974P |
| 1362601-1363000 | 956P |
| 1363001-1364000 | 992L |
| 1364001-1365000 | 975P |
| 1365001-800 | 956P |
| 1365801-1367000 | 974P |
| 1367001-1369400 | 992L |
| 1369401-1370000 | 996L |
| 1370001-1371000 | 974L |
| 1371001-600 | 996L |
| 1371601-1373000 | 992L |
| 1373001-1374000 | 975P |
| 1374001-1375000 | 992L |
| 1375001-1376000 | 950L |
| 1376001-1377000 | 992L |
| 1377001-1378300 | 974P |
| 1378301-1379000 | 956P |
| 1379001-1380200 | 972L |
| 1380201-1381000 | 978L |
| 1381001-500 | 956P |
| 1381501-1383000 | 974P |
| 1383001-1384000 | 992L |
| 1384001-1386100 | 974P |
| 1386101-1387000 | 956P |
| 1387001-1388000 | 992L |
| 1388001-400 | 978L |
| 1388401-1389000 | 978L |
| 1389001-300 | 956P |
| 1389301-1390000 | 956P |
| 1390001-1391000 | 992L |
| 1391001-500 | 956P |
| 1391501-1392000 | 974P |
| 1392001-1393000 | 992L |
| 1393001-1394000 | 974P |
| 1394001-1396000 | 992L |
| 1396001-500 | 972L |
| 1396501-1398000 | 974L |
| 1398001-400 | 974P |
| 1398401-1399000 | 956P |
| 1399001-1400000 | 992L |
| 1400001-1401000 | 936 |
| 1401001-1403000 | 924 |
| 1403001-1409000 | 940 |
| 1409001-500 | 946 |
| 1409501-1410000 | 940 |
| 1410001-1414000 | 924 |
| 1414001-300 | 941 |
| 1414501-1415000 | 925 |
| 1415001-1417000 | 924 |
| 1417001-1419000 | 940 |
| 1419001-1420000 | 924 |
| 1420001-1421000 | 940 |
| 1421001-1422000 | 924 |
| 1422001-1424000 | 940 |
| 1424001-1428000 | 924 |
| 1428001-1430000 | 940 |
| 1430001-200 | 924 |
| 1430201-400 | 948 |
| 1430401-1431000 | 924 |
| 1431001-1433000 | 940 |
| 1433001-1438000 | 924 |
| 1438001-500 | 926 |
| 1438501-1439500 | 924 |
| 1439501-1440000 | 926 |
| 1440001-1441000 | 940 |
| 1441001-1442000 | 924 |
| 1442001-500 | 926 |
| 1442501-1444000 | 924 |
| 1444001-1445000 | 940 |
| 1445001-1447000 | 924 |
| 1447001-1448200 | 940 |
| 1449001-1450500 | 924 |
| 1500001-600 | 974P |
| 1500601-1501200 | 956P |
| 1501201-1502000 | 974P |
| 1502001-1503000 | 993L |
| 1503001-1504000 | 996L |
| 1504001-500 | 974L |
| 1504501-1505200 | 972L |
| 1505201-700 | 978L |
| 1505701-1506000 | 974L |
| 1506001-1507000 | 975P |
| 1507001-1508000 | 992L |
| 1508001-400 | 974P |
| 1508401-1509000 | 956P |
| 1509001-1510000 | 992L |
| 1510001-1511000 | 974L |
| 1511001-1512000 | 975P |
| 1512001-1513200 | 992L |
| 1513201-600 | 992P |
| 1513601-1514000 | 992L |
| 1514001-200 | 956P |
| 1514201-1515000 | 974P |
| 1515001-1516000 | 992L |
| 1516001-1517000 | 974P |
| 1517001-1520000 | 992L |
| 1520001-1521200 | 974L |
| 1521201-1522000 | 978L |
| 1522001-600 | 974P |
| 1522601-1525000 | 956P |
| 1525001-1527000 | 996L |
| 1527001-1528000 | 992L |
| 1528001-1531000 | 974P |
| 1531001-1533000 | 992L |
| 1533001-600 | 974P |
| 1533601-1534000 | 956P |
| 1534001-100 | 975P |
| 1535101-200 | 975P |
| 1535201-600 | 975P |
| 1535601-1536000 | 993L |
| 1536001-1537000 | 972L |
| 1537001-1538000 | 992L |
| 1538001-800 | 956P |
| 1538801-1539000 | 974P |
| 1539001-1540000 | 992L |
| 1540001-500 | 992P |
| 1540501-1541000 | 992L |
| 1541001-1542200 | 992L |
| 1542201-800 | 956P |
| 1542801-1543000 | 974P |
| 1543001-1544000 | 996L |
| 1544001-1545000 | 992L |
| 1545001-400 | 978L |
| 1545401-1546000 | 974L |
| 1546001-1548000 | 992L |
| 1548001-600 | 974L |
| 1548601-1549000 | 972L |
| 1549001-1550000 | 974P |
| 1550001-500 | 972P |
| 1550501-1552000 | 974P |
| 1552001-1555000 | 992L |
| 1555001-1557000 | 993P |
| 1557001-800 | 972L |
| 1557801-1558000 | 974L |
| 1558001-500 | 956 |
| 1558501-1559700 | 956P |
| 1559701-1560000 | 974P |
| 1560001-1561000 | 975P |
| 1561001-1563000 | 992L |
| 1563001-1565000 | 978L |
| 1565001-1567000 | 992L |
| 1567001-1568000 | 974L |
| 1568001-1569000 | 992L |
| 1569001-1571000 | 972L |
| 1571001-1572000 | 974P |
| 1572001-1573000 | 975P |
| 1573001-1575000 | 974P |
| 1575001-400 | 950L |
| 1575401-1576000 | 950P |
| 1576001-1577000 | 950L |
| 1577001-1578000 | 975P |
| 1578001-1580000 | 992L |
| 1580001-1581200 | 974L |
| 1581201-1582000 | 956P |
| 1582001-1583000 | 974P |
| 1583001-1584000 | 992L |
| 1584001-1585000 | 978L |
| 1585001-1586000 | 972L |
| 1586001-1587000 | 992L |
| 1587001-500 | 992P |
| 1587501-1589000 | 992L |
| 1589001-500 | 956P |
| 1589501-1590000 | 974P |
| 1590001-1591000 | 974L |
| 1591001-1592000 | 992L |
| 1592001-1593000 | 974P |
| 1593001-1595000 | 992L |
| 1595001-200 | 974P |
| 1595201-900 | 956P |
| 1595901-1596000 | 974P |
| 1596001-1611000 | 992L |
| 1611001-1612100 | 974P |
| 1612101-1613000 | 956P |
| 1613001-600 | 996L |
| 1614001-900 | 956P |
| 1614901-1615000 | 974P |
| 1615001-1625000 | 992L |
| 1625001-200 | 950L |
| 1625201-1626000 | 952L |
| 1626001-1627000 | 974P |
| 1627001-1633000 | 992L |
| 1633001-1635000 | 950L |
| 1635001-1636000 | 992L |
| 1636001-1637000 | 956P |
| 1637001-1638000 | 974P |
| 1638001-1642800 | 992L |
| 1642801-1643000 | 992P |
| 1643001-1644000 | 992L |
| 1644001-1646000 | 974L |
| 1646001-1648000 | 972L |
| 1648001-1649000 | 992L |
| 1649001-1652000 | 974P |
| 1652001-1653000 | 950L |
| 1653001-1654000 | 956P |
| 1654001-1657000 | 974P |
| 1657001-1660000 | 992L |
| 1660001-1661000 | 978L |
| 1661001-1663000 | 974P |
| 1663001-1664000 | 974L |
| 1664001-1665000 | 950L |
| 1665001-1666000 | 974P |
| 1666001-1667000 | 956P |
| 1667001-1669000 | 974P |
| 1669001-1670000 | 978L |
| 1670001-1671000 | 992L |
| 1671001-300 | 992L |
| 1671301-900 | 992P |
| 1671901-1672000 | 992L |
| 1672001-1676000 | 974P |
| 1676001-1678000 | 992L |
| 1678001-1679000 | 974P |
| 1679001-1681000 | 974L |
| 1681001-1682000 | 974P |
| 1682001-1683000 | 956P |
| 1683001-1685000 | 974P |
| 1685001-1686000 | 992L |
| 1686001-1688000 | 974P |
| 1688001-500 | 978L |
| 1689001-600 | 975P |
| 1690001-1691000 | 956 |
| 1691001-1693000 | 992L |
| 1693001-1696000 | 956P |
| 1696001-1699000 | 992L |
| 1699001-1703000 | 974P |
| 1703001-1704000 | 992L |
| 1704001-1705000 | 956P |
| 1705001-1706000 | 992L |
| 1706001-1707100 | 974P |
| 1707101-1708000 | 992L |
| 1708001-1714000 | 992L |
| 1714001-1715000 | 974P |
| 1715001-1717000 | 992L |
| 1717001-800 | 956 |
| 1718001-1750000 | 992L |
| 1750001-1761000 | 900 |
| 1761001-1765000 | 914 |
| 1765001-1767000 | 920 |
| 1767001-1768000 | 914 |
| 1768001-1769000 | 900 |
| 1769001-1770000 | 920 |
| 1770001-1778200 | 914 |
| 1778201-1779000 | 910 |
| 1779001-1780000 | 920 |
| 1780001-1782000 | 910 |
| 1782001-500 | 920 |
| 1782501-1783000 | 900 |
| 1783001-1808000 | 910 |
| 1808001-1810000 | 914 |
| 1810001-1811000 | 910 |
| 1811001-1813000 | 900 |
| 1813001-1818000 | 910 |
| 1818001-1819000 | 914 |
| 1819001-1821000 | 910 |

| | | | | | | |
|---|---|---|---|---|---|---|
| 1821001-1822000 | 914 | 1989001-400 | 914 | 2475001-2476000 | 992L | |
| 1822001-1827000 | 910 | 2000001-2001700 | 988 | 2476001-2477000 | 974P | A-001 to A-8900 — 980B |
| 1827001-600 | 914 | 2001701-2002400 | 986 | 2477001-2490000 | 992L | 1B-001 to 1B-18500 — 999B |
| 1827601-1829100 | 910 | 2002401-800 | 988 | 2490001-2492000 | 974L | 2B-001 to 2B-700 — 999B |
| 1829101-500 | 914 | 2002801-2003100 | 986 | 2492001-2504000 | 992L | 2B-701 to 2B-800 — 950B |
| 1829501-1830000 | 910 | 2004001-2035000 | 910 | 2504001-2505000 | 950L | C-001 to C-308100 — 992B |
| 1830001-1831000 | 900 | 2035001-2037200 | 981 | 2505001-300 | 950L | E-001 to E-114000 — 989 |
| 1831001-1832000 | 920 | 2040001-2064900 | 986 | 2506001-2526000 | 992L | E-114001 to E-140400 — 989E |
| 1832001-700 | 910 | 2100001-2191300 | 986A | 2526001-2528000 | 974P | F-101 to F-57600 — 995 |
| 1832701-1833000 | 914 | 2200001-2248000 | 987 | 2528001-2533000 | 992L | F-57601 to F-59850 — 995A |
| 1833301-1834500 | 910 | 2248001-2300000 | 987F | 2533001-2534000 | 974P | F-59851 to F-62000 — 995 |
| 1834501-1835400 | 914 | 2300001-2311000 | 992L | 2534001-2535000 | 992L | F-62001 to F-63000 — 995A |
| 1835401-1836900 | 910 | 2311001-2312000 | 974L | 2535001-2536000 | 974P | F-63001 to F-63800 — 995 |
| 1836901-1837400 | 914 | 2312001-2321700 | 992L | 2536001-2537000 | 974L | F-63801 to F-286200 — 995A |
| 1837401-1839000 | 910 | 2321701-2323000 | 974L | 2537001-2538000 | 974P | G-001 to G-13600 — 980 |
| 1839001-500 | 914 | 2323001-2326000 | 992L | 2538001-2539000 | 974L | G-13601 to G-14600 — 980 & 980A |
| 1839501-1844700 | 910 | 2326001-2327000 | 974P | 2539001-2542000 | 974P | G-14601 to G-44500 — 980 |
| 1844701-1845700 | 914 | 2327001-2333000 | 992L | 2542001-2543000 | 992L | G-44501 to G-45000 — 980A |
| 1845701-1848300 | 910 | 2333001-2336000 | 974P | 2543001-2545000 | 974P | G-45001 to G-47400 — 980 |
| 1848301-1849500 | 914 | 2336001-2338000 | 992L | 2545001-2547000 | 992L | G-47401 to G-48400 — 980A |
| 1849501-1851900 | 910 | 2338001-2339000 | 974P | 2547001-2548400 | 974P | G-48401 to G-58200 — 980 |
| 1851901-1853100 | 914 | 2339001-2340000 | 974L | 2548401-2548600 | 974L | G-58201 to G-58700 — 980A |
| 1853101-1856800 | 910 | 2340001-2341000 | 974P | 2548601-2548700 | 974P | G-58701 to G-61600 — 980 |
| 1856801-1857900 | 914 | 2341001-2346000 | 992L | 2548701-2550000 | 974L | G-61601 to G-62500 — 980A |
| 1857901-1860300 | 910 | 2346001-2347000 | 974P | 2550001-2551000 | 992L | G-62501 to G-67500 — 980 |
| 1860301-1861000 | 914 | 2347001-2356000 | 992L | 2551001-2552000 | 974L | G-67501 to G-68600 — 980A |
| 1861001-1863000 | 900 | 2356001-2358000 | 974P | 2552001-2555000 | 992L | G-68601- to G-651700 — 980 |
| 1863001-700 | 920 | 2358001-2364000 | 992L | 2555001-2555600 | 974L | H-001 to H-1000 — 921 |
| 1863701-1864300 | 900 | 2364001-2365000 | 974P | 2555701-2557000 | 974L | H-1001 to H-1800 — 400 & 921 |
| 1864301-1865000 | 920 | 2365001-2374000 | 992L | 2558001-2560000 | 992L | H-1801 to H-2000 — 921 |
| 1865001-500 | 914 | 2374001-2375000 | 974P | 2560001-2561000 | 974L | H-2001 to H-2800 — 400 & 921 |
| 1865501-1870300 | 910 | 2375001-2378000 | 992L | 2561001-2563000 | 992L | H-2801 to H-3500 — 400 |
| 1870301-1871500 | 914 | 2378001-2380000 | 974L | 2563001-2564000 | 974L | H-3501 to H-45200 — 921 |
| 1871501-1875100 | 910 | 2380001-2383000 | 992L | 2564001-2566000 | 992L | H-50001 to H-57500 — 401 |
| 1875101-600 | 914 | 2383001-2384000 | 950L | 2566001-2566800 | 974L | J-001 to J-619000 — 982 |
| 1875601-1876500 | 910 | 2384001-2385000 | 992L | 2567001-2581000 | 992L | M-001 to M-167800 — 982M |
| 1876501-1877500 | 914 | 2385001-2396000 | 974P | 2581001-2583900 | 992E | N-001 to N-532200 — 721 |
| 1877501-1878700 | 910 | 2386001-2390000 | 992L | 2583901-2584300 | 992L | O-1 to O-486300 — 987A |
| 1878701-1880000 | 914 | 2390001-2391000 | 974P | 2584301-2596000 | 992E | R-001 to R-3600 — 923 |
| 1880001-300 | 920 | 2391001-2393000 | 992L | 2596001-2597000 | 974L | S-001 to S-10000 — 950B |
| 1880301-1881500 | 900 | 2393001-2395000 | 974P | 2597001-2608000 | 992E | SS-001 to SS-87400 — 987S |
| 1881501-700 | 920 | 2395001-2397000 | 992L | 2608001-2608900 | 974L | T-001 to T-783000 — 911 |
| 1881701-900 | 900 | 2397001-2398000 | 974L | 2609001-2611000 | 992E | V-001 to V-127200 — 911M |
| 1881901-1882900 | 920 | 2398001-2401000 | 992L | 2611001-2611400 | 950L | X-001 to X-179700 — 917 |
| 1882901-1885000 | 900 | 2401001-2402000 | 974P | 2611401-2613000 | 950E | Y-001 to Y-273400 — 747 |
| 1885001-1887400 | 910 | 2402001-2407000 | 992L | 2613001-2618000 | 992E | CY-001 to CY-86100 — 748 |
| 1887401-1888600 | 914 | 2407001-2409000 | 974P | 2618001-2619000 | 950E | O-01A to 167400-A — 750 |
| 1888601-1891000 | 910 | 2409001-2413000 | 992L | 2619001-2631000 | 992E | O-01C to 44200-C — 751 |
| 1891001-1892200 | 914 | 2413001-2414000 | 974P | 2631001-2631600 | 950E | |
| 1892201-1894600 | 910 | 2414001-2415000 | 974L | 2631801-2632000 | 950E | |
| 1894601-1895800 | 914 | 2415001-2418000 | 992L | 2632001-2639000 | 992E | |
| 1895801-1899000 | 910 | 2418001-2420000 | 974P | 2639001-2641000 | 950E | |
| 1899001-300 | 900 | 2420001-2422000 | 992L | 2641001-2649000 | 992E | |
| 1899301-1900000 | 920 | 2422001-2423000 | 974P | 2649001-2650000 | 950E | |
| 1900001-400 | 910 | 2423001-2432000 | 992L | 2651001-2655300 | 992E | |
| 1900401-1902100 | 914 | 2432001-2433000 | 974P | 2900001-2911500 | 979 | |
| 1902101-1907000 | 910 | 2433001-2434000 | 992L. | 2911601-2931900 | 979F | |
| 1907001-1909000 | 914 | 2434001-2435000 | 974P | 3000001-3002300 | 922 | |
| 1909001-1910000 | 910 | 2435001-2437000 | 992L | 3002301-3002500 | 922M.P. | |
| 1910001-500 | 920 | 2437001-2438000 | 974P | 3002501-3003000 | 922 | |
| 1910501-1911000 | 900 | 2438001-2442000 | 992L | 3003801-3004000 | 922M.P. | |
| 1911001-1913000 | 920 | 2442001-2445000 | 974P | 3004001-3006000 | 922 | |
| 1913001-1914000 | 900 | 2445001-2451000 | 992L | 3006101-3006300 | 922M.P. | |
| 1914001-1920000 | 910 | 2451001-2453000 | 974P | 3006301-3008000 | 922 | |
| 1920001-1922000 | 920 | 2453001-2455000 | 992L | 3008001-3008600 | 922M.P. | |
| 1922001-1924000 | 910 | 2455001-2456000 | 974P | 3008601-3010000 | 922 | |
| 1924001-1925000 | 900 | 2456001-2457000 | 992L | 3010001-3010500 | 922 | |
| 1925001-1936000 | 910 | 2457001-2458000 | 950L | 3010501-3010700 | 922M.P. | |
| 1936001-1937000 | 920 | 2458001-2459000 | 974L | 3010701-3011900 | 922 | |
| 1937001-900 | 900 | 2459001-2461000 | 992L | 3011901-3012500 | 922M.P. | |
| 1940001-1941000 | 914 | 2461001-2462000 | 974L | 3012501-3013100 | 922 | |
| 1941001-1949000 | 910 | 2462001-2464000 | 992L | 3013101-3013700 | 922M.P. | |
| 1949001-1950000 | 914 | 2464001-2466000 | 974P | 3013701-3015700 | 922 | |
| 1950001-1962000 | 910 | 2466001-2468000 | 992L | 3050001-3054800 | 902 | |
| 1962001-1963000 | 914 | 2468001-2469000 | 974P | 3054801-3056000 | 922 | |
| 1963001-1975000 | 910 | 2469001-2472000 | 992L | 3056001-3060800 | 902 | |
| 1975001-1976000 | 914 | 2472001-2473000 | 974P | 3061001-3065100 | 904 | |
| 1976001-1980000 | 910 | 2473001-2474000 | 992L | 3100001-3133800 | 916 | |
| 1980001-1981000 | 914 | 2474001-2475000 | 974P | 3135001-3152700 | 918 | |
| 1981001-1988500 | 910 | | | 3200001-3460900 | 912 | |
| | | | | 4000001-4447201 | 987F | |
| | | | | 4447301-4523000 | 987E | |

*Hamilton 36 size chronometer watch

* Hayden W. Wheeler model

**NOTE:** The above serial number and grade listing is an actual Hamilton factory list and is accurate in most cases. However, it has been brought to our attention that in rare cases the serial number and grade number do not match the list. One example is the Hayden W. Wheeler model.

(See Hamilton Watch Co. **Serial Numbers and Grades** section located at the end of the Hamilton Watch price section to identify the movement, size and grade of your watch.)

Grade 925, 18 size, 17 jewels, hunting case, serial number 101,495.

Grade 932, 18 size, 16 jewels, open face, serial number 6,888.

## HAMILTON
### 18 SIZE

| Grade or Name — Description | | Avg | Ex-Fn | Mint |
|---|---|---|---|---|
| 7J, OF, LS, FULL | ★ ★ | $1,200 | $1,500 | $2,000 |
| 11J, HC, LS, FULL | ★ ★ ★ | 1,400 | 1,700 | 2,100 |
| 11J, OF, LS, FULL | ★ ★ ★ ★ | 1,600 | 1,900 | 2,300 |
| 922, 15J, OF | ★ ★ | 450 | 550 | 700 |
| 923, 15J, HC | ★ ★ | 500 | 600 | 750 |
| 924, 17J, NI, OF, DMK | | 85 | 100 | 125 |
| 925, 17J, NI, HC, DMK | | 100 | 125 | 175 |
| 926, 17J, NI, OF, DMK, ADJ | | 85 | 100 | 125 |
| 927, 17J, NI, HC, DMK, ADJ | | 100 | 125 | 175 |
| 928, 15J, NI, OF | | 125 | 150 | 200 |
| 929, 15J, NI, HC, 14K | | 600 | 700 | 800 |
| 929, 15J, NI, HC | | 175 | 225 | 300 |
| 930, 16J, NI, OF | | 150 | 200 | 275 |
| 931, 16J, NI, HC | | 200 | 250 | 325 |
| 932 or 936, serial #s less than 50, OF | ★ ★ ★ | 1,500 | 1,900 | 2,500 |
| 932, 16J, NI, OF | ★ ★ | 400 | 450 | 525 |
|    932 (S#s less than 400 up to $1,200) | | | | |
| 933, 16J, NI, HC | ★ ★ | 500 | 550 | 625 |
|    933 ((Serial #s started at 1021, S#s less than 1,300 up to $1,400) | | | | |
| 934, 17J, NI, OF, DMK, ADJ | | 100 | 125 | 175 |
| 934, 17J, NI, OF, ADJ, Coin | | 85 | 100 | 150 |
| 935, 17J, NI, HC, DMK, ADJ. | ★ | 250 | 300 | 375 |
| 936, 17J, NI, OF, DMK, SR & DR | | 85 | 100 | 150 |
|    936 ( S#s less than 400 up to $1,200) | | | | |
| 937, 17J, NI, HC, DMK, SR & DR | | 150 | 200 | 275 |
|    937 (Serial #s started at 1001, S#s less than 1,300 up to $1,200) | | | | |

🕒 Watches listed in this book are priced at the collectable retail level, as **Complete** watches having an original 14k gold-filled case for Stem Wind and *Key Wind* with silver case, an original white enamel single sunk dial, and with the entire original movement in good working order with no repairs needed.

| Grade or Name — Description | | Avg | Ex-Fn | Mint |
|---|---|---|---|---|
| 938, 17J, NI, OF, DMK, DR | ★★ | $500 | $600 | $775 |
| 939, 17J, NI, HC, DMK, DR | ★★ | 600 | 700 | 875 |
| 940, 21J, NI, OF, Mermod Jaccards St. Louis Paragon Time Keeper & an hour glass on mvt. | | 350 | 450 | 550 |
| 940, 21J, NI, OF, DMK, SR & DR, Adj.5P, GJS | | 200 | 225 | 260 |
| 940, 21J, NI, OF, SR & DR, 2-Tone | | 300 | 325 | 375 |
| 940, 21J, NI, OF, DR, Marked Extra | ★ | 350 | 400 | 575 |
| 940, 21J, NI, OF, GF or Coin | | 200 | 225 | 260 |
| 940, 21J, NI, OF, DR, Marked Special | ★ | 350 | 400 | 575 |
| 941, 21J, NI, HC, DR, GJS, | | 250 | 300 | 350 |
| 941, 21J, NI, HC, DR, GJS, Marked Special | ★ | 425 | 475 | 550 |
| 941, 21J, NI, HC, DMK, SR & DR, Adj.5P, GJS | | 250 | 325 | 400 |
| 942, 21J, NI, OF, DMK, DR, Adj.5P, GJS | | 250 | 325 | 375 |
| 943, 21J, NI, HC, DMK, DR, Adj.5P, GJS | ★ | 400 | 450 | 500 |
| 943, 21J, Marked Burlington Special | ★ | 550 | 650 | 800 |
| 944, 19J, NI, OF, DMK, DR, Adj.5P, GJS | | 250 | 275 | 325 |
| 945, 19J, GJS, 2-Tone, HC | ★★ | 1,000 | 1,200 | 1,500 |
| 946, Anderson (jobber name on movement), 14K | | 800 | 1,000 | 1,300 |
| 946, 23J, Marked Extra, OF, GJS | ★ | 550 | 600 | 675 |
| 946, 23J, Marked "Loaner" on case | ★ | 500 | 550 | 625 |
| 946, 23J, NI, OF, DMK, DR, Adj.5P, GJS | | 500 | 550 | 625 |
| 946, 23J, NI, OF, DMK, Adj.5P, GJS, unmarked | | 500 | 550 | 625 |
| 947, 23J, NI, DMK, DR, Adj.5P, GJS, 14K, HC, not marked "947" | ★★★ | 3,500 | 4,000 | 5,000 |

MOVEMENTS WITH ODD GRADE NUMBERS ARE HUNTING CASE.
MOVEMENTS WITH EVEN GRADE NUMBERS ARE OPEN FACE.
Note: Some 18 size movements are marked with grade numbers, some are not. Collectors prefer marked movement.
Note: The first hunting case was a Model number 937 which begins with serial number 1001.

**Grade 947 (marked),** 18 size, 23 jewels, gold jewel settings, hunting case, Adj6p, serial number 163,219.

**Burlington Special,** 18 size, 21 jewels, Grade 943, open face, serial number 121,614.

🕐 Watches listed in this book are priced at the collectable retail level, as **Complete** watches having an original 14k gold-filled case for Stem Wind and *Key Wind* with silver case, an original white enamel single sunk dial, and with the entire original movement in good working order with no repairs needed.

| Grade or Name — Description | Avg | Ex-Fn | Mint |
|---|---|---|---|
| 947, 23J, GJS, Adj.5P, GJS, 14K, HC, marked "947" ..... ★★★★ | $6,000 | $7,000 | $8,000 |
| 947, 23J, GJS, Adj.5P, marked 947 Extra, 14K, HC ..... ★★★★★ | 6,500 | 7,500 | 8,500 |
| 948, 17J, NI, OF, DMK, DR, Adj.5P, GJS.............................. ★ | 300 | 350 | 425 |
| 948, 17J, NI, DMK, DR, Adj.5P, GJS, OF, Coin ..................... ★ | 300 | 350 | 425 |
| The Banner, 928, 15J, NI, OF ............................................. | 125 | 145 | 200 |
| The Banner, 940, 21J, NI, OF ............................................. | 250 | 300 | 365 |
| The Banner, 940 **special**, 21J, NI, OF................................ | 350 | 400 | 500 |
| The Banner, 941, 21J, NI, HC ............................................ | 300 | 350 | 410 |
| The Banner, 17J, M#927, HC, ADJ ..................................... | 125 | 150 | 200 |
| Burlington Special, 17J, Adj.5P, OF .................................. | 300 | 350 | 425 |
| Burlington Special, 17J, Adj.5P, HC .................................. | 350 | 400 | 475 |
| Burlington Special, 21J, Adj.5P, OF .................................. | 400 | 450 | 525 |
| Burlington Special, 21J, Adj.5P, HC .................................. | 450 | 500 | 575 |
| Imperial Canada, GRADE 922, OF ................................. ★ | 600 | 700 | 850 |
| Imperial Canada, GRADE 923, HC ................................ ★ | 700 | 850 | 975 |
| Inspectors Standard, 21J, OF ........................................... | 300 | 350 | 475 |
| RAILROAD watches with R.R. names as | | | |
|     Chesapeake & Ohio 23J .......................................... | 500 | 550 | 650 |
|     Special for Railroad Service 21J .............................. | 300 | 350 | 425 |
|     Official Standard, 17J, G#936 ................................ | 200 | 225 | 275 |
| The Union, 17J ................................................................ | 125 | 145 | 200 |
| The Union Special, 17J ..................................................... | 125 | 145 | 200 |
| The Union, 17J, G#925, HC .............................................. | 200 | 225 | 275 |

Grade 950, 16 size, 23 jewels, pendant set, gold train, gold jewel settings, serial number 1,020,650.

Grade 961, 16 size, 21 jewels, gold train, gold jewel settings, serial number 81,848.

## 16 SIZE

| Grade or Name — Description | Avg | Ex-Fn | Mint |
|---|---|---|---|
| 950, 23J, LS, BRG, DR, GT, 14K ..................................................... | $750 | $850 | $950 |
| 950, 23J, LS, DR, OF, BRG, GJS, Adj.5P, NI, GT ........................ | 475 | 525 | 575 |
| 950, 23J, PS, DR, OF, GJS, BRG, Adj.5P, NI, GT ........................ | 475 | 525 | 575 |
| 950B, 23J, LS, OF, Adj.6P, NI, DR, BRG .................................... | 500 | 550 | 575 |
| 950E, 23J, LS, OF, Adj.6P, NI, DR, BRG..................................... | 525 | 575 | 600 |
| 951, 23J, LS, BRG, Adj.5P, NI, GT, GJS, DR, HC ............. ★★★ | 5,000 | 5,500 | 6,000 |
| 951, 23J, PS, BRG, Adj.5P, NI, GT, GJS, DR, HC............. ★★★ | 5,000 | 5,500 | 6,000 |
| 951, 23J, PS, BRG, Adj.5P, NI, GT, GJS, DR, HC,14K ..... ★★★ | 5,500 | 6,000 | 6,500 |
| 952, 19J, LS or PS, OF, BRG, Adj.5P, NI, GJS, DR ....................... | 200 | 250 | 300 |
| 952, 19J, LS or PS, BRG, Adj.5P, OF, 14K .................................. | 475 | 525 | 600 |
| 953, 19J, LS or PS, BRG, HC, GJS, GT.................................. ★★ | 2,000 | 2,500 | 3,000 |

🕐 Watches listed in this book are priced at the collectable retail level, as **Complete** watches having an original 14k gold-filled case for Stem Wind and *Key Wind* with silver case, an original white enamel single sunk dial, and with the entire original movement in good working order with no repairs needed.

| Grade or Name — Description | Avg | Ex-Fn | Mint |
|---|---|---|---|
| 954, 17J, LS or PS, OF, 3/4, DR, Adj.5P | $85 | $100 | $150 |
| 956, 17J, PS, OF, 3/4, DR, Adj.5P | 85 | 100 | 150 |
| 960, 21J, PS, OF, BRG, GJS, GT, DR, Adj.5P ★ | 350 | 375 | 425 |
| 960, 21J, LS, OF, BRG, GJS, GT, DR, Adj.5P ★ | 375 | 400 | 450 |
| 961, 21J, PS & LS, HC, BRG, GJS, GT, DR, Adj.5P ★ | 400 | 450 | 525 |
| 962, 17J, PS, OF, BRG ★★ | 500 | 600 | 700 |
| 963, 17J, PS, HC, BRG ★★ | 550 | 650 | 750 |
| 964, 17J, PS, OF, BRG ★★ | 650 | 700 | 800 |
| 965, 17J, PS, HC, BRG ★★ | 500 | 550 | 650 |
| 966, 17J, PS, OF, 3/4 ★★ | 600 | 650 | 750 |
| 967, 17J, PS, HC, 3/4 ★★ | 625 | 675 | 775 |
| 968, 17J, PS, OF, 3/4 ★ | 325 | 375 | 475 |
| 969, 17J, PS, HC, 3/4 ★ | 425 | 450 | 500 |
| 970, 21J, PS, OF, 3/4 | 275 | 325 | 375 |
| 971, 23J, Adj.5P, **SWISS MADE** | 75 | 100 | 135 |
| 971, 21J, PS, HC, 3/4 | 225 | 275 | 325 |
| 972, 17J, PS & LS, OF, 3/4, NI, GJS, DR, Adj.5P, DMK | 150 | 170 | 200 |
| 973, 17J, PS & LS, HC, 3/4, NI, DR, Adj.5P | 175 | 200 | 250 |
| 974, 17J, LS, OF, 3/4, NI, Adj.3P | 90 | 125 | 140 |
| 974, 17J, OF, PS, Adj.3P | 70 | 90 | 120 |
| 974, 17J, OF, 2-tone | 150 | 175 | 250 |
| 2974B, 17J, OF, Adj.3P, **hacking**, U.S. GOV | 175 | 200 | 250 |
| 975, 17J, PS & LS, HC, 3/4, NI, Adj.3P | 100 | 125 | 150 |
| 976, 16J, PS, OF, 3/4 | 150 | 175 | 225 |
| 977, 16J, PS, HC, 3/4 | 150 | 175 | 225 |
| 978, 17J, LS, OF, 3/4, NI, DMK | 85 | 100 | 125 |
| 990, 21J, LS, OF, GJS, DR, Adj.5P, DMK, NI, 3/4, GT | 250 | 275 | 300 |
| 991, 21J, LS, HC, 3/4, GJS, Adj.5P, DMK, NI, GT | 275 | 300 | 325 |
| 992, 21J, OF, 3/4, Adj.5P, SR & DR, NI | 195 | 220 | 250 |
| 992, 21J, OF, 3/4, **gold center wheel**, GJS, Adj.5P, SR & DR, NI. | 200 | 225 | 265 |
| 992, 21J, OF, 3/4, PS & LS, GJS, Adj.5P, DR, NI, DMK, **2 -Tone** | 275 | 300 | 350 |
| 992, 21J, **Extra**, OF, 3/4, PS & LS, GJS, Adj.5P, DR, NI, DMK | 300 | 325 | 375 |

Grade 992B, 16 size, 21 jewels, Adj.6p.

Grade 4992B, 16 size, 22 jewels, Adj.6p.

MOVEMENTS WITH ODD GRADE NUMBERS ARE HUNTING CASE.
MOVEMENTS WITH EVEN GRADE NUMBERS ARE OPEN FACE.

Grade 992, 21 jewels, gold center wheel, gold jewel settings, Adj.5P, marked Elinvar on movement, serial #2,595,787.

Grade 3992B, 22J, Adj.6P, "Navigation Master", note outside chapter on dial 1–10.

| Grade or Name — Description | Avg | Ex-Fn | Mint |
|---|---|---|---|
| 992, 21J, marked **Elinvar,** gold center wheel, 3/4, GJS, Adj.5P ..... | $300 | $335 | $375 |
| 992, 21J, marked **Special,** OF, 3/4, PS & LS, GJS, Adj.5P, DR, NI, DMK, Adj. for RR Service' on dial................................... | 425 | 475 | 550 |
| 992B, 21J, Adj.6P, **2-Tone**................................................. | 400 | 450 | 500 |
| 992B, 21J, LS, Adj.6P, OF, 3/4............................................ | 300 | 335 | 400 |
| 992B, 21J, OF, Adj.6P, 3/4, military silver case ............................. | 265 | 300 | 350 |
| 3992B, 22J, Adj.6P, 12 hr. dial, (Canadian), silver case ..............★ | 350 | 400 | 465 |
| 3992B, 22J, Adj.6P, "Navigation Master", Silver case .................★ | 375 | 425 | 485 |
| 4992B, 22J, LS, OF, 3/4, 24-hr. dial, Greenwich Civil Time ......... | 200 | 225 | 260 |
| 993, 21J, PS, HC, GJS, Adj.5P, DR, NI, DMK............................ | 350 | 375 | 425 |
| 993, 21J, LS, HC, GJS, Adj.5P, DMK, DR, NI............................ | 350 | 375 | 425 |
| 993, 21J, marked **Special,** tu-tone, HC, GJS, Adj.5P, DMK, DR  ★ | 375 | 400 | 475 |
| 993, 21J, LS, HC, GJS, Adj.5P, DMK, DR, NI, **14K** ..................... | 750 | 800 | 875 |
| 993, 21J, LS, HC, GJS, Adj.5P, DMK, DR, ( GF multi color case ) | 500 | 550 | 600 |

ADMIRAL, 16 size, 16 jewels, Damaskeened on nickel 3/4 plate, serial no. 57821.

Chronograph, Grade 23, 16 size, 19 jewels, start-stop-reset to 0.

| Grade or Name — Description | Avg | Ex-Fn | Mint |
|---|---|---|---|
| 994, 21J, BRG, OF, GJS, GT, DR, Adj.5P, DMK, PS ............... ★ | $900 | $1,100 | $1,250 |
| 994, 21J, BRG, OF, GJS, GT, DR, Adj.5P, DMK, LS ............... ★ | 975 | 1,250 | 1,400 |
| 995, 19J, GJS, BRG, HC ............................................... ★ ★ | 1,200 | 1,300 | 1,500 |
| 996, 19J, LS, OF, 3/4 GJS, DR, Adj.5P, DMK .......................... | 200 | 235 | 275 |
| Admiral, 16J., Grade 977, 3/4 plate, OF, ........................ ★ ★ ★ | 120 | 135 | 155 |
| Admiral,16J,NI, ADJ., DMK, HC...................................... | 120 | 135 | 155 |
| DeLong Escapement, 21J, 992-B ...................................... | 1,500 | 1,700 | 2,000 |
| Electric Interurban, 17J, G#974, OF ................................ | 125 | 150 | 210 |
| Official Standard, 17J, OF........................................... | 175 | 200 | 275 |
| Union Special, 17J................................................... | 100 | 125 | 200 |
| Hayden W. Wheeler, 17J, OF.......................................★ | 400 | 475 | 600 |
| Hayden W. Wheeler, 17J, HC .......................................★ | 450 | 535 | 650 |
| Hayden W. Wheeler, 21J.............................................★ | 500 | 600 | 700 |
| Hayden W. Wheeler, 21J, 14K H.W.W. case ..........................★ | 900 | 1,000 | 1,100 |
| Limited, 17J, G#974 ................................................. | 125 | 150 | 225 |
| Swiss Mfg., 17J, Adj.2P, GF case.................................... | 85 | 100 | 125 |
| Swiss Mfg., 23J, Adj.3P, ( by Buren W. Co. G# 917 ), Ca. 1969-70s | 95 | 110 | 145 |

## CHRONOGRAPH
### Grade 23

| Grade or Name — Description | Avg | Ex-Fn | Mint |
|---|---|---|---|
| 16S, 19J, start-stop-reset to 0 ............................................. | $275 | $325 | $385 |

## 12 SIZE

(Some cases were octagon, decagon, cushion, etc.)

| Grade or Name — Description | Avg | Ex-Fn | Mint |
|---|---|---|---|
| 900, 19J, BRG, DR, Adj.5P, GJS, OF, 14K ..................................... | $275 | $300 | $375 |
| 900, 19J, BRG, DR, Adj.5P, GJS, OF ............................................ | 100 | 125 | 175 |
| 902, 19J, BRG, DR, Adj.5P, GJS....................................... | 100 | 125 | 200 |

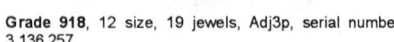

Grade 918, 12 size, 19 jewels, Adj3p, serial number 3,136,257.

Grade 920, 12 size, 23 jewels, gold train, gold jewel settings, serial number 1,863,381.

🕐 Watches listed in this book are priced at the collectable retail level, as **Complete** watches having an original 14k gold-filled case for Stem Wind and *Key Wind* with silver case, an original white enamel single sunk dial, and with the entire original movement in good working order with no repairs needed.

| Grade or Name — Description | Avg | Ex-Fn | Mint |
|---|---|---|---|
| 902, 19J, BRG, DR, Adj.5P, GJS, 14K.................... | $300 | $325 | $375 |
| 904, 21J, BRG, DR, Adj.5P, GJS, GT.................... | 100 | 125 | 175 |
| 910, 17J, 3/4, DR, ADJ.................... | 50 | 60 | 75 |
| 912, 17J, **Digital model, rotating seconds,** OF.................... | 80 | 110 | 150 |
| 912, 17J, 3/4, DR, ADJ.................... | 50 | 60 | 75 |
| 914, 17J, 3/4, DR, Adj.3P, GJS.................... | 50 | 60 | 75 |
| 914, 17J, 3/4, DR, Adj.3P, GJS, 14K.................... | 225 | 250 | 300 |
| 916, 17J, 3/4, DR, Adj.3P.................... | 50 | 60 | 75 |
| 916, 17J, Adj.3P, silver case .................... | 50 | 60 | 75 |
| 918, 19J, Adj.3P, WGF.................... | 75 | 100 | 150 |
| 918, 19J, 3/4, DR, Adj.3P, GJS, OF.................... | 75 | 100 | 150 |
| 920, 23J, BRG, DR, Adj.5P, GJS, GT, OF.................... | 200 | 250 | 325 |
| 920, 23J, BRG, DR, Adj.5P, GJS, GT, 14K.................... | 400 | 450 | 525 |
| 922, 23J, BRG, DR, Adj.5P, GJS, GT, 14K.................... | 400 | 450 | 525 |
| 922, 23J, BRG, DR, Adj.5P, GJS, GT, OF.................... | 200 | 250 | 325 |
| 922 MP, marked (MASTERPIECE), 18K case.................... ★ | 800 | 900 | 1,100 |
| 922 MP, marked (MASTERPIECE), Platinum case .................... ★ | 850 | 950 | 1,200 |
| 922 MP, GF, Hamilton case.................... | 300 | 400 | 550 |
| 400, 21J, (Illinois 12 size M#2, 5 tooth click) **Hamilton on dial.** ★ | 300 | 400 | 550 |

Grade 922MP, 12 size, 23 jewels, **marked** "masterpiece" serial number 3,013,390, c. 1930.

**Grade 912,** 12 size, 17 jewels, with Secometer dial, originally sold for $88.70.

## 10 SIZE

| Grade or Name — Description | Avg | Ex-Fn | Mint |
|---|---|---|---|
| 917, 17J, 3/4, DR, Adj.3P.................... | $40 | $50 | $70 |
| 917, 17J, 3/4, DR, Adj.3P, 14K.................... | 200 | 225 | 300 |
| 921, 21J, BRG, DR, Adj.5P.................... | 80 | 100 | 125 |
| 923, 23J, BRG, DR, Adj.5P.................... | 150 | 175 | 250 |
| 923, 23J, G.F.................... | 275 | 300 | 375 |
| 923, 23J, 18K, and box.................... | 500 | 600 | 700 |
| 945, 23J, Adj.5P, Masterpiece on DIAL.................... | 125 | 150 | 225 |

🕐 Watches listed in this book are priced at the collectable retail level, as complete watches having an original 14k goldfilled case & KW with a Silver case, an original white enamel single sunk dial, and with the entire original movement in good working order with no repairs needed, unless otherwise noted.

## 0 SIZE

| Grade or Name — Description | Avg | Ex-Fn | Mint |
|---|---|---|---|
| 981, 17J, 3/4, Adj.3P, DR, 18K, HC | $275 | $300 | $350 |
| 982, 17-19J, open face same as 981 & 983 HC but no seconds bit . | 75 | 100 | 135 |
| 983, 17J, Adj.3P, DR, GJS, 18K, HC | 275 | 300 | 350 |
| 985, 19J, BRG, Adj.3P, DR, GJS, GT, 18K, HC | 300 | 325 | 375 |
| Lady Hamilton, 14K case, OF | 200 | 225 | 300 |
| Lady Hamilton, 23J, GJS, gold filled OF | 125 | 150 | 200 |

*Above:* model 22, 21 jewels, 70mm, wind indicator, adjusted to 6 positions, base metal case.

*Right*: Chronometer in gimbals and box, 36 size, wind indicator.

## CHRONOMETER

| Grade or Name — Description | Avg | Ex-Fn | Mint |
|---|---|---|---|
| 35S, M#22, 21J, Wind Indicator, Adj.6P, in gimbals and box, lever | $550 | $650 | $750 |
| 35S, M#22, 21J, Wind Indicator, Adj.6P, in a large base metal OF case | 475 | 550 | 675 |
| 36S, M#36, 21J, Wind Indicator, in gimbals and box | 1,200 | 1,400 | 1,600 |
| 36S, M#36, 21J, 56 hr. W. Ind.,"SID" (sidereal), chrome case ..... ★ | 1,200 | 1,400 | 1,600 |
| 36S, M#36, 21J, Wind Indicator, in Hamilton sterling pocket watch case with bow (s# 1,260,001 to 1,260,970) | 2,000 | 2,400 | 3,000 |
| 85S, M#21, 14J, KW, KS, Fusee, Detent Escapement with helical hairspring, gimbals and box | 1,300 | 1,500 | 1,800 |

**CASE MODEL # A**
gold filled : $100 - $125 - $140

**CASE MODEL # 2**
gold filled : $100- $125 - $150
14K Gold : $350 - $400 - $500

**CASE MODEL # 3**
gold filled : $95- $115 - $130

This Tag Identifies
The Improved
992

**CASE MODEL # 4**
gold filled : $90 - $115 - $130

**CASE MODEL # 5**
gold filled : $100- $115 - $130

**CASE MODEL # 6**
gold filled : $110- $130 - $150

**CASE MODEL # 7**
White gold filled : $90 - $100 - $125

**CASE MODEL # 8**
gold filled : $110- $130 - $150

**CASE MODEL # 10**
gold filled : $100- $125 - $150

Model "A" was advertised in a Gold-filled Case & advertised with a grade 950 movement.
Models 2 & 17 came in 14K solid GOLD or gold-filled, model 2 advertised with 992 or 950.
Models 3, 4, 5, 6, (7 white G.F.), 8, 10, 11, Cross Bar, & Traffic Special II all gold-filled.
Model "16" gold plate and Model "15" & Traffic Special I was stainless steel case.

🕐 NOTE: Factory Advertised as a **complete** watch and was fitted with a certain matched, timed
and rated movement and sold in the factory designed case style as a complete watch. The factory
also sold _uncased_ movements to **JOBBERS** such as Jewelry stores & they cased the movement in
a case styles the **CUSTOMER requested.** All the factory advertised complete watches came with
the dial **SHOWN or CHOICE** of other **Railroad** dials.

**CASE MODEL # 11**
gold filled : $100 - $115 - $130

**CASE MODEL #14**
Nickel: $95- $110 - $120

**CASE MODEL #15**
S. steel : $30- $40 - $50

**CASE MODEL # 16**
gold plated : $80 - $90 - $110

**CASE MODEL #17**
gold filled : $100- $120 - $150
Gold : $400 - $450 - $500

**CASE MODEL Cross Bar**
gold filled : $100- $125 - $140

**TRAFFIC SPECIAL I**
S. Steel : $25 - $35 - $45

**TRAFFIC SPECIAL II**
gold plated : $45- $55 - $65

Railway Specials were packed & shipped in a plastic ivory cigarette style box and were sealed with a ribbon. To remove the watch break seal by cutting the ribbon which holds the watch in box.

Model "A" was advertised in a Gold-filled Case & advertised with a grade 950 movement.
Models 2 & 17 came in 14K solid GOLD or gold-filled, model 2 advertised with 992 or 950.
Models 3, 4, 5, 6, 8, 10, 11, & Cross Bar gold-filled.
Model "16" gold plate and Model "15" & Traffic Special I was stainless steel case.
Case Model 14 = Nickel-Chrome.

# HAMILTON W. CO. IDENTIFICATION OF MOVEMENTS

**How To Identify Your Watch:** Compare the movement with the illustration in this section. While comparing, note the location of the balance, jewels, screws, gears, and back plate (Full, 3/4, Bridge) which will be clues in identifying the movement you have. Having determined the size, the **GRADE** can also be found by looking up the serial number of your watch in the Hamilton Serial Number & Grades List. Illustrations of selected grades of the different size movements are shown to assist you in identifying movements. Hamilton movements which do not have grade numbers engraved on them <u>do</u> carry serial numbers which can be checked against the serial number list to secure the *grade number.*

**Grade 936,** <u>18 SIZE</u>, **Full Plate, OPEN FACE** SHOWN. Also grades 922, 924, 926, 928, 930, 932, 934, 938, 940, 942, 944, 946, & 948 All look SIMILAR to the above.

**Grade 925,** <u>18 SIZE</u>, **Full Plate, Hunting Case** SHOWN. Also grades 923, 927, 929, 931, 933, 935, 937, 939, 941, 943, 945, and 947 All look SIMILAR to the above.

NOTE: 18 Size Grades 924, 925, 926, 927, 928, 929, 930, 931, 932, 933, 934, & 935 use 90% same parts but not plates. 18 Size Grades 936, 937, 938, 939, & 948 use 90% same parts but not plates. Grades 940, 941, 942, & 943 use 90% same parts but not plates. 18 Size Grades 944 & 946 use 90% same parts.

**Grade 971,** <u>16 SIZE</u>, **Hunting Case,** 3/4 Plate, 21 jewels, Shown. Note; Crown Wheel with 2 Screws this movement uses a 4 Footed Dial. Also grades 969, 973, 975, 991, & 993 all look SIMILAR to the above. Note location of the larger ratchet wheel next to balance cock.

Grade 992, <u>16 SIZE</u>, **Open Face,** 3/4 Plate, 21 jewels, Shown. Note; Crown Wheel with 2 Screws this movement uses a 4 Footed Dial. Also grades 954, 968, 970, 972, 974, & 990 all look SIMILAR to the above. Note location of the smaller Crown wheel next to balance cock.

NOTE: 16 Size Grades 950, 952, & 996 use 90% same parts. 16 Size Grades 954, 962, 963, 966, 967, 972, & 973 use 90% same parts but not plates. 16 Size Grades 956, 964, 965, 968, 969, 974, 975, 976, 977, & 978 use 90% same parts. 16 Size Grades 960, 961, 970, 971, 990, 991, 992, 993, & 994 use 90% same parts but not plates. Grades 950E & 950B differ from grade 950. Grades 992E & 992B differ from grade 992.

Grade 992 Note: with narrow stripes, 16 size, 3/4 plate, 21 jewels, 5 positions. Note: Crown Wheel with 1 Screw.

Grade 992 E = wide stripes Damaskeening with ELINVAR under balance wheel. 16 size, 3/4 plate, 21J., 5 positions.

Grade 992 B, 16 size, 3/4 plate, 21J., **6 POSITIONS.**

Grade 950 16 size, BRIDGE, 23J., 5 positions. Note: with narrow stripes,

Grade 950 E = wide stripes Damaskeening with ELINVAR under balance wheel. 16 size, BRIDGE, 23J., 5 positions.

Grade 950 B, 16 size, BRIDGE, 23J., **6 POSITIONS.**

Grade 960, <u>16 SIZE</u>, BRIDGE, OPEN FACE SHOWN. Also GRADES 950, 952, 962, 964, 994 all look SIMILAR to the above. Note location of the smaller Crown wheel next to balance cock.

Grade 961, <u>16 SIZE</u>, BRIDGE, Hunting Case SHOWN. Also GRADES 951, 963, 965 all look SIMILAR to the above. Note location of the larger ratchet wheel next to balance cock.

SWISS MADE, 16 size, open face, 17 to 23 jewels, 3/4 plate.

**Grade 902, 12 size**
Open face, bridge movt., 19 jewels, double roller

**Grade 912, 12 size**
Open face, ¾ plate movt., 17 jewels, double roller

**Grade 918, 12 size**
Open face, ¾ plate movt., 19 jewels, double roller

**Grade 922, 12 size**
Open face, bridge movt., 23 jewels, double roller

**Grade 917, 10 size**
Open face, ¾ plate movt., 17 jewels, double roller

**Grade 921, 10 size**
Open face, bridge movt., 21 jewels, double roller

**Grade 923, 10 size**
Open face, bridge movt., 23 jewels, double roller

**Grade 983, 0 size**
Hunting, bridge movt., 17 jewels,
double roller

**Grade 979,6/0 size**
Hunting, ¾ plate movt., 19
jewels, double roller

**Grade 986, 6/0 size**
Open face, ¾ plate movt., 17
jewels, double roller

# HAMPDEN WATCH CO.
# (DUEBER WATCH CO.)
### Springfield, Massachusetts
### Canton, Ohio
### 1876 - 1930

The New York Watch Co. preceded Hampden, and before that Don J. Mozart (1864) produced his three-wheel watch. Mozart was assisted by George Samuel Rice of New York and, as a result of their joint efforts, the New York Watch Co. was formed in 1866 in Providence, Rhode Island. It was moved in 1867 to Springfield, Massachusetts. Two grades of watches were decided on, and the company started with a 18S, 3/4 plate engraved "Springfield." They were sold for $60 to $75. The 18S, 3/4 plate were standard production, and the highest grade was a "George Walker" that sold for about $200 and a 16S, 3/4 plate "State Street" which had steel parts and exposed balance and escape wheels that were gold plated.

John C. Dueber started manufacturing watch cases in 1864 and bought a controlling interest in a company in 1886. At about this time a disagreement arose between Elgin, Waltham, and the Illinois Watch companies. Also, at this time, an anti-trust law was passed, and the watch case manufacturers formed a boycott against Dueber. Dueber was faced with a major decision, whether to stay in business, surrender to the watch case companies or buy a watch company. He decided to buy the Hampden Watch Co. of Springfield, Mass. By 1889 the operation had moved to Canton, Ohio. By the end of the year the company was turning out 600 watches a day. The first 16 size watch was produced in 1890. In 1894 Hampden introduced the first 23J movement made in America. Hampden assigned serial numbers at random to the New York Watch Co. movements for years after they purchased the N.Y.W.Co.

## HAMPDEN ESTIMATED SERIAL NUMBER
## AND PRODUCTION DATES

| DATE–SERIAL NO. | DATE–SERIAL NO. | DATE–SERIAL NO. | DATE–SERIAL NO. |
|---|---|---|---|
| 1877--- 60,000 | 1889--- 555,500 | 1901---1,512,000 | 1913---3,048,000 |
| 1878--- 91,000 | 1890--- 611,000 | 1902---1,642,000 | 1914---3,176,000 |
| 1879---122,000 | 1891--- 666,500 | 1903---1,768,000 | 1915---3,304,000 |
| 1880---153,000 | 1892--- 722,000 | 1904---1,896,000 | 1916---3,432,000 |
| 1881---184,000 | 1893--- 775,000 | 1905---2,024,000 | 1917---3,560,000 |
| 1882---215,000 | 1894--- 833,000 | 1906---2,152,000 | 1918---3,680,000 |
| 1883---250,000 | 1895--- 888,500 | 1907---2,280,000 | 1919---3,816,000 |
| 1884---300,000 | 1896--- 944,000 | 1908---2,408,000 | 1920---3,944,000 |
| 1885---350,000 | 1897---1,000,000 | 1909---2,536,000 | 1921---4,072,000 |
| 1886---400,000 | 1898---1,128,000 | 1910---2,664,000 | 1922---4,200,000 |
| 1887---450,000 | 1899---1,256,000 | 1911---2,792,000 | 1923---4,400,000 |
| 1888---500,000 | 1900---1,384,000 | 1912---2,920,000 | 1924---4,600,000 |

The above list is provided for determining the **APPROXIMATE** age of your watch. Match serial number with date. Watches were not necessarily sold in the exact order of manufactured date.

**Chronology of the Development of Hampden Watch Co.:**
The Mozart Watch Co., Providence, R. I. ( 1864-1866 )
New York Watch Co., Providence, R. I. ( 1866-1867 )
New York Watch Co., Springfield, Mass. ( 1867-1875 )
New York Watch Mfg. Co., Springfield, Mass. ( 1875-1876 )
Hampden Watch Co., Springfield, Mass. ( 1877-1886 )
Hampden-Dueber Watch Co., Springfield, Mass. ( 1886-1888 )
Hampden Watch Co., Canton, Ohio. ( 1888–1923 )
Dueber Watch Co., Canton, Ohio. ( 1888–1923 )
Dueber-Hampden Watch Co., Canton, Ohio. ( 1923–1931 )
Amtorg, U.S.S.R ( 1930–Present )

Issued 1890

Issued 1892

Issued 1895

Dueber Watch Co., 18 size, 15 jewels, nickel movement. Model 3, hunting case.

Dueber Grand, 18 size, 17 jewels, open face, originally sold for $20.00.

## HAMPDEN
### 18 SIZE

| Grade or Name — Description | Avg | Ex-Fn | Mint |
|---|---|---|---|
| America, 7J, KW KS | $60 | $85 | $110 |
| Anchor, 17J, ADJ, GJS, DMK, OF | 75 | 100 | 150 |
| "3" Ball, 17J, ADJ, NI, DMK, OF | 150 | 175 | 200 |
| Champion, 7-11J, ADJ, FULL, gilded, or, NI, OF | 65 | 85 | 100 |
| Champion, 7-11J, ADJ, FULL, gilded, or, NI, HC | 100 | 125 | 150 |
| Champion, 15-17J, ADJ, FULL, gilded, or, NI, OF | 70 | 75 | 110 |
| Champion, 15-17J, ADJ, FULL, gilded, or, NI, HC | 125 | 135 | 165 |
| Correct Time, 15J, HC | 125 | 150 | 200 |
| Dueber, 16J, gilded, DMK, OF | 75 | 100 | 150 |
| Dueber, 17J, gilded, DMK, OF | 75 | 100 | 150 |
| John C. Dueber, 15J, gilded, DMK, OF | 75 | 100 | 150 |
| John C. Dueber, 17J, gilded, ADJ, DMK, OF | 75 | 100 | 150 |
| John C. Dueber, Special, 17J, ADJ, DMK, OF | 75 | 100 | 150 |
| John C. Dueber, Special, 17J, ADJ, DMK, HC | 100 | 135 | 195 |
| John C. Dueber, 17J, HC | 100 | 125 | 175 |
| John C. Dueber, 21J, HC | 250 | 300 | 375 |
| Dueber Grand, 17J, OF | 75 | 100 | 150 |
| Dueber Grand, 17J, ADJ, HC | 100 | 125 | 175 |
| Dueber Grand, 21J, ADJ, DMK, NI, HC | 250 | 300 | 375 |

🕐 Generic, nameless or unmarked grades for watch movements are listed under the Company name or initials of the Company, etc. by size, jewel count and description.

| | Avg | Ex-Fn | Mint |
|---|---|---|---|
| Dueber W. Co.,7-11J, OF | 75 | 100 | 125 |
| Dueber W. Co., 15J, DMK, OF | 75 | 100 | 135 |
| Dueber W. Co., 15J, DMK, HC | 100 | 125 | 175 |
| Dueber W. Co., 16J, OF | 75 | 100 | 150 |
| Dueber W. Co., 16J, HC | 100 | 125 | 175 |
| Dueber W. Co., 17J, DMK, ADJ, OF | 75 | 100 | 150 |
| Dueber W. Co., 17J, Gilded | 75 | 100 | 150 |
| Dueber W. Co., 17J, DMK, ADJ, HC | 100 | 125 | 175 |
| Dueber W. Co., 19J, ADJ, GJS, HC ★ | 400 | 475 | 575 |
| Dueber W. Co., 21J, Adj.5P, GJS, OF | 200 | 225 | 265 |
| Dueber W. Co., 21J, GJS, Adj.5P, HC | 250 | 275 | 350 |

John C. Dueber Special, 18 size, 17 jewels, serial number 949,097.

Oriental, 18 size, 15 jewels, open face, serial number 117,825.

| Grade or Name — Description | Avg | Ex-Fn | Mint |
|---|---|---|---|
| Homer Foot, gilded, KW, OF (Early) | $200 | $225 | $275 |
| Gladiator, KW, OF | 75 | 100 | 150 |
| Gladiator, 11J, NI, DMK, OF | 75 | 100 | 150 |
| Gulf Stream Sp., 21J, R.R. grade, OF, LS ★ | 400 | 500 | 625 |

⊕ Generic, nameless or unmarked grades for watch movements are listed under the Company name or initials of the Company, etc. by size, jewel count and description.

| | | | |
|---|---|---|---|
| Hampden W. Co., 7J, KW, KS, OF | 75 | 100 | 150 |
| Hampden W. Co., 7J, SW, OF | 60 | 75 | 100 |
| Hampden W. Co., 11J, OF, KW | 75 | 100 | 135 |
| Hampden W. Co., 11J, HC, KW | 100 | 125 | 150 |
| Hampden W. Co., 11J, OF, SW | 75 | 100 | 135 |
| Hampden W. Co., 11J, HC, SW | 100 | 125 | 175 |
| Hampden W. Co., 15J, OF, KW | 75 | 100 | 150 |
| Hampden W. Co., 15J, HC, KW | 100 | 125 | 175 |
| Hampden W. Co., 15J, HC, SW | 100 | 125 | 175 |
| Hampden W. Co., 15J, SW, Gilded, OF | 75 | 100 | 150 |
| Hampden W. Co., 15J, SW, NI, OF | 75 | 100 | 150 |
| Hampden W. Co., 15J, **Multi-color, 14K, HC** | 1,600 | 1,800 | 2,200 |
| Hampden W. Co., 16J, OF | 75 | 100 | 150 |
| Hampden W. Co., 17J, SW, Gilded | 75 | 100 | 150 |
| Hampden W. Co., 17J, SW, NI, OF | 75 | 100 | 150 |
| Hampden W. Co., 17J, HC, SW | 100 | 125 | 175 |
| Hampden W. Co., 17J, LS, HC, **14K** | 500 | 550 | 625 |
| Hampden W. Co., 17J, LS, HC, **10K** | 350 | 400 | 475 |
| Hampden W. Co., 21J, OF, HC, SW | 200 | 225 | 275 |
| John Hancock, 7J, Adj., OF | 60 | 75 | 100 |
| John Hancock, 15J, Adj.3P, OF | 70 | 90 | 135 |
| John Hancock, 17J, GJS, Adj.3P, OF | 75 | 100 | 150 |
| John Hancock, 17J, GJS, Adj.3P, HC | 125 | 150 | 200 |
| John Hancock, 21J, GJS, Adj.3P, OF | 200 | 225 | 275 |
| John Hancock, 23J, GJS, Adj.5P, OF | 235 | 265 | 325 |
| Hayward, 15J, KW | 100 | 125 | 200 |
| Hayward, 11J, SW | 75 | 100 | 125 |

⊕ Watches listed in this book are priced at the **collectable fair market value** at the RETAIL level, as complete watches having an original 14k gold filled case, KEY WIND with silver, an original white enamel single sunk dial, and with the entire original movement in good working order with no repairs needed, unless otherwise noted.

Menlo Park, 18 size, 17 jewels, serial number 1,184,116.

New Railway, 18 size, 23 jewels, open face only, gold jewel settings, originally sold for $50.00, Model 2.

| Grade or Name — Description | Avg | Ex-Fn | Mint |
|---|---|---|---|
| Lafayette, 11J, NI | $75 | $85 | $125 |
| Lafayette, 15J, NI, KW | 125 | 150 | 200 |
| Lafayette, 15J, NI | 100 | 125 | 175 |
| Lakeside, 15J, NI, SW | 100 | 125 | 175 |
| M. J. & Co. Railroad Watch Co., 15J, HC ★ | 300 | 400 | 525 |
| Menlo Park, 15-17J, NI, ADJ, OF | 100 | 125 | 175 |
| Mermod, Jaccard & Co., 15J, KW, HC | 125 | 150 | 200 |
| Metropolis, 15J, NI, SW, OF | 75 | 100 | 150 |
| Wm. McKinley, 17J, Adj.3P, OF | 75 | 100 | 150 |
| Wm. McKinley, 21J, GJS, Adj.5P | 200 | 225 | 265 |
| New Railway, 17J, GJS, Adj.5P, OF | 75 | 100 | 150 |
| New Railway, 19J, GJS, Adj.5P, OF | 150 | 175 | 225 |
| New Railway, 19J, GJS, Adj.5P, HC | 175 | 225 | 275 |

Railway, 18 size, 17 jewels, key wind & set, early railroad watch.

Special Railway, 18 size, 23 jewels, Adj5p, serial number 3,357,284.

Watches listed in this book are priced at the collectable retail level, as **complete** watches having an original 14k gold-filled case and *Key Wind* with silver, an original white enamel single sunk dial, and with the entire original movement in good working order with no repairs needed.

| Grade or Name — Description | Avg | Ex-Fn | Mint |
|---|---|---|---|
| New Railway, 21J, GJS, Adj.5P, HC | $200 | $245 | $300 |
| New Railway, 21J, GJS, Adj.5P, OF | 200 | 225 | 265 |
| New Railway, 23J, GJS, Adj.5P | 200 | 275 | 350 |
| New Railway, 23J, GJS, Adj.5P, 14K, OF | 700 | 750 | 800 |
| North Am. RR, 21J, GJS, Adj.5P, OF, LS | 200 | 225 | 250 |
| North Am. RR, 21J, GJS, Adj.3P, HC, PS | 200 | 275 | 325 |
| Pennsylvania Special, 17J, GJS, Adj.5P, DR, NI ★★ | 700 | 900 | 1,200 |
| J. C. Perry, 15J, KW, gilded, HC | 125 | 150 | 200 |
| J. C. Perry, 15J, NI, SW, OF | 75 | 90 | 100 |
| J. C. Perry, 15J, gilded, SW, OF | 75 | 100 | 150 |
| Railway, 15J, gilded, OF | 75 | 100 | 150 |
| Railway, 17J, NI, OF | 75 | 100 | 150 |
| Railway, 15J, KW, marked on mvt., HC ★★ | 500 | 600 | 800 |
| **Railroad with R.R. names on dial and movement:** | | | |
| Canadian Pacific RR, 17J, OF ★ | 500 | 600 | 800 |
| Canadian Pacific RR, 21J, OF ★ | 550 | 700 | 900 |
| Private Label R.R. 17J, OF ★ | 300 | 350 | 400 |
| Special Railway, 17J, GJS, Adj.5P, NI, DR, OF | 75 | 100 | 150 |
| Special Railway, 21J, GJS, Adj.5P, NI, DR, 2-Tone, OF | 200 | 225 | 250 |
| Special Railway, 23J, GJS, Adj.5P, NI, DR, 2-Tone, OF | 275 | 300 | 375 |
| Special Railway, 23J, Adj.5P, HC | 300 | 350 | 450 |
| Special Railway, 23J, 14K, HC | 800 | 850 | 950 |
| Springfield, 7-11J, KW, gilded, HC | 100 | 125 | 175 |
| Springfield, 7-11J, SW, NI, HC | 100 | 125 | 175 |
| Standard, 15J, gilded, HC | 100 | 125 | 175 |
| State Street, 15J, NI, LS, (Early KW) | 175 | 200 | 250 |
| Theo. Studley, 15J, KW, KS, HC | 125 | 150 | 200 |
| Tramway Special, 17J, NI | 175 | 200 | 250 |
| Woolworth, 11-15J, KW | 100 | 125 | 175 |
| Grade 31,45,46,49,65,66,69, 70,71, ALL =11J | 65 | 85 | 100 |
| Grade 32,33,34,35,36,40,41,55,56,58,59,60, All =15J | 75 | 95 | 125 |
| Grade, 43,44,47,48,63,64,67,68,80,81, ALL =16-17J | 85 | 100 | 150 |
| Grade 85, **19J**, GJS, 2-Tone, HC ★★ | 500 | 600 | 750 |
| Grade 95, **21J**, GJS, OF | 200 | 225 | 250 |
| Grade 125, **21J**, Adj.3P, OF | 175 | 200 | 235 |

## 16 SIZE

| Grade or Name — Description | Avg | Ex-Fn | Mint |
|---|---|---|---|
| Beacon, 7J, OF | $55 | $60 | $85 |
| Champion, 7J, NI, 3/4, gilded, coin, OF | 60 | 75 | 100 |
| Champion, 7J, NI, 3/4, gilded, OF | 60 | 75 | 100 |
| Champion, 7J, NI, 3/4, gilded, HC | 100 | 125 | 175 |
| Chronometer, 21J, detent escapement, NI, Adj.3P, GJS | 600 | 750 | 950 |
| John C. Dueber, 17J, GJS, NI, Adj.5P, 3/4 | 75 | 100 | 150 |
| John C. Dueber, 21J, GJS, NI, Adj.5P, 3/4 ★ | 300 | 375 | 450 |
| John C. Dueber, 21J, GJS, NI, Adj.5P, DR, BRG | 200 | 220 | 250 |
| Dueber Watch Co., 17J, ADJ, 3/4 | 75 | 100 | 150 |

🕐 Generic, nameless or unmarked grades for watch movements are listed under the Company name or initials of the Company, etc. by size, jewel count and description.

🕐 Some watch manufacturers personalize watches for jobbers or jewelry firms, with exclusive private signed or marked movements. The valuable collectable watches are listed under the signed or marked movement. Other exclusive private signed or marked movements will have equivalent value are only slightly higher value and should be compared to Generic or Nameless movements. Railroad signed or marked (dials & movements) are usually more collectable & higher in value.

Hampden W. Co., Bridge Model, 16 size, 23 jewels, 2-tone movement, serial number 1,899,430.

Hampden W. Co., 16 size, 17 jewels, gold jewel settings, serial number 3,075,235.

🕐 Generic, nameless or unmarked grades for watch movements are listed under the Company name or initials of the Company, etc. by size, jewel count and description.

| Grade or Name — Description | Av | Ex-Fn | Mint |
|---|---|---|---|
| Hampden W. Co., 7J, SW, OF | $60 | $75 | $125 |
| Hampden W. Co., 7J, SW, HC | 75 | 100 | 150 |
| Hampden W. Co., 11J, SW, OF | 60 | 75 | 125 |
| Hampden W. Co., 11J, SW, HC | 75 | 100 | 150 |
| Hampden W. Co., 15J, SW, OF | 50 | 75 | 125 |
| Hampden W. Co., 15J, SW, HC | 75 | 100 | 150 |
| Hampden W. Co., 17J, SW, OF | 60 | 75 | 125 |
| Hampden W. Co., 17J, **14K, Multi-color,** HC | 1,500 | 1,600 | 1,800 |
| Hampden W. Co., 17J, SW, HC | 75 | 100 | 150 |
| Hampden W. Co., 21J, SW, HC | 250 | 300 | 375 |
| Hampden W. Co., 21J, SW, OF | 200 | 220 | 250 |
| Hampden W. Co., 23J, Adj.5P, GJS, 3/4 | 300 | 350 | 425 |
| Hampden W. Co., 23J, Series 2, **Freesprung,** GJS GT, HC ★ ★ ★ | 500 | 650 | 800 |
| Masonic Dial, 23J, GJS, 2-Tone **porcelain dial** | 450 | 525 | 650 |

Hampden W. Co., Series 1, 16 size, 15 jewels, stem wind open face.

Railway, 16 size, 17 jewels, Adj.5P, gold jewel settings, serial number 2,271,866.

Grade 104, 16 size, 23 jewels, gold jewel settings, gold train, Adj5p, open face, serial number 2,801,184.

Hampden style watch produced in Russia with the machinery purchased by the Russian factory. This watch is a 16 size 7 jewel movement Ca. 1935

| Grade or Name — Description | Avg | Ex-Fn | Mint |
|---|---|---|---|
| Wm. McKinley, 17J, GJS, Adj.5P, NI, DR, 3/4 | $75 | $100 | $150 |
| Wm. McKinley, 21J, GJS, Adj.5P, NI, DR, 3/4 | 225 | 265 | 350 |
| Wm. McKinley, 21J, GJS, Adj.5P, NI, DR, 3/4, **Coin** | 200 | 235 | 295 |
| Wm. McKinley, 21J, GJS, Adj.5P, NI, DR, BRG | 200 | 225 | 250 |
| New Railway, 21J, GJS, Adj.5P | 250 | 275 | 325 |
| New Railway, 23J, GJS, Adj.5P, LS, HC | 375 | 400 | 450 |
| Ohioan, 21J, Adj.5P, GJS, 3/4 | 250 | 300 | 375 |
| Railway, 17-19J, GJS, Adj.5P, BRG, DR | 200 | 225 | 265 |
| Special Railway, 23J, Adj.5P, NI, BRG, DR | 275 | 325 | 375 |
| **Russian** made model, 7J, 16 size, 3/4 plate | 75 | 85 | 95 |
| Garfield, 21J., Adj.5P, OF | 200 | 220 | 250 |
| Gen'l Stark, 15J, DMK, BRG | 75 | 100 | 150 |
| Gen'l Stark, 17J, DMK, BRG | 75 | 100 | 150 |
| 95, 21J, marked ''95'', GJS, Adj.5P | 225 | 250 | 275 |
| 97 HC, 98 HC, 107 OF, 108 OF, **ALL = 17J**, Adj.3P, NI, 3/4 | 75 | 100 | 150 |
| 99, 15J, 3/4, HC | 100 | 125 | 175 |
| 103, 21J, GJS, Adj.5P, NI, BRG, DR | 225 | 250 | 300 |
| 104, 23J, GJS, Adj.5P, NI, 3\4 or BRG, DR, DMK, OF | 250 | 300 | 400 |
| 104, 23J, GJS, Adj.5P, NI, BRG, DR, DMK, HC | 300 | 375 | 475 |
| 105, 21J, GJS, Adj.5P, NI, 3/4, DR, DMK | 200 | 220 | 250 |
| 106, 107 OF, & 108, **17J**, SW, NI | 75 | 100 | 150 |
| 109, 15J, 3/4, OF | 75 | 100 | 150 |
| 110, 11J, 3/4 | 60 | 70 | 85 |
| 115, 21J, SW, NI, OF | 200 | 220 | 250 |
| 120, 21J, SW, NI, OF, **Chronometer on dial** | 225 | 250 | 275 |
| 340, 17J, SW, NI | 75 | 100 | 150 |
| 440, 15J, 2-tone | 100 | 125 | 175 |
| 555, 21J, GT, GJS, **Chronometer on dial & mvt.** | 300 | 350 | 400 |
| 555, 21J, GT, GJS, **Chronometer on dial ONLY** | 200 | 235 | 275 |
| 600, 17J, SW, NI | 75 | 100 | 150 |

🕘 Generic, nameless or unmarked grades for watch movements are listed under the Company name or initials of the Company, etc. by size, jewel count and description.

🕘 Some watch manufacturers personalize watches for jobbers or jewelry firms, with exclusive private signed or marked movements. The valuable collectable watches are listed under the signed or marked movement. Other exclusive private signed or marked movements will have equivalent value are only slightly higher value and should be compared to Generic or Nameless movements. Railroad signed or marked (dials & movements) are usually more collectable & higher in value.

Dueber Grand, 12 size, 17 jewels, gold jewel settings, hunting case, serial number 1,737,354.

Dueber Grand, 12 size, 17 jewels, gold jewel settings, open face, pin set, serial number 1,732,255.

## 12 SIZE
### ( SEE ALSO "12 SIZE " THIN MODEL )

| Grade or Name — Description | Avg | Ex-Fn | Mint |
|---|---|---|---|
| Champion, 7J, SW | $35 | $40 | $60 |
| Dueber Grand, 17J, BRG, OF | 50 | 60 | 80 |
| Dueber Grand, 17J, BRG, HC | 55 | 65 | 85 |
| Dueber Grand, 17J, 3/4 plate | 50 | 60 | 80 |
| Hampden W. Co., 7J, SW, OF | 40 | 50 | 75 |
| Hampden W. Co., 17J, 14K, Multi-color, HC | 700 | 800 | 1,000 |
| John Hancock, 21J, BRG | 90 | 110 | 140 |
| Gen'l Stark, 15J, BRG | 40 | 50 | 75 |
| Gen'l Stark, 15J, pin set | 40 | 50 | 75 |
| 207-300 HC & 302 OF, 7J, 3/4 (add $35 for HC) | 40 | 50 | 75 |
| 304 HC & 306 OF, 15J, 3/4 (add $35 for HC) | 40 | 50 | 75 |
| 305-308 HC & 310 OF, 17J, 3/4 (add $35 for HC) | 50 | 60 | 75 |
| 307, 17J | 40 | 50 | 75 |
| 310, 17J, gold filled OF case | 40 | 50 | 75 |
| 310, 17J, 14K OF case | 150 | 165 | 200 |
| 312, 21J, 3/4, Adj.5P, DMK, HC | 95 | 120 | 150 |
| 314, 21J, DR, Adj. 5P, DMK, OF | 75 | 95 | 125 |
| 31 OF, 17J, SW, 14K | 275 | 325 | 400 |

Paul Revere, Example of Hampden Watch Co.'s thin series showing face and movement, 12 size, 17-19 jewels, Adj5p.

## 12 SIZE (THIN MODEL)

| Grade or Name — Description | Avg | Ex-Fn | Mint |
|---|---|---|---|
| Aviator, 17J, Adj.4P | $60 | $75 | $95 |
| Aviator, 19J, Adj.4P | 65 | 80 | 110 |
| Beacon, 17J | 50 | 60 | 80 |
| Nathan Hale, 15J ★ | 50 | 75 | 100 |
| Minuteman, 17J ★ | 65 | 85 | 125 |
| Ohioan, 21J, Adj.3P, GJS, 3/4 | 50 | 60 | 75 |
| Paul Revere, 17J, OF, 14K | 275 | 325 | 400 |
| Paul Revere, 17J | 50 | 60 | 85 |
| Paul Revere, 19J | 75 | 90 | 125 |

Note: Some 12 Sizes came in cases of octagon, decagon, hexagon, triad, and cushion shapes.

## 6 SIZE

| Grade or Name — Description | Avg | Ex-Fn | Mint |
|---|---|---|---|
| 200, 7J (add $25 for HC) | $40 | $50 | $75 |
| 206, 11J (add $25 for HC) | 40 | 50 | 75 |
| 213, 15J (add $25 for HC) | 40 | 50 | 75 |
| 220, 17J (add $25 for HC) | 40 | 50 | 75 |
| Hampden W. Co., 15J, **multi-color Gold Filled, HC** | 200 | 245 | 300 |
| Hampden W. Co., 15J, **multi-color, 14K, HC** | 425 | 550 | 625 |

Molly Stark, 000 size, 7 jewels, hunting or open face, originally sold for $12.00.

## 000 SIZE

| Grade or Name — Description | Avg | Ex-Fn | Mint |
|---|---|---|---|
| Diadem, 11-15J, **14K**, OF Case | $100 | $135 | $200 |
| Diadem, 11-15J, **14K**, HC Case | 200 | 250 | 325 |
| Diadem, 11-15J, **Gold Filled**, HC Case | 95 | 125 | 175 |
| Molly Stark, 7J, **Gold Filled**, HC Case | 95 | 125 | 175 |
| Molly Stark, 7J, **14K**, HC Case | 200 | 250 | 325 |
| Molly Stark, 7J, Pin Set, OF | 50 | 75 | 125 |
| Four Hundred, 11, 15, 16, & 17J, HC | 95 | 125 | 175 |
| **14K Multi-color, HC** | 450 | 550 | 700 |

🕐 Watches listed in this book are priced at the collectable retail level, as **complete** watches having an original 14k gold-filled case and *Key Wind* with silver, an original white enamel single sunk dial, and with the entire original movement in good working order with no repairs needed.

# HAMPDEN WATCH CO.
## IDENTIFICATION OF MOVEMENTS

**How to Identify Your Watch Size & Model:** Compare the movement of your watch with the illustrations in this section. While comparing, note the location of the balance, jewels, screws, gears, and type of back plate (Full, 3/4, Bridge) which will be clues in identifying the movement you have.

**Series I, 18 size**
Hunting or open face, key wind & set

**Series II, 18 size**
Hunting, stem wind, pendant or lever set

**Series III, 18 size**
Hunting, stem wind, pendant or lever set

**Series IV, 18 size**
Open face, stem wind, lever set

**Series 1, 16 size**
Open face, stem wind, pendant or lever set

**Series II, 16 size**
Hunting, stem wind, pendant or lever set

**Series III, 16 size**
Open face, stem wind, pendant set

**Series IV, 16 size**
Hunting, stem wind, pendant or lever set

**Series V, 16 size**
Open face, stem wind, pendant or lever set

**Series VI, 16 size**
Hunting, stem wind, pendant set

**Series VII, 16 size**
Open face, stem wind, pendant set

**Series III, 12 size**
Open face, stem wind, pendant set

**Series I, 12 size**
Hunting, stem wind, lever set

**Series II, 12 size**
Open face, stem wind, lever set

**Series IV, 12 size**
Open face, stem wind, pendant

**Series V, 12 size**
Open face, stem wind, pendant set

**Series I, 6 size**
Open face, stem wind

**Series I, 3/0 size**
Hunting, stem wind

🕐 Characteristics of watches differ for the same age of both case and movement, because these features vary it may not be accurate to date a watch by one single influence. Example: the second hand was <u>not</u> commonly found on watches before 1750, but common about 1800. The first second hand appeared in 1665 and another in 1690. Therefore statements are broad rather than accurate.

**Series II, 3/0 size**
Open face, stem wind, pendant

**Series III, 3/0 size**
Hunting, lever or pendant

**Series IV, 3/0 size**
Hunting, stem wind, pendant

# HERMAN VON DER HEYDT
## CHICAGO SELF–WINDING WATCH CO.
### Chicago, Illinois
#### 1883

Herman von der Heydt patented a self-winding watch on Feb. 19, 1884. A total of 35 watches were hand-made by von der Heydt. The watches were 18S, full plate, lever escapement and fully-jeweled. The wind mechanism was a gravity type made of heavy steel and shaped like a crescent. The body motion let the heavy crescent move which was connected to a ratchet on the winding arbor, resulting in self-winding. Five movements were nickel and sold for about $90; the gilded model sold for about $75.

| Grade or Name — Description | | Avg | Ex-Fn | Mint |
|---|---|---|---|---|
| 18S, 19J, FULL, NI | ★★★★ | $12,000 | $14,000 | $16,000 |
| 18S, 19J, FULL, gilded | ★★★★ | 10,000 | 12,000 | 14,000 |

Herman Von Der Heydt, 18 size self winding watch. "Chicago S. W. Co." on dial.

Herman Von Der Heydt, 18 size, 19 jewels; America's only self winding pocket watch. Note crescent shaped winding weight.

# E. HOWARD & CO.
### Boston (Roxbury), Massachusetts
### December 11, 1858 - 1903

After the failure of the Boston Watch Company (1853 -57 ), Edward Howard decided to personally attempt the successful production of watches using the interchangeable machine-made parts system. He and Charles Rice, his financial backer, were unable to buy out the defunct watch company in Waltham, however, they did remove (per a prior claim) the watches in progress, the tools and the machinery to Howard and Davis' Roxbury factory (first watch factory in America), in late 1857. During their first year, the machinery was retooled for the production of a revolutionary new watch of Howard's design. Also, the remaining Boston Watch Co. movements were completed (E. Howard & Co. dials, Howard & Rice on the movement). By the summer of 1858, Edward Howard had produced his first watch. On December 11, 1858 the firm of E. Howard & Co. was formed for the manufacture of high-grade watches. Howard's first model was entirely different from any watch previously made. It introduced the more accurate "quick beat" train to American watchmaking. The top plate was in two sections and had six pillars instead of the usual four pillars in a full plate. The balance was gold or steel at first, then later it was a compensation balance loaded with gold screws. Reed's patented barrel was used for the first time. The size, based on the Dennison system, was a little larger than the regular 18 size. In 1861, a 3/4 plate model was put on the market. Most movements were being stamped with "N" to designate Howard's 18 size. On February 4, 1868 Howard patented a new steel motor barrel which was to supersede the Reed's, but not before some 28,000 had been produced. Also, in 1868 Howard introduced the stemwinding movement and was probably the first company to market such a watch in the U. S. By 1869, Howard was producing their "L" or 16 size as well as their first nickel movements. In 1870, G. P. Reed's micrometer regulator was patented for use by E. Howard & Co. The Reed style "whiplash" regulator has been used in more pocket watches, worldwide, than any other type. In 1878, the manufacturing of keywind movements was discontinued. Mr. Howard retired in 1882, but the company continued to produce watch movements of the grade and style set by him until 1903. This company was the first to adjust to all six positions. Their dials were always a hard enamel and always bore the name "E. Howard & Co., Boston." In 1903, the company transferred all rights to use the name "Edward Howard," in conjunction with the production of watches, to the Keystone Watch Case Co. Most of their models were stamped "Howard" on the dial and "E. Howard Watch Co., Boston. U.S.A." on the movement. Edward Howard's company never produced its own watch cases, the great majority of which were solid gold or silver. Keystone, however, produced complete watches, many of which were gold filled.

### CHRONOLOGICAL DEVELOPMENT OF E. HOWARD & CO.:
Howard, Davis & Dennison, Roxbury, Mass., ( 1850 )
American Horologue Company, Roxbury, Mass., ( 1851 )
Warren Manufacturing Company, Roxbury, Mass., ( 1851-53 )
Boston Watch Co., Roxbury, Mass., ( 1853-54 ) & Waltham, Mass., ( 1854-57 )
Howard & Rice, Roxbury, Mass., ( 1857-58) with  (E. Howard & Co. on dials)
E. Howard & Co., Roxbury, Mass., ( 1858-1903 )
Keystone Watch Case Co. (Howard line), Jersey City, N. J., ( 1903-30 )

**LEFT:** Balance cock unmarked =UNADJUSTED
**CENTER:** Balance cock marked heat &cold =adjusted to TEMPERATURE
**RIGHT:** Balance cock marked adjusted =FULLY  ADJUSTED

A List of initials for most of the Solid Gold watch case companies used with E. Howard & Co.

A.W.C. Co.=American Watch Case Co.
B & T = Booz & Thomas
B.W.C. Co.=Brooklyn Watch Case Co.
C & M =Crosby & Mathewson
C.E.H. & Co. = C.E. Hale & Co.
C.W. Mfg. Co. = Courvoisier Wilcox Mfg. Co.
D T W & Co.= D.T. Warren & Co.
E.H. & Co. = E. Hale & Co.
F & Co. = Fellows & Co.
F & S = Fellows & Shell
J M H = J.M. Harper
J S (intertwined)= Jeannot & Shiebler

K (inside) U = Keller & Untermeyer
K E & F. Co.= Keller, Ettinger & Fink N.Y.
M B = Margot Bros.
M & B = Mathey Bros.
N.Y.G.W.C.Co =New York Gold Watch Case Co.
P & B = Peters & Boss
S & D = Serex & Desmaison
S & M B = Serex Maitre Bros.
S & R = Serex & Robert
W & S = Warren & Spadone
W P & Co = Wheeler Parsons & Co.
W W C Mfg. Co =Western Watch Case Co.

Crescent Watch Case Co.
Dueber Watch Case Co.
Keystone Watch Case Co.

Ladd Watch Case Co.
Marsh= Marsh Watch Case Co.
Muhr Watch Case Co.

Roy = Roy Watch Case Co.

E. HOWARD & CO., Series I, helical hair-spring, detent escapement, KW KS, N (18)size, serial # 1120

E. HOWARD & CO., N (18) size, 15 jewels, chronometer escapement engraved on balance cock, Robin's escapement, serial # 3126.

E. HOWARD & CO., İ (10) size, KW KS, note compensating balance above center wheel, serial # 3363.

E. HOWARD & CO., İ (10) size, KW KS, **note** solid balance wheel below center wheel, serial # 3406.

## E. HOWARD & CO.
### APPROXIMATE DATES, SERIAL NOS., AND TOTAL PRODUCTION

| Serial No. | Date | Series | Total Prod. |
|---|---|---|---|
| 131-1,900— | 1858-1860— | I (18S)— | 1,800 |
| 1,901-3,000— | 1860-1861— | II (18S)— | 1,100 |
| 3,001-3,100— | 1861— | K (14S)— | 100 |
| 3,101-3,250— | 1861— | III (18S)— | 150 |
| 3,401-3,500— | 1861— | i (10S)— | 100 |
| 3,501-28,000— | 1861-1871— | III (18S)— | 4,500 |
| 30,001-50,000— | 1868-1883— | IV (18S)— | 20,000 |
| 50,001-71,000— | 1869-1899 — | V (16S)— | 21,000 |
| 100,001-105,500— | 1869-1899— | VI (6S)— | 5,500 |
| 200,001-227,000— | 1880-1899— | VII (18S)—27,000 |  |
| *228,001-231,000— | 1895— | VII (18S)— | 3,000 |
| 300,001-309,000— | 1884-1899— | VIII (18S)— | 9,000 |
| *309,001-310,000— | 1895— | VIII (18S)— | 1,000 |
| 400,001-405,000— | 1890-1895— | IX (18S)— | 5,000 |
| 500,001-501,500— | 1890-1899— | X (12S)— | 1,500 |
| *600,001-601,500—1896—1903— | | XI (16S)— | 1,500 |
| *700,001-701,500—1896—1903— | | XII (16S)— | 1,500 |

(*) = 3/4 Split Plates with 17 Jewels. **Total about-** 100,000

The above list is provided for determining the APPROXIMATE age of your watch. Match serial number with date. Watches were not necessarily sold in the exact order of manufactured date.

### E. HOWARD & CO. WATCH SIZES

| Letter | Inches | Approx. Size |
|---|---|---|
| N | 1 13/16 | 18 |
| L | 1 11/16 | 16 |
| K | 1 10/16 | 14 |
| J | 1 9/16 | 12 |
| I | 1 8/16 | 10 |
| H | 1 7/16 | 8 |
| G | 1 6/16 | 6 |
| F | 1 5/16 | 4 |
| E | 1 4/16 | 2 |
| D | 1 3/16 | 0 |

**Below Mershon's Patent** center wheel rack regulator (April 26 1859),

Standard Escapement

Coles Escapement

Deer
Adjusted to
Hcl6P

Horse
Adjusted to
HCI-No
positions

Hound
Unadjusted

**NOTE:** E. Howard & Co. movements will not fit standard cases properly.

**14 or K size**, 15 jewels, right angle lever escapement, experimental model, serial number 3,122.

**10 or I size**, 15 jewels; note cut-out to view escape wheel, experimental model, serial number 3,472.

### E. HOWARD & CO.
#### N SIZE (18)   (In Original Cases)

| Series or Name — Description | | Avg | Ex-Fn | Mint |
|---|---|---|---|---|
| E. Howard & Co. on dial and movement, 15-16J, 1857 Model, (Howard & Rice style), KW & KS, silver case ........... ★ ★ ★ | | $1,600 | $2,000 | $2,500 |
| I, II or III, Isochronism, 15J, gilded, KW, helical hairspring ......................................... ★ ★ ★ ★ | | 5,000 | 6,000 | 8,000 |

Series 1, 18 size, 15 jewels, note the compensating balance on this early movement, serial number 133.

Series II, 18 size, 15 jewels, key wind & set, serial number 2,477.

| Grade or Name — Description | Avg | Ex-Fn | Mint |
|---|---|---|---|
| I, 15J, with serial # below 100 ............................................................ | $5,000 | $6,000 | $7,500 |
| I, 15J, with serial # below 200............................................................. | 2,000 | 3,000 | 4,500 |
| I, 15J, with serial # below 300............................................................. | 1,000 | 2,000 | 3,000 |
| I, 15J, gilded, KW, 18K, HC or OF, upright pallets ................. ★ ★ | 3,000 | 4,000 | 5,000 |
| I, 15J, gilded, KW, 18K, HC or OF, horizontal pallets ................ ★ | 2,200 | 2,500 | 3,000 |
| I, 15J, gilded, KW, silver HC ........................................................ ★ | 1,500 | 1,900 | 2,400 |
| I, 15J, (movement only).................................................................... ★ | 500 | 600 | 700 |
| II, 15J, gilded, KW, 18K, HC or OF ............................................... ★ | 2,000 | 2,500 | 3,000 |
| II, 15J, gilded, KW, silver HC......................................................... ★ | 1,200 | 1,500 | 2,000 |
| II, 15J, (movement only) ................................................................. ★ | 450 | 550 | 650 |
| III, 15J, gilded, KW, 18K, HC ............................................................ | 1,300 | 1,500 | 1,800 |
| III, 15J, gilded, KW, silver case......................................................... | 600 | 800 | 1,000 |
| III, 15J, nickel, KW, silver case......................................................... | 700 | 900 | 1,100 |
| III, 15J, gilded, KW, 18K, Mershon's Patent .................................... | 1,500 | 1,800 | 2,000 |
| III, 15J, gilded, KW, 18K, Coles Escapement ......................... ★ ★ | 1,600 | 1,900 | 2,300 |
| III, 15J, NI, Private label .................................................................... | 800 | 1,000 | 1,200 |
| III, 15J , (movement only)................................................................... | 150 | 175 | 225 |
| IV, 15J, gilded or nickel, KW, 18K, HC............................................. | 1,200 | 1,400 | 1,700 |
| IV, 15J, gilded or nickel, SW, 18K, HC ............................................ | 1,000 | 1,200 | 1,400 |

Series III, 18 size, 15 jewels, note Mershon's Patent center wheel rack regulator (April 26 1859), serial number 22,693.

Series III, 18 size, 15 jewels, note high balance wheel over center wheel, serial number 7,000.

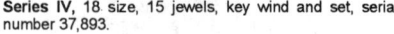

Series IV, 18 size, 15 jewels, key wind and set, serial number 37,893.

Series VII, 18 size, 15 jewels, nickel movement, note running deer on movement, "adjusted" on bridge, serial number 219,304.

| Series or Name — Description | | Avg | Ex-Fn | Mint |
|---|---|---|---|---|
| IV, personalized with jobber's name, silver | ★★ | $500 | $600 | $800 |
| IV, 15J, gilded, Cole's Escapement | ★★★★ | 1,500 | 1,600 | 1,700 |
| IV, 15J (movement only) | | 90 | 110 | 150 |
| VII, 15J, gilded or nickel, SW, 14K, HC | | 1,000 | 1,200 | 1,500 |
| VII, 17J, nickel, split plate, SW, 14K, HC | ★★★★ | 1,200 | 1,400 | 1,700 |
| VII, 17J, nickel, split plate, SW, silver, HC | ★ | 600 | 700 | 900 |
| VII, 19J, nickel, split plate, SW, 14K, HC | ★★★ | 2,500 | 3,000 | 4,000 |
| VII, 15J (movement only) | | 95 | 100 | 115 |
| VII, Ball, 17J, nickel, SW, 14K, HC | ★★★ | 3,500 | 4,000 | 6,000 |
| VII, Ball, 17J, nickel, SW, GF, HC | ★★★ | 2,200 | 2,800 | 3,500 |
| VIII, 15J, gilded or nickel, SW, 14K, OF | | 900 | 1,000 | 1,400 |
| VIII, 17J, nickel, split plate, SW, 14K, OF | ★ | 1,200 | 1,400 | 1,700 |
| VIII, 17J, nickel, split plate, SW, silver, OF | ★ | 425 | 525 | 650 |
| VIII, 15J (movement only) | | 85 | 90 | 100 |
| VIII, Ball, 17J, nickel, SW, 14K, OF | ★★ | 3,000 | 3,500 | 4,000 |
| VIII, Ball, 17J, nickel, SW, GF, OF | ★★ | 1,000 | 1,500 | 2,000 |

Series VII, 18 size, 17J, nickel, split plate, adjusted, Stem Wind, serial number 228,055.

Series VIII, 18 size, 15 jewels, serial number 308,455.

Series VIII, 18 size, 17 jewels, split plate model, gold jewel settings, serial number 309,904.

Series IX, 18 size, 15 jewels, hunting. This series is gilded only and hound grade exclusively, S # 402,873.

| Series or Name — Description | Avg | Ex-Fn | Mint |
|---|---|---|---|
| IX, 15J, gilded, SW, 14K, HC | $900 | $1,100 | $1,400 |
| IX, 15J, gilded, SW, silver, HC | 425 | 525 | 650 |
| IX, 15J (movement only) | 80 | 85 | 100 |

### L SIZE (16)
#### (In Original Cases)

| Series or Name — Description | Avg | Ex-Fn | Mint |
|---|---|---|---|
| V, 15J, gilded, KW, 18K, HC | $1,000 | $1,200 | $1,500 |
| V, 15J, gilded, KW, 18K, Coles Escapement ★★★★ | 1,300 | 1,500 | 1,800 |
| V, 15J, gilded or nickel, SW, 14K, HC | 800 | 1,000 | 1,300 |
| V, 15J, gilded, SW, 14K, Coles Escapement ★★★★ | 1,100 | 1,300 | 1,600 |
| Prescott, 15J., gilded, SW, (Series V movement only) ★★ | 1,000 | 1,500 | 2,000 |

Series V, 16 or L size, Prescott Model, 15 jewels, hunting, serial number 50,434.

Series XI, 16 size, 17 jewels, split plate model, nickel movement, gold jewel settings, serial number 600,021.

🕐 Watches listed in this book are priced at the collectable retail level, as **complete** watches having an original 14k gold-filled case and *Key Wind* with silver, an original white enamel single sunk dial, and with the entire original movement in good working order with no repairs needed.

Series XII, L-16 size, 21 jewels, split plate model, nickel movement, gold lettering, gold jewel settings, serial number 700,899.

Series K, 14 or K size, 15 jewels, key wind & set, serial number 3,004.

| Series or Name — Description | | Avg | Ex-Fn | Mint |
|---|---|---|---|---|
| V, 15J (movement only) | | $90 | $100 | $125 |
| XI, 17J, nickel, split plate, SW, 14K, HC | ★ | 1,100 | 1,300 | 1,600 |
| XI, 17J, nickel, split plate, SW, silver, HC | ★ | 400 | 500 | 650 |
| XI, 17J (movement only) | | 200 | 300 | 450 |
| XII, 17J, nickel, split plate, SW, 14K, OF | ★ | 1,000 | 1,200 | 1,500 |
| XII, 17J, nickel, split plate, SW, silver, OF | ★ | 375 | 475 | 625 |
| XII, 17J (movement only) | | 100 | 150 | 175 |
| XII, 21J, nickel, split plate, SW, 14K OF | ★★★ | 2,500 | 3,000 | 4,000 |

### K SIZE (14)
#### (In Original Cases)

| Series or Name — Description | | Avg | Ex-Fn | Mint |
|---|---|---|---|---|
| K, 15J, gilded, KW, 18K, HC | ★★★★ | $4,000 | $5,000 | $6,500 |

### J SIZE (12)
#### (In Original Cases)

| Series or Name – Description | | Avg | Ex-Fn | Mint |
|---|---|---|---|---|
| X, 15J, nickel, hound, SW, 14K, OF | ★ | $700 | $900 | $1,200 |
| X, 15J, nickel, horse, SW, 14K, OF | ★ | 800 | 1,000 | 1,300 |
| X, 15J, nickel, deer, SW, 14K, OF | ★ | 900 | 1,100 | 1,400 |
| X, 15J, hound (movement only) | ★ | 200 | 250 | 300 |

X, 15J, nickel, hound, SW, serial # 500,003

Series X, 12 or J size, 15 jewels, note deer on movement, serial number 501,361.

I size (10 size), 15 jewels, gilded, key wind, serial number 3,404.

### I SIZE (10)
#### (In Original Cases)

| Series or Name — Description | | Avg | Ex-Fn | Mint |
|---|---|---|---|---|
| I, 15J, gilded, KW, 18K HC | ★★★ | $2,800 | $3,400 | $4,200 |

### G SIZE (6)
#### (In Original Cases)

| Series or Name — Description | | Avg | Ex-Fn | Mint |
|---|---|---|---|---|
| VI, 15J, gilded, KW, 18K, HC | ★★ | $1,400 | $1,800 | $2,400 |
| VI, 15J, gilded or nickel, SW, 18K, HC | | 1,000 | 1,200 | 1,500 |
| VI, 15J, gilded or nickel, SW, 14K, HC | | 700 | 850 | 1,000 |
| VI, 15J (movement only) | | 175 | 200 | 300 |

Series VI, 6 or G size, 15 jewels, stem wind.

Series VI, 6 or G size, 15 jewels, stem wind, serial number 104,520.

🕐 Generic, nameless or unmarked grades for watch movements are listed under the Company name or initials of the Company, etc. by size, jewel count and description.

# E. HOWARD WATCH CO. (KEYSTONE)
## Waltham, Massachusetts
### 1902 - 1930

The Howard name was purchased by the Keystone Watch Case Co. in 1902. The watches are marked "E. Howard Watch Co. Boston, U. S. A." There were no patent rights transferred, just the Howard name. The "Edward Howard" chronometer was the highest grade, 16 size, and was introduced in 1912 for $350.

Keystone Howard also gained control of U. S. Watch Co. of Waltham and New York Standard Watch Company.

## ESTIMATED SERIAL NUMBERS
## AND PRODUCTION DATES

**Date    Serial No.**

1902— 850,000
1903— 900,000
1909— 980,000
1912—1,100,000
1915—1,285,000
1917—1,340,000
1921—1,400,000
1930—1,500,000

The arrows denote number of jewels and adjustments in each grade.

Cross =23 jewel, 5 positions

Star =21 jewel, Adj.5P, & 19J with V under star

Triangle =19 jewel, 5 positions

Circle =17 jewel, 3 positions

SERIES 1905, 16 size, 17 jewels, open face. This model can be identified by the slant parallel damaskeening. This represents the **top** grade with raised gold jewel settings double, roller, Adj.5P and sold for $115.00 in 1910.

1907 Model, Series 0, 23 jewels, HC, serial # 953,481. NOTE: The escape wheel bridge & the fourth wheel bridge is not notched out as is the Series 0 movement.

SERIES 9, 16 size, 17 jewels, open face. This model can be identified by the checkerboard damaskeening. This represents the **mid** grade, GJS, double roller, Adj.5P and sold for $105.00 in 1910.

SERIES 3, 16 size, 17 jewels open face. This model can be identified by the circular damaskeening. This represents the **lowest** grade of the three with single roller, Adj.3P and sold for $100.00 in 1910.

E. Howard Watch Co., Series 0, 16 size, 23 jewels, in original E. Howard Watch Co. swing-out movement Keystone Extra gold filled Open Face case.

E. HOWARD WATCH CO. Series 0 (not marked), 16S, 23J., Hunting Case,

🕒 unmarked Series, No., 0, 1, 2, 5 & 10 , also 1907 look the same as the 2 above illustrations, 1907 & Series or No. 0=23J, Series or No.1&10=21J, Series2=17J, 1905 & Series or No.=19J.

## E. HOWARD WATCH CO. (KEYSTONE)
### 16 SIZE

| Series or Name — Description | Avg | Ex-Fn | Mint |
|---|---|---|---|
| No. 0, & 1907, 23J, BRG, Adj.5P, DR, OF | $500 | $550 | $650 |
| 1907 model & No.0, 23J, BRG, Adj.5P, DR, HC | 550 | 600 | 685 |
| Unmarked, 23J, BRG, Adj.5P, DR, OF | 425 | 450 | 500 |
| Series 0, 23J, BRG, Adj.5P, DR, **Ruby banking pins** | 550 | 600 | 650 |
| Series 0, 23J, BRG, Adj.5P, DR, **jeweled barrel** | 550 | 600 | 650 |
| Series 0, 23J, BRG, Adj.5P, DR, OF, 14K | 850 | 950 | 1,200 |
| Series 0, 23J, BRG, Adj.5P, DR, HC, 14K | 1,000 | 1,200 | 1,500 |
| No. 1, 21J, BRG, Adj.5P, DR ............★ | 400 | 445 | 500 |
| Series 1, 21J, BRG, Adj.5P, DR | 400 | 445 | 500 |
| Series 2, 17J, BRG, Adj.5P, DR, HC | 200 | 245 | 300 |

Series II, Railroad Chronometer, 16 size, 21 jewels, Adj5p, serial number 1,217,534.

Edward Howard Model, 16 size, 23 blue sapphire jewels, frosted gold bridge, wolfteeth wind, serial # 77.

🕒 Watches listed in this book are priced at the **collectable fair market value** at the RETAIL level, as complete watches having an original 14k gold filled case, KEY WIND with silver, an original white enamel single sunk dial, and with the entire original movement in good working order with no repairs needed, unless otherwise noted.

E. Howard Watch Co., 16 size, 23 jewels, by Waltham, raised gold jewel settings, Adj5p, hunting case, bridge style movement.

E. Howard Watch Co., 16 size 19 jewels, by Waltham, gold jewel settings, Adj3p, hunting case, 3/4 plate movement.

| Series or Name — Description | Avg | Ex-Fn | Mint |
|---|---|---|---|
| Series 2, 17J, BRG, Adj.5P, DR, OF | $125 | $145 | $175 |
| Series 3, 17J, 3/4, Adj.3P, circular DMK | 100 | 120 | 150 |
| Series 3, 17J, OF, Adj.3P, 14K, circular DMK | 500 | 525 | 560 |
| No. 5, 19J, GJS, BRG, HC ★ | 400 | 425 | 475 |
| Series 5, 19J, BRG, Adj.5P, DR, 14K | 550 | 575 | 625 |
| Series 5, 19J, BRG, Adj.5P, DR, 1907 Model | 225 | 250 | 300 |
| 1905, 17J, 3/4, Adj.5P, DR, RGJS, slant parallel DMK, OF | 125 | 145 | 175 |
| 1905, 17J, 3/4, Adj.5P, DR, RGJS, slant parallel DMK, HC | 175 | 200 | 250 |
| Series 9, 17J, 3/4, Adj.5P, DR, LS, checkerboard DMK | 175 | 200 | 250 |
| Series 9, 17J, 3/4, Adj.5P, DR, 14K, checkerboard DMK (railroad grade) | 475 | 500 | 550 |
| Series 10, 21J, BRG, Adj.5P, DR Marked Non–Magnetic ★ | 375 | 425 | 475 |
| Series 10, 21J, BRG, Adj.5P, DR | 375 | 400 | 425 |
| No. 10, 21J, BRG, Adj.5P, DR | 350 | 375 | 400 |
| Series 11, 21J, R.R. Chrono., Adj.5P, DR | 375 | 425 | 475 |
| Edward Howard, 23 blue sapphire pressed J, Free Sprung, Adj.5P, DR, Serial numbers below 300, without box ★ ★ | 6,000 | 7,000 | 8,000 |
| Edward Howard, 23 blue sapphire pressed J, Free Sprung, Adj.5P, DR, Serial numbers below 300, with original box and papers, 18K Edward Howard case ★ ★ ★ | 8,000 | 9,000 | 10,000 |
| 23J, E. Howard W. Co. on movement (mfg. by Waltham), 14K, Brg model ★ ★ | 1,200 | 1,400 | 1,700 |
| 23J, E. Howard W. Co. on movement (mfg. by Waltham), OF, gold filled | 500 | 600 | 700 |
| 23J, E. Howard W. Co. on movement (mfg. by Waltham), HC, gold filled | 600 | 700 | 850 |
| 21J, Waltham Model, Bridge model, HC | 400 | 450 | 550 |
| 21J, Waltham Model, 3/4, OF | 275 | 300 | 350 |
| 19J, Waltham Model, Bridge model, HC | 275 | 300 | 375 |
| 19J, Waltham Model, 3/4, OF | 275 | 300 | 350 |
| 17J, Waltham Model, Bridge model, HC | 250 | 300 | 375 |
| 17J, Waltham Model, 3/4, OF | 225 | 250 | 300 |
| Climax,7J., (made for export ), gilded, OF | 60 | 70 | 90 |

## 12 SIZE

| Series or Name — Description | Avg | Ex-Fn | Mint |
|---|---|---|---|
| Series 6, 19J, BRG, DR, Adj.5P, 1908 Model, 14K, HC | $300 | $350 | $425 |
| Series 6, 19J, BRG, DR, Adj.5P, 14K, OF | 200 | 250 | 325 |
| Series 6, 19J, BRG, DR, Adj.5P, OF | 100 | 120 | 150 |
| Series 7, 17J, BRG, DR, Adj.3P, 14K, OF | 200 | 250 | 325 |
| Series 7, 17J, BRG, DR, Adj.3P, OF | 70 | 90 | 125 |
| Series 8, 21J, BRG, DR, Adj.5P, OF | 100 | 125 | 175 |
| Series 8, 23J, BRG, DR, Adj.5P, 14K, OF | 350 | 400 | 475 |
| Series 8, 23J, BRG, DR, Adj.5P, OF | 150 | 200 | 225 |
| Series 8, 23J, BRG, DR, Adj.5P, 14K, HC | 450 | 550 | 650 |
| 23J,Waltham Model, BRG, HC | 250 | 300 | 350 |
| 23J,Waltham Model, BRG, OF | 200 | 250 | 300 |
| 21J,Waltham Model, BRG, HC | 200 | 250 | 300 |
| 21J,Waltham Model, BRG, OF | 200 | 225 | 250 |
| 17J,Waltham Model, BRG, HC | 150 | 175 | 200 |
| 17J,Waltham Model, BRG, OF | 125 | 150 | 175 |
| 17J,Waltham Model, 3/4, HC | 125 | 150 | 175 |
| 17J,Waltham Model, 3/4, OF | 100 | 125 | 150 |

NOTE: First Serial # for **12 size** with 17J.=977,001; 19J.=977,451; 21J.=1,055,851.

**Series 8**, 12 size, 21 jewels, open face, stop works, extra thin.

**E. Howard Watch Co.,** 10 size, 17J, Adj3p, serial # 61,230. (Serial # started at about 1,001 on this model.)

SERIES 8 GOING BARREL =21J.    SERIES 6 GOING BARREL =19J.    SERIES 7 GOING BARREL =17J.

## 10 SIZE

NOTE: 10 Size Serial numbers start at about 1,001 on this model.

| Series or Name — Description | Avg | Ex-Fn | Mint |
|---|---|---|---|
| Thin Model, 21J, ADJ, 14K case, OF | $250 | $275 | $325 |
| Thin Model, 19J, ADJ, 14K case, OF | 225 | 250 | 300 |
| Thin Model, 17J, ADJ, 14K case, OF | 200 | 225 | 275 |

STYLE R.R. Chronometer

STYLE R.R. Antique Bow
note: Jointed- Inside Cap

STYLE R.R. Plain swing out

STYLE R.R. Engine Turned swing out

STYLE R.R. SWING OUT

Rail Road Chronometer = Gold Filled
Rail Road Antique Bow= solid gold 18K gold, 14K gold heavy, 14K gold, & 25 year **Gold Filled**
SWING OUT = Gold Filled and the swing out **Plain** also came 14K solid gold

🕐 NOTE: Factory Advertised as a **complete** watch and was fitted with a certain matched, timed and rated movement and sold in the factory designed case style as a **complete** watch. The factory adverised as _"Howard movements and cases are not sold separately"_. All the factory advertised **complete** watches came with a enamel dial SHOWN or <u>CHOICE</u> of other **Railroad** dials.

# ILLINOIS WATCH CO.
## Springfield, Illinois
### 1869 - 1927

The Illinois Watch Company was organized mainly through the efforts of J. C. Adams. The first directors were J. T. Stuart, W. B. Miller, John Williams, John W. Bunn, George Black and George Passfield. In 1879 the company changed all its watches to a quick train movement by changing the number of teeth in the fourth wheel. The first mainspring made by the company was used in 1882. The next year soft enamel dials were used.

The Illinois Watch Co. used more names on its movements than any other watch manufacturer. To identify all of them requires extensive knowledge by the collector plus a good working knowledge of watch mechanics. Engraved on some early movements, for example, are "S. W. Co." or "I. W. Co., Springfield, Ill." To the novice these abbreviations might be hard to understand, thus making Illinois watches difficult to identify. But one saving clue is that the location "Springfield, Illinois" appears on most of these watches. It is important to learn how to identify these type watches because some of them are extremely collectible. Examples of some of the more valuable of these are: the Benjamin Franklin (size 18 or 16, 25 or 26 jewels), Paillard's Non-Magnetic, Pennsylvania Special, C & O, and B & O railroad models.

The earliest movements made by the Illinois Watch Co. are listed below. They made the first watch in early 1872, but the company really didn't get off the ground until 1875. Going by the serial number, the first watch made was the Stuart. Next was the Mason, followed by the Bunn, the Miller, and finally the Currier. The first stem-wind was made in 1875.

STUART, FIRST Run was serial numbers ............ 1 to 100.
MASON, FIRST Run was serial numbers ............ 101 to 200.
BUNN, FIRST Run was serial numbers ................. 201 to 300.
MILLER, FIRST Run was serial numbers ............ 301 to 400.
CURRIER, FIRST Run was serial numbers........... 401 to 500.

The Illinois Watch Company was sold to Hamilton Watch Co. in 1927. The Illinois factory continued to produce Illinois watches under the new management until 1932. After 1933 Hamilton produced watches bearing the Illinois name in their own factory until 1939.

## CHRONOLOGY OF THE DEVELOPMENT OF ILLINOIS WATCH CO.:
Illinois Springfield Watch Co.................................... 1869-1879
Springfield Illinois Watch Co.................................... 1879-1885
Illinois Watch Co...................................................... 1885-1927
Illinois Watch Co. sold to Hamilton Watch Co. ....... 1927

ILLINOIS WATCH CO., Bates Model, 18 size, 7 jewels, key wind & set, serial number 43,876, c.1874.

BUNN, 18 size, 16 jewels, hunting case, NOTE: Chalmer patented regulator, serial number 1,185,809.

## ILLINOIS ESTIMATED SERIAL NUMBERS AND PRODUCTION DATES

| DATE – SERIAL NO. | DATE – SERIAL NO. | DATE – SERIAL NO. |
|---|---|---|
| 1872 – 5,000 | 1893 – 1,120,000 | 1914 – 2,600,000 |
| 1873 – 20,000 | 1894 – 1,160,000 | 1915 – 2,700,000 |
| 1874 – 50,000 | 1895 – 1,220,000 | 1916 – 2,800,000 |
| 1875 – 75,000 | 1896 – 1,250,000 | 1917 – 3,000,000 |
| 1876 – 100,000 | 1897 – 1,290,000 | 1918 – 3,200,000 |
| 1877 – 145,000 | 1898 – 1,330,000 | 1919 – 3,400,000 |
| 1878 – 210,000 | 1899 – 1,370,000 | 1920 – 3,600,000 |
| 1879 – 250,000 | 1900 – 1,410,000 | 1921 – 3,750,000 |
| 1880 – 300,000 | 1901 – 1,450,000 | 1922 – 3,900,000 |
| 1881 – 350,000 | 1902 – 1,500,000 | 1923 – 4,000,000 |
| 1882 – 400,000 | 1903 – 1,650,000 | 1924 – 4,500,000 |
| 1883 – 450,000 | 1904 – 1,700,000 | 1925 – 4,700,000 |
| 1884 – 500,000 | 1905 – 1,800,000 | 1926 – 4,800,000 |
| 1885 – 550,000 | 1906 – 1,840,000 | 1927 – 5,000,000 |
| 1886 – 600,000 | 1907 – 1,900,000 | (Sold to Hamilton) |
| 1887 – 700,000 | 1908 – 2,100,000 | 1928 – 5,200,000 |
| 1888 – 800,000 | 1909 – 2,150,000 | 1929 – 5,350,000 |
| 1889 – 900,000 | 1910 – 2,200,000 | 1930 – 5,400,000 |
| 1890 – 1,000,000 | 1911 – 2,300,000 | 1931 – 5,500,000 |
| 1891 – 1,040,000 | 1912 – 2,400,000 | 1932 – 5,600,000 |
| 1892 – 1,080,000 | 1913 – 2,500,000 | |

The above list is provided for determining the **APPROXIMATE** age of your watch. Match serial number with date. Watches were not necessarily sold in the exact order of manufactured date.

**NOTE:** It required several months for raw material to emerge as a finished movement. All the while the factory is producing all sizes, models and grades. The numbering system was basically "consecutive", due to demand a batch of movements could be side tracked, thus allowing a different size and model to move ahead to meet this demand. Therefore, the dates some movements were sold and delivered to the trade, may not be "consecutive".

(See Illinois Identification of Movements section located at the end of the Illinois price section to identify the movement, size and model number of your watch.)

## ILLINOIS
### 18 SIZE (ALL FULL PLATE)

| Grade or Name — Description | Avg | Ex-Fn | Mint |
|---|---|---|---|
| Alleghany, 11J, KW, gilded, OF | $100 | $120 | $150 |
| Alleghany, 11J, M#1, NI, KW | 125 | 145 | 175 |
| Alleghany, 11J, M#2, NI, Transition | 100 | 125 | 175 |
| America, 7J, M#3, Silveroid | 65 | 80 | 100 |
| America, 7J, M#1-2, KW | 100 | 125 | 175 |
| America Special, 7J, M#1-2, KW | 150 | 175 | 225 |
| Army & Navy, 19J, GJS, Adj.5P | 225 | 250 | 300 |
| Army & Navy, 21J, GJS, Adj.5P | 275 | 300 | 350 |
| Baltimore & Ohio R.R. Special, 17J, GJS, ADJ | 500 | 700 | 900 |
| Baltimore & Ohio R.R. Special, 21J, GJS, NI, ADJ | 1,000 | 1,200 | 1,400 |
| Baltimore & Ohio R.R. Standard, 24J, GJS, ADJ | 1,500 | 1,700 | 2,000 |
| Bates, 7J, M#1-2, KW | 125 | 150 | 185 |
| Benjamin Franklin U.S.A., 17J, ADJ, NI | 600 | 675 | 750 |

🕐 Watches listed in this book are priced at the **collectable fair market value** at the **retail** level, as **complete** watches having an original 14k gold filled case, *KEY WIND* with silver, an original white enamel single sunk dial, and with the entire original movement in good working order with no repairs needed, unless otherwise noted.

🕐 GENERIC, NAMELESS OR **UNMARKED GRADES** FOR WATCH MOVEMENTS ARE LISTED UNDER THE COMPANY NAME OR INITIALS OF THE COMPANY, ETC. BY SIZE, JEWEL COUNT AND DESCRIPTION.

🕐 Some watch manufacturers personalize watches for jobbers or jewelry firms, with exclusive private signed or marked movements. The valuable collectable watches are listed under the signed or marked movement. Other exclusive private signed or marked movements will have equivalent value are only slightly higher value and should be compared to Generic or Nameless movements. Railroad signed or marked (dials & movements) are usually more collectable & higher in value.

Illinois Watch Co., 18 size, railroad watch with a Ferguson dial with the numbers 1 through 12 in red.

Army and Navy, 18 size, 19 jewels, engraved on movement "Washington Watch Co.," serial number 1,606,612.

| Grade or Name — Description | | Avg | Ex-Fn | Mint |
|---|---|---|---|---|
| Benjamin Franklin U.S.A., 21J, GJS, **Adj.6P**, NI | ★ | $1,000 | $1,200 | $1,400 |
| Benjamin Franklin U.S.A., 21J, GJS, Adj.5P, NI | ★ | 900 | 1,100 | 1,300 |
| Benjamin Franklin U.S.A., 24J, GJS, Adj.6P, NI | ★ | 2,500 | 2,800 | 3,250 |
| Benjamin Franklin U.S.A., 25J, GJS, Adj.6P, NI | ★ | 6,000 | 6,500 | 7,500 |
| Benjamin Franklin U.S.A., 26J, GJS, Adj.6P, NI, | ★★★★★ | 6,500 | 7,000 | 7,500 |
| Bunn, 15J, M#1, KW, KS, **1st. run S# 201 to 300**, OF | ★★★ | 2,000 | 2,400 | 3,000 |
| Bunn, 15J, M#1, KW, KS, OF | ★ | 500 | 600 | 775 |
| Bunn, 15J, M#1, KW, KS, "ADJUSTED", | | 550 | 650 | 825 |
| Bunn, 15J, KW/SW transition | | 425 | 500 | 650 |
| Bunn, 15J, M#1, KW, Coin | | 500 | 600 | 775 |
| Bunn, 15J, KW, M#1, HC | | 550 | 650 | 825 |
| Bunn, 16J, KW, OF | | 500 | 600 | 775 |
| Bunn, 16J, KW, HC | | 550 | 650 | 825 |
| Bunn, 16J, SW, HC | | 550 | 650 | 825 |
| Bunn, 16J, SW, ADJ, HC | | 550 | 650 | 825 |
| Bunn, 17J, SW, M#1, HC | ★ | 650 | 750 | 925 |
| Bunn, 17J, M#2, SW, NI, ADJ, Chalmers patent reg., HC | ★ | 550 | 600 | 700 |
| Bunn, 17J, SW, NI, Coin | | 125 | 150 | 200 |
| Bunn, 17J, SW, M#3, 5th pinion, gilded, OF | | 350 | 400 | 475 |
| Bunn, 17J, M#4, SW, NI, OF | | 125 | 150 | 200 |
| Bunn, 17J, M#5, SW, NI, HC | | 150 | 200 | 275 |
| Bunn, 17J, M#6, SW, NI, OF | | 125 | 150 | 200 |
| Bunn, 18J, SW, NI, ADJ., OF | ★★★★ | 900 | 1,000 | 1,200 |
| Bunn, 19J, SW, NI, OF, DR, LS, GJS, Adj.5P, **J. barrel** | | 250 | 300 | 325 |
| Bunn, 19J, SW, OF, Adj.6P, DR, **J. barrel** | | 300 | 350 | 425 |
| Bunn, 19J, SW, GJS, HC, DR, Adj.5P, **J. barrel** | ★ | 350 | 400 | 500 |

⊕ Watches listed in this book are priced at the **collectable fair market value** at the RETAIL level, as complete watches having an original 14k gold filled case, KEY WIND with silver, an original white enamel single sunk dial, and with the entire original movement in good working order with no repairs needed, unless otherwise noted.

⊕ Some grades are not included. Their values can be determined by comparing with **similar** age, size, metal content, style, models and grades listed.

**Bunn Special**, 18 size, 24 jewels, adjusted, serial number 1,413,435

**Bunn Special**, 18 size, 26 Ruby jewels, "J: Home & Co." on dial, adjusted to six positions, gold jewel settings, serial number 2,019,415.

| Grade or Name — Description | Avg | Ex-Fn | Mint |
|---|---|---|---|
| Bunn Special, 21J, SW, **Coin** | $200 | $225 | $250 |
| Bunn Special, 21J, GJS, ADJ, HC | 400 | 450 | 500 |
| Bunn Special, 21J, GJS, ADJ, DR, OF | 200 | 225 | 265 |
| Bunn Special, 21J, GJS, DR, Adj.5P, OF | 200 | 230 | 275 |
| Bunn Special, 21J, GJS, DR, Adj.6P, OF | 225 | 250 | 285 |
| Bunn Special, 21J, GJS, Adj.5P, **HC, 14K** | 750 | 800 | 900 |
| Bunn Special, 21J, GJS, ADJ, 2-Tone | 250 | 285 | 325 |
| Bunn Special, 21J, GJS, Adj.5P, DR | 225 | 250 | 300 |
| Bunn Special, 21J," EXTRA", GJS ★ | 385 | 500 | 625 |
| Bunn Special, 23J, GJS, ADJ, DR, OF | 425 | 475 | 550 |
| Bunn Special, 23J, GJS, Adj.6P, DR, OF | 450 | 500 | 575 |
| Bunn Special, 23J, GJS, Adj.6P, DR, 2-Tone, OF ★★★ | 500 | 600 | 750 |
| Bunn Special, 23J, GJS, ADJ, DR, HC ★★ | 1,900 | 2,200 | 2,500 |
| Bunn Special, 24J, GJS, Adj.5P, DR, HC | 800 | 900 | 1,100 |
| Bunn Special, 24J, GJS, Adj.5P, DR, **14K, HC** | 1,450 | 1,600 | 1,800 |
| Bunn Special, 24J, GJS, Adj.5P, DR, OF | 700 | 775 | 850 |
| Bunn Special, 24J, GJS, Adj.6P, DR, OF | 725 | 800 | 875 |
| Bunn Special, 24J, GJS, Adj.6P, DR, HC | 800 | 900 | 1,200 |
| Bunn Special, 25J, GJS, Adj.6P, DR ★★★ | 5,000 | 5,500 | 6,500 |
| Bunn Special, 26J, GJS, Adj.6P, DR ★★ | 4,500 | 5,000 | 6,000 |
| Central Truck Railroad, 15J, KW, KS ★ | 350 | 400 | 475 |
| Chesapeake & Ohio, 17J, ADJ, OF ★ | 400 | 500 | 600 |
| Chesapeake & Ohio Special, 21J, GJS, 2-Tone ★ | 1,000 | 1,200 | 1,500 |
| Chesapeake & Ohio Special, 24J, NI, ADJ, GJS ★ | 1,700 | 1,900 | 2,200 |
| Chronometer, 11-15J, KW, OF | 125 | 150 | 185 |
| Chronometer, 15J, M#2, HC | 150 | 175 | 225 |
| Columbia, 11J, M#3, 5th Pinion | 100 | 125 | 175 |
| Columbia, 11J, M#1 & 2, KW | 100 | 125 | 175 |
| Columbia, 11J, M#1 & 2, Silveroid | 75 | 100 | 150 |
| Columbia Special, 11J, M#1-2-3, KW | 100 | 125 | 175 |
| Columbia Special, 11J, M#1-2-3, KW, transition | 75 | 100 | 125 |
| Comet, 11J, M#3, OF, LS, SW | 75 | 100 | 125 |
| Commodore Perry, 15-16J, HC | 150 | 175 | 225 |
| Criterion, 11-15J, HC | 100 | 125 | 150 |

🕐 Some watch manufacturers personalize watches for jobbers or jewelry firms, with exclusive private signed or marked movements. The valuable collectable watches are listed under the signed or marked movement. Other exclusive private signed or marked movements will have equivalent value are only slightly higher value and should be compared to Generic or Nameless movements. Railroad signed or marked (dials & movements) are usually more collectable & higher in value.

Diurnal, 18 size, 7 jewels, key wind & set, only one run, total production 2,000, serial number 86,757.

Emperor, 18 size, 21 jewels, Adj3p, serial number 2,396,628.

| Grade or Name — Description | Avg | Ex-Fn | Mint |
|---|---|---|---|
| Currier, 11-12J, KW, OF | $100 | $125 | $175 |
| Currier, 11-12J, KW, HC | 125 | 175 | 225 |
| Currier, 11-12J, **1st run S# 401 to 500** ★★★ | 300 | 400 | 550 |
| Currier, 11-12J, transition, OF | 75 | 95 | 125 |
| Currier, 13–15J, M#3, OF | 75 | 95 | 125 |
| Currier, 13–15J, M#3, HC | 100 | 130 | 165 |
| Dauntless, 11J | 75 | 95 | 125 |
| Dean, 15J, M#1, KW, HC ★ | 250 | 350 | 450 |
| Diurnal, 7J, KW, KS, HC, Coin ★ | 200 | 250 | 325 |
| Dominion Railway, with train on dial ★ | 900 | 1,000 | 1,300 |
| Eastlake, 11J, SW, KW, Transition | 100 | 125 | 175 |
| Emperor, 21J, M#6, LS, SW, ADJ | 200 | 225 | 275 |
| Enterprise, M#2, ADJ | 100 | 125 | 175 |
| Eureka, 11J | 100 | 125 | 175 |
| Favorite, 16J, LS, OF | 100 | 125 | 160 |
| Forest City, 7–11J, SW, LS, HC | 125 | 150 | 200 |
| Forest City, 17J, KW/SW, gilted, | 150 | 175 | 225 |
| General Grant or General Lee, 11J, M#1, KW | 225 | 250 | 300 |
| Hoyt, 7-9-11J, M#1-2, KW | 75 | 100 | 150 |

⊕ Generic, nameless, Personalized Jobber Watches or unmarked grades for watch movements are listed under the Company name or initials of the Company, etc. by size, jewel count and description.

| | Avg | Ex-Fn | Mint |
|---|---|---|---|
| Illinois Watch Co., 7-9J, | $75 | $95 | $125 |
| Illinois Watch Co., 11J, M#1-2, KW, | 75 | 95 | 125 |
| Illinois Watch Co., 11J, M#3 | 55 | 75 | 100 |
| Illinois Watch Co., 13J, M#1-2, KW, | 100 | 125 | 175 |
| Illinois Watch Co., 15J, M#1-2, KW, | 100 | 125 | 175 |
| Illinois Watch Co., 15J, KW, ADJ, NI | 125 | 150 | 200 |
| Illinois Watch Co., 15J, SW, ADJ, DMK, NI | 75 | 95 | 125 |
| Illinois Watch Co., 15J, transition | 60 | 75 | 100 |
| Illinois Watch Co., 15J, SW, **Silveroid** | 50 | 60 | 75 |
| Illinois Watch Co., 15J, SW, **9K, HC** | 300 | 400 | 550 |
| Illinois Watch Co., 16J, SW, ADJ, DMK, NI | 75 | 95 | 125 |
| Illinois Watch Co., 16J, SW, ADJ, DMK, NI, marked **ADJ** ★ | 200 | 250 | 325 |
| Illinois Watch Co., 17J, SW, **Silveroid** | 50 | 60 | 75 |
| Illinois Watch Co., 17J, M#3, **5th Pinion** | 200 | 220 | 250 |
| Illinois Watch Co., 17J, SW, 2 tone mvt, | 65 | 95 | 145 |

Ill. W. Co., 18 size, 17 jewels, adjusted, 2-tone movement, serial number 1,404,442.

Miller, 18 size, 17 jewels, 5th pinion model which changed hunting case to open face.

Generic, nameless, Personalized Jobber Watches or unmarked grades for watch movements are listed under the Company name or initials of the Company, etc. by size, jewel count and description.

| Grade or Name — Description | Avg | Ex-Fn | Mint |
|---|---|---|---|
| Illinois Watch Co., 17J, SW, ADJ............................................. | $75 | $95 | $125 |
| Illinois Watch Co., 17J, SW, "EXTRA", Adj.4P............................. | 85 | 110 | 135 |
| Illinois Watch Co., 17J, transition..................................... | 75 | 95 | 125 |
| Illinois Watch Co., 19J, ADJ. **J. Barrel**, OF................................... | 200 | 225 | 250 |
| Illinois Watch Co., 21J, Adj.3P, OF......................................... | 175 | 195 | 225 |
| Illinois Watch Co., 21J, ADJ5-6P, .......................................... | 300 | 335 | 375 |
| Illinois Watch Co., 24J, ADJ, ............................................... | 500 | 550 | 625 |
| Interior, 7J, KW & SW, OF................................................. | 100 | 125 | 175 |
| Interstate Chronometer, 17J, HC........................................ | 400 | 500 | 650 |
| Interstate Chronometer, 17J, OF ....................................... | 300 | 400 | 550 |
| Interstate Chronometer, 23J, Adj.5P, GJS, NI, OF.....................★ | 850 | 950 | 1,150 |
| Interstate Chronometer, 23J, Adj.5P, GJS, NI, HC ................ ★ ★ | 1,200 | 1,400 | 1,650 |
| Iowa W. Co., 7-11J, M#1-2, KW, ........................................ | 175 | 200 | 250 |
| King of the Road, 16 &17J, NI, OF & HC, LS, ADJ .................★ | 400 | 500 | 625 |
| King Special, 17J, 2-tone, OF ............................................. | 100 | 125 | 185 |
| King Philip Sp., 17J, ( RR spur line)...................................... | 275 | 350 | 425 |
| Lafayette, 24J, GJS, Adj.6P, NI, SW, OF............................... | 950 | 1,050 | 1,250 |
| Lafayette, 24J, GJS, Adj.6P, NI, SW, HC ............................. | 1,200 | 1,400 | 1,600 |
| Lakeshore, 17J, OF, LS, NI, SW .......................................... | 100 | 125 | 175 |
| Landis W. Co., 15-17J................................................... | 75 | 100 | 150 |
| Liberty Bell, 17J, LS, NI, SW, OF....................................... | 75 | 100 | 135 |
| Liberty Bell, 17J, LS, NI, SW, HC ...................................... | 100 | 125 | 175 |
| Lightning Express, 11-13J, KWKS, .................................... | 85 | 95 | 125 |
| A. Lincoln, 21J, Adj.5P, NI, DR, GJS, HC ............................... | 350 | 375 | 400 |
| A. Lincoln, 21J, Adj.5P, NI, DR, GJS,OF ............................... | 225 | 250 | 300 |
| Lincoln Park, 15-17J, LS, OF............................................ | 75 | 100 | 150 |
| Majestic Special, 17J, 2-tone, OF ...................................... | 100 | 125 | 150 |
| Maiden Lane, 16-17J, 5th Pinion ...................................... | 350 | 400 | 475 |
| Manhattan, 11-13J, NI, KW, LS, HC or OF ............................. | 125 | 140 | 185 |
| Manhattan, 15–17J, NI, KW, LS,HC or OF ............................ | 130 | 155 | 200 |
| Mason, 7J, KW, KS, HC ................................................ | 125 | 150 | 200 |
| Mason, 7J, KW, KS, HC, **1st run S# 101 to 200**................ ★ ★ ★ | 400 | 500 | 650 |
| Miller, 15J,**1st run S# 301 to 400**............................... ★ ★ ★ | 375 | 425 | 550 |
| Miller, 15J, M#1, HC, KW................................................ | 150 | 175 | 225 |
| Miller, 15J, M#1, HC, KW, ADJ......................................... | 175 | 200 | 250 |
| Miller, 15J, KW, OF ....................................................... | 125 | 150 | 200 |
| Miller, 17J, 5th Pinion, ADJ............................................. | 275 | 300 | 375 |

Paillard Non-Magnetic W. Co., 18 size, 24 jewels, gold jewel settings, serial number 1,397,812.

Pennsylvania Special, 18 size, 26 jewels, Adj6p, 2-tone movement, serial number 1,742,913.

| Grade or Name — Description | Avg | Ex-Fn | Mint |
|---|---|---|---|
| Monarch W. Co., 17J, NI, ADJ, SW | $125 | $150 | $200 |
| Montgomery Ward, 17J, OF, GJS | 125 | 150 | 200 |
| Montgomery Ward, 21J | 175 | 200 | 275 |
| Montgomery Ward Timer, 21J, ★ | 175 | 200 | 275 |
| Montgomery Ward, 24J, OF | 950 | 1,050 | 1,250 |
| Montgomery Ward, 24J, HC ★ | 1,200 | 1,400 | 1,700 |
| Muscatine W. Co., 15J, LS, NI, HC | 150 | 175 | 225 |
| The National, 11J, SW, LS, OF | 75 | 100 | 135 |
| Non-Magnetic W. Co., 21J, OF ★ | 225 | 275 | 350 |
| A.Norton,7J, KW, KS, | 100 | 125 | 150 |
| Paillard Non-Magnetic W. Co., 15J, NI, OF | 75 | 100 | 150 |
| Paillard Non-Magnetic W. Co., 17J, GJS, NI, Adj.5P, OF | 100 | 125 | 165 |
| Paillard Non-Magnetic W. Co., 21J, GJS, NI, Adj.5P, OF | 200 | 250 | 325 |
| Paillard Non-Magnetic W. Co., 23J, GJS, NI, Adj.5P, OF | 850 | 900 | 1,150 |
| Paillard Non-Magnetic W. Co., 24J, GJS, NI, Adj.5P, OF | 950 | 1,050 | 1,250 |
| Pennsylvania Special, 17J, GJS, ADJ ★ | 600 | 750 | 900 |
| Pennsylvania Special, 21J, DR, Adj.5P ★ | 1,200 | 1,400 | 1,800 |
| Pennsylvania Special, 24J, DR, GJS, ADJ ★ | 1,800 | 2,000 | 2,400 |
| Pennsylvania Special, 25J, DR, GJS, ADJ, NI ★★★★ | 5,000 | 5,500 | 6,500 |
| Pennsylvania Special, 26J, DR, GJS, ADJ, NI ★★ | 4,500 | 5,000 | 6,000 |
| Pierce Arrow, 17J, "automaker logo" ★ | 350 | 425 | 575 |
| Plymouth W. Co., 15-17J, SW | 65 | 95 | 125 |
| Potomac, 17J, OF, ADJ, NI | 125 | 150 | 200 |
| The President, 15J, NI, OF | 125 | 150 | 200 |
| The President, 17J, DMK, 14K gold case | 600 | 700 | 850 |
| Rail Road Construction, 17J, OF | 200 | 250 | 325 |
| Rail Road Dispatcher Extra, 17J, OF | 200 | 250 | 325 |
| Rail Road Employee's Special, 17J, HC | 250 | 300 | 350 |
| Rail Road Timer Extra, 17-21J, (Montgomery Ward), OF ★ | 300 | 350 | 450 |
| Rail Road King, 15J, NI, ADJ | 225 | 250 | 285 |
| Rail Road King, 16J, NI, ADJ ★ | 300 | 350 | 425 |
| Rail Road King, 17J, NI, ADJ ★ | 300 | 350 | 425 |
| The Railroader, 15J, OF, ADJ, NI | 250 | 300 | 375 |
| Railway , 11J, KW, KS, gilt ★ | 95 | 100 | 125 |
| Railway Engineer, 15J | 250 | 300 | 375 |
| Railway Regulator, 11-15J, KW, KS, gilt ★★ | 400 | 500 | 675 |

The President, 18 size, 17 jewels, chalmer patented regulator, serial number 1,240,909.

Railroad King, 18 size, 17 jewels, Fifth Pinion Model, adjusted. Note Chalmer patented regulator, S# 1,160,836.

| Grade or Name — Description | Avg | Ex-Fn | Mint |
|---|---|---|---|
| Remington W.Co. 17J, OF ........★ | $175 | $200 | $300 |
| Remington W.Co. 17J, HC ........★ | 200 | 250 | 375 |
| S. W. Co., 15J, M#1, KW, HC | 125 | 150 | 200 |
| R.W. Sears Watch Co. Chicago,"Defiance" model, 14K,HC | 650 | 750 | 900 |
| Sears & Roebuck Special, 17J, GJS, NI, DMK, Adj | 125 | 150 | 200 |
| Senate, 17J, NI, DMK | 125 | 150 | 200 |
| Southern R.R. Special, 21J, LS, ADJ, OF ........★ | 1,000 | 1,200 | 1,500 |
| Southern R.R. Special, 21J, M#5, LS, Adj., HC ........★ | 1,400 | 1,650 | 2,000 |
| Star Light, 17J, 5th pinion, Chalmers Reg. OF | 175 | 225 | 300 |
| Stewart Special, 21J, Adj. | 175 | 200 | 225 |
| Stewart Special, 17J, Adj. | 125 | 150 | 175 |
| Stewart Special, 11-15J, Adj. | 75 | 100 | 125 |
| Stuart, 15J, M#1, KW, KS | 500 | 600 | 750 |
| Stuart, 15J, M#1, KW, KS, transition ........★ | 300 | 350 | 450 |
| Stuart, 15J, M#1, KW, KS, marked Adj. ........★★ | 500 | 650 | 825 |
| Stuart, ADJ, KW, Abbotts Conversion, 18K, HC ........★★ | 1,500 | 1,700 | 2,000 |
| Stuart, 15J, M#1, KW, KS, Coin ........★ | 500 | 600 | 775 |
| Stuart, 15J, M#1, KW, KS, 1st run S# 1 to 10" ........★★★★ | 5,000 | 6,500 | 8,500 |
| Stuart, 15J, M#1, KW, KS, 1st run S# 11 to 100" ........★★★ | 3,000 | 3,500 | 4,500 |

Sears & Roebuck Special, 18 size, 17 jewels, serial number 1,481,879.

Washington W. Co., Lafayette model, 18 size, 24 Ruby jewels, gold jewel settings, adjusted, serial # 3,392,897.

| Grade or Name — Description | Avg | Ex-Fn | Mint |
|---|---|---|---|
| Stuart, 17J, M#3, 5th Pinion ................................ ★★ | $300 | $400 | $475 |
| Stuart, 17J, M#3, 5th Pinion, ADJ ......................... ★★ | 375 | 425 | 500 |
| Transition Models, 17J, OF.................................... | 100 | 125 | 155 |
| Train Dispatcher Special, 21J, (Montgomery Ward), Adj, OF ........ | 400 | 450 | 525 |
| Time King, 17J, OF, LS, NI................................... | 150 | 175 | 250 |
| Time King, 21J, OF, LS, ...................................... | 175 | 200 | 275 |
| Union Pacific Sp., 17J, OF ................................... ★ | 275 | 350 | 450 |
| **Vault Time Lock** for Mosler, 15J, 72 hr............................ | 100 | 125 | 155 |
| ☉ Washington W. Co. (See Army & Navy, Liberty Bell, Lafayette, Senate) | | | |
| Ward's Special, 15J, NI, FULL, LS, ......................... | 95 | 110 | 130 |
| George Washington,11J, HC.................................... | 100 | 125 | 165 |
| Washington,11-17J, ........................................... | 80 | 95 | 125 |
| N0. 5, 11J, KW KS, (**marked** No.5), HC....................... | 150 | 200 | 265 |
| 65, 15J, HC, LS, M#2............................................ | 75 | 100 | 135 |
| 89, 17-21J, nickel, ADJ, OF .................................. | 65 | 75 | 95 |
| 89, 21J, nickel, ADJ, HC...................................... | 75 | 100 | 135 |
| 101, 11J, SW, KW, OF........................................... | 75 | 100 | 135 |
| 101, 11J, SW, KW, Silveroid ................................... | 50 | 70 | 85 |
| 101, 11J, SW, KW, HC .......................................... | 75 | 100 | 150 |
| 102, 13J, SW, KW, Silveroid .................................. | 40 | 60 | 85 |
| 102, 13J, SW, KW, OF.......................................... | 75 | 100 | 135 |
| 102, 13J, SW, KW, HC.......................................... | 100 | 125 | 155 |
| 103, 15-16J, ADJ............................................... | 85 | 95 | 125 |
| 104, 15J, M#2, HC............................................. ★★ | 375 | 450 | 600 |
| 104, 17J, M#3, OF............................................. ★★★ | 450 | 550 | 700 |
| 105, 17J, M#3, OF............................................. ★★★ | 750 | 850 | 1,000 |
| 105, 15J, M#2, GJS, ADJ, KW, KS, HC .......................... ★★ | 700 | 775 | 895 |
| 106, 15J, ADJ, KW, KS ........................................ | 100 | 125 | 155 |
| 444, 17J, OF, NI, ADJ, ........................................ | 75 | 85 | 135 |
| 445, 19J, GJS, 2-Tone, HC.................................... ★★ | 1,000 | 1,200 | 1,500 |
| 1908 Special, 21J, OF, NI, Adj.5P,(**marked** 1908 special)............ | 300 | 400 | 550 |

STUART, 17 jewels, Model #3, 5th Pinion, Transition Model.

First Model in 14K white or green gold filled Wadsworth case, showing Montgomery numerical dial.

🕐 Watches listed in this book are priced at the collectable RETAIL level, as **complete** watches having an original 14k gold filled case, *KEY WIND* with silver, an original white enamel single sunk dial, and with the entire original movement in good working order with no repairs needed, unless otherwise noted.

🕐 Generic, nameless or unmarked grades for watch movements are listed under the Company name or initials of the Company, etc. by size, jewel count and description.

## ILLINOIS
### 16 SIZE

| Grade or Name — Description | Avg | Ex-Fx | Mint |
|---|---|---|---|
| Adams Street, 17J, 3/4, SW, NI, DMK | $175 | $225 | $300 |
| Adams Street, 21J, 3F brg, NI, DMK | 300 | 350 | 425 |
| Ak-Sar-Ben (Nebraska backward), 17J, OF, GCW | 150 | 175 | 225 |
| Ariston, 11J, OF | 60 | 75 | 125 |
| Ariston, 15J, OF | 60 | 75 | 125 |
| Ariston, 17J, 3F brg, HC | 175 | 225 | 300 |
| Ariston, 17J, Adj.3P, OF | 150 | 175 | 225 |
| Ariston, 19J, Adj.3P, OF | 150 | 175 | 225 |
| Ariston, 21J, GJS, Adj.6P, OF | 350 | 400 | 500 |
| Ariston, 23J, GJS, Adj.6P, OF | 500 | 600 | 750 |
| Ariston, 23J, GJS, Adj.6P, HC ★★ | 700 | 800 | 1,000 |
| Arlington Special, 17J, OF | 75 | 100 | 135 |
| Arlington Special, 17J, OF, Silveroid | 60 | 75 | 125 |
| Army & Navy, 19J, GJS, Adj.3P, NI, 1F brg | 200 | 250 | 325 |
| Army & Navy, 21J, GJS, Adj.3P, 1F brg | 300 | 375 | 450 |
| B & M Special, 17J, BRG, Adj.4P | 200 | 250 | 325 |
| B & O Standard, 21J | 450 | 500 | 625 |
| Benjamin Franklin, 17J, ADJ, DMK, | 300 | 325 | 400 |
| Benjamin Franklin, 21J, GJS, Adj.5P, DR, GT, | 550 | 625 | 700 |
| Benjamin Franklin, 25J, GJS, Adj.6P, DR, GT, OF ★★ | 3,000 | 3,500 | 4,000 |
| Benjamin Franklin, 25J, GJS, Adj.6P, DR, GT, HC ★★★ | 3,500 | 4,000 | 4,500 |
| Bunn, 17J, LS, OF, NI, 3/4, GJS, Adj.5P | 150 | 175 | 200 |
| Bunn, 17J, LS, NI, 3/4, Adj.5P, HC ★★★ | 650 | 800 | 1,000 |
| Bunn, 19J, LS, OF, NI, 3/4, GJS, Adj.5P | 175 | 225 | 250 |

**Ben Franklin**, 16 size, 25 jewels, gold jewel settings, gold train, **Getty Model**, serial number 2,242,138.

**Bunn Special**, Model 163, 16 size, 23J., gold jewel settings, gold train, 60 hour movement, serial # 5,421,504.

Note: Bunn Special original cases were marked Bunn Special except for Elinvars (Hamilton cased).

🕐 Generic, nameless or **unmarked grades** for watch movements are listed under the Company name or initials of the Company, etc. by size, jewel count and description.

🕐 Watches listed in this book are priced at the **collectable fair market value** at the RETAIL level, as complete watches having an original 14k gold filled case, KEY WIND with silver, an original white enamel single sunk dial, and with the entire original movement in good working order with no repairs needed, unless otherwise noted.

**Left:** Standard style escapement. **Right:** DeLong style escapement.

**Illinois Watch Co.**, 16 size, 25J., 3 fingered bridge Getty Model, gold train, HC, note serial number S731,870.

| Grade or Name — Description | Avg | Ex-Fn | Mint |
|---|---|---|---|
| Bunn, 19J, LS, NI, 3/4, Adj.5P, HC ..................................... ★ ★ ★ | $800 | $1,000 | $1,500 |
| Bunn, 19J, LS, OF, NI, 3/4, GJS, Adj.5P, 60 hour.......................... | 300 | 350 | 425 |
| Bunn, 19J, **marked Jeweled Barrel**............................................ | 200 | 225 | 275 |
| Bunn Special, 19J, LS, OF, NI, 3/4, Adj.6P, GT............................ | 175 | 200 | 235 |
| Bunn Special, 19J, LS, OF, NI, 3/4, Adj.5P, GT, 60 hour ............. | 300 | 350 | 425 |
| Bunn Special, 21J, NI, GJS, Adj.6P, GT, HC.............................. ★ | 500 | 595 | 700 |
| Bunn Special, 21J, LS, OF, NI, 3/4, GJS, Adj.6P, GT .................... | 250 | 275 | 325 |
| Bunn Special, 21J, LS, GJS, Adj.6P, GT, **gold plated Mvt.** .... ★ ★ | 500 | 600 | 800 |
| Bunn Special, 21J, LS,OF, NI, 3/4, GJS, Adj.6P, GT, 60 hour ...... | 300 | 375 | 400 |
| Bunn Special, 21J, LS, OF, NI, 3/4, GJS, Adj.6P, GT, 60 hr. **Elinvar**............................................................................ | 375 | 475 | 525 |
| Bunn Special, 21J, 60 hr., 14K, OF, Bunn Special case ............. ★ | 850 | 900 | 1,100 |
| Bunn Special, 23J, LS, OF, NI, 3/4, GJS, Adj.6P, GT .................... | 425 | 475 | 550 |
| Bunn Special, 23J, LS, OF, NI, 3/4, GJS, Adj.6P, GT, 60 hour ...... | 475 | 550 | 600 |
| Bunn Special, 23J, LS, OF, NI, 3/4, GJS, Adj.6P, GT, with 23J, 60-hour on dial...................................................... | 725 | 775 | 825 |
| Bunn Special, 23J, LS, NI, GJS, GT, Adj.6P, HC............ ★ ★ ★ ★ | 1,700 | 2,000 | 2,500 |
| 161 Bunn Special, 21J, 3/4, Adj.6P, 60 hour.................................. | 475 | 525 | 575 |
| 161A Bunn Special, 21J, 3/4, Adj.6P, 60 hour (**Elinvar** signed under balance or on top plate) .................................... | 550 | 600 | 700 |
| 161 Elinvar Bunn Special, 21J, 3/4, Adj.6P, 60 hour (**Elinvar** signed at bottom of bridge).................................... | 550 | 600 | 700 |
| 161B, Bunn Special, 21J, 60 hour, pressed jewels .......... ★ ★ ★ ★ | 4,000 | 5,000 | 6,500 |
| 163 Bunn Special, 23J, GJS, Adj.6P, 3/4, 60 hour.......................... | 700 | 800 | 900 |
| 163 Elinvar Bunn Special, 23J, GJS, Adj.6P, 60 hour (**Elinvar** signed at bottom of cock, uncut  balance)............ ★ | 950 | 1,100 | 1,250 |

◷ Generic, nameless  or  unmarked grades for watch movements  are listed under the Company name or initials of the Company, etc. by size, jewel count and description.

◷ Some grades are not included. Their values can be determined by comparing with **similar** age, size, metal content, style, models and grades listed.

| Grade or Name — Description | Avg | Ex-Fn | Mint |
|---|---|---|---|
| 163A Elinvar Bunn Special, 23J, GJS, Adj.6P, 3/4, 60 hour (**Elinvar** signed under balance) | $975 | $1,100 | $1,275 |
| 163A Elinvar Bunn Special, 23J, Adj.6P, 3/4, 60 hour (**Elinvar** signed on train bridge) | 975 | 1,100 | 1,275 |
| Burlington W. Co., 15J, OF | 50 | 75 | 125 |
| BurlingtonW. Co., 15J, HC | 125 | 150 | 200 |
| BurlingtonW. Co., 17J, OF | 50 | 75 | 125 |
| Burlington W. Co., 17J, HC | 125 | 150 | 200 |
| Burlington W. Co., 19J, 3/4, NI, Adj.3P | 100 | 125 | 165 |
| Burlington W. Co., 19J, BRG, NI, Adj.3P | 100 | 125 | 165 |
| Burlington W. Co., 19J, 3/4, HC | 150 | 175 | 225 |
| Burlington W. Co., 19J, 3F brg, NI, Adj.3P | 100 | 125 | 165 |
| Burlington W. Co., 21J, 3/4, NI, Adj.3P | 175 | 200 | 225 |
| Burlington W. Co., 21J, Adj.6P, GJS.............★★ | 300 | 350 | 450 |
| Burlington, Bull Dog- **on dial**, 21J, SW, LS, GJS, GT | 325 | 375 | 425 |
| C & O Special, 21J, 3/4, NI, ADJ.................★ | 900 | 1,100 | 1,250 |
| Capitol, 19J, OF, 3/4, NI, Adj.3P | 100 | 125 | 165 |
| Central, 17J, SW, PS, OF | 50 | 75 | 125 |
| Commodore Perry Special, 21J, Adj.6P, GT, OF | 350 | 375 | 425 |
| Craftsman, 17J, OF | 50 | 75 | 125 |
| DeLong Escapement, 21J, GJS, (Bunn Sp. or A. Lincoln) Adj.6P, 14K OF ............★★★★★ | 1,500 | 1,700 | 2,000 |
| Dependon, 17J, (J.V.Farwell) | 125 | 155 | 225 |
| Dependon, 21J, (J.V.Farwell) | 200 | 245 | 300 |
| Diamond, Ruby, Sapphire, 21J, GJS, GT, Adj.6P, BRG, OF ......★ | 1,000 | 1,200 | 1,400 |
| Diamond, Ruby, Sapphire, 23J, GJS, GT, Adj.6P, BRG, OF ★★★ | 2,000 | 2,200 | 2,500 |
| Diamond, Ruby, Sapphire, 23J, GJS, GT, Adj.6P, BRG, HC★★★ | 2,500 | 3,000 | 3,500 |
| Diamond, Ruby, Sapphire, 23J, GJS, GT, Adj.6P, 3/4 plate, OF ............★★★ | 1,400 | 1,600 | 2,000 |
| Dispatcher, 19J, Adj.3P | 175 | 200 | 225 |
| Fifth Ave.,19J, Adj.3P,GT,OF | 95 | 110 | 150 |
| Fifth Ave., 21J, Adj.3P,GT,OF | 150 | 175 | 200 |
| Franklin Street, 15J, 3/4, NI, ADJ | 75 | 100 | 150 |
| Grant, 17J, ADJ, LS, **Getty Model,** OF | 85 | 95 | 125 |
| Getty Model # 4 &5, 21J | 250 | 300 | 350 |
| Getty Model # 4 &5, 17J | 75 | 100 | 135 |

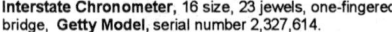

Interstate Chronometer, 16 size, 23 jewels, one-fingered bridge, **Getty Model**, serial number 2,327,614.

A. Lincoln, 16 size, 21 jewels, gold jewel settings, gold train, Adj5p, **Getty Model**, serial number 2,237,406.

| Grade or Name — Description | Avg | Ex-Fn | Mint |
|---|---|---|---|
| Great Northern Special, 17J, BRG, ADJ | $250 | $275 | $325 |
| Great Northern Special, 19J, BRG, ADJ | 275 | 300 | 350 |
| Great Northern Special, 21J, BRG, ADJ, Adj.3P | 325 | 365 | 425 |
| Greenwich, 23J, Washington W. Co. GT,GJS, ADJ.6P ....... ★★★ | 1,500 | 1,700 | 2,000 |
| Illinois Central, 17-21J, 2-Tone, Adj.3P, GT | 100 | 125 | 150 |

⊙ GENERIC, NAMELESS OR **UNMARKED GRADES** FOR WATCH MOVEMENTS ARE LISTED UNDER THE COMPANY NAME OR INITIALS OF THE COMPANY, ETC. BY SIZE, JEWEL COUNT AND DESCRIPTION.

| | | | |
|---|---|---|---|
| Illinois Watch Co., 7-9J, M#1-2-3 | $55 | $75 | $125 |
| Illinois Watch Co., 11-17J, (Rockland) | 75 | 95 | 150 |
| Illinois Watch Co., 11-13J, 3/4, OF | 55 | 75 | 125 |
| Illinois Watch Co., 11-13J, M#7, 3/4, OF | 55 | 75 | 125 |
| Illinois Watch Co., 11-13, M#6, 3/4, HC | 100 | 125 | 175 |
| Illinois Watch Co., 15J, M#2, OF | 55 | 75 | 125 |
| Illinois Watch Co., 15J, M#1, HC | 100 | 125 | 175 |
| Illinois Watch Co., 15J, M#3, OF | 55 | 75 | 125 |
| Illinois Watch Co., 15J, 3/4, ADJ | 55 | 75 | 125 |
| Illinois Watch Co., 15J, 3F brg, GJS | 55 | 75 | 125 |
| Illinois Watch Co., 16-17J, 14K, HC | 400 | 450 | 525 |
| Illinois Watch Co., 16-17J, Adj.3P, OF | 75 | 95 | 150 |
| Illinois Watch Co., 16-17J, M#2-3, SW, OF | 55 | 75 | 125 |
| Illinois Watch Co., 17J, M#6, SW, HC | 100 | 125 | 175 |
| Illinois Watch Co., 17J, M#7, OF | 75 | 100 | 135 |
| Illinois Watch Co., 17J, M#5, 3/4, ADJ, HC | 100 | 125 | 150 |
| Illinois Watch Co., 17J, M#4, 3F brg, GJS, Adj.5P, HC | 125 | 150 | 225 |
| Illinois Watch Co., 19J, 3/4, GJS, Adj.5P , **jeweled barrel** | 125 | 135 | 185 |
| Illinois Watch Co., 19J, 3/4, BRG, Adj.3-4P | 95 | 110 | 150 |
| Illinois Watch Co., 21J, Adj.3P, OF | 175 | 200 | 250 |
| Illinois Watch Co., 21J, ADJ, OF | 175 | 200 | 250 |
| Illinois Watch Co., 21J, GJS, HC | 200 | 225 | 275 |
| Illinois Watch Co., 21J, 3/4, GJS, Adj.5P | 175 | 200 | 225 |
| Illinois Watch Co., 21J, 3F brg, GJS, Adj.4P | 165 | 185 | 200 |
| Illinois Watch Co., 21J, 3F brg, GJS, Adj.5P | 200 | 250 | 275 |
| Illinois Watch Co., 23J, GJS | 250 | 300 | 375 |
| Illinois Watch Co., 25J, 4th model,3F brg, GJS, Adj.5P, HC ★★★ | 3,000 | 3,500 | 4,000 |
| Imperial Sp., 17J, SW, LS, Adj.4P, OF | 100 | 125 | 155 |
| Interstate Chronometer, 17J, GCW, Adj.3P, HC | 275 | 300 | 325 |
| Interstate Chronometer, 17J, GCW, Adj.3P, OF | 250 | 275 | 300 |
| Interstate Chronometer, 23J, 1F brg, ADJ, OF ★ | 700 | 800 | 950 |
| Interstate Chronometer, 23J, 1F brg, ADJ, HC ★★ | 1,000 | 1,100 | 1,300 |
| Lafayette, 23J, Washington W.Co., GJS, Adj.5P, GT, OF ....... ★★ | 850 | 950 | 1,100 |
| Lafayette, 23J, Washington W.Co., GJS, Adj.5P, GT, HC ... ★★★ | 1,200 | 1,400 | 1,700 |
| Lakeshore, 17J, OF | 75 | 100 | 135 |
| Lakeshore, 17J, HC | 150 | 175 | 225 |
| Landis W. Co., 15-17J | 75 | 100 | 135 |
| Liberty Bell, 17J, OF | 100 | 120 | 150 |
| Liberty Bell, 17J, HC ★★★ | 600 | 700 | 800 |
| A. Lincoln, 21J,3/4, GJS, Adj.5P, OF | 225 | 255 | 300 |
| A. Lincoln, 21J,3/4, GJS, Adj.5P, HC | 300 | 365 | 425 |
| Logan, 15, OF | 55 | 75 | 125 |
| Marvel, 19J, GT, GJS, Adj.3P, Of | 75 | 95 | 120 |
| Marine Special, 21J, 3/4, Adj.3P | 250 | 275 | 325 |
| Monarch W. Co., 17J, NI, ADJ, SW | 125 | 150 | 200 |
| Monroe, 17J, NI,3/4, OF (Washington W. Co.) | 100 | 120 | 150 |
| Monroe, 15J, 3/4, OF (Washington W. Co.) | 75 | 100 | 150 |
| Montgomery Ward, 17J, LS, Thin Model , OF | 75 | 95 | 135 |
| Our No. 1, 15J, HC, M#1 | 150 | 200 | 275 |
| Overland Special, 19J, Adj., OF | 150 | 175 | 225 |

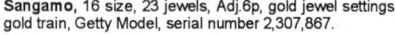

**Sangamo**, 16 size, 23 jewels, Adj.6p, gold jewel settings, gold train, Getty Model, serial number 2,307,867.

**Sangamo Special**, 16 S, 23J., marked 60 hr. movement, Adj.6p, gold jewel settings, gold train, S# 4,758,199.

| Grade or Name Description | Avg | Ex-Fn | Mint |
|---|---|---|---|
| Paillard Non-Magnetic Watch Co., 11J, 3/4 | $75 | $100 | $135 |
| Paillard Non-Magnetic Watch Co., 15J, 3/4 | 75 | 100 | 135 |
| Paillard Non-Magnetic Watch Co., 17J, 3/4, Adj.5P, DMK | 100 | 125 | 175 |
| Paillard Non-Magnetic Watch Co., 21J, 3/4, GJS, Adj.5P, DMK | 300 | 400 | 500 |
| Penn. Special, 17-19J, Adj.3P, OF | 95 | 110 | 135 |
| Pennsylvania Special, 23J, 3/4, GJS, Adj.5P ★ | 1,300 | 1,500 | 1,700 |
| Plymouth W. Co., 15-17J, OF (Add $25 for HC) | 75 | 100 | 125 |
| Precise, 21J, OF, LS, Adj.3P | 175 | 200 | 225 |
| Quincy Street, 17J, 3/4, NI, DMK, ADJ | 75 | 100 | 125 |
| Railroad Dispatcher, 11-15J, DMK, 3/4 | 150 | 175 | 225 |
| Railroad King, 17J, HC | 250 | 285 | 350 |
| Railroad Official, 23J, 3 Finger bridge ★★★★★ | 1,600 | 2,000 | 2,500 |
| Railway King, 17J, OF | 150 | 175 | 225 |
| Remington W.Co. 11-15J, OF | 100 | 125 | 160 |
| Remington W.Co. 17J, OF ★ | 175 | 200 | 300 |
| Remington W.Co. 17J, HC ★★ | 250 | 300 | 400 |
| Rockland, 17J, GJS, GT, 7th model, grade 305, OF | 55 | 75 | 100 |
| Sangamo, 19J, model # 4, GJS, GT, ADJ., HC ★★★★ | 4,000 | 5,000 | 6,000 |
| Sangamo, 21J, GJS, Adj.6P, HC | 325 | 375 | 400 |
| Sangamo, 21J, GJS, Adj.6P, EXTRA or SPECIAL, HC ★ | 500 | 600 | 750 |
| Sangamo, 21J, GJS, Adj.6P, EXTRA or SPECIAL, OF ★ | 500 | 600 | 750 |
| Sangamo, 21J, GJS, Adj., OF | 200 | 250 | 325 |
| Sangamo, 21J, 3/4, GJS, DR, Adj.6P, OF | 225 | 275 | 335 |
| Sangamo, 23J,3/4, GJS, DR, Adj.6P, OF | 325 | 385 | 450 |
| Sangamo, 23J, 3/4, GJS, DR, Adj.6P, HC | 525 | 575 | 625 |
| Sangamo, 25J, M#5, 3/4, GJS, DR, Adj.6P ★★★ | 4,000 | 5,000 | 6,500 |
| Sangamo, 26J, M#5, 3/4, GJS, DR, Adj.6P ★★★ | 5,000 | 6,000 | 7,500 |
| Sangamo Special, 19J, BRG, GJS, GT, Adj.6P, OF | 350 | 375 | 425 |
| Sangamo Special, 19J, BRG, GJS, GT, Adj.6P, HC ★★★ | 1,200 | 1,500 | 1,800 |
| Sangamo, Extra, 21J, Adj.6P, gold train, Of. | 400 | 465 | 525 |
| Sangamo Special, 21J, M#7, OF | 325 | 375 | 450 |
| Sangamo Special, 21J, M#8, BRG, HC ★★★ | 1,400 | 1,600 | 1,900 |
| Sangamo Special, 21J, M#9, BRG, GJS, GT, Adj.6P, OF | 325 | 375 | 450 |
| Sangamo Special, 21J, BRG, GJS, GT, Diamond end cap | 350 | 400 | 475 |
| Sangamo Special, 23J, M#9-10, BRG, GJS, GT, Adj.6P, Sangamo Special **HINGED** case | 600 | 650 | 750 |

| Grade or Name — Description | Avg | Ex-Fn | Mint |
|---|---|---|---|
| Sangamo Special, 23J, BRG, GJS, GT, Adj.6P, Diamond | | | |
|     end stone, **screw back,** Sangamo Special case ...................... | $575 | $625 | $700 |
| Sangamo Special, 23J, M#8, GJS, GT, Adj.6P, **HC** ........... ★★★ | 1,500 | 1,800 | 2,000 |
| Sangamo Special, 23J, BRG, GJS, GT, Adj.6P, **not marked** | | | |
|     60 hour, rigid bow, Sangamo Special case ............................. | 575 | 625 | 700 |
| Sangamo Special, 23J, BRG, GJS, GT, Adj.6P, | | | |
|     **marked 60 hour,** Sangamo Special case ................. ★★★★ | 1,000 | 1,200 | 1,500 |
| Sangamo Special, 23J, BRG, GJS, GT, Adj.6P, 60 hour, | | | |
|     rigid bow, Sangamo Special case **14K gold case**.................... | 1,200 | 1,350 | 1,600 |
| Santa Fe Special, 17J, BRG, Adj.3P.............................................. | 200 | 225 | 275 |
| Santa Fe Special, 21J, 3/4, Adj.5P, OF......................................... | 250 | 300 | 375 |
| Santa Fe Special, 21J, 3/4, Adj.5P, HC......................................... | 375 | 400 | 475 |
| Sears, Roebuck & Co. Special, 15-17J, ADJ............................... | 75 | 100 | 135 |
| Senate, 17J, (Washington W. Co.), NI, 3/4, ADJ...................... | 75 | 100 | 135 |
| Standard, 15J.................................................................................... | 50 | 75 | 125 |
| Sterling, 17J, SW, PS, Adj.3P, OF................................................ | 50 | 75 | 115 |
| Sterling, 19-21J, SW, PS, Adj.3P, OF .......................................... | 175 | 200 | 225 |
| Stewart, 17J..................................................................................... | 50 | 75 | 125 |
| Stewart Special, 21J, Adj., ............................................................ | 150 | 175 | 200 |
| Stewart Special, 19J, Adj.3P ......................................................... | 100 | 125 | 150 |
| Stewart Special, 15-17J, .................................................................. | 50 | 75 | 125 |
| The General, 15J, OF...................................................................... | 50 | 70 | 90 |
| Time King, 17J, OF ........................................................................ | 75 | 100 | 135 |
| Time King, 19J, Adj.3P, OF......................................................... | 100 | 125 | 150 |
| Union Pacific,17J, Adj.,DR, 2-tone, DMK, OF............................★ | 300 | 350 | 400 |
| Victor, 21J, 3/4, Adj.3P .................................................................. | 150 | 175 | 200 |

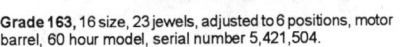

Grade 163, 16 size, 23 jewels, adjusted to 6 positions, motor barrel, 60 hour model, serial number 5,421,504.

LAFAYETTE, 23J, 16 size, WASHINGTON W.CO., GJS, Adj.5P, GT, HC.

| Grade or Name — Description | Avg | Ex-Fn | Mint |
|---|---|---|---|
| 161 through 163A —See Bunn Special | | | |
| 167L, 17J, marked ........................................................................... | $125 | $150 | $175 |
| 167, 17J .......................................................................................... | 50 | 75 | 125 |
| 169, 19J, Adj.3P, OF ..................................................................... | 100 | 125 | 150 |
| 174, 23J, LS, GJS, Adj., OF, marked ....................................... ★★ | 675 | 725 | 800 |
| 175, 17J, RR grade & a (RR inspectors name on dial &mvt.) ......... | 200 | 245 | 300 |
| 177, 19J, SW, LS, 60 hour, Adj.5P, OF......................................★ | 400 | 500 | 650 |

🕘 Generic, nameless or unmarked grades for watch movements are listed under the Company name or initials of the Company, etc. by size, jewel count and description.

| Grade or Name — Description | Avg | Ex-Fn | Mint |
|---|---|---|---|
| 179, 21J, HC, 3F brg, **marked** Ruby Jewels .................. ★ | $300 | $400 | $550 |
| 184, 19J, 3F brg, LS, OF .................................................... | 100 | 125 | 175 |
| 187, 17J, 3F brg, Adj.5P, GJS, GT, HC.............................. | 225 | 275 | 350 |
| 181-189, 21J, 3F brg, Adj.6P, GJS, GT, **marked** Ruby Jewels, HC | 400 | 450 | 525 |
| 333, 15J, HC .................................................................... | 100 | 125 | 175 |
| 555, 17J, 3/4, ................................................................. | 75 | 100 | 135 |
| 777, 17J, 3/4, ADJ .......................................................... | 75 | 100 | 135 |
| 805, 17J, BRG, GJS, GT, DR, OF ..................................... | 75 | 100 | 135 |
| 809, 23j, Adj.6P, GT, **marked 809** .................. ★★★ | 300 | 350 | 400 |
| 900, 19J, LS, Adj.3P........................................................ | 100 | 125 | 150 |

Illinois Watch Co., 14 size, 16 jewels, Adj5p.

Illinois Watch Co., 14 size, 21J., adjusted, nickel movement, gold jewel settings, serial number 1,029,204.

## ILLINOIS
### 14 SIZE

| Grade or Name — Description | Avg | Ex-Fn | Mint |
|---|---|---|---|
| Illinois Watch Co., 7J, M#1-2-3, SW, OF ....................... | $40 | $50 | $65 |
| Illinois Watch Co., 11J, M#1-2-3, SW, OF ..................... | 50 | 60 | 75 |
| Illinois Watch Co., 15J, M#1-2-3, SW, OF ..................... | 60 | 70 | 90 |
| Illinois Watch Co., 16J, M#1-2-3, SW, OF ..................... | 75 | 80 | 115 |
| Illinois Watch Co., 21J, M#1-2-3, SW, OF ............... ★ | 150 | 165 | 195 |
| Illinois Watch Co., 22J, ................................................ ★ | 200 | 275 | 375 |

NOTE: Add $25 for above watches in hunting case.

## ILLINOIS
### 12 SIZE and 13 SIZE

| Grade or Name — Description | Avg | Ex-Fn | Mint |
|---|---|---|---|
| Accurate, 21J, GJS, OF .................................................. | $60 | $75 | $125 |
| Aristocrat, 19J, OF........................................................ | 40 | 50 | 70 |
| Ariston, 11-17J, OF ....................................................... | 60 | 70 | 85 |
| Ariston, 19J, OF............................................................. | 75 | 100 | 150 |
| Ariston, 21J, OF............................................................. | 85 | 110 | 160 |
| Ariston, 23J, OF....................................................... ★ | 200 | 250 | 300 |
| Aluminum Watch, 17J, model #3, G#525, **made of aluminum** | | | |
| S# 3,869,251 to S# 3,869,300 ..................... ★★★★ | 2,000 | 2,500 | 3,000 |

Characteristics of watches differ for the same age of both case and movement, because these features vary it may not be accurate to date a watch by one single influence. Example: the second hand was not commonly found on watches before 1750, but common about 1800. The first second hand appeared in 1665 and another in 1690. Therefore statements are broad rather than accurate.

Ben Franklin, 12 size, 17 jewels, open face, gold train, serial number 2,366,286.

Illini, 13 size, 21 jewels, bridge model, serial number 3,650,129. Note five tooth click.

| Grade or Name — Description | Avg | Ex-Fn | Mint |
|---|---|---|---|
| Autocrat, 17J, Adj.3P, 3/4 | $60 | $70 | $85 |
| Autocrat, 19J, Adj.3P, 3/4 | 65 | 75 | 95 |
| Banker, 17-21J, Adj.3P, OF | 60 | 70 | 90 |
| Benjamin Franklin, 17J, OF | 200 | 250 | 325 |
| Bunn Special, 21J, Adj 3P, (by Hamilton), OF ★★ | 200 | 250 | 325 |
| Burlington Special, 19J, GT, OF | 50 | 60 | 75 |
| Burlington Special, 19J, GT, HC | 75 | 95 | 135 |
| Burlington W. Co., 21J, GT, OF | 70 | 80 | 100 |
| Burlington W. Co., 21J, GT, HC | 100 | 135 | 165 |
| Central, 17J, OF, 2-Tone | 50 | 60 | 80 |
| Commodore Perry Special, 17J., adj.3P | 80 | 100 | 125 |
| Criterion, 21J, OF | 70 | 80 | 95 |
| Dependon, 17, (J.V.Farwell), OF HC, | 100 | 125 | 185 |
| Diamond Ruby Sapphire, 21J, Adj.5P, GJS ★ | 300 | 350 | 425 |
| Elite, 19J, OF | 60 | 75 | 85 |
| Garland, 17J, Adj.,GT, OF | 60 | 70 | 80 |
| Gold Metal, 17J, OF | 60 | 70 | 80 |

Example of Illinois Thin Model, 12 size, 17 jewels, adjusted to 3 positions.

Maiden America, 12 size, 17 jewels, serial number 2,820,499.

Santa Fe Special, 12 size, 21 jewels, three-quarter plate, serial number 3,414,422.

| Grade or Name — Description | Avg | Ex-Fn | Mint |
|---|---|---|---|
| Illini, 13 Size, 21J, Adj.5P, BRG, GJS, five tooth click, OF | $75 | $100 | $135 |
| Illini **Extra,** 13 Size, 21J, Adj.5P, five tooth click, OF | 85 | 120 | 165 |
| Illini, 13 Size, 23J, Adj.5P, BRG, GJS, five tooth click, | 125 | 150 | 200 |
| Illini, 13 Size, 23J, Adj.6P, BRG, GJS, five tooth click, 14K | 275 | 335 | 425 |
| Illinois Watch Co., 7-11J | 50 | 65 | 75 |
| Illinois Watch Co., 15J | 40 | 65 | 75 |
| Illinois Watch Co., 16-17J, OF, 14K | 250 | 275 | 325 |
| Illinois Watch Co., 16-17J, OF, GF | 65 | 90 | 120 |
| Illinois Watch Co., 17J, HC, GF | 75 | 100 | 135 |
| Illinois Watch Co., 19J | 60 | 70 | 85 |
| Illinois Watch Co., 21J, OF | 80 | 90 | 125 |
| Illinois Watch Co., 21J, marked (21 SPECIAL), OF | 80 | 95 | 130 |
| Illinois Watch Co., 21J, HC | 100 | 125 | 150 |
| Illinois Watch Co., 23J, OF | 135 | 165 | 200 |
| Illinois Watch Co., 19J, OF, EXTRA THIN MODEL | 60 | 75 | 100 |
| Illinois Watch Co., 21J, OF, EXTRA THIN MODEL | 80 | 100 | 150 |
| Interstate Chronometer, 21J, GJS, OF | 150 | 175 | 225 |
| Interstate Chronometer, 21J, GJS, HC ★ | 200 | 225 | 275 |
| A. Lincoln, 19J, Adj.5P, GJS, DR, 3/4, marked on mvt. | 75 | 90 | 110 |
| A. Lincoln, 21J, Adj.5P, DR, GJS | 100 | 125 | 150 |
| Maiden America, 17J, ADJ | 60 | 70 | 85 |
| Marquis Autocrat, 17J, OF | 60 | 70 | 85 |
| Master, 21J, GT, GJS, OF | 80 | 90 | 110 |
| Masterpiece, 19J, Adj.3P, OF | 65 | 75 | 100 |
| A. Norton, 21J, OF | 75 | 90 | 110 |
| Plymouth Watch Co., 15-17J, OF, HC | 50 | 60 | 75 |
| Railroad Dispatch , 11-15J, | 40 | 45 | 55 |
| Railroad Dispatch , 17-19J, SW, GT | 80 | 95 | 125 |
| Rockland, 17J, | 50 | 80 | 95 |
| Roosevelt, 19J, Adj.3P, OF | 70 | 80 | 90 |
| Santa Fe Special, 21J | 100 | 125 | 150 |
| Sterling, 17J, OF | 50 | 60 | 75 |
| Sterling, 19-21J, OF | 55 | 65 | 85 |
| Stewart Special, 17J, SW, Adj.3P | 50 | 60 | 75 |
| Stewart Special, 19J, SW, OF, GT | 55 | 65 | 80 |
| Time King, 19J, SW, Adj.3P | 60 | 70 | 85 |
| Time King, 21J, SW, Adj.3P | 80 | 90 | 110 |
| Transit, 19J, OF, PS | 60 | 70 | 85 |

| Grade or Name — Description | Avg | Ex-Fn | Mint |
|---|---|---|---|
| Vim, 17J, ADJ, BRG, GJS, DR, OF | $50 | $60 | $75 |
| Washington W. Co., **Monroe**, 11J | 100 | 125 | 150 |
| Washington W. Co., **Army & Navy**, 19J | 100 | 125 | 150 |
| Washington W. Co., **Senate**, 17J, M#2, PS, | 60 | 70 | 85 |
| 121, 21J, Adj.3P | 70 | 85 | 95 |
| 127, 17J, ADJ | 60 | 70 | 85 |
| 129, 19J, Adj.3P | 60 | 70 | 85 |
| 219, 11J, M#1 | 50 | 60 | 75 |
| 403, 15J, BRG | 60 | 70 | 85 |
| 405, 17J, BRG, ADJ, OF | 60 | 70 | 85 |
| 409, 21J, BRG, Diamond, Ruby, Sapphire, Adj.5P, GJS ★ | 275 | 325 | 450 |
| 410, 23J, BRG, GJS, Adj.6P, DR | 150 | 200 | 275 |
| 410, 23J, BRG, GJS, Adj.6P, DR, 14K, OF | 250 | 300 | 375 |

## ILLINOIS
### 8 SIZE

| Grade or Name — Description | Avg | Ex-Fn | Mint |
|---|---|---|---|
| Arlington, 7J, ★ | $125 | $150 | $200 |
| Rose LeLand, 13J, ★★ | 225 | 250 | 300 |
| Stanley, 7J, ★★★ | 250 | 300 | 350 |
| Mary Stuart, 15J, ★★ | 200 | 250 | 300 |
| Sunnyside, 11J, ★ | 150 | 200 | 250 |
| 151, 7J, 3/4 | 40 | 50 | 65 |
| 152, 11J, 3/4 | 50 | 60 | 75 |
| 155, 11J, 3/4 | 60 | 70 | 85 |
| **Illinois W. Co.** , 11-15-16-17J, ( nameless unmarked grades ) | 30 | 40 | 55 |

Note: Add $10 more for above watches in hunting case.

Illinois Watch Co., 8 size, 7 jewels

Grade 144, 6 size, 15 jewels, serial number 5,902,290.

## ILLINOIS
### 6 SIZE

| Grade or Name — Description | Avg | Ex-Fn | Mint |
|---|---|---|---|
| Illinois W. Co., 7J, LS, HC, 14K | $200 | $225 | $300 |
| Illinois W. Co., 7J, HC | 50 | 75 | 125 |

🕐 Generic, nameless or unmarked grades for watch movements are listed under the Company name or initials of the Company, etc. by size, jewel count and description.

| Grade or Name — Description | Avg | Ex-Fn | Mint |
|---|---|---|---|
| Illinois W. Co., 7J, OF, Coin | $35 | $45 | $60 |
| Illinois W. Co., 11-12-13J, OF, HC | 50 | 75 | 125 |
| Illinois W. Co., 15J, OF, HC, 14K | 200 | 250 | 325 |
| Illinois W. Co., 17J, OF, HC | 50 | 75 | 125 |
| Illinois W. Co., 19J, OF, HC | 75 | 100 | 150 |
| Plymouth Watch Co., 17J, OF, HC | 50 | 60 | 75 |
| Washington W. Co., 15J, Liberty Bell, HC | 125 | 150 | 200 |
| Washington W. Co., 11J, Martha Washington, HC | 200 | 250 | 325 |

## ILLINOIS
### 4 SIZE

| Grade or Name — Description | Avg | Ex-Fn | Mint |
|---|---|---|---|
| Illinois W. Co., 7J, LS, HC | $50 | $55 | $95 |
| Illinois W. Co., 11J, LS, HC | 50 | 75 | 125 |
| Illinois W. Co., 15-16J, LS, HC | 50 | 75 | 125 |

## ILLINOIS
### 0 SIZE

| Grade or Name — Description | Avg | Ex-Fn | Mint |
|---|---|---|---|
| Accuratus, 17J, OF | $75 | $125 | $150 |
| Burlington Special, 15-17J, 3/4, OF | 75 | 95 | 150 |
| **Illinois W. Co.**, 7 to 17J, LS, HC, 14K | 175 | 225 | 300 |
| 201, 11J, BRG, NI | 75 | 100 | 150 |
| 203, 15J, BRG, NI | 75 | 100 | 150 |
| 204, 17J, BRG, NI | 75 | 100 | 150 |
| Interstate Chronometer, 15J, HC, SW | 175 | 200 | 275 |
| Interstate Chronometer, 17J, HC, SW | 185 | 210 | 285 |
| Plymouth Watch Co., 15-17J, HC | 50 | 60 | 75 |
| Santa Fe Special, 15-17J | 70 | 80 | 95 |
| Washington W. Co., Liberty Bell, 15J, ADJ | 150 | 175 | 250 |
| Washington W. Co., Mt. Vernon, 17J, ADJ | 160 | 185 | 275 |

Grade 201, 0 size, 11 jewels, originally sold for $8.10.

Grade 203, 0 size, 15 jewels, originally sold for $10.40

Grade 204, 0 size, 17 jewels, originally sold for $12.83.

🕐 Watches listed in this book are priced at the **collectable fair market value** at the **retail** level, as **complete** watches having an original 14k gold filled case, *KEY WIND* with silver, an original white enamel single sunk dial, and with the entire original movement in good working order with no repairs needed, unless otherwise noted.

# ILLINOIS SPRINGFIELD WATCH CO.
# IDENTIFICATION OF MOVEMENTS
### BY MODEL NUMBER

How to Identify Your Watch: Compare the movement of your watch with the illustrations in this section. Upon matching the movement exactly, the model number and size can be determined. While comparing, note the location of the balance, jewels, screws, gears, and type of back plate (Full, 3/4, Bridge) which will be clues in identifying the movement you have. Having determined the size and model number, you can now find your watch in the main price listing by name or number (which is engraved on the movement).

### THE ILLINOIS WATCH CO. GRADE AND MODEL CHART

| Size | Model | Plate Design | Setting | Hunting or Open Face | Type Barrel | Started w/ Serial No. | Remarks |
|------|-------|--------------|---------|----------------------|-------------|------------------------|---------|
| 18 | 1 | Full | Key | Htg | Reg | 1 | Course train |
| | 2 | Full | Lever | Htg | Reg | 38,901 | Course train |
| | 3 | Full | Lever | OF | Reg | 46,201 | Course train, 5th pinion |
| | 4 | Full | Pendant | OF | Reg | 1,050,001 | Fast train |
| | 5 | Full | Lever | Htg | Reg | 1,256,101 | Fast train, RR Grade |
| | 6 | Full | Lever | OF | Reg | 1,144,401 | Fast train, RR Grade |
| 16 | 1 | Full | Lever | Htg | Reg | 1,030,001 | Thick model |
| | 2 | Full | Pendant | OF | Reg | 1,037,001 | Thick model |
| | 3 | Full | Lever | OF | Reg | 1,038,001 | Thick model |
| | 4 | ¾ & brg | Lever | Htg | Reg | 1,300,001 | Getty model |
| | 5 | ¾ & brg | Lever | OF | Reg | 1,300,601 | Getty model |
| | 6 | ¾ & brg | Pendant | Htg | Reg | 2,160,111 | DR & Improved RR model |
| | 7 | ¾ & brg | Pendant | OF | Reg | 2,160,011 | DR & Improved RR model |
| | 8 | ¾ & brg | Lever | Htg | Reg | 2,523,101 | DR & Improved RR model |
| | 9 | ¾ & brg | Lever | OF | Reg | 2,522,001 | DR & Improved model |
| | 10 | Cent brg | Lever | OF | Motor | 3,178,901 | Also 17S Ex Thin RR gr 48 hr |
| | 11 | ¾ | Lever & Pen | OF | Motor | 4,001,001 | RR grade 48 hr |
| | 12 | ¾ | Lever & Pen | Htg | Motor | 4,002,001 | RR grade 48 hr |
| | 13 | Cent brg | Lever | OF | Motor | 4,166,801 | Also 17S RR grade 60 hr |
| | 14 | ¾ | Lever | OF | Motor | 4,492,501 | RR grade 60 hr |
| | 15 | ¾ | Lever | OF | Motor | 5,488,301 | RR grade 60 hr Elinvar |
| 14 | 1 | Full | Lever | Htg | Reg | 1,009,501 | Thick model |
| | 2 | Full | Pendant | OF | Reg | 1,000,001 | Thick model |
| | 3 | Full | Lever | OF | Reg | 1,001,001 | Thick model |
| 13 | 1 | brg | Pendant | OF | Motor | | Ex Thin gr 538 & 539 |
| 12 | 1 | ¾ | Pendant | OF | Reg | 1,685,001 | |
| Thin | 2 | ¾ | Pendant | Htg | Reg | 1,748,751 | |
| | 3 | Cent brg | Pendant | OF | Reg | 2,337,011 | Center bridge |
| | 4 | Cent brg | Pendant | Htg | Reg | 2,337,001 | Center bridge |
| | 5 | Cent brg | Pendant | OF | Motor | 3,742,201 | Center bridge |
| | 6 | Cent brg | Pendant | Htg | Motor | 4,395,301 | Center bridge |
| 12T | 1 | True Ctr brg | Pendant | OF | Motor | 3,700,001 | 1 tooth click, Also 13S |
| | 2 | True Ctr brg | Pendant | OF | Motor | 3,869,301 | 5 tooth click |
| | 3 | ¾ | Pendant | OF | Motor | 3,869,201 | 2 tooth click |
| 8 | 1 | Full | Key or lever | Htg | Reg | 100,001 | Plate not recessed |
| | 2 | Full | Lever | Htg | Reg | 100,101 | Plate is recessed |
| 6 | 1 | ¾ | Lever | Htg | Reg | 552,001 | |
| 4 | 1 | ¾ | Lever | Htg | Reg | 551,501 | |
| 0 | 1 | ¾ | Pendant | OF | Reg | 1,815,901 | |
| | 2 | ¾ | Pendant | Htg | Reg | 1,749,801 | |
| | 3 | Cent brg | Pendant | OF | Reg | 2,644,001 | |
| | 4 | Cent brg | Pendant | Htg | Reg | 2,637,001 | |

**Rigid** bow 60 HR. MODEL
gold filled: $175 - $225 - $275
14K gold: $375 - $450 - $500

Antique bow MODEL
gold filled: $90 - $110 - $125
14K gold: $300 - $350 - $400

FIRST MODEL
gold filled: $100 - $125 - $150

**Stiff** bow 60 HR. MODEL
gold filled: $200 - $250 - $275
14K gold: $400 - $475 - $550

Empire bow MODEL
gold filled: $90 - $110 - $130
14K gold: $300 - $350 - $420

MODEL 28
gold filled: $125 - $150 - $175
gold filled **2 tone**: $150 - $175 - $200

MODEL 29
gold filled: $100 - $125 - $150

MODEL 107
gold filled: $100 - $115 - $130

MODEL 28, 173 & 206=combination white & yellow gold-filled
models Solid Gold cases= rigid bow
Gold-filled cases (1st. model), (antique), (rigid bow), 28, 29, 107, 108, 128, 173, 181, 193, & 206

🕐 NOTE: Factory Advertised as a **complete** watch and was fitted with a certain matched, timed and rated movement and sold in the factory designed case style as a **complete** watch. The factory also sold _uncased_ movements to **JOBBERS** such as Jewelry stores & they cased the movement in a case styles the **CUSTOMER requested.** All the factory advertised **complete** watches came with the dial **SHOWN or CHOICE** of other Railroad dials.

MODEL 108
gold filled: $100 - $115 - $130

MODEL 128
gold filled: $70 - $80 - $100

MODEL 173
gold filled: $100 - $125 - $150
gold filled 2 tone: $150 - $175 - $200

MODEL 181
gold filled: $100 - $115 - $130

MODEL 193
gold filled: $100 - $125 - $150

MODEL 206
gold filled: $90 - $110 - $140
gold filled 2 tone: $110 - $140 - $160

BUNN SPECIALS were packed & shipped
in a ALUMINUM cigarette style box.

MODEL 28, 173 & 206=combination white & yellow gold-filled
models Solid Gold cases= rigid bow
Gold-filled cases (1st. model), (antique), (rigid bow), 28, 29, 107, 108, 128, 173, 181, 193, & 206

🕐 NOTE: Factory Advertised as a complete watch and was fitted with a certain matched, timed and rated movement and sold in the factory designed case style as a complete watch. The factory also sold _uncased_ movements to JOBBERS such as Jewelry stores & they cased the movement in a case styles the CUSTOMER requested. All the factory advertised complete watches came with the dial SHOWN or CHOICE of other Railroad dials.

**Model 1**, 18 size, hunting, key wind & set.

**Model 2**, 18 size, hunting, lever set, coarse train.

**Model 3**, 18 size, open face, lever set, coarse train, with fifth pinion.

**Model 4**, 18 size, open face, pendant set, fine train.

**Model 5**, 18 size, hunting, lever set, fine train.

**Model 6**, 18 size, open face, lever set, fine train.

**Model 1**, 16 size, hunting, lever set.

**Model 2**, 16 size, open face, pendant set.

**Model 3**, 16 size, open face, lever set

**Model 4**, 16 size, three-quarter plate, hunting, lever set.

**Model 4**, 16 size, three-quarter plate, bridge, hunting, lever set.

**Model 5**, 16 size, three-quarter plate, open face, lever set.

**Model 5**, 16 size, three-quarter plate, bridge, open face, lever set.

**Model 6**, 16 size - Pendant set
**Model 8**, 16 size - Lever set
hunting, three-quarter plate

**Model 6**, 16 size - Pendant set
**Model 8**, 16 size - Lever set
hunting, bridge model

**Model 7**, 16 size - Pendant set
**Model 9**, 16 size - Lever set
open face, three-quarter plate

**Model 7**, 16 size - Pendant set
**Model 9**, 16 size - Lever set
open face, bridge model

**Model 10**, 16 size, bridge, extra thin, open face, lever set, motor barrel.

**Model 11,** 16 size, three-quarter plate, open face, pendant set, motor barrel.

**Model 12,** 16 size, three-quarter plate, hunting, pendant set, motor barrel.

**Model 13,** 16 size, bridge, open face, lever set, motor barrel.

**Model 14,** 16 size, three-quarter plate, open face, lever set, 60-hour motor barrel.

**Model 15,** 60 Hr. Elinvar.

**Model B,** 16 size, hunting case.

**Model C**, 16 size, open face

**Model D**, 16 size, open face

**Model 1**, 14 size, hunting, lever set.

**Model 2**, 14 size, open face, pendant set.

**Model 3**, 14 size, open face, lever set.

**Model 1**, 13 size, bridge, extra thin, open face, pendant set, motor barrel.

Model 1, 12 size, three-quarter plate, open face, pendant set.

Model 1, 12 size, three-quarter plate, bridge, open face, pendant set.

Model 2, 12 size, three-quarter plate, hunting, pendant set.

Model 2, 12 size, three-quarter plate, bridge, hunting, pendant set.

Model 3, 12 size, Model 4, 12 & 14 size, bridge, open face, pendant set.

Model 4, 12 size, bridge, hunting, pendant set.

**Model 5**, 12 size, bridge, open face, pendant set, motor barrel.

**Model 1**, 12 size, extra thin, bridge, open face, pendant set, motor barrel.

**Model 2**, 12 size, extra thin, bridge, open face, pendant set, motor barrel.

**Model 3**, 12 size, extra thin, three-quarter plate, open face, pendant set, motor barrel.

**Model A**, 12 size, bridge, open face.

**Model 1**, 8 size, hunting, key or lever set.

**Model 2**, 8 size, hunting, lever set.

**Model 1**, 6 size, hunting, lever set.

**Model 1**, 4 size, hunting, lever set.

**Model 1**, 0 size, three-quarter plate, open face, pendant set.

**Model 2**, 0 size, three-quarter plate, hunting, pendant set.

**Model 3**, 0 size, bridge, open face, pendant set.

**Model 4**, 0 size, bridge, hunting, pendant set.

**Model 3**, 3/0 size, bridge, open face, pendant set.

**Model 4**, 3/0 size, bridge, hunting, pendant set.

**Model 1**, 6/0 size, three-quarter plate, open face, pendant set.

**Model 2**, 6/0 size, bridge, open face, pendant set.

284

# INDEPENDENT WATCH CO.
## Fredonia, New York
### 1875 - 1885

The California Watch Company was idle for two years before it was purchased by brothers E. W. Howard and C. M. Howard. They had been selling watches by mail for sometime and started engraving the Howard Bros. name on them and using American-made watches. Their chief supply came from Hampden Watch Co., Illinois W. Co., U. S. Watch Co. of Marion. The brothers formed the Independent Watch Co. in 1880, but it was not a watch factory in the true sense. They had other manufacturers engrave the Independent Watch Co. name on the top plates and on the dials of their watches. These watches were sold by mail order and sent to the buyer C. O. D. The names used on the movements were "Howard Bros.," "Independent Watch Co.," "FredoniaWatch Co.," and "Lakeshore Watch Co., Fredonia,N. Y."

The company later decided to manufacture watches and used the name Fredonia Watch Co., but they found that selling watches two different ways was not very good.The business survived until 1885 at which time the owners decided to move the plant to a new location at Peoria, Illinois. Approximately 350,000 watches were made that sold for $16.00.

### CHRONOLOGY OF THE DEVELOPMENT OF INDEPENDENT WATCH CO.

Independent Watch Co. .............................................. 1875–1881
Fredonia Watch Co. ..................................................... 1881–1885
Peoria Watch Co. ....................................................... 1885–1889

### 18 SIZE

| Grade or Name — Description | Avg | Ex-Fn | Mint |
|---|---|---|---|
| 18S, 7J, KW, KS, OF, by U.S. W. Co. Marion, with butterfly cutout.............................................★ | $450 | $550 | $675 |
| 18S, 11J, KW, KS, by Hampden........................................ | 250 | 325 | 375 |
| 18S, 11J, KW, KS, Coin.................................................. | 235 | 285 | 350 |
| 18S, 11J, KW, KS......................................................... | 235 | 285 | 350 |
| 18S, 15J, KW, KS......................................................... | 235 | 285 | 350 |
| 18S, Howard Bros., 11J, KW, KS..................................... | 350 | 425 | 475 |
| 18S, Independent W. Co., 11J......................................... | 235 | 285 | 350 |
| 18S, Lakeshore W. Co., 15J, KW, HC, by N.Y. W. Co. .......... | 250 | 325 | 375 |

Independent Watch Co. on movement, on dial Howard Bros. Fredonia N.Y., 18 size, 11 jewels, key wind & stem wind, improved April 10,1879, serial number 126,319.

Independent Watch Co., 18 size, 15 jewels, key wind, made by U.S. Marion Watch Co., note butterfly cutout, serial number 192,661.

🕐 Watches listed in this book are priced at the **collectable fair market value** at the RETAIL level, as complete watches having an original 14k gold filled case, KEY WIND with silver, an original white enamel single sunk dial, and with the entire original movement in good working order with no repairs needed, unless otherwise noted.

# ROBERT H. INGERSOLL & BROS.

### New York, New York
### 1892 - 1922

In 1892 this company published a catalog for the mail order trade. It listed men's watch chains and a "silverine" watch for $3.95. It was not a true Ingersoll but a "Universal," introduced that same year to the dealers. The first $1 watches were jeweled; "Reliance" had seven jewels. In 1916, Ingersoll's production was 16,000 a day. The slogan was "The Watch that Made the Dollar Famous." The first 1,000 watches were made by Waterbury Clock Co. By 1922 the Ingersoll line was completely taken over by Waterbury. U. S. Time Corp. acquired Waterbury in 1944 and continued to use the Ingersoll name on certain watches.

## ESTIMATED SERIAL NUMBERS
## AND PRODUCTION DATES

| DATE—SERIAL NO. | DATE—SERIAL NO. | DATE—SERIAL NO. | DATE—SERIAL NO. |
|---|---|---|---|
| 1892 – 150,000 | 1902 – 7,200,000 | 1912 – 38,500,000 | 1922 – 60,500,000 |
| 1893 – 310,000 | 1903 – 7,900,000 | 1913 – 40,000,000 | 1923 – 62,000,000 |
| 1894 – 650,000 | 1904 – 8,100,000 | 1914 – 41,500,000 | 1924 – 65,000,000 |
| 1895 – 1,000,000 | 1905 –10,000,000 | 1915 – 42,500,000 | 1925 – 67,500,000 |
| 1896 – 2,000,000 | 1906 –12,500,000 | 1916 – 45,500,000 | 1926 – 69,000,000 |
| 1897 – 2,900,000 | 1907 –15,000,000 | 1917 – 47,000,000 | 1927 – 70,500,000 |
| 1898 – 3,500,000 | 1908 –17,500,000 | 1918 – 47,500,000 | 1928 – 71,500,000 |
| 1899 – 3,750,000 | 1909 –20,000,000 | 1919 – 50,000,000 | 1929 – 73,500,000 |
| 1900 – 6,000,000 | 1910 –25,000,000 | 1920 – 55,000,000 | 1930 – 75,000,000 |
| 1901 – 6,700,000 | 1911 –30,000,000 | 1921 – 58,000,000 | 1944 – 95,000,000 |

The above list is provided for determining the APPROXIMATE age of your watch. Match serial number with date. Watches were not necessarily sold in the exact order of manufactured date.

Ingersoll Back Wind & Set, patent date Dec. 23, 1890 and Jan. 13, 1891, c. late 1890s.

Ingersoll, engraved movement also pin set..

Ingersoll, Celluloid Case in Black or White.

Ingersoll, Blind Man's Watch.

## INGERSOLL DOLLAR TYPE

NOTE: Prices are for complete watch in **good running order**. In some specialty markets, the comic character watches may bring higher prices in top condition.

| Grade or Name — Description | Avg | Ex-Fn | Mint |
|---|---|---|---|
| Ingersoll All **Back Wind** Models | $100 | $125 | $175 |
| Admiral Dewey, "Flagship Olympia" on back of case | 150 | 175 | 250 |
| American Pride | 75 | 100 | 125 |
| Are U My Neighbor | 35 | 45 | 65 |
| B. B. H. Special, Backwind | 65 | 75 | 95 |
| Blind Man Pocket Watch | 50 | 75 | 95 |
| Boer War, on dial **Souvenier of South African War 1900** .... ★ ★ ★ ★ | 900 | 1,100 | 1,400 |
| Buck | 25 | 30 | 40 |
| Calendar (on moveable calendar on back of case) | 75 | 85 | 125 |
| Celluloid Case in Black or White | 100 | 135 | 185 |
| Champion (many models) | 50 | 75 | 125 |
| Chancery | 50 | 75 | 125 |
| Chicago Expo. 1933 | 200 | 250 | 325 |
| Climax | 40 | 45 | 65 |
| Clock Watch, pat. 1878-90-91 | 75 | 85 | 125 |
| Cloverine | 60 | 70 | 85 |
| Colby | 25 | 30 | 40 |
| Columbus | 45 | 60 | 85 |
| Columbus (3 ships on back of case), 1893 ★ | 250 | 300 | 450 |
| Connecticut W. Co. | 30 | 40 | 50 |
| Cord | 20 | 30 | 45 |
| Crown | 25 | 30 | 40 |
| Dan Dee | 35 | 45 | 75 |
| Defiance | 30 | 40 | 55 |
| Delaware W. Co. | 25 | 30 | 40 |
| Devon Mfg. Co. | 25 | 30 | 40 |

Scout watch ( Be prepared )

Yankee watch with bicycle on dial.

NOTE : ADD $25 to $75 for original BOX and PAPERS

Ingersoll Premium, early back wind & set.

Ingersoll Triumph, note pin for setting.

| Grade or Name — Description | Avg | Ex-Fn | Mint |
|---|---|---|---|
| Eclipse (many models) | $25 | $30 | $40 |
| Eclipse Radiolite | 30 | 35 | 40 |
| Endura | 30 | 35 | 40 |
| Ensign | 30 | 35 | 40 |
| Escort | 25 | 30 | 40 |
| Fancy Dials ( unfaded to be mint ) | 100 | 145 | 200 |
| Freedom | 30 | 35 | 40 |
| Gotham | 25 | 30 | 40 |
| Graceline | 45 | 50 | 65 |
| Gregg | 25 | 30 | 40 |
| Junior (several models) | 25 | 30 | 40 |
| Junior Radiolite | 35 | 40 | 55 |
| Kelton | 25 | 30 | 40 |
| Lapel Watches | 35 | 55 | 75 |
| Leader | 35 | 40 | 50 |
| Leeds | 25 | 30 | 40 |
| Leonard Watch Co. | 25 | 30 | 40 |
| Liberty U.S.A., backwind | 75 | 100 | 150 |
| Liberty Watch Co. | 35 | 45 | 75 |
| Limited, LEVER SET ON CASE RIM OF WATCH | 50 | 60 | 80 |
| Major | 25 | 40 | 60 |
| Maple Leaf | 25 | 30 | 40 |
| Master Craft | 25 | 30 | 40 |
| Midget (several models) | 35 | 50 | 75 |
| Midget , 6 size, "patd. Jan. 29 -01," Damaskeened, fancy case | 75 | 100 | 150 |
| Monarch | 25 | 30 | 40 |
| New West | 30 | 45 | 65 |
| New York World's Fair, 1939 | 150 | 175 | 200 |
| Overland | 35 | 40 | 50 |
| Pan American Expo., Buffalo, 1901 | 200 | 275 | 350 |
| Paris World Expo., 1900 | 150 | 175 | 225 |
| Patrol | 35 | 45 | 65 |
| Perfection | 35 | 45 | 55 |
| Pilgram | 40 | 50 | 55 |
| Premier, back wind, eagle on back, c. 1894 ........★ | 95 | 125 | 200 |

NOTE : ADD $25 to $75 for original BOX and PAPERS

Left: Ingersoll Back Wind, c. 1895.          Right: Yankee Back Wind, c. 1893.

| Grade or Name — Description | Avg | Ex-Fn | Mint |
|---|---|---|---|
| Premium Back Wind and Set | $50 | $75 | $100 |
| Progress, 1933 World's Fair Chicago | 200 | 275 | 350 |
| Puritan | 35 | 50 | 75 |
| Quaker | 40 | 45 | 60 |
| Radiolite | 30 | 35 | 45 |
| Reliance, 7J | 50 | 70 | 95 |
| Remington W. Co. USA | 60 | 75 | 95 |
| Rotary International, c. 1920 | 50 | 65 | 80 |
| Royal | 25 | 30 | 40 |
| St. Louis World's Fair (two models) | 250 | 300 | 400 |
| St. Louis World's Fair, 1904 | 150 | 200 | 275 |
| The Saturday Post | 150 | 175 | 225 |
| Senator | 35 | 40 | 50 |
| Senior | 25 | 30 | 40 |
| Sir Leeds | 25 | 30 | 40 |
| Solar | 25 | 30 | 40 |
| Souvenir Special | 50 | 75 | 100 |
| Sterling | 35 | 40 | 50 |
| Ten Hune | 60 | 70 | 85 |
| The Yankee Bicycle Watch | 40 | 50 | 65 |
| Traveler with Bed Side Stand | 35 | 45 | 65 |
| Triumph | 100 | 125 | 150 |
| Triumph Pinset | 150 | 175 | 225 |
| True Test | 25 | 30 | 40 |
| Trump | 35 | 45 | 55 |
| USA (two models) | 50 | 75 | 100 |
| Universal, 1st model | 200 | 250 | 300 |
| Uncle Sam | 40 | 50 | 60 |
| George Washington | 150 | 175 | 225 |
| Waterbury (several models) | 40 | 60 | 90 |

NOTE : ADD $25 to $75 for original BOX and PAPERS

| Grade or Name — Description | Avg | Ex-Fn | Mint |
|---|---|---|---|
| Waterbury Back Wind, 35 Size | $100 | $150 | $200 |
| Winner | 30 | 40 | 50 |
| Winner with S.B.B. | 40 | 45 | 55 |
| Yankee Backwind | 85 | 95 | 150 |
| Yankee Bicycle Watch (sold for $1.00 in 1896) | 175 | 195 | 250 |
| Yankee Radiolite | 40 | 55 | 75 |
| Yankee Radiolite with S.B.B. | 45 | 50 | 60 |
| Yankee Special (many models) | 75 | 100 | 150 |
| Yankee, Perpetual calendar on back of case | 75 | 100 | 150 |

**Ingersoll** moveable calendar for years 1929-1951 located on back of case.

**Ingersoll** movement made in Great Britain.

## INGERSOLL LTD.
### (GREAT BRITAIN)

| Grade or Name — Description | Avg | Ex-Fn | Mint |
|---|---|---|---|
| Ingersoll Ltd. (many models) | $50 | $75 | $100 |
| Coronation, Elizabeth II on watch | 175 | 200 | 250 |
| Coronation, June 2, 1953 on dial | 175 | 200 | 250 |
| 16S, 7J, 3F Brg | 55 | 60 | 85 |
| 16S, 15J, 3F Brg | 75 | 85 | 110 |
| 16S, 17J, 3F Brg, ADJ | 115 | 145 | 175 |
| 16S, 19J, 3F Brg, Adj 5P | 250 | 300 | 375 |
| 12S, 4J | 35 | 40 | 65 |

🕐 Some grades are not included. Their values can be determined by comparing with **similar** age, size, metal content, style, models and grades listed.

INGRAHAM, Seven Seas, shows standard time, & Nautical time.

New York to Paris, airplane model commemorating Lindbergh's famous flight.

# E. INGRAHAM CO.

## Bristol, Connecticut

### 1912 - 1968

The E. Ingraham Co. purchased the Bannatyne Co. in 1912. They produced their first American pocket watch in 1913. A total of about 65 million American-made pocket watches and over 12 million wrist watches were produced before they started to import watches in 1968.

| Grade or Name — Description | Avg | Ex-Fn | Mint |
|---|---|---|---|
| Ingraham W. Co. (many models) | $25 | $35 | $50 |
| Allure | 30 | 40 | 55 |
| Aristocrat Railroad Special | 35 | 40 | 50 |
| Autocrat | 25 | 30 | 45 |
| Basket Ball Foot Ball Timer | 35 | 45 | 65 |
| Beacon | 25 | 30 | 45 |
| Biltmore | 25 | 30 | 45 |
| Biltmore Radium | 25 | 30 | 45 |
| Bristol | 25 | 30 | 45 |
| Clipper | 25 | 30 | 45 |
| Co-Ed | 20 | 25 | 30 |
| Comet | 25 | 30 | 45 |
| Companion, sweep second hand | 25 | 30 | 40 |
| Cub | 25 | 30 | 45 |
| Dale | 25 | 30 | 45 |
| Demi–hunter style cover | 30 | 40 | 55 |
| Digital seconds dial, (no second hand but a digital seconds on dial) | 30 | 40 | 55 |
| Dixie | 25 | 30 | 45 |
| Dot | 25 | 30 | 45 |
| Endura | 25 | 30 | 45 |
| Everbrite (all models) | 25 | 30 | 45 |
| Graceline, | 25 | 35 | 50 |
| Ingraham USA | 25 | 30 | 45 |
| Jockey | 25 | 30 | 40 |
| Laddie | 25 | 30 | 40 |
| Laddie Athlete | 40 | 45 | 55 |
| Lady's Purse Watch, with fancy bezel | 45 | 50 | 65 |
| Lendix Extra | 25 | 30 | 40 |

🕐 Prices are for complete watch in **good running order.** In some specialty markets, the comic character watches may bring higher prices in top condition.

NOTE : ADD $25 to $75 for original BOX and PAPERS

Pastor Stop Watch, Sterling W. Co. printed on dial, with start stop & fly back to zero function. The Sterling Watch Company. Inc. Waterbury, Conn. U.S.A. on movement

| Grade or Name — Description | | Avg | Ex-Fn | Mint |
|---|---|---|---|---|
| Pastor Stop Watch, (Sterling W. Co), fly back to zero | ★★★ | $150 | $200 | $275 |
| Pathfinder, compass on pendant | | 65 | 75 | 95 |

**Path Finder** showing compass in crown.     Printed on dial, "**Unbreakable crystal**," ca. 1924.

| Grade or Name — Description | Avg | Ex-Fn | Mint |
|---|---|---|---|
| Patriot | $125 | $150 | $250 |
| Peerless | 30 | 35 | 55 |
| Pilot | 30 | 40 | 55 |
| Pocket Pal | 25 | 30 | 40 |
| Pony | 25 | 30 | 40 |
| Pride | 20 | 25 | 35 |
| Princess | 20 | 30 | 45 |
| Prince | 25 | 35 | 45 |
| Professional | 30 | 35 | 45 |
| Pup | 25 | 30 | 40 |
| Reliance | 45 | 50 | 65 |
| Rex | 25 | 30 | 40 |
| Rite Time | 25 | 30 | 40 |
| St. Regis | 25 | 30 | 40 |
| Secometer | 20 | 25 | 35 |
| Sentinel | 25 | 30 | 40 |
| Sentinel Click | 20 | 25 | 35 |
| Sentinel Fold Up Travel | 45 | 50 | 65 |
| Sentry | 25 | 30 | 35 |
| Seven Seas, 24 hr. dial & nautical dial | 75 | 100 | 150 |
| Silver Star | 25 | 30 | 40 |

| Grade or Name — Description | Avg | Ex-Fn | Mint |
|---|---|---|---|
| Sturdy | $25 | $30 | $40 |
| Target | 25 | 30 | 40 |
| The Best | 20 | 25 | 30 |
| The Pal | 30 | 35 | 40 |
| Time Ball | 25 | 30 | 40 |
| Time & Time | 30 | 40 | 55 |
| Top Flight | 20 | 25 | 35 |
| Top Notch | 35 | 45 | 50 |
| Tower | 25 | 30 | 40 |

Trail Blazer, Commemorating Byrd's Antarctic Expedition.

Showing back side of Trail Blazer, also depicted on box.

FOB

BOX: Same as depicted on BACK of watch.

| Grade or Name — Description | Avg | Ex-Fn | Mint |
|---|---|---|---|
| Trail Blazer, Commemorating BYRD'S Antarctic Expedition | $175 | $225 | $300 |
| Trail Blazer watch, with fob (wings over the pole), + box . ★★★ | 400 | 500 | 750 |
| Treasure | 15 | 20 | 25 |
| Unbreakable Crystal | 45 | 50 | 65 |
| Uncle Sam (all models) | 50 | 75 | 95 |
| Uncle Sam Backwind & Set | 125 | 150 | 190 |
| United | 30 | 35 | 40 |
| Viceroy | 20 | 25 | 35 |
| Victory | 25 | 30 | 55 |
| Wings | 30 | 35 | 40 |

NOTE : ADD $25 to $75 for original BOX and PAPERS

**Left:** Example of a basic International Watch Co. movement with patent dates of Aug. 19, 1902, Jan. 27, 1903 & Aug. 11, 1903. **Right:** Example of a Highland.

## INTERNATIONAL WATCH CO.

### Newark City, New Jersey
### 1902 - 1907

This company produced only non-jeweled or low-cost production type watches that were inexpensive and nickel plated. Names on their watches include: Berkshire, Madison, and Mascot.

| Grade or Name — Description | | Avg | Ex-Fn | Mint |
|---|---|---|---|---|
| 18 Size, skeletonized, pinlever escape., first model | ★★ | $100 | $125 | $175 |
| Berkshire, OF | ★ | 75 | 100 | 150 |
| Highland | ★ | 65 | 90 | 140 |
| Madison, 18S, OF | ★ | 75 | 100 | 150 |
| Mascot, OF | ★ | 50 | 75 | 125 |

## KANKAKEE WATCH CO.

### Kankakee, Illinois
### 1900

This company reportedly became the McIntyre Watch Co. Little other information is available.

| Grade or Name — Description | | Avg | Ex-Fn | Mint |
|---|---|---|---|---|
| 16S, BRG, NI | ★★★★ | $5,500 | $6,000 | $7,000 |

🕐 Watches listed in this book are priced at the **collectable fair market value** at the RETAIL level, as complete watches having an original 14k gold filled case, KEY WIND with silver, an original white enamel single sunk dial, and with the entire original movement in good working order with no repairs needed, unless otherwise noted.

# KELLY WATCH CO.

### Chicago, Illinois
### c. 1900

| Grade or Name — Description | Avg | Ex-Fn | Mint |
|---|---|---|---|
| 16S, aluminum movement and OF case.............................★ ★ ★ ★ | $225 | $250 | $300 |

Kelly Watch Co., 16 size, aluminum movement, straight line lever, quick train, porcelain dial, stem set, reversible ratchet stem wind, originally sold for $2.20, Ca. 1900.

# KEYSTONE STANDARD WATCH CO.

### Lancaster, Pennsylvania
### 1886 - 1890

Abram Bitner agreed to buy a large number of stockholders' shares of the Lancaster Watch Co. at 10 cents on the dollar; he ended up with 5,625 shares out of the 8,000 that were available. Some 8,900 movements had been completed but not sold at the time of the shares purchase. The company Bitner formed assumed the name of Keystone Standard Watch Co. as the trademark but in reality existed as the Lancaster Watch Co. The business was sold to **Hamilton Watch Co.** in 1891. Total production was 48,000.

| Grade or Name — Description | Avg | Ex-Fn | Mint |
|---|---|---|---|
| 18S, 7-15J, OF, KW | $100 | $120 | $150 |
| 18S, 7-15J, OF, SW, 3/4, LS | 75 | 100 | 150 |
| 18S, 15J, dust proof, ADJ | 150 | 175 | 225 |
| 18S, 11-15J, dust proof, OF | 100 | 125 | 175 |
| 18S, 11-15J, dust proof, HC | 150 | 175 | 225 |
| 18S, West End, 15J, HC | 75 | 125 | 175 |
| 8S, 11J, dust proof | 100 | 125 | 175 |
| 6S, 7-10J, HC ★ | 175 | 200 | 250 |

Keystone Watch Co., dust proof model, 18 size, 15 jewels, serial number 352,766.

Knickerbocker movement, 16-18 size, 7 jewels, duplex escapement.

# KNICKERBOCKER WATCH CO.

### New York, New York
### 1890 - 1930

This company imported and sold Swiss and low-cost production American watches.

| Grade or Name — Description | Avg | Ex-Fn | Mint |
|---|---|---|---|
| 18S, 7J, OF, PS, NI, duplex escapement | $60 | $75 | $95 |
| 16S, 7J | 45 | 55 | 75 |
| 12S, 7J, OF | 45 | 55 | 85 |
| 10S, Barkley "8 Day" | 75 | 100 | 125 |
| 6S, Duplex | 50 | 60 | 75 |

🕒 Some grades are not included. Their values can be determined by comparing with **similar** age, size, metal content, style, models and grades listed.

🕒 Watches listed in this book are priced at the **collectable fair market value** at the RETAIL level, as complete watches having an original 14k gold filled case, KEY WIND with silver, an original white enamel single sunk dial, and with the entire original movement in good working order with no repairs needed, unless otherwise noted.

# LANCASTER WATCH CO.
## Lancaster, Pennsylvania
### 1877 - 1886

Work commenced on Sept. 1, 1877, at the Lancaster Watch Co. The watches produced there were designed to sell at a cheaper price than normal. They had a solid top, 3/4 plate, and a pillar plate that was fully ruby-jeweled (4 pairs). They had a gilt and nickel movement and a new stem-wind device, modeled by Mosly & Todd. By mid-1878 the Lancaster Watch Co. had produced 150 movements. Four grades of watches were made: Keystone, Fulton, Franklin, and Melrose. In September 1879 the company had made 334 movements. In 1880 the total was up to 1,250 movements, and by mid-1882 about 17,000 movements had been produced. All totaled, about 20,000 watch movements were made.

About 75, 8-size ladies' watches were also made.

## CHRONOLOGY OF THE DEVELOPMENT OF THE LANCASTER WATCH CO.

| | |
|---|---|
| Adams and Perry Watch Mfg. Co. | 1874-1876 |
| Lancaster Watch Co. | 1877-1878 |
| Lancaster Pa. Watch Co. | 1878-1879 |
| Lancaster Watch Co. | 1879-1886 |
| Keystone Standard Co. | 1886-1890 |
| Hamilton Watch Co. | 1892-1958 |

## LANCASTER
### 18 SIZE
#### (All 3/4 Plate)

| Grade or Name — Description | Avg | Ex-Fn | Mint |
|---|---|---|---|
| Chester, 7-11J, KW, dust proof, gilded | $125 | $150 | $200 |
| Comet, 7J, NI | 125 | 150 | 200 |
| Delaware, 20J, ADJ, SW, dust proof, gilded | 300 | 375 | 450 |
| Denver, 7J, dust proof, gilded | 75 | 100 | 125 |
| Denver, 7J, gilded, dust proof, Silveroid | 40 | 50 | 65 |
| Elberon, 7J, dust proof | 125 | 150 | 200 |
| Ben Franklin, 7J, KW, gilded | 250 | 300 | 375 |
| Ben Franklin, 11J, KW, gilded | 300 | 350 | 425 |
| Fulton, 7J, ADJ, KW, gilded | 125 | 150 | 200 |
| Fulton, 11J, ADJ, KW, gilded | 125 | 150 | 200 |
| Girard, 15J, ADJ, dust proof, gilded | 100 | 145 | 200 |
| Hoosac, 11J, OF | 125 | 175 | 225 |
| Keystone, 15J, ADJ, gilded, GJS, dust proof | 100 | 125 | 175 |
| Keystone, 15J, ADJ, gilded, GJS, Silveroid | 75 | 90 | 125 |
| Lancaster, 7J, SW | 75 | 90 | 120 |
| Lancaster, 15J, SW, Silveroid | 60 | 75 | 100 |
| Lancaster, 15J, OF | 75 | 100 | 150 |
| Lancaster Pa., 20J, ADJ, NI ★★★ | 400 | 500 | 650 |

🕐 Some grades are not included. Their values can be determined by comparing with similar age, size, metal content, style, models and grades listed.

🕐 Watches listed in this book are priced at the **collectable fair market value** at the RETAIL level, as complete watches having an original 14k gold filled case, KEY WIND with silver, an original white enamel single sunk dial, and with the entire original movement in good working order with no repairs needed, unless otherwise noted.

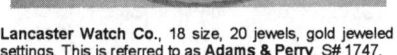

**Lancaster Watch Co.**, 18 size, 20 jewels, gold jeweled settings, This is referred to as **Adams & Perry** S# 1747.

**Stevens Model**, 18 size, 15 jewels, adjusted, dust proof model, swing-out movement, c.1886.

| Grade or Name — Description | Avg | Ex-Fn | Mint |
|---|---|---|---|
| Lancaster Watch Co., 20J, ADJ, GJS, | | | |
|     Referred to as **(Adams & Perry)** model ............... ★ ★ ★ | $1,000 | $1,500 | $2,200 |
| Malvern, 7J, dust proof, gilded............................................. | 90 | 110 | 130 |
| Melrose, 15J, NI, ADJ, GJS ................................................. | 100 | 125 | 175 |
| Nation Standard American Watch Co., 7J, HC ................. | 200 | 225 | 275 |
| New Era, 7J, gilded, KW, HC ............................................... | 75 | 100 | 150 |
| New Era, 7J, gilded, KW, Silveroid..................................... | 60 | 80 | 100 |
| Paoli, 7J, NI, dust proof, ...................................................... | 75 | 100 | 150 |
| Wm. Penn, 20J, ADJ, NI, dust proof ................................... | 400 | 500 | 650 |
| Radnor, 7J, dust proof, gilded ............................................ | 100 | 125 | 175 |
| Record, 7J, dust proof, Silveroid........................................ | 60 | 80 | 100 |
| Record, 15J, NI...................................................................... | 75 | 100 | 150 |

**West End**, 18 size, 15 jewels, key wind & set, serial number 158,080, c. 1878.

**Lancaster movement**, 8-10 size, 15 jewels, serial number 317,812.

🕐 Watches listed in this book are priced at the collectable **fair market** retail level, as **Complete** watches having an original 14k gold-filled case for Stem Wind and *Key Wind* with silver case, an original white enamel single sunk dial, and with the entire original movement in good working order with no repairs needed.

| Grade or Name — Description | Avg | Ex-Fn | Mint |
|---|---|---|---|
| Ruby, 7-16J, NI | $275 | $325 | $400 |
| Sidney, 15J, NI, dust proof, | 100 | 125 | 150 |
| Stevens, 15J, ADJ, NI, dust proof | 150 | 175 | 225 |
| West End, 19J, HC, KW, gilded | 450 | 500 | 550 |
| West End, 15J, HC, KW, KS | 175 | 200 | 250 |
| West End, 15J, SW | 175 | 200 | 250 |
| West End, 15J, SW, Silveroid | 60 | 80 | 100 |

## 8 SIZE

| Grade or Name — Description | Avg | Ex-Fn | Mint |
|---|---|---|---|
| Cricket, 11J | $65 | $70 | $80 |
| Diamond, 15J | 70 | 80 | 90 |
| Echo, 11J | 65 | 70 | 75 |
| Flora, 7-11J, gilded | 75 | 100 | 150 |
| Iris, 13J | 65 | 70 | 80 |
| Lady Penn, 20J, GJS, ADJ, NI | 300 | 350 | 425 |
| Lancaster W. Co., 7J | 75 | 100 | 125 |
| Pearl, 7J | 55 | 60 | 65 |
| Red Rose, of Lancaster, 15J | 75 | 80 | 90 |
| Ruby, 15J | 75 | 80 | 90 |

# MANHATTAN WATCH CO.

### New York, New York
### 1883 - 1891

The Manhattan Watch Co. made mainly low cost production watches. A complete and full line of watches was made, and most were cased and styled to be sold as a **complete** watch. The watches were generally 16S with full plate movements. The patented winding mechanism was different. These watches were in both in hunter and open-face cases and later had a sweep second hand. Total production was 160,000 or more watches.

Manhattan Watch Co., stop watch, 16 size, note the escapement uses upright "D"—shaped pallets (steel), serial number 117,480.

Manhattan Watch Co., 16 size, stop watch. Note the two buttons on top; the right (at 2 o'clock) one sets the hands, the left (at 10 o'clock) starts and stops the watch.

## 16 SIZE

| Grade or Name — Description | | Avg | Ex-Fn | Mint |
|---|---|---|---|---|
| OF, with back wind, base metal case | ★ | $250 | $300 | $400 |
| OF, 2 button stop watch, screw back & bezel, enamel dial, gold-filled case | ★ ★ | 200 | 250 | 350 |
| OF, 2 button stop watch, snap back & bezel, paper dial, base metal case | ★ | 100 | 125 | 150 |
| HC, 2 button stop watch, snap back & bezel, paper dial, base metal case | ★ | 200 | 250 | 300 |
| OF, 1 button, sweep sec., base metal case , paper dial | ★ | 125 | 175 | 225 |
| HC, 1 button, sweep sec., base metal case, paper dial | ★ | 200 | 250 | 300 |
| Ship's Bell Time Dial, OF or HC | ★ ★ ★ ★ | 300 | 400 | 500 |
| Twenty-Four Hour Dial, OF or HC | ★ ★ ★ ★ | 300 | 400 | 500 |
| Stallcup, 7J, OF | ★ | 150 | 200 | 250 |

## 12 SIZE

| Grade or Name — Description | | Avg | Ex-Fn | Mint |
|---|---|---|---|---|
| 12S | ★ | $125 | $200 | $275 |

Manhattan Watch Co., **16 size**, time only watch & note no second hand, the button at Right sets the hands.

Manhattan Watch Co., **16 size**, time only with Sweep-Second hand, the button at Right sets the hands.

Manhattan Watch Co., **16 size**, Ship's Bell Time DIAL for NAUTIAL USES & sweep second hand, Hunting Case.

Manhattan Watch Co., **16 size**, with a 24-HOUR DIAL.& sweep second hand, Hunting Case.

# MANISTEE WATCH CO.

### Manistee, Michigan
### 1908 - 1912

The Manistee watches, first marketed in 1909, were designed to compete with the low-cost production watches. Dials, jewels, and hairsprings were not produced at the factory. The first movement was 18S, 7J, and sold for about $5. Manistee also made 5J, 15J, 17J, and 21J watches in cheap cases in sizes 16 and 12. Estimated total production was 60,000. Most were sold by Star Watch Case Co.

## 18 SIZE

| Grade or Name —Description | | Avg | Ex-Fn | Mint |
|---|---|---|---|---|
| 18S, 7J, 3/4, LS, HC | ★ | $325 | $375 | $425 |
| 18S, 7J, 3/4, LS, OF | ★ | 275 | 325 | 375 |
| 18S, 7J, 3/4, LS, OF, gold train | ★ ★ | 375 | 400 | 450 |

## 16 TO 12 SIZE

| Grade or Name —Description | | Avg | Ex-Fn | Mint |
|---|---|---|---|---|
| 16S, 7J, OF | ★ | $200 | $250 | $325 |
| 16S, 15J, OF | ★ | 225 | 250 | 325 |
| 16S, 15J, HC | ★ | 250 | 275 | 350 |
| 16S, 17J, OF | ★ | 225 | 250 | 325 |
| 16S, 19J, HC | ★ | 300 | 350 | 425 |
| 16S, 21J, OF | ★ | 325 | 375 | 450 |
| 12S, 15J | ★ | 150 | 175 | 225 |

Manistee movement, 18 size, 7 jewels, 3/4 plate, open face, serial number 919.

Manistee movement, 16 size, 17 jewels, three-quarter plate, open face, serial number 39,052.

🕐 Watches listed in this book are priced at the collectable retail level, as **complete** watches having an original 14k gold-filled case and *Key Wind* with silver, an original white enamel single sunk dial, and with the entire original movement in good working order with no repairs needed.

🕐 Some grades are not included. Their values can be determined by comparing with **similar** age, size, metal content, style, models and grades listed.

# McINTYRE WATCH CO.

### Kankakee, Illinois

### 1905 - 1911

This company probably bought the factory from Kankakee Watch Co. In 1908 Charles DeLong was made master watchmaker, and he designed and improved the railroad watches. Only a few watches were made, estimated total production being about **eight watches**.

| Grade or Name — Description | | Avg | Ex-Fn | Mint |
|---|---|---|---|---|
| 16S, 21J, BRG, NI, WI | ★★★★ | $4,500 | $5,000 | $6,500 |
| 16S, 25J, BRG, NI, WI, Adj.5P, equidistant escapement | ★★★★ | 5,500 | 6,000 | 7,500 |
| 12S, 19J, BRG | ★★★★ | 2,000 | 2,500 | 3,500 |

McIntyre Watch Co., 16 size, 25 jewels, adjusted to 5 positions with wind indicator, with equidistant escapement, manufactured about 1909. Above illustration taken from a blue print.

EXAMPLE OF A BREGUET STYLE DIAL

EXAMPLE OF A BOX CAR STYLE DIAL

# MELROSE WATCH CO.

### Melrose, Massachusetts

### 1866 - 1868

Melrose Watch Co. began as Tremont Watch Co. and imported the expansion balances and escapements. In 1866 the Tremont Watch Co. moved, changed its name to Melrose Watch Co., and started making complete watch movements, including a new style 18S movement engraved "Melrose Watch Co." About 3,000 were produced. Some watches are found with "Melrose" on the dial and "Tremont" on the movement. Serial numbers start at about 30,000.

Example of a basic **Melrose Watch Co.** movement, 18 size, 15 jewels, key wind & set.

| Grade or Name — Description | | Avg | Ex-Fn | Mint |
|---|---|---|---|---|
| 18S, 7J, KW, KS | ★ ★ | $300 | $350 | $375 |
| 18S, 11J, KW, KS, OF | ★ ★ | 325 | 370 | 450 |
| 18S, 15J, KW, KS | ★ ★ | 350 | 400 | 475 |
| 18S, 15J, KW, KS, Silveroid | ★ ★ | 250 | 300 | 375 |

Note: Add $25.00 - $50.00 to values of above watches in hunting case.

# MOZART WATCH CO.

### Providence, Rhode Island

### Ann Arbor, Michigan

### 1864 - 1870

In 1864 Don J. Mozart started out to produce a less expensive three-wheel watch in Providence, R. I. Despite his best efforts, the venture was declared a failure by 1866. Mozart left Providence and moved to Ann Arbor, Mich. There, again, he started on a three-wheel watch and succeeded in producing thirty. The three-wheel watch was not a new idea except to American manufacturers. Three-wheel watches were made many decades before Mozart's first effort, but credit for the first American-made three-wheel watch must go to him. The size was about 18 and could be called a 3/4 or full plate movement. The balance bridge was screwed on the top plate, as was customary. The round bridge partially covered the opening in the top plate and was just large enough for the balance to oscillate. The balance was compensated and somewhat smaller in diameter than usual. Mozart called it a chronolever, and it was to function so perfectly it would be free from friction. That sounded good but was in no way true.

The watch was of the usual thickness for the American 18 size with a train that had a main wheel with the usual number of teeth and a ten-leaf center pinion, but it had a large center wheel of 108 teeth and a third wheel of 90 teeth, with a six-leaf third (escape) pinion. The escape wheel had 30 teeth and received its impulse directly from the roller on the staff, while the escape tooth locked on the intermediate lever pallet. The escape pinion had a long pivot that carried the second hand, which made a circuit of the dial, once in 12 seconds. The total number of Mozart watches produced was 165, and about 30 of these were the three-wheel type.

| Grade or Name — Description | | Avg | Ex-Fn | Mint |
|---|---|---|---|---|
| 18S, 3/4, KW, KS, 3-wheel ............................................ | ★★★★★ | $11,000 | $15,000 | $20,000 |
| 18S, 3/4, KW, KS .......................................................... | ★★★★ | 6,000 | 7,000 | 8,000 |

Mozart Watch Co. movement, 18 size, three-quarter plate, key wind & set, three-wheel train, "Patent Dec. 24th, 1868" engraved on back plate.

NASHUA WATCH CO. (marked), 20 size, 19 jewels, gold jewel settings, key wind & set from back, stop work, serial number 1,219.

# NASHUA WATCH CO.

### Nashua, New Hampshire

### 1859 - 1862

One of the most important contributions to the American Watch industry was made by the Nashua Watch Co. of Nashua, New Hampshire. Founded in 1859 by B. D. Bingham, the company hired some of the most innovative and creative watchmakers in America and produced an extremely high grade American pocket watch.

His company included N. P. Stratton, C. V. Woerd, Charles Moseley, James H. Gerry, and James Gooding, among others. Most of the people connected with the Nashua Watch Company became famous for various advances in watch manufacture, at one time or another. Many had extremely important American patents on various inventions that came to be regarded as a benchmark of the best watches America was capable of making at the time.

The Nashua Watch Co. is important for many reasons. It was the first American company to produce a truly superior high grade movement; the 3/4 plate design used by Nashua became the standard for over 40 years in the American marketplace. Perhaps most importantly, the watches designed by the Nashua Watch Co., and later by the Nashua division of the American Watch Co., became the leaders in the production of the highest quality watches made in America and forced the entire Swiss watch industry to change their technology to compete with the Nashua designs.

Nashua continually won awards for their various models of watches both here and in Europe. By virtue of their sheer technical superiority and classical elegance, Nashua became known universally as the most innovative producer of watches America ever knew.

The original Nashua company produced material for about 1,000 movements but, except for a handful, almost the entire production was finished by the American Watch Company at Waltham, Mass., after R. E. Robbins took over Nashua in 1862 when the company was in grave financial difficulty. Robbins was very happy about the arrangement since he got back almost all the watchmaking geniuses who had left him in 1859 to join Nashua. Robbins incorporated the Nashua Division into the American Watch Company as its high grade experimental division.

Over the years, many of the major advances were made by the Nashua division of Waltham, including the 1860 model 16-size keywind keyset, the 1862 model 20-size key wind keyset, the 1870 model 18-size keywind keyset, pin set, and lever set (which became the first American advertised Railroad watch), the 1868 model 16-size stem wind, and the 1872 model 17-size stemwind. The Nashua division also greatly influenced the 1888 model and the 1892 model by Waltham.

Since almost all the production material made by Nashua from 1859 until its incorporation into the American Watch Co. in 1862 was unfinished by Nashua, only about four examples of the 20-size keywind keyset from the back signed Nashua Watch Co. are known to exist.

| Grade or Name — Description | | Avg | Ex-Fn | Mint |
|---|---|---|---|---|
| Nashua (marked), 19J, KW, KS, 3/4, 18K | ★★★★★ | $18,000 | $22,000 | $28,000 |
| Nashua (marked), 15J, KW, KS, 3/4, silver case | ★★★★ | 9,000 | 11,000 | 13,000 |

# NEWARK WATCH CO.
### Newark, New Jersey
### 1864 - 1870

Arthur Wadsworth, one of the designers for Newark Watch Co., patented an 18 Size full plate movement. The first movements reached the market in 1867. This company produced only about 8,000 watches before it was sold to the Cornell Watch Co.

**CHRONOLOGY OF THE DEVELOPMENT OF NEWARK WATCH CO.:**
Newark Watch Co. 1864-1870; S#s 6,501 to 12,000;
Cornell Watch Co., Chicago, Ill. 1870-1874; S#s 12,001 to 25,000;
Cornell Watch Co., San Francisco, Calif. 1874-Jan. 1876; S#s 25,001 to 35,000;
California Watch Co., Jan. 1876-mid 1876.

Watches listed in this book are priced at the **collectable fair market value** at the RETAIL level, as complete watches having an original 14k gold filled case, KEY WIND with silver, an original white enamel single sunk dial, and with the entire original movement in good working order with no repairs needed, unless otherwise noted.

Newark Watch Co. Robert Fellows movement, 18 size, 15 jewels, key wind & set, serial number 12, 044.

| Grade or Name — Description | | Avg | Ex-Fn | Mint |
|---|---|---|---|---|
| 18S, 15J, KW, KS, HC | ★★ | $350 | $400 | $500 |
| 18S, 15J, KW, KS, OF | ★★ | 300 | 350 | 435 |
| 18S, 7J, KW, KS | ★★ | 300 | 350 | 435 |
| J. C. Adams, 11J, KW, KS | ★★ | 350 | 400 | 475 |
| J. C. Adams, 11J, KW, KS, Coin | ★★ | 350 | 400 | 475 |
| Edward Biven, 11-15J, KW, KS | ★★ | 350 | 400 | 475 |
| Robert Fellows, KW, KS | ★★ | 400 | 450 | 535 |
| Keyless Watch Co., 15J, LS, SW | ★★ | 300 | 350 | 435 |
| Newark Watch Co., 7-15J, KW, KS | ★★ | 350 | 400 | 475 |
| Arthur Wadsworth, SW | ★★★ | 400 | 500 | 600 |
| Arthur Wadsworth, 18S, 15J, 18K, HC ("Arthur Wadsworth, New York" on dial; "Keyless Watch, Patent #3655, June 19, 1866" engraved on movement) | ★★★ | 1,000 | 1,200 | 1,500 |

# NEW ENGLAND WATCH CO.

## Waterbury, Connecticut
### 1898 - 1914

The New England Watch Co., formerly the Waterbury Watch Co., made a watch with a duplex escapement, gilt, 16S, open faced. Watches with the skeletonized movement are very desirable. The company later became Timex Watch Co.

| Grade or Name — Description | | Avg | Ex-Fn | Mint |
|---|---|---|---|---|
| 16S, OF, duplex, **SKELETON**, good running order | ★ | $250 | $295 | $350 |
| 12S, 16S, 18S, OF, pictures on dial: ladies, dogs, horses, trains, flags, ships, cards, etc. | | 150 | 175 | 225 |
| 12S, 16S, 18S, OF, duplex escapement, good running order | | 50 | 65 | 95 |
| 12S, 16S, 18S, OF, pin lever escapement, good running order | | 35 | 45 | 60 |

🕐 Watches listed in this book are priced at the collectable **fair market** retail level, as **Complete** watches having an original 14k gold-filled case for Stem Wind and *Key Wind* with silver case, an original white enamel single sunk dial, and with the entire original movement in good working order with no repairs needed.

Front and back view of a **skeletonized** New England Watch Co. movement. This watch is fitted with a glass back and front, making the entire movement and wheels visible, 4 jewels, silver hands, black numbers, originally sold for $10-13.

| Grade or Name — Description | Avg | Ex-Fn | Mint |
|---|---|---|---|
| 6S, duplex | $35 | $40 | $55 |
| 0 S, 15-17 J, lever escapement | 50 | 65 | 85 |
| Addison, (all sizes ) | 35 | 40 | 55 |
| Alden | 35 | 40 | 55 |
| Ambassador, 12S, duplex | 25 | 30 | 40 |
| Americus, duplex | 20 | 25 | 30 |
| Avour, duplex escapement | 35 | 40 | 55 |
| Berkshire, duplex, 14K, GF | 60 | 70 | 85 |

**New England Watch Co.,** 16 size, 7 jewels, open face, double roller, Dan Patch stop watch.

**New England Watch Co.,** Scout, about 16 size, 4 jewels, duplex escapement, New England base metal case.

New England Watch Co., multi-colored paper dials, showing poker style playing cards. Watches complete with these type dials bring $150 - $400.00.

New England Watch Co., 0 size, 17 jewels, serial # 1,000,283

| Grade or Name — Description | Avg | Ex-Fn | Mint |
|---|---|---|---|
| Cadish, duplex escapement | $35 | $40 | $55 |
| Cavour, duplex escapement | 45 | 50 | 60 |
| Columbian | 20 | 30 | 45 |
| Chronograph, 7J, Start, Stop & Reset | 125 | 150 | 200 |
| Cruiser, duplex | 45 | 50 | 65 |
| Dan Patch, 7J ★ | 275 | 350 | 425 |
| Dominion, **0 size** | 20 | 30 | 45 |
| Excelsior, 7J | 65 | 70 | 95 |
| **Enamel**, full enamel cased watches back and bezel, blue red green, sizes from 6 size to 0 size | 75 | 100 | 150 |
| **Embossed**, base metal cases with duplex escapement | 45 | 65 | 95 |
| **Fancy**, **"unfaded dial"** | 100 | 145 | 200 |
| Gabour | 65 | 70 | 85 |
| General | 20 | 30 | 45 |
| Hale, 7J | 25 | 30 | 45 |
| Jockey, duplex | 55 | 60 | 75 |
| Oxford | 20 | 30 | 45 |
| Padishah, duplex | 45 | 50 | 65 |
| Putnam | 65 | 70 | 85 |
| Queen Mab, duplex escapemeny - **0 size, 4J** | 40 | 50 | 65 |
| Rugby, stop watch | 65 | 70 | 85 |
| Scout, 12 Size, duplex escapement, HC | 40 | 45 | 60 |
| Senator, duplex escapement | 40 | 45 | 55 |
| Trump, duplex | 40 | 45 | 55 |
| Tuxedo | 20 | 30 | 45 |
| Tuxedo, DUPLEX ESCAPEMENT | 45 | 50 | 65 |

🕐 Some grades are not included. Their values can be determined by comparing with **similar** age, size, metal content, style, models and grades listed.

# NEW HAVEN CLOCK AND WATCH CO.

### New Haven, Connecticut

### 1853 - 1956

The company started making watches in early 1880 in New Haven and produced the regular 16S, lever watch. These sold for $3.75. The company soon reached a production of about 200 watches per day, making a total of some 40 million watches.

NEW HAVEN Clock & Watch Co., Angelus, with rotating dials, patented Jan 23, 1900.

NEW HAVEN, Ships Time, Ben Franklin dial , Note this watch uses only one hand.

| Grade or Name – Description | Avg | Ex-Fn | Mint |
|---|---|---|---|
| Always Right | $45 | $55 | $75 |
| Angelus, 2 rotating dials | 125 | 175 | 250 |
| Beardsley Radiant | 45 | 50 | 65 |
| Buddy | 35 | 40 | 45 |
| Bull Dog | 40 | 45 | 60 |
| Compensated | 35 | 40 | 45 |
| Captain Scout | 85 | 100 | 150 |
| Celluloid case (bold colors) | 25 | 30 | 40 |
| Chronometer | 45 | 85 | 100 |
| Earl | 30 | 35 | 40 |
| Elite | 40 | 50 | 65 |
| Elm City | 30 | 35 | 40 |
| Fancy dials, no fading | 100 | 145 | 200 |
| Football Timer | 65 | 75 | 95 |
| Ford Special | 75 | 85 | 100 |
| Hamilton | 35 | 45 | 60 |
| Handy Andy | 50 | 60 | 75 |
| Jerome USA | 35 | 40 | 50 |

🕐 Note: Some styles, models and grades are not included. Their values can be determined by comparing with **similar** styles, size, age, models and grades listed.

NOTE : ADD $25 to $50 for original BOX and PAPERS

Example of Kaiser Wilhelm.

Example of Traveler.

| Grade or Name – Description | | Avg | Ex-Fn | Mint |
|---|---|---|---|---|
| Kaiser Wilhelm | ★ ★ | $200 | $275 | $350 |
| Kermit | | 40 | 45 | 55 |
| Laddie | | 25 | 30 | 40 |
| Lady Clare | | 20 | 25 | 30 |
| Leonard Watch Co. | | 25 | 40 | 50 |
| Leonard | | 25 | 35 | 45 |
| Mastercraft Rayolite | | 35 | 45 | 60 |
| Miracle | | 25 | 30 | 40 |
| Nehi | | 50 | 70 | 85 |
| New Haven, pin lever, SW | | 50 | 75 | 100 |
| New Haven, back wind | | 100 | 135 | 200 |
| Panama Official Souvenir, 1915 | | 200 | 250 | 350 |
| Pastor Stop Watch | | 65 | 85 | 100 |
| Paul Pry, 14 size with a Locomotive on back of case | | 25 | 30 | 35 |
| Pedometer, 14 size, OF | | 25 | 30 | 35 |
| Pentagon-shaped case | | 20 | 25 | 30 |
| Playing cards on dial | | 100 | 175 | 300 |
| Service | | 30 | 35 | 40 |
| Ships Time & Franklin dial | | 75 | 95 | 125 |
| Sports Timer | | 65 | 75 | 95 |
| Surity | | 20 | 25 | 35 |
| Tip Top | | 20 | 30 | 50 |
| Tip Top Jr. | | 20 | 30 | 50 |
| The American | | 45 | 50 | 60 |
| Tommy Ticker | | 30 | 35 | 40 |
| Tourist | | 25 | 30 | 35 |
| Traveler, with travel case | | 40 | 45 | 60 |
| True Time Teller Tip Top | | 40 | 45 | 60 |
| United | | 30 | 35 | 40 |
| USA | | 30 | 35 | 40 |
| Victor | | 25 | 30 | 35 |

NOTE : ADD $25 to $50 for original BOX and PAPERS

# NEW HAVEN WATCH CO.

### New Haven, Connecticut
### 1883 - 1887

This company was organized October 16, 1883 with the intention of producing W. E. Doolittle's patented watch; however, this plan was soon abandoned. They did produce a "Model A" watch, the first was marketed in the spring of 1884. Estimated total production is <u>200</u> and only **5 known to exist**. The original capital became absorbed by Trenton W. Co.

New Haven Watch Co., on movement "Alpha, 149, Pat. Dec. 27-81," lever escapement, open face, very rare watch.

| Grade or Name – Description | | Avg | Ex-Fn | Mint |
|---|---|---|---|---|
| "A" Model, about 18S, pat. Dec. 27, '81 ..................... ★ ★ ★ ★ | | $600 | $750 | $950 |
| Alpha Model, pat. Dec. 27, '81 ...................................... ★ ★ ★ ★ | | 600 | 750 | 900 |

### NEW YORK CITY WATCH CO.
### New York, New York
### 1890 - 1897

This company manufactured the Dollar-type watches, which had a pendant-type crank. The watch is wound by **cranking the pendant,** and has a pin lever escapement. The hands are set from the back of the watch movement. The" **patent number 526,871"**, is engraved on movement, patent is dated October 1894, and was held by S. Schisgall. The New York City Watch Co., 20 size watch has the words "Lever Winder" printed on the paper dial.

🕐 Watches listed in this book are priced at the **collectable fair market value** at the RETAIL level, as complete watches having an original 14k gold filled case, KEY WIND with silver, an original white enamel single sunk dial, and with the entire original movement in good working order with no repairs needed, unless otherwise noted.

| Grade or Name – Description | | Avg | Ex-Fn | Mint |
|---|---|---|---|---|
| 18-20S, no jewels, "**Lever Winder on dial**" .............. ★★★★★ | | $650 | $800 | $1,000 |
| 18-20S, no jewels, "**SUN DIAL on dial**" ................... ★★★★★ | | $650 | $800 | $1,000 |

**New York City Watch Co.**, about 18-20 size, "**Lever Winder**" printed on paper dial. This watch is <u>WOUND</u> by cranking the pendant back and forth , pin lever escapement, also **back set**, & *"New York City Watch Co., patent No. 526,871"* engraved on movement.

## NEW YORK CHRONOGRAPH WATCH CO.
### NEW YORK, NEW YORK
#### 1880 -1885

    This company sold about 800 watches marked "New York Chronograph Watch Co." The 18 size stop watch was manufactured by Manhattan Watch Co.

| Grade or Name –Description | | Avg | Ex-Fn | Mint |
|---|---|---|---|---|
| 18S, 7J, stop watch, HC ............................................................ ★ | | $125 | $150 | $200 |
| 18S, 7J, stop watch, OF ............................................................. ★ | | 100 | 125 | 175 |
| 16S, 7J, SW, time only, OF ........................................................ ★ | | 100 | 175 | 250 |
| 16S, 9-11J, SW, time only, OF.................................................... ★ | | 100 | 175 | 250 |
| 16S, 7-11J, SW, time only sweep sec., OF ................................. ★ | | 100 | 175 | 250 |
| 16S, 7-11J, SW, **true CHRONOGRAPH**, OF................ ★★★ | | 200 | 250 | 350 |

**N.Y. Chronograph Watch Co.**, dial and movement, 16 size, 7 jewels, open face, time only, sweep second hand.

**New York Chronograph Watch Co.** dial and movement, 7 jewels, open face, buttons at the top of case set hands and stop watch.

# NEW YORK STANDARD WATCH CO.

### Jersey City, New Jersey
### 1885 - 1929

The first watch reached the market in early 1888 and was a 18S. The most interesting feature was a straight line lever with a "worm gear escapement." This was patented by R. J. Clay. All watches were quick train and open-faced. The company also made its own cases and sold a complete watch. A prefix number was added to the serial number after the first 10,000 watches were made. Estimated total production was 7,000,000.

**New York Standard, Chronograph,** 18 size, 7 jewels, stem wind, second hand start-stop and fly back, three-quarter plate, serial number 5,334,322.

**New York Standard,** converts to a hunting case movement or a open face movement, serial number 602,506.

## N. Y. STANDARD
### 16 AND 18 SIZE

| Grade or Name – Description | Avg | Ex-Fn | Mint |
|---|---|---|---|
| 18S, 7J, N. Y. Standard, KW, KS ...................................... | $250 | $300 | $375 |
| 18S, 7J, N. Y. Standard, SW ........................................ | 40 | 50 | 65 |
| 18S, 15J, N. Y. Standard, SW, LS, HC........................... | 100 | 125 | 175 |
| Chronograph, 7J, 3/4, NI, DMK, SW, fly back hand ..................... | 125 | 175 | 250 |
| Chronograph, 10J, (marked 10J), fly back hand..........................★ | 135 | 185 | 275 |
| Chronograph, 13J, sweep sec., stop & fly back hand..................... | 135 | 185 | 260 |
| Chronograph, 15J, 3/4, NI, DMK, SW,fly back hand, .................. | 150 | 200 | 275 |
| Columbus, 7J....................................................................... | 40 | 50 | 65 |
| Convertible,15J.,16 Size, HC or OF...................................★★★★ | 300 | 425 | 600 |
| Crown W. Co., 7J, OF or HC ........................................... | 40 | 60 | 65 |
| Crown W. Co., 15J, HC ................................................... | 50 | 75 | 100 |
| Dan Patch, 7J, stop watch(pat. DEC. 22 '08 )...........................★ | 275 | 350 | 425 |
| Dan Patch, 17J, stop watch(pat. DEC. 22 '08 )........................★★ | 375 | 450 | 525 |
| Edgemere, 7J, OF & HC.................................................. | 40 | 50 | 65 |
| Excelsior, 7J, OF or HC.................................................... | 40 | 50 | 65 |

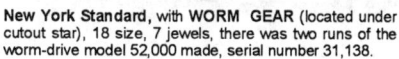

New York Standard, with WORM GEAR (located under cutout star), 18 size, 7 jewels, there was two runs of the worm-drive model 52,000 made, serial number 31,138.

Remington W. Co. (marked on movement & case), 16 size, 11 jewels, 2-tone damaskeening, NOTE crown wheel & ratchet ( no click), serial # CC021,331.

| Grade or Name – Description | Avg | Ex-Fn | Mint |
|---|---|---|---|
| Harvard W. CO., 7-11J., ................................................ | $30 | $40 | $50 |
| Hi Grade...................................................................... | 40 | 50 | 65 |
| Ideal............................................................................ | 40 | 50 | 65 |
| Jefferson, 7J., ............................................................. | 40 | 50 | 60 |
| La Salle, 7J.,................................................................ | 35 | 45 | 55 |
| New Era, 7J., OF or HC, skeletonized (Poor Man's Dudley) ........ | 250 | 275 | 325 |
| New Era,7-11J................................................................ | 30 | 40 | 55 |
| New York Standard W. Co., 11J, 3/4.................................... | 50 | 75 | 100 |
| New York Standard, 7J, 3/4 ........................................... | 50 | 75 | 100 |
| New York Standard, 15J, BRG ........................................ | 75 | 100 | 125 |
| N. Y. Standard, with (" WORM GEAR" )..............................★ | 400 | 450 | 500 |

🕐 Note: Some styles, models and grades are not included. Their values can be determined by comparing with **similar** styles, size, age, models and grades listed.

| Grade or Name – Description | Avg | Ex-Fn | Mint |
|---|---|---|---|
| Pan American, 7J, OF | $50 | $75 | $100 |
| Perfection, 7J, OF or HC | 40 | 50 | 65 |
| Perfection, 15J, OF or HC, NI | 50 | 75 | 100 |
| Remington W. Co., 11J, marked mvt. & case | 75 | 100 | 135 |
| Solar W. Co., 7J | 40 | 50 | 65 |
| Special USA, 7J | 35 | 45 | 55 |
| 18S Tribune USA, 23J, HC or OF, Pat. Reg. Adj. | 150 | 175 | 225 |
| Washington, 7-11J., | 40 | 50 | 65 |
| William Penn, 7-11J., | 40 | 50 | 65 |
| Wilmington | 40 | 50 | 65 |

For watches with **O'Hara Multi-Color Dials,** add $75 to value in **mint condition;** add $5 for Hunting Cases.

## 12 SIZE

| Grade or Name – Description | Avg | Ex-Fn | Mint |
|---|---|---|---|
| N. Y. Standard, 7J-11J, OF | $25 | $30 | $45 |
| N. Y. Standard, 7J-11J, HC | 30 | 45 | 50 |
| N. Y. Standard, 7J, HC, Multi-Color dial | 100 | 125 | 175 |
| N. Y. Standard, 15J, OF | 35 | 40 | 45 |
| N. Y. Standard, 15J, HC | 40 | 45 | 50 |
| Crown W. Co., 7J, OF or HC | 30 | 40 | 55 |

New York Standard Watch Co., 12 size, 7 jewels, open face, serial number 1021224.

New York Standard W.Co., 6 size G# 144, Hunting Case.

## 6 SIZE AND 0 SIZE

| Grade or Name – Description | Avg | Ex-Fn | Mint |
|---|---|---|---|
| Alton, 7-15J | $35 | $40 | $55 |
| American, 7J., | 35 | 40 | 55 |
| Empire State W. Co., 7J | 40 | 50 | 65 |
| Standard USA, 7J | 40 | 50 | 65 |
| 6S, Columbia, 7J, HC | 60 | 70 | 85 |
| 6S, N. Y. Standard, 7J, HC | 60 | 70 | 85 |
| 6S, Orient, SW | 30 | 40 | 55 |
| 6S, Progress, 7J, YGF | 40 | 50 | 65 |
| 6S or 0S, Crown W. Co., 7J, OF or HC | 20 | 30 | 45 |
| 0S, Ideal, 7J, HC | 60 | 70 | 85 |
| 0S, N. Y. Standard, 7J, HC | 60 | 70 | 85 |

# NEW YORK STANDARD WATCH CO.
## IDENTIFICATION OF MOVEMENTS

How to Identify Your Watch: Compare the movement of your watch with the illustrations in this section. Upon matching the movement exactly, the model number and size can be determined. While comparing, note the location of the balance, jewels, screws, gears, and type of back plate (Full, 3/4, Bridge) which will be clues in identifying the movement you have. Having determined the size and model number, you can now find your watch in the main price listing by name or number (which is engraved on the movement).

18 size, 5th model, hunting

18 size, 6th model, open face

18 size, No. 80

18 size, No. 64

18 size, No. 360

18 size, No. 60

18 size, No. 165

18 size, 4th Model

16 size, No. 94

16 size, No. 91

16 size, 1st Model,
converts to open
or hunting

16 size, No. 1516

16 size, No. 390

12 size, No. 170             12 size, No. 1570

12 size, hunting             12 size, No. 1512

12 size, No. 370     6 size, No. 146     6 size, No. 44

0 size, No. 300     3/0 size, No. 730     10/0 size, No. 1015

# NEW YORK SPRINGFIELD WATCH CO.
## Springfield, Massachusetts
### 1866 - 1876

The New York Watch Co. had a rather difficult time getting started. The name of the company was changed from the Mozart Watch Co. to the New York Watch Co., and it was located in Rhode Island. Before any watches had been produced, they moved to Springfield, Mass., in 1867. A factory was built there, but only about 100 watches were produced before a fire occurred on April 23, 1870. Shortly after the fire, in 1870, a newly-designed watch was introduced. The first movements reached the market in 1871, and the first grade was a fully-jeweled adjusted movement called "Frederick Billings." The standard 18S and the Swiss Ligne systems were both used in gauging the size of these watches. The New York Watch Co. used full signatures on its movements. The doors closed in the summer of 1876.

In January 1877, the Hampden Watch Co. was organized and commenced active operation in June 1877.

### CHRONOLOGY OF THE DEVELOPMENT OF NEW YORK WATCH CO.

| | |
|---|---|
| The Mozart Watch Co., Providence, R. I. | 1864-1866 |
| New York Watch Co., Providence, R. I. | 1866-1867 |
| New York Watch Co., Springfield, Mass. | 1867-1875 |
| New York Watch Mfg. Co., Springfield, Mass. | 1875-1876 |
| Hampden Watch Co., Springfield, Mass. | 1877-1886 |
| Hampden-Dueber Watch Co., Springfield, Mass. | 1886-1888 |
| Hampden Watch Co. Works, Canton, Ohio | 1888-1923 |
| Dueber-Hampden Watch Co., Canton, Ohio | 1923-1930 |
| Amtorg, U.S.S.R. | 1930 |

### NEW YORK WATCH CO. SPRINGFIELD
### ESTIMATED SERIAL NUMBERS
### AND PRODUCTION DATES

| DATE – SERIAL NO. | DATE – SERIAL NO. |
|---|---|
| 1866 – 1,000 | 1871 – 20,000 |
| 1867 – 3,000 | 1872 – 30,000 |
| 1868 – 5,000 | 1873 – 40,000 |
| 1869 – 7,000 | 1874 – 50,000 |
| 1870 – 10,000 | 1875 – 60,000 |

The above list is provided for determining the APPROXIMATE age of your watch. Match serial number with date. Watches were not necessarily sold in the exact order of manufactured date.

### N. Y. W. SPRINGFIELD
### 18 TO 20 SIZE

| Grade or Name – Description | | Avg | Ex-Fn | Mint |
|---|---|---|---|---|
| Aaron Bagg, 7J, KW, KS | ★ | $200 | $250 | $325 |
| Frederick Billings, 15J, KW, KS | ★ | 200 | 250 | 325 |
| E. W. Bond, 15J, 3/4 | ★★★ | 450 | 600 | 700 |
| J. A. Briggs, 11J, KW, KS, from back | ★★ | 300 | 350 | 425 |

Some grades are not included. Their values can be determined by comparing with **similar** age, size, metal content, style, models and grades listed.

Watches listed in this book are priced at the collectable retail level, as **complete** watches having an original 14k gold-filled case and *Key Wind* with silver, an original white enamel single sunk dial, and with the entire original movement in good working order with no repairs needed.

E.W. **Bond** movement, 18 size, 7 jewels, three-quarter plate.

**Chas. E. Hayward,** 18 size, 15 jewels, key wind & set, note the **hidden key,** serial number 18,733.

| Grade or Name – Description | | Avg | Ex-Fn | Mint |
|---|---|---|---|---|
| Albert Clark, 15J, KW, KS, from back, 3/4 | ★ ★ | $300 | $350 | $425 |
| Homer Foot, 15J, KW, KS, from back, 3/4 | ★ | 300 | 350 | 425 |
| Herman Gerz, 11J, KW, KS | ★ | 200 | 250 | 325 |
| John Hancock, 7J, KW, KS | | 100 | 200 | 275 |
| John Hancock, 7J, KW, KS, Silveroid | | 75 | 100 | 125 |
| John Hancock, 7J, KW, KS, Coin | | 150 | 200 | 275 |
| Chas. E. Hayward, 15J, KW, KS, long balance cock | | 150 | 200 | 275 |
| Chas. E. Hayward, 15J, KW, KS, Coin | | 150 | 200 | 275 |
| J. L. King, 15J, KW, KS, from back, 3/4 | ★ | 400 | 500 | 600 |
| New York Watch Co., 7J, KW, KS | ★ | 150 | 200 | 275 |
| New York Watch Co., 15-19J, KW, KS, Wolf's Teeth winding, **(Serial #s below 75)** | ★ ★ ★ ★ | 1,300 | 1,500 | 2,000 |
| New York Watch Co., 15-19J, KW, KS, Wolf's Teeth winding, all original | ★ ★ ★ | 1,000 | 1,200 | 1,500 |
| New York Watch Co., 11J, KW, KS | ★ ★ | 300 | 350 | 375 |
| H. G. Norton, 15J, KW, KS, from back, 3/4 | ★ | 300 | 350 | 425 |

**H.G. Norton,** 18 size, 15 jewels, three-quarter plate, gold escape wheel, serial number 6592.

**New York Watch Co.,** 18 size, 15-19 jewels, stem wind, hunting case, note wolf teeth winding, serial number 978.

**State Street** movement, 18 size, 11 jewels, three-quarter plate.

**Theo E. Studley** movement, 18 size, 15 jewels, key wind & set, full plate.

| Grade or Name – Description | | Avg | Ex-Fn | Mint |
|---|---|---|---|---|
| J. C. Perry, 15J | ★ | $150 | $200 | $275 |
| J. C. Perry, 15J, Silveroid | ★ | 100 | 125 | 175 |
| Railway, 15J, KW, FULL, Coin | ★ ★ | 600 | 650 | 725 |
| Railway, 15J, KW, KS, FULL | ★ ★ | 600 | 650 | 725 |
| William Romp,15J,KW,KS from back,3/4 | ★ ★ | 500 | 650 | 950 |
| Geo. Sam Rice, 7J, KW, KS | ★ | 300 | 350 | 425 |
| Springfield, 19J, KW, KS, from back, ADJ, Wolf teeth wind, serial Nos. below 1,000 | ★ ★ ★ | 1,300 | 1,500 | 1,800 |
| State Street, 11J, 3/4, SW | ★ ★ | 325 | 400 | 500 |
| State Street, 11J, 3/4, SW, Silveroid | ★ ★ | 325 | 425 | 550 |
| Theo E. Studley, 15J, KW, Coin | | 100 | 125 | 175 |
| Theo E. Studley, 15J, KW, KS | | 100 | 125 | 175 |
| George Walker, 17J, KW, 3/4, ADJ | ★ | 300 | 400 | 500 |
| Chester Woolworth, 15J, KW, KS | | 100 | 125 | 175 |
| Chester Woolworth, 11J, KW, KS | | 100 | 125 | 175 |
| Chester Woolworth, 11J, KW, KS, Silveroid | | 65 | 75 | 95 |
| Chester Woolworth, 11J, KW, KS, ADJ | | 150 | 175 | 225 |
| #4, 15J, ADJ, KW, KS | | 125 | 150 | 200 |
| #5, 15J, KW, KS | | 100 | 125 | 175 |
| #6, 11J, KW, KS | | 100 | 125 | 175 |
| #6, 11J, KW, KS, Silveroid | | 65 | 75 | 95 |

🕐 Some KW, KS watches made by the New York Watch Co. have a hidden key. If you unscrew the crown, and the crown comes out as a key, add $100 to the listed value.

🕐 Watches listed in this book are priced at the collectable retail level, as **complete** watches having an original 14k gold-filled case and *Key Wind* with silver, an original white enamel single sunk dial, and with the entire original movement in good working order with no repairs needed.

🕐 This book endeavours to be a GUIDE or helpful manual and offers a wealth of material to be used as a tool not as a absolute document. Price Guides are like watches the worst may be better than none at all, but at best cannot be expected to be 100% accurate.

🕐 Characteristics of watches differ for the same age of both case and movement, because these features vary it may not be accurate to date a watch by one single influence. Example: the second hand was _not_ commonly found on watches before 1750, but common about 1800. The first second hand appeared in 1665 and another in 1690. Therefore statements are broad rather than accurate.

# NON-MAGNETIC WATCH CO.

## Geneva and America
## 1887 - 1905

The Non-Magnetic Watch Co. sold and imported watches from the Swiss as well as contracted watches made in America. Geneva Non-Magnetic marked watches appear to be the oldest type of movement. This company sold a full line of watches, high grade to low grade, as well as repeaters and ladies watches. An advertisement appeared in the monthly journal of "Locomotive Engineers" in 1887. The ad states that the "Paillard's patent non-magnetic watches are uninfluenced by magnetism of electricity." Each watch contains the Paillard's patent non-magnetic, inoxidizable compensation balance and hairspring. An ad in 1888 shows prices for 16 size Swiss style watches as low as $15 for 7 jewels and as high as $135 for 20 jewels.

## 18 SIZE
### (must be marked Paillard's Patent)

| Grade or Name – Description | Avg | Ex-Fn | Mint |
|---|---|---|---|
| Elgin, 17J, FULL, SW, LS, OF | $100 | $125 | $175 |
| Elgin, 17J, FULL, SW, LS, HC | 125 | 150 | 225 |
| Elgin, 15J, FULL, SW, LS, OF | 75 | 100 | 150 |
| Elgin, 15-17J, FULL, SW, LS, HC | 100 | 125 | 175 |
| Illinois, 24J, GJS, NI, Adj.5P, OF | 900 | 950 | 1,000 |
| Illinois, 24J, GJS, NI, Adj.5P, HC ★★ | 950 | 1,100 | 1,300 |
| Illinois, 23J, GJS, NI, Adj.5P, OF | 700 | 750 | 925 |
| Illinois, 23J, GJS, NI, Adj.5P, HC ★★★ | 1,600 | 1,800 | 2,100 |
| Illinois, 21J, GJS, NI, Adj.5P, OF | 200 | 250 | 325 |
| Illinois, 21J, GJS, NI, Adj.5P, HC | 250 | 300 | 325 |
| Illinois, 17J, NI, ADJ, OF | 100 | 125 | 175 |
| Illinois, 17J, NI, ADJ, HC | 125 | 150 | 225 |
| Illinois, 15J, NI, OF | 75 | 100 | 150 |
| Illinois, 15J, NI, HC | 100 | 125 | 175 |
| Illinois, 11J, OF | 75 | 100 | 150 |

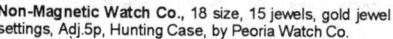

**Non-Magnetic Watch Co.**, 18 size, 15 jewels, gold jewel settings, Adj.5p, Hunting Case, by Peoria Watch Co.

**Non-Magnetic Watch Co.**, 18 size, 21 Ruby jewels, Adj.5p, note "Paillard" engraved on movement.

⊕ Watches listed in this book are priced at the collectable retail level, as **complete** watches having an original 14k gold-filled case and *Key Wind* with silver, an original white enamel single sunk dial, and with the entire original movement in good working order with no repairs needed.

Non-Magnetic Watch Co., 18 size, 16J., 3/4 plate, hunting, note "Geneva" engraved on movement, serial # 6113.

Non-Magnetic Watch Co., 18 size, 16 jewels, bridge model, example of a Swiss Ebauche.

| Grade or Name – Description | Avg | Ex-Fn | Mint |
|---|---|---|---|
| Illinois, 11J, HC | $100 | $125 | $175 |
| Peoria, 17J, FULL, SW, LS, Adj., OF | 325 | 350 | 400 |
| Peoria, 15J, FULL, SW, LS, Adj., OF | 300 | 325 | 375 |
| Peoria, 15J, FULL, SW, LS, Adj., HC | 400 | 425 | 475 |
| Peoria, 11J, FULL, SW, LS, OF | 100 | 125 | 175 |
| Peoria, 11J, FULL, SW, LS, HC | 175 | 200 | 250 |
| Swiss, 16J, 3/4 plate, SW, LS, Adj., OF | 60 | 70 | 85 |
| Swiss, 16J, 3/4 plate, SW, LS, Adj., HC | 75 | 100 | 150 |
| Swiss, 15J, bar bridge, SW, LS, Adj., OF | 55 | 65 | 80 |
| Swiss, 15J, bar bridge, SW, LS, Adj., HC | 75 | 100 | 150 |
| Swiss, 11J, 3/4 plate, SW, LS, OF, HC | 75 | 100 | 150 |
| Swiss, 11J, bar bridge, SW, LS, OF, HC | 75 | 100 | 150 |

Non-Magnetic Watch Co., 16 size, 21 Ruby jewels, adjusted, made by Illinois Watch Co.

Non-Magnetic Watch Co., 16 size, 20J., in gold jewel settings, stem wind, open or hunting. Swiss made.

🕐 Watches listed in this book are priced at the **collectable fair market value** at the RETAIL level, as complete watches having an original 14k gold filled case, KEY WIND with silver, an original white enamel single sunk dial, and with the entire original movement in good working order with no repairs needed, unless otherwise noted.

**Non-Magnetic Watch Co.**, 16 size, three-quarter plate, 16 jewels, hunting case, adjusted.

**Non-Magnetic Watch Co.**, 16 size, three-quarter plate, 15 jewels, note "Paillard's Patent, Balance And Spring" engraved on movement.

## 16 SIZE
### (must be marked Paillard's Patent)

| Grade or Name – Description | Avg | Ex-Fn | Mint |
|---|---|---|---|
| Illinois, 21J, GJS, 3/4, DR, Adj.6P, OF | $200 | $250 | $325 |
| Illinois, 21J, GJS, 3/4, DR, Adj.6P, HC | 300 | 350 | 425 |
| Illinois, 17J, 3/4, DR, ADJ, OF | 75 | 100 | 150 |
| Illinois, 17J, 3/4, DR, ADJ, HC | 100 | 125 | 175 |
| Illinois, 15J, HC | 75 | 100 | 125 |
| Illinois, 15J, OF | 65 | 80 | 135 |
| Illinois, 11J, OF | 55 | 75 | 125 |
| Illinois, 11J, HC | 75 | 100 | 150 |
| Swiss, 20J, GJS, DR, Adj.6P, NI, 1/2 ,OF | 75 | 100 | 150 |
| Swiss, 20J, GJS, DR, Adj.6P, NI, 1/2, HC | 100 | 125 | 175 |
| Swiss, 18J, GJS, DR, Adj.6P, NI, 1/2, OF | 75 | 100 | 150 |
| Swiss, 18J, GJS, DR, Adj.6P, NI, 1/2, HC | 100 | 125 | 175 |
| Swiss, 16J, GJS, DR, Adj.6P, NI, 1/2,OF | 75 | 100 | 150 |
| Swiss, 16J, GJS, DR, Adj.6P, NI, 1/2, HC | 75 | 100 | 150 |
| Swiss, 15J, DR, NI, 3/4, OF | 75 | 100 | 150 |
| Swiss, 15J, DR, NI, 3/4, HC | 100 | 125 | 175 |
| Swiss, 11J, NI, 3/4, OF | 60 | 70 | 95 |
| Swiss, 11J, NI, 3/4, HC | 100 | 125 | 175 |
| Swiss, 7J, OF & 3/4, HC | 55 | 65 | 85 |

🕐 Generic, nameless or unmarked grades for watch movements are listed under the Company name or initials of the Company, etc. by size, jewel count and description.

🕐 Some watch manufacturers personalize watches for jobbers or jewelry firms, with exclusive private signed or marked movements. The valuable collectable watches are listed under the signed or marked movement. Other exclusive private signed or marked movements will have equivalent value are only slightly higher value and should be compared to Generic or Nameless movements. Railroad signed or marked (dials & movements) are usually more collectable & higher in value.

🕐 Some grades are not included. Their values can be determined by comparing with **similar** age, size, metal content, style, models and grades listed.

# OTAY WATCH CO.
## Otay, California
### 1889 - 1894

This company produced about 1,000 watches with a serial number range of 1,000 to 1,500 and 30,000 to 31,000. The company was purchased by a Japanese manufacturer in 1894. Names on Otay movements include: Golden Gate, F. A. Kimball, Native Sun, Overland Mail, R. D. Perry, and P. H. Wheeler.

Otay Watch Co. Dial; note hunting case style and lever for setting hands.

Otay Watch Co., F.A. Kimball, 18 size, 15 jewels, lever set, hunting, serial number 1,264.

### 18 SIZE

| Grade or Name – Description | | Avg | Ex-Fn | Mint |
|---|---|---|---|---|
| California, 15J., LS, HC, NI | ★★★ | $2,000 | $2,200 | $2,500 |
| Golden Gate, 15J, LS, HC, OF, NI | ★★★ | 2,000 | 2,200 | 2,600 |
| F. A. Kimball, 15J, LS, HC, Gilt | ★★ | 1,200 | 1,400 | 1,700 |
| Native Son, 15J, LS, HC, NI | ★★ | 1,600 | 1,800 | 2,100 |
| Overland Mail, 15J, LS, HC, NI | ★★★ | 2,200 | 2,600 | 2,800 |
| R. D. Perry, 15J, LS, HC, Gilt | ★★ | 1,200 | 1,400 | 1,700 |
| P. H. Wheeler, 15J, LS, HC, Gilt | ★★ | 1,200 | 1,400 | 1,700 |
| Sunset, 7J, Gilt, HC | ★★ | 1,200 | 1,400 | 1,700 |

# D. D. PALMER WATCH CO.
## Waltham, Massachusetts
### 1864 - 1875

In 1858, at age 20, Mr. Palmer opened a small jewelry store in Waltham, Mass. Here he became interested in pocket chronometers. At first he bought the balance and jewels from Swiss manufacturers. In 1864 he took a position with the American Watch Co. and made the chronometers in his spare time (only about 25 produced). They were,18S, 3/4 plate, gilded, key wind, and some were nickel. At first they were fusee driven, but he mainly used going barrels. About 1870, Palmer started making lever watches and by 1875 he left the American Watch Co. and started making a 10S keywind, gilded movement, and a 16S, 3/4 plate, gilt and nickel, and a stem wind of his own invention (a vibrating crown wheel). In all he made about 1,500 watches. The signature appearing on the watches was "Palmer W. Co. Wal., Mass."

He basically had three grades of watches: Fine-Solid Nickel; Medium-Nickel Plated; and Medium-Gold Gilt. They were made in open-face and hunter cases.

D. D. Palmer Watch Co., 18 size, 15 jewels, Palmer's Pat.
Stem Winder on movement, serial number 1,098.

| Grade or name – Description | Avg | Ex-Fn | Mint |
|---|---|---|---|
| 10-14S, 15-17J, 3/4 plate, KW, spring detent chronometer ★★★★ | $4,000 | $4,500 | $6,000 |
| 16-18S, 17J, NI, OF, 18K...................................................... ★★★ | 1,800 | 2,100 | 2,500 |

## PEORIA WATCH CO.

### Peoria, Illinois
### 1885 - 1895

The roots of this company began with the Independent Watch Co. (1880 - 1883). These watches marked Marion and Mark Twain were made by the Fredonia Watch Co. (1883 - 1885) Peoria Watch Co. opened Dec. 19, 1885, and made one model of railroad watches in about 1887.

Peoria Watch Co., 18 size, 15 jewels, nickel damaskeening plates, hunting, note patented regulator, serial number 11,532.

🕐 Watches listed in this book are priced at the **collectable fair market value** at the RETAIL level, as complete watches having an original 14k gold filled case, KEY WIND with silver, an original white enamel single sunk dial, and with the entire original movement in good working order with no repairs needed, unless otherwise noted.

Peoria watches were 18S, quick train, 15 jewel, and all stem wind. These watches are hard to find, as only about 3,000 were made. Peoria also made railroad watches for A. C. Smith's Non-Magnetic Watch Co. of America, from 1884-1888. The 18S watches were full plate, adjusted, and had whiplash regulator.

The Peoria Watch Co. closed in 1889, having produced about 47,000 watches.

| Grade or Name – Description | Avg | Ex-Fn | Mint |
|---|---|---|---|
| 18S, 9-11J, SW, OF | $150 | $200 | $250 |
| 18S, 15J, SW, personalized name | 175 | 225 | 275 |
| 18S, Peoria W. Co., 15J, SW, OF | 200 | 250 | 300 |
| 18S, Peoria W. Co., 15J, SW, HC | 225 | 250 | 325 |
| 18S, Peoria W. Co., 15J, SW, low S# | 325 | 350 | 400 |
| 18S, Anti-Magnetic, 15J, SW | 325 | 350 | 400 |
| 18S, Anti-Magnetic, 15J, Made for Railway Service | 350 | 375 | 425 |
| 18S, Non-Magnetic Watch Co. of America, 15J, NI, SW, GJS, Adj.5P, OF | 350 | 375 | 425 |
| 18S, 15J, Non-Magnetic Watch Co. of America, NI, SW, GJS, Adj.5P, HC | 400 | 425 | 475 |
| 18S, Made for Railway Service, 15J, NI, GJS, Adj.5P, OF | 300 | 350 | 425 |
| 18S, Made for Railway Service, 15J, NI, GJS, Adj.5P, HC | 350 | 425 | 500 |

# PHILADELPHIA WATCH CO.

## Philadelphia, Pennsylvania

### 1874 - 1886

Eugene Paulus organized the Philadelphia Watch Co. about 1874. Most all the parts were made in Switzerland, and finished and cased in this country. The International Watch Co. is believed to have manufactured the movements for Philadelphia Watch Co. Estimated total production of the company is 12,000 watches.

Philadelphia Watch Co., 16 size, 15 jewels, gold jewel settings, hunting case model. "Paulus Patents 1868. Aug. 25th, Nov. 3rd" on movement, serial number 5,751.

| Grade or Name – Description | | Avg | Ex-Fn | Mint |
|---|---|---|---|---|
| 18S, 15J, SW, HC | ★ | $350 | $450 | $575 |
| 18S, 15J, KW, KS | ★ | 275 | 375 | 500 |
| 18S, 15J, SW, OF | ★ | 325 | 425 | 525 |
| 18S, HC, KW, KS, 18K original case marked Philadelphia Watch Co. | ★ ★ | 1,200 | 1,400 | 1,800 |
| 18S, 11J, KW, KS | ★ | 150 | 175 | 225 |
| 16S, 15J, KW, KS | ★ | 150 | 175 | 225 |
| 16S, 19J, KW, KS, GJS | ★ | 375 | 475 | 600 |
| 8S-6S, 11J, HC | ★ | 150 | 175 | 225 |
| 8S-6S, 15J, HC | ★ | 150 | 175 | 225 |
| 8S-6S, Paulus, 19J, KW, KS | ★ | 225 | 300 | 400 |
| 000/S, 7J, HC, PS | ★ | 125 | 200 | 300 |

# JAMES & HENRY PITKIN

### Hartford, Connecticut
### New York, New York
### 1838 - 1852

Henry Pitkin was the first to attempt to manufacture watches by machinery. The machines were of Pitkin's own design and very crude, but he had some brilliant ideas. His first four workers were paid $30 a year plus their board. After much hardship, the first watches were produced in the fall of 1838. The watches had going barrels, not the fusee and chain, and the American flag was engraved on the plates to denote they were American made and to exemplify the true spirit of American independence in watchmaking.

The first 50 watches were stamped with the name "Henry Pitkin." Others bore the firm name "H. & J. F. Pitkin." The movements were about 16S and 3/4 plate. The plates were rolled brass and stamped out with dies. The pinions were lantern style with eight leaves. The movement had a slow train of 14,400 beats per hour. Pitkin's first plan was to make the ends of the pinions conical and let them run in the ends of hardened steel screws, similar to the Marine clock balances. A large brass setting was put in the plates and extended above the surface. Three screws, with small jewels set in their ends, were inserted so that they closed about the pivot with very small end shake. This proved to be too expensive and was used in only a few movements. Next, he tried to make standard type movements extend above the plates with the end shake controlled by means of a screw running down into the end of the pivots, reducing friction. This "capped jewel train" was used for a while before he adopted the standard ways of jeweling. The escape wheels were the star type, English style. The balance was made of gold and steel. These movements were fire gilded and not interchangeable. The dials, hands, mainsprings and hairsprings were imported. The rounded pallets were manufactured by Pitkin, and the cases for his watches were made on the premises. As many as 900 watches could have been made by Pitkin.

| Grade or Name – Description | | Avg | Ex-Fn | Mint |
|---|---|---|---|---|
| Henry Pitkin S#1-50 | ★★★★★ | $15,000 | $20,000 | $25,000 |
| H. & J. F. Pitkin, S#50-377 | ★★★★ | 10,000 | 15,000 | 20,000 |
| Pitkin & Co., New York, S#378-900 | ★★★ | 4,500 | 6,000 | 7,500 |
| W. Pitkin, Hartford, Conn., S# approx. 40,000, fusee lever, KW, Coin | ★★ | 600 | 700 | 800 |

**H. & J. F. Pitkin,** about 16 size, engraved on movement
**"H. & J. F. PITKIN DETACHED LEVER",** key wind & set.

Movements marked with New York are English made imports.

# ALBERT H. POTTER WATCH CO.

### New York, New York
### 1855 - 1875

Albert Potter started his apprenticeship in 1852. When this was completed he moved to New York to take up watchmaking on his own. He made about 35 watches in all that sold for $225 to $350. Some were chronometers, some were lever escapements, key wind, gilded movements, some were fusee driven, both bridge and 3/4 plate. Potter was a contemporary of Charles Fasoldt and John Mulford, both horological inventors from Albany, N. Y. Potter moved to Cuba in 1861 but returned to New York in 1868. In 1872 he worked in Chicago and formed the Potter Brothers Company with his brother William. He moved to Geneva about 1876. His company produced a total of about 600 watches, but only about 40 of those were made in the U. S.

| Grade or Name – Description | Avg | Ex-Fn | Mint |
|---|---|---|---|
| 18S, 29J, 18K HC, 1 min. repeater, Geneva ......... ★★★ | $8,500 | $10,000 | $13,000 |
| 18S, BRG lever, Chronometer, signed A. H. Potter, New York, 18K Potter case, U.S. mfg. ...... ★★★★ | 10,000 | 12,000 | 16,000 |
| 18S, BRG lever with wind indicator, 18K Potter case ...... ★★★ | 6,500 | 8,500 | 9,500 |
| 18S-20S, Tourbillion, signed A. H. Potter, Boston, gilded, 18K Potter case, U.S. mfg. ...... ★★★★★ | 15,000 | 17,000 | 20,000 |
| 16S-18S, 22J, helical spring, detent chronometer escapement, Geneva, 18K ......... | 4,000 | 5,000 | 6,500 |
| 4S, 21J, hour repeater, Geneva, 18K Potter HC ......... | 3,000 | 3,500 | 4,500 |

Albert H. Potter, 18 size, 22 jewels, pat. Oct. 11, 1875 & June 4, 1876, helical hairspring, detent escapement, made in GENEVA, serial number 14.

A.H. Potter Watch Co., BOSTON, 18 size, about 6 jewels, detent escapement, note similarity to E.H. Howard & Co. early watches, serial number 5.

# GEORGE P. REED
## Boston, Massachusetts 1865 - 1885

In 1854, George P. Reed entered the employment of Dennison, Howard and Davis, in Roxbury, Mass., and moved with the company to Waltham, Mass. Here he was placed in charge of the pinion finishing room. While there he invented and received a patent for the mainspring barrel and maintiming power combination. This patent was dated February 18, 1857. Reed returned to Roxbury with Howard who purchased his patented barrel. He stayed with the Howard factory as foreman and adjuster until 1865, when he left for Boston to start his own account.

He obtained a patent on April 7, 1868, for an improved chronometer escapement which featured simplified construction. He made about 100 chronometers with his improved escapement, to which he added a stem-wind device. His company turned out about 100 watches the first three years. Most, if not all, of his watches run for two days and have up and down indicators on the dial. They are both 18S and 16S, 3/4 plate, nickel, and are artistically designed. Reed experimented with various combinations of lever and chronometer escapements. One was a rotary watch he made in 1862 and called the ''Monitor.'' It was the first rotary watch made in America. In all, Reed made a total of about 550 watches, and these are valuable to collectors.

| Grade or Name – Description | Avg | Ex-Fn | Mint |
|---|---|---|---|
| 18S, 15J, LS, OF or HC, Wind Indicator, chronometer escapement, 18K case ................................. ★ ★ ★ ★ | $9,000 | $11,500 | $15,000 |
| 16S, 15J, LS, OF or HC, not chronometer, 18K case .......... ★ ★ ★ | 6,500 | 7,000 | 9,000 |
| 16S, 15J, LS, OF, 31 day calendar, 18K case ...................... ★ ★ ★ | 6,500 | 7,000 | 9,000 |

George P. Reed, 18 size, 15 jewels, key & stem wind, key & lever set, lever escapement, 48 hour up and down wind indicator, serial number 262.

George P. Reed, 18 size, 15 jewels, key & stem wind, key & lever set, lever escapement, 48 hour up and down wind indicator, serial number 5.

George P. Reed Boston, 18 -16 size, 15 jewels, key & stem wind, key & lever set, lever escapement, serial # 282.

# ROCKFORD WATCH CO.

### Rockford, Illinois
### 1873 - 1915

The Rockford Watch Company's equipment was bought from the Cornell Watch Co., and two of Cornell's employees, C. W. Parker and P. H. Wheeler, went to work for Rockford. The factory was located 93 miles from Chicago on the Rock River. The first watch was placed on the market on May 1, 1876. They were key wind, 18S, full plate expansion balance & dials made by outside contract. By 1877 the company was making 3/4 plate nickel movements that fit standard size cases. Three railroads came through Rockford, and the company always advertised to the railroad and the demand was very popular with them. The company had some problems in 1896, and the name changed to Rockford Watch Co. Ltd. It closed in 1915.

## ROCKFORD ESTIMATED SERIAL NUMBERS AND PRODUCTION DATES

| DATE–SERIAL # | DATE–SERIAL # | DATE–SERIAL # | DATE–SERIAL # |
|---|---|---|---|
| 1874 – 22,200 | 1884 – 226,000 | 1895 – 450,000 | 1906 – 670,000 |
| 1875 – 42,600 | 1885 – 247,000 | 1896 – 470,000 | 1907 – 690,000 |
| 1876 – 63,000 | 1886 – 267,000 | 1897 – 490,000 | 1908 – 734,000 |
| 1877 – 83,000 | 1887 – 287,500 | 1898 – 510,000 | 1909 – 790,000 |
| 1878 – 103,000 | 1888 – 308,000 | 1899 – 530,000 | 1910 – 824,000 |
| 1879 – 124,000 | 1889 – 328,500 | 1900 – 550,000 | 1911 – 880,000 |
| 1880 – 144,000 | 1890 – 349,000 | 1901 – 570,000 | 1912 – 936,000 |
| 1881 – 165,000 | 1891 – 369,500 | 1902 – 590,000 | 1913 – 958,000 |
| 1882 – 185,000 | 1892 – 390,000 | 1903 – 610,000 | 1914 – 980,000 |
| 1883 – 206,000 | 1893 – 410,000 | 1904 – 630,000 | 1915-1,000,000 |
| | 1894 – 430,000 | 1905 – 650,000 | |

The above list is provided for determining the APPROXIMATE age of your watch. Match serial number with date. Watches were not necessarily sold in the exact order of manufactured date.

## ROCKFORD

### 18 SIZE

| Grade or Name – Description | Avg | Ex-Fn | Mint |
|---|---|---|---|
| Belmont USA, 21J, LS, OF, NI, M#7 ................................ | $250 | $300 | $375 |
| Chronometer, 17J, ADJ, OF, G925................................ | 275 | 350 | 500 |
| Dome Model, 9J, brass plates.................................★ | 150 | 175 | 225 |

Rockfork Watch Co., Enamel **Railroad** double sunk dial, with two hour hands for a second time zone the hour hand at 2 O'clock is **BLUE**, the hour hand at 3 O'clock is **RED**.

🕐 Watches listed in this book are priced at the collectable retail level, **as complete** watches having an original 14k gold-filled case and *Key Wind* with silver, an original white enamel single sunk dial, and with the entire original movement in good working order with no repairs needed.

**Rockford Watch Co.**, 18 size, 11 jewels, hunting, Model number 3, exposed escapement, serial number 190,564.

**Special Railway**, 18 size, 17 jewels, hunting, Model number 8, serial number 344,551.

| Grade or Name – Description | Avg | Ex-Fn | Mint |
|---|---|---|---|
| King Edward, 21J, **Plymouth W. Co.**, 14K HC | $850 | $950 | $1,100 |
| King Edward (Sears), 21J, GJS, ADJ, NI, OF | 350 | 475 | 525 |
| King Edward (Sears), 21J, GJS, ADJ, NI, HC | 375 | 475 | 575 |
| Paxton's, 21J, (**Special on dial**), OF | 235 | 285 | 350 |
| Pennsylvania Special, 25J, LS, Adj.6P, tu-tone, OF ★★★ | 3,000 | 4,000 | 6,000 |
| Railway King, 21J, OF | 550 | 650 | 775 |
| The Ramsey Watch, 11J, NI, KW or SW | 100 | 120 | 150 |
| The Ramsey Watch, 15J, NI, KW or SW | 100 | 120 | 150 |
| The Ramsey Watch, M#7, 21J, OF, NI, ADJ | 400 | 475 | 550 |

🕐 Generic, nameless or **unmarked** grades for watch movements are listed under the Company name or initials of the Company, etc. by size, jewel count and description.

| | Avg | Ex-Fn | Mint |
|---|---|---|---|
| Rockford Early KW-KS, M#1-2, with low Serial #s less than 500 ★ | $400 | $500 | $675 |
| Rockford Early KW-KS, M#1-2, with low Serial #s less than 500, Coin ★ | 400 | 500 | 675 |
| Rockford Early KW-KS, M#1-2, with reversible case | 300 | 400 | 500 |
| Rockford Early, 19J, KW-KS, M#1-2, S# less than 100 ★★ | 1,000 | 1,400 | 2,000 |
| Rockford, 7-9J, SW, FULL, OF | 70 | 85 | 135 |
| Rockford, 7J, KW, FULL, OF | 70 | 85 | 135 |
| Rockford, 7J, KW, FULL, Silveroid | 70 | 85 | 135 |
| Rockford, 9J, SW, FULL, HC | 100 | 125 | 175 |
| Rockford, M#1, 9J, KW, FULL, HC | 150 | 175 | 225 |
| Rockford, 11J, SW, FULL, OF | 75 | 100 | 150 |
| Rockford, 11-13J, M#6, exposed escape wheel, FULL, HC | 175 | 225 | 300 |
| Rockford, M#1-2, 11J, KW, FULL | 150 | 175 | 225 |
| Rockford, M#1-2, 11J, transition case, FULL | 100 | 125 | 175 |
| Rockford, 11J, KW, Coin HC | 150 | 175 | 225 |
| Rockford, 9J, KW, M#5, 3/4 Plate, HC Coin ★ | 225 | 300 | 450 |
| Rockford, 11J, KW, M#5, 3/4 Plate, HC Coin ★ | 250 | 325 | 500 |
| Rockford, 15J, KW, M#5, 3/4 Plate, HC Coin ★ | 275 | 350 | 550 |
| Rockford, 13J, HC | 100 | 125 | 175 |
| Rockford, 15J, SW, FULL | 75 | 100 | 150 |
| Rockford, 15J, KW, FULL, multi-color dial | 275 | 350 | 425 |
| Rockford, 15J, SW, 2-Tone movement | 100 | 125 | 175 |

🕐 Watches listed in this book are priced at the collectable retail level, as **complete** watches having an original 14k gold-filled case and *Key Wind* with silver, an original white enamel single sunk dial, and with the entire original movement in good working order with no repairs needed.

Rockford movement, 18 size, 7 jewels, model 5, hunting, lever set, three-quarter plate.

Grade 900, 18 size, 24J., Adj5p. Warning: 24J. fakes have been made from 21J movements. The fakes are missing the eliptical jewel setting on the barrel bridge.

| Grade or Name – Description | Avg | Ex-Fn | Mint |
|---|---|---|---|
| Rockford, 15J, KW, FULL, ADJ | $175 | $225 | $350 |
| Rockford, 15J, KW/SW | 100 | 150 | 200 |
| Rockford, 15J, KW/SW, Silveroid | 65 | 90 | 125 |
| Rockford, 15J, M#6, exposed escapement wheel, FULL, HC, LS, nickel mvt. | 275 | 300 | 350 |
| Rockford, 15J, M#6, exposed escapement wheel, FULL, HC, LS, gilded mvt. | 175 | 200 | 250 |
| Rockford, 15J, M#6, exposed wheel, nickel mvt., Coin | 175 | 200 | 250 |
| Rockford, M#1, 15J, KW, FULL | 100 | 125 | 175 |
| Rockford, 16J, GJS, NI, DMK, SW | 75 | 100 | 150 |
| Rockford, 16J, GJS, NI, DMK, SW, Silveroid | 75 | 90 | 135 |
| Rockford, 16J, GJS, NI, DMK, SW, Coin | 75 | 100 | 150 |
| Rockford, 17J, NI, DMK, SW, OF | 75 | 100 | 150 |
| Rockford, 17J, GJS, NI, DMK, SW, Adj.5P | 100 | 125 | 175 |
| Rockford, 17J, GJS, NI, SW, 2-Tone, OF | 125 | 150 | 200 |
| Rockford, M#1-2, 19J, KW, FULL, GJS, ADJ ★★★★ | 1,500 | 1,700 | 2,200 |
| Rockford, 19J, transition, HC, GJS ★ | 400 | 500 | 650 |
| Rockford, 21J, SW, Silveroid | 225 | 250 | 300 |
| Rockford, 21J, GJS, OF, Adj.5P, wind indicator ★★ | 2,500 | 3,000 | 3,500 |
| Rockford, 21J, SW, DMK, ADJ, HC | 375 | 450 | 475 |
| Rockford, 21J, NI, DMK, ADJ, OF | 300 | 350 | 400 |
| Rockford, 21J, GJS, NI, DMK, Adj.5P, marked "RG" | 300 | 350 | 400 |
| Rockford, 22J, GJS, NI, DMK, Adj.5P, marked "RG",2 tone ★★ | 1,400 | 1,600 | 1,800 |
| Rockford, 24J, GJS, SW, LS, Adj.5P, marked "RG," OF | 1,200 | 1,400 | 1,700 |
| Rockford, 24J, GJS, SW, LS, Adj.5P, marked "RG," HC ★ | 1,400 | 1,750 | 1,950 |
| Rockford, 25J, GJS, SW, LS, Adj.5P, NI, DMK ★★ | 3,500 | 5,000 | 6,500 |
| Rockford, 26J, GJS, SW, LS, Adj.5P, NI, DMK ★★★ | 8,000 | 10,000 | 16,000 |

🕐 Generic, nameless or **unmarked** grades for watch movements are listed under the Company name or initials of the Company, etc. by size, jewel count and description.

| | | | |
|---|---|---|---|
| R.W. Co., 7-9-11J, NI or Gilded | 65 | 75 | 95 |
| R.W. Co., 15J, NI or Gilded | 75 | 85 | 100 |
| R.W. Co., 16-17J, Adj, NI, SW | 75 | 100 | 150 |
| R.W. Co., 21J, Adj, NI, SW, | 150 | 175 | 225 |
| R.W. Co., 22J, Adj, NI, SW,"RG," OF | 450 | 550 | 650 |

**Rockford Watch Co.**, 18 size, 15 jewels, model # 5, 3/4 plate, key & stem wind.

**Rockford Watch Co.**, 18 size, 15 jewels, model 4, open face, lever set, serial number 227,430.

| Grade or Name – Description | Avg | Ex-Fn | Mint |
|---|---|---|---|
| Special Railway, 17J, ADJ, 2-tone, SW, HC | $400 | $500 | $650 |
| The Syndicate Watch Co., M#7, 15J, LS, NI, HC | 150 | 200 | 275 |
| Winnebago, 17J, LS, GJS, Adj.5P, DR, NI, DMK | 150 | 175 | 225 |
| Winnebago, 17J, LS, GJS, Adj.5P, DR, NI, DMK, Silveroid | 100 | 125 | 175 |
| 24 Hour Dial, 15J, SW or KW | 150 | 175 | 225 |
| 40, 15J, M#3, HC ★★ | 250 | 300 | 375 |
| 43, 15J, M#3, HC, 2-Tone | 100 | 125 | 175 |
| 66, 11J, M#7, OF | 75 | 100 | 150 |
| 66, 11J, M#7, OF, Silveroid | 50 | 65 | 80 |
| 66, 11J, M#7, HC | 75 | 100 | 150 |
| 72, 15J, KW-SW, exposed escapement, HC ★ | 600 | 700 | 850 |
| 81, 9J, M#3, HC, Gilt | 100 | 125 | 175 |
| 82, Special, 21J, SW ★★ | 400 | 500 | 650 |
| 83, 15J, M#8, HC, 2-Tone | 125 | 150 | 200 |
| 86, 15J, M#7, OF, NI | 55 | 75 | 125 |
| 93, 9J, M#8, HC, Gilt | 100 | 125 | 175 |
| 94, 9J, M#7, OF | 55 | 75 | 125 |
| 200-205, 17J, M#9, OF, NI, LS | 75 | 100 | 150 |
| 245, 19J, HC, GJS, 2-Tone ★ | 1,000 | 1,200 | 1,400 |
| 800, 24J, GJS, DR, Adj.5P, DMK, HC ★ | 1,200 | 1,400 | 1,600 |
| 805, 21J, GJS, Adj.5P, NI, DMK, HC, marked "RG" | 300 | 375 | 500 |
| 810, 21J, NI, DMK, ADJ, HC | 325 | 375 | 425 |
| 820, 17J, HC, SW ★★ | 300 | 350 | 425 |
| 825, 17J, HC, FULL | 125 | 150 | 200 |
| 830, 17J, HC, FULL | 100 | 125 | 175 |
| 835, 17J, HC, FULL | 100 | 125 | 175 |
| 835, 17J, HC, FULL, Silveroid | 80 | 95 | 125 |
| 845, 21J, HC, GJS, FULL ★ | 400 | 475 | 550 |
| 870, 7J, HC, FULL | 75 | 100 | 150 |

🕐 Watches listed in this book are priced at the collectable retail level, as **complete** watches having an original 14k gold-filled case and *Key Wind* with silver, an original white enamel single sunk dial, and with the entire original movement in good working order with no repairs needed.

| Grade or Name – Description | | Avg. | Ex-Fn | Mint |
|---|---|---|---|---|
| 890, 24J, GJS, DR, Adj.5P, **HC**, NI, DMK | ★★ | $1,500 | $1,700 | $1,950 |
| 900, 24J, GJS, DR, Adj.5P, OF, NI, DMK | ★★ | 1,400 | 1,550 | 1,800 |
| 900, 24J, GJS, DR, Adj.5P, 14K, OF case | ★★ | 2,000 | 2,400 | 3,000 |
| 905, 21J, GJS, DR, Adj.5P, OF, NI, DMK | | 300 | 350 | 400 |
| 910, 21J, NI, DMK, ADJ, OF | | 150 | 175 | 250 |
| 912, 21J, OF | ★★ | 425 | 475 | 600 |
| 915, 17J, M#9, OF, SW | ★★★ | 450 | 500 | 625 |
| 918, 24J, GJS, DR, Adj.5P, OF, NI, DMK | ★★ | 1,400 | 1,600 | 1,850 |
| 918, 21J, OF, NI, GJS, Adj.5P, DR | | 275 | 325 | 375 |
| 918, 21J, OF, NI, GJS, Adj.5P, DR, Coin | | 275 | 325 | 375 |
| 920 & 930 , 17J, OF | | 175 | 225 | 275 |
| 925 & 935, 17J, OF | | 75 | 100 | 135 |
| 945, 21J, M#9, OF, SW | | 200 | 250 | 300 |
| 950, 21J, OF, NI, GJS, Adj.5P, DR, Wind Indicator | ★★ | 2,500 | 3,000 | 4,000 |
| 970, 7J, OF | | 60 | 70 | 90 |
| 970, 7J, OF, Silveroid | | 40 | 50 | 70 |

## 16 SIZE

| Grade or Name – Description | | Avg | Ex-Fn | Mint |
|---|---|---|---|---|
| Commodore Perry, 21J, OF, GJS, GT, marked ''RG'' | ★ | $275 | $335 | $400 |
| Commodore Perry, 15-17J, ADJ | | 100 | 125 | 150 |
| Cosmos, 17J, OF, GJS, LS, DMK, marked dial & mvt. | | 225 | 300 | 400 |
| Cosmos, 17J, **HC**, GJS, LS, DMK, marked dial & mvt. | | 275 | 335 | 450 |
| Doll Watch Co., 17J, marked dial & mvt. | ★ | 235 | 300 | 400 |
| Doll Watch Co., 21J, marked dial & mvt. | ★ | 300 | 400 | 550 |
| Doll Watch Co., 23J, marked dial & mvt. | ★★★ | 1,000 | 1,200 | 1,500 |
| Dome Model, 15J | | 60 | 75 | 100 |
| Dome Model, 17J | | 65 | 80 | 120 |
| Dome Model, 17J, 2-tone, HC | | 200 | 250 | 325 |
| Herald Square, 7J, 3/4, OF | | 75 | 95 | 125 |
| Iroquois, 17J, DR, **14K, HC** | | 525 | 575 | 675 |
| Iroquois, 17J, DR, OF | | 150 | 175 | 225 |
| Peerless, 17J, OF, NI, LS, DMK | | 75 | 95 | 125 |
| Pocahontas, 17-21J, GJS, Adj.5P, DR | ★ | 225 | 250 | 375 |
| Prince of Wales (Sears), 21J, Plymouth W. Co. | | 300 | 350 | 400 |
| Prince of Wales (Sears), 21J, Plymouth W. Co.14K | | 600 | 675 | 750 |

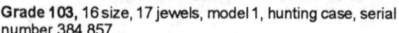

Grade 103, 16 size, 17 jewels, model 1, hunting case, serial number 384,857.

Cosmos movement, 16 size, 17 jewels, open face, gold jewel settings, grade 565, model 2.

**Grade 500-HC**, model 4, 16 size, 21 jewels, gold jewel settings, gold train, Adj6p, marked "RG," serial number 546,617, originally sold for about $100.00.

**Grade 505-OF**, model 5, 16 size, 21 jewels, gold jewel settings, gold train, Adj6p, marked "RG," serial number 593,929, originally sold for about $100.00.

Generic, **nameless** or **unmarked** grades for watch movements are listed under the Company name or initials of the Company, etc. by size, jewel count and description.

| Grade or Name – Description | Avg | Ex-Fn | Mint |
|---|---|---|---|
| Rockford, 7J, 3/4, HC | $100 | $125 | $175 |
| Rockford, 9J, 3/4, SW, OF | 60 | 85 | 95 |
| Rockford, 9J, SW, Silveroid | 40 | 60 | 80 |
| Rockford, 9J, SW, HC | 100 | 125 | 175 |
| Rockford, 11J, SW, Silveroid | 60 | 85 | 100 |
| Rockford, 11J, 3/4, HC | 100 | 125 | 175 |
| Rockford, 15J, 3/4, ADJ, OF | 75 | 100 | 135 |
| Rockford, 15J, 3/4, ADJ, Silveroid | 60 | 85 | 100 |
| Rockford, 15J, 3/4, ADJ, HC | 100 | 125 | 175 |
| Rockford, 16J, 3/4, SW, Silveroid | 60 | 85 | 100 |
| Rockford, 16J, 3/4, ADJ, NI, DMK | 75 | 100 | 135 |
| Rockford, 17J, 3/4 | 75 | 100 | 135 |
| Rockford, 17J, 3/4, 2-Tone, marked "RG" | 125 | 150 | 200 |
| Rockford, 17J, BRG, Adj.3P, DR | 100 | 125 | 175 |
| Rockford, 17J, GJS, Adj.5P, DR, **Wind Indicator** | 800 | 875 | 975 |
| Rockford, 17J, BRG, Silveroid | 65 | 90 | 110 |
| Rockford, 17J, 3/4, Silveroid | 60 | 85 | 100 |
| Rockford, 21J, 3/4, SW, Silveroid | 200 | 225 | 275 |
| Rockford, 21J, BRG, SW, Silveroid | 200 | 225 | 275 |
| Rockford, 21J, 3/4, GJS, Adj.5P | 250 | 275 | 325 |
| Rockford, 21J, BRG, GJS, Adj.5P, GT, DR | 275 | 300 | 375 |
| Rockford, 21J, GJS, Adj.5P, DR, **Wind Indicator** | 900 | 1,000 | 1,200 |
| Winnebago, 17J, BRG, GJS, Adj.5P, NI | 175 | 225 | 275 |
| Winnebago, 21J, BRG, GJS, Adj.5P, NI | 375 | 425 | 500 |
| 100, 16J, M#1, HC, 3/4, 2-Tone | 200 | 250 | 300 |
| 100S, 21J, Special, HC, 3/4, LS | 275 | 350 | 375 |
| 102, 15J, HC, M#1 ★ | 125 | 150 | 200 |
| 103, 15-17J, HC, M#1 ★ ★ | 250 | 300 | 375 |
| 104, 11J, HC, M#1 | 50 | 60 | 75 |
| 110, 17J, 2 tone dome style mvt.,HC | 300 | 335 | 400 |
| 115-125, 17J, Special, HC ★ ★ ★ | 500 | 600 | 750 |
| 120-130, 17J, HC ★ ★ ★ | 400 | 500 | 650 |

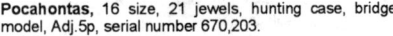

Pocahontas, 16 size, 21 jewels, hunting case, bridge model, Adj.5p, serial number 670,203.

Rockford movement, 16 size, 17 jewels, 3/4 plate, open face, grade 575, model 2, serial number 556,064.

| Grade or Name – Description | Avg | Ex-Fn | Mint |
|---|---|---|---|
| 400 & 405, 17J, NI, Adj.5P, GJS, DR, BRG | $100 | $125 | $175 |
| 445, 19J, HC, GJS, BRG ★★ | 850 | 1,000 | 1,200 |
| 500, 21J, BRG, NI, GJS, Adj.5P, GT, HC ★★ | 500 | 550 | 625 |
| 501, 21J, GJS, HC ★★★ | 900 | 1,100 | 1,250 |
| 505, 21J, BRG, NI, GJS, Adj.5P, GT, OF ★★ | 400 | 500 | 650 |
| 510, 21J, BRG, NI, GJS, Adj.5P, GT, HC ★ | 375 | 450 | 550 |
| 515 & 525, 21J, OF, 3/4 | 200 | 250 | 275 |
| 520, 21J, HC, 3/4 | 275 | 350 | 400 |
| 520, 21J, BRG, NI, GJS, Adj.5P, HC | 400 | 450 | 525 |
| 525, 21J. M#5, GT, Adj.5P ★ | 275 | 350 | 400 |
| 530, 21J, HC, GJS, Adj.5P, marked "RG" ★ | 300 | 350 | 425 |
| 535, 21J, OF, 3/4 ★ | 225 | 275 | 350 |
| 537, 21J, OF, GJS, Adj.5P ★★ | 500 | 600 | 775 |
| 545, 21J,GT,BRG, Adj.5P, OF | 250 | 300 | 350 |
| 561, 17J, BRG | 125 | 150 | 200 |
| 566, 17J, BRG | 125 | 150 | 200 |
| 572, 17J, BRG, NI, GJS, Adj.5P | 85 | 110 | 150 |
| 573, 17J, BRG, NI | 75 | 100 | 135 |
| 578-579, 17J, PS, GJS ★★ | 300 | 350 | 475 |
| 584 & 585, 15J, 3/4 NI | 40 | 60 | 85 |
| 620-625, 21J, HC, 3/4 ★ | 300 | 400 | 525 |
| 655, 21J, OF, **Wind Indicator,** marked 655 ★ | 850 | 900 | 1,000 |

🕐 Watches listed in this book are priced at the collectable retail level, as **complete** watches having an original 14k gold-filled case and *Key Wind* with silver, an original white enamel single sunk dial, and with the entire original movement in good working order with no repairs needed.

🕐 This book endeavours to be a GUIDE or helpful manual and offers a wealth of material to be used as a tool not as a absolute document. Price Guides are like watches the worst may be better than none at all, but at best cannot be expected to be 100% accurate

**Rockford Watch Co.**, 12 size, 15 jewels, model 1, hunting, pendant set.

**Rockford Watch Co.**, 12 size, 15 jewels, model 2, open face, pendant set.

## 12 SIZE
### All 3/4 Bridge

| Grade or Name – Description | Avg | Ex-Fn | Mint |
|---|---|---|---|
| Commodore Perry, 15-17J, ADJ. | $50 | $60 | $75 |
| Doll Watch Co., 21J, marked on dial & movement, OF ............★ | 300 | 350 | 425 |
| Iroquois, 17J, BRG, DR, ADJ. | 60 | 70 | 100 |
| Pocahontas, 21J, GJS, Adj.5P, BRG, DR | 150 | 175 | 200 |
| Rockford, 15J, BRG | 35 | 40 | 55 |
| Rockford, 17J, BRG, NI, DR, ADJ. | 50 | 60 | 75 |
| Rockford, 21J, BRG, NI, DR, ADJ. | 100 | 125 | 150 |
| Rockford, 21J, BRG, NI, DR, ADJ, Silveroid | 75 | 100 | 125 |
| Winona, 15J, BRG | 45 | 55 | 80 |
| 300, 23J, 3/4, GJS, Adj.5P, HC .............................★★★ | 300 | 350 | 425 |
| 305, 23J, BRG, NI, GJS, Adj.5P, GT, OF .................★★★ | 300 | 350 | 425 |
| 310(HC)-315(OF), 21J, BRG, NI, GJS, Adj.5P | 75 | 100 | 150 |
| 320(HC)-325(OF), 17J, BRG, NI, ADJ, DR | 40 | 60 | 85 |
| 330, 17J, BRG, NI, DR, OF | 40 | 60 | 85 |
| 335, 17J, BRG, NI, DR, HC | 40 | 60 | 85 |
| 340(HC)-345(OF), 21J, M#1 ...............................★ | 200 | 225 | 300 |
| 350, 17J, OF | 40 | 60 | 85 |
| 355, 17J, HC | 50 | 65 | 95 |

Note: Add $10 to $25 to above watches with hunting case.

## 8 SIZE

| Grade or Name – Description | Avg | Ex-Fn | Mint |
|---|---|---|---|
| 15J, 3/4, HC, LS, 14K, 40 DWT | $375 | $400 | $475 |
| 9–15J, 3/4, KW or SW, LS, OF or HC, | 100 | 125 | 175 |

## 6 SIZE

| Grade or Name – Description | Avg | Ex-Fn | Mint |
|---|---|---|---|
| 9J, HC, NI | $60 | $70 | $85 |

**Rockford movement,** 6 size, 17 jewels, quick train, straight line escapement, compensating balance, adjusted to temperature, micrometric regulator, three-quarter damaskeened plates.

### 6 SIZE

| Grade or Name – Description | Avg | Ex-Fn | Mint |
|---|---|---|---|
| 9J, HC, NI | $60 | $70 | $85 |
| 15J, 3/4, NI | 40 | 60 | 85 |
| 16J, 3/4, NI | 70 | 90 | 115 |
| 17J, 3/4, ADJ, NI | 80 | 100 | 125 |

### 0 SIZE

| Grade or Name – Description | Avg | Ex-Fn | Mint |
|---|---|---|---|
| Iroquois, 17J., HC | $200 | $225 | $275 |
| Plymouth Watch Co., 15-17J, HC | 200 | 225 | 275 |
| 7J, BRG, NI, DR, HC | 100 | 120 | 155 |
| 11J, BRG, NI, DR, HC | 110 | 130 | 165 |
| 15J, BRG, NI, DR, HC | 125 | 135 | 175 |
| 17J, BRG, NI, DR, HC | 175 | 200 | 250 |
| 17J, BRG, NI, DR, in marked Rockford HC ★ | 325 | 350 | 375 |

🕐 Watches listed in this book are priced at the collectable retail level, as **complete** watches having an original 14k gold-filled case and *Key Wind* with silver, an original white enamel single sunk dial, and with the entire original movement in good working order with no repairs needed.

🕐 This book endeavours to be a GUIDE or helpful manual and offers a wealth of material to be used as a tool not as a absolute document. Price Guides are like watches the worst may be better than none at all, but at best cannot be expected to be 100% accurate.

🕐 Characteristics of watches differ for the same age of both case and movement, because these features vary it may not be accurate to date a watch by one single influence. Example: the second hand was _not_ commonly found on watches before 1750, but common about 1800. The first second hand appeared in 1665 and another in 1690. Therefore statements are broad rather than accurate.

# ROCKFORD WATCH CO.
## IDENTIFICATION OF MOVEMENTS
### BY MODEL NUMBER

How to Identify Your Watch: Compare the movement of your watch with the illustrations in this section. Upon matching the movement exactly, the model number and size can be determined. While comparing, note the location of the balance, jewels, screws, gears, and type of back plate (Full, 3/4, Bridge) which will be clues in identifying the movement you have. Having determined the size and model number, you can now find your watch in the main price listing by name or number (which is engraved on the movement).

# The Rockford Watch Company, Ltd.

## NUMBER AND GRADE

### WITH

## DESCRIPTION OF MOVEMENTS MANUFACTURED TO DATE

| Number and Grade of Movement | GRADE | Size | Style | | | Jewels | Wind | Sett | Model |
|---|---|---|---|---|---|---|---|---|---|
| 1 to 114,000 | | 18 | Htg. | F. Pl. | | | Key | Key | 1 |
| 114,001 " 115,000 | | " | " | ¾ Pl. | | | Stem | Lever | 5 |
| 115,001 " 126,000 | | " | " | F. Pl. | | | " | " | 2 |
| 126,001 " 127,000 | | " | " | ¾ Pl. | | | " | " | 5 |
| 127,001 " 130,000 | | " | " | F. Pl. | | | " | " | 2 |
| 130,001 " 131,000 | | " | " | ¾ Pl. | | | " | " | 5 |
| 131,001 " 133,000 | | " | " | F. Pl. | | | " | " | 3 |
| 133,001 " 134,000 | | " | " | ¾ Pl. | | | " | " | 5 |
| 134,001 " 138,000 | | " | " | F. Pl. | | | " | " | 3 |
| 138,001 " 139,000 | | " | " | ¾ Pl. | | | " | " | 5 |
| 139,001 " 143,000 | | " | " | F. Pl. | | | " | " | 3 |
| 143,001 " 144,000 | | " | " | ¾ Pl. | | | " | " | 5 |
| 144,001 " 145,000 | | " | " | F. Pl. | | | " | " | 3 |
| 145,001 " 146,000 | | " | " | ¾ Pl. | | | " | " | 5 |
| 146,001 " 149,000 | | " | " | F. Pl. | | | " | " | 3 |
| 149,001 " 151,000 | | " | " | ¾ Pl. | | | " | " | 5 |
| 151,001 " 153,000 | | " | " | F. Pl. | | | " | " | 3 |
| 153,001 " 154,000 | | " | " | ¾ Pl. | | | " | " | 5 |
| 154,001 " 158,000 | | " | " | F. Pl. | | | " | " | 3 |
| 158,001 " 159,000 | | " | " | ¾ Pl. | | | " | " | 5 |
| 159,001 " 169,000 | | " | " | F. Pl. | | | " | " | 3 |
| 170,001 " 170,100 | | " | " | ¾ Pl. | | 15 | " | " | 5 |
| 170,101 " 177,000 | | " | " | F. Pl. | | | " | " | 3 |
| 177,001 " 177,800 | | " | " | " | | | " | " | 6 |
| 177,901 " 189,500 | | " | " | " | | | " | " | 3 |
| 189,601 " 190,900 | | " | " | " | | | " | " | 6 |
| 191,001 " 191,100 | | " | " | " | | | " | " | 3 |
| 191,101 " 196,400 | | " | O. F. | " | | | " | " | 4 |
| 196,501 " 197,000 | | " | Htg. | " | | | " | " | 6 |
| 197,101 " 197,500 | | " | " | " | | | " | " | 3 |
| 197,601 " 198,000 | | " | " | " | | | " | " | 6 |
| 198,101 " 199,100 | | " | O. F. | " | | | " | " | 4 |
| 199,201 " 199,500 | | " | Htg. | " | | | " | " | 6 |
| 199,600 " 200,000 | | " | " | ¾ Pl. | | | " | " | 5 |
| 200,001 " 213,100 | | 8 | " | " | | | " | " | 1 |
| 213,101 " 218,900 | | 6 | " | " | | | " | " | " |
| 219,001 " 219,500 | | 18 | " | " | | | " | " | 5 |
| 219,501 " 224,500 | | " | " | F. Pl. | | | " | " | 3 |
| 224,501 " 228,900 | | " | O. F. | " | | | " | " | 4 |
| 229,001 " 232,000 | | " | Htg. | " | | | " | " | 3 |
| 232,001 " 233,000 | | " | " | ¾ Pl. | | | " | " | 5 |
| 233,001 " 234,000 | 47 | " | O. F. | F. Pl. | Nickel | 15 | " | " | 4 |
| 234,001 " 235,000 | 45 | " | " | " | " | " | " | " | " |
| 235,001 " 236,000 | 43 | " | Htg. | F. Pl. | " | " | " | " | 3 |
| 236,001 " 237,000 | 44 | " | " | " | Gilt | " | " | " | " |
| 237,001 " 238,000 | 45 | " | O. F. | F. Pl. | " | " | " | " | 4 |
| 238,001 " 239,000 | | " | " | " | " | 9 | " | " | " |
| 239,001 " 240,000 | 45 | " | " | " | " | 15 | " | " | " |
| 240,001 " 241,000 | 46 | " | " | " | " | 11 | " | " | " |
| 241,001 " 241,800 | 47 | " | " | " | Nickel | 15 | " | " | " |
| 241,801 " 242,000 | 40 | " | Htg. | " | " | " | " | " | 3 |
| 242,001 " 243,000 | 43 | " | " | " | " | " | " | " | " |
| 243,001 " 244,000 | 44 | " | " | " | Gilt | " | " | " | " |
| 244,001 " 244,300 | 49 | " | " | " | Nickel | " | " | " | 6 |
| 244,301 " 244,400 | 72 | " | " | " | " | " | " | " | " |
| 244,401 " 245,000 | 62 | " | " | " | " | 11 | " | " | 8 |
| 245,001 " 246,000 | 81 | " | " | " | Gilt | 9 | " | " | 3 |
| 246,001 " 247,000 | 44 | " | " | " | " | 15 | " | " | " |
| 247,001 " 248,000 | 64 | " | O. F. | " | " | 11 | " | " | 4 |
| 248,001 " 249,000 | 46 | " | Htg. | " | " | 15 | " | " | 6 |
| 249,001 " 250,000 | 49 | " | " | " | Nickel | " | " | " | " |
| 250,001 " 250,500 | 62 | " | " | " | " | 11 | " | " | " |
| 250,501 " 251,000 | 60 | " | O. F. | " | " | " | " | " | 7 |
| 251,001 " 252,000 | 66 | " | " | " | " | " | " | " | " |
| 252,001 " 253,000 | 67 | " | " | " | Gilt | " | " | " | " |
| 253,001 " 253,500 | 83 | " | Htg. | " | Nickel | 15 | " | " | 8 |
| 253,501 " 253,700 | 77 | " | " | " | " | " | " | " | " |
| 253,701 " 254,000 | 68 | " | " | " | Gilt | 11 | " | " | " |
| 254,001 " 254,600 | 86 | " | O. F. | " | Nickel | 15 | " | " | 7 |
| 254,601 " 254,800 | 76 | " | " | " | " | " | " | " | " |
| 254,801 " 255,000 | 78 | " | " | " | Gilt | " | " | " | " |
| 255,001 " 256,000 | 89 | " | " | " | " | " | " | " | " |
| 256,001 " 257,000 | 68 | " | Htg. | " | " | 11 | " | " | 8 |
| 257,001 " 258,000 | 93 | " | " | " | " | 9 | " | " | " |
| 258,001 " 259,000 | 69 | " | " | " | Nickel | 11 | " | " | " |

## The Rockford Watch Company, Ltd.

| Number and Grade of Movement | GRADE | Size | | Style (F. Pl.) | Style | Jewels | Wind | Sett | Model |
|---|---|---|---|---|---|---|---|---|---|
| 259,001 to 260,000 | 66 | 18 | O. F. | F. Pl. | Nickel | 11 | Stem | Lever | 7 |
| 260,001 " 261,000 | 68 | " | Htg. | " | Gilt | " | " | " | 8 |
| 261,001 " 262,000 | 86 | " | O. F. | " | Nickel | 15 | " | " | 7 |
| 262,001 " 263,000 | 67 | " | " | " | Gilt | 11 | " | " | " |
| 263,001 " 264,000 | 83 | " | Htg. | " | Nickel | 15 | " | " | 8 |
| 264,001 " 265,000 | 69 | " | " | " | " | " | " | " | " |
| 265,001 " 266,000 | 68 | " | " | " | Gilt | 11 | " | " | " |
| 266,001 " 267,000 | 93 | " | " | " | " | 9 | " | " | 8 |
| 267,001 " 267,800 | 83 | " | " | " | Nickel | 15 | " | " | " |
| 267,801 " 268,000 | 77 | " | " | " | " | " | " | " | " |
| 268,001 " 269,000 | 68 | " | " | " | Gilt | 11 | " | " | " |
| 269,001 " 270,000 | 67 | " | O. F. | " | " | " | " | " | 7 |
| 270,001 " 270,800 | 85 | " | Htg. | " | " | 15 | " | " | 8 |
| 270,801 " 271,000 | 79 | " | " | " | " | " | " | " | " |
| 271,001 " 272,000 | 66 | " | O. F. | " | Nickel | 11 | " | " | 7 |
| 272,001 " 272,100 | 77 | " | Htg. | " | " | 15 | " | " | 8 |
| 272,101 " 272,200 | 83 | " | " | " | " | " | " | " | " |
| 272,201 " 272,300 | 77 | " | " | " | " | " | " | " | " |
| 272,301 " 272,600 | 83 | " | " | " | " | " | " | " | " |
| 272,601 " 272,700 | 77 | " | " | " | " | " | " | " | " |
| 272,701 " 272,900 | 83 | " | " | " | " | " | " | " | " |
| 272,901 " 273,000 | 77 | " | " | " | " | " | " | " | " |
| 273,001 " 274,000 | 69 | " | " | " | " | " | " | " | " |
| 274,001 " 275,000 | 83 | " | " | " | " | " | " | " | " |
| 275,001 " 276,000 | 69 | " | " | " | " | 11 | " | " | " |
| 276,001 " 277,000 | 83 | " | " | " | " | 15 | " | " | " |
| 277,001 " 278,000 | 85 | " | " | " | Gilt | " | " | " | " |
| 278,001 " 279,000 | 66 | " | O. F. | " | Nickel | 11 | " | " | 7 |
| 279,001 " 279,200 | 76 | " | Htg. | " | " | 15 | " | " | " |
| 279,201 " 280,000 | 86 | " | " | " | " | " | " | " | " |
| 280,001 " 281,000 | 66 | " | " | " | " | 11 | " | " | " |
| 281,001 " 282,000 | 85 | " | Htg. | " | Gilt | 15 | " | " | 8 |
| 282,001 " 283,000 | 83 | " | " | " | Nickel | " | " | " | " |
| 283,001 " 284,000 | 93 | " | " | " | Gilt | 9 | " | " | " |
| 284,001 " 285,000 | 89 | " | O. F. | " | " | 15 | " | " | 7 |
| 285,001 " 286,000 | 69 | " | Htg. | " | Hickel | 11 | " | " | 8 |
| 286,001 " 286,200 | 83 | " | " | " | Nick.& Gilt | 15 | " | " | " |
| 286,201 " 286,500 | 84 | " | " | " | " | " | " | " | " |
| 286,501 " 287,000 | 83 | " | " | " | Nickel | " | " | " | " |
| 287,001 " 288,000 | 66 | " | O. F. | " | " | 11 | " | " | 7 |
| 288,001 " 289,000 | 67 | " | " | " | Gilt | " | " | " | " |
| 289,001 " 289,500 | 84 | " | Htg. | " | Spot Gilt | 15 | " | " | 8 |
| 289,501 " 291,000 | 83 | " | " | " | Nickel | " | " | " | " |
| 291,001 " 292,000 | 69 | " | " | " | " | 11 | " | " | " |
| 292,001 " 293,000 | 67 | " | O. F. | " | Gilt | " | " | " | 7 |
| 293,001 " 294,000 | 85 | " | Htg. | " | " | 15 | " | " | 8 |
| 294,001 " 295,000 | 93 | " | " | " | " | 9 | " | " | " |
| 295,001 " 296,000 | 66 | " | O. F. | " | Nickel | 11 | " | " | 7 |
| 296,001 " 297,000 | 89 | " | " | " | Gilt | 15 | " | " | " |
| 297,001 " 298,000 | 69 | " | Htg. | " | Nickel | 11 | " | " | 8 |
| 298,001 " 299,000 | 67 | " | O. F. | " | Gilt | " | " | " | 7 |
| 299,001 " 300,000 | 93 | " | Htg. | " | " | 9 | " | " | 8 |
| 300,001 " 300,500 | 84 | " | " | " | Nick.& Gilt | 15 | " | " | " |
| 300,501 " 300,700 | 83 | " | " | " | Nickel | " | " | " | " |
| 300,701 " 301,000 | 70 | " | " | " | Nick.& Gilt | 16 | " | " | " |
| 301,001 " 302,000 | 66 | " | O. F. | " | Nickel | 11 | " | " | 7 |
| 302,001 " 303,000 | 93 | " | Htg. | " | Gilt | 9 | " | " | 8 |
| 303,001 " 304,000 | 69 | " | " | " | Nickel | 11 | " | " | " |
| 304,001 " 304,500 | 84 | " | " | " | Nick.& Gilt | 15 | " | " | " |
| 304,501 " 305,000 | 83 | " | " | " | Nickel | " | " | " | " |
| 305,001 " 305,500 | 84 | " | " | " | Nick.&Gilt | " | " | " | " |
| 305,501 " 306,000 | 83 | " | " | " | Nickel | " | " | " | " |
| 306,001 " 307,000 | 66 | " | O. F. | " | " | 11 | " | " | 7 |
| 307,001 " 308,000 | 83 | " | Htg. | " | " | 15 | " | " | 8 |
| 308,001 " 309,000 | 93 | " | " | " | Gilt | 9 | " | " | " |
| 309,001 " 310,000 | 83 | " | " | " | Nickel | 15 | " | " | " |
| 310,001 " 310,500 | 87 | " | O. F. | " | Nick.& Gilt | " | " | " | 7 |
| 310,501 " 310,700 | 88 | " | " | " | Nickel | 16 | " | " | " |
| 310,701 " 311,000 | 86 | " | " | " | " | 15 | " | " | " |
| 311,001 " 312,000 | 69 | " | Htg. | " | " | 11 | " | " | 8 |
| 312,001 " 313,000 | 93 | " | " | " | Gilt | 9 | " | " | " |
| 313,001 " 314,000 | 83 | " | " | " | Nickel | 15 | " | " | " |
| 314,001 " 317,000 | 93 | " | " | " | Gilt | 9 | " | " | " |
| 317,001 " 318,000 | 85 | " | " | " | " | 15 | " | " | " |
| 318,001 " 319,000 | 93 | " | " | " | " | 9 | " | " | " |
| 319,001 " 320,000 | 85 | " | " | " | " | 15 | " | " | " |
| 320,001 " 321,000 | 84 | " | " | " | Nick.& Gilt | " | " | " | " |
| 321,001 " 322,000 | 83 | " | " | " | Nickel | " | " | " | " |
| 322,001 " 323,000 | 84 | " | " | " | Nick.& Gilt | " | " | " | " |
| 323,001 " 325,000 | 83 | " | " | " | Nickel | " | " | " | " |
| 325,001 " 326,000 | 85 | " | " | " | Gilt | " | " | " | " |
| 326,001 " 327,000 | 93 | " | " | " | " | 9 | " | " | " |
| 327,001 " 328,000 | 83 | " | " | " | Nickel | 15 | " | " | " |
| 328,001 " 329,000 | 89 | " | O. F. | " | Gilt | " | " | " | 7 |
| 329,001 " 329,100 | 84 | " | Htg. | " | Nick.& Gilt | " | " | " | 8 |
| 329,101 " 329,200 | 83 | " | " | " | Special | ..... | " | " | " |
| 329,201 " 329,700 | 84 | " | " | " | Nick.& Gilt | 15 | " | " | " |
| 329,701 " 330,000 | 70 | " | " | " | " | 16 | " | " | " |
| 330,001 " 330,800 | 87 | " | O. F. | " | Nickel | 15 | " | " | 7 |

## The Rockford Watch Company, Ltd.

| Number and Grade of Movement | GRADE | Size | Style | | | Jewels | Wind | Sett | Model |
|---|---|---|---|---|---|---|---|---|---|
| 330,801 to 331,000 | 88 | 18 | O. F. | F. Pl. | Nick. & Gilt | 16 | Stem | Lever | 7 |
| 331,001 " 332,000 | 68 | " | Htg. | " | Gilt | 11 | " | " | 8 |
| 332,001 " 333,000 | 86 | " | O. F. | " | Nickel | 15 | " | " | 7 |
| 333,001 " 334,000 | 69 | " | Htg. | " | " | 11 | " | " | 8 |
| 334,001 " 335,000 | 66 | " | O. F. | " | " | " | " | " | 7 |
| 335,001 " 336,000 | 94 | " | " | " | Gilt | 9 | " | " | " |
| 336,001 " 337,000 | 68 | " | Htg. | " | " | 11 | " | " | 8 |
| 337,001 " 338,000 | 94 | " | O. F. | " | " | 9 | " | " | 7 |
| 338,001 " 338,500 | 88 | " | " | " | Nick. & Gilt | 16 | " | " | " |
| 338,501 " 339,000 | 86 | " | " | " | Nickel | " | " | " | " |
| 339,001 " 339,500 | 70 | " | Htg. | " | Nick. & Gilt | " | " | " | 8 |
| 339,501 " 340,000 | 84 | " | " | " | " | 15 | " | " | " |
| 340,001 " 341,000 | 66 | " | O. F. | " | Nickel | 11 | " | " | 7 |
| 341,001 " 342,000 | 85 | " | Htg. | " | Gilt | 15 | " | " | 8 |
| 342,001 " 343,000 | 89 | " | O. F. | " | " | " | " | " | 7 |
| 343,001 " 344,000 | 94 | " | " | " | " | 9 | " | " | " |
| 344,001 " 345,000 | 84 | " | Htg. | " | Nick. & Gilt | 15 | " | " | 8 |
| 345,001 " 346,000 | 68 | " | " | " | Gilt | 11 | " | " | " |
| 346,001 " 347,000 | 87 | " | O. F. | " | Nick. & Gilt | 15 | " | " | 7 |
| 347,001 " 348,000 | 94 | " | " | " | Gilt | 9 | " | " | " |
| 348,001 " 348,300 | 88 | " | " | " | Nick. & Gilt | 16 | " | " | " |
| 348,301 " 348,500 | 87 | " | " | " | " | 15 | " | " | " |
| 348,501 " 349,000 | 86 | " | " | " | Nickel | " | " | " | " |
| 349,001 " 349,500 | 67 | " | " | " | Gilt | 11 | " | " | " |
| 349,501 " 350,000 | 89 | " | " | " | " | 15 | " | " | " |
| 350,001 " 350,500 | 70 | " | Htg. | " | Nick. & Gilt | 16 | " | " | 8 |
| 350,501 " 351,000 | 85 | " | " | " | Gilt | 15 | " | " | " |
| 351,001 " 352,000 | 87 | " | O. F. | " | Nick & Gilt | " | " | " | 7 |
| 352,001 " 352,500 | 88 | " | " | " | " | 16 | " | " | " |
| 352,501 " 353,000 | 67 | " | " | " | Gilt | 11 | " | " | " |
| 353,001 " 353,500 | 100 | 16 | Htg. | ¾ Pl. | Nick. & Gilt | 16 | " | " | 1 |
| 353,501 " 353,800 | 101 | " | " | " | Nickel | 15 | " | " | " |
| 353,801 " 354,000 | 102 | " | " | " | " | " | " | " | " |
| 354,001 " 354,500 | 103 | " | " | " | " | " | " | " | " |
| 354,501 " 355,000 | 104 | " | " | " | " | 11 | " | " | " |
| 355,001 " 355,500 | 111 | " | " | " | Gilt | 15 | " | " | " |
| 355,501 " 356,000 | 112 | " | " | " | " | " | " | " | " |
| 356,001 " 356,500 | 113 | " | " | " | " | 11 | " | " | " |
| 356,501 " 357,000 | 114 | " | " | " | " | 9 | " | " | " |
| 357,001 " 358,500 | 68 | 18 | " | F. Pl. | " | 11 | " | " | 8 |
| 358,501 " 359,000 | 67 | " | O. F. | " | " | " | " | " | 7 |
| 359,001 " 359,500 | 87 | " | " | " | Nick. & Gilt | 15 | " | " | " |
| 359,501 " 360,000 | 86 | " | " | " | Nickel | " | " | " | " |
| 360,001 " 360,500 | 101 | 16 | Htg. | ¾ Pl. | Nick. & Gilt | " | " | " | 1 |
| 360,501 " 361,000 | 102 | " | " | " | Nickel | " | " | " | " |
| 361,001 " 361,500 | 103 | " | " | " | " | " | " | " | " |
| 361,501 " 362,000 | 104 | " | " | " | " | 11 | " | " | " |
| 362,001 " 364,000 | 67 | 18 | O. F. | F. Pl. | Gilt | " | " | " | 7 |
| 364,001 " 365,000 | 112 | 16 | Htg. | ¾ Pl. | " | 15 | " | " | 1 |
| 365,001 " 366,000 | 102 | " | " | " | Nickel | " | " | " | " |
| 366,001 " 367,000 | 103 | " | " | " | " | " | " | " | " |
| 367,001 " 368,000 | 67 | 18 | O. F. | F. Pl. | Gilt | 11 | " | " | 7 |
| 368,001 " 368,500 | 112 | 16 | Htg. | ¾ Pl. | " | 15 | " | " | 1 |
| 368,501 " 369,000 | 101 | " | " | " | Nick. & Gilt | " | " | " | " |
| 369,001 " 370,000 | 104 | " | " | " | Nickel | 11 | " | " | " |
| 370,001 " 370,500 | 86 | 18 | O. F. | F. Pl. | " | 15 | " | " | 7 |
| 370,501 " 371,000 | 87 | " | " | " | Nick. & Gilt | " | " | " | " |
| 371,001 " 371,500 | 89 | " | " | " | Gilt | " | " | " | " |
| 371,501 " 372,000 | 94 | " | " | " | " | 9 | " | " | " |
| 372,001 " 372,500 | 113 | 16 | Htg. | ¾ Pl. | " | 11 | " | " | 1 |
| 372,501 " 373,000 | 114 | " | " | " | " | 9 | " | " | " |
| 373,001 " 374,000 | 113 | " | " | " | " | 11 | " | " | " |
| 274,001 " 374,500 | 68 | 18 | " | F. Pl. | " | " | " | " | 8 |
| 374,501 " 375,000 | 94 | " | O. F. | " | " | 9 | " | " | 7 |
| 375,001 " 376,000 | 87 | " | " | " | Nick. & Gilt | 15 | " | " | " |
| 376,001 " 376,200 | 100 | 16 | Htg. | ¾ Pl. | " | 16 | " | " | 1 |
| 376,201 " 376,700 | 101 | " | " | " | " | 15 | " | " | " |
| 376,701 " 377,000 | 102 | " | " | " | Nickel | " | " | " | " |
| 377,001 " 377,500 | 104 | " | " | " | " | 11 | " | " | " |
| 377,501 " 378,000 | 103 | " | " | " | " | 15 | " | " | " |
| 378,001 " 379,000 | 94 | 18 | O. F. | F. Pl. | Gilt | 9 | " | ' | 7 |
| 379,001 " 379,500 | 86 | " | " | " | Nickel | 15 | " | " | " |
| 379,501 " 380,000 | 84 | " | Htg. | " | Nick. & Gilt | " | " | " | 8 |
| 380,001 " 380,500 | 101 | 16 | " | ¾ Pl. | " | " | " | " | 1 |
| 380,501 " 381,000 | 104 | " | " | " | Nickel | 11 | " | " | " |
| 381,001 " 381,300 | 102 | " | " | " | " | 15 | " | " | " |
| 381,301 " 382,000 | 103 | " | " | " | " | " | " | " | " |
| 382,001 " 382,200 | 111 | " | " | " | Gilt | " | " | " | " |
| 382,201 " 383,000 | 112 | " | " | " | " | " | " | " | " |
| 383,001 " 383,500 | 113 | " | " | " | " | 11 | " | " | " |
| 383,501 " 384,000 | 114 | " | " | " | " | 9 | " | " | " |
| 384,001 " 384,500 | 100 | " | " | " | Nick. & Gilt | 16 | " | " | " |
| 384,501 " 385,000 | 103 | " | " | " | Nickel | 15 | " | " | " |
| 385,001 " 385,500 | 104 | " | " | " | " | 11 | " | " | " |
| 385,501 " 386,000 | 103 | " | " | " | " | 15 | " | " | " |
| 386,001 " 387,000 | 112 | " | " | " | Gilt | " | " | " | " |
| 387,001 " 387,500 | 93 | 18 | " | F. Pl. | " | 9 | " | " | 8 |
| 387,501 " 388,000 | 68 | " | " | " | " | 11 | " | " | " |

# The Rockford Watch Company, Ltd.

| Number and Grade of Movement | GRADE | Size | | Style | | Jewels | Wind | Sett | Model |
|---|---|---|---|---|---|---|---|---|---|
| 388,001 to 388,500 | 94 | 18 | O. F. | F. Pl. | Gilt | 9 | Stem | Lever | 7 |
| 388,501 " 389,000 | 89 | " | " | " | " | 15 | " | " | " |
| 389,001 " 389,100 | 76 | " | " | " | Nickel | " | " | " | " |
| 389,101 " 390,000 | 86 | " | " | " | " | " | " | " | " |
| 390,001 " 391,000 | 69 | " | Htg. | " | " | 11 | " | " | 8 |
| 391,001 " 391,400 | 162 | 6 | " | ¾ Pl. | Gilt | 9 | " | " | 2 |
| 391,401 " 391,700 | 161 | " | " | " | " | 11 | " | " | " |
| 391,701 " 392,000 | 160 | " | " | " | " | 15 | " | " | " |
| 392,001 " 392,300 | 154 | " | " | " | Nickel | 9 | " | " | " |
| 392,301 " 392,500 | 153 | " | " | " | " | 11 | " | " | " |
| 392,501 " 392,700 | 152 | " | " | " | " | 15 | " | " | " |
| 392,701 " 392,900 | 151 | " | " | " | Nick.& Gilt | " | " | " | " |
| 392,901 " 393,000 | 150 | " | " | " | " | 16 | " | " | " |
| 393,001 " 393,500 | 154 | " | " | " | Nickel | 9 | " | " | " |
| 393,501 " 394,000 | 153 | " | " | " | " | 11 | " | " | " |
| 394,001 " 394,500 | 152 | " | " | " | " | 15 | " | " | " |
| 394,501 " 394,800 | 151 | " | " | " | Nick.& Gilt | " | " | " | " |
| 394,801 " 395,000 | 150 | " | " | " | " | 16 | " | " | " |
| 395,001 " 396,000 | 162 | " | " | " | Gilt | 9 | " | " | " |
| 396,001 " 396,500 | 161 | " | " | " | " | 11 | " | " | " |
| 396,501 " 397,000 | 160 | " | " | " | " | 15 | " | " | " |
| 397,001 " 397,800 | 162 | " | " | " | " | 9 | " | " | " |
| 397,801 " 398,600 | 161 | " | " | " | " | 11 | " | " | " |
| 398,601 " 399,000 | 160 | " | " | " | " | 15 | " | " | " |
| 399,001 " 400,200 | 153 | " | " | " | Nickel | 11 | " | " | " |
| 400,201 " 400,700 | 152 | " | " | " | " | 15 | " | " | " |
| 400,701 " 401,000 | 152 | " | " | " | Nick.& Gilt | " | " | " | " |
| 401,001 " 401,500 | 93 | 18 | " | F. Pl. | Gilt | 9 | " | " | 8 |
| 401,501 " 402,000 | 68 | " | " | " | " | 11 | " | " | " |
| 402,001 " 402,500 | 69 | " | " | " | Nickel | " | " | " | " |
| 402,501 " 403,000 | 85 | " | " | " | Gilt | 15 | " | " | " |
| 403,001 " 403,500 | 94 | " | O. F. | " | " | 9 | " | " | 7 |
| 403,501 " 404,000 | 86 | " | " | " | Nickel | 15 | " | " | " |
| 404,001 " 404,300 | 60 | " | " | " | Nick.& Gilt | 11 | " | " | " |
| 404,301 " 405,000 | 66 | " | " | " | Nickel | 17 | " | " | " |
| 405,001 " 405,500 | 86 | " | " | " | " | 15 | " | " | " |
| 405,501 " 406,000 | 83 | " | Htg. | " | " | " | " | " | 8 |
| 406,001 " 407,000 | 69 | " | " | " | " | 11 | " | " | " |
| 407,001 " 407,500 | 68 | " | " | " | Gilt | " | " | " | " |
| 407,501 " 408,000 | 85 | " | " | " | " | 15 | " | " | " |
| 408,001 " 408,500 | 93 | " | " | " | " | 9 | " | " | " |
| 408,501 " 409,000 | 94 | " | O. F. | " | " | " | " | " | 7 |
| 409,001 " 410,000 | 69 | " | Htg. | " | Nickel | 11 | " | " | 8 |
| 410,001 " 410,500 | 93 | " | " | " | Gilt | 9 | " | " | " |
| 410,501 " 411,000 | 68 | " | " | " | " | 11 | " | " | " |
| 411,001 " 411,500 | 94 | " | O. F. | " | " | 9 | " | " | 7 |
| 411,501 " 412,000 | 67 | " | " | " | " | 11 | " | " | " |
| 412,001 " 412,500 | 86 | " | " | " | Nickel | 15 | " | " | " |
| 412,501 " 413,000 | 69 | " | Htg. | " | " | 11 | " | " | " |
| 413,001 " 414,000 | 93 | " | " | " | Gilt | 9 | " | " | 8 |
| 414,001 " 415,000 | 94 | " | O. F. | " | " | " | " | " | 7 |
| 415,001 " 415,200 | 81 | " | Htg. | " | Plain | 17 | " | " | 8 |
| 415,201 " 415,500 | 83 | " | " | " | Nickel | 15 | " | " | " |
| 415,501 " 415,600 | 80 | " | " | " | Spot Gilt | 17 | " | " | " |
| 415,601 " 416,000 | 82 | " | " | " | Plain | " | " | " | " |
| 416,001 " 416,100 | 61 | " | O. F. | " | .......... | " | " | " | 7 |
| 416,101 " 416,500 | 86 | " | " | " | Nickel | 15 | " | " | " |
| 416,501 " 417,000 | 62 | " | " | " | Plain | 17 | " | " | " |
| 417,001 " 417,500 | 66 | " | " | " | Nickel | 11 | " | " | " |
| 417,501 " 418,000 | 83 | " | Htg. | " | " | 17 | " | " | 8 |
| 418,001 " 419,000 | 93 | " | " | " | Gilt | 9 | " | " | " |
| 419,001 " 419,500 | 94 | " | " | " | " | " | " | " | " |
| 419,501 " 420,500 | 153 | 6 | " | ¾ Pl. | Nickel | 11 | " | " | 2 |
| 420,501 " 421,500 | 161 | " | " | " | Gilt | " | " | " | " |
| 421,501 " 422,500 | 162 | " | " | " | " | 9 | " | " | " |
| 422,501 " 423,000 | 66 | 18 | " | F. Pl. | Nickel | 11 | " | " | 7 |
| 423,001 " 424,000 | 93 | " | Htg. | " | Gilt | 9 | " | " | 8 |
| 424,001 " 425,000 | 69 | " | " | " | Nickel | 11 | " | " | 8 |
| 425,001 " 425,500 | 94 | " | O. F. | " | Gilt | 9 | " | " | 7 |
| 425,501 " 426,000 | 66 | " | " | " | Nickel | 11 | " | " | " |
| 426,001 " 427,000 | 83 | " | Htg. | " | " | 15 | " | " | 8 |
| 427,001 " 428,000 | 69 | " | " | " | " | 11 | " | " | " |
| 428,001 " 429,000 | 66 | " | O. F. | " | " | " | " | " | 7 |
| 429,001 " 430,000 | 83 | " | Htg. | " | " | 15 | " | " | 8 |
| 430,001 " 431,000 | 68 | " | " | " | Gilt | 11 | " | " | " |
| 431,001 " 431,500 | 66 | " | O. F. | " | Nickel | " | " | " | 7 |
| 431,501 " 432,000 | 82 | " | Htg. | " | Plain | 17 | " | " | 8 |
| 432,001 " 433,000 | 67 | " | O. F. | " | Gilt | 11 | " | " | 7 |
| 433,001 " 433,100 | 83 | " | Htg. | " | Nickel | 15 | " | " | 8 |
| 433,101 " 433,140 | 82a | " | " | " | " | " | " | " | " |
| 433,141 " 433,400 | 82 | " | " | " | " | " | " | " | " |
| 433,401 " 433,500 | 82 | " | " | " | " | 17 | " | " | " |
| 433,501 " 433,600 | 82 | " | " | " | " | " | " | " | " |
| 433,601 " 433,700 | 83 | " | " | " | " | 15 | " | " | " |
| 433,701 " 433,750 | 82 | " | " | " | Plain | 17 | " | " | " |
| 433,751 " 433,800 | 80 | " | " | " | Spot Gilt | " | " | " | " |
| 433,801 " 434,000 | 81 | " | " | " | Plain | " | " | " | " |
| 434,001 " 434,500 | 83 | " | " | " | Nickel | 15 | " | " | " |
| | 69 | " | " | " | " | " | " | " | " |

# The Rockford Watch Company, Ltd.

| Number and Grade of Movement | GRADE | Size | | | Style | | Jewels | Wind | Sett | Model |
|---|---|---|---|---|---|---|---|---|---|---|
| | | | | | **Style** | | | | | |
| 434,501 to 434,600 | 86 | 18 | O.F. | F. Pl. | Nickel | | 15 | Stem | Lever | 7 |
| 434,601 " 434,700 | 62 | " | " | " | Plain | | 17 | " | " | " |
| 434,701 " 435,000 | 86 | " | O.F. | " | Nickel | | 15 | " | " | " |
| 435,001 " 435,500 | 85 | " | Htg. | " | Gilt | | " | " | " | 8 |
| 435,501 " 436,000 | 94 | " | O.F. | " | " | | 9 | " | " | 7 |
| 436,001 " 436,100 | 67 | " | " | " | " | | 11 | " | " | " |
| 436,101 " 436,200 | 89 | " | " | " | " | | 15 | " | " | " |
| 436,201 " 436,300 | 67 | " | " | " | " | | 11 | " | " | " |
| 436,301 " 437,000 | 89 | " | " | " | " | | " | " | " | " |
| 437,001 " 437,800 | 82 | " | Htg. | " | Nickel | | 17 | " | " | 8 |
| 437,801 " 438,000 | 81 | " | " | " | Plain | | " | " | " | " |
| 438,001 " 438,500 | 83 | " | " | " | " | | 15 | " | " | " |
| 438,501 " 438,900 | 62 | " | O.F. | " | " | | 17 | " | " | 7 |
| 438,901 " 439,000 | 86 | " | " | " | Nickel | | 15 | " | " | " |
| 439,001 " 439,500 | 82 | " | Htg. | " | " | | 17 | " | " | 8 |
| 439,501 " 439,550 | 80 | " | " | " | Nick.& Gilt | | " | " | " | " |
| 439,551 " 439,650 | 82a | " | " | " | Nickel | | " | " | " | " |
| 439,651 " 439,700 | 81 | " | " | " | " | | " | " | " | " |
| 439,701 " 439,750 | 62a | " | O.F. | " | " | | " | " | " | 7 |
| 439,751 " 439,850 | 62 | " | " | " | " | | " | " | " | " |
| 439,851 " 439,900 | 61 | " | " | " | " | | 15 | " | " | " |
| 439,901 " 439,950 | 86 | " | " | " | " | | 17 | " | " | " |
| 439,951 " 440,000 | 62a | " | " | " | " | | " | " | " | " |
| 440,001 " 441,000 | 93 | " | Htg. | " | Gilt | | 9 | " | " | 8 |
| 441,001 " 441,500 | 62 | " | O.F. | " | Nickel | | 17 | " | " | 7 |
| 441,501 " 442,000 | 83 | " | Htg. | " | Plain | | 15 | " | " | 8 |
| 442,001 " 442,050 | 80 | " | " | " | Nick.& Gilt | | 17 | " | " | " |
| 424,051 " 442,150 | 81 | " | " | " | Plain | | " | " | " | " |
| 442,151 " 442,500 | 82 | " | " | " | Nickel | | " | " | " | " |
| 500,001 " 500,054 | 930 | " | O.F. | " | " | | " | " | " | 9 |
| 500,055 | 935 | " | " | " | " | | " | " | " | " |
| 500,056 to 500,250 | 930 | " | " | " | " | | " | " | " | 7 |
| 500,251 " 500,260 | 920 | " | " | " | " | | " | " | " | 9 |
| 500,261 " 500,300 | 930 | " | " | " | " | | " | " | " | " |
| 500,301 " 500,400 | 935 | " | " | " | " | | " | " | " | 10 |
| 500,401 " 500,800 | 830 | " | Htg. | " | " | | " | " | " | " |
| 500,801 " 500,900 | 835 | " | " | " | " | | " | " | " | " |
| 500,901 " 501,100 | 830 | " | " | " | " | | " | " | " | " |
| 501,101 " 501,900 | 835 | " | " | " | " | | " | " | " | " |
| 501,901 " 502,400 | 830 | " | " | " | " | | " | " | " | " |
| 502,401 " 502,481 | 930 | " | O.F. | " | " | | " | " | " | 9 |
| 502,482 " 502,489 | 935 | " | " | " | " | | " | " | " | " |
| 502,490 " 502 592 | 930 | " | " | " | " | | " | " | " | " |
| 502,593 | 935 | " | " | " | " | | " | " | " | " |
| 502,594 to 502,700 | 930 | " | " | " | " | | " | " | " | " |
| 502,701 " 503,200 | 935 | " | " | " | " | | " | " | " | 10 |
| 503,201 " 503,460 | 830 | " | Htg. | " | " | | " | " | " | 8 |
| 503,461 " 503,470 | 820 | " | " | " | " | | " | " | " | 10 |
| 503,471 " 503,483 | 830 | " | " | " | " | | " | " | " | 8 |
| 503,484 " 503,489 | 820 | " | " | " | " | | " | " | " | 10 |
| 503,490 " 503,520 | 830 | " | " | " | " | | " | " | " | 8 |
| 503,521 " 503,531 | 820 | " | " | " | " | | " | " | " | 10 |
| 503,532 " 503,536 | 830 | " | " | " | " | | " | " | " | 8 |
| 503,537 " 503,540 | 820 | " | " | " | " | | " | " | " | 10 |
| 503,541 " 503,550 | 825 | " | " | " | " | | " | " | " | " |
| 503,551 " 503,610 | 830 | " | " | " | " | | " | " | " | 8 |
| 503,611 " 503,620 | 820 | " | " | " | " | | " | " | " | 10 |
| 503,621 " 503,700 | 830 | " | " | " | " | | " | " | " | " |
| 503,701 " 504,000 | 835 | " | " | " | " | | " | " | " | " |
| 504,001 " 504,100 | 830 | " | " | " | " | | " | " | " | " |
| 504,101 " 505,150 | 835 | " | " | " | " | | " | " | " | " |
| 505,151 " 505,200 | 830 | " | " | " | " | | " | " | " | " |
| 505,201 " 505,300 | 835 | " | " | " | " | | " | " | " | " |
| 505,301 " 505,350 | 830 | " | " | " | " | | " | " | " | " |
| 505,351 " 505,360 | 835 | " | " | " | " | | " | " | " | " |
| 505,361 " 505,370 | 830 | " | " | " | " | | " | " | " | " |
| 505,371 " 505,398 | 835 | " | " | " | " | | " | " | " | " |
| 505,399 " 505,400 | 830 | " | " | " | " | | " | " | " | " |
| 505,401 " 505,700 | 835 | " | " | " | " | | " | " | " | " |
| 505,701 " 506,000 | 830 | " | " | " | " | | " | " | " | " |
| 506,001 " 506,800 | 935 | " | O.F. | " | " | | " | " | " | 9 |
| 506,801 " 506,810 | 910 | " | " | " | " | | 21 | " | " | " |
| 506,811 " 507,600 | 930 | " | " | " | " | | 17 | " | " | 10 |
| 507,601 " 507,900 | 830 | " | Htg. | " | " | | " | " | " | " |
| 507,901 " 508,500 | 835 | " | " | " | " | | " | " | " | " |
| 508,501 " 509,000 | 830 | " | " | " | " | | " | " | " | " |
| 509,001 " 509,100 | 820 | " | " | " | " | | " | " | " | 8 |
| 509,101 " 509,700 | 925 | " | O.F. | " | " | | " | " | " | 9 |
| 509,701 " 509,729 | 920 | " | " | " | " | | " | " | " | 7 |
| 509,730 | 915 | " | " | " | " | | " | " | " | " |
| 509,731 to 509,759 | 920 | " | " | " | " | | " | " | " | " |
| 509,760 | 915 | " | " | " | " | | " | " | " | " |
| 509,761 to 509,791 | 920 | " | " | " | " | | " | " | " | " |
| 509,792 | 915 | " | " | " | " | | " | " | " | " |
| 509,793 to 509,900 | 920 | " | " | " | " | | " | " | " | 10 |
| 509,901 " 510,200 | 810 | " | Htg. | " | " | | 21 | " | " | " |
| 510,201 " 510,700 | 825 | " | " | " | " | | 17 | " | " | " |
| 510,701 " 511,300 | 830 | " | " | " | " | | " | " | " | " |
| 511,301 " 511,600 | 835 | " | " | " | " | | " | " | " | " |

# The Rockford Watch Company, Ltd.

| Number and Grade of Movement | GRADE | Size | Style | | Jewels | Wind | Sett | Model |
|---|---|---|---|---|---|---|---|---|
| 511,601 to 512,500 | 935 | 18 | O. F. | F. Pl. | Nickel | 17 | Stem | Lever | 9 |
| 512,501 " 512,600 | 910 | " | " | " | " | 21 | " | " | " |
| 512,601 " 512,700 | 920 | " | " | " | " | 17 | " | " | 7 |
| 512,701 " 512,800 | 930 | " | " | " | " | " | " | " | 9 |
| 512,801 " 512,850 | 920 | " | " | " | " | " | " | " | 7 |
| 512,851 " 512,872 | 830 | " | Htg. | " | " | " | " | " | 10 |
| 512,873 | 915 | " | O. F. | " | " | " | " | " | 7 |
| 512,874 to 512,875 | 920 | " | " | " | " | " | " | " | " |
| 512,876 | 915 | " | " | " | " | " | " | " | " |
| 512,877 to 512,900 | 920 | " | " | " | " | " | " | " | " |
| 512,901 " 513,101 | 830 | " | Htg. | " | " | " | " | " | 10 |
| 513,102 " 513,181 | 820 | " | " | " | " | " | " | " | 8 |
| 513,182 | 815 | " | " | " | " | " | " | " | " |
| 513,183 to 513,251 | 820 | " | " | " | " | " | " | " | " |
| 513,252 " 513,259 | 810 | " | " | " | " | 21 | " | " | 10 |
| 513,260 " 513,300 | 820 | " | " | " | " | 17 | " | " | 8 |
| 513,301 " 513,400 | 830 | " | " | " | " | " | " | " | 10 |
| 513,401 " 513,500 | 835 | " | " | " | " | " | " | " | " |
| 513,501 " 513,600 | 830 | " | " | " | " | " | " | " | " |
| 513,601 " 513,900 | 835 | " | " | " | " | " | " | " | " |
| 513,901 " 514,000 | 930 | " | O. F. | " | " | " | " | " | 9 |
| 514,001 " 514,100 | 935 | " | " | " | " | " | " | " | " |
| 514,101 " 514,150 | 825 | " | Htg. | " | " | " | " | " | 10 |
| 514,151 " 514,500 | 835 | " | " | " | " | " | " | " | " |
| 514,501 " 514,600 | 930 | " | O. F. | " | " | " | " | " | 9 |
| 514,601 " 514,900 | 935 | " | " | " | " | " | " | " | " |
| 514,901 " 515,100 | 835 | " | Htg. | " | " | " | " | " | 10 |
| 515,101 " 515,400 | 935 | " | O. F. | " | " | " | " | " | 9 |
| 515,401 " 515,500 | 810 | " | Htg. | " | " | 21 | " | " | 10 |
| 515,501 " 515,600 | 910 | " | O. F. | " | " | " | " | " | 9 |
| 515,601 " 516,000 | 935 | " | " | " | " | 17 | " | " | " |
| 516,001 " 516,300 | 925 | " | " | " | " | " | " | " | " |
| 516,301 " 516,400 | 935 | " | " | " | " | " | " | " | " |
| 516,401 " 516,500 | 925 | " | " | " | " | " | " | " | " |
| 516,501 " 517,200 | 825 | " | Htg. | " | " | " | " | " | 10 |
| 517,201 " 519,300 | 910 | " | O. F. | " | " | 21 | " | " | 9 |
| 519,301 " 519,400 | 900 | " | " | " | " | 24 | " | " | " |
| 519,401 " 519,500 | 800 | " | Htg. | " | " | " | " | " | 10 |
| 519,501 " 519,600 | 805 | " | " | " | " | 21 | " | " | " |
| 519,601 " 519,700 | 905 | " | O. F. | " | " | " | " | " | 9 |
| 519,701 " 520,000 | 835 | " | Htg. | " | " | 17 | " | " | 10 |
| 520,001 " 521,000 | 935 | " | O. F. | " | " | " | " | " | 9 |
| 521,001 " 522,000 | 870 | " | Htg. | " | " | 7 | " | " | 10 |
| 522,001 " 522,400 | 970 | " | O. F. | " | " | " | " | " | 9 |
| 522,401 " 523,500 | 870 | " | Htg. | " | " | " | " | " | 10 |
| 523,501 " 524,800 | 970 | " | O. F. | " | " | " | " | " | 9 |
| 524,801 " 525,000 | 935 | " | " | " | " | 17 | " | " | " |
| 525,001 " 525,100 | 900 | " | " | " | " | 24 | " | " | " |
| 525,101 " 525,400 | 935 | " | " | " | " | 17 | " | " | " |
| 525,401 " 525,900 | 925 | " | " | " | " | " | " | " | " |
| 525,901 " 526,700 | 825 | " | Htg. | " | " | " | " | " | 10 |
| 526,701 " 526,900 | 930 | " | O. F. | " | " | " | " | " | 9 |
| 526,901 " 527,900 | 935 | " | " | " | " | " | " | " | " |
| 527,901 " 528,800 | 930 | " | " | " | " | " | " | " | " |
| 528,801 " 529,800 | 935 | " | " | " | " | " | " | " | " |
| 529,801 " 530,800 | 925 | " | " | " | " | " | " | " | " |
| 530,801 " 531,800 | 835 | " | Htg. | " | " | " | " | " | 10 |
| 531,801 " 532,450 | 825 | " | " | " | " | " | " | " | " |
| 532,451 " 532,500 | 835 | " | " | " | " | " | " | " | " |
| 532,501 " 533,400 | 925 | " | O. F. | " | " | " | " | " | 9 |
| 533,401 " 534,000 | 935 | " | " | " | " | " | " | " | " |
| 534,001 " 534,012 | 920 | " | " | " | " | " | " | " | 7 |
| 534,013 | 915 | " | " | " | " | " | " | " | " |
| 534,014 to 534,035 | 920 | " | " | " | " | " | " | " | " |
| 534,036 | 915 | " | " | " | " | " | " | " | " |
| 534,037 to 534,039 | 920 | " | " | " | " | " | " | " | " |
| 534,040 | 915 | " | " | " | " | " | " | " | " |
| 534,041 to 534,064 | 920 | " | " | " | " | " | " | " | " |
| 534,065 | 915 | " | " | " | " | " | " | " | " |
| 534,066 to 534,112 | 920 | " | " | " | " | " | " | " | " |
| 534,113 " 534,115 | 915 | " | " | " | " | " | " | " | " |
| 534,116 " 534,119 | 920 | " | " | " | " | " | " | " | " |
| 534,120 | 915 | " | " | " | " | " | " | " | " |
| 534,121 | 920 | " | " | " | " | " | " | " | " |
| 534,122 to 534,123 | 915 | " | " | " | " | " | " | " | " |
| 534,124 " 534,127 | 920 | " | " | " | " | " | " | " | " |
| 534,128 | 915 | " | " | " | " | " | " | " | " |
| 534,129 to 534,130 | 920 | " | " | " | " | " | " | " | " |
| 534,131 | 915 | " | " | " | " | " | " | " | " |
| 534,132 | 920 | " | " | " | " | " | " | " | " |
| 534,133 | 915 | " | " | " | " | " | " | " | " |
| 534,134 | 920 | " | " | " | " | " | " | " | " |
| 534,135 | 915 | " | " | " | " | " | " | " | " |
| 534,136 to 534,138 | 920 | " | " | " | " | " | " | " | " |
| 534,139 | 915 | " | " | " | " | " | " | " | " |
| 534,140 to 534,144 | 920 | " | " | " | " | " | " | " | " |
| 534,145 | 915 | " | " | " | " | " | " | " | " |
| 534,146 to 534,147 | 920 | " | " | " | " | " | " | " | " |
| 534,148 | 915 | " | " | " | " | " | " | " | " |

## The Rockford Watch Company, Ltd.

| Number and Grade of Movement | GRADE | Size | Style | | Jewels | Wind | Sett | Model |
|---|---|---|---|---|---|---|---|---|
| | | | | | | | | **Description of Movement** |
| 534,149 | 920 | 18 | O. F. | F. Pl. | Nickel | 17 | Stem | Lever | 7 |
| 534,150 | 915 | " | " | " | " | " | " | " | " |
| 534,151 to 534,155 | 920 | " | " | " | " | " | " | " | " |
| 534,156 " 534,157 | 915 | " | " | " | " | " | " | " | " |
| 534,158 " 534,163 | 920 | " | " | " | " | " | " | " | " |
| 534,164 | 915 | " | " | " | " | " | " | " | " |
| 534,165 to 534,171 | 920 | " | " | " | " | " | " | " | " |
| 534,172 | 915 | " | " | " | " | " | " | " | " |
| 534,173 | 920 | " | " | " | " | " | " | " | " |
| 534,174 | 915 | " | " | " | " | " | " | " | " |
| 534,175 | 920 | " | " | " | " | " | " | " | " |
| 534,176 to 534,179 | 915 | * | " | " | " | " | " | " | " |
| 534,180 " 534,182 | 920 | " | " | " | " | " | " | " | " |
| 534,183 | 915 | " | " | " | " | " | " | " | " |
| 534,184 | 920 | " | " | " | " | " | " | " | " |
| 534,185 | 915 | " | " | " | " | " | " | " | " |
| 534,186 to 534,188 | 920 | " | " | " | " | " | " | " | " |
| 534,189 | 915 | " | " | " | " | " | " | " | " |
| 534,190 to 534,196 | 920 | " | " | " | " | " | " | " | " |
| 534,197 | 915 | " | " | " | " | " | " | " | " |
| 534,198 | 920 | " | " | " | " | " | " | " | " |
| 534,199 | 915 | " | " | " | " | " | " | " | " |
| 534,200 | 920 | " | " | " | " | " | " | " | " |
| 534,401 to 534,600 | 930 | " | " | " | " | " | " | " | 9 |
| 534,601 " 535,200 | 910 | " | " | " | " | 21 | " | " | " |
| 535,201 " 535,400 | 900 | " | " | " | " | 24 | " | " | " |
| 535,401 " 535,600 | 910 | " | " | " | " | 21 | " | " | " |
| 535,601 " 535,700 | 800 | " | Htg. | " | " | 24 | " | " | 10 |
| 535,701 " 535,800 | 805 | " | " | " | " | 21 | " | " | " |
| 535,801 " 536,300 | 910 | " | O. F. | " | " | " | " | " | 9 |
| 536,301 " 536,600 | 930 | " | " | " | " | 17 | " | " | " |
| 536,601 " 536,700 | 945 | " | " | " | " | 21 | " | " | Special |
| 536,701 " 537,400 | 910 | " | " | " | " | " | " | " | 9 |
| 537,401 " 539,400 | 935 | " | " | " | " | 17 | " | " | " |
| 539,401 " 540,400 | 910 | " | " | " | " | 21 | " | " | " |
| 540,401 " 541,400 | 935 | " | " | " | " | 17 | " | " | " |
| 541,401 " 541,500 | 905 | " | " | " | " | 21 | " | " | " |
| 541,501 " 542,000 | 835 | " | Htg. | " | " | 17 | " | " | 10 |
| 542,001 " 542,300 | 800 | " | " | " | " | 24 | " | " | " |
| 542,301 " 542,500 | 810 | " | " | " | " | 21 | " | " | " |
| 542,501 " 542,700 | 900 | " | O. F. | " | " | 24 | " | " | 9 |
| 542,701 " 542,800 | 905 | " | " | " | " | 21 | " | " | " |
| 542,801 " 543,300 | 805 | " | Htg. | " | " | " | " | " | 10 |
| 543,301 " 543,500 | 905 | " | O. F. | " | " | " | " | " | 9 |
| 543,501 " 544,000 | 835 | " | Htg. | " | " | 17 | " | " | 10 |
| 544,001 " 544,100 | 560 | 16 | " | ¾ Pl. | " | " | " | " | 3 |
| 544,101 " 544,200 | 570 | " | " | " | " | " | " | " | " |
| 544,201 " 544,400 | 560 | " | " | " | " | " | " | " | " |
| 544,401 " 544,500 | 530 | " | " | " | " | 21 | " | " | " |
| 544,501 " 544,800 | 550 | " | " | " | " | 17 | " | " | 4 |
| 544,801 " 545,000 | 540 | " | " | " | " | 21 | " | " | " |
| 545,001 " 545,500 | 535 | " | O. F. | " | " | " | " | " | 2 |
| 545,501 " 546,500 | 570 | " | Htg. | " | " | 17 | " | " | 3 |
| 546,501 " 546,600 | 540 | " | " | " | " | 21 | " | " | 4 |
| 546,601 " 546,700 | 500 | " | " | " | " | " | " | " | " |
| 546,701 " 546,800 | 510 | " | " | " | " | " | " | " | " |
| 546,801 " 546,900 | 520 | " | " | " | " | " | " | " | " |
| 546,901 " 547,000 | 530 | " | " | " | " | " | " | " | 3 |
| 547,001 " 548,000 | 560 | " | " | " | " | 17 | " | " | " |
| 548,001 " 549,000 | 565 | " | O. F. | " | " | " | " | " | 2 |
| 549,001 " 550,000 | 575 | " | " | " | " | " | " | " | " |
| 550,001 " 550,500 | 560 | " | Htg. | " | " | " | " | " | 3 |
| 550,501 " 550,600 | 515 | " | O. F. | " | " | 21 | " | " | 5 |
| 550,601 " 550,700 | 525 | " | " | " | " | " | " | " | " |
| 550,701 " 550,900 | 545 | " | " | " | " | " | " | " | " |
| 550,901 " 551,200 | 555 | " | " | " | " | 17 | " | " | " |
| 551,201 " 551,700 | 530 | " | Htg. | " | " | 21 | " | " | 3 |
| 551,701 " 552,700 | 575 | " | O. F. | " | " | 17 | " | " | 2 |
| 552,701 " 553,200 | 565 | " | " | " | " | " | " | " | " |
| 553,201 " 554,200 | 570 | " | Htg. | " | " | " | " | " | 3 |
| 554,201 " 554,700 | 565 | " | O. F. | " | " | " | " | " | 2 |
| 554,701 " 554,900 | 555 | " | " | " | " | " | " | " | 5 |
| 554,901 " 554,920 | 535 | " | " | " | " | 21 | " | " | 2 |
| 554,921 " 554,927 | 570 | " | Htg. | " | " | " | " | " | 3 |
| 554,928 " 554,930 | 575 | " | O. F. | " | " | 17 | " | " | 2 |
| 554,931 " 554,940 | 560 | " | Htg. | " | " | " | " | " | 2 |
| 554,941 " 554,960 | 605 | " | O. F. | " | " | 11 | " | Pend. | Special |
| 554,961 | | " | " | " | Gilt | " | " | " | " |
| 554,962 | | " | " | " | " | " | " | " | " |
| 554,963 | | " | " | " | " | " | " | " | " |
| 554,964 | | " | Htg. | " | Nickel | 17 | " | " | " |
| 554,965 | | " | " | " | Gilt | " | " | " | " |
| 554,966 | | " | " | " | " | " | " | " | " |
| 554,967 | | " | " | " | Nickel | " | " | " | " |
| 554,968 | | " | " | " | Gilt | 15 | " | " | " |
| 554,699 | | " | O. F. | " | ......... | " | " | " | " |
| 554,970 | | " | " | " | ......... | " | " | " | " |
| 554,971 | | " | Htg. | " | ......... | " | " | " | " |
| 554,972 | | | " | " | ......... | " | " | " | " |

# The Rockford Watch Company, Ltd.

| Number and Grade of Movement | GRADE | Size | | Style | | Jewels | Wind | Sett | Model |
|---|---|---|---|---|---|---|---|---|---|
| 554,973 | | 16 | Htg. | ¾ Pl. | Gilt | 11 | Stem | Pend. | Special |
| 554,974 | 935 | 18 | O. F. | F. Pl. | Nickel | 17 | " | Lever | 9 |
| 554,975 | | 16 | Htg. | ¾ Pl. | Nickel | 11 | " | Pend. | Special |
| 554,976 | | " | " | " | | " | " | " | " |
| 554,977 | | " | " | " | | " | " | " | " |
| 554,978 | | " | O. F. | " | Nickel | 17 | " | " | " |
| 554,979 | | " | " | " | " | " | " | " | " |
| 554,981 to 554,992 | 25 | 18 | " | F. Pl. | " | 25 | " | Lever | " |
| 555,001 " 556,000 | 560 | 16 | Htg. | ¾ Pl. | " | 17 | " | " | 3 |
| 556,001 " 558,000 | 575 | " | O. F. | " | " | " | " | " | 2 |
| 558,001 " 558,500 | 550 | " | Htg. | " | " | " | " | " | 4 |
| 558,501 " 559,000 | 540 | " | " | " | " | 21 | " | " | " |
| 559,001 " 560,000 | 560 | " | " | " | " | 17 | " | " | 3 |
| 560,001 " 560,500 | 545 | " | O. F. | " | " | 21 | " | " | 5 |
| 560,501 " 561,000 | 555 | " | " | " | " | 17 | " | " | " |
| 561,001 " 562,000 | 835 | 18 | Htg. | F. Pl. | " | " | " | " | 10 |
| 562,001 " 563,000 | 935 | " | O. F. | " | " | " | " | " | 9 |
| 563,001 " 565,000 | 570 | 16 | Htg. | ¾ Pl. | " | " | " | " | 3 |
| 565,001 " 566,000 | 575 | " | O. F. | " | " | " | " | " | 2 |
| 566,001 " 566,500 | 918 | 18 | " | F. Pl. | " | 24 | " | " | 9 |
| 566,501 " 566,600 | 930 | " | " | " | " | 17 | " | " | " |
| 566,601 " 566,800 | 935 | " | " | " | " | " | " | " | " |
| 566,801 " 566,900 | 830 | " | Htg. | " | " | " | " | " | 10 |
| 566,901 " 566,940 | 500 | 16 | " | ¾ Pl. | " | 21 | " | " | 4 |
| 566,941 " 567,000 | 501 | " | " | " | " | " | " | " | " |
| 567,001 " 568,000 | 575 | " | O. F. | " | " | 17 | " | " | 2 |
| 568,001 " 570,000 | 570 | " | Htg. | " | " | " | " | " | 3 |
| 570,001 " 571,000 | 575 | " | O. F. | " | " | " | " | " | 2 |
| 571,001 " 571,300 | 545 | " | " | " | " | 21 | " | " | 5 |
| 571,301 " 571,500 | 575 | " | " | " | " | 17 | " | " | 2 |
| 571,501 " 571,530 | 505 | " | " | " | " | 21 | " | " | 5 |
| 571,531 " 571,600 | 515 | " | " | " | " | " | " | " | " |
| 571,601 " 571,700 | 570 | " | Htg. | " | " | 17 | " | " | 3 |
| 571,701 " 571,900 | 575 | " | O. F. | " | " | " | " | " | 2 |
| 571,901 " 572,000 | 585 | " | " | " | " | 15 | " | " | " |
| 572,001 " 572,700 | 565 | " | " | " | " | 17 | " | " | " |
| 572,701 " 573,000 | 560 | " | Htg. | " | " | " | " | " | 3 |
| 573,001 " 573,500 | 810 | 18 | " | F. Pl. | " | 21 | " | " | 10 |
| 573,501 " 573,510 | 590 | 16 | " | ¾ Pl. | " | 11 | " | " | 3 |
| 573,511 " 574,000 | 584 | " | " | " | " | 15 | " | " | " |
| 574,001 " 574,500 | 905 | 18 | O. F. | F. Pl. | " | 21 | " | " | 9 |
| 574,501 " 575,000 | 835 | " | Htg. | " | " | 17 | " | " | 10 |
| 575,001 " 577,000 | 570 | 16 | " | ¾ Pl. | " | " | " | " | 3 |
| 577,001 " 577,500 | 584 | " | " | " | " | 15 | " | " | " |
| 577,501 " 577,800 | 565 | " | O. F. | " | " | 17 | " | " | 2 |
| 577,801 " 577,900 | 520 | " | Htg. | " | " | 21 | " | " | 4 |
| 577,901 " 578,000 | 525 | " | O. F. | " | " | " | " | " | 5 |
| 578,001 " 579,150 | 835 | 18 | Htg. | F. Pl. | " | 17 | " | " | 10 |
| 579,201 " 579,370 | 935 | " | O. F. | " | " | " | " | " | 9 |
| 579,401 " 579,500 | 570 | 16 | Htg. | ¾ Pl. | " | " | " | " | 3 |
| 579,501 " 579,600 | 575 | " | O. F. | " | " | " | " | " | 2 |
| 579,601 " 579,700 | 560 | " | Htg. | " | " | " | " | " | 3 |
| 579,701 " 579,735 | 565 | " | O. F. | " | " | " | " | " | 2 |
| 579,801 " 579,900 | 830 | 18 | Htg. | F. Pl. | " | " | " | " | 10 |
| 579,901 " 580,000 | 930 | " | O. F. | " | " | " | " | " | 9 |
| 580,001 " 580,200 | 560 | 16 | Htg. | ¾ Pl. | " | " | " | " | 3 |
| 580,201 " 580,300 | 565 | " | O. F. | " | " | " | " | " | 2 |
| 580,301 " 580,500 | 570 | " | Htg. | " | " | " | " | " | 3 |
| 580,501 " 580,600 | 575 | " | O. F. | " | " | " | " | " | 2 |
| 580,601 " 581,000 | 930 | 18 | " | F. Pl. | " | " | " | " | 9 |
| 581,001 " 582,000 | 585 | 16 | " | ¾ Pl. | " | 15 | " | " | 2 |
| 582,001 " 583,000 | 584 | " | Htg. | " | " | " | " | " | 3 |
| 583,001 " 584,000 | 560 | " | " | " | " | 17 | " | " | " |
| 584,001 " 585,000 | 584 | " | " | " | " | 15 | " | " | " |
| 585,001 " 585,500 | 935 | 18 | O. F. | F. Pl. | " | 17 | " | " | 9 |
| 585,501 " 585,600 | 515 | 16 | " | ¾ Pl. | " | 21 | " | " | 5 |
| 585,601 " 585,700 | 525 | " | " | " | " | " | " | " | " |
| 585,701 " 585,800 | 830 | 18 | Htg. | F. Pl. | " | 17 | " | " | 10 |
| 585,801 " 585,900 | 930 | " | O. F. | " | " | " | " | " | 9 |
| 585,901 " 586,000 | 835 | " | Htg. | " | " | " | " | " | 10 |
| 586,001 " 588,000 | 584 | 16 | " | ¾ Pl. | " | 15 | " | " | 3 |
| 588,001 " 590,000 | 835 | 18 | " | F. Pl. | " | 17 | " | " | 10 |
| 590,001 " 591,000 | 570 | 16 | " | ¾ Pl. | " | " | " | " | 3 |
| 591,001 " 592,000 | 584 | " | " | " | " | 15 | " | " | " |
| 592,001 " 593,000 | 835 | 18 | " | F. Pl. | " | 17 | " | " | 10 |
| 593,001 " 593,100 | 560 | 16 | " | ¾ Pl. | " | " | " | " | 3 |
| 593,101 " 593,200 | 570 | " | " | " | " | " | " | " | " |
| 593,201 " 593,300 | 100 | " | " | " | " | 21 | " | Pend. | Special |
| 593,301 " 593,400 | 101 | " | O. F. | " | " | " | " | " | " |
| 593,401 " 593,600 | 925 | 18 | " | F. Pl. | " | 17 | " | Lever | 9 |
| 593,601 " 593,700 | 835 | " | Htg. | " | " | " | " | " | 10 |
| 593,701 " 593,800 | 825 | " | " | " | " | " | " | " | " |
| 593,801 " 593,900 | 520 | 16 | " | ¾ Pl. | " | 21 | " | " | 4 |
| 593,901 " 594,000 | 505 | " | O. F. | " | " | " | " | " | 5 |
| 594,001 " 596,000 | 590 | " | Htg. | " | " | 11 | " | Pend. | 3 |
| 596,001 " 597,000 | 595 | " | O. F. | " | " | " | " | " | 2 |
| 597,001 " 598,000 | 590 | " | Htg. | " | " | " | " | " | 3 |
| 598,001 " 599,000 | 586 | " | " | " | " | 15 | " | " | 5 |
| 599,001 " 599,500 | 587 | " | O. F. | " | " | " | " | " | 2 |

## The Rockford Watch Company, Ltd.

| Number and Grade of Movement | GRADE | Size | | Style | | Jewels | Wind | Sett | Model |
|---|---|---|---|---|---|---|---|---|---|
| 599,501 to 599,502 | 575 | 16 | O. F. | ¾ Pl. | Nickel | 17 | Stem | Lever | 2 |
| 599,503 " 599,504 | 565 | " | " | " | " | " | " | " | " |
| 599,505 | 575 | " | " | " | " | " | " | " | " |
| 599,506 to 600,000 | 587 | " | " | " | " | 15 | " | Pend. | " |
| 600,001 " 601,000 | 935 | 18 | " | F. Pl. | " | 17 | " | Lever | 9 |
| 601,001 " 602,000 | 590 | 16 | Htg. | ¾ Pl. | " | 11 | " | Pend. | 3 |
| 602,001 " 603,000 | 595 | " | O. F. | " | " | " | " | " | 2 |
| 603,001 " 605,000 | 561 | " | Htg. | " | " | 17 | " | " | 4 |
| 605,001 " 605,700 | 573 | " | O. F. | " | " | " | " | " | 5 |
| 605,701 " 605,850 | 845 | 18 | Htg. | F. Pl. | " | 21 | " | Lever | Special |
| 605,851 " 605,900 | 945 | " | O. F. | " | " | " | " | " | " |
| 605,901 " 605,950 | 540 | 16 | Htg. | ¾ Pl. | " | " | " | " | 4 |
| 606,001 " 608,000 | 935 | 18 | O. F. | F. Pl. | " | 17 | " | " | 9 |
| 608,001 " 609,000 | 572 | 16 | O. F. | ¾ Pl. | " | " | " | Pend. | 4 |
| 609,001 " 610,000 | 566 | " | O. F. | " | " | " | " | " | 5 |
| 610,001 " 613,000 | 605 | " | " | " | " | 11 | " | " | 2 |
| 613,001 " 614,000 | 587 | " | " | " | " | 15 | " | " | " |
| 614,001 " 615,000 | 600 | " | Htg. | " | " | 11 | " | " | 3 |
| 615,001 " 617,000 | 605 | " | O. F. | " | " | " | " | " | 2 |
| 617,001 " 617,500 | 586 | " | Htg. | " | " | 15 | " | " | 3 |
| 617,501 " 617,800 | 845 | 18 | | F. Pl. | " | 21 | " | Lever | Special |
| 617,801 " 618,000 | 810 | " | " | " | " | " | " | " | 10 |
| 618,001 " 618,500 | 587 | 16 | O. F. | ¾ Pl. | " | 15 | " | Pend. | 2 |
| 618,501 " 618,600 | 578 | " | Htg. | " | " | 17 | " | " | 3 |
| 618,601 " 618,700 | 579 | " | O. F. | " | " | " | " | " | 2 |
| 618,701 " 618,800 | 600 | " | Htg. | " | " | 11 | " | " | 3 |
| 618,801 " 618,900 | 586 | " | " | " | " | 15 | " | " | " |
| 618,901 " 618,950 | 120 | " | " | " | " | 17 | " | " | Special |
| 618,951 " 619,000 | 125 | " | O. F. | " | " | " | " | " | " |
| 619,001 " 619,300 | 525 | " | " | " | " | 21 | " | Lever | 5 |
| 619,301 " 619,700 | 600 | " | Htg. | " | " | 11 | " | Pend. | 3 |
| 619,701 " 619,900 | 565 | " | O. F. | " | " | 17 | " | Lever | " |
| 619,901 " 620,000 | 101 | " | " | " | " | 21 | " | Pend. | Special |
| 620,001 " 621,000 | 545 | " | " | " | " | " | " | Lever | 5 |
| 621,001 " 622,000 | 935 | 18 | " | F. Pl. | " | 17 | " | " | 9 |
| 622,001 " 622,300 | 160 | 0 | Htg. | ¾ Pl. | " | 15 | " | Pend. | 1 |
| 622,301 " 622,350 | 140 | " | " | " | " | 17 | " | " | " |
| 622,351 " 622,500 | 150 | " | " | " | " | " | " | " | " |
| 622,501 " 623,000 | 160 | " | " | " | " | 15 | " | " | " |
| 623,001 " 623,100 | 200 | 18 | O. F. | F. Pl. | " | 17 | " | Lever | 10 |
| 623,101 " 623,500 | 605 | 16 | " | ¾ Pl. | " | 11 | " | Pend. | 2 |
| 623,501 " 624,000 | 160 | 0 | Htg. | " | " | 15 | " | " | 1 |
| 624,001 " 624,200 | 205 | 18 | O. F. | F. Pl. | " | 17 | " | Lever | 10 |
| 624,201 " 624,300 | 945 | " | " | " | " | 21 | " | " | Special |
| 624,301 " 624,400 | 930 | " | " | " | " | 17 | " | " | 9 |
| 624,401 " 624,450 | 110 | 16 | Htg. | ¾ Pl. | " | " | " | Pend. | Special |
| 624,451 " 624,500 | 115 | " | O. F. | " | " | " | " | " | " |
| 624,501 " 624,525 | 130 | " | Htg. | " | Gilt | " | " | " | " |
| 624,526 " 624,550 | 135 | " | O. F. | " | " | " | " | " | " |
| 624,601 " 624,800 | 540 | " | Htg. | " | Nickel | 21 | " | Lever | 4 |
| 625,001 " 625,400 | 400 | " | " | " | " | 17 | " | Pend. | " |
| 626,001 " 626,200 | 405 | " | " | " | " | 21 | " | " | 5 |
| 626,201 " 626,400 | 510 | " | " | " | " | " | " | Lever | 4 |
| 626,401 " 626,600 | 515 | " | O. F. | " | " | " | " | " | 5 |
| 626,601 " 626,700 | 520 | " | Htg. | " | " | " | " | " | 4 |
| 626,701 " 626,900 | 525 | " | O. F. | " | " | " | " | " | 5 |
| 626,901 " 627,000 | 845 | 18 | Htg. | F. Pl. | " | " | " | " | Special |
| 627,001 " 627,300 | 572 | 16 | | ¾ Pl. | " | 17 | " | Pend. | 4 |
| 628,001 " 628,100 | 500 | " | " | " | " | 21 | " | Lever | " |
| 628,101 " 628,300 | 520 | " | " | " | " | " | " | " | " |
| 628,301 " 628,500 | 515 | " | O. F. | " | " | " | " | " | 5 |
| 628,501 " 628,600 | 505 | " | " | " | " | " | " | " | 5 |
| 628,601 " 628,800 | 510 | " | Htg. | " | " | " | " | " | 4 |
| 628,801 " 628,950 | 100 | " | " | " | " | " | " | Pend. | Special |
| 628,951 " 629,000 | 101 | " | O. F. | " | " | " | " | " | " |
| 629,001 " 630,000 | 935 | 18 | " | F. Pl. | " | 17 | " | Lever | 9 |
| 630,001 " 630,600 | 835 | " | Htg. | " | " | " | " | " | 10 |
| 630,601 " 630,700 | 162 | 0 | " | ¾ Pl. | " | " | " | Pend. | 1 |
| 630,701 " 630,800 | 150 | " | " | " | " | " | " | " | " |
| 630,801 " 631,000 | 160 | " | " | " | " | 15 | " | " | " |
| 631,001 " 632,000 | 586 | 16 | " | " | " | " | " | " | 3 |
| 632,001 " 632,500 | 825 | 18 | " | F. Pl. | " | 17 | " | Lever | 10 |
| 633,001 " 633,500 | 925 | " | O. F. | " | " | " | " | " | 9 |
| 634,001 " 635,000 | 587 | 16 | " | ¾ Pl. | " | 15 | " | Pend. | 2 |
| 635,001 " 636,000 | 935 | 18 | " | F. Pl. | " | 17 | " | Lever | 9 |
| 636,001 " 636,500 | 160 | 0 | Htg. | ¾ Pl. | " | 15 | " | Pend. | 1 |
| 636,501 " 636,600 | 150 | " | " | " | " | 17 | " | " | " |
| 636,601 " 638,000 | 160 | " | " | " | " | 15 | " | " | " |
| 638,001 " 639,000 | 600 | 16 | " | " | " | 11 | " | " | 3 |
| 639,001 " 640,000 | 160 | 0 | " | " | " | 15 | " | Pend. | 1 |
| 640,001 " 641,000 | 162 | " | " | " | " | " | " | " | " |
| 641,001 " 642,000 | 610 | 16 | " | " | " | 7 | " | " | Special |
| 642,001 " 643,000 | 615 | " | O. F. | " | " | " | " | " | 3 |
| 643,001 " 644,000 | 587 | " | " | " | " | 15 | " | " | 2 |
| 644,001 " 644,500 | 142 | 0 | Htg. | " | " | 17 | " | " | " |
| 645,001 " 646,600 | 162 | " | " | " | " | 15 | " | " | 1 |
| 646,001 " 647,000 | 610 | 16 | " | " | " | 7 | " | " | Special |
| 647,001 " 648,000 | 615 | " | O. F. | " | " | " | " | " | 3 |
| 648,001 " 649,000 | 160 | 0 | Htg. | " | " | 15 | " | Pend. | 1 |
| 649,001 " 650,000 | 605 | 16 | O. F. | " | " | 11 | " | " | 2 |

## The Rockford Watch Company, Ltd.

| Number and Grade of Movement | GRADE | Size | | Style | | Jewels | Wind | Sett | Model |
|---|---|---|---|---|---|---|---|---|---|
| | | | | Description of Movement | | | | | |
| 650,001 " 651,000 | 573 | 16 | O. F. | ¾ Pl. | Nickel | 17 | Stem | Pend. | 5 |
| 651,001 to 656,000 | 160 | 0 | Htg. | " | " | 15 | " | " | 1 |
| 656,001 " 656,100 | 152 | " | " | " | " | 17 | " | " | Special |
| 657,001 " 657,200 | 182 | " | " | " | " | 7 | " | " | " |
| 658,001 " 659,000 | 600 | 16 | " | " | " | 11 | " | " | 3 |
| 659,001 " 659,200 | 930 | 18 | O. F. | F. Pl. | " | 17 | " | Lever | 9 |
| 660,001 " 660,100 | 910 | " | " | " | " | 21 | " | " | " |
| 661,101 " 661,200 | 810 | " | Htg. | " | " | " | " | " | 10 |
| 662,001 " 662,600 | 100 | 16 | " | ¾ Pl. | " | " | " | Pend. | Special |
| 663,001 " 663,100 | 101 | " | O. F. | " | " | " | " | " | " |
| 664,001 " 664,100 | 845 | 18 | Htg. | F. Pl. | " | " | " | Lever | " |
| 665,001 " 665,100 | 830 | " | " | " | " | 17 | " | " | 10 |
| 666,001 " 666,100 | 900 | " | O. F. | " | " | 24 | " | " | 9 |
| 667,001 " 667,100 | 905 | " | " | " | " | 21 | " | " | " |
| 668,001 " 669,000 | 605 | 16 | " | ¾ Pl. | " | 11 | " | Pend. | 2 |
| 669,001 " 669,100 | 912 | 18 | " | F. Pl. | Spot Gilt | 21 | " | Lever | 9 |
| 670,001 " 670,100 | 537 | 16 | " | ¾ Pl. | " | " | " | " | 2 |
| 671,001 " 671,300 | 200 | 18 | " | F. Pl. | Nickel | 17 | " | " | 10 |
| 672,001 " 673,000 | 205 | " | " | " | " | " | " | " | " |
| 674,001 " 675,000 | 405 | 16 | " | ¾ Pl. | " | " | " | Pend. | 5 |
| 675,001 " 675,500 | 525 | " | " | " | " | 21 | " | Lever | " |
| 676,001 " 677,000 | 566 | " | " | " | " | 17 | " | Pend. | " |
| 677,001 " 678,000 | 573 | " | " | " | " | " | " | " | 3 |
| 678,001 " 678,500 | 586 | " | " | " | " | 15 | " | " | 2 |
| 679,001 " 680,500 | 587 | " | " | " | " | " | " | " | 3 |
| 681,001 " 682,000 | 600 | " | Htg. | " | " | 11 | " | " | 2 |
| 682,001 " 686,000 | 605 | " | O. F. | " | " | " | " | " | " |
| 686,001 " 693,000 | 615 | " | " | " | " | 7 | " | " | " |
| 693,001 " 694,000 | 610 | " | Htg. | " | " | " | " | " | 3 |
| 694,001 " 694,500 | 935 | 18 | O. F. | F. Pl. | " | 17 | " | Lever | 9 |
| 695,001 " 695,500 | 945 | " | " | " | " | 21 | " | " | Special |

## STYLE & NAMES OF U.S.A. HANDS

Cresent    Light Spade    HR. Spade, Min. Whip    Ex. Heavy Spade

Moon    Breguet Moon    Diamond    Open Diamond

Louis XIV    Louis XIV    Gothic    Kite

Triangle    Open Square    Cross Bar Diamond    Double Hour

Whip    Demi-Hunter    Skeleton    Luminous

Cathedral    Morning Glory Open    Morning Glory    Fleur de Lis

SERIAL NUMBER - GRADE, Size, Style, Jewels, MODEL

695501-696000=945,18S.O.F.21J,M#SP.
696001-697000=838,18S.H.C.17J,M#10
697001-698000=938,18S.O.F.17J,M# 9
698001-699000=150, 0S. H.C.17J,M# 1
699001-700000=140, 0S. H.C.17J,M# 1
700001-702100=180, 0S. H.C. 7J,M# 1
702101-703000=160, 0S. H.C.15J,M# 1
703001-703500=170, 0S. H.C.17J,M# 1
703501-704000=160, 0S. H.C.15J,M# 1
704001-704300=935,18S.O.F.17J,M# 9
704301-704400=930,18S.O.F.17J,M# 9
704401-704500=935,18S.O.F.17J,M# 9
704501-704600=930,18S.O.F.17J,M# 9
704601-705000=935,18S.O.F.17J,M# 9
705001-706000=572,16S.H.C.17J,M# 4
706001-707000=600,16S.H.C.11J,M# 3
707001-708000=918,16S.O.F.21J,M# 9
708001-709000=586,16S.H.C.15J,M# 4
709001-710000=587,16S.O.F.15J,M# 3
710001-710100=930,18S.O.F.17J,M# 9
710101-710600=935,18S.O.F.17J,M# 9
710601-710700=930,18S.O.F.17J,M# 9
710701-711000=935,18S.O.F.17J,M# 9
711001-711100=830,18S.H.C.17J,M# 9
711101-711500=835,18S.H.C.17J,M#10
711501-711600=830,18S.H.C.17J,M#10
711601-712000=835,18S.H.C.17J,M#10
712001-712700=573,16S.O.F.17J,M# 5
712701-713000=635,16S.O.F.17J,M# 5
713001-714000=610,16S.O.F. 7J,M#SP.
714001-715000=572,16S.H.C.17J,M# 4
715001-716000=586,16S.O.F.15J,M# 3
716001-717000=587,16S.O.F.15J,M# 2
717001-718000=600,16S.O.F.11J,M# 3
718001-719000=605,16S.O.F.11J,M# 2
719001-720000=615,16S.O.F. 7J,M# 3
720001-721000=610,16S.O.F. 7J,M#SP.
721001-721500=600,16S.H.C.11J,M# 3
721501-722000=586,16S.H.C.15J,M# 3
722501-722700=573,16S.O.F.17J,M# 5
722701-722800=635,16S.O.F.17J,M# 5
722801-722900=573,16S.O.F.17J,M# 5
722901-723000=635,16S.O.F.17J,M# 5
723001-724000=935,18S.O.F.17J,M#10
724001-725000=205,18S.O.F.17J,M# 9
724501-725100=930,18S.O.F.17J,M# 9
725101-726000=935,18S.O.F.17J,M# 9
726001-727000=405,16S.O.F.17J,M# 5
727001-728000=587,16S.O.F.15J,M# 2
728001-728500=573,16S.O.F.17J,M# 5
728501-728600=635,16S.O.F.17J,M# 5
728601-728800=573,16S.O.F.17J,M# 5
728801-729000=635,16S.O.F.17J,M# 5
729001-729800=600,16S.H.C.11J,M# 3
729801-730000=586,16S.O.F.15J,M# 3
730001-730700=610,16S.O.F. 7J,M#SP.
730701-731000=586,16S.O.F.15J,M# 3
731001-732000=615,16S.O.F. 7J,M# 3
732001-732500=162, 0S.H.C.17J,M# 1
732501-733000=150, 0S.H.C.17J,M# 1
733001-734000=572, 6S.H.C.17J,M# 4
734001-735000=586,16S.O.F.15J,M# 2
735001-735200=610,16S.H.C. 7J,M#SP.
735201-736000=586,16S.O.F.15J,M# 2
736001-738000=935,18S.O.F.17J,M# 9
738001-739000=938,18S.O.F.17J,M#10
739001-740000=925,18S.O.F.17J,M# 9
740001-740200=830,18S.H.C.17J,M#10
740201-741000=835,18S.H.C.17J,M#10
741001-741100=600,16S.H.C.17J,M# 3
741101-742000=586,16S.H.C.15J,M# 3
742001-742500=605,16S.O.F.11J,M# 2
742501-743000=587,16S,O,F.15J,M# 2
743001-745000=935,18S.O.F.17J,M# 9
745001-746000=930,18S.O.F.17J,M# 9
746001-747000=586,16S.O.F.15J,M# 2
747001-748000=935,18S.O.F.17J,M# 9
748001-749000=938,18S.O.F.17J,M#10
749001-749600=572,16S.H.C.17J,M# 4
749601-750000=630,16S.H.C.17J,M# 4
750001-750200=573,16S.O.F.17J,M# 5
750201-750600=635,16S.O.F.17J,M# 5
750601-751000=573,16S.O.F.17J,M# 5
751001-751200=605,16S.O.F.15J,M# 2
752001-752100=572,16S.H.C.17J,M# 4
752101-752200=630,16S.H.C.17J,M# 4
752201-753000=572,16S.H.C.17J,M# 4
753001-754000=573,16S.H.C.17J,M# 5
754001-755000=586,16S.H.C.15J,M# 3
755001-756000=587,16S.O.F.15J,M# 2
756001-757000=935,18S.O.F.17J,M# 9
757001-758000=925,18S.O.F.17J,M# 9
758001-759000=150, 0S.H.C.17J,M# 1
759001-759500=572,16S.H.C.17J,M# 4

759501-756000=620,16S.H.C.21J,M# 5
760001-760500=573,16S.O.F.17J,M# 5
760501-761000=625,16S.O.F.21J,M# 5
761001-762000=160, 0S.H.C.15J,M# 1
762001-762500=400,16S.H.C.17J,M# 4
762501-764000=405,16S.O.F.17J,M# 5
764001-765000=205,18S.O.F.17J,M#10
765001-765500=515,16S.O.F.21J,M# 5
765501-766000=545,16S.O.F.21J,M# 5
766010-767000=930,18S.O.F.17J,M# 9
767001-768000=572,16S.H.C.17J,M# 4
768001-769000=935,18S.O.F.17J,M# 9
769001-770000=918,18S.O.F.21J,M#10
770001-770500=938,18S.O.F.17J,M#10
770501-771000=835,18S.H.C.17J,M#10
771001-772000=586,16S.O.F.15J,M# 3
772001-772100=320,12S.H.C.17J,M# 1
772001-772200=330,12S.H.C.17J,M# 1
772201-772300=310,12S.H.C.21J,M# 1
772301-772400=300,12S.O.F.23J,M# 1
772401-772600=325,12S.O.F.17J,M# 2
772601-772800=335,12S.O.F.17J,M# 2
772801-772900=315,12S.O.F.21J,M# 2
772901-773000=305,12S.O.F.23J,M# 2
773001-773100=300,12S.H.C.23J,M# 1
773101-773200=310,12S.H.C.21J,M# 1
773201-773400=320,12S.H.C.17J,M# 1
773401-773500=305,12S.O.F.23J,M# 2
773501-773600=315,12S.O.F.21J,M# 2
773601-773800=325,12S.O.F.17J,M# 2
773801-774000=330,12S.H.C.17J,M# 1
774001-774500=335,12S.O.F.17J,M# 2
774501-774700=325,12S.O.F.17J,M# 2
774701-774000=330,12S.H.C.17J,M# 1
774901-775000=320,12S.H.C.17J,M# 1
775001-776000=587,16S.O.F.15J,M# 2
776001-777000=630,16S.H.C.17J,M# 5
777001-778000=635,16S.O.F.17J,M# 5
778001-779000=838,18S.H.C.17J,M#10
779001-779500=938,18S.H.C.17J,M#10
779501-780000=935,18S.O.F.17J,M# 9
780001-781000=835,18S.H.C.17J,M#10
781001-782000=545,16S.O.F.21J,M# 5
782001-783000=404,16S.O.F.17J,M# 5
783001-784000=561,16S.H.C.17J,M# 4
784001-785000=930,18S.O.F.17J,M# 9
785001-786000=205,18S.O.F.17J,M# 9
786001-787000=935,18S.O.F.17J,M# 9
787001-787200=310,12S.H.C.21J,M# 1
787201-788000=335,12S.O.F.17J,M# 2
788001-788100=315,12S.O.F.21J,M# 2
788101-789000=335,12S.O.F.17J,M# 2
789001-789100=330,12S.O.F.17J,M# 1
789001-789500=320,12S.H.C.17J,M# 1
789501-790000=330,12S.H.C.17J,M3 1
790001-791000=325,12S.O.F.17J,M# 2
791001-792000=330,12S.H.C.17J,M# 1
792001-792900=335,12S.O.F.17J,M# 2
722901-793000=355,12S.O.F.17J,M# 2
793001-796000=935,18S.O.F.17J,M# 9
796001-797000=930,18S.O.F.17J,M# 9
797001-798000=938,18S.O.F.17J,M# 9
798001-799000=830,18S.H.C.17J,M# 8
799001-800000=587,16S.O.F.15J,M# 2
800001-801000=572,16S.H.C.17J,M# 4
801001-802000=573,16S.O.F.17J,M# 5
802001-802500=573,16S.O.F.17J,M# 5
802501-803000=566,16S.O.F.17J,M# 5
803001-804000=573,16S.O.F.17J,M# 5
804001-805000=150, 0S.H.C.17J,M# 1
805001-806000=335,12S.O.F.17J,M# 2
806001-806100=300,12S.H.C.23J,M# 1
806101-807000=335,12S.O.F.17J,M# 2
807001-807100=305,12S.O.F.23J,M# 2
807101-808000=335,12S.O.F.17J,M# 2
808001-810000=573,16S.O.F.17J,M# 5
810001-811000=572,16S,H.C.17J,M# 4
811001-811200=160, 0S.H.C.15J,M# 1
811201-813000=330,12S.H.C.17J,M# 1
813001-814000=355,12S.O.F.17J,M# 2
814001-814500=350,12S.H.C.17J,M# 1
814501-814600=345,12S.H.C.21J,M# 1
814601-814700=340,12S.O.F.21J,M# 2
814701-815000=350,12S.H.C.17J,M# 1
815001-816000=335,12S.O.F.17J,M# 2
816001-817000=190, 0S.H.C.15J,M# 1
817001-818000=185 0S.H.C.17J,M# 1
818001-819000=335,12S.O.F.17J,M# 2
819001-820000=355,12S.O.F.17J,M# 2
820001-821000=190, 0S.H.C.15J,M# 1
821001-822000=335,12S.O.F.17J,M# 1
822001-823000=350,12S.H.C.17J,M# 1
823001-824000=330,12S.H.C.17J,M# 1

SERIAL NUMBER - GRADE, Size, Style, Jewels, MODEL

695505-696000=945,18S.O.F.21J.
696001-697000=838,18S.H.C.17J.
697001-698000=938,18S.O.F.17J.
698001-699000=150, 0S. H.C.17J.
699001-700000=140, 0S. H.C.17J.
700001-702100=180, 0S. H.C. 7J.
702101-703000=160, 0S. H.C.15J.
703001-703500=170, 0S. H.C.11J.
703501-704000=160, 0S. H.C.15J.
704001-704300=935,18S.O.F.17J.
704301-704400=930,18S.O.F.17J.
704401-704500=935,18S.O.F.17J.
704501-704600=930,18S.O.F.17J.
704601-705000=935,18S.O.F.17J.
705001-706000=572,16S.H.C.17J.
706001-707000=600,16S.H.C.11J.
707001-708000=918,18S.O.F.21J.
708001-709000=586,16S.H.C.15J.
709001-710000=587,18S.O.F.15J.
710001-710100=930,18S.O.F.17J.
710101-710600=935,18S.O.F.17J.
710601-710700=930,18S.O.F.17J.
710701-711000=935,18S.O.F.17J.
711001-711100=830,18S.H.C.17J.
711101-711500=835,18S.H.C.17J.
711501-711600=830,18S.H.C.17J.
711601-712000=835,18S.H.C.17J.
712001-712700=573,16S.O.F.17J.
712701-713000=635,16S.O.F.17J.
713001-714000=610,16S.O.F. 7J.
714001-715000=572,16S.H.C.17J.
715001-716000=586,16S.O.F.15J.
716001-717000=587,16S.O.F.15J.
717001-718000=600,16S.O.F.11J.
718001-719000=605,16S.O.F.11J.
719001-720000=615,16S.O.F. 7J.
720001-721000=610,16S.O.F. 7J.
721001-721500=600,16S.H.C.11J.
721501-722000=586,16S.H.C.15J.
722501-722700=573,16S.O.F.17J.
722701-722800=635,16S.O.F.17J.
722801-722900=573,16S.O.F.17J.
722901-723000=635,16S.O.F.17J.
723001-724000=935,18S.O.F.17J.
724001-725000=205,18S.O.F.17J.
725001-725100=930,18S.O.F.17J.
725101-726000=935,18S.O.F.17J.
726001-727000=405,18S.O.F.17J.
727001-728000=587,16S.O.F.15J.
728001-728500=573,16S.O.F.17J.
728501-728600=635,16S.O.F.17J.
728601-728800=573,16S.O.F.17J.
728801-729000=635,16S.O.F.17J.
729001-729800=600,16S.H.C.11J.
729801-730000=586,16S.O.F.15J.
730001-730700=610,16S.O.F.17J.
730701-731000=586,16S.O.F.15J.
731001-732000=615,16S.O.F. 7J.
732001-732500=162, 0S.H.C.17J.
732501-733000=150, 0S.H.C.17J.
733001-734000=572, 6S.H.C.17J.
734001-735000=586,16S.O.F.15J.
735001-735200=610,16S.H.C. 7J.
735201-736000=586,16S.H.C.15J.
736001-738000=935,18S.O.F.17J.
738001-739000=938,18S.O.F.17J.
739001-740000=925,18S.O.F.17J.
740001-740200=830,18S.H.C.17J.
740201-741000=835,18S.O.F.17J.
741001-741100=600,16S.H.C.11J.
741101-742000=586,16S.H.C.15J.
742001-742500=605,16S.O.F.11J.
742501-743000=587,16S.O,F.15J.
743001-745000=935,18S.O.F.17J.
745001-746000=930,18S.O.F.17J.
746001-747000=586,16S.O.F.15J.
747001-748000=935,18S.O.F.17J.
748001-749000=938,18S.O.F.17J.
749001-749600=572,16S.H.C.17J.
749601-750000=630,16S.H.C.17J.
750001-750200=573,16S.O.F.17J.
750201-750600=635,16S.O.F.17J.
750601-751000=573,16S.O.F.17J.
751001-751200=605,16S.O.F.15J.
751201-752100=572,16S.H.C.17J.
752101-752200=605,16S.H.C.17J.
752201-753000=572,16S.H.C.17J.
753001-754000=573,16S.O.F.17J.
754001-755000=586,16S.H.C.15J.
755001-756000=587,16S.O.F.15J.
756001-757000=935,18S.O.F.17J.
757001-758000=925,18S.O.F.17J.
758001-759000=150, 0S.H.C.17J.
759001-759500=572,16S.H.C.17J.

SERIAL NUMBER - GRADE, Size, Style, Jewels, MODEL

759501-756000=620,16S.H.C.21J.
760001-760500=573,16S.O.F.17J.
760501-761000=625,16S.O.F.21J.
761001-762000=160, 0S.H.C.15J.
762001-762500=400,16S.H.C.17J.
762501-764000=405,16S.O.F.17J.
764001-765000=205,18S.O.F.17J.
765001-765500=515,16S.O.F.21J.
765501-766000=545,16S.O.F.21J.
760010-767000=930,18S.O.F.17J.
767001-768000=572,16S.H.C.17J.
768001-769000=935,18S.O.F.17J.
769001-770000=918,18S.O.F.21J.
770001-770500=938,18S.O.F.17J.
770501-771000=835,18S.H.C.17J.
771001-772000=586,16S.O.F.15J.
772001-772100=320,12S.H.C.17J.
772001-772200=330,12S.O.F.17J.
772201-772300=310,12S.H.C.21J.
772301-772400=300,12S.H.C.23J.
772401-772600=325,12S.O.F.17J.
772601-772800=335,12S.O.F.17J.
772801-772900=315,12S.O.F.21J.
772901-773000=305,12S.O.F.23J.
773001-773100=300,12S.H.C.23J.
773101-773200=310,12S.H.C.21J.
773201-773400=320,12S.H.C.17J.
773401-773500=305,12S.O.F.23J.
773501-773600=315,12S.O.F.21J.
773601-773800=325,12S.O.F.17J.
773801-774000=330,12S.H.C.17J.
774001-774500=335,12S.O.F.17J.
774501-774700=325,12S.O.F.17J.
774701-774000=330,12S.H.C.17J.
774901-775000=320,12S.H.C.17J.
775001-776000=587,16S.O.F.15J.
776001-777000=630,16S.H.C.17J.
777001-778000=635,16S.O.F.17J.
778001-779000=838,18S.H.C.17J.
779001-779500=938,18S.H.C.17J.
779501-780000=935,18S.O.F.17J.
780001-781000=835,18S.H.C.17J.
781001-782000=545,16S.O.F.21J.
782001-783000=404,16S.O.F.17J.
783001-784000=561,16S.H.C.17J.
784001-785000=930,18S.O.F.17J.
785001-786000=205,18S.O.F.17J.
786001-787000=935,18S.O.F.17J.
787001-787200=310,12S.H.C.21J.
787201-788000=335,12S.O.F.17J.
788001-788100=315,12S.O.F.21J.
788101-789000=335,12S.O.F.17J.
789001-789100=335,12S.H.C.17J.
789001-789500=320,12S.H.C.17J.
789501-790000=330,12S.H.C.17J.
790001-791000=325,12S.O.F.17J.
791001-792000=330,12S.O.F.17J.
792001-792900=335,12S.O.F.17J.
722901-793000=355,12S.O.F.17J.
793001-796000=935,18S.O.F.17J.
796001-797000=930,18S.O.F.17J.
797001-798000=938,18S.O.F.17J.
798001-799000=830,18S.H.C.17J.
799001-800000=587,16S.O.F.15J.
800001-801000=572,16S.H.C.17J.
801001-802000=573,16S.O.F.17J.
802001-802500=573,16S.O.F.17J.
802501-803000=566,16S.O.F.17J.
803001-804000=573,16S.O.F.17J.
804001-805000=150, 0S.H.C.17J.
805001-806000=335,12S.O.F.17J.
806001-806100=300,12S.H.C.23J.
806101-807000=335,12S.O.F.17J.
807001-807100=305,12S.O.F.23J.
807101-808000=335,12S.O.F.17J.
808001-810000=573,16S.O.F.17J.
810001-811000=572,16S.H.C.17J.
811001-812000=160, 0S.H.C.15J.
812001-813000=330,12S.H.C.17J.
813001-814000=355,12S.O.F.17J.
814001-814500=350,12S.H.C.17J.
814501-814600=345,12S.H.C.21J.
814601-814700=340,12S.O.F.21J.
814701-815000=350,12S.H.C.17J.
815001-816000=335,12S.O.F.17J.
816001-817000=190, 0S.H.C.15J.
817001-818000=185 OS.H.C.17J.
818001-819000=335,12S.O.F.17J.
819001-820000=355,12S.O.F.17J.
820001-821000=190, 0S.H.C.15J.
821001-822000=335,12S.H.C.17J.
822001-823000=350,12S.H.C.17J.
823001-824000=330,12S.H.C.17J.

**Model 1**, 18 size, full plate, hunting, key wind & set.

**Model 2**, 18 size, full plate, hunting, lever set.

**Model 3**, 18 size, full plate, hunting, lever set.

**Model 4**, 18 size, full plate, open face, lever set.

**Model 5**, 18 size, three-quarter plate, hunting, lever set.

**Model 6**, 18 size, full plate, hunting, lever set, exposed escapement.

**Model 7**, 18 size, full plate, open face, lever set.

**Model 8**, 18 size, full plate, hunting, lever set.

**Model 9**, 18 size, full plate, open face, lever set.

**Model 10**, 18 size, full plate, hunting, lever set.

**Model 1**, 16 size, three-quarter plate, hunting, lever set.

**Model 2**, 16 size, three-quarter plate, open face, pendant & lever set.

Model 3, 16 size, three-quarter plate, hunting, pendant & lever set.

Model 4, 16 size, three-quarter plate, bridge, hunting, pendant & lever set.

Model 5, 16 size, three-quarter plate, bridge, open face, pendant & lever set.

Model 1, 12 size, three-quarter plate bridge, hunting, pendant set.

Model 2, 12 size, three-quarter plate bridge, open face, pendant set.

Model 1, 6 & 8 size, three-quarter plate, hunting, lever set.

Model 2, 6 size, three-quarter plate, hunting, lever set.

Model 1, 0 size, three-quarter plate, bridge, hunting, pendant set.

Model 2, 0 size, three-quarter plate, bridge, open face, pendant set.

354

# SAN JOSE WATCH CO.
### California 1891

Very few watches were made by the San Jose Watch Co., and very little is known about them. The company purchased the Otay Watch Company and machinery and remaining watch movements. The San Jose Watch Co. produced about a dozen watches. Engraved on a San Jose Watch Co. movement S# 30,656 (First watch manufactured by San Jose Watch Co. November 1891).

| Grade or Name – Description | | Avg | Ex-Fn | Mint |
|---|---|---|---|---|
| 18S, 15J, LS, SW | ★★★★ | $1,500 | $2,000 | $2,500 |

SAN JOSE WATCH CO. movement 18 size 15 jewels, Otay W. Co. material & machinery used to produce movement.

M.S. Smith & Co. movement, 18 size, 19 jewels, three-quarter plate, key wind & set.

# M. S. SMITH & CO.
### Detroit, Michigan 1870 - 1874

Eber B. Ward purchased the M. S. Smith & Co. which was a large jewelry firm. These watches carried the Smith name on them. A Mr. Hoyt was engaged to produce these watches and about 100 were produced before the Freeport Watch Co. purchased the firm. These watches are very similar to the J.H.Allison movements.

| Grade or Name – Description | | Avg | Ex-Fn | Mint |
|---|---|---|---|---|
| 18S, 19J, 3/4, KW, KS, Freeport Model, 18K case | ★★★ | $2,500 | $3,000 | $3,600 |
| 18S, 19J, 3/4, KW, KS, Freeport Model | ★★★ | 1,200 | 1,500 | 2,300 |
| 18S, 15J, 3/4, wolf's tooth -wind, Swiss, 14K HC | ★ | 800 | 900 | 1,100 |
| 6S, 15J, KW, KS, HC 18K case | ★ | 700 | 800 | 1,000 |
| 6S, 15J, SW | ★ | 400 | 500 | 700 |

M. S. Smith & Co., 18S, 15J, 3/4, wolf's tooth -wind, Swiss, Ca. 1874.

M. S. Smith, 6-8 size, 15 jewels, KW KS, Swiss, 18K HC, Ca. 1870.

# SOUTH BEND WATCH CO.

### South Bend, Indiana
### March 1903 - December 1929

Three brothers, George, Clement and J. M. Studebaker, purchased the successful Columbus Watch Co. The first South Bend watches were full plate and similar to the Columbus watches. The serial numbers started at 380,501 where as the Columbus serial numbers stopped at about 500,000. The highest grade watch was a "Polaris," a 16S, 3/4 plate, 21 jewels, and with an open face. This watch sold for about $100. The 227 and 229 were also high grade. The company identified its movements by model numbers 1, 2, and 3, and had grades from 100 to 431. The even numbers were hunting cases, and the odd numbers were open-faced cases. The lowest grade was a 203, 7J, that sold for about $6.75. The company closed on Dec. 31, 1929.

## SOUTH BEND ESTIMATED SERIAL NUMBERS
## AND PRODUCTION DATES

| DATE – SERIAL NO. | DATE – SERIAL NO. | DATE – SERIAL NO. | DATE – SERIAL NO. |
|---|---|---|---|
| 1903 – 380,501 | 1910 – 620,000 | 1917 – 865,000 | 1924 – 1,110,000 |
| 1904 – 410,000 | 1911 – 655,000 | 1918 – 900,000 | 1925 – 1,145,000 |
| 1905 – 445,000 | 1912 – 690,000 | 1919 – 935,000 | 1926 – 1,180,000 |
| 1906 – 480,000 | 1913 – 725,000 | 1920 – 970,000 | 1927 – 1,215,000 |
| 1907 – 515,000 | 1914 – 760,000 | 1921 – 1,005,000 | 1928 – 1,250,000 |
| 1908 – 550,000 | 1915 – 795,000 | 1922 – 1,040,000 | 1929 – 1,275,000 |
| 1909 – 585,000 | 1916 – 825,000 | 1923 – 1,075,000 | |

The above list is provided for determining the APPROXIMATE age of your watch. Match serial number with date. Watches were not necessarily sold in the exact order of manufactured date.

## SOUTH BEND
### 18 SIZE (Lever set)

| Grade or Name – Description | Avg | Ex-Fn | Mint |
|---|---|---|---|
| South Bend, 15J, OF | $75 | $100 | $150 |
| South Bend, 15J, HC | 100 | 125 | 175 |
| South Bend, 17J, OF | 75 | 100 | 150 |
| South Bend, 17J, HC | 100 | 125 | 175 |
| South Bend, 21J, OF | 225 | 250 | 300 |
| South Bend, 21J, HC, 14K | 700 | 800 | 900 |
| South Bend, 21J, OF, HC, Silveroid | 225 | 250 | 275 |
| South Bend, 21J, SW, HC | 300 | 365 | 435 |
| *The Studebaker*, G#323, 17J, GJS, NI, Adj.5P, OF | 250 | 325 | 400 |
| *The Studebaker*, G#328, 21J, GJS, NI, FULL, Adj.5P, HC ★ | 500 | 650 | 825 |
| *The Studebaker*, G#329, 21J, GJS, NI, FULL, Adj.5P, OF | 400 | 475 | 525 |
| 304, 15J, HC | 100 | 125 | 175 |

🕐 Generic, nameless or **unmarked** grades for watch movements are listed under the Company name or initials of the Company, etc. by size, jewel count and description.

🕐 Watches listed in this book are priced at the collectable retail level, as **complete** watches having an original 14k gold-filled case and *Key Wind* with silver, an original white enamel single sunk dial, and with the entire original movement in good working order with no repairs needed.

**South Bend** movement, 18 size, 17 jewels, stem wind, hunting, serial number 426,726.

The Studebaker in (SCRIPT), 18 size, 21 jewels, gold jewel settings, marked 329, stem wind.

| Grade or Name – Description | Avg | Ex-Fn | Mint |
|---|---|---|---|
| 305, 15J, OF...................................................................................... | $75 | $100 | $150 |
| 305, 15J, OF, Silveroid................................................................... | 50 | 60 | 75 |
| 309, 17J, OF...................................................................................... | 75 | 100 | 150 |
| 312, 17J, HC, NI, ADJ..................................................................... | 100 | 125 | 175 |
| 313, 17J, OF, NI, ADJ, marked 313...........................................★ | 200 | 250 | 325 |
| 315, 17J, OF, NI, Adj.3P................................................................. | 75 | 100 | 150 |
| **G#s 323, 328 & 329 see "The Studebaker"** | | | |
| 327, 21J, OF, Adj.5P, marked 327..............................................★ | 275 | 325 | 425 |
| 327, 21J, OF, Adj.5P, marked 327, Silveroid...........................★ | 200 | 225 | 275 |
| 330, 15J, M#1, LS, HC.................................................................... | 100 | 135 | 200 |
| 331, 15J, M#1, LS, OF.................................................................... | 75 | 100 | 150 |
| 332, 15J, HC.................................................................................... | 175 | 225 | 300 |
| 333, 15J, OF.................................................................................... | 75 | 100 | 150 |
| 337, 17J, OF.................................................................................... | 75 | 100 | 150 |
| 340, 17J, M#1, Adj.3P, NI, HC...................................................... | 125 | 150 | 200 |
| 341, 17J, M#1, ADJ, NI, Adj.3P, OF............................................. | 100 | 125 | 175 |
| 342, 17J, M#1, LS............................................................................ | 75 | 100 | 150 |
| 343, 17J, M#1, LS, OF.................................................................... | 75 | 100 | 150 |
| 344, 17J, HC, NI, Adj.3P.........................................................★ ★ | 300 | 350 | 425 |
| 345, 17J, OF, NI, Adj.3P..........................................................★ ★ | 275 | 325 | 400 |
| 346, 17J, HC, NI......................................................................★ ★ | 300 | 350 | 425 |
| 347, 17J, OF, NI.............................................................................. | 75 | 100 | 125 |
| 355, 19J, GJS, 2-Tone, HC......................................................★ ★ | 1,000 | 1,200 | 1,500 |

🕐 Generic, nameless or **unmarked** grades for watch movements are listed under the Company name or initials of the Company, etc. by size, jewel count and description.

🕐 Watches listed in this book are priced at the collectable retail level, as **complete** watches having an original 14k gold-filled case and *Key Wind* with silver, an original white enamel single sunk dial, and with the entire original movement in good working order with no repairs needed.

Grade 211, 16 size, 17 jewels, three-quarter plate, serial number 703,389.

Grade 295, 16 size, 21 jewels, first model, gold jewel settings, gold train, open face, serial number 518,022.

## 16 SIZE
### M#1 Lever set

| Grade or Name – Description | Avg | Ex-Fn | Mint |
|---|---|---|---|
| Polaris, 21J, M#1, Adj.5P, 3/4, NI, DR, GJS, GT, | | | |
| 14K South Bend case with Polaris dial ........................... ★ ★ | $1,800 | $2,000 | $2,400 |
| South Bend, 7J, OF........................................................................ | 50 | 75 | 125 |
| South Bend, 7J, HC ...................................................................... | 75 | 100 | 150 |
| South Bend, 9J, OF........................................................................ | 50 | 75 | 125 |
| South Bend, 9J, HC........................................................................ | 75 | 100 | 150 |
| South Bend, 15J, OF...................................................................... | 50 | 75 | 125 |
| South Bend, 15J, HC...................................................................... | 75 | 100 | 150 |
| South Bend, 15J, OF, Silveroid.................................................... | 50 | 60 | 85 |
| South Bend, 17J, OF...................................................................... | 50 | 75 | 125 |
| South Bend, 17J, HC, ADJ............................................................ | 100 | 125 | 175 |
| South Bend, 17J, 14K HC ............................................................ | 475 | 500 | 575 |
| South Bend, 21J, OF, Adj, 5P ...................................................... | 200 | 225 | 250 |
| South Bend, 21J, HC, ADJ............................................................ | 300 | 350 | 400 |
| The Studebaker 223, 17J, M#2, Adj.5P, GJS, DR, GT ......... ★ ★ | 300 | 350 | 425 |
| The Studebaker 229, 21J, M#2, Adj.5P, GJS, DR, GT .......... ★ ★ | 400 | 450 | 525 |
| Studebaker, 21J, OF, PS, Adj.5P.................................................. | 275 | 325 | 375 |
| 203, 7J, 3/4, NI, OF ...................................................................... | 50 | 75 | 125 |
| 204, 15J, 3/4, NI, HC.................................................................... | 75 | 100 | 150 |
| 207, 15J, OF, PS ............................................................................ | 50 | 75 | 125 |
| 209, 9J, M#2, OF, PS..................................................................... | 50 | 75 | 125 |
| 211, 17J, M#2, 3/4, NI, OF........................................................... | 50 | 75 | 125 |
| 212, 17J, M#2, HC, LS, heat & cold.............................................. | 100 | 125 | 175 |
| 215, 17J, M#2, OF, LS, heat & cold.............................................. | 50 | 75 | 125 |
| 215, 17J, M#2, OF, SILVEROID.................................................. | 50 | 60 | 75 |
| 217, 17J, M#2, OF, NI, BRG, DR, GT, ADJ.3P. ........................... | 75 | 100 | 150 |
| 219, 19J, OF, NI, PS, BRG, DR, ADJ.4P...................................... | 125 | 150 | 200 |

⊕ Generic, nameless or unmarked grades for watch movements are listed under the Company name or initials of the Company, etc. by size, jewel count and description.

**South Bend Watch Co. Polaris,** 16 size, 21 jewels, model number 1, Adj5p, gold jewel setting, gold train, open face, serial number,518,236.

**Grade 227,** 16 size, 21 jewels, RR approved, gold jewel settings, Adj5p, serial number 1,222,843.

| Grade or Name – Description | | Avg | Ex-Fn | Mint |
|---|---|---|---|---|
| 223, 17J, M#2, OF, LS, ADJ.5P | | $50 | $75 | $125 |
| 227, 21J, M#2, BRG, NI, LS, DR, ADJ.5P, OF | | 200 | 225 | 275 |
| 245, 19J, GJS, BRG, HC | ★★ | 600 | 700 | 850 |
| 260, 7J, M#1, HC | | 75 | 95 | 125 |
| 261, 7J, M#1, OF | | 50 | 75 | 100 |
| 280, 15J, M#1, HC | | 80 | 100 | 150 |
| 281, 15J, M#1, OF | | 60 | 75 | 125 |
| 290, 17J, M#1, LS, ADJ.3P, HC | ★★ | 200 | 250 | 325 |
| 291, 17J, M#1, OF, ADJ.3P | ★★ | 175 | 200 | 275 |
| 292, 19J, M#1, HC, 3/4, GJS, NI, DR, Adj,5P | ★ | 250 | 300 | 375 |
| 293, 19J, M#1, OF, 3/4, GJS, NI, DR, Adj,5P | ★ | 175 | 225 | 275 |
| 294, 21J, M#1, ADJ.5P, GJS, GT, HC, marked 294 | ★★ | 300 | 350 | 475 |
| 295, 21J, M#1 OF, LS, ADJ.5P, GJS, GT, marked 295 | ★ | 350 | 400 | 475 |
| 298, 17J, M#1, HC, ADJ.3P | ★★ | 200 | 250 | 325 |
| 299, 17J, M#1, OF, ADJ.3P | ★★ | 175 | 225 | 275 |

## 12 SIZE
### (OF Only)

| Grade or Name – Description | | Avg | Ex-Fn | Mint |
|---|---|---|---|---|
| Chesterfield, 15J, BRG, NI, DR, G#407 | | $50 | $60 | $75 |
| Chesterfield, 17J, BRG, NI, DR, GJS, ADJ.3P,G#419 | | 60 | 70 | 85 |
| Chesterfield, 21J, BRG, NI, DR, GJS, ADJ.5P,G#431 | ★ | 100 | 120 | 150 |
| Digital,Studebaker, 21J, BRG, NI, DR, GJS, ADJ.5P, | ★★ | 200 | 250 | 325 |
| South Bend, 15J | | 35 | 45 | 60 |
| South Bend, 17J | | 40 | 50 | 65 |
| South Bend, 17J, Silveroid | | 35 | 40 | 55 |
| South Bend, 19J | | 75 | 90 | 110 |
| South Bend, 21J | | 100 | 135 | 175 |
| Studebaker, 21J, PS, 3/4, NI, Adj.5P, GJS | | 150 | 175 | 200 |
| 407, 15J, Silveroid | | 35 | 45 | 55 |
| 407, 15J | | 45 | 55 | 65 |
| 411, 17J, DR, GJS | | 75 | 100 | 125 |

Grade 411, 12 size, 17 jewels, open face, double roller.

Chesterfield, 12 size, 21 jewels, open face only, bridge, gold jewel settings, pendant set, double roller, Adj5p.

| Grade or Name – Description | | Avg | Ex-Fn | Mint |
|---|---|---|---|---|
| 415, 17J, ADJ to temp. | ★ ★ | $125 | $150 | $200 |
| 419, 17J, Adj.3P | ★ ★ | 125 | 150 | 200 |
| 429, 19J, Adj.4P, GT, GJS | ★ | 75 | 100 | 125 |
| 431, 21J, Adj.5P, DR, GJS | ★ ★ | 125 | 150 | 200 |
| 431, 21J, Adj.5P, Silveroid | | 75 | 100 | 125 |

## 6 SIZE

| Grade or Name – Description | | Avg | Ex-Fn | Mint |
|---|---|---|---|---|
| South Bend, 11J, G#160, HC | ★ | $75 | $85 | $150 |
| South Bend, 15J, G#170, HC | ★ | 100 | 125 | 200 |
| South Bend, 17J, G#180, HC | ★ ★ | 100 | 125 | 200 |
| South Bend, 17J, G#180, 14K | ★ ★ | 200 | 250 | 325 |

South Bend, 6 size, grade # 170, 15 jewels.

Grade 120-HC, 121-OF, 0 size, 17 jewels, bridge, nickel, double roller, pendant set.

## 0 SIZE

| Grade or Name – Description | | Avg | Ex-Fn | Mint |
|---|---|---|---|---|
| South Bend, 15J, M# 1 & 2, OF, PS | | $50 | $60 | $75 |
| Grade 100 HC & 101 OF, 7J, PS | | 75 | 100 | 150 |
| Grade 110 HC & 111 OF, 15J, 3F Brg, DR | ★ | 100 | 125 | 150 |
| Grade 120 HC & 121 OF, 17J, BRG, NI, DR, PS | ★ ★ | 125 | 150 | 200 |
| Grade 150 HC & 151 OF, 17J, M# 3, BRG, NI, PS | ★ ★ | 125 | 150 | 200 |

# Record of Serial and Grade Numbers of South Bend Watch Movements

| Serial Number | Grade | Size | Model | Jewels |
|---|---|---|---|---|
| 1000 to 4000... | Htg. | 18 | 1 | 7 |
| 4001 to 7000... | " | 18 | 1 | 7 |
| 7001 to 10000... | " | 16 | 1 | 15 |
| 10001 to 21000... | " | 18 | 1 | 15 |
| 21001 to 29500... | " | 16 | 1 | 7 |
| 29501 to 37000... | " | 18 | 1 | 7 |
| 37001 to 41000... | " | 16 | 1 | 15 |
| 41001 to 52000... | " | 18 | 1 | 15 |
| 52001 to 61000... | " | 18 | 1 | 7 |
| 61001 to 76000... | " | 18 | 1 | 15 |
| 76001 to 83000... | " | 16 | 1 | 15 |
| 83001 to 92000... | " | 16 | 1 | 7 |
| 92001 to 97000... | " | 18 | 1 | 7 |
| 97001 to 105000... | " | 18 | 1 | 15 |
| 105001 to 114000... | " | 16 | 1 | 17 |
| 114001 to 127000... | " | 18 | 1 | 15 |
| 127501 to 138000... | " | 18 | 1 | 17 |
| 138001 to 156000... | " | 16 | 1 | 7 |
| 156001 to 165000... | " | 18 | 1 | 15 |
| 165001 to 171000... | " | 16 | 1 | 7 |
| 171001 to 196000... | " | 16 | 1 | 17 |
| 196001 to 201000... | " | 18 | 1 | 7 |
| 201001 to 214000... | " | 16 | 1 | 15 |
| 214001 to 218000... | " | 16 | 1 | 7 |
| 218001 to 220000... | " | 18 | 1 | 15 |
| 220001 to 232000... | " | 16 | 1 | 15 |
| 232001 to 250000... | " | 18 | 1 | 7 |
| 250001 to 261000... | " | 16 | 1 | 7 |
| 261001 to 267000... | " | 16 | 1 | 15 |
| 267001 to 271000... | " | 18 | 1 | 15 |
| 271001 to 274000... | " | 16 | 1 | 15 |
| 274001 to 281000... | " | 16 | 1 | 7 |
| 281001 to 292000... | " | 16 | 1 | 7 |
| 292001 to 294000... | " | 16 | 1 | 17 |
| 294001 to 295500... | " | 18 | 1 | 17 |
| 295501 to 299100... | " | 16 | 1 | 7 |
| 299101 to 302000... | " | 18 | 1 | 7 |
| 302001 to 311000... | " | 16 | 1 | 7 |
| 311001 to 314000... | " | 16 | 1 | 15 |
| 314001 to 321000... | " | 18 | 1 | 15 |
| 321001 to 329000... | " | 16 | 1 | 7 |
| 329001 to 334000... | " | 18 | 1 | 7 |
| 334001 to 341000... | " | 16 | 1 | 15 |
| 341001 to 347000... | " | 16 | 1 | 7 |
| 347001 to 349500... | " | 16 | 1 | 17 |
| 349501 to 354000... | " | 16 | 1 | 15 |
| 354001 to 361000... | " | 18 | 1 | 7 |
| 361001 to 366000... | " | 16 | 1 | 7 |
| 366001 to 368000... | " | 18 | 1 | 17 |
| 368001 to 371000... | " | 16 | 1 | 15 |
| 371001 to 374000... | " | 18 | 1 | 15 |
| 374001 to 376000... | " | 16 | 1 | 17 |
| 376001 to 377000... | " | 16 | 1 | 15 |
| 377001 to 378000... | " | 18 | 1 | 17 |
| 378001 to 379000... | " | 18 | 1 | 15 |
| 379501 to 380500... | " | 16 | 1 | 15 |
| 380501 to 381000... | 160 | 6 | 1 | 11 |
| 381001 to 381500... | 170 | 6 | 1 | 15 |
| 381501 to 382500... | 330 | 18 | 1 | 15 |
| 382501 to 383000... | 160 | 6 | 1 | 11 |
| 383001 to 383500... | 170 | 6 | 1 | 15 |
| 383501 to 384000... | 302 | 18 | 1 | 15 |
| 384001 to 384500... | 160 | 6 | 1 | 11 |
| 384501 to 384900... | 291 | 16 | 1 | 17 |
| 384901 to 385200... | 281 | 16 | 1 | 17 |
| 385201 to 385500... | 291 | 16 | 1 | 17 |
| 385501 to 386400... | 290 | 16 | 1 | 17 |
| 386401 to 386900... | 280 | 16 | 1 | 15 |
| 386901 to 387400... | 170 | 6 | 1 | 15 |
| 387401 to 387900... | 330 | 18 | 1 | 15 |
| 387901 to 388400... | 331 | 18 | 1 | 15 |
| 388401 to 389400... | 180 | 6 | 1 | 17 |
| 389401 to 389900... | 170 | 6 | 1 | 15 |
| 389901 to 390400... | 341 | 18 | 1 | 17 |
| 390401 to 390900... | 331 | 18 | 1 | 15 |
| 390901 to 391200... | 330 | 18 | 1 | 15 |
| 391201 to 391700... | 341 | 18 | 1 | 17 |
| 391701 to 392600... | 330 | 18 | 1 | 15 |
| 392601 to 394100... | 331 | 18 | 1 | 15 |
| 394101 to 396000... | 330 | 18 | 1 | 15 |
| 396001 to 400000... | 340 | 18 | 1 | 17 |

| Serial Number | Grade | Size | Model | Jewels |
|---|---|---|---|---|
| 400001 to 401200... | 331 | 18 | 1 | 15 |
| 401201 to 403200... | 330 | 18 | 1 | 15 |
| 403201 to 407200... | 341 | 18 | 1 | 17 |
| 407201 to 408500... | 340 | 18 | 1 | 17 |
| 408501 to 408700... | 342 | 18 | 1 | 17 |
| 408901 to 409200... | 342 | 18 | 1 | 17 |
| 409201 to 412200... | 330 | 18 | 1 | 15 |
| 412201 to 413800... | 290 | 16 | 1 | 17 |
| 413801 to 414800... | 342 | 18 | 1 | 17 |
| 414801 to 415800... | 291 | 16 | 1 | 17 |
| 415801 to 417700... | 331 | 18 | 1 | 15 |
| 417701 to 418700... | 342 | 18 | 1 | 17 |
| 418701 to 419700... | 343 | 18 | 1 | 17 |
| 419701 to 420600... | 290 | 16 | 1 | 17 |
| 420601 to 421900... | 291 | 16 | 1 | 17 |
| 421901 to 422400... | 281 | 16 | 1 | 15 |
| 422401 to 423200... | 280 | 16 | 1 | 15 |
| 423201 to 423800... | 313 | 18 | 1 | 17 |
| 423801 to 425800... | 261 | 16 | 1 | 7 |
| 425801 to 426100... | 281 | 16 | 1 | 15 |
| 426101 to 428100... | 342 | 18 | 1 | 17 |
| 428101 to 431100... | 260 | 16 | 1 | 7 |
| 431101 to 431600... | 280 | 16 | 1 | 15 |
| 431601 to 432100... | 281 | 16 | 1 | 15 |
| 432101 to 433300... | 342 | 18 | 1 | 17 |
| 433101 to 435100... | 340 | 18 | 1 | 17 |
| 435101 to 436600... | 280 | 16 | 1 | 15 |
| 436601 to 437900... | 281 | 16 | 1 | 15 |
| 437901 to 438200... | 280 | 16 | 1 | 15 |
| 438201 to 438500... | 290 | 16 | 1 | 17 |
| 438501 to 439500... | 293 | 16 | 1 | 19 |
| 439501 to 440500... | 280 | 16 | 1 | 15 |
| 440501 to 441500... | 290 | 16 | 1 | 17 |
| 441501 to 441600... | 260 | 16 | 1 | 7 |
| 441601 to 441700... | 261 | 16 | 1 | 7 |
| 441701 to 441800... | 290 | 16 | 1 | 17 |
| 441801 to 441850... | 293 | 16 | 1 | 17 |
| 441901 to 445900... | 280 | 16 | 1 | 15 |
| 445901 to 446000... | Htg. | 16 | 1 | 21 |
| 446001 to 447000... | 261 | 16 | 1 | 7 |
| 447001 to 450000... | 260 | 16 | 1 | 7 |
| 450001 to 451000... | 261 | 16 | 1 | 7 |
| 451001 to 453000... | 260 | 16 | 1 | 7 |
| 453001 to 455000... | 261 | 16 | 1 | 7 |
| 455001 to 457000... | 343 | 18 | 1 | 17 |
| 457001 to 461000... | 260 | 16 | 1 | 7 |
| 461001 to 462500... | 331 | 18 | 1 | 15 |
| 462501 to 464000... | 281 | 16 | 1 | 15 |
| 464001 to 466300... | 331 | 18 | 1 | 15 |
| 466301 to 467300... | 261 | 16 | 1 | 7 |
| 467301 to 468800... | 331 | 18 | 1 | 15 |
| 468801 to 469300... | 290 | 16 | 1 | 17 |
| 469301 to 469800... | 294 | 16 | 1 | 21 |
| 469801 to 470100... | 295 | 16 | 1 | 21 |
| *470101 to 470200... | 295 | 16 | 1 | 21 |
| 470201 to 470300... | 295 | 16 | 1 | 21 |
| 470301 to 471300... | 281 | 16 | 1 | 15 |
| 471301 to 472300... | 280 | 16 | 1 | 15 |
| 472301 to 473300... | 281 | 16 | 1 | 15 |
| 473301 to 474800... | 330 | 18 | 1 | 15 |
| 474801 to 475800... | 331 | 18 | 1 | 15 |
| 475801 to 476800... | 290 | 16 | 1 | 17 |
| 477001 to 478000... | 261 | 16 | 1 | 7 |
| 478001 to 479000... | 330 | 18 | 1 | 15 |
| 479001 to 480000... | 261 | 16 | 1 | 7 |
| 480001 to 480200... | 295 | 16 | 1 | 21 |
| *480201 to 480500... | 295 | 16 | 1 | 21 |
| 480501 to 481500... | 290 | 16 | 1 | 17 |
| 481501 to 483500... | 291 | 16 | 1 | 17 |
| 483501 to 485000... | 280 | 16 | 1 | 15 |
| 485001 to 486000... | 331 | 18 | 1 | 15 |
| 486001 to 487000... | 330 | 18 | 1 | 15 |
| 487001 to 489000... | 331 | 18 | 1 | 15 |
| 489001 to 490000... | 341 | 18 | 1 | 17 |
| *490001 to 490500... | 294 | 16 | 1 | 21 |
| 490501 to 490800... | 293 | 16 | 1 | 19 |
| *490R01 to 490900... | 293 | 16 | 1 | 19 |
| 490901 to 491000... | 293 | 16 | 1 | 19 |
| 491001 to 492000... | 281 | 16 | 1 | 15 |
| 492001 to 493000... | 330 | 18 | 1 | 15 |
| 493001 to 494000... | 340 | 18 | 1 | 17 |

Although grade numbers appear in this list some of the earlier watches did not have grade numbers stamped upon them. In all instances odd grade numbers indicate open face movement, even grade numbers indicate hunting movement.

*Watches with these serial numbers have double roller.

| Serial Number | Grade | Size | Model | Jewels | Serial Number | Grade | Size | Model | Jewels |
|---|---|---|---|---|---|---|---|---|---|
| 494001 to 495000... | 290 | 16 | 1 | 17 | 570001 to 571000... | 261 | 16 | 1 | 7 |
| 495001 to 497000... | 331 | 18 | 1 | 15 | *571001 to 572000... | 313 | 18 | 2 | 17 |
| 497001 to 498000... | 261 | 16 | 1 | 7 | 572001 to 573000... | 280 | 16 | 1 | 15 |
| 498001 to 499000... | 291 | 16 | 1 | 17 | 573001 to 574000... | 347 | 18 | 2 | 17 |
| 499001 to 500000... | 261 | 16 | 1 | 7 | *574001 to 575000... | 323 | 18 | 2 | 17 |
| 500001 to 501000... | 281 | 16 | 1 | 15 | *575001 to 576000... | 217 | 16 | 2 | 17 |
| 501001 to 502000... | 290 | 16 | 1 | 17 | 576001 to 577000... | 333 | 18 | 2 | 15 |
| 502001 to 503000... | 331 | 18 | 1 | 15 | 577001 to 578000... | 281 | 16 | 1 | 15 |
| 503001 to 503500... | 341 | 18 | 1 | 17 | *578001 to 579000... | 223 | 16 | 2 | 17 |
| 503501 to 504000... | 343 | 18 | 1 | 17 | *579001 to 580000... | 329 | 18 | 2 | 21 |
| 504001 to 505000... | 290 | 16 | 1 | 17 | *580001 to 581000... | 212 | 16 | 2 | 17 |
| 505001 to 505100... | 293 | 16 | 1 | 19 | *581001 to 582000... | 333 | 18 | 2 | 15 |
| *505101 to 505500... | 293 | 16 | 1 | 19 | 582001 to 583000... | 261 | 16 | 1 | 7 |
| 505501 to 506500... | 261 | 16 | 1 | 7 | *583001 to 584000... | 227 | 16 | 2 | 21 |
| 506501 to 507500... | 280 | 16 | 1 | 15 | *584001 to 585000... | 229 | 16 | 2 | 21 |
| 507501 to 508500... | 261 | 16 | 1 | 7 | 585001 to 586000... | 207 | 16 | 2 | 15 |
| 508501 to 509500... | 280 | 16 | 1 | 15 | 586001 to 587000... | 211 | 16 | 2 | 17 |
| 509501 to 510500... | 281 | 16 | 1 | 15 | *587001 to 588000... | 215 | 16 | 2 | 17 |
| 510501 to 511000... | 291 | 16 | 1 | 17 | 588001 to 589000... | 260 | 16 | 1 | 7 |
| 511401 to 511500... | 299 | 16 | 1 | 17 | *589001 to 590000... | 217 | 16 | 2 | 17 |
| 511501 to 511900... | 292 | 16 | 1 | 19 | 590001 to 591000... | 204 | 16 | 2 | 15 |
| *511901 to 512000... | 292 | 16 | 1 | 19 | 591001 to 592000... | 203 | 16 | 2 | 7 |
| 512001 to 513000... | 333 | 18 | 2 | 15 | 592001 to 593000... | 207 | 16 | 2 | 15 |
| 513001 to 514000... | 280 | 16 | 1 | 15 | *593001 to 594000... | 212 | 16 | 2 | 17 |
| 514001 to 515000... | 261 | 16 | 1 | 7 | 594001 to 595000... | 203 | 16 | 2 | 7 |
| 515001 to 516000... | 260 | 16 | 1 | 7 | 595001 to 596000... | 332 | 18 | 2 | 15 |
| 516001 to 516500... | 298 | 16 | 1 | 17 | *596001 to 597000... | 215 | 16 | 2 | 17 |
| *516501 to 516600... | 298 | 16 | 1 | 17 | *597001 to 598000... | 223 | 16 | 2 | 17 |
| 516601 to 516800... | 298 | 16 | 1 | 17 | *598001 to 599000... | 229 | 16 | 2 | 21 |
| 516801 to 516900... | 298 | 16 | 1 | 17 | 599001 to 600000... | 260 | 16 | 1 | 7 |
| 516901 to 517000... | 298 | 16 | 1 | 17 | 600001 to 601000... | 211 | 16 | 2 | 17 |
| 517001 to 517700... | 345 | 18 | 2 | 17 | *601001 to 602000... | 313 | 18 | 2 | 17 |
| *517701 to 518000... | 345 | 18 | 2 | 17 | 602001 to 603000... | 203 | 16 | 2 | 7 |
| *518001 to 518500... | 295 | 16 | 1 | 21 | 603001 to 604000... | 204 | 16 | 2 | 15 |
| *518501 to 519000... | 294 | 16 | 1 | 21 | 604001 to 605000... | 207 | 16 | 2 | 15 |
| 519001 to 520000... | 347 | 18 | 2 | 17 | 605001 to 606000... | 333 | 18 | 2 | 15 |
| 520001 to 521000... | 332 | 18 | 2 | 15 | 606001 to 607000... | 347 | 18 | 2 | 17 |
| *521001 to 522000... | 329 | 18 | 2 | 21 | *607001 to 608000... | 215 | 16 | 2 | 17 |
| *522001 to 523000... | 293 | 16 | 1 | 19 | 608001 to 609000... | 211 | 16 | 2 | 17 |
| 523001 to 523400... | 299 | 16 | 1 | 17 | 609001 to 610000... | 203 | 16 | 2 | 7 |
| *523401 to 524000... | 299 | 16 | 1 | 17 | *610001 to 611000... | 215 | 16 | 2 | 17 |
| 524001 to 524300... | 344 | 18 | 2 | 17 | 611001 to 612000... | 207 | 16 | 2 | 15 |
| *524301 to 524800... | 344 | 18 | 2 | 17 | 612001 to 613000... | 203 | 16 | 2 | 7 |
| 524801 to 525000... | 344 | 18 | 2 | 17 | *613001 to 614000... | 212 | 16 | 2 | 17 |
| 525001 to 526000... | 346 | 18 | 2 | 17 | 614001 to 615000... | 305 | 18 | 2 | 15 |
| 526001 to 527000... | 333 | 18 | 2 | 15 | 615001 to 616000... | 204 | 16 | 2 | 15 |
| 527001 to 528000... | 347 | 18 | 2 | 17 | 616001 to 617000... | 207 | 16 | 2 | 15 |
| *528001 to 529000... | 345 | 18 | 2 | 17 | 617001 to 618000... | 203 | 16 | 2 | 7 |
| *529001 to 530000... | 292 | 16 | 1 | 19 | *618001 to 619000... | 415 | 12 | 1 | 17 |
| 530001 to 531000... | 260 | 16 | 1 | 7 | *619001 to 620000... | 431 | 12 | 1 | 21 |
| 531001 to 532000... | 281 | 16 | 1 | 15 | 620001 to 621000... | 211 | 16 | 2 | 17 |
| 532001 to 533000... | 333 | 18 | 2 | 15 | *621001 to 622000... | 223 | 16 | 2 | 17 |
| *533001 to 534000... | 323 | 18 | 2 | 17 | *622001 to 623000... | 229 | 16 | 2 | 21 |
| *534001 to 535000... | 345 | 18 | 2 | 17 | *623001 to 624000... | 411 | 12 | 1 | 17 |
| 535001 to 536000... | 347 | 18 | 2 | 17 | *624001 to 625000... | 215 | 16 | 2 | 17 |
| 536001 to 537000... | 333 | 18 | 2 | 15 | 625001 to 626000... | 203 | 16 | 2 | 7 |
| 537001 to 538000... | 312 | 18 | 2 | 17 | 626001 to 627000... | 305 | 18 | 2 | 15 |
| 538001 to 539000... | 332 | 18 | 2 | 15 | 627001 to 628000... | 207 | 16 | 2 | 15 |
| *539001 to 539500... | 298 | 16 | 1 | 17 | *628001 to 629000... | 419 | 12 | 1 | 17 |
| 539501 to 539700... | 298 | 16 | 1 | 17 | 629001 to 630000... | 260 | 16 | 1 | 7 |
| *539701 to 540000... | 298 | 16 | 1 | 17 | *630001 to 631000... | 407 | 12 | 1 | 16 |
| *540001 to 540400... | 299 | 16 | 1 | 17 | *631001 to 632000... | 217 | 16 | 2 | 17 |
| 540401 to 541000... | 299 | 16 | 1 | 17 | 632001 to 633000... | 204 | 16 | 2 | 15 |
| *541001 to 542000... | 328 | 18 | 2 | 21 | 633001 to 634000... | 347 | 18 | 2 | 17 |
| *542001 to 543000... | 313 | 18 | 2 | 17 | *634001 to 635000... | 329 | 18 | 2 | 21 |
| 543001 to 544000... | 261 | 16 | 1 | 7 | 635001 to 636000... | 203 | 16 | 2 | 7 |
| 544001 to 545000... | 260 | 16 | 1 | 7 | *636001 to 637000... | 217 | 16 | 2 | 17 |
| 545001 to 546000... | 333 | 18 | 2 | 15 | *637001 to 638000... | 411 | 12 | 1 | 17 |
| 546001 to 547000... | 332 | 18 | 2 | 15 | 638001 to 639000... | 211 | 16 | 2 | 17 |
| 547001 to 548000... | 333 | 18 | 2 | 15 | *639001 to 640000... | 212 | 16 | 2 | 17 |
| 548001 to 549000... | 346 | 18 | 2 | 17 | *640001 to 641000... | 217 | 16 | 2 | 17 |
| 549001 to 550000... | 261 | 16 | 1 | 7 | *641001 to 642000... | 415 | 12 | 1 | 17 |
| 550001 to 551000... | 280 | 16 | 1 | 15 | 642001 to 643000... | 203 | 16 | 2 | 7 |
| 551001 to 552000... | 281 | 16 | 1 | 15 | *643001 to 644000... | 229 | 16 | 2 | 21 |
| 552001 to 553000... | 347 | 18 | 2 | 17 | 644001 to 645000... | 260 | 16 | 1 | 7 |
| *553001 to 554000... | 313 | 18 | 2 | 17 | *645001 to 646000... | 215 | 16 | 2 | 17 |
| *554001 to 555000... | 323 | 18 | 2 | 17 | 646001 to 647000... | 207 | 16 | 2 | 15 |
| 555001 to 556000... | 327 | 18 | 2 | 21 | *647001 to 648000... | 407 | 12 | 1 | 15 |
| *556001 to 557000... | 298 | 16 | 1 | 17 | *648001 to 649000... | 419 | 12 | 1 | 17 |
| *557001 to 558000... | 299 | 16 | 1 | 17 | 649001 to 650000... | 207 | 16 | 2 | 15 |
| 558001 to 559000... | 347 | 18 | 2 | 17 | 650181 to 655200... | Htg. | 0 | 1 | 7 |
| 559001 to 560000... | 346 | 18 | 2 | 17 | 655201 to 656200... | " | 0 | 1 | 15 |
| *560001 to 561000... | 313 | 18 | 2 | 17 | 656201 to 659700... | " | 0 | 1 | 7 |
| 561001 to 562000... | 333 | 18 | 2 | 15 | 659701 to 662400... | " | 0 | 1 | 7 |
| 562001 to 563000... | 332 | 18 | 2 | 15 | 662401 to 662500... | O.F. | 0 | 2 | 7 |
| 563001 to 564000... | 261 | 16 | 1 | 7 | 662501 to 665400... | Htg. | 0 | 2 | 7 |
| 564001 to 565000... | 347 | 18 | 2 | 17 | 665401 to 665500... | O.F. | 0 | 2 | 7 |
| 565001 to 566000... | 260 | 16 | 1 | 7 | 665501 to 666000... | Htg. | 0 | 2 | 7 |
| 566001 to 567000... | 211 | 16 | 2 | 17 | 666001 to 666500... | " | 0 | 2 | 17 |
| 567001 to 569000... | 333 | 18 | 2 | 15 | 666501 to 666600... | " | 0 | 2 | 15 |
| *569001 to 570000... | 215 | 18 | 2 | 17 | 666601 to 666650... | O.F. | 0 | 2 | 15 |

Although grade numbers appear in this list some of the earlier watches did not have grade numbers stamped upon them. In all instances odd grade numbers indicate open face movement, even grade numbers indicate hunting movement.
*Watches with these serial numbers have double roller.

| Serial Number | Grade | Size | Model | Jewels | | Serial Number | Grade | Size | Model | Jewels |
|---|---|---|---|---|---|---|---|---|---|---|
| 666651 to 667500... | Htg. | 0 | 2 | 15 | | *739001 to 740000... | 217 | 16 | 2 | 17 |
| 667501 to 671500... | " | 0 | 2 | 7 | | *740001 to 740200... | 101 | 0 | 2 | 7 |
| 671501 to 671600... | O. F. | 0 | 2 | 7 | | *740201 to 741000... | 100 | 0 | 2 | 7 |
| 671601 to 672800... | Htg. | 0 | 2 | 7 | | *741001 to 741200... | 111 | 0 | 2 | 15 |
| 672801 to 672900... | O. F. | 0 | 2 | 7 | | *741201 to 742000... | 110 | 0 | 2 | 15 |
| 672901 to 673000... | Htg. | 0 | 2 | 7 | | 742001 to 743000... | 207 | 16 | 2 | 15 |
| 673001 to 674000... | " | 0 | 2 | 15 | | 743001 to 744000... | 203 | 16 | 2 | 7 |
| 674001 to 675000... | " | 0 | 2 | 17 | | *744001 to 745000... | 212 | 16 | 2 | 17 |
| 675001 to 676000... | " | 0 | 2 | 7 | | *745001 to 746000... | 227 | 16 | 2 | 21 |
| 676001 to 679400... | " | 0 | 2 | 15 | | *746001 to 746100... | 111 | 0 | 2 | 15 |
| 679401 to 679500... | O. F. | 0 | 2 | 15 | | *746101 to 747000... | 110 | 0 | 2 | 15 |
| 679501 to 680400... | Htg. | 0 | 2 | 15 | | *747001 to 748000... | 305 | 18 | 2 | 16 |
| 680401 to 680500... | O. F. | 0 | 2 | 15 | | 748001 to 749600... | 309 | 18 | 2 | 17 |
| 680501 to 681000... | Htg. | 0 | 2 | 15 | | *749601 to 750000... | 223 | 16 | 2 | 17 |
| 681001 to 682000... | " | 0 | 2 | 17 | | 750001 to 751000... | 207 | 16 | 2 | 15 |
| 682001 to 682800... | " | 0 | 2 | 15 | | *751001 to 751100... | 101 | 0 | 2 | 7 |
| 682801 to 682900... | O. F. | 0 | 2 | 15 | | *751101 to 752000... | 100 | 0 | 2 | 7 |
| 682901 to 683000... | Htg. | 0 | 2 | 15 | | 752001 to 753000... | 211 | 16 | 2 | 17 |
| 683001 to 684000... | " | 0 | 2 | 17 | | *753001 to 754000... | 229 | 16 | 2 | 21 |
| 684001 to 684600... | " | 0 | 2 | 7 | | 754001 to 755000... | 203 | 16 | 2 | 7 |
| 684601 to 684700... | O. F. | 0 | 2 | 7 | | *755001 to 756000... | 215 | 16 | 2 | 17 |
| 684701 to 685000... | Htg. | 0 | 2 | 7 | | *756001 to 757000... | 313 | 18 | 2 | 17 |
| 685001 to 686000... | ' | 0 | 2 | 15 | | *757001 to 758000... | 323 | 18 | 2 | 17 |
| 686001 to 686100... | 101 | 0 | 2 | 7 | | 758001 to 759000... | 204 | 16 | 2 | 15 |
| 686101 to 687000... | 100 | 0 | 2 | 7 | | *759001 to 759500... | Htg. | 0 | 2 | 17 |
| 687001 to 687100... | 111 | 0 | 2 | 15 | | 759501 to 759510... | 150 | 0 | 3 | 17 |
| 687101 to 688000... | 110 | 0 | 2 | 15 | | 759511 to 759520... | 103 | 0 | 3 | 7 |
| 688001 to 688100... | 101 | 0 | 2 | 7 | | 759521 to 759530... | 102 | 0 | 3 | 7 |
| 688101 to 689000... | 100 | 0 | 2 | 7 | | 759531 to 759540... | 151 | 0 | 3 | 17 |
| 689001 to 689100... | 111 | 0 | 2 | 15 | | 759541 to 760000... | Htg. | 0 | 2 | 15 |
| 689101 to 690000... | 110 | 0 | 2 | 15 | | 760001 to 761000... | 305 | 18 | 2 | 15 |
| 690001 to 690100... | 101 | 0 | 2 | 7 | | 761001 to 762000... | 207 | 16 | 2 | 15 |
| 690101 to 691000... | 100 | 0 | 2 | 7 | | *762001 to 762100... | 111 | 0 | 2 | 15 |
| 691001 to 691100... | 101 | 0 | 2 | 7 | | 762101 to 763000... | 110 | 0 | 2 | 17 |
| 691101 to 692000... | 100 | 0 | 2 | 7 | | 763001 to 764000... | 203 | 16 | 2 | 7 |
| 692001 to 692100... | 111 | 0 | 2 | 15 | | *764001 to 765000... | 215 | 16 | 2 | 17 |
| 692101 to 693000... | 110 | 0 | 2 | 15 | | *765001 to 766000... | 217 | 16 | 2 | 17 |
| 693001 to 693100... | 101 | 0 | 2 | 7 | | 766001 to 767000... | 211 | 16 | 2 | 17 |
| 693101 to 694000... | 100 | 0 | 2 | 7 | | *767001 to 768000... | 217 | 16 | 2 | 17 |
| *694001 to 695000... | 217 | 16 | 2 | 17 | | *768001 to 769000... | 212 | 16 | 2 | 17 |
| 695001 to 696000... | 305 | 18 | 2 | 15 | | *769001 to 770000... | 217 | 16 | 2 | 17 |
| 696001 to 696100... | 111 | 0 | 2 | 15 | | *770001 to 771000... | 151 | 0 | 3 | 17 |
| 696101 to 697000... | 110 | 0 | 2 | 15 | | *771001 to 772000... | 217 | 16 | 2 | 17 |
| 697001 to 697100... | 101 | 0 | 2 | 7 | | *772001 to 773000... | 150 | 0 | 3 | 17 |
| 697101 to 698000... | 100 | 0 | 2 | 7 | | *773001 to 774000... | 215 | 16 | 2 | 17 |
| *698001 to 699000... | 215 | 16 | 2 | 17 | | *774001 to 775000... | 107 | 0 | 3 | 15 |
| *699001 to 700000... | 415 | 12 | 1 | 17 | | *775001 to 776000... | 106 | 0 | 3 | 15 |
| *700001 to 701000... | 431 | 12 | 1 | 21 | | 776001 to 777000... | 207 | 16 | 2 | 15 |
| *701001 to 702000... | 313 | 18 | 2 | 17 | | *777001 to 778000... | 102 | 0 | 3 | 7 |
| 702001 to 702100... | 111 | 0 | 2 | 15 | | *778001 to 779000... | 103 | 0 | 3 | 7 |
| 702101 to 703000... | 110 | 0 | 2 | 15 | | 779001 to 780000... | 211 | 16 | 2 | 17 |
| 703001 to 704000... | 211 | 16 | 2 | 17 | | 780001 to 781000... | 203 | 16 | 2 | 7 |
| *704001 to 705000... | 212 | 16 | 2 | 17 | | 781001 to 782000... | 305 | 18 | 2 | 16 |
| *705001 to 706000... | 305 | 18 | 2 | 15 | | *782001 to 783000... | 217 | 16 | 2 | 17 |
| *706001 to 707000... | 215 | 16 | 2 | 17 | | *783001 to 784000... | 215 | 16 | 2 | 17 |
| 707001 to 708000... | 203 | 16 | 2 | 7 | | 784001 to 785000... | 207 | 16 | 2 | 15 |
| *708001 to 709000... | 407 | 12 | 1 | 15 | | *785001 to 786000... | 215 | 16 | 2 | 17 |
| 709001 to 710000... | 204 | 16 | 2 | 15 | | *786001 to 787000... | 227 | 16 | 2 | 21 |
| 710001 to 711000... | 305 | 18 | 2 | 15 | | *787001 to 788000... | 407 | 12 | 1 | 15 |
| 711001 to 712000... | 260 | 16 | 1 | 7 | | *788001 to 789000... | 217 | 16 | 2 | 17 |
| 712001 to 713000... | 207 | 16 | 2 | 16 | | 789001 to 790000... | 211 | 16 | 2 | 17 |
| *713001 to 713100... | 111 | 0 | 2 | 15 | | *790001 to 791000... | 215 | 16 | 2 | 17 |
| *713101 to 714000... | 110 | 0 | 2 | 15 | | *791001 to 792000... | 217 | 16 | 2 | 17 |
| *714001 to 715000... | 227 | 16 | 2 | 21 | | *792001 to 793000... | 407 | 12 | 1 | 15 |
| 715001 to 716000... | 211 | 16 | 2 | 17 | | *793001 to 794000... | 215 | 16 | 2 | 17 |
| *716001 to 717000... | 411 | 12 | 1 | 17 | | *794001 to 795000... | 212 | 16 | 2 | 17 |
| *717001 to 717100... | 101 | 0 | 2 | 7 | | *795001 to 796000... | 411 | 12 | 1 | 17 |
| *717101 to 718000... | 100 | 0 | 2 | 7 | | 796001 to 797000... | 203 | 16 | 2 | 7 |
| *718001 to 719000... | 215 | 16 | 2 | 17 | | *797001 to 798000... | 407 | 12 | 1 | 15 |
| 719001 to 720000... | 309 | 18 | 2 | 17 | | *798001 to 799000... | 429 | 12 | 1 | 19 |
| 720001 to 721000... | 203 | 16 | 2 | 7 | | *799001 to 800000... | 411 | 12 | 1 | 19 |
| *721001 to 722000... | 227 | 16 | 2 | 21 | | *800001 to 801000... | 219 | 16 | 2 | 19 |
| 722001 to 723000... | 204 | 16 | 2 | 15 | | *801001 to 802000... | 429 | 12 | 1 | 19 |
| 723001 to 724000... | 207 | 16 | 2 | 15 | | *802001 to 804000... | 219 | 16 | 2 | 19 |
| 724001 to 725000... | 211 | 16 | 2 | 17 | | *804001 to 805000... | 411 | 12 | 1 | 17 |
| *725001 to 726000... | 217 | 16 | 2 | 17 | | *805001 to 806000... | 407 | 12 | 1 | 15 |
| *726001 to 727000... | 227 | 16 | 2 | 21 | | *806001 to 808000... | 429 | 12 | 1 | 19 |
| *727001 to 728000... | 223 | 16 | 2 | 17 | | *808001 to 809000... | 219 | 16 | 2 | 19 |
| *728001 to 729000... | 212 | 16 | 2 | 17 | | *809001 to 810000... | 411 | 12 | 1 | 17 |
| 729001 to 730000... | 305 | 18 | 2 | 15 | | *810001 to 811000... | 429 | 12 | 1 | 19 |
| 730001 to 731000... | 304 | 18 | 2 | 15 | | *811001 to 812000... | 211 | 16 | 2 | 17 |
| *731001 to 732000... | 313 | 18 | 2 | 17 | | *812001 to 814000... | 219 | 16 | 2 | 19 |
| 732001 to 733000... | 309 | 18 | 2 | 17 | | *814001 to 815000... | 429 | 12 | 1 | 19 |
| 733001 to 734000... | 211 | 16 | 2 | 17 | | *815001 to 816000... | 407 | 12 | 1 | 15 |
| *734001 to 735000... | 215 | 16 | 2 | 17 | | *816001 to 817000... | 219 | 16 | 2 | 19 |
| *735001 to 736000... | 217 | 16 | 2 | 17 | | *817001 to 818000... | 429 | 12 | 1 | 19 |
| *736001 to 737000... |  | 0 | 2 | 17 | | *818001 to 819000... | 219 | 16 | 2 | 19 |
| *737001 to 738000... | 227 | 16 | 2 | 21 | | *819001 to 820000... | 429 | 12 | 1 | 19 |
| *738001 to 739000... | 215 | 16 | 2 | 17 | | | | | | |

Although grade numbers appear in this list some of the earlier watches did not have grade numbers stamped upon them. In all instances odd grade numbers indicate open face movement, even grade numbers indicate hunting movement.

*Watches with these serial numbers have double roller.

### 18 SIZE—MODEL 1
#### Open Face and Hunting Lever Set

No. 341—Open Face, 17 Jewels, Lever Set, Adjusted to Temperature & 3 Positions.
No. 340—Hunting, 17 Jewels, Lever Set, Adjusted to Temperature & 3 Positions.
No. 343—Open Face, 17 Jewels, Lever Set.
No. 342—Hunting, 17 Jewels, Lever Set.
No. 331—Open Face, 15 Jewels, Lever Set.
No. 330—Hunting, 15 Jewels, Lever Set.

Model 1, Full Plate, Open face.                    Model 1 , Full Plate, Hunting

### 18 SIZE—MODEL 2
#### Open Face and Hunting, Lever Set

No. 329—21J, Open Face, "Studebaker," Adjusted to Temperature and 5 Positions.
No. 328—21J, Hunting,  "Studebaker," Adjusted to Temperature and 5 Positions.
No. 327—21J, Open Face, Adjusted to Temperature and 5 Positions.
No. 323—17J, Open Face, "Studebaker," Adjusted to Temperature and 5 Positions.
No. 345—17J, Open Face, Adjusted to Temperature and 3 Positions.
No. 344—17J, Hunting, Adjusted to Temperature and 3 Positions.
No. 313—17J, Open Face, Adjusted to Temperature.
No. 312—17J, Hunting, Adjusted to Temperature.
Nos. 309, 337, 347—17J, Open Face.
No. 346—17J, Hunting.
Nos. 333, 305—15J, Open Face.
Nos. 332, 304—15J, Hunting.

Model 2, Full Plate, Open face.                    Model 2, Full Plate, Hunting.

## 16 SIZE—MODEL 1
### Open Face and Hunting, Lever Set

No. 295—Open Face, 21 Jewels, Adjusted to Temperature and 5 Positions.
No. 294—Hunting, 21 Jewels, Adjusted to Temperature and 5 Positions.
No. 293—Open Face, 19 Jewels, Adjusted to Temperature and 5 Positions.
No. 292—Hunting, 19 Jewels, Adjusted to Temperature and 5 Positions.
No. 299—Open Face, 17 Jewels, Adjusted to Temperature and 3 Positions.
No. 298—Hunting, 17 Jewels, Adjusted to Temperature and 3 Positions.
No. 291—Open Face, 17 Jewels, Adjusted to Temperature and 3 Positions.
No. 290—Hunting, 17 Jewels, Adjusted to Temperature and 3 Positions.
No. 281—Open Face, 15 Jewels, & No. 280—Hunting, 15 Jewels.
No. 261—Open Face, 7 Jewels, & No. 260—Hunting, 7 Jewels.

Model 1, 3/4 Plate, Open Face.     Model 1, 3/4 Plate, Hunting.

## 16 SIZE—MODEL 2
### Open Face and Hunting, Pendant and Lever Set.

No. 229—21J, Open Face, Lever Set, "Studebaker," Adjust. to Temp. and 5 Positions.
No. 227—21J, Open Face, Lever Set, Adjusted to Temperature and 5 Positions.
No. 219—19J, Open Face, Pendant Set, Adjusted to Temperature and 4 Positions.
No. 223—17J, Open Face, Lever Set, "Studebaker," Adjust. to Temp. and 5 Positions.
No. 217—17J, Open Face, Lever Set, Adjusted to Temperature and 3 Positions.
No. 215—17J, Open Face, Pendant Set, Adjusted to Temperature.
No. 212—17J, Hunting, Lever Set, Adjusted to Temperature.
No. 211—17J, Open Face, Pendant Set
No. 207—15J, Open Face, Pendant Set, & No. 204—15J, Hunting, Lever Set.
No. 209—9J, Open Face, Pendant Set, & No. 203—7J, Open Face, Pendant Set.

Model 2, 3/4 Plate, HC.        Model 2, 3/4 Plate, OF.

Model 2, Bridges, Open Face.

## 12 SIZE—MODEL 1
### Chesterfield Series  and Grade 429 Special
### Made in Pendant Set, Open Face Only

No. 431—21J, Adjusted to Temperature and 5 Positions.
No. 429—19J, Adjusted to Temperature and 4 Positions.
No. 419—17J, Adjusted to Temperature and 3 Positions.
No. 415—17J, Adjusted to Temperature.
No. 411—17J.
No. 407—15J.

Model 1, Bridges, Open Face.

Model 1, Lower Plate, Dial Side.

### 6 SIZE— MODEL 1
#### Hunting
Grade No. 180, 17 Jewels
Grade No. 170, 15 Jewels
Grade No. 160, 11 Jewels

Serial Number Range
380,501 to 389,900

Model 1, 3/4 Plate, 6 size

### 0 SIZE—MODEL 1
#### Open Face, No second hand, Hunting has second hand

Model numbers 1 & 2 serial numbers under 659,700. All open face and hunting parts for this model except dial and fourth pinion are interchangeable.

Model 1, Open Face, 3/4 Plate, 7 jewels.

Model 1, Hunting, Bridges, 15-17 jewels.

## 0 SIZE—MODEL 2
### Open Face, No second hand, Hunting has second hand

No. 100— 7 Jewels, Hunting, 3/4 Bridge.
No. 101— 7 Jewels, Open Face, 3/4 Plate.
No. 110— 15 Jewels, Hunting, 3/4 Bridge.
No. 111— 15 Jewels, Open Face, 3/4 Plate.
No. 120— 17 Jewels, Hunting, 3/4 Bridge.
No. 121— 17 Jewels, Open Face, 3/4 Plate.

Model 2, Open Face, 3/4 Plate.        Model 2, Hunting, 3/4 Bridge.

Model numbers 1 & 2 serial numbers under 659,700. All open face and hunting parts for this model except dial and fourth pinion are interchangeable.

## 0 SIZE—MODEL 3
### Both Open Face and Hunting have second hand

No. 151— 21J, Open Face, Bridge Model.
No. 150— 21J, Hunting, Bridge Model.
No. 121— 17J, Open Face, Bridge Model.
No. 120— 17J, Hunting, Bridge Model.

Model 3, Open Face, Bridges.        Model 3, Hunting, Bridges.

# J. P. STEVENS & CO.

## J. P. STEVENS & BRO.
## J. P. STEVENS WATCH CO.
### Atlanta, Georgia
### 1882 - 1887

In mid-1881 J. P. Stevens bought part of the Springfield Watch Co. of Massachusetts; and some unfinished watch components from E. F. Bowman. He set up his watchmaking firm above his jewelry store in Atlanta, Ga., and started to produce the Bowman unfinished watches which were 16 size and 18 size, to which was added the "Stevens Patent Regulator." This regulator is best described as a simple disc attached to the plate which has an eccentric groove cut for the arm of the regulator to move in. This regulator is a prominent feature of the J. P. Stevens, and only the top is jeweled. These watches were 16S, 3/4 plate, stem wind and had a nickel plate with damaskeening. The pallets were equidistant locking and needed greater accuracy in manufacturing. About 50 of these watches were made. A line of gilt movements was added. The pallet and fork are made of one piece aluminum. The aluminum was combined with 1/10 copper and formed an exceedingly tough metal which will not rust or become magnetized. The lever of this watch is only one-third the weight of a steel lever. The aluminum lever affords the least possible resistance for overcoming inertia in transmitting power from the escape wheel to the balance. In 1884, the company was turning out about ten watches a day at a price of $20 to $100 each. In the spring of 1887 the company failed. Only 174 true Stevens watches were made, but other watches carried the J. P. Stevens name.

Original J. P. **Stevens** movement, 16-18 size, 15 jewels, note patented eccentric style regulator, serial number 65.

J.P. **Stevens Watch Co.** movement by **Columbus** Watch Co., 18 size, 11-15 jewels.

## 16 TO 18 SIZE

| Grade or Name – Description | | Avg | Ex-Fn | Mint |
|---|---|---|---|---|
| Original Model, Serial Nos. 1 to 174,(recased) ★ ★ ★ | | $2,000 | $2,500 | $3,000 |
| Original Model, Serial Nos. 1 to 174 with original J. P. Stevens dial & 18K case ★ ★ ★ ★ | | 7,000 | 8,000 | 9,500 |
| Aurora, 15-17J ★ | | 350 | 400 | 525 |
| Chronograph, 17J, Swiss made, fly back hand ★ | | 500 | 600 | 750 |
| Columbus W. Co., 15-17J ★ | | 400 | 450 | 575 |

J. P. **Stevens & Bro.**, on movement & dial, made by **Aurora**, 18 size, 15 jewels, Hunting Case, S # 39806.

J. P. **Stevens & Bro.**, Swiss chronograph movement, about 18 size, with fly back hand.

| Grade or Name – Description | | Avg | Ex-Fn | Mint |
|---|---|---|---|---|
| Elgin, 15-17J | ★ | $300 | $350 | $425 |
| Hamilton, 17J | ★ | 400 | 450 | 525 |
| Hampden, 15-17J | | 300 | 350 | 425 |
| Illinois, 15-17J | ★ | 600 | 650 | 725 |
| N. Y. W. Co., 17J, Full Plate, S#s range in 500s | ★ | 700 | 750 | 825 |
| N. Y. W. Co. "Bond" Model, S#s range in 500s | ★ ★ | 850 | 950 | 1,100 |
| A. Potter, 14K case, Swiss made | ★ ★ | 2,000 | 3,000 | 4,000 |
| Rockford, 15J, Full Plate, HC | ★ | 400 | 450 | 625 |
| 18S Swiss, 15-17J, bar style movement, wolf teeth winding | | 400 | 500 | 650 |
| 16S Swiss, 15-17J, Longines | ★ | 175 | 200 | 250 |
| 16S Swiss, 15-17J, 3/4 plate | ★ | 175 | 200 | 250 |
| Waltham, 11-15-17J | ★ | 400 | 450 | 625 |

**J.P. Stevens & Bro.**, about 18 size, 17 jewels, wolf teeth winding, Ca. about 1889.

**J.P. Stevens Watch Co.** movement by **Waltham**, 18 size, 11 jewels, serial number 1,240,058.

J.P. **Stevens** movement made by Hampden, 18 size, 17 jewels, note eccentric style regulator, serial # 1695.

J.P. **Stevens & Bro.**, movement made by Hampden, model 4, 18 size, 17jewels, model 4, S#732,085.

## 6 SIZE

| Grade or Name – Description | Avg | Ex-Fn | Mint |
|---|---|---|---|
| Ladies Model, 15J, LS, HC, 14K .................................................... | $500 | $575 | $650 |
| Ladies Model, 15J, LS, GF case, HC............................................. | 225 | 275 | 350 |
| Ladies Model, 15J, LS, GF cases, OF............................................ | 200 | 250 | 325 |
| Ladies Model, 15J, LS, GF cases, Swiss made ............................. | 175 | 225 | 325 |

J.P. **Stevens Watch Co.**, 16 size, 15 jewels, Adjusted to temperature & positions, serial number 21,814.

J.P. **Stevens Watch Co.**, 6 size, 11 jewels, exposed winding gears.

🕐 Generic, nameless or **unmarked** grades for watch movements are listed under the Company name or initials of the Company, etc. by size, jewel count and description.

🕐 Watches listed in this book are priced at the collectable retail level, as **complete** watches having an original 14k gold-filled case and *Key Wind* with silver, an original white enamel single sunk dial, and with the entire original movement in good working order with no repairs needed.

# SUFFOLK WATCH CO.

## Waltham, Massachusetts 1899 - 1901

The Suffolk Watch Company officially succeeded the Columbia Watch Company in March 1901. However, the Suffolk 0-size, 7-jewel nickel movement with lever escapement was being manufactured in the Columbia factory before the end of 1899. More than 25,000 movements were made . The factory was closed after it was purchased by the Keystone Watch Case Company on May 17, 1901. The machinery was moved to the nearby factory of the United States Watch Company (purchased by Keystone in April 1901), where it was used to make the United States Watch Company's 0-size movement,introduced in April 1902. Both the Columbia Watch Company and the Suffolk Watch Company made 0-size movements only.

| Grade or Name – Description | Avg | Ex-Fn | Mint |
|---|---|---|---|
| 0S, 7J, NI, HC ............................................................★ | $100 | $135 | $175 |

Suffolk Watch Co., 0 Size, 7 jewels, serial number 216,841.   Seth Thomas, *Colonia U.S.A.* on movement, 18 size, 7 jewels, model # 11.

# SETH THOMAS WATCH CO.

## Thomaston, Connecticut

## 1883 - 1915

Seth Thomas is a very prominent clock manufacturer, but in early 1883, the company made a decision to manufacture watches. The watches were first placed on the market in 1885. They were 18S, open face, stem wind, 3/4 plate, and the escapement was between the plates. The compensating balance was set well below the normal. They were 11J, 16,000 beats per minute train, but soon went to 18,000 or quick train. In 1886, the company started to make higher grade watches and produced four grades: 7J, 11J, 15J, and 17J. That year the output was 100 watches a day.

### SETH THOMAS ESTIMATED SERIAL NUMBERS AND PRODUCTION DATES

| DATE – SERIAL NO. | DATE – SERIAL NO | DATE–SERIAL NO. | DATE – SERIAL NO. |
|---|---|---|---|
| 1885 – 5,000 | 1893 – 510,000 | 1901 – 1,230,000 | 1909 – 2,500,000 |
| 1886 – 20,000 | 1894 – 600,000 | 1902 – 1,320,000 | 1910 – 2,725,000 |
| 1887 – 40,000 | 1895 – 690,000 | 1903 – 1,410,000 | 1911 – 2,950,000 |
| 1888 – 80,000 | 1896 – 780,000 | 1904 – 1,500,000 | 1912 – 3,175,000 |
| 1889 – 150,000 | 1897 – 870,000 | 1905 – 1,700,000 | 1913 – 3,490,000 |
| 1890 – 235,000 | 1898 – 960,000 | 1906 – 1,900,000 | 1914 – 3,600,000 |
| 1891 – 330,000 | 1899 – 1,050,000 | 1907 – 2,100,000 | |
| 1892 – 420,000 | 1900 – 1,140,000 | 1908 – 2,300,000 | |

The above list is provided for determining the APPROXIMATE age of your watch.  Match serial number with date.  Watches were not necessarily sold in the exact order of manufactured date.

Seth Thomas movement, 18 size,17 jewels, Molineux model, 2 tone yellow gold, heavy damaskeening, H. C.

Seth Thomas 18 size,"Molineux" 17 J., 2 tone yellow gold gilt & nickel heavy damaskeening model #2 ,HC

## 18 SIZE

| Grade or Name – Description | Avg | Ex-Fn | Mint |
|---|---|---|---|
| Century, 7J, OF | $50 | $75 | $125 |
| Century, 7J, HC | 75 | 100 | 150 |
| Century, 15J, OF | 50 | 75 | 125 |
| Century, 15J, HC | 75 | 100 | 150 |
| Chautauqua, 15J, GJS, M#5 | 125 | 150 | 225 |
| Colonia U.S.A., 7J, model # 11 | 50 | 65 | 100 |
| Eagle Series, No. 36, 7J, OF | 75 | 100 | 125 |
| Eagle Series, No. 37, 7J, HC | 100 | 125 | 150 |
| Eagle Series, No. 106, 11J, OF | 75 | 100 | 125 |
| Eagle Series, No. 107, 11J, HC | 100 | 125 | 150 |
| Eagle Series, No. 206, 15J, OF | 75 | 100 | 125 |

Liberty, Eagle Series,18 size, 7 jewels, hunting or open face, eagle on movement.

Maiden Lane, 18 size, 28 jewels, gold jewel settings, Adj5p, engraved dated as =8,1,99. No serial number.

Henry Molineux, 18 size, 17 jewels, "Corona W. Co. USA" on dial, open face, serial number 54,951.

Seth Thomas, 18 size, 23 jewels, gold jewel settings, adjusted, serial number 298,333.

| Grade or Name – Description | Avg | Ex-Fn | Mint |
|---|---|---|---|
| Eagle Series, No. 207, 15J, HC | $125 | $150 | $175 |
| Eagle Series, 15J, M# 2, HC | 100 | 125 | 175 |
| Eagle Series, No. 210, 17J, OF | 100 | 125 | 150 |
| Eagle Series, No. 211, 17J, HC | 150 | 175 | 225 |
| Eagle Series, 17J, NI, 3/4, OF | 100 | 125 | 150 |
| Edgemere, 11J | 75 | 100 | 125 |
| Edgemere, 17J | 75 | 100 | 150 |
| Keywind M#2, 7J, 11J, & 15J, 3/4 | 150 | 200 | 300 |
| Keywind M#4, 7J, 11J, & 15J, 3/4 | 150 | 200 | 300 |
| Lakeshore, 17J, GJS, ADJ, NI | 200 | 250 | 300 |
| Liberty, 7J, 3/4, eagle on back plate | 75 | 100 | 125 |
| Maiden Lane, 17J, GJS, DR, Adj.6P, NI, marked ★★ | 900 | 1,100 | 1,400 |
| Maiden Lane, 19J, GJS, DR, Adj.6P, NI, marked ★★★ | 1,000 | 1,200 | 1,500 |
| Maiden Lane, 21J, GJS, DR, Adj.6P, NI, marked ★ | 1,200 | 1,500 | 1,700 |
| Maiden Lane, 24J, GJS, DR, Adj.6P, marked ★★★ | 1,700 | 2,000 | 2,200 |
| Maiden Lane, 25J, GJS, DR, Adj.6P, NI, marked ★★ | 2,500 | 2,800 | 3,200 |
| Maiden Lane, 28J, GJS, DR, Adj.5P, NI, marked ★★★★★ | 15,000 | 18,000 | 25,000 |
| Henry Molineux, M#3, 17J, 3/4, GJS, ADJ ★★ | 550 | 600 | 700 |
| Henry Molineux, M#2, 17J, GJS, ADJ ★★ | 550 | 600 | 700 |
| Henry Molineux, M#2, 20-21J, GJS, ADJ ★★★ | 1,000 | 1,200 | 1,500 |
| Monarch Watch Co., 7-15J, 2-tone | 75 | 100 | 150 |
| Republic USA, 7J, OF | 75 | 100 | 125 |

🕐 Generic, nameless or **unmarked** grades for watch movements are listed under the Company name or initials of the Company, etc. by size, jewel count and description.

| | Avg | Ex-Fn | Mint |
|---|---|---|---|
| S. Thomas, 7J, 3/4, multi-color dial | 150 | 200 | 275 |
| S. Thomas, 7J, 3/4 | 75 | 100 | 125 |
| S. Thomas, 11J, 3/4, HC | 75 | 100 | 150 |
| S. Thomas, 11J, 3/4, OF | 75 | 100 | 125 |
| S. Thomas, 15J, 3/4, HC | 100 | 125 | 175 |
| S. Thomas, 15J, 3/4, gilded, OF | 75 | 100 | 125 |
| S. Thomas, 15J, 3/4 , OF | 75 | 100 | 125 |
| S. Thomas, 16J, 3/4 | 75 | 100 | 150 |
| S. Thomas, 17J, 3/4, OF, nickel | 100 | 125 | 175 |

| Grade or Name – Description | Avg | Ex-Fn | Mint |
|---|---|---|---|
| S. Thomas, 17J, 3/4, 2-Tone........................................ | $125 | $150 | $200 |
| S. Thomas, 17J, 3/4, OF, gilded............................... | 75 | 100 | 150 |
| S. Thomas, 17J, 3/4, HC............................................. | 125 | 150 | 175 |
| S. Thomas, 19J, GJS, DR, Adj.5P, OF .................... ★★ | 500 | 600 | 850 |
| S. Thomas, 21J, GJS, DR, Adj.5P.............................. | 325 | 400 | 475 |
| S. Thomas, 23J, GJS, DR, Adj.5P .......................... ★★ | 1,000 | 1,300 | 1,500 |
| Special Motor Service,17J, 2 tone, LS, OF................ | 275 | 300 | 350 |
| 20th Century (Wards), 11J.......................................... | 75 | 100 | 150 |
| 20th Century (Wards), 11J, 2-Tone............................ | 100 | 125 | 175 |
| Wyoming Watch Co., 7J, OF ..................................... | 125 | 150 | 200 |
| S. Thomas, G# 33, 7J, 3/4, gilded, OF....................... | 75 | 100 | 125 |
| S. Thomas, G# 37, 7J, 3/4, NI, HC ........................... | 75 | 100 | 150 |
| S. Thomas, G# 44, 11J, 3/4, gilded, OF..................... | 75 | 100 | 125 |
| S. Thomas, G# 47, 7J, gilded, FULL, OF .................. | 75 | 100 | 125 |
| S. Thomas, G# 58, 11J, FULL, gilt, OF ..................... | 75 | 100 | 125 |
| S. Thomas, G# 70, 15J, 3/4, gilded, OF..................... | 75 | 100 | 125 |
| S. Thomas, G# 80, 17J, 3/4, gilded, ADJ, HC ........... | 75 | 100 | 150 |
| S. Thomas, G# 101, 15J, 3/4, gilded, ADJ, OF .......... | 75 | 100 | 125 |
| S. Thomas, G# 149, 15J, gilded, FULL, OF................ | 75 | 100 | 125 |
| S. Thomas, G# 159, 15J, NI, FULL, OF...................... | 75 | 100 | 125 |
| S. Thomas, G# 169, 17J, NI, FULL, OF...................... | 75 | 125 | 150 |
| S. Thomas, G# 170, 15J, 3/4, NI, OF......................... | 75 | 100 | 125 |
| S. Thomas, G# 179, 17J, 3/4, NI, ADJ, OF ................ | 75 | 125 | 150 |
| S. Thomas, G# 180, 17J, 3/4, NI, HC ........................ | 75 | 125 | 150 |
| S. Thomas, G# 182, 17J, DR, NI, FULL, OF .............. | 100 | 125 | 175 |
| S. Thomas, G# 201, 15J, 3/4, NI, ADJ, OF ................ | 100 | 130 | 175 |
| S. Thomas, G# 245, 19J, GJS, 2-Tone, HC ................ | 1,000 | 1,200 | 1,500 |
| S. Thomas, G# 260, 21J, DR, Adj.6P, NI, FULL, OF.... | 350 | 400 | 450 |
| S. Thomas, G# 281-282, 17J, FULL, DR, Adj.3P, OF, 2-tone ...... | 175 | 225 | 275 |
| S. Thomas, G# 382, 17J, FULL, DR, Adj.5P, OF, 2-tone .............. | 175 | 225 | 275 |
| Trainsman Special, **fake 23J Adj**, seen in model 10 or 12.............. | 65 | 75 | 95 |

**Trainsman Special, fake 23 jewels,** Adjusted, Chicago U.S.A., jewels made of glass, seen in model 10 or 12.

**Grade 36,** 16 size, 7 jewels, open face, three-quarter nickel plate.

🕑 Generic, nameless or **unmarked** grades for watch movements are listed under the Company name or initials of the Company, etc. by size, jewel count and description.

🕑 Watches listed in this book are priced at the collectable retail level, as **complete** watches having an original 14k gold-filled case and *Key Wind* with silver, an original white enamel single sunk dial, and with the entire original movement in good working order with no repairs needed.

## 16 SIZE
### (OF Only)

| Grade or Name – Description | Avg | Ex-Fn | Mint |
|---|---|---|---|
| Centennial, 7J, 3/4, NI, OF | $60 | $75 | $95 |
| Locust, 7J, NI, 3/4, OF | 60 | 75 | 95 |
| Locust, 17J, NI, ADJ, 3/4, OF | 100 | 135 | 175 |
| Republic USA, 7J, OF | 60 | 75 | 95 |

🕐 Generic, nameless or **unmarked** grades for watch movements are listed under the Company name or initials of the Company, etc. by size, jewel count and description.

| | | | |
|---|---|---|---|
| S. Thomas, G# 25, 7J, BRG, OF | $60 | $75 | $95 |
| S. Thomas, G# 26, 15J, BRG, GJS, OF | 60 | 75 | 95 |
| S. Thomas, G# 27, 17J, BRG, GJS, OF | 60 | 75 | 95 |
| S. Thomas, G# 28, 17J, BRG, Adj.3P, GJS, OF | 100 | 125 | 150 |
| S. Thomas, G# 326, 7J, 3/4, NI, OF | 60 | 75 | 95 |
| S. Thomas, G# 328, 15J, 3/4, NI, OF | 60 | 75 | 95 |
| S. Thomas, G# 332, 7J, 3/4, NI, OF | 60 | 75 | 95 |
| S. Thomas, G# 334, 15J, NI, ADJ,3/4, DMK, OF | 75 | 100 | 150 |
| S. Thomas, G# 336, 17J, ADJ, 3/4, DMK, OF | 100 | 120 | 150 |

Seth Thomas, 12 size, 7 jewels, open face, pendant set.

Seth Thomas, 12 size, 17 jewels, gold jewel settings, gold center wheel, open face, Adj3p.

## 12 SIZE
### (OF Only)

| Grade or Name – Description | Avg | Ex-Fn | Mint |
|---|---|---|---|
| Centennial, 7J | $40 | $45 | $60 |
| Republic USA, 7J, OF | 45 | 60 | 80 |
| S. Thomas, G# 25, 7J, BRG, OF | 50 | 65 | 90 |
| S. Thomas, G# 26, 15J, BRG, GJS, OF | 55 | 70 | 90 |
| S. Thomas, G# 27, 17J, BRG, GJS, OF | 60 | 75 | 95 |
| S. Thomas, G# 28, 17J, OF, BRG, Adj.3P, GJS | 75 | 80 | 95 |
| S. Thomas, G# 326, 7J, OF, 3/4, NI | 50 | 60 | 75 |
| S. Thomas, G# 328, 15J, OF, 3/4, NI | 55 | 65 | 85 |

🕐 Watches listed in this book are priced at the collectable retail level, as complete watches having an original 14k gold-filled case and Key Wind with silver, an original white enamel single sunk dial, and with the entire original movement in good working order with no repairs needed.

🕐 Generic, nameless or unmarked grades for watch movements are listed under the Company name or initials of the Company, etc. by size, jewel count and description.

Seth Thomas movement, 6 size, 7 jewels, serial number 441,839. Sometimes appears in a 12 size case.

SETH THOMAS, 0 size, 15 jewels, pendant set, hunting case, serial number 200,449.

## 6 SIZE

### (Some 6 Size were used to fit 12 Size cases)

| Grade or Name – Description | Avg | Ex-Fn | Mint |
|---|---|---|---|
| Century, 7J, NI, 3/4 | $45 | $50 | $65 |
| Countess Janet, 17J, Adj., HC | 65 | 75 | 85 |
| Eagle Series, 7J, No. 45, 3/4, NI, DMK, OF | 55 | 60 | 75 |
| Eagle Series, 7J, No. 205, 3/4, HC | 75 | 100 | 150 |
| Eagle Series, 15J, No. 35, 3/4, NI, DMK, OF | 65 | 70 | 85 |
| Eagle Series, 15J, No. 245, 3/4, HC | 75 | 100 | 150 |
| Edgemere, 7-11J, | 55 | 60 | 75 |
| Republic USA, 7J | 45 | 50 | 65 |
| Seth Thomas, 7J, 3/4, HC, 14K, 26 DWT | 250 | 275 | 325 |
| Seth Thomas, 11J, 3/4, HC | 75 | 100 | 150 |
| Seth Thomas, 11J, 3/4, OF | 45 | 55 | 65 |
| S. Thomas, G# 35, 7J, HC, NI, DMK,3/4 | 45 | 55 | 65 |
| S. Thomas, G# 119, 16J, HC, GJS, NI, DMK, 3/4 | 100 | 125 | 175 |
| S. Thomas, G# 205, 15J, HC | 75 | 100 | 150 |
| S. Thomas, G# 320, 7J, OF, NI, DMK, 3/4 | 50 | 65 | 85 |
| S. Thomas, G# 322, 15J, OF | 55 | 60 | 70 |

NOTE: Add $25 to $50 for HC.

## 0 SIZE

| Grade or Name – Description | Avg | Ex-Fn | Mint |
|---|---|---|---|
| Seth Thomas, 7J, OF, No. 1 | $60 | $70 | $85 |
| Seth Thomas, 7J, HC, No. 1 | 75 | 100 | 150 |
| Seth Thomas, 15J, OF, GJS, No. 3 | 60 | 70 | 85 |
| Seth Thomas, 15J, HC, No. 3 | 75 | 100 | 150 |
| Seth Thomas, 17J, OF, GJS, PS, No. 9 | 60 | 70 | 85 |
| Seth Thomas, 17J, HC, GJS, PS, No. 9 | 75 | 100 | 150 |

NOTE: Add $25 to $50 for HC.

# SETH THOMAS WATCH CO.
## IDENTIFICATION OF MOVEMENTS
### BY MODEL NUMBER

How to Identify Your Watch: Compare the movement of your watch with the illustrations in this section. Upon matching the movement exactly, the model number and size can be determined. While comparing, note the location of the balance, jewels, screws, gears, and type of back plate (Full, 3/4, Bridge) which will be clues in identifying the movement you have. Having determined the size and model number, you can now find your watch in the main price listing by name or number (which is engraved on the movement).

**Model 1, 18 size, Open Face**

**Model 2, 18 size, Hunting**

**Model 3, 18 size, Open Face**

**Model 4, 18 size, Key Wind**

Model 5, 18 size, Maiden Lane Series, Open Face.

Model 6, 18 Size, Open Face

Model 7 & 9, 18 size

Model 8, 18 size

Model 10, 18 size, Open Face

Model 11, 18 size, Hunting

🕐 This book endeavours to be a GUIDE or helpful manual and offers a wealth of material to be used as a tool not as a absolute document. Price Guides are like watches the worst may be better than none at all, but at best cannot be expected to be 100% accurate.

🕐 Characteristics of watches differ for the same age of both case and movement, because these features vary it may not be accurate to date a watch by one single influence. Example: the second hand was not commonly found on watches before 1750, but common about 1800. The first second hand appeared in 1665 and another in 1690. Therefore statements are broad rather than accurate.

Model 13, 18 size, Hunting

16 Size

16 Size, Open Face

12 Size, Open Face

6 Size, Open face

Model 14, 6 size

Model 16 & 17, 6 size

# TREMONT WATCH CO.

## Boston, Massachusetts
### 1864 - 1866

In 1864 A. L. Dennison thought that if he could produce a good movement at a reasonable price, there would be a ready market for it. Dennison went to Switzerland to find a supplier of cheap parts, as arbors were too high in America. He found a source for parts, mainly the train and escapement and the balance. About 600 sets were to be furnished. Dials were first made by Mr. Gold and Mr. Spurr, then later by Mr. Hull and Mr. Carpenter. Tremont had hoped to produce 600 sets of trains per month. In 1865, the first movements were ready for the market. They were 18S, key wind, fully jeweled, and were engraved "Tremont Watch Co." In 1886, the company moved from Boston to Melrose. Another 18S was made, and the company made its own train and escapement. The watches were engraved "Melrose Watch Co., Melrose, Mass." The Tremont Watch Co. produced about 5,000 watches before being sold to the English Watch Co.

Tremont Watch Co., with "Washington Street Boston" engraved on movement, 18 size, 15 jewels, key wind and set, serial number 5,264.

Tremont movement, 18 size, 15 jewels, key wind & set, serial number 8,875.

| Grade or Name – Description | Avg | Ex-Fn | Mint |
|---|---|---|---|
| 18S, 7J, KW, KS......★ | $250 | $275 | $350 |
| 18S, 11J, KW, KS...... | 250 | 275 | 350 |
| 18S, 7-11-15J, KW, KS, gilded Silveroid...... | 200 | 235 | 275 |
| 18S, 7-11-15J, KW, KS, gilded, marked LONDON ...... | 200 | 235 | 275 |
| 18S, 15J, KW, KS, gilded...... | 250 | 275 | 350 |
| 18S, 15J, KW, KS, HC, 14K...... | 650 | 675 | 750 |
| 18S, 15J, KW, KS, gilded, Washington Street ......★ ★ | 450 | 550 | 700 |
| 18S, 17J, KW, KS, gilded...... | 300 | 325 | 400 |
| 18S, 15J, KW, KS from back, 3/4 plate ......★ ★ ★ | 1,500 | 1,700 | 2,000 |

🕐 Watches listed in this book are priced at the collectable retail level, as **complete** watches having an original 14k gold-filled case and *Key Wind* with silver, an original white enamel single sunk dial, and with the entire original movement in good working order with no repairs needed.

# TRENTON WATCH CO.
### Trenton, New Jersey
### 1885 - 1908

Trenton watches were marketed under the following labels: Trenton, Ingersoll, Fortuna, Illinois Watch Case Company, Calumet U.S.A., Locomotives Special, Marvel Watch Co., and Reliance Watch Co.

Serial numbers started at 2,001 and ended at 4,100,000. Total production was about 1,934,000.

## CHRONOLOGY OF THE DEVELOPMENT OF TRENTON WATCH CO.:

New Haven Watch Co., New Haven, Conn. ............. 1883-1887
Trenton Watch Co., Trenton, N. J. ........................... 1887 -1908
Sold to Ingersoll ....................................................... 1908-1922

### TRENTON MODELS AND GRADES
#### With Years of Manufacture and Serial Numbers

| Date | Numbers | Size | Model | Date | Numbers | Size | Model |
|------|---------|------|-------|------|---------|------|-------|
| 1887-1889 | 2,001- 61,000 | 18 | 1 | 1900-1903 | 2,000,001-2,075,000 | 6 | 2 |
| 1889-1891 | 64,001- 135,000 | 18 | 2 | 1902-1905 | 2,075,001-2,160,000 | 6 | 3 LS |
| 1891-1898 | 135,001- 201,000 *¹ | 18 | 3 | | | 12 | 2 LS |
| 1899-1904 | 201,001- 300,000 | 18 | 6 | 1905-1907 | 2,160,001-2,250,000 | 6 | 3 PS |
| 1891-1900 | 300,001- 500,000 | 18 | 4 | | | 12 | 2 PS |
| 1892-1897 | 500,001- 600,000 | 6 | 1 | 1899-1902 | 2,500,001-2,600,000 | 3/0 | 1 |
| 1894-1899 | 650,001- 700,000 | 16 | 1 | ca. 1906 | 2,800,001-2,850,000 | 6 | 3 PS |
| 1898-1900 | 700,001- 750,000 | 6 | 2 | | | 12 | 2 PS |
| 1900-1904 | 750,001- 800,000 *² | 18 | 4 | 1900-1904 | 3,000,001-3,139,000 | 16 | 2 |
| 1896-1900 | 850,001- 900,000 | 12 | 1 | 1903-1907 | 3,139,001-3,238,000 | 16 | 3 OF |
| 1898-1903 | 900,001-1,100,000 | 18 | 5 | 1903-1907 | 3,500,001-3,600,000 | 16 | 3 HC |
| 1902-1907 | 1,300,001-1,400,000 | 18 | 6 | 1905-1907 | 4,000,001-4,100,000 | 0 | 1 |

1—7 jewel grades made only during 1891; 9 jewel chronograph Pat. Mar.,17, 1891, made 1891-1898.
2—A few examples are KWKS for export to England.

**Trenton** movement, 18 size, 4 jewels, model # 1, serial number 4,744.

**Trenton** movement, 18 size, 7 jewels, 4th model, serial number 788,313.

**18 SIZE**

| Grade or Name – Description | Avg | Ex-Fn | Mint |
|---|---|---|---|
| Trenton W. Co., M#1-2, gilded, OF ............................★ | $150 | $175 | $250 |
| Trenton W. Co., M#3, 7J, 3/4 ............................... | 50 | 75 | 125 |
| Trenton W. Co., M#3, 9J, 3/4 ............................... | 50 | 75 | 125 |
| Trenton W. Co., M#4, 7J, FULL ............................ | 50 | 75 | 125 |
| Trenton W. Co., M#4, 11J, FULL .......................... | 50 | 75 | 125 |
| Trenton W. Co., M#4, 15J, FULL .......................... | 50 | 75 | 125 |
| Trenton W. Co., M#4-5, FULL, OF, NI ................... | 50 | 75 | 125 |
| Marvel W. Co. Fake 23 jewels ............................ | 100 | 125 | 150 |
| New Haven Watch Co. style, M#1, 4J .........★★★ | 250 | 325 | 450 |
| Railroad Special, fake 23J, tu-tone, locomotive on dial & mvt. ★★ | 150 | 185 | 235 |
| Trenton, 7J, KW, KS ......................................★ | 225 | 300 | 425 |

Note: Add $25 to value of above watches in hunting case.

**Trenton** movement, 18 size, 7 jewels, model #3, serial number 148,945.

**Chronograph,** 16 size, 9 jewels, **third model**; start, stop & fly back, sweep second hand.

**16 SIZE**

| Grade or Name – Description | Avg | Ex-Fn | Mint |
|---|---|---|---|
| Trenton W. Co., M#1-2, 7J, 3/4, NI, OF ...................... | $50 | $75 | $125 |
| Trenton W. Co., M#3, 7J, 3F BRG ........................... | 50 | 75 | 125 |
| Trenton W. Co., M#3, 11J, 3F BRG ......................... | 50 | 75 | 125 |
| Trenton W. Co., M#3, 15J, 3F BRG ......................... | 50 | 75 | 125 |
| Trenton W. Co., 7,11,15J, 3F BRG, NI ...................... | 50 | 75 | 125 |
| Chronograph, 9J, start, stop, & fly back, **DMK** ....★★★ | 250 | 325 | 450 |
| Chronograph, 9J, start, stop, & fly back, **GILDED** ....★★★ | 250 | 325 | 450 |
| Convertible Model, 7J, OF ...............................★ | 100 | 125 | 175 |
| Trenton W. Co., Grade #30 & 31, 7J ....................... | 50 | 75 | 125 |
| Trenton W. Co., Grade #35, 36 & 38, 11J ................. | 50 | 75 | 125 |
| Trenton W. Co., Grade #45, 16J ........................... | 75 | 100 | 150 |
| Trenton W. Co., Grade #125, 12J .......................... | 50 | 75 | 125 |
| Ingersoll Trenton, 7J, 3F BRG ............................. | 50 | 75 | 125 |

🕐 Generic, nameless or **unmarked** grades for watch movements are listed under the Company name or initials of the Company, etc. by size, jewel count and description.

🕐 Watches listed in this book are priced at the collectable retail level, as **complete** watches having an original 14k gold-filled case and *Key Wind* with silver, an original white enamel single sunk dial, and with the entire original movement in good working order with no repairs needed.

Ingersoll Trenton movement, 16 size, 19 jewels, three fingered bridge, adjusted, serial number 3,419,771.

Ingersoll Trenton movement, 16 size, 12 jewels; "Edgemere" engraved on movement.

| Grade or Name – Description | Avg | Ex-Fn | Mint |
|---|---|---|---|
| Ingersoll Trenton, 15J, 3F BRG, NI, ADJ | $75 | $100 | $150 |
| Ingersoll Trenton, 17J, 3F BRG, NI, ADJ | 75 | 100 | 150 |
| Ingersoll Trenton, 19J, 3F BRG, NI, Adj.5P ★ | 150 | 250 | 300 |
| Peerless, 7J, SW, LS | 50 | 65 | 80 |
| Railroad Reliance, 17J, OF ★ | 100 | 125 | 150 |
| Reliance, 7J | 50 | 65 | 80 |

Note: Add $25 to value of above watches in hunting case.

Railroad Special, 18 size, 23 jewels, tu-tone, locomotive on dial & movement, model # 6, S# 1,3660,044.

Trenton movement, convertible model converts to open face or hunting case, 16 size, 7 J.

### 10 - 12 SIZE

| Grade or Name – Description | Avg | Ex-Fn | Mint |
|---|---|---|---|
| "Fortuna," 7J, 3 finger BRG | $40 | $50 | $65 |
| Trenton W. Co., M#1, 7J, 3/4 | 40 | 50 | 65 |
| Monogram, 7J, SW | 30 | 40 | 55 |

Note: Add $25 to value of above watches in hunting case.

Trenton Watch Co. movement, 6 size, 7 jewels, open face & hunting, nickel damaskeened.

### 6 SIZE

| Grade or Name – Description | Avg | Ex-Fn | Mint |
|---|---|---|---|
| Trenton W. Co., 7J, 3/4, NI | $30 | $40 | $55 |
| Trenton W. Co., 7J, 3Finger BRG | 30 | 40 | 55 |
| Trenton W. Co., 15J, 3Finger BRG | 40 | 50 | 65 |
| "Fortuna," 7J, 3 Finger Bridge | 30 | 40 | 55 |

Note: Add $25 to value of above watches in hunting case.

### 0 SIZE

| Grade or Name – Description | Avg | Ex-Fn | Mint |
|---|---|---|---|
| Trenton W. Co., 7J, 3F BRG | $40 | $50 | $65 |
| Trenton W. Co., 15J, 3F BRG | 50 | 60 | 75 |

Note: Add $25 to value of above watches in hunting case.

Trenton Chronograph, 9J, start, stop, & fly back, **Model # 3.**

# UNITED STATES WATCH CO.

## Marion, New Jersey

### 1865 - 1877

The United States Watch Company was chartered in 1865, and the factory building was started in August 1865 and was completed in 1866. The first watch, called the "Frederic Atherton," was not put on the market until July 1867. It was America's first mass produced stem winding watch. This first grade was 18S, 19J, full plate and a gilt finish movement. A distinctive feature of the company's full plate movements was the butterfly shaped patented opening in the plate which allowed escapement inspection. That same year a second grade called the "Fayette Stratton" was introduced. It was also a gilt finish, full plate movement.

Most of these were 15J, but some of the very early examples have been noted in 17J. In 1868 the "George Channing," "Edwin Rollo," and "Marion Watch Co." grades were introduced. All were 18S, 15J, full plate movements in a gilt finish. In February 1869 the gilt version of the "United States Watch Co." grade was introduced. It was 18S, 19J, full plate and was the company's first entry into the prestige market. Later that year the company introduced their first nickel grade, a 19J, 18S, full plate movement called the "A. H. Wallis." About this same time, in December 1869, they introduced America's most expensive watch, the first nickel, 19J, 18S, full plate "United States Watch Co." grade. Depending on case weight, these prestige watches retailed between $500 and $600, more than the average man earned in a year at that time. The company also introduced damaskeening to the American market; first on gilt movements and later on the nickel grades. The damaskeening process was later improved by using **IVORY** disc in place of wooden disc. The United States and Wallis 19J prestige grades were beautifully finished with richly enameled engraving including a variety of unique designs on the balance cock. It is significant to note that no solid gold trains have been seen with these prestige items in the extant examples presently known.

FREDERIC ATHERTON & CO. movement, 18 size, 19 jewels, gold jewel settings, key wind & pin set. Note butterfly cut-out.

In 1870 the company introduced their first watch for ladies, a 10S, 15J, plate, cock & bridge movement which was made to their specifications in Switzerland. This model was first introduced in two grades, the "R. F. Pratt" and "Chas. G. Knapp," both in a 15J, gilt finish movement. Later it was offered in a high grade, 19J "I. H. Wright" nickel finish movement. During 1870 and 1871 several other full plate grades in both gilt and nickel finish were introduced. In 1871 development on a new line of full plate, 3/4, plate, and plate & bridge was started but not introduced to the market until late in 1872 and early in 1873. The 10S and 16S new grades in plate and bridge were probably delayed well into 1873 and were not available long before the "Panic of 1873" started in September; this explains their relative scarcity.

By July 1874 the "Panic" had taken its toll and it was necessary for the company to reorganize as the Marion Watch Company, a name formerly used for one of their grades. At this time jewel count, finish standards, and prices were lowered on the full plate older grades, but this proved to be a mistake. That same year they introduced a cased watch called the "North Star", their cheapest watch at $15 retail.

The year of 1875 hit the watch industry the hardest; price cutting was predatory and the higher priced watches of the United States Watch Co. were particulary vulnerable. Further lowering of finish standards and prices did not help and in 1876 the company was once again reorganized into the Empire City Watch Co. and their products were displayed at the Centennial that year. The Centennial Exhibition was not enough to save the faltering company and they finally closed their doors in 1877. The Howard brothers of Fredonia, New York (Independent and Fredonia Watch Co.) purchased most of the remaining movement stock and machinery. In the ten year period of movement production, current statistical studies indicate an estimated production of only some 60,000 watches, much smaller than the number deduced from the serial numbers assigned up to as high as 289,000.

NOTE: The above historical data and estimated production figures are based on data included in the new NAWCC book **MARION, A History of the United States Watch Company,** by William Muir and Bernard Kraus. This definitive work is available from NAWCC, Inc., 514 Poplar St., Columbia, PA. (Courtesy, Gene Fuller, MARION book editor.) This book is recommended by Mr. Shugart and Mr. Gilbert for your library.

## EMPIRE CITY W. CO. & EQUIVALENT U.S.W. CO. GRADES

| Empire City W. Co. | United States W. Co. |
|---|---|
| W. S. Wyse | A. H. Wallis |
| L. W. Frost | Henry Randel |
| Cyrus H. Loutrel | Wm. Alexander |
| J. L. Ogden | S. M. Beard |
| E. F. C. Young | John W. Lewis |
| D. C. Wilcox | George Channing |
| Henry Harper | Asa Fuller |
| Jesse A. Dodd | Edwin Rollo |
| E. C. Hine | J. W. Deacon |
| New York Belle | A. J. Wood |
| The Champion | G. A. Read |
| Black Diamond | Young America |

## NOTE: Courtesy Gene Fuller, NAWCC "MARION" book editor.

Empire City W. Co., Henry Harper, note:
movement does not have **Butterfly Cut-out**.

United States Watch Co. movement, 18 size, 19 jewels, gold jewel settings, key wind. Their highest grade watch.

United States Watch Co., Henry Randel, 15jewels, KWKS, FROSTED plates, S.# 24,944

## MARION

### 18 SIZE

#### (All with Butterfly Cut-out Except for 3/4 Plate)

| Grade or Name – Description | Avg | Ex-Fn | Mint |
|---|---|---|---|
| Wm. Alexander, 15J, NI, KW, HC | $275 | $350 | $425 |
| Wm. Alexander, 15J, NI, KW, OF | 200 | 250 | 325 |
| Wm. Alexander, 15J, NI, SW, OF | 225 | 275 | 350 |
| Frederic Atherton & Co., 15J, SW, gilded | 250 | 325 | 400 |
| Frederic Atherton & Co., 17J, KW, gilded, HC | 300 | 350 | 425 |
| Frederic Atherton & Co., 17J, KW, gilded, OF | 250 | 300 | 375 |
| Frederic Atherton & Co., 17J, SW, gilded, HC | 300 | 350 | 425 |
| Frederic Atherton & Co., 17J, SW, gilded, OF | 250 | 325 | 400 |

U.S. Watch Co., dial and movement, 18 size, 20 jewels, hunting case, 3/4 plate, engraved on movement "N.D. Godfrey," serial number 72,042. Painted on the dial "New York 1873." The dial consists of day-date-month and moon phases.

| Grade or Name – Description | Avg | Ex-Fn | Mint |
|---|---|---|---|
| Frederic Atherton & Co., 19J, SW, gilded, ...................... ★★★★ | $800 | $1,000 | $1,300 |
| Frederic Atherton & Co., 19J, KW, gilded .............................. ★★ | 600 | 700 | 850 |
| BC&M R.R., 11J, KW.....................................................★★★★ | 1,600 | 1,800 | 2,100 |
| BC&M R.R., 15J, gilded, KW .......................................★★★★ | 1,600 | 1,800 | 2,100 |
| S. M. Beard, 15J, KW, NI, OF........................................ | 250 | 300 | 375 |
| S. M. Beard, 15J, SW, NI, OF........................................ | 250 | 300 | 375 |
| S. M. Beard, 15J, SW or KW, HC ................................. | 300 | 350 | 425 |
| Centennial Phil., 11-15J, SW or KW, NI ......................... ★★★★ | 1,800 | 2,000 | 2,300 |
| George Channing, 15J, KW, NI..................................... | 250 | 300 | 375 |
| George Channing, 15J, KW, gilded............................... | 225 | 275 | 325 |
| George Channing, 15J, KW, NI, 3/4 Plate ............................. ★★ | 350 | 400 | 475 |
| George Channing, 17J, KW, NI...................................... | 275 | 325 | 400 |
| J. W. Deacon, 11-13J, KW, gilded............................... | 175 | 225 | 300 |
| J. W. Deacon, 15J, KW, gilded ................................... | 175 | 225 | 300 |
| J. W. Deacon, 11-15J, KW, 3/4 Plate............................ ★ | 275 | 325 | 400 |
| Empire City Watch Co., 11J, SW, **no butterfly cut-out** ...... ★★★ | 175 | 225 | 300 |
| Empire City Watch Co., 15J, SW, NI, **no butterfly cut-out** ★★★ | 200 | 250 | 325 |
| Empire Combination Timer, 11J, FULL, time & distance |  |  |  |
|   on dial............................................................... ★★★ | 400 | 500 | 650 |
| Empire Combination Timer, 15J, 3/4, time & distance |  |  |  |
|   on dial................................................................ ★★★ | 600 | 750 | 1,000 |
| Fellows, 15J, NI, KW ................................................. | 400 | 450 | 525 |
| Benjamin Franklin, 15J, KW........................................ | 400 | 450 | 525 |
| Asa Fuller, 7-11J, gilded, KW..................................... | 200 | 225 | 275 |
| Asa Fuller, 15J, gilded, KW ....................................... | 200 | 225 | 275 |
| Asa Fuller, 15J, gilded, KW, 3/4 Plate.....................................★★ | 300 | 325 | 350 |
| N. D. Godfrey, 20J, NI, 3/4 plate, day date month, moon |  |  |  |
|   phases, c. 1873, HC, 18K ......................................... ★★★★ | 4,000 | 5,000 | 6,000 |
| John W. Lewis, 15J, NI, KW ...................................... | 225 | 275 | 350 |
| John W. Lewis, 15J, NI, SW ...................................... | 250 | 300 | 375 |

**Edwin Rollo,** 18 size, 15 jewels, gilded, key wind & set, note butterfly cut-out, serial number 110,214.

**Marion Watch Co.** personalized Watch, 18 size, about 15J., pin set, note butterfly cut-out, serial # 106,761.

🕐 Watches listed in this book are priced at the collectable retail level, as **complete** watches having an original 14k gold-filled case and *Key Wind* with silver, an original white enamel single sunk dial, and with the entire original movement in good working order with no repairs needed.

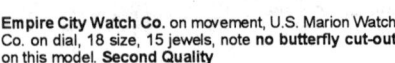

Empire City Watch Co. on movement, U.S. Marion Watch Co. on dial, 18 size, 15 jewels, note **no butterfly cut-out** on this model. **Second Quality**

United States Watch Co., 18 size, 19 jewels, gold jewel settings, key wind & pin set, serial number 24,054.

| Grade or Name – Description | Avg | Ex-Fn | Mint |
|---|---|---|---|
| John W. Lewis, 15J, NI, 3/4 Plate ............................ ★★ | $350 | $400 | $475 |
| Marion Watch Co., 11J, KW, gilded................................. | 200 | 250 | 325 |
| Marion Watch Co., 15J, KW, gilded................................. | 200 | 250 | 325 |
| Marion Watch Co., 15J, SW, gilded, 3/4 Plate ................. ★★ | 300 | 350 | 425 |
| Marion Watch Co., 17-19J, KW, gilded ......................... ★ | 300 | 350 | 425 |
| N.J. R.R.&T. Co., 15J, gilded, KW................................. ★ | 1,200 | 1,400 | 1,700 |
| Newspaper Special Order, 11-15J, gilded, SW or KW ................. | 325 | 375 | 450 |
| North Star, 7J, KW, NI case ......................................... | 300 | 350 | 425 |
| North Star, 7J, SW, KS ............................................... | 300 | 350 | 425 |
| North Star, 7J, 3/4 Plate............................................. | 325 | 375 | 450 |
| Pennsylvania R.R., 15J, NI, KW ......................... ★★★★ | 2,500 | 2,700 | 2,900 |
| Personalized Watches, 7-11J, KW, 3/4 Plate................. ★ | 250 | 300 | 375 |
| Personalized Watches, 11J, KW, gilded ......................... ★ | 250 | 300 | 375 |
| Personalized Watches, 15J, KW, gilded ......................... ★ | 250 | 300 | 375 |
| Personalized Watches, 15J, KW, NI .............................. ★ | 275 | 325 | 400 |
| Personalized Watches, 15J, KW, 3/4 Plate ..................... ★ | 300 | 350 | 425 |
| Personalized Watches, 19J, KW, Full Plate.................... ★ | 400 | 450 | 525 |
| Henry Randel, 15J, KW, NI .......................................... | 250 | 300 | 375 |
| Henry Randel, 15J, KW, frosted plates............................ | 265 | 325 | 395 |
| Henry Randel, 15J, SW, NI .......................................... | 250 | 300 | 375 |
| Henry Randel, 15J, 3/4 Plate ................................... ★★ | 350 | 400 | 475 |
| Henry Randel, 17J, KW, NI .......................................... ★ | 275 | 325 | 400 |
| G. A. Read, 7J, gilded, KW.......................................... | 200 | 250 | 325 |
| G. A. Read, 7J, 3/4 Plate ............................................ | 300 | 350 | 425 |
| Edwin Rollo, 11J, KW, gilded........................................ | 200 | 250 | 325 |
| Edwin Rollo, 15J, KW, gilded........................................ | 200 | 250 | 325 |
| Edwin Rollo, 15J, SW, gilded ....................................... | 200 | 250 | 325 |
| Edwin Rollo, 15J, 3/4 Plate ...................................... ★ | 300 | 350 | 425 |
| Royal Gold, 11J, KW.................................................. | 200 | 250 | 300 |
| Royal Gold, 15J, KW.................................................. | 300 | 350 | 425 |
| Royal Gold, 15J, 3/4 Plate....................................... ★★ | 400 | 450 | 525 |

🕑 Watches listed in this book are priced at the collectable retail level, as **complete** watches having an original 14k gold-filled case and *Key Wind* with silver, an original white enamel single sunk dial, and with the entire original movement in good working order with no repairs needed.

**A.H. Wallis** on movement, Empire City Watch Co. on dial, 18 size, 19 jewels, three-quarter plate, hunting. This combination timer has listed on the dial, 16 cities showing the time of day and distance in comparison with New York City, serial number 54,409.

| Grade or Name – Description | | Avg | Ex-Fn | Mint |
|---|---|---|---|---|
| Rural New York, 15J, gilded | | $250 | $300 | $375 |
| Fayette Stratton, 11J, gilded | | 250 | 300 | 375 |
| Fayette Stratton, 15J, KW, gilded | | 250 | 300 | 375 |
| Fayette Stratton, 15J, SW, gilded | | 250 | 300 | 325 |
| Fayette Stratton, 17J, KW, gilded | | 275 | 325 | 400 |
| Fayette Stratton, 17J, SW, gilded | | 300 | 350 | 425 |
| Union Pacific R.R., 15J, KW, gilded | ★★★ | 1,800 | 2,000 | 2,300 |
| United States Watch Co., 15J, NI, KW | | 500 | 550 | 625 |
| United States Watch Co., 15J, NI, SW | | 600 | 650 | 725 |
| United States Watch Co., 15J, 3/4 Plate, NI | | 600 | 650 | 725 |
| United States Watch Co., 15J, 3/4 Plate, gilded | | 600 | 650 | 725 |
| United States Watch Co., 19J, GJS, Adj.5P, 18K HC, dial mvt. & case all marked, Pin Set, SW | ★★★ | 3,500 | 4,000 | 4,500 |
| United States Watch Co., 19J, NI, KW | ★★ | 750 | 950 | 1,200 |
| United States Watch Co., 19J, NI, SW | ★★ | 900 | 1,100 | 1,350 |
| A. H. Wallis, 15J, KW, NI | | 250 | 300 | 375 |
| A. H. Wallis, 15J, SW, NI | | 250 | 300 | 375 |
| A. H. Wallis, 17J, KW, NI | | 275 | 325 | 400 |
| A. H. Wallis, 17J, SW, NI | | 300 | 350 | 425 |
| A. H. Wallis, 19J, KW, NI | ★★★ | 600 | 650 | 725 |
| A. H. Wallis, 19J, SW, NI | ★★★ | 650 | 700 | 775 |
| D. C. Wilcox, 15J, SW, no butterfly cut-out | | 250 | 300 | 375 |
| I. H. Wright, 11J, KW, gilded | | 225 | 275 | 350 |
| I. H. Wright, 15J, KW, gilded | | 225 | 275 | 350 |

🕐 Watches listed in this book are priced at the collectable retail level, as **complete** watches having an original 14k gold-filled case and *Key Wind* with silver, an original white enamel single sunk dial, and with the entire original movement in good working order with no repairs needed.

🕐 Some grades are not included. Their values can be determined by comparing with **similar** age, size, metal content, style, models and grades listed.

## 16 SIZE
### 1/4 Plate

| Grade or Name – Description | | Avg | Ex-Fn | Mint |
|---|---|---|---|---|
| S. M. Beard, 15J, NI, KW, .................................... ★ ★ ★ ★ | | $400 | $450 | $525 |
| John W. Lewis, 15J, NI, KW ............................... ★ ★ ★ ★ | | 400 | 450 | 525 |
| Personalized Watches, 15J, NI, SW ..................... ★ ★ ★ ★ | | 400 | 450 | 525 |
| Edwin Rollo, 15J, KW .......................................... ★ ★ ★ ★ | | 400 | 450 | 525 |
| United States Watch Co., 15J, NI, SW ............... ★ ★ ★ ★ | | 600 | 700 | 850 |
| A. H. Wallis, 19J, NI, SW, ................................. ★ ★ ★ ★ | | 600 | 700 | 850 |

Note: 16S, 1/4 plate are the scarcest of the U.S.W.Co.–Marion watches.

**Asa Fuller,** 16 size, 15 jewels, stem wind, one-quarter plate, serial number 280,018. Note: 3 screws on barrel bridge.

**United States Watch Co.,** 14 size, 15 jewels, three-quarter plate, engraved on movement "Royal Gold American Watch, New York, Extra Jeweled."

## 14 SIZE
### 3/4 Plate

| Grade or Name – Description | | Avg | Ex-Fn | Mint |
|---|---|---|---|---|
| Centennial Phil., 11J, KW, gilded ..................................... | | $400 | $500 | $750 |
| J. W. Deacon, 11J, ............................................... ★ ★ | | 250 | 300 | 375 |
| Asa Fuller, 15J, ................................................... ★ ★ | | 350 | 400 | 475 |
| John W. Lewis, 15J, NI ........................................ ★ ★ | | 300 | 350 | 400 |
| North Star, 15J, .......................................................... | | 250 | 300 | 375 |
| Personalized Watches, 7-11J, ............................ ★ ★ | | 350 | 400 | 475 |
| Edwin Rollo, 15J, ...................................................... ★ | | 300 | 350 | 425 |
| Royal Gold, 15J, ........................................................ ★ | | 350 | 400 | 475 |
| Young America, 7J, gilded............................................. | | 300 | 350 | 425 |

🕐 Watches listed in this book are priced at the collectable retail level, as **complete** watches having an original 14k gold-filled case and *Key Wind* with silver, an original white enamel single sunk dial, and with the entire original movement in good working order with no repairs needed.

🕐 Some grades are not included. Their values can be determined by comparing with **similar** age, size, metal content, style, models and grades listed.

## 10 SIZE
### 1/4 Plate

| Grade or Name – Description | Avg | Ex-Fn | Mint |
|---|---|---|---|
| Wm. Alexander, 15J, KW, NI | $200 | $250 | $325 |
| S. M. Beard, 15J, KW, NI, 1/4 Plate | 200 | 250 | 325 |
| Empire City Watch Co., 15J, KW ★ | 200 | 250 | 325 |
| Chas. G. Knapp, 15J, Swiss, 1/4 Plate, KW | 100 | 150 | 225 |
| Personalized Watches, 11-15J, 1/4 Plate | 200 | 250 | 325 |
| R. F. Pratt, 15J, Swiss, 1/4 Plate, KW | 100 | 150 | 225 |
| Edwin Rollo, 11-15J, 1/4 Plate ★ | 250 | 300 | 375 |
| A. H. Wallis, 17-19J, KW, 1/4 Plate | 225 | 275 | 350 |
| A. J. Wood, 15J, 1/4 Plate, KW ★★★★ | 300 | 350 | 425 |
| I. H. Wright, 19J, Swiss, NI, Plate, KW ★★★ | 500 | 550 | 625 |

**S. M. Beard**, 10 size, 15 jewels, key wind, quarter plate, serial number 248,407. Note: 2 screws on barrel bridge.  **Chas. G. Knapp**, 10 size, 15 jewels, Swiss, quarter plate, key wind.

# U. S. WATCH CO.
## OF WALTHAM
### Waltham, Massachusetts
#### 1884 - 1905

The business was started as the Waltham Watch Tool Co. in 1879. It was organized as the United States Watch Co. in 1884. The first watches were 16S, 3/4 plate pillar movement in three grades. They had a very wide mainspring barrel (the top was thinner than most) which was wedged up in the center to make room for the balance wheel. These watches are called dome watches and are hard to find. The fork was made of an aluminum alloy with a circular slot and a square ruby pin. The balance was gold at first, as was the movement which was a slow train, but the expansion balance was changed when they went to a quick train. The movement required a special case which proved unpopular. By 1887, some 3,000 watches had been made. A new model was then produced, a 16S movement that would fit a standard case. These movements were quick train expansion balance with standard type lever and 3/4 plate pillar movement. This Company reached a top production of 10 watches a day for a **very short period.** The company was sold to the E. Howard Watch Co. ( Keystone ) in 1903. The United States Watch Co. produced some 890,000 watches total. Its top grade watch movement was the **"President."**

## U. S. WATCH CO. OF WALTHAM
### ESTIMATED SERIAL NUMBERS AND PRODUCTION DATES

| Date | Serial No. | | Date | Serial No. |
|------|-----------|---|------|-----------|
| 1887 | 3,000 | | 1896 | 300,000 |
| 1888 | 6,500 | | 1897 | 350,000 |
| 1889 | 10,000 | | 1898 | 400,000 |
| 1890 | 30,000 | | 1899 | 500,000 |
| 1891 | 60,000 | | 1900 | 600,000 |
| 1892 | 90,000 | | 1901 | 700,000 |
| 1893 | 150,000 | | 1902 | 750,000 |
| 1894 | 200,000 | | 1903 | 800,000 |
| 1895 | 250,000 | | | |

**U.S. Watch Co. of Waltham,** The President , 18 size, 17 jewels, hunting, serial number 150,000.

**U.S. Watch Co. of Waltham,** The President, 18 size, 17 jewels, open face, 2-tone, adj., note regulator, serial number 150,350.

### 18 SIZE

| Grade or Name – Description | Avg | Ex-Fn | Mint |
|----------------------------|-----|-------|------|
| Express Train, 15J, OF, ADJ................................................. | $275 | $325 | $400 |
| Express Train, 15J, HC, ADJ ............................................... | 375 | 425 | 500 |
| The President, 17J, HC.............................................. ★ ★ | 500 | 550 | 625 |
| The President, 21J, GJS, Adj.6P, DR, 14K .............................. ★ ★ | 900 | 950 | 1,025 |
| The President, 17J, GJS, Adj.6P, DR, NI, DMK, OF .................. ★ | 500 | 550 | 625 |
| U. S. Watch Co., 15J, OF, **2-tone, stem attached** ..................... ★ | 250 | 300 | 375 |
| Washington Square, 15J, HCH........................................ ★ | 150 | 200 | 275 |
| U. S. Watch Co., 39 (HC) & 79 (OF), 17J, GJS, ADJ, NI, DMK, Adj.5P, BRG ......................................... | 100 | 125 | 175 |
| U. S. Watch Co., 40 (HC) & 80 (OF), 17J, GJS............................ | 100 | 125 | 175 |
| U. S. Watch Co., 48 (HC) & 88 (OF), 7J, gilded, FULL ............... | 100 | 125 | 175 |
| U. S. Watch Co., 48 (HC) & 88 (OF), 7J, gilded, FULL, Silveroid | 60 | 70 | 85 |
| U. S. Watch Co., 52 (HC)........................................................ | 125 | 150 | 200 |
| U. S. Watch Co., 92 (OF), 17J, Silveroid ...................................... | 60 | 70 | 85 |

🕐 Generic, nameless or unmarked grades for watch movements are listed under the Company name or initials of the Company, etc. by size, jewel count and description.

🕐 Some grades are not included. Their values can be determined by comparing with **similar** age, size, metal content, style, models and grades listed.

| Grade or Name – Description | Avg | Ex-Fn | Mint |
|---|---|---|---|
| U. S. Watch Co., 52 (HC) & 92 (OF), 17J........................ | $100 | $125 | $175 |
| U. S. Watch Co., 53 (HC) & 93 (OF), 15J, NI, FULL, DMK......... | 100 | 125 | 175 |
| U. S. Watch Co., 54 (HC) & 94 (OF), 15J........................ | 100 | 125 | 175 |
| U. S. Watch Co., 56 (HC) & 96 (OF), 11J........................ | 100 | 125 | 175 |
| U. S. Watch Co., 57 (HC) & 97 (OF), 15J........................ | 100 | 125 | 175 |
| U. S. Watch Co., 58 (HC) & 98 (OF), 11J, NI, FULL, DMK......... | 100 | 125 | 175 |

U.S. Watch Co. of Waltham, 16 size, 7 jewels, gilded, note raised dome on center of movement, engraved on movement "Chas. V. Woerd's Patents," serial number 3,564.

U.S. Watch Co. of Waltham, 16 size, 7 jewels, "A New Watch Company At Waltham, Est'd 1885" on movement, serial number 770,771.

### 16 SIZE

| Grade or Name – Description | Avg | Ex-Fn | Mint |
|---|---|---|---|
| Dome Plate Model, 7J, gilded ............................... | $125 | $150 | $200 |
| U. S. Watch Co., Early KW-KS, 7J, S# below 100........... | 500 | 700 | 1,000 |
| U. S. Watch Co., 103, 17J, NI, 3/4, ADJ .................... | 65 | 75 | 125 |
| U. S. Watch Co., 104, 17J, NI, 3/4........................ | 65 | 75 | 125 |
| U. S. Watch Co., 104, 17J, NI, 3/4, Silveroid.............. | 55 | 60 | 85 |
| U. S. Watch Co., 105, 15J, NI, 3/4, HC .................... | 125 | 150 | 200 |
| U. S. Watch Co., 105, 15J, NI, 3/4, OF .................... | 55 | 75 | 125 |
| U. S. Watch Co., 105, 15J, NI, 3/4, Silveroid.............. | 45 | 65 | 115 |
| U. S. Watch Co., 106, 15J, gilded,3/4, Silveroid.......... | 45 | 65 | 115 |
| U. S. Watch Co., 106, 15J, gilded,3/4...................... | 55 | 75 | 125 |
| U. S. Watch Co., 108, 11J, gilded, 3/4.................... | 55 | 75 | 125 |
| U. S. Watch Co., 109, 7J, NI, 3/4......................... | 55 | 75 | 125 |
| U. S. Watch Co., 110, 7J, 3/4, HC........................ | 65 | 75 | 125 |
| U. S. Watch Co., 110, 7J, 3/4, OF........................ | 55 | 60 | 75 |

Note: Add $20 - $40 to value of above watches in hunting case.

🕐 Generic, nameless or **unmarked** grades for watch movements are listed under the Company name or initials of the Company, etc. by size, jewel count and description.

🕐 Watches listed in this book are priced at the collectable retail level, as complete watches having an original 14k gold-filled case and Key Wind with silver, an original white enamel single sunk dial, and with the entire original movement in good working order with no repairs needed.

U.S. Watch Co., 16 size, 15 jewels, three-quarter plate.

### 6 SIZE

| Grade or Name – Description | Avg | Ex-Fn | Mint |
|---|---|---|---|
| U. S. Watch Co., 60, 17J, GJS, NI, 3/4, Adj.3P | $40 | $60 | $85 |
| U. S. Watch Co., 60, 17J, GJS, NI, 3/4, Adj.3P, HC, 14K | 225 | 275 | 350 |
| U. S. Watch Co., 62, 15J, NI, 3/4 | 40 | 60 | 85 |
| U. S. Watch Co., 63, 15J, gilded | 40 | 60 | 85 |
| U. S. Watch Co., 64, 11J, NI | 40 | 60 | 85 |
| U. S. Watch Co., 65, 11J, gilded | 20 | 30 | 40 |
| U. S. Watch Co., 66, 7J, gilded | 20 | 30 | 40 |
| U. S. Watch Co., 66, 7-11J, NI, 3/4 | 40 | 60 | 85 |
| U. S. Watch Co., 68, 16J, GJS, NI, 3/4 | 50 | 75 | 125 |
| U. S. Watch Co., 69, 7J, NI, HC | 75 | 100 | 150 |
| U. S. Watch Co., 69, 7J, NI, OF | 20 | 30 | 40 |

Grade 64, 6 size, 11 jewels

U.S. Watch Co. of Waltham, 0 size, 7 jewels, serial number 808,231.

### 0 SIZE

| Grade or Name – Description | Avg | Ex-Fn | Mint |
|---|---|---|---|
| Betsy Ross, HC, GF case | $125 | $150 | $200 |
| U. S. Watch Co., 15J, HC, GF case | 100 | 125 | 175 |
| U. S. Watch Co., 7-11J, HC, GF case | 100 | 125 | 175 |

# THE WASHINGTON WATCH CO.

## Washington, D. C.

### 1872 - 1874

J. P. Hopkins, though better known as the inventor of the Auburndale Rotary Watch, was also connected with the Washington Watch Co. they may have produced about 50 watches. They were 18S, key wind, 3/4 plate and had duplex escapements. Before Hopkins came to Washington Watch Co. he had handmade about six fine watches. Most of the materials used to produce the watch movements were purchased from the Illinois Watch Co. The company had a total production of 45 movements with duplex escapements.

| Grade or Name – Description | | Avg | Ex-Fn | Mint |
|---|---|---|---|---|
| 18S, 15J, 3/4, KW, KS...................................................... ★ ★ ★ ★ | | $3,500 | $4,500 | $5,500 |

# WATERBURY WATCH CO.

## Waterbury, Connecticut

### 1880 - 1898

The Waterbury Watch Co. was formed in 1880, and D. A. A. Buck made its first watch. The watches were simple and had only 50 parts. The mainspring was about nine feet long and coiled around the movement. It had a two-wheel train rather than the standard four-wheel train. The Waterbury long wind movement revolved once every hour and had a duplex escapement. The dial was made of paper, and the watch was priced at $3.50 to $4.00. Some of these watches were used as give aways.

Waterbury Watch Co., skeletonized movement; "A poor man's tourbillon," c. 1890.

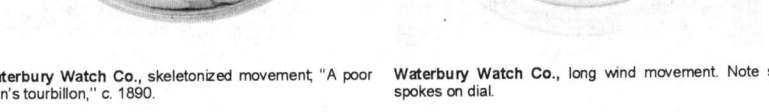

Waterbury Watch Co., long wind movement. Note six spokes on dial.

## CHRONOLOGY OF THE DEVELOPMENT OF THE WATERBURY WATCH CO.:

Waterbury Watch Co., Waterbury, Conn. ................. 1880-1898
New England Watch Co. ............................................ 1898-1912
Purchased Ingersoll. .................................................... 1914
Became U. S. Time Corp. (maker of Timex) ............ 1944

Waterbury Watch Co. movement, Series C.

Series L, Waterbury W. Co. Duplex Escapement, about 16 size.

### 18 TO 0 SIZES

| Grade or Name – Description | Avg | Ex-Fn | Mint |
|---|---|---|---|
| 35S, 1890-1891, back wind................................................. | $100 | $150 | $200 |
| Long wind, skeletonized, 3 spokes................................. ★ | 350 | 400 | 550 |
| Long wind, skeletonized, 4 spokes............................. ★ ★ | 600 | 750 | 1,000 |
| Long wind, skeletonized, 6 spokes................................. ★ | 400 | 450 | 700 |
| Long wind, skeletonized, 6 spokes, **celluloid case**....................... ★ | 500 | 600 | 750 |
| Series A, long wind, skeletonized ................................. ★ | 350 | 400 | 550 |
| Series B, long wind................................................ | 200 | 225 | 300 |
| Series C, long wind................................................ | 200 | 225 | 300 |
| Series D, long wind................................................ | 225 | 250 | 350 |
| Series E, long wind (discontinued 1890) ........................ | 275 | 300 | 400 |
| Series F, Duplex escapement.................................... | 75 | 85 | 100 |

⏱ Some grades are not included. Their values can be determined by comparing with **similar** age, size, metal content, style, models and grades listed.

⏱ Watches listed in this book are priced at the collectable retail level, as **complete** watches having an original 14k gold-filled case and *Key Wind* with silver, an original white enamel single sunk dial, and with the entire original movement in good working order with no repairs needed.

⏱ This book endeavours to be a GUIDE or helpful manual and offers a wealth of material to be used as a tool not as a absolute document. Price Guides are like watches the worst may be better than none at all, but at best cannot be expected to be 100% accurate.

⏱ Characteristics of watches differ for the same age of both case and movement, because these features vary it may not be accurate to date a watch by one single influence. Example: the second hand was not commonly found on watches before 1750, but common about 1800. The first second hand appeared in 1665 and another in 1690. Therefore statements are broad rather than accurate.

**Series I, The Trump**, about 18 size, no jewels, pin lever escapement.

**Series T, Oxford Duplex Escapement**, about 18 size, no jewels.

| Grade or Name – Description | Avg | Ex-Fn | Mint |
|---|---|---|---|
| Series G, 3/4 lever escapement.................................................★ | $200 | $225 | $300 |
| Series H, Columbian Duplex...........................................★★ | 250 | 275 | 350 |
| Series I, Trump, duplex, ................................................ | 85 | 95 | 110 |
| Series I, Trump, 3/4 ...................................................... | 85 | 95 | 110 |
| Series J, Americus Duplex .............................................. | 85 | 95 | 110 |
| Series K, Charles Benedict Duplex................................. | 125 | 150 | 200 |
| Series L, Waterbury W. Co. Duplex ............................... | 85 | 100 | 125 |
| Series N, Addison Duplex .............................................. | 60 | 80 | 95 |
| Series P, Rugby Duplex.................................................. | 100 | 125 | 150 |
| Series R, Tuxedo Duplex................................................ | 80 | 100 | 125 |
| Series S, Elfin .............................................................. | 65 | 75 | 85 |
| Series T, Oxford Duplex................................................ | 65 | 75 | 85 |
| Series W, Addison ........................................................ | 85 | 125 | 135 |
| Series Z ....................................................................... | 65 | 85 | 95 |
| Free Press Watch, Series E............................................. | 200 | 225 | 250 |
| Old Honesty, Series C, longwind, .................................. | 250 | 300 | 400 |
| Oxford, ....................................................................... | 55 | 80 | 95 |
| The Trump.................................................................... | 50 | 75 | 90 |
| Waterbury W. Co., 7J, 3/4, low Serial No. ...................... | 300 | 375 | 500 |

NOTE: Dollar -watches must be in **Running** condition to bring these prices.

🕒 Some grades are not included. Their values can be determined by comparing with **similar** age, size, metal content, style, models and grades listed.

🕒 Watches listed in this book are priced at the collectable retail level, as **complete** watches having an original 14k gold-filled case and *Key Wind* with silver, an original white enamel single sunk dial, and with the entire original movement in good working order with no repairs needed.

🕒 This book endeavours to be a GUIDE or helpful manual and offers a wealth of material to be used as a tool not as a absolute document. Price Guides are like watches the worst may be better than none at all, but at best cannot be expected to be 100% accurate.

# E. N. WELCH MFG. CO.

### Bristol, Connecticut
### 1834 - 1897

Elisha Welch founded this company about 1834. His company failed in 1897, and the Sessions Clock Co. took over the business in 1903. E. N. Welch Mfg. Co. produced the large watch which was displayed at the Chicago Exposition in 1893. This watch depicted the landing of Columbus on the back of the case.

E.N. Welch Mfg. Co., 36 size, back wind & set, made for the Chicago Exposition in 1893. Die debossed back depicting the landing of Columbus in America, Oct, 12th, 1492.

| Grade or Name – Description | Avg | Ex-Fn | Mint |
|---|---|---|---|
| 36S, Columbus Exhibition watch | $350 | $435 | $500 |

# WESTCLOX

### United Clock Co. – Western Clock Mfg. Co.– General Time Corp.
### Athens, Georgia
### 1899 - Present

The first Westclox pocket watch was made about 1899; however, the Westclox name did not appear on their watches until 1906. In 1903 they were making 100 watches a day, and in 1920 production was at 15,000 per day. This company is still in business in Athens, Georgia.

| Grade or Name – Description | Avg | Ex-Fn | Mint |
|---|---|---|---|
| M#1, SW, push to set, GRO | $75 | $100 | $125 |
| M#2, SW, back set, GRO | 50 | 60 | 75 |
| 18S, Westclox M#4, OF, GRO | 50 | 60 | 75 |
| 1910 Models to 1920, GRO | 35 | 45 | 60 |
| Anniversary | 35 | 45 | 60 |
| Antique | 20 | 30 | 45 |
| Boy Proof | 45 | 50 | 75 |
| Bingo | 30 | 40 | 55 |
| Bulls Eye (several models) | 15 | 20 | 25 |
| Campus | 15 | 20 | 25 |
| Celluloid case, 70mm | 30 | 35 | 45 |
| Coronado | 15 | 20 | 25 |
| Country Gentleman | 40 | 50 | 60 |

Boy Proof Model, about 16 size, designed to be tamper proof.

Westclox movement, stem wind, back set.

| Grade or Name – Description | Avg | Ex-Fn | Mint |
|---|---|---|---|
| Dax (many models) | $10 | $15 | $20 |
| Dewey | 10 | 15 | 20 |
| Elite | 25 | 35 | 40 |
| Everbrite (several models) | 15 | 20 | 30 |
| Explorer | 225 | 275 | 325 |
| Farm Bureau | 65 | 85 | 100 |
| Glo Ben | 65 | 85 | 100 |
| Glory Be | 20 | 25 | 30 |
| Johnny Zero (several models) | 65 | 75 | 95 |
| Ideal | 30 | 35 | 40 |
| Lighted Dial | 25 | 30 | 40 |
| Magnetic | 20 | 25 | 30 |
| Major | 25 | 30 | 35 |
| Man Time | 15 | 20 | 25 |
| Mark IV | 35 | 45 | 55 |
| Mascot | 20 | 25 | 30 |
| Maxim | 30 | 40 | 50 |

Zep, about 16 size with radiant numbers and hands, c. 1929.

Explorer, back of case and dial, "Wings Over The Pole, The Explorer" on back of case.

**World's Fair watch & fob,** (1982 -Knoxville Tn.){Wagner Time Inc.}, total production for watch 4,200 and 200 for the FOB, Ca. 1982 .

| Grade or Name – Description | Avg | Ex-Fn | Mint |
|---|---|---|---|
| Military Style, 24 hour | $65 | $85 | $100 |
| Monitor | 15 | 20 | 25 |
| Mustang | 40 | 45 | 60 |
| NAWCC, TOTAL PRODUCTION = 1,000 | 60 | 75 | 100 |
| Panther | 45 | 50 | 60 |
| Pasture Stop Watch, (fly back hand) Sterling Watch Co. | 65 | 75 | 90 |
| Pocket Ben (many models) | 20 | 35 | 60 |
| Ruby | 25 | 30 | 45 |
| Scepter | 20 | 25 | 30 |
| Scotty (several models) | 15 | 20 | 25 |
| Silogram | 15 | 20 | 25 |
| Smile | 25 | 30 | 40 |
| Solo | 15 | 20 | 25 |
| St. Regis | 20 | 25 | 35 |
| Sterling Watch Co. **(see Pasture Stop Watch )** | | | |
| Sun Mark | 30 | 35 | 40 |
| Team Mate (various major league teams) | 25 | 35 | 40 |
| Tele Time | 25 | 35 | 45 |
| Texan | 35 | 45 | 65 |
| The Airplane | 45 | 55 | 65 |
| The American, **back SET** | 50 | 60 | 75 |
| The Conductor | 45 | 55 | 65 |
| Tiny Tim | 150 | 200 | 275 |
| Trail Blazer | 40 | 45 | 55 |
| Uncle Sam | 40 | 50 | 60 |
| Victor | 80 | 100 | 130 |
| Vote | 25 | 35 | 45 |
| Westclox | 15 | 20 | 25 |
| World's Fair (1982 -Knoxville Tn.){Wagner Time Inc.} | 75 | 85 | 100 |
| Zep, (Zepplin) | 225 | 275 | 375 |
| Zodiak Time | 35 | 40 | 45 |

# WESTERN WATCH CO.

## Chicago, Illinois
## 1880

Albert Trotter purchased the unfinished watches from the California Watch Co. Mr. Trotter finished and sold those watches. Later he moved to Chicago and, with Paul Cornell and others, formed the Western Watch Company. Very few watches were completed by the Western Watch Co.

| Grade or Name – Description | | Avg | Ex-Fn | Mint |
|---|---|---|---|---|
| Western Watch Co., 18S, FULL ................................... ★★★★ | | $2,500 | $3,000 | $4,000 |

Western Watch Co. movement, 18 size, 15 jewels, key wind & set.

# WICHITA WATCH CO.

## Wichita, Kansas
## July, 1887 - 1888

This company completed construction of their factory in Wichita, Kansas in June 1888, and only a half dozen watches were produced during the brief period the company was in operation. The president was J. R. Snively. These watches are 18S, half plate, adjusted, 15 jewels.

| Grade or Name – Description | | Avg | Ex-Fn | Mint |
|---|---|---|---|---|
| 18S, 15J, plate, ADJ .......................................... ★★★★ | | $3,500 | $4,500 | $5,500 |

🕐 Watches listed in this book are priced at the collectable retail level, as **complete** watches having an original 14k gold-filled case and *Key Wind* with silver, an original white enamel single sunk dial, and with the entire original movement in good working order with no repairs needed.

# COMIC AND CHARACTER WATCHES

When discussing the topic of watches and someone mentions Comic Character Watches, we immediately picture a watch with Mickey Mouse. Isn't Mickey Mouse the most famous of all watches in the world? Before Mickey appeared in the 1930's there were a handful of lesser known comic watches with characters like Skeezix, Smitty and Buster Brown, but it was the Mickey Mouse Watch that paved the way for all other comic character watches. As a collaboration between Walt Disney (the creator of Mickey Mouse) and Robert Ingersoll and his brother the founders of the Ingersoll-Waterbury Watch Company. The Mickey Mouse Watch was one of this century's greatest marketing concepts. In a two year period Ingersoll had sold nearly 2.5 million Mickey Mouse wrist and pocket watches. Throughout the 1930's they also introduced other watches with Disney characters such as Big Bad Wolf in 1934, as well as, the Donald Duck wrist watch. The Donald Duck pocket watch was produced several years later in 1939. The Mickey Lapel and Mickey Deluxe Wrist were produced in the late 1930's.

Ingersoll dominated the character watch market in the early 1930's due to the incredible popularity of the Disney characters, however by the mid 1930's other companies mainly Ingraham and New Haven secured the rights to other popular characters. Throughout the 1930's kids fell in love with these watches featuring their favorite comic character or hero, such as, Popeye, Superman, Buck Rogers, Orphan Annie, Dick Tracy and The Lone Ranger. There was also a couple of other well known characters, Betty Boop and Cowboy Tom Mix produced but for some reason these watches did not become popular like all the others, so very small quantities were produced.

During World War II production of comic watches ceased, but after the war comic watches came back stronger than ever. Once again Disney was the overall leader. The Ingersoll name only appeared on some of the watches to keep the trade name still familiar, as Ingersoll was sold to U.S. Time Watch Company.

The late 1940's was very good to the character watch market and proof being the many character watches produced as the Twentieth Birthday Series for Mickey in 1948 that included with Mickey, Donald Duck, Pinocchio, Pluto, Bambi, Joe Carioca, Jiminy Cricket, Bongo Bear and Daisy Duck. Other watches from this time include Porky Pig, Puss-N-Boots, Joe Palooka, Gene Autry, Captain and Mary Marvel and others featuring characters of the comic and cartoons, space and western heroes.

The early to mid 1950's was also a vibrant time for character watch production with more Disney characters, western heroes and comic characters than ever before, but by 1958 manufacturing of character watches had almost completely stopped as manufacturing costs went up, popularity of some characters faded and many other circumstances led to a complete stop of any of these watches until the late 1960's. The watches were never the same again.

In the 1970's the Comic Character Watch once again made it's come back with the Bradley Watch Company (Elgin W. Co.) leading the way just as Ingersoll did in the first years of comic watches.

Today there are hundreds of character watches to choose from, Disney Super Hero movie characters like E.T., and Roger Rabbit and a wealth of others, but today's fascination is not just with the new but with the old as we see in the re-issue of the original Mickey watches. There is a growing awareness and appreciation for all the originals. It is a very unusual attraction that draws people to love and collect the character watches of the past. Collectors appreciate the original boxes (that are fascinating works of art) and the face of the watch that features the character that we love. The manufacturing method of these simple pin lever movements were not the best of timekeepers, but were solidly constructed.

All in all, when you put together the watches and boxes they are pieces of functional art and history that brings back memories of our youth. Something that no other kind of watch can do.

Babe Ruth, by Exact Time, ca. 1948.

Betty Boop, by Ingraham, ca. 1934.

| Style or Grade – Description | Avg | Ex-Fn | Mint | Mint +Box |
|---|---|---|---|---|
| Alice in Wonderland, WW, c. 1951, by U.S. Time | $30 | $35 | $50 | $275 |
| Alice, Red Riding Hood, & Marjory Daw, WW, c. 1953, by Bradley | 30 | 35 | 55 | 150 |
| Alice in Wonderland, WW, c. 1958, by Timex | 30 | 35 | 50 | 300 |
| Alice in Wonderland & Mad Hatter, WW, c. 1948, by New Haven | 60 | 85 | 125 | 250 |
| Annie Oakley, WW, (Action Gun) c. 1951, by New Haven | 150 | 195 | 275 | 425 |
| Archie, WW, c.1970s, Swiss, | 45 | 60 | 100 | 150 |
| Babe Ruth, WW, c. 1948, by Exact Time, box baseball pledge card | ★175 | 275 | 400 | 1,300 |
| Ballerina, WW, c.1955, Ingraham, Action legs, | 30 | 35 | 45 | 60 |
| Bambi, WW, c. 1949, by U.S. Time, Birthday series | 100 | 175 | 250 | 450 |
| Barbie, WW, c.1964 (blue dial),by Bradley | 30 | 40 | 50 | 125 |
| Barbie, WW, c.1970, by Bradley, action arms | 30 | 35 | 45 | 70 |
| Batman, WW, c. 1970 by Gilbert (band in shape of bat) | 100 | 175 | 225 | 300 |
| Batman, WW, c. 1978, by Timex | 100 | 125 | 175 | 250 |
| Betty Boop, PW, c. 1934, by Ingraham (with diedebossed back) | ★★★★350 | 750 | 1,000 | 1,800 |
| Betty Boop, WW, c.1980s, with hearts on dial & band | 30 | 35 | 50 | 75 |
| Bert & Ernie, WW, c.1970s, swiss | 30 | 35 | 40 | 70 |
| Big Bad Wolf & 3 Pigs, PW, c. 1936, by Ingersoll | 300 | 450 | 700 | 1,200 |
| Big Bad Wolf & 3 Pigs, WW, c. 1936, by Ingersoll | 300 | 550 | 850 | 1,800 |
| Big Bird, WW, c.1970s, Swiss, action arms, (pop up box) | 30 | 35 | 45 | 60 |
| Blondie & Dagwood, WW, c.1950s, Swiss | 150 | 200 | 250 | 475 |
| Bongo Bear, WW, c.1946, Ingersoll, Birthday series | 100 | 150 | 200 | 300 |
| Boy Scout,PW, c.1937, by Ingersoll, be prepared hands | 250 | 275 | 350 | 600 |
| Boy Scout,WW, c.1938, by New Haven | 75 | 85 | 100 | 150 |
| Buck Rogers, PW, c.1935, Ingraham (lightning bolt hands) | 300 | 400 | 650 | 1,000 |
| Bud Man, WW, Swiss, c.1970s | 40 | 50 | 60 | 75 |
| Bugs Bunny, WW, c. 1951, Swiss, (carrot shaped hands) | 100 | 175 | 275 | 550 |
| Bugs Bunny, WW, c. 1951, Swiss, (without carrot hands) | 70 | 100 | 175 | 400 |
| Bugs Bunny, WW, c. 1970, Swiss, (standing bugs) | 45 | 50 | 60 | 75 |

⊕ NOTE: Beware ( **COLOR COPY DIALS** ) are being faked as Buck Rodgers, Babe Ruth, Hopalong Cassidy and others. *BUYER BEWARE*

BIG BAD WOLF & 3 PIGS, + FOB INGERSOLL

BUSTER BROWN, INGERSOLL, Ca. 1925

BUGS BUNNY, EXACT TIME, Ca. 1949

BUCK ROGERS, INGRAHAM, Ca. 1935

BIG BAD WOLF & 3 PIGS

– DICK TRACY, NEW HAVEN, Ca.1948

– DICK TRACY, (six shooter action arm) Ca.1952

DIZZY DEAN, By Everbright W. Co.

DONALD, with mickey seconds hand, 3 grades.

DONALD DUCK, by INGERSOLL, C. 1942.

DALE EVANS, INGRAHAM

DAN DARE, INGERSOLL made in England

FROM OUTER SPACE, INGERSOLL made in England

| Style or Grade – Description | Avg | Ex-Fn | Mint | Mint +Box |
|---|---|---|---|---|
| Buster Brown, PW, c. 1928, by Ingersoll | $125 | $175 | $250 | $450 |
| Buster Brown, PW, c. 1928, by Ingersoll (Buster in circle) | 125 | 175 | 300 | 450 |
| Buster Brown, WW, c.1930, engraved case | 125 | 145 | 180 | 225 |
| Buzz Corey, WW, c. 1952, by U.S. Time | 75 | 125 | 200 | 450 |
| Buzzy the Crow, in red hat | 30 | 35 | 40 | 55 |
| Captain Liberty, WW, c. 1950, by U.S. Time. | 50 | 80 | 150 | 450 |
| Captain Marvel, PW, c. 1945, by New Haven | 175 | 250 | 400 | 700 |
| Captain Marvel,WW, c.1948, New Haven (small w.w.) | 65 | 95 | 175 | 350 |
| Captain Marvel, WW, c. 1948, by New Haven (larger size ) | 90 | 125 | 200 | 475 |
| Captain Marvel, WW, c. 1948, Swiss made | 95 | 140 | 225 | 350 |
| Captain Midnight, PW, c. 1948, by Ingraham | 250 | 300 | 400 | 600 |
| Casper, WW, c.1970s, Swiss, action arms | 25 | 30 | 35 | 55 |
| Cat In The Hat, WW, c.1970s, Swiss, Action arms | 25 | 30 | 35 | 70 |
| Cinderella, WW, c. 1950, by U.S. Time (slipper box) | 40 | 45 | 65 | 225 |
| Cinderella, WW, c. 1955, by Timex ( box with imitation cel) | 30 | 40 | 60 | 225 |
| Cinderella, WW, c. 1958, by Timex (box with plastic statue) | 20 | 30 | 60 | 225 |
| Cinderella, WW, c. 1958, by Timex (box &porcelain statue) | 40 | 50 | 75 | 225 |
| Coca Cola, PW, c. 1948, by Ingersoll | 125 | 150 | 200 | 300 |
| Cub Scout, WW, by Timex | | | | |
| Daisy Duck, WW, c. 1947, by Ingersoll (tonneau style) | 100 | 175 | 250 | 500 |
| Daisy Duck, WW, c. 1948, by U.S. Time (fluted bezel, birthday series) | 100 | 175 | 250 | 450 |
| Dale Evans, WW, c.1949,by Ingraham,Dale standing | 80 | 100 | 125 | 250 |
| Dale Evans, WW, c. 1950, by Bradley (western style leather band & necklace &lucky horseshoe) | 75 | 85 | 100 | 350 |
| Dale Evans, WW, c. 1960, by Bradley ( round ) | 35 | 40 | 65 | 150 |
| Dan Dare, PW, c. 1950, by Ingersoll Ltd. (made in England) (action arm) | 200 | 300 | 400 | 700 |
| Davy Crockett, WW, c. 1951, by Bradley (round dial) | 35 | 50 | 90 | 250 |
| Davy Crockett, WW, c. 1955, by U.S. Time (& powder horn) | 75 | 85 | 110 | 350 |
| Davy Crockett, WW, c. 1956, by Bradley (barrel shaped dial) | 30 | 55 | 100 | 225 |
| Dennis the Menace, WW, c. 1970, by Bradley | 35 | 45 | 75 | 100 |
| Dick Tracy, PW, c. 1948, by Ingersoll | 250 | 350 | 500 | 800 |
| Dick Tracy, WW, c. 1948, by New Haven (round dial) | 95 | 110 | 140 | 325 |
| Dick Tracy, WW, c. 1948, by New Haven (small tonneau) | 75 | 100 | 150 | 275 |
| Dick Tracy, WW, c. 1935, by New Haven (large) | 150 | 225 | 300 | 500 |
| Dick Tracy, WW, c. 1951, by New Haven (6 shooter action) | 195 | 275 | 350 | 575 |
| Dizzy Dean, PW, c. 1935, by Ingersoll ★★ | 200 | 350 | 500 | 1,000 |
| Dizzy Dean, WW, c. 1938, by Everbright W.Co. ★★ | 200 | 300 | 500 | 1,000 |

🕐Note: To be mint condition, character watches must have **unfaded dials**, and boxes must have ALL inserts. (PW=Pocket Watch; WW=Wrist Watch)

NOTE: Beware ( **COLOR COPY DIALS** ) are being **FAKED** as Buck Rogers, Babe Ruth, Ho-palong Cassidy and others. *BUYER BEWARE*

COCA COLA, PW, Ca. 1948, by Ingersoll.

ADOLF HITLER, character wrist watch, Swiss movement "Roskopf" caliber, Ca. 1935.

Dizzy Dean, Ingersoll, ca. 1935

Donald Duck, Ingersoll, ca. 1940.

| Style or Grade – Description | | Avg | Ex-Fn | Mint | Mint +Box |
|---|---|---|---|---|---|
| Donald Duck, PW, c. 1939, by Ingersoll (Mickey on back) | ★ | $200 | $400 | $700 | $1,500 |
| Donald Duck, WW, c. 1935, by Ingersoll (Mickey on second hand) | ★★ | 500 | 800 | 1,200 | 3,000 |
| Donald Duck, WW, c. 1942, by U.S. Time (tonneau style, silver tone) | | 100 | 150 | 250 | 500 |
| Donald Duck, WW, c. 1948, by U.S. Time (tonneau style, gold tone) | | 150 | 200 | 300 | 500 |
| Donald Duck, PW, , c. 1954, Swiss made | | 75 | 150 | 250 | 400 |
| Donald Duck, WW, c. 1948, by Ingersoll (fluted bezel, birthday series) | | 150 | 175 | 250 | 450 |
| Donald Duck, WW, c. 1955, by U.S. Time, (plain bezel, pop-up in box) | | 65 | 85 | 145 | 420 |
| Dopey, WW, c. 1948, by Ingersoll (fluted bezel, birthday series) | | 100 | 150 | 250 | 450 |
| Dudley Do-Right, WW, 17J (Bullwinkle & Rocky) | | 65 | 85 | 150 | 225 |
| Elmer Fudd, WW, c.1970s, Swiss | | 55 | 75 | 100 | 150 |
| Elvis, WW, c.1970s, Bradley | | 55 | 60 | 75 | 125 |
| Flash Gordon, PW, c. 1939, by Ingersoll | | 350 | 475 | 650 | 950 |
| Flash Gordon,WW, c.1970, Precision | | 100 | 225 | 350 | 500 |
| From Outer Space, PW, Ingersoll G.Britian, | | 100 | 150 | 225 | 350 |
| Fred Flintstone, WW, (Fred on dial ) | | 100 | 125 | 150 | 250 |
| Garfield,WW, (The Cat Jumped Over The Moon) | | 40 | 45 | 65 | 75 |
| Gene Autry, WW, c. 1939, by Ingersoll (Gene and Champion on dial) | | 100 | 150 | 250 | 400 |

Donald Duck, Ingersoll, ca.1947.    – Gene Autry, (action gun), by Ingersoll, ca.1950.    – Gene Autry (Swiss made), ca.1956.

MICKEY MOUSE, by Ingersoll, original band, Ca.1938

MICKEY MOUSE, by Ingersoll,

MICKEY MOUSE by Ingersoll, center LUGS.

MICKEY MOUSE, by Bradley, 1972 -1985

MICKEY MOUSE, made in England by Ingersoll, Ca.1934

Who's afraid of the Big Bad Wolf

Hopalong Cassidy, U.S. Time, ca. 1950s.            Hopalong Cassidy, Ingersoll, ca. 1955.

| Style or Grade – Description | Avg | Ex-Fn | Mint | Mint +Box |
|---|---|---|---|---|
| Gene Autry, WW, c. 1939, by Ingersoll | $95 | $125 | $200 | $400 |
| Gene Autry, WW, c. 1950, by New Haven, (action gun) | 200 | 275 | 350 | 425 |
| Gene Autry, WW, c. 1956, Swiss made | 65 | 75 | 95 | 225 |
| Girl Scouts, WW, c.1955, by Timex | 25 | 30 | 35 | 45 |
| Goofy, WW, c. 1972, by Helbros, 17J (watch runs backward) | 385 | 500 | 750 | 950 |
| Hopalong Cassidy, WW, by U.S. Time (metal watch, box with saddle) | 30 | 35 | 65 | 225 |
| Hopalong Cassidy, WW, by U.S. Time (plastic watch, box with saddle) | 45 | 55 | 75 | 235 |
| Hopalong Cassidy, WW, by U.S. Time (small watch, leather Western band, flat rectangular box) | 35 | 45 | 75 | 300 |
| Hopalong Cassidy, WW, by U.S. Time (regular size watch, black leather cowboy strap) | 35 | 45 | 85 | 325 |
| Hopalong Cassidy, PW, c. 1955, by U.S. Time (rawhide strap and fob) | 125 | 225 | 300 | 450 |
| Howdy Doody, WW, c. 1954, by Ingraham (with moving eyes) | 100 | 125 | 175 | 400 |
| Howdy Doody, WW, c. 1954, by Ingraham (with friends) | 75 | 100 | 150 | 550 |
| Jamboree, PW, c. 1951, by Ingersoll, Ltd. | 75 | 100 | 250 | 400 |

Howdy Doody (& friends)  —   BUD MAN  Ca.1970s  —   Li'l Abner (waving flag)

LONE RANGER, New Haven, ca.1939

LONE RANGER, New Haven, ca.1939

MICKEY MOUSE Ingersoll, ca.1933

MICKEY MOUSE Ingersoll, ca.1933

**LEFT:** Mickey Mouse, Ingersoll, w/ Mickey seconds, ca.1939. **CENTER:** Mickey Mouse, Ingersoll, no seconds, ca.1939.. **RIGHT:** Mickey Mouse, Ingersoll, birthday series, ca.1948

Note: To be **mint** condition, character watches must have unfaded dials, and boxes must have all inserts. (PW=Pocket Watch; WW=Wrist Watch)

| Style or Grade – Description | Avg | Ex-Fn | Mint | Mint +Box |
|---|---|---|---|---|
| James Bond 007, WW, c. 1972, by Gilbert | $70 | $125 | $200 | $300 |
| Jeff Arnold, PW, c. 1952, by Ingersoll (English watch with moving gun) | 150 | 200 | 325 | 550 |
| Jiminy Cricket, WW, c.1946, Ingersoll, action arms | 75 | 100 | 200 | 450 |
| Joe Carioca, WW, c. 1948, by U.S. Time (fluted bezel, birthday series) | 115 | 165 | 265 | 460 |
| Joe Palooka, WW, c. 1948, by New Haven | 150 | 200 | 300 | 550 |
| Li'l Abner, WW, c. 1948, by New Haven (waving flag) | 150 | 175 | 250 | 500 |
| Li'l Abner, WW, c. 1948, by New Haven (moving mule) | 150 | 175 | 200 | 400 |
| Little King, WW, c. 1968, by Timex | 55 | 125 | 225 | 425 |
| Little Pig Fiddler, WW, c.1947, by Ingersoll | 125 | 200 | 300 | 450 |
| Lone Ranger, PW, c. 1939, by New Haven (with fob) | 150 | 250 | 400 | 600 |
| Lone Ranger, WW, c. 1938, by New Haven (large) | 95 | 185 | 295 | 475 |
| Lone Ranger, WW, c. 1948, New Haven, (Fluted lugs) | 75 | 125 | 200 | 400 |
| Louie, WW, c.1940s, by Ingersoll, (Donalds nephew) | 100 | 150 | 200 | 400 |
| Mary Marvel, WW, c. 1948, by U.S. Time (paper box) | 65 | 85 | 125 | 315 |
| Mary Marvel, WW, c. 1948, by U.S. Time (plastic box) | 65 | 85 | 125 | 325 |
| Mickey Mouse, PW, c.1933, by Ingersoll, #1&2 (tall stem) | 285 | 350 | 450 | 650 |
| Mickey Mouse, PW, c. 1936, by Ingersoll, #3&4 (short stems) | 200 | 275 | 400 | 650 |
| Mickey Mouse, PW, c. 1938, by Ingersoll (Mickey decal on back) | 275 | 400 | 700 | 1,000 |
| Mickey Mouse, PW, c. 1933, by Ingersoll Ltd. (English) | 300 | 450 | 750 | 1,400 |
| Mickey Mouse, PW, c. 1934, by Ingersoll, (Foreign) | 275 | 325 | 450 | 650 |
| Mickey Mouse, PW, c.1976, by Bradley (bicentennial model) | 40 | 50 | 75 | 125 |
| Mickey Mouse, PW, c. 1974, by Bradley (no second hand) | 30 | 35 | 50 | 85 |
| Mickey Mouse, PW, c. 1974, by Bradley ("Bradley" printed at 6) | 25 | 30 | 40 | 65 |

MICKEY MOUSE, Ingersoll, model no.3 on the left.     Right: Model no.4 is shown with lapel button

NOTE: Beware ( COLOR COPY DIALS ) are being FAKED as Buck Rodgers, Babe Ruth, Hopalong Cassidy and others. *BUYER BEWARE*

| Style or Grade – Description | Avg | Ex-Fn | Mint | Mint +Box |
|---|---|---|---|---|
| Mickey Mouse, WW, c. 1933, by Ingersoll (metal band with 3 Mickeys' on seconds disc) | $200 | $300 | $375 | $750 |
| Mickey Mouse, WW, c. 1938-9, by Ingersoll (one Mickey for second hand) | 125 | 200 | 295 | 900 |
| Mickey Mouse, WW, c. 1938-9, by Ingersoll, plain seconds | 85 | 125 | 200 | 350 |
| Mickey Mouse, WW, c. 1938-9, by Ingersoll (girl's watch, 1 Mickey for second hand) | 175 | 200 | 275 | 900 |
| Mickey Mouse, WW, c. 1948, by Ingersoll (fluted bezel, birthday series) | 150 | 175 | 200 | 450 |
| Mickey Mouse, WW, c. 1946, by U.S. Time (10k gold plated) | 100 | 125 | 200 | 300 |
| Mickey Mouse, WW, c. 1947, by U.S. Time (tonneau, plain, several styles) | 75 | 95 | 150 | 325 |
| Mickey Mouse, WW, c. 1947, by U.S. Time (same as above, gold tone) | 85 | 100 | 160 | 350 |
| Mickey Mouse, WW, c. 1950s, by U.S. Time (round style) | 35 | 45 | 55 | 275 |
| Mickey Mouse, WW, c. 1958, by U.S. Time (statue of Mickey in box) | 35 | 45 | 75 | 250 |
| Mickey Mouse, WW, c. 1965 to 1970, by Timex (Mickey Mouse electric) | 85 | 100 | 150 | 250 |
| Mickey Mouse, WW, c. 1965-70s, Timex (manual wind) | 55 | 65 | 90 | 140 |
| Mickey Mouse, WW, c. 1970s, by Bradley | 20 | 25 | 35 | 80 |
| Mickey Mouse, WW, c. 1980, by Bradley (colored min. chapter) | 60 | 70 | 85 | 150 |
| Mickey Mouse, WW, c. 1983, by Bradley (limited commemorative model) | 60 | 75 | 100 | 150 |

Mickey Mouse, Bradley, ca. 1969.

Mickey Mouse, with wide bezel, Ingersoll, it is believed dealers have used a Wrist Watch dial in a Hopalong case, ca. 1955.

Note: To be **mint** condition, character watches must have unfaded dials, and boxes must have all inserts. (PW=Pocket Watch; WW=Wrist Watch)

**Left:** Captain Marvel, Ca. 1948. **Center:** Minnie Mouse, U.S.Time, Ca.196. **Right:** Orphan Annie, New Haven, Ca.1939

ORPHAN ANNIE, New Haven, Ca. 1940                2 styles of POPEYE & friends, New Haven, Ca. 1936

POPEYE, New Haven, ( with friends ), Ca. 1935     POPEYE, New Haven, Ca. 1940

🕐Note: To be **mint** condition, character watches must have unfaded dials, and boxes must have all inserts. (PW=Pocket Watch; WW=Wrist Watch)

LEFT: GOOFY watch runs backward.    CENTER: Little Pig & fiddle.    RIGHT: Porky Pig

Left: Pluto, Birthday Series, by Ingersoll.    Center: Rocky Jones, Ca. 1955.    Right: Speedy Gonzales, Swiss

DONALD DUCK, on face with MICKEY on back side of watch.

| Style or Grade – Description | Avg | Ex-Fn | Mint | Mint +Box |
|---|---|---|---|---|
| Mickey Mouse, WW, c. 1985, by ETA (clear plastic bezel and band) | $30 | $35 | $45 | $85 |
| Mickey Mouse, WW, c.1980s, Bradley, (Tachemeter dial) | 45 | 50 | 60 | 75 |
| Mighty Mouse, WW, c.1980s, Swiss, (Plastic case) | 25 | 30 | 35 | 40 |
| Minnie Mouse, WW, c. 1958, by U.S. Time (statue of Minnie in box) | 35 | 45 | 65 | 225 |
| Moon Mullins, PW, c. 1930, by Ingersoll | ★ 200 | 300 | 500 | 750 |
| Orphan Annie, WW, c. 1939, by New Haven (fluted bezel) | 75 | 95 | 125 | 350 |
| Orphan Annie, WW, c. 1935, by New Haven (large style) | 100 | 120 | 155 | 400 |
| Orphan Annie, WW, c. 1948, by New Haven smaller model) | 50 | 65 | 100 | 300 |
| Orphan Annie, WW, c. 1968, by Timex | 45 | 55 | 75 | 110 |
| Peter Pan, PW, c. 1948, by Ingram | 150 | 200 | 300 | 600 |
| Pinocchio, WW, c. 1948, by Ingersoll (fluted bezel, birthday series) | 125 | 150 | 250 | 400 |
| Pinocchio, WW, c. 1948, by U.S. Time (Happy Birthday cake box) | 125 | 150 | 250 | 450 |
| Pluto, WW, c. 1948, by U.S. Time( birthday series) | 100 | 150 | 250 | 450 |
| Popeye, PW, c. 1935, by New Haven (with friends on dial) | ★ 275 | 450 | 650 | 1,100 |
| Popeye, PW, c. 1936, by New Haven (plain dial) | 225 | 375 | 500 | 1,000 |
| Popeye, WW, c. 1936, by New Haven (tonneau style, with friends on dial) | ★ 250 | 375 | 650 | 1,200 |
| Popeye, WW, c. 1966, by Bradley (round style) | 75 | 100 | 125 | 200 |
| Popeye, WW, c. 1948, Swiss, Olive Oyl at 3 | 75 | 150 | 250 | 400 |
| Porky Pig, WW, c. 1948, by Ingraham (tonneau) | 100 | 175 | 250 | 450 |
| Porky Pig, WW, c. 1949, by U.S. Time (round) | 95 | 185 | 265 | 465 |
| Puss-N-Boots, WW, c. 1959, by Bradley | 100 | 175 | 250 | 400 |
| Quarterback, WW, c.1965, Swiss, (Football action arm) | 65 | 75 | 85 | 125 |
| Robin, WW, c. 1978, by Timex | 40 | 45 | 65 | 90 |
| Robin Hood, WW, c. 1955, by Bradley (tonneau style) | 85 | 125 | 195 | 350 |
| Robin Hood, WW, c. 1958, by Viking (round) | 75 | 150 | 200 | 400 |
| Rocky Jones Space Ranger, WW, c. 1955, by Ingraham | 125 | 235 | 350 | 700 |
| Roy Rogers, PW, c. 1960, by Ingraham, rim set | 70 | 85 | 100 | 150 |
| Roy Rogers, WW, c. 1954, by Ingraham (Roy and rearing Trigger) | 75 | 95 | 125 | 250 |

Joe Palooka, Ca.1948.

— Snow White U.S.Time. —

Roy Rogers, Ingraham, ca. 1954.

ROY ROGERS, Ingraham, note rim set, Ca. 1960.

ROY ROGERS, Ingraham ( large ), Ca. 1951.

ROY ROGERS, Ingraham, Ca. 1951

SKEEZIX, Ingraham, Ca. 1936.

**Left:** Smitty, New Haven, Ca.1936. **Center:** Superman, New Haven, Ca.1939. **Right:** Superman, New Haven, Ca.1939.

| Style or Grade – Description | Avg | Ex-Fn | Mint | Mint +Box |
|---|---|---|---|---|
| Roy Rogers, WW, c. 1954, by Ingraham (Roy and Trigger) ..... | $60 | $75 | $100 | $250 |
| Roy Rogers, WW, c. 1954, by Ingraham (expansion band)......... | 60 | 75 | 100 | 250 |
| Roy Rogers, WW, c. 1956, by Ingraham (round dial).................. | 60 | 75 | 100 | 200 |
| Rudy Nebb, PW, c. 1930, by Ingraham ..................................... | 150 | 200 | 275 | 500 |
| Shirley Temple, PW, c.1958, by Westclox......................★★ | 275 | 375 | 450 | 550 |
| Skeezix, PW, c. 1928, by Ingraham ......................................... | 225 | 275 | 350 | 650 |
| Sky King, WW, ( action gun )................................................... | 75 | 100 | 150 | 200 |
| Smitty, PW, c. 1928, by New Haven ........................................ | 225 | 275 | 350 | 650 |
| Smitty, WW, c. 1936, by New Haven........................................ | 150 | 200 | 300 | 550 |
| Smokey Stover, WW, c. 1968, by Timex .................................. | 75 | 100 | 150 | 225 |
| Snoopy, WW, c. 1958 (tennis racket) ...................................... | 30 | 35 | 50 | 85 |
| Snoopy, WW, c. 1958 (Woodstock)......................................... | 30 | 35 | 50 | 85 |
| Snow White, WW, c. 1938, by Ingersoll (tonneau)................... | 100 | 125 | 200 | 400 |
| Snow White, WW, c. 1952, by U.S. Time (round)...................... | 45 | 50 | 65 | 275 |
| Snow White, WW, c. 1956, by U.S. Time (statue in box) ........... | 40 | 45 | 70 | 285 |
| Snow White, WW, c. 1962, by U.S. Time (plastic watch).......... | 40 | 45 | 65 | 275 |
| Speedy Gonzales, WW, Swiss .................................................. | 75 | 95 | 150 | 225 |
| Spiro Agnew, WW,c.1970s, Swiss ............................................ | 25 | 30 | 35 | 45 |
| Superman, PW, c. 1956, by Bradley ........................................ | 150 | 250 | 350 | 600 |
| Superman, WW, c. 1938, by New Haven .................................. | 200 | 250 | 325 | 600 |
| Superman, WW, c.1946, by Ingraham(lightning bolt hands).... | 150 | 175 | 250 | 450 |
| Superman, WW, c. 1978, by Timex (large size)......................... | 50 | 65 | 95 | 150 |
| Superman, WW, c. 1978, by Timex (small size)........................ | 45 | 50 | 75 | 125 |
| Superman, WW, c.1975, Dabs & Co., yellow min. chapter........ | 45 | 50 | 75 | 150 |
| Superman, WW, c.1965, Swiss, rotating superman.................. | 55 | 75 | 125 | 225 |
| Superman, WW, c.1976, Timex, sweep sec. hand...................... | 60 | 65 | 95 | 150 |
| Three Little Pigs, PW, c. 1936, by Ingersoll.................★★ | 400 | 600 | 850 | 1,200 |
| Tom Corbett, WW, c. 1954, by New Haven............................... | 75 | 100 | 150 | 450 |
| Tom Mix, PW, c. 1936, by Ingersoll (with fob) ...........★★★ | 450 | 750 | 1,000 | 2,500 |
| Tom Mix, WW, c. 1936, by Ingersoll ...........................★★★ | 400 | 600 | 900 | 3,000 |
| Winnie the Pooh Bear, c.1970s, Swiss..................................... | 30 | 35 | 45 | 65 |
| Wizard of Oz, c.1972, swiss, ................................................... | 30 | 45 | 70 | 120 |
| Wonder Woman,WW, c.1975, stars at 1,2,4,5,7,8,10,11 ........... | 65 | 70 | 95 | 160 |
| Wonder Woman,WW, c.1975, Dabs & Co. ................................. | 50 | 65 | 95 | 150 |
| Woody Woodpecker, WW, c. 1948, by Ingersoll (town)............ | 85 | 125 | 250 | 450 |
| Woody Woodpecker, WW, c. 1952, by Ingraham (round dial)................................................................... | 100 | 125 | 175 | 400 |
| Yogi Bear, WW, c. 1964, by Bradley ........................................ | 50 | 55 | 75 | 100 |
| Zorro, WW, c. 1956, by U.S. Time............................................ | 55 | 60 | 85 | 250 |

**Left:** Tom Corbett, Space Cadet, New Haven, ca. 1935. **Center:** Tom Mix, Ingersoll, ca. 1936. **Right:** Woody Woodpecker, U.S. Time, ca. 1948.

**Moon Mullins,** by Ingersoll, ca. 1928

**Rudy Nebb,** by Ingersoll, ca. 1928

**Shirley Temple,** by Westclox, ca. 1958

**Lone Ranger,** New Haven, complete with leather cord.

CUB SCOUT by Timex    BOY SCOUT by New Haven    DAVY CROCKETT, by Ingraham

**MICKEY MOUSE WRIST WATCH** with metal or leather strap bearing Mickey's picture. The watch itself is smartly styled ... round and therefore entirely practical for a very little girl's wrist. Packed in Mickey Mouse display carton. Retails $2.75. List . . . . . . $3.90

**MICKEY MOUSE WATCH AND FOB—** a wonderful buy at $1.50 complete. Mickey on the dial of the watch pointing out the time—Mickey on the fob—three little Mickies on the second-circle chasing each other around. List . . . . $2.20

New Mickey Mouse Lapel Watch. A handsome lapel model with Mickey's hands telling time on small dial. Mickey on dial and back of a black glossy finished case with nickel trim. Black lapel cord and button. Each in a display box.

No. 1W61. Each......................$2.10

**LONE RANGER FOB WATCH**

New De Luxe Mickey Mouse Wrist Watch. A smarter thinner chromium plated rectangular case. Mickey appears in bright colors on the dial. Fitted with a perspiration proof leather band. Each in display box.

No. 11W440. Each.................. $5.54

# EARLY ANTIQUE WATCHES

The early antique watches looked quite similar to small table clocks. These drum-shaped watches were about two inches in diameter and usually over one-half inch thick. The drum-shaped watch lost popularity in the late 1500s. The earliest portable timepieces did not carry the maker's name, but initials were common. The cases generally had a hinged lid which covered the dial. This lid was pierced with small holes to enable ready identification of the position of the hour hand. They also usually contained a bell. The dial often had the numbers "I" to "XII" engraved in Roman numerals and the numbers "13" to "24" in Arabic numbers with the "2" engraved in the form of a "Z." Even the earliest of timepieces incorporated striking. The oldest known watch with a date engraved on the case was made in 1548. A drum-shaped watch with the initials "C. W.," it was most likely produced by Casper Werner, a protege of Henlein.

Early pocket watches were designed to run from 12 to 16 hours. The pinions usually bore five leaves, the great wheel 55 teeth, the second wheel 45 teeth, the third wheel 40 teeth, and the escape wheel 15 teeth. With one less pinion and wheel the escape wheel ran reverse to a standard four-wheel watch. During the 1500s, 1600s, and much of the 1700s, it was stylish to decorate not only the case and balance cock but all parts including the clicks, barrel, studs, springs, pillars, hands, and stackfreed. The plates themselves were decorated with pierced and engraved metal scrolls, and in some instances the maker's name was engraved in a style to correspond with the general decoration of the movement. During these periods the most celebrated artists, designers, and engravers were employed. The early watches were decorated by famous artists such as Jean Vauquier 1670, Daniel Marot 1700, Gillis l'Egare 1650, Michel Labon 1630, Pierre Bourdon 1750, and D. Cochin 1750. Most of the artists were employed to design and execute pierced and repousse cases.

Alarm watch made by Bockel of London Ca. 1648.

## THE MID-1700s

In the mid-1700s relatively minor changes are noticed. Decoration became less distinctive and less artistic. The newer escapements resulted in better time keeping, and a smaller balance cock was used. The table and foot became smaller. The foot grew more narrow, and as the century and the development of the watch advanced, the decoration on the balance cock became smaller and less elaborate. About 1720 the foot was becoming solid and flat. No longer was it hand pierced; however, some of the pierced ones were produced until about 1770. Thousands of these beautiful hand pierced watch cocks have been made into necklaces and brooches or framed. Sadly, many of the old movements were destroyed in a mad haste to cater to the buyers' fancy.

## THE 1800s

As the 1800s approached the balance cocks became less artistic as the decoration on movements gradually diminished. Breguet and Berthoud spent very little time on the beauty or artistic design on their balance cocks or pillars. But the cases were often magnificent in design and beauty, made with enamels in many colors and laden with precious stones. During this period the movements were plain and possessed very little artistic character.

As early as 1820 three-quarter and one-half plate designs were being used with the balance cock lowered to the same level as the other wheels. The result was a slimmer watch.

Exposed illustration of an early watch movement, c. 1800-1850. Note that movement is key wind and set from the dial side. The illustrated example is a chain driven fusee with a verge escapement: a- Main spring barrel and chain. b- Fusee. c - Verge escapement. d- Balance wheel. e- Dial. f - Hour hand. g- Minute hand. h- Winding arbor. i- Setting arbor.

⊕ Characteristics of watches differ for the same age of both case and movement, because these features vary it may not be accurate to date a watch by one single influence. Example: the second hand was not commonly found on watches before 1750, but common about 1800. The first second hand appeared in 1665 and another in 1690. Therefore statements are **broad** rather than accurate.

# MOVEMENTS " IN THE GRAY "
Movements in an early stage of manufacture.

ABOUT MID 1600'S

ABOUT 1700'S

ABOUT 1790 — 1830

EBAUCHE style movement with verge, chain driven fusee, under sprung, KW, ABOUT 1810 — 1860.

BAR STYLE movement, cylinder, ABOUT 1840–80.

🕐 **Multi-color** cases became popular by 1800, 1st. used in 1760 & **Engine Turning** rarely found before early 1760s. **Tortoise Shell** 1st. used in 1620, but did not become popular till about 1780.

The ebauche makers and the cottage industry made different models designed to conform or answer the needs of each country to which they were trying to do business with such as French style, English style, Chinese style etc. This makes it hard to determine the origin of the ebauche watch. The case may be made in England, the movement Swiss, and the dial French.

Below are some of the principle workmen employed in the sub-divided production of plain parts or ebauche simple watch movements (in the rough)from about 1800s. Some of these were small family specialist which formed a *cottage industry* (some being females) they usually produced only one product as: verge-makers, hairspring-makers, fusee-makers, wheel-makers, dial-makers, chain-makers, balance-makers, hand-makers & etc..

1. Cock-maker (made brass blanks )
2. Pillar-maker (turn the pillars etc.)
3. Frame-maker (two full plates, bars, bridges etc.)
4. Fusee-maker
5. Verge-makers
6. Chain-makers
7. Wheel-maker (small and large )
8. Wheel-cutter (cuts the teeth on the wheels)
9. Pinion- maker
10. Escapement-maker
11. Balance-makers (made of steel or brass)
12. Spring-maker(hair & main springs)
13. Hand-maker
14. Dial-maker

The following is a list of craftsman employed to make the cases.

1. Case-maker (makes cupped lids for cases)
2. Side-maker (makes the side of the case)
3. Cap-maker (makes the lids of the case)
4. The joint-finisher (joints for cases)
5. Glass-maker (made the crystal for the bezels)
6. Bezel-makers
7. Pendant-maker

These blank movements, dials and cases were then shipped on to the final destination the *watch-maker* or *finisher* as the house of (CARTIER). The Finisher would often house or contract decorators to finish the cases. The Finisher completed, polished, engraved, timed, regulated and made all the adjustments to the movements. They added and fitted the case to the movement. They added and fitted the complications such as repeaters to the movements.

This type of system of producing watches left time for the Master watch-makers or famous watch-makers to invent, design new and better ways to make watches such as did Abraham Louis Breguet. Thus the more famous the maker the higher the price of the watch even though the watch-maker may not have **made** the smallest piece for the *finished* watch.

🕐 **Multi-color** cases became popular by 1800, 1st. used in 1760 & **Engine Turning** rarely found before early 1760s. **Tortoise Shell** 1st. used in 1620, but did not become popular till about 1780.

## CLUES TO DATING YOUR WATCH

To establish the age of a watch there are many points to be considered. The dial, hands, pillars, balance cock and pendant, for example, contain important clues in determining the age of your watch. However, no one part alone should be considered sufficient evidence to draw a definite conclusion as to age. The watch as a whole must be considered. For example, an English-made silver-cased watch will have a hallmark inside the case. It is quite simple to refer to the London Hallmark Table for hallmarks after 1697. The hallmark will reveal the age of the case only. This does not fix the age of the movement. Many movements are housed in cases made years before or after the movement was produced.

An informed collector will note that a watch with an **enamel dial**, for instance, could not have been made before 1635. **A pair of cases** indicates it could not have been made prior to 1640. The **minute hand** was introduced in 1687. The presence of a **cylinder escapement** would indicate it was made after 1710. **1750 the duplex escapement** was first used. A **dust cap** first appeared in 1774. *1776 LePine introduced the thin watch.* **Keyless winding** came into being after 1820, but did not gain widespread popularity until *after* about 1860. All of these clues and more must be considered before accurately assessing the age of a watch. *Some watches were also updated such as minute hand added or new style escapement added.*

Example of an early pocket watch with a stackfreed design to equalize power much as a fusee does. Note dumbbell shaped foliot which served as a balance for verge escapement, and the tear shaped cam which is part of the stackfreed.

Characteristics of watches differ for the same age of both case and movement, because these features vary it may not be accurate to date a watch by one single influence. Example: the second hand was <u>not</u> commonly found on watches before 1750, but common about 1800. The first second hand appeared in 1665 and another in 1690. Therefore statements are **broad** rather than accurate.

# PILLARS

Pillars are of interest and should be considered as one of the elements in determining age. Through the years small watches used round pillars, and the larger watches generally used a square type engraved pillar.

(*Illus.* 1) This pillar is one of the earliest types and used in the 1800s as well. This particular pillar came from a watch which dates about 1550. It is known that this type pillar was used in 1675 by Gaspard Girod of France and also in 1835 by James Taylor of England.

(*Illus.* 2) This style pillar is called the tulip pattern. Some watchmakers preferred to omit the vertical divisions. This style was popular between 1660 and 1750 but may be found on later watches. It was common practice to use ornamentation on the tulip pillar.

(*Illus.* 3) The ornament shown was used by Daniel Quare of London from 1665 to 1725 and by the celebrated Tompion, as well as many others.

(*Illus.* 4) This type pillar is referred to as the Egyptian and dates from 1630 to the 1800s. The squared Egyptian pattern was introduced about 1630 and some may be found with a wider division with a head or bust inserted. This style was used by D. Bouquet of London about 1640 and by many other watchmakers.

Illus. 3

Illus. 1          Illus. 2                                      Illus. 4

(*Illus.* 5) This pillar was used by Thomas Earnshaw of London about 1780. The plain style was prominent for close to two hundred years 1650 to 1825.

Illus. 5          Illus. 6          Illus. 7                    Illus. 8

(Illus. 6) This style was popular and was used by many craftsmen. Nathaniel Barrow of London put this in his watches about 1680.

(Illus. 7) This pillar may be seen in watches made by Pierre Combet of Lyons, France, about 1720. It was also used by many others.

(Illus. 8) This style pillar and the ornament were used by John Ellicott of England and other watchmakers from 1730 to 1770.

These illustrations represent just a few of the basic pillars that were used. Each watchmaker would design and change details to create his own individual identity. This sometimes makes it more difficult to readily determine the age of watches.

## BALANCE COCKS OR BRIDGES

The first balance cocks or bridges used to support the balance staff were a plain "S" shape. The cocks used on the old three-wheel watches were very elaborate; hand-pierced and engraved. At first no screws were used to hold the cock in place. It is noteworthy that on the three wheel watch the regulator was a ratchet and click and was used on these earlier movements to adjust the mainspring. About 1635 the balance cock was screwed to the plate and pinned on its underside, which helped steady the balance. The first cock illustrated is a beautifully decorated example made by Josias Jeubi of Paris about 1580. Note that it is pinned to a stud which passes through a square cut in the foot of the cock. Next is a balance cock made by Bouquet of London about 1640. The third balance cock is one made by Jean Rousseau and dates around 1650. The fourth one dates around 1655.

The next two bridges are supported on both sides of the balance cock by means of screws or pins. They are strikingly different and usually cover much of the plate of the movement. This style of balance cock was used around 1675 and was still seen as late as 1765.

The beautiful balance cock below at left, with the ornate foot, dates about 1660. The next illustrated balance cock with the heavy ornamentation was used from about 1700 to 1720 or longer. By 1720 a face was added to the design. The face shows up where the table terminates on most balance cocks.

1680–1700 NOTE wavy edge to the foot & two ears on the table

D shaped foot
Ca. 1690–1720

1750–1780 NOTE the ballon shape table & "pierced" fan shaped foot on this cock.

1760–1830, NOTE solid foot

1810 - 1835

1810–1830

1810–1865, look for barrel bridge

1850 NOTE under-sprung

🕐 Characteristics of watches differ for the same age of both case and movement, because these features vary it may not be accurate to date a watch by one single influence. Example: the second hand was <u>not</u> commonly found on watches before 1750, but common about 1800. The first second hand appeared in 1665 and another in 1690. Therefore statements are **broad** rather than accurate.

**LePine** style movement Ca. 1790-1820, with free standing barrel, also note the horse shoe shaped bridge, this denotes center seconds.

**LePine**, or FRENCH style ebauche caliber, NOTE the step shaped and tapered bridges, also note the free standing barrel, Ca. 1800--1825.

**LePine**, or FRENCH style ebauche caliber, NOTE the step shaped and tapered bridges, also note the COVERED barrel bridge, this style movement was popular from Ca.1820–1835.

**LePine**, or FRENCH style ebauche caliber, NOTE the step shaped and tapered bridges, also note the CURVED barrel bridge, this style movement was popular from Ca.1830–1845.

🕐 Characteristics of watches differ for the same age of both case and movement, because these features vary it may not be accurate to date a watch by one single influence. Example: the second hand was not commonly found on watches before 1750, but common about 1800. The first second hand appeared in 1665 and another in 1690. Therefore statements are **broad** rather than accurate.

🕐 **Multi-color** cases became popular by 1800, 1st. used in 1760 & **Engine Turning** rarely found before early 1760s. **Tortoise Shell** 1st. used in 1620, but did not become popular till about 1780.

Bar (Le Coultre) SWISS style ebauche caliber, NOTE the flat straight bridges and parallel design, also the CURVED barrel bridge this movement was popular Ca.1830–1850.

Bar (Le Coultre) SWISS style ebauche caliber, NOTE the flat straight bridges and parallel design, also the STRAIGHT barrel bridge this movement was popular Ca.1840–1885.

JULES JURGENSEN Style Bar SWISS La Chaux de Fonds ebauche caliber, Ca.1870–1895.

**Duplex escapement**

Invented in 1750

**Virgule Escapement**

**Rack and lever escapement**

Invented in 1722

An informed collector will note that a watch with an enamel dial, for instance, could not have been made before 1635. A pair of cases indicates it could not have been made prior to 1640. The minute hand was introduced in 1650. The presence of a cylinder escapement would indicate it was made after 1710. 1750 the duplex escapement was first used. A dust cap first appeared in 1774. 1776 Lepine introduced the thin watch. Keyless winding came into being after 1820 but did not gain widespread popularity until after about 1860. All of these clues and more must be considered before accurately assessing the age of a watch. Some watches were also **updated** such as minute hand added or new style escapement added.

# EARLY EUROPEAN WATCHMAKERS

Achard, J. Francois (Geneva, ca. 1750)
Addison, J. (London, 1760-1900)
Adamson, Gustave (Paris, 1775-1790)
Alfred, W. Humphreys (London, ca. 1905)
Alibut (Paris, ca. 1750s)
Alliez, Buchelard & Teron Co. (French, ca. 1830)
Amabric, Abraham (Geneva, ca. 1750-1800)
Amabric, Freres (Geneva, ca. 1760-1795)
Amon (Paris, 1913)
Andre, Jean (enamel) (Geneva, 1660-1705)
Anthony, Willams (London, 1785-1840)
Antram, J. (London, ca. 1700-1730)
Appleby, Edward (London, ca. 1675)
Appleby, Joshua (London, ca. 1720-1745)
Ardin, Coppet (ca. 1710)
Arlaud, Benjamin (London, c. 1680)
Arlaud, Louis (Geneva, ca. 1750)
Arnold & Frodsham, Charles (London, 1845)
Arnold, Henery (London, ca. 1770-1780)
Arnold, John (London, ca. 1760-1790)
Arnold, John Roger, son of (London, ca. 1800-1830)
Arnold, Nicolas (ca. 1850)
Arnold & Lewis, Lote Simmons (Manchester, ca. 1860)
Arnold & Son (London, ca. 1787-1799)
Assman, Julius (Glasshutte, 1850-1885)
Auber, Daniel (London, ca. 1750)
Aubert, D. F. (Geneva, ca. 1825)
Aubert, Ferdinand (1810-1835)
Aubert & Co. (Geneva, ca. 1850)
Aubry, Irenee (Geneva, 1885-1910)
Audebert (Paris, 1810-1820)
Audemars, Freres (Swiss, 1810 until Co. splits in 1885)
Audemars, Louis-Benjamin (Swiss, 1811-1867)
Aureole (Swiss, 1921)
Auricoste, Jules (Paris, ca. 1910)
Bachhofen, Felix (Swiss, 1675-1690)
Badollet, Jean-Jacques (Geneva, 1779-1891)
Baillon, Jean-Hilaire (Paris, ca. 1727)
Baird, Wm. (London, 1815-1825)
Balsiger & Fils (ca. 1825)
Barberet, J. (Paris, ca. 1600)
Barbezat, Bole (Swiss, 1870)
Baronneau, Jean-Louis (France, 1675-1700)
Barraud & Lunds (1812-1840)
Barraud, Paul-Philip (London, 1752-1820)
Barrow, Edward (London, ca. 1650-1710)
Barrow, Nathaniel (London, 1653-1689)
Barry, M. (French, ca. 1620)
Bartholony, Abraham (Paris, 1750-1752)
Barton, James (London, 1760-1780)
Barwise (London, 1800)
Bassereau, Jean-Hilaire (Paris, ca. 1800-1810)
Bautte, Jean-Francois (Geneva, 1800-1835)
Bautte & Moynier (Geneva, ca. 1825)
Beaumarchais, Caron (Paris, 1750-1795)
Beauvais, Simon (London, ca. 1690)
Beckman, Daniel (London, 1670-1685)
Beckner, Abraham (London, ca. 1640)
Beliard, Dominique (Paris, ca. 1750)
Bell, Benj. (London, 1650-1668)
Bennett, John (London, 1850-1895)
Benson, J. W. (London, 1825-1890)
Benson, J. W. (London, 1850-1900)
Bergstein, L. (London, ca. 1840)
Bernard, Nicholas (Paris, 1650-1690)
Bernoulli, Daniel (Paris, 1720-1780)
Berrollas, J. A. (Denmark, 1800-1830)
Berthoud, Augusta-Louis (Paris, ca. 1875)

Berthoud, Ferdinand (Paris, 1750-1805)
Beihler & Hartmann (Geneva, ca. 1875)
Blanc, Henri (Geneva, ends 1964)
Blanc, Jules (Geneva, 1929-1940)
Blanc & Fils (Geneva, 1770-1790)
Bock, Johann (German, 1700-1750)
Bockel (London, ca. 1650)
Bolslandon, Metz (ca. 1780)
Bolviller, Moise (Paris, 1840-1870)
Bommelt, Leonhart (Nuremburg, Ger., ca. 1690)
Bonney (London, ca. 1790)
Bonniksen, Bahne (England, 1890-1930) invented karrusel
Booth, Edward (name change to Barlow)
Bordier, Denis (France, ca. 1575)
Bordier, Freres (Geneva, 1787-1810)
Bordier, Jacques (enamel) (ca. 1670)
Bornand, A. (Geneva, 1895-1915)
Boubon (Paris, 1810-1820)
Bouquet, David (London, ca. 1630-1650)
Bovet, Edouard (Swiss, 1820-1918)
Bovier, G. (enamel painter) (Paris, c. 1750)
Brandt, Iacob (Swiss, ca. 1700)
Brandt, Robert & Co. (Geneva, ca. 1820)
Breitling, "Leon" (Swiss, since 1884)
Brockbank (London, 1776-present)
Brocke (London, ca. 1640)
Brodon, Nicolas (Paris, 1674-1682)
Bronikoff, a Wjatka (Russia, 1850 "watches of wood")
Bruguier, Charles A. (Geneva, 1800-1860)
Bull, Rainulph (one of the first British) (1590-1617)
Burgis, Eduardus (London, 1680-1710)
Burgis, G. (London, 1720-1740)
Burnet, Thomas (London, ca. 1800)
Busch, Abraham (Hamburg, Ger., ca. 1680)
Buz, Johannes (Augsburg, Bavaria, ca. 1625)
Cabrier, Charles (London, ca. 1690-1720)
Capt, Henry Daniel (Geneva, 1802-1880)
Caron, Augustus (Paris, ca. 1750-1760)
Caron, Francois-Modeste (Paris, 1770-1788)
Caron, Pierre (Paris, ca. 1700)
Caron, Pierre Augustin (pat. virgule escapement) (Paris, 1750-1795)
Carpenter, William (London, 1750-1800)
Carte, John (England, 1680-1700)
Champod, P. Amedee (enamel) (Geneva, 1850-1910)
Chapponier, Jean (Geneva, 1780-1800)
Charman (London, 1780-1800)
Charrot (Paris, 1775-1810)
Chartiere (enamel) (France, ca. 1635)
Chaunes (Paris, ca. 1580-1600)
Chavanne & Pompejo (Vienna, 1785-1800)
Cheneviere, Louis (Geneva, 1710-1740)
Cheneviere, Urbain (Geneva, 1730-1760)
Cheriot or Cherioz, Daniel (ca. 1750-1790)
Cheuillard (Blois, France, ca. 1600)
Chevalier & Co. (Geneva, 1795-1810)
Cisin, Charles (Swiss, 1580-1610)
Clark, Geo. (London, 1750-1785)
Clerc (Swiss, ca. 1875)
Clouzier, Jacques (Paris, 1690-1750)
Cochin, D. (Paris, ca. 1800)
Cocque, Geo. (ca. 1610)
Cogniat (Paris, ca. 1675)
Coladon, Louis (Geneva, 1780-1850)
Cole, James Ferguson (London, 1820-1875)
Cole, Thomas (London, 1820-1864)
Collins, Clement (London, ca. 1705)
Collins, John (London, ca. 1720)

Collins, R. (London, ca. 1815)
Colondre & Schnee (ca. 1875)
Combret, Pierre (Lyons, France, ca. 1610-1625)
Cotton, John (London, ca. 1695-1715)
Coulin, Jaques & Bry, Amy (Paris & Geneva, 1780-1790)
Court, Jean-Pierre (ca. 1790-1810)
Courvosier, Freres (Swiss, 1810-1852)
Courvoisier & Houriet (Geneva, ca. 1790)
Cox, James (London, 1760-1785)
Crofswell J.N. (London), ca. 1825
Csacher, C. (Prague, Aus., ca. 1725)
Cumming, Alexander (London, 1750-1800)
Cummins, T. (London, 1820)
Cuper, Barthelemy (French, 1615-1635)
Curtis, John (London, ca. 1720)
Cusin, Charles (Geneva, ca. 1587)
Darling, William (British, ca. 1825)
De Baghyn, Adriaan (Amsterdam, ca. 1750)
Debaufre, Peter (French, 1690-1720) (Debaufre escap.)
Debaufre, Pierre (Paris, London, Geneva, 1675-1722)
De Bry, Theodore (German, 1585-1620)
De Charmes, Simon (London, France, 1690-1730)
De Choudens (Swiss & French, 1760-1790)
Decombaz, Gedeon (Geneva, 1780-1820)
Degeilh & Co. (ca. 1880-1900)
De Heca, Michel (Paris, ca. 1685)
De L Garde, Abraham (Paris, "Blois," ca. 1590)
Delynne, F. L. (Paris, ca. 1775)
Dent, Edward John (London, 1815-1850)
Derham, William (English, ca. 1677-1730)
Deroch, F. (Swiss, 1730-1770)
Des Arts & Co. (Geneva, 1790-1810)
Desquivillons & DeChoudens (Paris, ca. 1785)
Destouches, Jean-Francois-Albert (Holland, ca. 1760)
Devis, John (London, 1770-1785)
Dimier & Co. (Geneva, 1820-1925)
Dinglinger (enamel) (Dresden, Ger., ca. 1675)
Ditisheim & Co. "Maurice" (Swiss, 1894)
Ditisheim, Paul (Swiss, 1892)
Dobson, A. (London, 1660-1680)
Droz, Daniel (Chaux-de-Fonds, Sw., ca. 1760)
Droz, Henri (Chaux-de-Fonds, Sw., ca. 1775)
Droz, Pierre Jacquet (Chaux-de-Fonds, Sw., 1750-1775)
Droz, Pierre (Swiss, 1740-1770)
Droz & Co. (Swiss, ca. 1825)
Dubie (enamel) (Paris, ca. 1635)
Dubois & Fils (Paris, ca. 1680)
Duchene & Co. "Louis" (Geneva, 1790-1820)
Ducommun, Charles (Geneva, ca. 1750)
Duduict, Jacques (Blois, France, ca. 1600)
Dufalga, Philippe (Geneva, 1730-1790)
Dufalga, P. F. (Geneva, ca. 1750)
Dufour, Foll & Co. (Geneva, 1800-1830)
Dufour, J. E. & Co. (ca. 1890)
Dufour & Ceret (Ferney, Fr., ca. 1770-1785)
Dufour & Zentler (ca. 1870)
Duhamel, Pierre (Paris, ca. 1680)
Dupin, Paul (London, 1730-1765)
Dupont (Geneva, ca. 1810-1830)
Dupont, Jean (enamel) (Geneva, 1800-1860)
Duru (Paris, ca. 1650)
Dutertre, Baptiste (ca. 1730) (pat. duplex escapement)
Dutton, William (London, 1760-1840)
Earnshaw, Thomas (London, 1760-1842)
East, Edward (London, 1630-1670)
Edmonds, James (London to U.S.A., 1720-1766)
Edward, George & Son (London, ca. 1875)
Ekegren, Henri-Robert (Geneva, 1860)
Ellicott, John (London, 1728-1810)
Emery, Josiah (Geneva, 1750-1800)
Esquivillon & De Choudens (Paris, 1710-1780)
Ester, Jean Henry (Geneva, 1610-1665)
Etherington, George (London, 1680-1730)
Etienne Guyot & Co. (Geneva, ca. 1880)

Facio De Duillier, Nicholas (British, 1665-1710)
Fallery, Jacques (Geneva, ca. 1760)
Farmer, G. W. (wooden watches) (Germany, 1650-1675)
Fatio, Alfred (Geneva, 1920-1940)
Fatton, Frederick Louis (London, ca. 1822)
Favre Marius & Fils (Geneva, 1893)
Fenie, M. (ca. 1635)
Ferrero, J. (ca. 1854-1900)
Fiarce, Clement (Paris, ca. 1700)
Fitter, Joseph (London, ca. 1660)
Fontac (London, ca. 1775)
Forfaict, Nicolas (Paris, 1573-1619)
Fowles, Allen (Kilmarnock, Scot., ca. 1770)
French (London, 1810-1840)
Fureur (Swiss, 1910)
Gallopin "Henri Capt" (Geneva, 1875)
Garnod, G. (Paris, ca. 1640)
Garnier, Paul (Paris, 1825) (pat. Garnier escapement)
Garrault, Jacobus (Geneva, ca. 1650)
Garty & Constable (London, ca. 1750)
Gaudron, Antoine (Paris, 1675-1707)
Gaudron, Pierre (Paris, 1695-1740)
Geissheim, Smod (Augsburg, Ger., ca. 1625)
Gent, James & Son (London, 1875-1910)
Gerbeau, V. (Paris, 1900-1930)
Gerrard (British, 1790-1820)
Gibs, William (Rotterdam, ca. 1720)
Gibbons Joshua (London), ca. 1825
Gibson & Co., Ltd. (Ireland, ca. 1875-1920)
Gidon (Paris, ca. 1700)
Gillespey, Charles (Ireland, 1774-1171)
Girard, Perregaux (Swiss, 1856)
Girard, Theodore (Paris, 1623-1670)
Girardier, Charles (Geneva, 1780-1815)
Girod, B. (Paris, ca. 1810)
Girod, Gaspard (Paris, ca. 1670-1690)
Godod, E. (Paris, ca. 1790)
Godon, F. L. (Paris, ca. 1787)
Golay, A. Leresche & Fils (Geneva, 1844-1857)
Golay, H. (Swiss, 1969-1911)
Golay, Stahl & Fils (1878-1914)
Gollons (Paris, ca. 1663)
Gounouilhou, P. S. (Geneva, 1815-1840)
Gout, Ralph (London, 1790-1830)
Graham, George (London, 1715-1750)
Grandjean, Henri (Swiss, 1825-1880)
Grandjean, L. C. (Swiss, 1890-1920)
Grant, John & Son (English, 1780-1867)
Grantham, William (London, ca. 1860)
Grasset, Isaac (Geneva, ca. 1896)
Gray & Constable (London, ca. 1750)
Grazioza (Swiss, ca. 1901)
Grebauval, Hierosme (ca. 1575)
Gregory, Jermie (London, ca. 1652-1680)
Gregson, Jean P. (Paris, 1770-1790)
Griblin, Nicolas (French, 1650-1716)
Griessenback, Johann G. (Bavaria, ca. 1660)
Grignion "family" (London, 1690-1825)
Grignion, Daniel & Thomas (London, 1780-1790)
Grosclaude, Ch. & Co. (Swiss, ca. 1865)
Grosjean, Henry (French, ca. 1865)
Gruber, Hans (Nurnberg, Ger., ca. 1520-1560)
Gruber, Michel (Nurnberg, Ger., ca. 1605)
Gruet (Geneva, Sw., ca. 1664)
Gubelin, E. (Lucern, Switzerland, ca. 1832)
Guillaume, Ch. (pat. Invar, Elinvar)
Haas Nevevx & Co. (founder B. J. Haas) (Geneva, 1828-1925)
Hagen, Johan (German, ca. 1750)
Haley, Charles (London, 1781-1825)
Hallewey (London, 1695-1720)
Hamilton & Co. (London, 1865-1920)
Hamilton G.(London), Ca.1800s
Harper, Henry (London, ca. 1665-1700)

Harrison, John (England, 1710-1775) (pat. comp. balance)
Hasluck Brothers (London, ca. 1695)
Hautefeuille, Jean (Paris, 1670-1722)
Hautefeuille, John (Paris, 1660-1700)
Hawley, John (London, ca. 1850)
Hebert, Juliette (enamel) (Geneva, ca. 1890)
Helbros (Geneva, since 1918)
Hele or Henlein, Peter (Nurnberg, 1510-1540)
Heliger, J. (Zug, Sw., ca. 1575)
Henner, Johann (Wurtzburg, Ger., ca. 1730)
Henry, F. S. (Swiss, ca. 1850)
Hentschel, J. J. (French, ca. 1750)
Hess, L. (Zurich, Sw., ca. 1780)
Hessichti, Dionistus (ca. 1630)
Higgs & Evans (London, 1775-1825)
Hill, Ben. (London, 1640-1670)
Hoguet, Francois (Paris, ca. 1750)
Hooke, Robert (England, 1650-1700)
Hoseman, Stephen (London, ca. 1710-1740)
Houghton, James (England, ca. 1800-1820)
Houghton, Thomas (Chorley, England, ca. 1820-1840)
Houriet, Jacques Frederic (Paris 1810-1825)
Huaud, Freres (enamel) (Geneva, ca. 1685)
Huber, Peter (German, ca. 1875)
Hubert, David (London, 1714-1747)
Hubert, Oliver (London, ca. 1740)
Hubert, Etienne (French, 1650-1690)
Hues, Peter (Augsburg, Ger., ca. 1600)
Huguenin, David L. (Swiss, 1780-1835)
Humbert-Droz, David (Swiss, ca. 1790)
Huygens, Christian (Paris, 1657-1680)
Iaquier or Jacquier, Francois (Geneva, 1690-1720)
Ilbery, William (London, 1800-1835)
Ingold, Pierre-Frederic (Swiss, Paris, London, 1810-1870)
Invicta ("R. Picard") (Swiss, 1896)
Jaccard, E. H. & Co. (Swiss, ca. 1850)
Jacot, Charles-Edouard (Swiss, 1830-1860) (pat. Chinese duplex)
Jaeger, Edmond (Paris, 1875-1920)
Jaeger Le Coultre & Co. (Swiss, since 1833)
Jamison, Geo. (London, 1786-1810)
Janvier, Antide (Paris, 1771-1834)
Japy, Frederic & Sons "family" (French, Swiss, ca. 1776)
Jaquet, Pierre (Swiss, 1750-1790)
Jean Richard, Daniel (Swiss, 1685-1740)
Jean Richard, Edouard (Swiss, 1900-1930)
Jeannot, Paul (ca. 1890)
Jefferys & Gildert (London, 1790)
Jessop, Josias (London, 1780-1794)
Jeubi, Josias (Paris, ca. 1575)
Joly, Jacques (Paris, ca. 1625)
Jovat (London, ca. 1690)
Johnson Josh. Liverpool (English), ca.1810-1850
Jones, Henry (London, ca. 1665-1690)
Jump, Joseph (English, ca. 1827-1850)
Junod, Freres (Geneva, ca. 1850)
Jurgensen, Urban & Jules (Copenhagen, Swiss,1745-1912)
Just & Son (London, 1790-1825)
Juvet, Edouard (Swiss, 1844-1880)
Juvet, Leo (Swiss, 1860-1890)
Keates, William (London, ca. 1780)
Keely, W. (London, ca. 1790)
Kendall, Larcum (London, ca. 1786)
Kendall, James (London, 1740-1790)
Kessels, H. J. (Holland, 1800-1845)
Kirkton, R. (London, ca. 1790)
Klein, Johann Heinr (Copenhagen, Den., ca. 1710)
Klentschi, C. F. (Swiss, 1790-1840)
Koehn, Edward (Geneva, 1860-1908)
Kreizer, Conard (German, 1595-1658)
Kuhn, Jan Hendrik (Amsterdam, 1775-1800)
Kullberg, Victor (Copenhagen to London, 1850-1890)
Lamy, Michel (Paris, 1767-1800)
Lang & Padoux (ca. 1860)

Larcay (Paris, ca. 1725)
Lardy, Francois (Geneva, ca. 1825)
Larpent, Isacc & Jurgensen (Copenhagen, 1748-1811)
Laurier, Francois (Paris, 1654-1675)
Le Baufre (Paris, ca. 1650)
Lebet (Geneva, ca. 1850)
Lebet & Fils (Swiss, 1830-1892)
Le Coultre, Ami (Geneva, ca. 1887)
Le Coultre, Eugene (Geneva, ca. 1850)
Leekey, C. (London, ca. 1750)
Leeky, Gabriel (London, ca. 1775-1820)
Lepaute, Jean-Andre (Paris, 1750-1774)
Le Pine', Jean-Antoine (Paris, 1744-1814)
Le Prevost (Swiss), ca.1810
Leroux, John (England, 1758-1805)
Le Roy & Co. (Paris, ca. 1853)
Le Roy, Charles (Paris, 1733-1770)
Le Roy, Julien (Paris, 1705-1750)
Le Roy, Pierre (French, 1710-80) (improved duplex escap.)
Levy, Hermanos (Hong Kong, "Swiss," 1880-1890)
L'Hardy, Francois (Geneva, 1790-1825)
Lichtenauer (Wurzberg, Ger., ca. 1725)
Lindesay, G. (London, ca. 1740-1770)
Lindgren, Erik (England, 1735-1775) (pat. rack lever)
Litherland, Peter (English, 1780-1876)
Loehr, (Von) (Swiss, ca. 1880)
Long & Drew (enamel) (London, ca. 1790-1810)
Losada, Jose R. (London, 1835-1890)
Lowndes, Jonathan (London, ca. 1680-1700)
MacCabe, James (London, 1778-1830)
Maillardet & Co. (Swiss, ca. 1800)
Mairet, Sylvain (Swiss, 1825-1885) (London, 1830-1840)
Malignon, A. (Geneva, ca. 1835)
Marchand, Abraham (Geneva, 1690-1725)
Margetts, George (London, 1780-1800)
Markwick Markham, "Perigal" "Recordon" (London, 1780-1825)
Marshall, John (London, ca. 1690)
Martin (Paris, ca. 1780)
Martin, Thomas (London, ca. 1870)
Martineau, Joseph (London, 1765-1790)
Martinot, "family" (Paris, 1570-1770)
Martinot, James (London, ca. 1780)
Mascarone, Gio Batt (London, ca. 1635)
Massey, Edward (England, 1800-1850)
Massey, Henry (London, 1692-1745)
E. Mathey-Tissot & Co. (Swiss, 1886-1896)
Matile, Henry (Swiss, ca. 1825)
Maurer, Johann (Fiessna, Ger., ca. 1640-1650)
May, George (English, 1750-1770)
Mayr, Johann Peter (Augsburg, Ger., ca. 1770)
McCabe, James (London, 1780-1710)
McDowall, Charles (London, ca. 1820-1860)
Meak, John (London, ca. 1825)
Mecke, Daniel (ca. 1760)
Melly, Freres (Geneva, Paris, 1791-1844)
Mercier, A. D. (Swiss, 1790-1820)
Mercier, Francois David (Paris, ca. 1700)
Meuron & Co. (Swiss, ca. 1784)
Meylan, C. H. "Meylan W. Co." (Swiss, ca. 1880)
Michel, Jean-Robert (Paris, ca. 1750)
Miller, Joseph (London, ca. 1728)
Milleret & Tissot (Swiss, ca. 1835)
Miroir (London, ca. 1700-1725)
Mistral (Swiss, ca. 1902)
Mobilis (Swiss, ca. 1910)
Modernista (Swiss, ca. 1903)
Moillet, Jean-Jacques (Paris, 1776-1789)
Molina, Antonio (Madrid, Spain, ca. 1800)
Molinie (Swiss, ca. 1840)
Molyneux, Robert (London, ca. 1825-1850)
Montandon, Chs. Ad. (Swiss, 1800-1830)
Morand, Pierre (Paris, ca. 1790)

Moricand & Co. (Swiss, ca. 1780)
Moricand & Desgranges (Geneva, 1828-1835)
Moricand, Christ (Geneva, 1745-1790)
Morin, Pierre (English, French & Dutch style, ca. 1700)
Morliere (enamel) (Blois, Fr., ca. 1636-1650)
Moser, George Michael (London, ca. 1716-1730)
Motel, Jean Francois (French, 1800-1850)
Moulineux, Robert (London, 1800-1840)
Moulinier, Aine & Co. (Swiss, 1828-1851)
Moulinier, Freres & Co. (Swiss, ca. 1822)
Mudge, Thomas (London, 1740-1790)
Mulsund (enamel) (Paris, ca. 1700)
Munoz, Blas (Madrid, Spain, ca. 1806-1823)
Mussard, Jean (Geneva, 1699-1727)
Musy Padre & Figlo (Paris, 1710-1760)
Myrmecide (Paris, ca. 1525)
Nardin, Ulysse (Swiss, ca. 1846)
Nelson, W. (London, 1777-1818)
Nocturne (ca. 1920)
Noir, Jean-Baptiste (Paris, 1680-1710)
Norris, J. (Dutch, 1680-1700)
Norton (London), ca.1805
Nouwen, Michael (1st English, 1580-1600)
Noyean (ca. 1850)
Oldnburg, Johan (German, ca. 1648)
Oudin, Charles (Paris, 1807-1900)
Owen, John (English, ca. 1790)
Palmer, Samuel (London, ca. 1790-1810)
Panier, Iosue "Josue" (Paris, ca. 1790)
Papillon (ca. 1690)
Papillon, Francesco (Florence, ca. 1705)
Parr, Thomas (London, ca. 1735-1775)
Payne, H. & John (London, ca. 1735-1775)
Pellaton, Albert (Swiss, ca. 1873)
Pellaton, James (Swiss, 1903) (Tourbillon)
Pendleton, Richard (London, 1780-1805)
Pennington, Robert (English, 1780-1816)
Perigal, Francis (English, 1770-1790)
Pernetti, F. (Swiss, ca. 1850)
Perrelet, Abram (Swiss, 1780) (self wind)
Perret, Edouard (Swiss, 1850)
Perrin, Freres (Swiss, 1810)
Phillips, Edouard (Paris, ca. 1860)
Phleisot (Dijon, Fr., ca. 1540)
Piaget, George (Swiss, ca. 1881)
Picard, James (Geneva, ca. 1850)
Piguet & Capt (Geneva, 1802-1811)
Piguet & Meylan (Geneva, 1811-1828)
Piguet, Victorin-Emile (Geneva, 1870-1935)
Plairas, Solomon (Blois, Fr., ca. 1640)
Plumbe, David (ca. 1730)
Poitevin, B. (Paris, 1850-1935)
Poncet, J. F. (Dresden, 1750)
Poncet, Jean-Francois (Swiss, 1740-1800)
Potter, Harry (London, 1760-1800)
Pouzait, Jean-Moise (Geneva, 1780-1800)
Poy, Gottfrey (London, ca. 1725-1730)
Prest, Thomas (English, 1820-1855)
Prevost, Freres (ca. 1820)
Prior, Edward (London, 1825-1865)
Prior, George (London, 1800-1830)
Pyke, John (English, 1750-1780)
Quare, Daniel (London, 1700-1724)
Quarella, Antonio (ca. 1790)
Racine, Cesar (Swiss, ca. 1902)
Racine, Charles Frederic (Chaux-de-Fonds, Swiss, ca. 1810-1832)
Raillard, Claude (Paris, 1662-1675)
Raiss (1890-1910) (enamel)
Rait, D. C. (German, ca. 1866)
Ramsay, David (Scotland, France, London, 1590-1654)
Ramuz, Humbert U. & Co. (Swiss, ca. 1882)
Ratel, Henri (Paris, 1850-1900)
Recordon, Louis (London, 1778-1824)

Redier, Antoine (Paris, 1835-1883)
Renierhes (London, ca. 1850)
Rey, Jn. Ante, & Fils (Paris, 1790-1810)
Reynaud, P. & Co. (1860)
Rich, John (Geneva, London, 1795-1825)
Richard, Daniel Jean (1685-1740)
Richter, Jean Louis (enamel) (Geneva, 1786-1840)
Rigaud, Pierre (Geneva, 1750-1800)
Rigot, Francois (Geneva, ca. 1825)
Robert & Courvoisier & Co. (Paris, 1781-1832)
Robin, Robert (Paris, 1765-1805)
Robinet, Charles (Paris, ca. 1640)
Robinson, Olivier & Fredmahn (Naples, 1727-1790)
Robinson William (Liverpool), ca.1850
Rogers, Isaac (London, 1770-1810)
Romilly, Sieur (Geneva, ca. 1750-1775)
Rooker, Richard (London, 1790-1810)
Rose, Joseph (London, 1752-1795)
Rosier, John (Geneva, ca. 1750)
Roskell, Robert (London, 1798-1830) (rack-lever)
Roskopf, G. (German to Swiss, 1835-1885)
Rosselet, Louis (Geneva, 1855-1900) (enamel)
Rousseau, Jean (Paris, 1580-1642)
Roux, Bordier & Co. (Geneva, ca. 1795)
Ruegger, Jacques (ca. 1800-1840)
Ruel, Samuel (Rotterdam, ca. 1750)
Rugendas, Nicholas (Augsburg, Ger., ca. 1700-1750)
Rundell & Bridge (London, ca. 1772-1825)
Sailler, Johann (Vienna, Aus., ca. 1575)
Sanchez, Cayetano (Madrid, Spain, c. 1790-1800)
Sandoz, Henri F. (Tavannes W. Co.) (ca. 1840)
Savage, George (London, 1808-1855) (Inv. pin lever)
Savage, William (London (1800-1850)
Savile, John (London, ca. 1656-1679)
Schatck, Johann Engel (Prague, ca. 1650)
Schultz, Michael (ca. 1600-1650)
Schuster, Caspar (Nunburg, ca. 1570)
Sermand, J. (Geneva, ca. 1640)
Sherman De Neilly (Belfort, ca. 1910)
Sherwood, J. (London, ca. 1750-1775)
Solson (London, 1750)
Soret (Geneva, ca. 1810)
Soret, Frederic II (1735-1806)
Soret, Isaac & Co. (1690-1760)
Spencer & Perkins (London, 1790-1808)
Stadlin, Francois (Swiss, 1680-1735)
Staples, James (1755-1795)
Stuffer, M. T. (Swiss, 1830-1855)
Stauffer "Stauffer Son & Co." (London, 1880)
Strasser & Rohde (Glashutte, 1875)
Sudek, J. (ca. 1850)
Sully, Henry (French, London, 1700-1725)
Swift, Thomas (London, ca. 1825-1865)
Tavan, Antoine (Geneva, 1775-1830)
Tavernier, Jean (Paris, 1744-1795)
Tempor Watch Co. (1930) (Masonic watch)
Terond, Allier & Bachelard (ca. 1805-1830)
Terrot & Fazy (ca. 1767-1775)
Terrot, Philippe (Geneva, ca. 1732)
Terroux (ca. 1776)
Theed & Pikett (ca. 1750)
Thierry, J. (London, ca. 1760)
Thierry, Niel (ca. 1810)
Thiout, Antoine (Paris, 1724-1760)
Thorne, Robert (London, 1850)
Thoroton, James (London, 1860)
Thuret, Jacques (Paris, ca. 1695)
Thomason J.N. (Edinburgh), ca.1830
Timing & Repeating W. Co. (Geneva, 1900)
Tompion, Thomas (English, 1671-1713)
Tonkin, Tho. (London, ca. 1760)
Toutaia, Henri (French, 1650) (enamel)
Toutin, Jean (enamel) (Blois, Fr., ca. 1630)
Treffler, Sebastain (ca. 1750)

Tregent, J. (English, 1765-1800)
Truitte, Louis & Mourier (Geneva, ca. 1780)
Tyrer, Thomas (London, ca. 1782)
Uhren Fabrik Union (Glashutte, 1893-1970)
Ullman, J. & Co. (Swiss, 1893)
Ulrich, Johann (London, 1820-1870)
Upjohn, W. J. (London, 1815-1824)
Vacheron, Abraham Girod (German, 1760-1843)
Valere (Paris, 1860)
Vallier, Jean (Lyons, Fr., ca. 1630)
Valove, James (London, ca. 1740)
Vanbroff, James (Germany, ca. 1600)
Van Ceule, J. (ca. 1799-1725)
Vandersteen (ca. 1725)
Vaucher, C. H. (Geneva, ca. 1835)
Vaucher, Daniel (Paris, 1767-1790)
Vaucher, Freres (Swiss, 1850)
Vauquer, Robert (French, ca. 1650) (enamel)
Veigneur, F. I. (ca. 1780)
Verdiere A. (Paris), ca.1810
Vernod, Henriette (Paris, ca. 1790)
Vigne, James (London, ca. 1770)
Vrard, L., & Co. (Pekin, 1860-1872)

Vulliamy, Justin (London, ca. 1830-1854)
Vully, Jaques (ca. 1890-1900)
Vuolf (Swiss, ca. 1600)
Waldron, John (London, 1760)
Wales, Giles & Co. (Swiss, ca. 1870)
Waltrin (Paris, ca. 1820)
Weston, D. & Willis (enamel) (London, ca. 1800-1810)
Whitthorne, James (Dublin, since 1725)
Willats, John (London, ca. 1860)
Williamson, Timothy (London, 1770-1790)
Wilter, John (London, ca. 1760)
Winckles, John (London, 1770-1790)
Winnerl, Joseph Thaddeus (Paris, 1829-1886)
Wiss, Freres & Menu (Swiss, ca. 1787-1810)
Wiss, G. (Geneva, ca. 1750)
Wright, Charles (London, 1760-1790)
Wright, Thomas (English, ca. 1770-1790)
Young, Richard (London, 1765-1785)
Zech, Jacob (Prague, Aus. 1525-1540)
Zolling, Ferdinand (Frankfurt, Ger. ca. 1750)

**Tambour style case**, probably Nuremburg, ca. 1575, hinged cover, pierced to reveal engraved Roman chapter I-XII and Arabic 13-24 Central chapter, 60mm.

# HALLMARKS OF LONDON

Hallmarks were used on gold and silver cases imported from England. These marks, when interpreted, will give you the age of the case and location of the assay office.

The date-marks used 20 letters of the alphabet, A-U, never using the letters W, X, Y, or Z. The letters J & I or U & V, because of their similarity in shape, were never used together within the same 20-year period. A total of four marks can be found on English cases, which are:

The **MAKER'S MARK** was used to denote the manufacturer of the case.
The **STANDARD MARK** was used to denote a guarantee of the quality of the metal.
The **ASSAY OFFICE MARK** (also known as the town mark) was used to denote the location of the assay office.
The **DATE LETTER MARK** was a letter of the alphabet used to denote the year in which the article was stamped.
The stamp was used on gold and silver cases by the assay office.

The Maker's Mark      The Standard Mark

The Assay Office Mark      The Date Letter Mark

1822-up     1478 to 1821

Chester     Birmingham     Edinburgh     Dublin     Glasgow

## SWISS HALLMARKS

18k .750     14k .585     Platinum .950

Sterling Silver

Sterling Silver .925     Silver .800

Lucerne     Neuchatel.
Poinçons d'essai
de décembre 1852.

German silver mark     German gold mark

.800

TROY WEIGHT = 24 grains=1dwt., 1 Grain= 0.0648 grams, 20dwt = 1 OZ., 12oz = 1 LB.
NOTE: Gold & Silver Standards Vary from Country to Country. U.S.A. Coin Gold =.900 or 21 3/5K, Silver Coin=.900.
Gold Standards: 24K=1,000%or 1.0, 23K=.958 1/3, 22K=.916 2/3, 21K=.875, 20K=.833 1/3, 19K=.791 2/3, 18K=.750,
17K=.708 1/3, 16K=.666 2/3, 15K=.625, 14K=.583 1/3, 13K=.541 2/3, 12K=.500, 11=.458 1/3, 10K=.416 2/3, 9K= .375.
8K=.333 1/3, 7K=.291 2/3, 6K=.250, 5K=.208 1/3, 4K=.166 2/3, 3K=.125, 2K=.83 1/3, 1K=.41 2/3.

# LONDON HALLMARKS

| Letter | Year | Letter | Year | Letter | Year | Letter | Year | Letter | Year | Letter | Year | Letter | Year | Letter | Year | Letter | Year |
|---|---|---|---|---|---|---|---|---|---|---|---|---|---|---|---|---|---|
| O | 1551 | M | 1589 | k | 1627 | J | 1666 | a | 1709 | a | 1752 | B | 1797 | f | 1841 | i | 1884 |
| P | 1552 | N | 1590 | l | 1628 | K | 1667 | b | 1710 | b | 1753 | C | 1798 | g | 1842 | k | 1885 |
| Q | 1553 | O | 1591 | m | 1629 | L | 1668 | c | 1711 | c | 1754 | D | 1799 | h | 1843 | l | 1886 |
| R | 1554 | P | 1592 | n | 1630 | M | 1669 | d | 1712 | d | 1755 | E | 1800 | i | 1844 | m | 1887 |
| S | 1555 | Q | 1593 | o | 1631 | N | 1670 | e | 1713 | e | 1756 | F | 1801 | k | 1845 | n | 1888 |
| T | 1556 | R | 1594 | p | 1632 | O | 1671 | f | 1714 | f | 1757 | G | 1802 | l | 1846 | o | 1889 |
| V | 1557 | S | 1595 | q | 1633 | P | 1672 | g | 1715 | g | 1758 | H | 1803 | m | 1847 | p | 1890 |
| a | 1558 | T | 1596 | r | 1634 | Q | 1673 | A | 1716 | h | 1759 | I | 1804 | n | 1848 | q | 1891 |
| b | 1559 | V | 1597 | s | 1635 | R | 1674 | B | 1717 | i | 1760 | K | 1805 | o | 1849 | R | 1892 |
| C | 1560 | W | 1598 | t | 1636 | S | 1675 | C | 1718 | k | 1761 | L | 1806 | p | 1850 | S | 1893 |
| d | 1561 | B | 1599 | u | 1637 | T | 1676 | D | 1719 | l | 1762 | M | 1807 | q | 1851 | T | 1894 |
| e | 1562 | U | 1600 | A | 1638 | V | 1677 | E | 1720 | m | 1763 | N | 1808 | r | 1852 | U | 1895 |
| f | 1563 | D | 1601 | b | 1639 | a | 1678 | F | 1721 | n | 1764 | O | 1809 | s | 1853 | a | 1896 |
| g | 1564 | E | 1602 | c | 1640 | b | 1679 | G | 1722 | o | 1765 | P | 1810 | t | 1854 | b | 1897 |
| h | 1565 | F | 1603 | d | 1641 | c | 1680 | H | 1723 | p | 1766 | Q | 1811 | u | 1855 | c | 1898 |
| i | 1566 | G | 1604 | e | 1642 | d | 1681 | I | 1724 | r | 1767 | R | 1812 | a | 1856 | d | 1899 |
| k | 1567 | h | 1605 | f | 1643 | e | 1682 | K | 1725 | r | 1768 | S | 1813 | b | 1857 | e | 1900 |
| l | 1568 | I | 1606 | g | 1644 | f | 1683 | L | 1726 | s | 1769 | T | 1814 | c | 1858 | f | 1901 |
| m | 1569 | K | 1607 | h | 1645 | g | 1684 | M | 1727 | t | 1770 | U | 1815 | d | 1859 | g | 1902 |
| n | 1570 | L | 1608 | i | 1646 | h | 1685 | N | 1728 | u | 1771 | a | 1816 | e | 1860 | h | 1903 |
| o | 1571 | M | 1609 | k | 1647 | i | 1686 | O | 1729 | a | 1772 | b | 1817 | f | 1861 | i | 1904 |
| p | 1572 | N | 1610 | l | 1648 | k | 1687 | P | 1730 | b | 1773 | c | 1818 | g | 1862 | k | 1905 |
| q | 1573 | O | 1611 | m | 1649 | l | 1688 | Q | 1731 | c | 1774 | d | 1819 | h | 1863 | l | 1906 |
| r | 1574 | P | 1612 | n | 1650 | m | 1689 | R | 1732 | d | 1775 | e | 1820 | i | 1864 | m | 1907 |
| s | 1575 | Q | 1613 | o | 1651 | n | 1690 | S | 1733 | a | 1776 | f | 1821 | k | 1865 | n | 1908 |
| t | 1576 | R | 1614 | p | 1652 | o | 1691 | T | 1734 | b | 1777 | g | 1822 | l | 1866 | o | 1909 |
| u | 1577 | S | 1615 | q | 1653 | p | 1692 | V | 1735 | c | 1778 | h | 1823 | m | 1867 | p | 1910 |
| A | 1578 | T | 1616 | r | 1654 | q | 1693 | a | 1736 | d | 1779 | i | 1824 | n | 1868 | q | 1911 |
| B | 1579 | V | 1617 | s | 1655 | r | 1694 | b | 1737 | e | 1780 | k | 1825 | o | 1869 | r | 1912 |
| C | 1580 | a | 1618 | t | 1656 | s | 1695 | c | 1738 | f | 1781 | l | 1826 | p | 1870 | s | 1913 |
| D | 1581 | b | 1619 | u | 1657 | t | 1696 | d | 1739 | g | 1782 | m | 1827 | q | 1871 | t | 1914 |
| E | 1582 | C | 1620 | B | 1658 | u | 1697 | d | 1739 | h | 1783 | n | 1828 | r | 1872 | u | 1915 |
| F | 1583 | d | 1621 | b | 1659 | A | 1698 | e | 1740 | i | 1784 | o | 1829 | s | 1873 | a | 1916 |
| G | 1584 | e | 1622 | C | 1660 | B | 1699 | f | 1741 | k | 1785 | p | 1830 | t | 1874 | b | 1917 |
| H | 1585 | f | 1623 | D | 1661 | C | 1700 | g | 1742 | l | 1786 | q | 1831 | u | 1875 | c | 1918 |
| I | 1586 | g | 1624 | E | 1662 | ff | 1701 | h | 1743 | m | 1787 | r | 1832 | A | 1876 | d | 1919 |
| K | 1587 | h | 1625 | F | 1663 | G | 1702 | i | 1744 | n | 1788 | s | 1833 | B | 1877 | e | 1920 |
| L | 1588 | i | 1626 | G | 1664 | h | 1703 | k | 1745 | o | 1789 | t | 1834 | C | 1878 | f | 1921 |
|  |  |  |  | H | 1665 | b | 1704 | l | 1746 | p | 1790 | u | 1835 | D | 1879 | g | 1922 |
|  |  |  |  |  |  | k | 1705 | m | 1747 | q | 1791 | a | 1836 | E | 1880 | h | 1923 |
|  |  |  |  |  |  | l | 1706 | n | 1748 | r | 1792 | B | 1837 | F | 1881 | i | 1924 |
|  |  |  |  |  |  | V | 1707 | o | 1749 | s | 1793 | C | 1838 | G | 1882 | k | 1925 |
|  |  |  |  |  |  | R | 1708 | p | 1750 | t | 1794 | B | 1839 | H | 1883 | l | 1926 |
|  |  |  |  |  |  |  |  | q | 1751 | u | 1795 | e | 1840 |  |  |  |  |
|  |  |  |  |  |  |  |  |  |  | A | 1796 |  |  |  |  |  |  |

# DATE LETTER MARKS FOR
# BIRMINGHAM & CHESTER

## BIRMINGHAM ASSAY OFFICE DATE LETTERS

| | | | | | | | | | |
|---|---|---|---|---|---|---|---|---|---|
| A 1773 | a 1798 | A 1824 | A 1849 | a 1875 |
| B 1774 | b 1799 | B 1825 | B 1850 | b 1876 |
| C 1775 | C 1800 | C 1826 | C 1851 | c 1877 |
| D 1776 | d 1801 | D 1827 | D 1852 | d 1878 |
| E 1777 | e 1802 | E 1828 | E 1853 | e 1879 |
| F 1778 | f 1803 | J 1829 | F 1854 | f 1880 |
| G 1779 | g 1804 | G 1830 | G 1855 | g 1881 |
| H 1780 | h 1805 | h 1831 | H 1856 | h 1882 |
| I 1781 | i 1806 | J 1832 | I 1857 | i 1883 |
| K 1782 | j 1807 | K 1833 | J 1858 | k 1884 |
| L 1783 | k 1808 | T 1834 | K 1859 | l 1885 |
| M 1784 | l 1809 | M 1835 | L 1860 | m 1886 |
| N 1785 | m 1810 | N 1836 | M 1861 | n 1887 |
| O 1786 | n 1811 | D 1837 | N 1862 | o 1888 |
| P 1787 | O 1812 | P 1838 | O 1863 | p 1889 |
| Q 1788 | P 1813 | Q 1839 | P 1864 | q 1890 |
| R 1789 | q 1814 | R 1840 | Q 1865 | r 1891 |
| S 1790 | r 1815 | S 1841 | R 1866 | s 1892 |
| T 1791 | s 1816 | T 1842 | S 1867 | t 1893 |
| U 1792 | t 1817 | U 1843 | T 1868 | u 1894 |
| V 1793 | u 1818 | W 1844 | U 1869 | v 1895 |
| W 1794 | v 1819 | m 1845 | V 1870 | w 1896 |
| X 1795 | w 1820 | X 1846 | W 1871 | x 1897 |
| Y 1796 | X 1821 | y 1847 | X 1872 | y 1898 |
| Z 1797 | Y 1822 | Z 1848 | Y 1873 | z 1899 |
| | Z 1823 | | Z 1874 | |

## CHESTER ASSAY OFFICE DATE LETTERS

| | | | | | | | |
|---|---|---|---|---|---|---|---|
| A 1701 | a 1726 | a 1751 | a 1776 | A 1797 | A 1818 | N 1839 | a 1864 |
| B 1702 | b 1727 | b 1752 | b 1777 | B 1798 | B 1819 | O 1840 | b 1865 |
| C 1703 | c 1728 | C 1753 | c 1778 | C 1799 | C 1820 | C 1841 | c 1866 |
| D 1704 | d 1729 | d 1754 | d 1779 | D 1800 | D 1821 | D 1842 | N 1867 |
| E 1705 | e 1730 | e 1755 | e 1780 | E 1801 | E 1822 | e 1843 | e 1868 |
| F 1706 | f 1731 | f 1756 | f 1781 | F 1802 | F 1823 | f 1844 | f 1869 |
| G 1707 | g 1732 | G 1757 | g 1782 | G 1803 | F 1824 | g 1845 | g 1870 |
| H 1708 | h 1733 | h 1758 | h 1783 | H 1804 | G 1825 | h 1846 | h 1871 |
| I 1709 | i 1734 | i 1759 | i 1784 | I 1805 | H 1826 | J 1847 | i 1872 |
| K 1710 | k 1735 | k 1760 | k 1785 | K 1806 | I 1827 | S 1848 | k 1873 |
| L 1711 | l 1736 | l 1761 | l 1786 | L 1807 | K 1828 | C 1849 | l 1874 |
| M 1712 | m 1737 | m 1762 | m 1787 | M 1808 | L 1829 | m 1850 | m 1875 |
| N 1713 | n 1738 | n 1763 | n 1788 | N 1809 | M 1830 | n 1851 | n 1876 |
| O 1714 | o 1739 | o 1764 | O 1789 | O 1810 | N 1831 | o 1852 | O 1877 |
| P 1715 | p 1740 | p 1765 | p 1790 | P 1811 | O 1832 | p 1853 | p 1878 |
| Q 1716 | q 1741 | q 1766 | q 1791 | Q 1812 | P 1833 | q 1854 | q 1879 |
| R 1717 | r 1742 | r 1767 | r 1792 | R 1813 | Q 1834 | R 1855 | r 1880 |
| S 1718 | s 1743 | s 1768 | s 1793 | S 1814 | R 1835 | S 1856 | s 1881 |
| T 1719 | t 1744 | t 1769 | t 1794 | T 1815 | S 1836 | t 1857 | t 1882 |
| U 1720 | u 1745 | u 1770 | u 1795 | U 1816 | T 1837 | u 1858 | u 1883 |
| V 1721 | v 1746 | v 1771 | V 1796 | V 1817 | U 1838 | v 1859 | A 1884 |
| W 1722 | w 1747 | V 1772 | | | | W 1860 | B 1885 |
| X 1723 | X 1748 | w 1773 | | | | X 1861 | C 1886 |
| Y 1724 | w 1749 | X 1774 | | | | y 1862 | D 1887 |
| Z 1725 | z 1750 | Y 1775 | | | | z 1863 | E 1888 |
| | | | | | | | F 1889 |

# REPEATING WATCHES

Repeating watches or repeaters are those watches which will sound the time at the wish of the user. The repeating mechanism is operated by either a slide, plunger, or button in the case of the watch. There are basically five types of repeating mechanisms, some more common than others:

(1). **QUARTER REPEATERS**– The quarter repeater strikes the previous hour and quarter hour. In the older watches usually verge the striking is on a single bell attached to the inside of the case and the hour and quarter striking uses the same tone. There is first a series of hammer blows on the bell to indicate the hours, followed, after a short pause, by up to three twin strikes to denote the number of quarters elapsed. In later watches the striking is on wire gongs attached to the movement itself. The hours are struck on a single deep gong and the quarters on a higher-pitched gong followed by the deeper gong, producing a "ting-tang" sound.

(2). **HALF-QUARTER REPEATERS** -These strike the hours, the last quarter (ting-tang) and the previous half-quarter; i.e., seven and a half minutes. Half-quarter repeaters are mostly all verge escapement watches and are rarely seen by the average collector.

(3). **FIVE-MINUTE REPEATERS**– These fall into two types. One system is similar to the half-quarter repeater but follows the quarter "ting-tang" by a single higher-pitched strike for each five minute interval elapsed since the last quarter. The other system strikes the hours on a deep gong and follows this with a single higher note for each five minute period after the hour, omitting a quarter striking.

(4).**MINUTE REPEATERS**– The most complicated of the repeater is similar to the 1/4 repeater with the addition of the minutes. The minute repeater strikes the last recorded hour, quarter and minutes. At 10:52; a minute repeater will strike 10 deep chimes for the hour, 3 double chimes (deep & high) producing a "ting-tang for 3/4 hours & 7 high pitched chimes for 7 minutes (45+7=52).

(5). **CLOCK WATCHES**– The clock watch is essentially a repeater with the features of a striking clock. Where as the above-mentioned repeaters are all operated by a plunger or slide which winds the repeating function and which runs down after the last strike, the clock watch is wound in the same way as the going train usually with a key and is operated by the touch of a button in the case. The repeat function can be operated many times before the watch needs to be rewound. The CLOCK part of the name comes from the watch also striking the hours and sometimes the quarters or half hour in passing. The clock watch is easily recognizable by the two winding holes in either the case or the dial.

In addition to the five types described above, the features of striking are sometimes found with not only two but three and even four gongs, this producing a peal of notes. These repeaters are known as **"CARILLONS."**

At the other end of the scale from the carillon is the "dumb" repeater. This strikes on a block of metal in the case or on the movement and is felt rather than heard. It is said that the idea was to produce a watch that would not embarrass its owner when he wished to know when to slip away from boring company. Although the dumb repeater is less desirable for the average collector, it certainly should not be avoided–Breguet himself made dumb repeaters.

**Grande Sonnerie** and **Petite Sonnerie** have been used since early 1700's. The clock watch striking system at first was called *Dutch Striking* because it was used in clock making in about 1665. The older system used striking on bells and struck the hours of the day. Then came the Dutch Striking which also struck the half-hour. This system later developed into a chiming function called **Grande Sonnerie** (grand strike or tone) which struck both the hour and quarter hours are struck ever 15 minutes (thus the hour is repeated ever 15 minutes). The **Petite Sonnerie** is a simpler variation of *Grande Sonnerie* in which the 1/4 hour are struck, but the hour is struck only at the o'clock (not repeated).

L.Audemars 2 train Grande or Petite Sonnerie minute repeating clock watch. Note: Marked on bezel sonne & silence at 12 o'clock also Petite Sonnerie & Grande Sonnerie at 6 o'clock, Ca. 1870's.

L. Audemars 2 train Grande or Petite Sonnerie 1/4 repeating clock watch. Note: The push button in the pendant that activate the repeating gongs, Ca. 1850.

## A BIT OF HISTORY

Now that we have seen what repeaters are supposed to do, it might be in order to look briefly at their origins. Before the days of electric light, it was a major project to tell the time at night, since striking a tinderbox was said to have taken up to fifteen minutes to accomplish. Clocks, of course, had striking mechanisms, but they tended to keep the occupants of the house awake listening for the next strike. The repeating addition to the clock meant that the master of the house could silence the passing strike at night and, at his whim, simply pull a cord over his bed to activate the striking in another part of the house and thus waking everyone. To silence those members of the household who did not appreciate a clock booming out in the early hours of the morning, the horologists of the day turned their thoughts to the idea of a repeating watch.

The first mention of repeating watches is in the contest between Daniel Quare (1649-1724) and the Rev. Edward Barlow (1639-1719) to miniaturize the repeating action of a clock. Barlow, who for some reason had changed his name from Booth, was a theoretical horologist of outstanding ability. Barlow's design made for him by Thomas Tompion and Quare's watch were both submitted to King James II and the Privy Council for a decision as to whom should be granted a patent. The King chose Quare's design because the repeating mechanism was operated by a single push-button, whereas Barlow's required two. Quare was granted a patent in 1687. Barlow had had his share of fame earlier, however, with the invention of rack-striking for clocks in 1676.

Quare went into production with his new repeater watches, but changed the design to replace the push-button in the case with a pendant that could be pushed in. The first of these watches showed a fault that is still found on the cheaper repeaters of this century – that is, if the pendant was not pushed fully in, then the incorrect hours were struck. To overcome this problem, he invented the so-called "all-or-nothing" piece. This is a mechanism whereby if the pendant was not pushed fully home, then the watch would not strike at all.

The half-quarter appeared shortly after the all-or-nothing piece, and then by about 1710 the five-minute repeater was on the market. Some five years after this, a "deaf-piece" was often fitted to the watch. This was a slide or pin fitted to the case which, when activated, caused the hammers to be lifted away from the bell and had the same effect as a dumb repeater.

Sometime around 1730, Joseph Graham decided to dispense with the idea of a bell and arranged for the hammers to strike a dust-cover, thus making the watch slimmer and preventing dust from entering the pierced case.

About the middle of the century, the French master Le Roy carried the idea a stage further and dispensed with both bells and dust covers, and used a metal block which revolutionized the thickness of the repeating watch and introduced the dumb repeater. Breguet used wire gongs around 1789 and the pattern for the modern repeater was set. The minute repeater came into more common use after 1800, and earlier examples are definitely very rare, although it is known that Thomas Mudge made a complicated watch incorporating minute repeating for Ferdinand VI of Spain about 1750.

By the last quarter of the 1700s, Switzerland had gone for the repeater in a big way and the center of fine craftsmanship for complicated watches was in the Valley of Joux. Here the principle of division of labor was highly refined and whole families were hard at work producing parts for repeating and musical watches. Since one person concentrated only on one part of the watch, it is hardly surprising that parts of excellent quality were turned out. The basic movements were then sold to watchmakers/finishers all over the Continent and even to England, where the principle of one man, one watch, among the stubborn majority eventually led to the downfall of what had once been the greatest watchmaking nation in history.

The greatest popularity of the repeater came, however, in the last quarter of the 1800s, when Switzerland turned them out in the tens of thousands. Although there were many different names on the dials of the watches, most seem to have been produced by the company "Le Phare" and only finished by the name on the dial. The production of repeaters in quantity seems to have ground to a finish in about 1921 due to (a) the invention of luminous dials and universal electric or gas lighting, and (b) a lack of watchmakers willing to learn the highly demanding skills. The interest in horology over the past decade has, however, revived the idea of the repeater and several companies in Switzerland are now producing limited editions of expensive models.

## BUYING A REPEATER

Since so many repeaters seem to have been repaired at some time in the past by incompetent watchmakers, it is often too expensive a purchase if the buyer does not know what he is doing.

Rule One should be: if it does not work perfectly, avoid it like the plague unless a competent repairer first gives you an estimate which suits your pocket. All too often in the past the repairer was under the impression that metal grows with age and he has filed the teeth of a rack in order to get the full striking to work again. When it dawned on him that the problem was a worn bearing, the tooth was stretched with a punch and refiled, making it weak. It was then goodbye to a fine piece of craftsmanship.

A better quality repeater is usually one which is "jeweled to the hammers." This simply means that the hammers have jeweled bearing which can be seen by searching the movement for the hammers, locating the pivots around which they swing, and looking for the jeweled bearing in which they sit.

All repeaters have some system for regulating the speed of the repeating train. On the older fusee types, there was usually a rather primitive arrangement of a pinion in an eccentric bushing which could be turned to increase or decrease the depth of engagement of the pinion with the next wheel. Another system, a little better, uses an anchor and a toothed wheel as in an alarm clock. This system is usually located under the dial but can be detected by the buzzing sound it makes when the train is operated. The far superior system is the centrifugal governor which can be seen whizzing around in the top plate of the watch when the repeating action is operated. On the whole, the watch with the centrifugal governor is more desirable, although it must be mentioned that the Swiss turned out some inferior watches with this system.

Minute repeating movement by Dent of London. Minute repeating on two gongs and slide activated. Also note the watch has a split second chronograph, Ca. early 1900s.

Test the watch by operating the repeating train over a full hour, seeing that the quarters and minutes function correctly, then test each individual hour. Finally, set the hands to just before 1 o'clock (about 12:45) and test the striking. Any defect due to dirt or worn bearings will show up by the final blow(s), being either sluggish or not striking at all. If there is incorrect striking, have an expert look at it before you buy.

Try a partial operation of the slide or push-piece. If the watch has an all-or-nothing piece (as a reasonable grade movement should have), then the watch will not strike. Partial striking indicates either a low grade watch or a non-functioning all-or-nothing piece.

Note: Additional features such as chronograph functions, calendar, moon phase, etc., and will obviously affect the price of the watch.

Important note: Remember Rule One, if any function does not work, **BUYER BEWARE!**

# TOURBILLON

Breguet invented the tourbillon in 1795. A tourbillon is a device designed to reduce the position errors of a watch. This device has the escape wheel, lever and balance wheel all mounted in a carriage of light frameworks. This carriage makes one complete turn every minute. The fourth wheel is fixed and is concentric with the carriage pinion and arbor. The escape wheel pinion meshes with the fourth wheel and will roll around the fixed fourth wheel. The escape wheel and lever are mounted on the carriage, and the third wheel drives the carriage pinion, turning the carriage once every minute. This rotation of the escapement will help reduce the position errors of a watch. One of the major objections is that the carriage and escapement weight mass must be stopped and started at each release of the escapement. The tourbillon design requires extreme skill to produce and is usually found on watches of high quality. Somewhat similar to the tourbillon is the karrusel, except it rotates about once per hour and the fourth wheel is not fixed. It also takes less skill to produce.

**Charles Frodsham,** TOURBILLON escapement, minute repeating, split second chronograph, about 600 to 700 tourbillons are known exist. About 85 % of the tourbillon movements were made by Nicole Nielson & Co. as in this watch.

444

**Tourbillon**

A. Fixed fourth wheel
B. Third wheel
C. Carriage (one revolution per minute)
D. Carriage pinion
E. Escape Wheel & pinion
F. Arbor for seconds hand
G. Escape cock
H. Lever & pallets

# MUSICAL WATCHES
(Three basic types)

**Stacked Tooth**

**Disc Type with individual teeth**

**Pinned Cylinder & Comb**

# EUROPEAN POCKET WATCH LISTINGS
## Pricing at Collectable Fair Market Retail Level
### (Complete Watches Only)

Unless otherwise noted, watches listed in this section are priced at the collectable **fair market** retail level and as **complete** watches having an original 14k gold-filled case with an original white enamel single sunk dial, and the entire original movement in good working order with no repairs needed. Watches listed as 14k and 18k are solid gold cases. Coin or silveroid type and stainless steel cases will be listed as such. Keywind and keyset pocket watches are listed as having original coin silver cases. Dollar type watches, or low cost production watches, are listed as having a base metal type case and a composition dial.

The prices shown were averaged from dealers' lists just prior to publication and are an indication of the retail level or what collectors will pay. Prices are provided in three categories: average condition, extra fine, and mint condition, and are shown in whole dollar amounts only. The values listed are a guide for the *collectable* retail level and are provided for your information only. Dealers will not necessarily pay FULL RETAIL PRICE. Prices listed are for watches with *original cases* and *dials*.

☺ Descriptions and serial number ranges listed for early watches cannot be considered 100 percent accurate due to the manner in which records were kept by these companies. Watches were not necessarily sold in the exact order of manufactured date.

**Important Notice.** All of the information, including valuations, in this book has been compiled from the most reliable sources, and every effort has been made to eliminate errors and questionable data. Nevertheless, the possibility of error, in a work of such immense scope, always exists. The publisher or authors will not be held responsible for losses which may occur in the purchase, sale, or other transaction of items, because of information contained herein. Readers who feel they have discovered errors are invited to write and inform us, so they may be corrected in subsequent editions.

## INFORMATION NEEDED

This price guide is interested in any facts and information you might have that should possibly be considered for future editions. Documented facts are needed. Please send photo or sources of information to:

### COOKSEY SHUGART
### P.O. BOX 3147
### CLEVELAND, TENNESSEE
### 37320-3147

*( WHEN CORRESPONDING, PLEASE INCLUDE A*
*SELF-ADDRESSED, STAMPED ENVELOPE. )*

# AGASSIZ
Swiss

Auguste Agassiz of Saint Imier & Geneva started manufacturing quality watches in 1832. They later became interested in making a flat style watch which proved to be very popular. Some of these movements can be fitted inside a $20 gold piece.

The company was inherited by Ernest Francillion who built a factory called **Longines.** The Longines factory continued the Agassiz line until the Great Depression.

Agassiz, 43mm, 17 jewels, World Time, 42 Cities, ca. 1940.     Agassiz, 40mm, 21 jewels, 8 day with wind indicator.

| TYPE – DESCRIPTION | Avg | Ex-Fn | Mint |
|---|---|---|---|
| Early, KW KS, Swiss bar Mvt., time only, Ca.1870, Silver case ... | $80 | $100 | $135 |
| Time only, gold, 40–44mm, 10-12 size, OF | 200 | 275 | 325 |
| HC | 350 | 400 | 450 |
| Time only, gold, 45- 50mm, OF | 250 | 350 | 450 |
| Time only, gold & **enamel**, 45- 50mm, OF | 1,000 | 1,200 | 1,500 |
| HC | 400 | 500 | 600 |

Agassiz, Time only, gold & enamel, 45- 50mm, OF     Agassiz, $20 gold  22 / 18K coin watch, Ca. 1950s.

| TYPE – DESCRIPTION | Avg | Ex-Fn | Mint |
|---|---|---|---|
| 8 day, 21J, wind indicator, gold, 40mm, OF | $900 | $1,200 | $1,600 |
| $20 gold 22 / 18K coin watch, 34mm, Ca. 1950s | 1,900 | 2,000 | 2,300 |
| World Time, 42 Cities, gold, 43mm, OF | 4,800 | 5,800 | 7,000 |
| Chronograph, gold, 45-50mm, OF | 450 | 550 | 650 |
| HC | 650 | 750 | 850 |
| Split second chronograph, gold, OF | 800 | 900 | 1,000 |
| HC | 900 | 1,000 | 1,200 |
| 1/4 hr. repeater, gold, 46-52mm, OF | 800 | 900 | 1,000 |
| HC | 1,200 | 1,400 | 1,600 |
| Minute repeater, gold, 46-52mm, OF | 1,500 | 1,800 | 2,500 |
| OF w/chrono. | 1,800 | 2,000 | 2,800 |
| Minute repeater, gold, 46-52mm, HC | 2,000 | 2,200 | 3,000 |
| HC w/chrono. | 2,500 | 2,800 | 3,500 |

# ASSMANN
### Glasshute

Julius Assmann began producing watches with the help of Adolf Lange in 1852. His watches are stylistically similar to those produced by Lange. Later on he adopted his own lever style. Assmann made highly decorative watches for the South American market that are highly regarded by some collectors.

Assmann, 50mm, 19 jewels, diamond cap jewels, gold jewel settings, gold lever escapement, serial number 3,086, BRIDGE MODEL, ca. 1875.

Assmann, 50mm, 19 jewels, diamond cap jewels, gold jewel settings, gold lever escapement, serial number 3,739, ca. 1877.

| TYPE – DESCRIPTION | Avg | Ex-Fn | Mint |
|---|---|---|---|
| Time only, gold, 45- 50mm, OF | $1,200 | $1,400 | $1,600 |
| HC | 1,800 | 2,000 | 2,200 |
| Chronograph, gold, 45-50mm, OF | 2,200 | 2,500 | 2,800 |
| HC | 3,500 | 4,000 | 4,500 |
| Split second chronograph, gold, 45-52mm, OF | 3,000 | 3,500 | 4,000 |
| HC | 3,500 | 4,000 | 4,500 |
| 1/4 hr. repeater, gold, 46-52mm, OF | 2,500 | 2,800 | 3,200 |
| HC | 3,500 | 4,000 | 4,500 |
| Minute repeater, gold, 46-52mm, OF | 4,000 | 4,500 | 5,000 |
| HC | 6,000 | 6,500 | 7,500 |
| Perp. moonph. cal. w/min. repeater, gold, HC | 40,000 | 45,000 | 50,000 |

🕐 Some models and grades are not included. Their values can be determined by comparing with similar age, size, metal content, style, models and grades listed.

🕐 Watches listed in this book are priced at the collectable fair market value at the retail level, as complete watches having an original case, an original white enamel dial, and with the entire original movement in good working order with no repairs needed, unless otherwise noted.

# AUDEMARS, PIGUET & CIE
Swiss

Audemars, Piguet & Cie was founded in 1875 by Jules Audemars and Edward Piguet, both successors to fine horological families. This company produced many fine high grade and complicated watches, predominantly in nickel and, with a few exceptions, fully jeweled. Their complicated watches are sought after more than the plain timepieces. They also produced some very handsome wristwatches.

Audemars Piguet, 40mm, about 10 size, 19 jewels, cabochon on winding stem, Platinum, OF.

Audemars, Piguet, 43mm., 18 jewels, adj.6P, jumping hour, day-date-month windows, ca. 1925.

| TYPE – DESCRIPTION | Avg | Ex-Fn | Mint |
|---|---|---|---|
| Early, KW KS, Swiss bar Mvt., time only, Ca.1870, **Gold case** .... | $800 | $900 | $1,200 |
| Time only, gold, 40-44mm, OF............................................................. | 700 | 900 | 1,000 |
|     HC ........................................................................................ | 1,000 | 1,200 | 1,400 |
|     Platinum, OF ............................................................................. | 1,000 | 1,200 | 1,400 |
| Time only, gold, 45- 50mm, OF......................................................... | 1,500 | 1,800 | 2,000 |
|     HC ........................................................................................ | 2,800 | 3,500 | 4,000 |
| Jumping hour w/ day-date-month, gold, 43mm., ca. 1925. ............ | 6,000 | 8,000 | 10,000 |
| Rising Arms, 44mm, one arm points to the hours &the other to the minute, 18K, OF.............................................................. | 8,000 | 10,000 | 12,000 |

Audemars Piguet, pressure on a push-piece on rim of watch, lifts the arms of the bronze, one points to the hour and the other points to the minutes, 44mm, 18K, OF.

Audemars Piguet, Perpetual moon phase calendar, Astronomic watch showing the moon phases, and perpetual calendar showing day, date, & month, Ca.1920s.

AUDEMARS PIGUET, 46mm, 36 jewels, minute repeater, split-second chronograph, serial # 3853, Ca.1888.

AUDEMARS PIGUET, 46mm, Min. repeater, moon-phase, Chronograph, 18K, HC, Ca.1928.

| TYPE – DESCRIPTION | Avg | Ex-Fn | Mint |
|---|---|---|---|
| Chronograph, gold, 45-50mm, OF | $3,000 | $3,500 | $4,000 |
| HC | 3,500 | 4,000 | 4,500 |
| OF w/register | 3,000 | 3,500 | 4,000 |
| HC w/register | 5,000 | 6,000 | 7,000 |
| Split second chronograph, gold, 45-52mm, OF | 4,500 | 5,000 | 5,500 |
| HC | 6,000 | 6,500 | 7,000 |
| OF w/register | 5,000 | 5,500 | 6,000 |
| HC w/register | 7,000 | 7,500 | 8,000 |
| 5 minute repeater, gold, 46-52mm, OF | 6,000 | 6,500 | 7,000 |
| HC | 7,000 | 7,500 | 8,000 |
| Minute repeater, gold, 46-52mm, OF | 8,000 | 8,500 | 9,000 |
| HC | 10,000 | 11,000 | 12,000 |
| OF w/chrono. | 10,000 | 11,000 | 12,000 |
| HC w/chrono. | 11,000 | 12,000 | 13,000 |
| OF w/chrono. & register | 11,000 | 12,000 | 13,000 |
| HC w/chrono. & register | 12,000 | 13,000 | 14,000 |
| OF w/split chrono. & register | 15,000 | 18,000 | 20,000 |
| HC w/split chrono. & register | 18,000 | 20,000 | 22,000 |
| Perpetual moonphase calendar, gold, OF | 20,000 | 25,000 | 30,000 |
| HC | 25,000 | 30,000 | 35,000 |
| Perp. moonphase cal. w/min.repeater, chronograph, gold, OF | 50,000 | 55,000 | 60,000 |
| HC | 75,000 | 85,000 | 100,000 |

## PRODUCTION TOTALS

| Date- Serial # | Date- Serial # |
|---|---|
| 1882 - 2,000 | 1935 - 42,000 |
| 1890 - 4,000 | 1940 - 44,000 |
| 1895 - 5,350 | 1945 - 48,000 |
| 1900 - 6,500 | 1950 - 55,000 |
| 1905 - 9,500 | 1955 - 65,000 |
| 1910-13,000 | 1960 - 75,000 |
| 1915-17,000 | 1965 - 90,000 |
| 1920-25,000 | 1970-115,000 |
| 1925-33,000 | 1975-160,000 |
| 1930-40,000 | 1980-225,000 |

🕐 Some models and grades are not included. Their values can be determined by comparing with similar age, size, metal content, style, models and grades listed.

🕐 Watches listed in this book are priced at the collectable fair market value at the retail level, as complete watches having an original case, an original white enamel dial, and with the entire original movement in good working order with no repairs needed, unless otherwise noted.

# BARRAUD & LUNDS
## LONDON (CORNHILL)

The Barraud family ( of which ) there were several makers, one of them being Paul Philip Barraud. Paul was in the trade at 86 Cornhill from about 1796 to 1813. His sons John and James, traded at 41 Cornhill as Barraud & Sons from 1813 till 1838. After 1838 the firm became known as Barraud & Lunds.

| TYPE – DESCRIPTION | Avg | Ex-Fn | Mint |
|---|---|---|---|
| Time only, gold, 45- 50mm, OF | $650 | $750 | $900 |
| HC | 1,000 | 1,250 | 1,400 |
| Chronograph, gold, 45-50mm, OF | 1,200 | 1,300 | 1,450 |
| HC | 1,500 | 1,700 | 1,850 |
| Split second chronograph, gold, 45-52mm, OF | 1,800 | 2,000 | 2,300 |
| HC | 2,500 | 2,800 | 3,250 |
| 1/4 hr. repeater, gold, 46-52mm, OF | 1,850 | 2,000 | 2,300 |
| HC | 2,200 | 2,500 | 2,800 |
| Minute repeater, gold, 46-52mm, OF | 3,000 | 3,400 | 4,000 |
| HC | 3,800 | 4,000 | 4,400 |
| OF w/chrono. | 3,500 | 3,800 | 4,250 |
| HC w/chrono. | 4,250 | 4,500 | 4,800 |

# BARWISE
## LONDON

John Barwise a leading watchmaker born 1790 died 1843. Dealer at 29 St.Martin's Lane, and with Weston Barwise from 1820 to 1842. John Barwise was also the chairman of British Watch Co. 1842 to 1843. Then Barwise moved back to 29 St.Martin's Lane, 1845 to 1851, and 69 Piccadilly from 1856 to 1875.

| TYPE – DESCRIPTION | Avg | Ex-Fn | Mint |
|---|---|---|---|
| Time only, gold, 45- 50mm, OF | $900 | $1,250 | $1,400 |
| HC | 1,200 | 1,500 | 1,800 |
| Chronograph, gold, 45-50mm, OF | 1,200 | 1,500 | 1,800 |
| HC | 1,500 | 1,800 | 2,000 |
| Split second chronograph, gold, 45-52mm, OF | 2,000 | 2,400 | 2,700 |
| HC | 3,000 | 3,250 | 3,500 |
| 1/4 hr. repeater, gold, 46-52mm, OF | 1,800 | 2,000 | 2,300 |
| HC | 2,500 | 2,800 | 3,200 |
| Minute repeater, gold, 46-52mm, OF | 3,500 | 4,000 | 4,500 |
| HC | 4,250 | 4,600 | 5,000 |
| OF w/chrono. | 4,000 | 4,500 | 5,250 |
| HC w/chrono. | 4,500 | 5,250 | 5,750 |
| Dent Chronometer, gold, 48-52mm, OF | 6,000 | 6,600 | 7,500 |
| HC | 7,000 | 8,000 | 9,000 |

🕐 Some models and grades are not included. Their values can be determined by comparing with similar age, size, metal content, style, models and grades listed.

🕐 Watches listed in this book are priced at the collectable fair market value at the retail level, as complete watches having an original case, an original white enamel dial, and with the entire original movement in good working order with no repairs needed, unless otherwise noted.

# J. W. BENSON
## London

The Benson signature is found on many medium to high grade gilt movements produced for the English market circa 1870-1900. "Makers to the Admiralty" & "Makers to the Queen" are usually signed on the Benson movements.

| TYPE – DESCRIPTION | Avg | Ex-Fn | Mint |
|---|---|---|---|
| KWKS, side lever, Silver hallmarked, 48-52mm, OF, C. 1875 | $100 | $150 | $175 |
| SW, 17J, Silver, 49mm, Demi-hunter, C. 1885 | 130 | 150 | 200 |
| Fusee w/indicator, KWKS, side lever, Silver, 54mm, OF, C.1870.. | 400 | 450 | 500 |
| Fusee, lever escape., high grade, SW, 18K, 54mm, OF, C.1875 .... | 700 | 900 | 1,000 |
| Fusee, w/indicator, free spring, lever escape.,18K, 50mm, OF | 1,200 | 1,300 | 1,400 |
| Time only, gold, 45-48mm, OF | 500 | 550 | 600 |
| HC | 700 | 800 | 900 |
| Split second chronograph, gold, 45-52mm, OF | 4,500 | 5,000 | 5,500 |
| HC | 6,000 | 6,500 | 7,000 |
| Minute repeater, gold, 46-52mm, OF | 4,000 | 4,500 | 5,000 |
| HC | 4,500 | 5,000 | 5,500 |

J. W. Benson, 45mm, Split Second Chronograph, 20 jewels, 3/4 plate, free sprung, hunting case, Ca. 1890.

## COMPARISON OF WATCH SIZES

| U. S. A. | EUROPEAN |
|---|---|
| 10-12 SIZE | 40—44 MM |
| 16    SIZE | 45—48 MM |
| 18    SIZE | 50—54 MM |

# BOVET
### FRENCH & SWISS

Edouard Bovet starts a company in the village of Fleuier Switzerland about 1818 and another firm in Besancon in 1832. The Bovet firm specialized in watches for the chinese market. The Bovet Companies was purchased by Leuba Freres (Cesar & Charles). The new Bovet firm discontinued making watches for the Chinese market. The company was purchased by the Ullmann & Co. in 1918.

**Above:** *Superior quality* finely painted turquoise enamel watch set in pearls, 18K, 58mm, time only, Duplex Escapement, signed BOVET, Ca. 1845.

| TYPE – DESCRIPTION | Avg | Ex-Fn | Mint |
|---|---|---|---|
| Time only, LEVER escapement, KW, Silver, 58mm, OF | $250 | $300 | $350 |
| HC | 350 | 395 | 450 |
| Time only, DUPLEX escapement, KW, Silver, 58mm, OF | 300 | 350 | 400 |
| HC | 395 | 425 | 475 |
| Time only, DUPLEX escapement, KW, GOLD, 58mm, OF | 1,000 | 1,200 | 1,400 |
| HC | 1,500 | 1,600 | 1,850 |
| Enamel, Time only, DUPLEX escap., KW, Silver, 58mm, OF | 900 | 1,200 | 1,500 |
| HC | 1,200 | 1,400 | 1,750 |
| ( below *SUPERIOR QUALITY* Gold & Enamel, on OF & HC watches ) | | | |
| Gold &Enamel, Time only, Duplex escap., KW, 55- 58mm, OF | 8,000 | 15,000 | 18,000 |
| HC | 15,000 | 20,000 | 25,000 |

🕐 Some models and grades are not included. Their values can be determined by comparing with similar age, size, metal content, style, models and grades listed.

🕐 Watches listed in this book are priced at the collectable retail level, as complete watches having an original case, an original dial, and with the entire original movement in good working order with no repairs needed.

# ABRAHAM-LOUIS BREGUET
# also BREGUET ET FILS
Paris

**Abraham-Louis Breguet,** one of the worlds most celebrated watchmakers.

ABRAHAM-LOUIS BREGUET was born at Neuchatel in 1747 and died in 1823. He was perhaps the greatest horologist of all time in terms of design, elegance, and innovation. He is responsible for the development of the tourbillion, the perpetual calendar, the shock-proof parachute suspension, the isochronal overcoil, and many other improvements. It is difficult to include him in this section because of the complexity surrounding identification of his work which was frequently forged, and the fact that so many pieces produced by his shop were unique. Suffice it to say that the vast majority of watches one encounters bearing his name were either marketed only by his firm or are outright fakes made by others for the export market. Much study is required for proper identification.

**Abraham-Louis Breguet,** PRODUCTION TOTALS

| Date — | Serial # | Date — | Serial # |
|---|---|---|---|
| 1795 --- | 150 | 1815 --- | 2700 |
| 1800 --- | 600 | 1820 --- | 3500 |
| 1805 --- | 1600 | 1825 --- | 4500 |
| 1810 --- | 2000 | 1830 --- | 5000 |

Abraham-Louis Breguet died on 17th day of September, 1823. The Breguet firm continues today with the tradition started by Abraham-Louis. At first in the hands of his immediate successors and later under the guidance of the "Browns", when the interest of the Breguet family diversified. Today the firm of Breguet continues to produce high quality and exclusive range of watches based on the *classic style* that has made the Breguet name so famous. The Company makes jewelry, wrist watches, clocks, as well as, fine pocket watches. They produce choice examples, with complicated movements and should be signed on dial, case and movement.

⊕ This book endeavors to be a GUIDE or helpful manual and offers a wealth of material to be used as a tool not as a absolute document. Price Guides are like watches the worst may be better than none at all, but at best cannot be expected to be 100% accurate.

⊕ Characteristics of watches differ for the same age of both case and movement, because these features vary it may not be accurate to date a watch by one single influence. Example: the second hand was not commonly found on watches before 1750, but common about 1800. The first second hand appeared in 1665 and another in 1690. Therefore statements are broad rather than accurate.

61mm. Example of Breguet souscription style face and movement. Gilt movement with central winding arbor, balance with parachute suspension, HANGING ruby cylinder escapement. White enamel dial with secret signature at 12 o'clock.

| TYPE – DESCRIPTION | Avg | Ex-Fn | Mint |
|---|---|---|---|
| 1/4 repeater, Brequet & Fils, silver, OF, KWKS, 54mm C.1820..... | $700 | $900 | $1,100 |
| 1/4 repeater, Brequet & Fils, KWKS, 18K, 54mm, OF, C.1820...... | 2,000 | 2,500 | 3,000 |
| 1/4 repeater, Brequet & Fils, verge, automated, 18K, 55mm, OF ... | 3,500 | 4,500 | 5,500 |
| Ruby cylinder, parachute, KW, 18K, 49mm, OF, C. 1800 .............. | 5,000 | 6,500 | 8,500 |
| Repeater Horologer De La Marine , silver dial, ruby cylinder escapement ......................................... | 14,000 | 17,000 | 20,000 |
| Min. repeater, split sec. chrono., min. register 18K, 2 tone case, 53mm, OF, C. 1945 ...................................... | 12,000 | 15,000 | 20,000 |
| Jump hr.w/ aperture, revolving min.disc, 18K, 46mm, OF, C.1930 | 8,000 | 10,000 | 12,000 |
| Hanging ruby cylinder, enamel "souscription" dial, center wind, all original,18K, 61mm, OF, C. 1795 ................. | 14,000 | 16,000 | 22,000 |
| Montre'a tact, 6J ruby cylinder, "souscription" , pearl & enamel case, 18K, 36mm, C. 1810 ........................... | 20,000 | 25,000 | 30,000 |

Abraham Louis Breguet, repeating, ruby cylinder watch. Left: gilt movement with standing barrel. Note jeweled parachute suspension. Right: Dial side of movement, repeating train with exposed springs.

Important repeater Horologer De La Marine by Breguet. Left: Guilloche silver dial with roman numerals and typical Breguet hands. Right: Gilt brass movement with ruby cylinder escapement and triple arm balance.

Breguet "montre a tact" or touch time watch, 36mm. Case embellished with 12 pearls for tactile hours (Braille style watch). The arrow on case revolves. Souscription movement with 6 jewels, central barrel, ruby cylinder escapement.

BREGUET, 51mm, chronograph with perpetual calendar and minute repeater. Note sector style wind indicator.

BREGUET, 53mm, minute repeating, split-second chronograph. Chronograph activated by crown and button on band. Repeater activated by slide.

Breguet, 45-48mm, ruby cylinder, KW KS, Swiss bar Mvt., time only, Ca.1830, 18K case

| TYPE – DESCRIPTION | Avg | Ex-Fn | Mint |
|---|---|---|---|
| Min. repeater, perpetual calendar chronograph, wind indicator, 18K, OF, 51mm, C. 1932 | $40,000 | $50,000 | $60,000 |
| Min. repeater, split sec. chronograph, two tone gold case, 53mm, C.1948 | 12,000 | 16,000 | 20,000 |
| Perpetual calendar, thin digital watch, 18K case, 45mm | 9,000 | 11,000 | 14,000 |
| Tactile braille watch, 18K enamel case w/ pearls, 36mm | 22,000 | 27,000 | 32,500 |
| Small keyless watch, platinum balance, gold case, 18mm | 20,000 | 25,000 | 32,000 |
| Early, KW KS, Swiss bar Mvt., time only, Ca.1830, 18K case | 3,000 | 3,500 | 4,000 |

# BULOVA
## U. S. A. & Swiss

Bulova was a leader in the mass production of quality wristwatches; however, their pocket watch output was small and limited to mostly basic time only varieties. The ultra thin "Phantom" was one of their limited production models.

Joseph Bulova started with a wholesale jewelry business in 1875. The first watches were marketed in the early 1920s. Bulova manufactured millions of movements in their own Swiss plant. The company cased these movements in the U.S.A. and imports all production today. The ACCUTRON was introduced in 1960 and sold about 5 million watches.

🕐 Some models and grades are not included. Their values can be determined by comparing with similar age, size, metal content, style, models and grades listed.

🕐 Watches listed in this book are priced at the collectable retail level, as complete watches having an original case, an original dial, and with the entire original movement in good working order with no repairs needed.

| TYPE – DESCRIPTION | Avg | Ex-Fn | Mint |
|---|---|---|---|
| GF, 17J, 42mm, OF, C. 1940 | $40 | $50 | $65 |
| Rose GF, art deco, 17J, 42mm, OF, C. 1930 | 60 | 80 | 100 |
| 14K, 17J, 42mm, OF, C. 1950 | 175 | 200 | 225 |
| Platinum, ultra-thin, "Phantom", 18J, 43mm, OF, C. 1920 | 600 | 700 | 800 |
| Accutron, date, GF, 43mm, HC | 100 | 125 | 155 |

BULOVA  Accutron, with date, gold filled hunting case, about 43mm, ca. 1970s.

HENRY CAPT, 52mm, 32 jewels, minute repeater, serial number 34,711, ca. 1900.

# HENRY CAPT
Geneva

Henry Daniel Capt of Geneva was an associate of Isac Daniel Piguet for about 10 years from 1802 to 1812. Their firm produced quality watches and specialized in musicals, repeaters and chronometers. By 1844, his son was director of the firm and around 1880 the firm was sold to Gallopin.

| TYPE – DESCRIPTION | Avg | Ex-Fn | Mint |
|---|---|---|---|
| Early, KW KS, Swiss bar Mvt., time only, Ca.1870, Silver case ... | $85 | $95 | $135 |
| Early, KW KS, Swiss bar Mvt., time only, Ca.1870, Gold | 600 | 750 | 1,000 |
| Time only, gold, 45- 50mm, OF | 700 | 800 | 900 |
| HC | 900 | 1,000 | 1,200 |
| Chronograph, gold, 45-50mm, OF | 850 | 950 | 1,100 |
| HC | 1,000 | 1,200 | 1,400 |
| Split second chronograph, gold, 45-52mm, OF | 1,200 | 1,400 | 1,600 |
| HC | 1,500 | 1,800 | 2,000 |
| 1/4 hr. repeater, gold, 46-52mm, OF | 1,800 | 2,200 | 2,500 |
| HC | 2,500 | 3,000 | 3,500 |
| Minute repeater, gold, 46-52mm, OF | 2,500 | 3,500 | 4,000 |
| HC | 3,500 | 4,000 | 4,500 |
| OF, w/split chrono. | 6,500 | 7,500 | 8,500 |
| HC, w/split chrono. | 12,000 | 14,000 | 16,000 |
| Perpetual moonphase calendar, gold, OF | 10,000 | 12,000 | 14,000 |
| HC | 13,000 | 15,000 | 16,000 |
| Perp. moonphase cal., w/min.repeater, gold, OF | 25,000 | 30,000 | 35,000 |
| Perp. moonphase cal. ,w/min.repeater and chrono., gold, HC | 35,000 | 40,000 | 45,000 |

# CARTIER

Paris

CARTIER was a famous artisan from Paris who first made powder flasks. By the mid-1840s the family became known as the finest goldsmiths of Paris. Around the turn of the century the Cartier firm was designing watches and in 1904 the first wrist watches were being made. In 1917 Cartier created a watch design that was to become known as the tank-style case. The tank-style case was made to look like tank caterpillars of the U. S. A and is still popular today.

Cartier, 52mm, 40 jewels, triple complicated-perpetual calendar, minute repeater, split-second chronograph.

Cartier, 45mm, 18 jewels, flat, astronomic with moon phases triple calendar, platinum watch, Ca. 1930s.

| TYPE – DESCRIPTION | Avg | Ex-Fn | Mint |
|---|---|---|---|
| Time only, gold, 40- 44mm, OF | $1,600 | $1,800 | $2,000 |
| HC | 2,000 | 2,200 | 2,500 |
| Time only, gold, 45- 50mm, OF | 2,500 | 3,000 | 3,500 |
| HC | 3,500 | 4,000 | 4,500 |
| Flat, astronomic w/ moon ph. triple calendar, platinum,OF | 10,000 | 12,000 | 15,000 |
| Chronograph, gold, 45-50mm, OF | 4,500 | 5,000 | 5,500 |
| 5 minute repeater, gold, 46-52mm, OF | 6,000 | 7,000 | 8,000 |
| HC | 7,000 | 8,000 | 9,000 |
| Minute repeater, gold, 46-52mm, OF | 10,000 | 12,000 | 14,000 |
| HC | 12,000 | 14,000 | 16,000 |
| Triple complicated, astronomical moon ph. perpetual triple cal., min. repeater, split sec. chron. w/min. recorder, signed European Watch & Clock Co., 18K case, c. 1930 | 100,000 | 110,000 | 120,000 |

Above: **Cartier,** 43mm, 18 jewels, dial has raised gold Arabic numbers, 18k, OF, Ca.1930s.

# T. F. COOPER
Liverpool

The Cooper name is usually marked on inner dust covers which protect Swiss ebauche keywind bar movements. Numerous watches produced from 1850-1890 are found with this Liverpool name. The T.F. Cooper firm also supplied the U.S. market with low cost silver-cased keywinds.

| TYPE – DESCRIPTION | Avg | Ex-Fn | Mint |
|---|---|---|---|
| KWKS, "full-jeweled" , Silver, 44-48mm, OF, Ca.1850-1875...... | $70 | $80 | $100 |
| KWKS, 15J, Silver, 46-50mm, HC, Ca.1850-1870........................ | 75 | 90 | 130 |
| KW, Fusee, lever, silver, 48mm, OF, C. 1870................................. | 130 | 150 | 175 |
| KW, 15J, metal dust cover, gilt dial, 18K, OF, C. 1875.................. | 250 | 325 | 375 |
| KW, 15J. Lady's , 18K, 44mm, fancy HC, C. 1875....................... | 300 | 350 | 400 |
| KW, gold dial, bar movement w/side lever escap.,<br>    parachute shock on balance, 18K, 50mm, OF, C. 1870 ......... | 275 | 350 | 400 |
| Captains double time, 15J., KWKS, silver, 48mm, OF, C.1865...... | 400 | 465 | 550 |

T.F. Cooper, KW, bar movement with right angle lever escapement, parachute shock on balance, 18K, 50mm, OF, Ca. 1852.

# COURVOISER, Freres
SWISS (La Chaux de Fonds )

Started as Courvoiser & Cie in 1810-11, by 1845 Henri-Louis and Philippe-Auguste became owners. In 1852 name changes to Courvoiser, Freres. The watches circa 1810 are signed with the older signature. They exported very ornate pieces for the Chinese market (LePine bar caliber).They also obtained a Chinese *TRADEMARK* for their signature.

Courvoiser- Freres, 37mm, cylinder escap. with wolf-tooth winding, 18K, HC, Ca.1880.

| TYPE – DESCRIPTION | Avg | Ex-Fn | Mint |
|---|---|---|---|
| Time only, KW, **SILVER**, 45- 50mm, OF | $250 | $300 | $375 |
| HC | 300 | 375 | 450 |
| Time only, KW, **Gold**, 45- 50mm, OF | 750 | 850 | 1,000 |
| HC | 1,000 | 1,200 | 1,500 |
| Captains Watch, **SILVER**, 2 hour dials, 2 trains, Key Wind, | | | |
| center seconds, 50mm, OF | 600 | 700 | 800 |
| HC, (SAME AS ABOVE) | 700 | 800 | 1,000 |
| Captains Watch, **GOLD**, 2 hour dials, 2 trains, Key Wind, | | | |
| center seconds, 50mm, OF | 1,200 | 1,500 | 1,800 |
| HC, (SAME AS ABOVE) | 1,800 | 2,250 | 2,800 |
| 1/4 hr. repeater, **SILVER**, 46-52mm, OF | 900 | 1,000 | 1,200 |
| 1/4 hr. repeater, **GOLD**, 46-52mm, OF | 1,600 | 1,800 | 2,000 |
| Dent Chronometer, gold, 48-52mm, OF | 4,000 | 4,500 | 5,000 |
| HC | 6,000 | 6,500 | 7,000 |

# DENT (M. F. & Co.)
## LONDON

Edward John Dent, born in 1790 died in 1853. Edward worked for J.R. Arnold, at 84 Strand from 1830-1840 and worked alone at 82 Strand from 1841 to 1849. Then moved to 61 Strand 1850 till 1853. The year before his death the Westminster Place gave Dent the contract for making BIG BEN with a big bell weighing over 13 tons. The clock was built by Frederick Rippon Dent. The Dent firm was in business until 1920.

| TYPE – DESCRIPTION | Avg | Ex-Fn | Mint |
|---|---|---|---|
| Time only, gold, 45- 50mm, OF | $1,100 | $1,200 | $1,400 |
| HC | 1,400 | 1,700 | 2,000 |
| Chronograph, gold, 45-50mm, OF | 1,500 | 1,800 | 2,200 |
| HC | 1,800 | 2,200 | 2,600 |
| Split second chronograph, gold, 45-52mm, OF | 2,300 | 2,700 | 3,200 |
| HC | 3,500 | 4,000 | 5,000 |
| 1/4 hr. repeater, gold, 46-52mm, OF | 2,000 | 2,500 | 3,000 |
| HC | 3,000 | 3,500 | 4,250 |
| HC w/chrono., cal. & moonphase | 5,700 | 6,700 | 8,000 |
| Minute repeater, gold, OF | 4,000 | 5,000 | 6,000 |
| HC | 5,500 | 6,500 | 7,500 |
| OF w/chrono. | 5,000 | 5,500 | 6,750 |
| HC w/split chrono. | 12,000 | 14,000 | 17,000 |
| HC w/cal. & moonphase | 14,000 | 17,000 | 20,000 |
| Detent chronometer, gold, 48-52mm, OF | 8,000 | 10,000 | 12,000 |
| Perpetual moonphase calendar, gold, OF | 15,000 | 20,000 | 25,000 |
| HC | 20,000 | 25,000 | 32,500 |
| Perp. moonphase cal. w/min. repeater, OF | 35,000 | 40,000 | 50,000 |
| HC | 50,000 | 55,000 | 65,000 |

🕐 Some models and grades are not included. Their values can be determined by comparing with similar age, size, metal content, style, models and grades listed.

🕐 Watches listed in this book are priced at the collectable fair market value at the retail level, as complete watches having an original case, an original white enamel dial, and with the entire original movement in good working order with no repairs needed, unless otherwise noted.

# DUBOIS et FILS

La Locle (SWISS)

Dealer and Watchmaker, one of the most active in the LA LOCLE region. Founded in 1785 by Philippe (1738-1808 ). They exported all over the world and specialized in automaton watches, skeleton watches and watches with false pendulums. The company is still in business today.

| TYPE – DESCRIPTION | Avg | Ex-Fn | Mint |
|---|---|---|---|
| Verge, KW, pair case, silver, 48-52mm | $450 | $500 | $550 |
| Verge, enamel w/scene, silver or gilt, 48-52mm | 1,500 | 1,800 | 2,000 |
| Verge w/mock pendulum, silver, OF, 48-52mm | 1,200 | 1,500 | 1,800 |
| Verge, KW, GOLD, OF, 50-54mm | 1,000 | 1,250 | 1,500 |
| Verge, KW, GOLD w/enamel, OF,52mm | 2,250 | 2,500 | 2,850 |
| 1/4 hr. repeater, SILVER, OF, 50-54mm | 900 | 1,100 | 1,300 |
| 1/4 hr. repeater, GOLD, OF, 50-54mm | 1,500 | 1,700 | 2,000 |
| 1/4 hr. repeater w/automaton, 18K, OF, 50-52mm | 5,000 | 5,500 | 6,000 |

**Dubois et Fils,** Verge with mock pendulum, silver, OF, enamel dial, 48-52mm, Ca. 1830.

**Dubois et Fils,** Verge, enamel w/scene, silver or gilt, OF, painted enamel scene, 48-52mm. Ca. 1810.

## COMPARISON OF WATCH SIZES

| U. S. A. | EUROPEAN |
|---|---|
| 10-12 SIZE | 40—44 MM |
| 16 SIZE | 45—48 MM |
| 18 SIZE | 50—54 MM |

MILLIMETERS 10    20    30    40    50    60

# DUCHENE L., & Fils
## GENEVA

Watchmaker, well known for their large and small pieces, including coach clocks, calendar watches and minute repeater watches. The firm was known also for decorative work with polychrome champleve enamel and painted enamel, and fantasy watches. The movements are classically-designed, with fusee & verge escapements. Cases are in "Empire-style", engraved or guilloche.

| TYPE – DESCRIPTION | Avg | Ex-Fn | Mint |
|---|---|---|---|
| KW, cylinder, silver, 46mm, OF | $175 | $225 | $275 |
| HC | 250 | 300 | 375 |
| KW, verge fusee, silver, 46-52mm, OF | 375 | 425 | 500 |
| KW, verge fusee, enamel case ,gilt, 52mm, OF | 1,500 | 1,600 | 1,700 |
| 1/4 hr. repeater, silver, 54mm, OF | 1,200 | 1,350 | 1,500 |
| 1/4 hr. repeater, gold, 52mm, OF | 1,500 | 1,700 | 2,000 |
| Ball form, KWKS, cylinder, 29mm, OF | 1,500 | 1,650 | 1,800 |

Duchene L. & Fils, 1/4 Hour Repeater, fusee and cylinder escapement, repeats on gongs, 52mm, Ca. 1820.

# DUNAND
## Swiss

The Dunand factory produced repeaters, timers & chronographs during the 1890-1930 time period. (Also see Timers and Chrono. section.)

| TYPE – DESCRIPTION | Avg | Ex-Fn | Mint |
|---|---|---|---|
| Time only, gold, 45-50mm, OF | $350 | $400 | $500 |
| HC | 450 | 500 | 600 |
| Chronograph, gold, 45-50mm,OF | 500 | 600 | 700 |
| HC | 700 | 800 | 900 |
| Split second chronograph, gold, 45-52mm, OF | 900 | 1,000 | 1,100 |
| HC | 1,000 | 1,100 | 1,200 |
| 1/4 hr. repeater, gold, 46-52mm, OF | 800 | 900 | 1,000 |
| HC | 1,000 | 1,200 | 1,400 |
| OF w/chrono. | 1,100 | 1,200 | 1,300 |
| HC w/chrono. | 1,200 | 1,400 | 1,600 |
| Minute repeater, gold, 46-52mm, OF | 1,500 | 1,800 | 2,200 |
| HC | 2,000 | 2,200 | 2,500 |

# EARNSHAW, THOMAS
LONDON

Thomas Earnshaw born in 1749 died in 1829. In about 1781 he improves the spring detent. Earnshaw also contributed to the development of the chronometer. He pioneered the method of fusing brass and steel together to form a laminate of the compensation rims as in the modern method of today. Known for his chronometers he also made 1/4 and 1/2 hour repeaters with cylinder and duplex escapements.

THOMAS EARNSHAW, chronometer, KWKS, spring detent, Z or S balance with trapezoidal weights, helical hairspring, serial # 589, silver case, Ca.1810.

| TYPE – DESCRIPTION | Avg | Ex-Fn | Mint |
|---|---|---|---|
| Time only, KW, **SILVER**, 45- 48mm, OF | $1,000 | $1,500 | $2,000 |
| HC | 2,000 | 2,500 | 3,000 |
| Time only, KW, **GOLD**, 45- 48mm, OF | 2,500 | 3,000 | 3,500 |
| HC | 3,000 | 3,500 | 4,000 |
| 1/4 hr. repeater, **GOLD**, 46-52mm, OF | 6,000 | 7,000 | 8,000 |
| HC | 7,500 | 8,500 | 9,500 |
| Spring detent escapement, chronometer, gold, 48-54mm, OF | 7,000 | 8,000 | 9,000 |
| HC | 10,000 | 12,000 | 14,000 |

# H. R. EKEGREN
Copenhagen & Geneva

Henry Robert Ekegren, a Swiss maker of quality watches, started in business around 1870. The firm specialized in flat watches, chronometers and repeaters. Ekegren became associated with F. Koehn in 1891.

| TYPE – DESCRIPTION | Avg | Ex-Fn | Mint |
|---|---|---|---|
| Time only, gold, 45- 50mm, OF | $600 | $800 | $1,000 |
| HC | 800 | 1,200 | 1,500 |
| Chronograph, gold, 45-50mm, OF | 1,000 | 1,200 | 1,500 |
| HC | 1,200 | 1,500 | 1,800 |
| Split second chronograph, gold, 45-52mm, OF | 1,500 | 1,800 | 2,000 |
| HC | 1,800 | 2,000 | 2,200 |
| FIVE-Minute repeater, gold, 46-52mm, OF | 2,000 | 2,200 | 2,500 |
| HC | 2,500 | 3,000 | 3,500 |

🕐 Some models and grades are not included. Their values can be determined by comparing with similar age, size, metal content, style, models and grades listed.

🕐 Watches listed in this book are priced at the collectable fair market **value** at the **retail** level, as complete watches having an original case, an original white enamel dial, and with the entire original movement in good working order with no repairs needed, unless otherwise noted.

H.R. EKEGREN 46mm, minute repeater, slide activated, jeweled through hammers, open face, serial no. 78,268.

H.R. EKEGREN, 47mm, minute repeater, jeweled through hammers, hunting case.

| TYPE – DESCRIPTION | Avg | Ex-Fn | Mint |
|---|---|---|---|
| Minute repeater, gold, 46-52mm, OF | $3,000 | $3,200 | $4,000 |
| HC | 3,500 | 4,000 | 4,600 |
| OF w/chrono. | 2,500 | 3,000 | 3,500 |
| HC w/chrono. | 4,000 | 4,500 | 5,000 |
| OF w/split chrono. | 4,500 | 5,000 | 5,500 |
| HC w/split chrono. | 7,500 | 8,500 | 9,500 |
| Perpetual moonphase calendar, gold, OF | 12,000 | 15,000 | 18,000 |
| Perpetual moonphase cal. w/ min. repeater, OF | 25,000 | 30,000 | 35,000 |
| HC | 30,000 | 35,000 | 40,000 |
| Perp. moonphase cal. w/min. rep. and chrono., OF | 40,000 | 45,000 | 50,000 |
| HC | 45,000 | 50,000 | 55,000 |
| Karrusel, gold, 48-55mm, OF | 8,000 | 9,000 | 10,000 |
| Tourbillion, gold, 48-55mm, OF | 40,000 | 45,000 | 50,000 |
| Detent chronometer, gold, 48-52mm, OF | 6,000 | 7,000 | 8,000 |
| World time watch, gold, 48-52mm, OF | 15,000 | 18,000 | 20,000 |

# FAVRE–LEUBE
## Le Locle & Geneva

Founded in 1737, this firm is still active and production has covered more than eight generations of watchmakers. The firm name had a name change when Abraham Favre married Miss Leube. The company has make some very fine quality watches.

FAVER-LEUBE, 53mm, Minute repeater, 15 jewels, slide on rim activates the repeater mechanism, Ca.1895.

| TYPE – DESCRIPTION | Avg | Ex-Fn | Mint |
|---|---|---|---|
| Early, KW KS, Swiss bar Mvt., time only, Ca.1870, Silver case ... | $75 | $85 | $100 |
| KW, Gold w/enamel, 35-40mm, HC | 1,700 | 1,800 | 2,000 |
| KW, silver w/enamel, 45mm, HC | 375 | 450 | 500 |
| KW, Gold w/enamel, 45-48mm, OF | 1,200 | 1,500 | 1,700 |
| Chronograph, gold, 45-50mm, OF | 2,200 | 2,500 | 2,800 |
| HC | 3,500 | 4,000 | 4,500 |
| Split second chronograph, gold, 45-52mm, OF | 3,000 | 3,500 | 4,000 |
| HC | 3,500 | 4,000 | 4,500 |
| 1/4 hr. repeater, gold, 46-52mm, OF | 2,500 | 2,800 | 3,200 |
| HC | 3,500 | 4,000 | 4,500 |
| Minute repeater, gold, 46-52mm, OF | 4,000 | 4,500 | 5,000 |
| HC | 6,000 | 6,500 | 7,500 |

# CHARLES FRODSHAM
London

Charles Frodsham followed in the footsteps of his father, William, whose father was close with Earnshaw. Charles became the most eminent of the family, producing very fine chronometers and some rare tourbillon and complicated watches. He died in 1871. His quality movements endorse the letters A.D. FMSZ. Originally Arnold & **Frodsham** was located at 84 Strand, London until 1858. He later moved to New Bond Street, London.

Frodsham, 84 Strand, London engraved on movement, 16-18 jewels, platinum balance screws, Ca. 1850s

Chas. Frodsham, 84 Strand London, 25 jewels, Fusee, Freesprung, Diamond end stone, serial number 3520.

| TYPE – DESCRIPTION | Avg | Ex-Fn | Mint |
|---|---|---|---|
| Early, KW KS, **Swiss bar Mvt.,** time only, Silver case | $125 | $150 | $225 |
| Time only, early mvt. **84 Strand,** silver, 45- 48mm, OF, C.1850 ... | 350 | 400 | 500 |
| Time only, early mvt. **84 Strand,** gold, 45- 48mm, OF, C.1850 ..... | 1,000 | 1,200 | 1,500 |
| Time only, gold, 45- 50mm, OF | 1,000 | 1,200 | 1,500 |
| HC | 1,200 | 1,500 | 1,800 |
| Chronograph, gold, 45-50mm, OF | 1,500 | 1,800 | 2,000 |
| HC | 1,800 | 2,000 | 2,200 |
| Split second chronograph, gold, 45-52m, OF | 3,000 | 3,200 | 3,500 |
| HC | 3,500 | 4,000 | 4,500 |

Frodsham, 46-50mm, jeweled through the center wheel, stem wind, 18K case, Ca. 1895.

Frodsham, 59mm, 60 minute Karrusel, 15 jewels, stem wind, open face, 18K gold case, Ca. 1895.

| TYPE – DESCRIPTION | Avg | Ex-Fn | Mint |
|---|---|---|---|
| Minute repeater, gold, 46-52mm,OF | $6,000 | $7,000 | $8,000 |
| HC | 10,000 | 12,000 | 14,000 |
| OF w/split chrono. | 18,000 | 20,000 | 22,000 |
| HC w/split chrono. | 20,000 | 23,000 | 25,000 |
| Perpetual moonphase calendar, gold, OF | 25,000 | 30,000 | 35,000 |
| Perp. moonphase cal. w/min. repeater, OF | 45,000 | 55,000 | 60,000 |
| HC | 65,000 | 70,000 | 75,000 |
| Karrusel, 16J, 59-60 Min karrusel, 18K, C.1895 | 4,500 | 5,000 | 6,250 |
| Tourbillion, gold, 48-55mm, OF | 50,000 | 55,000 | 65,000 |
| Marine chronometer, Parkinson-Frodsham, helical hairspring, w/ detent escape., 48 hr. WI, C. 1840, 97mm deck box | 2,000 | 3,000 | 3,500 |
| Detent chronometer, w/wind ind., silver, OF, KWKS, C. 1850 | 2,800 | 3,000 | 3,300 |

# GIRARD-PERREGAUX
## Swiss

In 1856, The Constant Girard and Henry Perregaux families founded the Swiss firm of Girard-Perregaux. About 1880, the firm made a tourbillon with three golden bridges. A replica of this watch was made in 1982. Both were a supreme expression of horological craftsmanship. In 1906, the company purchased the Hecht factory in Geneva. Girard-Perregaux has been recognized many times and still makes prestigious quartz and mechanical watches.

| TYPE – DESCRIPTION | Avg | Ex-Fn | Mint |
|---|---|---|---|
| Skeletonized "Shell" (Shell Oil advertising watch),7J., Base metal display case, 45mm, C.1930 | $100 | $150 | $175 |
| Time only, gold 40-44mm, OF | 250 | 300 | 350 |
| HC | 350 | 450 | 550 |
| Time only, gold 45- 50mm, OF | 600 | 850 | 900 |
| HC | 950 | 1,250 | 1,500 |

GIRARD-PERREGAUX, three golden bridges movement patented March 25th, 1884.

GIRARD-PERREGAUX, Chronometer, with pivoted dentent, gold train, 20 jewels, nickel movement, Ca. 1878.

| TYPE – DESCRIPTION | Avg | Ex-Fn | Mint |
|---|---|---|---|
| 3 gold bridges, with **silver** case, C. 1884, | $4,000 | $5,000 | $6,000 |
| with **gold** case | 4,500 | 5,500 | 7,500 |
| Chronometer, pivoted detent, 20J., gold train, 18K, C.1878 | 13,000 | 15,000 | 17,000 |
| Chronograph, gold, 45-50mm, OF | 1,200 | 1,400 | 1,600 |
| HC | 1,500 | 1,800 | 2,000 |
| 1/4 hr. repeater, gold, 45-52mm, OF | 2,000 | 2,200 | 2,500 |
| HC | 3,000 | 3,200 | 3,500 |
| HC w/chrono., cal. & moonphase | 6,000 | 6,500 | 7,500 |
| Minute repeater, gold, 46-52mm, OF | 3,500 | 4,500 | 5,000 |
| HC | 4,500 | 5,000 | 6,000 |
| OF w/chrono. | 4,500 | 5,000 | 5,500 |
| OF w/split chrono. | 6,500 | 7,000 | 7,500 |
| HC w/cal. & moonphase | 10,000 | 12,000 | 15,000 |
| Detent chronometer, gold, 48-54mm, OF | 6,000 | 7,000 | 8,000 |
| HC | 8,000 | 9,000 | 10,000 |

# GOLAY A., LERESCHE & Fils
## SWISS

Manufactured under the name Golay-Leresche from 1844-1857, then his son changed the name to Golay A., Leresche & Fils, he worked until the beginning of the 20th Century. Watches were primarily exported to U.S.A., he was well known for watches of all kinds and "grande complications".

| TYPE – DESCRIPTION | Avg | Ex-Fn | Mint |
|---|---|---|---|
| Time only, gold, 45- 50mm, OF | $900 | $1,000 | $1,100 |
| HC | 1,200 | 1,500 | 1,800 |
| Chronograph, gold, 45-50mm, OF | 1,200 | 1,500 | 1,800 |
| HC | 1,500 | 1,800 | 2,100 |
| Split second chronograph, gold, 45-52mm, OF | 1,800 | 2,000 | 2,500 |
| HC | 3,000 | 3,500 | 4,000 |

Golay A., **Leresche & Fils**, 1/4 hour repeater, 47mm, 41 jewels, key wind, Ca. 1855.

Golay A., **Leresche & Fils**, minute repeater, split seconds chonograph, moon phases, day date month, open face, Ca. 1896.

| TYPE – DESCRIPTION | Avg | Ex-Fn | Mint |
|---|---|---|---|
| 1/4 hr. repeater, gold, 46-52mm, OF | $1,800 | $2,000 | $2,200 |
| HC | 2,200 | 2,500 | 2,800 |
|     HC w/chrono., cal. & moonphase | 5,500 | 6,000 | 6,500 |
| Minute repeater, gold, OF | 3,000 | 3,500 | 4,000 |
|     HC | 4,500 | 5,000 | 5,500 |
|     OF w/chrono. | 4,000 | 4,500 | 5,000 |
|     HC w/split chrono. | 10,000 | 12,000 | 14,000 |
|     HC w/cal. & moonphase | 10,000 | 12,000 | 15,000 |
| Detent chronometer, gold, 48-52mm, OF | 8,000 | 9,000 | 10,000 |
| Perpetual moonphase calendar, gold, OF | 10,000 | 15,000 | 18,000 |
|     HC | 14,000 | 17,000 | 20,000 |
| Perp. moonphase cal. w/min. repeater, OF | 25,000 | 30,000 | 35,000 |
|     HC | 45,000 | 50,000 | 55,000 |

Note: Some models and grades are not included. Their values can be determined  by comparing with similar age, size, metal content, style, models and grades listed.

Watches listed in this book are priced at the collectable fair market **value** at the **retail** level, as complete watches having an original case, an original white enamel dial, and with the entire original movement in good working order with no repairs needed, unless otherwise noted.

# H. GRANDJEAN

The son of David-Henri (1774-1845), this respected maker produced high quality complicated watches, chronometers and ornately decorated watches for the South American market. A Grandjean specialty was magnificent enamel and gem set ladies watches.

| TYPE – DESCRIPTION | Avg | Ex-Fn | Mint |
|---|---|---|---|
| Time only, gold, 45- 50mm, OF | $900 | $1,000 | $1,100 |
| HC | 1,200 | 1,500 | 1,800 |
| Chronograph, gold, 45-50mm, OF | 1,200 | 1,500 | 1,800 |
| HC | 1,500 | 1,800 | 2,100 |
| Split second chronograph, gold, 45-52mm, OF | 1,800 | 2,000 | 2,500 |
| HC | 3,000 | 3,500 | 4,000 |
| 1/4 hr. repeater, gold, 46-52mm, OF | 1,800 | 2,000 | 2,200 |
| HC | 2,200 | 2,500 | 2,800 |
| HC w/chrono., cal. & moonphase | 4,500 | 5,000 | 5,500 |
| Minute repeater, gold, OF | 3,000 | 3,500 | 4,000 |
| HC | 4,500 | 5,000 | 5,500 |
| OF w/chrono. | 3,500 | 4,000 | 4,500 |
| HC w/split chrono. | 10,000 | 12,000 | 14,000 |
| HC w/cal. & moonphase | 10,000 | 12,000 | 15,000 |
| Detent chronometer, gold, 48-52mm, OF | 8,000 | 9,000 | 10,000 |
| Perpetual moonphase calendar, gold, OF | 10,000 | 15,000 | 18,000 |
| HC | 14,000 | 17,000 | 20,000 |
| Perp. moonphase cal. w/min. repeater, OF | 25,000 | 30,000 | 35,000 |
| HC | 45,000 | 50,000 | 55,000 |
| Grande & Petite Sonnniere repeating clock watch, 38J, fancy dial, 18k gold, 53mm, HC | 35,000 | 40,000 | 45,000 |

H. GRANDJEAN, Grande & Petite Sonnniere repeating clock watch, 38J, with tandem wind mechanism, fancy dial, 18k gold, 53mm, HC

# GRUEN WATCH CO.
Swiss & U. S. A. (1894 - 1953 )

The early roots of the Gruen Company are found in Columbus, Ohio where Dietrich Gruen and W.J. Savage formed a partnership in 1876. The D. Gruen & Son legacy began in 1894 and flourished with the introduction of fine quality "Precision" movements. Curvex movements, ultra-thins and the prestigious 50th anniversary model are highlights of this prolific company.

D. Gruen & Son, 44mm, jeweled through center wheel, made for railroad service, serial number 62,428.

Gruen 50th Anniversary Watch, 40mm or 10 size, 21 jewels, (two diamonds) placed in a five-sided pentagon case, solid gold bridges.

| TYPE – DESCRIPTION | Avg | Ex-Fn | Mint |
|---|---|---|---|
| 17J, veri-thin or precision, GF, 40-43mm, OF, C. 1920's | $50 | $65 | $85 |
| 17J, veri-thin-precision, 14K, 40-43mm, C.1930 | 200 | 250 | 300 |
| Pentagon case ,17J, GF, 40-43mm, OF, C.1920's | 100 | 125 | 165 |
| Pentagon case, 17-19J, precision, 14K, 40-43mm, C. 1930 | 250 | 300 | 375 |
| 21-23J, D. Gruen, Swiss, Gold, 45-54mm, OF, C. 1900-20 | 200 | 300 | 425 |
| 21J, D. Gruen, (by Assmann),14K, OF, C. 1905 | 400 | 500 | 600 |
| 21J, D. Gruen, (by Assmann),14K, HC, C. 1910 | 700 | 900 | 1,100 |
| **50th anniversary** , 12K gold movement, 21J & 2 diamonds, pentagon case, 18K, 40mm, OF, C. 1924 | 2,200 | 2,500 | 3,000 |

Gruen W. Co., Swiss made, 23 jewels in screwed settings, 47mm, wind indicator, micrometer regulator, Ca.1900's.

Gruen W. Co., 40mm, Precision V1 1/2 verithin, 21 jewels, 8 positions, serial number 535,203.

# E. GUBELIN

Swiss

Jacques Edouard Gubelin joined the firm of Mourice Brithschmid in Lucerne around 1854. By 1919, Edouard Gubelin headed the firm. In 1921 they opened an office in New York & produced fine jewelry and watches for 5 generations.

E. GUBELIN, 50mm, 29J., minute repeater, chronograph, day-date-month-moon phase.

E. GUBELIN, 48mm, world time with 68 cities on outside bezel 24 hour on inter bezel, 18k open face.

| TYPE – DESCRIPTION | Avg | Ex-Fn | Mint |
|---|---|---|---|
| Time only, gold, 40- 44mm, OF | $450 | $500 | $650 |
| HC | 500 | 625 | 750 |
| Time only, gold, 45- 50mm, OF | 800 | 900 | 1,000 |
| HC | 1,000 | 1,200 | 1,500 |
| Chronograph, gold, 45-50mm, OF | 1,200 | 1,300 | 1,400 |
| HC | 1,800 | 2,000 | 2,500 |
| Split second chronograph, gold, 45-52mm, OF | 2,000 | 2,200 | 2,500 |
| HC | 2,500 | 3,000 | 3,500 |
| 1/4 hr. repeater, gold, 46-52mm, OF | 2,000 | 2,500 | 2,800 |
| HC | 2,500 | 2,800 | 3,000 |
| OF w/chrono. | 2,500 | 2,800 | 3,000 |
| HC w/chrono. | 2,800 | 3,000 | 3,500 |
| HC w/chrono., calendar & moonphase | 4,000 | 4,500 | 5,000 |
| 5 minute repeater, gold, 46-52mm, OF | 3,500 | 3,800 | 4,000 |
| HC | 4,000 | 4,300 | 4,500 |
| Minute repeater, gold, 46-52mm, OF | 4,000 | 4,500 | 5,000 |
| OF w/chrono. | 4,500 | 5,000 | 5,500 |
| OF w/split chrono. | 6,000 | 6,500 | 7,500 |
| OF w/chrono., calendar & moonphase | 8,500 | 9,500 | 11,000 |
| World time watch, gold, 48-52mm, OF | 4,500 | 5,000 | 5,500 |
| Perpetual moonphase calendar, gold, OF | 15,000 | 18,000 | 20,000 |
| Perp. moonphase cal. w/min. repeater, OF | 40,000 | 45,000 | 50,000 |
| Perp. moonphase cal. w/min.rep. and chrono., OF | 45,000 | 50,000 | 55,000 |

472

# C. L. GUINAND & CO.
### Swiss

| TYPE – DESCRIPTION | Avg | Ex-Fn | Mint |
|---|---|---|---|
| Timer with register, base metal, OF, 46mm | $40 | $50 | $65 |
| Timer, split second, register, base metal, OF, 46mm | 55 | 65 | 75 |
| Chronograph, 30 min. register,14K, 50mm, OF, C. 1910 | 500 | 600 | 700 |
| Split sec. chrono., 30 min. register, 14K, OF, 50mm, C. 1915 | 1,000 | 1,300 | 1,600 |
| Minute repeater, split sec. chrono., 18K, OF, 50mm, C. 1915 | 4,000 | 4,500 | 5,200 |

C.L. Guinand, 50mm, split-second chronograph, serial number 44,109.

Haas, Neveux & Co., 40mm, 31 jewels, minute repeater, 18k open face case, serial number 11,339.

# HAAS, NEVEUX
### Swiss

The Haas Neveux factory is one of the oldest in Switzerland, producing from 1828-1925. High grade precision timepieces and chronometers were characteristic of this reputable firm's output.

| TYPE – DESCRIPTION | Avg | Ex-Fn | Mint |
|---|---|---|---|
| Time only, gold, 40- 44mm, OF | $300 | $400 | $500 |
| HC | 450 | 500 | 600 |
| Time only, gold, 45- 50mm, OF | 400 | 500 | 600 |
| HC | 600 | 800 | 900 |
| Chronograph, gold, 45-50mm, OF | 800 | 850 | 900 |
| HC | 900 | 1,000 | 1,100 |
| Split second chronograph, gold, 45-52mm, OF | 1,200 | 1,800 | 2,000 |
| HC | 1,500 | 2,000 | 2,500 |
| 1/4 hr. repeater, gold, 46-52mm, OF | 1,500 | 1,800 | 2,200 |
| HC | 1,200 | 1,500 | 1,800 |
| Minute repeater, gold, 46-52mm, OF | 1,500 | 2,000 | 2,500 |
| OF w/split chrono. | 4,000 | 4,500 | 5,000 |
| OF w/cal. & moonphase | 4,000 | 4,500 | 5,000 |
| Perpetual moonphase calendar, gold, OF | 8,000 | 9,000 | 10,000 |
| Perp. moonphase cal. w/min. repeater, OF | 25,000 | 30,000 | 35,000 |
| HC | 28,000 | 32,000 | 37,000 |
| Perp. moonphase cal. w/min. rep. and chrono., OF | 30,000 | 35,000 | 40,000 |

# HEBDOMAS
### Swiss

The Hebdomas name is commonly found on imported Swiss novelty "8" day watches. Produced from the early 1900's to the 1960's, these popular timepieces featured fancy colored dials with an opening at the bottom of dial to expose the balance wheel and pallet-fork.

Hebdomas, 8 day ( JOURS ) 6 jewels, balance seen from the face of the watch, Ca.1920s. This style watch is now being made by Arnex Time Corp. (Lucien Piccard).

Hebdomas, 8 day ( JOURS ), 6 jewels, 1 adjustment, exposed balance, day date, center seconds, Ca.1920s

| TYPE – DESCRIPTION | Avg | Ex-Fn | Mint |
|---|---|---|---|
| 8 day, exposed balance, 7J, gun metal, 50mm, OF, C. 1920............ | $75 | $85 | $100 |
| 8 day, exposed balance, 7J, fancy dial, 50mm, OF, C. 1920............ | 95 | 110 | 130 |
| 8 day, exposed balance, 7J, silver, 50mm, HC, C. 1920's ............... | 200 | 250 | 275 |
| 8 day, exposed balance, 7J, day date calendar, center sec., with fancy dial, silver, 55mm, OF, C. 1920's......................... | 200 | 250 | 300 |

🕐 Note: Some models and grades are not included. Their values can be determined by comparing with similar age, size, metal content, style, models and grades listed.

🕐 Watches listed in this book are priced at the collectable fair market **value** at the **retail** level, as complete watches having an original case, an original white enamel dial, and with the entire original movement in good working order with no repairs needed, unless otherwise noted.

### COMPARISON OF WATCH SIZES

| U. S. A. | EUROPEAN |
|---|---|
| 10-12 SIZE | 40—44 MM |
| 16   SIZE | 45—48 MM |
| 18   SIZE | 50—54 MM |

# HUGUENIN & CO.
Swiss

Huguenin & Co., 2-Train 1/4 second jump watch, center sweep hand, enamel dial, 54mm, KW KS, 18K, Ca. 1880.

Huguenin & Co., 2-Train 1/4 second jump watch, 2 main barrels & 2 gear trains, 54mm, KW KS, Ca. 1880.

| TYPE – DESCRIPTION | Avg | Ex-Fn | Mint |
|---|---|---|---|
| KW, cylinder, silver, 46- 48mm, OF, C. 1870s | $75 | $85 | $100 |
| KW, silver, 46- 48mm, HC, C. 1870s | 100 | 125 | 150 |
| KW, cylinder escapement, 18K, 48mm, OF, C.1870s | 225 | 300 | 375 |
| KW, fancy engraved, 18K, 47mm, HC, C. 1870s | 400 | 450 | 525 |
| 1/4 Sec. Jump, 2-train, gold, 50-54mm | 2,000 | 2,400 | 2,800 |
| Chronograph, gold, 45-52mm, OF | 1,000 | 1,200 | 1,500 |
| HC | 1,300 | 1,500 | 1,800 |
| 1/4 hr. repeater, gold, 46-52mm, OF | 1,500 | 1,800 | 2,000 |
| HC | 2,000 | 2,200 | 2,400 |
| Minute repeater, gold, 46-52mm, OF | 2,000 | 2,500 | 2,800 |
| HC | 3,500 | 4,000 | 4,500 |
| OF, w/ chrono. | 2,300 | 2,500 | 2,800 |
| OF, w/ split chrono. | 5,500 | 6,000 | 6,500 |
| HC, w/ split chrono. | 6,500 | 7,000 | 7,500 |
| HC, w/ chrono., cal. & moonphase | 6,000 | 6,500 | 7,000 |

Huguenin & Co., Chronograph, enamel dial, 51mm, 18K, Hunting Case, Ca. 1890.

Huguenin & Co., Chronograph, 3/4 plate movement, 51mm, 18K, Hunting Case, Ca. 1890.

# International Watch Co.
### Swiss

The founder of the prestigious Swiss International Watch Co. was an American engineer F.A. Jones from Boston and earlier had worked for E. Howard Watch & Clock company. The company began in 1868 and in 1879 was sold to Mr. J. Rauschenbach. The company today is still making precision, hand crafted watches. IWC is well known for its super-light watch constructed of titanium.

International W. Co., apertures for jump hour and minute disc, 16 jewels, enamel dial,

International Watch Co., 54mm, 17 jewels, adj.6P, serial number 741,073.

| TYPE – DESCRIPTION | Avg | Ex-Fn | Mint |
|---|---|---|---|
| Early, KW, Time only, Swiss bar, silver case | $125 | $150 | $185 |
| Time only, gold, 40-44mm, OF | 400 | 475 | 550 |
| HC | 650 | 750 | 850 |
| Time only, gold, 45-50mm, OF | 600 | 700 | 800 |
| HC | 900 | 1,200 | 1,500 |
| Jump hour and minute disc, 16 jewels, 14K, HC | 1,800 | 2,000 | 2,500 |
| Chronograph, gold, 45-50mm, OF | 1,800 | 2,000 | 2,500 |
| HC | 2,000 | 2,500 | 3,000 |
| Split second chronograph, gold, 45-52mm, OF | 3,000 | 3,500 | 4,000 |
| HC | 4,000 | 4,500 | 5,000 |
| Minute repeater, gold, 46-52mm, OF | 3,000 | 3,200 | 3,500 |
| HC | 3,500 | 4,500 | 5,500 |
| OF, w/split chrono. | 7,000 | 7,500 | 8,500 |
| HC, w/split chrono. | 9,000 | 10,000 | 11,000 |
| OF, w/cal. & moonphase | 8,000 | 9,000 | 10,000 |
| HC, w/chrono., cal. & moonphase | 9,000 | 10,000 | 11,000 |
| Detent chronometer, gold, 48-52mm, OF | 7,000 | 8,000 | 9,000 |
| World Time watch, gold, 48-52mm, OF | 12,000 | 15,000 | 18,000 |
| Perpetual moonphase calendar, gold, OF | 7,000 | 8,000 | 9,000 |
| Perpetual moonphase calendar, w/minute repeater, HC | 30,000 | 35,000 | 40,000 |

⊕ Some models and grades are not included. Their values can be determined by comparing with similar age, size, metal content, style, models and grades listed.

⊕ Watches listed in this book are priced at the collectable fair market **value** at the retail level, as complete watches having an original case, an original white enamel dial, and with the entire original movement in good working order with no repairs needed, unless otherwise noted.

# INVICTA
Swiss

| TYPE – DESCRIPTION | Avg | Ex-Fn | Mint |
|---|---|---|---|
| 1/4 hr. repeater, gun metal ,48mm, OF, C. 1900s | $400 | $450 | $500 |
| 1/4 hr. repeater, silver, 48mm, OF, C. 1900s | 500 | 600 | 700 |
| 1/4 hr. repeater, silver, 50mm, HC, C. 1900s | 700 | 800 | 900 |
| Min. repeater, gun metal, 52mm, HC, C. 1900s | 1,000 | 1,200 | 1,300 |
| Min. repeater, silver, 52mm, HC, C. 1900s | 1,100 | 1,300 | 1,400 |

# JACOT, HENRI
PARIS

Henri Jacot settled in Paris in 1820 and developed the carriage clock industry. He also invented and improved watchmaking and clock making tools. Henri Jacot died July 31, 1867.

| TYPE – DESCRIPTION | Avg | Ex-Fn | Mint |
|---|---|---|---|
| KW, cylinder, silver, 46mm, OF | $75 | $85 | $100 |
| HC | 100 | 125 | 150 |
| KW, LADIES, 18K, 40-44mm, OF | 200 | 250 | 300 |
| HC | 275 | 325 | 375 |
| KW, GENTS, 18K, 48mm, OF | 375 | 425 | 475 |
| HC | 475 | 525 | 600 |
| 1/4 hr. repeater, SILVER, 50mm, OF | 900 | 1,000 | 1,200 |
| 1/4 hr. repeater, GOLD, 50mm, OF | 1,700 | 1,800 | 2,000 |

# JULES JURGENSEN
Swiss

The firm of Jules Jurgensen was an extension of the earlier firm of Urban Jurgensen & Sons, which was located, at various times, in Copenhagen and Le Locle. Jules ultimately established his firm in Le Locle after his father's death in the early 1830's. From that time forward the company produced, generally speaking, very fine watches that were high grade and complicated. It appears that by 1850 the company had already established a strong market in America, offering beautiful heavy 18K gold watches of exemplary quality. Until around 1885, most stem-winding watches exhibited the **bow-setting feature.**

The **Jules Jurgensen** famous bow setting feature.

Jules Jurgensen, 27 jewels, 1/5 second jump watch, 2 main barrels & 2 gear trains, 54mm, Ca. 1890.

Almost any collectible Jurgensen watch will be fully signed on the dial and movement, with an impressively embossed "JJ" stamping on all covers of the case. Watches not so marked should be examined carefully; and untypical or inelegant stamping should be viewed suspiciously, as there have been some forgeries of these fine watches. Frequently one finds the original box and papers accompanying the watch, which enhances the value. After 1885, as the firm started to buy movements from other companies, we begin to see variations in Jurgensen watches. By 1930, Jurgensen watches barely resembled the quality and aesthetics of the early period, and they are not as desirable to the collector.

JULES JURGENSEN, 46mm, 21J., hands set by inclination of pendant ring, serial # 14,492, ca.1890.

JULES JURGENSEN, 40mm, flat time only, digital watch, windows for hours and minutes, Ca.1930s.

| TYPE – DESCRIPTION | Avg | Ex-Fn | Mint |
|---|---|---|---|
| Time only, gold, 40- 44mm, OF | $225 | $275 | $350 |
| HC | 550 | 600 | 650 |
| Time only, gold, 45- 50mm, OF | 2,000 | 2,500 | 3,000 |
| HC | 3,000 | 3,500 | 4,000 |
| Flat digital watch, 18J., gold, 40-44mm, OF, C. 1930 | 5,500 | 6,000 | 7,000 |
| 1/5 second jump watch, 2 main barrels & 2 gear trains, 18K OF | 3,500 | 4,500 | 6,000 |
| Chronograph, gold, 45-50mm, OF | 2,500 | 3,000 | 3,500 |
| HC | 4,000 | 4,500 | 5,000 |
| HC w/register | 4,500 | 5,000 | 5,500 |
| Split second chronograph, gold, 45-52mm, OF | 5,500 | 6,000 | 6,500 |
| HC | 6,500 | 7,000 | 7,500 |
| 5 minute repeater, gold, 46-52mm, OF | 6,000 | 6,500 | 7,000 |
| HC | 7,500 | 8,500 | 9,000 |
| Minute repeater, gold, 46-52mm, OF | 10,000 | 11,000 | 12,000 |
| HC | 15,000 | 18,000 | 20,000 |
| OF, w/ chrono. | 12,000 | 13,000 | 14,000 |
| HC, w/ chrono. | 16,000 | 18,000 | 22,000 |
| OF, w/split chrono. | 18,000 | 20,000 | 22,000 |
| HC, w/split chrono. | 20,000 | 25,000 | 30,000 |
| Detent chronometer, gold, 48-52mm, OF | 10,000 | 12,000 | 15,000 |
| Perpetual moonphase calendar, gold, OF | 20,000 | 25,000 | 30,000 |
| HC | 25,000 | 30,000 | 35,000 |
| Perp. moonphase cal. w/min. repeater, OF | 45,000 | 55,000 | 65,000 |
| HC | 55,000 | 60,000 | 70,000 |

# EDWARD KOEHN

Swiss

Koehn was an innovative watchmaker and a specialist in the design of thin calibre watches. Formerly associated with Patek Phillipe and H. R. Ekegren, he produced watches under his own name from 1891-1930.

| TYPE – DESCRIPTION | Avg | Ex-Fn | Mint |
|---|---|---|---|
| Time only, gold, 40- 44mm, OF | $375 | $450 | $500 |
| HC | 500 | 650 | 800 |
| Time only, gold, 45- 50mm, OF | 800 | 900 | 1,000 |
| HC | 1,000 | 1,200 | 1,500 |
| Chronograph, gold, 45-50mm, OF | 1,200 | 1,500 | 1,800 |
| HC | 1,500 | 1,800 | 2,000 |
| Split second chronograph,gold, 45-52mm, OF | 1,800 | 2,000 | 2,200 |
| HC | 2,500 | 2,800 | 3,200 |
| 5 minute repeater, gold, 45-52mm, OF | 3,000 | 3,500 | 4,000 |
| HC | 3,500 | 4,000 | 4,500 |
| Minute repeater, gold, 46-52mm, OF | 3,000 | 3,500 | 3,800 |
| HC | 3,500 | 4,000 | 4,500 |
| OF, w/split chrono. | 4,500 | 5,000 | 5,500 |
| HC, w/split chrono. | 6,500 | 7,000 | 7,500 |

**E. Koehn,** of Geneve, 46mm, 18 jewels, note: **free standing barrel,** lever escapement, Ca. 1900.

Note: Some models and grades are not included. Their values can be determined by comparing with similar age, size, metal content, style, models and grades listed.

Watches listed in this book are priced at the collectable fair market **value** at the retail level, as complete watches having an original case, an original white enamel dial, and with the entire original movement in good working order with no repairs needed, unless otherwise noted.

### COMPARISON OF WATCH SIZES

| U. S. A. | EUROPEAN |
|---|---|
| 10-12 SIZE | 40—44 MM |
| 16 SIZE | 45—48 MM |
| 18 SIZE | 50—54 MM |

# A. LANGE & SOHNE
### Swiss

A. Lange & Sohne was established with the aid of the German government at Glashutte, Germany in 1845. Lange typically produced 3/4 plate lever watches in gilt finish for the domestic market, and in nickel for the export market. High grade and very practical, these watches had a banking system for the pallet that was later used briefly by E. Howard in America. Lange complicated watches are scarce and very desirable.

## PRODUCTION TOTALS

| DATE– SERIAL # | DATE– SERIAL # | DATE– SERIAL # |
|---|---|---|
| 1870— 5,000 | 1895— 35,000 | 1920— 75,000 |
| 1875— 10,000 | 1900— 40,000 | 1925— 80,000 |
| 1880— 20,000 | 1905— 50,000 | 1930— 85,000 |
| 1885— 25,000 | 1910— 60,000 | 1935— 90,000 |
| 1890— 30,000 | 1915— 70,000 | 1940—100,000 |

| TYPE – DESCRIPTION | Avg | Ex-Fn | Mint |
|---|---|---|---|
| Time only, first grade, gold, 45- 50mm, OF | $2,000 | $2,200 | $2,500 |
| HC | 3,000 | 3,200 | 3,500 |
| World War II model, wind indicator, 52mm, OF | 1,500 | 1,800 | 2,200 |
| Chronograph, gold, 45-50mm, OF | 4,000 | 4,500 | 5,000 |
| HC | 5,000 | 5,500 | 6,000 |
| Split second chronograph, gold, 45-52mm, OF | 10,000 | 12,000 | 15,000 |
| HC | 12,000 | 15,000 | 18,000 |
| 1/4 hr. repeater, gold, 45-52mm, OF | 8,000 | 9,000 | 10,000 |
| HC | 10,000 | 12,000 | 15,000 |
| Minute repeater, gold, 45-52mm, OF | 10,000 | 12,000 | 15,000 |
| HC | 15,000 | 18,000 | 20,000 |
| OF, w/split chrono. | 15,000 | 18,000 | 20,000 |
| HC, w/split chrono. | 20,000 | 25,000 | 30,000 |
| Detent chronometer, gold, 48-52mm, OF | 30,000 | 35,000 | 40,000 |
| Perpetual moonphase calendar, gold, OF | 30,000 | 35,000 | 40,000 |
| Perp. moonphase cal. w/min. repeater, OF | 45,000 | 55,000 | 65,000 |
| Perp. moonphase cal. w/min. rep. and chrono., HC | 65,000 | 75,000 | 85,000 |

A. LANGE & SOHNE, 52mm, wind indicator, World War II model, open face.

A. LANGE & SOHNE, 48mm, three-quarter plate, engraved on movement "Deutsche Uhren Fabrikation Glashutte," serial number 58,398.

# LE COULTRE & CO.
### Swiss

Le Coultre and Co. was founded by Antoine Le Coultre in 1833. A fine clock maker, he created a machine to cut pinions from solid steel as well as other machines for manufacturing clocks and watches. By 1900 they were making flat or thin watches. They made parts for Patek Philippe & Co., Tissot, Vacheron & Constantin, Omega, Paul Ditisheim, Agassiz, Longines and others.

| TYPE – DESCRIPTION | Avg | Ex-Fn | Mint |
| --- | --- | --- | --- |
| Early, KW, Time only, Swiss bar, Pre. 1870, silver case | $125 | $150 | $225 |
| Time only, gold, 40- 44mm, OF | 300 | 400 | 500 |
| HC | 450 | 550 | 650 |
| Time only, gold, 45- 50mm, OF | 400 | 500 | 600 |
| HC | 600 | 750 | 900 |
| Roulette wheel style bezel, gold, 40mm, OF | 400 | 450 | 500 |
| World time watch, gold, 48-52mm, OF | 12,000 | 15,000 | 17,000 |
| Chronograph, gold, 45-50mm, OF | 900 | 1,200 | 1,500 |
| HC | 1,200 | 1,500 | 1,800 |
| OF, w/register | 1,000 | 1,400 | 1,650 |
| Split second chronograph, gold, 45-52mm, OF | 2,000 | 2,200 | 2,400 |
| HC | 2,500 | 2,700 | 3,000 |

Le Coultre & Co., 52mm, 32 jewels, minute repeater, exposed winding gears, 14k hunting case.

Le Coultre & Co., Roulette wheel style bezel, gold, 40mm, OF

| TYPE – DESCRIPTION | Avg | Ex-Fn | Mint |
| --- | --- | --- | --- |
| 1/4 hr. repeater, gold, 46-52mm, OF | $1,500 | $1,800 | $2,000 |
| HC w/chrono., cal. & moonphase | 3,000 | 3,500 | 4,000 |
| Minute repeater, gold, 46-52mm, OF | 2,700 | 2,900 | 3,200 |
| HC | 3,200 | 3,400 | 3,600 |
| OF, w/chrono. & register | 3,200 | 3,400 | 3,600 |
| HC, w/chrono. & register | 3,500 | 3,800 | 4,000 |
| HC, w/split chrono. | 9,000 | 10,000 | 12,000 |
| HC w/chrono., cal. & moonphase | 10,000 | 12,000 | 15,000 |
| Perpetual moonphase calendar, gold, OF | 8,000 | 9,000 | 10,000 |
| HC | 9,000 | 10,000 | 12,000 |
| Perp. moonphase cal. w/min. repeater, OF | 15,000 | 18,000 | 20,000 |
| HC | 18,000 | 20,000 | 22,000 |
| Perpetual moonphase cal. w/ min. rep. & chrono., OF | 18,000 | 20,000 | 22,000 |
| HC | 22,000 | 25,000 | 30,000 |

Caliber 30

Caliber 31

Caliber 46

Caliber 33

Caliber 32

Caliber 48

Caliber 43 A

Caliber 43 B

Caliber 49

# LE PHARE

Swiss

**Le Phare specialized in the production of repeater ebauches from 1880-1940.**

| TYPE – DESCRIPTION | Avg | Ex-Fn | Mint |
|---|---|---|---|
| Chronograph, gold, 45-50mm, OF | $600 | $800 | $1,000 |
| HC | 700 | 900 | 1,100 |
| Split second chronograph, gold, 45-52mm, OF | 1,200 | 1,400 | 1,600 |
| HC | 1,400 | 1,600 | 1,800 |
| 1/4 hr. repeater, gold, 46-52mm, OF | 1,200 | 1,400 | 1,500 |
| HC | 1,400 | 1,600 | 1,800 |
| HC w/chrono., cal. & moonphase | 2,500 | 3,000 | 3,500 |
| Minute repeater, gold, 46-56mm, OF | 1,800 | 2,000 | 2,200 |
| HC | 2,000 | 2,200 | 2,400 |
| OF w/chrono. & register | 2,000 | 2,200 | 2,400 |
| HC w/chrono. | 2,200 | 2,400 | 2,600 |
| HC w/chrono., cal. & moonphase | 3,500 | 4,000 | 4,500 |

**Le Phare,** 56mm, minute repeater, chronograph and calendar with moon phases.

**Le Phare,** 57mm, 1/4 repeater, chronograph , Ca. 1905.

**Le Phare, Minute repeater,** gold, 54mm, HC, 17 jewels, 3/4 plate, push button , Ca. 1895.

Caliber OV      Caliber LV      Caliber OF

Caliber E      Caliber 115 V      Caliber EV

Caliber D      Caliber DV      Caliber J

Caliber 110 M      Caliber ZM      Caliber 105

# LE ROY ET CIE
Paris

Le Roy et Cie was the final product of a dynasty of great watchmakers, starting with Julien Le Roy and his son Pierre, whose credits are numerous in the development of horology in the 18th century. There is, however, much confusion and hoopla over "Le Roy" watches. Frequently, you will see watches signed "Le Roy" that have nothing to do with the original family. These watches are unimportant. You have to distinguish between the works of Julien, of Pierre, of Charles, and of their contemporary namesakes. The modern firm, Le Roy et Cie., established in the late 19th century, contracted and finished some very fine and, in some cases, extremely important complicated watches, using imported Swiss ebauches.

| TYPE – DESCRIPTION | Avg | Ex-Fn | Mint |
|---|---|---|---|
| Verge, KW, paircase, silver, 49-50mm, C. 1775 | $300 | $400 | $500 |
| Verge, fusee, Enamel w/scene, 18K, 38- 40mm, C. 1760 | 2,000 | 2,500 | 3,000 |
| Miniature, 22mm, diamonds & pearls on enamel, OF | 1,000 | 1,200 | 1,500 |
| Time only, gold, 45- 50mm, OF | 800 | 900 | 1,000 |
| 1/4 hr. repeater, gold, 46-52mm, OF | 1,800 | 2,200 | 2,600 |
| Min. repeater, two train, tandem winding wheels, fully jeweled jump center seconds, gold, 50mm | 8,000 | 9,000 | 10,500 |

Le Roy, 50mm, minute repeater, two train, tandem winding wheels, jump center seconds.

Le Roy, 22mm, miniature watch with enamel, pearls, with a Diamond on the pin, 18K, OF, Ca. 1910.

🕐 This book endeavours to be a GUIDE or helpful manual and offers a wealth of material to be used as a tool not as a absolute document. Price Guides are like watches the worst may be better than none at all, but at best cannot be expected to be 100% accurate.

🕐 Characteristics of watches differ for the same age of both case and movement, because these features vary it may not be accurate to date a watch by one single influence. Example: the second hand was not commonly found on watches before 1750, but common about 1800. The first second hand appeared in 1665 and another in 1690. Therefore statements are broad rather than accurate.

# LONGINES
### Swiss

The beautiful Fabrique des Longines is situated in St. Imier, Switzerland.
The company was founded by Ernest Francillon in 1866. They manufacture all grades of watches.

## PRODUCTION TOTALS
### LONGINES DATE OF MOVEMENT MANUFACTURE

| DATE– SERIAL # | DATE– SERIAL # | DATE– SERIAL # |
|---|---|---|
| 1867 --- 1 | 1911 - 2,500,000 | 1937 - 5,500,000 |
| 1870 --- 20,000 | 1912 - 2,750,000 | 1938 - 5,750,000 |
| 1875 --- 100,000 | 1913 - 3,000,000 | 1940 - 6,000,000 |
| 1882 ---250,000 | 1915 - 3,250,000 | 1945 - 7,000,000 |
| 1888 --- 500,000 | 1917 - 3,500,000 | 1950 - 8,000,000 |
| 1893 --- 750,000 | 1919 - 3,750,000 | 1953 - 9,000,000 |
| 1899 - 1,000,000 | 1922 - 4,000,000 | 1956-10,000,000 |
| 1901 - 1,250,000 | 1925 - 4,250,000 | 1959-11,000,000 |
| 1904 - 1,500,000 | 1926 - 4,500,000 | 1962-12,000,000 |
| 1905 - 1,750,000 | 1928 - 4,750,000 | 1966-13,000,000 |
| 1907 - 2,000,000 | 1929 - 5,000,000 | 1967-14,000,000 |
| 1909 - 2,250,000 | 1934 - 5,250,000 | 1969-15,000,000 |

The above list is provided for determining the APPROXIMATE age of your watch. Match serial number with date. Watches were not necessarily sold in the exact order of manufactured date.

LONGINES, 44mm, 21 jewels, U.S. Army AC, adjusted to temp. & 5 positions, World War II model.

LONGINES, 59mm, 26 jewels, minute repeater, chronograph, one register, ca. 1910.

| TYPE – DESCRIPTION | Avg | Ex-Fn | Mint |
|---|---|---|---|
| 15 -17J, GF, 44- 50mm, OF, C. 1930 | $45 | $55 | $75 |
| 15 -17J, silver, 48- 50mm, HC, C. 1890 | 90 | 100 | 150 |
| 15 -17J, for Tiffany, Sterling, 45- 50mm OF, C. 1905 | 125 | 150 | 175 |
| KW, for Turkish market, .800 silver, HC, C. 1900 | 125 | 150 | 175 |
| 21J, RR "Express Monarch", LS, GF, 48- 50mm, OF, C.1910 | 175 | 200 | 250 |
| U.S. Army AC, World War II, 21J., silver, 44mm, OF | 600 | 700 | 850 |
| Time only, gold, 40- 44mm, OF | 250 | 325 | 425 |
|     HC | 350 | 400 | 475 |
| Time only, gold, 45- 48mm, OF | 300 | 400 | 500 |
|     HC | 450 | 600 | 750 |
| World time watch, gold, 48-52mm, OF | 8,000 | 9,000 | 10,000 |
| Chronograph w/register, silver, OF, 48- 50mm, C. 1905 | 250 | 300 | 400 |
| Chronograph, gold, 45-50mm, OF | 500 | 600 | 700 |
|     HC | 700 | 800 | 900 |

Longines, 46mm, Min. repeater, 24 jewels, 3/4 plate design, open face, Ca. 1915.

| TYPE – DESCRIPTION | Avg | Ex-Fn | Mint |
|---|---|---|---|
| Split second chronograph, gold, 45-52mm, OF | $1,000 | $1,200 | $1,400 |
| HC | 1,200 | 1,500 | 1,800 |
| Chronograph, Lugrin's Pat., fly back, silver OF case | 375 | 400 | 475 |
| 1/4 hr. repeater, gold, 46-52mm, OF | 1,200 | 1,500 | 1,800 |
| HC | 1,500 | 1,800 | 2,000 |
| HC w/chrono., cal. & moonphase | 4,000 | 5,000 | 6,000 |
| Minute repeater, gold, 46-52mm, OF | 2,000 | 2,200 | 2,500 |
| HC | 2,500 | 2,800 | 3,000 |
| OF w/chrono. | 2,200 | 2,500 | 2,700 |
| HC w/chrono. | 3,000 | 3,500 | 3,750 |
| OF w/split chrono. | 3,500 | 4,000 | 4,500 |
| HC w/split chrono. | 6,500 | 7,000 | 7,500 |
| HC w/cal. & moon- phase | 9,000 | 10,000 | 12,000 |
| Perpetual moonphase calendar, gold, OF | 6,000 | 8,000 | 10,000 |
| Perp. moonphase cal. w/min.repeater & chrono., OF | 15,000 | 18,000 | 20,000 |
| HC | 18,000 | 20,000 | 22,000 |

Longines , Chronograph, H.A. Lugrin's Pat. June 13, Oct. 3, 1976, Start, Stop, Fly Back.

Longines, 50mm Chronograph, Minute repeater, 18K hunting case, Ca. 1930.

# MARKWICK, MARKHAM
LONDON (1725-1825)

He enjoyed selling clocks and watches to the Turkish Market. Watches can be found with his name & that of another maker added, Example: Markwick, Markham "Perigal", or "Recordon". Also watches with the names "Story" Ca.1780, "Borrel" Ca.1813 and "Perigal" Ca.1825 are known.

| TYPE – DESCRIPTION | Avg | Ex-Fn | Mint |
|---|---|---|---|
| VERGE, pair case, silver plain, 50mm, OF | $400 | $425 | $475 |
| VERGE, pair case, silver w/ repousee, 50mm, OF | 800 | 1,000 | 1,200 |
| VERGE, triple cased, Tortoise shell on outer case, 56mm, OF | 1,200 | 1,500 | 2,000 |
| VERGE, GOLD, 48-52mm, OF | 1,000 | 1,200 | 1,400 |
| VERGE, GOLD, W/ repousee pair case, 46-50mm, OF | 2,000 | 2,500 | 3,000 |
| 1/4 hr. repeater, SILVER, 54mm, OF | 1,500 | 2,000 | 2,500 |
| 1/4 hr. repeater, GOLD, 54mm, OF | 2,500 | 3,000 | 3,500 |

**Markwick, Markham,** Triple cased , 18K gold cases, Painted enamel on first & second case, made for Turkish Market, Ca. 1800.

## COMPARISON OF WATCH SIZES

| U. S. A. | EUROPEAN |
|---|---|
| 10-12 SIZE | 40—44 MM |
| 16 SIZE | 45—48 MM |
| 18 SIZE | 50—52 MM |

MILLIMETERS 10    20    30    40    50    60

# MATHEY – TISSOT
Swiss

| TYPE – DESCRIPTION | Avg | Ex-Fn | Mint |
|---|---|---|---|
| Early, KW, Time only, Swiss bar, Pre 1870, silver | $100 | $125 | $175 |
| Time only, gold, 40- 44mm, OF | 275 | 350 | 425 |
| HC | 400 | 500 | 575 |
| Time only, gold, 45- 50mm, OF | 400 | 500 | 600 |
| HC | 600 | 750 | 900 |
| 1/4 hr. repeater, gold, 46-52mm, OF | 1,200 | 1,400 | 1,600 |
| HC | 1,500 | 1,800 | 2,000 |
| OF w/chrono., cal. & moonphase | 2,000 | 2,200 | 2,400 |
| HC w/chrono., cal. & moonphase | 2,500 | 3,500 | 4,500 |

Mathey-Tissot, 52mm, 27 jewels, quarter jump sweep second chronograph, two train, 18k HC.

Mathey-Tissot, min. repeater with chronograph, day date month & moon phases, HC.

| TYPE – DESCRIPTION | Avg | Ex-Fn | Mint |
|---|---|---|---|
| Minute repeater, gold, 46-52mm, OF | $2,400 | $2,600 | $2,800 |
| HC | 3,000 | 3,500 | 4,000 |
| OF w/chrono. & register | 3,000 | 3,500 | 4,000 |
| HC w/chrono. & register | 3,500 | 4,000 | 4,500 |
| HC w/chrono. & moon ph,. day date month, | 8,000 | 9,000 | 10,000 |
| OF w/split chrono. | 6,000 | 7,000 | 7,500 |
| HC w/split chrono. | 8,000 | 9,000 | 10,000 |
| OF w/cal. & moonphase | 7,000 | 8,000 | 9,000 |
| HC w/cal. & moonphase | 9,000 | 10,000 | 12,000 |
| World time watch, gold, 48-52mm, OF | 12,000 | 15,000 | 18,000 |
| Perpetual moonphase calendar, gold, OF | 8,000 | 10,000 | 12,000 |
| Perp. moonphase cal. w/min. repeater, OF | 20,000 | 25,000 | 30,000 |
| HC | 25,000 | 30,000 | 35,000 |
| Perp. moonphase cal. w/min. rep. and chrono., OF | 22,000 | 27,000 | 32,000 |
| HC | 27,000 | 32,000 | 37,000 |

🕐 Note: Some models and grades are not included. Their values can be determined by comparing with **similar** age, size, metal content, style, models and grades listed.

# MEYLAN WATCH CO.

Swiss

Meylan Watch Co., founded by C.H. Meylan in 1880, manufactured fine watches, with complications, in Le Brassus, Switzerland.

| TYPE – DESCRIPTION | Avg | Ex-Fn | Mint |
|---|---|---|---|
| Time only, gold, 40- 44mm, OF | $375 | $425 | $500 |
| HC | 600 | 675 | 750 |
| Time only, gold, 40- 44mm, 18K case & **enamel on bezel**, OF | 1,500 | 1,800 | 2,200 |
| Time only, gold, 45- 50mm, OF | 500 | 600 | 700 |
| HC | 850 | 950 | 1,100 |
| Chronograph, gold, 45-50mm, OF | 700 | 800 | 900 |
| HC | 900 | 1,000 | 1,200 |
| Split second chronograph, gold, 45-52mm, OF | 1,200 | 1,400 | 1,600 |
| HC | 1,800 | 2,000 | 2,200 |
| 1/4 hr. repeater, gold, 46-52mm, OF | 1,500 | 1,800 | 2,000 |
| HC | 2,000 | 2,200 | 2,400 |
| HC w/chrono., cal. & moonphase | 3,000 | 3,500 | 4,000 |

C. H. Meylan, 42mm, 21 jewels, straight line lever escapement, 18K case with enamel on bezel.

C. H. Meylan, Minute Repeater, split second Chronograph, minute register, 18K gold OF case, Ca. 1895

| TYPE – DESCRIPTION | Avg | Ex-Fn | Mint |
|---|---|---|---|
| 5 minute repeater, gold, 46-52mm, OF | $2,500 | $2,700 | $3,000 |
| HC | 2,750 | 3,000 | 3,250 |
| Minute repeater, gold, OF | 3,000 | 3,200 | 3,500 |
| HC | 4,000 | 4,500 | 5,000 |
| OF w/chrono. | 3,500 | 4,000 | 4,200 |
| HC w/chrono. | 4,500 | 5,000 | 5,500 |
| OF w/split chrono. | 5,000 | 5,500 | 6,000 |
| HC w/split chrono. | 8,000 | 9,000 | 10,000 |
| OF w/cal. & moonphase | 8,000 | 9,000 | 10,000 |
| HC w/cal. & moonphase | 12,000 | 14,000 | 15,000 |
| HC w/chrono., cal. & moonphase | 13,000 | 15,000 | 16,000 |
| Tourbillion, gold, 48-55mm, OF | 25,000 | 30,000 | 35,000 |
| Detent chronometer, gold, 48-52mm, OF | 4,000 | 5,000 | 5,500 |
| World time watch, gold, 48-52mm, OF | 8,000 | 9,000 | 10,000 |
| Perpetual moonphase calendar, gold, OF | 12,000 | 14,000 | 15,000 |
| HC | 13,000 | 15,000 | 16,000 |
| Perp. moonphase cal. w/min. rep. and chrono., OF | 20,000 | 22,000 | 24,000 |
| HC | 25,000 | 30,000 | 35,000 |

# MORICAND, CH.
## GENEVA

Firm specialized in making verge watches with cases highly decorated with stones and enameled portraits. Associates with brother Benjamin and Francois Colladon from 1752 to 1755, with a firm name of Collardon & Moricand. Later, with Jean Delisle then later in 1780 as Moricand.

Delisle & Moricand, 36MM, 1/4 hour repeater pendant activated, two-footed balance bridge, Ca.1775.

Ch. Moricand, 46mm, gilt and enamel with two ladies in a floral garden, KW KS, Ca.1800.

| TYPE – DESCRIPTION | Avg | Ex-Fn | Mint |
|---|---|---|---|
| Verge, KW, paircase, **silver**, 50mm, OF | $375 | $450 | $500 |
| Verge, enamel w/ portrait, **silver/ gilt**, 49-52mm, OF | 1,000 | 1,200 | 1,400 |
| Verge, KW, **gold**, 50-54mm, OF | 1,000 | 1,250 | 1,500 |
| Verge, KW, **gold** w/ enamel, 52mm, OF | 2,500 | 3,000 | 3,500 |
| 1/4 hr. repeater, **silver**, 54mm, OF | 1,000 | 1,200 | 1,500 |
| 1/4 hr. repeater, **gold**, 50-54mm, OF | 2,000 | 2,500 | 3,000 |
| 1/4 hr. repeater, **gold** w/ enamel, 54mm, OF | 5,000 | 5,500 | 6,000 |

# C. MONTANDON
## Swiss

This 19th century maker was associated with Perret & Company as well as other Le Locle and Chaux-de-Fonds factories. Montandon specialized in low cost keywind watches for the American market.

| TYPE – DESCRIPTION | Avg | Ex-Fn | Mint |
|---|---|---|---|
| KW, cylinder escap., silver, 46mm, OF, C. 1870 | $75 | $85 | $100 |
| KW, silver, 46-48mm, HC, C. 1875 | 90 | 100 | 120 |
| KW, 15J, lady's , 18K, 40-44mm, OF, C. 1870 | 150 | 175 | 225 |
| KW, 15J, lady's, 18K, 40-44mm, HC, C. 1870 | 225 | 300 | 375 |
| KW, 15J, gent's, 18K, 48mm, OF, C. 1875 | 225 | 300 | 375 |
| Chronograph, gold, 45-50mm, OF | 1,000 | 1,200 | 1,400 |
| HC | 1,800 | 2,000 | 2,200 |
| 1/4 hr. repeater, gold, 46-52mm, OF | 2,000 | 2,200 | 2,600 |
| HC | 2,500 | 3,000 | 3,500 |
| Minute repeater, gold, 46-52mm, OF | 2,500 | 3,000 | 3,500 |
| OF w/cal. & moonphase | 3,500 | 4,000 | 4,500 |
| HC | 3,000 | 3,500 | 4,000 |
| HC w/cal. & moonphase | 5,500 | 6,000 | 6,500 |
| HC w/chrono., cal. & moonphase | 6,000 | 6,500 | 7,000 |

# MOVADO
Swiss

L. A. I. Ditesheim & Freres (L.A.I. the initials of the 3 Ditesheim brothers) formed their company in 1881. The name Movado ("always in motion") was adopted in 1905. The Swiss company invented a system of watch making which they called "Polyplan." This was an arrangement of three different angles to the watch movement which produced a curve effect to the case so as to fit the curvature of the arm. Another unusual watch produced by this company in 1926 was the "Ermeto." This watch was designed to be protected while inside a purse or pocket and each time the cover was opened to view the time, the watch was partially wound.

Movado, 40mm, SW, lever escapement calibre 540.　　Movado, 44mm, 15J., J.settings, Adj.4P, calibre 800M.

| TYPE – DESCRIPTION | Avg | Ex-Fn | Mint |
|---|---|---|---|
| SW, 17J, LS, Silver, 43mm, OF, C. 1920 | $100 | $150 | $175 |
| SW, 15J, LS, Silver, 47mm, HC, C. 1920 | 125 | 150 | 200 |
| Time only, gold, 40-44mm, OF | 200 | 250 | 325 |
| HC | 350 | 425 | 500 |
| Time only, gold, 45-50mm, OF | 400 | 500 | 600 |
| HC | 800 | 900 | 1,000 |
| Purse watch, black leather, 50 x 33mm, C. 1930's | 275 | 300 | 350 |
| Purse watch with moonph. & calendar, 50 x 33mm, C.1930's | 1,000 | 1,200 | 1,300 |
| Coin form, 17J, St. Christopher coin, 18K, closed case, 29mm | 800 | 900 | 1,000 |
| Chronograph, gold, 45-50mm, OF | 1,500 | 1,800 | 2,000 |
| Minute repeater, gold, 46-52mm, OF | 3,500 | 4,000 | 4,500 |
| HC | 4,000 | 4,500 | 5,000 |
| HC w/split chrono. & register | 8,000 | 8,500 | 9,000 |

🕐 Some models and grades are not included. Their values can be determined by comparing with similar age, size, metal content, style, models and grades listed.

## COMPARISON OF WATCH SIZES

| U. S. A. | EUROPEAN |
|---|---|
| 10-12 SIZE | 40—44 MM |
| 16    SIZE | 45—48 MM |
| 18    SIZE | 50—54 MM |

# ULYSSE NARDIN
### Swiss

Ulysse Nardin was born in 1823. The company he started in 1846 produced many fine timepieces and chronometers, as well as repeaters and more complicated watches. This firm, as did Assmann, found a strong market in South America as well as other countries. Ulysse's son, Paul David Nardin, succeeded him, as did Paul David's sons after him.

Ulysse Nardin, Key wind, 18 jewels, pivoted detent, bridge movement, 48mm, Ca. 1860.

Ulysse Nardin, pocket chronometer with date, 19J. pivoted detent, gold jewel settings, Ca.1890.

| TYPE – DESCRIPTION | Avg | Ex-Fn | Mint |
|---|---|---|---|
| Early KW, 18J., pivoted detent, bar style mvt., gold, HC, C.1860 .. | $3,000 | $3,500 | $4,000 |
| Time only, gold, 40-44mm, OF | 300 | 400 | 500 |
| HC | 450 | 550 | 650 |
| Time only, gold, 45- 50mm, OF | 600 | 650 | 700 |
| HC | 750 | 800 | 850 |
| Chronograph, gold, 45-50mm, OF | 1,200 | 1,300 | 1,400 |
| HC | 1,500 | 1,700 | 1,900 |
| Deck chronometer w/box, detent chronometer, C. 1905 | 1,500 | 1,800 | 2,000 |
| Pocket chronometer, lever escape., 21J., GJS, 18K, HC, C.1910.... | 1,200 | 1,500 | 1,800 |
| Pocket chronometer, pivoted detent, with date, gold, 57mm | 4,000 | 4,500 | 5,000 |
| World time watch, gold, 48-52mm, OF | 12,000 | 15,000 | 18,000 |
| Karrusel, 52 Min. karrusel, free sprung balance, silver case............ | 6,000 | 7,000 | 8,000 |

Ulysse Nardin, 53mm, 52 minute karrusel, free sprung balance, ca. 1905.

Ulysse Nardin, pocket chronometer, lever escapement, 21 jewels, gold jewel settings, Ca. 1910

| TYPE – DESCRIPTION | Avg | Ex-Fn | Mint |
|---|---|---|---|
| 1/4 hr. repeater, gold, 46-52mm, OF | $1,500 | $2,000 | $2,500 |
| OF w/chrono., cal. moonphase | 2,000 | 2,200 | 2,500 |
| HC | 1,800 | 2,300 | 2,850 |
| HC w/chrono., cal. & moonphase | 3,500 | 4,000 | 4,500 |
| Minute repeater, gold, 46-52mm, OF | 3,000 | 3,200 | 3,500 |
| HC | 4,000 | 4,200 | 4,500 |
| OF w/split chrono. | 4,500 | 4,800 | 5,500 |
| HC w/split chrono. | 7,000 | 8,000 | 9,000 |
| OF w/cal. & moonphase | 10,000 | 12,000 | 15,000 |
| HC w/cal. & moonphase | 10,000 | 12,000 | 14,000 |
| HC w/chrono., cal. & moonphase | 12,000 | 13,000 | 15,000 |
| Perpetual moonphase calendar, gold, OF | 12,000 | 14,000 | 15,000 |
| HC | 13,000 | 15,000 | 17,000 |
| Perp. moonphase cal. w/min . repeater, OF | 25,000 | 28,000 | 30,000 |
| HC | 27,000 | 30,000 | 32,000 |
| Perp. moonphase cal. w/min. rep. and chrono. , OF | 28,000 | 30,000 | 32,000 |
| HC | 30,000 | 32,000 | 35,000 |

# NICOLE, NIELSEN & CO.
## London

Adolphe Nicole in 1840 came to London from Switzerland and joined Henry Capt. In 1876 Emil Nielsen became a partner in the firm. The company was purchased by S. Smith & Sons in 1904. Tourbillons were made by V. Kullberg and Nicole, Nielsen for the England market.

**( Made ebauche for Dent, Frodsham, and Smith )**

Nicole, Nielsen, 50mm, chronograph, 15 jewels, 3/4 plate, gilded movement, Ca. 1890.

Nicole, Nielsen, 64mm, min. repeater, split-second chronograph, tourbillon, free sprung escapement.

| TYPE – DESCRIPTION | Avg | Ex-Fn | Mint |
|---|---|---|---|
| Time only, gold, 45- 50mm, OF | $900 | $1,000 | $1,200 |
| HC | 1,200 | 1,500 | 1,800 |
| Chronograph, gold, 45-50mm, HC | 2,000 | 2,400 | 2,900 |
| Minute repeater, gold, 46-52mm, OF | 2,700 | 3,000 | 3,500 |
| HC | 3,500 | 3,800 | 4,000 |
| OF w/chrono. & register | 3,850 | 4,250 | 4,750 |
| HC w/chrono. & register | 4,000 | 4,400 | 5,000 |

| TYPE – DESCRIPTION | Avg | Ex-Fn | Mint |
|---|---|---|---|
| Minute repeater, tourbillon, split-second chronograph, free sprung escapement, gold, 64mm, | $100,000 | $125,000 | $150,000 |
| Karrusel, gold, 48-55mm, OF | 9,000 | 10,000 | 12,000 |
| Tourbillion, gold, 48-55mm, OF | 25,000 | 30,000 | 35,000 |
| Perpetual moon phase calendar, gold, OF | 22,000 | 24,000 | 26,000 |
| HC | 25,000 | 26,000 | 28,000 |
| Perp. moonphase cal. w/min.rep. and chrono., OF | 35,000 | 38,000 | 40,000 |
| HC | 38,000 | 40,000 | 42,000 |

# NON–MAGNETIC WATCH CO.
Swiss

| TYPE – DESCRIPTION | Avg | Ex-Fn | Mint |
|---|---|---|---|
| Time only, gold, 45- 50mm, OF | $400 | $500 | $600 |
| HC | 600 | 800 | 1,000 |
| Chronograph, gold, 45-50mm, OF | 900 | 1,000 | 1,200 |
| HC | 1,000 | 1,200 | 1,400 |
| Split second chronograph, gold, 45-52mm, OF | 1,100 | 1,200 | 1,500 |
| HC | 1,350 | 1,500 | 1,750 |
| 1/4 hr. repeater, gold, 46-52mm, OF | 1,500 | 1,800 | 2,200 |
| HC | 1,800 | 2,000 | 2,400 |
| Minute repeater, gold, 46-52mm, OF | 2,500 | 2,800 | 3,000 |
| HC | 2,800 | 3,200 | 3,500 |
| OF w/split chrono. | 4,500 | 5,000 | 5,500 |
| HC w/split chrono. | 5,000 | 5,500 | 6,000 |
| HC w/chrono., cal. & moonphase | 8,000 | 9,000 | 10,000 |

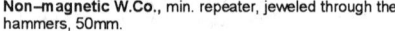

Non–magnetic W.Co., min. repeater, jeweled through the hammers, 50mm.

Omega pocket watch movement, 45-48mm, 15 jewels, serial number 9,888,934.

🕐 Watches listed in this book are priced at the collectable fair market **value** at the retail level, as complete watches having an original case, an original white enamel dial, and with the entire original movement in good working order with no repairs needed, unless otherwise noted.

# OMEGA WATCH CO.

Swiss

Omega Watch Co. was founded by Louis Brandt in 1848. They produced watches of different grades. In 1930, they began to produce different lines with Tissot under the name Societe Sussie pour l'Industrie Horlogere. The firm has been part of the ESTH group since 1971.

PRODUCTION TOTALS

| DATE– SERIAL # | DATE– SERIAL # |
|---|---|
| 1895 – 50,000 | 1940-12,500,000 |
| 1900 – 500,000 | 1945-14,000,000 |
| 1905 -1,000,000 | 1950-15,500,000 |
| 1910 -2,500,000 | 1955-16,500,000 |
| 1915 -4,500,000 | 1960-18,000,000 |
| 1920 -6,000,000 | 1965-23,000,000 |
| 1925 -7,500,000 | 1970-28,000,000 |
| 1930 -9,500,000 | 1975-35,000,000 |
| 1935-11,000,000 | |

The above list is provided for determining the APPROXIMATE age of your watch. Match serial number with date. Watches were not necessarily sold in the exact order of manufactured date.

| TYPE – DESCRIPTION | Avg | Ex-Fn | Mint |
|---|---|---|---|
| 15J, gilt, silver, 48mm, OF, C. 1905 | $60 | $75 | $90 |
| 15J, SW, silver 47mm, HC, C. 1910 | 85 | 100 | 125 |
| 21J, R.R. model, GF, 52mm, OF, C. 1915 | 150 | 175 | 200 |
| Time only, gold, 45- 48mm, OF | 400 | 500 | 600 |
| HC | 500 | 600 | 700 |
| Chronograph, gold, 45-50mm, OF | 900 | 1,000 | 1,100 |
| HC | 1,200 | 1,400 | 1,600 |
| Chronograph, gold, 45-50mm, **Double-Dial,** OF | 3,000 | 4,000 | 4,500 |
| Minute repeater, gold, 46-52mm, OF | 2,200 | 2,500 | 2,750 |
| HC | 2,750 | 3,000 | 3,250 |
| OF w/split chrono. | 4,200 | 4,700 | 5,000 |
| HC w/split chrono. | 4,500 | 5,000 | 5,250 |
| HC w/chrono., cal. & moonphase | 7,500 | 8,000 | 8,500 |

Omega, **Chronograph,** gold, 45-50mm, **Double-Dial,** open face, Multi-color enamel dials.

# CHARLES OUDIN
### PARIS

Oudin was a pupil of Breguet and became a talented maker from 1807-1830. He produced quality timepieces and invented an early "keyless" watch.

Charles Oudin, Dial & Movement, 51mm, 32J., Minute repeater with Chronograph, Ca.1910.

| TYPE – DESCRIPTION | Avg | Ex-Fn | Mint |
|---|---|---|---|
| Verge, KW, silver single case, 45mm, OF, C. 1865 | $300 | $400 | $500 |
| Early, KW, Time only, Swiss bar, silver , OF | 75 | 85 | 100 |
| GOLD, OF | 400 | 500 | 700 |
| Split sec. chrono., 29J, w/ register,18K, 51mm, HC, C. 1900 | 1,800 | 2,000 | 2,500 |
| Minute repeater, gold, 46-52mm, OF | 3,000 | 3,500 | 3,700 |
| HC | 3,500 | 3,750 | 4,000 |
| OF w/chrono. & register | 4,000 | 4,250 | 4,500 |
| HC w/chrono. & register | 4,700 | 4,900 | 5,000 |

"CHs. OUDIN, Paris," engraved on movement, Key Wind, cylinder escapement, Swiss bar, Ca. 1865.

# PATEK, PHILIPPE & CIE.

### Swiss

Patek, Philippe & Cie. has produced some of the world's most desirable factory-made watches. Antoine Norbert de Patek began contracting and selling watches in the 1830's, later became partners with Francois Czapek and generally produced lovely decorative watches for a high class of clientele. In 1845 Adrien Philippe, inventor of the modern stem-winding system, joined the firm of Patek & Cie., and in 1851, the firm established its present name. Between Philippe's talent as a watchmaker and Patek's talent as a businessman with a taste for the impeccable, the firm rapidly established an international reputation which lasts to this day. Early Patek, Philippe & Cie. watches are generally signed only on the dust cover, but some are signed on the dial and cuvette. It was not until the 1880's that the practice began of fully signing the dial, movement and case-perhaps in response to some contemporary forgery but more likely a necessity to conform to customs' regulations for their growing international market. Many early and totally original Patek watches have suffered from the misconception that all products of the company are fully signed. Never the less, collectors find such pieces more desirable. It requires more experience, however, to determine the originality of the earlier pieces. As with Vacheron & Constantin, some watches were originally cased in U.S.A., but this lowers their value in general.

## PRODUCTION TOTALS

| DATE—SERIAL # | DATE—SERIAL # | DATE—SERIAL # |
|---|---|---|
| 1840— 100 | 1950—700,000 | 1940— 900,000 |
| 1845— 1,200 | 1955—725,000 | 1945— 915,000 |
| 1850— 3,000 | 1960—750,000 | 1950— 930,000 |
| 1855— 8,000 | 1965—775,000 | 1955— 940,000 |
| 1860— 15,000 | 1970—795,000 | 1960— 960,000 |
| 1865— 22,000 | | 1965— 975,000 |
| 1870— 35,000 | | 1970— 995,000 |
| 1875— 45,000 | DATE—SERIAL # | |
| 1880— 55,000 | 1920— 800,000 | |
| 1885— 70,000 | 1925— 805,000 | DATE—SERIAL # |
| 1890— 85,000 | 1930— 820,000 | 1960—1,100,000 |
| 1895—100,000 | 1935— 824,000 | 1965—1,130,000 |
| 1900—110,000 | 1940— 835,000 | 1970—1,250,000 |
| 1905—125,000 | 1945— 850,000 | 1975—1,350,000 |
| 1910—150,000 | 1950— 860,000 | 1980—1,450,000 |
| 1915—175,000 | 1955— 870,000 | 1985—1,600,000 |
| 1920—190,000 | 1960— 880,000 | 1990—1,850,000 |
| 1925—200,000 | 1965— 890,000 | |
| | 1970— 895,000 | |

The above list is provided for determining the APPROXIMATE age of your watch. Match serial number with date. Watches were not necessarily sold in the exact order of manufactured date.

Patek, Philippe & Cie. 43mm, time only, 18K, open face.

Patek, Philippe & Cie., 18 jewels, engraved gold dial with enamel center, 18K, 43mm, Ca. 1920's.

Patek, Philippe & Cie. , KWKS, lever escapement, gilt movement, signed on 18K case, 47mm, Ca. 1865.

Patek, Philippe & Co., Perpetual calendar, moonphase, min. repeater & split second chronograph, 18K, OF.

Patek, Philippe & Co., "Chronometro Gondolo", 19 jewels, signed, lever escapement, 51mm, Ca. 1908.

Patek, Philippe & Co., dial & movement, min. repeater, 29J, perpetual calendar, day, date, month, moon-phases, 18K.

| TYPE – DESCRIPTION | Avg | Ex-Fn | Mint |
|---|---|---|---|
| Time only, gold, 25- 30mm, ladies, OF | $800 | $900 | $1,100 |
| HC | 1,000 | 1,500 | 1,800 |
| Time only, gold, 32- 44mm, OF | 1,800 | 2,000 | 2,500 |
| HC | 2,500 | 3,000 | 3,500 |
| Time only, **enameled bezel,** gold, 32- 44mm, OF | 2,000 | 2,500 | 3,200 |
| Time only, gold, 45- 50mm, OF | 2,000 | 2,200 | 2,500 |
| HC | 3,000 | 3,200 | 3,500 |
| EARLY Time only, KWKS, gilt mvt., lever or cylinder escapement pre 1865, signed on gold case, 40-45mm, | 1,500 | 1,800 | 2,000 |
| Time only, Chronometre Gondolo, gold, 38mm, OF | 2,000 | 2,500 | 3,000 |
| Time only, Chronometre Gondolo, gold, 50mm, OF | 2,500 | 3,000 | 3,500 |

Patek, Philippe & Co., enameled bezel, 18K OF, 42mm

Patek, Philippe & Co., perpetual calendar with moon phases, signed, 18 jewels, 49mm, Ca. 1949

| TYPE – DESCRIPTION | Avg | Ex-Fn | Mint |
|---|---|---|---|
| Chronograph, gold, 45-50mm, OF | $3,500 | $4,000 | $4,500 |
| HC | 5,000 | 5,250 | 5,500 |
| OF w/register | 4,000 | 4,250 | 4,750 |
| HC w/register | 5,500 | 5,750 | 6,000 |
| Split second chronograph, gold, 45-52mm, OF | 7,000 | 7,500 | 8,000 |
| HC | 9,000 | 9,500 | 10,000 |
| OF w/register | 7,500 | 8,000 | 8,500 |
| HC w/register | 9,500 | 10,000 | 11,000 |
| 1/4 hr. repeater, gold, 46-52mm, OF | 4,500 | 4,750 | 5,000 |
| HC | 5,500 | 6,000 | 6,500 |
| 5 minute repeater, gold, 46-52mm, OF | 6,000 | 6,500 | 7,000 |
| HC | 8,500 | 9,500 | 10,000 |
| OF w/split chrono. | 12,000 | 14,000 | 16,000 |
| HC w/split chrono. | 15,000 | 18,000 | 20,000 |
| Minute repeater, gold, 46-52mm, OF | 9,000 | 10,000 | 11,000 |
| HC | 12,000 | 15,000 | 18,000 |
| OF w/chrono. | 14,000 | 16,000 | 18,000 |
| HC w/chrono. | 18,000 | 20,000 | 22,000 |
| OF w/chrono. & register | 15,000 | 18,000 | 20,000 |
| HC w/chrono. & register | 20,000 | 22,000 | 24,000 |

| TYPE – DESCRIPTION | Avg | Ex-Fn | Mint |
|---|---|---|---|
| Minute repeater, w/split chrono., gold, 46-52mm, OF | $15,000 | $18,000 | $20,000 |
| HC w/split chrono. | 20,000 | 22,000 | 24,000 |
| OF w/split chrono. & register | 18,000 | 20,000 | 23,000 |
| HC w/split chrono. & register | 25,000 | 30,000 | 32,000 |
| OF w/cal. & moonphase | 20,000 | 25,000 | 30,000 |
| HC w/cal. & moon phase | 25,000 | 30,000 | 35,000 |
| OF w/chrono., cal. & moonphase | 22,000 | 27,000 | 32,000 |
| HC w/chrono., cal. & moonphase | 30,000 | 35,000 | 40,000 |
| Perpetual moonphase calendar, gold, OF | 35,000 | 40,000 | 45,000 |
| HC | 45,000 | 50,000 | 55,000 |
| Perp. moonphase cal. w/min. repeater, OF | 60,000 | 65,000 | 70,000 |
| HC | 70,000 | 75,000 | 80,000 |
| Perpetual moonphase cal. w/ min. rep. & chrono. , OF | 80,000 | 85,000 | 90,000 |
| HC | 90,000 | 95,000 | 100,000 |
| Perpetual moonphase cal. w/ min. rep. & split sec. chrono. , OF | 100,000 | 110,000 | 125,000 |
| HC | 150,000 | 175,000 | 200,000 |

Patek, Philippe & Co., Digital Jump Hour, with minute hand & second hand, 18 jewels, 45mm, 18K.

Patek, Philippe & Co., gold coin watch, 100 pesetas, secret push-piece opens lid to disclose dial, 35mm, Ca.1928.

| TYPE – DESCRIPTION | Avg | Ex-Fn | Mint |
|---|---|---|---|
| Lady's pendant watch w/ brooch,18K & small diamonds, 27mm | $2,400 | $2,800 | $3,300 |
| Gold Coin, 100 pesetas 18K, 18J., coin opens to disclose dial | 4,000 | 4,500 | 5,000 |
| Digital Jump Hour, W/minute hand & sec. hand, 45mm, 18K | 30,000 | 40,000 | 50,000 |
| Karrusel, gold, 48-55mm, OF | 90,000 | 95,000 | 100,000 |
| Tourbillion, gold, 48-55mm, OF | 125,000 | 130,000 | 135,000 |
| HC | 140,000 | 145,000 | 150,000 |
| Detent chronometer, gold, 48-52mm, OF | 65,000 | 70,000 | 75,000 |
| HC | 75,000 | 80,000 | 85,000 |
| World time watch, gold, 48-52mm, OF | 90,000 | 95,000 | 100,000 |

## COMPARISON OF WATCH SIZES

| U. S. A. | EUROPEAN |
|---|---|
| 10-12 SIZE | 40—44 MM |
| 16 SIZE | 45—48 MM |
| 18 SIZE | 50—54 MM |

# PICARD, JAMES
## GENEVA
Watch dealer and finisher in the latter part of the 19th Century. Known for his complicated watches and pocket chronometers of high quality.

| TYPE – DESCRIPTION | Avg | Ex-Fn | Mint |
|---|---|---|---|
| Time only, gold, 45- 50mm, OF | $500 | $600 | $700 |
| HC | 650 | 750 | 850 |
| Chronograph, gold, 45-50mm, OF | 800 | 850 | 900 |
| Split second chronograph, gold, 45-52mm, OF | 1,800 | 2,000 | 2,200 |
| HC w/register | 2,850 | 3,250 | 3,500 |
| 5 minute repeater, gold, 45-52mm, OF | 3,250 | 3,500 | 3,750 |
| HC | 3,500 | 3,750 | 4,000 |
| Minute repeater, gold, 45-52mm, OF | 3,500 | 3,750 | 4,000 |
| HC | 3,750 | 4,000 | 4,250 |
| OF w/split chrono. | 5,000 | 5,500 | 6,000 |
| HC w/split chrono. | 7,500 | 8,000 | 8,500 |
| OF w/cal. & moonphase | 9,000 | 9,500 | 10,000 |
| HC w/chrono., cal. & moonphase | 10,000 | 12,000 | 14,000 |
| Tourbillion, gold, 48-55mm, OF | 30,000 | 35,000 | 40,000 |
| Detent chronometer, gold, 48-52mm , OF | 4,000 | 5,000 | 6,000 |
| HC | 5,500 | 6,500 | 7,500 |
| Perp. moonphase cal. w/min.rep. and chrono, OF | 20,000 | 25,000 | 30,000 |
| HC | 30,000 | 35,000 | 40,000 |

# ALBERT H. POTTER & CO.
(Note: For further information on Potter timepieces, see U.S. Watch Section.)

**Albert Potter**, 22 jewels, hunting case, helical hair spring, detent escapement.

| TYPE – DESCRIPTION | Avg | Ex-Fn | Mint |
|---|---|---|---|
| Time only, gold, 45- 48mm, OF | $4,000 | $5,000 | $6,000 |
| HC | 5,000 | 6,000 | 7,000 |
| Pocket chronometer, pivoted detent ,free-spring balance, porcelain dial, bridge mvt., re-cased (silver), 58mm, C.1879. | 5,500 | 6,500 | 7,500 |
| Calendar, nickel, offset seconds and days of week dials, SW, 18K, 50mm, OF, C.1800 | 8,000 | 9,000 | 10,000 |
| Rare lever, SW, 19J, nickel mvt., 1/2 moon-shaped plate for barrel & train, white enamel dial, triple signed, lever with counterpoise on pallet,18k, 52mm, HC, C.1882 | 100,000 | 120,000 | 140,000 |

Watches listed in this book are priced at the collectable fair market **value** at the retail level, as complete watches having an original case, an original white enamel dial, and with the entire original movement in good working order with no repairs needed, unless otherwise noted.

| TYPE – DESCRIPTION | Avg | Ex-Fn | Mint |
|---|---|---|---|
| Regulator dial (center minute hand, offset hours, offset seconds), | | | |
| half moon- shaped nickel mvt., 18K, 50mm, OF, C.1880 | $18,000 | $23,000 | $30,000 |
| Minute repeater, gold, 46-52mm, OF | 15,000 | 18,000 | 20,000 |
| HC | 20,000 | 22,000 | 25,000 |
| Detent chronometer, gold, 48-52mm, OF | 15,000 | 18,000 | 20,000 |
| HC | 18,000 | 20,000 | 22,000 |
| Perp. moonphase cal. w/min. repeater, HC | 28,000 | 35,000 | 40,000 |
| Perp. moonphase cal. w/min. rep. & chrono.,HC | 32,000 | 35,000 | 38,000 |

# PRIOR, GEORGE
### LONDON

George Prior born in 1793 and died in 1830. He was a recipient of two prestigious awards and well known for his pieces for the turkish market. He also produced tortoise shell and triple-case watches with the outer case featuring wood with silver inlay. He made gold watches with Oriental chased cases, watches with pierced outer cases and triple-cased enamel engraved and repeaters.

| TYPE – DESCRIPTION | Avg | Ex-Fn | Mint |
|---|---|---|---|
| Verge, pair case, plain silver, 50mm, OF | $500 | $550 | $600 |
| Verge, pair case w/ repousee, silver, 50mm, OF | 1,000 | 1,200 | 1,500 |
| Verge, triple case w/ tortoise shell, silver, 56mm, OF | 1,500 | 1,800 | 2,000 |
| Verge, pair case, GOLD, 48-52mm, OF | 2,000 | 2,300 | 2,800 |
| Verge, pair case, GOLD & enamel, 48-54mm, OF | 2,800 | 3,000 | 3,500 |
| 1/4 hr. repeater, pair case, GOLD & enamel, 50mm, OF | 6,000 | 7,000 | 8,000 |

**George Prior,** 52mm, dial and engine turned silver hunter's case, verge fusee, KW KS, white porcelain signed dial, Ca. 1830.

# ROLEX WATCH CO.
Swiss

Rolex was founded by Hans Wilsdorf in 1905 & in <u>1908</u> the trade-mark **"Rolex"** was officially registered. In 1926, they made the first real waterproof wrist watch and called it the **"Oyster."** In 1931, Rolex introduced a self-wind movement which they called **"Perpetual"**. In 1945, they introduced the **"Date-Just"** which showed the day of the month. The **"Submariner"** was introduced in 1953 and in 1954 the **"GMT Master"** model. In 1956, a "Day-Date" model was released which indicates the day of the month (in numbers) and the day of the week (in letters.)

Rolex, 42-43mm, 17 jewels, three adjustments, cam regulator, exposed winding gears.

## ROLEX ESTIMATED PRODUCTION DATES

| DATE–SERIAL # | DATE–SERIAL # | DATE–SERIAL # |
|---|---|---|
| 1925 — 25,000 | 1949 — 608,000 | 1973— 3,741,000 |
| 1926 — 27,500 | 1950 — 673,500 | 1974— 4,000,000 |
| 1927 — 30,500 | 1951 — 735,500 | 1975— 4,260,000 |
| 1928 — 33,000 | 1952 — 804,000 | 1976— 4,530,000 |
| 1929 — 35,500 | 1953 — 869,000 | 1977— 5,000,000 |
| 1930 — 38,000 | 1954 — 935,000 | 1978— 5,480,000 |
| 1931 — 40,000 | 1955—1,010,000 | 1979— 5,960,000 |
| 1932 — 43,000 | 1956—1,095,000 | 1980— 6,430,000 |
| 1933 — 49,000 | 1957—1,167,000 | 1981— 6,910,000 |
| 1934 — 55,000 | 1958—1,245,000 | 1982— 7,380,000 |
| 1935 — 62,000 | 1959—1,323,000 | 1983— 7,860,000 |
| 1936 — 82,000 | 1960—1,401,000 | 1984— 8,340,000 |
| 1937 — 98,000 | 1961—1,485,000 | 1985— 8,810,000 |
| 1938—118,000 | 1962—1,557,000 | 1986— 9,300,000 |
| 1939—136,000 | 1963—1,635,000 | 1987— 9,760,000 |
| 1940—165,000 | 1964—1,713,000 | 1987 1/2-9,999,999 |
| 1941—194,000 | 1965—1,791,000 | 1987 3/4-R000,001 |
| 1942—224,000 | 1966—1,870,000 | 1988 — R999,999 |
| 1943—253,000 | 1967—2,164,000 | 1989 — L000,001 |
| 1944—284,000 | 1968—2,426,000 | 1990 — L999,999 |
| 1945—348,000 | 1969—2,689,000 | 1990 1/2-E000,001 |
| 1946—413,000 | 1970—2,952,000 | 1991 1/4-E999,999 |
| 1947—478,000 | 1971—3,215,000 | 1991 1/2-X000,001 |
| 1948—543,000 | 1972—3,478,000 | 1991 3/4-N000,001 |
| | | 1992 1/4-C000,001 |

The above list is provided for determining the APPROXIMATE age of your watch. Match serial number with date. Watches were not necessarily sold in the exact order of manufactured date.The above list was furnished with the help of TOM ENGLE.

Hans Wilsdorf started in 1905 with his brother-in-law using the name of Wilsdorf & Davis. They used movement supplier Aegler in Bienne and bought cases in London. In 1919 Wilsdorf started the "Manufacture des Montres Rolex", the movements were manufactured in Bienne but finished in Geneva. 1950 the **Turn-o-graph** was used, the forerunner of the **SUBMARINER.**

ROLEX, split seconds Chronograph, register, S.S. case.

ROLEX, Masonic watch, mother of pearl dial, 15J.

| TYPE – DESCRIPTION | Avg | Ex-Fn | Mint |
|---|---|---|---|
| 17J, silver, 45mm, OF, C. 1920's.......................................................... | $200 | $250 | $325 |
| 17J, 3 adj., CAM regulator, 14K, 43mm, OF, C. 1920 ..................... | 500 | 600 | 750 |
| 1/4 Century Club, 17J, 14K, 41mm, OF, C. 1940 .......................... | 700 | 800 | 900 |
| Thin line, 17J, 18K, 42mm, OF, C. 1940.................................... | 700 | 800 | 950 |
| Time only, gold, 40-44mm, 18K, OF......................................... | 500 | 700 | 900 |
| HC .......... | 700 | 900 | 1,000 |
| Time only, gold, 45-50mm, 18K, OF......................................... | 800 | 900 | 1,000 |
| HC .......................................................................... | 1,200 | 1,400 | 1,600 |
| Duo dial, fancy-shaped, 17J, 18K/WG, OF, 41mm, C. 1930.......... | 2,000 | 2,500 | 3,000 |
| $20 dollar coin watch in closed case, triple signed, C.1950............ | 2,500 | 3,000 | 3,500 |
| World time watch, gold, 45-52mm ................................................. | 9,000 | 10,000 | 11,000 |
| Chronograph, split seconds, register, S.S. case, 50mm................... | 3,000 | 4,000 | 5,000 |
| Masonic, mother of pearl dial, silver triangler case, Ca.1930s ........ | 3,500 | 4,000 | 4,500 |

**Romilly**, Gold , verge, pair case with polychrome enamel & scene, 52mm, OF, Ca.1730.

## ROMILLY, JEAN
PARIS

Became a master Watchmaker in 1752 after studying in Geneva and Paris. In 1755, he completed a repeater with beating seconds and a large balance (at one oscillation per second ). He also made watches with a 8 day power reserve. Also known for his very ornate paintings on enamel.

| TYPE – DESCRIPTION | Avg | Ex-Fn | Mint |
|---|---|---|---|
| Time only, KW, verge, silver, 46-52mm OF | $700 | $900 | $1,200 |
| Time & Calendar, verge, silver, 50mm, OF | 1,500 | 1,650 | 1,800 |
| Gold , verge, pair case, plain, 48mm, OF | 2,000 | 2,200 | 2,400 |
| Gold , verge, pair case w/ enamel & scene, Ca.1730, 52mm, OF.... | 4,000 | 4,500 | 5,500 |
| 1/4 repeater, **SILVER**, 52mm, OF | 2,500 | 2,800 | 3,500 |
| 1/4 repeater, **GOLD**, 54mm, OF | 3,500 | 4,000 | 4,500 |

## ROBERT ROSKELL
Liverpool

Roskell was active from 1798-1830 and worked in both Liverpool and London. He made fine rack lever fusees and gold dial watches. Other family members also produced watches for many years in Liverpool.

R. Roskell, 47mm, bar style movement, cylinder escapement, Ca. 1850.

Roskell, fusee, table pierced & "engraved" & note the foot of balance cock is not pierced ,KW KS, Ca. 1830.

| TYPE – DESCRIPTION | Avg | Ex-Fn | Mint |
|---|---|---|---|
| KW, (Swiss ebauche) 15J, silver, 48mm, OF, C. 1830-70 | $65 | $90 | $110 |
| KW, (Swiss) 15J, silver, 46-48mm, HC, C. 1830-70 | 75 | 90 | 130 |
| KW, 13J, dust cover, fancy gold dial, 18K, 47mm, OF, C.1830-70 | 250 | 325 | 375 |

Roskell, 48mm, lever escapement, KW KS, Ca.1830.          Roskell, 55mm, KW KS, Ca. 1825

| TYPE – DESCRIPTION | Avg | Ex-Fn | Mint |
|---|---|---|---|
| Rack lever fusee, porcelain dial, silver, hallmarked, OF, C.1870.... | $375 | $435 | $500 |
| 2 day marine chronometer fusee, spring detent escapement, helical hairspring, 54 hr. wind ind., gimbal & box ................ | 1,800 | 2,000 | 2,500 |
| Debaufre escapement, KW KS, silver, 55mm, OF................... ★ ★ | 3,000 | 3,200 | 3,500 |

**Debaufre escapement,**
D-shaped & inclined pallet

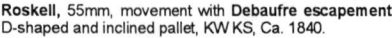

Roskell, 55mm, movement with **Debaufre escapement,**
D-shaped and inclined pallet, KW KS, Ca. 1840.

Robert Roskell, 52mm, London, fusee, spring detent escapement, helical hairspring, 54 hr. wind ind., KW KS.

# ROSKOPF
## Swiss

Maker of pin lever, early low cost stem wind watches, often found with fancy dials. A **true** Roskopf watch has only *3 wheels* in its train of gears.

Roskopf, multi-colored blue enamel dial, nail set.

Roskopf, 45mm, pin lever escapement, 3 wheel train.

| TYPE – DESCRIPTION | Avg | Ex-Fn | Mint |
|---|---|---|---|
| 4J, pin lever, 3 wheel train, nail set, base metal, OF, Ca. 1885 ...... | $45 | $55 | $80 |
| Fancy dial, oversize plain case, 55mm, OF, Ca. 1880 .................... | 60 | 75 | 95 |
| Fancy enamel dial, fancy enamel case, 55mm, OF, Ca. 1880 ........ | 100 | 135 | 175 |

**Roskopf,** multi-colored enamel with blue & purple Butterflies & silver case, nail set.

# SANDOZ & FILS
### SWISS

Large family of watchmakers in the La Chaux-de-Fonds area. Known for repeating watches and pocket chronometers of fine quality.

| TYPE – DESCRIPTION | Avg | Ex-Fn | Mint |
|---|---|---|---|
| Time only, gold, 40- 44mm, OF | $300 | $375 | $450 |
| HC | 450 | 500 | 600 |
| Time only, gold, 45- 50mm, OF | 500 | 600 | 700 |
| HC | 650 | 750 | 850 |
| Chronograph, gold, 45-50mm, OF | 700 | 750 | 800 |
| Split second chronograph, gold, 45-52mm, OF | 1,600 | 1,800 | 2,000 |
| HC w/register | 2,250 | 2,500 | 2,750 |
| 5 minute repeater, gold, 45-52mm, OF | 2,500 | 2,650 | 2,850 |
| HC | 3,000 | 3,300 | 3,750 |
| Minute repeater, gold, 45-52mm, OF | 2,500 | 2,800 | 3,000 |
| HC | 3,000 | 3,500 | 4,000 |
| OF w/split chrono. | 5,000 | 5,500 | 6,000 |
| HC w/split chrono. | 7,500 | 8,000 | 8,500 |
| OF w/cal. & moonphase | 9,000 | 9,500 | 10,000 |
| HC w/chrono., cal. & moonphase | 10,000 | 12,000 | 14,000 |
| Tourbillion, gold, 48-55mm, OF | 25,000 | 30,000 | 35,000 |
| Detent chronometer, gold, 48-52mm , OF | 5,000 | 6,000 | 7,000 |
| HC | 5,500 | 6,500 | 7,500 |
| World time watch, gold, 48-52mm, OF | 8,000 | 10,000 | 12,000 |
| Perp. moonphase cal. w/min.rep. and chrono, OF | 25,000 | 30,000 | 35,000 |
| HC | 30,000 | 35,000 | 40,000 |

**Sandoz,** 52mm, KW, nickel bridge, gold train, Ca.1880.

# THOMAS RUSSELL & SONS
### London

Thomas Russell & Sons produced quality early keyless watches including Karrusels and chronometers. (Circa 1870-1910 )

| TYPE – DESCRIPTION | Avg | Ex-Fn | Mint |
|---|---|---|---|
| Time only, gold, 45-48mm, OF | $600 | $800 | $900 |
| Chronograph, gold, 45-50mm, OF | 1,250 | 1,400 | 1,650 |
| Split second chronograph, gold, 45-52mm, OF | 1,800 | 2,000 | 2,500 |
| Minute repeater, gold, 46-52mm, OF | 3,500 | 3,800 | 4,000 |
| HC | 3,850 | 4,250 | 4,500 |
| Karrusel, 18K, 51mm, OF, C. 1890 | 4,000 | 4,500 | 5,000 |

# TAVANNES
Swiss

| TYPE – DESCRIPTION | Avg | Ex-Fn | Mint |
|---|---|---|---|
| 15J, GF, 35mm, HC, C. 1910 | $90 | $100 | $125 |
| 15J, 14K, 35mm, HC, C. 1910 | 225 | 250 | 300 |
| 17J, 14K, 45mm, OF, C. 1915 | 225 | 250 | 300 |
| 21J, 14K, 45mm, OF, C. 1920 | 250 | 275 | 325 |
| Enamel & gold, 14K, 45mm, OF, C. 1925 | 275 | 300 | 375 |

# TIFFANY & CO.

In 1837 Charles Lewis Tiffany opened a store with John P. Young. They enlarged this operation in 1841, with the help of J.L. Eliss, and imported fine jewelry, watches and clocks from Europe. They incorporated as Tiffany & Co. in 1853. Tiffany made clocks, on special order, in New York around the mid-1800's. About 1874 Tiffany & Co. started a watch factory in Geneva but with little success. Four years later Patek, Philippe & Co. assumed the management of their Geneva watch business. The watch machinery was returned to America. Tiffany, Young & Ellis had been a client of Patek, Philippe & Co. since 1849. Tiffany & Co. introduced Patek, Philippe to the American market in 1885. Audemars, Piguet and International Watch Co. also made watches for this esteemed company. Tiffany & Co. sells watches of simple elegance as well as watches with complications such as chronographs, moon phases, repeaters, etc.

| TYPE – DESCRIPTION | Avg | Ex-Fn | Mint |
|---|---|---|---|
| Time only, gold, 40- 44mm, OF | $375 | $425 | $500 |
| HC | 525 | 625 | 700 |
| Time only, gold, 40-44mm, 18K case & enamel on bezel, OF | 1,500 | 1,800 | 2,200 |
| Time only, gold, 45- 50mm, OF | 800 | 850 | 900 |
| HC | 900 | 950 | 1,000 |
| Chronograph, gold, 45-50mm, OF | 1,450 | 1,600 | 1,800 |
| HC | 1,800 | 1,900 | 2,000 |
| OF w/register | 1,600 | 1,700 | 1,900 |
| Split second chronograph, gold, 45-52mm, OF | 2,800 | 3,000 | 3,250 |
| HC | 3,500 | 3,800 | 4,000 |

Tiffany & Co., 43mm, enamel on bezel, 18K.

Tiffany & Co., 50mm, 25J., split-second chronograph, made by Ekegren.

Tiffany & Co., flat minute repeater, 45mm, 29 jewels, made by Patek, Philippe & Co., ca. 1911.

| TYPE – DESCRIPTION | Avg | Ex-Fn | Mint |
|---|---|---|---|
| 5 minute repeater, gold, 46-52mm, OF | $3,500 | $4,000 | $4,500 |
| HC | 4,000 | 4,500 | 5,000 |
| OF w/split chrono. | 6,000 | 6,500 | 7,000 |
| HC w/split chrono. | 6,850 | 7,250 | 7,500 |
| Minute repeater, gold, 46-52mm, OF | 3,500 | 3,750 | 4,000 |
| HC | 4,500 | 5,000 | 5,500 |
| by P. P. & Co., flat, 29J., gold, 45mm, OF, C.1912 | 9,000 | 12,000 | 15,000 |
| OF w/split chrono. & register | 8,000 | 9,000 | 10,000 |
| HC w/split chrono. & register | 9,000 | 10,000 | 12,000 |
| HC w/chrono., cal. & moonphase | 12,000 | 14,000 | 16,000 |
| World time watch, gold, 48-52mm, OF | 12,000 | 14,000 | 16,000 |
| Perpetual moonphase calendar, gold, OF | 9,000 | 10,000 | 12,000 |
| Perp. moonphase cal. w/min. rep. and chrono, OF | 35,000 | 40,000 | 45,000 |
| HC | 40,000 | 45,000 | 50,000 |

# TIMING & REPEATING WATCH CO.
### Geneva

Timing & Rerpeating W. Co., chronograph movement Patented Sept. 23, 1880 - England Pat. # 3224.

Timing & Repeating W. CO., chronograph movement Patented Sept. 23, 1880 - England Pat. # 3224.

| TYPE – DESCRIPTION | Avg | Ex-Fn | Mint |
|---|---|---|---|
| Chronograph, 17J, GF, 48mm, OF, C. 1900 | $150 | $175 | $250 |
| Chronograph w/register, 17J, GF, 48mm, OF, C. 1900 | 200 | 250 | 275 |
| Chronograph, 17J, gilt mvt., silver, 49mm, HC, C. 1900 | 250 | 300 | 325 |

# TISSOT

Swiss

The firm of Chs. Tissot & Fils was founded in 1853 in Le Locle by Charles Tissot. This skilled watchmaker worked from his home and in 1907 a factory was started. In 1971 the worlds first plastic wrist watch was made.

| TYPE – DESCRIPTION | Avg | Ex-Fn | Mint |
|---|---|---|---|
| Time only, gold, 40- 44mm, OF | $350 | $425 | $500 |
| HC | 475 | 550 | 650 |
| Time only, gold, 45- 50mm, OF | 500 | 600 | 700 |
| HC | 650 | 750 | 850 |
| 2-Train 1/4 second jump watch, silver, 50mm, | 700 | 800 | 900 |
| 2-Train 1/4 second jump watch, gold, 50mm, | 1,700 | 2,000 | 2,500 |
| Chronograph, gold, 45-50mm, OF | 800 | 850 | 900 |
| Split second chronograph, gold, 45-52mm, OF | 1,800 | 2,000 | 2,200 |
| HC w/register | 2,850 | 3,250 | 3,500 |
| 5 minute repeater, gold, 45-52mm, OF | 3,250 | 3,500 | 3,750 |
| HC | 3,500 | 3,750 | 4,000 |
| Minute repeater, gold, 45-52mm, OF | 3,500 | 3,750 | 4,000 |
| HC | 3,750 | 4,000 | 4,250 |
| OF w/split chrono. | 5,000 | 5,500 | 6,000 |
| HC w/split chrono. | 7,500 | 8,000 | 8,500 |
| OF w/cal. & moonphase | 9,000 | 9,500 | 10,000 |
| HC w/chrono., cal. & moonphase | 10,000 | 12,000 | 14,000 |
| Tourbillion, gold, 48-55mm, OF | 38,000 | 45,000 | 50,000 |
| Detent chronometer, gold, 48-52mm , OF | 5,000 | 6,000 | 7,000 |
| HC | 5,500 | 6,500 | 7,500 |
| World time watch, gold, 48-52mm, OF | 12,000 | 14,000 | 15,000 |
| Perp. moonphase cal. w/min.rep. and chrono, OF | 25,000 | 30,000 | 35,000 |
| HC | 30,000 | 35,000 | 40,000 |

Tissot, 2-Train 1/4 second jump watch, center sweep hand, enamel dial, 28 J., gold train, 54mm, KWKS, 18K, Ca. 1880.

Tissot, Minute repeater, with chronograph, day date month, moonphase, 27 jewels, 18K, HC, Ca. 1910.

Watches listed in this book are priced at the collectable fair market **value** at the retail level, as complete watches having an original case, an original white enamel dial, and with the entire original movement in good working order with no repairs needed, unless otherwise noted.

# TOBIAS & CO.

M. I. Tobias started a watchmaking career in Liverpool, about 1810 and exported watches to America. About 1820 the company started using movements made in Switzerland the watches were engraved, *Liverpool*. The Tobias family exported watches from about 1810 to 1868. The script *M.I. Tobias* can be misleading the script letter( I) may look like a **(J)**. The watches with a (J) are Swiss made & used a club-tooth escape-wheel made of steel, the Liverpool watches used a (I) & a "ratchet" (sharp-pointed ) escape wheel made of brass.

M. I. Tobias, Liverpool, Fusee, Right angle lever, 15 jewels, diamond end stone, S # 41,383, Ca. 1855.

M. I. Tobias, multi-color gold dial & thin gold case, 52mm.

| TYPE – DESCRIPTION | Avg | Ex-Fn | Mint |
|---|---|---|---|
| KW, 7-15J, silver, 47mm, OF | $75 | $85 | $125 |
| KW,7- 15J, silver, 47mm, HC | 90 | 125 | 175 |
| KW,7-15J, swiss, **gilt dial,** fancy case, **18K,** 48mm,OF | 250 | 300 | 375 |
| KW, lever, fusee, **gold dial, Heavy 18K,** 52mm, HC | 900 | 1,200 | 1,500 |
| KW, rack lever escapement, **Silver,** 56mm, OF | 400 | 500 | 600 |
| HC | 500 | 600 | 700 |
| KW, rack lever escapement, **Gold,** 56mm, OF | 900 | 1,000 | 1,200 |
| HC | 1,100 | 1,300 | 1,500 |
| KW, verge fusee, **multi-color gold dial & THIN case,** 52mm, OF | 500 | 600 | 700 |
| HC | 700 | 800 | 950 |
| Captain's watch, center sec., sub-sec., gold dial, **18K,** 51mm, OF.. | 1,500 | 1,800 | 2,000 |
| **18K,** 51mm, HC | 1,800 | 2,200 | 2,500 |

**Tobias**, (Liverpool), 51mm, OF, 18K, Captain's watch, center sec., subseconds, gold dial.

# TOUCHON & CO.

Swiss

Touchon & Co. started using this name as a trade mark in 1907. They manufactured complex and simple watches. In 1921 they associated with the firm of Wittnauer & Co.

Touchon & Co., 47mm, 29 jewels, minute repeater, open face, jeweled through hammers.

Touchon & Co., 47mm, 29 jewels, split-second chronograph and minute repeater, ca. 1910.

| TYPE – DESCRIPTION | Avg | Ex-Fn | Mint |
|---|---|---|---|
| Time only, gold, 45- 50mm, OF | $450 | $500 | $600 |
| HC | 550 | 650 | 750 |
| 1/4 hr. repeater, gold, 46-52mm, OF | 1,000 | 1,200 | 1,400 |
| HC | 1,500 | 1,800 | 2,000 |
| OF w/chrono. | 1,200 | 1,400 | 1,500 |
| HC w/chrono. | 1,700 | 2,000 | 2,200 |
| OF w/chrono., cal. & moonphase | 3,000 | 3,500 | 4,000 |
| HC w/chrono., cal. & moonphase | 4,500 | 5,500 | 6,500 |
| 5 minute repeater, gold, 46-52mm, OF | 3,000 | 3,500 | 4,000 |
| HC | 3,500 | 4,000 | 4,500 |
| Minute repeater, gold, 46-52mm, OF | 3,500 | 4,000 | 4,500 |
| HC | 4,500 | 5,000 | 5,500 |
| OF w/chrono. & register | 3,750 | 4,250 | 4,750 |
| HC w/chrono. & register | 5,000 | 5,500 | 6,000 |
| OF w/split chrono. | 4,750 | 5,500 | 5,750 |
| HC w/split chrono. & register | 9,000 | 9,500 | 10,000 |
| HC w/chrono., cal. & moonphase | 10,000 | 12,000 | 13,000 |
| World time watch, gold, 48-52mm, OF | 12,000 | 14,000 | 16,000 |
| Perpetual moonphase calendar, gold, OF | 10,000 | 11,000 | 12,000 |
| Perp. moonphase cal. w/min.repeater, HC | 25,000 | 30,000 | 35,000 |
| Perp. moonphase cal. w/min.rep. and chrono., HC | 35,000 | 38,000 | 40,000 |

### COMPARISON OF WATCH SIZES

| U. S. A. | EUROPEAN |
|---|---|
| 10-12 SIZE | 40—44 MM |
| 16 SIZE | 45—48 MM |
| 18 SIZE | 50—52 MM |

# VACHERON & CONSTANTIN

Swiss

The firm of Vacheron & Constantin was officially founded by Abraham Vacheron in 1785, but the association bearing the name today did not come into being until 1819. In these early periods, different grades of watches produced by Vacheron & Constantin bore different names.

## ESTIMATED PRODUCTION DATES

| DATE–SERIAL # | DATE–SERIAL # | DATE–SERIAL # |
|---|---|---|
| 1830 - 30,000 | 1880-170,000 | 1930-410,000 |
| 1835 - 40,000 | 1885-180,000 | 1935-420,000 |
| 1840 - 50,000 | 1890-190,000 | 1940-440,000 |
| 1845 - 60,000 | 1895-223,000 | 1945-464,000 |
| 1850 - 75,000 | 1900-256,000 | 1950-488,000 |
| 1855 - 95,000 | 1905-289,000 | 1955-512,000 |
| 1860-110,000 | 1910-322,000 | 1960-536,000 |
| 1865-125,000 | 1915-355,000 | 1965-560,000 |
| 1870-140,000 | 1920-385,000 | 1970-585,000 |
| 1875-155,000 | 1925-400,000 | |

The above list is provided for determining the APPROXIMATE age of your watch. Match serial number with date. Watches were not necessarily sold in the exact order of manufactured date.

Early movements manufactured with the machines invented by George-Auguste Leschot. The machines were built in the Vacheron Constantin factory Ca. 1839 to 1940. In about 1863 to 1865 V. & C. manufactured a inexpensive watch using the names Abraham Vacheron or Abm. Vacheron also the name of Chossat & Cie.

The association with Leschot, around 1840, catapulted the firm into its position as a top quality manufacturer. Before that time, their watches were typical of Genevese production. Vacheron & Constantin exported many movements to the United States to firms such as Bigelow, Kennard & Co., which were cased domestically, typically in the period 1900-1935. In its early period the firm produced some lovely ladies' enameled watches, later it produced high grade timepieces and complicated watches, & to this day produces fine watches.

Vacheron & Constantin, 44mm, 18 jewels, enamel bezel, 18K, Ca. 1930.

Early bar movement, lever escap., **signed "VACHERON & CONSTANTIN"** time only, KW KS, silver case, Ca.1840-1875.

| TYPE – DESCRIPTION | Avg | Ex-Fn | Mint |
|---|---|---|---|
| Early bar movement, lever escap., **signed Vacheron & Constantin** | | | |
| time only, KW KS, silver case, 30-39mm, OF | $125 | $150 | $200 |
| (same as above) 40-44mm, OF | 175 | 225 | 250 |
| (same as above) 45-48mm, OF | 200 | 250 | 325 |
| Early Le-Pine bar movement, duplex escap., GOLD & ENAMEL | | | |
| KW KS, **signed Vacheron & Constantin**, 49mm, OF | 4,500 | 5,000 | 5,500 |
| Time only, 18K gold & **enamel bezel**, 40-44mm, OF | 1,200 | 1,300 | 1,500 |

Vacheron & Constantin, 49mm, Early Le-Pine bar style movement, duplex escapement, GOLD & ENAMEL, KW KS, **signed Vacheron & Constantin**, 49mm, OF, Ca. 1840.

**Vacheron & Constantin,** Gold coin 50 pesos 900 fine, coin hollowed out to receive watch, LEFT view shows dial & movement.

| TYPE – DESCRIPTION | Avg | Ex-Fn | Mint |
|---|---|---|---|
| Time only, 18K gold, 40-44mm, OF | $700 | $800 | $900 |
| HC | 1,000 | 1,200 | 1,500 |
| Time only, gold, 45-50mm, OF | 1,200 | 1,500 | 1,800 |
| HC | 1,800 | 2,000 | 2,200 |
| X-thin, 17J., **Aluminum,** weight =20 grains, OF, C. 1940 | 2,500 | 3,000 | 3,500 |
| Desk chronometer, wooden box, 21J., silver, 60mm,OF, C.1943 | 2,200 | 2,500 | 2,800 |
| Gold coin 50 pesos 900 fine, coin hollowed out to receive watch | 3,000 | 3,500 | 4,000 |

V. & C., Chronograph, for the corps of engineers USA, 20 jewels, enamel dial, nail set, 50mm, Ca.1919.

V. & C., Astronomic with moon phases, perpetual calendar, minute repeater, split-second chronograph, 1905.

| TYPE – DESCRIPTION | Avg | Ex-Fn | Mint |
|---|---|---|---|
| Chronograph, **SILVER**, 45-50mm, OF | $1,200 | $1,500 | $1,800 |
| Chronograph, **GOLD**, 45-50mm, OF | 2,500 | 2,750 | 3,000 |
| HC | 3,000 | 3,500 | 4,000 |
| OF w/register | 2,750 | 3,000 | 3,250 |
| HC w/register | 3,500 | 4,000 | 4,500 |

V. & C., 40mm, wolf tooth winding, open face.

V. & C., 40mm, 31J., Min. repeater, slide activated, OF.

| TYPE – DESCRIPTION | Avg | Ex-Fn | Mint |
|---|---|---|---|
| Split second chronograph, gold, 45-52mm, OF | $5,500 | $5,750 | $6,000 |
| HC | 6,500 | 7,000 | 7,500 |
| OF w/register | 6,000 | 6,500 | 7,000 |
| HC w/register | 7,500 | 7,750 | 8,000 |
| Minute repeater, gold, 46-52mm, OF | 6,500 | 7,500 | 8,000 |
| HC | 12,000 | 14,000 | 16,000 |
| OF w/chrono. | 8,000 | 9,000 | 10,000 |
| HC w/chrono. | 13,000 | 15,000 | 17,000 |
| OF w/chrono. & register | 8,500 | 9,500 | 10,500 |
| HC w/chrono. & register | 14,000 | 16,000 | 18,000 |
| OF w/split chrono. | 11,000 | 12,000 | 13,000 |
| HC w/split chrono. | 16,000 | 18,000 | 20,000 |
| OF w/split chrono. & register | 12,000 | 14,000 | 15,000 |
| HC w/split chrono. & register | 17,000 | 19,000 | 22,000 |
| OF w/chrono., cal. & moonphase | 18,000 | 20,000 | 22,000 |
| Tourbillion, gold, 48-55mm, OF | 65,000 | 75,000 | 85,000 |
| World time watch, gold, 48-52mm, OF | 55,000 | 65,000 | 75,000 |
| Perp. moonphase cal. w/min. repeater, OF | 65,000 | 75,000 | 85,000 |
| HC | 70,000 | 80,000 | 90,000 |
| Perp. moonphase cal. w/min. rep. and split sec. chrono., OF | 70,000 | 80,000 | 90,000 |
| Perp. moonphase cal. w/min. rep. and split sec. chrono., HC | 100,000 | 110,000 | 120,000 |

V. & C., extra thin and light weight (20 grains), about 12 size, 44mm, OF, 17 jewels, Ca. 1940.

V. & C., World time, revolving 24 hour dial, 31 citys of the world, 18 jewels, 45mm, Ca. 1945

# ZENITH
## Swiss

Zenith watch and clock factory was founded in 1865 by George Farvre Jacot. They mass produced watches of different grades in large quantities. By 1920 they had manufactured 2,000,000 watches.

ZENITH, Gold alarm watch, enamel dial, 17 jewels, 50mm, Ca. 1930

| TYPE – DESCRIPTION | Avg | Ex-Fn | Mint |
|---|---|---|---|
| Time only, gold, 40-44mm, OF | $275 | $325 | $400 |
| HC | 400 | 450 | 500 |
| Time only, gold, 40-44mm, with enamel on bezel, 18K, OF | 600 | 700 | 800 |
| Time only, gold, 45-50mm, OF | 400 | 500 | 600 |
| HC | 500 | 600 | 700 |
| Alarm watch, 17J., nail set, two barrels, gold, 50mm, C.1930 | 1,500 | 1,600 | 1,750 |
| Chronograph, gold, 45-50mm, OF | 900 | 1,000 | 1,100 |
| HC | 1,000 | 1,100 | 1,200 |
| Minute repeater, gold, 46-52mm, OF | 2,800 | 3,000 | 3,200 |
| HC | 3,500 | 3,750 | 4,000 |
| OF w/split chrono. | 4,500 | 5,000 | 5,500 |
| HC w/split chrono. | 7,000 | 7,500 | 8,000 |
| OF w/chrono., cal. & moonphase | 6,500 | 7,000 | 7,500 |
| HC w/chrono., cal. & moonphase | 9,000 | 9,500 | 10,000 |
| Perp. moonphase cal. w/min. rep. and chrono., OF | 22,000 | 25,000 | 27,000 |
| HC | 25,000 | 28,000 | 30,000 |

ZENITH, 44mm, 18K, enamel on case, open face, 17 jewels, signed ZENITH, Ca. 1930's.

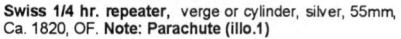

Swiss 1/4 hr. repeater, verge or cylinder, silver, 55mm, Ca. 1820, OF. **Note: Parachute (illo.1)**    Swiss 1/4 hr. rep., pump, verge or cylinder, 18K, 52mm, OF, Ca.1800s. **(illo.2)**

## PRE–1850 REPEATERS

| TYPE – DESCRIPTION | Avg | Ex-Fn | Mint |
|---|---|---|---|
| Swiss 1/4 hr. rep., verge or cylinder, silver, 55mm, OF (illo.1)...... | $1,000 | $1,200 | $1,500 |
| Swiss 1/4 hr. rep., pump, verge or cylinder, 18K, 52mm, OF, C.1800s (illo.2) ............................................. | 1,500 | 2,000 | 2,500 |
| Swiss 1/4 hr., automaton on dial (2 figures), gilt, verge, KW, 55mm, OF, early 1800s ..................................... | 2,500 | 3,000 | 3,500 |
| Swiss 1/4 hr. musical repeater disc-driven, KW KS, cylinder,18k, 57mm, OF, C. 1825, (illo.3)............................. | 4,000 | 5,500 | 6,000 |
| Swiss 1/4 hr. repeater, 32-35mm, KW KS, gold, Ca. 1850, (illo.4) | 1,800 | 2,000 | 2,500 |

Swiss 1/4 hr. musical repeater disc-driven, cylinder, Kw KS, 18k, 57mm, OF, C. 1825, **(illo.3)**    Swiss 1/4 hr. repeater, 32-35mm, cylinder escapement, Swiss bar movement, KW KS, gold, Ca. 1850, **(illo.4)**

French, 1/4 hr. repeater, gold and enamel superior quality, enameled scene, outer case with pearls, verge, 20K, 52mm, OF, C.1785. (illo.5)

1/4 hr. repeater, Virgule escap., KW, 18K, 46mm, OF, Ca. 1840. (illo.6)

| TYPE – DESCRIPTION | Avg | Ex-Fn | Mint |
|---|---|---|---|
| Skeletonized 1/4 hr., cylinder, Swiss, 18K, 58mm, OF, C.1810...... | $4,000 | $4,500 | $5,000 |
| French 1/4 hr. repeater, 18K gold and enamel, verge, enameled scene, superior quality, outer pearls, 52mm, OF, C.1785 (illo.5) ...... | 6,000 | 7,000 | 7,500 |
| 1/4 hr. repeater, Virgule escap., KW, 18K, 46mm, OF (illo.6)........ | 3,000 | 3,200 | 3,500 |
| 1/4 hr. rep., erotic scene (concealed in cuvette), automated, multi-color gold figures, verge, pump 1/4 hr., 18K, 54mm, OF, C.1800... | 3,500 | 4,000 | 4,250 |
| French or Swiss pump 1/4 hr. repeater, free standing barrel, **Thin gold** case, cylinder escape., tapered bridges , Ca.1790-1835, (illo.7) ..... | 2,000 | 3,000 | 3,500 |
| 1/4 hr. repeater, repousse pair case, verge, 22K, 49mm (illo.8) ..... | 5,500 | 6,000 | 7,000 |
| 1/4 hr. repeater, musical, 25 musical tines, cylinder, center seconds, KW, 18K, 58mm,OF, C. 1820 (illo.9) .......... | 5,000 | 6,000 | 7,500 |

French or Swiss pump 1/4 hr. repeater, free standing barrel, cylinder escapement, tapered bridges, Thin gold engine turned case, Ca. 1790-1835. (illo.7)

**1/4 hour verge repeater,** 49mm, 22K gold repousse pair case, repeating on an inner bell, repeat mechanism is activated from the pendant, ca. 1750-1780, **(illo.8)**

**1/4 hour repeater, musical,** 25 musical tines, cylinder, center seconds, KW, 18K, 58mm, OF, Ca.1820, **(illo.9 )**

**1/4 hour repeater,** verge (London, Dutch), pierced inner case, repousee outer case, gold, 49mm, C.1750, **(illo.10)**

**1/4 Hr. repeating coach watch,** with alarm,120mm diameter, verge fusee, silver repousse case, ca.1730-40. **(illo. 11)**

| TYPE – DESCRIPTION | Avg | Ex-Fn | Mint |
|---|---|---|---|
| Early 1/4 hr. rep., Paris (Clouzier) gilt dial w/ enamel hour cartouches, verge, gilt & shagreen case, 58mm, OF, C.1700 | $7,000 | $8,000 | $8,500 |
| 1/4 hr. rep., verge (London, Dutch), pierced inner case, repousee outer case, gold, 49mm, C.1750 (illo.10) | 5,500 | 6,000 | 7,000 |
| 1/4 hr. repeating coach watch w/alarm, verge, fusee, silver repousee case, 120mm, C. 1730 (illo. 11) | 8,000 | 9,000 | 11,000 |
| 1/4 hr. repeater with automaton dial, verge, Swiss, KW, 3 automated figures on dial and carillon chimes, silver, 52mm, OF, C. 1790. | 2,500 | 3,000 | 3,250 |
| 1/4 hr. repeater, London, gilt & shagreen paircase, verge, extremely fine, 56mm, OF, C.1700s | 4,000 | 4,250 | 4,500 |
| Gold & enamel. 1/4 hr. repeater, London, cylinder, Fusee, paircase, enamel on outer case, 18K, 48mm, C. 1790 | 4,000 | 4,500 | 5,000 |
| Swiss, 1/4 hr. pump repeater, w/ automaton, verge, 18K, 54mm, OF, C. 1800 | 4,500 | 5,500 | 6,000 |
| Virgule escapement, 1/4 hr. repeater, fancy gold & multi-dial, London, KW, 18K, OF, C. 1840 | 2,800 | 3,000 | 3,500 |

# REPEATERS

1/4 hour repeater, 17 jewels, nail set, gun metal case, 49mm, C. 1910. (illo.12)

1/4 hour repeater with chronograph, gun metal base-metal or gold filled, 49-50mm, (illo.13)

| TYPE – DESCRIPTION | Avg | Ex-Fn | Mint |
|---|---|---|---|
| 1/4 hr. repeater, 17J, gun metal, 49-50mm, C. 1910 (illo.12) | $400 | $500 | $600 |
| 1/4 hr. repeater, 17J, silver, 49-50mm, OF, C. 1910 | 500 | 600 | 700 |
| 1/4 hr. repeater, 17J, silver, 49-50mm, HC, C. 1910 | 600 | 700 | 900 |
| 1/4 hr. rep. w/chrono.,17J, base metal gun metal or GF, OF 49-50mm, C.1910 (illo.13) | 600 | 750 | 950 |
| 1/4 hr. rep. w/chrono.,17J, base metal, gun metal or GF, HC 49-50mm, C.1910 | 700 | 800 | 1,000 |

1/4 hr. repeater with Calendar, 17J, gold filled, 3/4 plate,   1/4 hour repeater, 55mm, 2 Jacquemarts, gilt case. (illo.15)
open face, 50mm, C. 1910 (illo.14)

| TYPE – DESCRIPTION | Avg | Ex-Fn | Mint |
|---|---|---|---|
| 1/4 hr. repeater with Calendar, 17J, gun metal or gold filled, 3/4 plate, OF, 49-50mm, C. 1910 (illo.14) | $600 | $700 | $800 |
| Swiss 1/4 hr. repeater w/moonphase & calendar, 17J, 18K, 53mm, HC, C. 1900 | 3,000 | 3,500 | 4,000 |
| 55mm, 1/4 repeater, 2 Jacquemarts, gilt case, (illo.15) | 2,000 | 2,300 | 2,800 |
| Swiss 1/4 hr. repeater, **Erotic Scene**, 14K, HC, 50-54mm, ALL ORIGINAL, ( note: beware of fakes ), (illo.16) | 2,000 | 3,000 | 4,000 |

Swiss 1/4 hour repeater, **Erotic Scene** with automaton action dial, 14K, HC, 50-54mm, **all original,** (illo.16)

## COMPARISON OF WATCH SIZES

| U. S. A. | EUROPEAN |
|---|---|
| 10-12  SIZE | 40—44 MM |
| 16     SIZE | 45—48 MM |
| 18     SIZE | 50—54 MM |

**Minute Repeater**, 20J, Swiss, gilt mvt., gun metal, 52mm, HC, C.1910. (illo.17)

**Swiss minute repeater**, 54mm, jeweled through hammers, 14k case. (illo.18)

| TYPE – DESCRIPTION | Avg | Ex-Fn | Mint |
|---|---|---|---|
| Min. rep., 20J, Swiss, gilt mvt., gun metal, 52mm, **OF**, 1910 ......... | $1,000 | $1,100 | $1,200 |
| Min. rep., 20J, Swiss, gilt mvt., gun metal, 52mm, **HC**, Ca.1910 (illo.17)................................................. | 1,200 | 1,300 | 1,500 |
| Min. rep., 17J, Swiss, gilt, 18K, 52mm, HC, C. 1910 ...................... | 2,000 | 2,300 | 2,500 |
| Min. rep., 32 J, Swiss, gilt, 18K, 54mm, HC, C. 1910 ..................... | 2,200 | 2,400 | 2,800 |
| Min. rep., 32 J, Swiss, porcelain dial, 14K, OF, C. 1905 (illo.18).. | 2,000 | 2,300 | 2,600 |
| Min. rep., 32 J, Swiss, porcelain dial, 18K, OF, C. 1905 (illo.19).. | 2,300 | 2,500 | 3,000 |
| Min. repeater, Self contained, (activated from button on crown) 25J, 14K, OF, C. 1915............................................................. | 3,500 | 4,000 | 4,500 |
| Min. repeater, Swiss, ultra thin,32J, 18K, OF, C. 1930.................... | 4,000 | 5,000 | 6,000 |
| Min. repeater, automated Father & Baby Time, 18K, 54mm,(illo.20) ................................................................ | 5,000 | 5,500 | 6,000 |

**Minute Repeater**, 32 J, Swiss, porcelain dial, wolf tooth winding, 18K, OF, C. 1905. (illo.19)

**Father & Baby Time**, automated min. repeater, 54mm, note father and baby striking bell, 18K. (illo.20)

Minute repeating **Clock Watch**, 3/4 plate, a on or off strike activated mechanism, three gongs, tandem-winding barrels, 18K, 48-50mm, HC, Ca.1900 (illo.21)

**Minute repeater**, split second chronograph, Swiss, 18K, 47-50mm, OF, Ca.1900 . (illo.22)

| TYPE – DESCRIPTION | Avg | Ex-Fn | Mint |
|---|---|---|---|
| Min. repeating Clock Watch, 18K, 48-50mm, HC, Ca.1900 (illo.21) | $7,000 | $8,000 | $9,000 |
| Min.rep. w/ chrono, Swiss ,SW, 18K, large 58mm, OF, C.1900..... | 2,500 | 3,000 | 3,500 |
| Min. repeater w/chrono. register, 32J, nickel, very high quality, 18K, 50mm, OF, C. 1900 ......................................................... | 3,000 | 3,500 | 4,000 |
| Min. rep.w/chrono, 30 min. register, Swiss, 36J, 18K ,HC, C.1895 | 3,500 | 4,000 | 4,500 |
| Min. rep., split sec. chrono, Swiss, 18K, 47-50mm, OF, C.1900  (illo.22) ................................................................ | 5,000 | 6,500 | 7,000 |
| Min. rep., split sec. chrono, Swiss, 18K, 47-50mm, HC,C.1900 ................................................................................ | 6,000 | 7,000 | 8,500 |
| Swiss min. repeater, chrono, moonphase and calendar, 30J or more, 18K, 60mm, HC, C. 1895 (illo.23)............................................ | 5,000 | 6,000 | 7,000 |
| Swiss min. repeater, chrono, moonphase and **perpetual calendar,** 30J or more, 18K, 60mm, HC, C. 1895  (illo.24)................ ★ | 12,000 | 14,000 | 18,000 |
| Swiss  min. rep., Grand Sonnerie, clockwatch w/ carillon chimes, 2 train, nickel, tandem wind, 30J, 3 hammers, ornate case, 18K, 55mm, HC, C. 1900...................................................... | 10,000 | 12,000 | 15,000 |

**Swiss minute repeater**, chronograph, start - stop - return to zero, moonphase and calendar, 30J or more, 18K, 60mm, HC, C. 1895.  (illo.23)

**Swiss minute repeater**, chronograph, moonphase and **perpetual calendar**, 30J or more, 18K, 60mm, HC, C. 1895. (illo.24)

# PRE–1850 ALARMS

| TYPE – DESCRIPTION | Avg | Ex-Fn | Mint |
|---|---|---|---|
| Alarm, ( **Blois France** ), double silver case pierced and engraved, gilt mvt., cut gut cord fusee, 2 wheel train + verge escape. w/foliot, silver balance cock, 44mm, Ca. 1640, (illo.25) | $15,000 | $17,000 | $20,000 |
| Alarm, 2 cases pierced, 3 wheel train, Egyptian pierced pillers, verge & foliot, 51mm, Ca. 1675 (illo.26) | 7,000 | 9,000 | 12,000 |

ALARM, **from BLOIS** FRANCE, double silver case pierced and engraved, silver crown dial with roman numbers, alarm center dial with arabic numbers, gilt movement, cut gut cord fusee, 2 wheel train plus verge escapement with foliot, silver balance cock, 44mm, Ca. 1640. It is believed French watch-making started in the town of **Blois France.** (illo.25)

ALARM, 2 cases pierced & engraved, roman outer dial, alarm center dial, blued hands , 3 wheel train, Egyptian pierced pillers, verge & foliot, endless screw adjustment, Paris, 51mm, Ca. 1675. (illo.26)

ALARM, strikes on bell, pair cased, verge, C. 1650. (illo.27)

Alarm, pair cased, first case pique nailed skin, second case pierced, 4 wheel train, verge, amphora pillers, 56mm, Ca. 1680. (illo.28)

| TYPE – DESCRIPTION | Avg | Ex-Fn | Mint |
|---|---|---|---|
| Alarm, strikes on bell, pair cased, verge, C. 1650. (illo.27) | $6,000 | $6,500 | $7,000 |
| Alarm, pair cased, first case pique nailed skin, 4 wheel train, verge, 56mm, Ca. 1680. (illo.28) | 9,000 | 11,000 | 13,000 |
| Alarm, Rotterdam, silver pierced case, gilt, tulip pillars, verge, fusee, 48mm, Ca. 1685 (illo.29) | 6,000 | 6,500 | 7,000 |
| Alarm, "oignon", verge, fusee, large pierced bal. bridge (illo.30) | 6,000 | 7,000 | 8,000 |

ALARM, Rotterdam, silver pierced case, gilt, tulip pillars, verge, fusee, 48mm, Ca. 1685. (illo.29)

ALARM, "oignon", verge, fusee, large pierced balance bridge. (illo.30)

ALARM, nailed pique shagreen skin, second case pierced silver, balance cock has short feet, 4 wheel train verge, 60mm, London, Ca. 1685. (illo.31)

ALARM, nailed pique shagreen skin, triple cases, entirely pierced throughout, richly decorated, 4 wheel train, verge, fusee, English-Swiss, Ca. 1700. (illo.32)

| TYPE – DESCRIPTION | Avg | Ex-Fn | Mint |
|---|---|---|---|
| Alarm, nailed pique shagreen skin, second case pierced silver, 4 wheel train verge, 60mm, London, Ca. 1685 (illo.31) ......... | $6,500 | $7,500 | $8,500 |
| Alarm, nailed pique shagreen skin, English-Swiss, verge, fusee, Ca.1700s, (illo.32)............................................................ | 6,000 | 6,500 | 7,500 |
| Oignon alarm, verge, French, silver and animal skin cover, movement wound from center arbor on dial, silver champleve dial, 60mm, OF, C. 1760 ........................... | 5,000 | 5,500 | 6,000 |

## ALARMS

The most common Swiss and German alarms are usually in base metal or gun metal cases. Early makes with porcelain dials are more desirable than later (post 1920's) metal dial alarms.

| TYPE – DESCRIPTION | Avg | Ex-Fn | Mint |
|---|---|---|---|
| Swiss alarm sounding on bell,7J, base metal, 49mm,OF, C.1915 ... | $80 | $90 | $120 |
| Swiss alarm sounding on gongs, 15J, tandem wind, gun metal, 50mm, OF, C. 1900 ............................................. | 150 | 200 | 275 |
| Cricket alarm, w/cricket design, Swiss , SW, silver case, 48mm, OF, C.1890............................................. | 500 | 700 | 800 |

## COMPARISON OF WATCH SIZES

| U. S. A. | EUROPEAN |
|---|---|
| 10-12  SIZE | 40—44 MM |
| 16     SIZE | 45—48 MM |
| 18     SIZE | 50—54 MM |

# TIMERS & CHRONOGRAPHS
Gallet, Racine & other names are commonly found on timers & chronographs.

Timer, 1/5 sec., 7J, register, base metal, 48mm, OF.   Timer, **split second**, register, base metal, 46mm, OF.

| TYPE – DESCRIPTION | Avg | Ex-Fn | Mint |
|---|---|---|---|
| Timer, 1/5 sec., register,7J, base metal, 48mm, OF, C. 1940 | $35 | $45 | $55 |
| Timer, 1/5 sec. register, **17J**, base metal, 48mm, OF, C. 1940 | 45 | 55 | 65 |
| Timer, **split sec.**, register, base metal, 46mm, OF, C. 1940 | 60 | 75 | 100 |
| Timer or Stop Watch, **silver,** 48mm, HC, 1925 | 130 | 150 | 175 |
| Chronograph, **7J, GF or silver,** 48mm, OF, C. 1905 | 130 | 150 | 185 |
| HC | 150 | 175 | 200 |
| Chronograph, **15-17J, porcelain** dial, GF or silver, 50mm, OF, | 225 | 250 | 300 |
| HC, | 250 | 300 | 350 |
| Chronograph, **20J, 18K,** 52mm, OF, C. 1895 | 500 | 600 | 700 |
| HC | 600 | 700 | 850 |

Timer or Stop Watch, **silver,** 48mm, HC.     Chronograph, 7-17J, GF, 48mm, OF, C. 1905.

Chronograph, w/register, porc. dial, **20J, 14K,** 52mm, HC, Ca. 1890.

Chronograph, Split Seconds, w/register, porc. dial, **20J, 18K,** 52mm, OF, Ca. 1910.

| TYPE – DESCRIPTION | Avg | Ex-Fn | Mint |
|---|---|---|---|
| Chronog. w/register, porc. dial, **15J, silver,** 52mm, OF, C. 1890.... | $250 | $300 | $350 |
| HC ......................................................................................... | 300 | 325 | 375 |
| Chronog. w/register, porc. dial, **20J, 14K,** 52mm, OF, C. 1890...... | 400 | 500 | 600 |
| HC ......................................................................................... | 500 | 600 | 750 |
| Chronog. w/register, porc. dial, **20J, 18K,** 52mm, OF, C. 1890...... | 600 | 700 | 800 |
| HC ......................................................................................... | 800 | 900 | 1,200 |
| Split sec. chronograph, 15-17J, **.800 silver,** 52mm, OF, C. 1900.. | 275 | 300 | 325 |
| Split sec. chronograph, 19-32J, **18K,** 52mm, OF, C. 1900 ............. | 800 | 900 | 1,200 |
| HC ......................................................................................... | 1,000 | 1,200 | 1,500 |
| Double dial (time on front, chrono. on back), Swiss , 17J, | | | |
| 14K display case , 51mm, OF, Ca. 1885................................. | 900 | 1,100 | 1,250 |
| 1/4 second jump watch, 26J, two gear train, KW , **18K,** HC, C.1880 | 2,200 | 2,500 | 3,000 |

Double dial (time on front, chrono. on back), Swiss , 17J, 14K display case , 51mm, OF, Ca. 1885.

1/4 second jump watch, 26J, two gear train, two main spring barrels, KW , 18K, 53mm, HC, C.1880.

# POCKET CHRONOMETER

JOHN ARNOLD, chronometer, KWKS, spring detent, Z balance with adjustable weights, helical hair spring, 18K case, serial # 14, upright escape wheel, "INV ET FECT" engraved on movement (made by), his chronometer factory was located in Chigwell (London), #36 pocket chronometers sold for about $500.00 in 1776. (illo.33)

| TYPE – DESCRIPTION | Avg | Ex-Fn | Mint |
|---|---|---|---|
| Chronometer, KWKS, spring detent, Z bal., helical hair-spring, "JOHN ARNOLD", 18K case, C. 1776 (illo.33) | $10,000 | $12,000 | $15,000 |
| Chronometer, KWKS, spring detent, Z bal., helical hair-spring, silver case, C. 1795 (illo.34) | 5,000 | 6,000 | 7,000 |
| Chronometer, KWKS, spring detent, Z bal., helical hair-spring, "R. ARNOLD", 18K case, C. 1805 (illo.35) | 8,000 | 10,000 | 12,000 |

Chronometer,13 jewels, KWKS, spring detent, Z balance with screw counterpoise on terminal curves, helical hair-spring, silver case, Ca. 1795. (illo.34)

R. ARNOLD, chronometer, KWKS, spring detent, Z balance with screw counterpoise on terminal curves, helical hair-spring, 18K case, 58mm, C. 1805. (illo.35)

JOHANNES KESSELS "ALTON", deck chronometer, KWKS, spring detent, fusee, silver case, C. 1830 . (illo.36)

Detent chronometer, Helical hairspring, Swiss, SW, 18K, 56mm, HC, C. 1900. (illo.37)

| TYPE – DESCRIPTION | Avg | Ex-Fn | Mint |
|---|---|---|---|
| Chronometer, KWKS, spring detent, Z bal., helical hair-spring, "KESSELS", **silver case**, C. 1830. (illo.36) | $2,000 | $3,000 | $4,000 |
| Chronometer, KW, spring detent, **coin**, OF, C. 1875 | 600 | 700 | 900 |
| Detent chronometer, Swiss, SW, **18K**, 56mm, HC, Ca.1900 (ill0.37) | 1,500 | 1,700 | 2,000 |
| Detent chronometer, English, w/ wind indicator, **18K**, 48mm, OF . | 3,500 | 4,000 | 5,000 |
| Chronometer, pivoted detent, helical hairspring, (French), SW, **silver**, 56mm, OF, (illo.38) | 300 | 400 | 550 |
| Pocket chronometer, Swiss, 20 jewel, fancy case, silver and gilt dial, detent, w/ helical spring,**18K**, 49mm, HC, C. 1890 | 8,000 | 9,000 | 10,000 |

Engraved on movement "*Chronome'tre*" (French), 16 jewels, pivoted detent, helical hairspring, stem wind, manufactured by **LIP** in **Besancon France**, silver, 56mm, OF, Ca. 1910-30. (illo.38)

Detent chronometer, English, w/ fusee, helical hairspring, note: Trapezoidal weights on balance.

🕐 Note: Some models and grades are not included. Their values can be determined by comparing with **similar** age, size, metal content, style, models and grades listed.

🕐 Note: Watches listed in this book are priced at the **collectable retail** level, as **complete** watches having an original case, an original dial, and with the entire original movement in good working order with no repairs needed.

# TOURBILLION, KARRUSEL,
# RARE & UNUSUAL MOVEMENTS

One minute so called "Poor Man's Tourbillon", center seconds silver watch with centered dial & visible system. Swiss, 54mm. (illo.39)

Visible Tourbillon, 53mm, 13 jewels, tourbillon system is visible from dial side, ca. 1913. (illo.40)

| TYPE – DESCRIPTION | Avg | Ex-Fn | Mint |
|---|---|---|---|
| Tourbillion, Swiss, base metal, 54mm, OF (illo.39) | $1,200 | $1,500 | $1,800 |
| Tourbillon, 53mm, 13J, visible from dial, Ca. 1913 (illo.40) | 1,600 | 1,700 | 2,000 |
| Tourbillon, In 4 min., 15J, enamel dial, silver, C.1930 (illo.41) | 3,000 | 3,200 | 3,500 |
| Karrusel, in 52 min., English, 3/4, gilt, 16J, SW, silver case, 56mm, OF, C.1885, (illo.42) | 3,300 | 3,850 | 4,250 |
| Helicoil mainspring, Swiss, 15J, cylinder esc., base metal, 51mm, OF, C. 1910 (illo.43) | 1,000 | 1,200 | 1,500 |

TOURBILLON, in 4 minutes, 15 jewels, enamel dial, silver case, Ca.1930. (illo.41)

52 minute KARRUSEL, 57mm, 14J., English, silver case, Ca.1885. (illo.42)

## COMPARISON OF WATCH SIZES

| U. S. A. | EUROPEAN |
|---|---|
| 10-12 SIZE | 40—44 MM |
| 16  SIZE | 45—48 MM |
| 18  SIZE | 50—54 MM |

Helicoil Mainspring, 51mm, 15J., rare winding system, cylindrical spring replaces standard mainspring. (illo.43)

Lever with Fusee, KW KS, (Liverpool), hallmarked, silver, **undersprung**, 46mm, OF, Ca. 1850-70.(illo.44)

## EARLY PRE–1850 NON—GOLD

| TYPE – DESCRIPTION | Avg | Ex-Fn | Mint |
|---|---|---|---|
| Lever, Fusee, (Liverpool ), silver, 46mm, OF, Ca. 1850-70 (illo.44) | $150 | $200 | $250 |
| Lever or cylinder, BAR, KW KS, silver, 46-52mm,OF( illo.45)..... | 125 | 150 | 175 |
| Lever or cylinder, BAR, KW KS, silver, 46-52mm, OF, Ca. 1840-85 | 125 | 150 | 175 |
| Lever or cylinder, **engraved** BAR, KW KS, silver, 46-52mm, OF, Ca. 1840-85 ( illo.46)...................................................... | 150 | 200 | 250 |
| Lever or cylinder, **Le-PINE,** KW KS, silver, 46-52mm (illo.46)... | 150 | 200 | 250 |
| Rack & pinion lever escap., KW KS, silver, 46-52mm, OF (illo.48) | 250 | 300 | 350 |

Lever, KW KS, bar style movement, note **curved barrel bridge,** silver, 46-52mm, OF, C. 1830-50. (illo.45)

Lever, **Le-PINE style bar, engraved,** KW KS, silver, 46-52mm, OF, Ca. 1840-85. (illo.46)

Lever, **Le-PINE style tapered bar movement,** KW KS, silver, 46-52mm, OF, Ca. 1820-35. (illo.47)

**Rack & pinion** lever escapement, KW KS, silver, 46-52mm, Ca. 1830. (illo.48)

Verge, chain driven fusee, (English) paircase, 52mm, OF, C.1800- 40. (illo.49)

Verge, fusee, (English) paircase, hallmarked, KW, 52mm, OF, Ca. 1780-90. (illo.50)

| TYPE – DESCRIPTION | Avg | Ex-Fn | Mint |
|---|---|---|---|
| Verge, Fusee (Swiss), KW, (unmarked) single case, | | | |
|    silver, 49mm, OF, C. 1810-40 | $300 | $350 | $400 |
| Verge (English) paircase, 52mm, OF, C.1800- 40 (illo.49) | 300 | 350 | 400 |
| Painted "farmer's dial," verge, Swiss / London, | | | |
|    silver, 52-55m, OF | 400 | 500 | 600 |
| Rack &lever, Fusee, silver, 52mm, OF, C. 1830-50 | 300 | 400 | 500 |
| Cylinder, Fusee, silver, 48-52mm, OF, C. 1830s | 300 | 400 | 500 |
| Verge, Fusee (Swiss), KW, silver single case, 49mm | | | |
|    OF, C. 1810-1840 | 300 | 350 | 400 |
| Verge (English) paircase, hallmarked, KW, | | | |
|    52mm, OF, C. 1780-90-(illo.50) | 300 | 350 | 400 |
| Miniature, verge, lady's, plain, porcelain dial, hallmarked | | | |
|    silver, 24mm, OF, C. 1810 | 800 | 900 | 1,000 |
| Gilt & enamel, verge, Swiss or French, 46mm, OF, C. 1800 | 900 | 1,100 | 1,300 |
| Skeletonized, verge, Swiss, double case, hand-carved movement, | | | |
|    case silver & horn, 53mm,OF, C. 1800 | 600 | 700 | 800 |
| Repouse paircase, fancy dial, verge, London, | | | |
|    hallmarked silver, 49mm, OF, C. 1800, (illo.51) | 1,200 | 1,400 | 1,600 |
| Erotic Repousee paircase, Swan & Lady, verge, London, (illo.52). | 1,300 | 1,500 | 2,000 |

Repousee paircase, fancy dial, verge, English hallmarked silver case, 49mm, OF, C. 1800. (illo.51)

Erotic Repousee silver paircase, Swan & Lady, verge, Fusee, London. (illo.52)

OIGNON watch with mock pendulum, 58mm, Ca. 1700-1720. (illo.53)

Lady & mock pendulum, mock pendulum can be seen at top of Ladies head , 58mm, Ca. 1690 (illo.54)

| TYPE – DESCRIPTION | Avg | Ex-Fn | Mint |
|---|---|---|---|
| Oignon watch with mock pendulum, 58mm, ca. 1700-20 (illo.53) . | $3,500 | $4,500 | $5,000 |
| Lady & mock pendulum, enamel Lady, 58mm, Ca. 1690 (illo.54) . | 4,000 | 5,000 | 6,000 |
| Verge w/ calendar, repousee paircase, London hallmarked, 51mm, OF, C. 1690 | 3,500 | 4,000 | 4,500 |
| Dublin, early verge, silver paircase, champleve silver dial (signed), 54mm, OF, C. 1720 | 2,500 | 3,000 | 3,500 |
| Early verge, large winged cock, signed silver dial, London, Egyptian pillars, silver, 55mm, OF, C. 1700 (illo.55) | 2,500 | 3,000 | 3,200 |
| Viennese enamel on gilt, verge, fusee, multi-scenes on case, KW, 55mm, HC, C. 1780 | 2,800 | 3,500 | 3,800 |
| English, verge w/ calendar, signed champleve dial, silver & horn, 54mm OF, C. 1680 | 3,500 | 4,000 | 4,500 |

Early verge, large D shaped foot on the cock, London, signed silver dial, Egyptian pillars, silver, 55mm, OF, C. 1700 . (illo.55)

Tortoise shell case, verge with chain driven fusee, calendar, D shaped foot balance cock, C. 1700, (illo.56)

English, verge, hand pierced cock, fusee, silver, note face on balance cock, C. 1720, (illo.57)

| TYPE – DESCRIPTION | Avg | Ex-Fn | Mint |
|---|---|---|---|
| Tortoise shell, verge, calendar, Ca. 1700, (illo.56) | $3,000 | $3,500 | $4,500 |
| English, verge, hand pierced cock, fusee, silver, Ca. 1720, (illo.57) | 2,500 | 3,000 | 3,500 |
| Pumpkin Form Case, verge, silver, 40mm, Ca. 1775 (illo.58) | 3,000 | 3,500 | 4,000 |
| Garooned Case, verge, fusee, 44mm, silver, Ca. 1650 (illp.59) | 9,000 | 10,000 | 12,000 |
| Painted scene on horn, verge, gilt, 57mm, OF, Ca. 1780, (illo.60) | 2,000 | 2,500 | 3,500 |

Pumpkin Form Case, verge, silver, Ca. 1775. (illo.58)

Garooned Case, verge, fusee, 44mm, Ca. 1650. (illp.59)

Painted horn (full scene in color) London, verge, gilt, 57mm, OF, C. 1780. (illo.60)

Early Astronomic watch with day date month calendar, lunar calendar, 57mm, Ca. 1680. (illo.61)

| TYPE – DESCRIPTION | Avg | Ex-Fn | Mint |
|---|---|---|---|
| Early Astronomic watch with day date month calendar, lunar calendar, 57mm, Ca. 1680. (illo.61) | $10,000 | $15,000 | $18,000 |
| Early Astronomic watch with moon phases and triple date, fusee with cut-gut cord, 3 gear train, foliot, Ca.1660. (illo.62) | 15,000 | 17,000 | 20,000 |

Early Astronomic watch with moon phases and triple date, fusee with, cut-gut cord, 3 gear train, 6 armed foliot, Ca.1660. (illo.62)

Early German made silver watch, verge and foliot, silver pierced dial, "Hamburg", Ca. 1660. (illo.63)

| TYPE – DESCRIPTION | Avg | Ex-Fn | Mint |
|---|---|---|---|
| Early German made silver watch, verge and foliot, silver pierced dial, "Hamburg", Ca. 1660 (illo.63) | $8,000 | $9,000 | $10,000 |
| Early silver watch, blued steel hand, cut-gut fusee, foliot, rosette for adj., 53mm, Ca.1660 (illo.64) | 16,000 | 18,000 | 20,000 |

Early silver watch, silver dial with blued steel hand, cut gut fusee, 3 wheel train, foliot, rosette for adjustment of the motor-spring tension, 53mm, Ca.1660. (illo.64)

Pair cased, first case silver covered with nailed skin, verge, cut-gut cord fusee, 3 wheel train, foliot, pierced cock, endless screw adjustment for main spring tension, 45mm, Ca. 1660. (illo.65)

Early French watch movement with hour and minute hand, striking bell each hour, hand pierced case & gilt brass movement, cut-gut fusee, c. 1600s. (illo.66)

| TYPE – DESCRIPTION | Avg | Ex-Fn | Mint |
|---|---|---|---|
| Pair cased, first case silver & nailed skin, verge, fusee, 3 wheel train, foliot, pierced cock, 45mm, Ca. 1660 (illo.65) | $5,500 | $6,500 | $7,500 |
| Early French watch hour and minute hand, striking on bell, cut-gut fusee, c. 1600s (illo.66) | 15,000 | 18,000 | 20,000 |
| Early Drum Clock, iron plates, 4 wheel train, brass fusee on a steel great wheel, steel contrate wheel with brass teeth, steel verge and foliot balance w/ T-shaped ends, 34mm high (illo.67) | 28,000 | 35,000 | 45,000 |

43mm, Early Drum Clock, iron plates, 4 wheel train, brass fusee on a steel great wheel, steel contrate wheel with brass teeth, steel verge and foliot balance with T-shaped ends . The cylindrical gilt brass case is finely engraved and is 34mm high, Ca. 1550—1560. (illo.67)

# PRE–1850 *GOLD*

Lever or verge, (Liverpool), 18K, multi-colored gold dial, 52mm, OF, C.1845-75. (illo.68).

Lever or cylinder, BAR style movement, GOLD, 45-52mm, OF, 1840-1865. (illo.69)

| TYPE – DESCRIPTION | Avg | Ex-Fn | Mint |
|---|---|---|---|
| Lever or verge, (Liverpool), 18K, 52mm, OF, C.1845-75 (illo.68). | $600 | $700 | $800 |
| Lever or verge, (Liverpool), 15J, 18K, 52mm, HC, C. 1845-75 | 700 | 900 | 1,100 |
| Lever or cylinder, BAR, GOLD, 45-52mm, OF(illo.69) | 325 | 375 | 450 |
| (same as above) w / skeletonized movement,18K, (illo.70) | 600 | 700 | 800 |
| Lever or cylinder, Le-Pine, GOLD, 45-52mm, OF(illo.71) | 325 | 375 | 450 |
| Cylinder Fusee, paircase, London, plain case, porcelain dial,18K, 48mm, OF, C. 1880 | 1,600 | 1,800 | 1,900 |
| Verge, multi-color case, Swiss/ French, porcelain dial, 18K, 42mm,OF, Ca. 1770-1800 | 1,500 | 1,800 | 2,000 |
| Verge, French, gold & enamel patterns on case, KWKS, OF, C. 1805 | 1,800 | 2,200 | 2,500 |
| Verge, (Swiss), 18K, 52-54mm, plain case, OF, C. 1790-1820 | 750 | 950 | 1,200 |
| Verge ,Swiss, gold scene, high quality ,18K, 50mm, OF, C.1790 | 2,000 | 2,200 | 2,500 |

Lever or cylinder, skeletonized & engraved bar movement, Swiss, 45-52mm, OF,18K. (illo.70)

Lever or cylinder escapement, Le-Pine style movement, Ca. 1820-1835, GOLD, 45-52mm, OF. (illo.71)

Verge, repousee paircase, 20K gold case, 43mm, Open Face, Ca.1780, (illo.72)

Early verge, ID shaped balance cock, signed dial, London, Egyptian pillars, gold, 55mm, OF, Ca. 1760. (illo.73)

| TYPE – DESCRIPTION | Avg | Ex-Fn | Mint |
|---|---|---|---|
| Verge, repousee paircase, 20K, 43mm, OF, C.1780, (illo.72) | $2,500 | $3,000 | $3,500 |
| Early verge, large winged cock, signed dial, London,Egyptian pillars, gold, 55mm, OF, C. 1760 (illo.73) | 2,800 | 3,200 | 3,700 |
| Virgule, Fusee, Swiss or French, 18K, 50-55mm, OF, C. 1790 | 1,200 | 1,500 | 1,650 |
| Virgule, signed Le-Pine Paris, 18K, Ca.1790, 60mm, OF, (illo.74) | 1,600 | 1,800 | 2,000 |
| Skeletonized French, diamonds on bezel, 39mm, C.1780,(illo.75) | 2,000 | 2,400 | 2,800 |
| Rack & Pinion lever escapement, 18K, OF, Ca. 1830 (illo.76) | 650 | 700 | 850 |

Virgule escapement, signed "Le-Pine (Paris)," horse-shoe shaped centerbridge, 18K, Ca.1790, 60mm, OF, (illo.74)

Skeletonized French watch, diamonds on bezel, 39mm, C.1780,(illo.75)

Rack and Lever Escapement, 18K, OF, Ca. 1830. (illo.76)

CHATELAINE, verge, fusee, 22k pair case, 45mm, (illo.76)

| TYPE – DESCRIPTION | Avg | Ex-Fn | Mint |
|---|---|---|---|
| Chatelaine, verge, fusee, 22k pair case, (illo.76)............................. | $3,500 | $4,000 | $4,500 |
| Early gold & nailed double case watch, foliot, C.1670 (illo.77)...... | 22,000 | 25,000 | 28,000 |

Early gold & nailed double case watch, Champleve gold dial, 3 wheel train, verge, foliot, rosette adjustment and endless screw, 50mm, C.1670 (illo.77)

GOLD KEYS, the tops are all gold and the bottom key shaft is base metal, PRICES= **$85 to $150** each.

# MISC. MEN'S GF / SILVER / BASE METAL

Dollar watch **German**, base metal ,OF, C.1895. (illo.78)

Dollar watch **German**, back wind, **waterproof model**, base metal, OF, C.1885. (illo.79)

| TYPE – DESCRIPTION | Avg | Ex-Fn | Mint |
|---|---|---|---|
| Dollar watch **German**, base metal ,OF, C.1895 (illo.78) ............... | $35 | $45 | $65 |
| Dollar watch **German,** back wind, **waterproof,** OF, C.1885 (illo.79) | 300 | 350 | 400 |
| Base metal, 7-17J, SW, 43-48mm, OF, C. 1900-1930 ..................... | 35 | 45 | 65 |
| GF or silver, 7-17J, SW, 43-48mm, OF, C. 1895-1940 .................. | 55 | 65 | 85 |
| GF/silver, 7-17J, SW, 43-52mm, HC, C. 1895-1940 ...................... | 75 | 95 | 130 |
| Swiss Fakes , 7J, KW, base metal, OF, 52mm, C. 1870-90............. | 65 | 85 | 100 |
| Non-magnetic, pat.# 7546/780, **Moeris**, base metal, (illo.80) ......... | 100 | 125 | 150 |
| Cylinder, (Liverpool), 1/2 plate design, (illo.81)............................. | 100 | 125 | 150 |

Non-magnetic, pat.#7546/780, **Moeris**, base metal, thumb-nail set, SW, OF. (illo.80)

Cylinder escapement, (Liverpool), 1/2 plate design, marked 4 hole jeweled=8 jewels. (illo.81)

## COMPARISON OF WATCH SIZES

| U. S. A. | EUROPEAN |
|---|---|
| 10-12 SIZE | 40—44 MM |
| 16    SIZE | 45—48 MM |
| 18    SIZE | 50—54 MM |

KW KS, **Chinese Duplex** escapement, 3/4 plate design, OF. (illo.82)

KW KS, with a **Compass** on movement, lever escapement. (illo.83)

| TYPE – DESCRIPTION | Avg | Ex-Fn | Mint |
|---|---|---|---|
| KWKS, **Chinese Duplex**, 3/4 plate design, OF, (illo.82) | $300 | $350 | $400 |
| KWKS, **Compass** on movement, lever escap., (illo.83) | 125 | 150 | 195 |
| KWKS, 6-15J, silver, 45-52mm, OF, C. 1860-85 | 65 | 90 | 100 |
| KWKS, 8-17J, silver, 45-52mm, HC, C. 1860-85 | 75 | 100 | 130 |
| Engraved movement, KWKS, 15J, silver, 46mm, HC, C.1870 | 100 | 130 | 150 |
| KWKS, marked railway, pin lever, Swiss, (illo.84) | 45 | 65 | 85 |
| 21J, RR type, GF, 48mm, OF, C. 1910-30 | 80 | 100 | 130 |
| 25J, Waltham (Swiss made), GF, 48mm, OF, C. 1950 | 100 | 150 | 175 |
| Niello enamel, 17J, SW, silver, 45mm, HC, C. 1940 | 125 | 175 | 225 |
| Niello enamel & embossed hunting scene on case, enamel dial, 3/4 plate, made in **Beaucourt France**, OF, (illo.85) | 200 | 225 | 265 |

KWKS, marked railway, pin lever, Swiss. (illo.84)

Niello enamel & embossed hunting scene on case, enamel dial, 3/4 plate, made in Beaucourt France, OF, Ca. 1890. (illo.85)

1/4 repeater early rim activated, Swiss or French, silver, OF, Ca.1820. (illo.86)

Automaton, **Adam & Eve**, note snake circles Adam & Eve, hand painted enamel dial, KW KS, OF. (illo. 87)

| TYPE – DESCRIPTION | Avg | Ex-Fn | Mint |
|---|---|---|---|
| 1/4 repeater early rim activated, silver, OF, Ca.1820 (illo.86)......... | $900 | $1,000 | $1,200 |
| Automaton, **Adam & Eve**, w/ snake, KW KS, OF (illo. 87)........... | 5,000 | 6,000 | 7,000 |
| Spring detent chronometer w/Tandem wind, fusee, 56mm, Ca.1875 (illo.88)............................................... | 700 | 800 | 900 |
| Gamblers playing card dial, Swiss, silver, OF (illo.89) .................. | 400 | 450 | 500 |

Spring Detent chronometer with Tandem wind, chain driven fusee, Helical hair spring, 56mm, Ca.1875. (illo.88)

Gamblers playing card porcelain dial, Swiss, silver, OF. (illo.89)

Exposed Skeletonized Balance from dial, enamel painted dial, verge, fusee, KW KS, large advance-retard index, Ca.1790. (illo.90)

| TYPE – DESCRIPTION | Avg | Ex-Fn | Mint |
|---|---|---|---|
| Exposed Balance from dial, enamel painted dial, Ca.1790 (illo.90) | $1,500 | $2,000 | $2,400 |
| Wandering Digital Jump Hour Hand, 45mm, Ca. 1880 (illo.91).... | 6,000 | 7,000 | 8,000 |
| Jump Digital Hour, W/ Date, at 6, sec. hand at 3, Ca. 1820 (illo.92) | 3,000 | 3,500 | 4,000 |

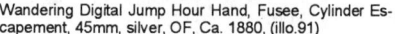

Wandering Digital Jump Hour Hand, Fusee, Cylinder Escapement, 45mm, silver, OF, Ca. 1880, (illo.91)

Jump Digital Hour, W/ Date, at 6, sec. hand at 3, silver, engine turned dial, OF, Ca. 1820 (illo.92)

## COMPARISON OF WATCH SIZES

| U. S. A. | EUROPEAN |
|---|---|
| 10-12 SIZE | 40—44 MM |
| 16    SIZE | 45—48 MM |
| 18    SIZE | 50—54 MM |

Day, date, moon phases, Swiss, fancy dial GF, 46mm lever set at rim of case. (illo.93)

Mock pendulum (seen from face side), duplex escap. Multicolor dial. (illo.94)

| TYPE – DESCRIPTION | Avg | Ex-Fn | Mint |
|---|---|---|---|
| Day, date, moon phases, Swiss, fancy dial, **GF**, 46mm (illo.93)..... | $300 | $350 | $425 |
| Day, date, moon phases, Swiss, fancy dial, **gun metal**, 46mm ...... | 200 | 250 | 300 |
| Mock pendulum (seen from face side), duplex escap. (illo.94)....... | 400 | 500 | 600 |
| Self winding, (Loehr patent), KW, set from back, (illo.95)............. | 450 | 500 | 575 |
| Shell Oil Co., by Giard Perregaux, 40mm (illo.96)......................... | 125 | 150 | 175 |

Self winding, (Loehr patent), KW, set from back. (illo.95)

Shell Oil Co., by Giard Perregaux, 40mm. (illo.96)

## MISC. MEN'S *GOLD* / PLATINUM

| TYPE – DESCRIPTION | Avg | Ex-Fn | Mint |
|---|---|---|---|
| SW, 17J, 14K, 43-46mm, OF, C. 1910-1940.................................... | $175 | $225 | $275 |
| SW, 17J-19J, 18K, 43-46mm, OF, C. 1910-1940............................ | 225 | 275 | 350 |
| SW, 17J, 14K, 48mm, HC, C. 1910-1940....................................... | 375 | 425 | 500 |
| SW, 17J, Platinum, 42mm, OF, C. 1940's...................................... | 475 | 550 | 650 |
| KWKS, 15J, lever, fancy ,gilt dial, 18K, 45mm, C. 1870.............. | 250 | 300 | 400 |
| KWKS, 15-20J, lever 18K, 49-53mm, C. 1870-1885 ..................... | 400 | 500 | 650 |
| Lever, Fusee, (Liverpool), 15J, porcelain dial, 18K, 52mm, C.1860 | 450 | 550 | 700 |

# UNUSUAL NON—GOLD

Skull (miniature) form watch, fusee, cylinder escapement, 25mm. (illo.97)

Blinking Eyes, pin set animated eyes, 46mm. (illo.98)

| TYPE – DESCRIPTION | Avg | Ex-Fn | Mint |
|---|---|---|---|
| Skull (miniature) form, fusee, cylinder escape., 25mm, (illo.97) .... | $550 | $700 | $950 |
| Blinking Eyes, pin set animated eyes, 46mm, (illo.98) ..................... | 200 | 250 | 300 |
| 8 day, exposed balance, 7J, gun metal, 50mm, C. 1920s (illo.99)... | 75 | 85 | 125 |
| 8 day, exposed balance, 7J, Swiss, **DAY & DATE,** gun metal, 50mm, C. 1920s ...................................................... | 130 | 150 | 195 |
| Roulette wheel dial, 7J, SW, base metal, 46mm, OF, C.1915 ......... | 130 | 150 | 200 |
| Game spin wheel novelty watch, 6 horses, gun metal, (illo.100)..... | 300 | 350 | 400 |

8 day, exposed balance, 7J, by Hebdomas but with other name, gun metal, 50mm, C. 1920s. (illo.99)

Game spin wheel novelty watch, 6 horses, gun metal. (illo.100)

⊕ Note: Some models and grades are not included. Their values can be determined by comparing with **similar** age, size, metal content, style, models and grades listed.

⊕ Note: Watches listed in this book are priced at the collectable retail level, as **complete** watches having an original case, an original dial, and with the entire original movement in good working order with no repairs needed.

Chinese market, KWKS, duplex esc. silver, 58mm, OF, C.1870. (illo.101)

Chinese market, KW, duplex esc. silver, 58mm, OF, C.1870. (illo.102)

| TYPE – DESCRIPTION | Avg | Ex-Fn | Mint |
|---|---|---|---|
| For Chinese market, lever esc., 12J, KWKS, silver, 55mm, OF, C. 1880 | $250 | $300 | $325 |
| Chinese market, KW, duplex esc. silver, 58mm, OF, C.1870 (illo.101) | 300 | 350 | 400 |
| Chinese market, KW, duplex esc. silver, 58mm, OF, C.1870 (illo.102) | 300 | 350 | 425 |
| Chinese market, KW, duplex esc. silver, carved movement, 58mm, OF, C.1870 (illo.103) | 375 | 425 | 475 |
| Carved movement, lever escap., KWKS, silver, 58mm, OF(illo.104) | 125 | 150 | 175 |
| KW, for Turkish market, 15J, .800 silver, 47mm, HC, C. 1880 | 100 | 150 | 175 |

Chinese market, KW, duplex esc. silver, carved movement,58mm, OF, C.1870. (illo.103)

Carved movement, lever escap., KWKS, silver, 58mm, OF. (illo.104)

Oversize, moon phase & calendar, silver, 65-70mm, Ca.1900. (illo.105)

Moonphase triple cal., Swiss, gun metal , 50mm, OF, C.1905. (illo.106)

| TYPE – DESCRIPTION | Avg | Ex-Fn | Mint |
|---|---|---|---|
| Oversize PW, 15J, base metal, 65-70mm, C. 1900-1915 ................ | $150 | $200 | $225 |
| Oversize, moon ph. & calendar, silver,65-70mm, Ca.1900 (illo.105) | 900 | 1,200 | 1,500 |
| Moonphase triple cal., Swiss, gun metal , 50mm, OF, C.1905(illo.106) | 250 | 350 | 400 |
| Moonphase triple cal., Swiss, silver or GF, 50mm, OF, C.1905...... | 300 | 400 | 500 |
| Moonphase triple cal., Swiss, silver, 52-54mm, **HC**, C. 1905......... | 700 | 800 | 850 |
| Moonphase calendar, sterling, , oversize 65mm, OF, C. 1895......... | 600 | 750 | 800 |
| Verge (Swiss) skeletonized KW movement, silver & horn. paircase, 61mm, C. 1800.......................................................................... | 600 | 700 | 800 |
| Captain's watch, 2 hour dials, 1 train, KW KS, center second, silver, 50mm, HC, C. 1870 (illo.107) ...................................... | 600 | 700 | 800 |
| Digital dial (porcelain), 15J, SW, Swiss, jump hr. & min. discs, silver,HC, C. 1900 (illo.108) ............. | 400 | 500 | 650 |

Captain's watch, 2 hour dials, 1 train, KW KS, center second, silver, 50mm, HC, C. 1870. (illo.107)

Digital dial (porcelain), 15J, SW, Swiss, jump hr. & min. discs, silver,HC, C. 1900. (illo.108)

Automated with moving windmill on dial, Swiss, colored scene, exposed balance, 8 day , base metal, OF, C.1910. (illo.109)

Masonic triangular watch, Swiss ,17J, **mother of pearl** masonic dial, sterling, C. 1920's. (illo.110)

| TYPE – DESCRIPTION | Avg | Ex-Fn | Mint |
|---|---|---|---|
| Automated w/moving windmill on dial, Swiss, colored scene, exposed balance, 8 day , base metal, OF, C.1910 (illo.109)... | $475 | $500 | $575 |
| Masonic triangular watch, Swiss ,17J, **mother of pearl** masonic dial, sterling, C. 1920's (illo.110)............................. | 1,800 | 2,500 | 2,800 |
| World time w/ 6 zones, Swiss, silver, 52mm, OF, C. 1900 (illo.111) | 600 | 700 | 1,000 |
| World time, 24 Cities, w/ coded color rotating dial, 61mm(illo.112) | 3,000 | 3,500 | 4,000 |

World time, with 6 zones, Swiss, silver, 52mm, OF, Ca.1900. (illo.111)

World time, 24 Cities, with coded color rotating dial, Ca. 1895, 61mm. (illo.112)

Note: Some models and grades are not included. Their values can be determined by comparing with **similar** age, size, metal content, style, models and grades listed.

Note: Watches listed in this book are priced at the collectable retail level, as **complete** watches having an original case, an original dial, and with the entire original movement in good working order with no repairs needed.

| TYPE – DESCRIPTION | Avg | Ex-Fn | Mint |
|---|---|---|---|
| Sector watch, fan-shaped, fly back hour & min. hands, 17J, "Record Watch Co.," silver, 49x34mm, Ca. 1900 (illo.113).. | $1,800 | $2,500 | $3,000 |
| Mysterieuse watch, Swiss, see-through dial, hidden movement silver, 52mm, OF, Ca. 1895 (illo.114)..................................... | 2,000 | 2,500 | 2,850 |
| Wooden works, wooden wheels, wooden case, 50mm (illo.115).... | 1,400 | 1,800 | 2,400 |
| Self-wind, Swiss, cylinder escape., self-wind, gun metal (illo.116) | 300 | 350 | 400 |
| Musical, play's 2 tunes, silver, HC, 50mm, Ca. 1900 (illo.117)...... | 3,000 | 3,500 | 4,000 |

Sector watch, fan-shaped, fly back hour & min. hands, 17J, "Record Watch Co.," silver, 49x34mm, Ca. 1900. (illo.113)

Mysterieuse watch, Swiss, see-through dial, hidden movement silver, 52mm, OF, Ca. 1895. (illo.114)

Wooden works, wooden wheels, wooden case, all wooden watch, 50mm, made in Russia in, Ca. 1860. (illo.115)

Self-wind, Swiss, cylinder escapement, self-wind, gun metal. (illo.116)

Musical, play's 2 tunes, silver, 30 Tynes, HC, 50mm, 1900. (illo.117)

Rock crystal & enamel, star shape case, champleve enameled dial, verge, French, gilt & crystal case, 57x27mm, original French form Ca. 1600-1660, Viennese form Ca. 1780-1800. (illo.118)

| TYPE – DESCRIPTION | Avg | Ex-Fn | Mint |
|---|---|---|---|
| Rock crystal & enamel, star shape case, champleve enameled dial, verge, French, gilt & crystal case, 57x27mm, C.1800 (illo.118) | $5,000 | $5,500 | $6,000 |
| Crucifix form 1/4 hr. repeater & musical, crystal & silver form case, (illo.119) | 10,000 | 13,000 | 15,000 |

Crucifix form 1/4 hr. repeater & musical, crystal & silver form case, original French form Ca. 1600-1660, Viennese form Ca. 1780-1800. (illo.119)

# MEN'S UNUSUAL *"GOLD"*

Extra flat watch, **1.5mm thick,** Swiss, 18K, HC, 50mm. (illo.120)

| TYPE – DESCRIPTION | Avg | Ex-Fn | Mint |
|---|---|---|---|
| Extra flat watch, 1.5mm thick, Swiss, 18K, HC, 50mm (illo.120) .. | $7,000 | $8,000 | $9,000 |
| Jump 1/4 seconds, 2 train, 30J, KW, nickel, by August Saltzman (Swiss), 18K, 56mm, HC, C. 1870 ......................................... | 2,000 | 2,500 | 3,000 |
| Captain's watch, enameled portraits on case, Maharaja & Queen Victoria, KW, lever movement, 18K, 44mm, HC, C.1870 ..... | 2,500 | 3,000 | 3,500 |
| Captain's watch, KW, 15J, engraved case & gold dial, 18K, 52-58mm, OF, C. 1870 (illo.121)................................... | 1,200 | 1,400 | 1,500 |
| 1776-1876 centennial watch, H.O. Stauffer, bridges in 1776 form, 17J, 18K, 53mm, HC, C. 1876, (illo.122)............................... | 2,500 | 2,800 | 3,000 |

Captain's watch, KW, 15J, engraved case & gold dial, 18K, 52-58mm, OF, Ca. 1870. (illo.121)

1776-1876 centennial watch, H.O. Stauffer, bridges in 1776 form, 17J, 18K, 53mm, HC, Ca. 1876. (illo.122)

Double dials double lids, back side cal., front time & moon phases, 18K, HC, Ca. 1910. (illo.123)

| TYPE – DESCRIPTION | Avg | Ex-Fn | Mint |
|---|---|---|---|
| Captain's watch, KW KS, 15J, ornate case, Swiss, 18K, 52mm, HC, C. 1870 | $1,500 | $1,700 | $2,000 |
| Digital dial, hrs. & min. on digital jump discs, Swiss, 15J, SW, 18K, 51mm, HC, C. 1905 | 1,500 | 1,600 | 1,900 |
| Moonphase, double dial, calendar, Swiss, 17J, back lid opens to reveal full moon w/cal. dial, 14K, HC, C.1890 (illo.123) | 3,000 | 3,500 | 3,750 |
| Two train, center independent sec.,2 going barrels, lever escap., KW KS, GOLD, 42mm, Ca. 1880, HC (illo. 124) | 1,800 | 2,000 | 2,500 |
| Art Deco dial, Swiss, 18K, 45mm,OF (illo.125) | 1,000 | 1,200 | 1,500 |
| Double dials, world time & moon ph. triple date,18K, (illo.126) | 8,000 | 9,000 | 10,000 |
| Perpetual calendar with moonphase and chrono., Swiss , 20J, porcelain dial, 3/4 plate, 18K, 51mm, OF, C.1890-1900 | 8,000 | 9,000 | 10,000 |
| Rare verge, w/ automaton "Serpent, Adam & Eve" on dial with moving serpent, verge, French , 18K, OF, C. 1800 | 5,000 | 6,000 | 6,500 |
| Musical, two train of gears, pin cylinder & 24 blades, one tune, 18K, (illo.127) | 6,500 | 7,000 | 7,500 |
| Waterproof watch w/wind ind. 17J., C.1885, (illo.128) | 1,875 | 2,000 | 2,300 |
| Cigarette lighter & Swiss watch, Dunhill, Silver, C.1926, (illo.129) | 300 | 400 | 500 |
| 9K case | 1,200 | 1,400 | 1,500 |
| 14K case | 1,700 | 1,800 | 2,000 |
| $20.00 U.S. gold coin, 17J, mvt. in coin, 35mm, Ca.1920's (illo.130) | 1,500 | 1,600 | 1,800 |

Two train, center independent sec.,2 going barrels, lever escap.,KW KS, GOLD, 42mm, Ca. 1880, HC. (illo. 124)

Art Deco dial, Swiss, 18K, 45mm,OF. (illo.125)

Double dials, world time & moon ph. triple date,18K. (illo.126)

Musical, two train of gears, pin cylinder & 24 blades, one tune, 18K. (illo.127)

Waterproof watch w/wind ind. 17J., C.1885. (illo.128)

Cigarette lighter & Swiss watch, Dunhill, Silver, Ca.1926. (illo.129)

$20.00 U.S. gold coin, 17J, Swiss mvt. in coin, 35mm, Ca.1920's. (illo.130)

558

## MISC. SWISS LADY'S  Ca. 1850–1950  SILVER or GOLD FILLED

| TYPE – DESCRIPTION | Avg | Ex-Fn | Mint |
|---|---|---|---|
| GF or silver, 7-17J, SW, 35mm, OF, C. 1900-1930 | $40 | $45 | $55 |
| GF or silver, 10-15J, SW, 35mm, fancy dial, OF, C. 1910 | 55 | 75 | 90 |
| GF or silver, 7-17J, SW, 35- 40mm, HC, C. 1890-1930 | 65 | 85 | 110 |
| Enamel or silver, cylinder, pinset, 35mm, OF, C. 1910 | 75 | 80 | 100 |
| KWKS, silver, 40- 45mm, OF, C. 1865-1885 | 65 | 80 | 100 |
| KWKS, silver, 37- 45mm, HC, C. 1865-1885 | 75 | 90 | 125 |
| Ball shaped, 17J, 35mm, SW, GF or silver with chain | 80 | 100 | 155 |

## MISC. LADYS  Ca. 1850–1950  *GOLD*  (NO ENAMEL)

| TYPE – DESCRIPTION | Avg | Ex-Fn | Mint |
|---|---|---|---|
| SW, 7-15J, 14K, 35- 40mm, OF, C. 1910-1930 | $85 | $100 | $150 |
| SW, 7-15J, 14K, 35- 40mm, HC, C. 1910-1930 | 225 | 275 | 300 |
| KWKS, 10J, cylinder, 18K, 34- 40mm, OF, C.1865-90 | 145 | 165 | 225 |
| KWKS, 10J, cylinder, 18K, 38- 43mm, HC, C. 1865-85 | 230 | 275 | 325 |
| Fusee, lever, fancy dial, 18K, 38- 43mm, OF, C. 1845-75 | 300 | 400 | 500 |
| Fusee, lever, fancy dial, 18K, 38- 43mm, HC, C. 1850s | 400 | 500 | 600 |
| Ball shaped w/pin, 10J, 14K, 25mm, OF, C. 1890 | 500 | 600 | 650 |

## MISC. LADYS  Ca. 1850–1950  ENAMEL ON  *GOLD*

| TYPE – DESCRIPTION | Avg | Ex-Fn | Mint |
|---|---|---|---|
| KW, enamel (black outlines) 18K, 40- 42mm HC, C. 1860 | $450 | $550 | $650 |
| KW, enamel & dia., Swiss, 10J, 18K, OF, C. 1860 | 450 | 550 | 650 |
| Pattern enamel & demi-hunter, 15J, 18K , 35mm, HC, C.1885 | 500 | 650 | 800 |
| Portrait enamel, KWKS, Swiss, 14K, 34- 42mm, HC, C. 1870 | 550 | 700 | 850 |
| Enamel , with pearls and/ or dia., 10-17J, w/ matching pin, 18K, 23-26mm, OF | 900 | 1,100 | 1,300 |
| Enamel, w/dia. or pearls, w/ pin, 18K, 26-30mm, HC, C. 1895 | 1,400 | 1,500 | 1,700 |
| Miniature verge, gold & enamel w/ pearls, superior enamel, Swiss, KW, gold case, 27mm, OF, C. 1770, | 4,000 | 4,500 | 5,000 |
| Miniature HC enamel & dia., 17J, Swiss, with orig. pin, 18K, 23mm, HC, C. 1890 | 1,500 | 2,000 | 2,300 |
| Ball-shaped (Duchene) Geneva, verge, KW, enamel and gold, 25mm, C. 1800 | 1,800 | 2,200 | 2,500 |

Note: Some models and grades are not included. Their values can be determined by comparing with similar age, size, metal content, style, models and grades listed.

Note: Watches listed in this book are priced at the collectable retail level, as complete watches having an original case, an original dial, and with the entire original movement in good working order with no repairs needed.

### COMPARISON OF WATCH SIZES

| U. S. A. | EUROPEAN |
|---|---|
| 10-12 SIZE | 40—44 MM |
| 16   SIZE | 45—48 MM |
| 18   SIZE | 50—54 MM |

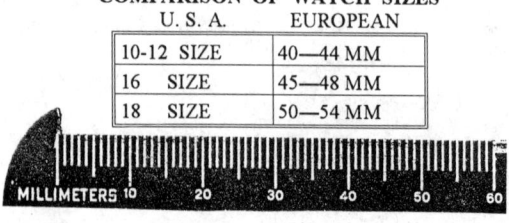

# LADY'S UNUSUAL *GOLD* & ENAMEL

LEFT; Ball-shaped, bezel wind, 18K, enamel & diamonds, Swiss, 18K, 16mm, OF, C. 1920. (illo.131) CENTER: Ring watch w/enamel & dia., Swiss, 18K, 18mm, C.1910. (illo.132) RIGHT: Padlock form enamel and gold, Swiss, KW. (illo.133)

| TYPE – DESCRIPTION | Avg | Ex-Fn | Mint |
|---|---|---|---|
| Ball-shaped, bezel wind, Swiss, enamel & diamondson 18K case, 16mm, OF, C. 1920 (illo.131) | $1,200 | $1,400 | $1,600 |
| Ring watch w/enamel & dia., Swiss, 18K, 18mm, C.1910 (illo.132) | 1,200 | 1,800 | 2,000 |
| Cherry form enamel & 18K, 17J, closed case, bezel wind, Swiss, 18K, 22mm, | 2,500 | 3,000 | 3,500 |
| Flower basket form, enamel and 18K, Swiss, KWKS, with heart form movement, 10J, 18K, 30x24mm, HC, C. 1860 | 3,000 | 3,500 | 4,000 |
| Padlock form enamel and gold, Swiss, KW (illo.133) | 2,000 | 2,250 | 2,500 |
| Padlock form enamel and gold (cover over dial,) Swiss, KW, diamonds on case, heart shaped mvt.,18K, 28x51mm, HC, C.1870 | 3,000 | 3,500 | 4,000 |
| Form watch in shape of **leaf**, gold & enamel, Bar mvt. (illo.134) | 3,000 | 3,250 | 3,500 |

 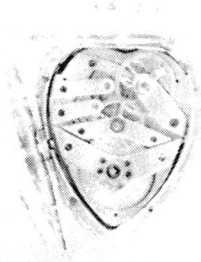

Form watch in shape of **leaf**, gold & enamel, cylinder escapement, Bar movement., KW KS, Ca.1865. (illo.134)

Scarab form gold & enamel, 10J, cylinder, diamonds, closed case w/wings that open, 18K, 54x23mm, C.1885. (illo.135)

Rare enamel & gold harps, matched pair w/ music, verge, diamonds, lapis and enameled scenes, 3 3/4 high, C.1830. (illo.136)

| TYPE – DESCRIPTION | Avg | Ex-Fn | Mint |
|---|---|---|---|
| Scarab form gold & enamel, 10J, cylinder, diamonds, closed case w/wings that open, 18K, 54x23mm, C.1885 (illo.135) | $5,000 | $6,000 | $7,000 |
| Lorgnette with enamel & gold, KW, 10J, Swiss, 3 1/4" x 1" cover ornamented w/dia., 18K | 4,000 | 5,000 | 6,000 |
| Rare enamel & gold harps, matched pair w/ music, verge, diamonds, lapis and enameled scenes, 3 3/4 high, C.1830 (illo.136) | 25,000 | 30,000 | 35,000 |
| Rock crystal case, silver dial, Viennese made, C. 1730 (illo.137) | 10,000 | 12,000 | 15,000 |

Rock crystal case, silver dial, Viennese made, C. 1830. (illo.137)

# ENAMEL WATCHES

Floral enamel watch. Bouquet of flowers within a champleve border of scrolls enclosing panels of flowers. (illo.E-2)

Floral enamel watch. Finely painted floral enamel panel within border of seed pearls. (illo.E-1)

| SIZE AND DESCRIPTION | Avg | Ex-Fn | Mint |
|---|---|---|---|
| 55mm, finely painted floral, seed pearls, (Bovet also Ilbery),18K (illo.E.1) | $6,000 | $7,500 | $9,000 |
| 47mm, gold enamel repeater, with chatelaine of pierced gold links & enamel plaques with enamel key & fob seals (illo.E.2) | 3,500 | 4,500 | 5,500 |
| Enamel & pearls, hunting scene of lion, for China market, duplex escapement, 62mm, Ca. 1845 (illo.E-3) | 5,000 | 6,000 | 7,000 |
| Enamel and 18K case, automated horseman and windmill also horse drinks water (illo.E-4) | 35,000 | 37,500 | 40,000 |
| Enamel floral scene, enamel and pearls on gold case, finely painted floral bouquet, 55mm (illo.E-5) | 30,000 | 35,000 | 40,000 |
| VIENNESE enamel watch, the front cover shows a lady and gentleman in a scene, the back cover pictures three boys in a scene, 55mm (illo.E-6 & E-6A) | 2,000 | 2,500 | 3,000 |
| 54mm, 29J., 1/4 repeater, pearls & enamel, silver case (illo.E-8) | 2,200 | 2,800 | 3,500 |
| VIENNESE Lapis Lazuli enamel watch, verge fusee, top and bottom covers are finely cut solid lapis stone, champleve enamel dial, Ca. 1800 (illo.E-9) | 3,500 | 4,500 | 5,000 |

🕐 French watch-making believed to have started in town of Blois, France. French Enamel Watches also believed to have started in Blois, in early 1600's.

Enamel & pearls, hunting scene of lion, for China market,
duplex escapement, 62mm, Ca. 1845. (illo.E-3)

Enamel and 18K case, automated horseman and windmill
also fountain, horse drinks water. (illo.E-4)

Enamel floral scene, enamel and pearls on gold case, finely
painted floral bouquet, 55mm. (illo.E-5)

VIENNESE enamel watch, the front cover shows a lady and gentleman in a scene, the back cover pictures three boys in a scene, 55mm. (illo.E-6)

VIENNESE enamel watch, same watch as above, two-footed balance bridge, the inner lids are decorated with polychrome enamelled scenes. (illo.E-6A)

54mm, 29J, 1/4 hour repeater, Pearls and enamel on a silver case, ca. 1885. (illo.E-8)

VIENNESE Lapis Lazuli enamel watch, verge fusee, top and bottom covers are finely cut solid lapis stone, champleve enamel dial, ca. 1800. (illo.E-9)

Floral enamel watch, 57mm, bouquet of flowers within a gold case set with split pearls. (illo.E-10)

Enamel scene watch, 58mm, finely painted scene of ships in harbor. (illo.E-11)

| SIZE AND DESCRIPTION | Avg | Ex-Fn | Mint |
|---|---|---|---|
| 57mm, floral enamel, duplex, (Bovet), pearls, 18K, (illo.E-10) ...... | $8,000 | $9,000 | $10,000 |
| 58mm, harbor scene enamel, duplex, 18k, Ca. 1790 (illo.E-11) .... | 20,000 | 26,000 | 32,000 |
| 43mm, basket form champleve enamel, 18k, Ca.1800 (illo.E.12)... | 3,000 | 3,500 | 4,000 |
| 42mm, champleve border, finely painted flowers, (Le Roy), gold case & chain.................... | 2,500 | 3,000 | 3,500 |
| 37mm, rose gold guilloche enamel demi-hunter................ | 400 | 500 | 600 |
| 36mm, gold enamel & champleve enamel, verge, Ca. 1800 .......... | 1,800 | 2,200 | 2,800 |
| 35mm, gold champleve enamel, (L'Epine), cylinder .............. | 800 | 1,000 | 1,200 |
| 35mm, gold enamel & seed pearls, rose cut diamonds .............. | 400 | 500 | 600 |
| 34mm, gold egg-shaped form enamel, verge, (Austrian) .............. | 2,000 | 2,200 | 2,500 |
| 30mm, gold miniature enamel, verge, seed pearls, Ca. 1800 .......... | 2,000 | 2,400 | 2,800 |
| 27mm, gold enamel lapel brooch with seed pearls & rose cut diamonds, Ca. 1890 ...... | 700 | 800 | 900 |
| 27mm, gold fine enamel lapel brooch with cut diamonds by C. H. Meylan (illo.E.13) ...... | 1,500 | 2,000 | 2,500 |

Enamel form tapered oval basket with rising rope handle, enhanced with panels of flowers, 18K case. (illo.E-12)

A chased enamel gold lady's pendant watch. Enamel portrait of a lady. (illo.E-13)

( ILLO. A )          (ILLO. B )                    ( ILLO. D)

| Size and Description | Avg | Ex-Fn | Mint |
|---|---|---|---|
| 27mm, Art Noveau design, multi-colored flowers gold & diamond pendant watch & pin, 18K, OF, Ca.1890 (illo. A)................... | $1,000 | $1,200 | $1,400 |
| 25mm, Enamel & pearls & diamonds, star shaped gold settings , pendant and pen, 18K, OF, Ca. 1890 ( illo. B )....................... | 800 | 900 | 1,000 |
| 25mm, enamel pendant with pin, golden frame of vines around a scene of a lady , 14K, OF, Ca. 1900 ...................................... | 900 | 1,100 | 1,400 |
| 24mm, pearl pendant watch with pin, seed pearls also on classic fleur-de-lis designed pin, 14K OF, Ca.1885 ( illo. C )............ | 800 | 1,000 | 1,200 |
| 24mm, enamel and gold pendant watch with a starburst gold and pearl pin, 10 J, cylinder movement, 18K, OF, Ca.1900 ( illo. D )... | 1,100 | 1,300 | 1,600 |
| 22mm, ball-shaped enamel & pearl pendant watch, exposed balance, lever escapement can be seen back crystal ( illo. E ).............. | 1,400 | 1,700 | 2,200 |
| 20mm, 17J, three-finger bridge miniature movement, Adj.5P, by Didsheim platinum OF case, Ca.1930s ( illo. F ).............. | 1,500 | 1,600 | 1,800 |

( ILLO. E )

( ILLO. C )                          ( ILLO. F )

## Am. Waltham W. Co.

| Date | Serial # |
|---|---|
| 1852 | 50 |
| 1853 | 400 |
| 1854 | 1,000 |
| 1855 | 2,500 |
| 1856 | 4,000 |
| 1857 | 6,000 |
| 1858 | 10,000 |
| 1859 | 15,000 |
| 1860 | 20,000 |
| 1861 | 30,000 |
| 1862 | 45,000 |
| 1863 | 65,000 |
| 1864 | 110,000 |
| 1865 | 180,000 |
| 1866 | 260,000 |
| 1867 | 330,000 |
| 1868 | 410,000 |
| 1869 | 460,000 |
| 1870 | 500,000 |
| 1871 | 540,000 |
| 1872 | 590,000 |
| 1873 | 680,000 |
| 1874 | 730,000 |
| 1875 | 810,000 |
| 1876 | 910,000 |
| 1877 | 1,000,000 |
| 1878 | 1,150,000 |
| 1879 | 1,350,000 |
| 1880 | 1,500,000 |
| 1881 | 1,670,000 |
| 1882 | 1,835,000 |
| 1883 | 2,000,000 |
| 1884 | 2,350,000 |
| 1885 | 2,650,000 |
| 1886 | 3,000,000 |
| 1887 | 3,400,000 |
| 1888 | 3,800,000 |
| 1889 | 4,000,000 |
| 1890 | 4,700,000 |
| 1891 | 5,200,000 |
| 1892 | 5,800,000 |
| 1893 | 6,300,000 |
| 1894 | 6,700,000 |
| 1895 | 7,100,000 |
| 1896 | 7,450,000 |
| 1897 | 8,100,000 |
| 1898 | 8,400,000 |
| 1899 | 9,000,000 |
| 1900 | 9,500,000 |
| 1901 | 10,200,000 |
| 1902 | 11,100,000 |
| 1903 | 12,100,000 |
| 1904 | 13,500,000 |
| 1905 | 14,300,000 |
| 1906 | 14,700,000 |
| 1907 | 15,500,000 |
| 1908 | 16,400,000 |
| 1909 | 17,600,000 |
| 1910 | 17,900,000 |
| 1911 | 18,100,000 |
| 1912 | 18,200,000 |
| 1913 | 18,900,000 |
| 1914 | 19,500,000 |
| 1915 | 20,000,000 |
| 1916 | 20,500,000 |
| 1917 | 20,900,000 |
| 1918 | 21,800,000 |
| 1919 | 22,500,000 |
| 1920 | 23,400,000 |
| 1921 | 23,900,000 |
| 1922 | 24,100,000 |
| 1923 | 24,300,000 |
| 1924 | 24,550,000 |
| 1925 | 24,800,000 |
| 1926 | 25,200,000 |
| 1927 | 26,100,000 |
| 1928 | 26,600,000 |
| 1929 | 26,900,000 |
| 1930 | 27,100,000 |
| 1931 | 27,300,000 |
| 1932 | 27,550,000 |
| 1933 | 27,750,000 |
| 1934 | 28,100,000 |
| 1935 | 28,400,000 |
| 1936 | 29,100,000 |
| 1937 | 29,400,000 |
| 1938 | 29,750,000 |
| 1939 | 30,050,000 |
| 1940 | 30,250,000 |
| 1941 | 30,750,000 |
| 1942 | 31,050,000 |
| 1943 | 31,400,000 |
| 1944 | 32,100,000 |
| 1945 | 32,350,000 |
| 1946 | 32,350,000 |
| 1947 | 32,750,000 |
| 1948 | 33,100,000 |
| 1949 | 33,500,000 |
| 1950 | 33,560,000 |
| 1951 | 33,600,000 |
| 1952 | 33,700,000 |
| 1953 | 33,800,000 |
| 1954 | 34,100,000 |
| 1955 | 34,450,000 |
| 1956 | 34,700,000 |
| 1957 | 35,000,000 |

## Aurora W. Co.

| Date | Serial # |
|---|---|
| 1884 | 10,001 |
| 1885 | 60,000 |
| 1886 | 101,000 |
| 1887 | 160,000 |
| 1888 | 200,000 |
| 1889 | 215,000 |
| 1890 | 230,901 |

## Columbus W. Co.

| Date | Serial # |
|---|---|
| 1875 | 1,000 |
| 1876 | 3,000 |
| 1877 | 6,000 |
| 1878 | 9,000 |
| 1879 | 12,000 |
| 1880 | 15,000 |
| 1881 | 18,000 |
| 1882 | 21,000 |
| 1883 | 25,000 |
| 1884 | 30,000 |
| 1885 | 40,000 |
| 1886 | 53,000 |
| 1887 | 75,000 |
| 1888 | 97,000 |
| 1889 | 119,000 |
| 1890 | 141,000 |
| 1891 | 163,000 |
| 1892 | 185,000 |
| 1893 | 207,000 |
| 1894 | 229,000 |
| 1895 | 251,000 |
| 1896 | 273,000 |
| 1897 | 295,000 |
| 1898 | 317,000 |
| 1899 | 339,000 |
| 1900 | 361,000 |
| 1901 | 383,000 |

### SPECIAL BLOCK OF SERIAL NOS.

| Date | Serial # |
|---|---|
| 1894 | 500,001 |
| 1895 | 501,500 |
| 1898 | 503,000 |
| 1900 | 504,300 |
| 1902 | 506,000 |

## Elgin Watch Co.

| Date | Serial # |
|---|---|
| 1867 | 10,000 |
| 1868 | 30,000 |
| 1869 | 60,000 |
| 1870 | 100,000 |
| 1871 | 150,000 |
| 1872 | 200,000 |
| 1873 | 250,000 |
| 1874 | 300,000 |
| 1875 | 400,000 |
| 1876 | 450,000 |
| 1877 | 500,000 |
| 1878 | 550,000 |
| 1879 | 600,000 |
| 1880 | 750,000 |
| 1881 | 900,000 |
| 1882 | 1,000,000 March, 9th |
| 1883 | 1,250,000 |
| 1884 | 1,500,000 |
| 1885 | 1,750,000 |
| 1886 | 2,000,000 June 20th |
| 1887 | 2,500,000 |
| 1888 | 3,000,000 Aug 4th |
| 1889 | 3,500,000 |
| 1890 | 4,000,000 Aug 16th |
| 1891 | 4,300,000 |
| 1892 | 4,600,000 |
| 1893 | 5,000,000 July 1st |
| 1894 | 5,500,000 |
| 1895 | 6,000,000 Nov.26th |
| 1896 | 6,500,000 |
| 1897 | 7,000,000 Oct. 28th |
| 1898 | 7,500,000 |
| 1899 | 8,000,000 Jan.18th |
| 1900 | 9,000,000 Nov.14th |
| 1901 | 9,300,000 |
| 1902 | 9,600,000 |
| 1903 | 10,000,000 May 15th |
| 1904 | 11,000,000 April 4th |
| 1905 | 12,000,000 Oct 6th |
| 1906 | 12,500,000 |
| 1907 | 13,000,000 April 4th |
| 1908 | 13,500,000 |
| 1909 | 14,000,000 Feb 9th |
| 1910 | 15,000,000 April 2nd |
| 1911 | 16,000,000 July 11th |
| 1912 | 17,000,000 Nov.6th |
| 1913 | 17,500,000 |
| 1914 | 18,000,000 |
| 1915 | 18,500,000 |
| 1916 | 19,000,000 |
| 1917 | 20,000,000 |
| 1918 | 21,000,000 |
| 1919 | 22,000,000 |
| 1920 | 23,000,000 |
| 1921 | 24,000,000 |
| 1922 | 25,000,000 |
| 1923 | 26,000,000 |
| 1924 | 27,000,000 |
| 1925 | 28,050,000 |
| 1926 | 29,120,000 |
| 1927 | 30,050,000 |
| 1928 | 31,500,000 |
| 1929 | 32,500,000 |
| 1930 | 32,500,000 |
| 1931 | 33,000,000 |
| 1932 | 33,700,000 |
| 1933 | 34,000,000 |
| 1934 | 35,000,000 |
| 1935 | 35,650,000 |
| 1936 | 36,200,000 |
| 1937 | 37,100,000 |
| 1938 | 37,900,000 |
| 1939 | 38,200,000 |
| 1940 | 39,100,000 |
| 1941 | 40,200,000 |
| 1942 | 41,100,000 |
| 1943 | 42,200,000 |
| 1944 | 42,620,000 |
| 1945 | 43,200,000 |
| 1946 | 44,000,000 |
| 1947 | 45,000,000 |
| 1948 | 46,000,000 |
| 1949 | 47,000,000 |
| 1950 | 48,000,000 |
| 1951 | 49,500,000 |
| 1952 | 52,000,000 |
| 1953 | 53,500,000 |
| 1954 | 54,000,000 |
| 1955 | 54,500,000 |
| 1956 | 55,000,000 |

## Hamilton Watch Co.

| Date | Serial No. |
|---|---|
| 1893 | 1-2,000 |
| 1894 | 5,000 |
| 1895 | 11,500 |
| 1896 | 16,000 |
| 1897 | 27,000 |
| 1898 | 50,000 |
| 1899 | 74,000 |
| 1900 | 104,000 |
| 1901 | 143,000 |
| 1902 | 196,000 |
| 1903 | 260,000 |
| 1904 | 340,000 |
| 1905 | 425,000 |
| 1906 | 590,000 |
| 1907 | 756,000 |
| 1908 | 921,000 |
| 1909 | 1,087,000 |
| 1910 | 1,150,500 |
| 1911 | 1,250,000 |
| 1912 | 1,331,000 |
| 1913 | 1,370,000 |
| 1914 | 1,410,000 |
| 1915 | 1,450,500 |
| 1916 | 1,517,000 |
| 1917 | 1,580,000 |
| 1918 | 1,650,000 |
| 1919 | 1,700,000 |
| 1920 | 1,760,000 |
| 1921 | 1,900,000 |
| 1922 | 1,900,000 |
| 1923 | 1,950,000 |
| 1924 | 2,000,000 |
| 1925 | 2,150,000 |
| 1926 | 2,200,000 |
| 1927 | 2,250,000 |
| 1928 | 2,300,000 |
| 1929 | 2,350,000 |
| 1930 | 2,400,000 |
| 1931 | 2,450,000 |
| 1932 | 2,500,000 |
| 1933 | 2,600,000 |
| 1934 | 2,700,000 |
| 1935 | 2,900,000 |
| 1936 | 2,900,000 |
| 1937 | 3,000,000 |
| 1938 | 3,300,000 |
| 1939 | 3,400,000 |
| 1940 | 3,600,000 |
| 1941 | 3,900,000 |
| 1942 | 4,025,000 |

DATE LETTERS
B on 950B=1942-50
C on 992B=1942-59
S on 950B=1950-55
OTHER DATE LETTERS = 1930s to 1950s

## Hampden W. Co.

| Date | Serial # |
|---|---|
| 1877 | 60,000 |
| 1878 | 91,000 |
| 1879 | 122,000 |
| 1880 | 153,000 |
| 1881 | 184,000 |
| 1882 | 215,000 |
| 1883 | 250,000 |
| 1884 | 300,000 |
| 1885 | 350,000 |
| 1886 | 400,000 |
| 1887 | 450,000 |
| 1888 | 500,000 |
| 1889 | 555,500 |
| 1890 | 611,000 |
| 1891 | 666,500 |
| 1892 | 722,000 |
| 1893 | 775,000 |
| 1894 | 833,000 |
| 1895 | 888,500 |
| 1896 | 944,000 |
| 1897 | 1,000,000 |
| 1898 | 1,128,000 |
| 1899 | 1,256,000 |
| 1900 | 1,384,000 |
| 1901 | 1,512,000 |
| 1902 | 1,642,000 |
| 1903 | 1,768,000 |
| 1904 | 1,896,000 |
| 1905 | 2,024,000 |
| 1906 | 2,152,000 |
| 1907 | 2,280,000 |
| 1908 | 2,408,000 |
| 1909 | 2,536,000 |
| 1910 | 2,664,000 |
| 1911 | 2,792,000 |
| 1912 | 2,920,000 |
| 1913 | 3,048,000 |
| 1914 | 3,176,000 |
| 1915 | 3,304,000 |
| 1916 | 3,432,000 |
| 1917 | 3,560,000 |
| 1918 | 3,680,000 |
| 1919 | 3,816,000 |
| 1920 | 3,944,000 |
| 1921 | 4,072,000 |
| 1922 | 4,200,000 |
| 1923 | 4,400,000 |
| 1924 | 4,600,000 |

## E. Howard & Co.

| Date | Serial # |
|---|---|
| 1858-60 | 131-1,900 |
| 1860-61 | 1,901-3,000 |
| 1861 | 3,001-3,100 |
| 1861 | 3,101-3,250 |
| 1861 | 3,401-3,500 |
| 1861-71 | 3,501-28,000 |
| 1868-83 | 30,001-50,000 |
| 1869-99 | 50,001-71,000 |
| 1880-99 | 100,001-105,000 |
| 1880-90 | 200,001-227,000 |
| 1885-99 | 228,001-231,000 |
| 1884-99 | 300,001-309,000 |
| 1895 | 309,001-310,000 |
| 1890-95 | 400,001-405,000 |
| 1890-95 | 500,001-501,500 |
| 1896-1903 | 600,001-601,500 |
| 1896-1903 | 700,001-701,500 |

## Howard Watch Co. (Keystone)

| Date | Serial # |
|---|---|
| 1902 | 850,000 |
| 1905 | 900,000 |
| 1909 | 980,000 |
| 1912 | 1,100,000 |
| 1915 | 1,285,000 |
| 1917 | 1,340,000 |
| 1921 | 1,400,000 |
| 1930 | 1,500,000 |

## Illinois Watch Co.

| Date | Serial # |
|---|---|
| 1872 | 5,000 |
| 1873 | 20,000 |
| 1874 | 50,000 |
| 1875 | 75,000 |
| 1876 | 100,000 |
| 1877 | 145,000 |
| 1878 | 210,000 |
| 1879 | 250,000 |
| 1880 | 300,000 |
| 1881 | 350,000 |
| 1882 | 400,000 |
| 1883 | 400,000 |
| 1884 | 500,000 |
| 1885 | 550,000 |
| 1886 | 600,000 |
| 1887 | 700,000 |
| 1888 | 800,000 |
| 1889 | 960,000 |
| 1890 | 1,000,000 |
| 1891 | 1,040,000 |
| 1892 | 1,090,000 |
| 1893 | 1,120,000 |
| 1894 | 1,160,000 |
| 1895 | 1,220,000 |
| 1896 | 1,250,000 |
| 1897 | 1,290,000 |
| 1898 | 1,330,000 |
| 1899 | 1,370,000 |
| 1900 | 1,410,000 |
| 1901 | 1,450,000 |
| 1902 | 1,500,000 |
| 1903 | 1,650,000 |
| 1904 | 1,700,000 |
| 1905 | 1,800,000 |
| 1906 | 1,840,000 |
| 1907 | 1,900,000 |
| 1908 | 2,100,000 |
| 1909 | 2,150,000 |
| 1910 | 2,300,000 |
| 1911 | 2,320,000 |
| 1912 | 2,400,000 |
| 1913 | 2,500,000 |
| 1914 | 2,600,000 |
| 1915 | 2,700,000 |
| 1916 | 2,800,000 |
| 1917 | 3,000,000 |
| 1918 | 3,200,000 |
| 1919 | 3,400,000 |
| 1920 | 3,600,000 |
| 1921 | 3,750,000 |
| 1922 | 3,900,000 |
| 1923 | 4,000,000 |
| 1924 | 4,500,000 |
| 1925 | 4,700,000 |
| 1926 | 4,800,000 |
| 1927 | 5,000,000 |

(Sold to Hamilton)

| Date | Serial # |
|---|---|
| 1928 | 3,500,000 |
| 1929 | 3,400,000 |
| 1930 | 5,400,000 |
| 1931 | 5,500,000 |
| 1932 | 5,600,000 |

## Rockford W.Co.

| Date | Serial # |
|---|---|
| 1874 | 22,200 |
| 1875 | 42,450 |
| 1876 | 63,000 |
| 1877 | 83,000 |
| 1878 | 103,000 |
| 1879 | 124,000 |
| 1880 | 144,000 |
| 1881 | 165,000 |
| 1882 | 185,000 |
| 1883 | 206,000 |
| 1884 | 226,000 |
| 1885 | 247,000 |
| 1886 | 267,000 |
| 1887 | 287,500 |
| 1888 | 308,000 |
| 1889 | 328,500 |
| 1890 | 349,000 |
| 1891 | 369,500 |
| 1892 | 390,000 |
| 1893 | 410,000 |
| 1894 | 430,000 |
| 1895 | 450,000 |
| 1896 | 470,000 |
| 1897 | 490,000 |
| 1898 | 510,000 |
| 1899 | 530,000 |
| 1900 | 550,000 |
| 1901 | 570,000 |
| 1902 | 590,000 |
| 1903 | 610,000 |
| 1904 | 630,000 |
| 1905 | 650,000 |
| 1906 | 670,000 |
| 1907 | 690,000 |
| 1908 | 734,000 |
| 1909 | 790,000 |
| 1910 | 824,000 |
| 1911 | 880,000 |
| 1912 | 936,000 |
| 1913 | 958,000 |
| 1914 | 980,000 |
| 1915 | 1,000,000 |

## South Bend W. Co.

| Date | Serial # |
|---|---|
| 1903 | 380,501 |
| 1904 | 410,000 |
| 1905 | 445,000 |
| 1906 | 460,000 |
| 1907 | 515,000 |
| 1908 | 550,000 |
| 1909 | 585,000 |
| 1910 | 620,000 |
| 1911 | 655,000 |
| 1912 | 690,000 |
| 1913 | 725,000 |
| 1914 | 760,000 |
| 1915 | 795,000 |
| 1916 | 825,000 |
| 1917 | 865,000 |
| 1918 | 900,000 |
| 1919 | 935,000 |
| 1920 | 970,000 |
| 1921 | 1,005,000 |
| 1922 | 1,040,000 |
| 1923 | 1,075,000 |
| 1924 | 1,110,000 |
| 1925 | 1,145,000 |
| 1926 | 1,180,000 |
| 1927 | 1,215,000 |
| 1928 | 1,245,000 |
| 1929 | 1,275,000 |

## Seth Thomas W. Co.

| Date | Serial # |
|---|---|
| 1885 | 5,000 |
| 1886 | 20,000 |
| 1887 | 40,000 |
| 1888 | 80,000 |
| 1889 | 150,000 |
| 1890 | 235,000 |
| 1891 | 320,000 |
| 1892 | 420,000 |
| 1893 | 510,000 |
| 1894 | 600,000 |
| 1895 | 690,000 |
| 1896 | 780,000 |
| 1897 | 870,000 |
| 1898 | 960,000 |
| 1899 | 1,050,000 |
| 1900 | 1,140,000 |
| 1901 | 1,230,000 |
| 1902 | 1,320,000 |
| 1903 | 1,410,000 |
| 1904 | 1,500,000 |
| 1905 | 1,700,000 |
| 1906 | 1,900,000 |
| 1907 | 2,100,000 |
| 1908 | 2,300,000 |
| 1909 | 2,525,000 |
| 1910 | 2,725,000 |
| 1911 | 2,950,000 |
| 1912 | 3,175,000 |
| 1913 | 3,490,000 |
| 1914 | 3,600,000 |

## Ball Watch Co. (Hamilton)

| Date | Serial # |
|---|---|
| 1895 | 13,000 |
| 1897 | 20,500 |
| 1900 | 42,000 |
| 1902 | 170,000 |
| 1905 | 462,000 |
| 1910 | 600,000 |
| 1915 | 603,000 |
| 1920 | 610,000 |
| 1925 | 620,000 |
| 1930 | 637,000 |
| 1935 | 641,000 |
| 1938 | 647,000 |
| 1939 | 650,000 |
| 1940 | 651,000 |
| 1941 | 652,000 |
| 1942 | 654,000 |

(Waltham)

| Date | Serial # |
|---|---|
| 1900 | 060,700 |
| 1905 | 202,000 |
| 1910 | 216,000 |
| 1915 | 250,000 |
| 1920 | 260,000 |
| 1925 | 270,000 |

(Illinois)

| Date | Serial # |
|---|---|
| 1929 | 800,000 |
| 1930 | 801,000 |
| 1931 | 803,000 |
| 1932 | 804,000 |

(Elgin)
1904-1906
S # range
11,853,000-12,282,000

(E. Howard & Co.)
1893-1895
S # range
226,000-308,000

(Hampden)
1891-1892
S # range
626,750-657,960-759,720

## Audemars Piguet

| Date | Serial # |
|---|---|
| 1882 | 2,000 |
| 1890 | 4,000 |
| 1895 | 5,350 |
| 1900 | 6,500 |
| 1905 | 9,500 |
| 1910 | 13,000 |
| 1915 | 17,000 |
| 1920 | 25,000 |
| 1925 | 33,000 |
| 1930 | 40,000 |
| 1935 | 42,000 |
| 1940 | 44,000 |
| 1945 | 48,000 |
| 1950 | 55,000 |
| 1955 | 65,000 |
| 1960 | 75,000 |
| 1965 | 90,000 |
| 1970 | 115,000 |
| 1975 | 160,000 |
| 1980 | 225,000 |

## International W.Co. (Schaffhausen)

| Date | Serial # |
|---|---|
| 1875 | 4,000 |
| 1885 | 10,000 |
| 1890 | 15,000 |
| 1895 | 100,000 |
| 1900 | 300,000 |
| 1905 | 500,000 |
| 1910 | 500,000 |
| 1915 | 600,000 |
| 1920 | 700,000 |
| 1925 | 750,000 |
| 1930 | 800,000 |
| 1935 | 850,000 |
| 1940 | 900,000 |
| 1945 | 955,000 |
| 1950 | 1,000,000 |
| 1955 | 1,200,000 |
| 1960 | 1,500,000 |

## A. Lange & Sohne

| Date | Serial # |
|---|---|
| 1870 | 5,000 |
| 1875 | 10,000 |
| 1880 | 20,000 |
| 1885 | 25,000 |
| 1890 | 30,000 |
| 1895 | 35,000 |
| 1900 | 40,000 |
| 1905 | 50,000 |
| 1910 | 60,000 |
| 1915 | 70,000 |
| 1920 | 75,000 |
| 1925 | 80,000 |
| 1930 | 85,000 |
| 1935 | 90,000 |
| 1940 | 100,000 |

## Longines

| Date | Serial # |
|---|---|
| 1867 | 1 |
| 1870 | 20,000 |
| 1877 | 100,000 |
| 1882 | 250,000 |
| 1888 | 500,000 |
| 1893 | 750,000 |
| 1899 | 1,000,000 |
| 1901 | 1,250,000 |
| 1904 | 1,500,000 |
| 1905 | 1,750,000 |
| 1907 | 2,000,000 |
| 1909 | 2,250,000 |
| 1911 | 2,500,000 |
| 1912 | 2,750,000 |
| 1913 | 3,000,000 |
| 1915 | 3,250,000 |
| 1917 | 3,500,000 |
| 1919 | 3,750,000 |
| 1922 | 4,000,000 |
| 1925 | 4,250,000 |
| 1926 | 4,500,000 |
| 1928 | 4,750,000 |
| 1929 | 5,000,000 |
| 1934 | 5,250,000 |
| 1937 | 5,500,000 |
| 1938 | 5,750,000 |
| 1940 | 6,000,000 |
| 1945 | 7,000,000 |
| 1950 | 8,000,000 |
| 1953 | 9,000,000 |
| 1956 | 10,000,000 |
| 1959 | 11,000,000 |
| 1962 | 12,000,000 |
| 1966 | 13,000,000 |
| 1967 | 14,000,000 |
| 1969 | 15,000,000 |

## Omega

| Date | Serial # |
|---|---|
| 1895 | 50,000 |
| 1900 | 500,000 |
| 1905 | 1,000,000 |
| 1910 | 2,500,000 |
| 1915 | 4,500,000 |
| 1920 | 6,000,000 |
| 1925 | 7,500,000 |
| 1930 | 9,500,000 |
| 1935 | 11,000,000 |
| 1940 | 12,500,000 |
| 1945 | 14,000,000 |
| 1950 | 15,500,000 |
| 1960 | 18,000,000 |
| 1970 | 28,000,000 |
| 1975 | 35,000,000 |

## Patek Philippe & Co.

| Date | Serial # |
|---|---|
| 1840 | 100 |
| 1845 | 1,200 |
| 1850 | 3,000 |
| 1855 | 8,000 |
| 1860 | 15,000 |
| 1865 | 22,000 |
| 1870 | 35,000 |
| 1875 | 45,000 |
| 1880 | 55,000 |
| 1885 | 70,000 |
| 1890 | 85,000 |
| 1895 | 100,000 |
| 1900 | 110,000 |
| 1905 | 125,000 |
| 1910 | 150,000 |
| 1915 | 175,000 |
| 1920 | 190,000 |
| 1925 | 200,000 |
| 1930 | 250,000 |
| 1935 | 700,000 |
| 1940 | 750,000 |
| 1945 | 760,000 |
| 1950 | 700,000 |
| 1955 | 725,000 |
| 1960 | 750,000 |
| 1965 | 775,000 |
| 1970 | 795,000 |
| 1975 | 900,000 |

## Rolex (Case S #)

| Date | Serial # |
|---|---|
| 1925 | 25,000 |
| 1926 | 27,500 |
| 1927 | 30,500 |
| 1928 | 33,000 |
| 1929 | 35,500 |
| 1930 | 38,000 |
| 1931 | 40,000 |
| 1932 | 43,000 |
| 1933 | 49,000 |
| 1934 | 55,000 |
| 1935 | 62,000 |
| 1936 | 82,000 |
| 1937 | 98,000 |
| 1938 | 118,000 |
| 1939 | 136,000 |
| 1940 | 165,000 |
| 1941 | 194,000 |
| 1942 | 224,000 |
| 1943 | 253,000 |
| 1944 | 284,000 |
| 1945 | 348,000 |
| 1946 | 413,000 |
| 1947 | 478,000 |
| 1948 | 543,000 |
| 1949 | 608,000 |
| 1950 | 673,500 |
| 1951 | 735,500 |
| 1952 | 804,000 |
| 1953 | 860,000 |
| 1954 | 935,000 |
| 1955 | 1,010,000 |
| 1956 | 1,095,000 |
| 1957 | 1,167,000 |
| 1958 | 1,245,000 |
| 1959 | 1,323,000 |
| 1960 | 1,401,000 |
| 1961 | 1,485,000 |
| 1962 | 1,557,000 |
| 1963 | 1,635,000 |
| 1964 | 1,713,000 |
| 1965 | 1,791,000 |
| 1966 | 1,870,000 |
| 1967 | 2,164,000 |
| 1968 | 2,426,000 |
| 1969 | 2,689,000 |
| 1970 | 2,952,000 |
| 1971 | 3,215,000 |
| 1972 | 3,478,000 |
| 1973 | 3,741,000 |
| 1974 | 4,004,000 |
| 1975 | 4,260,000 |
| 1976 | 4,530,000 |
| 1977 | 5,000,000 |
| 1978 | 5,480,000 |
| 1979 | 5,960,000 |
| 1980 | 6,430,000 |
| 1981 | 6,910,000 |
| 1982 | 7,380,000 |
| 1983 | 7,860,000 |
| 1984 | 8,340,000 |
| 1985 | 8,810,000 |
| 1986 | 9,300,000 |
| 1987 1/2 | 9,999,999 |
| 1987 3/4 | R000,001 |
| 1988 | R999,999 |
| 1989 | L000,001 |
| 1990 | L999,999 |
| 1990 1/2 | E000,001 |
| 1991 1/4 | E999,999 |
| 1991 1/2 | X000,001 |

## Vacheron

| Date | Serial # |
|---|---|
| 1830 | 30,000 |
| 1835 | 40,000 |
| 1840 | 50,000 |
| 1845 | 60,000 |
| 1850 | 75,000 |
| 1855 | 95,000 |
| 1860 | 110,000 |
| 1865 | 125,000 |
| 1870 | 140,000 |
| 1875 | 150,000 |
| 1880 | 170,000 |
| 1885 | 180,000 |
| 1890 | 190,000 |
| 1895 | 223,000 |
| 1900 | 256,000 |
| 1905 | 280,000 |
| 1910 | 322,000 |
| 1915 | 355,000 |
| 1920 | 395,000 |
| 1925 | 400,000 |
| 1930 | 410,000 |
| 1935 | 420,000 |
| 1940 | 440,000 |
| 1945 | 468,000 |
| 1950 | 498,000 |
| 1955 | 512,000 |
| 1960 | 536,000 |
| 1965 | 560,000 |
| 1970 | 585,000 |

The above list is provided for determining the **approximate** age of your watch. Match serial number with date. Watches were not necessarily sold in the exact order of manufactured date.

# ROMANCING THE WRIST WATCH

The wrist watch is considered by many watch collectors to be "today's collectable." This phenomenon is due, in part, to the development of the quartz movement which began in the 1970's and virtually revolutionized the watch market. Although these quartz watches are quiet, accurate timekeepers, and are inexpensive to manufacture, the watches of the past hold a special fascination in the heart of the collector. They enjoy collecting the timepieces with jeweled and moving parts that produce a rhythmic heartbeat inside their gold cases.

The watch collector has seen the prices of wrist watches soar in the past years, as wrist watches have become more and more in demand as an object of fashion, function and jewelry. A Patek, Philippe man's platinum minute repeater wrist watch sold for the record price of 345,000 Swiss francs, about $250,000 U.S. Not far behind this record setting sale was a Patek, Philippe "Calatrava" that brought $198,000. A Patek, Philippe enameled white gold "World Time" man's wrist watch sold for about $130,000. Some collectors have seen the values of their wrist watches double and, in many cases, triple in recent years. For example, in the early 1980s, a Patek, Phillipe perpetual calendar chronograph watch would have sold for $10,000. In 1987, the same watch would have sold for $50,000, and in 1988 for $80,000. In 1989, the price was up to $100,000. Such dramatic increases in values have brought about a feverish demand for wrist watches. The Swiss wrist watch has the attention of the wealthiest collectors, with Patek, Philippe & Co. at the top of their list and Audemars Piguet, Cartier, Rolex, and Vacheron & Constantin close behind. Other wrist watches showing appreciable value are Ebel, A. Lange, Gubelin, International Watch Co., Le Coultre, Ulysse Nardin, and Piaget. Next are Jules Jurgensen, Baume & Mercier, Gerard Perregaux, Movado, and Omega; then Benrus, Bulova, Agassiz, Elgin, Gruen, Hamilton, Illinois, Longines, and Waltham, the character watches, chronographs, and complicated watches.

Many wrist watch collectors have focused on fashion and take pride in wearing their unique watches. Women have been buying high fashion men's watches to wear, making women candidates for collecting. Young men appear to enjoy collecting wrist watches rather than pocket watches. The intense competition within their increasing numbers has influenced the rising prices.

*     *     *

European and Japanese collectors are making the biggest impact on the wrist watch market with their volume of buying, as well as the higher prices being paid. The American collector has been inspired by the heated market which has been, in part, fueled by the weakened U.S. dollar. The general appearance of a wrist watch seems to be the main factor in the price of the watch, but high mechanical standards, along with the various functions of the watch, also determine the price. Some of these features include repeaters, chronographs, duo-dials, bubble backs, curvex, flip-up tops, reverso, day-date-month moon phase, jump hour, diamond dial, world time, sector, skeletonized, character, first versions as early auto winds, very early electronics, unusual shapes, and enamel bezels.

EBEL WATCH CO., chronograph with triple day & moon phases, outside chapter shows tachymetre, 18k gold.

Today's watches are a "mixed bag," ranging from gold luxury watches priced at $10,000, and mid-priced watches at $1,000, to the low-end plastic quartz watches at $30, and all keep time equally well. The gold watch is still a status symbol today; a mark of affluence and of appreciation for the finer things in life. The Swiss control about 85 percent of the luxury watch market, while the Japanese have about the same percentage of the market for more moderately-priced watches. The predominant companies producing the "top of the line" watches are Patek, Philippe & Co., Cartier, Gubelin, Audemars Piguet, Piaget, Vacheron Constantin. Just below in price, but higher in volume, are names like Rolex, International Watch Co., Girard Perregaux, and Le Coultre. Collectors are also wearing high grade new watches by Ebel, Blancpain, Gerald Genta, Hublot, Raymond Weil, and watches produced for and bearing the names of Chanel, Christian Dior, and Dunhill. Prices of Ebel watches start at about $1,000 and go upward to $24,000. This company also manufactures watches for Cartier. Patek, Philippe watches range in price from $3,000 to $100,000.

Audemars Piguet produces a tourbillon wrist watch that retails for about $28,000. Blancpain, owned by Omega, produces only about 100 ultra-thin handmade watches per year. Rolex is the most recognizable name in today's luxury wrist watch market. The Rolex 18k gold President with fluted bezel, champagne cabochon dial, and 18k gold bracelet, sells for $9,400, while the same watch with diamond bezel and dial sells for $14,400. Rolex makes the Oyster Quartz day-date, 18k gold, pave diamond dial with sapphire, bezel case, and bracelet set with 107 diamonds totaling 8.06 carats, which bears a price tag of $100,000.

The Warhol collection, which included about 200 watches, was sold on April 27, 1988 at Sotheby's for a reported price of $461,000. The artist collected watches of various styles and types. A set of three vinyl quartz character watches brought the price of $2,400. A stainless steel Gene Autry watch listed and pre-determined to bring about $100 sold for $1,700. The so-called "heavy weight" wrist watches such as Patek Philippe, Cartier, Rolex, and Vacheron Constantin sold for two to three times the estimated prices.

The trend or vogue for older watches has motivated some watch companies to reproduce favorite watches from their past models. Companies have searched their archives to find older models that sold well, and are now marketing replicas of those watches. Hamilton Classics Authentic Reproductions From America's Past include the Ventura (1957), Wilshire City (1939), Cabot (1935), and Ardmore (1934). Jaeger LeCoultre's Reverso has been reintroduced, as well as Longines' hour angle watch developed and worn by Charles Lindbergh. Also, the Lorus Company has marketed a close look-a-like to the Mickey Mouse wrist watch first sold by Ingersoll in the early 1930s.

The romancing of the wrist watch is moving at a steady upward pace. Price adjustments may be needed, but should hold for a few more years. The quality American movements may still be undervalued, and the novelty or comic character wrist watches may still be a good value for the investor.

**Left:** Movado designed by Andy Warhol the "Times Five" were made in Quartz and limited to 205 pieces. The dials have New York scenes are in black and white with red hands. The five time zones cases are black with black links Ca. 1987.

# A SHORT HISTORY OF WRIST WATCHES

In the late 1700s, Queen Elizabeth adorned her wrist with a watch heavily decorated with jewels and gold. While no one is sure who invented the wrist watch Queen Elizabeth was wearing, or even the first wrist watch ever, as few appeared around 1790. Small miniature watches had been made earlier than this, however. David Rosseau made a watch which was about 18mm in diameter (the size of a dime) in the late 1600s.

Miniaturized wrist watch by WALTHAM. Model number 400. Note size comparison to dime.

Miniaturization was a great challenge to many of the famous watch makers including Louis Jaquet, Paul Ditisheim, John Arnold and Henri Capt. The smallest watch in semi-mass production was 12mm by 5mm. In early 1930, the American Waltham Watch Co. made a 9mm by 20mm Model 400 watch.

Wrist watches were at first thought to be too small and delicate to be practical for men to wear. However, during World War I a German officer was said to have strapped a small pocket watch to his wrist with a leather webbed cup. This arrangement freed both hands and proved to be most useful. After the war, the wrist watch gained in popularity. Mass production of wrist watches was started around 1880 by the Swiss industry. The Swiss introduced them to the United States around 1895, but they did not prove to be very popular at first. Around 1907 the Elgin and Illinois watch companies were manufacturing wrist watches and by 1912 Hampden and Waltham had started.

BREGUET self-winding pocket watch, Ca. 1785.     ROTOR for self winding wrist watch.     HARWOOD self-winding wrist watch, Ca.1928.

By 1920 the round styles were being replaced with square, rectangular and tonneau shapes and decorated with gems. By 1928 wrist watches were outselling pocket watches, and, by 1935, over 85 percent of the watches being produced were wrist watches.

Self-wind pocket watches were first developed by Abraham Louis Perrelet in 1770 and by Abraham Louis Breguet about 1777. Louis Recordon made improvements in 1780, but is was not until 1923 that the principle of self-winding was adapted to the wrist watch by John Harwood, an Englishman who set up factories to make his patented self-wind wrist watches in Switzerland, London, France, and the United States. His watches first reached the market about 1929. The firm A. Schild manufactured about 15,000 watches in Switzerland. Mr. Harwood's watch company removed the traditional stem or crown to wind the mainspring, but in order to set the hands it was necessary to turn the bezel. The Harwood Watch Co. failed around 1931 and the patent expired.

Early in 1930 the Rolex Watch Co. introduced the Rolex Oyster Perpetual, the first waterproof and self-winding wrist watch. In 1933 the first "Incabloc" shock protection device was used. By 1940 wrist watches came in all shapes and types including complicated chronographs, calendars, and repeaters. Novelties, digital jump hour and multi-dial were very popular, as well.

A dramatic change occurred in 1957 when the Hamilton Watch Co. eliminated the mainspring and replaced it with a small battery that lasted well over one year. In 1960 the balance wheel was removed in the Accutron by Bulova and replaced by a tuning fork with miniature pawls.

1. Case number.    2. Movement serial number.    3. Caliber number.    4. Caliber number.

NOTE: Some wrist watches have a grade or caliber number engraved on the movement. For example, Patek, Phillipe & Co. has a caliber number 27-460Q. The '27' stands for 27mm; the '460Q' is the grade; the 'Q' designates Quantieme (Perpetual calendar and moon phases).

# AUTOMATIC WINDING

The self-winding watch uses the movements of the body in order to wind up the mainspring slowly and nearly continuously. The first pocket self-winding watches were executed by a watchmaker from Le Locle, Abraham-Louis Perrelet, around 1770.

Early self wind pocket watch by Breguet.

**ETERNA-MATIC** automatic winding mechanism with rotor oscillating on *5 ball bearings 1st introduced in 1949*. 1.–Oscillating weight. 2. –Oscillating gear. 3. –Upper wheel of auxiliary pawl-wheel. 4. –Lower wheel of auxiliary pawl-wheel. 5. –Pawl-wheel with pinion. 6. –Lower wheel of pawl wheel with pinion. 7. –Transmission-wheel with pinion. 8. –Crown-wheel yoke. 9. –Winding pinion. 10. –Crown-wheel. 11. –Ratchet-wheel. 12. –Barrel. 13. –Driving runner for ratchet-wheel. 14. –Winding stem. 15. –Winding button.

They were improved soon after by Abraham-Louis Breguet. In the case of the pocket watch, the movements causing the winding of the watch were essentially the result of walking. This system of winding was never widely adopted. The watch was a fancy model and not a really useful one. Herman von der Heydt was the only maker in America to work with the self-winding pocket watch. However, inventors always kept the idea of the self-winding watch in mind.

In 1923, the British firm Harwood took up once again the solution of the problem of automatic winding, for wrist watches. This was the spark which rapidly resulted in research to improve and simplify this type of mechanism. A company was formed in London to manufacture Harwood's watch, and before long over 500 jewelers in the United Kingdom were selling his automatic watch. A second company was formed in France, and a third in the United States. The business flourished about two and one-half years. Then, in 1931, these companies were liquidated.

Early self-winding wrist watch by FREY W. Co., Ca. 1930's.
NOTE: The pendulum style weight for self-winding.

Early self-winding wrist watch by AUTORIST W. Co.
Ca.1930's. Winding by moving flexible lugs.

574

CHRONOGRAPH with ONE push piece.          CHRONOGRAPH with TWO push pieces.

## Chronograph with two push pieces:

*Action and movement of hands :* The pusher No .1 sets the hands in action and second action stops the same hands.

Pusher No. 2 brings the hands back to zero. During their movement this pusher is a fixture, thus preventing the accidental return of the hands to zero. The double pusher chronograph permits an interruption in the reading, the hands are set going again from the position they stopped, thus indispensable for any time lost during a control of any description.

## HOW TO READ THE TACHY-TELEMETER DIAL

### Tachometer

The spiral scale around center of dial indicates miles per hour, based on a trial over one mile. It indicates speeds from 400 to 20 miles per hour on three turns. Each turn of spiral corresponds to one minute (scale for first 8 seconds being omitted), the outer turn from 400 to 60 (0 to 1 minute) and the center turn from 30 to 20 miles per hour (2 to 3 minutes).

When passing the first marker of mile zone, start chronograph hand by pressing push piece. When passing following mile marker, press push piece again. The chronograph hand now indicates the speed in miles per hour on the spiral. If a mile has been made in less than one minute the speed will be indicated on outside turn of spiral; from 1 to 2 minutes on middle turn and 2 to 3 minutes on center turn.

EXAMPLE: If a mile has been made in 1 minute and 15 seconds the chronograph hand indicates 48 miles per hour on middle turn of spiral.

### Telemeter

The Telemeter scale around margin of dial is based on the speed of sound compared with the speed of light. Each small division is 100 meters. The scale is read in kilometers and hundreds of meters. Approximately 16 divisions equal 1 mile.

*To determine the distance of a storm:* When you see the flash of lightning press push piece of chronograph. When hearing thunder press again, the chronograph hand will indicate on the Telemeter scale the distance in kilometers and hundreds of meters. One kilometer equals 5/8 of a mile.

Dial No. 1 is a simple stop watch and chronograph dial. Graduated into fifths of seconds.

Dial No. 2 is used to time a car over a quarter-mile track and read the numbers of miles per hour directly from dial.

Dial No. 3 is used to measure speed in kilometers per hour over a course of one fifth of a kilometer.

Dial No. 4 used by physicians to count the pulse beats of a patient.

Dial No. 5 is used by artillery officers for determining distance by means of sound in kilometers.

Dial No. 6 shows a tachometer: many watches are made with several scales on the same dial in order to cover a greater range of functions. The figures are sometimes grouped in a spiral form or in several circles, thus the hand may make more than one complete revolution.

# CHRONOGRAPH MECHANISM
### NUMBERS & NAMES USED IN THE EBAUCHE BOOK
### " TECHNOLOGICAL DICTIONARY OF WATCH PARTS " Ca. 1953

8000  Chronograph central wheel, w/ finger
8020 = Minute-recording wheel, register
8060 = Driving wheel
8070 = Pillar  or Crown wheel, 3 functions
8080 = Coupling clutch w/ transmission wheel, 2 functions
8100 = Sliding or star gear, 2 functions
8140 = Operating or starting lever, 2 functions
8180 = Fly-back lever, reset to zero
8200 = Blocking lever, 2 functions
8220 = Hammer or heart piece striker, 2 functions
8270 = Minute-recording jumper spring
8290 = Friction spring , for chronograph central wheel
8320 = Coupling clutch spring
8325 = Sliding gear spring, 2 functions
8335 = Operating  or starting lever spring
8345 = Blocking lever spring
8350 = Hammer or heartpiece lever spring, 2 functions
8355 = Pillar or crown wheel jumper or block
8500 = Chronograph bridge, for center & min. recording wheels

# CHRONOGRAPH

The term chronograph is derived from the Greek words chronos which means "time" and grapho which means "to write." The first recording of intervals of time was around 1822 by the inventor Rieussec. His chronograph made dots of ink on a dial as a measure of time. Around 1862 Adolph Nicole introduced the first chronograph with a hand that returned to zero. The split second chronograph made its appearance around 1879. Today a chronograph can be described as a timepiece that starts at will, stops at will, and can return to zero at will. A mechanical chronograph had a sweep or center second hand that will start, stop, and fly back to zero. The term chronometer should not be confused with chronograph. A chronometer is a timepiece that has superior time keeping qualities at the time it is made. The CHRONOGRAPH **1 button** wrist watch was 1st. advertised in 1910 & a 2 **button** CHRONOGRAPH in 1939 by Breitling.

**A.** Day window. **B.** Split second hand. **C.** Calendar pusher. **D.** Register for seconds. **E.** Calendar pusher. **F.** Date hand. **G.** Register for total hours. **H.** Sweep center second hand. **I.** Month window. **J.** Start/stop pusher. **K.** Register for total minutes. **L.** Return pusher. **M.** Day of month.

| TRADE MARK | MANUFACTURER | TRADE MARK | MANUFACTURER |
|---|---|---|---|
| | VALJOUX<br>Now part of the ETA group | | LANDERON |
| | VENUS | | FONTAINEMELON |

# WRIST WATCH CASE AND DIAL STYLES

Barrel      Maxine      Square

Round    Square Cut Corner    Cushion    Rectangle

Flared      Tank

**Round**
(Ladies style; converts to lapel or wrist)

Curved or Curvex

Rectangle Cut Corner    Tonneau    Baguette    Oval

Caliber number

Coded number

Coded symbol

Company name

MERCEDES

TRYLON    BATON (RECTILINE)    BATON

MOON    REGATE    POINTEX    LEAF

## HOUR and MINUTE HANDS

ALPHA    INDEX

DAUPHINE    MODERN

DAUPHINE PITCHED    FUSEAUX

DIAMOND    LANCE

FILS    RADIUM DAUPHINE

RADIUM

### SECOND HANDS

ALPHA    DAUPHINE    INDEX    MODERN

FILS    (REGULAR)

---

---

580

# SWISS CODE INITIALS

Some Swiss watches have three initials on the balance bridge. These initials are not model identification but are for house identification. Following is a list of import initials with the name of the Swiss company maker.

AOC–Roamer
AOL–Adolph Schwarcz & Son
AOX–Alstate W. Co.
AXA–Wittnauer
AXZ–Benrus
AYP-Audemars Piguet
BOL–Lemania
BXC–Avia
BXJ–Midland
BXN–Benrus
BXP–Imperial, Bayer, Pretzfelder & Mills
BXW–Bulova
COC–Crawford
COW–Croton
CXC–Concord
CXD–Cypres
CXH–Clinton
CXV–Cort
CXW–Central; Benrus
DOB–Dreffa W. Co.
DOW–Deauville
EOE–Elrex
EON–Avalon
EOP–Harvel
EOT–Lavina
EXC–Everbrite
FXE–Provis
FXU–Louis Aisenstein & Bros.
FXW–Louis
GXC–Gruen
GXI–Gotham (Ollendorff)
GXM–Girard-Perregaux
GXR–Grant
GXW–Gothic
HOM–Homis
HON–Tissot; A. Hirsch
HOR–Lanco; Langendorf

HOU–Oris
HXF–Harman
HXM–R. H. Macy & Co.
HXN–Harvel
HXO–Harold K. Oleet
HXW–Helbros
HYL– Hamilton
HYO–Hilton W Co.
JXE–Normandie
JXJ–Jules Jurgensen
JXR–Gallet
KOT–Landau
KXJ–Wm. J. Kappel
KXV–Louis
KXZ–Kelton; Benrus, Central
LOA–Emil Langer
LOD–Latham
LOE–Packard
LXA–Laco, Winton, Elbon
LXE–Evkob
LXJ–LeCoultre
LXW–Longines
MOG–Mead & Co.; Boulevard
MOU–Tower; Delbana
MXE–Monarch
MXH–Seeland
MXI–Movado
MXT–Mathey-Tissot
NOA–U.Nardin
NOS–Heritage
NOU–Louvic
NXJ–National Jewelers Co.
NXO–Oris
OXG–Omega
OXL–Wyler
OYT–Shriro (Sandoz)
POY–Camy; Copley
PXA–Pierce
PXP–Patek, Philippe

PXT–Paul Breguette
PXW–Parker
PYS–Langel
QXO–Kelbert
ROC–Raleigh
ROL–Ribaux
ROP–Rodania
ROR-Audemars Piguet
ROW–Rolex
RXG–R. Gsell & Co.
RXM–Galmor
RXW–Rima
RXY–Liengme
RYW–Ritex
SOA–Felca
SOE–Semca
SOW–Seeland
SOX–Cortebert, Orvin
SXE–Savoy; Banner
SXK–S. Kocher & Co.
SXS–Franco
UOA–Actua
UOB–Aero
UOW–Universal
UXM–Medana
UXN–Marsh
UYW–Stanley W. Co.
VOS–Sheffield
VXN–Vacheron & Constantin
VXT–Kingston
WOA–Tower
WOB–Wyler
WOG–Breitling
WOR–Creston
WXC–Buren
WXE–Welsbro
WXW–Westfield
ZFX–Zenith W.Co.
ZOV–Titus
ZYV–Hampden (new company)

To determine your wrist watch band size use the above gauge and measure between the lugs. The band sizes are listed on each side of the gauge.

When performing any underwater activity, the dynamic pressure generated through movement is greater than the static pressure. Below a ranking of water resistance for most watches.

1 **meter** = 3.28 ft., 330 ft. =about 100 **meters.**

33.89 ft. =1 **atmosphere**, 100 ft. = about 3 **atmospheres**.

50M = shower only, rain, sweat-resistant (1 AT. )
100M = swimming (**no diving**) -330 ft.
200M = snorkeling, skin diving -600 ft.
1000M =scuba diving -3,300 ft.

# WRIST WATCH LISTINGS

## Pricing At Collectable Fair Market Value At Retail Level
### (Complete Watches Only)

Unless otherwise noted, wrist watches listed in this section are priced at the *collectable* fair market RETAIL level (What a **collector** may expect to pay for a watch from a watch dealer) and as **complete** watches having an original gold-filled case and stainless steel back, also with original dial, and the entire original movement in good working order with no repairs needed. They are also priced as having a watch band made of **leather** except where a bracelet is described. Watches listed as 14k and 18k are solid gold cases. Coin or silveroid type and stainless steel cases will be listed as such. Dollar-type watches, or low cost production watches, are listed as having a base metal type case and a composition dial.

Many of the watch manufacturers were commissioned to put jewelers' or jobbers' **names** on their movements in place of their own. Because of this practice, the true manufacturers of these movements are difficult to identify.

The prices shown were averaged from dealers' lists just prior to publication and are an indication of the retail level or what collectors will pay. **Prices** are provided in three categories: **average condition, extra fine, and mint condition,** and are shown in whole dollar amounts only. The values listed are a guide for the *collectable* retail level and are provided for your information only. **Dealers** will not necessarily **pay full retail** price. Prices listed are for watches with **original** cases, movement and dials and in good running order.

**Warning:** There are currently fake wrist watches being sold on the worldwide market. These watches have the appearance of authenticity but are merely cheap imitations of prestigious companies such as Rolex (all types), Gucci, Cartier, & Piaget.

**Important Notice.** All of the information, including valuations, in this book has been compiled from the most reliable sources, and every effort has been made to eliminate errors and questionable data. Nevertheless, the possibility of error, in a work of such immense scope, always exists. The publisher or authors will not be held responsible for losses which may occur in the purchase, sale, or other transaction of items, because of information contained herein. Readers who feel they have discovered errors are invited to write and inform us, so they may be corrected in subsequent editions.

---

**INFORMATION NEEDED** — The authors are interested in any facts and information you might have that should possibly be considered for future editions. Documented facts are needed, so please send photo or sources of information. Send to:

### COOKSEY SHUGART
### P.O. BOX 3147
### CLEVELAND, TN. 37320-3147

When **CORRESPONDING**, Please send a ✉ self addressed, stamped **ENVELOPE**.

ABERCROMBIE & FITCH, 17J., chronog.by Valj.,3 reg.
14K..........................................$900    $1,000    $1,100
s.steel .........................................$360    $400    $500

**Abercrombie & Fitch**, 17J., **Sea Farer**, chronog., waterproof
18k ........................................$1,000    $1,200    $1,400
s. steel ...................................$325    $375    $475

**Abercrombie & Fitch**, 17J., chronog.by Valj.,3 reg., Ca.1950
s.steel .......................................$350    $400    $500

ABRA, 17J., step case, c.1930s
base metal ...............................$35    $45    $55

🕐 Some grades are not included. Their values can be
determined by comparing with similar age, size, metal
content, style, grades, or models such as time only,
chronograph, repeater etc. listed.

ABRA,17J., carved case, c.1930s
base metal................................$30    $40    $50

ABRA, 17J., engraved case
base metal................................$35    $45    $55

ABRA,15J., curved case, c.1930s
base metal................................$35    $45    $55

ABRA,15J., engraved case, c.1930s
gold plate..................................$35    $45    $55

'ABRA, 17J., **jump hour**
s. steel .....................................$250    $300    $350

ACRO W. CO., 17 jewels, **hinged back**
18k .......................................... $250    $300    $350

ADMES, 17 jewels, self wind, waterproof, center sec.,
14K.............................................$85    $100    $135
gold filled................................. $25    $30    $40

AGASSIZ, 17 jewels, **World Time**
18k .......................................$4,000    $5,000    $6,000

AGASSIZ, 17 jewels, fancy bezel,
18k ...........................................$500    $600    $750

AGASSIZ, 18 jewels, for Tiffany & Co., 48mm, oversize
18k ...........................................$800    $900    $1,000

AGASSIZ,17J., C. 1940s
18K(W)...................................$600    $700    $800

AGASSIZ, 18 jewels, barrel shaped dial, 40mm,
18k ...........................................$400    $500    $600

AGASSIZ, 17 jewels, for Tiffany & Co., 45mm
18k ...............,........................$700    $800    $950

ALPHA, 17J., chrono. 2 reg., cal.48, c.1950s
14K .......................................$400    $450    $550
s.steel ...................................$150    $175    $225

ALPHA, 17J., **Fancy lugs**, sweep sec., c. 1948
18k ...........................................$250    $275    $300

ALPHA, 17J, autowind, c.1950s
18K.....................................$175   $200   $250

ALSTA, 17 jewels, **wrist alarm**
gold filled ................................$95   $125   $150

ALPINA, 15 jewels, automatic, water proof, center sec.
gold filled...................................$50   $60   $75

ALTON, 17J., fancy lugs, c.1950s
14K .......................................$150   $175   $225

ALPINA, 17 jewels, automatic, water proof, aux. sec.
18k ..........................................$175   $200   $250

ALTUS, 17 jewels, ref. 827
18k ..........................................$150   $175   $200

AM. WALTHAM, 17J.,c.1930s
14k ..........................................$150   $175   $250

ALSTA, 17J., **chronograph**, 3 reg.
14K..........................................$425   $475   $500
base metal ...............................$200   $250   $300

WALTHAM, 17J., aux. sec. c.1930s
14k ..........................................$150   $175   $250

AM. WALTHAM, 17J., aux.sec., c.1930s
14k ...................................$140    $165    $240

AM. WALTHAM, 21J., cal.750B, GJS, c.1950s
14k ...................................$150    $175    $250

AM. WALTHAM, 17J., cal.750B, c.1951
gold filled...................................$75    $100    $125

AM. WALTHAM, 15J., "Masonic" model, c.1925
14k ...................................$600    $700    $800

AM. WALTHAM, 15-17J, **solid lugs**, c.1920s
sterling silver .........................$200    $250    $325

AM. WALTHAM, 15-17J, "Ruby"model, c.1920s
gold filled ...............................$125    $150    $175

AM. WALTHAM, 17 J, barrel shaped dial, c. 1920
14k ...................................$175    $200    $250

AM. WALTHAM, 17 jewels, "Cromwell"
gold filled ...............................$50    $65    $85

AM. WALTHAM, 17 jewels, "Oberlin"
gold filled ...............................$50    $65    $95

AM. WALTHAM, 15 jewels, engraved bezel
gold filled ...............................$100    $125    $175

AM. WALTHAM, 17J., for Tiffany & Co.
14k ...........................................$300      $350      $400

AM.WALTHAM, 19J., **enamel dial**, C. 1905
silver ......................................$135      $165      $225

AM. WALTHAM, 17 jewels, wire lugs
14k ...........................................$450      $500      $600

AM. WALTHAM, 17 jewels, "Duxbury"
gold filled...................................$50      $75      $100

AM. WALTHAM, 21 jewels, curved back
14k ...........................................$225      $275      $300

AM. WALTHAM, 7-15 jewels, wandering sec., c. 1930
gold filled ...........................$150      $200      $275

AM. WALTHAM, 17 jewels, **wandering sec.**, c. 1930
gold filled ...............................$175      $225      $295

AM. WALTHAM, 17 jewels, "Fairmont"
gold filled .................................$75      $100      $135

AM. WALTHAM, 17 jewels, "Stan Hope"
gold filled .................................$50      $75      $100

AM. WALTHAM, 17 jewels, "Winfield"
gold filled .................................$50      $75      $100

AM. WALTHAM, wandering min., **jumping hour.**, c. 1933
gold filled ...............................$500      $600      $750

AM. WALTHAM, 15J., aux. sec.
gold filled...................................$30     $50     $75

AM. WALTHAM, 15 J., case by Rolland Fischer
silver ......................................$300     $350     $450

AM. WALTHAM, 21 jewels, "Albright"
14k .........................................$100     $125     $150

AM. WALTHAM, 21 jewels, "Sheraton"
14k .........................................$100     $125     $150

AM. WALTHAM, 15J., **enamel dial, center lugs,** c.1915
silver ......................................$250     $300     $350

AM. WALTHAM, 17 jewels, center sec.
gold filled...................................$35     $45     $60

AM. WALTHAM, 15J., **wire lugs,** engraved, S#16,952,060
14K .........................................$250     $300     $350

AM. WALTHAM, 15 jewels, **winds at 12,** wire lugs, c. 1916
silver ......................................$200     $250     $300

AM. WALTHAM, 15 jewels, **enamel dial,** Ca. 1920
base metal ...............................$250     $300     $375

AM. WALTHAM, 7-15J., **pulsations**, solid lugs, c.1925
silver ........................................$300      $350      $400

AM. WALTHAM, 17J.,**"Riverside", GJS**, c.1918
silver ........................................$450      $500      $600

AM. WALTHAM, 15 jewels, c. 1930
gold filled................................. $60      $70      $85

AM. WALTHAM, 7J., **oxidized case**, c.1930s
gold filled................................$75      $100      $125

AM. WALTHAM, 7-15J., **cut conner dial**, c.1930s
gold filled................................$75      $100      $125

AM. WALTHAM, 15 jewels,
gold filled ................. $80      $90      $100

AM. WALTHAM, 15J., **engraved oxidized case**,c.1930s
gold filled ................................$75      $100      $125

AM. WALTHAM, 15J.,**engraved case**
gold filled ................................$75      $85      $100

AM. WALTHAM, 17 jewels, 18K applied #s
silver ........................................$175      $200      $235

AM. WALTHAM, 7-15 jewels, engraved case
gold filled ................................$75      $100      $135

AM. WALTHAM, 7-15 jewels, **carved** case
gold filled ................................$80      $95      $125

AM. WALTHAM, 15 jewels, **curved back**
14k ............................................$200     $225     $250

AM. WALTHAM, 7-15 jewels, engraved case
gold filled...................................$80     $100     $125

AM. WALTHAM, 17 jewels, tank style, **18K applied #s**
14kw ........................................$200     $225     $250

AM. WALTHAM, 15-17 jewels,
gold filled...................................$60     $70     $85

AM. WALTHAM, 7-15 jewels,
gold filled...................................$80     $90     $100

AM. WALTHAM, 15-17J, Premier, note **screwed on case**
14K...........................................$300     $350     $400

AM. WALTHAM, 15J., case by Rolland Fischer,
silver .......................................$400     $500     $625

AM. WALTHAM, 15 jewels, "Depollier," **early water
proof, (Canteen style)**, c. 1917
silver .......................................$500     $600     $750

AM. WALTHAM, 15 jewels, protective grill, c. 1907
gold filled ..............................$250     $300     $365
14k .........................................$750     $850     $1,000

AM. WALTHAM, 17 jewels, military with **hack setting**
s. steel ....................................$85     $100     $135

AM. WALTHAM, 17 jewels, **cut-corner dial**
14k .........................................$200    $250    $300

🕐 Some grades are not included. Their values can be
determined by comparing with **similar** age, size, metal
content, style, grades, or models such as **time only**,
chronograph, repeater etc. listed.

AM. WALTHAM, 17 jewels, luminous dial
14k .........................................$175    $225    $275

AM. WALTHAM, 17 jewels, **wire lugs**
gold filled..............................$125    $150    $175

AM. WALTHAM, 17 jewels, **center lugs**
14k .......................................$185    $225    $275

AM. WALTHAM, 17 jewels, "**Allen**"
gold filled..................................$50    $75    $100

AM. WALTHAM, 17 jewels, "**Penton**"
gold filled ................................$50    $75    $100

AM. WALTHAM, 9-17 jewels, "**Side-wrist**"
gold filled ..............................$125    $150    $200

AM. WALTHAM, 17 jewels, **curvex, 42mm**
14k .........................................$300    $350    $400

AM. WALTHAM, 17 jewels, **curvex, 52mm**
14k .......................................$400    $500    $700

AM. WALTHAM, 17 jewels, **curvex, 42mm**
gold filled ...............................$100    $150    $175

🕐 Some grades are not included. Their values can be
determined by comparing with **similar** age, size, metal
content, style, grades, or models such as **time only**,
chronograph, repeater etc. listed.

AM. WALTHAM, 17-21 jewels, curved
14k ......................................$175     $225     $300
gold filled..................................$65     $75     $100

AM. WALTHAM, 15J., **note bow swings, screw back case,
solid lugs, enamel dial, early water proof** , c. 1920s
14K ................................... ★★$450     $550     $750

AM. WALTHAM, 17 jewels, curved, aux. sec.
gold filled..................................$65     $80     $100

AM. WALTHAM, 17 jewels, enamel bezel
14k ............................................$650     $750     $950
14k (w) ...................................$500     $600     $800
gold filled .............................$150     $200     $250

AM. WALTHAM, 17 jewels, curved
gold filled..................................$65     $75     $120

AM. WALTHAM,17J., enamel bezel,**"ruby"** model,c.1928
14k(w)....................................$550     $650     $800

AM. WALTHAM, 21 jewels, C.1938
14K............................................$150     $200     $250

AM. WALTHAM,17J., **stepped case**
gold filled ...............................$75     $100     $125

AM. WALTHAM, 17 jewels, curved
gold filled..................................$75     $85     $125

AM. WALTHAM, 17 jewels, **"Jeffrey"**
gold filled ...............................$75     $100     $125

AM. WALTHAM, 17 jewels, curved
gold filled..................................$65     $75     $100

AM. WALTHAM, 21 jewels, "**Tulane**"
gold filled.....................................$40      $50      $80

AM. WALTHAM, 17J., triangular, masonic symbols
fancy hands, **mother of pearl dial**, Ca. 1950
gold filled............................$1,000      $1,200      $1,500

AM. WALTHAM, 7-15J., luminous dial, c.1928
base metal ...............................$40      $50      $75

AM. WALTHAM, 7-15J., cushion case, c.1928
gold filled.....................................$50      $75      $100

AM. WALTHAM, 7-15J., tonneau case, c. 1928
gold filled.....................................$50      $75      $100

AM. WALTHAM, 7J., luminous dial, c.1928
base metal...............................$60      $70      $90

AM. WALTHAM, 7J., luminous dial, c. 1928
gold filled ...............................$75      $100      $125

AM. WALTHAM, 17J., luminous dial, c.1929
gold filled ...............................$60      $70      $80
14k(w)......................................$175      $200      $275

AM. WALTHAM, 17J., aux. sec., c. 1928
14k(w)......................................$175      $200      $275

AM. WALTHAM,7-15J., **lugless case**, c.1928
gold filled ...............................$60      $75      $125

AM. WALTHAM,15J., luminous dial, c.1928
14k ...........................................$175      $225      $300

AM. WALTHAM,15J., brush finish, c.1928
14k ...........................................$175      $225      $300

AM. WALTHAM,7J., luminous dial, c.1928
gold plate ....................................$75      $85      $125

AM. WALTHAM,17J.,GJS, ca.1940
14K...........................................$150      $175      $200

AM. WALTHAM,7-15J., cut corner case, c.1929
gold filled.................................$75      $85      $95

AM. WALTHAM,15J., **fluted case**, GJS, c.1925
14k(w)+enamel........................$95      $110      $150

AM. WALTHAM,7-15J., **Butler finish** = (smooth), c.1928
gold filled .................................$75      $100      $125

AM. WALTHAM, 7-15J., GJS, Ca.1927
14K(w)....................................$175      $225      $300

AM. WALTHAM,7-15J., engraved case, etched dial, c.1929
14k(w)...................................... $60      $70      $100
gold filled ................................. $25      $35      $55

AM. WALTHAM,15J., engraved case, etched dial, c.1928
14K(W)..................................... $50      $65      $75
gold filled ................................ $25      $35      $50

AM. WALTHAM,7-15J., enamel case, c. 1928
14k(w)...................................... $75      $90      $120

AM. WALTHAM,15J., enamel case, c.1929
gold filled (w)..........................$40      $55      $75

## AMERICAN WALTHAM WATCH CO. IDENTIFICATION BY MOVEMENT

Model 1900, 0 size

Model 1907, 0 size

Jewel Series

Model 1900, 0/3 size,
open face

Model 1907, 0/3 size,
hunting

Model 1898 & 1912,
0/6 size, hunting

Model 1898 & 1912,
0/6 size, open face

10½ ligne

10 ligne

7½ ligne

5¼ ligne

Model 400

Model 450

Model 650

Model 675

Model 750

AMERICUS, 17 jewels, **8 day** movement, c. 1933
| | | | |
|---|---|---|---|
| 18k | $1,000 | $1,200 | $1,500 |
| gold filled | $400 | $500 | $600 |
| s. steel | $300 | $400 | $500 |

AMERICUS, 7 jewels, curved, c.1935
| | | | |
|---|---|---|---|
| gold filled | $100 | $125 | $150 |

ANGELUS, 17 jewels, chronograph, 2 reg., c. 1943
| | | | |
|---|---|---|---|
| 18k | $600 | $700 | $800 |
| 14k | $400 | $500 | $600 |
| gold filled | $150 | $200 | $250 |

ANGELUS, 17J., chronograph, **triple date**, C. 1949
| | | | |
|---|---|---|---|
| s. steel | $350 | $400 | $500 |
| 14k | $700 | $900 | $1,000 |
| 18k | $1,300 | $1,400 | $1,500 |

ANGELUS, 17J., day, date, moon ph.,C. 1949
| | | | |
|---|---|---|---|
| s. steel | $250 | $300 | $375 |

ANGELUS, 17 jewels, chronograph, 2 reg., water proof
| | | | |
|---|---|---|---|
| 14k | $500 | $600 | $700 |
| 18k | $700 | $800 | $900 |
| s. steel | $200 | $250 | $300 |

ANGELUS, 17J., **date and alarm**, c.1955
| | | | |
|---|---|---|---|
| s. steel | $150 | $175 | $200 |

ANGELUS, 27 jewels, **1/4 hour repeater**
| | | | |
|---|---|---|---|
| s. steel | $2,700 | $3,000 | $3,500 |

ARAMIS, 15 jewels, **early self wind, lug action winding by back & forth motion of watch case**, c. 1933
s. steel .......................................$600     $700     $900

ARBU, 17 jewels, triple date, moon phase
18k ............................................$800    $1,000    $1,200
s. steel .....................................$300     $350     $400

ARBU, 17 jewels, chronograph, 3 reg., day-date-month
18k ............................................$700     $850    $1,000
s. steel .....................................$350     $400     $450

ARBU, 17 jewels, **split second chronograph**
18k ........................................$3,000    $3,300    $3,700

ARCTOS, 17J., "PARAT", **unique dial**, c.1955
base metal...............................$100     $125     $150

ARDATH, 17J., chronograph, triple date, c.1947
s. steel....................................$250     $300     $350

ARISTO, 17 jewels, chronog., water proof
14k...........................................$500     $600     $750
s. steel....................................$150     $175     $225

ARISTO, 17J., chronog., 3 reg., **triple date**
14k........................................$1,500    $1,750    $2,000
s. steel....................................$400     $500     $625

ARISTO, 17 jewels, day-date-month, moon phase
s. steel ......................................$275     $300      $375

ARMADILLO, by DAVE WALDO, flip top, coin
silver coin ...............................$450     $550      $650
18k plate ................................$500     $600      $700

ARSA, 17 jewels, day-date-month, moon phase
18k ...........................................$800     $900      $1,000
s. steel ...................................$250     $300      $350

ARSA, 15 jewels, day-date-month, moon phase
18k ...........................................$800     $900      $1,000
s. steel ...................................$250     $300      $375

ASPREY, 16 jewels, **curved hinged back**
9k..............................................$175     $225      $350

ASPREY, 17J., **date**, ca. 1930s
14k...........................................$375     $425      $475
gold filled .............................$150     $200      $275

ASPREY, 15 jewels, **duo dial**
18k.........................................$1,700     $2,000      $2,500

ASPREY, 17 jewels, **enamel dial, center lugs**
9k.............................................$200     $250      $300

AUDAX, 15J., Ca.1938
9k..............................................$100     $135      $185

🕐 Some grades are not included. Their values can be
determined by comparing with **similar** age, size, metal
content, style, grades, or models such as **time only**,
chronograph, repeater etc. listed.

AUDEMARS PIGUET, 33J., **minute** repeater, gold train, platinum & 18K with **40** diamond bezel, diamond dial & diamonds on band
18K & platinum ................$70,000   $80,000   $90,000

AUDEMARS PIGUET, 29 J., **minute repeater**, c. 1907
18k ....................................$60,000   $70,000   $80,000

AUDEMARS PIGUET, 29 J., **minute repeater**, c. 1925
platinum ............................$70,000   $80,000   $90,000

AUDEMARS PIGUET, 19 J., **tourbillon**, self-winding tourbillon can be seen from dial side
18k .......................................$9,000   $10,000   $12,000

AUDEMARS PIGUET, 36 J., octogonal shaped case, triple date, moon phase, perpetual
18k C&B ..........................$12,000   $13,000   $14,000

AUDEMARS PIGUET, 33J., day date, moon ph., c.1989
18k........................................$3,000   $3,500   $4,000

AUDEMARS PIGUET, day date, moon ph., C. 1980s
18k........................................$3,000   $3,500   $4,000

AUDEMARS PIGUET, chronograph, triple date, moon ph., tear drop lugs, Ca. 1940s
18k......................................$25,000   $35,000   $45,000

AUDEMARS PIGUET, 36 jewels, gold rotor, day-date
month, moon phase, perpetual
18 k C&B..............................$9,000    $10,000    $11,000

AUDEMARS PIGUET, skeletonized, triple date,
moon phase,  perpetual , C. 1980s
platinum.............................$14,000    $16,000    $18,000

AUDEMARS PIGUET, 17 J., chronog., 3 reg., c. 1945
s.steel ..................................$17,000    $20,000    $25,000
18k .......................................$20,000    $25,000    $30,000

AUDEMARS PIGUET, 18 J., "Le Brassus," **chronog.**
skeletonized
18k C&B...........................$20,000    $22,000    $25,000

AUDEMARS PIGUET, 22 jewels, chronog., 2 reg.,
s.steel ..................................$12,000    $15,000    $18,000
18k .......................................$18,000    $20,000    $22,000

AUDEMARS PIGUET, 18 jewels, skeletonized
18k .......................................$5,000    $6,000    $7,000

AUDEMARS PIGUET, 17 jewels, thin skeletonized
18k .......................................$5,000    $6,000    $7,000

🕐 Some grades are not included. Their values can be
determined by comparing with **similar** age, size, metal
content, style, grades, or models such as **time only**,
chronograph, repeater etc. listed.

AUDEMARS PIGUET, 18 J., triple date, moonphase
18k .......................................$4,000    $5,000    $6,000

AUDEMARS PIGUET, 36 jewels, skeletonized
18k .......................................$5,500    $6,500    $8,000

AUDEMARS PIGUET, 17 J., center lugs, skeletonized
18k ...............................$7,000    $7,500    $8,500

AUDEMARS PIGUET, 17J., Dodecagonal, black dial
18k .......................................$1,200    $1,400    $1,600

AUDEMARS PIGUET, 17J., diamond dial, c. 1970
18k .......................................$2,000    $2,200    $2,500

AUDEMARS PIGUET, 12 diamond dial c.1960
platinum ...............................$2,000    $2,200    $2,500

AUDEMARS PIGUET, 11 diamond dial
18k .......................................$1,600    $1,800    $2,000

AUDEMARS PIGUET, 12 sapphire dial, c.1950
18k .......................................$2,500    $2,700    $3,000

AUDEMARS PIGUET, 17 jewels, 12 diamond dial
18k (w) ...............................$2,500    $2,700    $3,000

AUDEMARS PIGUET, 36 jewels, self-winding
18k .......................................$1,400    $1,600    $1,900

AUDEMARS PIGUET, 17 jewels, adj. to 5 positions
18k C&B............................$1,200    $1,400    $1,600

AUDEMARS PIGUET, 17 jewels, rope style bezel
18k C&B ..............................$1,500     $1,800     $2,000

AUDEMARS PIGUET, 36 jewels, self-winding
18k .......................................$1,800     $2,000     $2,400

AUDEMARS PIGUET, 17J., diamond bezel, center lugs
18k .......................................$2,000     $2,200     $2,400

AUDEMARS PIGUET, 36 jewels, lazuli dial
18k C&B............................$2,200     $2,400     $2,800

AUDEMARS PIGUET, 20J., rope style bezel, c. 1980s
18k case, 14k band ..............$1,000     $1,100     $1,200

AUDEMARS PIGUET, 17 jewels, thin style
18k C&B............................$2,000     $2,200     $2,500

AUDEMARS PIGUET, 20J., "Le Brassus," c. 1970
18k C&B............................$2,000     $2,200     $2,400

AUDEMARS PIGUET, 17 jewels, fancy bezel, c. 1950
18k .......................................$2,000     $2,400     $2,800

AUDEMARS PIGUET, fancy shaped, c.1960s
18k .......................................$2,500     $3,000     $3,500

AUDEMARS PIGUET, 17J., "Philosopher", hour hand
18k .......................................$2,200     $2,500     $2,800

AUDEMARS PIGUET, 20 jewels, thin model
18k .........................................$1,100    $1,200    $1,300

AUDEMARS PIGUET, 17J., engraved bezel, c. 1963
18k .........................................$1,500    $2,000    $2,200

AUDEMARS PIGUET, 17J., wide bezel, thin model
14k C&B.............................$1,500    $1,600    $1,800

AUDEMARS PIGUET, 21J., auto wind, center sec.
18k .........................................$1,600    $1,800    $2,000

🕀 Some grades are not included. Their values can be
determined by comparing with similar age, size, metal
content, style, grades, or models such as time only,
chronograph, repeater etc. listed.

AUDEMARS PIGUET, **world time**, fancy lugs
s. steel ................................$10,000    $12,000    $15,000

AUDEMARS PIGUET, **world time** , c. 1940s
14k .........................................$12,000    $14,000    $17,000

AUDEMARS PIGUET, 18 jewels, gold train
18k ...................................... $2,500    $3,000    $3,500

AUDEMARS PIGUET, 18J., **hidden lugs**, Ca. 1950
18k ...................................... $1,200    $1,400    $1,700

AUDEMARS PIGUET, 18 jewels, aux. sec. c. 1940
18k .........................................$2,000    $2,200    $2,500

AUDEMARS PIGUET, 17 jewels, for Tiffany & Co.
18k C&B.............................$2,000     $2,200     $2,400

AUDEMARS PIGUET, 18J., no second hand, Ca. 1965
18k ........................................$800     $950     $1,100

AUDEMARS PIGUET, 18 jewels, aux. sec.
18k ......................................$2,000     $2,100     $2,300

AUDEMARS PIGUET, 18 jewels, center sec., c. 1950
18k ......................................$1,500     $1,800     $2,200

AUDEMARS PIGUET, 18 jewels, tank style, c. 1960
18k (w)..............................$1,500     $1,600     $1,800

AUDEMARS PIGUET,18J., straight line lever escape.
18k ......................................$1,200     $1,400     $1,700

AUDEMARS PIGUET, 18 jewels, hooded lugs
18k ......................................$1,500     $1,600     $1,800

AUDEMARS PIGUET, 17 jewels, mid-size
18k ........................................$500     $600     $750

AUDEMARS PIGUET, 17J., engraved bezel, c.1966
18k ......................................$1,400     $1,600     $1,800

AUDEMARS PIGUET, 18J., mid size,  **flat bezel**, Ca. 1969
18k ......................................$1,200     $1,400     $1,700

AUDEMARS PIGUET, gold textured dial, c.1960s
18k ..............................$1,000    $1,100    $1,200

AUDEMARS PIGUET, 18J., aux. sec., c. 1950s
18k ..............................$1,200    $1,500    $1,800

AUDEMARS PIGUET, 18J., auto wind, waterproof
18k ..............................$1,600    $1,800    $2,000

AUDEMARS PIGUET, 18 jewels, **painted dial**, c. 1970
18k ..............................$1,000    $1,100    $1,300

AUDEMARS PIGUET, 21 jewels, 18k gold rotor
18k ..............................$1,700    $1,900    $2,300

AUDEMARS PIGUET, 19J., center sec.
18k ..............................$1,500    $2,000    $2,500

AUDEMARS PIGUET, 18J., screw back, waterproof
18k ..............................$1,600    $1,800    $2,000

AUDEMARS PIGUET, 17 jewels, gold train
18k ..............................$1,000    $1,200    $1,500

AUDEMARS PIGUET, **triple date, moon ph.**, c.1930s
18k ..............................$30,000    $35,000    $40,000

AUDEMARS PIGUET, 18 J.," **top hat**", aux. sec., c. 1950
platinum ..............................$3,000    $3,500    $4,000

🕐 Some grades are not included. Their values can be determined by comparing with **similar** age, size, metal content, style, grades, or models such as **time only**, chronograph, repeater etc. listed.

AUDEMARS PIGUET, 17J., gold train, 2 tone case in platinum & gold
18k (w) C&B ......................$2,500    $2,700    $3,000

AUDEMARS PIGUET, large bezel, c.1940s
18k C&B............................$3,000    $3,500    $4,000

AUDEMARS PIGUET, 17 jewels, gold train
14k C&B..............................$1,600    $1,800    $2,200

AUDEMARS PIGUET, 18 J., textured bezel, c. 1950
18k .......................................$1,700    $1,900    $2,000

AUDEMARS PIGUET, 2 tone dial, c.1930s
18k .......................................$2,500    $3,000    $3,500

🕐 Some grades are not included. Their values can be determined by comparing with **similar** age, size, metal content, style, grades, or models such as **time only**, chronograph, repeater etc. listed.

AUDEMARS PIGUET, 17 jewels, gold train, c. 1940
18k (w) ................................$2,200    $2,500    $2,800

AUDEMARS PIGUET, 18J, curvex, large bezel, c. 1950
18k .......................................$2,000    $2,200    $2,500

AUDEMARS PIGUET, 18 jewels, tank style, c. 1950's
18k .......................................$2,000    $2,200    $2,500

AUDEMARS PIGUET, Royal Oak, **date**, auto wind, c.1973
s.steel & Quartz...................$1,500    $1,700    $2,000
18k C&B.............................$6,000    $7,000    $8,000

AUDEMARS PIGUET, quartz, 12 diamonds, c. 1981
s. steel .................................$1,200    $1,400    $1,600

AUDEMARS PIGUET,ladys, 72 small diamonds, c.1930s
plat.case & band ................. $1,500    $1,700    $2,000

AUSTIN, 17J., fancy bezel,
gold filled.................................... $75    $80    $95

AUTOMATIQUE, 17J., cal.F699, c. 1955
s. steel ......................................... $55    $60    $75

AUTORIST, 15 jewels, **lug action wind**, enamel dial
s. steel ......................................... $400    $500    $600

AUTORIST, 15 jewels, **lug action wind**, c. 1930
s. steel ......................................... $400    $500    $600

🕐 Some grades are not included. Their values can be
determined by comparing with **similar** age, size, metal
content, style, grades, or models such as **time only**,
chronograph, repeater etc. listed.

AUTORIST, 15 jewels, **lug action wind**, c. 1930
gold filled ............................... $500    $600    $700

AUTORIST, 15 jewels, **lug action wind**, (lady's)
s. steel .................................... $200    $300    $400

AVALON,17J., aux.sec.
gold filled ............................... $35    $40    $50

AVALON,17J., aux.sec.
gold filled ............................... $50    $60    $70

BALL W. CO., 25 jewels, auto wind, adj. to 5 pos., E.T.A.
10k .......................................... $375    $400    $450

BALL W. CO., 25 jewels, auto wind, adj. to 5 pos., E.T.A.
gold filled...............................$250     $275     $325

BALL W. CO., 25 jewels, auto wind, adj. to 5 pos., E.T.A.
s. steel ....................................$200     $235     $300

BAUME & MERCIER, 18J., triple date, moon phase
s. steel ....................................$400     $500     $600

BAUME & MERCIER, 17J., chronog., 2 reg., c.1949
gold filled...............................$225     $250     $325

BAUME & MERCIER, 17J., chronog., 2 reg.,c.1950s
18k .........................................$500     $600     $700

BAUME & MERCIER, 18J., chronog., 3 reg. & dates
s. steel ....................................$400     $500     $625

BAUME & MERCIER, 18 J., chronog., 3 reg. & dates
18k .........................................$1,200     $1,400     $1,700

BAUME & MERCIER, 18 jewels, tachymeter, c. 1940
s. steel, black dial ...................$400     $500     $600

BAUME & MERCIER, 17J., triple date, chronog.
moon ph., c.1950s
18k .........................................$1,500    $1,700    $2,000

BAUME & MERCIER, 17J., 2 dials, 2 time zones &
2 movements
18k .........................................$600    $700    $800

BAUME & MERCIER, 18 J., chronog., fancy lugs
18k .........................................$1,800    $2,200    $2,600

BAUME & MERCIER, 18 jewels, gold dial, date
14k C&B..................................$400    $450    $500

BAUME & MERCIER, 17J., chronog., triple date
18k .........................................$1,200    $1,400    $1,600

BAUME & MERCIER, 18 jewels, thin model
14k C&B..................................$400    $450    $500

BAUME & MERCIER, 18J., triple date, moon phase
18k .........................................$800    $900    $1,000

BAUME & MERCIER, 17 jewels, center sec., c. 1956
14k .........................................$175    $200    $250

BAUME & MERCIER, 17 jewels, aux. sec., c. 1955
14k ..........................................$175      $225      $250

BAUME & MERCIER, 17J., RF#49300, c. 1965
14k ..........................................$150      $175      $225

BAUME & MERCIER, 18 J., "Riviera", date, c. 1980s
18k & s. steel .........................$500      $600      $700

BAUME & MERCIER, quartz, enamel dial, tank, c.1990s
14k ..........................................$300      $350      $400

BAUME & MERCIER, 17J., curved, c. 1990s
14k C&B.................................$500      $600      $700

BAUME & MERCIER,17J., sec. window, auto-w., c.1950s
base metal...............................$100      $125      $150

BAUME & MERCIER, 17J.,diam. dial, cal#1080, c.1950s
14k(W)....................................$500      $600      $750

BAYLOR, 17J., hidden lugs
gold filled ...............................$40       $55       $75
14k ..........................................$125      $150      $175

BAYLOR, 17J., diamond on bezel & dial, c.1948
14k ..........................................$300      $350      $400

BELTONE, 17J., fancy hidden lugs
14k ..........................................$175      $200      $250

BEMONTOIR, 15J., enamel dial, c.1920
14k .............................. $125     $150     $175

BENRUS,17J., day date
base metal ............................... $20     $30     $40

BENRUS, 18J., mystery-diamond dial
18k ......................................... $350     $400     $475
gold filled............................... $100     $150     $200

BENRUS, 15 jewels, day, date, c. 1948
s. steel ...................................... $75     $90     $110

🕐 Some grades are not included. Their values can be
determined by comparing with **similar** age, size, metal
content, style, grades, or models such as **time only**,
chronograph, repeater etc. listed.

BENRUS, 15 jewels, quick change date
gold filled ................................ $80     $100     $125

BENRUS,17J.,"Sky Chief", chronog., c.1945
s. steel ..................................... $300     $350     $425

BENRUS,17J.,"Sky Chief", chronog., center lugs, c.1945
gold filled .............................. $325     $375     $450

BENRUS,17J.,"Sky Chief",triple date,chronog.,c.1940s
s. steel ...................................... $400     $475     $575

BENRUS, 15 jewels, auto wind, fancy lugs, c. 1950
14k ..................................$150     $200     $250
gold filled..................................$60     $75     $90

BENRUS, 15J., auto wind, fancy bezel, by ETA, c. 1950
gold filled..................................$60     $75     $90
14k ..........................................$115     $135     $200

BENRUS,17J., jumping hour, wandering min.
gold filled..................................$125     $160     $200

BENRUS,17J., dial-0-rama, direct read, c. 1958
gold filled..................................$95     $150     $185

🕐 Some grades are not included. Their values can be determined by comparing with **similar** age, size, metal content, style, grades, or models such as **time only**, chronograph, repeater etc. listed.

BENRUS, 15 jewels, jumping hour, wandering min.
gold filled ..............................$100     $120     $140
s. steel .....................................$60     $70     $85

BENRUS,17J., fancy lugs
gold filled ..................................$55     $65     $80

BENRUS,17J., fancy lugs
gold filled ..................................$40     $50     $70

BENRUS,17J., center sec., heavy lugs,
gold filled ..................................$40     $50     $65

🕐 Some grades are not included. Their values can be determined by comparing with **similar** age, size, metal content, style, grades, or models such as **time only**, chronograph, repeater etc. listed.

BENRUS, 15 jewels, fancy lugs, c. 1948
14k .........................................$325    $375    $425
gold filled............................$125    $150    $175

BENRUS, 15J., auto-wind, **water-proof**
gold filled.................................$30    $40    $55

BENRUS, 15 jewels, fancy bezel, cal. BB14
14k ..........................................$250    $300    $375
gold filled.................................$100    $135    $175

BENRUS, 21J., aux. sec., c. 1950s
14k ..........................................$125    $150    $175

🕐 Some grades are not included. Their values can be
determined by comparing with similar age, size, metal
content, style, grades, or models such as time only,
chronograph, repeater etc. listed.

BENRUS, 17J., **wind indicator,** c. 1955
gold filled...............................$100    $125    $155

BENRUS, 21J., aux. sec., fancy lugs, c.1950
gold filled.................................$60    $70    $95

BENRUS, 17J., hidden lugs
14K .........................................$125    $150    $185

BENRUS, 17J., cadillac logo, c.1950s
gold plate..................................$80    $90    $100

BENRUS, 17J., by ETA, c.1955
gold filled..................................$60    $70    $80

BENRUS, 15J., engraved bezel, c.1935
14k ..........................................$175     $200     $250

BENRUS, 17J., Rhinestone dial, c. 1945
gold filled...................................$75     $85     $100

BENRUS, 17J., date, fancy lugs, c.1950
gold filled...............................$100     $125     $150

BENRUS, 17J., aux. sec., c.1940
14k ..........................................$100     $125     $150

BENRUS, 15J.,aux sec.
gold filled...................................$50     $70     $90

BENRUS,17J., flared case, cal.180, c. 1951
gold filled .................................$75     $100     $150

BENRUS, 7J., rhinestone dial, fancy lugs, c. 1948
base metal.................................$50     $60     $85

BENRUS,17J., rhinestone dial, cal. bb1, c. 1945
gold plate ..................................$60     $70     $90

BENRUS, 15J.,stepped case
gold filled .................................$50     $60     $80

BENRUS, 15J.,fancy lugs
14kC&B..................................$500     $550     $650

BENRUS, 17J., hidden lugs, cal.11ax, Ca.1951
14k .........................................$250      $275      $325

BENRUS, 15J., hooded lugs, cal#bb3
gold filled.................................$50      $75      $100

BENRUS, 15J., **enamel bezel**, c. 1930
14k (w)....................................$350      $450      $525

BENRUS, 15 jewels, 26 diamond bezel
14k (w)....................................$350      $450      $550

BENRUS,17J., aux sec., Ca.1935
gold filled.................................$50      $70      $100

BENRUS, 15 jewels, **flip-top case**, c. 1940
gold filled .............................$175      $200      $250

BENRUS,17J., hooded lugs, c.1948
14k ...........................................$150      $175      $225

BENRUS,17J., hooded lugs, cal.AX11, c. 1950
14k ...........................................$225      $250      $300

BENRUS, 15 jewels, hooded lugs
gold filled ...............................$60      $70      $100

BENRUS, 15 jewels, cal. AX, fancy bezel
14k ...........................................$175      $200      $275

🕐 Some grades are not included. Their values can be determined by comparing with **similar** age, size, metal content, style, grades, or models such as **time only**, chronograph, repeater etc. listed.

# BENRUS ( continued )

BENRUS, 17 jewels, curved, rhinestones , hooded lugs
14k ...........................................$175      $225      $350

BENRUS, 15 jewels, curved back, c. 1942
gold filled...................................$60      $75      $90

BENSON, 15 jewels, by Landon, aux sec. c.1930s
9k ...........................................$175      $200      $250

BENSON, 15J., Ca.1938
9k ...........................................$150      $175      $200

BENSON, 15 jewels, enamel dial, tank style case
9k ...........................................$200      $250      $300

🕐 Some grades are not included. Their values can be
determined by comparing with similar age, size, metal
content, style, grades, or models such as time only,
chronograph, repeater etc. listed.

BENSON, 15 jewels, enamel dial, flared case
9k ...........................................$200      $250      $300

BENSON, 15 jewels, enamel dial, 2-tone flared case
9k ...........................................$275      $325      $375

BERG, 25J., auto-wind, c.1959
14k ...........................................$125      $150      $175

BLANCPAIN, 23J, day-date-month, moon ph., auto-wind
18k ...........................................$2,000      $2,500      $3,000
18K—perpetual ...................$6,000      $7,000      $8,000

BLANCPAIN, 17J.,hooded lugs, c.1945
14k ...........................................$200      $250      $300

BLANCPAIN, 16J., c.1925
silver .........................................$100     $125     $150

BOILLAT FRERES, 17 jewels, "Blita," waterproof
s. steel .......................................$30     $40     $50

E. BOREL, 17 jewels, chronometer, aux. sec.
18k .........................................$200     $300     $375
gold filled.................................$50     $60     $75

E. BOREL, 17J., cocktail style, c.1960s
gold filled.................................$100     $150     $200
s. steel .......................................$75     $85     $100

E. BOREL, 17J., cocktail dial, date, c. 1969
base metal ...................................$60     $75     $95

E. BOREL, 15J., hour dial, min. dial, center sec., c.1940
s. steel .......................................$250     $325     $375

E. BOREL, 17 jewels, auto wind, date
gold filled ...................................$70     $80     $110

BOUCHERON, 17J., c.1930s
18k ...........................................$500     $600     $750

🕐 Some grades are not included. Their values can be determined by comparing with **similar** age, size, metal content, style, grades, or models such as **time only**, chronograph, repeater etc. listed.

🕐 Some grades are not included. Their values can be determined by comparing with **similar** age, size, metal content, style, grades, or models such as **time only**, chronograph, repeater etc. listed.

BOULEVARD, 17J., "STOP", c.1950s
s. steel .......................................$75    $100    $125

BOVET, 17 jewels, chronog., 2 reg., c. 1940
s. steel .....................................$125    $150    $200

BOVET, 17 jewels, chronog., triple date & 3 reg.
14k .........................................$600    $700    $800
gold filled...............................$250    $300    $350

BREGUET, 21 jewels, skeletonized
18k C&B.............................$7,000    $7,500    $8,000

BREGUET, 17J., chronog., triple date, Ca.1950
s. steel .................................$6,000    $7,000    $8,000

BREGUET, auto-w., triple date, moon ph., **leap year**
18k.....................................$12,000    $14,000    $16,000

BREGUET, jump hour, c.1980s, **total made =50**
18k ......................................$8,000    $9,000    $10,000

BREGUET, 37J., auto-w., date, moon ph., 60 hr. wind ind.
18k ....................................$12,000    $13,000    $14,000

BREGUET, 17 jewels, silver dial, thin model
18k ........................................$1,200   $1,400   $1,600

P. BREGUETTE, 17 jewels, diamond dial, c. 1940
14k .........................................$400   $500   $600

BREGUET, 17 jewels, curvex
platinum..................................$3,000   $4,000   $5,000

P. BREGUETTE, 17J., gold jewel settings, date, Ca.1948
gold filled ...............................$100   $125   $150

P. BREGUETTE, 17J., gold jewel settings, Ca.1948
14k ..........................................$150   $175   $225

P. BREGUETTE, 17J., triple date, c.1960s
s. steel .....................................$100   $125   $175

P. BREGUETTE, 17J., gold jewel settings, flared case
14k .........................................$200   $225   $250

Breitling, 17 J., "Chronomat," slide rule bezel
18k .......................................$2,000   $2,250   $2,500
gold filled ..............................$900   $1,000   $1,200
s. steel .....................................$800   $900   $1,100

P. BREGUETTE, 17J., gold jewel settings, date, Ca.1948
gold filled..................................$60   $80   $100

BREITLING (continued)

BREITLING, 17J., chronog., RF#769, sq.button, c.1942
18k .......................................$1,800    $2,000    $2,200

BREITLING, 17J., chronog., RF#1199, sq. button, c.1958
s. steel ....................................$375    $400    $450

BREITLING, 17J., chronog., "Navitimer," **24 hour**, 3 reg.
18k .......................................$4,000    $4,500    $4,750
s. steel ....................................$900    $1,000    $1,200

BREITLING, 17 jewels, split sec. chronog., 2 reg.
s. steel ....................................$3,000    $4,000    $5,000

BREITLING, 18J., date, moon ph., split chronog. 3 reg.
18k .......................................$8,000    $9,000    $10,000

BREITLING, 17 jewels, chronog., "Navitimer," date
s. steel ....................................$400    $450    $500

BREITLING, 17 J., chronog., "Cosmonaute," date
s. steel ....................................$400    $525    $575

🕐 Some grades are not included. Their values can be
determined by comparing with **similar** age, size, metal
content, style, grades, or models such as **time only**,
chronograph, repeater etc. listed.

BREITLING, 17 J., chronog., "Chronomat," 3 reg.
s. steel ......................................$450     $500        $575

BREITLING, 17 J., telemeter, 1 button, hinged lugs
s. steel- 44mm........................$750      $850        $950

BREITLING, 17 J., chronog., Navitimer, Ca. 1952
s. steel ......................................$900     $1,000      $1,200

BREITLING, 17 jewels, tachymeter, Ca.1925
s. steel ..................................$1,200     $1,300      $1,400

BREITLING, 17 jewels, chronog., pulsations
s. steel ......................................$500     $600        $700

BREITLING, 17 jewels, chronog., 2 reg.
s. steel ..................................$1,200     $1,300      $1,400

BREITLING, 17 jewels, tachymeter, center hinged lugs
s. steel - 35mm .......................$800     $1,000      $1,200

BREITLING, 17J., chronog., RF#765, c.1960
14k ............................................$800     $1,000      $1,200
s. steel ......................................$300     $350        $400

BREITLING, 17 jewels, chronog., Toptime
s. steel ....................................$350      $400      $450

BREITLING, 17 jewels, chronog., 2 reg. RF#790
18K refinished dial.............$1,000      $1,200      $1,400
18K original dial.................$1,200      $1,400      $1,700

BREITLING, 17J., chronog., 2 reg., "Premier", RF#790
18k ......................................$1,200      $1,400      $1,700

BREITLING, 17J., chronog., 3 reg., RF#787, c.1942
14k C&B.............................$1,200      $1,400      $1,600

BREITLING, 17 jewels, chronog., "Premier," 3 reg.
s. steel ....................................$400      $500      $600

BREITLING, 17 J., chronog., day-date-month, 3 reg.
18k ......................................$1,600      $2,000      $2,250
s. steel ....................................$700      $800      $900

BREITLING, 17 jewels, chronog., 2 reg.
s. steel ....................................$250      $300      $375

BREITLING, 17 jewels, chronog., 2 reg.
18k ......................................$1,000      $1,250      $1,500
s. steel ....................................$275      $325      $400

BREITLING, 17 J., split sec. chronog., "Duograph"
18k .......................................$6,000    $7,000    $8,000
s. steel ...............................$3,000    $4,000    $5,000

BREITLING, 17J., chronog., 3 reg., RF#815, c.1968
gold filled...............................$300    $375    $425

BREITLING, 17J., chronog., Toptime, RF#810, c.1968
s. steel ....................................$300    $350    $400

BREITLING, 17J., chronog., RF#2110, c. 1970
s. steel ....................................$250    $300    $350

BREITLING, 17J., chronog., Datora, RF#2031, c.1970
s. steel ....................................$275    $350    $375

BREITLING, 17J., chronog., RF#2110, c.1970
s. steel ....................................$300    $350    $400

BREITLING, 17J., chronog., RF#2009-33, c. 1975
s. steel ....................................$275    $325    $375

BREITLING, 17J., chronog., auto w., date, c. 1969
s. steel ....................................$250    $300    $375

BREITLING, 17J., chronog., RF#1450, 3 reg., c.1970
s. steel .............................$275    $350    $400

BUCHERER,17 jewels, **note day date in lugs**
18k .........................$900    $1,200    $1,400

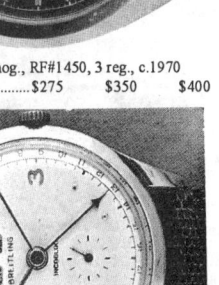

BREITLING, 17J., day date month,
18k .............................$300    $400    $500

BUCHERER,17 jewels, chronog., 2 reg.
18k .........................$475    $500    $550

BREITLING, 21J., "UNITIME", date, 24 hour, c.1958
gold filled.....................$500    $600    $700
18k ............................$1,000    $1,100    $1,250

BUCHERER, 17J., chronog., 2 reg., C.1959
18k .........................$500    $600    $750
s. steel .....................$275    $325    $375

BREITLING, 21J., auto-wind, rf#2528, c.1959
s. steel .............................$75    $85    $95

BUCHERER, 25 J., triple date moon ph., cal.693, c.1950
18k .........................$1,000    $1,200    $1,400

BUCHERER, 21J., 3 dates, moon ph., diamond dial
18k ........................................$2,400    $2,600    $2,800

BUCHERER, 15 jewels, 8 day movement
18k .......................................$1,000    $1,200    $1,400
gold filled................................$500     $600     $700

BUECHE-GIROD, 17 J., day-date-month, moon ph.
s. steel .....................................$250    $300     $375

BUECHE-GIROD, 17J., by Piguet, cal.99, c.1975
18k .............................................$400    $500     $600

⊕ Some grades are not included. Their values can be
determined by comparing with **similar** age, size, metal
content, style, grades, or models such as **time only**,
chronograph, repeater etc. listed.

BUECHE-GIROD, 17J., dual time movements,
18k ......................................... $500      $600     $700

BUECHE-GIROD, 17 jewels, tank style case
18k ......................................... $500      $550     $600

BUECHE-GIROD, 17 jewels
18k C&B................................ $600      $700     $800

P. BUHRE, 17 jewels, aux. sec.
gold filled ................................. $40      $50      $65

P. BUHRE, 17J., alarm, C.1956
s. steel ........................................ $90     $120     $155

BULOVA, Accutron, "RF # 210" **gold bezel** & s.steel case
s.steel &**14k**..............................$250     $285     $375

BULOVA, Accutron, "Spaceview Alpha"
14k ..........................................$500    $600    $750

BULOVA, Accutron, "RF # 213"
s.steel .....................................$150    $200    $250

BULOVA, Accutron, "Spaceview B"
s.steel .....................................$150    $200    $250

BULOVA, Accutron, "RF # 214"
s.steel .....................................$150    $200    $250

BULOVA, Accutron, "Spaceview H"
gold filled................................$175    $225    $275

BULOVA, Accutron, "RF # 216"
s.steel .....................................$150    $200    $250

BULOVA, Accutron, "RF # 202"
gold filled................................$175    $225    $275

BULOVA, Accutron, "RF # 218" center lugs
s.steel .....................................$175    $225    $275

BULOVA, Accutron, "RF # 223"
s.steel ........................................$175      $225      $275
14k ..........................................$425      $475      $575

BULOVA, Accutron, "RF # 412" gold filled bezel & s.steel
gold filled & s.steel case ........$175      $225      $275

BULOVA, Accutron, "RF # 400"
gold filled..............................$175      $225      $275

BULOVA, Accutron, "RF # 413" gold filled bezel & s.steel
gold filled & s.steel case ........$175      $225      $275

BULOVA, Accutron, "RF # 401"
s.steel ........................................$150      $200      $250

BULOVA, Accutron, "RF # 417"
gold filled ..............................$175      $225      $275

BULOVA, Accutron, "RF # 403"
gold filled................................$175      $225      $275

BULOVA, Accutron, "RF # 420"
gold filled ..............................$175      $225      $275

BULOVA, Accutron, "RF # 411"
gold filled................................$175      $225      $275

BULOVA, Accutron, "RF # 500" center lugs
14k ..........................................$400      $450      $550

# BULOVA / Accutron (continued)

BULOVA, Accutron, "RF # 505"
14k yellow or white ...............$425    $475    $585

BULOVA, Accutron, "RF # 513"
14k .........................................$400    $450    $550

BULOVA, Accutron, "RF # 514" Florentine engraved case
14k .........................................$425    $475    $585

BULOVA, Accutron, "RF # 560"
14k .........................................$400    $450    $550

BULOVA, Accutron, "RF # 602"
18k .........................................$500    $550    $650

BULOVA, Accutron, "Mickey" day & date
14k .........................................$550    $650    $775

BULOVA, Accutron, date, "M 8" on back - Ca. 1968
14k .........................................$400    $425    $475

BULOVA, Accutron, "Spaceview"
s. steel ....................................$150    $200    $250

BULOVA, Accutron, **"converted dial"**, cal. 214, c.1963
gold filled ...............................$125    $150    $225
Note Below: Bulova Accutron regulator, to regulate use a
tooth pick and move regulator up or down.

🕐 NOTE: Some Bulova cases are stamped with a year date
code letter & number .L=1950s, M=1960s, N=1970s
example: L3=1953, M4=1964, N5=1975, etc.

🕐 NOTE: Some Bulova cases are stamped with a year date code letter & number .L=1950s, M=1960s, N=1970s example: L3=1953, M4=1964, N5=1975, etc.

BULOVA, Accutron, cal. 214, c. 1963
s. steel .................................... $150    $200    $250

BULOVA, Accutron, "Spaceview," c. 1960
14k ......................................... $400    $450    $600
gold filled................................ $175    $225    $275
s. steel .................................... $150    $200    $250

BULOVA, Accutron, "Spaceview"
s. steel .................................... $150    $200    $250

BULOVA, Accutron, "Spaceview"
18k ......................................... $600    $700    $800
14k ......................................... $400    $500    $600
s. steel .................................... $150    $200    $250

BULOVA, Accutron, "Spaceview," c. 1965
gold filled ............................... $175    $225    $275

BULOVA, Accutron, "Spaceview," c. 1961
gold filled ............................... $175    $225    $275

BULOVA, Accutron, "Spaceview," c. 1967
gold filled ............................... $225    $275    $350
s. steel .................................... $175    $225    $275
14k ......................................... $500    $600    $700

BULOVA, Accutron, **converted dial,** Alpha, waterproof
14k ......................................... $250    $300    $375

**Accutron,** reached 1/2 million in sales by 1966, 3/4 by 1968, by 1970 1 million watches, and by 1976, 2 million watches.

BULOVA, Accutron, "Spaceview," center lugs
gold filled................................$200     $225     $300

BULOVA, Accutron, "Spaceview," center lugs
s. steel ....................................$200     $235     $275

BULOVA, Accutron, center lugs
gold filled................................$200     $225     $300

BULOVA, Accutron, "Spaceview," center lugs
14k C & B...............................$500     $600     $700

BULOVA, Accutron, **converted** dial, date, cal.218
14k 2 tone ...............................$200     $250     $300

BULOVA, Accutron, 2 tone, Ca. 1967
gold filled ...............................$200     $250     $300

BULOVA, Accutron, Skeletonized, date, cal.218, Ca.1967
14k ...........................................$350     $400     $500

BULOVA, Accutron, oval, "Spaceview"
s. steel ....................................$150     $200     $250

BULOVA, Accutron, two tone, date
14k 2 tone ...............................$225     $250     $350

BULOVA, Accutron, "Spaceview,"
s. steel ......................................$150      $200      $250

BULOVA, Accutron, RR approved, 24 hr. dial in red, date
gold filled ...............................$175      $200      $235

BULOVA, Accutron, "Spaceview,"
s. steel ......................................$150      $200      $250

BULOVA, Accutron, **quartz**, RR approved, day date
gold plate ................................... $75      $85      $150

BULOVA, Accutron, "Spaceview," gold bezel
14k ...........................................$400      $500      $650
gold bezel & s. steel case .......$200      $250      $300

BULOVA, Accutron, RR approved
s. steel ......................................$125      $145      $200

BULOVA, Accutron, railroad approved, C. 1960s
gold filled................................$150      $185      $225
s. steel ......................................$125      $150      $200

🕐 NOTE: Some Bulova cases are stamped with a year date
code letter & number. L=1950s, M=1960s, N=1970s
example: L3=1953, M4=1964, N5=1975, etc.

BULOVA, Accutron, **Mark II / RR approved,** date
Crown at 2 sets the hour hand, Crown at 4 sets Time & Date
s. steel ......................................$200      $250      $350

BULOVA, Accutron, cal. 214," Pulsation", c. 1966
gold filled.................................$125      $150      $195
14k .........................................$500      $550      $600

BULOVA, Accutron, masonic dial
14k ...........................................$235      $300      $375

BULOVA, Accutron, cal. 214," Pulsation", c. 1966
14k .........................................$500      $550      $600

BULOVA, Accutron, asymmetric
14k .........................................$450      $500      $575

BULOVA, Accutron, cal. 214, diamond dial
14k .........................................$450      $550      $700
18K..........................................$500      $600      $800

BULOVA, Accutron, asymmetric, 2- tone dial, Ca.1963
14k .........................................$500      $575      $650

BULOVA, Accutron, sweep sec. hand
gold filled...............................$75      $95      $100

BULOVA, Accutron, "ASTRONAUT A", 24 hour dial
18kC&B............................$1,200      $1,400      $1,800
14k .........................................$800      $1,000      $1,200
gold filled ...........................$250      $300      $375
s. steel ....................................$175      $225      $300

BULOVA, Accutron, "ASTRONAUT B", rotating bezel
s. steel .........................................$195    $250    $295

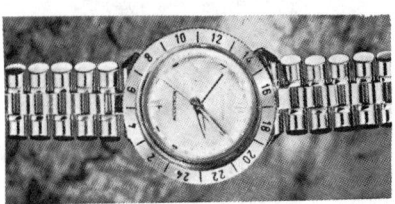

BULOVA, Accutron, "ASTRONAUT C", 18k case & band,
retail price in June, 1964 was $1,000.00.
**18k C & B** ...........................$1,400    $1,600    $2,000

BULOVA, Accutron, "Astronaut Mark II", time zone, window
at six o'clock, date at 12, note: red dial, on back N2 = 1972
14k .........................................$400    $495    $600
s. steel ....................................$150    $175    $240

BULOVA, Accutron, "Astronaut Mark II", time zone, original sales price was $275.00 in S. Steel.
14k .........................................$400    $495    $600
gold filled...............................$200    $275    $350
s. steel ....................................$195    $235    $275

BULOVA, Accutron, "Astronaut Mark II", time zone window
at 6-o'clock & date at 12-o'clock.
14k ..........................................$475    $525    $600

BULOVA, Accutron, "Astronaut Mark II", time zone with a
extra red hour hand, date at 3 o'clock, on back M9 = 1969
gold filled ..............................$200    $275    $350

BULOVA, Accutron
gold filled ..............................$100    $125    $150

BULOVA, Accutron, Ca. 1966
gold filled ..................................$75    $100    $135

BULOVA, Accutron, fancy lugs
gold filled................................$100    $125    $150

BULOVA, Accutron, date, gold filled bezel
s. steel ......................................$65    $75    $95

BULOVA, Accutron
gold filled................................$175    $200    $250

BULOVA, Accutron, date, Ca. 1967
s. steel ......................................$85    $100    $135

BULOVA, Accutron, 4 diamond dial, Ca. 1967
gold filled................................$150    $200    $250

BULOVA, Accutron, date
gold filled ...............................$125    $150    $200

BULOVA, Accutron, day date
14k ..........................................$175    $225    $300

BULOVA, Accutron, date, "M 7" on back = Ca. 1967
14k ..........................................$400    $425    $475

BULOVA, (Accu- quartz), quartz & tuning fork, day date
gold filled...................................$75      $100      $125

BULOVA, Accutron, cushion spaceview, Ca. 1970
s. steel .....................................$150      $200      $250

BULOVA, Accutron,  model 2183,
s. steel .........................................$60      $70      $80

BULOVA, Accutron, **wood bezel**, day date
gold filled .................................$75      $100      $150

BULOVA, Accutron, date, Ca.1972
base metal ...................................$65      $75      $85

BULOVA, Accutron, red dial, date
gold filled .................................$75      $100      $125

BULOVA, Accutron,  faceted crystal, day date
gold filled...................................$75      $85      $100

BULOVA, Accutron,  numbered bezel, day date
14k ...........................................$350      $400      $475

BULOVA, Accuquartz, diamond bezel, day date
14k .................................................. $350      $400      $450

BULOVA, Accuquartz, note band with **accutron symbol**
18k C&B.................................... $600      $700      $850

BULOVA, Accutron, day date
gold filled................................. $100      $125      $150

BULOVA, Accutron, day date, c. 1970
s. steel ...................................... $50      $60      $70

BULOVA, Accutron, day date, Ca.1972
gold filled................................. $100      $125      $150

BULOVA, Accutron, model 2186, direct read
gold filled ................................. $75      $100      $150

BULOVA, Accutron, day date
14k C&B.................................... $500      $550      $600

BULOVA, Accutron, **Accutron 14k Gold Band**, Ca.1972
14k C & B.................................... $500      $600      $700

BULOVA, Accutron, diamond on bezel
14k(w) C&B ............................$400      $500      $600

BULOVA, Accutron, date
gold filled................................$100      $125      $150

BULOVA, Accutron, divers 660 ft.depth, 24 hr.dial,
rotating outside chapter, day  date
s. steel ......................................$175      $200      $225

BULOVA, Accutron, day date,
14k C&B..................................$400      $450      $500

BULOVA, Accutron, date.
14k C&B................................$400      $450      $500

BULOVA, Accutron, fancy bezel
14k C&B................................$400      $450      $525

BULOVA, Accutron, lady accutron
14k ..........................................$100      $110      $120

BULOVA, Accutron, note links in accutron band
gold plate ................................ $60      $75      $95

BULOVA, Accutron, date, Ca. 1968
gold filled ..............................$100      $125      $150

🕐 NOTE: Some Bulova cases are stamped with a year date code letter & number .L=1950s, M=1960s, N=1970s example: L3=1953, M4=1964, N5=1975, etc.

BULOVA, Accutron, wide oval bezel
gold filled....................................$40    $50    $60

BULOVA, digital,
s. steel ........................................$95    $125    $165

BULOVA, Accutron, 32 small diamond bezel
14k(w)......................................$250    $275    $300

BULOVA, enamel bezel
s. steel ....................................$100    $125    $150

BULOVA, Accutron, cal. #221, textured bezel
sterling & 14k ..........................$75    $100    $125

BULOVA, 15J., one button chronog.,1/5 sec.,C.1946
gold filled ...............................$300    $335    $375

BULOVA, Accutron, pendant style watch
14k ...........................................$100    $125    $150

BULOVA, 17J., one button chronog., cal.10BK, c.1947
gold filled ...............................$300    $325    $375

BULOVA, 17J., chronog., "660 feet" dive watch, c.1972
s. steel .....................................$100      $125      $150

BULOVA, 16 jewels, military style
s. steel ...................................$250      $300      $350

BULOVA, 17J., Alarm, cal.11aerc, c.1967
s. steel ....................................$100      $125      $150

BULOVA, self winding, c. 1960
14k ..........................................$100      $125      $150
gold filled.................................$40      $50      $60

BULOVA, 17J., fancy lugs
gold filled ..................................$75      $90      $125

BULOVA, 23 jewels, waterproof
14k .........................................$175      $200      $250

BULOVA, 23 jewels, date, 6 adj., c. 1951
gold filled ..............................$100      $125      $175

BULOVA, 17J., 1 button chronograph, cal.9arc, ca.1952
gold filled ..............................$300      $325      $375
14K .......................................$500      $550      $600

BULOVA, fancy long lugs, c. 1942
gold filled.................................$65    $80    $100

BULOVA, 17J., fancy lugs, c.1958
14k .............................................$275    $325    $375

BULOVA, 21J., fancy lugs, c.1950
gold filled.................................$65    $80    $100

BULOVA, 17J., center sec., c.1942
gold filled.................................$45    $55    $65

BULOVA, 15J., military style, c.1940
s. steel .......................................$65    $75    $85

BULOVA, cal. 700, canteen style, c. 1946
s. steel ....................................$300    $400    $500

BULOVA, 15J., military style, cal.10 bnch, c.1940
s. steel .......................................$95    $125    $150

BULOVA, 17J., U.S.A. military, c.1945
s. steel .......................................$90    $110    $130

BULOVA, 17J., 20 diamond dial
14k(w)....................................$250    $300    $375

BULOVA, 23J., 12 diamond dial, c. 1959
14k(w)..................................$250    $300    $375

BULOVA, 30J., diam. dial, cal#10B2AC, C.1960s
14k(w)..................................$200    $250    $300

BULOVA, early auto wind movement by Champ

BULOVA, early auto wind, by Champ, c. 1930
gold filled..................................$400    $500    $600

BULOVA, diamond dial, c. 1939
platinum..................................$900    $1,100    $1,250
14k (w)..................................$600    $700    $800

BULOVA, 21 jewels, hidden lugs, diamond dial, c. 1935
14k..................................$600    $700    $800

BULOVA, hidden lugs, diamond dial, c. 1945
14k..................................$500    $600    $700

BULOVA, 21 jewels, diamond dial, long lugs, c. 1941
14k (w)..................................$250    $300    $375

BULOVA, 17J., 3 diamond dial, cal.8ae, c.1949
14k..................................$200    $250    $325

BULOVA, 17 jewels, curved, cal. 7AP, c. 1939
14k..................................$250    $300    $375

BULOVA, 17J., drivers watch, c.1935
gold filled.................................$300  $350  $400

BULOVA, 17J., engraved, Ca. 1928
gold filled.................................$80  $90  $110

BULOVA, 17J., 5th ave., cal.6am, engraved bezel, c.1935
gold filled.................................$90  $110  $150

BULOVA, 21J., stepped bezel, curved,
gold filled.................................$100  $125  $165

BULOVA, 21J., plain bezel, curved,
gold filled.................................$100  $125  $165

BULOVA, 17J., cal. 7ap, c.1937
gold filled.................................$100  $125  $165

BULOVA, 17J., curved, cal.7ap, c.1936
gold filled.................................$75  $100  $150

BULOVA, 17J., cal.13al, c.1935
14k.................................$165  $185  $225

BULOVA, 17J., cal.9af, c.1929
s. steel.................................$65  $75  $100

BULOVA, 17J., cal.7ap, c.1934
gold filled.................................$100  $125  $175

BULOVA, 15J., cal.10ae, c.1938
gold filled.................................$65  $75  $90

BULOVA, 17 jewels, curved, c. 1939
gold filled.................................$75  $100  $125

BULOVA, 21 jewels, curved, c. 1939
gold filled..................................$75    $100    $125

BULOVA, 21J., cal# 6AE,
14k .........................................$175    $225    $300

BULOVA, 17 jewels, duo dial, c. 1935
gold filled...............................$475    $550    $625
s. steel ...................................$375    $425    $475

BULOVA, 17 jewels, 2 tone duo dial
s. steel ...................................$400    $450    $500

BULOVA, 17 jewels, 2 tone dial, fancy bezel
s. steel .......................................$75    $85    $100

🕐 Some grades are not included. Their values can be determined by comparing with **similar** age, size, metal content, style, models and grades listed.

BULOVA, 17 J., **President,** wandering sec., c. 1932
gold filled ..............................$150    $200    $250

BULOVA, 17 jewels, cal. 10GM, fancy lugs, c. 1953
gold filled ................................$80    $90    $100
14k .........................................$250    $300    $350

BULOVA, 15J., fancy lugs, c.1952
gold filled ................................$80    $90    $100

BULOVA, 21J., fancy lugs, c.1952
14k .........................................$225    $250    $325
gold filled ................................$80    $90    $100

BULOVA, 17J., fancy lugs, cal.8an, c.1951
14k ..........................................$375    $425    $475
gold filled ..............................$150    $175    $225

BULOVA, 17J., cal.8ad, fancy lugs, c.1939
gold plate .................................$80    $90    $100

BULOVA, 17J., fancy lugs, c.1950 code on case=(LO)
gold filled ...............................$50    $60    $70

BULOVA, 21J., cal. 7ak, c.1945
gold filled................................$60    $70    $80

BULOVA, 17J., gold jewel settings, Ca.1923
gold filled ...............................$100    $125    $150

BULOVA, 21J., c.1950s
gold filled................................$80    $100    $130

BULOVA, 21J., **carved case**, c.1948
14k .........................................$165    $185    $235

BULOVA, 21J., scalloped case, c.1950s
gold filled ...............................$100    $125    $150

BULOVA, 21J., cal.7ak, c.1945
gold filled .................................$60    $70    $80

BULOVA, 7J., c.1945
gold filled.................................$40    $50    $75

BULOVA, 17J., cal.8ae, fancy hidden lugs, c.1941
gold filled ..................................$75    $100    $125

BULOVA, 21J., hooded lugs, c.1945
14k ........................................$175      $200      $250

BULOVA, 21 jewels, hooded lugs, cal. 8AC, c. 1952
14k ..........................................$300      $350      $400

BULOVA, 17 jewels, fancy long lugs, c. 1942
14k ..........................................$200      $250      $300

BULOVA, 15 jewels, engraved bezel, c. 1925
gold filled..............................$100      $125      $150

BULOVA, 17J., cal. 8AC, **flip top, photo watch,** c. 1940
gold filled..............................$150      $200      $225
14k ..........................................$300      $375      $450

🕐 Some grades are not included. Their values can be determined by comparing with **similar** age, size, metal content,
style, models and grades listed.

BULOVA, 15 jewels, wandering hr. min. sec., c. 1928
s. steel ....................................$200      $235      $275

BULOVA, 17J., right angle, cal. 8AZ, c. 1938
gold filled ..............................$125      $150      $175
14k ..........................................$300      $350      $400

BULOVA, 17 jewels, aux. sec.
14k ..........................................$175      $200      $250

BULOVA, 17 jewels, fancy bezel
gold filled ..............................$100      $120      $140

BULOVA, 17 jewels, bell shaped lugs
14k ..........................................$225      $275      $300

BULOVA, 17 jewels, fancy lugs
14k ...............................................$200     $250     $300

BULOVA, 21J., hidden lugs, c.1950s
14k ...........................................$250     $300     $350

BULOVA, 17J., center sec., cal.10bac, c.1935
gold filled....................................$75     $100     $125

BULOVA, 21J., hidden lugs, c.1945
gold filled ...................................$75     $85     $125

BULOVA, 17J., cal.8ac, fancy lugs, c.1940
gold plate ....................................$50     $60     $70

BULOVA, 17J., FORD logo, c.1947
gold plate ...................................$90     $110     $135

BULOVA, 17J., flared top of case & sides,
gold filled....................................$70     $80     $90

BULOVA, 17J., FORD logo, c.1947
base metal ...............................$70     $80     $90

BULOVA, 21J., hidden lugs, c.1961
gold filled....................................$65     $80     $125

BULOVA, 17J., engraved lugs & bezel, cal.10an,c.1928
s. steel .........................................$40     $50     $60

BULOVA, 17J., engraved bezel only
base metal ...................................$40      $50      $60

BULOVA, 17 jewels, cal#11AF
10k ...........................................$120      $140      $175

BULOVA, 15J., cal.11ac, c.1958
gold filled..................................$90      $110      $135

BULOVA, 17 jewels , engraved bezel
gold filled ...................................$50      $60      $75

BULOVA, 15J., cal.10ae, c.1935
gold filled..................................$50      $60      $70

BULOVA, 17 jewels, engraved, tank style, hinged case
chrome plate .............................. $40      $50      $60

BULOVA, 7J., cal.10bc, c.1949
gold filled..................................$40      $50      $60

BULOVA, 17 jewels, engraved bezel,
gold filled ...................................$40      $50      $60

BULOVA, 15J., cal.10an, c.1929
base metal ...................................$40      $50      $60

BULOVA, 17 jewels, ''The Governor''
14k ...........................................$225      $275      $350

BULOVA, 17J., right angle case
gold filled...................................$175    $225    $275

BULOVA, 17 jewels, "The Ambassador"
gold filled...................................$40    $50    $60

BULOVA, 17 jewels, "The Curtis," tank style
gold filled...................................$100    $125    $150

BULOVA, 15 jewels, "The Athelete"
gold filled...................................$100    $115    $125

BULOVA, 17 jewels, "The Lone Eagle," fancy bezel
gold filled...................................$130    $150    $175

BUREN, 17 jewels, day-date-month, moon phase
s. steel.....................................$225    $275    $325

BUREN, 17 jewels, long lugs
14k.........................................$150    $170    $200

BUREN, 17 jewels, center lugs, c.1940
9k..........................................$250    $275    $325

BUTEX, 17J., triple date, moon ph.
gold filled ...............................$250    $300    $375

CARLTON, 15 jewels, stepped case, c. 1939
gold filled ...............................$100    $125    $175
14k.........................................$275    $325    $375

CARTIER, 18 J., 8 day Mvt., tank style, by E. W. Co.
18k ....................................$30,000    $35,000    $40,000

CARTIER, 18 J., sapphire crown & bezel, c. 1970
18k ......................................$2,500    $3,000    $3,500

CARTIER, 18 jewels, curved, tank style
18k ......................................$7,000    $8,000    $9,000

CARTIER, 18 jewels, curved, signed E. W. Co., c.1930s
18k ......................................$6,000    $7,000    $8,000

CARTIER, 18 J., tank style, platinum case & band
platinum C&B....................$10,000    $12,000    $14,000

CARTIER, 18 jewels, tank style case, c. 1970s
18k ......................................$1,200    $1,400    $1,600

CARTIER, 20 jewels, tank style case, c. 1950
18k ......................................$1,800    $2,000    $2,200

CARTIER, Must de, **quartz,** tank style case, c.1980s
Vermeil =(gold over sterling)
G.P. vermeil............................$200    $250    $300
SAME STYLE CASE AS ABOVE
CARTIER, Must de, **Mechanical,** tank style case, c.1980s
Vermeil =(gold over sterling)
G.P. vermeil............................$200    $250    $300

CARTIER, 18 jewels, tank style, European W. Co.
platinum...............................$4,000    $5,000    $6,000

CARTIER, 18 jewels, by Movado
14k ......................................$1,000    $1,200    $1,400

CARTIER, 18 jewels, duo plan, European W. Co.
18k C&B ............................ $2,500    $3,000    $3,500

CARTIER, 18J., by Le Coultre, long lugs
18k ........................................ $1,200    $1,400    $1,600

CARTIER, 18 jewels, curved, hidden lugs
18k ........................................ $3,500    $4,000    $4,500

CARTIER, 18 jewels, by Universal, c. 1960
18k ........................................ $800    $1,000    $1,200

CARTIER, 18 jewels, center lugs, c. 1930
18k ........................................ $2,800    $3,200    $3,600

CARTIER, 18 J., Prince, by Le Coultre, C.1930
18k ........................................ $30,000    $40,000    $50,000

time zone
18k ........................................ $25,000    $30,000    $35,000

CARTIER, 18 jewels, c. 1960
18k ........................................ $1,400    $1,600    $1,800

CARTIER, 18 J., early E.W.Co., C. 1928
18k ........................................ $4,000    $5,000    $6,000

CARTIER, 18 J., lady's watch by European W. Co.
18kC&B ............................ $2,000    $2,500    $3,000

CARTIER, 18 J., sovonnette H.C.style, C. 1928
18k ........................................ $10,000    $11,000    $12,000

CARTIER, 18 J., tank for Chinese mkt., E.W.Co., Ca. 1925
18k ........................................ $3,500    $4,000    $4,500

CARTIER,18 J., guichet tank, jump hr. & min. by E.W.Co.
18k .....................................$30,000    $35,000    $40,000

CARTIER, 18 J., jump hr. & min., E. W. Co. c. 1930
platinum..............................$35,000    $40,000    $45,000

CARTIER, 18 J.,"Santos", cal.21
mens18k...............................$1,800    $2,000    $2,200
ladies 18k ............................$1,600    $1,800    $2,000

CARTIER, 18 J., "Santos," 18k & s. steel case, band
platinum & 18k C&B ........$12,000    $14,000    $16,000
18k & s. steel C&B................$800    $1,000    $1,200

CARTIER, Panthere, large, date, water resistant
18k C & B ...........................$4,000    $5,000    $6,500

CARTIER, 18 jewels, "Santos," date
18k & s. steel C&B ...............$800    $1,000    $1,200

CARTIER, 18 jewels, "Santos," octagonal, date
18k & s. steel C&B ...............$600    $800    $1,000

CARTIER, 18 jewels, "Santos," lady's, date
18k & s. steel C&B ...............$500    $600    $700

CARTIER, 25 jewels, chronog., European W. Co.
18k ....................................$60,000    $70,000    $80,000

CARTIER, 29 jewels, min. repeater, c. 1925
18k ....................................$100,000    $125,000    $150,000

CARTIER, 18 jewels, c. 1925
18k .........................................$3,500    $4,000    $4,500

CARTIER, 18 jewels, asymmetric, E. W. Co., c. 1928
18k .........................................$8,000    $9,000    $10,000

CARTIER, 18 J., oval maxi, C. 1968
18k .................................$10,000    $12,000    $14,000

CARTIER, 18 jewels, by Le Coultre
18k .........................................$2,000    $2,500    $3,000

CARTIER, 18 J., bamboo style bezel, C.1970s
18k .........................................$4,000    $4,500    $5,000

CARTIER, 18 J., large cut corner bezel, C.1970s
18k .......................................$3,000    $3,500    $4,000

CARTIER, 18 J., "Helm", single lug, C. 1950s
18k ...................................$20,000    $25,000    $30,000
platinum..............................$60,000    $70,000    $80,000

CARTIER, 18 J.,by E.W.CO., single lug, C. 1949
18k ......................................$15,000    $18,000    $22,000

CARTIER, 29 J., min. repeater, by Le Coultre, c. 1930
platinum..............................$80,000    $90,000    $100,000

CARTIER, 18 J., by ESKA
18k(w) C&B .........................$1,000    $1,200    $1,500

CARTIER, 18 jewels, date chapter, by Le Coultre
14k .........................................$1,000    $1,200    $1,400

CARTIER,Quartz, 296 factory diamonds on bezel & 18k Band
18k .......................................$12,000    $13,000    $14,000

CARTIER, 18 J., lady's, E.W.CO., c.1948
18k .......................................$2,000    $2,500    $3,000

CARTIER, 18J., tonneau, Ca. 1920
platinum ...............................$4,000    $5,000    $6,000

CARTIER, 18 J., lady's, E.W.Co., C.1949
14k(w) C&B .........................$400    $500    $600

CERTINA, 17J., auto-wind, c.1950s
s. steel .......................................$70    $80    $90

CERTINA, 17J., "NEWART", auto-wind, date, c.1965
14k ..........................................$150    $175    $200

CENTRAL, 7J., cal.39, c.1937
gold filled ..................................$60    $70    $80

CHEVROLET, 6J., in form of car radiator, C. 1927
silver .......................................$400    $500    $650

CHOPARD, 18 J., 2 dial , 2 time zones, diam.bezel
18k C&B..........................\$2,000      \$2,500      \$3,000

CHOPARD, 18 J., skeletonized, diamond dial &hands
18k .......................................\$3,500      \$4,000      \$4,500

CHOPARD, 28J., triple date moon ph., cal.900, c.1980
18k .............................................\$800      \$900      \$1,000

CHOPARD, 20 J., RF#2113, c.1978
18k ..............................................\$300      \$400      \$500

CHOPARD, 17J., RF#2134, c.1978
18k ..............................................\$300      \$400      \$500

CLEBAR, 17 jewels, chronog., 2 reg., cal.2248, c.1952
gold filled ...............................\$250      \$275      \$325
base metal................................\$200      \$250      \$300

CLEBAR, 17 jewels, chronog., 3 reg. c.1950s
gold filled ...............................\$275      \$325      \$375
s. steel ....................................\$250      \$300      \$350

CLEBAR, 17J., chronog.,triple date, moon ph.
gold filled ...............................\$550      \$650      \$800
s. steel ....................................\$500      \$600      \$750

CLEBAR, 17 jewels, center lugs, chronog., c. 1938
s. steel .....................................\$350      \$400      \$475

CONCORD, 17J., aux. sec., ca. 1947
14k ........................................$200     $250     $300

CONCORD, 17 jewels, center sec.
14k ........................................$200     $250     $325

CONCORD, 17 jewels, chronog. 2 reg., c.1940s
s. steel ..................................$250     $300     $350

CONDAL,15J. hunter style, flip top, C.1928
silver ......................................$400     $500     $600

CONTINENTAL, 17J., 3 diamond dial
14k ........................................$150     $175     $200

CORNAVIN, 17J., day date, c. 1960
gold filled ..............................$100     $125     $150

CORNAVIN, 17J., date, auto, RF#1243, C.1963
gold filled ..............................$60     $75     $110
s. steel ..................................$50     $65     $100

CORONET, 17J., chronog.
s. steel ..................................$175     $200     $250

CORTEBERT, 15 jewels, c. 1940s
gold filled ..............................$40     $50     $60

CORTEBERT, 15 jewels, c. 1941
gold filled ..............................$50     $60     $75

CORTEBERT, 17 J., "Sport," triple date, moon phase
18k .......................................$600   $700   $800
gold filled................................$200   $250   $350

CORTEBERT, 17 jewels, center sec.
s. steel ......................................$30   $40   $50

CORTEBERT, quartz, U.K. military, (CWC)
s. steel ......................................$75   $100   $125

CORTEBERT, (CWC), chronog., by Valjoux, c.1971
s. steel ......................................$300   $350   $400

CORUM, 17 J., twenty dollar gold piece
18k & 22k .........................$3,000   $3,500   $4,000

CORUM, 24k gold ingot, GR.15
24k .....................................$1,200   $1,400   $1,600

CORUM, 17 J., in form of Rolls-Royce car radiator
18k .......................................$2,200   $2,500   $2,800

CORUM, 17 jewels, peacock feather dial
18k ...........................................$800   $900   $1,000

CORUM, 17 jewels, rope style bezel
18k C&B..............................$1,000   $1,200   $1,500

CORUM, 17 jewels, in form of book
18k ........................................$600    $700    $900

CRAWFORD, 17J., hooded lugs, c. 1940
14k ............................................$150    $175    $225

CORUM, 21 jewels, "pave" diamond dial,  c.1990
18k C&B..............................$2,200    $2,500    $3,000

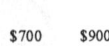

CRAWFORD, 17J., pendant watch
base metal ...............................$50    $75    $100

CORUM, 21 jewels, gold dial
18k ............................................$400    $500    $600

CROTON, 17 jewels, day date
gold filled ................................$40    $50    $60

CRAWFORD, 17J., triple date, c. 1942
s. steel ........................................$80    $110    $150

CROTON, 17 jewels, diamond bezel & dial
14k (w) ....................................$300    $375    $500

CRAWFORD, 17J., chronog.engraved bezel
base metal ...............................$125    $150    $175

CROTON, 17 jewels, chronog., c. 1948
s. steel ......................................$175    $200    $250

CROTON, 17 jewels, chronog., c. 1946
s. steel ................................... $185   $225   $275

CROTON, 17 jewels, cal.630, c.1943
gold filled................................ $30   $40   $55

CROTON, 17 jewels, fancy lugs
14k ......................................... $175   $225   $275

CROTON, 17 jewels, fancy lugs
14k ......................................... $250   $300   $375

CROTON, 7 jewels, drivers style, c.1938
gold filled................................ $175   $225   $275

CROTON, 17 jewels, swinging lugs, cal.f3x, c.1940
14k ......................................... $125   $150   $175

CROWN, 7J., luminous dial
base metal ............................... $30   $40   $55

CROWN, 7J., luminous dial
gold filled ............................... $50   $75   $100

CRYSLER, 17J., aux. sec., ca. 1950s
gold filled ............................... $50   $70   $90

CYMA,7J.,enamel dial, wire lugs,(signal corp.USA),c.1928
silver ...................................... $250   $300   $350

CYMA, 17 jewels, aux. sec.
| | | | |
|---|---|---|---|
| 18k | $200 | $250 | $300 |
| 14k | $175 | $200 | $250 |
| gold filled | $65 | $75 | $85 |

CYMA, 15J., enamel dial, (Tacy W. Co.), c. 1925
silver ................................$65   $75   $100

CYMA, 15J., military style, cal.234, Ca.1945
s. steel ................................$75   $100   $150

CYMA, 15J.,
base metal ................................$40   $50   $60

CYMA, 15J., engraved case
chromium................................$50   $60   $70

CYMA, 15J., engraved case
chromium................................$50   $60   $70

CYMA, 15J., 2-tone case
chromium................................$60   $70   $80

CYMA, 15J., engraved case
chromium................................$60   $70   $80

CYMA, 15J.,
chromium................................$50   $60   $70

Some grades are not included. Their values can be determined by comparing with **similar** age, size, metal content, style, models and grades listed.

CYMA, 15J., engraved case
chromium..................................$60      $70      $80

DAU, 15J., wire lugs, c.1915
14k ...........................................$80      $90      $100

DAYNITE, 7 jewels, 8 day movement, c. 1925
s. steel ....................................$250      $300      $400

DELBANA, 17J., fancy hooded lugs, c.1951
14k ...........................................$150      $175      $225

DIDISHEIM, 15J., "Winton", enamel art deco bezel, c.1927
14k(w)....................................$250      $300      $350

P. DITISHEIM, 17 J., "Solvil," diamond dial, c. 1947
18k .......................................$300      $350      $400

P. DITISHEIM, 17 J., "Solvil," diamond dial, c. 1947
platinum..................................$600      $700      $800

P. DITISHEIM, 17 J., "Solvil," diamond dial, c. 1948
platinum..................................$600      $700      $800

P. DITISHEIM, 17 J., "Solvil," curved, diamond dial
platinum...............................$1,000      $1,200      $1,400

P. DITISHEIM, 17 jewels, diamond dial, curved
platinum...............................$1,000      $1,200      $1,400

P. DITISHEIM, 17 J., baguette diamonds, fancy bezel
platinum ............................... $1,400    $1,600    $1,800

P. DITISHEIM, 17 jewels, hinged lugs, enameled bezel
14k ......................................... $700    $800    $900

DOME, 25 jewels, triple dates, auto wind
18k ......................................... $400    $500    $600

DORIC, 17J., fancy lugs, two tone case, c.1935
gold filled.................................. $60    $70    $85

DOXA, 17 jewels, aux sec.
gold filled.................................. $40    $50    $60

DOXA, 17 jewels, center sec., fancy lugs
14k .......................................... $150    $200    $250

DOXA, 17 jewels, chronog., fluted lugs
14k .......................................... $350    $400    $475

DOXA, 17J., chronog., date, 3 reg., by Valjoux
gold filled ................................ $325    $375    $450
14k .......................................... $600    $700    $800

DOXA, 17 jewels, chronog., triple dates, moon phase
14k ......................................... $1,100    $1,200    $1,500

DOXA, 17 jewels, chronog., 2 reg., c. 1942
gold filled..................................$250    $300      $400

DOXA, 17 jewels, chronog., cal. 1220, c. 1940
gold filled..................................$225    $275      $325
s. steel ......................................$175    $225      $275

DOXA, 17 jewels, center sec
s. steel ..........................................$50    $65      $85

DOXA, 17 jewels, center sec., c. 1949
gold filled..................................$70    $85      $125

DOXA, 17J., "Grafic" date,
14k ...........................................$200    $250      $300

DOXA, 17J., cal. 1361, c.1948
14k ...........................................$200    $250      $300

DRIVA, 15 jewels, repeater, repeats on gong, repeater
wound by bolt above hand, c. 1930
s. steel ...................................$3,500    $4,000      $4,500

DRIVA, 15 jewels, 5 min. repeater
14k ...........................................$3,000    $3,500      $4,000

DRIVA, 17 jewels, double teardrop lugs, c.1945
14k ...........................................$300    $350      $400

DUGENA, 17J., cal.985, c.1960
14k ........................................$150    $200    $250

DUNHILL, 17J., date, alarm by Le Coultre, c. 1965
s. steel ....................................$350    $400    $450

DUNHILL, 15J., by Bulwark W.Co., engraved bezel,c.1930
gold filled................................$75    $125    $185

DUODIAL, 15 jewels, c. 1934
9k ...........................................$900    $1,000    $1,200

EBEL, 21 jewels, chronog., self winding, perpetual cal.
18k ........................................$8,000    $9,000    $10,000

EBEL, 18 jewels, Ca.1959
18k .........................................$200    $250    $300

EBEL, 18 jewels, applied gold numbers, c. 1950
18k .........................................$400    $450    $500

EBEL, 17 jewels, slide open to wind
leather ....................................$200    $250    $300

EBEL, 17 jewels, chronog., 2 reg., enamel dial
s. steel ....................................$200    $250    $300

🕐 Some grades are not included. Their values can be determined by comparing with similar age, size, metal content, style, grades, or models such as time only, chronograph, repeater etc. listed.

EBEL, 17 jewels, chronog., c. 1955
14k ............................................$400      $500      $550
gold filled....................................$200      $250      $325

EBEL, 17 jewels, chronog., "pulsation", c. 1943
s. steel ......................................$300      $350      $400

EBEL, 17 jewels, chronog., 3 reg., c. 1941
14k ............................................$500      $575      $650
s. steel ......................................$300      $350      $400

EBEL, 17J., "sport", c.1949
gold filled....................................$60       $70       $80

EBEL, 17J., cal.119, auto-wind, c.1950
s. steel ....................................$100      $125      $155

EBEL, 17J., cal.93, center sec., c.1950
18k ............................................$300      $350      $400

EBEL, 17J., lady's watch, c.1948
14k C&B....................................$200      $225      $250

EBERHARD, 18 jewels, split sec. chronog., 3 reg.
18k ............................................$5,500    $6,500    $7,500

🕐 Some grades are not included. Their values can be determined by comparing with **similar** age, size, metal content, style, grades, or models such as **time only**, chronograph, repeater etc. listed.

EBERHARD, 17 J., tele-tachymeter, enamel dial, c. 1930
18k ......................................$1,500    $1,700    $2,000

EBERHARD, 17 jewels, chronog., 2 reg.
18k ...........................................$800    $900    $1,000

EBERHARD, 17 J., chronog., center lugs, 1 button, enamel
dial
s. steel ......................................$550    $650    $800

EBERHARD, 17 J., wire lugs, enamel dial, c.1928
early waterproof case
silver ........................................$700    $800    $900

EBERHARD, 17J., water proof, auto wind, triple date, moon
phases
18k rose ..............................$3,000    $3,200    $3,500

EKEGREN, 18 jewels, **jumping hr.**, c. 1920
platinum...............................$8,000    $9,000    $10,000
18k .......................................$6,000    $7,000    $8,000

ELECTRA W. Co., 17J, chronog., 1 button, hinged back,
enamel dial
silver ......................................$600    $700    $850

ELECTRA W. Co., 17J, chronog., 1 button, hinged back,
wire lugs, enamel dial
silver ........................................$600    $700    $850

ELECTION, 17J., cal. 4019, c.1940
s. steel .......................................$60      $70      $80

ELGIN, 21J., Lord Elgin, extended lugs, Ca.1955
14k ..........................................$200     $225     $275

ELGIN, 21J., Lord Elgin, extended lugs,
gold filled................................$125     $150     $175

ELGIN, 23J., fancy bezel, Lord Elgin
gold filled................................$40      $50      $60

ELGIN, 19J., fancy bezel, c.1950s
gold filled................................$125     $150     $200

🕐 Some grades are not included. Their values can be
determined by comparing with similar age, size, metal
content, style, grades, or models such as time only,
chronograph, repeater etc. listed.

ELGIN, 19J., U shaped lugs
gold filled ................................$50      $60      $70

ELGIN, 21J., Lord Elgin, hinged lugs
gold filled ................................$100     $125     $150

ELGIN, 15-17J., hooded lugs, gold jewel settings, Ca. 1925
14k(w)....................................$700     $800     $1,000

ELGIN, 17J., Shockmaster, auto-wind,
gold filled ................................$50      $60      $70

ELGIN, 21J., Lord Elgin, 3 diamonds, cal.626, c.1950
14k(w)....................................$150     $175     $225

ELGIN, 21J., cal.626, Ca.1950's
14k .............................................$150      $175      $225

ELGIN, 17J., stepped hooded lugs, c.1925
gold filled ...............................$100      $125      $175

ELGIN, 17J., stepped case, Ca. 1935
gold filled...................................$60      $75      $100

ELGIN, 17J., side lugs, Ca. 1958
gold filled ...............................$150      $175      $200

ELGIN, 15J., cal. 554, Ca. 1950's
gold filled...................................$50      $65      $100

ELGIN, 15J., stepped case,
gold filled ................................. $40      $50      $60

ELGIN, 15J., spur lugs, embossed dial, Ca.1929
gold filled...................................$50      $60      $75

ELGIN, 15J., hinged case, engraved bezel, c.1928
gold filled(w)............................ $60      $70      $80

ELGIN, 15J., Crown Guard, Ca.1929
gold filled...................................$50      $65      $85

ELGIN, 21J., bevelled lugs,
14k ...........................................$150      $200      $250

ELGIN, 19J., cal. 626, Ca. 1946
14k ............................................. $200      $225      $250

ELGIN, 7J., tear drop lugs,
gold filled................................. $40       $50       $60

ELGIN, 17J., long fluted lugs,
gold filled................................. $50       $60       $70

ELGIN, 21J., Lord Elgin,
gold filled................................. $40       $50       $60

ELGIN, 15J., Legionnaire, Ca. 1929
gold filled................................. $50       $60       $70

ELGIN, engraved case, Ca. 1924
14k ............................................ $200      $225      $250

ELGIN, 21J., Lord Elgin, cal.625, c.1950
14k ............................................ $175      $225      $275

ELGIN, 21J., Lord Elgin, cal. 713, GJS, c.1958
14k ............................................ $225      $250      $300

ELGIN, 17J., carved case,
gold filled ................................ $50       $60       $70

ELGIN, 21J., Lord Elgin, cal.559, c.1942
gold filled ................................ $50       $60       $70

🕐 Some grades are not included. Their values can be
determined by comparing with similar age, size, metal
content, style, grades, or models such as time only,
chronograph, repeater etc. listed.

ELGIN, 21J., Lord Elgin, GJS, c. 1936
14k ............................................. $175      $200      $250

ELGIN, 21J., Lord Elgin, GJS, cal.626, c.1940
14k ............................................. $175      $200      $250

ELGIN, 17J., **Adonis**, engraved, Ca. 1929
gold filled ................................... $70      $80      $100

ELGIN, 17J., "Dura Power" mainspring LOGO,
gold plate ................................... $60      $70      $80

ELGIN, 7J., hinged case, engraved case, c.1920s
gold filled ................................... $75      $95      $125

ELGIN,15J., fancy bezel, G#554
gold filled ............................... $50      $60      $70

ELGIN, 17 jewels, raised numbers
14k ......................................... $150      $175      $225

LORD ELGIN, 21 jewels, curved, raised numbers
14k ......................................... $175      $200      $250

ELGIN, 17 jewels, embossed dial
14k ......................................... $175      $225      $250

LORD ELGIN, 21 jewels, curved
gold filled ............................... $75      $100      $125

ELGIN, 17 jewels, curved, "Streamlined"
gold filled ............................... $100      $120      $140

⏱ Some grades are not included. Their values can be
determined by comparing with **similar** age, size, metal
content, style, grades, or models such as **time only**,
chronograph, repeater etc. listed.

ELGIN, 17 jewels, raised numbers
gold filled..................................$60     $70     $80

ELGIN, 15 jewels, curved, fancy bezel
gold filled..................................$100     $120     $140

LORD ELGIN, 21 jewels, curved
platinum..................................$400     $500     $600

LORD ELGIN, 21 jewels, curved
14k ..................................$225     $275     $350

ELGIN, 17 jewels, curved
gold filled..................................$75     $100     $125

ELGIN, 17 jewels, curved
gold filled..................................$60     $70     $80

ELGIN, 15 jewels, drivers style
gold filled ..................................$175     $200     $250

ELGIN, 17 jewels, "Ristflo"
gold filled ..................................$150     $175     $225

ELGIN, 17 jewels
gold filled ..................................$80     $90     $100

ELGIN, 17 jewels, hidden lugs
gold filled ..................................$80     $90     $100

ELGIN, 17 jewels, embossed dial
gold filled ..................................$60     $70     $80

🕐 Some grades are not included. Their values can be determined by comparing with **similar** age, size, metal content, style, grades, or models such as **time only**, chronograph, repeater etc. listed.

ELGIN, 17 jewels, curved, thin model
gold filled.................................$60      $70      $80

ELGIN, 17 jewels, stepped case
gold filled.................................$75      $90      $120

ELGIN, 17J., center sec., cal.11553, c.1928
gold filled.................................$200     $250     $300

ELGIN, 15 jewels, "William Osler" recess crown
gold filled.................................$225     $275     $350

ELGIN, 7 jewels, center sec., recess crown
gold filled.................................$225     $275     $350

ELGIN, 17J., engraved case, c.1928
gold filled.................................$100     $125     $175

ELGIN, 15J., 2 tone case, recessed crown
gold filled.................................$100     $125     $150

ELGIN,7-15J., engraved case, c. 1928
14K .........................................$200     $250     $325
gold filled .................................$70      $90      $110

ELGIN, 15J., engraved mermaid design case, c.1928
gold filled .................................$150     $200     $250

ELGIN, 15J., engraved case, c. 1928
gold filled .................................$100     $125     $150

ELGIN, 15J., curved engraved case, c. 1928
gold filled .................................$90      $100     $125

ELGIN, 15J., engraved case, c.1928
gold filled................................$75     $100     $125

ELGIN, 15J., engraved case, hooded lugs, c.1928
gold filled................................$175     $200     $250

ELGIN, 15 jewels, center lugs
gold filled................................$100     $120     $150

ELGIN, 7 jewels, fancy bezel
s. steel ...................................$50     $60     $70

ELGIN, 7 jewels, fancy bezel
gold filled................................$90     $100     $125

⏱ Some grades are not included. Their values can be
determined by comparing with **similar** age, size, metal
content, style, grades, or models such as **time only**,
chronograph, repeater etc. listed.

ELGIN, 17 jewels, "Crusade"
gold filled ...............................$100     $120     $140

ELGIN, 7 jewels
gold filled ...............................$40     $50     $60

ELGIN, 7 jewels, stepped bezel
s. steel ...................................$50     $60     $70

ELGIN, 15J., wire lugs, stem at "12", c.1920s
silver ......................................$150     $200     $275

ELGIN, 7J., "Recased", c.1920s
base metal ...............................$40     $50     $65

ELGIN, 15J., engraved case, c.1925
gold filled..................................$90     $100     $125

ELGIN, 21J., Lord Elgin, stepped case, c.1930
gold filled...................................$75     $85     $95

ELGIN, 21J., Lord Elgin, stepped case, c.1930
gold filled...................................$70     $80     $90

ELGIN, 7J., stepped case, c.1925
gold filled...................................$50     $60     $70

ELGIN, 15J., stepped case, c.1930
gold filled..................................$50     $60     $70

ELGIN, 21J., Lord Elgin, GJS, c.1937
14k ..........................................$175     $225     $275

ELGIN, 17J., stepped case, c.1930
gold filled .................................$65     $75     $90

ELGIN, 17J., curved, stepped case, c.1927
gold filled .................................$70     $80     $90

ELGIN, 17 jewels, raised numbers
gold filled .................................$50     $60     $70

ELGIN, 17 jewels, c. 1927
14k ..........................................$150     $175     $225

🕐 Some grades are not included. Their values can be determined by comparing with **similar** age, size, metal content,
style, models and grades listed.

LORD ELGIN, 21 jewels, diamond dial
14k (w)................................$200    $275    $325

LORD ELGIN, 21 jewels, flared case
14k ................................$250    $300    $350

Elgin, 19 jewels, c. 1947
14k.....................................$175    $225    $275
gold filled...................................$70    $80    $90

ELGIN, 19 jewels, flared case, fancy lugs
14k ................................$250    $300    $350

LORD ELGIN, 21 jewels, diamond dial
14k (w).................................$235    $300    $365

ELGIN, 7J., cushion case, c.1930
gold filled .................................$70    $90    $125

LORD ELGIN, 21 jewels, aux. sec., fancy lugs
14k ...........................................$250    $300    $325

ELGIN, 7-15J., cushion case, c.1930
chromium................................$40    $50    $60

ELGIN, 21J., Lord Elgin, cal.670, c.1948
14k ...........................................$225    $250    $300

🕐 Some grades are not included. Their values can be determined by comparing with **similar** age, size, metal content, style, models and grades listed.

ELGIN, 7-15J., solid lugs, Ca. 1925
s. steel ....................................$100    $125    $150

ELGIN, 15J., pierced shield, wire lugs, c.1918
silver ........................................$400     $450     $500

ELGIN, 15J., U.S.GOV'T grade II, c.1960s
s. steel ......................................$75     $100     $125

ELGIN, 15J., pierced shield, c.1918
silver ........................................$500     $550     $600

ELGIN, 15J., military style, 24 hr. dial, c.1942
s. steel ....................................$100     $125     $150

ELGIN, 15J., canteen style case, wire lugs, c.1919
nickel........................................$275     $325     $375

ELGIN, 15J., military style, cal.539, c.1940
s. steel ......................................$75     $100     $150

ELGIN, 15 jewels, "Official Boy Scout" model
s. steel ....................................$100     $125     $175

ELGIN, 16J., canteen style case, U.S.N.234C, c.1930s
s. steel ....................................$275     $325     $375

🕐 Some grades are not included. Their values can be
determined by comparing with **similar** age, size, metal
content, style, grades, or models such as **time only**,
chronograph, repeater etc. listed.

ELGIN, 7 jewels, "Official Boy Scout" model
s. steel .....................................$70      $85      $120

ELGIN, 15 jewels, enamel dial, wire lugs, c. 1915
silver ........................................$100     $125     $150

ELGIN, 15 jewels, enamel dial, wire lugs, c. 1915
silver ........................................$100     $125     $150

ELGIN, 15 jewels, center lugs
gold filled...............................$100     $125     $150

ELGIN, 15 jewels, center lugs, c. 1922
silver ........................................$125     $150     $200

ELGIN, 15J., case by Rolland Fischer, c. 1928
silver ........................................$250     $300     $375

ELGIN, 17J., center sec., c.1950
base metal................................$40      $45      $50

ELGIN, 21 jewels, "Black Knight"
14k ............................................$175     $200     $250

ELGIN, 7 jewels, "Avigo ", Ca. 1929
base metal .................................$60      $75      $95

🕐 Some grades are not included. Their values can be determined by comparing with **similar** age, size, metal content, style, grades, or models such as **time only**, chronograph, repeater etc. listed.

ELGIN, 21J., center sec., wire lugs, cal. 680, c.1952
gold filled..................................$50      $60      $70

ELGIN, 30J., auto-wind, grade 760,
gold filled ..................................$60      $70      $80

ELGIN, 17 jewels, **Alarm**, Ca. 1960
gold filled..................................$175      $200      $275

ELGIN, 19J.,cal.681 , c.1959
gold filled ..................................$40      $50      $60

ELGIN, 21J., Lord Elgin, **enamel bezel**, cal.688, c.1948
gold filled ..................................$75      $100      $125

ELGIN, 21J., water-proof, c.1952
s. steel .......................................$50      $60      $70

ELGIN, 23 J., "B. W. Raymond," R.R. approved
14k ...........................................$350      $400      $450
gold filled ..............................$175      $200      $275
s. steel ....................................$150      $175      $200

ELGIN, 17J., aux. sec., center lugs
gold filled..................................$60      $70      $80

🌐 Some grades are not included. Their values can be
determined by comparing with **similar** age, size, metal
content, style, grades, or models such as **time only**,
chronograph, repeater etc. listed.

LORD ELGIN, 21 jewels, diamond dial, c. 1958
14k (w)..................................$325    $375    $450

LORD ELGIN, 21 jewels, mystery dial, c. 1957
14k (w)..................................$190    $240    $275

LORD ELGIN, 21 J., direct reading, cal#719, C.1957
gold filled...............................$250    $325    $400

ELGIN, 17 J., in form of golf ball, rotating hr. & min.
gold filled...............................$325    $400    $500

LORD ELGIN, 21 jewels, applied numbers, c. 1946
14k ..........................................$175    $200    $300

LORD ELGIN, 21 jewels, curved, applied numbers
14k ..........................................$200    $250    $300

LORD ELGIN, 21 jewels, diamond dial, faceted crystal
14k ..........................................$300    $350    $400

ELGIN, 17 jewels, hinged back
14k (w) ..................................$150    $175    $250

ELGIN, 17 jewels, enamel bezel, Ca. 1930
14k (w) ..................................$500    $600    $700

ELGIN, 15 jewels, Art Deco bezel, c. 1935
gold filled ..............................$125    $150    $175

🕐 Some grades are not included. Their values can be
determined by comparing with **similar** age, size, metal
content, style, grades, or models such as **time only**,
chronograph, repeater etc. listed.

ELGIN, 15 jewels, 2 tone, c. 1930
gold filled..................................$80    $100    $120

ELGIN, 15 jewels, enamel bezel, c. 1920
14k (w)....................................$550    $650    $800

ELGIN, 17 jewels, raised numbers
gold filled...................................$60    $70    $80

ELGIN, 21 jewels, enamel bezel, 2 tone, c. 1931
14k ........................................$600    $700    $800
    gold filled............................$150    $200    $300

ELGIN, 7 jewels, fancy bezel
s. steel ......................................$50    $60    $70

ELGIN, 7 jewels, engraved bezel
s. steel ......................................$45    $55    $65

ELGIN, 17 jewels, aux. sec., curved
gold filled .................................$75    $95    $120

ELGIN, 17 jewels, curved
gold filled .................................$75    $90    $125

ELGIN, 17 jewels, curved
gold filled .................................$90    $100    $110

ELGIN, 21 jewels, blue enamel bezel, c. 1920
14k .......................................$1,000    $1,200    $1,400

ELGIN, 21 jewels, enamel bezel
18k ...........................................$800      $900      $1,100

LORD ELGIN, 21J, model 670, large lugs, anniversary of
50,000,000th watch (small run of watches), c. 1953
18k .......................................$1,250      $1,500      $1,800

LORD ELGIN, 21 jewels, wandering hr. & min., curved
gold filled................................$375      $425      $500

ELGIN, 17 jewels, double dial
gold filled................................$600      $675      $750

LORD ELGIN, 21 jewels, hooded lugs, c. 1952
14k ...........................................$275      $325      $375

LORD ELGIN, 21 jewels, curved, c. 1957
14k ...........................................$225      $275      $325

LORD ELGIN, 21 jewels, hooded lugs, c. 1950s
14k ...........................................$200      $250      $300

ELGIN, 15 jewels, waterproof
s. steel .......................................$30      $40      $50

ELGIN, 15 jewels, center sec.
gold filled .................................$35      $45      $55

ELGIN, 7 jewels, aux. sec.
gold filled .................................$30      $40      $55

LORD ELGIN, 21 jewels, stepped case
18k ...........................................$375      $425      $500

LORD ELGIN, 21 jewels, stepped case, curved
14k ..........................................$200    $250    $350

ELGIN, 17 jewels, stepped case
14k ..........................................$200    $250    $300

LORD ELGIN, 21 jewels, curved
gold filled.................................$70    $80    $90

ELGIN, 17 jewels, curved, fancy bezel
gold filled.................................$90    $125    $150

ELGIN, 17 jewels, curved, stepped case
gold filled.................................$90    $100    $120

ELGIN, 17 jewels, curved, stepped case
gold filled.................................$90    $100    $120

ELGIN, 17 jewels, curved
gold filled .................................$90    $100    $120

ELGIN, 19 jewels, stepped case
gold filled ................................$100    $125    $150

ELGIN, 15 jewels
gold filled .................................$60    $70    $80

ELGIN, 7 jewels, fancy bezel
s. steel ......................................$40    $50    $60

ELGIN, 7 jewels, fancy bezel
gold filled ................................$60    $70    $80

LORD ELGIN, 21 jewels, curved, c. 1938
14k ...........................................$200    $250    $350

ELGIN, 15 jewels, fancy bezel
gold filled.................................$80    $90    $100

ELGIN, 21 jewels, curved
gold filled.................................$50    $60    $70

LORD ELGIN, 21 jewels, raised numbers
14k ...........................................$175    $200    $275

LORD ELGIN, 21 jewels, curved
14k ...........................................$175    $200    $275

LORD ELGIN, 21 jewels, curved
14k ...........................................$200    $250    $300

LORD ELGIN, 21 jewels, aux. sec.
gold filled.................................$80    $90    $100

LORD ELGIN, 21 jewels, curved
14k ...........................................$200    $250    $300

ELGIN, 17 jewels, curved
gold filled.................................$70    $80    $90

ELGIN, 17 Jewels, raised numbers
14k ...........................................$200    $225    $250

LORD ELGIN, 15jewels, **electric**, 6 adj., Ca. 1962, (sold for $89.50, July of 1962), grade 725, in **good running order**
gold filled ..............................$200    $250    $325

**Elgin pioneering effort in electric watches started in 1955.**

LORD ELGIN, 15 jewels, **electric**, c. 1962
(back–set)
s. steel ..................................$200      $250      $325

LORD ELGIN, 15 jewels, **electric**, c.1962
( grade 725,  6 adj.)
gold filled...............................$200      $250      $325

ELGIN, 17 Jewels, Lady Elgin, flared case, cal. 650, c.1950
14k ..........................................$100      $125      $150

ELGIN, 15 Jewels, art deco, c.1925
gold filled..................................$40      $50      $60

ELGIN, 15 Jewels, art deco, c.1928
14k ...........................................$60      $70      $90

ELGIN, 17 Jewels, art deco, c.1928
18k(w).......................................$75      $90      $110

ELGIN, 15 jewels, art deco, Ca. 1928
gold filled..................................$25      $30      $45

ELGIN, 15 jewels, art deco, Ca. 1928
gold filled..................................$25      $30      $45

ELGIN, 15 jewels, art deco, Ca. 1928
gold filled..................................$25      $30      $45

ELGIN, 15 jewels, sports model, Ca. 1928
14k..............................................$60      $70      $85

ELGIN, 17J., 20 diamonds, art deco, Ca. 1928
18k.............................................$225      $250      $350

ELGIN, 15 jewels, 2 diamonds, art deco, Ca. 1928
gold filled..................................$75      $85      $125

**Model 3**, 3-0 size, three-quarter plate, open face, pendant set, first serial number 18,179,001, Grade 414, March, 1915.

**Model 1**, 5-0 size, three-quarter plate, hunting, pendant set, first serial number 14,699,001, Grade 380, Feb., 1910.

**Model 2**, 5-0 size, three-quarter plate, open face, pendant set, first serial number 17,890,001, Grade 399, Feb., 1914.

**Model 2**, 8-0 size, Grade 532, 539, sweep second.

**Model 7**, 8-0 size, Grades 554, 555,

**Model 20**, 8-0 size, Grades 681, 682.

**Model 1**, 10-0 size, three-quarter plate,

**Model 2**, 15-0 size, Grades 623, 624, 626.

**15-0 Size**, movement, Grades 670, 672, 673.

**15-0 size**, movement. Grade 674.

**15-0 size**, movement, Grades 557, 558, 559.

**Model 2**, 21-0 size, Grade 541, 533, 535.

**Model 3**, 21-0 size, Grade 547, sweep second.

**Model 4**, 21-0 size, Grades 617, 617L, 619, 619L.

**Model 9**, 21-0 size, Grades 650, 651.

**Model 9**, 21-0 size, Grades 655, 656.

GRADE 725, 15 jewels,"electric" model movement

"ELECTRIC", case showing back—set

Grade 607, self wind.

Grade 630, sweep second.

Grade 641, 642

Grade 643, self wind.

Grades 644, 645, self wind.

Grade 647, sweep second.

Grade 661

Grade 666, sweep second.

Grade 668, sweep second.

Grade 685

Grade 687

Grade 700

GRADE 710 & 719
719 = DIRECT READ
TRAIN SIDE

719 = DIAL SIDE
OF MOVEMENT

Grade 716

ENICAR, 17 jewels, center sec.
s. steel.......................................$20     $30     $50

ELOGA, triple calendar,
base metal ..................................$50     $65     $85

ENICAR, 17 jewels, triple date, moon phase
gold filled...............................$250     $300     $350

EMERSON, 17J., hooded lugs,
gold filled.................................$50     $60     $70

ENICAR, 15 jewels, egg shaped with compass, c. 1918
silver........................................$400     $450     $500

ENICAR, 17 jewels, center sec.
18k .............................................$200     $250     $300

ENICAR, 17J., autow., date, 24 hour dial, C.1970
s. steel.....................................$100     $125     $150

ENICAR, 17J., chronograph, 2 reg. Ca. 1955
s. steel ....................................$200     $250     $300

ESKA, 17J.,chronog., triple date, moon phase
14k.........................................$1,500     $1,700     $2,000

ESKA, 17 jewels, chronog., 2 reg., C. 1950s
s. steel ......................................$200    $250    $300

ESKA, 17 jewels, chronog., 2 reg., c. 1940
s. steel ......................................$1,200    $1,400    $1,600

ESKA, 17 jewels, multi-colored enamel dial
18k ..........................................$2,500    $2,700    $3,000

ETERNA, quartz, date, by ETA, cal#954, C.1975
s. steel ......................................$50    $75    $100

🕐 Some grades are not included. Their values can be
determined by comparing with similar age, size, metal
content, style, grades, or models such as time only,
chronograph, repeater etc. listed.

ETERNA, 19 jewels, day-date-month
18k.............................................$250    $300    $350

ETERNA, 17 jewels, chronog., triple date, 3 reg.
s.steel.........................................$375    $425    $500
18k...............................................$800    $900    $1,000

ETERNA, 21 jewels, date, cal. 14390, c.1960
18k...............................................$250    $300    $350

ETERNA, 19 jewels, c.1944
14k...............................................$150    $175    $200

ETERNA, 16 jewels, aux. sec., c.1945
gold filled.................................$80      $90      $100

ETERNA, 19 jewels, c.1938
gold filled.................................$50      $60      $70

ETERNA, 17 jewels, gold jewel settings, c.1935
14k .........................................$175     $225     $275

EVANS, 17 jewels, rhinestones on bezel, c. 1948
gold plate .................................$70      $80      $125

EVANS, 17 jewels, chronog., 2 reg., c. 1940
18k .........................................$350     $400     $475

EXACTUS, 17 J., chronog.,triple-date, moon ph.
s. steel....................................$500     $600     $700

EXCELSIOR, 17 jewels, chronog., 2 reg.
14k.........................................$375     $450     $500
gold filled.................................$175     $200     $235

EXCELSIOR, 17 jewels, chronog.
gold filled.................................$200     $225     $275
s. steel....................................$200     $225     $250

EXCELSIOR PARK, 17 jewels, chronog.
s. steel....................................$175     $225     $275

FAIRFAX, 6J, engraved case, c.1929
base metal ...................................$40     $50     $65

FAIRFAX, 6J, engraved case, c.1929
base metal ...................................$50     $60     $70

FAIRFAX, 6J, butler finish case, c.1929
base metal ...................................$40     $50     $60

FAIRFAX, 6J, engraved case, c.1929
gold filled...................................$50     $60     $70

FAITH, 17J, flip top case, by Hyde Park, c.1950
gold filled...................................$150     $175     $225

⏱ Some grades are not included. Their values can be
determined by comparing with **similar** age, size, metal
content, style, grades, or models such as **time only**,
chronograph, repeater etc. listed.

FAVRE LEUBA,17J., altimeter or aneroid barometer
s. steel.......................................$200     $250     $300

FAVRE LEUBA,17J., triple date, cal.Valj.89, c.1948
s. steel.......................................$150     $175     $200

FERRARI, quartz, chronog., c.1988
base metal...............................$200     $250     $300

FELCA, 17 jewels, auto wind
gold filled...................................$50     $60     $75
14k...........................................$125     $150     $200
18k...........................................$175     $225     $275

FONTAINEMELON, S. A., 17 J., gold train, digital
14k .........................................$1,500      $1,700      $2,000

FRAMONT, 17J, timer, date, cal. 290, c.1970
s. steel ......................................$100      $125      $150

FREY, 25J., rotating outside chapter, c.1970
s. steel .......................................$75      $100      $125

FREY,17J., GJS, c.1970
s. steel .......................................$30      $40      $55

🕐 Note: Some models and grades are not included. Their
values can be determined by comparing with **similar** age,
size, metal content, style, models and grades listed.

FREY,15J., engraved case, c.1933
base metal..................................$30      $40      $55

FREY,15J., engraved stepped case, c.1933
base metal..................................$40      $50      $65

FREY,15J., engraved case, c.1933
base metal..................................$50      $60      $70

FRIEDLI, 17 jewels, auto wind, center sec.
gold filled..................................$40      $45      $55
18k..........................................$175      $225      $275

FRODSHAM, 17J., Ca. 1935
18k(w)....................................$400      $500      $600

GALLET, 15 jewels, wire lugs, Ca. 1925
silver .........................................$100     $150        $200

GALLET, 15 jewels, waterproof, auto wind
s. steel ......................................$50        $60        $70

GALLET, 17 jewels, chronog., single button, c. 1950
s. steel ...................................... $350     $400        $465

GALLET, 17J., chronog., by Racine, US air force, c. 1978
s. steel ...................................... $150      $200        $250

GALLET, 17 jewels, chronog., 3 reg., c. 1945
s. steel......................................$300      $350        $400

GALLET, 17 jewels, chronog., 3 reg., c. 1942
gold filled................................$350      $400        $475

GALLET, 17J., chronog., 2 reg.,single button, C.1925,
silver"small size" ...................$800       $1,000     $1,200

GALLET, 17J., chronog., 3 reg.,triple date, moon ph.
18k.........................................$2,000      $2,500     $3,000

GALLET, 17J., chronog., 3 reg.,triple date,
14k .........................................$700      $800      $900
s. steel ....................................$400      $500      $600

GALLET, 17 jewels, chronog., 3 reg., c. 1955
s. steel ....................................$300      $350      $400

GALLET, 17 jewels, day-date-month, c. 1941
gold filled................................$400      $500      $600

GALLET, 17 jewels, chronog., 2 reg.
14k .........................................$425      $525      $575
s. steel ....................................$200      $235      $275

GALLET, 17 jewels, chronog., mid size, c. 1940
s. steel ....................................$300      $350      $400

GALLET, 17J., chronog., flying officer, cal.149, c. 1958
s. steel ....................................$400      $500      $600

GALLET, 17 jewels, chronog., waterproof
s. steel ....................................$300      $400      $500

GALLET, 17 jewels, chronog., 2 reg.
s. steel ....................................$200      $250      $300

🕐 Some grades are not included. Their values can be
determined by comparing with **similar** age, size, metal
content, style, grades, or models such as **time only**,
chronograph, repeater etc. listed.

GALLET, 17 jewels, oval, chronog., 2 reg.
s. steel ........................................$300     $400     $500

GALLET, 17 jewels, chronog., 2 reg.
gold filled.................................$200     $225     $275

GALLET, 17 jewels, chronog., 2 reg.
s. steel .......................................$175     $225     $275

GALLET, 17 jewels, time dial at 12 , chronog.
s. steel........................................$300     $350     $400

P. GARNIER, 17 jewels, minu-stop, c. 1965
s. steel......................................  $90     $125     $150

P. GARNIER, 17 jewels, world time,  c. 1968
s. steel......................................  $100     $125     $150

GARLAND, 17J., center sec., water-proof.
s. steel........................................$30     $40     $50

GALLET, 17 jewels, chronog., 2 reg., c. 1939
s. steel .......................................$200     $300     $350

Some grades are not included. Their values can be determined by comparing with similar age, size, metal content, style, grades, or models such as time only, chronograph, repeater etc. listed.

GENEVE, 15 jewels, dual dial, c. 1939
s. steel ................................$400    $550    $650

GENEVE, 15 jewels, dual dial, c. 1937
s. steel ................................$350    $400    $550

GENEVE, 17 jewels, curly lugs, c.1950
14k ................................$250    $325    $375

GERMINAL, 17 J., "Voltaire"
14k ................................$150    $175    $200

GERMINAL, 15 J., early auto wind, lug action, c. 1933
s. steel ................................$500    $600    $700

GERALD GENTA, 29J., skeletonized, auto wind,
perpetual calendar
18k C&B ................................$15,000    $17,000    $20,000

GIRARD-PERREGAUX, 17J., auto wind, C.1951
s. steel ................................$60    $80    $100

GIRARD-PERREGAUX, 17J., alarm, c.1960
gold filled................................$100    $125    $150

GIRARD-PERREGAUX, 39J., center sec. c.1955
14k................................$200    $225    $275

⊕ Some grades are not included. Their values can be
determined by comparing with **similar** age, size, metal
content, style, grades, or models such as **time only**,
chronograph, repeater etc. listed.

GIRARD-PERREGAUX, 17J., center sec., c.1948
18k ..........................................$250     $275     $300

GIRARD-PERREGAUX, 17J., center sec., c.1960
s. steel ........................................$60     $70     $85

GIRARD-PERREGAUX, 17J., cal.47ae, c.1953
14k ..........................................$200     $235     $300

GIRARD-PERREGAUX, 17J., Sea Hawk., c.1960
gold filled..................................$50     $60     $75

GIRARD-PERREGAUX, 17J., aux. sec., c.1958
gold filled..................................$50     $60     $75

GIRARD-PERREGAUX, 17J., aux. sec., c.1950
s. steel........................................$80     $90     $110

GIRARD-PERREGAUX, 17J., date, c.1960
gold filled..................................$50     $60     $75

GIRARD-PERREGAUX, 39J., auto-matic, date, c.1960
18k............................................$225     $275     $325

🕐 Some grades are not included. Their values can be
determined by comparing with **similar** age, size, metal
content, style, grades, or models such as **time only**,
chronograph, repeater etc. listed.

GIRARD-PERREGAUX, 39J., chronometre HF, c.1970
s. steel ......................................$70     $80     $95

GIRARD-PERREGAUX, 39 jewels, center sec.
14k...........................................$175    $200    $300

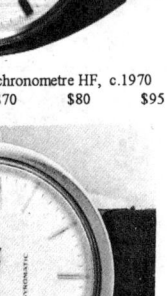

GIRARD-PERREGAUX,17J.,"Gyromatic",date
gold filled..................................$60     $70     $80

GIRARD-PERREGAUX, 17J., chronog., 2 reg.
s. steel....................................$300    $350    $400

GIRARD-PERREGAUX, 17J.,"Gyromatic",date
18k ............................................$200    $225    $275

GIRARD-PERREGAUX, 17J., by Valjoux cal.72, c.1955
s. steel....................................$400    $475    $550

GIRARD-PERREGAUX, 17J., triple date, autow.
s. steel ....................................$150    $175    $200

GIRARD-PERREGAUX, 17J., chronog cal.285, c.1940
gold filled................................$300    $350    $400

GIRARD-PERREGAUX, 17J., pulsations, c.1948
14k ........................................$500    $550    $600

GIRARD-PERREGAUX, 17 J., chronog., 3 reg., c. 1952
s. steel ....................................$350    $400    $500

GIRARD-PERREGAUX, 17J, chronog., triple date, moon phase
18k ........................................$1,800    $2,000    $2,200

GIRARD-PERREGAUX, 39 J., Ca. 1955
14k ........................................$200    $225    $300
18k ........................................$250    $300    $375

GIRARD-PERREGAUX, 17J., aux. sec., Ca.1960
14k ........................................$200    $225    $265

GIRARD-PERREGAUX, 17J., "gyromatic",
14k ........................................$200    $225    $250

GIRARD-PERREGAUX, 17J., RF#2459, c.1970
14k ........................................$150    $175    $200

GIRARD-PERREGAUX, 17J., cal.a6 3606, GJS, c.1955
14k ........................................$150    $175    $200

GIRARD-PERREGAUX, 17J., recess crown, GJS, c.1954
14k ........................................$200    $225    $250

GIRARD-PERREGAUX, 17J., cal.86, GJS, c.1948
14k .........................................$100      $125      $165

GIRARD-PERREGAUX, 17J., recess crown, GJS, c.1947
gold filled................................$50      $60      $75

GIRARD-PERREGAUX, 17J., cal.86ae, GJS, c.1940
s. steel .......................................$50      $60      $75

GIRARD-PERREGAUX, 17J., "1791", GJS, c.1942
s. steel...................................$100      $125      $150

GIRARD-PERREGAUX, 17J., two tone case, GJS, c.1942
14k .........................................$250      $275      $350

GIRARD-PERREGAUX, 17J., cal.91ae220, GJS, c.1948
gold filled................................$60      $70      $85

GIRARD-PERREGAUX, 17J., GJS, c.1953
14k .........................................$150      $175      $200

GIRARD-PERREGAUX, 17J., GJS, c.1936
gold filled................................$80      $90      $110

GIRARD-PERREGAUX, 17J., cal. 86ae, GJS, c.1942
s. steel .......................................$50      $60      $75

GIRARD-PERREGAUX, 17J., cal.86ae, GJS, c.1942
14k...........................................$150      $175      $200

🕐 Some grades are not included. Their values can be
determined by comparing with **similar** age, size, metal
content, style, grades, or models such as **time only**,
chronograph, repeater etc. listed.

GIRARD-PERREGAUX, 39 jewels, aux. sec.
14k .......................................... $200     $225     $300

GIRARD-PERREGAUX, 17 jewels, aux. sec.
gold filled ................................... $60     $70     $80

GIRARD-PERREGAUX, 17 jewels, tank style, c. 1948
14k .......................................... $200     $250     $300

GIRARD-PERREGAUX, 17 J., C. 1948
14k .......................................... $200     $225     $300

GIRARD-PERREGAUX, 17 J., date, stepped case,
18k .......................................... $600     $700     $850
14k .......................................... $450     $525     $650

GLASHUTTE, 17J., 2 reg., fluted bezel, c.1942
s. steel .................................... $800     $900     $1,100

GLASHUTTE, 17J., signed Uhrenfabrik Glashutte, c.1935
18k .......................................... $600     $750     $950

GLASHUTTE, 15J., signed "GUB", Ca.1950's
gold filled ............................... $300     $350     $400

GLYCINE, 17J., **Airman** ,auto-wind, 24hr., date, c.1970
s. steel .................................... $200     $250     $275

GLYCINE, 17J., 15 diamond dial, cal.4645, c.1945
14k .......................................... $700     $800     $900

GLYCINE, 17J., 3 diamond dial, c.1950
14k(w).....................................$175    $200    $275

GLYCINE, 17 jewels, airman, 24 hr. dial, date, C.1960s
s. steel ...................................$250    $300    $375

GLYCINE, 17 jewels, **curved,** c. 1938
18k ..........................................$350    $400    $500

GLYCINE, 17 jewels, aux. sec., c. 1934
14k (w).....................................$200    $250    $275

GLYCINE, 18 jewels, faceted crystal & bezel
gold filled.................................$80    $90    $100

GOERING W. Co.,jump hr., wandering sec.,C.1935
14k.......................................$1,000    $1,300    $1,700

GOERING W. Co.,jump hr., wandering sec.,C.1935
chrome...................................$200    $250    $300

GOERING W. Co., 15J., center sec., C.1935
base metal...............................$50    $60    $75

GOERING W. Co., 15J., engraved case, C.1935
gold filled...............................$50    $60    $75

GOERING W. Co., 15J., engraved case, C.1935
gold filled...............................$80    $90    $110

GOERING W. Co., 15J., engraved case, C.1935
gold filled...............................$80    $90    $110

GOERING W. Co., 15J., rectangular, C.1935
gold filled..................................$70    $80    $95

GOERING W. Co., 15J., ladies engraved case, C.1935
gold filled..................................$30    $40    $55

GOLAY, 18 jewels, aux. sec., c. 1928
18k & platinum...................$1,500    $1,800    $2,200

GOLAY, 32 jewels, min. repeater, adj. to 5 positions
18k .........................$20,000    $25,000    $30,000

GRANA, 16J., **Masonic dial**, GJS, ca. 1948
14k .............................................$175    $225    $250

GRUEN, 17J., curved, precision, cal. 330, Ca. 1937
platinum.................................$900    $1,000    $1,200

GRUEN, 15J., enamel dial, wire lugs, c. 1915
silver ...................................... $150    $175    $250

GRUEN, 17J.,driver's watch, winds at 12, cal.400, c.1938
gold filled ...............................$250    $300    $350

GRUEN,17J., curved, drivers, cal.401, RF#352, c.1932
gold filled ............................. $450    $500    $650

GRUEN, 17J., extremely curved, drivers, c. 1932 , and
side view of watch
gold filled ............................. $500    $600    $750

GRUEN, 17 J., extremely curved, driver's watch
gold filled..............................$550    $650    $800

GRUEN, 17J., driver's watch , flexible long lugs
gold filled..............................$700    $800    $950

GRUEN, 17 jewels, curvex, c. 1949
gold filled..............................$250    $300    $350

GRUEN, 17 jewels, curvex, 35mm long
gold filled..............................$250    $300    $400

GRUEN, 17 jewels, curvex, 55mm long, C.1937
14k ..........................................$900   $1,000   $1,200

GRUEN, 17J.,curvex, precision, C. 1936
14k ..........................................$500    $600    $700

GRUEN, 17 jewels, curvex, c. 1937
gold filled..............................$250    $300    $350

GRUEN, 17 jewels, curvex, c. 1945
gold filled ..............................$300    $350    $400

GRUEN, 17 jewels, curvex, 50mm long, c. 1937
gold filled ..............................$400    $500    $650

GRUEN, 17 jewels, curvex, c. 1937
s. steel ....................................$175    $200    $250

GRUEN, 17 jewels, curvex, aux. sec.
gold filled ..............................$275    $350    $400

GRUEN, 17J., note bezel,curvex, ca.1936
gold filled ..............................$250    $300    $350

GRUEN, 17 jewels, curvex
gold filled ..............................$250    $300    $350

🕐 First **CURVEX** was introduced on October 26, 1935 it
was series # 311, the 2nd. series was 330 in 1939 and in 1940
series # 440 was issued.

GRUEN, 17 jewels, curvex
gold filled.................................$175    $200    $250

GRUEN, 17 jewels, curvex
gold filled.................................$175    $200    $250

GRUEN, 17J., curvex, RF#202, cal.311, c. 1936
gold filled............................... $250    $300    $350

GRUEN, 15J., curvex, RF#226, c. 1936
gold filled............................... $175    $200    $300

GRUEN, 15J., curvex, stepped case, RF#278, c. 1936
s. steel ..................................... $250    $300    $350

GRUEN, 15J., curvex, RF#255, cal.500, c. 1936
gold filled............................... $250    $300    $350

GRUEN, 17J., curvex, RF#266, cal.165, c. 1935
gold filled ............................. $100    $150    $200

GRUEN, 17J., curvex, RF#280, cal.330, c. 1936
gold filled ............................. $250    $300    $350

GRUEN, 17J., curvex, stepped case, RF#280,  c. 1937
14k ........................................ $550    $650    $750
gold filled ............................. $250    $300    $350

GRUEN, 17J., curvex, precision, RF#292, cal.330, c. 1937
gold filled ............................. $350    $400    $450

GRUEN, 15J., curvex, RF#324, cal.500, c. 1936
gold filled ............................. $275    $325    $400

GRUEN, 17J., curvex, RF#308, cal.330, c. 1936
14k ........................................ $550    $650    $750
gold filled ............................. $250    $300    $350

GRUEN, 17J., curvex, RF#339, cal.330, c. 1939
gold filled.............................. $250      $300        $350

GRUEN, 17J., curvex, aux. sec.
gold filled.............................. $100      $150        $200

GRUEN, 17J., curvex, cal#440, hooded lugs, ca.1943
14k ......................................... $200      $250        $300

GRUEN, 17 jewels, curvex, fancy lugs
14k ......................................... $300      $350        $400

GRUEN, 17 jewels, curvex, long lugs
14k ......................................... $300      $350        $450

GRUEN, 15 jewels, **tu-tone case**, double dial, Ca. 1937
14k W & Y ......................... $2,500      $3,000        $3,500

GRUEN, 17 jewels, **jumping hr**., double dial
14k ...................................... $2,500      $3,000        $3,500

GRUEN, 17 jewels, double dial
gold filled .............................. $800      $900        $1,200

GRUEN, 17 jewels, double dial, curved, c.1930s
gold filled .............................. $350      $400        $450

GRUEN, 17 jewels, double dial, curved, c. 1938
gold filled .............................. $800      $900        $1,100

GRUEN, 17 jewels, double dial
gold filled .............................. $700      $800        $1,000

GRUEN, 17 jewels, double dial, c. 1932
gold filled .............................. $800      $900        $1,000

GRUEN, 15 jewels, in form of car radiator, curved
nickel........................................$800    $1,000    $1,250

GRUEN, 17 jewels, curvex, diamond dial, c. 1946
14k ...........................................$300    $400    $500

GRUEN, 17J., curvex, 3 diam., RF#568, cal.440, c. 1945
14k(w)...................................... $275    $325    $400

GRUEN, 17J., curvex, 5 diam., RF#615, cal.370c. 1945
14k(w)...................................... $275    $375    $400

GRUEN, 17J., stepped case, 3 diam., RF#798, c. 1950
14k(w)...................................... $300    $350    $425

GRUEN, 17J., curvex, diamond dial, faceted crystal
14k ...........................................$375    $450    $500

GRUEN, 17 jewels, veri thin model, fancy lugs
14k ...........................................$300    $350    $450

GRUEN, 17 jewels, auto wind, cal. 840, c. 1952
18k ...........................................$300    $350    $400

GRUEN, 17 jewels, curvex, fancy lugs
gold filled ...............................$150    $175    $200

GRUEN, 17 jewels, curvex, diamond dial, fancy lugs
14k (w) ...................................$200    $250    $325

GRUEN, 21 jewels, diamond dial, fancy center lugs
14k ......................................... $375     $425     $500

GRUEN, 21 jewels, fancy lugs, c. 1945
14k .......................................... $350     $400     $500

GRUEN, 17 jewels, curvex, fancy lugs, c. 1943
gold filled.................................. $90     $125     $150
14k .......................................... $300     $350     $450

GRUEN, 17 jewels, curvex, diamond dial, c. 1945
14k .......................................... $350     $400     $450

GRUEN, 17J., flared, diamond dial,
14k(w)..................................... $400     $450     $500

GRUEN, 17 jewels, curvex, diamond dial, c.1945
14k ......................................... $250     $300     $375

GRUEN, 17 jewels, curvex, diamond dial, c. 1951
14k(w)C&B ............................ $550     $650     $800

GRUEN, 17J., so called **50th Anniversary, with a engraved**
quadron precision extra **mvt. G# 119**, Adj., also used **G# 123.**
14k(w)..................................... $300     $350     $450

GRUEN, 17 jewels, curvex, c.1951
14k .......................................... $275     $325     $450

GRUEN, 17 jewels, curvex
14k .......................................... $400     $500     $600

GRUEN, 21J., veri-thin, precision, swinging lugs
gold filled................................$150    $175    $200

GRUEN, 15J., RF#467, cal.431, c. 1948
gold filled ................................ $60    $70.    $95

GRUEN, 15J., RF#93, cal.179, c. 1925
gold filled................................. $75    $100    $125

GRUEN, 17J., precision, RF#498, cal.440, c. 1945
gold filled ................................ $60    $70    $95

GRUEN, 17J., stepped lugs, RF#449, cal.440, c. 1945
gold filled............................. $100    $125    $150

GRUEN, 17J., curvex, RF#498, cal.440, c. 1945
gold filled ............................. $100    $125    $175

GRUEN, 17J., large lugs, RF#449, cal.440, c. 1945
gold filled.............................. $125    $150    $200

GRUEN, 17J., curvex, RF#530, cal.335, c. 1948
gold filled ................................ $60    $70    $95

GRUEN, 17J., RF#449, cal.440, c. 1943
gold filled.............................. $100    $125    $175

GRUEN, 17J., veri-thin, RF#530, cal.430, c. 1945
14k ........................................ $200    $250    $300

GRUEN, 17J.,  curvex, RF#544, cal.440, c. 1942
gold filled.............................. $100        $125        $150

GRUEN, 17J., veri-thin 3 diam., RF#558, cal.335, c. 1945
14k(w)................................... $200        $275        $325

GRUEN, 17J.,  curvex, RF#576, cal.440, c. 1942
gold filled..............................$125        $150        $185
14k ......................................... $250        $300        $375

GRUEN, 17J.,  3 diam.curvex, RF#587, cal.430, c. 1948
gold filled.............................. $125        $150        $225

GRUEN, 17J.,  curvex, RF#607, cal.370, c. 1943
gold filled.............................. $125        $150        $200

GRUEN, 17J., fancy lugs, curvex, RF#610, c. 1945
14k ......................................... $475        $550        $625

GRUEN, 17J.,  curvex, RF#610, cal.1370, c. 1945
14k ......................................... $400        $475        $575

GRUEN, 17J., 3 diam., curvex, RF#615, cal.370, c. 1945
14k ......................................... $200        $250        $350

GRUEN, 17J.,  curvex, RF#642, cal.370, c. 1945
gold filled .............................. $100        $125        $150

GRUEN, 17J.,  curvex, RF#650, cal.370, c. 1948
gold filled .............................. $100        $125        $150

GRUEN, 17J., twisted bezel, RF#657, cal.335, c. 1953
gold filled............................... $150        $175        $225

GRUEN, 17J., curvex, faceted crystal, cal.440, c. 1947
14k ........................................ $250        $300        $375

GRUEN, 21J., precision, RF#674, cal.430, c. 1947
gold filled................................. $60        $70        $95

GRUEN, 21J., precision, RF#801, cal335., c. 1953
14k ......................................... $200        $250        $300

GRUEN, 21J., precision, RF#738, cal.335, c. 1948
14k ......................................... $225        $275        $325

GRUEN, 17J., veri-thin, large lugs, c. 1950
14k ......................................... $200        $235        $300

GRUEN, 17J., curvex, RF#750, cal.370, c. 1940
gold filled............................... $100        $135        $175

GRUEN, 17J., center wheel not jeweled, c. 1938
gold filled ............................... $90        $110        $150

GRUEN, 17J., curvex, RF#773, cal.370, c. 1945
gold filled...............................$100        $125        $165

GRUEN, 17J., stepped case, ca.1930
gold filled ............................... $80        $90        $110

GRUEN, 19 jewels, precision, c. 1920
14k ...........................................$300    $400    $500

GRUEN, 17 jewels, curvex
14k ...........................................$300    $350    $400

GRUEN, 17J., curvex, cal#440, ca.1940s
gold filled.................................$100    $125    $175

GRUEN, 17 jewels, curvex, c. 1943
14k ...........................................$400    $450    $500

GRUEN, 17 jewels, cal. 440, RF#449, Ca. 1945
gold filled................................$150    $175    $200

⊕ Some grades are not included. Their values can be
determined by comparing with **similar** age, size, metal
content, style, grades, or models such as **time only**,
chronograph, repeater etc. listed.

GRUEN, 17 jewels, Curvex, RF#610, 3 diam.dial, Ca.1945
14k(w) 6 diam.case ................$400    $450    $500

GRUEN, 21J., "Precision", RF#709, cal.335, Ca.1945
gold filled .................................$75    $85    $125

GRUEN, 15 jewels, RF#8w, cal.157, Ca. 1929
gold filled .................................$75    $100    $150

GRUEN, 15 jewels, 3 Adj., Ca.1930
gold filled .................................$60    $70    $95

GRUEN, 17J., veri-thin, cal.405, c. 1946
gold filled .................................$70    $90    $125

GRUEN, 17J., curvex, RF#450, cal.440, c. 1938
gold filled.............................. $150      $200      $275

GRUEN, 17J., curvex, RF#448, cal.440, c. 1941
gold filled.............................. $150      $200      $250

GRUEN, 17J., curvex, RF#450, cal.440, c. 1938
14k ......................................... $250      $300      $375

GRUEN, 17J., curvex, RF#879, cal.370, c. 1942
14k ......................................... $300      $350      $400

GRUEN, 17J., curvex, RF#450, cal.440, c. 1942
14k .........................................$ 225      $265      $350

GRUEN, 17J., curvex, RF#448, cal.440, c. 1944
14k ......................................... $350      $400      $450

GRUEN, 17J., curvex, RF#364, cal.400, c. 1935
gold filled.............................. $150      $175      $225

GRUEN, 17J., curvex, RF#293, cal.330, c. 1940
gold filled.............................. $150      $175      $225

GRUEN, 17J., precision, RF#271, cal., c. 1936
gold filled.............................. $125      $150      $200

GRUEN, 17J., fluted bezel, RF#240, cal.335, c. 1935
14k ......................................... $200      $250      $325

GRUEN, 17J., curvex, RF#602, cal.370, c. 1943
14k ........................................... $300      $350      $400

GRUEN, 17 jewels, curvex, c. 1947
14k ........................................... $300      $350      $450

GRUEN, 17J., curvex, RF#449, cal.440, c. 1945
14k ........................................... $250      $300      $350

GRUEN, 17 jewels, curvex, c. 1937
gold filled ................................ $185      $225      $275

GRUEN, 17J., veri-thin, cal.420, c. 1948
gold filled................................ $65        $75        $95

GRUEN, 17 jewels, curvex, fancy lugs
14k ........................................... $250      $300      $350

GRUEN, 17 jewels, curvex, c. 1936
gold filled................................$200      $250      $300

GRUEN, 17 jewels, curvex, c. 1939
14k ........................................... $400      $450      $500
gold filled ................................ $300      $350      $400

GRUEN, 17 jewels, precision, fancy lugs
14k ........................................... $300      $400      $500

🕐 Some grades are not included. Their values can be
determined by comparing with **similar** age, size, metal
content, style, grades, or models such as **time only**,
chronograph, repeater etc. listed.

GRUEN, 17 jewels, curvex, fancy lugs, c. 1961
14k ........................................... $400      $500      $600

**Gruen Quadron rectangular movement**

GRUEN, 15-17J., enamel on nickel, Ca. 1927
nickel........................................$200   $225   $275

GRUEN, 17J., crown-guard, quadron mvt., Ca. 1927
18k ........................................$225   $300   $350

GRUEN, 15-17J., enamel art Deco, Ca. 1927
gold filled................................$250   $275   $300

GRUEN, 15-17J., inlaid enamel case, quadron mvt., Ca. 1927
gold filled................................$100   $125   $175

GRUEN, 15-17J., center sec., radium dial, Ca. 1927
14k........................................$200   $225   $275

GRUEN, 15-17J., engraved case, quadron mvt., Ca. 1927
gold filled................................$65   $80   $100

GRUEN, 15-17J., engraved case, radium dial, Ca. 1927
nickel........................................$75   $95   $125

GRUEN, 15-17J., crown-guard, quadron mvt., Ca. 1927
14k ........................................$200   $225   $275

GRUEN, 15-17J., tank w/crown guard, Ca. 1927
14k........................................$200   $250   $325

GRUEN, 15-17J., crown-guard, quadron mvt., Ca. 1927
gold filled................................$125   $150   $175

GRUEN, 15-17J., tank engraved, Ca. 1927
14k........................................$200   $225   $275

GRUEN, 17J., pulsemeter,
s. steel ...................................$400    $500    $600

GRUEN, 17 jewels, physicians chronog., screw back
18k ....................................$1,500   $1,700   $2,000

GRUEN, 17J., jump 24 hour, c. 1970
s. steel ...................................... $70    $80    $100

GRUEN, 17J., alarm, date, c. 1964
s. steel ..................................... $125    $150    $175

GRUEN, 17J., triple date, cal.415, c. 1953
gold filled............................... $150    $175    $225

GRUEN, 17 jewels, rope style bezel with diamonds
14k...........................................$250    $300    $375

GRUEN, 17J., center sec., cal.n510, c. 1960
base metal................................. $40    $50    $60

GRUEN, 17 jewels, day-date-month, c. 1948
s. steel.....................................$150    $175    $225

GRUEN, 17 jewels, veri thin model, fancy lugs
14k ......................................... $250     $300     $350

GRUEN, 17J., mystery dial, cal#215, ca.1965
gold filled................................ $200     $250     $300

GRUEN, 17J., veri thin model, fancy lugs, 24 hr. dial
14k ........................................... $225     $300     $400

GRUEN, 17J., **Airflight**, jumping hours, c. 1960
gold filled................................ $200     $235     $300

GRUEN, 17J., engraved case, cal.117, c. 1929
14k(w)................................... $250     $325     $375

GRUEN, 15J., cushion, luminous dial, c. 1930s
gold filled................................. $85     $95     $150

GRUEN, 15-17J., barrel shaped, Ca. 1939
gold filled............................... $100     $150     $175

GRUEN, 17J., veri-thin, fancy bezel, Ca. 1948
gold filled............................... $125     $150     $175

GRUEN, 15-17J., RF# 544, Ca. 1949
gold filled............................... $125     $150     $175

GRUEN, 17J., fluted center lugs, cal.343, c. 1936
gold filled.............................. $100      $125      $150

GRUEN, 17J., nurse style double dial, ca.1937
s. steel ...................................$175      $225      $300

E. GUBELIN, 17 jewels, chronog. 3 reg., Valj.72, c. 1950
18k ......................................$1,000      $1,100      $1,200

E. GUBELIN, 19 jewels, chronog., day-date-month
18k ......................................$1,250      $1,500      $1,800

E. GUBELIN, 19J., chronog.by Valjoux, waterpf, 3 reg.
18k ......................................$1,000      $1,250      $1,400

E. GUBELIN, 29 jewels, min. repeater
18k C&B ...........................$25,000      $30,000      $35,000

E. GUBELIN, 25J., ipso-matic, triple date, moon ph.
14k & steel back .................$1,250      $1,350      $1,550
18k.........................................$2,000      $2,250      $2,500

E. GUBELIN, 15J., triple date, c.1945
s. steel....................................$300      $350      $400

E. GUBELIN, 19 jewels, 18k case, 14k band
18k & 14k C&B......................$600      $700      $900

E. GUBELIN, 17J., ca. 1970s
18k ..........................................$200      $250      $300

E. GUBELIN,17J., cal#F690, center sec., ca. 1950s
18k ..........................................$250      $300      $350
s. steel ....................................$100      $125      $175

E. GUBELIN, 17J., ca. 1952
s. steel ....................................$150      $200      $250

E. GUBELIN, 25J., ipso-matic, c.1955
14k ..........................................$300      $350      $400

E. GUBELIN, 17J., alarm, ipso-vox, c.1960
18k..............................................$800      $1,000      $1,200

E. GUBELIN, 17J., ipso-vox, date, alarm, c.1960
s. steel ....................................$350      $400      $450

E. GUBELIN, 17J., carved lugs, center sec., c.1944
18k..............................................$400      $450      $500

E. GUBELIN, 17J., 8 baguettes, 3 diamonds, c.1948
platinum ................................$500      $550      $600

E. GUBELIN, 15J., duoplan, c.1935
s. steel..........................................$300      $350      $400

E. GUBELIN, 15J., ca. 1935
18k(W)..................................$700    $800    $900

E. GUBELIN, 19 J., hunter style pop-up lid, c. 1930
18k (w)..................................$4,500    $5,500    $6,000

E. GUBELIN, 17jewels, jumping hr., c. 1924
14k .......................................$8,000    $9,000    $10,000

E. GUBELIN, 25J., triple date, moon phase, c. 1950
18k .......................................$2,500    $3,000    $3,500

E. GUBELIN, 19 jewels, fancy bezel, enamel dial
18k .......................................$1,500    $1,600    $1,800

E. GUBELIN, 19 jewels, fancy lugs, center sec.
18k.........................................$500    $600    $800

E. GUBELIN, 19 jewels, fancy hooded lugs
18k.........................................$1,000    $1,200    $1,500

E. GUBELIN, 19 jewels, curvex, 2 tone
18k.........................................$1,000    $1,100    $1,200

E. GUBELIN, 19J., center sec., flared case, c. 1950
18k.........................................$350    $450    $550

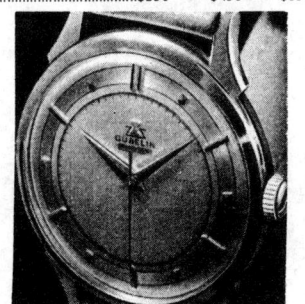

E. GUBELIN, 21 jewels, center sec.
18k.........................................$300    $350    $425

E. GUBELIN, 17 jewels, by Vacheron & Constantin
18k ...........................................$2,000    $2,500    $3,000

E. GUBELIN, 18 jewels, curved, stepped case, c. 1940
18k .........................................$1,000    $1,200    $1,500

GUINAND, 17J., chronog., day-date-month, 3 reg.
18k ........................................$700    $800    $950
s. steel .....................................$300    $350    $400

GUINAND, 17 J., chronog., triple date, moon phase
18k .........................................$1,000    $1,200    $1,400
s. steel .....................................$600    $700    $800

HAFIS, 15J., center sec., cushion style
gold plate ...................................$50    $60    $75

HAFIS, 15J., luminous dial
gold plate...................................$50    $60    $75

HAFIS, 15J., engraved case
gold plate...................................$70    $80    $95
14k...........................................$150    $200    $275

HAFIS, 15J., engraved case
gold plate...................................$50    $60    $75

HAFIS, 15J., engraved case
gold plate...................................$60    $70    $85

HAFIS, 15J., engraved case
gold plate...................................$50    $60    $75

HAFIS, 15J., engraved case
gold plate ..................................$60    $70    $85

HAFIS, 15J., engraved case
gold plate ..................................$60    $70    $85

HAFIS, 15J., engraved case
gold plate ..................................$60    $70    $85

HAFIS, 15J., luminous dial
gold plate ..................................$50    $55    $65

HAFIS, 15J., curved case
gold plate ..................................$50    $60    $75
14k .........................................$125    $150    $200

HAFIS, 17 jewels, carved lugs
14k .........................................$150    $175    $200

HAFIS, 15J., engraved case, curved
gold plate ..................................$60    $70    $85
14k .........................................$150    $175    $200

HAFIS, 17J., 'Queen Druga", 52 diamonds
Platinum..................................$350    $400    $450

HAFIS, 15J., "Queen Marie", 26 diamonds
18k .........................................$200    $250    $300

HAFIS, 15J., "Queen Charlotte", 22 diamonds
18k .........................................$175    $200    $225

HALLMARK, 17 jewels, day-date-month, auto wind
gold filled ..............................$150    $175    $200

HAMILTON, electric, "Altair"
gold filled...................................$800    $1,000    $1,300

HAMILTON, electric, "Aquatel"
gold filled...................................$100    $125    $200

HAMILTON, electric, "Aquatel B"
gold filled...................................$100    $125    $200

HAMILTON, electric, "Atlantis"
gold filled...................................$100    $125    $200

HAMILTON, electric, "Centaur"
gold filled...................................$125    $175    $225

HAMILTON, electric, "Clearview", **display back**
gold filled...................................$200    $250    $300

HAMILTON, electric, "Converta I", 18k bezel & s.s. case
18k &S.S. ...............................$175    $225    $275

HAMILTON, electric, "Converta II", 14k bezel & s.s. case
14k &S.S. ...............................$150    $175    $225

HAMILTON, electric, "Converta III", 10k bezel & s.s. case
10k &S.S. ...............................$100    $125    $200

HAMILTON, electric, "Converta IV", S.S. bezel & case
s. steel ....................................$100    $125    $150

HAMILTON, electric, "Everest"
gold filled ...............................$175    $225    $275

HAMILTON, electric, "Everest II"
gold filled ...............................$125    $165    $235

HAMILTON, electric, "Gemini" Ca.1963
gold filled...................................$85    $100    $150

HAMILTON, electric, "Gemini II" Ca.1965
gold filled...................................$85    $100    $150

HAMILTON, electric, "Lord Lancaster E," 12 diamonds
14k ............................................$450    $500    $600

HAMILTON, electric, "Lord Lancaster J," 8 diamonds
gold filled...................................$225    $275    $350

HAMILTON, electric, "Meteor," c. 1959
gold filled...................................$275    $325    $400

HAMILTON, electric, "Nautilus" 200, single lugs
14k ............................................$200    $250    $325

HAMILTON, electric, "Nautilus" 201
14k ...........................................$175    $200    $225

HAMILTON, electric, "Nautilus" 202
14k ...........................................$225    $250    $275

HAMILTON, electric, "Nautilus" 400
gold filled ..................................$80    $90    $100

HAMILTON, electric, "Nautilus" 401
gold filled ..................................$80    $90    $100

HAMILTON, electric, "Nautilus" 402
gold filled ..................................$80    $90    $100

HAMILTON, electric, "Nautilus" 403, pocket watch
gold filled ..................................$150    $200    $275

HAMILTON, electric, "Nautilus" 404
gold filled..................................$80    $90    $100

HAMILTON, electric, "Nautilus" 405
gold filled..................................$60    $70    $80

HAMILTON, electric, "Nautilus" 450, gold filled bezel
gold filled..................................$60    $70    $80

HAMILTON, electric, "Nautilus" 500
s. steel ......................................$60    $70    $80

HAMILTON, electric, "Nautilus" 501
s. steel ......................................$60    $70    $80

HAMILTON, electric, "Nautilus" 502
s. steel ......................................$60    $70    $80

HAMILTON, electric, "Nautilus" 503
s. steel ......................................$60    $70    $80

HAMILTON, electric, "Nautilus" 506
s. steel ......................................$70    $80    $90

HAMILTON, electric, "Nautilus" 507
s. steel ......................................$70    $80    $90

HAMILTON, electric, "Nautilus" 508
s. steel ......................................$60    $70    $80

HAMILTON, electric, "Nautilus" 509
s. steel ......................................$70    $80    $90

HAMILTON, electric, "Nautilus" 600
gold plate ..................................$60    $70    $80

HAMILTON, electric, "Nautilus" 601
gold plate ....................................$60　　$70　　$80

HAMILTON, electric, "Nautilus" 602
gold plate ....................................$60　　$70　　$80

HAMILTON, electric, "Nautilus" 604
gold plate ....................................$70　　$80　　$90

HAMILTON, electric, "Nautilus" 605
gold plate ....................................$60　　$70　　$80

HAMILTON, electric, "Pacer," 2 tone
14k .........................................$700　　$950　　$1,100
gold filled................................$275　　$300　　$350

HAMILTON, electric, "Pegasus", engraved bezel
gold filled ...............................$100　　$135　　$200

HAMILTON, electric, "Polaris"
14k .........................................$300　　$350　　$400

HAMILTON, electric,"Polaris", diamond dial
14k .........................................$400　　$450　　$500

HAMILTON, electric,"Polaris II"
14k .........................................$300　　$350　　$400

HAMILTON, electric, "Regulus"
s. steel .....................................$200　　$300　　$400

HAMILTON, electric, "Regulus" II
s. steel ......................................$80    $90    $125

HAMILTON, electric, "Sea-Lectric I", GF bezel
s. steel ....................................$100    $125    $175

HAMILTON, electric, "R. R. Special"
model#52 =10k GF case.........$150    $200    $250
model#51 =GF bezel .............$100    $150    $200·
model#50 =s. steel....................$90    $125    $150

HAMILTON, electric, "Sea-Lectric II"
s. steel ....................................$100    $125    $150

HAMILTON, electric, "Saturn"
gold filled..............................$175    $225    $300

HAMILTON, electric, "Skip Jack"
s. steel ...................................... $70    $80    $100

HAMILTON, electric, "Savitar"
14k ..........................................$350    $400    $450

HAMILTON, electric, "Spectra"
18k **Rose gold** .....................$1,000    $1,100    $1,250
14k ..........................................$450    $550    $625

HAMILTON, electric, "Savitar 11", ca.1966
gold filled...............................$175    $200    $250

HAMILTON, electric, "Spectra" II
gold filled ..............................$100    $125    $175

HAMILTON, electric, "Summit"
14k ............................................$150    $175    $225

HAMILTON, electric, "Summit" II
gold filled..................................$125    $150    $200

HAMILTON, electric, "Taurus"
gold filled..................................$100    $125    $175

HAMILTON, electric, "Titan"
gold filled..................................$100    $125    $175

HAMILTON, electric, "Titan II"
gold filled..................................$125    $150    $200

HAMILTON, electric, "Titan III"
gold filled ...............................$125    $150    $200

HAMILTON, electric, "Titan IV-B"
14kC&B...................................$350    $400    $500

HAMILTON, electric, "Uranus"
gold filled ...............................$125    $150    $175

HAMILTON, electric, "Van Horn", Ca.1957
14k ...........................................$200    $250    $350
14k +diam. dial......................$250    $300    $400

HAMILTON, electric, Vantage , ca.1959
gold filled ...............................$125    $150    $200

🕐 Some grades are not included. Their values can be determined by comparing with similar age, size, metal content, style, grades, or models such as time only, chronograph, repeater etc. listed.

HAMILTON, electric, "Vega"
gold filled..............................$275     $325     $400

HAMILTON, electric, "Vela"
gold filled..............................$100     $125     $175

HAMILTON electric, "Ventura"
18k .......................................$1,300    $1,500    $1,800
14k .......................................$800      $1,000    $1,200

HAMILTON electric, "Ventura", 6 diamond dial
14K.........................................$850     $1,100    $1,250

HAMILTON, electric,"Victor", ca.1958
gold filled..............................$125     $150     $200

Hamilton, electric, "Victor II"
gold filled ..............................$150     $200     $250

HAMILTON, 17 jewels, "Seckron," dual dial, c. 1935
gold filled ..............................$700     $800     $950

HAMILTON, 17 jewels, dual dial
gold filled ..............................$700     $800     $900

HAMILTON, "Flint Ridge," flip top is lug activated Grade
987=17J., Grade 979=19J.
14k .......................................$2,250    $2,500    $3,000

HAMILTON, 17 jewels, "Cross Country," c. 1962
14k .........................................$250     $300     $400
gold filled...............................$150     $200     $250

HAMILTON, 17J., chronog., by Valjoux cal.7733, c.1971
s. steel .....................................$275     $300     $350

HAMILTON, 17J., "Transcontinental," auto-wind, Ca. 1963
14k .........................................$350     $400     $500
gold filled...............................$175     $225     $300

HAMILTON, 17J., chronog., DATE, by Valjoux cal.7732,
s. steel ..................................... $200     $250     $350

HAMILTON, Golden Tempus, 18J., time zones, Ca. 1961
14k .........................................$400     $450     $550
14k +diamonds ......................$450     $500     $650

HAMILTON, 17J., chronog, screw -back,
s. steel .....................................$100     $125     $175

HAMILTON, 22J., above Flight I =14k MARKERS,
14k case ...............................$1,400     $1,600     $2,000

HAMILTON, 22J., above Flight II =14k dots & #s,
gold filled case........................$600     $700     $900

HAMILTON, 22J., auto-wind, Ca. 1970
gold filled ................................$50     $65     $95
s. steel ......................................$40     $50     $80

HAMILTON, 17J., auto-wind,day date, c.1971
s. steel ........................................$40        $50        $75

HAMILTON, 17J., hinged lugs, "Tuxedo", cal., c.1940
gold filled................................$125        $150        $200

HAMILTON, 17J., hinged lugs, cal., c.1940
gold filled................................$125        $150        $200

HAMILTON, 17J., drivers,cal.907, c.1938
gold filled................................$125        $150        $200

HAMILTON,17J., drivers, **winds at 12**, ca. 1938
gold filled................................$350        $400        $450

HAMILTON, 19 jewels, "Otis," reversible, c. 1946
gold filled ..............................$750        $900        $1,200

HAMILTON, 19 J., "Coronado," black enamel bezel
14k ..........................................$900        $1,100        $1,300

HAMILTON, 19 jewels, "Piping Rock," enamel bezel
14k yellow or white................$800        $900        $1,100

HAMILTON, 19 jewels, "Spur," enamel bezel
14k ....................................$1,800        $2,000        $2,500
14k(w)................................$1,200        $1,500        $2,000

HAMILTON, 17J., enamel on white gold bezel & case yellow
14k ..........................................$900        $1,000        $1,200

HAMILTON, 15J., "Oval", c. 1920s
14k ..........................................$400    $500    $650

HAMILTON, 17 jewels, cal. 987, GJS, ca. 1932
gold filled................................$175    $200    $225

HAMILTON, 17 jewels, "Alan"
gold filled................................$90    $125    $175

HAMILTON, 22 jewels, " Aldrich", Ca, 1961
14k ..........................................$150    $185    $250

HAMILTON, 19 jewels, "Allison" , Ca. 1940
14k ..........................................$300    $350    $450

HAMILTON,17J., " Amherst", 14k markers
gold filled................................$80    $90    $100

HAMILTON, 19 jewels, "Andrews"
14k .........................................$300    $375    $500

HAMILTON, 22J., " Ansley" , 14k markers
gold filled .................................$80    $90    $100

HAMILTON, 17J., "Aqualine ", 14k markers, Ca. 1961
gold filled .................................$55    $65    $85

HAMILTON, 17J., " Ardmore", Ca. 1935
14k .........................................$300    $375    $475

HAMILTON, 17J., " Arnold", Ca. 1961
gold plate .................................$50    $60    $75

HAMILTON, 19J., " Ashley", Ca. 1951
gold plate .................................$60    $75    $95

HAMILTON, 22J., "Attache", 14k markers, c.1961
gold filled................................$150      $175      $225

HAMILTON, 22J., " Baron II" , 5 diamond dial, c. 1961
14k ..........................................$200      $225      $275

HAMILTON, 17J.," Austin ", c. 1951
gold filled................................$100      $125      $175

HAMILTON, 17J.," Bartley' ", , Ca.1936
gold filled ..............................$100      $125      $175

HAMILTON, 17J, "Bagley," applied numbers, c. 1941
gold filled................................$125      $150      $200

HAMILTON, 19J.,"Barton", tu tone dial, c.1951
14k ..........................................$275      $350      $425

HAMILTON, 19J.," Bailey ", c.1951
gold filled................................$100      $125      $175

HAMILTON, 22J., "Baton",  14k markers
14k ..........................................$250      $300      $350

HAMILTON, 22J., " Barbizon",  diam. bezel, Ca.1957
18k(w)....................................$500      $600      $800

HAMILTON,17J.,"Beldon", 2 tone dial, sealed case, c.1951
gold filled ...............................$80      $100      $150

HAMILTON, 22J., " Baron" , 5 diam. dial, BIG lugs, c.1961
14k ..........................................$225      $275      $325

HAMILTON, 22J., " Bentley",  14k markers, c. 1961
gold filled ...............................$80      $100      $135

HAMILTON, 19J., " Bentley", 14k markers, Ca. 1938
14k .................................$400      $450      $575

HAMILTON, 17J., " Benton", 14k markers, c. 1954
10k ............................................$200      $250      $300

HAMILTON, 17J., " Berkshire", 14k markers, Ca. 1952
gold filled................................$100      $125      $175

HAMILTON, 17J.," Blake ", 4 diam. dial, Ca.1961
gold filled................................$125      $150      $200

HAMILTON, 17-21J.," Blake ", c.1951
gold filled................................$90      $100      $135

HAMILTON, 17J., " Boatswain", center sec., c. 1961
gold plate ...................................$50      $60      $75

HAMILTON, 17J., " Boatswain II" , c. 1961
gold plate ...................................$60      $70      $85

HAMILTON, 17J.," Boone ", Ca.1937
gold filled .............................$100      $125      $175

HAMILTON, 19 jewels, "Boulton" , Ca. 1941
gold filled .............................$100      $125      $175

HAMILTON, 22J., " Boulton II" , 14k markers, c. 1961
gold filled .................................$90      $100      $135

HAMILTON, 17J.,"Boyd", c.1951
gold filled .............................$100      $135      $185

HAMILTON, 22J., "Bradford B" , 14k markers, c. 1961
14k ...........................................$125      $150      $200

HAMILTON, 22J., "Bradford B" , 11 diam. dial, c. 1961
14k .........................................$200      $225      $250

HAMILTON, 17J., "Brandon", swing lugs, c. 1951
gold filled.................................$100      $125      $165

HAMILTON, 17 jewels, "Brandon", Ca. 1951
gold filled.................................$100      $125      $175

HAMILTON, 19J.,"Brent ", **faceted** crystal, c.1951
gold filled.................................$100      $135      $185

HAMILTON, 19 jewels, "Brock" , c. 1941
14k .........................................$200      $250      $300

HAMILTON, 19 jewels, "Brock" , c. 1951
14k .........................................$200      $250      $300

HAMILTON, 19J.," Brooke ", Ca.1951
gold filled ...............................$250      $300      $400

HAMILTON, 19 jewels, "Byrd"
18k .........................................$550      $650      $800
14k .........................................$400      $500      $650

HAMILTON, 17J.,"Cabot", cal.960, Ca. 1938
gold filled ...............................$90      $100      $150

HAMILTON, 17J.,"Cambridge"
14k .........................................$450      $550      $700

HAMILTON, 19J.," Cambridge ", c.1951
platinum...................................$700      $800      $1,000

# HAMILTON (continued) 733

HAMILTON, 19 jewels, "Cameron" , c. 1941
14k ...........................................$250    $300    $400

HAMILTON, 17J.,"Captain Rice"
14k ...........................................$250    $300    $375

HAMILTON, 17J.," Carl ", Ca.1953
gold filled..................................$90    $100    $135

HAMILTON, 17J.," Carlisle ", cal. 937, Ca.1937
gold filled..................................$150    $200    $250

HAMILTON, 17J.," Carson ", Ca.1935
gold filled..................................$125    $150    $175

HAMILTON, 17J., " Carson", c. 1961
gold plate ...................................$80    $100    $120

HAMILTON, 17J.," Carlton ", c.1951
gold filled ...............................$100    $125    $165

HAMILTON, 17J., " Carlyle", c. 1961
gold plate...................................$50    $60    $75

HAMILTON, 17J., " Carteret"   14k markers
14k ...........................................$175    $200    $250

HAMILTON, 19J.," Cedric ", c.1951
gold filled ...............................$100    $125    $165

HAMILTON, 22J., "Chadwick ", 14k markers, c. 1961
14k ...........................................$125    $150    $185

HAMILTON, 22J., "Chapman ", 14k markers, c. 1961
gold filled..................................$90      $100      $135

HAMILTON, 17J., " Chattam",Ca. 1953
gold filled..................................$100      $125      $175
14k ...........................................$250      $300      $375

HAMILTON, 17J., " Clark", Ca. 1937
gold filled..................................$150      $200      $275

HAMILTON, 18J., "Clearview " , 14k markers, c. 1961
14k ...........................................$175      $200      $235

HAMILTON, 17J.," Clinton ", c.1951
s. steel .......................................$50      $60      $70

HAMILTON, 17J.," Clyde ", c.1951
gold filled..................................$90      $115      $150

HAMILTON, 17J., c. 1961
gold plate ..................................$60      $70      $85

HAMILTON, 17J., "Contour " , c. 1937
gold filled ..............................$350      $400      $450

HAMILTON, 17J., "Conway ", c. 1961
gold plate ..................................$70      $85      $120

HAMILTON, 17J., " Cordell", Ca. 1961
14k C&B..............................$275      $300      $325

HAMILTON, 22J., "Corvet " , 14k markers, c. 1961
gold filled ..............................$100      $125      $165

HAMILTON, 17J., "Courtney" , 14k markers, c. 1961
gold filled..................................$80      $90      $125

HAMILTON, 22J., "Courtney" , 6 diamond dial, c. 1961
14k .......................................$200      $225      $250

HAMILTON, 17J.," Craig ", c.1951
gold filled..................................$90      $100      $135

HAMILTON, 22J., " Cullen" , 14k markers, c. 1961
gold filled..................................$80      $90      $100

HAMILTON, 22J., " Curtiss", Ca. 1956
14k ............................................$200      $250      $350

HAMILTON, 19J., " Custer", Ca. 1937
14k ............................................$200      $250      $350

HAMILTON, 17J., "Darrell", cal#747, c. 1951
gold filled ...............................$120      $160      $180

HAMILTON, 17J., "Dawson " , c. 1961
gold filled ..................................$80      $90      $100

HAMILTON, 17J., "Dean " , c. 1961
gold filled ..................................$50      $60      $70

HAMILTON, 17J., "Deauville ", c. 1961
gold plate ..................................$60      $70      $80

HAMILTON, 17J.," Dennis ", Ca.1961
14k .........................................$150      $175      $200

HAMILTON, 17J.," Dennis ", Ca.1951
gold filled ...............................$100      $150      $200

HAMILTON, 17J.," "Dewitt ", c.1951
gold filled...............................$100      $125      $150

HAMILTON, 17J., " Dexter" , c. 1961
gold plate ...................................$80      $90      $100

HAMILTON, 17J.," "Dexter ", c.1951
gold filled...............................$100      $125      $175

HAMILTON, 17J.," "Dickens ", Ca.1937
gold filled...............................$175      $200      $250

HAMILTON, 17J.," "Dixon ", Ca.1937
gold filled.................................$100      $135      $200

HAMILTON, 17 jewels, "Dodson" , c. 1937
gold filled...............................$150      $175      $225

HAMILTON, 19J.," Donald ", c.1951
14k ........................................$275      $325      $400

HAMILTON, 17J.," Donavan ", center lugs
14k .........................................$350      $450      $550

HAMILTON, 22J.," Donavan II", Ca.1961
14k .........................................$200      $225      $275

HAMILTON, 17J.," Dorsey ", Ca.1937
14k .........................................$200      $250      $325

HAMILTON, 17J.," Doublet ", Ca.1961
14k .........................................$125      $150      $200

HAMILTON, 17J.," Drake ", Ca.1951
gold filled .............................$100      $125      $175

HAMILTON, 17J.," Drake ", Ca.1935
gold filled .............................$125      $150      $195

HAMILTON, 17J., "Drummond ", 14k markers, c. 1961
gold filled.................................\$75       \$85       \$120

HAMILTON, 17J.," Dunham ", c.1951
gold filled...............................\$100      \$125      \$175

HAMILTON, 19 jewels, "Dunkirk", c. 1941
14k ...........................................\$250      \$300      \$400

HAMILTON, 17 jewels, "Dyson", c. 1951
gold filled..................................\$95      \$125      \$165

HAMILTON, 17J.," Eaton ", c.1951
gold filled.................................\$100      \$135      \$200

HAMILTON, 17J.," Eliott ", Cal.980
gold filled.................................\$100      \$125      \$150

HAMILTON, 17J.," Emery ", c.1951
gold filled .................................\$90      \$100      \$135

HAMILTON, 17 jewels, "Eric", c. 1951
gold filled .................................\$85      \$95      \$125

HAMILTON, 17 jewels, "Ericsson"
14k ...........................................\$275      \$350      \$450

HAMILTON, 17 jewels, "Emerson", c. 1941
gold filled .................................\$100      \$125      \$175

HAMILTON, 17 jewels, "Endicott", c. 1941
gold filled .................................\$80      \$125      \$150

HAMILTON, 17 jewels, "Essex", c. 1941
gold filled ...............................\$125      \$150      \$175

HAMILTON, 17J., " Farrell", 14k # s, c.1961
gold plate ....................................$60      $70      $80

HAMILTON, 17J., " First Mate", c.1961
gold plate ....................................$60      $70      $80

HAMILTON, 18J.,"Fleetwood ", c.1951
14k ...........................................$125      $175      $200

HAMILTON, 17 jewels, "Forbes" , c. 1951
gold filled..............................$100      $125      $175

HAMILTON, 19 jewels, "Foster" , c. 1941
14k ...........................................$325      $400      $475

HAMILTON, 17J.," Franklin ", c.1951
gold filled .................................$90      $120      $165

HAMILTON, 17J., " Gardner", c.1961
gold plate ..................................$60      $75      $90

HAMILTON, 17J.," Gary ", c.1951
gold filled ...............................$100      $125      $165

HAMILTON, 17J.," Gary ", fluted lugs, Ca.1951
gold filled .................................$80      $95      $125

HAMILTON, 19J.," Gilbert ", c.1951
14k ...........................................$225      $275      $350

🕐 Some grades are not included. Their values can be
determined by comparing with **similar** age, size, metal
content, style, grades, or models such as **time only**,
chronograph, repeater etc. listed.

HAMILTON, 19 jewels, "Gilman" , c. 1941
14k ...........................................$350      $400      $450

HAMILTON, 17J.,"Gladstone", cal.981, c.1951
gold filled...............................$100      $125      $175

HAMILTON, 17J.," Glendale ", engraved case,
14K...........................................$600      $750      $900

HAMILTON, 17J., " Glendon",  c.1961
gold plate ...................................$70      $80      $90

HAMILTON, 17J.," Glenn ", c.1951
14k ...........................................$200      $250      $300

HAMILTON, 19 jewels, "Glenn Curtis"
14k ..........................................$300      $350      $450

HAMILTON, 18J., " Golden Tempus II", 14k #s, c.1961
gold filled .................................$70      $80      $90

HAMILTON, 19J.," Gordon ", c.1951
18k .......................................... $325      $400      $550

HAMILTON, 22J., " Gramercy", 14k #s, c.1961
gold filled .................................$80      $90      $120

HAMILTON, 17 jewels, "Grant"
sterling ....................................$125      $150      $185

HAMILTON, 17 jewels, "Greenwich"
gold filled ...............................$100      $125      $175

HAMILTON, 17J.," Grover ", c.1951
gold filled..................................$90      $100      $135

HAMILTON, 17J., " Howard", on dial & movement
gold filled .............................$425      $525      $675

HAMILTON, 17J.," Harris ",  Ca.1937
gold filled..................................$60      $80      $100

HAMILTON, 17J.," Jeffrey ", c.1951
gold filled ..............................$100      $125      $175

HAMILTON, 17J.," Hastings ", cal.987
gold filled...............................$125      $150      $200

HAMILTON, 19 jewels, "Judson"
gold filled ..............................$100      $125      $150

HAMILTON, 19J.," Hayden ", c.1951
gold filled...............................$100      $125      $175

HAMILTON, 17J., " Keane", c.1961
gold plate ..................................$60      $75      $100

HAMILTON, 18J., " Holden", c.1961
gold filled...................................$70      $80      $90

HAMILTON, 19J.," Keith ", c.1951
14k .........................................$250      $275      $350

HAMILTON, 17J.," Huntley ", Ca.1961
gold filled................................$100      $120      $150

HAMILTON, 22J.," Kevin ",  hidden lugs, Ca.1951
14k ...........................................$350      $400      $500

HAMILTON, 17J., " Khyber", 14k #s, c.1961
gold filled.................................$120    $140    $165

HAMILTON, 17J.,"Lambert ", c.1951
gold filled .................................$90    $100    $135

HAMILTON, 17J.," Kinematic II ", Ca.1961
gold plate ...................................$60    $70    $95

HAMILTON, 17J,( Lange is =14k), Langdon is =G. filled
14k .........................................$150    $175    $200
gold filled .................................$75    $100    $150

HAMILTON, 19J.," Kirby ", c.1951
gold filled.................................$90    $100    $135

HAMILTON, 17J.," Langford ", Ca.1937
14k .........................................$200    $250    $350

HAMILTON, 17J.," Kirk ", c.1951
14k ...........................................$125    $150    $200

HAMILTON, 17 jewels, "Langley"
18k ...........................................$425    $525    $675

HAMILTON, 17J.," Lawrence ", Ca.1937
gold filled ...............................$100    $125    $165

HAMILTON, 17J., " Lakeland", c.1961
s. steel .........................................$50    $60    $70

🕐 Some grades are not included. Their values can be determined by comparing with similar age, size, metal content, style, grades, or models such as time only, chronograph, repeater etc. listed.

HAMILTON, 17 jewels, "Lee"
gold filled..................................$125          $150          $200

HAMILTON, 17 & 19 jewels, "Linwood" Ca. 1937
gold filled................................$150          $200          $250

HAMILTON, 19 jewels, "Livingston"
14k ...........................................$250          $300          $375

HAMILTON, 17J., " Lord Lancaster", Ca.1965
14k W.......................................$300          $400          $500

HAMILTON, 19J., " Lowell", Ca.1935
14k ...........................................$200          $250          $300

HAMILTON, 17J., " Lowell", Ca.1961
gold plate .................................$50          $60          $75

HAMILTON, 17 jewels, "Martin"
gold filled ..................................$80          $95          $125

HAMILTON, 17J., "Masterpiece", Ca.1955
14k ..........................................$175          $200          $275

HAMILTON, 17J.,"Meadowbrook"
14k ...........................................$600          $700          $800
18k ...........................................$800          $900          $1,100
Platinum....................................$1,400          $1,600          $1,800

HAMILTON, 17J., " Merritt", Ca.1937
gold filled .................................$100          $125          $150

HAMILTON, 19 jewels, "Midas," hidden lugs , c. 1941
14k rose .....................................$250          $300          $375

HAMILTON, 19J.," Milton ", c.1951
gold filled ................................$100          $125          $165

HAMILTON, 17J., "Montclair", 14k #s, c.1961
gold filled..................................$75      $100      $125

HAMILTON, 17J.," Morley ", c.1937
gold filled..................................$90      $125      $150

HAMILTON, 17J., "Mount Vernon", Ca.1932
gold filled..................................$200     $250      $325

HAMILTON, 17J.," Myron ", c.1951
gold filled..................................$90      $125      $150

HAMILTON, 22J., "Newlin", 14k #s, c.1961
gold filled..................................$60      $75       $90

HAMILTON, 17J.," Neil ", c.1951
gold filled ...............................$80        $90       $100

HAMILTON, 17J., "Nelson", Ca.1937
gold filled ...............................$100       $125      $175

HAMILTON, 17J., "Newton", cal.747, Ca.1951
gold filled ...............................$100       $125      $175

HAMILTON, 17J, Norde is 14k, Nordon,18J, is gold filled
14k .......................................$175        $200      $250
gold filled ...............................$75        $100      $125

HAMILTON, 19 jewels, "Norman" , c. 1951
14k .......................................$175        $225      $275
gold filled ...............................$100       $125      $175

HAMILTON, 17J., " Norman", 14k #s, c.1961
gold filled....................................$70      $80      $95

HAMILTON, 17 jewels, "Norfolk"
14k ...........................................$450      $550      $700

HAMILTON, 22J., " Norton", 14k #s, c.1961
gold filled................................$100      $125      $150

HAMILTON, 19 jewels, "Oakmont"
14k ...........................................$450      $550      $700

HAMILTON, 17J., "Orson ", c.1961
gold filled................................$50      $60      $70

HAMILTON,17J., " Pacermatic", auto-wind,14k #s, c.1961
gold filled................................$500      $575      $700

HAMILTON, 19 jewels, "Paige" , c. 1941
gold filled ................................$80      $100      $150

HAMILTON, 22J., " Parker B", 14k #s, c.1961
gold filled ................................$100      $125      $150

HAMILTON, 17 jewels, "Perry"
gold filled ................................$125      $150      $175

HAMILTON, 19J.," Perry ", c.1951
gold filled ................................$85      $100      $135

HAMILTON, 22J., "Peyton ", c.1961
gold filled ................................$60      $70      $80

HAMILTON, 19 jewels, "Pierre" Ca. 1937
14k ...........................................$400      $500      $600

HAMILTON, 17J.," Pinehurst "
14k .............................................$900      $1,000      $1,200

HAMILTON, 17J., " Prentice", c.1961
gold plate ...................................$60      $75      $100

HAMILTON, 17J., "Prescott ", Ca. 1937
gold filled.................................$100      $135      $175

HAMILTON, 17 jewels, "Putnam"
14k ..............................................$400      $450      $525

HAMILTON, 17 jewels, "Putnam"
gold filled..................................$200      $275      $325

HAMILTON, 22J., " Radburn", 14k #s, c.1961
14k ...............................................$175      $200      $225

HAMILTON, 17J.," Raleigh ", Plain
14k ...........................................$300      $350      $425

HAMILTON, 17J.,"Raleigh", Engraved
gold filled.............................$150      $175      $225

HAMILTON, 17J., " Ramsey", c.1961
gold plate ...................................$50      $60      $75

HAMILTON, 17 jewels, "Randolph" , c. 1937
gold filled .................................$90      $125      $155

HAMILTON, 18J., " Randolph", 14k #s, c.1961
14k ........................................$150      $175      $200

HAMILTON, 17 jewels, "Reagan" , c. 1941
gold filled ..................................$90      $125      $155

HAMILTON, 17J., " Richman", 14k #s, Ca.1935
18k ..........................................$300     $350     $450

HAMILTON, 17J., " Robert", Ca.1953
14k ..........................................$250     $300     $400

HAMILTON, 18J., " Rodney", 14k #s, Ca.1961
gold filled....................................$60     $70     $80

HAMILTON, 17J., "Roland", Ca.1937
gold filled..................................$100     $125     $175

HAMILTON, 22J., " Romanesque M", c.1961
14k ..........................................$150     $175     $225

HAMILTON, 17J., "Romanesque N ", c.1961
gold filled..................................$50     $60     $75

HAMILTON, 22J., " Romanesque R", c.1961
gold filled ...................................$50     $60     $75

HAMILTON, 22J., "Romanesque S ", c.1961
gold filled ..................................$75     $80     $100

HAMILTON, 17J., " Romanesque T", c.1961
gold plate.....................................$75     $80     $100

HAMILTON, 19 jewels, "Ross", c. 1941
gold filled ...................................$75     $95     $150

HAMILTON, 17 jewels, "Russell", hinged lugs , c. 1941
gold filled ...............................$125     $150     $175

HAMILTON, 19 jewels, "Rutledge", c. 1941
platinum...................................$700     $800     $1,000

HAMILTON, 17J., " Sawyer", 14k #s, c.1961
gold filled..................................$80      $100      $120

HAMILTON, 17J.," Scott ", GJS, Ca..1935
gold filled..................................$70      $80      $100

HAMILTON, 19J.," Scott ", GJS, 982, Ca.1951
14k ...........................................$300      $400      $500

HAMILTON, 17J., " Sea Breeze", c.1961
gold plate ..................................$60      $70      $80

HAMILTON, 17J., " Seabrook", c.1961
gold plate ..................................$60      $70      $80

HAMILTON, 17J., " Sea-cap ", c.1961
gold plate ..................................$70      $80      $90

HAMILTON, 22J., " Sea Cliff ", 14k #s, c.1961
gold filled ................................$80      $90      $100

HAMILTON, 17J., " Sea - crest", c.1961
s. steel ......................................$40      $50      $65

HAMILTON, 17J., " Sea- glo ", c.1961
s. steel ......................................$50      $60      $75

HAMILTON, 17J., " Sea - guard", c.1962
s. steel ......................................$50      $60      $75

⊕ Some grades are not included. Their values can be
determined by comparing with similar age, size, metal
content, style, grades, or models such as time only,
chronograph, repeater etc. listed.

HAMILTON, 17J., " Sea - mate ", c.1961
gold plate ...................................$60      $80      $100

HAMILTON, 17J., " Sea - skip ", c.1962
s. steel ......................................$60      $70      $80

HAMILTON, 22J., " Sea Ranger " , 14K #s, c.1961
gold filled................................. $80      $90      $100

HAMILTON, 17J., " Seaview ", 14k #s, c.1961
14k ..........................................$125      $150      $175

HAMILTON, 17J., " Sea Rover B ", c.1961
s. steel .....................................$60      $70      $80

HAMILTON, 18J.,"Sectometer B ", c.1951
gold filled ...................................$70      $80      $90

HAMILTON, 17J., " Sea- scape ",  c.1961
gold plate ...................................$60      $70      $80

HAMILTON, 18J.," Sectometer C ", c.1951
14k ...........................................$150      $175      $225

HAMILTON, 17J., " Sea- scout B ", c.1961
s. steel .....................................$70      $80      $90

HAMILTON, 17J., " Sedgman", Ca. 1952
gold filled ...................................$65      $75      $95

HAMILTON, 17 jewels, "Sentinel," hack setting , Ca. 1941
gold filled.................................$100      $120      $140

HAMILTON, 18J., " Seville", c.1961
gold filled..................................$60      $75      $90

HAMILTON, 19J., " Sherwood", Ca.1935
14k ............................................$200      $250      $300

HAMILTON, 22J., " Sherwood M", 14k #s, wood dial,
American walnut wood dial, c.1961
14k ...........................................$500      $600      $900

HAMILTON, 17J., " Sherwood N", 14k #s, wood dial,
Mexican Mahogany wood dial, c.1961
14k .............................................$500      $600      $850

HAMILTON, 22J.," Sherwood R",  dial is made of wood,
(dial is American walnut) c.1961
14k ...........................................$600      $700      $1,000

HAMILTON, 19J.," Sherwood", c.1951
gold filled.................................$90      $100      $150

HAMILTON, 17J.," Sheryll ", small size, c.1951, also
matched styling to the Sherwood, ladies watch
gold filled.................................$80      $90      $125

HAMILTON, 17 jewels, "Sidney" , c. 1941
gold filled.................................$125      $175      $225

HAMILTON, 22J., " Sir Echo" ,14K #s, 6 diamond, c.1961
14k .........................................$225      $250      $300

HAMILTON, 22J., " Sir Echo", 2 diamonds, 14K #s, c.1961
14k ...........................................$200      $225      $250

HAMILTON, 22J., " Sir Echo" , 14K #s, c.1961
14k ...........................................$150      $175      $200

HAMILTON, 17J., "Sloane", c.1961
gold plate ................................. $60      $70      $95

HAMILTON, 17J.," Spencer ", c.1951
10k ........................................ $140      $160      $200

HAMILTON, 22J., " Stafford" , 14K #s, c.1961
14k ........................................ $225      $250      $300

HAMILTON, 18 jewels, "Steeldon", c. 1951
s. steel ..................................... $50      $60      $95

HAMILTON, 17 jewels, "Stanford" , c. 1941
gold filled................................. $90      $100      $135

HAMILTON, 19 jewels, "Stanley"
gold filled ............................. $125      $165      $225

HAMILTON, 18J., " Stormking IV" , 14K #s, c.1961
gold filled ............................... $70      $80      $90

HAMILTON, 18J., " Stormking VI" , c.1961
gold filled ............................... $80      $90      $100

HAMILTON, 18J., " Stormking VII" , c.1961
gold filled ............................... $60      $70      $80

HAMILTON, 18J., " Stormking VIII" , 14K #s, c.1961
10k .......................................... $100      $120      $150

HAMILTON, 17J., " Stormking IX" , 14K #s, c.1961
14k .......................................... $150      $175      $200

HAMILTON, 19J.," Stuart ", c.1951
gold filled.................................$90      $100      $135

HAMILTON, 17-19 jewels, "Sutton" , Ca. 1941
gold filled.................................$125      $165      $200

HAMILTON, 22 jewels, "Sutton II" , Ca. 1961
14k ..........................................$150      $175      $200

HAMILTON, 17J., " Talbot" , Ca.1937
gold filled.................................$90      $120      $165

HAMILTON, 17J., " Talbot" , c.1961
gold filled.................................. $80      $100      $120

HAMILTON, 17J., " Taylor" , Ca.1936
gold filled .............................. $150      $175      $200

HAMILTON, 22J., " Thor" , 14K #s, c.1961
gold filled .............................. $175      $200      $250

HAMILTON, 22J., " Trent" , 14K #s, c.1961
gold filled ................................ $90      $100      $125

HAMILTON, 18J.," Todd ", c.1951
gold filled ............................... $75      $90      $110

HAMILTON, 19 jewels, "Touraine" , c. 1941
14k rose ................................... $200      $245      $295

HAMILTON, 17J., " Turner" , Ca.1937
gold filled ............................... $90      $120      $165

HAMILTON,22J., "Tuxedo B ", 44 diamonds,14K #s,
14k(w)..................................... $350      $400      $525

HAMILTON, 22J., " Tuxedo II", 44 diamonds,14K #s,
14k(w)..................................... $350      $400      $525

HAMILTON, 17J.," Raymon ", c.1951
s. steel ........................................$60      $70      $80

HAMILTON, 17J.," Vardon ", sealed. c.1951
s. steel ........................................$50      $60      $70

HAMILTON, 22J., " Valiant" , 14K #s,c.1961
gold filled................................ $150      $175      $200

HAMILTON, 17J.," " Viking", c.1961
gold plate ................................. $70      $80      $90

HAMILTON, 17J., " Viking II" , c.1961
gold plate ................................. $60      $70      $80

HAMILTON, 17 jewels, "Vincent" , c. 1941
gold filled ...............................$125      $150      $175

HAMILTON, 17 jewels, "Watson", Ca. 1930
gold filled ...............................$100      $125      $175

HAMILTON, 19 jewels, "Wayne", Ca. 1935
14k .............................................$200      $250      $300

HAMILTON, 17 jewels, "Whitford", Ca. 1960
14k .............................................$175      $200      $250

HAMILTON, 17 jewels, "Webster"
gold filled..............................$125     $150     $200

HAMILTON, 19J.," Wesley ", c.1951
14k ............................................$200     $250     $300

HAMILTON, 17 jewels, "Whitman" , c. 1941
gold filled................................$100     $125     $150

HAMILTON, 17 jewels, "Wilson", flared, Ca. 1956
gold filled................................$125     $150     $175

HAMILTON, 17 jewels, "Whitney"
gold filled.....................★ ★ $200     $265     $350

HAMILTON, 19 jewels, "Wilshire" , c. 1941
gold filled ................................$125     $150     $175

HAMILTON, 19 jewels, "Winthrop" , c. 1941
gold filled ................................$100     $125     $150

HAMILTON, 17 jewels, "Yorktown" , c. 1941
gold filled ................................$100     $125     $175

HAMILTON,18J., cal.735 , c.1960
gold filled ................................$100     $125     $165

HAMILTON,18J., cal.748 , c.1950
gold filled ................................$85     $95     $125

HAMILTON,17J., pierced lugs
14k ...........................................$200      $225      $250

Hamilton acquired Buren Watch Factory of
Switzerland in 1966 & adapted a ultra thin
self-winding movement for the Thin-o-matic
series.

HAMILTON, 17 jewels, ''Accumatic X''
s. steel ...........................................$50      $60      $70

HAMILTON, 17 jewels, ''Accumatic XI''
s. steel ...........................................$50      $60      $70

HAMILTON, 17 jewels, ''Accumatic A-575'', date
s. steel ...........................................$50      $60      $75

HAMILTON, 17 jewels, ''Accumatic A-600''
gold plate ...................................$50      $60      $70

HAMILTON, 17 jewels, ''Accumatic A-650''
gold plate ...................................$50      $60      $75

HAMILTON, 17 jewels, ''Accumatic A-651''
gold plate ...................................$50      $60      $75

HAMILTON, 17 jewels, ''Automatic K-203''
14k ...........................................$150      $175      $200

HAMILTON, 17 jewels, ''Automatic K-303''
10k ...........................................$100      $125      $150

HAMILTON, 17 jewels, ''Automatic K-304''
10k ...........................................$100      $125      $150

Hamilton acquired Buren Watch Factory of
Switzerland in 1966 & adapted a ultra thin
self-winding movement for the Thin-o-matic
series.

HAMILTON, 17 jewels, "Automatic **K-414**"
gold filled..................................$60      $75      $95

HAMILTON, 17 jewels, "Accumatic **VII**"
gold plate ..................................$50      $60      $75

HAMILTON, 17 jewels, "Automatic **K-415**"
gold filled..................................$60      $75      $95

HAMILTON, 17 jewels, "Automatic **K-416**"
gold filled..................................$60      $75      $95

HAMILTON, 17 jewels, "**Kinematic II**"
gold plate ..................................$50      $60      $75

HAMILTON, 17 jewels, "Automatic **K-417**"
gold filled ..................................$60      $75      $95

HAMILTON, 17 jewels, "Automatic **K-418**"
gold filled ..................................$60      $75      $95

HAMILTON, 17 jewels, "Automatic **K-419**"
gold filled ..................................$60      $75      $95

HAMILTON, 17 jewels, "Automatic **K-420**"
gold filled ..................................$60      $75      $95

HAMILTON, 17 jewels, "Automatic **K-458**"
gold filled ..................................$60      $75      $95

🕐 Some grades are not included. Their values can be
determined by comparing with **similar** age, size, metal
content, style, grades, or models such as **time only**,
chronograph, repeater etc. listed.

HAMILTON, 17 jewels, "Automatic K-459"
gold filled....................................$60      $75      $95

HAMILTON, 17 jewels, "Automatic K-650"
gold plate ...................................$50      $60      $75

HAMILTON, 17 jewels, "Automatic K-460"
gold filled....................................$60      $75      $95

HAMILTON, 18 jewels, "Thincraft II"
gold filled ..................................$60      $75      $95

HAMILTON, 17 jewels, "Automatic K-475", DATE
gold filled..................................$225      $275      $350

HAMILTON, 17 jewels, "Thinline 2000"
14k ...........................................$125      $150      $185

HAMILTON, 17 jewels, "Automatic K-503" Ca.1962
s. steel .......................................$60      $75      $85

HAMILTON, 17 jewels, "Thinline 2001"
14k ...........................................$125      $150      $185

HAMILTON, 17 jewels, "Automatic K-507"
s. steel .......................................$50      $60      $70

HAMILTON, 17 jewels, "Thinline 3000"
10k ...........................................$100      $125      $150

HAMILTON, 17 jewels, "Thinline **4000**"
gold filled..................................$60    $70    $85

HAMILTON, 17 jewels, "Thinline **4001**"
gold filled..................................$60    $70    $85

HAMILTON, 17 jewels, "Thin-o-matic", **date**
gold plate ..................................$70    $80    $95

HAMILTON, 17 jewels, "Thin-o-matic", **Masterpiece**
14k .........................................$150   $175   $200

HAMILTON, 17 jewels, "Thin-o-matic **T-200**"
14k .........................................$125   $150   $200

HAMILTON, 17 jewels, "Thin-o-matic **T-201**", 6- diamonds
14k .........................................$150   $200   $250

HAMILTON, 17 jewels, "Thin-o-matic **T-201**"
14k .........................................$125   $150   $200

HAMILTON, 17 jewels, "Thin-o-matic **T-202**"
14k .........................................$125   $150   $200

HAMILTON, 17 jewels, "Thin-o-matic **T-300**"
10k .........................................$100   $125   $165

HAMILTON, 17 jewels, "Thin-o-matic **T-400**"
gold filled ..................................$60   $70    $95

HAMILTON, 17 jewels, "Thin-o-matic T-401"
gold filled...............................$90     $100     $125

HAMILTON, 17 jewels, "Thin-o-matic T-450"
gold filled...............................$60     $70     $95

HAMILTON, 17 jewels, "Thin-o-matic T-402"
gold filled...............................$60     $70     $95

HAMILTON, 17 jewels, "Thin-o-matic T-451"
gold filled...............................$60     $70     $95

HAMILTON, 17 jewels, "Thin-o-matic T-403"
gold filled...............................$195     $225     $265

HAMILTON, 17 jewels, "Thin-o-matic T-475"
gold filled...............................$60     $70     $95

HAMILTON, 17 jewels, "Thin-o-matic T-404"
gold filled...............................$60     $70     $95

HAMILTON, 17 jewels, "Thin-o-matic T-476", date
gold filled...............................$70     $80     $100

HAMILTON, 17 jewels, "Thin-o-matic T-405"
gold filled...............................$60     $70     $95

HAMILTON, 17 jewels, "Thin-o-matic T-500"
s. steel.......................................$50     $60     $70

🕐 Some grades are not included. Their values can be
determined by comparing with **similar** age, size, metal
content, style, grades, or models such as **time only**,
chronograph, repeater etc. listed.

HAMILTON, 17 jewels, "Thin-o-matic **T-501"**
s. steel .................................... $50     $60     $70

HAMILTON, 17 jewels, "Thin-o-matic **T-502"**
s. steel ........................................ $50     $60     $70

HAMILTON, 17 jewels, "Thin-o-matic **T-575"** date
s. steel ......................................... $55     $65     $75

HAMILTON, 17 jewels, "Thin-o-matic **T-650"**
gold plate .................................... $50     $60     $70

HAMILTON, 17 jewels, "Thinline **5000"**
s. steel ......................................... $50     $60     $70

HAMILTON, 17 jewels, "Cushion B"
gold filled ................................. $80     $100     $120

HAMILTON, 17 jewels, " Cushion "  plain or engraved
14k .......................................... $225     $250     $275
gold filled ................................. $80     $100     $125

HAMILTON, 17 jewels, tonneau engraved
14k .......................................... $225     $275     $350
gold filled ................................. $85     $100     $125

HAMILTON, 17J.,"Tonneau" plain
14k .......................................... $200     $250     $300
gold filled ................................. $100     $125     $165

HAMILTON, 17J., " Square " cal.986 cut corner
gold filled ................................. $90     $100     $135
14k .......................................... $150     $200     $250

HAMILTON, 17J., Square cut corner, engraved lugs
gold filled ................................. $100      $125      $150

HAMILTON, 17 jewels, 2 tone dial, engraved fancy
14k ........................................... $250      $300      $350
gold filled ................................. $100      $125      $150

HAMILTON, 17 jewels, 2 tone dial, aux. sec.
14k ........................................... $200      $250      $295

HAMILTON, 17J., cal.986, c.1928
gold filled ................................. $90      $100      $135

HAMILTON, 19J., gold jewel settings, cal.982, c.1943
platinum .................................... $700      $800      $1,000

HAMILTON, 17J., cal.987, enamel on case, c.1930
gold filled ................................. $100      $125      $165

HAMILTON, 17J., GJS, Ca.1940
gold filled ................................. $125      $150      $185

HAMILTON, 17J., aux. sec.,
14k ........................................... $225      $250      $275

HAMILTON, 19J., gold seal on movement, cal.982
14k ........................................... $200      $235      $300

HAMILTON, 19J., cal.982, c.1938
14k ........................................... $250      $275      $325

HAMILTON, 17J., curvex style, Ca. 1935
14k ........................................... $225      $250      $350

HAMILTON,17J., cal.980 , c.1938
gold filled.................................$175 $225 $265

HAMILTON,17J., cal.989E , c.1936
gold filled.................................$90 $100 $135

HAMILTON,17J., cal. 989E, c.1938
gold filled.................................$90 $100 $135

HAMILTON, 17 jewels, engraved bezel, hinged back
14k(w).....................................$400 $500 $600

HAMILTON, 22J., "Viscount", cal.770, Ca.1959
14k .........................................$250 $300 $350

HAMILTON, 17J., cal. 980, Ca.1937
gold filled.................................$125 $150 $185

HAMILTON, 17J., Ca.1950
gold filled .................................$125 $150 $185

HAMILTON, 17 jewels, hidden lugs
14k ........................................$325 $375 $425

HAMILTON, 17 jewels, long lugs
14k .........................................$225 $250 $285

HAMILTON, 17 jewels, engraved bezel, c. 1920
14k .........................................$300 $350 $400

HAMILTON, 17 jewels, "Hamilton Illinois" on dial
gold filled .................................$100 $150 $175

HAMILTON, 19 jewels
platinum..................................$650      $750      $850

HAMILTON, 19 jewels
platinum C&B.....................$1,100      $1,200      $1,300

HAMILTON, 19 jewels, applied numbers
platinum...................................$700      $800      $1,000

HAMILTON, 17J., cal.987, Ca.1932
gold filled................................$100      $125      $150

HAMILTON, 19J.,"bomb timer", c.1944
base metal ...............................$300      $350      $400

HAMILTON, 15 J., military frogman style, waterproof
(USN BU SHIPS on dial), canteen  style
s. steel....................................$275      $350      $450

HAMILTON, 21 J., military  issue, hack setting, c.1960s
base metal................................$75      $80      $95

HAMILTON, 17-19 jewels, top hat, diamond dial
14k .........................................$700      $800      $1,000

HAMILTON, 17-19 jewels, Top Hat, diamond dial
14k...........................................$700      $800      $950

HAMILTON, 17-19 jewels, diamond dial, hooded lugs
14k .............................$700     $800     $900

HAMILTON, 17-19 jewels, diamond dial
14k(w).............................$700     $800     $900

HAMILTON, 17-19 jewels, diamond dial , curved
14k .............................$1,000     $1,100     $1,250

HAMILTON, 17-19 jewels, diamond dial, c. 1940
14k .............................$1,000     $1,100     $1,250

HAMILTON, 17-19 jewels, diamond dial
14k .............................$600     $700     $800

HAMILTON, 17-19 jewels, diamond dial, hooded lugs
14k .............................$800     $900     $1,000

HAMILTON, 17-19 jewels,diamond dial
14k.............................$800     $900     $1,000

HAMILTON, 17-19 jewels, diam. dial, c.1948, top hat
platinum .............................$1,200     $1,300     $1,400
14k (w).............................$1,100     $1,200     $1,300

HAMILTON, 17-19 jewels, diamond dial
14k (w).............................$600     $700     $800

HAMILTON, 17-19 jewels, diamond dial, hooded lugs
14k.............................$600     $700     $800

HAMILTON, 17-19 jewels, diamond dial
platinum .............................$1,100     $1,200     $1,300
14k (w).............................$900     $1,000     $1,100

HAMILTON, 17-19J., mystery dial with diamonds & **bezel**
18k ............................................$550      $650      $800
14k ............................................$450      $550      $650

HAMILTON, 17-19 jewels, diamond dial
14k .........................................$300      $350      $400

HAMILTON, 17-19 jewels, diamond dial
14k (w)....................................$300      $350      $400

HAMILTON, 19 jewels, diamond dial, fancy *knoted* lugs
14k (w)...................................$300      $350      $400

HAMILTON,17J., " Belmont ", cal.955 , c.1933
gold filled................................$30      $40      $50

HAMILTON,17J., " Ladies Tonneau "cal.987 , c.1933
gold filled..............................$40      $50      $60

HAMILTON,17J., "Bianca", diamond & sapphire, c.1933
18k(w)...................................$150      $175      $250

HAMILTON,17J., " Bryn Mawr ", c.1933
14k...........................................$60      $80      $100

HAMILTON,17J., " Briarcliffe ",  c.1933
gold filled................................$30      $40      $50

HAMILTON,17J., " Caroline ", cal.955, c.1933
gold filled................................$20      $30      $40

HAMILTON,17J., " Cedarcrest ", cal.955, c.1933
14k...........................................$50      $60      $70

HAMILTON,17J., " Chevy Chase A ", cal. , c.1933
14k(w).....................................$60      $70      $85

HAMILTON,17J., " Chevy Chase B ", cal.989 , c.1933
14k ...........................................$70       $80        $90

HAMILTON,17J., " Chevy Chase C ", cal. , c.1933
14k(w).......................................$60        $70        $80

HAMILTON,17J., " Chevy Chase E ", c.1933
14k(w).......................................$70        $80        $90

HAMILTON,17J., " Diane ", c.1933
14k .........................................$60        $70        $85

HAMILTON,17J., " Drexel ", cal.955 , c.1933
14k .........................................$70        $95       $135

HAMILTON,17J., " Edgewood ", c.1933
gold filled.................................$30        $40        $45

HAMILTON,17J., " Eugenie ", 44 diamonds,  c.1933
platinum..................................$350       $400       $550

HAMILTON,17J., " Glenwood ", cal.955, c.1933
gold filled.................................$30        $40        $50

HAMILTON,17J., " Linden Hall ", c.1933
gold filled.................................$30        $40        $50

HAMILTON,17J.," Maritza ", 8 diamonds, cal.955 , c.1933
18k(w)......................................$95       $125       $150

HAMILTON,17J., " Mayfield ", cal.955 , c.1933
gold filled.................................$40        $45        $60

HAMILTON,17J., " Newcomb ", cal.989, c.1933
gold filled.................................$40        $45        $60

HAMILTON,17J., " Nightingale ", 40 diamonds, c.1933
18k(w)......................................$300       $350       $450

HAMILTON,17J., " Portia ", 8 diamonds, c.1933
18k(w)......................................$200       $250       $350

HAMILTON,17J., " Trudy ", c.1948
14k..........................................$75       $100       $135

**Grade 986A, 6/0 size**
Open face, ¾ plate movt., 17 jewels, double roller

**Grade 987, 6/0 size**
Hunting, ¾ plate movt., 17 jewels, double roller

**Grade 987A, 6/0 size**
Open face, ¾ plate movt., 17 jewels, double roller

**Grade 987S, 6/0 size**
Hunting, ¾ plate movt., 17 jewels, double roller

**Grade 747, 8/0 size**
Open face, ¾ plate movt., 17 jewels, double roller

**Grade 980, 14/0 size**
Open face, ¾ plate movt., 17 jewels, double roller

**Grade 982, 14/0 size**
Open face, ¾ plate movt., 19 jewels, double roller

**Grade 982M, 14/0 size**
Open face, ¾ plate movt., 19 jewels, double roller

**Grade 989, 18/0 size**
Open face, ¾ plate movt., 17 jewels, double roller

**Grade 997, 20/0 size**
Open face, ¾ plate movt., 17 jewels, double roller

**Grade 721, 21/0 size**
Open face, ¾ plate movt., 17 jewels, double roller

**Grade 995, 21/0 size**
Open face, ¾ plate movt., 17 jewels, double roller

**Grade 911, 22/0 size**
Open face, ¾ plate movt., 17 jewels, double roller

**Grade 911M, 22/0 size**
Open face, ¾ plate movt., 17 jewels, double roller

**Grade 780, 21/0 size**
17 jewels

**Grade 770, 12/0 size**
22 jewels

**Grade 761, 21/0 size**
22 jewels

**Grade 757, 21/0 size**
22 jewels

**Grade 753, 12/0 size, 19 jewels**
**Grade 752, 12/0 size, 17 jewels**

**Grade 754, 12/0 size, 19 jewels**
**Grade 770, 12/0 size, 17 jewels**

**Grade 750 & 751, 21/0 size**
17 jewels

**Grade 748, 8/0 size**
18 jewels

**Grade 747, 8/0 size**
17 jewels

## LIGNE GAUGE

**Grade 735, 8/0 size**
18 jewels

**Grade 730, 8/0 size**
17 jewels

**Grade 679**, 17 jewels
**Grade 692, 694 - calendar**

**Grade 666 & 663**, 17 jewels
**Grade 668** - calendar

**Grade 658, 661, 667**, 17 jewels
**Grade 665, 23J, Grade 664, 25J**
**Grade 662, 690** - calendar, 17J

**Grade 623 & 624**, 17 jewels

**Grade 505**, electric, 11 jewels

☞ **Note: Hamilton acquired Buren Watch Factory of Switzerland in 1966 and adapted a ultra thin self-winding movement for the " THIN-O-MATIC " series.**

HAMPDEN, 15J., engraved case, c.1925
gold filled................................$100    $125    $150

HAMPDEN, 17J., art deco style, c. 1936
14k ..........................................$150    $175    $200

HAMPDEN, 17J., by Lonville W. Co., c. 1936
gold filled................................$100    $125    $175

HAMPDEN, 17 jewels, double dial, c. 1930
gold filled................................$175    $225    $275

HAMPDEN, 15 jewels, c. 1928
14k ..........................................$175    $200    $250
gold filled................................$60     $70     $80

⊕ Some grades are not included. Their values can be
determined by comparing with similar age, size, metal
content, style, grades, or models such as time only,
chronograph, repeater etc. listed.

HAMPDEN,11J., "LEVER SET" , 3/0 size, c.1928
silver......................................$200    $250    $300

HAMPDEN, 15 jewels, c. 1928
14k ..........................................$175    $200    $225
gold filled................................$50     $60     $70

HAMPDEN, 11J., Molly Stark, c. 1928
base metal................................$60     $70     $80

HAMPDEN, 7J., tonneau shaped, c. 1928
gold filled................................$40     $60     $70

HARMAN,7J.,doctor style duo-dial,
gold filled................................$450    $500    $550

HARMAN,17J.,one button chronog., mid size, c.1940s
s. steel .......................................$250      $300      $350

HARVARD, 17 jewels, chronog., tach-telemeter
s. steel .......................................$250      $300      $350

HARVARD, 17 jewels, 1/5 sec. chronog.
s. steel .......................................$275      $300      $375

HARVEL, 17 jewels, date-o-graph
s. steel .......................................$125      $150      $175

🕐 Some grades are not included. Their values can be
determined by comparing with **similar** age, size, metal
content, style, grades, or models such as **time only**,
chronograph, repeater etc. listed.

HARVEL, 17J.,center sec.
gold filled...................................$20      $30      $45

HARWOOD, 15 jewels, early self winding, c. 1928
18k (w)......................................$700      $800      $900
14k...........................................$600      $650      $700
gold filled................................$300      $350      $400
s. steel....................................$200      $250      $300

HARWOOD, 15 J., rim set by turning bezel clockwise
9k.............................................$500      $550      $600

HARWOOD, 15 jewels, back set, c. 1925
18k............................................$500      $600      $700

HASTE, 17J., triple calendar moon ph.
gold filled...............................$200      $250      $300

HAYDEN, 7J., by Solomax W.Co., hinged case
gold filled..................................$60     $70     $85

HEBDOMAS, 7 J., visible escapement, 8 day movement
s. steel ......................................$400     $500     $600

HELBROS, 17 jewels, aux.sec., alarm
gold filled..............................$100     $125     $150

HELBROS, 7 jewels, fancy bezel, curvex
gold filled..............................$100     $120     $140

HELBROS, 7 jewels, aux. sec., ca. 1962
gold filled..................................$40     $50     $65

HELBROS, 17 jewels, aux. sec.
gold filled..............................$40     $50     $65

HELBROS, 17 jewels,
14k............................................$175     $200     $225

HELBROS, 7J., " Falcon ", c. 1929
base metal..............................$40     $50     $65

HELBROS, 7J., " Fairfax ", c. 1929
base metal................................$40     $50     $65

HELBROS, 7J., " Federal ", c. 1929
base metal................................$40     $50     $65

HELBROS, 7J., " Filmore ", c. 1929
base metal..................................$40     $50     $65

HELBROS, 7J., " Fletcher ", c. 1929
base metal ................................$40    $50    $65

HELBROS, 7J., " Franklin ", c. 1929
base metal................................$40    $50    $65

HELBROS, 7J., " Flint ", c. 1929
gold plate ................................$50    $60    $75

HELBROS, 7J., " Frigate ", c. 1929
base metal................................$40    $50    $65

HELBROS, 7J., " Forbes ", c. 1929
base metal ................................$40    $50    $65

HELBROS, 7J., " Fulton ", c. 1929
base metal................................$40    $50    $65

HELBROS, 7J., " Forrest ", c. 1929
base metal ................................$40    $50    $65

HELBROS, 17J., 24 hour dial
base metal................................$50    $60    $75

HELBROS, 7J., " Fortress ", c. 1929
gold plate ................................$40    $50    $65

HENDA, 15J., direct read, c. 1930
nickel ........................................$250    $300    $350

HERMES, 17J., big wire lugs, enamel dial
14k ............................................ $350      $400      $450

HELVETIA, 15 jewels, Ca. 1935
9k ............................................ $100      $125      $150

HELVETIA, 21 jewels, auto wind
gold filled ................................ $30      $40      $50

HEUER, 15 jewels, chronog., 2 reg., one button,
14k ...................................... $1,000      $1,300      $1,600

HEUER, 17J., chronog., 3 reg., 3 dates, moon phase
18k ................................... $1,500      $1,800      $2,200
s. steel ................................ $600      $700      $900

HEUER, 17 J., chronog., 3 reg., "Carrera, c.1960
s. steel .................................. $250      $300      $375

HEUER, 17 jewels, chronog., 3 dates, 3 reg. c.1948
14k ..................................... $500      $650      $800
s. steel ................................ $300      $350      $400

HEUER, 17 jewels, "Carrera," chronog., 2 reg., c.1960s
14k ..................................... $400      $500      $550
s. steel ................................ $200      $250      $325

🕐 Some grades are not included. Their values can be
determined by comparing with **similar** age, size, metal
content, style, grades, or models such as **time only**,
chronograph, repeater etc. listed.

HEUER,17J., " Seafarer ", by Valjoux # 72, c. 1972
14k .......................................$650      $700      $850
s. steel .....................................$400      $450      $500

HEUER,17J., " Monaco ", date, c. 1974
base metal...............................$150      $175      $200

HEUER,17J., "Camro ", by Valjoux #7730, c. 1965
14k .........................................$350      $450      $475
s. steel .....................................$100      $150      $200

HEUER,17J., **TAG**, split sec., date, 600 ft., gold & s. steel,
sold new for $1,895.00 in Ca.1991
14k.........................................$800      $900      $1,000
s. steel & 14k .......................$600      $700      $850

HEUER,17J., " Autavia ", cal.72, micro rotor, c. 1972
s. steel .....................................$100      $125      $150

HEUER, 17 jewels, day-date-month, moon phase
s. steel...................................$275      $325      $375

🕐 Some grades are not included. Their values can be
determined by comparing with **similar** age, size, metal
content, style, grades, or models such as **time only**,
chronograph, repeater etc. listed.

HEUER, 17 jewels, day-date-month
14k...........................................$500      $600      $700
s. steel.....................................$125      $150      $175

HILTON W. Co.,17J., chronog. by Venius W.Co.
18k ..........................................$375    $450    $500

HIRCO, 17J., center sec. auto-w.
gold filled..................................$30    $40    $50

HOWARD, 17J. engraved on movement, (Howard
Watch USA, Lancaster, PA, HW138, 17J. H980)

🕐 ..(see HAMILTON W. CO.)

E. HUGUENIN, 17 jewels, "Black Star," c. 1940
14k ..........................................$500    $600    $700

🕐 Some grades are not included. Their values can be
determined by comparing with similar age, size, metal
content, style, grades, or models such as time only,
chronograph, repeater etc. listed.

HUGEX, 17J., chronog., 2 reg.
gold filled ..............................$150    $175    $225

HYDEPARK, 17 jewels, flip up top
14k ..........................................$400    $500    $600

ILLINOIS, 17J., **Aluminum** case & band, direct read
Aluminum........ ★★★★★ $2,000    $2,200    $2,500

ILLINOIS, 15J., " Arlington", C. 1920s
gold filled ..............................$175    $200    $250

ILLINOIS, 17J., "Ardsley "
gold filled ..............................$150    $175    $200

ILLINOIS, 17 jewels, "Aviator"
gold filled................................$175    $225    $275

ILLINOIS, 17J., " Beau Monde ",  RF#212, c.1929
gold filled ..............................$225    $275    $350

ILLINOIS, 21J., " BARONET ", GJS, cal.601, c.1925
gold filled................................$400    $450    $500

ILLINOIS, 15J., "Beau Royal "
gold filled ..............................$225    $275    $350

ILLINOIS, 19J., " Beau Brummel"
18k ..........................................$600    $700    $850

ILLINOIS, 17J., ". Blackstone"
gold filled ..............................$125    $150    $195

ILLINOIS, 19 jewels, "Beau Brummel"
gold filled................................$250    $275    $375

ILLINOIS, 15J., " Bostonian "
gold filled ..............................$125    $150    $195

ILLINOIS, 17J., " Beau Brummel ", c.1929
gold filled................................$200    $250    $365

ILLINOIS, 17J., " Cavalier "
gold filled ............................$195    $235    $295

ILLINOIS, 17 jewels, "Champion"
gold filled..............................$150        $175        $250

ILLINOIS, 19 jewels, "Consul"
14k .........................................$350        $450        $575

ILLINOIS, 15 jewels, "Chatham"
gold filled..............................$150        $175        $225

ILLINOIS, 21 jewels, "Consul"
14k .........................................$350        $425        $575

ILLINOIS, 17J., " The  Chief's", chased bezel
gold filled (w).......................$185        $225        $275

ILLINOIS, 17J., " Derby "
gold filled ..............................$125        $150        $200

ILLINOIS, 17 jewels, "Chieftain"
gold filled..............................$350        $450        $575

ILLINOIS, 15 jewels,  "Ensign"
gold filled ..............................$225        $300        $395

ILLINOIS, 17J., " Commodore "
gold filled..............................$125        $150        $185

ILLINOIS, 15 jewels, "Ensign"
gold filled ..............................$225        $300        $395

ILLINOIS, 17J., " Fontenac "
gold filled................................$175      $200      $250

ILLINOIS, 17J., " Finalist "
gold filled................................$225      $250      $275

ILLINOIS, 17J., " Futura "
gold filled................................$200      $225      $250

ILLINOIS, 17J., " Guardsman ", plain, rotor second dial
gold filled............................$350      $400      $450

ILLINOIS, 17J., "Guardsman ", engraved, cal.307, c.1929
gold filled................................$350      $400      $450

ILLINOIS, 17 jewels, "Jolly Roger"
gold filled ...............................$300      $400      $550

ILLINOIS, 17J., " Kenilworth "
gold filled ...............................$175      $225      $275

ILLINOIS, 19 jewels, "Major"
gold filled ...............................$250      $325      $400

ILLINOIS, 17 jewels, "Major",
gold filled ...............................$250      $325      $400

ILLINOIS, 17 jewels, "Major"
gold filled ...............................$250      $325      $400

ILLINOIS, 17-21J., "Manhattan", aux. sec. at 9
14k ........................................$300   $375   $475

ILLINOIS, 17-21 jewels, "New Yorker", aux. sec. at 9
gold filled................................$200   $235   $300

ILLINOIS, 17-21J., "Manhattan", aux. sec. at 6
14k ........................................$300   $375   $475

ILLINOIS, 17-21 jewels, "New Yorker", aux. sec. at 6
gold filled................................$200   $235   $300

ILLINOIS, 19 jewels, "Marquis", engraved, curved case
gold filled................................$250   $300   $375

ILLINOIS, 17J., "Marquis", plain, curved case
gold filled................................$200   $235   $350

ILLINOIS, 17J., "Mate", engraved
gold filled................................$175   $200   $275

ILLINOIS, 17J., "Mate", plain
gold filled................................$150   $175   $225

ILLINOIS, 17J., engraved case in Maxine, plain, ladies
gold filled................................$100   $125   $150

ILLINOIS, 17 jewels, "Maxine", wire lugs, ladies
14k ........................................$150   $175   $200

ILLINOIS, 17J., " Medalist ", curved back, c.1929
gold filled................................$150    $175    $250

ILLINOIS, 17 jewels, "Piccadilly" in white or yellow G.F.
came with Luminous or Modern as a option
gold filled plain.......................$650    $750    $900
gold filled engraved...............$750    $875    $1,100

ILLINOIS, 17 jewels, "Pilot"
gold filled................................$200    $250    $300

ILLINOIS, 17 jewels, "Prince"
gold filled................................$175    $200    $225

ILLINOIS, 17J., "Ritz", white bezel & yellow center case
also called "Valedictorian"
gold filled................................$375    $450    $550

ILLINOIS, 15 jewels, "Rockingham"
gold filled................................$200    $250    $325

ILLINOIS, 17J., " Rockliffe ", cal.805, c.1925
14k............................................$350    $400    $495

ILLINOIS, 15 jewels, "Sangamo"
gold filled................................$100    $150    $200

ILLINOIS, 17J., " Skyway ", engraved case, G#307
gold filled................................$350    $475    $550

ILLINOIS, 17J., " Special ", c.1929
silver.........................................$250    $300    $450

ILLINOIS, 17 jewels, "Speedway"
gold filled...............................$225　　$275　　$375

ILLINOIS, 15 jewels, "Standish"
gold filled...............................$150　　$195　　$250

ILLINOIS, 17J., " Sterling ", direct read, c.1929
sterling silver .........................$200　　$225　　$325

ILLINOIS, 17J., " Townsman ", carved case
gold filled...............................$150　　$175　　$225

ILLINOIS, 17J., " Trophy "
gold filled...............................$100　　$125　　$175

ILLINOIS, 15 jewels, "Urbana"
gold filled............................$125　　$150　　$200

ILLINOIS, 17J., " Viking "
gold filled..............................$200　　$250　　$300

ILLINOIS, 17J., engraved side of case
base metal...............................$100　　$135　　$175

ILLINOIS, 17 jewels, engraved bezel, grade 807, c. 1920
14k .........................................$300　　$350　　$450

ILLINOIS, 17 jewels, "Off Duty", stars on bezel, Ca. 1927
gold filled ..............................$175　　$200　　$250

ILLINOIS, 15J., "Bennett", aux. sec. at 9 o'clock, c. 1925
gold filled................................$150     $195     $275

ILLINOIS, 19 jewels, aux. sec at 9
14k(W).....................................$400     $450     $550

ILLINOIS, 17 jewels, hand engraved, wire lugs
14k (W)...................................$150     $200     $250

ILLINOIS, 17J., maxine style, hand engraved, wire lugs,
14k (W)...................................$150     $200     $250

ILLINOIS, 15J., seconds at "9" c.1929
gold filled................................$200     $250     $300

ILLINOIS, 17J., engraved case, c.1929
gold filled ..............................$150     $200     $275

ILLINOIS, 17J., art deco, cal.207, c.1925
gold filled ..............................$135     $175     $250

ILLINOIS, 17J., double hinged, GJS, c.1929
gold filled ..............................$150     $175     $250

ILLINOIS, 15J., contract case, gold train, c.1929
14k ..........................................$100     $125     $175

ILLINOIS, 17J., engraved bezel, Ca.1929
gold filled ..............................$150     $175     $225

ILLINOIS, 17J., Shock-Proof Model,
nickel.........................................$100    $125    $175

ILLINOIS, 17J., engraved case
gold filled.................................$125    $150    $200

ILLINOIS, 15J.,engraved bezel, GJS, c.1926
14k (w)....................................$275    $300    $350

ILLINOIS, 15J., **winds at 12:00 o'clock**
silver .......................................$250    $300    $400

ILLINOIS, 15-17J., lady's watch, black enamel on bezel
14k ..........................................$100    $120    $140
gold filled.................................$30    $40    $50

ILLINOIS, 15J., " Antoinette ", c.1929
gold filled.................................$50    $60    $75

ILLINOIS, 17J., " Babette ", c.1929
14k ..........................................$80    $90    $120

ILLINOIS, 17J., " Bar Harbor ", c.1929
14k ..........................................$85    $95    $130

ILLINOIS, 17J., " Beverly=14k, Biloxi=gold filled ",c.1929
14k ..........................................$80    $90    $120
gold filled.................................$50    $60    $85

ILLINOIS, 17J., " Coronado ", black enamel, c.1929
14k ..........................................$85    $95    $110

ILLINOIS, 17J., " Daytona ", c.1929
14k ..........................................$90    $100    $110

ILLINOIS, 17J., " Debette ", c.1929
gold filled.................................$55    $65    $75

ILLINOIS, 17J., " Del Monte ", c.1929
gold filled.................................$55    $60    $75

ILLINOIS, 17J., " Eliza ", c.1929
gold filled.................................$65   $75   $90

ILLINOIS, 17J., " Long Beach ", c.1929
gold filled.................................$55   $65   $80

ILLINOIS, 17J., " Lynette ", c.1929
gold filled.................................$50   $60   $75

ILLINOIS, 17J., " Mariette ", c.1929
gold filled.................................$50   $60   $75

ILLINOIS, 17J., " Marionette ", c.1929
gold filled.................................$50   $60   $75

ILLINOIS, 17J., " Marlette ", c.1929
gold filled.................................$50   $60   $75

ILLINOIS, 16J., " Mary Todd ", c.1929
18k(w).................................$150   $200   $250

ILLINOIS, 16J., " Mary Todd ", black enamel bezel, c.1929
18k(w).................................$150   $200   $250

ILLINOIS, 16J., " Mary Todd ", c.1929
18k .................................$150   $200   $250

ILLINOIS, 17J., " Mateel ", c.1929
14k(w).................................$90   $100   $140

ILLINOIS, 17J., " Miami ", c.1929
gold filled .................................$55   $65   $85

ILLINOIS, 17J., " Narragansett ", c.1929
14k .................................$85   $95   $110

ILLINOIS, 17J., " Newport ", engraved case, c.1929
gold filled .................................$55   $65   $80

ILLINOIS, 16J., " Queen Wilhelmina ", 22 diamonds and
8 synthetic sapphires
18k(w).................................$200   $275   $350

ILLINOIS, rectangular, Grade 207,17 jewels

ILLINOIS, rectangular, 1st, 2nd & 3rd model

ILLINOIS, Model #4, 3/0 size, bridge, hunting,movement.

IMPERIAL,17J.,fancy lugs
14k(W) .....................................$250      $300      $350

IMPERIAL, 17J., center sec.
s. steel .......................................$30      $40      $55

⊕ Some grades are not included. Their values can be
determined by comparing with similar age, size, metal
content, style, grades, or models such as time only,
chronograph, repeater etc. listed.

INGERSOLL, 2 J.," Rist-Arch",  stepped case
base metal .................................$20      $30      $45

INGERSOLL, "Swagger",
base metal .................................$20      $25      $35

INGERSOLL, 7 jewels
base metal .................................$10      $15      $25

INGERSOLL, 7 jewels, radiolite dial wire lugs
W/ original band .....................$30      $40      $55
base metal .................................$15      $20      $35

INGERSOLL, 7 J., military style, **protective grill cover
wire lugs, all original band and cover**
base metal ...............................$50      $75      $125

INGRAHAM, 7 jewels, "Wristfit"
base metal ..................................... $5      $10     $15

INTERNATIONAL W. CO., 17 jewels, c. 1925
18k ............................................. $400    $500    $600

INTERNATIONAL W. CO., 16J., enamel dial, c. 1920
silver ........................................ $300    $350    $400

INTERNATIONAL W. CO., 17 jewels
14k ............................................. $400    $500    $600

INTERNATIONAL W. CO., 16J., cal.53, c. 1920
18k .......................................... $400    $450    $500

INTERNATIONAL W. CO., 21 J., center sec., c. 1920
18k .......................................... $600    $700    $800

INTERNATIONAL W. CO., 17 jewels, c. 1920
18k ............................................. $400    $500    $600

INTERNATIONAL W. CO., 17J., "Art Deco", Ca. 1955
TU-TONE case w/ enamel on bezel
18k ............................................. $800    $900   $1,100

INTERNATIONAL W. CO., **17 jewels, curved**
**14k**.............................................**$800**   **$900**  **$1,000**

INTERNATIONAL W. CO., 17 jewels
14k C&B................................. $700    $800    $900

INTERNATIONAL W. CO., 17 jewels, c. 1940
18k .................................$500      $600      $700

INTERNATIONAL W. CO., 17J., c. 1946
18k .................................$300      $400      $450

INTERNATIONAL W. CO., 17J., c. 1945
14k .................................$350      $400      $450

INTERNATIONAL W. CO., 17J., tank style, c. 1937
18k .................................$600      $700      $800

INTERNATIONAL W. CO., 17J., Tiffany on dial, c. 1942
14k .................................$600      $650      $700

INTERNATIONAL W. CO., 17J., c. 1926
s. steel .................................$300      $400      $450

INTERNATIONAL W. CO., 17 jewels, hidden lugs
14k .................................$700      $800      $900

INTERNATIONAL W. CO., 17 J., on dial "Yard"
18k .................................$1,000      $1,200      $1,400

INTERNATIONAL W. CO., 17J., aux. sec.
14k .................................$400      $500      $600

🕐 Some grades are not included. Their values can be determined by comparing with similar age, size, metal content, style, grades, or models such as time only, chronograph, repeater etc. listed.

INTERNATIONAL W. CO., 17 J., curved, on dial, "Yard"
platinum .................................$1,800      $2,000      $2,200

INTERNATIONAL W. CO., 17 jewels, hinged back
14k ..........................................$600    $700    $800

INTERNATIONAL W. CO., 17 jewels, curved
14k ..........................................$700    $800    $900

INTERNATIONAL W. CO., 17J, date, auto-wind, waterproof
18k ......................................$1,000    $1,200    $1,400

INTERNATIONAL W. CO., 21 jewels, auto wind, date
18k ...........................................$900    $1,000    $1,200

INTERNATIONAL W. CO., 17 jewels, center sec.
18k ..........................................$600    $700    $800

INTERNATIONAL W. CO., 17 jewels, center sec.
18k ..........................................$600    $700    $800

INTERNATIONAL W. CO., 17J., cen. sec., date,
platinum..............................$1,400    $1,600    $1,800

INTERNATIONAL W. CO.,17J., RF# 802a, cal.8541, c.1920
s. steel .....................................$300    $350    $400

INTERNATIONAL W. CO., 21J., "Ingeneur",  date, c.1976
non-magnetic................... ★ $400    $500    $650

🕐 Some grades are not included. Their values can be
determined by comparing with similar age, size, metal
content, style, grades, or models such as time only,
chronograph, repeater etc. listed.

INTERNATIONAL W. CO., 21J., date, c. 1960
18k ...........................................$900    $1,000    $1,100

INTERNATIONAL W. CO., 17J., center sec.cal.89, c.1957
18k ...........................................$500    $600    $700

INTERNATIONAL W. CO., 21J., cal.853, c. 1961
18k ...........................................$600    $700    $800

INTERNATIONAL W. CO., 17J., wide lugs, c. 1960
18k ...........................................$600    $700    $800

INTERNATIONAL W. CO.,17J.,fancy lugs,cal.C89, c.1952
18k ...........................................$700    $800    $900

INTERNATIONAL W. CO., 21J., cal.C852, c. 1952
18k ...........................................$600    $700    $800

INTERNATIONAL W. CO., 21J., cal.853, c. 1958
18k ...........................................$600    $700    $800

INTERNATIONAL W. CO., 17J., cal.89, c. 1962
s. steel ...................................$300    $350    $400

INTERNATIONAL W. CO., 17J., ca.1960s
18k C & B ...........................$1,100     $1,200     $1,400

INTERNATIONAL W. CO., 17J., auto wind,  Ca. 1960
18k...........................................$800     $700     $850

INTERNATIONAL W. CO., 17J., center sec.
18k ........................................$800     $900     $1,000

INTERNATIONAL W. CO., 17 jewels, center sec.
18k...........................................$600     $700     $800

INTERNATIONAL W. CO., 17J., fancy lugs, cen. sec.
18k ...........................................$700     $800     $900

INTERNATIONAL W. CO., 17 jewels, center sec., cal.402
18k...........................................$600     $700     $800

INTERNATIONAL W. Co., 18 jewels, center sec.
18k ...........................................$600     $700     $800

INTERNATIONAL W. CO., 17 jewels, center sec., cal. 89
18k...........................................$600     $700     $800

🕐 Some grades are not included. Their values can be
determined by comparing with **similar** age, size, metal
content, style, grades, or models such as **time only**,
chronograph, repeater etc. listed.

INTERNATIONAL W. CO., 17 jewels, center sec., cal.89
14k ...........................................$450      $500      $600

INTERNATIONAL W. CO., 17J, for Royal Navy, ca.1950
s. steel....................................$400      $500      $600

INTERNATIONAL W. CO., 36J., "Da Vinci," chronog.
auto wind, triple date, moon ph., center lugs
18k .........................................$7,500      $8,500      $9,500

INTERNATIONAL W. CO., 17J., winds at 12 o'clock
s. steel....................................$500      $600      $650

INTERNATIONAL W. CO., 17 jewels, c. 1953
18k.........................................$500      $600      $700

INTERNATIONAL W. CO., 17 jewels, aux. sec.
18k.........................................$600      $700      $800

INTERNATIONAL W. CO., "Porsche Design", date, auto-
wind, compass, sapphire mirror, RF#3510-LMW, Ca.1988
Titanium...................................$700      $800      $950

INTERNATIONAL W. CO., 17 jewels, c. 1948
18k ............................................$600    $700    $800

INTERNATIONAL W. CO., 17J.,date, 30 ATM=1,000 ft.
s. steel ......................................$300    $400    $450

INTERNATIONAL W. CO., 17J., aux sec., cal.83, c.1938
14k ............................................$500    $550    $600

INTERNATIONAL W. CO., 17J., ca.1940s
18k............................................$500    $600    $750

INTERNATIONAL W. CO., 17J., aux. sec., cal., c.1948
s. steel ......................................$275    $300    $350

INTERNATIONAL W. CO., 15J., cal. 83, ca.1945
14k............................................$400    $450    $500

INTERNATIONAL W. CO., 17J., cal.461, c.1962
18k ............................................$600    $700    $800

INTERNATIONAL W. CO., 21J., cal.44, mid-size, ca.1962
18k............................................$400    $450    $500

INTERNATIONAL W. CO., 17J., 36 small diamonds
platinum ...................................$600    $700    $800

# INTERNATIONAL WATCH CO.
## MOVEMENT IDENTIFICATION

Caliber 51N

Caliber 51

Caliber 41

Caliber 93, Baguette

Caliber 92

Caliber 431

Caliber 91

Caliber 90

Caliber 96

Caliber 94

Caliber 84

Caliber 44

Caliber 85

Caliber 852
Calendar - 8521

Caliber 853
Calendar - 8531

Caliber 401

Caliber 60

Caliber 62

Caliber 61

Caliber 86

Caliber 75 & 76

Caliber 87

Caliber 89

Caliber 88

Caliber 70

Caliber 83

Caliber 64

Caliber 63

Caliber 64

INVICTA, 15 jewels, chronog., min. reg. at 6 o'clock,
decimal aperture for sec. at 12 o'clock
18k ........................................ $5,000   $6,000   $7,500

INVICTA, 17 jewels, date, center sec.
18k ........................................ $200   $250   $300
s. steel .................................. $50   $75   $100

INVICTA, 17 jewels, day-date, waterproof
18k ........................................ $150   $175   $225
s. steel .................................. $60   $70   $80

INVICTA, 17 jewels, day-date-month
18k ........................................ $200   $250   $300
s. steel .................................. $70   $80   $95

🕐 Some grades are not included. Their values can be
determined by comparing with **similar** age, size, metal
content, style, grades, or models such as **time only**,
chronograph, repeater etc. listed.

INVICTA, 17 jewels, day-date-month, moon phase
18k ........................................ $350   $400   $450
s. steel .................................. $100   $120   $140

INVICTA, 17 jewels, waterproof
18k ........................................ $150   $200   $250
s. steel .................................. $40   $50   $60

INVICTA, 17 jewels, auto wind, waterproof
18k ........................................ $150   $200   $250
s. steel .................................. $50   $60   $70

JAEGER W. CO., 17J., RF#5184, chronog., Ca.1942
s.steel .................................... $500   $600   $700

JAEGER W. CO., 15J., duoplan, backwind, c.1935
s steel .....................................$400      $450      $500

JOHNSON-MATTHEY, 15 J., 5 gram ingot 24k gold
24k...........................................$200      $250      $300

JARDUR W. CO., 17J., RF#29840, c.1950
s. steel .....................................$200      $250      $300

JUNGHANS, 16J., chronometer, c.1965
14k............................................$135      $165      $200

JEAN LOUIS, 17 jewels, double dial, c. 1930
14k ............................................$300      $350      $425

JUNGHANS, electronic "Ato Chron" , C.1978
14k............................................$125      $150      $185

J. E. Watch Co., 17J., tank style, c.1950
gold plate ...............................$100      $125      $150

JUNGHANS , 17J., cal.J88, c.1980
s. steel.....................................$100      $125      $175

JEWEL, 15 jewels, dual dial, c. 1938
gold filled...............................$300      $350      $400

🕐 Some grades are not included. Their values can be
determined by comparing with **similar** age, size, metal
content, style, grades, or models such as **time only**,
chronograph, repeater etc. listed.

J. JURGENSEN, 31J, 5 min. repeater, enamel bezel, c.1906
18k ......................................$25,000    $30,000    $35,000

J. JURGENSEN, 15J, jumping hr., revolving min., c.1930s
18k ......................................$4,000    $5,000    $6,000

J. JURGENSEN,17J., large lugs, recess crown, c.1950
14k ......................................$300    $350    $400

J. JURGENSEN,17J., long lugs, c.1948
18k ......................................$150    $175    $200

J. JURGENSEN,17J., recess crown, fancy lugs, c.1952
14k ......................................$200    $225    $250

J. JURGENSEN,17J., 2 tone, center lugs, c.1940
14k......................................$400    $450    $500

J. JURGENSEN, 17 jewels, fancy lugs, ca.1949
14k......................................$300    $350    $450

J. JURGENSEN, 17 jewels, fancy lugs
14k......................................$300    $350    $400

J. JURGENSEN, 17 jewels, extra fancy lugs, c. 1946
18k......................................$500    $575    $650

J. JURGENSEN, 17 jewels, c. 1950
18k......................................$250    $300    $350

J. JURGENSEN, 17 jewels
18k ...........................................$175    $200    $225

J. JURGENSEN,17J., center sec., c.1946
14k ...........................................$150    $175    $200

J. JURGENSEN,17J., aux. sec., c.1948
14k ...........................................$150    $175    $200

J. JURGENSEN,17J., aux. sec., c.1940
14k ...........................................$150    $175    $200

J. JURGENSEN,17J., textured bezel, c.1960
14k ...........................................$125    $150    $175

J. JURGENSEN,17J., hidden lugs, c.1948
14k ...........................................$175    $200    $225

J. JURGENSEN,17J., hidden lugs, c.1940
14k...........................................$150    $175    $200

J. JURGENSEN,17J., hidden lugs, c.1952
14k...........................................$300    $350    $400

J. JURGENSEN,17J., hidden lugs, c.1950
14k...........................................$300    $350    $400

J. JURGENSEN,17J., hidden lugs, c.1948
14k...........................................$150    $175    $200

J. JURGENSEN, 17 J., small size chronog., ca. 1945
14k......................................$1,200    $1,400    $1,800

⏱ Some grades are not included. Their values can be determined by comparing with **similar** age, size, metal content, style, grades, or models such as **time only**, chronograph, repeater etc. listed.

J. JURGENSEN,17J., by Valjoux, cal. 69, c.1944
s. steel ....................................$800     $900     $1,000

J. JURGENSEN, 17 J., auto-w., cen. sec., ca. 1954
14k .........................................$250     $300     $350

J. JURGENSEN,17J., cal.8273, extended lugs, c.1958
14k .........................................$250     $275     $300

J. JURGENSEN,17J., aux, sec., c.1968
14k .........................................$125     $150     $175

J. JURGENSEN,17J., extended bezel, c.1950
14k..........................................$350     $375     $400

J. JURGENSEN,17J., cal.1139, c.1950
18k..........................................$225     $250     $300

J. JURGENSEN,17J., center sec., date, c.1960
14k..........................................$150     $175     $200

J. JURGENSEN,17J., center sec., mid size, c.1940
14k..........................................$175     $200     $225

🕐 Some grades are not included. Their values can be
determined by comparing with **similar** age, size, metal
content, style, grades, or models such as **time only**,
chronograph, repeater etc. listed.

J. JURGENSEN,17J., 12 diamond dial, date, c.1960
14k(w)....................................$200      $250      $300

J. JURGENSEN,17J., 40 diamond bezel, c.1960
14k(w)....................................$350      $375      $400

J. JURGENSEN, 17 J., 12 diamond dial, ca. 1960s
14k(W)....................................$200      $250      $300

JUVENIA,17J.,3 dates, moon ph., screw on back c. 1950s
18k ..........................................$500      $600      $700

JUVENIA, 21 jewels, **gold movement**
18k.........................................$350      $400      $450

JUVENIA, 17J.,
s. steel.....................................$50      $60      $75

JUVENIA, 17J.,
s. steel.....................................$55      $65      $85

JUVENIA, 17J.,
s. steel.....................................$75      $85      $110

🕐 Some grades are not included. Their values can be
determined by comparing with similar age, size, metal
content, style, grades, or models such as time only,
chronograph, repeater etc. listed.

JUVENIA, 17J.,
s. steel .............................$100      $125      $150

KELEK,17J., tachymeter, auto-wind, c.1970
s. steel ...................................$100      $150      $200

JUVENIA, 17J.,
s. steel ......................................$85      $100      $125

Kelton, 7 jewels, curved, stepped case
gold filled ................................ $30      $35      $40

JUVENIA, 17J.,
s. steel ......................................$80      $100      $120

KELTON, 7 jewels, "Drake"
gold filled ............................... $30      $35      $40

KELBERT, 17J., triple date, moon ph., ca.1945
s. steel ...................................$325      $365      $400

KENT W. CO.,17J., Continental W.Co.(french),chronog.
s. steel ...................................$100      $125      $150

KELBERT, 17 jewels, fancy lugs, c. 1949
gold filled.................................$70      $80      $100

KINGSTON, 17 jewels, day-date-month, moon phase
gold filled ..............................$225      $275      $325

KINGSTON,17J., cal.G10, hidden lugs, c.1943
gold filled..................................$60     $70     $85

KORD, day date month, moon ph.
s. steel .....................................$200     $250     $300

KURTH, 17 jewels, ''Certina''
gold filled....................................$20     $30     $40

LACO, 17J., center sec., c.1955
gold plate ..................................$25     $35     $50

LANCEL (Paris),17J., one button chronog. by Nicolet, c.1960
gold filled ...............................$225     $250     $285

A.LANGE & SOHNE,17J., 55mm., c.1940
s. steel ................................$1,000     $1,200     $1,400

A.LANGE & SOHNE, 17J, (Glashutte), c.1936
14k ........................................$1,200     $1,400     $1,600

LANGE ''UHR'' (Glashutte),15J., c.1936
14k ...........................................$800     $900     $1,000

LANGE ''UHR'' (Glashutte),17J., c.1937
s. steel .....................................$600     $700     $800

🕐 Some grades are not included. Their values can be
determined by comparing with **similar** age, size, metal
content, style, grades, or models such as **time only**,
chronograph, repeater etc. listed.

LANGE, 17J., (Glashutte), date, auto wind, waterproof
18k ..............................$800    $900    $1,000

LANGENDORF, 17J., "Lanco-Matic," waterproof
gold filled....................................$40    $50    $65

LAVINA, 17J., ca.1937
9K.............................................$125    $150    $175

LE COULTRE, 18J., skeletonized,
18k ...........................$1,200    $1,400    $1,600

LE COULTRE, 19 jewels, alarm
18k ..............................$800    $1,000    $1,200
gold filled.............................$250    $300    $400
s. steel ....................................$225    $275    $375

LE COULTRE, 19 jewels, alarm, c. 1950
18k .....................................$1,000    $1,100    $1,200
gold filled ...............................$300    $350    $400
s. steel .....................................$250    $300    $375

LE COULTRE, 17J., , alarm, cal.815, c.1960
gold filled ...............................$250    $300    $350

LE COULTRE, 17J., ruby dial, alarm, c.1960
gold filled ...............................$300    $350    $400

LE COULTRE, 17J.,cal.814, memovox,  alarm, c.1960
14k ...........................................$700    $1,000    $1,150
gold filled ...............................$225    $275    $375

LE COULTRE, 17J., cal.p815, alarm, c.1960
gold filled.................................$300     $350     $400

LE COULTRE, 17J.,memvox , alarm, auto wind,c.1973
14k & s.s.................................$450     $500     $550

LE COULTRE, 17J., RF#3025, wrist-alarm, c.1948
gold filled................................$300     $350     $400

LE COULTRE, 17J., RF#2676, cal.911, memvox, c.1960
gold filled ..............................$300     $350     $400

LE COULTRE, 17J., wrist alarm, Ca.1949
gold filled................................$300     $350     $400

LE COULTRE, 17J., date, memvox, c.1975
s. steel .......................................$175     $200     $250

LE COULTRE, 17J., "Polaris", underwater alarm tested to
600 feet, date, Ca. 1968
s. steel .....................................$350     $400     $475

LE COULTRE, 17J., auto wind, date, memvox, c.1976
gold filled ..............................$250     $300     $350

LE COULTRE, 19J., date, Memovox, ca. 1959
18k .....................................$900      $1,000      $1,200
gold filled.............................$300      $350        $400
s. steel ................................$175      $225        $300

LE COULTRE, 17J., powermatic, auto-wind, c.1950
gold filled ..............................$225      $250        $300

LE COULTRE, 19J., alarm, date, autowind
14k ........................................$1,000     $1,100     $1,200

LE COULTRE, 17J., cal 481, auto-wind, c.1954
gold filled ..............................$200      $225        $275

LE COULTRE, 19 jewels, alarm, date, autowind, ca. 1950
18k ......................................$1,200     $1,400     $1,600
gold filled.............................$275       $325        $400
s. steel .................................$250       $300        $350

LE COULTRE, 17J., auto wind, wind indicator
14k .........................................$550      $625        $700

LE COULTRE, 15 jewels, wire lugs, c. 1919
silver ......................................$200      $225        $250

LE COULTRE, 17 jewels, screw back
18k ...........................................$350      $400        $450

LE COULTRE, 17J., "Master Mariner, c.1960
14k .........................................$250 $300 $350

LE COULTRE, 17J., auto-wind, cal.p812, c.1955
gold filled ...............................$100 $125 $150

LE COULTRE, 17J., cal.p478, center sec.c.1947
s. steel .....................................$200 $225 $250

LE COULTRE, 17J., cal.818, aux. sec., c.1962
gold filled ...............................$100 $125 $150

LE COULTRE, 17J., "Master Mariner", c.1952
14k ..........................................$250 $300 $350

LE COULTRE, 17J., RF#2013, cal.480cw, c.1950
14k .........................................$250 $275 $325

LE COULTRE, 17J., "Master Mariner", auto-wind, c.1960
s. steel ...................................$100 $125 $150

LE COULTRE, 17J., RF#555-149, c.1955
14k .........................................$250 $350 $400

LE COULTRE, 17J., cal812, auto-wind, c.1952
s. steel ......................................$100    $125    $150

LE COULTRE, 17J.,"Coronet", cal.480cw, c.1951
gold filled................................$300    $350    $400

LE COULTRE, 17J., cal.480, wide bezel, c.1958
gold filled................................$100    $125    $150

LE COULTRE, 17J., cal.480, c.1955
14k ...........................................$250    $300    $350

LE COULTRE, 17J., RF#7534, c.1960
14k .............................................$400    $500    $550

LE COULTRE, 17J., 11 diamond dial, RF#197, c.1955
14k(w)......................................$200    $225    $250

LE COULTRE, 17 jewels, center lugs, c. 1960
18k ...........................................$400    $450    $500

LE COULTRE, 17 jewels, fancy lugs, c. 1950
14k ...........................................$400    $450    $500

🕐 Some grades are not included. Their values can be
determined by comparing with **similar** age, size, metal
content, style, grades, or models such as **time only**,
chronograph, repeater etc. listed.

LE COULTRE, 17J., fancy lugs
14k ...................................$400      $450      $500

LE COULTRE, 17J., fancy lugs, ca. 1950s
18k .........................................$500      $600      $700

LE COULTRE, 17 jewels, fancy lugs, c. 1952
14k .........................................$300      $400      $500

LE COULTRE, 17 jewels, fancy bezel & lugs
14k .........................................$600      $650      $700

LE COULTRE, 17 jewels, fancy bezel & lugs, Ca. 1953
14k .........................................$400      $450      $500

LE COULTRE, 17J., fancy bezel, Ca.1952
gold filled ...............................$150      $175      $225

LE COULTRE, 17J., auto wind, textured bezel, c. 1950
18k .........................................$250      $350      $450

LE COULTRE, 17 jewels, center sec., c. 1949
18k .........................................$400      $500      $600
s. steel ....................................$125      $150      $200

LE COULTRE, 17J., cen. sec., 24 hr dial, c. 1940
s. steel ....................................$225      $275      $325

This book endeavours to be a GUIDE or helpful manual and offers a wealth of material to be used as a tool not as a absolute document. Price Guides are like watches the worst may be better than none at all, but at best cannot be expected to be 100% accurate.

LE COULTRE, 17J., "Quartermaster", 24 hr dial, RF#114
s.steel ........................................$350    $375    $500

LE COULTRE, 17J., alarm, date, ca.1964
s. steel ...................................$150    $175    $225

LE COULTRE, 17J., cal.813, RF#388-870, Ca.1959
gold filled................................$100    $125    $150

LE COULTRE, 17J., quartz, cal.352, c.1970
gold filled ................................$50    $60    $75

LE COULTRE, 17J., center sec., Ca.1959
s.steel ........................................$100    $125    $150

LE COULTRE, 17J., date alarm, c.1975
gold filled ...............................$125    $150    $200

LE COULTRE, 17J., center sec., ca. 1930s
silver ........................................$350    $400    $450

LE COULTRE, 17 jewels, alarm, date, auto wind
14k ...........................................$400    $450    $500

LE COULTRE, 17J., chronog., 2 reg.
14k .......................................$1,000    $1,200    $1,350
s. steel ...................................$500    $600    $700

LE COULTRE, 17 jewels, chronog., 3 reg.
18k ........................................$3,000    $3,500    $4,000

LE COULTRE, 17J., chronog., cal.281, c.1940
s. steel ...................................$400    $450    $500

LE COULTRE, 17 jewels, mystery dial, c. 1955
14k .........................................$400    $500    $600

LE COULTRE, 17J., chronog., FR#2644, blue dial,
s. steel ...................................$450    $500    $550

LE COULTRE, 17J., diamond mystery dial & bezel
platinum..............................$1,500    $1,750    $2,000
14k(W) C&B .....................$1,200    $1,400    $1,600

LE COULTRE, 17J., chronog. 3 reg., ca. 1958
14k .......................................$1,800    $2,000    $2,200
s. steel ...................................$900    $1,000    $1,200

LE COULTRE, 17J., diamond mystery dial,
14k .........................................$400    $500    $600

LE COULTRE, 17J., diamond mystery dial, waterp.
platinum .............................$1,200    $1,400    $1,650
14k .........................................$900    $1,000    $1,200

LE COULTRE, 15 jewels, triple-date, c. 1945
s. steel .....................................$400    $500    $600
14k .........................................$900    $1,000    $1,100
18k .......................................$1,200    $1,300    $1,500

LE COULTRE, 17J, diamond dial, textured bezel, c. 1960s
14k (w).....................................$350    $400    $450

LE COULTRE, 17J, astronomic ,moon ph., c. 1940s
18k ......................$2,000    $2,200    $2,500
gold filled ..............................$700    $800    $900

LE COULTRE, 17J., date, cal.810, c.1952
14k .........................................$450    $500    $550

LE COULTRE, 17J., triple date, moon ph., fancy lugs
gold filled ..............................$800    $900    $1,000

LE COULTRE, 17J., date, center sec., c.1950
14k .........................................$450    $500    $550

🕐 Some grades are not included. Their values can be
determined by comparing with **similar** age, size, metal
content, style, grades, or models such as **time only**,
chronograph, repeater etc. listed.

LE COULTRE, 17J., time in 24 cities,  c.1960
14k .........................................$1,300    $1,500    $1,750

LE COULTRE, 17J., weems style, cal.450, c.1942
s. steel ........................................$800      $900      $1,000

LE COULTRE, 17J., rotating chapters, date,  c.1960
s. steel ......................................$700      $750      $800

LE COULTRE, 17J., "Futurematic", cal.817, c.1952
14k ............................................$850      $950      $1,150

LE COULTRE, 17 jewels, "Futurematic"
18k ............................................$1,200    $1,400    $1,650
14k ............................................$1,000    $1,200    $1,350

LE COULTRE, 17J, auto wind,power reserve window
gold filled ...............................$400      $475      $525
s. steel ............................... ★ $450      $500      $575

LE COULTRE, 23 J., auto-w., date cen. sec.
14k ...........................................$300      $350      $400

LE COULTRE, 17J., auto-w., date
14k ...........................................$300      $350      $400

LE COULTRE, 17J., day date, mid size, ca. 1940s
gold filled ...............................$300      $350      $400

🕐 Some grades are not included. Their values can be
determined by comparing with **similar** age, size, metal
content, style, grades, or models such as **time only**,
chronograph, repeater etc. listed.

LE COULTRE, 17J., fancy lugs, aux. sec., ca. 1948
14k .................................. $500       $600       $600

LE COULTRE, 17J., auto-w., ca. 1950s
14k .................................. $300       $350       $400

LE COULTRE, 17J., fancy lugs
14k .................................. $350       $400       $450

LE COULTRE, 17J., aux. sec. ca.1950s
14k .................................. $200       $250       $300

LE COULTRE, 17 jewels, fancy wide bezel, ca.1955
14k (W).................................. $400       $500       $600

LE COULTRE, 17J., alarm, date,
14k .................................. $400       $500       $600

LE COULTRE, 15J., drivers style wind at 12, c.1960s
s. steel .................................. $350       $400       $500

LE COULTRE,17J.,drivers style crown at 6,  RF#9041
s. steel .................................. $350       $400       $500

LE COULTRE, 17J.,RF#9041, cal.818, c.1960s
18k .................................. $500       $700       $800

LE COULTRE, 17J, ''Reverso,'' center sec., c. 1930
18k ....................................$5,500    $6,500    $7,500
s. steel ................................$1,500    $1,700    $2,200

LE COULTRE, 17J., ''Reverso,'' c. 1940s
18k ....................................$5,500    $6,500    $7,500
s. steel ................................$1,500    $1,700    $2,200

LE COULTRE, 17 jewels, fancy hooded lugs, c. 1952
14k ............................................$600    $650    $700

LE COULTRE, 17 jewels, fancy lugs
14k ............................................$500    $600    $700

LE COULTRE, 17 jewels, fancy lugs
14k ............................................$800    $900    $1,000

LE COULTRE, 17J., curvex,
14k ............................................$400    $500    $600

LE COULTRE, 17J., curvex, ca. 1940s
14k ............................................$500    $600    $700

LE COULTRE, 17J., stepped lugs, ca. 1944
gold filled ..............................$150    $175    $200

LE COULTRE, 17J.,  aux. sec., ca. 1940s
gold filled ..............................$150    $175    $200

LE COULTRE, 17J., square lugs, ca. 1948
14k ............................................$500    $600    $700

LE COULTRE, 17J., extended lugs, c.1938
gold filled..............................$100      $125      $150

LE COULTRE, 17J., aux. sec., c.1940
14k ........................................$250      $300      $350

LE COULTRE, 17J., tu tone dial, c.1940
gold filled..............................$100      $125      $150

LE COULTRE, 17J., large lugs, c.1938
gold filled..............................$125      $150      $200

LE COULTRE, 17J.,hidden lugs, c.1942
14k .........................................$400      $450      $500
gold filled..............................$175      $225      $300

LE COULTRE, 17J., hooded lugs, ca. 1940s
14k .........................................$500      $600      $700

LE COULTRE, 17J., swing lugs, cen. sec.
s. steel ....................................$300      $350      $400

LE COULTRE, 17J., fancy bezel, ca. 1940s
14k ........................................$800      $900      $1,000

LE COULTRE, 17J., Asymmetric, Ca. 1960s
gold filled ..............................$200      $225      $275

LE COULTRE, 17J., Asymmetric, cal.438.4cw, Ca.1957
gold filled ..............................$200      $225      $275

LE COULTRE, 17J., Asymmetric, diamond dial, RF#2406,
Ca.1960
14k ........................................$325      $375      $450

LE COULTRE, 17 jewels, long lugs, c. 1944
18k ...................................$300    $350    $400

LE COULTRE, 17 jewels, uniplan, c. 1938
14k (w)...................................$350    $400    $500

LE COULTRE, 15 jewels, duoplan, c. 1940
14k ...................................$1,000    $1,100    $1,200

LE COULTRE, 17 jewels, fancy lugs, c. 1948
14k ...................................$400    $450    $600

LE COULTRE, 17J., fancy lugs, cal.438-4cw, c.1951
18k ...................................$500    $600    $700

LE COULTRE, 17 jewels, fancy lugs
14k ...................................$600    $675    $750

LE COULTRE, 17 jewels, diamond dial, fancy lugs
14k ...................................$700    $800    $1,000

LE COULTRE, 17J., diamond dial, ca.1940s
14k ...................................$400    $500    $600

LE COULTRE, 17J., 12 diamond dial, cal.4870cw, c.1958
14k(w)...................................$250    $275    $325

LE COULTRE, 17J., diamond mystery dial ca.1940s
14k ...................................$800    $900    $1,000

LE COULTRE, 15J., hinged case, c.1920
14k ...................................$400    $450    $500

LE COULTRE, 17J., stepped case & lugs, cal., c.1950
gold filled..............................$100    $125    $150

LE COULTRE, 17J., aux. sec., c.1940
14k .........................................$200    $250    $275

LE COULTRE, 17J., cal.493, c.1955
10k ...........................................$200    $225    $275

LE COULTRE, 17J., cal.438-4cw, wide bezel, c.1950
14k .........................................$400    $450    $500

LE COULTRE, 17J., textured bezel, c.1952
14k .........................................$400    $450    $500

LE COULTRE, 17J., textured bezel, c.1950
14k .........................................$400    $450    $500

LE COULTRE, 17J., RF#7540,engraved bezel, cal., c.1960
14k .........................................$400    $450    $500

LE COULTRE, 17J., cal.p812, c.1948
gold filled ...............................$150    $200    $250

LE COULTRE, 17 jewels, tank style, c.1958
18k .........................................$400    $500    $600

LE COULTRE, 17J., textured bezel, cen. sec.
18k .........................................$500    $600    $750

LE COULTRE, 17J., aux. sec., ca. 1930s
14k ................................................$300      $400      $500

LE COULTRE, 17J, triple date, moon ph., fancy bezel
18k ........................ ★ ★ ★ $3,000     $4,000     $5,000
gold filled.............................$1,800     $2,000     $2,200

LE COULTRE, 17 jewels, c. 1945
18k ............................................$300      $350      $400

LE COULTRE, 17 jewels, fancy lugs, c. 1948
14k ............................................$400      $500      $600

LE COULTRE, 17 jewels, center lugs, c. 1945
14k ............................................$400      $500      $600

LE COULTRE, 17 jewels, center lugs, c. 1945
14k ............................................$400      $500      $600

LE COULTRE, 17 jewels, c. 1950s
14k ............................................$400      $500      $600

LE COULTRE, 17 jewels, 18k case & band
18k C&B.............................$1,000     $1,200     $1,400

LE COULTRE, 17 jewels, date cal. 810, c. 1952
14k ............................................$600      $700      $800

LE COULTRE, 17 jewels, two tone dial
14k ............................................$300      $400      $500
18k ............................................$400      $500      $600

🕐 Some grades are not included. Their values can be
determined by comparing with **similar** age, size, metal
content, style, grades, or models such as **time only**,
chronograph, repeater etc. listed.

LE COULTRE, 15 jewels, by Blancpain, c.1925
gold filled.............................$100      $125      $175

LE COULTRE, 15J., lady's
14k(W)...................................$200      $250      $300

LE COULTRE, 15J., lady's art deco, by Blancpain, c.1925
silver .......................................$300      $350      $400

LE COULTRE, quartz, date, waterproof, c. 1960s
18k .........................................$300      $350      $400

LE COULTRE, 15J., lady's REVERSO, c.1940
s. steel ....................................$800      $900      $1,000

LE COULTRE, 17J., lady's, cal.490bw, c.1950
gold filled ................................$40      $50      $65

LE COULTRE, electric, digital calendar
silver & gold..........................$300      $400      $500

LE COULTRE, 17J., lady's MYSTERY dial, c.1959
gold filled ...............................$100      $125      $150

LE COULTRE, 17 jewels, Asymmetric, c. 1953
gold filled...............................$350      $425      $550

LE COULTRE, 17 jewels, small, Asymmetric, c. 1953
gold filled...............................$200      $250      $300

LE JOUR, 17J., by Valjoux, cal.7750, c.1973
s. steel ....................................$150      $200      $250

LEMANIA, 17 jewels, auto wind
s. steel ..........................................$50      $60      $70

LEMANIA, 17 jewels, chronog., military, ca.1970s
s. steel ......................................$350      $400      $450

LEMANIA,17J., chronog., 3 reg., c.1946
14k ...........................................$500      $600      $700

LEONIDAS,17J., chronog., triple date, c.1945
gold filled ...............................$400      $450      $500

LEMANIA, 17 jewels, chronog., c. 1950
18k ...........................................$500      $600      $700

LEONIDAS, 17 jewels, triple date, 3 reg.
18k .......................................$1,200      $1,300      $1,500
s. steel ....................................$350      $400      $450

LEMANIA, 17 jewels, chronog., waterproof
s. steel .....................................$300      $350      $400

LEONIDAS, 17 jewels, auto wind, triple date, moon phase
s. steel .....................................$300      $350      $400

LEONIDAS, 17 jewels, chronog., 2 reg.
s. steel .....................................$150      $200      $275

LE PHARE, 17 jewels, chronog., triple date, 3 reg.
18k ............................................$900      $1,000      $1,250

LE PHARE, 17 jewels, chronog., 2 reg.
18k ............................................$375      $450      $500
14k ............................................$275      $325      $375
s. steel .....................................$100      $150      $200

LE PHARE, 17J., triple date, moon ph., waterproof
18k ............................................$800      $1,100      $1,250
gold filled.................................$400      $475      $550

LEVRETTE,17J., chronog., (fly back), center lugs, c.1935
18k ............................................$1,500      $1,600      $1,800

LIBELA,7J., direct read, c.1952
base metal .................................$150      $200      $250

LIP,15J., chronog., tu-tone, center lugs, (French), c.1940
gold filled & s.steel. ...............$550      $650      $750

LIP, electric, bulbous crown, (French)
s. steel .....................................$200      $250      $350

⏱ Some grades are not included. Their values can be
determined by comparing with **similar** age, size, metal
content, style, grades, or models such as **time only**,
chronograph, repeater etc. listed.

LONGINES, 15J., center lugs, enamel dial, ca.1923
silver .........................................$325     $400     $475

LONGINES,15J., enamel dial, pierced shield , c.1923
silver .........................................$325     $375     $475

LONGINES,15J., enamel dial, GJS, c.1925
14k .........................................$250     $300     $400

LONGINES, 18J.,wire lugs, ca.1928
14k .........................................$400     $500     $600

🕐 Some grades are not included. Their values can be
determined by comparing with **similar** age, size, metal
content, style, grades, or models such as **time only**,
chronograph, repeater etc. listed.

LONGINES, 15J., wire lugs, enamel dial, c.1927
silver .........................................$250     $300     $375

LONGINES, 15J., wire lugs, ca. 1930s
silver .........................................$250     $300     $375

LONGINES,17J., tu-tone, GJS, c.1936
14k & s.s. .........................................$175     $200     $325

LONGINES,17J., double dial, cal.932, c.1937
s. steel .........................................$700     $800     $1,000

LONGINES,17J., large & curved, GJS,
gold filled .........................................$175     $225     $325

LONGINES, 15J., GJS, c.1922
silver .......................................$250      $300      $375

LONGINES, 17J., GJS, cal.940, c.1931
18k ...........................................$500      $550      $700

LONGINES, 17J., GJS, cal.1086, c.1928
14k ...........................................$400      $500      $700

LONGINES, 17J., cal.101, c.1947
14k ...........................................$200      $225      $325

LONGINES, 17J., large Lindberg model 47mm., movable
bezel & center dial (weem's second setting), Ca. 1930s
18k .....................★ ★ ★ $20,000   $25,000   $30,000
silver ...................................$3,000   $4,000   $5,000
nickel...................................$2,000   $3,000   $4,400

LONGINES, 17J., small Lindberg model, original retail price
$97.50, Ca. 1930s
18k ..............................★ ★ $8,000   $9,000   $10,000
14k ...............................$7,000   $8,000   $9,000
gold filled ...........................$1,200   $1,400   $1,700
s. steel ...............................$1,200   $1,400   $1,700

LONGINES, 17J., Weems U.S. Patent 2008734 on dial
s. steel ...................................$450      $550      $650
14k ...........................................$800      $900   $1,000

LONGINES, 17J., "Weems", revolving bezel, Ca. 1940s
s. steel ...................................$475      $550      $650

LONGINES, 17J., 1 button, fly back hand, c.1940
10K .........................................$700      $800      $900

LONGINES,17J., 1 button, fly back hand, c.1945
center recording
s. steel ....................................$400    $500    $600

LONGINES, 17 jewels, chronog., 1 button, c. 1923
silver ....................................$1,400   $1,600   $1,800

LONGINES,17J., 1 button chronog., c.1946
14k ..........................................$2,000   $2,200   $2,400

LONGINES, 17J., chronog., one button
14k ..........................................$1,000   $1,100   $1,200

LONGINES,17J., 1 button, fly back hand, center recording,
RF# 5034, Ca. 1940
s. steel .....................................$200    $300    $400

LONGINES, 17J. chronog., ref. 1333, enamel dial
silver ....................................$1,300   $1,500   $1,800

LONGINES, 17J., chronog. 2 reg., tach.,
14k ..........................................$2,200   $2,400   $2,800

LONGINES, 17 jewels, chronog., 2 reg.
18k ..........................................$2,000   $2,200   $2,400

LONGINES,17J., chronog., c.1942
s. steel ..................................$700      $800      $900

LONGINES,17J., RF#6474, c.1955
s. steel ..................................$800      $1,000      $1,200

LONGINES, 17 jewels, chronog., 2 reg.
18k ..................................$1,500      $1,700      $2,000

LONGINES, 17 jewels, chronog., 2 reg.
14k ..................................$1,200      $1,400      $1,650
s. steel ..................................$800      $900      $1,000

LONGINES, 17J., chronog., ca. 1945
gold filled ..................................$300      $350      $400

LONGINES, 17 jewels, chronog. 1 button
14k ..................................$1,000      $1,200      $1,300

LONGINES,17J., chronog., cal.539, c.1969
s steel ..................................$200      $225      $275

LONGINES,17J., Valjoux 726, cal.332, c.1972
s. steel ..................................$225      $275      $325

LONGINES, 16J., military issue, waterpr., ca. 1940s
s. steel ....................................$400      $500      $600

LONGINES,17J., GJS, cal.352, c.1960
14k ............................................$225      $250      $350

LONGINES,17J., GJS, c.1965
18k ......................................$225      $250      $275

LONGINES,17J., GJS, cal., c.1960
14k ............................................$225      $250      $350

LONGINES,17J., GJS, cal.23z, c.1958
gold filled..................................$75      $100      $125

LONGINES,17J., aux. seconds, Ca. 1960
gold filled ................................$75      $100      $125

LONGINES, 17J., GJS, cal.194, c.1963
gold filled...................................$75      $100      $125

LONGINES,17J., Aux. seconds, gold jewel settings, Ca. 1957
14k ............................................$200      $235      $300

⊕ Some grades are not included. Their values can be
determined by comparing with **similar** age, size, metal
content, style, grades, or models such as **time only**,
chronograph, repeater etc. listed.

LONGINES,17J., RF#2033p, GJS, cal., c.1958
14k .........................................$225    $250    $300

LONGINES,17J., RF#2021, GJS, cal.23z, c.1955
14k .........................................$400    $500    $600

LONGINES,17J., GJS, cal.23z, c.1955
14k .........................................$250    $275    $300

LONGINES,17J., large fluted lugs, GJS, c.1940
14k .........................................$300    $375    $475

LONGINES,17J., large lugs, GJS, c.1952
18k .........................................$350    $400    $450

LONGINES,17J., GJS, cal.18LN, c.1952
14k .........................................$250    $300    $350

LONGINES,17J., one lug at 11 & one at 5, GJS, 1955
14k .........................................$350    $400    $450

LONGINES,17J., GJS, cal.22a, auto-wind, c.1958
14k .........................................$275    $350    $400

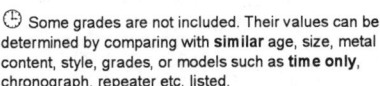

Some grades are not included. Their values can be
determined by comparing with **similar** age, size, metal
content, style, grades, or models such as **time only**,
chronograph, repeater etc. listed.

Some grades are not included. Their values can be
determined by comparing with **similar** age, size, metal
content, style, grades, or models such as **time only**,
chronograph, repeater etc. listed.

LONGINES,17J., GJS, cal.10L, c.1952
14k .............................................$200    $250    $300

LONGINES, 17 jewels, fancy lugs, c. 1954
14k .............................................$450    $550    $600

LONGINES,17J., GJS, cal.23z, c.1954
18k .............................................$250    $300    $350

LONGINES, 17 jewels, fancy lugs, c. 1949
14k .............................................$350    $400    $450

LONGINES, 15 jewels, c. 1940s
18k .............................................$400    $450    $500
14k .............................................$300    $350    $400
s. steel .......................................$100    $125    $150

LONGINES, 19J.,"Conquest", auto-wind,
14k .............................................$500    $600    $700

LONGINES,17J., GJS, cal.22ls, c.1950
14k .............................................$250    $300    $350

LONGINES, 17J., fancy lugs, diamond dial,
14k .............................................$500    $600    $700

🕐 Some grades are not included. Their values can be
determined by comparing with **similar** age, size, metal
content, style, grades, or models such as **time only**,
chronograph, repeater etc. listed.

LONGINES,17J., "Flagship", GJS, cal.340, c.1960
18k ...................................... $200    $250    $300

LONGINES,17J., RF#3759, GJS, cal.22as, c.1949
14k .......................................... $225    $275    $350

LONGINES,17J., center sec., GJS, c.1948
14k .......................................... $150    $200    $250

LONGINES,17J., GJS, center sec., c.1958
gold filled .............................. $100    $125    $175

LONGINES,17J., GJS, cal.19as, c.1955
gold filled................................. $75    $100    $125

LONGINES,17J., center sec., GJS, cal., c.1940
14k .......................................... $200    $250    $300

LONGINES,17J., GJS, cal.340, c.1960
14k .......................................... $150    $200    $250

LONGINES,17J., GJS, center sec., c.1943
14k .......................................... $180    $230    $300

⊕ Some grades are not included. Their values can be
determined by comparing with **similar** age, size, metal
content, style, grades, or models such as **time only**,
chronograph, repeater etc. listed.

LONGINES, 17J., military, Ca.1942
s. steel .....................................$150      $175      $200

LONGINES,17J., GJS, "Flagship", date, c.1964
gold filled...................................$80      $90      $100

LONGINES,17J., 36,000 (beat), auto-wind, "Ultra-Chron"
14k ...........................................$200      $250      $300

LONGINES,17J., RF#9003, GJS, "Conquest", c.1958
18k ...........................................$450      $525      $600

LONGINES,17J., a-wind, "Grand Prize", date, Ca.1960
gold filled ...................................$60      $80      $100

LONGINES,17J., oval textured bezel, cal.506, c.1965
14k ...........................................$200      $250      $300

LONGINES,17J., high frequency, date, c.1972
s. steel ........................................$60      $70      $90

LONGINES, 17 jewels, ''Flagship''
14k ...........................................$200      $250      $300

LONGINES, 17 jewels, gold jewel settings, Ca. 1950
s. steel .......................................$75    $100    $135

LONGINES, 17J., "Grand Prize", auto-w., date
14k ...........................................$400    $450    $500

LONGINES, 17 jewels, center seconds
14k ...........................................$200    $250    $350

LONGINES, 17J., "Conquest", auto-w., date, w.-indicator
s. steel ....................................$300    $350    $400

LONGINES, 17J., aux. seconds, large lugs
14k ...........................................$150    $200    $250

LONGINES, 17J., date, ca. 1940s
14k ...........................................$275    $325    $375

LONGINES, 17J., auto wind
14k ...........................................$150    $200    $250

LONGINES,17J., mystery dial, cal.232 c.1960
gold filled ...............................$125    $150    $175

LONGINES, 19J., "Conquest", auto-w., date, ca.1962
s. steel ....................................$125    $175    $225

LONGINES, 17J., mystery dial,
gold filled.................................$125    $150    $175

LONGINES, 17 jewels, mystery hand, ca.1962
gold filled.................................$100    $125    $150

LONGINES, 17 jewels, mystery hand,
14k ..........................................$300    $375    $475

LONGINES, 17 jewels, mystery hand, 12 diamond dial
14k ..........................................$500    $600    $750

LONGINES,17J., mystery 39 diamond dial, RF#1017
14k(w).....................................$650    $750    $850

LONGINES, 17 jewels, diamond dial, center lugs
14k ..........................................$600    $700    $800

LONGINES, 17 jewels, "Ultra Chrono," diamond dial
14k ..........................................$350    $375    $425

LONGINES, 17 jewels, "Ultra Chrono," date, c.1949
14k ..........................................$200    $250    $300

LONGINES, 17J., auto-w., aux. sec.
14k ..........................................$200    $250    $300

🕐 Some grades are not included. Their values can be
determined by comparing with **similar** age, size, metal
content, style, grades, or models such as **time only**,
chronograph, repeater etc. listed.

LONGINES, 17J., auto-w., aux. sec.
14k ...........................................$175    $200    $250

LONGINES, 17J., aux sec.
14k ...........................................$175    $200    $250

LONGINES, 17J., diamond dial
14k(W)....................................$200    $225    $300

LONGINES, 17J.,diamond bezel
gold filled................................$150    $200    $250

LONGINES, 17J.,3 diamond dial
gold filled ..............................$150    $175    $200

LONGINES, 17J., diamond dial,
14k(W)....................................$250    $300    $350

LONGINES, 17 jewels, cocktail style, 36 diamond dial
14k(W)....................................$275    $325    $375

LONGINES, 17 jewels, 12 diamond dial
14k (w) ..................................$300    $350    $425

LONGINES,17J., GJS, 34 diamond dial, date, c.1962
14k ...........................................$300    $350    $400

LONGINES,17J., 36 diamonds, GJS, cal.194, c.1955
14k(w)........................................$300      $350      $400

LONGINES, 17J., 14 diamond dial, Ca. 1960
14k ..........................................$275      $350      $400

LONGINES,17J., 14 diamonds,GJS, cal.370, c.1960
14k .........................................$250      $300      $350

LONGINES,17J., "Admiral", GJS, auto-wind, Ca. 1960
14k ..........................................$325      $350      $450

LONGINES,17J., 4 diamonds,  cal.194, c.1958
gold filled................................$150      $175      $200

LONGINES, 17J., GJS, tank style
14k C&B.................................$550      $600      $650

LONGINES, 17J., GJS, faceted crystal, Ca.1951
gold filled ..............................$125      $150      $185

LONGINES,17J., 37 diamonds on bezel 24 on dial, c.1958
14k(w)....................................$400      $450      $500

LONGINES, 17J., GJS, cal.9L, Ca.1939
gold filled ..............................$100      $125      $150

LONGINES, 17J., 4 diamonds, GJS, cal.23z, c.1948
14k ..........................................$250      $300      $350

LONGINES, 17J., 5 diamonds, GJS, c.1953
gold filled ..............................$150      $175      $200

LONGINES, 17J., 5 diamonds, GJS, cal.8ln, c.1940
14k(w)....................................$200      $250      $300

LONGINES, 17J., 17 diamonds, GJS, c.1951
14k ..........................................$350      $400      $500

LONGINES, 17J., 8 diamonds, GJS, cal.22L, c.1958
14k ..........................................$275      $300      $350

LONGINES, 17J., 15 diamonds, GJS, cal.9L, c.1945
platinum.................................$675      $775      $925
14k ..........................................$350      $400      $500

LONGINES,17J.,4 diamonds, textured bezel,cal.194, c.1955
gold filled................................$125      $150      $175

LONGINES, 17J., 18 diamonds, RF#176, GJS, c.1950
14k(w)....................................$400      $500      $600

LONGINES, 17J., 6 diamonds, GJS
14k ..........................................$250      $300      $350

LONGINES, 17J., 16 diamonds, cal.9LT, c.1958
14k(w)....................................$300      $400      $450

LONGINES, 17J., 4 diamonds, GJS, cal.L8474, c.1960
gold filled................................$100      $125      $175

LONGINES, 17J., 6 diamonds, RF#2763, GJS, c.1955
14k ..........................................$250      $300      $350

LONGINES, 17J., 8 diamonds, GJS, cal.9LT, c.1958
14k(w)....................................$250      $300      $350

LONGINES, 17J., 5 diamonds, GJS,  c.1945
14k C&B................................$450      $500      $550

LONGINES, 17J., 5 diamonds, GJS, cal.9L, c.1952
14k ..........................................$250      $300      $375

LONGINES, 17 jewels, diamond dial, c. 1944
14k ..........................................$400      $500      $600

LONGINES, 17 jewels, diamond dial, hidden lugs, c. 1938
s. steel .....................................$125      $150      $225

LONGINES, 17 jewels, fancy hidden lugs, diamond dial
14k (w) ...................................$600      $700      $800

LONGINES, 17 jewels, diamond dial, c. 1944
14k ........................................$400      $450      $500

LONGINES, 17 jewels, diamond dial, c. 1949
14k ........................................$350      $400      $450

LONGINES, 17 jewels, diamond dial, c. 1935
platinum..............................$1,100      $1,200      $1,400
14k ..........................................$750      $850      $1,000

LONGINES, 17 jewels, 18 diamond dial
14k (w) ...................................$250      $300      $375

LONGINES, 17 jewels, flared, 6 diamond dial
14k ............................................$500    $600    $700

LONGINES, 17 jewels, 4 diamond dial
14k ............................................$225    $275    $325

LONGINES, 17 jewels, 12 diamond dial
s.steel ......................................$250    $300    $400

LONGINES, 17 jewels, "Advocat", fancy lugs, Ca. 1951
14k ............................................$300    $350    $400

LONGINES, 17 jewels, c. 1923
gold filled...............................$125    $150    $175

LONGINES, 17 jewels, flared, c. 1959
14k ............................................$450    $500    $600

LONGINES, 17 jewels, flared
14k C&B................................$750    $850    $950

LONGINES, 17 jewels, fancy lugs, c. 1943
14k ............................................$350    $400    $450

LONGINES, 17 jewels, torpedo shaped numbers
14k ............................................$250    $300    $350

LONGINES, 17 jewels, curved, fancy lugs, c. 1939
14k ............................................$350    $400    $500

LONGINES, 17 jewels, center lugs, c. 1937
14k ............................................$250    $275    $350

LONGINES, 17 jewels, hooded lugs, diamond dial
14k(w)...................................$700    $800    $950

LONGINES, 17 jewels, hooded lugs
14k ...........................................$200      $250      $275

LONGINES, 17 jewels, 20 diamond dial, Ca. 1932
platinum....................................$800      $900      $1,100

LONGINES, 17 jewels, diamond dial, fancy lugs
14k .........................................$675      $750      $850

LONGINES, 17 jewels, diamond dial
14k(W)....................................$400      $450      $500

LONGINES, 17 jewels, diamond dial, c. 1944
14k .........................................$250      $300      $350

LONGINES, 17J.,curved,
14k ........................................$300      $350      $400

LONGINES, 17 jewels, fancy lugs
14k .........................................$250      $300      $350

LONGINES, 17J., stepped case,
14k .........................................$300      $350      $400

LONGINES, 17 jewels, c. 1930
18k .........................................$800      $900      $1,000
14k .........................................$450      $550      $700
gold filled..............................$150      $175      $200

LONGINES, 17J., curvex, 52mm, ca. 1930
gold filled ..............................$500      $600      $700

LONGINES, 15J., tonneau, GJS, c.1925
silver .......................................$350      $400      $450

LONGINES, 17J., stepped case, GJS, cal.9L, c.1939
14k ...........................................$275      $300      $325

LONGINES, 17J., extended lugs, GJS, cal.9L, c.1942
14k ...........................................$250      $300      $350

LONGINES, 17J., cut corner, cal.94w, c.1929
gold filled..............................$100      $125      $150

LONGINES, 17J., tonneau, cal.9L, c.1948
gold filled..............................$150      $175      $200

LONGINES, 17J., carved bezel, GJS, cal.9LT, c.1950
gold filled ..............................$100      $125      $150

LONGINES, 17J., butler finish, GJS, cal., c.1951
gold filled ..............................$100      $125      $150

LONGINES, 17J., beveled bezel, GJS, cal., c.1935
gold filled ..............................$100      $125      $150

LONGINES, 17J., aux. sec., GJS, cal.9L, c.1948
gold filled ..............................$100      $125      $150

LONGINES, 17J., carved case, GJS, cal.9LT, c.1950s
14k ...........................................$225      $275      $325

Some grades are not included. Their values can be
determined by comparing with similar age, size, metal
content, style, grades, or models such as time only,
chronograph, repeater etc. listed.

LONGINES, 17J., butler finish, GJS, cal.9LT, c.1957
14k ...................................$200     $250     $300

LONGINES, 17J., fluted lugs, GJS, cal.9L, c.1949
gold filled ..............................$125     $150     $175

LONGINES, 15J., butler finish, c.1926
gold filled................................$100     $125     $150

LONGINES, 17J., carved case, GJS, cal.9LT, c.1959
gold filled ..............................$125     $150     $185

LONGINES, 17J., stepped case, GJS, cal.9LT, c.1958
14k .............................................$250     $300     $350

LONGINES, 17J., spur lugs, GJS, cal., c.1948
gold filled ...............................$125     $150     $185

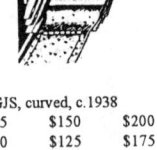

LONGINES, 17J., stepped case, GJS, curved, c.1938
gold filled................................$125     $150     $200
s. steel ....................................$100     $125     $175
14k ............................................$275     $300     $350

LONGINES, 17J., extended lugs, GJS, cal.9LT, c.1955
14k .........................................$300     $350     $400

LONGINES, 17J., fancy lugs, GJS, cal.9LT, c.1957
14k .........................................$225     $275     $325

LONGINES, 17J., fancy bezel, GJS, Ca. 1950
14k .........................................$450     $500     $550

LONGINES, 17J., fluted sides, GJS, cal.9LT, c.1950
gold filled..............................$125    $150    $185

LONGINES,17J., GJS, c.1958
14k ........................................$175    $225    $275

LONGINES, 17J., carved case, GJS, cal.9LT, c.1955
14k ..........................................$300    $350    $400

LONGINES, 17J., RF#3327, GJS, cal.,10L c.1948
14k ..........................................$250    $300    $350

LONGINES, 17J., U shaped lugs, GJS
14k ..........................................$400    $450    $500

LONGINES, 17J., extended lugs, GJS, cal.9LT, c.1951
14k ..........................................$250    $300    $350

LONGINES, 17J., gold jewel settings, Ca. 1951
gold filled..............................$100    $125    $150
14k (w)..................................$175    $200    $250

LONGINES, 17J., aux. sec., GJS, Ca.1951
14k ..........................................$175    $200    $275

LONGINES, 17J., RF#8475, GJS, cal.10L, c.1948
14k ..........................................$250    $300    $350

LONGINES, 17J., butler finish, GJS, cal.9L, c.1955
14k ..........................................$175    $200    $275

⊕ Some grades are not included. Their values can be
determined by comparing with similar age, size, metal
content, style, grades, or models such as time only,
chronograph, repeater etc. listed.

LONGINES, 17J., aux. sec., GJS, cal.9LT, c.1950
14k ..........................................$225      $275       $325

LONGINES, 17J., butler finish, GJS, cal.8LN, c.1942
14k ..........................................$200      $250       $350

LONGINES, 17J., beveled lugs, GJS, cal.8LN, c.1947
14k ..........................................$150      $200       $250

LONGINES, 17J., wide bezel, GJS, cal.23z, c.1950
gold filled..............................$125      $150       $175

LONGINES, 17J., tank style, GJS, cal.23z, c.1957
14k ..........................................$200      $250       $300

LONGINES, 17J., crab leg lugs, GJS, cal.10L, c.1951
gold filled.................................$75      $100       $125

LONGINES, 17J., GJS, cal. 23Z, Ca. 1950
gold filled.................................$70      $80       $90

LONGINES, 17J., bezeled case, GJS, cal.9LT, c.1955
gold filled.................................$75      $100       $125

LONGINES, 17J., curly lugs, GJS, cal.23z, c.1950
gold filled..............................$100      $135       $200

LONGINES, 17J., checked dial, GJS, cal.22L, c.1957
14k ..........................................$225      $275       $325

LONGINES, 17J., RF#1050, mystery dial, cal.23z, c.1960
14k .........................................$300        $350        $400

LONGINES, 17J., stepped lugs, GJS, cal.10L, c.1948
gold filled...............................$125        $150        $185

LONGINES, 17J., textured bezel, GJS, cal.22L, c.1950
14k .........................................$300        $350        $400

LONGINES, 17J., stepped case, GJS, cal.23z, c.1955
14k .........................................$250        $300        $350
gold filled...............................$100        $125        $150

LONGINES, 17J., carved case, GJS,
gold filled...............................$100        $125        $150

LONGINES, 17J., hooded lugs, GJS, cal.8LN, c.1942
gold filled ...............................$100        $125        $150

LONGINES, 17J., RF#2288, hidden lugs, GJS, c.1955
14k .........................................$400        $450        $500

LONGINES, 17J., hidden lugs
14k .........................................$600        $700        $800

LONGINES, 17J., contract case or recent case,
14k .........................................$400        $450        $500

LONGINES, 17 jewels, 42mm
14k (w) ...................................$275        $300        $400

🕐 Some grades are not included. Their values can be
determined by comparing with **similar** age, size, metal
content, style, grades, or models such as **time only**,
chronograph, repeater etc. listed.

LONGINES, 17 jewels, fancy lugs
14k .............................................$300      $350      $400

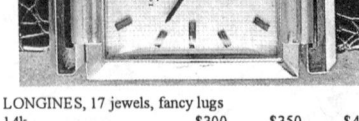

LONGINES, 17 jewels, c. 1939
14k .............................................$350      $400      $500

LONGINES, 17 jewels, curvex, slanted lugs
14k (w)....................................$250      $300      $350

LONGINES, 17 jewels, fancy lugs, c. 1942
14k .............................................$300      $350      $375

LONGINES, 17 jewels, fancy lugs, c. 1947
14k .............................................$275      $325      $375

LONGINES, 17 jewels, curved, flared
14k .............................................$275      $300      $350

LONGINES, 15 jewels, chased bezel
14k .........................................$700      $800      $900

LONGINES, 15 jewels, engraved bezel, c. 1928
14k (w) ...................................$450      $500      $650

LONGINES, 17J., faceted crystal,
14k .........................................$150      $200      $250

LONGINES, 17J., fancy lugs & diamond bezel
14k(W)...................................$500      $600      $700

LONGINES, 17J., curved case, Ca. 1930s
14k .........................................$250      $300      $350

LONGINES, 17J., fancy lugs
14k .................................\$400    \$450    \$500

LONGINES, 17J., cal#10L, center sec.,
14k .................................\$250    \$300    \$350

LONGINES, 17J., fancy lugs,
14k .................................\$325    \$350    \$400

LONGINES, 17J., center sec., fancy lugs, ca.1946
14k .................................\$250    \$300    \$350

LONGINES, 17J., cal#232, ca. 1948
14k .................................\$250    \$300    \$350

LONGINES, 17J., fancy lugs, cal#10L
14k .................................\$200    \$250    \$300

LONGINES, 17J., aux. sec.
14k .................................\$250    \$300    \$350

LONGINES, 17J., aux. sec.
14k .................................\$200    \$250    \$275

LONGINES, 17J., ca. 1952
14k .................................\$200    \$250    \$300

⊕ Some grades are not included. Their values can be
determined by comparing with **similar** age, size, metal
content, style, grades, or models such as **time only**,
chronograph, repeater etc. listed.

LONGINES, 17J., offset lugs
14k .................................\$250    \$300    \$350

LONGINES, 17J., fancy lugs, ca. 1951
14k ...........................................$400    $500    $600

LONGINES, 17J., Flared
14k .........................................$400    $450    $500

LONGINES, 17J., fancy bezel
14k ...........................................$200    $250    $300

LONGINES, 17 jewels, enameled bezel, c. 1928
14k .........................................$400    $450    $500

LONGINES, 17J., flared case, GJS, c.1955
gold filled...............................$175    $200    $275

LONGINES, 17 jewels, formed case
14k .........................................$350    $400    $475

LONGINES, 17J., flared case, GJS, cal.9LT, c.1950
gold filled...............................$150    $200    $250

LONGINES, 17J., flared, textured dial
14k ...........................................$400    $450    $550

LONGINES, 17J.,antimagnetic
s. steel ....................................$150    $200    $250

🕐 Some grades are not included. Their values can be
determined by comparing with similar age, size, metal
content, style, grades, or models such as time only,
chronograph, repeater etc. listed.

## LONGINES MOVEMENT IDENTIFICATION

Cal. No. 4.21, Ca.1930

Cal. No. 5.16, Ca.1922

Cal. No. 6.22, Ca.1932

Cal. No. 7.45, Ca.1916

Cal. No. 7.48, Ca.1925

Cal. No. 8.23, Ca.1931

Cal. No. 8.47, Ca.1916

Cal. No. 9.32, Ca.1932

Cal. No. 9.47, Ca.1922

Cal. No. 12.19, Ca.1934

Cal. No. 13.15, Ca.1936

Cal. No. 25.17, Ca.1935

## PRODUCTION TOTALS
### LONGINES DATE OF MOVEMENT MANUFACTURE

| DATE– SERIAL # | DATE– SERIAL # | DATE– SERIAL # |
|---|---|---|
| 1867 ---        1 | 1911 - 2,500,000 | 1937 - 5,500,000 |
| 1870 ---   20,000 | 1912 - 2,750,000 | 1938 - 5,750,000 |
| 1875 --- 100,000 | 1913 - 3,000,000 | 1940 - 6,000,000 |
| 1882 --- 250,000 | 1915 - 3,250,000 | 1945 - 7,000,000 |
| 1888 --- 500,000 | 1917 - 3,500,000 | 1950 - 8,000,000 |
| 1893 --- 750,000 | 1919 - 3,750,000 | 1953 - 9,000,000 |
| 1899 - 1,000,000 | 1922 - 4,000,000 | 1956-10,000,000 |
| 1901 - 1,250,000 | 1925 - 4,250,000 | 1959-11,000,000 |
| 1904 - 1,500,000 | 1926 - 4,500,000 | 1962-12,000,000 |
| 1905 - 1,750,000 | 1928 - 4,750,000 | 1966-13,000,000 |
| 1907 - 2,000,000 | 1929 - 5,000,000 | 1967-14,000,000 |
| 1909 - 2,250,000 | 1934 - 5,250,000 | 1969-15,000,000 |

The above list is provided for determining the APPROXIMATE age of your watch. Match serial number with date. Watches were not necessarily sold in the exact order of manufactured date.
LONGINES date of movement manufacture

Movement number

Caliber number

Caliber number

Reference number

Cal. No. 10.68, Ca.1932

Cal. No. 10.68, Lindburg

Cal. No. 12.68, Ca.1938

Cal. No. 12.68 Z, Ca.1939

Cal. No. 14.16, Ca.1951

Cal. No. 14.16 S, Ca.1954

Cal. No. 14.17, Ca.1952

Cal. No. 15.18, Ca.1941

Cal. No. 19 A, Ca.1952

Cal. No. 19.4, Ca.1953

Cal. No. 19.4 S, Ca.1953

Cal. No. 22 A, Ca.1945

Cal. No. 22 L, Ca.1946

Cal. No. 23 Z, Ca.1948

Cal. No. 23 ZD, Ca.1954

Cal. No. 25.17, Ca.1935

Cal. No. RR 280, Ca.1963

Cal. No. 290, Ca.1958

Cal. No. 310

Cal. No. 312

Cal. No. 380

Cal. No. 420

Cal. No. 430, Ca.1967

Cal. No. 320

Cal. No. 450

Cal. No. 460

Cal. No. 470

Cal. No. 30 CH, Ca.1947

Cal. No. 30 ZN

Cal. No. 330

LONGINES, 17J., "COMET", cal.702, c.1972
s. steel ........................................$75    $100    $125

LONGINES, 17J., lady's style, center lugs, c.1948
14k C&B ...................................$200    $250    $275

LONGINES, 15J., lady's style,
14k C&B ...................................$200    $250    $300

LORTON, 17 jewels, chronog., c. 1950
s. steel .....................................$150    $175    $200

LOUIS, 17J., center sec.,
14k ...........................................$100    $125    $150

LOUVIC, 17J., mystery dial, long triangular case, c.1950
base metal ...............................$75    $100    $135

LOUVIC, 17J., hunter style case, ca. 1965
s. steel ....................................$125    $150    $200

LOUVIC, 17J., mystery diamond dial, ca.1960
s. steel .....................................$60    $70    $80

LUCERNE, 17 jewels, 14k case & band
14k C&B ...................................$350    $400    $450

LUCIEN PICCARD, 17J., movement by Ditisheim
14k ...........................................$200    $250    $325

LUCIEN PICCARD, 17 jewels, gem set bezel
gold filled..............................$200     $250     $300

LUCIEN PICCARD, 17 jewels, "Seahawk," auto wind
18k C&B..............................$400     $450     $550

LUCIEN PICCARD, 17 jewels, wind indicator, c. 1958
s. steel .....................................$100     $125     $175

LUCIEN PICCARD, 17 jewels, skeletonized
18k ...........................................$800     $900     $1,000

🕐 Some grades are not included. Their values can be
determined by comparing with **similar** age, size, metal
content, style, grades, or models such as **time only**,
chronograph, repeater etc. listed.

LUSINA, 17 jewels, aux. sec., fancy lugs
gold filled ..................................$65     $80     $95

LYCEUM, 17J., beveled case, aux. sec.
14k ...........................................$125     $150     $175

MARLYS, 15J., G.J.S., c.1935
14k ...........................................$200     $225     $250

MAPPIN, 15 jewels, duo dial, c. 1930
9k ...........................................$1,000     $1,150     $1,350

MARS, 17 jewels, "Dateur," hinged back, c. 1934
gold filled ...............................$350     $400     $500

MARVIN, 17J., center sec., cal.520s, c.1943
14k ...............................................$100     $125     $150

MARVIN, 17J., non magnetic,
gold filled.....................................$40     $50     $75

MASTER, 17J., engraved case, c.1943
gold plate ...................................$40     $45     $55

MASTER, 17J., tonneau case, c.1943
gold plate ...................................$40     $45     $55

MASTER, 17J., stepped case, c.1943
gold plate ...................................$50     $55     $65

C.H. MEYLAN, 17 jewels, c. 1940s
18k ...........................................$700     $800     $900

C.H. MEYLAN, 18 jewels, jumping hr., c. 1920
18k ...........................................$8,000     $9,000     $10,000

C.H. MEYLAN, 16 jewels, wire lugs
14k ...........................................$700     $800     $900

C.H. MEYLAN, 27 jewels, 1 button chronog., 2 reg.
18k ...........................................$2,500     $3,000     $3,500

C.H. MEYLAN, 18J., ladies , Octagon case, c.1917
platinum...................................$300     $350     $400

J.E. MEYLAN, 17J., chronograph, 2 reg., ca. 1937
14k .....................................$1,000      $1,200      $1,400
s. steel ..................................$300        $350        $400

J.E. MEYLAN,17J., stop watch,
s. steel ..................................$175        $200        $250

MIDO, 15 jewels, in form of car radiator, c. 1940s
silver ...................................$1,700      $2,000      $2,500

MIDO, 17 jewels, chronog., "Multi-centerchrono", c. 1952
s. steel ..................................$300        $375        $450

⊕ Some grades are not included. Their values can be
determined by comparing with similar age, size, metal
content, style, grades, or models such as time only,
chronograph, repeater etc. listed.

MIDO, 17 jewels, chronog., "Multi-centerchrono"
s. steel ..................................$400        $450        $500
with telemeter dial ..................$425        $475        $525

MIDO, 17J., choronog., cal.1300, c.1954
gold filled ..............................$250        $300        $375
14k .........................................$650        $750        $800
18k .....................................$1,000      $1,250      $1,500

MIDO, 17J., choronog., pulsations, c.1955
18k .....................................$1,100      $1,300      $1,600

MIDO, 17J., carved case, cal.2m, c.1947
14k .........................................$150        $200        $250

MIDO, 17 jewels, diamond dial
platinum .................................$500    $600    $675
14k .......................................$250    $300    $350

MIDO, 17 jewels "Multifort," diamond dial
s. steel ..................................$125    $150    $225

MIDO, 17 jewels, fancy lugs, c. 1945
14k .......................................$250    $300    $350

MIDO, 15 jewels, mystery dial, c. 1935
s. steel ..................................$500    $550    $650

MIDO, 17J., multifort grand luxe, date, ca. 1950s
18k C&B................................$600    $700    $800

MIDO, 17J., RF#7204, cal.d917b, c.1958
s. steel ..................................$100    $125    $175

MIDO, 17J., RF#228, mid size case, c.1943
s. steel ..................................$100    $125    $150

MIDO, 17J., mid size case, c.1940
gold filled ..............................$100    $125    $175

MIDO, 17J., mid size case, cal.917r, c.1949
s. steel ..................................$100    $125    $150

🕐 Some grades are not included. Their values can be
determined by comparing with similar age, size, metal
content, style, grades, or models such as time only,
chronograph, repeater etc. listed.

MIDO, 17J., super auto-wind, muiltfort extra,
14k .................................... $175    $225    $300
s. steel ................................... $85    $100    $125

MIDO, 17J., "power wind", c.1955
s. steel ................................... $60    $80    $100

MIDO, 17J., rotating bezel, c.1960
s. steel ................................... $250    $300    $350

MIDO, 17J., multifort grand luxe, extra-flat
s. steel ................................... $100    $125    $150

MILDIA, 17 jewels
s. steel ................................... $30    $40    $50

MIMO, 15 jewels, date
gold filled ............................... $200    $225    $250

MIMO, 17J., "De Frece", date, c.1935
14k(w) .................................... $300    $350    $400

MIMO, 17 jewels, jumping hr., wandering min. & sec.
gold filled ............................... $300    $350    $450

MIMO, 17 jewels, 8 day, 6 gear train, c. 1950s
gold filled ............................... $800    $900    $1,000

MIMO, 17 jewels, duo dial
s. steel ..................................$400      $465      $575

MIMO, 15 jewels, engraved bezel
gold filled..................................$40      $50      $60

MIMO, 15 jewels, "Mimomatic," c. 1932
s. steel .......................................$75      $90      $110

MINERVA, 29J., min. repeater, repeats on 2 gongs
18k ..................................$20,000    $25,000    $30,000

MINERVA, 17 jewels, chronog., 2 reg.
18k ..........................................$900      $1,000      $1,400
s. steel .....................................$275      $350      $450

MINERVA, 17 jewels, 2 reg.
18k ........................................$500      $600      $700

MINERVA, 17 jewels, waterproof, c. 1950s
14k .........................................$400      $450      $575
s. steel ....................................$250      $300      $350

MINERVA, 17J., Valjoux cal.723, c.1955
14k .........................................$750      $850      $1,000
s. steel ....................................$500      $600      $700

MINERVA, 19 jewels, chronog., 3 reg.
s. steel .....................................$300      $350      $400

MINERVA, 17 jewels, one button chronog., c. 1942
s. steel ..................................$275    $325    $365

MISC. SWISS, 15J., shield cover, enamel dial, ca. 1927
silver ......................................$500    $600    $700

MINERVA, 17J., chronog., day-date-month, 3 reg.
18k ........................................$1,000    $1,200    $1,400

MISC. SWISS,15J., **rim wind**, wire lugs, cal., c.1920
s. steel ..................................$250    $300    $375

MINERVA, 17 jewels, center sec., auto wind
gold filled..................................$70    $80    $100

MISC. SWISS,15J., enamel dial, c.1925
s. steel ..................................$300    $350    $400

MISC. SWISS,15J., wire lugs, c.1925
silver ......................................$250    $325    $400

MISC. SWISS, 15J., hunter style, wire lugs, ca. 1926
silver ......................................$450    $525    $600

Some grades are not included. Their values can be determined by comparing with **similar** age, size, metal content, style, grades, or models such as **time only**, chronograph, repeater etc. listed.

MISC. SWISS, 15J., wire lugs, Ca. 1918
silver .....................................$150     $200     $250

MISC. SWISS, 15J., wire lugs, Ca. 1917
silver .........................................$75     $100     $125

MISC. SWISS, 15J., wire lugs, Ca. 1918
silver .......................................$200     $250     $300

MISC. SWISS, 15J., wire lugs, Ca. 1917
silver .......................................$100     $125     $150

MISC. SWISS, 15J., wire lugs, Ca. 1917
base metal ...............................$100     $200     $300

MISC. SWISS, 15J., wire lugs, Ca. 1917
silver .......................................$100     $200     $300

MISC. SWISS, 15J., wire lugs, Ca. 1917
silver .......................................$100     $200     $300

MISC. SWISS, 15J., wire lugs, Ca. 1917
silver .......................................$800     $900     $1,000

MISC. SWISS, 15J., wire lugs, Ca. 1917
base metal ...............................$150     $250     $350

MISC. SWISS, 15J., wire lugs, Ca. 1919
base metal ...............................$300     $400     $500

🕐 Some grades are not included. Their values can be determined by comparing with **similar** age, size, metal content, style, grades, or models such as **time only**, chronograph, repeater etc. listed.

MISC. SWISS, 15J., wire lugs, Ca. 1917
silver ....................................$100     $150     $200

MISC. SWISS, 15J., wire lugs, Ca. 1917
14K............................................$100     $150     $200

MISC. SWISS, 15J., wire lugs, Ca. 1917
14K............................................$200     $300     $400

MISC. SWISS, 15J., wire lugs, Ca. 1917
14K............................................$100     $200     $300

MISC. SWISS, 15J., wire lugs, Ca. 1917
14K............................................$100     $200     $300

MISC. SWISS, 15J., wire lugs, Ca. 1917
14K............................................$100     $200     $300

MISC. SWISS, 15J., wire lugs, Ca. 1917
14k ...........................................$100     $200     $300

MISC. SWISS, 15J., wire lugs, Ca. 1917
14K ...........................................$200     $300     $400

MISC. SWISS, 15J.,  Ca. 1935
base metal................................$150     $200     $250

MISC. SWISS, 17J., nail set, 31 X 43mm, ca.1915
14k ...........................................$1,200     $1,400     $1,600

MISC. SWISS, 15J.,  ca.1916
18k .........................................$1,200     $1,400     $1,600

MISC. SWISS, 15J., Ca.1916
18K......................................$1,200     $1,400     $1,600

MISC. SWISS, 15J., Ca.1916
18K......................................$500     $600     $800

MISC. SWISS, 15J., Ca.1916
18K......................................$800     $900     $1,200

MISC. SWISS, 15J., Ca.1916
18K......................................$1,400     $1,600     $1,800

MISC. SWISS, 15J., Ca.1916
14K......................................$300     $400     $500

MISC. SWISS, 15J., wire lugs, Ca.1916
silver......................................$100     $200     $300

MISC. SWISS, 15J., Ca.1916
18K......................................$800     $1,000     $1,200

MISC. SWISS, 15J., Ca.1916
silver......................................$100     $150     $200

MISC. SWISS, 15J., wire lugs, Ca.1916
14K......................................$200     $300     $400

MISC. SWISS, 15J., wire lugs, Ca.1917
silver......................................$100     $200     $300

MISC. SWISS, 15J., wire lugs, Ca.1917
silver .........................................$100    $200    $300

MISC. SWISS, 15J., wire lugs, Ca.1917
silver .........................................$100    $200    $300

MISC. SWISS, 15J., wire lugs, Ca.1917
silver .........................................$150    $250    $350

MISC. SWISS, 15J., Ca.1925
14K.............................................$250    $350    $450

MISC. SWISS, 15J., Ca.1925
14K.............................................$275    $375    $475

MISC. SWISS, 15J., Ca.1925
14K .............................................$250    $350    $450

MISC. SWISS, 15J., Ca.1925
14K .............................................$250    $350    $450

MISC. SWISS, 15J., Ca.1925
14K .............................................$250    $350    $450

MISC. SWISS, 15J., Ca.1925
14K .............................................$200    $300    $400

MISC. SWISS, 15J., Ca.1925
14K .............................................$200    $300    $400

🕐 Some grades are not included. Their values can be determined by comparing with **similar** age, size, metal content, style, grades, or models such as **time only**, chronograph, repeater etc. listed.

MISC. SWISS, 15J., Ca.1925
14K.........................................$300    $400    $500

MISC. SWISS, 15J., Ca.1930
18K.........................................$400    $600    $800

MISC. SWISS, 15J., Ca.1925
14K.........................................$200    $300    $400

MISC. SWISS, 15J., Ca.1930
14K.........................................$300    $400    $500

MISC. SWISS, 15J., Ca.1930
14K.........................................$400    $600    $800

MISC. SWISS, 15J., Ca.1930
18K.........................................$400    $600    $800

MISC. SWISS, 15J., Ca.1930
18K.........................................$400    $600    $800

MISC. SWISS, 15J., Ca.1930
18K.........................................$300    $400    $500

MISC. SWISS, 15J., Ca.1930
18K.........................................$300    $400    $500

MISC. SWISS, 15J., flex lugs, Ca.1930
18K .........................................$750    $850    $950

🕐 Some grades are not included. Their values can be
determined by comparing with similar age, size, metal
content, style, grades, or models such as time only,
chronograph, repeater etc. listed.

MISC. SWISS, 15J., Ca.1930
18K.........................................$600    $800    $1,000

MISC. SWISS, 15J., wire lugs, ca. 1925
silver ........................................$150    $175    $225

MISC. SWISS, 15J., wire lugs, nail set, ca.1925
silver ........................................$200    $250    $300

MISC. SWISS, 15J., aux. sec., ca. 1930s
gold filled...................................$75    $100    $125

MISC. SWISS, 17 jewels, picture watch "Flip up"
gold filled...................................$200    $250    $300

MISC. SWISS, 17J, **Flip Top** winds by opening lid, Ca.1932
base metal ..........................$1,000    $1,200    $1,500

MISC. SWISS, 17J., watch top flips up to view photo, c.1950
gold filled ..............................$200    $250    $300

MISC. SWISS, 17J.,  day date month moon phzse, Ca. 1955
gold filled ..............................$300    $350    $400
14K ....................................... $500    $700    $1,000

MISC. SWISS, 17J., jump hr., wandering min., c. 1930
9k ............................................$700    $900    $1,100

MISC. SWISS, 17J., wandering min., hr. by red mark
s. steel ....................................$250    $300    $350

MISC. SWISS, 17 jewels, fancy bezel
14k ............................................$275    $300    $350

MISC. SWISS, 17 jewels, masonic symbols, c. 1950s
s. steel & gold filled .............. $900      $1,100      $1,200

MISC. SWISS, 17 jewels, masonic symbols, c. 1975
base metal .............................. $200      $350      $450

MISC. SWISS, 15 jewels, early auto wind, c. 1930s
s. steel .................................... $400      $500      $650

MISC. SWISS, 15 jewels, 8 day movement , (8 JOURS)

MISC. SWISS, 15 jewels, 8 day watch, Ca. 1935
base metal .............................. $200      $300      $400
silver ...................................... $300      $400      $500

MISC. SWISS, 17 jewels, digital hr., min., sec.
gold filled .............................. $325      $375      $450
s. steel .................................... $300      $350      $400

MISC. SWISS, 15 jewels, double dial, c.1935
9K ............................................ $575      $675      $825

MISC. SWISS, 15 jewels, center lugs, c.1936
9K ............................................ $150      $175      $200

MISC. SWISS, 1 jewel, "Chevrolet Corvette", c.1970
base metal .............................. $150      $200      $250

MISC. SWISS, 1 jewel, "Mercedes Benz", c.1970
base metal .............................. $150      $200      $250

MISC. SWISS, 29 jewels, repeater, 2 jacquemart
18k ........................................$4,000   $4,500   $5,000

MISC. SWISS, 17J., silver coin, Ca. 1960
silver ........................................$300   $400   $500

MISC. SWISS, 17J., world time, date, Ca. 1965
s. steel ........................................$150   $175   $225

MISC. SWISS, 17J., golfers scorer, Ca. 1950
base metal ........................................$100   $150   $200

MISC. SWISS, 17J., jump hour at 12:00, Ca. 1930
14K ........................................$2,500   $3,500   $4,500

MISC. SWISS,15J., one button chronog. wind and sets at 12,
center hinged lugs, enamel dial, c.1920s
silver ........................................$1,000   $1,100   $1,350

MISC. SWISS,15J., 1 button chronog., enamel dial, wire
lugs, Ca.1923
silver ........................................$750   $900   $1,200

MISC. SWISS, 15-17J, enamel dial, one button chronog.
s. steel ........................................$650   $750   $900

MISC. SWISS, 17J.,early chronog., ca.1929
18k ......................................$1,400    $1,600    $1,800

MISC. SWISS, 15J., one button chronog., ca. 1925
silver ........................................$600    $700    $800

MISC. SWISS,15-17J, enamel dial, 1 button chronog.,  2 reg.
s. steel .....................................$500    $600    $700

MISC. SWISS, 17J., one button, chronog., ca. 1950
gold filled................................$300    $400    $475

MISC. SWISS, 17J., 2 reg.,  chronograph
s. steel ....................................$175    $200    $225

MISC. SWISS, 17J, chronog., 2 reg.
gold filled ..............................$225    $275    $350

MISC. SWISS,17J., "chronographe" on dial, c.1940
base metal ..............................$125    $150    $175

MISC. SWISS,17J., by Venus
s. steel ......................................$150    $175    $200
14k ...........................................$325    $375    $425
18K ...........................................$375    $425    $500

MISC. SWISS, 17J., triple date, chronog., 2 reg., c.1955
s. steel .....................................$300      $350      $400

MISC. SWISS, 17J., triple date, moon ph., ca. 1967
gold filled ...............................$250      $300      $350

MISC. SWISS, 17J., chronog., triple date, moon ph., c. 1945
14k ......................................$1,500    $1,600    $1,800
s. steel .....................................$500      $600      $750

MISC. SWISS, 17 jewels, early auto wind, c. 1930s
14k ...........................................$400      $500      $600

MISC. SWISS, 17J., diamond dial, Ca. 1945
14K ...........................................$450      $550      $650

MISC. SWISS, 17 jewels, **split sec.** chronog., 2 reg.
18k ......................................$3,000    $4,000    $5,000
s. steel .....................................$1,800    $2,000    $2,500

MISC. SWISS, 17J., diamond dial, top hat, Ca. 1945
platinum...............................$1,200    $1,400    $1,600

MISC. SWISS, 18 jewels, Jaeger, chronog., c. 1930s
18k ............................................$600      $700      $900

MISC. SWISS, 17J., mystery diamond dial, Ca. 1960
gold filled ...............................$200      $250      $300

MISC. SWISS, 17J., Rhinestone dial & bezel, Ca. 1950
gold filled..............................$300      $350      $400

MISC. SWISS, 17J., Rhinestone dial & bezel, Ca. 1950
gold filled..............................$200      $250      $300

MISC. SWISS, 17J., hidden lugs, Ca. 1934
gold filled..............................$150      $175      $200

MISC. SWISS, 17J., fancy lugs, Ca. 1945
14K...........................................$550      $650      $750

MISC. SWISS, 17J., fancy lugs, Ca. 1940
gold filled..............................$100      $150      $200

MISC. SWISS, 17J., fancy bezel, Ca. 1938
14K .........................................$350      $450      $550

MISC. SWISS, 17J., fancy bezel, Ca. 1947
gold filled ..............................$200      $250      $300
14K ..........................................$600      $700      $800

MISC. SWISS, 17J., fancy bezel, Ca. 1930
18K (W)...............................$1,500      $1,800      $2,200

MISC. SWISS, 7J., stepped case, Ca. 1935
gold filled ..............................$100      $175      $250

MISC. SWISS, 17J., wandering hour, Ca. 1938
base metal ..............................$250      $350      $450

MISC. SWISS, 15J., Ca. 1938
14K.................................$250    $300    $350

MISC. SWISS, 17J., Fancy lugs, Ca. 1950
gold filled ..............................$175    $250    $300

MISC. SWISS, 15J., Ca. 1925
silver ......................................$100    $150    $200

MISC. SWISS, 17J., Fancy lugs, Ca. 1950
14K .........................................$600    $650    $700

MISC. SWISS, 21J., curved, Ca. 1938
gold filled................................$200    $250    $300

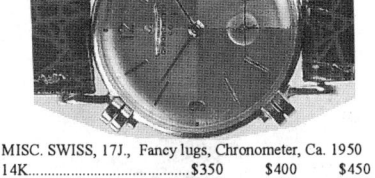

MISC. SWISS, 17J., Fancy lugs, Chronometer, Ca. 1950
14K..........................................$350    $400    $450

MISC. SWISS, 21J., Fancy lugs, Ca. 1955
18K ....................................$1,000    $1,400    $1,800

MISC. SWISS, 17J., Fancy lugs, Ca. 1948
gold filled ..............................$175    $200    $225

MISC. SWISS, 17J., Fancy lugs & bezel, Ca. 1950
gold filled................................$200    $250    $300

⊕ Some grades are not included. Their values can be
determined by comparing with **similar** age, size, metal
content, style, grades, or models such as **time only**,
chronograph, repeater etc. listed.

MISC. SWISS, 22J., Military, Ca. 1941
base metal ..............................$400    $450    $550

MISC. SWISS, 15J., Military, Ca. 1942
s. steel ....................................$150    $200    $250

MISC. SWISS, 16J., Military, Ca. 1940
base metal ..............................$150    $200    $250

MISC. SWISS, 17J., enamel & gold bezel, pin set, c.1925
18k ..........................................$275    $300    $350

MISC. SWISS,  15J., wire lugs, Ca. 1930
14K rose ..................................$100    $150    $200

MISC. SWISS,  15J., ,Ruby on case,  Ca. 1950
14K ........................................$100    $200    $300

MISC. SWISS,  15J., Ca. 1930
14K  case & band..................$200    $300    $400

MISC. SWISS,  15J., Ring watch, Ca. 1955
14K  .........................................$200    $300    $400

MISC. SWISS,  21J., horse shoe shsped, Ca. 1939
gold filled ..............................$200    $250    $300

MONARCH, 7 jewels, stepped case
gold filled..................................$40     $50     $60

MONARCH, 7 jewels,
gold filled..................................$40     $50     $60

MONARCH, 7 jewels, engraved bezel, curved
gold filled..................................$50     $60     $70

MONARCH, 7 jewels , curved
14k ..........................................$125     $150     $200
gold filled..................................$75     $95     $125

MONTBRILLANT, 15J., one button chronog. ca 1925
18k ..........................................$1,500     $2,000     $2,500

MONTE, 16J., "ancre", ca.1938
14k ..........................................$150     $175     $200

MORIVA,17J., auto-w. with wind indicator,
s. steel .....................................$100     $125     $150

HY. MOSER & CIE., 14J., "Signal Corps USA", ctr. lugs
silver ........................................$300     $350     $400

HY. MOSER & CIE., 14-18J., one button chronograph, wind
and set at 12, center lugs, 2 reg. Ca. 1920s
silver ........................................$2,000     $2,250     $2,500

MOVADO, 15J., polyplan, winds at 12 o'clock, 46mm, curved, c. 1910
18k .......................................$4,000     $5,000     $6,000

MOVADO, 15J., polyplan, winds at 12 o'clock,
14k .......................................$3,000     $4,000     $5,000

MOVADO, 17J., 50mm long, Calendarmeto, moon ph.
leather .....................................$675     $775     $975

MOVADO, 17J., RAY SKIN COVER
silver .......................................$250     $275     $325

MOVADO, 17J.,
silver .......................................$200     $225     $275

MOVADO, 15J., "Chronometre", c.1930
14k .........................................$250     $300     $350

MOVADO, 17J., day date month, "Sportsman"
14k .........................................$300     $400     $500

MOVADO, 17J., day date month,snap back
18k .........................................$500     $600     $700

MOVADO, 17J., triple date,  snap back ," calendomatic"
18k .......................................$700     $800     $900

MOVADO, 28J., date, "Kingmatic", c.1950
s. steel ......................................$80     $100     $120
14k(w)...........................................$250     $300     $350

MOVADO, 17J., month date, ca. 1950s
14k ...........................................$250    $300    $450

MOVADO, 17J., 1 button chronog., c.1948
s. steel .....................................$400    $500    $600

MOVADO, 17 jewels, day-date-month, c. 1945
18k ...........................................$700    $800    $900
gold filled...............................$350    $400    $500
s. steel ....................................$300    $350    $400

MOVADO, 17J., chronog., 2 reg., c.1940
14k ....................................$1,200    $1,400    $1,600

MOVADO, 17J, triple date, moon phases, Ca. 1950
s. steel .....................................$900    $1,000    $1,200

MOVADO, 17J., 3 reg. chronog.
s. steel .....................................$850    $1,100    $1,200

MOVADO, 17J., 3 reg. chronog.,
18k ....................................$2,500    $3,000    $3,500
14k ....................................$2,000    $2,500    $3,000
s. steel .....................................$800    $900    $1,200

MOVADO, 17J., "tempograf, chronog., 2 reg., c.1935
s. steel .....................................$750    $850    $950

MOVADO, 17J., 3 reg. chronog., date
s. steel ......................................$200      $300      $400

MOVADO, 17J., El Primero date at 5, c.1972
s. steel ......................................$300      $350      $400

MOVADO,17J., RF#2652, rotating chapter,cal.352, c.1958
s. steel ......................................$200      $250      $300

MOVADO, 17J., center sec., cal.261, c.1948
18k ..........................................$300      $350      $400

MOVADO, 17J., center sec., c.1942
14k ..........................................$250      $300      $350

MOVADO, 17J., center sec., c.1948
14k ..........................................$275      $300      $350

MOVADO, 17J., "Cronoplan", Ca. 1940s
s. steel ......................................$200      $250      $300

MOVADO, 15J., aux. sec., cal.75, c.1946
s. steel ......................................$100      $150      $200

⏰ Some grades are not included. Their values can be
determined by comparing with similar age, size, metal
content, style, grades, or models such as time only,
chronograph, repeater etc. listed.

MOVADO, 17J., aux. sec., cal.135, c.1955
s. steel ......................................$100    $125    $150

MOVADO, 17J., center sec.
14k ...........................................$250    $300    $350

MOVADO, 17J., auto-wind, cal.8577, c.1957
14k ...........................................$250    $300    $350

MOVADO, 17., center sec.
s. steel ......................................$100    $150    $200

MOVADO, 17J., Tiffany & Co. on dial, center sec.,
14k ...........................................$300    $350    $400

MOVADO, 20J., auto-wind,
14k ...........................................$250    $300    $350

MOVADO, 28J., center sec.," Kingmatic",
14k ...........................................$250    $300    $350

MOVADO, 15J., 2 colors of gold, tonneau, Ca. 1940
18k ...........................................$500    $600    $700

🕐 Some grades are not included. Their values can be determined by comparing with **similar** age, size, metal content, style, models and grades listed.

MOVADO, 17J., aux. sec.
18k ...........................................$300    $400    $500

MOVADO, 15 jewels, aux. sec.
14k C&B...............................$300    $400    $500

MOVADO, 17J., auto-w., ca. 1949
14k ...........................................$300    $350    $400

MOVADO, 17 jewels, aux. sec., center lugs
14k ...........................................$300    $350    $400

MOVADO, 17J., nonmagnetic
s. steel ....................................$150    $200    $250

MOVADO, 17J., cal. 7025, GJS, c.1964
18k ...........................................$250    $300    $350

MOVADO, 15 jewels, center lugs, c. 1930
18k ...........................................$500    $600    $700

MOVADO, 17J., hidden lugs, tu-tone dial, c.1960
18k ...........................................$450    $550    $600

MOVADO, 17J., textured 18k dial
18k ...........................................$300    $400    $500

MOVADO, 17 jewels, date at 12 o'clock
14k C&B...............................$400    $500    $600

MOVADO, 15 jewels, fancy lugs
18k ...................................... $400      $450      $500

MOVADO, 17J., wide bezel, c.1958
gold filled................................ $100      $125      $150

MOVADO, 17J., diamond bezel,
18k .......................................... $250      $300      $350

MOVADO, 17J., RF#621, c.1932
gold filled................................ $150      $175      $225

MOVADO, 17J., stepped case, "Curviplan", GJS, c.1942
14k .......................................... $600      $700      $800

MOVADO, 17J., aux. sec., c.1940
14k .......................................... $300      $350      $400

MOVADO, 17J., extended lugs, c.1945
14k .......................................... $400      $450      $500

MOVADO, 17J., aux. sec., c.1945
14k .......................................... $300      $350      $425

MOVADO, 17J., extended lugs, GJS, c.1940
14k .......................................... $300      $350      $400

MOVADO, 17J., tu-tone case, RF#13906, Ca.1948
14k .......................................... $300      $350      $400

Some grades are not included. Their values can be determined by comparing with similar age, size, metal content, style, grades, or models such as time only, chronograph, repeater etc. listed.

MOVADO, 15 jewels, curved, chronometre
14k ...........................................$600    $650    $700

MOVADO, 15 jewels, c. 1929
18k ...........................................$400    $500    $600

MOVADO, 17J., cal#510, ca.1941
14k ...........................................$400    $450    $500

MOVADO, 17 jewels
14k ...........................................$250    $300    $375

MOVADO, 17J., curviplan,
gold filled................................$300    $400    $500

MOVADO, 17 jewels, automatic, tank style
18k ...........................................$400    $500    $600

MOVADO, 17J., curviplan, ca.1941
14k ...........................................$500    $600    $700

MOVADO, 17 jewels, fancy lugs, c. 1947
14k ...........................................$300    $350    $400

MOVADO, 17J., fancy lugs, ca.1942
14k ...........................................$500    $550    $600

🕐 Some grades are not included. Their values can be determined by comparing with **similar** age, size, metal content, style, grades, or models such as **time only**, chronograph, repeater etc. listed.

MOVADO, 17J., Ca. 1940s
14k ...........................................$250    $300    $375

MOVADO, 17 jewels
18k ...........................................$400      $500      $600

MOVADO, 17 jewels, day date, Ca.1948
18k ...........................................$400      $500      $600

MOVADO, 17 jewels, hidden lugs, Ca.1940
14k ...........................................$425      $500      $600

MOVADO,17 jewels, stepped & hidden lugs, GJS, Ca.1937
14k ...........................................$450      $500      $600

MOVADO, 17 jewels, ladies, alarm, Ca.1950
18k ...........................................$400      $500      $600

SIDE VIEW

Mt. VERNON, 15 & 21 jewels, curvex style
gold plate...................................$60      $70      $85

Mt. VERNON, 15 jewels, curvex style
gold plate...................................$60      $70      $85

Mt. VERNON, 15 jewels, stepped case
s. steel......................................$60      $70      $85

Mt. VERNON, 17 jewels
gold filled..................................$60      $70      $85

Mt. VERNON, 15 jewels
gold filled..................................$35      $40      $55

## MOVADO MOVEMENT IDENTIFICATION

Caliber 35

Caliber 65

Caliber 575

Caliber25, 27-Sweep Second

Caliber 28

Caliber 575, Ermeto-Baby

Caliber 578, Ermeto Calendine

579, Calendoplan Baby

Caliber 5

Caliber 15

Caliber 50SP

Caliber 105, 107-Center Second

Caliber 190

Caliber 375, 377-Center Second

Caliber 440, 443-Center Second

Caliber 510

Caliber 260M, 261

Caliber 150MN, 157-Sweep Second

Caliber 155, Calendermeto

Caliber 470, 477-Center Second

Caliber 473, 473SC-Calendar/Moon phase

Caliber 475, 475SC-Center Second

Caliber 225, 255M

Caliber 115

Caliber 118

Caliber 220, 220M

Caliber 221, 226

Caliber 223, 228

Caliber 224, 224A

U. NARDIN, 29 J., "Astrolabium," self wind, waterproof, local time, equinoctial time, months, signs of zodiac, elevation & azimuth of sun & moon, aspect in which sun & moon stand to each other
18k .......................................$6,000     $7,000     $9,000

U. NARDIN, 17J., one button pulsations. ca.1920
18k .......................................$1,800     $2,000     $2,200

U. NARDIN, 17 jewels, chronog., c. 1950s
18k.......................................$2,500     $2,700     $3,000

U. NARDIN, 17 jewels, split sec. chronog., c. 1910
silver...................................$7,000     $8,000     $9,000

U. NARDIN, 17 jewels, chronog., 3 reg. c. 1940s
18k.......................................$2,000     $2,500     $3,000

U. NARDIN, 25 jewels, date
14k...........................................$350     $400     $450

U. NARDIN, 17J., chronog., "Pulsations," c. 1920
18k .......................................$3,000     $3,500     $4,000

⏰ Some grades are not included. Their values can be determined by comparing with **similar** age, size, metal content, style, grades, or models such as **time only**, chronograph, repeater etc. listed.

U. NARDIN, 17 jewels, auto wind, c. 1952
14k ............................................$250      $300      $350

U. NARDIN,21J.,auto-wind
18k............................................$300      $350      $400

U. NARDIN, 17J., center sec., chronometer, c.1950
gold filled................................$100      $125      $150

U. NARDIN, 17J., aux sec.
s. steel......................................$100      $150      $200

U. NARDIN, 17J., center sec., auto-wind, c.1950
14k .............................................$250      $300      $350

U. NARDIN, 17J., aux. sec.
18k...............................................$275      $325      $375

U. NARDIN, 17J., center sec., auto-wind, c.1950
18k ...........................................$250      $300      $375

U. NARDIN, 17J., fancy lugs
18k............................................$400      $500      $600

U. NARDIN, 17J., aux. sec., carved lugs, c.1950
14k .............................................$400    $450    $500

U. NARDIN, 17J., aux. sec., chronometer, c.1950
14k .............................................$250    $300    $350

U. NARDIN, 17J., aux. sec., chronometer, c.1947
18k .............................................$250    $300    $350

U. NARDIN, 17J., aux. sec., chronometer, C.1951
14k .............................................$200    $250    $300

U. NARDIN, 17J., aux. sec., chronometer, c.1964
gold plate.................................$100    $125    $150

U. NARDIN, 17J., aux. sec., chronometer, c.1948
gold filled.................................$100    $125    $150

U. NARDIN, 17J., fancy lugs
14k.............................................$250    $300    $350

U. NARDIN, 25J., chronometer, date, c.1975
s. steel.....................................$150    $175    $200

🕐 Some grades are not included. Their values can be
determined by comparing with **similar** age, size, metal
content, style, grades, or models such as **time only**,
chronograph, repeater etc. listed.

U. NARDIN, 17J., fluted case
14k ............................................$300      $400      $500

U. NARDIN, 17 jewels, c. 1920
18k................................$550      $600      $700

U. NARDIN, 17J., aux. sec., chronometer, c.1949
14k ..........................................$250      $300      $350

U. NARDIN, 17 jewels, WW I military style
s. steel......................................$450      $525      $600

U. NARDIN, 17J., aux. sec., chronometer, c.1950
18k ........................................$300      $350      $400

U. NARDIN, 17J., lady's chronometer, c.1947
14k C&B ................................$400      $450      $500

U. NARDIN, 17J., extended side lugs, chronometer, c.1951
14k ..........................................$250      $300      $350

NATIONAL, 17 jewels,
gold filled................................$40      $50      $65

U. NARDIN, 17 jewels, faceted crystal & bezel
s. steel .....................................$175      $225      $300

Some grades are not included. Their values can be determined by comparing with **similar** age, size, metal content, style, grades, or models such as **time only**, chronograph, repeater etc. listed.

NATIONAL, 15 jewels, day-date-month
gold filled................................$50      $60      $85

NATIONAL, 17 jewels, center sec., waterproof
s. steel ........................................$20      $30      $45

NATIONAL, 17 J., auto wind, center sec., waterproof
gold filled.................................$20      $30      $45

NEW ENGLAND W. Co., 7J.,  Addison, Alden, Cavour,
Hale, and other models, Ca.1915, colored dial add ( $25 )
14k ...........................................$100      $125      $150
gold filled.................................$50      $70      $90

NEW HAVEN, 7 jewels, engraved bezel
base metal ................................$15      $20      $30

NEW HAVEN, 7 jewels, stepped case
base metal ................................$15      $20      $30

NEW HAVEN, 7 jewels
base metal................................$10      $15      $25

NEW HAVEN,2 jewels, "Elf" ladies, etched case
base metal.................................. $5      $10      $15

NEW HAVEN, 7 jewels, "Duchess" ladies, etched case
gold plate....................................$5      $10      $15

NEWMARK, 17J., military chronog., c.1979
s. steel..................................... $150      $200      $250

NEW YORK STANDARD, 7 jewels
gold filled.................................$15      $25      $40
base metal.................................$10      $15      $20

NICE WATCH Co., 17J., one button chronog., c.1930
base metal ..............................$250      $300      $375

NICOLET W. CO., 17J., one button chronog., Ca. 1960
gold filled...............................$275      $325      $375

CHARLES NICOLET, 17J., chronog., ca. 1945
18k ...........................................$375      $425      $475

MARC NICOLET, 17J., aux. seconds
14k ...........................................$150      $165      $195

NITON, 18J., jump hr., (showing dial and movement)
(made ebauche for P.P.&CO.)
18k(W) ..............................$3,500      $4,500      $5,500

NIVADA, 21J., center sec., c.1960
base metal.................................$50      $65      $80

NIVADA, 21J., center sec., date, auto-w, c.1965
s. steel......................................$40      $60      $85

NIVADA, 25 jewels, waterproof, c. 1940
14k.............................................$500      $550      $625
gold filled...............................$275      $350      $425

NORMANDIE, 17 jewels, compass, c. 1945
s. steel ........................................$50      $60      $70

NORMANDIE, 17J., gold train, hidden lugs, cal.4873
14k ...........................................$150     $175     $200

OCTO, 17J., fluted lugs,
14k ...........................................$275     $325     $395

OFAIR, 17J., chronog., cal. Valjoux 72c, c.1948
gold filled................................$300     $350     $400
14k .........................................$600     $700     $775
18k .........................................$750     $850     $950

🕐 Some grades are not included. Their values can be
determined by comparing with similar age, size, metal
content, style, grades, or models such as time only,
chronograph, repeater etc. listed.

OGIVAL, 17 jewels, auto wind
gold filled................................$30      $40      $50

OLLENDORFF, 17 jewels, fancy lugs
14k...........................................$300     $350     $425

OLLENDORFF, 17 jewels, movement plates made of gold
14k............................................$500     $600     $700

OLLENDORFF, 7J., direct read, stepped case, c.1930
base metal................................$200     $250     $300

OLLENDORFF, 15J., engraved bevel,
chrome plated............................$40      $45      $55

OLMA, 17J., auto-wind, by Wyler, c.1932
s. steel ....................................$150     $175     $200

OLMA, 17J., large crab legs style lugs
gold plate ..................................$50     $75     $100

OLYMPIA, 15 jewels, double dial, c. 1938
s. steel ....................................$300     $350     $400

OMEGA, 15J., center lugs, enamel dial, Ca. 1930
18k ..........................................$500     $600     $750

OMEGA, 15J., wire lugs, Ca. 1925
silver ........................................$250     $350     $475

OMEGA, 15J., wire lugs, ca. 1930s
18k........................................$700     $800     $950

OMEGA, 15J., wire lugs,
14k........................................$350     $400     $450

OMEGA, 17 jewels, center sec.
14k........................................$225     $250     $300

OMEGA, 17 jewels, chronog., c. 1935
18k........................................$2,000     $2,500     $3,000

⏱ Some grades are not included. Their values can be
determined by comparing with similar age, size, metal
content, style, grades, or models such as time only,
chronograph, repeater etc. listed.

OMEGA, 17J., 2 reg. chronog., ca. 1940s
s. steel ................................$300      $400      $500
14k ......................................$600      $700      $800
18k ......................................$900      $1,000    $1,200

OMEGA, 17J., "Speedmaster", chronog., c. 1970
s. steel.................................$450      $550      $650

OMEGA, 17J., 2 reg., chronog., c. 1958
18k ......................................$900      $1,000    $1,200

OMEGA, 17J., "Speedmaster Pro.", chronog., c. 1969
"the first watch worn on the moon" on back of watch
18k C&B ...........................$2,500    $3,000    $3,500
s. steel.................................$600      $700      $800

OMEGA, 17 jewels, chronog., "Seamaster," c. 1963
14k ......................................$1,000    $1,250    $1,500
s. steel ...............................$500      $600      $700

OMEGA, 17J., "Speedmaster Pro. Mark II", c.1975
s. steel.................................$300      $375      $450

🕐 Some grades are not included. Their values can be
determined by comparing with **similar** age, size, metal
content, style, grades, or models such as **time only**,
chronograph, repeater etc. listed.

OMEGA, 17J., "Seamaster", chronog., cal.321, c. 1962
s. steel ...............................$500      $600      $750
14k ......................................$1,000    $1,250    $1,500
18k ......................................$1,400    $1,600    $1,950

OMEGA, 22J., "Seamaster", date, 2 reg., auto-wind, c.1975
s. steel ......................................$250      $300      $350

OMEGA, 17J., "Seamaster", chronostop, cal.865, c.1965
s. steel.....................................$125      $150      $200

OMEGA, 17J., Speedmaster Pro. MarkIII,cal.1040,c.1978
s. steel ...................................$350      $400      $475

OMEGA, 17J., "Seamaster", chronostop., rotating bezel
s. steel.....................................$150      $175      $275

OMEGA, 17J., Speedmaster, auto-wind, chronog., c.1975
s. steel ...................................$300      $375      $450

OMEGA, 17J., "Seamaster", chronog., cal.321, c.1970
s. steel.....................................$250      $300      $350

🕐 Some grades are not included. Their values can be
determined by comparing with **similar** age, size, metal
content, style, grades, or models such as **time only**,
chronograph, repeater etc. listed.

OMEGA, 17 jewels, chronog., "Seamaster," 3 reg.
14k ...............................$600     $700     $800

OMEGA, 17 jewels, chronog., "Flightmaster," 3 reg.
18kC&B ..............................$3,000     $3,500     $4,500
s. steel ......................................$350     $400     $500

OMEGA, 17 jewels, day-date-month, moon phase
18k .........................................$1,200     $1,400     $1,600
14k .........................................$1,000     $1,100     $1,200

OMEGA, 17J., day-date-month, moon phase, c. 1940
14k .........................................$1,000     $1,100     $1,200

OMEGA, 17J., day-date-month, moon phase, c. 1950s
18k..........................................$2,500     $3,000     $3,500

OMEGA, 17J.,date, "Constellation", chronometer
18k............................................$600     $700     $800
14k............................................$400     $450     $500

OMEGA, 24J., "Constellation", auto-wind, c.1960
14k............................................$500     $575     $625
s. steel....................................$225     $250     $300

OMEGA, 24J., "Constellation", auto-wind, c.1968
gold filled...............................$225     $250     $300

OMEGA, 24J., "Constellation", auto-wind, c.1969
s. steel .....................................$175     $200     $225

OMEGA, 17 jewels, "Constellation," auto wind, date
gold filled................................$225     $275     $350

OMEGA, 7J., "Constellation", quartz, cal.1342, c.1970
18k & s. s. ...............................$300     $350     $400

OMEGA, 24 jewels, "Constellation," auto wind
18k C&B ..............................$900     $1,000     $1,200

OMEGA, 17J.,  Chronometre, auto-w.,
14k .........................................$400     $450     $500

OMEGA, 24 jewels, "Constellation," c. 1959
18k............................................$550     $625     $675

OMEGA, electronic, "F300," c. 1950s
18k C&B.................................$600     $700     $800

OMEGA, 17 jewels, "Seamaster," date, waterproof
18k............................................$400     $450     $500

OMEGA, 24J., "Seamaster", auto-wind, c.1962
14k ...........................................$275    $350    $400
s. steel .....................................$100    $125    $150

Omega, 17 jewels, "Seamaster," auto wind
14k...........................................$300    $350    $400

OMEGA, 24J., "Seamaster", auto-wind, cal.562, c.1962
gold filled................................$100    $125    $150

OMEGA, 17J.,"Seamaster",chronometer
18k..........................................$350    $400    $450

OMEGA, 23J.,"Seamaster", auto-wind, cal.1022, c.1978
s. steel .......................................$85    $100    $150

OMEGA, 17J., "Seamaster", c.1953
gold filled................................$100    $125    $150

OMEGA, 17 jewels, automatic, date
14k ...........................................$200    $225    $275

OMEGA, 17J., "Seamaster Deluxe",
18k..........................................$350    $400    $450

OMEGA, 20J., "Seamaster", auto-wind, cal.501, c.1957
s. steel ........................................$100      $125      $150

OMEGA, 24J., "Constellation", auto-wind, cal.551, c.1962
14k...........................................$400      $450      $525

OMEGA, 17J., "Seamaster", auto-wind, cal.1570, c.1955
gold filled................................$100      $125      $150

OMEGA, 16-18J., gold train, center seconds
s. steel......................................$100      $125      $200

OMEGA, 17J., "Constellation", chronometer
18k ...........................................$475      $525      $600

OMEGA, 16J., center sec., c.1940
s. steel......................................$100      $125      $200

OMEGA, 24J., "Constellation", auto-wind, cal.505, c.1958
18k ...........................................$475      $525      $600

OMEGA, 16J., U.S. Army, cal., c.1948
s. steel......................................$150      $175      $250

OMEGA, 16J., center sec., c.1948
s. steel ...................................$125     $150     $175

OMEGA, 17J., auto-wind, center sec., c.1946
s. steel...................................$100     $125     $150

OMEGA, 15J., Military (England),  c.1946
s. steel .................................$175     $200     $235

OMEGA, 17J., Seamaster, diamond dial, cal.563, c.1955
s. steel...................................$150     $175     $200

OMEGA, 17J., "Railmaster", center sec.
s. steel ...................................$200     $250     $300

OMEGA, 17J., 12 diamond dial, center sec.
14k(W) ...................................$200     $250     $300

OMEGA, 15-17J., 24 hour marked, Ca. 1930
s. steel ...................................$200     $250     $300

OMEGA, 17J., fancy lugs, ca.1948
14k...........................................$350     $450     $500

🕐 Some grades are not included. Their values can be
determined by comparing with similar age, size, metal
content, style, grades, or models such as time only,
chronograph, repeater etc. listed.

OMEGA, 17J., aux.sec., cal.266, c.1956
s. steel ........................................$80      $100      $125

OMEGA, 17J., aux. sec., cal.360, c.1950
14k............................................$200      $235      $275

OMEGA, 17J., aux. sec., cal.266, c.1945
14k ...........................................$250      $300      $350

OMEGA, 17J., auto-wind, c.1949
18k............................................$250      $275      $300

OMEGA, 17J., auto-wind, cal.342, c.1955
gold filled................................$80      $100      $125

OMEGA, 17J., auto-wind, c.1952
18k ...........................................$300      $350      $400

OMEGA, 17J., seamaster, auto-wind
s. steel........................................$90      $120      $140

OMEGA, 17J., auto-wind, c.1949
18k ............................................$300      $350      $400

OMEGA, 17J., aux. sec., cal.302, c.1948
gold filled...............................$100    $125    $150

OMEGA, 15J., small lugs, c.1937
s. steel..................................$125    $150    $175

OMEGA, 15J., extended lugs, c.1939
14k .........................................$350    $375    $425
gold filled...............................$150    $175    $200

OMEGA, 17J., fancy lugs, ca. 1950s
14k............................................$300    $350    $400

OMEGA, 15J., aux. sec., c.1937
s. steel .....................................$100    $125    $150

OMEGA, 17J., faceted crystal,
14k(W).....................................$250    $300    $350

OMEGA, 15J., small lugs, c.1935
gold filled...............................$125    $150    $175

OMEGA, 17J., fancy lugs, ca. 1948
14k...........................................$400    $450    $500

OMEGA, 17J., beveled case, c.1936
s. steel ....................................$100    $150    $175

⌚ Some grades are not included. Their values can be
determined by comparing with **similar** age, size, metal
content, style, grades, or models such as **time only**,
chronograph, repeater etc. listed.

OMEGA, 17J., 9 diamond dial, ca. 1955
14k(W).....................................$200    $250    $300

OMEGA, 17J., wide bezel, center sec.,cal.470, c.1955
14k ...........................................$200      $250      $300

OMEGA, 17J., RF#347sc, cal.471, c.1956
18k .........................................$250      $300      $350

OMEGA, 17J., wide bezel & lugs, cal.369, c.1947
platinum...............................$1,000      $1,100      $1,200

OMEGA, 17J., "De Ville",
18k ...........................................$200      $250      $300

OMEGA, 17J., cal.620, c.1960
14k ...........................................$175      $225      $275

OMEGA, 17 jewels, aux. sec.
18k...........................................$300      $350      $400

OMEGA, 17 jewels, c. 1937
s. steel.....................................$200      $225      $250

OMEGA, 17 jewels
14k...........................................$300      $350      $400

OMEGA, 15J., sliding case, winds at 12, Ca.1930s
18k.......................................$1,500      $2,000      $2,500

OMEGA, 15 jewels, hidden winding stem, c. 1930
14k.......................................$1,200      $1,400      $1,600
s. steel....................................$800      $900      $1,000

🕐 Some grades are not included. Their values can be
determined by comparing with **similar** age, size, metal
content, style, grades, or models such as **time only**,
chronograph, repeater etc. listed.

OMEGA, 15J., engraved case, c.1925
14k .........................................$275     $325     $400

OMEGA, 15J., ladies, wire lugs, c.1925
silver.....................................$60     $75     $95

OMEGA, 19J., alarm,"Memomatic", c.1975
s. steel ....................................$175     $225     $275

OMEGA, 17J., ladies center sec., c.1938
silver.....................................$150     $200     $250

OMEGA, 17J., ladies flip open, 16 diamonds, c.1955
14k C&B ...............................$700     $800     $1,000

OMEGA, "Chrono-quartz, cal.1611, c.1975
s. steel ...................................$175     $200     $250

OMEGA, 15J., ladies, non-magnetic, c.1945
s. steel....................................$50     $65     $80

OMEGA, 17J., ladies, sapphire stones on lugs, c.1950
14k C&B ...............................$500     $600     $800

OMEGA, quartz, marine chronometer
s. steel ....................................$250     $300     $350

OMEGA, 17J., ladies, RF#8065, c.1965
18k C&B ...............................$500     $600     $700

## OMEGA BASIC CALIBRE IDENTIFICATION

Cal. No. 100, Ca.1943

Cal. No. 210, Ca.1946

Cal. No. 220, Ca.1941

Cal. No. 230, center seconds

Cal. No. 240, Ca.1939

Cal. No. 250, center seconds

Cal. No. 260, Ca.1943

Cal. No. 280, center seconds

Cal. No. 300, Ca.1944

Cal. No. 310, center seconds

Cal. No. 330, Ca.1943

Cal. No. 360, Ca.1944

Cal. No. 440

Cal. No. 372, jumping seconds

Cal. No. 410, Ca.1951

Cal. No. 420, center seconds

Cal. No. 455, Ca.1955

## OMEGA PRODUCTION TOTALS

| DATE-SERIAL # | DATE-SERIAL # | DATE-SERIAL # |
|---|---|---|
| 1895 – 50,000 | 1920 - 6,000,000 | 1950-15,500,000 |
| 1900 – 500,000 | 1925 - 7,500,000 | 1955-16,500,000 |
| 1905 - 1,000,000 | 1930 - 9,500,000 | 1960-18,000,000 |
| 1910 - 2,500,000 | 1935-11,000,000 | 1965-23,000,000 |
| 1915 - 4,500,000 | 1940-12,500,000 | 1970-28,000,000 |
| | 1945-14,000,000 | 1975-35,000,000 |

🕐 The above list is provided for determining the APPROXIMATE age of your watch. Match serial number with date. Watches were not necessarily sold in the exact order of manufactured date.

Cal. No. 470, Ca.1955

Cal. No. 480, Ca.1955

Cal. No. 490, Ca.1956

Cal. No. 500, Ca.1956

Cal. No. 510, Ca.1956

Cal. No. 520, center seconds

Cal. No. 540, Ca.1957

Cal. No. 550, Ca.1959

Cal. No. 570, Ca.1959

Cal. No. 590, Ca.1960

Cal. No. 600, Ca.1960

Cal. No. 620, Ca.1961

Cal. No. 580, Ca. 1959

Cal. No. 660, Ca.1963

Cal. No. 670, Ca.1963

Cal. No. 690, Ca.1962

Cal. No. 700, Ca.1964

Cal. No. 711, Ca.1966

Cal. No. 730, Ca.1967

Cal. No. 980, Ca.1969

Cal. No. 1040, Ca. 1971

Cal. No. 320, chronograh

Cal. No. 321, chronograh

Cal. No. 1010, Ca.1973

Cal. No. 1250-1260, Ca.1970

OPEL, 21 jewels, waterproof
gold filled..................................$50      $75      $100

ORATOR, 17 jewels, auto wind
s. steel .......................................$25     $35      $50

ORFINA, 17 jewels, triple date, moon phase, **bombe' lugs**
gold filled..................................$225     $275     $375

ORFINA, 17 jewels, triple date, moon phase, **carved lugs**
gold filled..................................$225     $275     $375

ORFINA, 17 jewels, day-date-month
gold filled ................................$70      $80      $100

ORFINA, 17 jewels, date
s. steel ......................................$50      $60      $70

ORVIN, 17 jewels, day-date, c. 1945
s. steel ......................................$70      $80      $90

PABRO, 17J., ladies 76 diamond watch, c.1930
platinum..................................$600     $700     $800

PARKER, 17J., 2 reg. chronog.,ca.1948
s. steel ......................................$150     $185     $225

" PATEK PHILIPPE" watches should be signed on the case, dial & movement to bring the prices listed in this book.
( **triple signed P.P.CO.**)

PATEK PHILIPPE, 29 jewels, min. repeater, c. 1920
platinum ..........................$125,000    $150,000    $175,000

PATEK PHILIPPE, 29J., min. repeater, 30 x 34mm
18k ...................................$150,000    $175,000    $200,000

PATEK PHILIPPE, 39J., auto-wind, min. repeater,
perpetual day date month calendars, moon ph., 24 hr. ind.,
leap year ind., RF#3974,  5 year waiting list, c.1989
18K....................................$225,000    $250,000    $275,000

PATEK PHILIPPE, 29, min. repeater, RF#2524
18k ...................................$100,000    $120,000    $150,000

PATEK PHILIPPE, 29 jewels, min. repeater, six watches finished by E. Gublin, 18k case & band, triple signed
18k C&B..........................$130,000    $140,000    $150,000

PATEK PHILIPPE, 50 sec. tourbillon, 57 hr. power reserve 5
gear train, 28 x 38mm, RF#3834
18k ...................................$150,000    $170,000    $190,000

PATEK PHILIPPE,18J., horizontal case, RF#504, 2 tone
18k ...................................$10,000    $11,000    $12,000

PATEK PHILIPPE,18 J., horizontal case, RF#139
18k ........................................$6,000    $7,000    $8,000

" PATEK PHILIPPE" watches should be signed on the case, dial & movement to bring the prices listed in this book.
( **triple signed P.P.CO.**)

PATEK PHILIPPE, 18J., designed by Gilbert Albert,
RF#3412, c. 1958
18k ....................................$18,000    $20,000    $22,000

PATEK PHILIPPE, 18J., asymmetric case designed by
Gilbert Albert, RF#3413, c. 1958
18k ....................................$20,000    $22,000    $25,000

PATEK PHILIPPE,18J., fluted hooded lugs, RF#2517
18k ........................................$4,000    $5,000    $6,000

PATEK PHILIPPE, 18 J., RF#3497, diamond set case
platinum C&B...................$10,000    $12,000    $14,000

PATEK PHILIPPE, 18J., RF#3424, asymmetric, c. 1960
18k ....................................$12,000    $14,000    $17,000

PATEK PHILIPPE, 18J., asymmetric,  diamond set
platinum............................$18,000    $20,000    $22,000

PATEK PHILIPPE, 18 J., Cal.#  9, hinged back, c. 1920s
18k ........................................$3,500    $4,000    $4,500

PATEK PHILIPPE, 18 jewels, Cal.#  9, curved, c. 1926
18k ........................................$3,500    $4,000    $4,500

PATEK PHILIPPE, 18 J., Cal.# 10, hinged back, c. 1920s
18k ........................................$3,500    $4,000    $5,000

PATEK PHILIPPE, 18 jewels, Cal.# 9, c. 1940s
18k ......................................$3,800    $4,200    $4,800

PATEK PHILIPPE, 18 jewels, Cal.# 9
18k .......................................$3,000    $3,500    $4,000

PATEK PHILIPPE, 18 jewels, Cal.. 9, c. 1950s
18k ......................................$3,500    $4,000    $4,500

PATEK PHILIPPE, 18 jewels, RF# 1560
18k .......................................$4,500    $4,700    $5,000

PATEK PHILIPPE,18J., cal.990, c.1936
18K..............................$4,000    $4,250    $4,500

PATEK PHILIPPE, 18 jewels, c. 1940s
18k .......................................$3,500    $4,000    $4,500

PATEK PHILIPPE,18J., RF#409, cal. c.1934
18K......................................$3,500    $3,700    $4,000

PATEK PHILIPPE, 18 jewels, c. 1943
18k ......................................$3,500    $4,000    $4,500

PATEK PHILIPPE, 18 J., stepped case, Cal.# 9, c. 1940s
18k .......................................$3,500    $4,000    $4,500

PATEK PHILIPPE, 18 jewels, c. 1930s
18k ......................................$3,000    $3,500    $4,000

PATEK PHILIPPE, 18 jewels, c. 1950s
18k .......................................$3,000    $3,500    $4,000

PATEK PHILIPPE, 18 jewels, c. 1945
18k .......................................$5,000    $5,500    $6,000

PATEK PHILIPPE, 18 jewels
18k .............................$3,500    $4,000    $4,500

PATEK PHILIPPE, 18 jewels, Cal.# 9, c. 1960s
18k .........................................$3,500    $4,000    $4,500

PATEK PHILIPPE, 18 jewels, curved, Cal.# 9
18k .........................................$5,500    $6,500    $7,500

PATEK PHILIPPE, 18J., decorated enamel case, c. 1920s
18k .........................................$8,000    $9,000    $10,000

PATEK PHILIPPE,18J., RF#2334,
18K.........................................$3,500    $3,800    $4,200

PATEK PHILIPPE,18J., extended lugs, two tone case,
cal.885, c.1943
18K.........................................$4,000    $4,500    $5,000

PATEK PHILIPPE,18J., diamond on dial & case
18K C&B...........................$3,000    $3,500    $4,000

PATEK PHILIPPE, 18 jewels, hidden lugs, c. 1930s
18k .........................................$2,500    $3,000    $3,750

PATEK PHILIPPE, 18 jewels, c. 1940s
18k .........................................$4,000    $4,500    $5,000

PATEK PHILIPPE, 18 jewels, hinged back, c. 1920s
18k .........................................$4,500    $5,000    $5,500

PATEK PHILIPPE, 18 jewels, applied gold numbers
18K .....................................$6,000    $7,000    $8,000

" PATEK PHILIPPE" watches should be signed on the case,
dial & movement to bring the prices listed in this book.
**( triple signed P.P.CO.)**

PATEK PHILIPPE, 18J., Cal.#9, fancy lugs
18k ..................................$6,000   $7,000   $8,000

PATEK PHILIPPE,18J., engraved bezel,hinged back,c.1920
18k ......................................$5,000   $5,500   $6,500

PATEK PHILIPPE, 18J., curved, hooded satin lugs
18k ..................................$8,000   $9,000   $10,000

PATEK PHILIPPE, 18J., ribbed case & fancy lugs
18k ......................................$3,000   $3,500   $4,000

PATEK PHILIPPE, 18 jewels, ''Staybrite,'' curved case
s. steel ..............................$3,000   $3,200   $3,400

PATEK PHILIPPE, 18 jewels, large lugs, c. 1960s
18k ......................................$4,000   $4,500   $5,000

PATEK PHILIPPE, 18 jewels, Cal.# 9, hooded lugs
18k ..................................$2,500   $3,000   $3,500

PATEK PHILIPPE, 18 jewels, M#9, c.1930
18k ......................................$4,000   $5,000   $6,000

PATEK PHILIPPE, 18 jewels, curved
18k ......................................$4,000   $4,500   $5,000

PATEK PHILIPPE, 18 jewels, c. 1930s
18k ......................................$3,000   $3,500   $4,000

PATEK PHILIPPE, 18J., Cal.# 9, center lugs, c. 1940s
18k .......................................$3,500     $4,000     $4,500

PATEK PHILIPPE, 18 jewels, c. 1940s
18k .......................................$4,000     $4,500     $5,000

PATEK PHILIPPE, 18J., triple lugs, RF#2471, ca.1951
18k .......................................$15,000     $20,000     $25,000

PATEK PHILIPPE, 18 jewels, triple lugs, RF#1482
18k .......................................$8,000     $9,000     $10,000

PATEK PHILIPPE, 18 jewels, curved, c. 1940s
18k .......................................$3,500     $4,000     $4,500

PATEK PHILIPPE, 18 jewels, Cal.#9, c. 1940s
18k .......................................$3,500     $4,000     $4,500

PATEK PHILIPPE, 18 jewels, curved, c. 1950s
18k .......................................$3,500     $4,000     $5,000

PATEK PHILIPPE, 18 jewels, hinged back, c. 1920s
18k .......................................$4,000     $4,500     $5,000

PATEK PHILIPPE, 18J., hinged back, stepped case
18k .......................................$4,000     $4,500     $5,000

PATEK PHILIPPE, 18J., RF#2520, M# 9, extended lugs
18k C&B.............................$7,000     $8,000     $9,000

PATEK PHILIPPE, 18J., fancy lugs, ca.1949
18k .......................................$6,000     $7,000     $8,000

PATEK PHILIPPE, 18 jewels, Cal.# 9, concave lugs
18k .................................$6,000    $7,000    $8,000

PATEK PHILIPPE, 18 J., Cal.#9, tank model, c.1940
18k .......................................$3,500    $3,800    $4,250

PATEK PHILIPPE, 18 jewels, moveable lugs
18K..................................$6,000    $7,000    $9,000

PATEK PHILIPPE, 18 jewels, lapidated lugs
18k ....................................$4,500    $5,000    $5,500

PATEK PHILIPPE, 18 jewels, fancy lugs, RF#1480
18k .......................................$4,250    $4,700    $5,300

PATEK PHILIPPE, 18 jewels, fancy lugs
18k .......................... $5,000    $5,500    $6,000

PATEK PHILIPPE, 18J., stylized hooded lugs, RF#2441
18k .......................................$5,000    $6,000    $7,000

PATEK PHILIPPE, 18 jewels, Cal.# 9, c. 1940s
18k.................................$4,000    $4,500    $5,000

PATEK PHILIPPE, 18J., 2 tone, hooded & stepped lugs
18k .......................................$8,000    $9,000    $10,000

PATEK PHILIPPE, 18 jewels, ''Reverso''
18k ....................................$20,000    $25,000    $30,000
s. steel ...................................$6,000    $8,000    $10,000

PATEK PHILIPPE, 18 jewels, top hat style, c. 1940s
18k ........................................$5,000    $5,500    $6,500
platinum ...............................$6,000    $7,000    $8,000

PATEK PHILIPPE, 18 jewels, top hat style
18k C&B .............................$5,500    $6,000    $7,000

PATEK PHILIPPE, 18 jewels, top hat style, diamond dial
platinum ...............................$7,000    $8,000    $9,000

PATEK PHILIPPE, 18 jewels, M# 9, curved, tank style
18k ........................................$6,000    $6,500    $7,000

PATEK PHILIPPE, 18J., inclined & curved case, Ca.1940s
18k ........................................$20,000    $24,000    $28,500

PATEK PHILIPPE, 18 jewels, Adj. to 8 positions
18k ........................................$4,000    $4,500    $5,000

PATEK PHILIPPE, 18 jewels, curvex, c. 1940s
18k ........................................$4,000    $4,500    $5,000

PATEK PHILIPPE, 18 J., converted to jump hr., recased
18k ........................................$4,000    $4,500    $5,000

PATEK PHILIPPE, 18 jewels, flared case, c. 1940s
18k ........................................$6,500    $7,000    $8,000

PATEK PHILIPPE, 18 jewels, Cal.# 9, c. 1950s
platinum ...............................$12,000    $14,000    $16,000

PATEK PHILIPPE, 18J., Cal.# 9, flared case, c. 1950s
18k ........................................$6,500    $7,500    $8,500

PATEK PHILIPPE, 18 jewels, massive flared case
18k ....................................$14,000   $16,000   $18,000
platinum.............................$18,000   $20,000   $22,000

PATEK PHILIPPE, 18J., RF#2441, curved, flared case
18k .......................................$8,000   $9,000   $10,000

PATEK PHILIPPE,18J., RF#2441, Eiffel tower, c. 1945
18k .......................................$8,000   $9,000   $10,000

PATEK PHILIPPE, 18 jewels, flared case
18k .......................................$5,000   $5,500   $6,500

PATEK PHILIPPE, 18 jewels, flared case, c. 1950s
18k .......................................$6,000   $6,500   $7,000

PATEK PHILIPPE, 18 jewels, c. 1950s
18k ....................................$6,000   $6,500   $7,000

PATEK PHILIPPE, 18J., 16 diamond on bezel, ca.1960
18k C&B.............................$6,000   $7,000   $8,000

PATEK PHILIPPE, 18 jewels, diamond dial, c. 1945
18k ....................................$5,000   $5,500   $6,000

PATEK PHILIPPE, 18 jewels, diamond dial
platinum...............................$6,000   $6,500   $7,000

PATEK PHILIPPE, 18 jewels, diamond dial, c. 1935
platinum...............................$6,000   $6,500   $7,000

PATEK PHILIPPE, 18 jewels, diamond dial & bezel
platinum...............................$7,000   $7,500   $8,000

PATEK PHILIPPE, 18J., hinged back, diamond bezel
18k ........................................$6,000    $7,000    $8,000

PATEK PHILIPPE,18J.,  RF#2493, c.1953
18K ..................................$2,500    $2,800    $3,200

PATEK PHILIPPE, 18 jewels, c. 1940s
18k ........................................$3,500    $4,000    $4,500

PATEK PHILIPPE,18J., RF#1431, cal., c.1940
18K ..................................$2,200    $2,500    $3,000

PATEK PHILIPPE, 18J., diamond dial, flared case
18k ........................................$7,500    $8,000    $9,000

PATEK PHILIPPE,18J., RF#2447,  c.1950
18K ..................................$2,200    $2,500    $2,850

PATEK PHILIPPE, 18J, Cal.# 9, diamond dial, starbrite case
s. steel ..................................$3,000    $3,500    $4,000

PATEK PHILIPPE,18J., carved lugs, RF#2423, c.1949
18K ..................................$3,000    $3,600    $4,200

PATEK PHILIPPE, 30 J., rf#2540, ca. 1957
18k ........................................$3,000    $3,200    $3,600

PATEK PHILIPPE,18J., RF#2424, c.1951
18K ..................................$3,000    $3,600    $4,200

PATEK PHILIPPE,18J., stepped lugs, c.1940
18K.....................................$3,200    $3,600    $4,200

PATEK PHILIPPE, 18 J., 18k band & case, c. 1950s
18k C&B..............................$3,000    $3,500    $4,000

PATEK PHILIPPE, 18 jewels, textured bezel, c. 1940s
18k ......................................$2,000    $2,500    $3,000

PATEK PHILIPPE, 18J., fancy off set lugs, thick crystal
18k ......................................$2,700    $3,100    $3,700

PATEK PHILIPPE, 18 jewels
18k ......................................$2,000    $2,500    $3,000

PATEK PHILIPPE, 18 jewels, M# 9, c. 1963
18k ......................................$2,000    $2,500    $3,000

PATEK PHILIPPE, 18 jewels, c. 1947
18k ......................................$2,500    $3,000    $3,500

PATEK PHILIPPE, 18 jewels, c. 1960s
18k ......................................$1,800    $2,000    $2,200

PATEK PHILIPPE, 18 jewels, oval lugs
18k ......................................$3,500    $4,000    $4,500

PATEK PHILIPPE, 18 jewels
18k ......................................$2,000    $2,200    $2,500

PATEK PHILIPPE, 18 jewels, Cal.# 9, c. 1948
18k ......................................$3,000    $3,500    $4,000

PATEK PHILIPPE, 18 jewels, diamond bezel , tank style
platinum..............................$6,500    $7,500    $8,500

PATEK PHILIPPE, 18 J., hooded & fluted lugs
18k ......................................$8,000    $9,000    $10,000

PATEK PHILIPPE, 18J., Cal.# 9, hidden dial, gold & plat.
18k & platinum..................$20,000    $22,000    $24,000

PATEK PHILIPPE, 18 jewels, Cal.# 9, c. 1980s
18k C&B..............................$2,500    $3,000    $3,500

PATEK PHILIPPE, 18 jewels, Cal.# 9, c. 1970s
18k C&B..............................$2,000    $2,200    $2,500

PATEK PHILIPPE, 18 jewels
18k (w) ................................$1,800    $2,000    $2,400

PATEK PHILIPPE, 18 jewels
18k C&B..............................$2,800    $3,200    $3,800

PATEK PHILIPPE, 18 jewels, textured dial & bezel
18k ......................................$3,000    $3,500    $4,000

PATEK PHILIPPE, 18 jewels, c. 1950s
18k ......................................$3,000    $3,200    $3,800

⊕ Some grades are not included. Their values can be determined by comparing with **similar** age, size, metal content, style, grades, or models such as **time only**, chronograph, repeater etc. listed.

PATEK PHILIPPE, 18 jewels, center sec., c. 1960s
18k C&B..............................$3,500   $4,000   $4,500

PATEK PHILIPPE, 18 J., tank, RF#2530-1, Ca. 1959
18k C&B..............................$3,500   $4,000   $4,500

PATEK PHILIPPE, 18J., tank, Cal.# 9, c. early 1910s
18k C&B..............................$4,000   $4,500   $5,000

PATEK PHILIPPE, 18 jewels, c. 1950s
18k ..............................$2,300   $2,500   $2,800

PATEK PHILIPPE, 18 jewels, c. 1950s
18k ..............................$2,200   $2,800   $3,200

PATEK PHILIPPE, 18 jewels, c. 1950s
18k ..............................$2,500   $2,800   $3,200

PATEK PHILIPPE, 18 jewels, c. 1960s
18k ..............................$3,000   $3,500   $4,000

PATEK PHILIPPE, 18 J., guilloche bezel, thick lugs
18k ..............................$3,000   $3,500   $4,000

PATEK PHILIPPE, 18 jewels, hidden lugs, c. 1945
18k ..............................$3,000   $3,500   $4,000

PATEK PHILIPPE, 18J., fluted cylindrical hooded lugs
18k ..............................$6,000   $7,000   $8,000

PATEK PHILIPPE, 18 jewels, hidden lugs
18k ........................................$2,000    $2,300    $2,800

PATEK PHILIPPE, 18 jewels, hooded lugs, c. 1940s
18k ........................................$2,400    $2,800    $3,300

PATEK PHILIPPE, 18 jewels, blue sapphire bezel
platinum ..............................$7,000    $8,000    $9,000

PATEK PHILIPPE, 18 jewels, overhanging lugs
18k ........................................$5,000    $5,500    $6,500

PATEK PHILIPPE, 18 jewels, fluted dropped lugs
18k ........................................$4,500    $5,000    $5,500

⊕ Some grades are not included. Their values can be
determined by comparing with **similar** age, size, metal
content, style, grades, or models such as **time only**,
chronograph, repeater etc. listed.

PATEK PHILIPPE, 18 jewels, c. 1940s
18k ........................................$3,000    $3,500    $4,000

PATEK PHILIPPE, 18 jewels, large bezel
18k ........................................$2,000    $2,500    $3,000

PATEK PHILIPPE, 18 jewels, c. 1940s
18k ........................................$2,000    $2,200    $2,500

PATEK PHILIPPE, 15J.,for Baily,Banks & Biddle, ca.1920
18k ........................................$4,000    $4,500    $5,000

PATEK PHILIPPE, 16J.,  ca.1923
18k ........................................$4,000    $4,800    $5,500

PATEK PHILIPPE, 18 jewels, c. 1910
18k ........................................$3,000     $3,500     $4,000

PATEK PHILIPPE, 18 jewels, c. 1930s
18k ........................................$3,500     $4,000     $5,000

PATEK PHILIPPE, 18 jewels, c. 1920s
18k ........................................$4,000     $4,500     $5,000

PATEK PHILIPPE, 18 jewels, c. 1930s
18k ........................................$4,000     $4,500     $5,500

PATEK PHILIPPE, 18 jewels, c. 1920s
18k ........................................$3,000     $3,500     $4,000

PATEK PHILIPPE, 18 jewels, **contract case, not signed**
18k (w) ...............................$1,800     $2,000     $2,500

PATEK PHILIPPE, 18 jewels, enamel dial,c. 1920s
18k ........................................$5,000     $5,500     $6,000

PATEK PHILIPPE, 18 jewels, Cal.# 9, c. 1925
18k ........................................$3,500     $4,000     $4,500

PATEK PHILIPPE, 18 jewels, Cal.# 9, c. 1910
platinum ...............................$7,000     $8,000     $9,000

PATEK PHILIPPE, 18 jewels, M# 9, c. 1920s
18k ........................................$5,000     $5,500     $6,000

PATEK PHILIPPE, 18J, diamond dial, curved, 42mm, c. 1919
platinum .............................. $7,000    $8,000    $9,000

PATEK PHILIPPE, 18 jewels
18k ......................................... $2,500    $3,000    $3,500

PATEK PHILIPPE, 18 jewels, made for E. Gublin
18k ......................................... $4,000    $4,500    $5,000

PATEK PHILIPPE, 18 jewels, ''Chronometro Gondolo''
18k ......................................... $5,000    $6,000    $7,000

PATEK PHILIPPE, 18jewels, RF#515, world time zone, 24 hr. rotating outside chapter, **tu-tone** case and band
18K C&B ........................ $200,000    $250,000    $300,000

PATEK PHILIPPE, 18 jewels, RF#2523, ''World Time,'' cloisonne polychrome enamel map on dial, **41 cities**
18k ..................................... $70,000    $80,000    $90,000

PATEK PHILIPPE, 18J., ''World Time,'' **41 cities**, RF#1415
18k ..................................... $35,000    $40,000    $45,000

PATEK PHILIPPE, 18 jewels, landscape cloisonne polychrome enamel dial
18k ..................................... $30,000    $35,000    $40,000

PATEK PHILIPPE, 18 jewels, **2 hour hands**, 2 time zones
18k ..................................... $18,000    $20,000    $24,000

PATEK PHILIPPE, 18J., traveling watch, hr. hand moves forward or backward to time zone, steps 1 hr. at a time
18k ......................................$20,000   $25,000   $30,000

PATEK PHILIPPE, 18J., chronog., RF#1579, fancy lugs
18k ......................................$16,000   $18,000   $20,000

PATEK PHILIPPE, 18J., RF#130, chronog., 1940s
18k ......................................$15,000   $18,000   $22,000

PATEK PHILIPPE, 18J., chronog., RF#591, 2 reg., c.1943
18k ......................................$22,000   $24,000   $26,000

PATEK PHILIPPE, 18J., RF#530, chronog.
18k ......................................$15,000   $18,000   $22,000

PATEK PHILIPPE, 18J., RF#130, chronog.," 2 tone"
18k & s. steel ......................$22,000   $24,000   $26,000

PATEK PHILIPPE, 18J., calatrava style, chronog., 2 reg., RF#130, c. 1940s
18k ......................................$20,000   $22,000   $25,000

Some grades are not included. Their values can be determined by comparing with **similar** age, size, metal content, style, grades, or models such as **time only**, chronograph, repeater etc. listed.

PATEK PHILIPPE, 32J., split sec. chronog.
18k ......................................$200,000   $225,000   $250,000

PATEK PHILIPPE, 18J., rf#3970E, chronog,triple date
moon ph., 24 hr. indicator, leap year indicator
18k ...................................$38,000    $42,000    $50,000

PATEK PHILIPPE, 26J., split sec. chronog. one button, for
Cartier, Sq. button for Rattrapante hand, crown for start stop
functions, RF#130, 8 adj., ca.1938
18k ...................................$110,000    $130,000    $150,000

PATEK PHILIPPE,18J., RF#130,split sec. chronog.,c.1958
18k ...................................$100,000    $115,000    $130,000

PATEK PHILIPPE, 18 jewels,  chronog., day-date month,
moon phase, made for E. Gueblin
18k C&B..........................$60,000    $70,000    $80,000

PATEK PHILIPPE,18J., RF#1506, chronog., waterproof
18k ...................................$24,000    $27,000    $30,000

PATEK PHILIPPE, 18J., chronog., triple date, moon ph.
perpetual calendar,RF# 1518, Calatrava case, Ca.1941-54
18k ............................ ★★ $70,000    $80,000    $90,000

PATEK PHILIPPE, 18J., chronog., pulsometer, c. 1965
18k ...................................$26,000    $29,000    $32,000

PATEK PHILIPPE, 23 J., chronog., triple date, moon ph.
perpetual calendar,ref.2499 (1 series) square button
18K ...................................$70,000    $75,000    $85,000

" PATEK PHILIPPE" watches should be signed on the case, dial & movement to bring the prices listed in this book.
**( triple signed P.P.CO.)**

PATEK PHILIPPE, 23 J., chronog., triple date, moon ph. perpetual calendar, ref.2499 (2 series)
18K.....................................$60,000    $65,000    $70,000

PATEK PHILIPPE, 23J., chronog., triple date, moon ph. perpetual calendar, ref.2499 (3 series)glass crystal
18k .....................................$60,000    $65,000    $70,000

PATEK PHILIPPE, 23J., chronog., triple date, moon ph. perpetual calendar,ref.2499 (3 series)only 2 in platinum
platinum...........................$150,000    $170,000    $200,000

⏰ Some grades are not included. Their values can be determined by comparing with **similar** age, size, metal content, style, grades, or models such as **time only**, chronograph, repeater etc. listed.

PATEK PHILIPPE, 23J., chronog., triple date, moon ph. perpetual calendar, ref.2499 (4 series)sapphire crystal
18k .....................................$50,000    $55,000    $60,000

PATEK PHILIPPE, 18 jewels, date, mid-sized, auto wind
platinum...............................$6,000    $7,000    $8,000

PATEK PHILIPPE, 18 jewels, auto wind, date, c. 1970s
18k C&B.............................$3,000    $3,500    $4,000

PATEK PHILIPPE,18J., RF#3514/1, date,c.1967
18K C&B.............................$2,000    $2,200    $2,400

PATEK PHILIPPE,18J., date, RF#3445, auto-wind, c.1961
18K.....................................$3,200    $3,500    $4,000

PATEK PHILIPPE,18J., date, RF#3604, textured dial, c.1977
18K(w)................................$2,000    $2,200    $2,400

PATEK PHILIPPE,18J., (day, date, month, at 9-12-3 ),
3 known to exist, manual wind, Ca.1934
18K.................★★★★★$200,000    $250,000    $300,000

PATEK PHILIPPE, 18J., RF#96, Calatrava, triple date note
moon phases at 12,  Ca.1936
18K....................................$125,000    $150,000    $175,000
platinum..........................$225,000    $250,000    $275,000

PATEK PHILIPPE, 18J., RF#3450, day-date-month, moon
phase, waterproof, **perpetual date at 3**
18k .....................................$22,000    $24,000    $28,000

PATEK PHILIPPE, 37J., RF#3448, cal.27-460q c.1968
18K .....................................$25,000    $27,000    $30,000

PATEK PHILIPPE, 37J., triple date, moon ph. RF #3448
platinum............................$35,000    $40,000    $45,000

PATEK PHILIPPE,18J., triple date, moon ph., RF#2438,
c.1962
18k .....................................$35,000    $40,000    $45,000

PATEK PHILIPPE, 15 jewels, enamel dial, c. 1910
18k ........................................$7,000    $8,000    $9,000

PATEK PHILIPPE,18J., "Officer", RF#3960, c.1992
18k 2,000 made, 18k(w) 150 made, platinum 50 made
18K.....................................$13,000    $14,000    $15,000
18k(w)...............................$15,000    $16,000    $17,000
platinum.............................$25,000    $27,000    $30,000

PATEK PHILIPPE, 15J., enamel dial, c. 1910
18k ........................................$7,000    $8,000    $9,000

PATEK PHILIPPE, 18 jewels, RF#1461
18k ........................................$2,500    $3,000    $3,500

PATEK PHILIPPE, 18 jewels
18k ........................................$2,000    $2,500    $3,000

PATEK PHILIPPE, 18 jewels, aux. sec.
18k ........................................$2,300    $2,700    $3,200

PATEK PHILIPPE, 18J., *Amagnetic* on dial, ca. 1960
18k ........................................$3,000    $4,000    $5,000

PATEK PHILIPPE, 18J.,"Calatrava", aux. sec., c. 1940
18k ........................................$3,000    $3,200    $3,500

PATEK PHILIPPE, 18 jewels, c. 1955
18k ......................................$2,200    $2,400    $2,600

PATEK PHILIPPE, 18 jewels, man's half size, c. 1920
18k ......................................$3,000    $4,000    $4,500
s. steel ................................$2,600    $2,800    $3,000

PATEK PHILIPPE, 18 jewels, RF# 2429, Ca. 1950s
18k ......................................$4,000    $4,200    $4,500

PATEK PHILIPPE, 18 jewels, aux. sec., c. 1950s
18k ......................................$2,500    $2,800    $3,200

PATEK PHILIPPE, 37J., RF#3429, self-winding
18k ......................................$3,600    $4,000    $4,500

PATEK PHILIPPE, 18J., aux. sec., RF#2526, ca. 1957
18k auto-w..........................$7,000    $8,000    $9,000

PATEK PHILIPPE,18J., **CLASSIC Calatrava**,  RF# 96
18k ......................................$3,200    $3,500    $4,000
s. steel ................................$2,200    $2,500    $2,800
platinum...............................$7,000    $7,500    $8,000
platinum + diam. dial ..........$7,500    $8,000    $8,500

The **CLASSIC Calatrava** model 96 was 1st used in 1932. It was designed at a time of transition from pocket watches to wrist watches. The coin was used as a perfect geometric shape to design a wrist watch case that has harmony and balance. Many varations from the classic model 96 have been used, but to most collectors the **CLASSIC** model 96 is known as the **Calatrava** model. The original 96 Calatrava model used a flat bezel, 31mm one piece case (lugs are not soldered on), manual wind, white dial, barrette-shaped hour markers, dauphine hands and aux. seconds chapter with a inside and outside circle and long 5 sec. markers. A Hobnail bezel was added in 1934, a black dial in 1937. To date there are many Calatrava models. The recent Calatrava is RF # 3796.

PATEK PHILIPPE, 18J., ''Calatrava,'' RF#96, c. 1950s
18k .....................................$3,000    $3,500    $4,000

PATEK PHILIPPE,18J., aux. sec., c.1943
18K ......................................$2,500    $2,700    $2,900

PATEK PHILIPPE, 18 J., auto wind, RF#1536, c.1950s
18k .....................................$4,000    $4,500    $5,000

PATEK PHILIPPE,37J., auto wind, RF#3429, c.1961
18K ......................................$3,700    $4,000    $4,400

PATEK PHILIPPE,18J., auto wind, RF#1516, c.1950
18K.......................................$3,800    $4,000    $4,500

PATEK PHILIPPE,18J., aux. sec., RF#96, cal.12-20, c.1937
18K ......................................$3,000    $3,200    $3,400

PATEK PHILIPPE,18J., aux. sec., RF#2445,
18K.......................................$2,400    $2,600    $2,800

PATEK PHILIPPE,18J.,  RF#1543, c.1947
18K ......................................$2,600    $2,800    $3,000

🕐 Some grades are not included. Their values can be determined by comparing with **similar** age, size, metal content, style, grades, or models such as **time only**, chronograph, repeater etc. listed.

PATEK PHILIPPE,18J., RF#1590, c.1951
18K.....................................$2,600     $2,800     $3,000

PATEK PHILIPPE, 18 jewels, waterproof, c. 1940s
18k .....................................$2,800     $3,200     $3,600

PATEK PHILIPPE, 18J., auto-w, extra long lugs, c. 1950
18k .....................................$3,000     $3,300     $3,600

PATEK PHILIPPE, 18J.,"Calatrava" waterproof, c. 1950s
18k .....................................$3,500     $4,000     $4,500

PATEK PHILIPPE, 18 jewels, aux. sec., c. 1950s
18k .....................................$2,200     $2,400     $2,600

PATEK PHILIPPE, 30J.,"Calatrava", auto wind, gold rotor
18k .....................................$7,000     $7,500     $8,000

PATEK PHILIPPE, 18 jewels, aux. sec.
18k .....................................$2,500     $2,700     $2,900

PATEK PHILIPPE,18J.,"Calatrava,"**enamel dial**, Ca.1940s
18k .....................................$5,000     $5,500     $6,000

" PATEK PHILIPPE" watches should be signed on the case,
dial & movement to bring the prices listed in this book.
**( triple signed P.P.CO.)**

PATEK PHILIPPE, 18J.,waterproof, "Calatrava," rf#2545
18k .......................................$3,500     $4,500     $5,000

PATEK PHILIPPE, 18J., fancy lugs, ca. 1948
18k ........................................$7,000     $8,000     $9,000

PATEK PHILIPPE, 18 jewels, "Calatrava," waterproof
platinum .................................$6,000     $7,000     $8,000

PATEK PHILIPPE, 18 jewels, curled lugs
18k .........................................$3,800     $4,000     $4,500

PATEK PHILIPPE, 18 jewels, aux. sec.
18k C&B ...............................$7,000     $8,000     $9,000

PATEK PHILIPPE, 18 jewels, "Calatrava," c. 1950s
18k .........................................$2,800     $3,200     $3,500

PATEK PHILIPPE, 18J., RF#2526, fancy lugs, c. 1940s
18k .........................................$4,000     $4,500     $5,000

PATEK PHILIPPE, 18 jewels, "Calatrava," c. 1940s
18k-rose ...............................$3,200     $4,000     $4,500

PATEK PHILIPPE, 18J., ''Calatrava,'' black dial, w/proof
18k .....................................$3,800     $4,200     $4,700

PATEK PHILIPPE, 18 jewels, center sec., waterproof
s. steel ................................$2,500     $2,800     $3,200

PATEK PHILIPPE, 21J., ''Calatrava,'' Breguet #s, c.1950s
18k .....................................$3,500     $4,000     $4,500

PATEK PHILIPPE, 18 jewels, center sec., c. 1950s
18k .....................................$3,000     $3,200     $3,500

PATEK PHILIPPE, 18J., center sec., rf#2466, ca.1949
18k .....................................$3,000     $3,500     $4,000

PATEK PHILIPPE, 18 jewels, conical lugs, center sec.
18k .....................................$3,300     $3,600     $4,000

PATEK PHILIPPE, 18 jewels, center sec., c. 1950s
18k .....................................$2,500     $2,700     $3,000

PATEK PHILIPPE, 20 jewels, center sec.
18k .....................................$2,500     $2,700     $3,000

PATEK PHILIPPE, 18 jewels, textured dial & bezel
18k .........................................$2,600    $2,800    $3,100

PATEK PHILIPPE,18J., center sec., RF#3411, c.1960
18K .....................................$2,200    $2,400    $2,700

PATEK PHILIPPE, 18 jewels, center sec., c. 1952
18k .......................................$2,600    $2,800    $3,100

PATEK PHILIPPE, 18 jewels, center sec., c. 1950s
18k.......................................$2,200    $2,400    $2,700

PATEK PHILIPPE, 18 jewels, center sec., waterproof
18k .......................................$3,000    $3,500    $4,000

PATEK PHILIPPE,18J., RF#3495, cal.27sc, c.1969
18K .....................................$2,000    $2,200    $2,400

PATEK PHILIPPE, 20 jewels, center sec.
18k .......................................$2,200    $2,400    $2,700

PATEK PHILIPPE, 18 jewels, center sec., c. 1960s
18k C&B.............................. $3,600    $4,000    $4,400

PATEK PHILIPPE, 18 jewels, auto wind, back set
18k ......................................$3,000　$3,200　$3,500

PATEK PHILIPPE, 18 jewels
18k C&B.............................$2,500　$3,000　$3,500

PATEK PHILIPPE, 18 jewels
18k ......................................$1,800　$2,000　$2,200

PATEK PHILIPPE,18J., RF#2501, c.1954
18K ......................................$1,600　$1,800　$2,000

PATEK PHILIPPE, 18 jewels, "Calatrava," c. 1940s
18k ......................................$3,500　$4,000　$4,500

PATEK PHILIPPE,18J., RF#2592, c.1956
18K ......................................$1,500　$1,700　$1,900

PATEK PHILIPPE, 36 jewels, auto-w.,c. 1970s
18k ......................................$2,800　$3,000　$3,200

PATEK PHILIPPE,18J., RF#3574, c.1960
s. steel ................................$1,000　$1,200　$1,400

PATEK PHILIPPE, 18J., ''Calatrava,'', rf#2588, c.1940s
18k .......................................$3,000    $3,500    $4,000

PATEK PHILIPPE, 18 jewels, unusual shape, c. 1940s
18k .......................................$6,000    $7,000    $8,000

PATEK PHILIPPE, 36J., "Nautilus", date,gold & steel
18K...................................$11,000    $12,000    $13,000
18k&s. steel ........................$5,000    $5,500    $6,000
s. steel .................................$3,000    $3,500    $4,000

PATEK PHILIPPE, mid size, quartz, rf#3900/1, date
s. steel .................................$2,000    $2,200    $2,600

PATEK PHILIPPE,  quartz, rf#3900/101, date
paved diamonds=.50ct., ruby hour markers
18k ....................................$6,000    $8,000    $10,000

PATEK PHILIPPE,  quartz, rf#3900/5,  date, dia-
monds=2.27ct.
18k C&B............................$9,000    $10,000    $13,000

PATEK PHILIPPE,  quartz, rf#3900/3, date, Carran dial
diamonds=.68ct.
platinum............................$20,000    $22,000    $24,000

PATEK PHILIPPE,  quartz, rf#3900/103, date
diamonds=.68ct, paved diamonds=.50, ruby markers
18k .......................................$7,000    $9,000    $11,000

333

3333

333

PATEK PHILIPPE, quartz, rf#3900/105, date,
diamonds=2.27, paved diamonds=.50, ruby markers
18k C&B............................$10,000  $12,000  $14,000

PATEK PHILIPPE, auto wind, rf#3800/103, date
diamonds=.91ct., paved diamonds=63ct., ruby markers
18kC&B............................$17,000  $20,000  $23,000

PATEK PHILIPPE, auto wind, rf#3800/105, date
diamonds=2.40ct., paved diam.=.63ct., ruby markers
18kC&B............................$22,000  $24,000  $26,000

" PATEK PHILIPPE" watches should be signed on the case,
dial & movement to bring the prices listed in this book.
( triple signed P.P.CO.)

Some grades are not included. Their values can be
determined by comparing with **similar** age, size, metal
content, style, grades, or models such as **time only**,
chronograph, repeater etc. listed.

PATEK PHILIPPE, auto wind, rf#3800/108, date,
diamonds=7.46ct.,paved diam.=1.50ct.,sapphire markers
18k C&B............................$30,000  $35,000  $40,000

PATEK PHILIPPE, 36J., "Nautilus," date, large size
s. steel ................................$4,000  $4,500  $5,000

PATEK PHILIPPE, 36 J. "Nautilus," diamond bezel
18k ....................................$13,000  $14,000  $15,000

PATEK PHILIPPE, skeleton, rf# 3885
18k ........................................$5,000  $6,000  $7,000

PATEK PHILIPPE, skeleton, rf# 3878
18k ........................................$6,000    $7,000    $8,000

PATEK PHILIPPE, skeleton, rf# 3886
18k ........................................$5,000    $6,000    $7,000

PATEK PHILIPPE, skeleton, diamonds=.62ct., rf# 3885
18k ........................................$6,000    $7,000    $8,000

PATEK PHILIPPE, skeleton, diamonds=.85ct., rf# 3884
18k ........................................$7,000    $8,000    $9,000

PATEK PHILIPPE, 36 jewels, diamond dial & bezel
18k ........................................$4,000    $4,500    $5,000

PATEK PHILIPPE, 18J., diamond dial, ca. 1952
platinum...............................$6,000    $7,000    $8,000

PATEK PHILIPPE, 18J., "Calatrava", diamond dial
platinum...............................$8,000    $9,000    $10,000

PATEK PHILIPPE, 18J., ''Calatrava,'' mid-sized, dia. dial
platinum...............................$8,000    $8,500    $9,000

🕐 Some grades are not included. Their values can be
determined by comparing with **similar** age, size, metal
content, style, grades, or models such as **time only**,
chronograph, repeater etc. listed.

PATEK PHILIPPE, 18 jewels, c. 1980s
18k C&B..............................$2,500    $2,800    $3,200

PATEK PHILIPPE, quartz, c. 1980s
18k C&B..............................$2,300    $2,500    $2,800

PATEK PHILIPPE, 18 jewels, c. 1960s
18k C&B..............................$3,500    $4,000    $4,500

PATEK PHILIPPE, 18 jewels, c. 1980s
18k C&B..............................$3,000    $3,200    $3,500

PATEK PHILIPPE, 18 jewels, massive lugs
18k...........................................$4,000    $4,500    $5,000

PATEK PHILIPPE, 18 jewels, concave & hooded lugs
18k...........................................$4,000    $4,300    $4,800

PATEK PHILIPPE, 18 jewels, hooded lugs, c.1930s
18K..........................................$4,500    $5,000    $5,500

PATEK PHILIPPE, 18 jewels, mid-sized, 2 tone
18k (y & w).........................$8,000    $9,000    $10,000

🕐 Some grades are not included. Their values can be
determined by comparing with **similar** age, size, metal
content, style, grades, or models such as **time only**,
chronograph, repeater etc. listed.

🕐 Some grades are not included. Their values can be
determined by comparing with **similar** age, size, metal
content, style, grades, or models such as **time only**,
chronograph, repeater etc. listed.

PATEK PHILIPPE, 18 J., extended lugs, 2 tone, rf#497
18k (y & w) ..........................$8,000    $9,000    $10,000

PATEK PHILIPPE, 18 jewels, lady's watch
18k ......................................$1,200    $1,400    $1,700

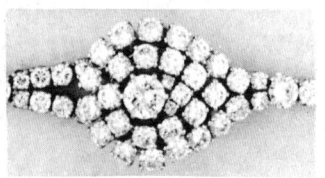

PATEK PHILIPPE,18 J., lady's, hinged lid set in diamonds
18k ......................................$3,500    $4,000    $4,500

PATEK PHILIPPE, 18 jewels, lady's watch
18k C&B..............................$2,500    $3,000    $3,500

PATEK PHILIPPE,  18 J., lady's watch, diamond bezel
platinum................................$3,000    $3,500    $4,000

PATEK PHILIPPE, 18 jewels, lady's watch, c. 1950s
18k ......................................$3,000    $3,500    $4,000

PATEK PHILIPPE, 18 jewels, lady's watch, c. 1940s
18k C&B ............................$3,500    $4,000    $4,500

PATEK PHILIPPE, 18J., lady's watch, min. repeater
18k......................................$40,000    $50,000    $60,000

PATEK PHILIPPE, 18 jewels, lady's watch, c. 1950s
18k......................................$1,800    $2,000    $2,500

PATEK PHILIPPE, 18 jewels, lady's watch, c. 1940s
18k......................................$1,000    $1,200    $1,400

PATEK PHILIPPE, 18 jewels, lady's watch, c. 1940s
18k......................................$1,500    $1,700    $2,000

PATEK PHILIPPE, 18 jewels, lady's watch, c. 1950s
18k......................................$1,000    $1,200    $1,500

# PATEK, PHILIPPE
## MOVEMENT IDENTIFICATION

**Caliber 6¾, no. 60**
S.no. 865000-869999
(1940-1955)

**Caliber 7, no. 70**
S.no. 943300-949999
(1940-1960)

**Caliber 8, no. 80**
S.no. 840000-849999
(1935-1960)

**Caliber 8, no. 85**
S.no. 850000-859999
(1935-1968)

**Caliber 9, no. 90**
S.no. 833150-839999
S.no. 970000-979999
(1940-1950)

**Caliber 9, no. 90a**
830000-833149
(1940-1950)

**Caliber 10, no. 105**
S.no. 900000-909999
(1940-1945)

**Caliber 10, no. 110**
S.no. 910000-919999
(1940-1950)

**Caliber 10, no. 200**
S.no. 740000-759999
(1952-1965)
S.no. 950000-959999
(1945-1955)

**Caliber 23, no. 300**
S.no. 780000-799999
(1955-1965)

**Caliber 12, no. 600AT**
S.no. 760000-779999
(1952-1960)

**Caliber 12, no. 400**
S.no. 720000-739999
(1950-1965)

**Caliber 12, no. 120**
826900-829999 (1935-1940)

**Caliber 12, no. 120A**
92000-929999 (1940-1950)
960000-969999 (1946-1952)
938000-939999 (1952-1954)

**Caliber 12 , center seconds**

**Caliber 13, no. 130A**

**Caliber 13, no. 130B**

**Caliber 13, no. 130C**

Chronograph, no. 862000-863995 (1940-1950); no. 867000-869999 (1950-1970)

**Caliber 12-600 AT,** S.no. 760,000-779,999 (1960-1970)

## PRODUCTION TOTALS

| DATE – SERIAL # | DATE – SERIAL # | DATE – SERIAL # |
|---|---|---|
| 1840 – 100 | 1950 – 700,000 | 1940 – 900,000 |
| 1845 – 1,200 | 1955 – 725,000 | 1945 – 915,000 |
| 1850 – 3,000 | 1960 – 750,000 | 1950 – 930,000 |
| 1855 – 8,000 | 1965 – 775,000 | 1955 – 940,000 |
| 1860 – 15,000 | 1970 – 795,000 | 1960 – 960,000 |
| 1865 – 22,000 | | 1965 – 975,000 |
| 1870 – 35,000 | DATE – SERIAL # | 1970 – 995,000 |
| 1875 – 45,000 | 1920 – 800,000 | |
| 1880 – 55,000 | 1925 – 805,000 | DATE – SERIAL # |
| 1885 – 70,000 | 1930 – 820,000 | 1960 – 1,100,000 |
| 1890 – 85,000 | 1935 – 824,000 | 1965 – 1,130,000 |
| 1895 – 100,000 | 1940 – 835,000 | 1970 – 1,250,000 |
| 1900 – 110,000 | 1945 – 850,000 | 1975 – 1,350,000 |
| 1905 – 125,000 | 1950 – 860,000 | 1980 – 1,450,000 |
| 1910 – 150,000 | 1955 – 870,000 | 1985 – 1,600,000 |
| 1915 – 175,000 | 1960 – 880,000 | 1990 – 1,850,000 |
| 1920 – 190,000 | 1965 – 890,000 | |
| 1925 – 200,000 | 1970 – 895,000 | |

The above list is provided for determining the APPROXIMATE age of your watch. Match serial number with date. Watches were not necessarily sold in the exact order of manufactured date.

PATRIA, 7 jewels, enamel dial, compass, Ca. 1920
s. steel ....................................$300      $350      $400

PATRIA, 7 jewels, enamel dial,
silver ......................................$100      $150      $200

PERFINE, 17 jewels, chronog., 2 reg.
gold filled................................$150      $175      $195
s. steel ....................................$75      $100      $125

PERPETUAL W. CO., 15 jewels, rim wind & set,
original retail price in 1933 was $31.50
14k ...........................................$700      $800      $900
gold filled................................$300      $350      $400
s. steel ....................................$200      $250      $300
base metal .............................$150      $200      $265

PERPETUAL W. CO., 15 jewels, c. 1930s
14k.........................................$600      $700      $800
gold filled..............................$350      $400      $450

PERPETUAL W. CO., 15J., fluted bezel, and sold for
"$37.50" in1933
base metal...............................$150      $200      $250

PERPETUAL W. CO., 15 jewels, fluted bezel
gold filled..............................$300      $350      $400

PERPETUAL W. CO., 15 J., diamond bezel, c. 1930s
platinum ..................................$400      $500      $600

PHILLIPE W. CO., 17J., RF#2501, chronog., c.1950
s. steel....................................$175      $200      $250

PIAGET,18J., cal.9p2 , c.1980
18k(w).....................................$500　　$600　　$700

PIAGET,18J., center sec., RF#1176, cal.f1560, c.1952
18k ..........................................$400　　$500　　$600

PIAGET,18J., center sec., c.1950
18k ..........................................$400　　$500　　$600

PIAGET, 18 jewels, 1904 $20 dollar gold piece, flip top
22k ..........................................$800　　$1,000　　$1,400

PIAGET, 18 jewels, 2 movements, 2 dials,
18k...........................................$700　　$800　　$900

PIAGET, 18 jewels, black dial
18k...........................................$500　　$600　　$700

PIAGET, 18 jewels, center sec., auto wind
18k...........................................$500　　$600　　$700

PIAGET, 18 jewels, ref. #8177, auto wind
18k...........................................$500　　$600　　$800

🕐 Some grades are not included. Their values can be
determined by comparing with similar age, size, metal
content, style, grades, or models such as time only,
chronograph, repeater etc. listed.

PIAGET, 18 jewels
18k ............................................$500    $600    $700

PIAGET, 30 jewels, auto wind, gold rotor
18k ............................................$500    $600    $700

PIAGET, 18 jewels, 18k case, 14k band
18k & 14k C&B......................$600    $700    $900

PIAGET, 18J., for Van Cleef,  center lugs, thin model
18k ............................................$500    $600    $700

PIAGET,18J., RF#9821 , c.1975
18k C&B................................$700    $800    $900

PIAGET, 18 jewels, oval style
18k C&B ................................$400    $450    $550

PIAGET, 18 jewels, oval style
18k...........................................$400    $450    $500

PIAGET, 18 jewels, textured bezel
18k...........................................$700    $800    $900

PIAGET, 18 jewels, textured bezel, classic 90 model
18k.....................................$1,100    $1,200    $1,400

PIAGET, 30 jewels, textured bezel
18k...........................................$500    $600    $700

PIAGET, 18J., rf#9298, c. 1970
18k .................................$1,000    $1,200    $1,400

PIAGET, 18 jewels, tank style
18k .................................$500    $550    $650

PIAGET, 18 jewels, "Executive", rf#7131C516
18k plain dial ......................$4,000    $4,500    $5,500
18k pave dial.......................$5,000    $5,500    $6,000

PIAGET, "Polo", rf#7131C701, quartz
18kC&B..............................$4,500    $5,000    $5,500

PIAGET, "Polo", rf#15562C701, quartz
18k .................................$4,000    $4,500    $5,000
NOTE: PIAGET identification # the first 3 to 5 = case design, a letter as A, B, C, =bracelet design. All models beginning with 7, 8,15 may be worn while swimming.

PIAGET, "Polo", rf#15562C701, quartz
18kC&B ..............................$4,000    $4,500    $5,000

PIAGET, rf#8065D4
18kC&B ..............................$1,500    $1,800    $2,100

PIAGET, 17 jewels, Ca. 1957
18k.................................$500    $600    $700

PICARD,17J., chronog., reg at 12 ,
base metal..................................$75    $100    $125

Some grades are not included. Their values can be
determined by comparing with **similar** age, size, metal
content, style, grades, or models such as **time only**,
chronograph, repeater etc. listed.

PIERCE, 17J., early auto wind, **"Parashock,"** Ca. 1930s
waterproof, back secured by four screws.
s. steel ..................................$400      $550      $750

PIERCE, 17J., triple date, moon ph.
gold filled ................................$225      $275      $350

PIERCE, 17 jewels, auto wind, c. 1948
gold filled..................................$40      $50      $60

POBEDA, 15J., tonneau, Ca. 1930s
14k **rose**....................................$300      $400      $500

PIERCE, 17 jewels, chronog. one button
s. steel ......................................$225      $250      $300

PONTIFA, 17 jewels, chronog. day-date-month, 3 reg.
14k ............................................$575      $650      $750
s. steel ....................................$350      $400      $450

PIERCE, 17 jewels, chronog., c. 1940s
s. steel ......................................$100      $135      $185
14k ............................................$350      $400      $450
18k ............................................$425      $475      $525

PORTA, 17J., antimagnetic, c.1955
gold plate ..................................$30      $40      $60

PRAESENT, 17J., triple date, moon ph., mid size, c.1948
gold filled.................................$250     $300     $375

PULSAR, L.E.D. (light emitting diode), ca.1975
14k ...........................................$300     $350     $400
gold filled ...............................$100     $150     $250

PREXA, 17 jewels, auto wind
gold filled.................................$30     $40     $50

PULSAR, L.E.D. (light emitting diode)
18k ...........................................$400     $450     $500
14k ...........................................$300     $375     $450
gold filled ...............................$125     $150     $185
s. steel .......................................$75     $95     $125

PROVITA, 17J., cal.1525, c.1973
18k ...........................................$150     $200     $250

RADO, 7J., double dial, c.1938
gold filled ...............................$350     $400     $450

PRONTO, 17 jewels, triple date, auto wind, waterproof
s. steel .......................................$60     $70     $85

Some grades are not included. Their values can be determined by comparing with **similar** age, size, metal content, style, grades, or models such as **time only**, chronograph, repeater etc. listed.

RADO, 17J., date, ca.1960
gold plate...............................$40     $50     $60

RAPID, 17J., on mvt. PATHE W. CO.
gold filled..................................$50      $75      $85

RECORD, 17J., split sec. chronog., date, moon phase
18k ........................................$5,000    $5,500    $6,000

RECORD, 17 jewels, split sec. chronog.
18k ........................................$6,000    $7,000    $8,000
s. steel ....................................$2,200    $2,500    $3,000

RECORD, 17 J., triple date, moon ph., auto wind,
2 reg. chronograph,
18k ........................................$1,500    $1,700    $2,000

RECORD, 17 jewels, triple date, moon phase, c. 1940s
18k ........................................$800      $900     $1,000

RECORD, 17 jewels, day-date-month, moon phase
s. steel ....................................$275     $325      $375

RECORD, 17 J., triple date, moon phase, auto wind
18k ........................................$1,000    $1,100    $1,200

REGINA, enamel dial, center lugs, c.1929
silver ........................................$150     $175      $200

Some grades are not included. Their values can be
determined by comparing with **similar** age, size, metal
content, style, grades, or models such as **time only**,
chronograph, repeater etc. listed.

REMBRANT, 17J., chronog., c.1942
18k ..........................................$425     $475     $550
s. steel ...................................$100     $125     $150

REVUE, 17J., beveled case, cal.54, c.1940
nickel.........................................$35     $50     $75

RIMA, 17J., aux. sec.,
14k .............................................$80     $100     $125

A. RIVALLE, 17J., chronog., c.1970
s. steel ......................................$50     $60     $70

ROAMER, 17 jewels, date, auto wind
gold filled .................................. $40     $50     $60

ROAMER, 17 jewels, auto wind, aux. sec.
gold filled ................................. $25     $30     $35

ROAMER, 23 jewels, ref. #4346
gold filled .................................. $30     $40     $50

ROAMER, 17 jewels, hidden lugs
gold filled ................................. $30     $40     $50

ROCAIL, 15J., auto-wind, c.1930s
s. steel ....................................$200        $250        $350

ROLEX,15 jewels, enamel dial, ca.1920
silver .....................................$500        $600        $800

ROCKFORD,15J., wire lugs, enamel dial, made in USA
s. steel ....................................$150        $200        $250

ROLEX, 15 jewels, enamel dial, flip top, c. 1918
silver .....................................$1,000      $1,200      $1,500

ROCKFORD,15J., "Winona", made in USA, S#761074
gold filled..............................$200          $250        $300
s. steel ....................................$150        $200        $250

ROLEX, 17J., RF# 2940, back is flat & tin can shaped
non-magnetic ........... ★★★ $1,000        $1,200      $1,400

ROCKFORD, 17J., "Iroquois", gold train
gold filled..............................$200          $250        $300

ROLEX, 26J., "Milgauss", RF#1019, c.1960s
s.steel ....................................$1,350      $1,650      $2,250

ROLEX, 25 jewels, Milgauss, oyster, perpetual, RF#6541
s. steel ...................................$1,200    $1,650    $2,000

ROLEX, 17 jewels," Century Club", c. 1960s
18k .........................................$1,200    $1,400    $1,600
14k .........................................$1,000    $1,200    $1,400

ROLEX, 17 jewels, ''Precision,'' center sec.
18k .........................................$900    $1,000    $1,200

ROLEX, 17 jewels, center sec., large lugs
18k .........................................$1,000    $1,200    $1,400

ROLEX, 17J., "Precision"
s. steel ...................................$400    $500    $600

ROLEX,17J., center sec., RF#9829, cal.1210
s. steel ...................................$300    $400    $500

ROLEX, 17J., rf#3562 , c.1955
14k .........................................$800    $900    $1,000

ROLEX,17J., center sec., RF#9659, c.1960
14k .........................................$800    $900    $1,000

ROLEX,17J., "Chronometer", RF# 4222, Ca.1945
18k ...........................................$900    $1,000    $1,200

ROLEX, 19J., rf#8443 , c.1965
14k ,..........................................$900    $1,000    $1,100

ROLEX, 17J., "Precision", fancy lugs,
9k ............................................$500    $600    $700

ROLEX, 17 jewels, ''Precision''
18k ...........................................$900    $1,000    $1,200

⊕ Some grades are not included. Their values can be
determined by comparing with **similar** age, size, metal
content, style, grades, or models such as **time only**,
chronograph, repeater etc. listed.

ROLEX, 15 jewels, wire lugs
9k .............................................$700    $800    $900

ROLEX, 15 jewels, early waterproof, (case within a case)
silver ......................................$1,600    $1,800    $2,000

ROLEX, 17 jewels, ref. #9659
14k C&B.............................$1,200    $1,400    $1,600

ROLEX, 17 jewels, ''Precision''
gold filled ...............................$400    $475    $550

ROLEX,15J., wire lugs, c.1925
silver .......................................$500    $600    $700

ROLEX, 15J., oyster, royal, c. 1930s
9k ...........................................$1,000    $1,400    $1,600

ROLEX,15J.,"Aqua", RF#2136, c.1928
s. steel .....................................$400    $500    $600

ROLEX, 15J., oyster, ca. 1930
silver .......................................$600    $700    $800

ROLEX,15J., RF#6071, c.1926
s. steel .....................................$400    $500    $600

ROLEX, 15 jewels, oyster, center sec.
18k ........................................$3,000    $3,400    $3,800
14k ........................................$2,200    $2,600    $3,000
9k ..........................................$1,400    $1,600    $1,800
silver .......................................$900    $1,000    $1,200
s. steel .....................................$800    $900    $1,000

ROLEX,15J., by OYSTER W. CO., c. 1927
s. steel .....................................$400    $500    $700

ROLEX, 17 jewels, oyster, ref. #2081
gold filled ...............................$600    $700    $900

ROLEX, 17 jewels, oyster, c. 1934
18k ........................................$3,000    $3,200    $3,400
14k ........................................$2,200    $2,500    $2,800
9k ..........................................$1,400    $1,600    $1,800
silver .......................................$800    $900    $1,000
s. steel .....................................$600    $700    $800

Some grades are not included. Their values can be determined by comparing with **similar** age, size, metal content, style, grades, or models such as **time only**, chronograph, repeater etc. listed.

ROLEX, 17 jewels, oyster, center sec.
| | | | |
|---|---|---|---|
| 18k ........................................$2,500 | $2,700 | $3,000 |
| 14k ........................................$2,000 | $2,200 | $2,500 |
| 9k ..........................................$1,400 | $1,500 | $1,700 |
| s. steel ....................................$600 | $700 | $800 |

ROLEX, 18J., center sec. ca. 1937
s. steel ....................................$500        $600        $700

ROLEX, 17 jewels, graduated bezel, c. 1928
silver ......................................$900        $1,000        $1,200

ROLEX,17J., RF#4647, c.1943
s. steel ....................................$450        $550        $650

ROLEX, 18J., note dial top half & bottom, RF#3139
s. steel ....................................$500        $600        $750

ROLEX,17J., RF#3139, c.1942
s. steel ....................................$450        $550        $650

ROLEX,17J., RF#4647, c.1948
s. steel ....................................$500        $600        $750

ROLEX, 17 jewels, oyster, ref. #4547
s. steel ....................................$600        $700        $800

ROLEX, 17 jewels, oyster, c. 1930s
18k ...........................................$2,500   $2,800   $3,400
14k .......................................$2,200   $2,400   $2,600

ROLEX,17J., "Viceroy", RF#3359, c.1943
14k & s. steel......................$1,200   $1,400   $1,800

ROLEX,17J., "Observatory", RF#3386, c.1940
gold filled................................$550   $650   $750

ROLEX, 17 jewels, oyster, extra prima "Viceroy"
18k ......................................$2,500   $2,800   $3,300

ROLEX,17J., RF#3116, c.1942
14k ........................................$2,200   $2,500   $2,800

ROLEX, 26 jewels, "Viceroy", center sec.
9k ..........................................$1,600   $1,800   $2,000

ROLEX, 17 jewels, oyster, "Viceroy," 2 tone, c. 1943
14k & s. steel ......................$1,200   $1,400   $1,800

ROLEX,17J., "Skyrocket", RF#, c.1944
gold filled ...............................$400   $500   $600

🕐 Some grades are not included. Their values can be determined by comparing with **similar** age, size, metal content, style, grades, or models such as **time only**, chronograph, repeater etc. listed.

ROLEX,17J., 28mm, small one button chronog., RF# 2303
9k .......................................$20,000    $22,000    $25,000

ROLEX,17J., Chronograph, triple date & **moon-phases**,
about **12 made**, rf# 81806 also rf# 2508, Valjoux caliber 72C,
This chronograph is being **FAKED** so beware.
18k ....................  ★ ★ ★ ★ $65,000    $75,000    $85,000

ROLEX,17J., split second chronog., RF# 4113, **15 examples**,
large 43mm, Valjoux caliber 55 VBR, Ca.1943
s. steel ................ ★ ★ ★ ★ $30,000    $40,000    $50,000

ROLEX, 17 J., chronog., 70-made, flat, tachometer,
rf#8206,c.1940s
18k ...........................................$15,000    $20,000    $25,000

ROLEX, 17J., one button chronog. 2 reg., curved back
18k .......................................$25,000    $28,000    $32,000

ROLEX, 17 J., chronog., center lugs, RF#3233, c. 1940s
18k ...................................$9,000    $10,000    $11,000
14k ..................................$5,000    $6,000    $7,000
9k ......................................$3,600    $4,000    $4,500
s. steel ................................$2,500    $3,000    $3,500

🕐 **Note: Rolex chronographs must have original dial, de-
duct 30% for refinished dial.**

ROLEX,17J., rf#3055 , Antimagnetique, 200 made, c.1956
18k .....................................$20,000    $22,000    $25,000

ROLEX, 17 jewels, chronog., mid-sized, c. 1950s
18k .......................................$8,000    $9,000    $10,000
14k .......................................$7,000    $8,000    $9,000

ROLEX,17J., Valjoux cal.23, RF#4062, c.1940
18k .......................................$6,000    $7,000    $8,000

ROLEX, 17 jewels, chronog., 3 reg. oyster, RF#6238
s. steel ...............................$3,000    $3,500    $4,000

ROLEX, 17J., chronog, 3 reg., RF#6234, Valjoux 72bc
s. steel ...................................$4,000    $4,500    $5,000
14k .........................................$8,000    $9,000    $10,000

ROLEX,17J., triple date, RF#4767, c.1948
s. steel ...................................$9,000    $10,000    $11,000

ROLEX, 17J., chronog., triple-date, diamond style chapter,
RF# 6036, about 175 made in Y. gold , 144 made pink gold
18k .....................................$22,000    $24,000    $26,000
14k .....................................$16,000    $18,000    $21,000
s. steel ..................................$8,000    $9,000    $10,000

ROLEX, 17J., **pulsation** chronog., 3 reg., rf# 6234, Ca. 1960
s. steel ...............................$10,000    $12,000    $14,000

ROLEX,17J., Antimagnetic chronog., 3 reg., rf#6034, about
45 made, Ca.1950s
18k .......................................$10,000    $12,000    $14,000

🕒 Some grades are not included. Their values can be
determined by comparing with **similar** age, size, metal
content, style, grades, or models such as **time only**,
chronograph, repeater etc. listed.

ROLEX, 17J., RF#6238, 3 reg., c. 1950s, rect. markers
18k .......................................$8,000    $9,000    $10,000

ROLEX,17J., exotic dial, RF#6239, Valjoux 727, c.1965
**"PAUL NEWMAN",** (*beware of reproduction dials*)
s. steel ................................$6,000    $7,000    $8,500

ROLEX, 17J., chronog., 3 reg., tear drop lugs, c. 1940s
18k .......................................$10,000    $11,000    $12,000
14k .......................................$8,000    $9,000    $10,000
s. steel ................................$4,000    $5,000    $6,000

ROLEX,17J., "Daytona", RF#6263, c.1978
s. steel ................................$4,000    $4,400    $4,800

ROLEX, 17J., triple-date, 3 reg., square markers
s. steel ................................$8,000    $9,000    $10,000

ROLEX,17J., screw down pusher 1st used 1976, RF#6265,
s. steel ................................$4,000    $4,400    $4,800

ROLEX, 17J.,  Daytona, red outside chapter exotic dial
RF# 6241, **"PAUL NEWMAN"**
s. steel ................................$6,000    $7,000    $8,500

ROLEX, 17 jewels, "Daytona," chronog., waterproof
18k .......................................$8,000    $9,000    $10,000
14k .......................................$6,000    $7,000    $8,000
s. steel ................................$3,200    $3,500    $3,800

ROLEX, 17 J., tachometer, 3 reg., RF#6239, c.1960s

| 18k | $10,000 | $12,000 | $14,000 |
|---|---|---|---|
| 14k | $8,000 | $9,000 | $10,000 |
| s. steel | $3,500 | $4,000 | $4,500 |

ROLEX,17J., triple-date, moon ph., RF#8171, **1,000 made**

| 18k | $12,000 | $15,000 | $18,000 |
|---|---|---|---|
| 14k | $9,000 | $10,000 | $12,000 |
| s. steel | $6,000 | $7,000 | $8,500 |

ROLEX,17J., day-date-month, moon ph.,oyster, RF#6062

| s. steel C&B | $6,000 | $7,000 | $8,000 |
|---|---|---|---|

ROLEX,17J., STARS on dial, triple date, rf#6062, about 50 made gold & 350 in s. steel, Ca. 1945

| 18k | $20,000 | $22,000 | $25,000 |
|---|---|---|---|

ROLEX,17J., day-date-month, moon ph., RF#6062,c.1945

| 18k | $12,000 | $15,000 | $18,000 |
|---|---|---|---|

ROLEX, 15J., jumping hr., duo dial, RF#4402, c. 1930s

| platinum | $14,000 | $16,000 | $19,000 |
|---|---|---|---|
| 18k | $12,000 | $14,000 | $16,000 |
| 14k | $10,000 | $11,000 | $12,000 |
| 9k | $7,000 | $8,000 | $9,000 |
| silver | $6,000 | $7,000 | $8,000 |
| gold filled | $4,000 | $5,000 | $6,500 |
| s. steel | $5,000 | $6,000 | $7,500 |

ROLEX,17J.,jump hr., duo dial, stepped case, RF#1521

| 18k 2 tone | $15,000 | $18,000 | $22,000 |
|---|---|---|---|
| 18k | $12,000 | $14,000 | $16,000 |
| 14k | $9,000 | $10,000 | $12,000 |
| 9k | $7,000 | $8,000 | $10,000 |
| s. steel | $6,000 | $7,000 | $8,000 |

ROLEX, 17 jewels, "Prince," duo dial, RF#1490

| 18k C&B | $6,000 | $7,000 | $8,000 |
|---|---|---|---|

ROLEX, 17 jewels, flared, duo dial, c. 1930s
9k ........................................$3,500    $4,000    $4,500

ROLEX, 15 jewels, "Prince," duo dial, c. 1930s
s. steel ..................................$3,000    $3,500    $4,000

ROLEX, 17J., 2 tone case tiger stripe, beware of FAKES
18k ....................................$12,000    $14,000    $16,000

ROLEX, 15 jewels, chronometer, duo dial, c. 1930s
s. steel ..................................$3,000    $3,500    $4,000

ROLEX, 17 jewels, "Prince," duo dial, stepped case
18k ......................................$6,000    $7,000    $8,000
14k ......................................$4,500    $5,000    $6,000
9k ........................................$3,500    $4,000    $4,500
silver ....................................$3,500    $4,000    $4,500
s. steel ..................................$3,000    $3,500    $4,000
gold filled.............................$2,800    $3,200    $3,500

ROLEX, 15 jewels, "Railway," stepped case, c. 1930s
18k 2 tone ........................$12,000    $14,000    $16,000
18k ....................................$10,000    $12,000    $14,000
14k 2 tone ..........................$9,000    $10,000    $11,000
14k ......................................$7,000    $8,000    $9,000
9k 2 tone ............................$5,000    $6,000    $7,000
9k ........................................$4,000    $4,500    $5,500
s. steel ..................................$4,000    $4,500    $5,000

ROLEX, 17J., RF#971, 2 tone stripes, Adj. to 6 pos.
18k ....................................$12,000    $14,000    $16,000
14k ....................................$10,000    $11,000    $12,500
9k ........................................$7,000    $7,500    $8,500

ROLEX, 15 jewels, "Prince," center sec., c. 1930s
18k ......................................$8,000    $9,000    $10,000

ROLEX, 15 jewels, flared, duo dial, Adj. to 6 pos.
9k ........................................$3,500    $4,000    $4,500

ROLEX, 15 jewels, 1/4 century club, RF#2541
14k ......................................$5,000    $5,500    $6,000

ROLEX, 15 jewels, 1/4 century club,
14k ........................................$5,000    $5,500    $6,000

ROLEX, 15 jewels, "Prince," RF#1343, c. 1935
platinum............................$10,000    $11,000    $12,000
18k ......................................$6,000    $7,000    $8,000
14k ......................................$5,000    $5,500    $6,500
gold filled............................$3,000    $3,200    $3,500

ROLEX, 17J., "Observatory", c.1938
gold filled............................$1,000    $1,100    $1,200

ROLEX, 15 jewels, stepped case, RF#1527
18k ........................................$8,000    $9,000    $10,000

ROLEX, 17J., date, mid size,
s. steel ....................................$400    $450    $550

ROLEX, 25J., rf#6604 , date, c.1958
s. steel ....................................$500    $550    $625

ROLEX, 25J., rf#1500 , date, c.1963
s. steel ....................................$600    $700    $800

ROLEX, 26J., rf#6694 , date, c.1971
s. steel ....................................$400    $450    $500

ROLEX, 17J., rf#6094 , date, Ca.1951
s. steel ....................................$400    $450    $550

ROLEX, 26J., rf#1501 , c.1970
s. steel .................................$600    $700    $800

ROLEX, 17 jewels, oyster, perpetual, date, ca.1950s
14k .......................................$1,700    $1,900    $2,200

ROLEX,25J., date, **marked gold bezel**, 2 tone case, rf#6305
s. steel/gold bezel ..................$800    $900    $1,000

ROLEX, 25J., **Oval Toni**, *about 2,000 made,* RF#6105, auto
wind, oyster, Ca.1953
14k .......................................$3,000    $3,200    $3,500

ROLEX, 17J., date, RF#6964, ca.1953
s. steel .......................................$400    $500    $600

ROLEX, 25J., oyster, perpetual, date, **Oval Toni**, RF#4467,
Ca. 1950s
18k .......................................$3,500    $3,700    $4,000

ROLEX, 26J., center sec., date just, RF# 1601, Ca.1968
s. steel / gold .......................$1,300    $1,500    $1,600

ROLEX, 17 jewels, ''Speed King''
s. steel .....................................$450    $500    $550

ROLEX, 17 jewels, ref. #4325
14k ...........................................$800    $900    $1,000

ROLEX, 19J., center sec.,gold & s. steel 2 tone case,
Gold & steel...........................$600    $700    $800

ROLEX, 25 jewels, "Explorer", RF#1016
s. steel .....................................$900    $1,100    $1,400

ROLEX, 17J., marked bezel, rose gold, c.1940s
18k ......................................$2,000    $2,200    $2,500

ROLEX, 17 jewels, oyster, manual wind
18k ......................................$1,000    $1,100    $1,250
14k .........................................$800    $900    $1,000
9k ...........................................$500    $550    $700
gold filled................................$350    $400    $450
s. steel ....................................$300    $350    $400

ROLEX, 17J., marked bezel 2 tone, ca. 1955
gold & s. steel........................$600    $650    $700

ROLEX, 17J., center sec., precision, rf#6422
s. steel .....................................$350    $400    $450

ROLEX, 25J., rf#6202, marked bezel, ca.1962
14k & s.s.............................$1,400    $1,800    $2,200

ROLEX, 26J.,  RF#1002, c.1965
14k .....................................$1,400     $1,500     $1,600

ROLEX, 25J., rf#5500 , Air King, c.1969
s. steel ....................................$450     $500     $550

ROLEX, 25J., marked bezel, textured dial, ca. 1949
14k .....................................$1,400     $1,600     $1,800

ROLEX, 16J., rf#6082 , c.1950
s. steel ....................................$400     $450     $500

ROLEX, 25J., rf#6565 , c.1958
s. steel ....................................$700     $800     $950

ROLEX, 25J., RF#1025, c.1960
14k .....................................$1,200     $1,400     $1,600

ROLEX, 25J., rf#6024 , c.1953
s. steel ....................................$450     $500     $600

ROLEX, 17J., rf#6424 , c.1965
s. steel ....................................$400     $450     $500

ROLEX, 25J., rf#6518 , c.1956
s. steel ....................................$400     $450     $500

ROLEX, 26J., perpetual oyster, **recent**
s. steel ....................................$400     $500     $600

ROLEX, 17J., rf#6284 , c.1955
18k ........................................$2,000     $2,200     $2,400

ROLEX, 25J., rf#6098 , star dial, c.1956
18k rose ...............................$2,500     $2,700     $3,000

ROLEX, 17J., rf#6024 , c.1952
s. steel ....................................$400     $450     $500

ROLEX, 25J., "Air King", RF#5500, c.1962
s. steel ....................................$400     $500     $550

ROLEX, 26J., rf#1005 , c.1964
14k & S.S..............................$600     $700     $800

ROLEX, 25J., "Air King",RF#5504, c.1959
s. steel ....................................$400     $500     $600

ROLEX, 17J., RF#6084, c.1951
14k .........................................$1,500      $1,700      $1,900

ROLEX, 25J., RF#6568, c.1956
s. steel ....................................$400      $450      $500

ROLEX, 25J., RF#6084, c.1953
14k .........................................$1,800      $2,000      $2,200

ROLEX, 18J.,  RF#8405, c.1950
18k ...........................................$900      $1,000      $1,100

ROLEX, 25J., RF#6564, c.1955
s. steel ....................................$400      $450      $500

ROLEX, 17J., center sec.
14k ...........................................$700      $800      $900

ROLEX, 25J., marked bezel, RF#6581, c.1954
14k .........................................$1,400      $1,600      $1,800

ROLEX, 15J.,  center sec., ca. 1939
14k ...........................................$700      $800      $900

ROLEX,17J., RF#6144, c.1948
18k & s.steel ..........................$600     $700     $800

ROLEX, 25J., "Bomb'e"12 diamond dial, RF#1030, c.1958
s. steel ....................................$600     $700     $800

ROLEX, 17J.,  Linz 1877, oyster, "Bomb'e", c. 1950s
18k ......................................$1,800     $2,000     $2,200

ROLEX, 26 jewels, "Bomb'e", rf#6590, c. 1950
14k ......................................$1,400     $1,600     $1,800

ROLEX, 25 jewels, "Bomb'e", rf. #6102, c.1953
14k ......................................$1,500     $1,700     $1,900

ROLEX, 26 jewels, "Bomb'e", rf#6102, c. 1950
18k ......................................$1,600     $1,800     $2,000

ROLEX, 19 jewels, "Bomb'e", center sec., c. 1950s
18k ......................................$1,400     $1,600     $1,800
14k ......................................$1,200     $1,400     $1,600
9k ........................................$800     $900     $1,000
s. steel ....................................$500     $600     $700

ROLEX, 17J.,  precision, center sec.
14k ............................................$600     $700     $800

ROLEX, 17 jewels, center sec., gold bezel
18k & s. steel .........................$600       $700         $800

ROLEX, 26J., bubble back, hooded lugs, rf#3595

| | | | |
|---|---|---|---|
| 18k ......................................$8,000 | $9,000 | $10,000 |
| 14k ......................................$6,000 | $6,500 | $7,000 |
| 9k ........................................$3,500 | $4,000 | $4,500 |
| s. steel ....................... ★ ★$12,000 | $14,000 | $16,000 |

ROLEX, 17 jewels, center sec., c. 1945

| | | |
|---|---|---|
| 18k ................................$2,000 | $2,200 | $2,500 |
| 14k .......................................$1,000 | $1,200 | $1,500 |
| 9k ........................................$900 | $1,000 | $1,100 |
| s. steel ....................................$400 | $450 | $550 |

ROLEX, 17J., Pall Mall, manual wind, Ca. 1949
14k .........................................$500       $600        $700

ROLEX, 18J., center sec.
s. steel ....................................$400       $450        $500

ROLEX, 17J., "Royal Observatory", RF#3121, c.1937
s. steel ....................................$450       $500        $600

ROLEX, 18J., aux. sec.
s. steel ....................................$400       $450        $500

ROLEX, 17J., "Record", manual wind, c.1940
s. steel ....................................$400       $500        $600

ROLEX, 17J., "Neptune", mid-size, manual wind, c.1939
gold filled.................................$400    $500    $600

ROLEX, 17J., "Victory", mid size, **Tudor**, c.1940
s. steel .....................................$400    $475    $550

ROLEX, 17J., sky-rocket, mid size, ca.1949, **steel back**
gold filled & s. steel ...............$400    $500    $600

ROLEX, 26 jewels, bubble back, hooded lugs, 2 tone
18k & s. steel ......................$6,000    $7,000    $8,000

ROLEX, 26 jewels, bubble back, hooded scalloped lugs
18k & s. steel ......................$5,000    $6,500    $8,000

ROLEX, 17J., RF#2280, manual wind, c.1951
s. steel ....................................$400    $500    $600

ROLEX, 15J., RF#2574, manual wind, tu-tone dial,
c.1940
s. steel ....................................$800    $900    $1,000

ROLEX, 18J., mid size, RF#3767, c.1940
chrome ....................................$300    $400    $500

ROLEX, 17J., mid size, RF#3478, c.1940
gold filled ...............................$300    $400    $500
s. steel ....................................$300    $400    $500

🕐 Some grades are not included. Their values can be
determined by comparing with **similar** age, size, metal
content, style, grades, or models such as **time only**,
chronograph, repeater etc. listed.

ROLEX, 17J., "Speed King", RF#4220, c.1945
s. steel ...................................$475      $575      $650

ROLEX, 18J., "Royal", mid size, aux. sec.
s. steel ...................................$400      $500      $600

ROLEX, 17J., "Speed King", RF#6056, c.1952
s. steel ...................................$400      $500      $600

ROLEX, 18J., "Speed King", mid size, center sec.
s. steel ...................................$400      $500      $600

ROLEX, 17J., mid size,RF#6066, c.1951
s. steel ...................................$400      $500      $600

ROLEX, 18J., B.B., hooded 2 tone yellow gold
Gold & steel.......................$3,500      $4,000      $4,500

ROLEX, 17J., mid size, RF#6466, c.1957
s. steel ...................................$400      $500      $600

ROLEX, 18J., B.B., hooded 2 tone **rose gold**
Gold & steel.......................$3,800      $4,200      $4,700

⊕ Some grades are not included. Their values can be
determined by comparing with **similar** age, size, metal
content, style, grades, or models such as **time only**,
chronograph, repeater etc. listed.

ROLEX, 18J., B.B., center sec.
s. steel .................................$1,000    $1,200    $1,400

ROLEX, 18J., B.B., marked bezel,
18k .......................................$4,000    $5,000    $6,000

ROLEX, 18J., B.B., not 2 tone, rf#3131
14k .......................................$2,700    $3,200    $3,700

ROLEX, 18J., B.B., chronometer, RF#3131, cal#600
14k .......................................$3,700    $4,000    $4,500
s. steel .................................$1,000    $1,200    $1,400

ROLEX, 18J., B.B., marked bezel,
s. steel .................................$1,000    $1,200    $1,400

ROLEX, 18J., B.B., cal#600, aux. sec., ca. 1945
s. steel .................................$1,000    $1,200    $1,400

ROLEX, 25J., rf#2764, B.B., marked bezel, 2 tone, c.1945
14k & S.S............................$1,500    $1,800    $2,300

🕐 Some grades are not included. Their values can be
determined by comparing with **similar** age, size, metal
content, style, grades, or models such as **time only**,
chronograph, repeater etc. listed.

ROLEX, 18J., B.B., self winding on dial
14k .......................................$3,300    $3,500    $3,900

ROLEX, 17J., BB, RF#3131, c.1948
14k ........................................$2,800    $3,000    $3,300

ROLEX, 17J., BB, RF#3725, ROSE GOLD case, c.1945
14k rose ...............................$3,500    $4,000    $4,500

ROLEX, 17J., BB, RF#3133, tu-tone, c.1940
14k &s.s. .............................$1,500    $1,700    $2,000

ROLEX, 17J.,  RF#3725, B.B., marked bezel, c.1945
12k ........................................$3,200    $3,400    $3,600

ROLEX, 17J., BB, RF#3372,  marked bezel, c.1954
s. steel ..................................$1,100    $1,400    $1,600

ROLEX, 17J.,  RF#5015, marked bezel, c.1949
s. steel ..................................$1,200    $1,400    $1,800

ROLEX, 17J., BB, RF#3372,  tu-tone, c.1940
14k & s.s. .............................$1,700    $2,000    $2,300

ROLEX, 18J., B.B., center sec. ca. 1940s
14k ........................................$2,800    $3,000    $3,200

ROLEX, 19J., B.B.,ca. 1940s
14k ........................................$3,000     $3,300     $3,600

ROLEX, 26J., bubble back, graduated bezel , aux. sec.
14k ........................................$3,000     $3,500     $4,000

ROLEX, 19 jewels, bubble back, 2 tone
18k & s. steel .......................$1,600     $1,800     $2,000

ROLEX, 26 jewels, bubble back, Arabic & Roman no.'s
14k ........................................$3,000     $3,500     $4,000

ROLEX, 26 J., bubble back, aux. sec., RF#3458, c1940s
18k ...................................$3,500     $4,000     $4,500
14k ...................................$3,000     $3,300     $3,600
9k .....................................$1,800     $2,000     $2,500
gold filled ..........................$1,100     $1,300     $1,500
s. steel ...............................$1,000     $1,200     $1,400

ROLEX, 26 J., bubble back, RF#2940, c. 1940s
18k ...................................$3,500     $4,000     $4,500
14k ...................................$3,000     $3,300     $3,600
9k .....................................$1,800     $2,000     $2,200
gold filled ..........................$1,100     $1,300     $1,500
s. steel ...............................$1,000     $1,200     $1,400

ROLEX, 26 J., bubble back, mercedes hands, c. 1930s
18k ...................................$3,500     $4,000     $4,500
14k ...................................$3,000     $3,300     $3,600
9k .....................................$1,800     $1,900     $2,200
gold filled ..........................$1,100     $1,300     $1,500
s. steel ...............................$1,000     $1,200     $1,400

⊕ Some grades are not included. Their values can be determined by comparing with similar age, size, metal content, style, grades, or models such as time only, chronograph, repeater etc. listed.

ROLEX, 26J., bubble back, marked bezel, c. 1940s
18k .......................................$4,000     $4,500     $5,000
14k .......................................$3,500     $4,000     $4,500
9k .........................................$3,000     $3,200     $3,500
gold filled............................$1,200     $1,400     $1,600
s. steel ................................$1,200     $1,400     $1,600

ROLEX, 26 jewels, bubble back, c. 1940s
s. steel ................................$1,000     $1,200     $1,400

ROLEX, 26 jewels, bubble back, c. 1940s
14k .......................................$2,800     $3,200     $3,600

ROLEX, 19 jewels, bubble back, center sec., rf#1453
18k .......................................$3,800     $4,000     $4,500
14k .......................................$3,000     $3,200     $3,500
s. steel ................................$1,000     $1,200     $1,400

ROLEX, 25J., rare  gold #s on black dial, rf#3133, B.B., 14k
bezel, c.1945
14k & s. steel. ......................$3,000     $3,200     $4,000

ROLEX, 26 jewels, bubble back
18k .......................................$4,000     $5,000     $6,000
s. steel ................................$1,000     $1,200     $1,400

ROLEX, 26 jewels, bubble back, 2 tone, c. 1940s
18k & s. steel ......................$1,600     $1,800     $2,000

ROLEX, 26 jewels, bubble back, c. 1945
14k .......................................$2,900     $3,200     $3,600

ROLEX, 26 jewels, bubble back, c. 1940s

| | | | |
|---|---|---|---|
| 18k | $3,700 | $4,000 | $4,500 |
| 14k | $2,800 | $3,200 | $3,600 |
| s. steel | $1,000 | $1,200 | $1,400 |

ROLEX, 18 jewels, bubble back, rf# 2940, c. 1940s

| | | | |
|---|---|---|---|
| s. steel | $1,000 | $1,200 | $1,400 |

ROLEX, 18 jewels, bubble back, c. 1942

| | | | |
|---|---|---|---|
| 18k | $3,700 | $4,000 | $4,500 |
| 14k | $2,800 | $3,200 | $3,600 |
| s. steel | $1,000 | $1,200 | $1,400 |

ROLEX, 18 jewels, bubble back, gold & s. steel band

| | | | |
|---|---|---|---|
| 14k & s. steel C&B | $2,200 | $2,500 | $3,000 |

ROLEX, 18 J., date, left hand winds at 9 o'clock

| | | | |
|---|---|---|---|
| s. steel | $1,400 | $1,600 | $1,800 |

ROLEX, 30 jewels, ''Presidential,'' 44 diamonds on dial & bezel, day-date, oyster, perpetual, RF#8038

| | | | |
|---|---|---|---|
| 18k C&B | $7,500 | $8,500 | $9,500 |

ROLEX, 26 jewels, day-date, 10 diamond dial, old model RF#1803

| | | | |
|---|---|---|---|
| 18k C&B | $5,000 | $5,500 | $6,000 |
| 18k (w) | $4,000 | $4,500 | $5,000 |

ROLEX, 26 jewels, ''Presidential,'' diamond dial, day-date, perpetual, oyster, RF#1804, quick set

| | | | |
|---|---|---|---|
| 18k C&B | $6,000 | $6,500 | $7,000 |

ROLEX, 30 jewels, ''Presidential,'' (Tridor), oyster, daydate, diamond dial, perpetual, oyster
18k (y & w) ........................$8,000     $8,500     $9,000

ROLEX, 26 Jewels, ''Presidential,'' day-date, single quick set model RF#18038, double quick-set RF#18238

| | | | |
|---|---|---|---|
| 18kC&B double quick-set... | $6,500 | $7,000 | $7,500 |
| 18k C&B single quick-set... | $5,500 | $6,000 | $6,500 |
| old model 18k..................... | $4,000 | $4,500 | $5,000 |

ROLEX, 30J., ''Presidential,'' bark finish, RF#1803, c.1971
18k C&B.............................$5,500     $6,000     $6,500

ROLEX, 26J., ''Presidential,'' day-date, perpetual, note textured dial, rose gold, RF#1803 old model
18k C & B ...........................$4,500     $5,000     $5,500

ROLEX, 30 jewels, ''Presidential,'' day-date, perpetual, oyster, diamond bezel, bark finish, RF#18078
18k C&B..............................$7,000     $7,500     $8,500

ROLEX, quartz, RF#19018
diamond dial & diamond bezel add $1,000-$1,200
18k .......................................$4,000     $5,000     $6,000

ROLEX, 26 Jewels, ''Presidential,'' day-date, perpetual, oyster, old model, RF#1803
18k C&B..............................$4,000     $4,500     $5,000

ROLEX, 26 J., jubilee band, 10 diamond dial, date just
18k C&B..............................$4,500    $5,500    $6,500
14k C&B..............................$3,500    $4,000    $5,000
gold & s. steel C&B ...........$2,000    $2,500    $3,000

ROLEX, 26 jewels, date, perpetual, oyster
18k ........................................$2,500    $2,700    $3,000
14k ........................................$1,600    $1,800    $2,200
s. steel ..................................$450       $550       $650

ROLEX, 26J., quick set, date, Oyster bracelet, c.1965
14k C&B..............................$2,800    $3,000    $3,200

ROLEX, 21 jewels, date just, center sec., c. 1965
18k ......................................$3,000    $3,500    $4,000

ROLEX, 26 jewels, date, oyster, mid-size
s. steel C&B...........................$500      $600       $700

ROLEX, 17J., RF#6694, c.1961
s. steel ...................................$400       $500       $600

ROLEX, 17J., RF#6426, c.1961
s. steel ...................................$400       $500       $600

ROLEX, 26 jewels, perpetual, oyster, date just
18k ........................................$4,000    $4,500    $5,500
18k & s. steel ......................$1,400    $1,600    $2,000
14k ........................................$2,800    $3,200    $4,000
14k & s. steel ......................$1,200    $1,400    $1,600
s. steel ...................................$600       $700       $900

ROLEX, 26J., perpetual, oyster, date, graduated bezel
14k .................................$2,600    $2,800    $3,000
s. steel ...............................$600    $700    $850

ROLEX, 21 jewels, perpetual, oyster
18k .................................$1,800    $1,900    $2,000
18k & s. steel ......................$800    $900    $1,200
14k .................................$1,400    $1,500    $1,600
14k & s. steel ......................$700    $800    $1,000
s. steel ...............................$500    $600    $700

ROLEX, 26 jewels, oyster, date, ref. #1625
18k & s. steel ....................$2,800    $3,200    $3,600
14k & s. steel C&B.............$1,000    $1,200    $1,500

ROLEX, 25J., **gold bezel**, "Explorer," rf#6610, Ca. 1956
s. steel & gold bezel ...........$1,000    $1,200    $1,400

ROLEX, 21 J., "Thunderbird," perpetual, oyster, date just
18k .................................$4,000    $4,500    $5,000
s. steel ...............................$800    $900    $1,100

ROLEX, 26 jewels, "Explorer," rf#1016, perpetual, oyster
s. steel ...............................$900    $1,000    $1,100

ROLEX, 21 jewels, perpetual, oyster date just, 2 tone
Gold & steel........................$1,200    $1,400    $1,600

ROLEX, 17J., **"Luminor Panerai,"** Italian military diving,
RF# 6151-1, Ca. **1940s**, Note: look for reproduction 1992
s. steel ...............................$1,500    $1,700    $2,000

ROLEX, 26 jewels, "GMT-Master," perpetual, oyster, date ruby & diamond dial
18k .......................................$5,500    $6,500    $7,500

ROLEX, 26 J., "Submariner," rf#5513
s. steel .................................$1,000    $1,200    $1,500

ROLEX, 26 J., "GMT-Master II," perp., oyster, date
18k .......................................$5,000    $6,000    $7,000
s. steel .................................$800    $900    $1,100

ROLEX, 26 J., "Submariner," perpetual, oyster, date
18k C&B...............................$7,000    $8,000    $9,000
18k & s. steel C&B .............$2,600    $2,800    $3,400
s. steel .................................$1,000    $1,200    $1,500

ROLEX, 26 J., "GMT-Master", rf#6542, c.1957
s. steel ......................................$900    $1,100    $1,300
Single quick set Presidential & Jubilee use 6 screws.
Double quick set Presidential & Jubilee use 7 screws.
Presidential or Jubilee gold link ....    $250.00
Jubilee or Oyster s. steel link .........    $40.00
Oyster gold link ..............................    $200.00
ROLEX first used **HACK** system in Ca. 1972
ROLEX first used the Quick Set feature Ca. 1977
Sapphire crystals were added in U.S.A. Ca.1989= gents $100.
steel screw-on crown=$20., gold screw-on crown=$35.

ROLEX, 26J., "Sea-Dweller," rf#1665, 2,000 ft, date
s. steel .................................$1,200    $1,400    $1,600

ROLEX factory only, mens diamond dials & bezels
Bezel 18k or platinum, W/44 full cut    $3,000    $5,000
Dial W/8 brilliants & 2 baguetts for Oyster Perpetual &
DAY DATE..................................    $1,000    $1,600
Dial W/ 10 baguettes for Oyster Perpetual &
DAY DATE..................................    $2,000    $3,500
Dial W/ 10 brilliants for Oyster Perpetual &
DATEJUST or DATE....................    $700    $1,500

ROLEX, 21J., "Sea-Dweller," up to 4,000 ft., rf# 16660, date
s. steel ...................$1,600    $1,800    $2,000

ROLEX, 26J., "Submariner", rf# 6536,100M,c.1958
s. steel ...................................$500    $600    $900

ROLEX, 26 jewels, "Explorer II," rf# 1665, date
s. steel ...................................$1,000    $1,200    $1,500

ROLEX, 15J., ca. 1935
s. steel ...................................$650    $750    $850

ROLEX,18J., hooded lugs
14k ...........................................$1,000    $1,200    $1,400

ROLEX, 26 jewels, "Submariner,"  rf# 5512, 200M
s. steel ......................................$800    $900    $1,100

ROLEX, 18J., stepped case, 2 tone, ca. 1940s
G & steel.............................$1,200    $1,500    $1,800

ROLEX, 15J., ca. 1937
s. steel .......................................$500      $600      $700

ROLEX, 15J., engraved case, c.1930
s. steel ......................................$500      $600      $700

ROLEX, 15J., GJS, c.1935
9K............................................$700      $800      $900

ROLEX, 18J., rf#4029, c.1945
18k .........................................$1,200      $1,400      $1,800

ROLEX, 17J., rf#619, ROSE gold,c.1948
18k .........................................$1,100      $1,200      $1,500

ROLEX, 18J., rf#2537,adj.6 pos. 2 tone,ca. 1940s
gold & steel .......................$2,000      $2,500      $3,000

ROLEX,15J.,  stepped case, c.1938
18k ....................................$1,800      $2,000      $2,200

ROLEX, 17J.,  center lug "Standard", c.1940
14k & s.s.............................$1,000      $1,200      $1,400

ROLEX, 17J.,  "Standard", c.1940
gold filled .............................$600      $700      $900

ROLEX, 15J.,  beveled case, c.1927
s. steel ....................................$400      $450      $500

Some grades are not included. Their values can be determined by comparing with similar age, size, metal content, style, grades, or models such as time only, chronograph, repeater etc. listed.

ROLEX, 17J., hidden lugs,
14k ........................................$1,500    $1,700    $2,000

ROLEX, 17J., "31 Victories",
18k ........................................$1,200    $1,400    $1,600

ROLEX, 18J., fluted bezel, rf#3737
18k ........................................$1,200    $1,500    $1,800

ROLEX, 18J., 3 diamond dial , ca. 1940s
18kC&B.............................$1,500    $1,800    $2,000

ROLEX, 18J., ca. 1940s
s. steel ...................................$500    $650    $800

ROLEX, 18J., round movement, ca. 1947
18k ........................................$1,000    $1,200    $1,500

ROLEX, 17 jewels, "Precision"
18k ........................................$1,200    $1,500    $1,800

ROLEX, 17 jewels, curvex
18k C&B.............................$3,000    $4,000    $5,000

ROLEX, 17 jewels, curved, c. 1940s
gold filled .............................$500    $600    $800

ROLEX, 17 jewels, "Ultra Prima," gold train
18k ........................................$1,800    $2,000    $2,400

ROLEX, 17 jewels, hooded lugs, 2 tone
rose & white gold ...............$3,000    $4,000    $5,000

ROLEX, 17 jewels, "Precision," c. 1940s
18k .......................................$1,200    $1,500    $1,800
14k .......................................$1,000    $1,200    $1,400

ROLEX, 17 jewels, "Standard," c. 1939
14k .......................................$2,000    $2,500    $3,000

ROLEX, 17 J. , "Precision," tank style, faceted bezel
18k .......................................$1,200    $1,500    $1,800

ROLEX, 17 jewels, "Benvenuto Cellini," thin model
18k .......................................$1,000    $1,100    $1,200

ROLEX, 17 jewels, extra flat, c. 1950s
18k .......................................$1,200    $1,500    $1,800

ROLEX, 21 jewels, "Cellini"
18k .......................................$900    $1,000    $1,200

ROLEX, 21 jewels, perpetual, oyster, c. 1945
18k .......................................$2,500    $3,000    $3,500

ROLEX, 21 jewels, "Cellini"
18k .......................................$1,000    $1,100    $1,300

ROLEX, 21 jewels, "Cellini"
18k C&B..............................$1,500     $1,800     $2,200

ROLEX, 21 jewels, "Cellini," diamond bezel
18k C&B..............................$2,500     $2,800     $3,200

ROLEX, 17J., "Cellini",  RF#4017, c.1988
18k .......................................$1,500     $1,700     $2,000

ROLEX, 21 jewels, "Benvenuto Cellini," diamonds on bezel
& band
18k .......................................$6,000     $7,000     $8,000

ROLEX, "Tudor," (Prince)
s. steel .................................$185     $250     $300

ROLEX,17J., "Tudor", auto-wind, RF#7909, c.1955
s. steel .....................................$125     $150     $195

ROLEX,  25J., "Tudor", rf# 7016,  submariner, by ETA
s. steel .....................................$275     $325     $400

ROLEX,  25J., "Tudor", submariner, date, by ETA,
rf# 76100, Ca.1985
s. steel .....................................$325     $400     $500

ROLEX, 25J., "Tudor", rf#7809, auto-wind, c.1978
s. steel .....................................$100     $125     $150

ROLEX, 17J., "Tudor", auto-wind, c.1955
18k ..........................................$600      $700      $800

ROLEX, "Tudor," chronog., date, rf#9420,
s. steel model sold for $1,200 retail Ca. 1992
s. steel ....................................$700      $800      $900

ROLEX, 17J., "Tudor", SOLAR, rf4463, c.1955
s. steel ....................................$200      $250      $300

ROLEX, quartz, "Tudor," date, 2 tone
18k & s. steel ..........................$250      $300      $400

ROLEX, 17J., "Tudor", rf#2765, TURTLE, Zell Bros
Gold filled...............................$250      $300      $350

ROLEX, quartz, "Tudor," date, Ca. 1992
s. steel & gold plate...............$300      $350      $400

ROLEX, "Tudor," chronog., date, 165 ft., **auto-wind**
s. steel ....................................$800      $900      $1,100

ROLEX, 15J., ladies, c.1930s
9k .............................................$250      $300      $375

ROLEX, 18J., lady's, Ca. 1948
18k ...........................................$350      $425      $495
14k ...........................................$225      $295      $350

ROLEX, 17J., ladies, "Oyster",
14k .......................................$1,000    $1,200    $1,400

ROLEX, 29J., ladies, "Oyster", RF#67003
s. steel &14k,C&B.............$1,000    $1,100    $1,200

ROLEX, 17J., ladies, "Oyster", RF#4486, c.1957
14k & s.s.case .........................$400    $500    $600

ROLEX, 17J., ladies, "Oyster", c.1948
18k .......................................$1,800    $2,000    $2,250

ROLEX, 17J., ladies,"Centergraph"
14k .......................................$1,000    $1,100    $1,200

ROLEX, 17J., ladies, "Oyster", RF#3492
s. steel.....................................$300    $350    $400

ROLEX, 17J., ladies, RF#4593, c.1954
s. steel.....................................$250    $300    $350

ROLEX, 15J., 54 diamonds, 9k band 18k(w) case, c.1930
9k & 18k .............................$1,200    $1,400    $1,600

ROLEX, 17J., ladies, c.1945
gold filled................................$125    $150    $200

ROLEX, 15J., lady's, curved, ca.1925
9k...........................................$200    $250    $300

ROLEX, 15J., lady's, center lugs, ca.1925
9k...........................................$300    $400    $500

ROLEX, 18J., lady's, ca. 1930s
18k .........................................$400     $500     $600

ROLEX, 15J., lady's, Ca.1925
15k band................................$400     $500     $600

ROLEX, 18J., wire lugs, diamond bezel, ca. 1940s
18k(W)...................................$500     $600     $700

ROLEX, Oyster Perpetual Datejust, diamond dial &bezel
18k C&B ............................$6,000     $6,500     $7,000

ROLEX, 18J., lady's,
14k .........................................$300     $350     $400

ROLEX, Oyster Perpetual Datejust
18k C&B ............................$4,500     $5,000     $5,500

ROLEX, 18J., lady's,
14k(W) C&B .........................$400     $500     $600

ROLEX, Oyster Perpetual Datejust
18k & s. steel ......................$1,500     $1,700     $2,000

ROLEX, 18J., lady's, bubble back
18k ......................................$1,600     $1,800     $2,200

ROLEX, Oyster Perpetual
18k & s. steel ......................$1,200     $1,400     $1,600

## ROLEX ESTIMATED PRODUCTION DATES

| DATE–SERIAL# | DATE– SERIAL# | DATE– SERIAL# | DATE– SERIAL# |
|---|---|---|---|
| 1925– 25,000 | 1943 – 270,000 | 1961– 1,500,000 | 1979– 5,650,000 |
| 1926– 27,500 | 1944 – 316,000 | 1962– 1,600,000 | 1980– 6,000,000 |
| 1927– 30,000 | 1945 – 362,000 | 1963– 1,680,000 | 1981– 6,500,000 |
| 1928– 33,000 | 1946 – 408,000 | 1964– 1,750,000 | 1982– 7,000,000 |
| 1929– 35,500 | 1947 – 454,000 | 1965– 1,830,000 | 1983– 7,500,000 |
| 1930– 38,000 | 1948 – 500,000 | 1966– 1,910,000 | 1984– 8,000,000 |
| 1931– 40,000 | 1949 – 571,000 | 1967– 2,000,000 | 1985– 8,500,000 |
| 1932– 43,000 | 1950 – 642,000 | 1968– 2,250,000 | 1986– 9,000,000 |
| 1933– 50,000 | 1951 – 714,000 | 1969– 2,500,000 | 1987– 9,750,000 |
| 1934– 62,000 | 1952 – 785,000 | 1970– 2,750,000 | 1987 1/2–9,999,999 |
| 1935– 75,000 | 1953 – 857,000 | 1971– 3,000,000 | 1987 1/2–R000,001 |
| 1936– 87,000 | 1954 – 928,000 | 1972– 3,300,000 | 1988– R999,999 |
| 1937–100,000 | 1955–1,000,000 | 1973– 3,650,000 | 1989– L000,001 |
| 1938–125,000 | 1956–1,080,000 | 1974– 4,000,000 | 1990– L999,999 |
| 1939–150,000 | 1957–1,160,000 | 1975– 4,300,000 | 1990 1/2–E000,001 |
| 1940–175,000 | 1958–1,250,000 | 1976– 4,650,000 | 1991 1/4–E999,999 |
| 1941–200,000 | 1959–1,320,000 | 1977– 5,000,000 | 1991 1/2–X000,001 |
| 1942–225,000 | 1960–1,440,000 | 1978– 5,300,000 | 1991 3/4–N000,001 |
|  |  |  | 1992 1/4–C000,001 |

The above list is provided for determining the APPROXIMATE age of your watch. Match serial number with date. Watches were not necessarily sold in the exact order of manufactured date. The above list was furnished by **TOM ENGLE** and **KEN SPECHT**

6694

Reference number, four figures engraved between the lugs

### Check the reference number of the case

On recent OYSTER models the number is engraved on the outside of the case between the lugs. Reference number of earlier models will be found engraved on the inside of the back of the case.

1705215

Serial number, six or seven figures engraved between the lugs

Reference number for NON-OYSTER models will be found engraved on the inside of the back of the case.

NON-OYSTER CASE

INSIDE OF BACK
Reference number
in four figures ·

OUTSIDE OF BACK
Serial number
in six or seven figures

# ROLEX
## MOVEMENT IDENTIFICATION

Ref. 90          Ref. 100          Ref. 150          Ref. 160          Ref. 161

(All without seconds)

**Ref. 170**          **Ref. 180**          **Ref. 200**          **Ref. 210**
without seconds     without seconds     without seconds     sweep seconds

**Ref. 250**               **Ref. 270**               **Ref. 300**
without seconds          without seconds          ordinary seconds

**Ref. 310**               **Ref. 350**               **Ref. 360**
sweep second            jump hour               ordinary second

**Ref. 400**          **Ref. 420**          **Ref. 420**          **Ref. 500**
ordinary seconds     ordinary seconds     rotor               ordinary seconds
**Ca. 1941**         **Ca. 1941**         **Ca. 1941**         **Ca. 1936**

Ref. 510
sweep second
Ca. 1936

Ref. 520
sweep second
Ca. 1936

Ref. 520
rotor
Ca. 1936

Ref. 530
self wind, sweep sec.
Ca. 1936

Ref. 600  Ca. 1931
ordinary seconds

Ref. 620  Ca. 1931
ordinary seconds

Ref. 620  Ca. 1931
rotor

Ref. 630  Ca. 1931
self wind, sweep sec.

Ref. 700  Ca. 1940
ordinary seconds

Ref. 710  Ca. 1940
sweep seconds

Ref. 720  Ca. 1940
ordinary seconds

Ref. 720  Ca. 1940
rotor

Ref. 730  Ca. 1945
self wind, sweep sec.

Ref. 740 **Ca. 1945**
self wind, calendar, sweep sec.

Ref. 800
ordinary seconds

**Ref. 850**
ordinary seconds

**Ref. 72**
chronograph, 3 registers

**Ref. 23**
chronograph, 2 registers

**Above:** Oyster style bracelet. **Below:** Presidential style band with hidden clasp.
**Right:** Jubilee style bracelet.

Current *double quick set* Presidential and Jubilee bracelets use **7 screws** for adjustment links.
The older models *Single quick set* Presidential and Jubilee bracelets use **6 screws** for adjustment links.

ROLLS, 15J., early auto wind, by Leon Hatot, movement inside case moves back & forth to wind, c. 1920s
s. steel ..................................$600    $700    $900

ROLLS, 15 jewels, early auto wind, c. 1920s
s. steel ..................................$700    $800    $1,000

ROLLS, 15 jewels, "ATO," flip top
s. steel ..................................$600    $700    $900

ROLLS, 15 jewels, ladies, "ATO," flip top, by Blancpain
18k ..........................................$800    $900    $1,000

ROTARY, 15J., aux. sec., ca.1934
9k ..............................................$125    $150    $175

ROXY, 8 day, engraved case, ca. 1930s
s. steel ....................................$200    $250    $300

RULON, ca. 1940s
gold filled ................................$60    $70    $80

RULON, 17J., 3 diamonds on dial
gold plate ................................$100    $125    $150

SCHILD, 17J., "Aqua lung", tach.chronog., ca.1972
s. steel ..................................$80    $100    $120

SCHULTZ, 17J., diamond dial, c.1930
platinum................................$1,800    $2,000    $2,200

J. SCHULTZ, 17J., enamel hunter style, ca. 1949
18k ........................................$1,500    $1,800    $2,000

SEELAND, 17J., aux. sec., Ca. 1955
14k ..........................................$90    $120    $165

SEELAND, 7J., ca. 1950s
gold filled...................................$50    $60    $70

SEELAND, 17J., "Quadramatic" auto-wind, c.1947
s. steel ......................................$25    $30    $40

SEELAND, 17J., manual wind, c.1947
chrome ......................................$25    $30    $40

SEIKO, 6J., wire lugs, on dial "LAUREL", ca.1925
s. steel ......................................$40    $50    $60

SEIKO, quartz, rope style bezel
14k ..........................................$175    $200    $225

SEMCA, 17J.,  day-date-month, moon phase, c. 1950s
18k ......................................$1,000    $1,300    $1,400

SEMCA, 17J., day-date-month, moon phase, c. 1950s
14k ..........................................$700    $800    $1,200

SETH THOMAS, day date, moon phases, ca. 1949
s. steel ......................................$250    $325    $375

🕐 Some grades are not included. Their values can be
determined by comparing with similar age, size, metal
content, style, grades, or models such as time only,
chronograph, repeater etc. listed.

SHEFFIELD,17J., chronog., by Venus, cal.189
s. steel ......................................$125    $150    $175

SIMGA,17J., textured dial,c.1940
18k ...........................................$200    $250    $300

SMITH, 17J., military , Ca.1969
s. steel ......................................$125    $150    $175

SPERINA, 7 jewels, day & date on lugs
s. steel .....................................$100    $125    $165

SOUTH BEND,17J., multi-color dial, made U.S.A.
base metal .............................$250    $300    $400

STANDARD,17J., 24 hr. dial, world time, c.1965
s. steel ....................................$100    $125    $165

SUIZO, 17J., one button chronog. ca. 1930s
gold filled ..............................$200    $250    $300

**SWATCH** ( see listings at the end of wrist watch section )

TAVANNES, 15J., enamel dial, flip top, c.1915
silver ......................................$300    $350    $400

TAVANNES, 17J., chronog., c.1940
s. steel ....................................$200     $250     $300

TAVANNES, 17J., extended lugs, c.1955
gold filled...............................$50     $60     $75

TAVANNES, 17J., aux. sec., c.1935
14k ..........................................$125     $150     $175

TAVANNES, 17J., GJS, cal.365k, c.1938
14k ..........................................$175     $200     $250

TAVANNES, 17 jewels, hour glass dial, **curved**
14k ..........................................$200     $250     $300

TAVANNES, 15 jewels, "334," c. 1939
14k (w) ...................................$200     $250     $300

TAVANNES, 17 jewels, aux. sec. ca. 1940s
s. steel ......................................$80     $100     $125

TAVANNES, 17 jewels, aux. sec.
14k ..........................................$225     $250     $275

TECHNOS, 17J., "Sky Diver", auto-wind, 500m., c.1970
s. steel ......................................$40     $50     $65

Some grades are not included. Their values can be determined by comparing with **similar** age, size, metal content, style, grades, or models such as **time only**, chronograph, repeater etc. listed.

TELDA, 17J., chronog.,3 reg, date,  moon ph., c.1980s
s. steel ..................................... $500      $600      $700

TELDA, 17J., center sec., c.1948
gold filled................................. $40      $50      $65

TEVO, 17J., hidden lugs
14k .......................................... $100      $135      $175

NOTE: Examples of Tiffany made up
watches are listed but were not sold by Tiffany & Co.. These off-brand watches will be
listed but not priced as true Tiffany & Co.
watches. EXAMPLES: *Kingston, Emerson,
Banner*, ETC. were not sold by Tiffany.

TIFFANY & CO.,17J., wire lugs, c.1920
silver ..................................... $400      $500      $600

TIFFANY & CO., 18J., by P.P.& CO., CA. 1920s
18K ..................................... $4,000      $5,000      $6,000

TIFFANY & CO., 17J., curved, mvt. by P.P. & Co., c. 1910
18k ......................................$6,000      $6,500      $7,000

TIFFANY & CO.,17J., by Banner"?", c.1926
18k .......................................... $300      $350      $400

TIFFANY & CO.,17J., by Wheeler "?", c.1930
14k .......................................... $150      $175      $200

TIFFANY & CO., 26 jewels, min. repeater, slide repeat,
automaton, 40mm
18k ..................................... $8,000      $9,000      $10,000

TIFFANY & CO., 15J., wire lugs, ca. 1928
silver ........................................$300      $350      $400

TIFFANY & CO.,17J., by P.P. & Co., wire lugs, c.1915
18k ........................................$3,500      $4,000      $4,500

TIFFANY & CO.,17J., by I.W.C., wire lugs, c.1918
14k ........................................$600      $700      $800

TIFFANY & CO., 15J., enamel dial, ca. 1930s
silver ........................................$500      $550      $600

TIFFANY & CO., 17J., Concord W. C0.
14k ........................................$600      $700      $800

TIFFANY & CO., 18J., by P.P.& Co., Ca. 1930s
platinum..............................$5,000      $6,000      $7,000

TIFFANY & CO., 15 jewels, Swiss, Ca. 1926
18k ........................................$500      $600      $700

TIFFANY & CO.,17J., by Longines, c.1928
14k ........................................$400      $500      $600

TIFFANY & CO.,17J., aux. sec., Swiss, c.1926
18k(w)....................................$700      $850      $1,000

TIFFANY & CO.,17J., by Fidea "?", c.1930
14k ........................................$200      $225      $250

TIFFANY & CO.,17J., GJS, by Movado, c.1940
14k ..........................................$600      $700      $800

TIFFANY & CO.,17J., by Kingston "?", hidden lugs, c.1943
14k ..........................................$150      $200      $250

TIFFANY & CO.,17J., by Charlin W. Co. "?", GJS, c.1940
14k ..........................................$150      $175      $200

TIFFANY & CO.,17J., by Emerson "?", c.1940
14k ..........................................$100      $125      $150

TIFFANY & CO.,17J., by Hampden "?", c.1949
14k ..........................................$100      $135      $175

TIFFANY & CO.,17J., by I.W.C., c.1942
14k ..........................................$600      $650      $750

TIFFANY & CO.,17J., by I.W.C., hidden lugs, c.1942
14k ..........................................$600      $700      $800

TIFFANY & CO., 17J., top hat, by I. W. CO.
14K ..........................................$1,000    $1,200    $1,400

TIFFANY & CO.,15J., one button chronog., by Goering,
69 mvt., c.1925
silver ......................................$1,000    $1,200    $1,400

TIFFANY & CO.,17J., Valjoux cal.72c., c.1948
s. steel ....................................$550      $650      $750
14k ..........................................$1,200    $1,300    $1,500
18k ..........................................$1,400    $1,600    $1,750

🕐 Some grades are not included. Their values can be
determined by comparing with **similar** age, size, metal
content, style, grades, or models such as **time only**,
chronograph, repeater etc. listed.

TIFFANY & CO.,17J., by Movado, c.1947
14k .......................................$2,000   $2,200   $2,500

TIFFANY & CO.,17J., by Bovet"?", c.1940
18k .......................................$600   $700   $800

TIFFANY & CO.,17J., by Tourneau , Valjoux 72c, c.1950
s. steel .....................................$500   $600   $650

TIFFANY & CO., 31J., chronog., triple date, moon ph. screw-
back, note window for date at 4 & 5
18k .......................................$2,500   $2,700   $3,000

TIFFANY & CO., 17J., chronog., day-date-month
14k .................................... $1,200   $1,400   $1,600

TIFFANY & CO., 21J., mvt. by P.P. & Co., c. 1950
18k ....................................$3,000   $3,500   $4,000

TIFFANY & CO., 17J., curved , ca.1920s
platinum...............................$1,000   $1,200   $1,500

TIFFANY & CO.,15J., engraved bezel, c.1919
18k .......................................$1,200   $1,500   $1,700

🕐 Some grades are not included. Their values can be
determined by comparing with similar age, size, metal
content, style, grades, or models such as time only,
chronograph, repeater etc. listed.

# TIFFANY & CO. (continued)

999

TIFFANY & CO., 15J., ca. 1920s
14k .........................................$500    $600    $700

TIFFANY & CO.,17J., by Hampden "?", c.1945
gold filled................................$75    $100    $125
14k .........................................$175    $200    $250

TIFFANY & CO.,17J., by Ollendorf "?", c.1945
14k .........................................$200    $250    $300

TIFFANY & CO.,17J., by Crawford "?", c.1947
14k .........................................$150    $175    $200

TIFFANY & CO.,17J., by Tissot, c.1948
14k .........................................$300    $350    $400

TIFFANY & CO.,17J., by Zodiac "?", c.1942
14k .........................................$150    $175    $200

TIFFANY & CO.,17J., by Glycine "?",  c.1945
gold filled................................$75    $100    $125
14k .........................................$200    $235    $275

TIFFANY & CO.,17J., extended bezel, c.1942
14k .........................................$400    $500    $600

TIFFANY & CO.,17J., by Wyler "?", c.1950
gold filled..............................$100    $125    $150

TIFFANY & CO., 17J., fancy lugs & bezel,ca.1950s
14k .........................................$300    $400    $500

TIFFANY & CO., 17J., applied numbers, ca. 1950s
14k ...........................................$400      $500      $600

TIFFANY & CO., 17J., flared & stepped, ca.1950s
14k ...........................................$300      $400      $500

TIFFANY & CO., 17 jewels, Swiss, c. 1935
18k ...........................................$700      $800      $900

TIFFANY & CO., 17 jewels, fancy bezel, c. 1942
14k ...........................................$400      $450      $500

TIFFANY & CO., 17 jewels, sculptured lugs, c. 1948
14k ...........................................$800      $900      $1,000

TIFFANY & CO.,17J., 3 diamond dial, by Lathin "?",
14k(w).....................................$200      $225      $250

TIFFANY & CO.,15J., rhinestones "?", c.1948
base metal .................................$40      $50      $75

TIFFANY & CO., 17J., "Movado", triple date, center sec.
s. steel ....................................$350      $450      $500

TIFFANY & CO.,17J., by Movado, triple date, c.1948
gold filled ...............................$400      $450      $500
14k & s.s..................................$500      $600      $700

TIFFANY & CO.,17J.,by Tissot,triple date moon ph.,
14k ...............................$1,000    $1,100    $1,200

TIFFANY & CO.,17J., by Helvetia , c.1948
gold filled ...............................$100    $125    $150
14k .........................................$250    $275    $300

TIFFANY & CO., 17J., triple date, moon ph.
s. steel ......................................$400    $450    $500

TIFFANY & CO.,17J., "?", c.1940
gold filled ................................$75    $100    $125

TIFFANY & CO.,17J., by Ardath "?", auto-wind, c.1950
14k ...........................................$100    $125    $150

TIFFANY & CO.,17J., by Mepa "?", GJS, c.1949
gold filled ...............................$50    $65    $80
14k .........................................$100    $135    $175

TIFFANY & CO.,17J., by Nicolet "?", c.1955
gold filled..................................$50    $60    $75

TIFFANY & CO.,17J., by Zenith, c.1939
14k ...........................................$200    $250    $300

TIFFANY & CO.,17J.,  c.1948
18k .............................................$500          $600          $700

TIFFANY & CO.,17J., carved lugs, c.1950
18k .........................................$300          $350          $400

TIFFANY & CO.,17J., ladies, by Longines, c.1920
18k .........................................$250          $300          $350

TIFFANY & CO.,17J., by I.W.C., c.1948
18k .........................................$300          $400          $500

TIFFANY & CO.,17J., I.W.C., c.1955
18k .........................................$200          $250          $300

TIFFANY & CO., 15J., 2 tone , ladies, ca. 1939
18k C&B..................................$400          $450          $500

TIFFANY & CO., 15J., early ladies, wire lugs ca.1925
14k .........................................$400          $450          $500

TIFFANY & CO., 17J., ladies, aux. sec.,  Ca.1940
gold filled ................................ $40          $45          $55

TIMECRAFT, 17 jewels, chronog., Ca. 1950
s. steel ....................................$125          $150          $175

TIMEX,chronog., slide to start, stop & return to zero
base metal ................................$50          $60          $70

TISSOT, 17 jewels, 1898 USA 20 dollar gold piece
24k .........................................$1,000    $1,500    $2,000

TISSOT,17J., military, chronog., Valjoux cal.225, c.1955
s. steel ....................................$325    $375    $425

TISSOT, 21 jewels, world time, 24 hr. dial, 24 cities
s. steel ....................................$700    $800    $900
18k .........................................$2,000    $2,500    $3,000

TISSOT,17J., Valjoux cal.726, c.1965
18k .........................................$800    $900    $1,100
14k .........................................$700    $800    $900

TISSOT, 21J, world time, 24 hr. dial, 24 cities, mid-size
18k .........................................$2,500    $3,000    $3,500

TISSOT,17J., auto-wind,"Navigator", date, c.1972
s. steel ....................................$150    $175    $225

TISSOT, 17J., "Stadium", tachymeter, c.1960
gold plate .................................$150    $175    $200

TISSOT, 17 jewels, chronog., 3 reg., c. 1956
s. steel ....................................$325    $375    $450

TISSOT, 17 jewels, chronog., 3 reg.
gold filled..............................$325    $450    $500
s. steel .................................$275    $325    $400

TISSOT, 17 jewels, chronog., 3 reg.
18k ......................................$700    $800    $900
s. steel .................................$250    $300    $350

TISSOT, 17 jewels, chronog., 3 reg., c. 1940s
14k ....................................$1,200    $1,400    $1,600

TISSOT, 17 jewels, chronog., triple date, moon phase
s. steel ..................................$900    $1,000    $1,250
14k .....................................$2,300    $2,500    $2,900
18k .....................................$2,750    $3,000    $3,300

TISSOT, 17J., day-date-month, moon phase, ctr. sec.
18k ......................................$1,200    $1,500    $1,800

TISSOT, 17J., "UHF", date, auto-wind, c.1960
14k ..........................................$200    $250    $300

TISSOT, 17J., auto-wind, date, c.1958
s. steel ....................................... $60    $70    $80

TISSOT, 17J., hidden lugs, c.1938
14k ......................................$300    $350    $425

TISSOT, 17J., 4 diamonds on dial, GJS, hooded lugs
gold filled...............................$125    $150    $200

TISSOT,17J., aux. sec., c.1951
18k ...................................$300  $350  $400

TISSOT, 15 jewels, wire lugs, aux. sec., Ca. 1915
silver ...................................$250  $300  $350

TISSOT,17J., hidden lugs, c.1950
14k ...................................$400  $450  $500

TITUS, 17 jewels, chronog., 2 reg.
18k ...................................$300  $350  $400
14k ...................................$200  $250  $300
s. steel ...................................$100  $150  $200

TISSOT,17J., aux. sec., c.1942
s. steel ...................................$90  $120  $150
18k ...................................$200  $250  $300

TISSOT, 17 jewels, large lugs,
14k ...................................$250  $300  $350

TORNEX-RAYVILLE,17J., military, "SEAL", auto-wind, water-proof, 150M or 490 ft., Ca. 1966
s. steel ...................................$200  $250  $300

TISSOT, 17J., open shutters to reveal dial
base metal ...................................$200  $250  $300

TOUCHON,17J., tonneau case, c.1928
18k(w)...................................$40

TOUCHON, 17J., jump hr., wandering min., c. 1930s
18k ........................................$4,000    $5,000    $6,000

TOURNEAU,17J, triple date, 3 reg., moon ph., c. 1952
s. steel .......................................$700    $800    $900

TOURNEAU,17J.,chronog. by Valjoux cal.886, c.1965
18k ........................................$2,500    $2,700    $3,000

TOURNEAU,17J., day date , c.1945
s. steel .......................................$250    $300    $350

TOURNEAU,17J., beveled lugs, c.1945
14k ..........................................$150    $200    $250

TOURIST, 17J., by MEPA, c.1958
s. steel ........................................ $50    $60    $70

TREBEX, 15 jewels,cut corner dial, c. 1940
gold filled ...................................$40    $50    $60

TREBEX, 15 jewels, c. 1940
gold filled ...................................$30    $40    $50

TREBEX, 15 jewels, c. 1940s
gold filled ...................................$30    $40    $50

TURLER, 15-17J., duo-dial, Ca.1930s
18k .......................................$2,000    $2,500    $3,000

UNITAS, 17 jewels, triple date, moon phase, c. 1948
s. steel ....................................$250    $300    $375

TURLER, 17 jewels, chronog., triple date, 3 reg.
18k ..........................................$900    $1,100    $1,300

URANIA, 15 jewels, military style grill, c. 1915
silver ......................................$150    $200    $250

UHRENFABRIK GLASHUTTE, 17J., chronog., c. 1940s
s. steel ....................................$450    $500    $600

UNIVER, 17J., triple date , moon ph., chronog.
14k .......................................$1,200    $1,400    $1,700

ULTIMOR, 17J., chronog., cal.51, c.1945
18k ..........................................$275    $325    $400

UNIVERSAL,17J.,"medico compax", c.1949
18k ..........................................$800    $900    $1,000

UNIVERSAL,17J., "uni compax", c.1942
s. steel .................................$300    $350    $400

UNIVERSAL,17J., tri-compax, day date moon ph.,c.1955
s. steel .................................$1,200    $1,300    $1,400
14k .................................$1,700    $2,000    $2,300

UNIVERSAL, 17J., chronog., triple date, moon phase
18k .................................$1,600    $1,800    $2,000
14k .................................$1,400    $1,600    $1,800

UNIVERSAL, 17J., chronog., aero compax, diff. meridian,
square pushers
14k .................................$1,800    $2,000    $2,400

UNIVERSAL, 17J. chronog., tri-compax, day date
s. steel .................................$1,000    $1,100    $1,200

UNIVERSAL, 17 jewels, chronog., M. #281, c. 1950s
18k .................................$2,200    $2,500    $2,800

UNIVERSAL, 17J., chronog., tri-compax, moon phase
s. steel .................................$1,100    $1,200    $1,300

UNIVERSAL, 17J., chronog., aero compax, diff. meridian,
round pushers
18k .................................$2,000    $2,200    $2,600

UNIVERSAL, 17J., chronog., compax, massive case
18k ........................................$2,500    $2,700    $3,000

UNIVERSAL, 17 jewels, c. 1952
14k ..........................................$275    $325    $375

UNIVERSAL, 17J., chronog., dato-compax, c. 1950s
14k ........................................$1,500    $1,800    $2,000
s. steel ......................................$500    $600    $700

UNIVERSAL, 17 jewels, day-date-month
14k ..........................................$600    $700    $800

UNIVERSAL,17J., compax, RF#885107, Valj.cal.72,c.1965
s. steel ......................................$600    $700    $800

UNIVERSAL,17J., "Polerouter Sub", date, auto-w., c.1960
14k ..........................................$250    $400    $550
s. steel ......................................$100    $135    $175

UNIVERSAL, 17J. chronog., 10 ligne size,uni-compax
s. steel ................................$ 1,000    $1,200    $1,400

UNIVERSAL,17J.,"Polerouter Sub",rotating bezel, c.1980s
s. steel ......................................$150    $200    $250

UNIVERSAL, 17 jewels, "Polerouter", auto wind, day date
18k .......................................$500     $600     $700

UNIVERSAL, 23J., auto-wind, date, c.1965
14k .........................................$250     $300        $350

UNIVERSAL, 28J., center sec., date, c.1958
18k ..........................................$400     $450     $500

UNIVERSAL,17J., cal. 138c, date, c.1952
18k ...........................................$300     $350     $400

UNIVERSAL,17J., cal.52, date, c.1965
18k ...........................................$200     $250     $300

UNIVERSAL, 17 jewels, day-date-month, moon phase
18k .......................................$1,200     $1,350     $1,500

UNIVERSAL,17J., Unisonic chronometer, date, c.1968
s. steel ....................................$125     $150     $175

UNIVERSAL,17J., m#264, large lugs, c.1957
gold filled ..............................$100     $125     $150

UNIVERSAL,17J., cal.267g, date, center sec. c.1948
18k .............................................$400      $450      $500

UNIVERSAL,17J., center sec., cal.263, c.1950
18k .............................................$300      $350      $400

UNIVERSAL, 16J., cal#230,ca. 1940s
s. steel ......................................$150      $200      $250

UNIVERSAL, 17J., aux. sec. tank style,ca. 1948
14k .............................................$400      $450      $500

UNIVERSAL,17J., center sec., cal.138, c.1950
s. steel ......................................$100      $125      $175

UNIVERSAL, 17J., fancy lugs
14k .............................................$350      $400      $450

UNIVERSAL,17J., center sec., cal.236, c.1955
18k .............................................$300      $350      $400

UNIVERSAL, 17 jewels, "Cabriolet," reverso, c. 1930s
s. steel ......................................$3,000     $3,500    $4,000

UNIVERSAL,17J., aux. sec., Ca.1955
s. steel ......................................$125      $150      $175

UNIVERSAL, 17 jewels, auto wind, c. 1955
14k .............................. $300    $350    $400
gold filled............................... $100    $120    $140

UNIVERSAL, quartz, day-date, center sec., c. 1960s
18k ............................................ $400    $500    $600

UNIVERSAL, quartz, , c.1981
18k ............................................ $300    $350    $400

UNIVERSAL, 17 jewels, auto wind
gold filled................................... $80    $90    $100

🕐 Some grades are not included. Their values can be determined by comparing with **similar** age, size, metal content, style, models and grades listed.

VACHERON, 36J., skeletonized, triple date, moon phase, leap year, gold rotor
18k ..................... $16,000    $17,000    $18,000

VACHERON, 36J., diamond bezel, triple date, moon ph., leap year, gold rotor
18k C&B............................ $12,000    $13,000    $14,000

VACHERON, 17J., triple date, moon phase, c. 1947
18k ..................................... $12,000    $14,000    $16,000

VACHERON, 17J., triple date, moon phase, c. 1945
18k ........................................ $8,000    $9,000    $10,000

VACHERON, 17J., triple date, moon phase, c. 1950s
18k ......................................$6,000    $7,000    $8,000

VACHERON, 29 jewels, waterproof, auto-w, c. 1960s
18k ......................................$2,200    $2,500    $2,750

VACHERON,17J., triple date, fancy lugs, moon ph.,
c. 1940s
18k ......................................$7,000    $8,000    $9,000

VACHERON, 29 jewels, auto wind, c. 1960s
18k ......................................$1,800    $2,000    $2,200

VACHERON, 17J., triple date, fancy lugs, c. 1940s
18k ......................................$3,000    $3,800    $4,000

VACHERON, 36 jewels, gold rotor, date
18k ......................................$1,600    $1,800    $2,000

VACHERON, 17 jewels, day-date-month, c. 1940s
18k ......................................$3,000    $3,500    $4,000

VACHERON, 29 jewels, center sec., auto wind, date
18k ......................................$2,200    $2,500    $2,750

VACHERON, 29 jewels, gold rotor, date
18k .......................................$1,800    $2,200    $2,600

VACHERON, 18J., chronog. 2 reg., ca.1942
s. steel ...................................$5,000    $6,000    $7,000

VACHERON, 33J., auto-wind 21k rotor, cal.1124 , c.1980s
18k & s.s. ............................$1,200    $1,400    $1,600

VACHERON, 17 jewels, chronog., 2 reg. Ca. 1934
18k & 14k band................$18,000    $20,000    $23,000

VACHERON,17J., enamel dial,1 button chronog.,c. 1910s
18k .......................................$25,000    $30,000    $35,000

VACHERON, 19 jewels, chronog., 2 reg., c. 1950s
18k C&B..............................$9,000    $10,000    $11,000

VACHERON, 15J., early chronog.,2 reg.,one button,
ca. 1921, large in size
18k .......................................$18,000    $20,000    $22,000

VACHERON, 17 jewels, chronog., 2 reg., c. 1945
18k .......................................$8,000    $9,000    $10,000

VACHERON, 29J., min. repeater, slide repeat, c. 1950
18k .................................$60,000    $70,000    $80,000

VACHERON, 29J., min. slide repeater, diamond dial
platinum...............................$80,000    $90,000    $100,000

VACHERON, 29J., min. slide repeater, ca. 1950s
18k ....................................$60,000    $70,000    $80,000

VACHERON, 18J., diamond set case, skeletonized
18k(W)................................$5,000    $5,500    $6,000

VACHERON, 18J., skeletonized, diamond bezel
18k ......................................$3,500    $4,000    $4,500

VACHERON, 17 jewels, skeletonized
18k......................................$3,000    $3,500    $4,000

VACHERON, 17 jewels, skeletonized, c. 1960s
18k ......................................$3,000    $3,500    $4,000

VACHERON, 17 jewels, mystery dial with diamonds
18k C&B...............................$1,200    $1,400    $1,600

VACHERON, 17 jewels, textured bezel
18k ......................................$1,300    $1,500    $1,800

VACHERON, 18 jewels, center sec., c. 1940s
18k .......................................$1,400     $1,600     $2,000

VACHERON, 18 jewels, center sec.
18k .......................................$1,300     $1,500     $1,800

VACHERON, 18J., fancy graduated bezel, c. 1950s
18k .......................................$4,000     $5,000     $6,000

VACHERON, 18 jewels, center sec.
18k .......................................$1,400     $1,600     $2,000

VACHERON, 18 jewels, auto wind, center sec., Ca. 1945
18k .......................................$1,700     $1,900     $2,200

VACHERON, 18 J., center sec., waterproof, c. 1950s
18k .......................................$1,700     $2,000     $2,200

VACHERON, 18 jewels, center sec., Ca. 1945
18k .......................................$1,200     $1,400     $1,700

VACHERON, 21J., auto wind, gold rotor, center sec.
18k .......................................$2,200     $2,400     $2,800

VACHERON, 18J., center sec., ca.1940s
18k .................................$1,500    $1,700    $2,000

VACHERON,17J., center sec., c.1940
s. steel ...............................$600    $700    $800

VACHERON, 18J., rf#6903, center sec., ca.1958
18k .................................$1,300    $1,500    $1,900

VACHERON,17J., center sec., large lugs, c.1949
18k .................................$2,400    $2,600    $2,900

VACHERON, 18J., center sec., ca.1953
18k .................................$1,600    $1,800    $2,000

VACHERON,17J., center sec., c.1940
s. steel ...............................$600    $700    $800

VACHERON, 18J., textured dial center sec.
18k .................................$1,600    $1,700    $2,000

VACHERON,17J., center sec., c.1940
18k .................................$1,500    $1,700    $2,000

Some grades are not included. Their values can be determined by comparing with **similar** age, size, metal content,
style, models and grades listed.

VACHERON, 18J., center sec.
s. steel ...................................... $500      $600      $700

VACHERON, 18J., fancy large lugs, center sec., ca.1953
18k ...................................... $2,200      $2,500      $2,800

VACHERON, 18J., center sec.
18k ...................................... $1,500      $1,700      $1,900

VACHERON, 18J., rf#4730, fancy lugs, ca. 1950s
18k ...................................... $1,800      $2,000      $2,400

VACHERON, 18J.,textured dial, center sec.,ca.1947
18k ...................................... $2,200      $2,400      $2,600

VACHERON, 18J.,textured dial, fancy lugs
18k ...................................... $1,800      $2,000      $2,400

VACHERON, 18J., rf#4824, ca.1950s
18k(W)................................ $1,400      $1,500      $1,700

VACHERON, 18J., center sec., ca.1944
14k ...................................... $1,500      $1,700      $1,900

VACHERON, 18J., royal chronometer, ca.1950s
18k .......................................$1,500   $1,700   $2,000

VACHERON, 17J., center sec.auto-w., ca.1945
18k .......................................$1,500   $1,700   $2,000

VACHERON, 29J., center sec., auto wind, c. 1950s
18k .......................................$2,200   $2,400   $2,700

VACHERON, 29 jewels, center sec., auto wind, c. 1949
18k .......................................$2,200   $2,500   $3,000

VACHERON, 29 jewels, textured dial, c. 1948
18k .......................................$1,800   $2,000   $2,200

VACHERON, 29 jewels, 2 tone dial, center sec.
18k .......................................$1,500   $1,700   $1,900

VACHERON, 29 jewels, center sec., center lugs,c. 1950s
18k .......................................$1,400   $1,600   $1,800

VACHERON, 29 jewels, center sec.
18k .......................................$1,300   $1,500   $1,800

VACHERON,17J., diamond dial, aux. sec., fancy lugs
platinum...............................$2,500   $2,700   $3,000

VACHERON, 17J., aux. sec., c.1945
18k ......................................$1,400    $1,600    $1,900

VACHERON, 17J., aux. sec., RF#4073, c.1942
s. steel ....................................$700    $800    $900

VACHERON, 17J., aux. sec., tear drop lugs, c.1945
18k ......................................$1,600    $1,800    $2,200

VACHERON, 17J., aux. sec, fluted lugs, c.1950s
18k ......................................$2,000    $2,200    $2,500

🕐 Some grades are not included. Their values can be determined by comparing with **similar** age, size, metal content, style, models and grades listed.

VACHERON, 18J., aux. sec., fancy lugs, ca. 1944
18k ......................................$1,600    $1,800    $2,200

VACHERON, 18J., aux. sec.
18k ......................................$1,600    $1,800    $2,200

VACHERON, 18J., fancy lugs
18k ......................................$1,600    $1,900    $2,300

VACHERON, 18J., cal#p453/3b, aux. sec.
18k ......................................$2,000    $2,200    $2,400

VACHERON, 18J., aux. sec.,
s. steel .....................................$500     $600     $700

VACHERON, 18J., aux. sec.
18k(W)................................$1,500     $1,700     $1,900

VACHERON, 18J., center sec.,fancy lugs, ca.1942
18k ...................................$1,500     $1,700     $1,900

VACHERON, 18J., aux. sec., ca.1951
18k ...................................$1,600     $1,800     $2,000

VACHERON, 18J., **winds at 12**, ca. 1928
18k .........................$3,000     $3,500     $4,000

VACHERON, 15J., champagne dial, long lugs, ca.1935
18k .........................$1,700     $1,800     $2,000

VACHERON, 17 jewels, aux. sec., fancy lugs
18k .........................$1,600     $1,900     $2,300

VACHERON, 17 jewels, aux. sec., Ca. 1950
18k .........................$1,600     $1,800     $2,200

VACHERON, 17 jewels, aux. sec., stepped lugs
18k .........................$1,800     $2,200     $2,500

VACHERON, 17 jewels, 2 tone dial, aux. sec.
18k .....................................$1,500    $1,800    $2,200

VACHERON, 17 jewels, aux. sec., c. 1940s
18k .......................................$1,600    $1,800    $2,200

VACHERON, 17 jewels, aux. sec.
18k .......................................$1,600    $1,800    $2,200

VACHERON, 17 jewels, aux. sec., c. 1940s
18k .......................................$1,500    $1,700    $1,900

VACHERON, 17 jewels, aux. sec.
s. steel ......................................$500    $600    $700

VACHERON, 17 jewels, aux. sec., large lugs, c. 1950s
18k .......................................$2,400    $2,600    $2,800

VACHERON, 17 jewels, aux. sec.
14k C&B..............................$1,000    $1,200    $1,400

VACHERON, 17 jewels, aux. sec.
18k .......................................$1,400    $1,600    $1,800

VACHERON, 17 jewels, aux. sec., c. 1940s
18k ......................................$1,500    $1,700    $1,900

VACHERON, 17 jewels, aux. sec.
18k ......................................$1,500    $1,700    $2,000

VACHERON, 17 jewels
18k C&B..............................$1,800    $2,200    $2,600

VACHERON, 17J., RF# 6498, Ca. 1965
18k ......................................$1,500    $1,700    $2,000

VACHERON, 17 jewels
18k ......................................$1,400    $1,600    $1,800

VACHERON, 18J., no sec. hand,
18k ......................................$1,300    $1,500    $1,700

VACHERON, 17J., RF#6099, cal.1003, c.1960
18k ......................................$1,200    $1,400    $1,600

VACHERON, 17J., RF#6335, wide bezel, c.1962
18k ......................................$1,300    $1,400    $1,600

VACHERON, 16J., barrel shaped silver dial, ca. 1916
18k ......................................$3,000    $3,500    $4,000

🕐 Some grades are not included. Their values can be determined by comparing with **similar** age, size, metal content, style, models and grades listed.

VACHERON, 16J., wire lugs, silver dial, ca.1917
14k ....................................$3,000    $3,500    $4,000

VACHERON, 18J., tonneau shaped, ca. 1930s
18k ....................................$2,500    $3,000    $3,500

VACHERON, 15J., lady's with wire lugs,ca.1920
18k(W)....................................$500    $600    $750

VACHERON, 15 jewels
18k C&B............................$2,000    $2,200    $2,600

VACHERON, 17 jewels
18k ....................................$2,200    $2,400    $2,600

VACHERON, 36 jewels, auto wind
18k C&B............................$1,500    $1,800    $2,200

VACHERON, 21 J., date, auto-w. ca. 1980s
s. steel ....................................$1,000    $1,200    $1,400

VACHERON, 15J., shutters with center slide to view dial, 2 tone case, ca. 1933
18k ....................................$10,000    $12,000    $14,000

VACHERON, 17J, with shutters, crowns at 3 & 9
18k ....................................$12,000    $14,000    $16,000

🕐 Some grades are not included. Their values can be determined by comparing with **similar** age, size, metal content, style, models and grades listed.

VACHERON, 18J., heavy case, ca.1930s
18k(W) ..................................$2,500    $3,000    $3,500

VACHERON, 18J., hidden lugs, ca.1940s
18k ........................................$2,200    $2,400    $2,800

VACHERON, 18J., silver dial, ca.1941
18k .......................................$2,000    $2,500    $3,000

VACHERON, 18J., applied numbers,  ca.1940
18k .......................................$2,000    $2,200    $2,400

VACHERON, 18J., off set lugs,
18k ...................................$2,000    $2,200    $2,500

VACHERON, 18J., black dial, aux. sec., ca.1937
18k .......................................$2,200    $2,400    $2,600

VACHERON, 18J., off set lugs,
18k .......................................$2,000    $2,200    $2,500

VACHERON, 18J., silver dial, ca.1942
18k .......................................$2,000    $2,500    $3,000

VACHERON, 18J., aux .sec.,
s. steel .................................$1,200    $1,400    $1,600

VACHERON, 18J., textured dial, large lugs, ca.1951
18k .......................................$4,000    $4,500    $5,000

VACHERON, 18J., fancy lugs,ca.1938
18k ...................................$2,800    $3,000    $3,200

VACHERON, 17 jewels, aux. sec., c. 1945
18k .......................................$1,600    $1,800    $2,000

VACHERON, 18J., textured bezel,ca.1950s
18k ...................................$2,000    $2,200    $2,500

VACHERON, 17 jewels, applied gold numbers
18k .......................................$1,400    $1,600    $1,800

VACHERON, 18 jewels, aux. sec., c. 1950s
18k .......................................$1,600    $1,800    $2,000

VACHERON, 17 jewels, fancy lugs
18k .......................................$1,800    $2,000    $2,200

VACHERON, 18 jewels, aux. sec., c. 1940s
18k .......................................$1,600    $1,800    $2,000

VACHERON, 17 jewels, c. 1950s
18k .......................................$1,800    $2,000    $2,200

VACHERON, 17J., applied gold numbers, c. 1940s
18k .......................................$1,600    $1,800    $2,100

VACHERON, 17 jewels, fancy lugs
14k .......................................$1,800    $2,100    $2,400

VACHERON, 17 jewels, stars on dial
18k C&B .............................$2,000    $2,300    $2,600

VACHERON, 17 jewels, stepped bezel, fancy lugs, Ca. 1940
18k ...................................$2,700    $2,900    $3,200

VACHERON,17J., hidden barrel shaped lugs, c.1943
14k .......................................$1,500    $1,700    $2,000

VACHERON,17J., aux. sec., c.1947
18k ...................................$1,600    $1,800    $2,000

VACHERON,17J., aux. sec., c.1942
18k ...................................$1,600    $1,700    $1,900

VACHERON,17J., RF#6249, aux. sec. c.1963
18k ......................................$1,800    $2,000    $2,200

VACHERON,17J., aux. sec., c.1934
18k .......................................$2,200    $2,400    $2,600

VACHERON, 17 jewels, aux. sec.
c. 1946
18k .......................................$2,200    $2,400    $2,600

VACHERON, 17 jewels, Art Deco bezel, c. 1925
18k .......................................$5,000    $5,500    $6,000

VACHERON, 17 jewels, long lugs, applied numbers
18k .......................................$2,200    $2,500    $2,800

VACHERON, 17 jewels, aux. sec.,
18k ...................................$2,200    $2,500    $2,800

VACHERON, 15J., hinged back, ca. 1930
18k ...................................$2,500    $2,700    $3,000

VACHERON, 18 jewels, aux. sec.
18k C&B..............................$2,300    $2,500    $2,800

VACHERON, 18J., large 2 tone mans watch, ca.1928
18k .....................................$5,000    $6,000    $7,000

VACHERON, 15 jewels, heavy bezel, c.1925
18K C&B ............................$3,500    $3,800    $4,200

VACHERON, 18J.,long curved case, ca.1929
platinum...............................$4,000    $4,500    $5,000

VACHERON, 17 jewels, curved, hooded lugs, c. 1930s
18k .....................................$3,000    $3,200    $3,500

VACHERON, 18J., ca. 1926
18k .....................................$2,000    $2,200    $2,500

VACHERON,15J., curvex,wire lugs,33mm long,ca.1923
18k .......................................$2,500    $2,700    $3,000

VACHERON, 18J., ca. 1950s
18k .....................................$1,500    $1,700    $1,900

VACHERON, 15J., early movement, ca.1925
18k .....................................$1,500    $1,700    $2,000

VACHERON, 17 jewels, aux. sec.
14k ......................................$1,800    $1,900    $2,000

VACHERON, 15J.,2 tone case, ca. 1926
18k .....................................$2,000    $2,400    $2,600

VACHERON, 17 jewels, flat & thin model, c. 1960s
18k ......................................$1,000    $1,200    $1,500

VACHERON, 18J., tank style, ca.1960s
18k .....................................$1,300    $1,500    $1,800

VACHERON, 17 jewels
18k C&B.............................$1,500    $1,600    $1,700

VACHERON, 17 jewels, hinged back
18k .....................................$1,400    $1,600    $1,800

VACHERON, 18 jewels, stepped case & beveled lugs
18k ......................................$1,600    $1,800    $2,000

VACHERON, 15J., wire lugs, enamel dial, Ca.1920s
18k .....................................$2,000    $2,200    $2,500

VACHERON, 15 jewels, c. 1920s
18k ......................................$1,200    $1,400    $1,600

VACHERON, 17 jewels, 2 tone, 24mm, c. 1920s
18k ......................................$2,000     $2,200     $2,500

VACHERON, 17 jewels, 68 diamond bezel
18k ......................................$1,800     $2,000     $2,500

VACHERON,17J., RF#7252, c.1962
18k ......................................$1,200     $1,400     $1,600

VACHERON, 17 jewels, flared, curvex, c. 1940s
18k ......................................$5,000     $5,500     $6,000

VACHERON, 17J., flared,12 diam. dial, aux. sec., c. 1948
platinum ...............................$5,000     $5,500     $6,000

VACHERON, 17 jewels, flared, c. 1948
18k ......................................$4,000     $4,500     $5,000

VACHERON, 17 jewels, flared, c. 1940s
18k ......................................$4,000     $4,500     $5,000

VACHERON, 17 jewels, "Chronoscope," jumping hr.,
revolving ruby min. indicator, c. 1930s
18k ......................................$20,000     $22,000     $24,000

VACHERON, 20 jewels, Adj. to 5 Pos., c. 1970s
18k ......................................$2,000     $2,200     $2,500

VACHERON, 22 jewels, lady's watch, c. 1970s
18k ......................................$1,000     $1,100     $1,200

VACHERON, 17 jewels, aux. sec., ruby dial
18k ........................................$2,200    $2,500    $2,800

VACHERON,16J., black star & forrest, wire lugs, c.1919
18k ........................................ $400    $500    $600

VACHERON, 21 jewels, center sec., c. 1950s
18k ........................................$3,000    $3,500    $4,000

VACHERON, 17 jewels, heavy bezel
18k ........................................$1,500    $1,700    $2,000

VACHERON, 17 jewels, aux. sec., fancy lugs, c. 1947
18k ........................................$2,200    $2,600    $3,000

VACHERON,17J., ladies, c.1948
18k ........................................$800    $900    $1,000

VACHERON, 15 J., lady's, wire lugs, ca.1919
18k ........................................ $400    $500    $600

VACHERON, 17 jewels , swinging lugs
14k ........................................$1,200    $1,500    $1,800

VACHERON, 17 jewels, lady's watch, c. 1960s
18k C&B............................$1,200    $1,400    $1,600

VACHERON, 17J., cased & timed in U.S.A. by Vacheron &
Constantine , heavy 14k gold bracelet, Ca.1950s
14k heavy C&B ...................$1,000    $1,200    $1,400

VAN CLEEF & ARPELS,17J., center lugs, c.1970
18k .......................................$500    $600    $700

VULCAIN,17jewels
s. steel .....................................$50    $75    $100

VERNO, 15 jewels, chased bezel
gold filled (w)...........................$75    $100    $125

VULCAIN,17J., "Cricket", alarm, c.1960
base metal.................................$90    $100    $125

VULCAIN, 17 jewels, "Cricket," alarm
s. steel ......................................$100    $125    $150

VULCAIN,17J., "Cricket", alarm, c.1948
s. steel ....................................$125    $150    $175

VULCAIN, 17 jewels, "Cricket", alarm
14k ...............................$225    $275    $325

VULCAIN,17J., center sec., alarm, c.1940
s. steel ...................................$120    $135    $165

VULCAIN, 17 jewels, "Cricket," alarm
gold filled...............................$150    $175    $200

WAKMANN,17J., "Gigandet" Valjoux cal.72, c.1955
18k .......................................$1,200    $1,400    $1,600

VULCAIN, 17 jewels, "Minstop"
s. steel .......................................$90    $125    $145

WAKMANN, 17J., chronog., 3 reg., triple date
14k ...........................................$500    $600    $700

WAKMANN,17J., 24 hr. dial, c.1955
s. steel .......................................$100    $125    $150

WAKMANN,17J., chronog., 3 reg., triple date, sq.buttons
s. steel .....................................$200    $250    $325

WAKMANN, 17 jewels, chronog., 3 reg., c. 1958
s. steel .....................................$200    $250    $325

WAKMANN,17J., chronog., Valjoux cal.188, c.1960
s. steel .....................................$175    $200    $225

WAKMANN,17J., chronog., Valjoux cal.236, c.1968
s. steel ...................................$175      $200      $250

WAKMANN,17J., chronog., c.1955
18k .......................................$600      $650      $700
s. steel ...................................$175      $200      $225

WAKMANN,17J., chronog., c.1970s
s. steel .......................................$90      $125      $155

WARWICK, 6J., hinged back, 1930s
gold plate ..................................$65      $85      $100

WARWICK, 15J., 1930s
gold plate ..................................$40      $50      $60

WARWICK, 15J., 1930s
gold plate ..................................$40      $50      $60

WARWICK, 6-15J., 1930s
gold plate ..................................$40      $50      $60

WARWICK, 6-15J., 1930s
gold plate ..................................$40      $50      $60

WARWICK, 6-15J., 1930s
gold plate ..................................$40      $50      $60

WARWICK, 6-15J., 1930s
gold plate ....................................$40     $50     $60

WARWICK, 15J., 1930s
gold plate ....................................$40     $50     $60

WARWICK, 15J., 1930s
base metal ..................................$20     $25     $35

WATEX, 7J., fluted case, c.1940
gold filled...................................$175     $200     $250

WEISCO, 7J., aux. sec., wire lugs, c. 1928
base metal ...................................$20     $30     $45

WELDON,17J., aux. sec., large lugs c.1950s
gold filled ...................................$75     $100     $125

WELSBRO ,17J., single button chronog., c.1940
s. steel .......................................$75     $100     $125

WELTALL W. Co., floral enamel on case, cylinder escp.
wire lugs, Ca. 1910
14k ...........................................$200     $225     $250

WEST END, 17 jewels, "Keepsake," c. 1925
silver .......................................$300     $400     $500

WEST END, 17 jewels, center lugs
18k ...........................................$300     $350     $400

WHITE STAR, 17J., triple date, moon phase, c. 1948
s. steel .......................................$400      $500      $600

WINTON, 17J., hooded lugs
14k ...........................................$125      $150      $175

WINTON, 16J., curvex, hinged back, c.1930s
silver .......................................$125      $150      $200

WITTNAUER, 17 jewels, fancy lugs
14k ...........................................$175      $200      $225

WITTNAUER, 17 jewels, chronog., day-date-month
s. steel .......................................$385      $475      $550

WITTNAUER, 17 jewels, chronog., c. 1948
s. steel .......................................$350      $400      $450

WITTNAUER,17J., "Professional", RF#6002, c.1955
18k ...........................................$600      $650      $725
s. steel .......................................$350      $395      $450

WITTNAUER,17J., chronog., waterproof, c.1958
18k ...........................................$550      $600      $650
s. steel .......................................$325      $375      $425

WITTNAUER,17J., chronog., by Venius, **Time Zone Bezel**,
Ca. 1955
s. steel .......................................$335      $385      $450

# WITTNAUER ( continued )

WITTNAUER,17J., chronog., by Valjoux, #72, cal.13w1
s. steel ....................................$175    $200    $225

WITTNAUER,7J., mid size , stop watch, c.1940
s. steel ....................................$150    $185    $225

WITTNAUER, 17 J., day date, set year by button
s. steel ....................................$75    $100    $125

WITTNAUER,17J., perpetual calendar
base metal .............................$125    $150    $200

WITTNAUER,7J., "Electronic", day date, c.1968
s. steel ....................................$40    $50    $60

WITTNAUER,17J., direct read, c.1970
s. steel ....................................$60    $70    $85

WITTNAUER,17J., Zircon on dial, direct read,  c.1970
base metal .................................$65    $75    $95

WITTNAUER, 17 jewels, auto wind, sector, date
s. steel ....................................$400    $450    $500

WITTNAUER, 17 jewels, c. 1950s
14k .............................................$225     $250     $300

WITTNAUER, 17 jewels, curved case, c.1950
14k .........................................$200     $250     $300

WITTNAUER,17J., aux. sec., c.1958
gold filled...............................$100     $125     $150

WITTNAUER, 17 jewels, cal.9wn, fancy lugs, c.1954
gold filled ...............................$100     $125     $150

WITTNAUER,17J., aux. sec., c.1950
14k .............................................$175     $200     $275

WITTNAUER, 17 jewels, fancy lugs, GJS
14k .........................................$175     $200     $275

WITTNAUER,17J., aux. sec., GJS, c.1948
14k .............................................$175     $200     $275

WITTNAUER,17J., aux. sec., GJS, large lugs, c.1950
14k .........................................$200     $225     $250

WITTNAUER,17J., aux. sec., fancy lugs, c.1955
gold filled...............................$60     $70     $80

WITTNAUER,17J., aux. sec., fancy case, c.1950
gold filled ...............................$80     $90     $125

WITTNAUER,17J., aux. sec., flared case
14k ...........................................$250    $275    $325

WITTNAUER,17J., aux. sec.
gold filled.................................$75    $85    $100

WITTNAUER, 17 jewels, fancy lugs, c. 1950s
14k ...........................................$200    $250    $300

WITTNAUER,17J., aux. sec., GJS, c. 1955
14k ...........................................$150    $200    $250

WITTNAUER,17J., aux. sec., tu-tone dial, c. 1950
gold filled.................................$60    $70    $80

WITTNAUER,17J., aux. sec., c. 1950
gold filled ...............................$50    $60    $70

WITTNAUER,15J., aux. sec., tonneau case, c.1945
gold plate .................................$50    $60    $70

WITTNAUER,17J., aux. sec.
gold filled ...............................$50    $60    $70

WITTNAUER,17J., aux. sec.
14k ...........................................$125    $150    $175

WITTNAUER,17J., flared case, Ca.1949
14k ...........................................$150    $175    $200

🕐 Some grades are not included. Their values can be determined by comparing with **similar** age, size, metal content, style, models and grades listed.

WITTNAUER,17J., RF#2067, c.1950
gold filled.................................$50      $60      $75

WITTNAUER,17J., auto-wind, c.1960
base metal ................................$40      $50      $60

WITTNAUER,17J., cal.7630, aux. sec., c.1955
14k ..........................................$140     $160    $180

WITTNAUER,17J., "Alarm", c.1960
gold filled.................................$100     $125    $150

WIG WAG, 15 jewels, early auto wind, c. 1932
s. steel ....................................$500     $600    $700

WYLER, 17 jewels, early auto wind, watch winds by using
the muscular movement of the wrist, back set
gold filled ..............................$400     $500    $600

WYLER, 17 jewels, early auto wind, back set
gold filled ..............................$400     $500    $600

WYLER, 17 jewels, center sec.
s. steel ........................................ $40      $50      $60

WYLER, 17 jewels, aux. sec.
s. steel ........................................ $40      $50      $60

🕐 Some grades are not included. Their values can be determined by comparing with **similar** age, size, metal content,
style, models and grades listed.

WYLER, 17 jewels
s. steel ..................................$40      $50      $60

WYLER, 17 jewels, diamond dial, c. 1946
s. steel ..................................$60      $70      $80

WYLER,17J., center sec., c.1945
s. steel ..................................$50      $60      $70

WYLER,17J., center sec., waterproof, ca.1941
s. steel ..................................$50      $60      $80

WYLER,17J., aux. sec., c.1938
s. steel ..................................$40      $50      $60

WYLER,17J., auto-wind, c.1932
chrome ...................................$50      $60      $70

WYLER,17J., day date month, c.1946
gold filled ...........................$100      $125      $175

WYLER, 17 jewels, chronog., c. 1940s
14k ....................................$400      $475      $525
s. steel ..............................$200      $225      $300

YALE, 15 jewels, calendar, c. 1939
14k ....................................$400      $450      $500
gold filled ...........................$100      $135      $200

🕐 Some grades are not included. Their values can be determined by comparing with **similar** age, size, metal content, style, models and grades listed.

ZELIA, 17 jewels, chronog.
18k ................................$375    $425    $475

ZENITH, 19 jewels, 33mm, c. 1950s
gold filled ................................ $50    $60    $75

ZENITH,15J., enamel dial, wire lugs, c. 1918
silver ........................................$250    $300    $350

ZENITH, 17 jewels, chronog.
18k ............................................$500    $600    $700

ZENITH,15J., signal corps on enamel dial, center lug, 1918
silver ........................................$275    $325    $375

ZENITH, 36 jewels, chronog., auto wind, c. 1969
s. steel ....................................$225    $275    $325

ZENITH,19J., Date at six, c.1962
s. steel ....................................$40    $60    $80

ZENITH,17J., Chronograph 3 reg., Ca.1965
14k ............................................$500    $575    $675
s. steel ....................................$250    $300    $350

ZENITH, 36J., "El Primero", RF#502,auto wind, c. 1970
18k .........................................$1,200    $1,400    $1,600

ZENITH, 17J., auto-wind, date at 5, Ca. 1959
18k .........................................$200    $250    $300

ZENITH, 36 jewels, "El Primero," chronog., triple date
moon phase, c. 1970s
18k .........................................$2,400    $2,600    $2,800

ZENTRA, 24 jewels, ladies,auto wind, c. 1958
14k ..............................................$75    $90    $125

ZODIAC, 17J., chronog., 2 reg., c.1948
gold filled ...............................$200    $250    $300
14k .........................................$425    $475    $525
18k .........................................$500    $575    $675

ZENITH,36J., chronog., auto-wind, triple date
base metal ..............................$400    $450    $550

ZODIAC, 17J., chronog., auto-wind, date, c.1971
s. steel .....................................$150    $200    $265

ZENITH, 17 jewels, fancy bezel
18k ............................................$200    $300    $350

ZODIAC, 17J., center sec., auto-wind, c.1959
s. steel .......................................$50    $60    $75

ZODIAC, 17J., day-date-month, moon phase, c. 1957
14k .........................................$500    $600    $700

ZODIAC, 17 jewels, 24 hour dial
s. steel ....................................$150    $175    $225

ZODIAC, 17J., center sec., power reserve, cal. 1094, c. 1959
s. steel ......................................$75    $90    $110

ZODIAC, 17 jewels, ref. #8088
14k .........................................$125    $150    $175

ZODIAC, 21J., date, "Olympos", date, auto-wind,c.1965
s. steel ......................................$60    $80    $100

ZODIAC, 17J., auto wind with reserve power indicator
14k .........................................$175    $200    $250
gold filled...............................$85    $100    $120

ZODIAC, 17J., center sec., Ca.1948
s. steel .....................................$50    $60    $75

Some grades are not included. Their values can be determined by comparing with **similar** age, size, metal content, style, grades, or models such as **time only**, chronograph, repeater etc. listed.

# SWATCH WATCH CODES

❑ REFERENCE CODES : Numbers may be found on the BAR-CODE sticker on the box.
(1.) The first letter of the reference code of a standard style SWATCH is a "G or L" the
**G=Gentleman** and the **L=LADY'S** .
(2.) The second letter is the COLOR of the CASE, the codes are as follows:

| | |
|---|---|
| A=Anthracite (hard coal) | O=Orange |
| B=Black | P=Pink |
| C=Chocolate or Coffee | R=Red |
| F=Amber or Feathers | S=Surf Blue |
| G=Green | T=Tan |
| I =Indigo Blue | V=Violet |
| J= Yellow | W=White |
| K=Clear or Transparent | X=Metal Surface |
| L=Light Blue | Y=Expanding Metal Bracelet |
| M=Metal Gray (light) | Z=SPECIAL or ART Models |
| N=Navy Gray or Blue | |

The FIRST number is technical reference.
    0=2 HANDS, hour & min.
    1=3 HANDS, Hour, Min. & Second
    4= DATE & 3 hands
    7=DAY +DATE & 3 hands
The POP, CHRONO, SCUBA & AUTOMATIC codes.
    POP SWATCH first letter code is" B"=BIG was used for 1986/1987.
    PW=POP WATCH used starting from1988.
    CHRONO SWATCH=SC, S=SWATCH, C=CHRONO
    SCUBA 200 =SD, S=SWATCH, D=DIVING
    AUTOMATIC SWATCH=SA, S=SWATCH, A=AUTOMATIC.
NOTE: ORIGINAL JELLY FISH, PUFF and the KIKI PICASSO have no reference codes.
    When a SWATCH is re-issued (even years later) the same reference code is used. To date
    the Swatch use date codes.

❑ **DATE CODES:** Date codes may be found on the case above the battery.
(1.) In 1983/84/85 a 3 digit date code was used.
    First # the MONTH 1 -9 was used and for October=A, November=B, December=C.
    The second & third #=year.
(2.) In 1984 a four digit date code was used.
    The first digit=year of manufacture
    The second & third digit=week (1=week 1 & 52=week 52)
    The fourth digit =day (1=Monday & 7=Sunday)
NOTES: The ESA symbol was used from 1982 to 1985.
    The ETA symbol was used from 1985 on.
    Between 1982 and mid 1984 a smaller battery cover was used.

❑ **COUNTRY CODES:** The country code is found on the case between the stem & battery.

| | | |
|---|---|---|
| Argentina = 7345 | Greece = 7342 | Portugal = 7267 |
| Australia = 6103 | Hong Kong = 5284 | Spain = 6129 |
| Austria = 2355 | Ireland = 6546 | Sweden = 4573 |
| * Belgium = 5753 | Italy = 6549 & 549 | Switzerland = 9003 |
| Canada = 6107 | Japan = 6131 | Switzerland = 541 |
| Canada = 7683 | Kenya = 6730 | |
| Denmark = 6449 | * Luxembourg = 5753 | |
| Dutch Antilles =7347 | Malta = 7398 | USA = 5755 & 755 |
| England = 5629 | Malta = 7700 | USA = 7400 |
| Finland = 6052 | Netherlands = 4301 | |
| France = 7448 | New Zealand = 6538 | |
| Germany = 5742 & 742 | Norway =6108 | |

🕐 **NOTE**: The first models (1983 ) were produced in small quantities, about 20,000 of each model.
By early 1984 the total production was 1 million, and mid -1992 over 100 million.
**THIS SWATCH PRICE LIST IS MORE USEFUL WHEN USED
WITH ANY FULL COLOR SWATCH CATALOG BY "SWATCH".**

🕐 Watches listed in this book are priced at the collectable **GOOD VALUE fair market** retail
level, as **complete** watches having an original case, an original dial, and with the entire original
movement in good working order with no repairs needed.

## 1983

| Name & Model # — Description | New + Box |
|---|---|
| Tennis Grid — GW-100 | $250 |
| Tennis Stripes — GW-101 | 1,300 |
| Tennis Grid —LW-100 | 150 |
| GB-001 (also w/ date ) | 400 |
| GB-100 | 700 |
| GB-101 (Later as Black Magic 1984=small SWATCH logo) | 350 |
| GB-103, (9 to 3) "first designer style watch" | 700 |
| GB-402 | 400 |
| GB-700 (also w/date only=GB-400 ) | 450 |
| GB-701 (also w/date only=GB-401-$800 ) | 550 |
| GB-702 | 450 |
| GB-703, (Classique) | 700 |
| GC-100 | 550 |
| GC-101 | 550 |
| GC-700 | 300 |
| GG-100 | 800 |
| GG-700, (also w/date only=GG-400-$800 ) | 250 |
| GG-701 | 800 |
| GG-702 | 300 |
| GM-700 | 175 |
| GN-001 | 300 |
| GN-100 | 700 |
| GN-101 | 800 |
| GN-700 (also w/date only=GN-400 ) | 250 |
| GN-701 | 250 |
| GR-100 | 400 |
| GR-101 | 550 |
| GR-102 | 850 |
| GR-103 | 250 |
| GR-700 | 300 |
| GT-100 | 900 |
| GT-101 | 650 |
| GT-403 | 300 |
| GT-700 | 800 |
| GT-701 | 800 |
| GT-702 (also w/date only=GT-402 ) | 450 |
| LB-100 | 800 |
| LM-100 | 1,000 |
| LN-100 | 600 |
| LR-100 | 1,000 |
| LR-101 | 1,000 |
| Fachhandel Logo | From $1,000.00 to $1,500.00 |

found on GB-001, GB-700, GB-101, GC-100, GC-101,GG-100, GG-700, GG-701, GN-100, GN-700, GR-100, GR-700, GT, GT-702, GT-101.

The Fachhandel Logo can be found on some older bands & dials.

## 1984

| Name & Model # — Description | New + Box |
|---|---|
| Art Deco — LM-103 | $175 |
| Beige Arabic — GT-102 | 200 |
| Beige Arabic — LT-100 | 145 |
| Black Divers — GB-704 | 270 |
| Black Magic — GB-101 [re-issue] | 280 |
| Classique — GB-703 [re-issue] | 235 |
| Classique — LB-103 | 175 |
| Compass — GR-400 | 525 |
| Compass — LR-102 | 400 |
| Compu-Tech — GR-401 | 700 |
| Chrono-Tech — GB-403 | 375 |
| Chrono-Tech — LB-104 | 125 |
| Don't Be Too Late — GA-100 | 850 |
| 4 Flags — GS-100 | 800 |
| 4 Flags — LS-100 | 350 |
| 12 Flags — GS-101 | 300 |
| 12 Flags —LS-101 | 150 |
| Grey Markers — GM-400 | 360 |
| Grey Memphis — GM-100 | 1,200 |
| Golden Tan — GT-103 | 250 |
| High Tech — GB-002 | 375 |
| High Tech —LB-102 | 140 |
| High Tech II — GA-101 | 550 |
| Mah-Jong — LA-101 | 175 |
| Miss Channel — LA-100 | 75 |
| Navy Roman — GN-702 | 275 |
| Navy Roman — LN-102 | 150 |
| Pirelli — GM-101 | 500 |
| Pirelli — LM-102 | 225 |
| Red 12-3-6-9 — LR-103 | 300 |
| Squiggly — LR-104 | 200 |
| White Memphis — LW-102 | 200 |
| Windrose — GW-103 | 475 |
| Windrose — LW-103 | 275 |
| Yellow Racer — GJ-400 | 600 |
| Yellow Racer — LJ-100 | 300 |

## 1985

| Name & Model # — Description | New + Box |
|---|---|
| Banana — LW-106 | $100 |
| BC/BG — LT-102 | 35 |
| Black Magic — LB-106 | 75 |
| Black Out — LB-105 | 350 |
| Calypso Diver — GM-701 | 160 |
| Classic — GB-706 | 125 |
| Classic — LB-107 | 80 |
| Dotted Swiss — GW-104 | 125 |
| Dotted Swiss — LW-104 | 75 |
| Golden Tan — LT-101 | 100 |
| Grey Flannel — GM-401 | 300 |
| Grey Flannel — LM-104 | 90 |
| Ice Mint — LW-105 | 75 |
| INC. — GA-103 | 225 |
| Jaegermeister — GB-404 | 300 |
| Jelly Fish — GK-100 | 275 |
| McGregor —GJ-100 | 300 |
| McSwatch — LR-105 | 140 |
| Neo-Quad — LB-109 | 80 |
| Nicholson — GB-705 (also w/date only=GB-401 ) | 275 |
| Nicholette — LB-105 | 90 |
| Oxford Navy — GN-401 | 325 |
| Oxford Navy — LN-103 | 100 |
| Pinstripe — GA-102 | 175 |
| Raspberry — LW-107 | 75 |
| Sheherazade — LM-105 | 35 |
| Techno-Sphere — GK-101 | 325 |
| Tri-Color Racer — LS-102 | 75 |
| Velvet Underground — LB-108 | 75 |
| Yamaha Racer — GJ-700 | 200 |

This SWATCH price list is more useful when used with any full color SWATCH catalog by "SWATCH".

Watches listed in this book are priced at the collectable **fair market** retail level, as **complete** watches having an original case, an original dial, and with the entire original movement in good working order with no repairs needed.

NOTE: The (1983 ) first models were produced in small quantities, about 20,000 of each model. By early 1984 the total production was 1 million, and by mid-1992 over 100 million.

## 1986

| Name & Model # — Description | New + Box |
|---|---|
| Aqua Dream — LK-100 | $50 |
| Black Coral — LK-101 | 35 |
| Carlisle — LG-103 | 35 |
| Chelsea — LB-112 | 35 |
| Club Stripe — GG-401 | 125 |
| Club Stripe — GG-101 (no date) | 150 |
| Cosmic Encounter — GS-102 | 200 |
| Emerald Diver — GG-703 | 200 |
| Gambela — LG-102 | 35 |
| Horus — LL-101 | 35 |
| Lancelot — GB-110 | 175 |
| Lionheart — LK-102 | 35 |
| Little Jelly — LK-103 | 75 |
| Mezza Luna — GB-107 | 85 |
| Nautilus — GK-102 | 225 |
| Osiris — GM-102 | 250 |
| Pink Dots — LL-100 | 45 |
| Ping Pong Blue — GW-106 | 75 |
| Ping Pong White — GW-105 | 75 |
| Pink Flamingo — LP-100 | 40 |
| Radar — LP-106 | 95 |
| Ritz — GA-400 | 225 |
| Rotor — GS-400 | 175 |
| Ruffled Feathers — GF-100 | 125 |
| Running Water — LS-103 | 55 |
| Sir Swatch — GB-111 | 175 |
| Soto — GB-109 | 125 |
| Tonga — GL-100 | 200 |
| Valkyrie — LP-101 | 35 |
| Vasily — LW-111 | 35 |

This SWATCH price list is more useful when used with any full color SWATCH catalog by "SWATCH".

Watches listed in this book are priced at the collectable **fair market** retail level, as **complete** watches having an original case, an original dial, and with the entire original movement in good working order with no repairs needed.

## 1987

| Name & Model # — Description | New + Box |
|---|---|
| Bandos Diver — GB-710 | $70 |
| Belvedere — LK-105 | 30 |
| Big Eclipse — GW-400 | 125 |
| Black Pearl — LB-114 | 30 |
| Blue Bay — LK-106 | 30 |
| Blue Cassata — LP-103 | 30 |
| Blue Horizon — LF-100 | 30 |
| Blue Note — GI-400 (also no date =GI-100 ) | 125 |
| Blue Racer — LR-107 | 30 |
| Borgo Nuovo — GF-102 | 300 |
| Calafatti — GK-105 | 100 |
| Classic Two — GB-709 | 60 |
| Classic Two — LB-115 & LB-116 | 30 |
| Commander — GB-115 | 100 |
| Follow Me — GJ-101 | 150 |
| Grey Flannel — GA-104 | 100 |
| High Moon — GA-107 | 200 |
| Kasumir — LW-114 | 75 |
| Kir Royale — LW-113 | 40 |
| Lazuli — GF-101 | 325 |
| Little Eclipse — LW-112 | 50 |
| Mackintosh — GB-116 | 200 |
| Marmorata — GB-119 | 100 |
| Nafea — LK-104 | 30 |
| Navigator — GB-707 | 165 |
| Newport — LW-115 | 30 |
| Newport Two — GW-108 | 85 |
| Nikolai — LW-116 | 30 |
| Nine To Six — GB-117 | 85 |
| Pago Pago — GL-400 (also no date ) | 400 |
| Pink Cassata — LL-102 | 30 |
| Pulsometer — GA-106 (manual to explain the dial function ) | 85 |
| Raspberry Shortcake — LP-102 | 40 |
| Silver Circle — GA-105 (also w/date =GA-401 ) | 135 |
| Skyracer — GK-106 | 125 |
| Snowwhite — GK-104 | 95 |
| Speed Limit — LW-117 | 30 |
| Spiga — LF-101 | 50 |
| Trevi — LB-117 | 50 |
| Turquoise Bay — GK-103 | 150 |
| Tutti Frutti — GW-109 | 75 |
| Vulcano — GB-114 | 275 |
| Waipitu — LB-113 | 75 |
| White Out — GW-107 | 100 |
| X-Rated — GB-406 | 125 |

## 1988

| Name & Model # — Description | New + Box |
|---|---|
| Albatross — GX-700 | $85 |
| Andromeda — GK-111 | 80 |
| Antibes — LW-120 | 75 |
| Backslash — GS-700 | 80 |
| Backslash — GS-103 (no date) | 95 |
| Beauchamps Place — LF-102 | 30 |
| Biarritz — LN-104 | 40 |
| Black Hawk — GX-702 | 80 |
| Blue Lolly — LP-105 | 30 |
| Camouflage—LP-106 | 100 |
| Coconut Grove — GB-120 | 200 |
| Coloured Love — GB-122 | 150 |
| Coral Gables — GB-407 | 120 |
| Courier — GX-703 | 80 |
| Dark Vader — GK-110 | 100 |
| Deauville — GW-401 | 85 |
| Deauville — GW-111 (no date) | 125 |
| Disque Bleu — GK-113 | 125 |
| Flamingo Deli — LK-107 | 125 |
| Flumotions — GN-102 | 30 |
| Frontloop — LK-110 | 30 |
| Frozen Dreams — LB-120 | 30 |
| Golden Sphere — GX-102 | 80 |
| Green Wave — GW-402 | 80 |
| Heartbreak — GX 101 | 50 |
| Heartstone — GX-100 | 55 |
| Hot Racer — LK-115 | 50 |
| Kailua Diver — GB-712 | 150 |
| Liquid Sky — LG-104 | 30 |
| Little Snowwhite—LK-116 | 30 |
| Luna Di Capri — LK-109 | 30 |
| Midas Touch — LK-112 | 30 |
| Moneypenny — LB-118 | 30 |
| Nab Light — LW-118 | 30 |
| Needles — GB-408 | 100 |
| Neo Rider — GB-103 | 150 |
| Notebook—LR-108 | 40 |
| Old Bond — GG-102 | 85 |
| O'Sole Mio — LK-108 | 30 |
| Paint By Numbers—LW-122 | 85 |
| Pink Lolly — LL-104 | 30 |
| Red Wave — LW-121 | 55 |
| Seventeen Seven—LW-123 | 50 |
| Sign Of Samas — GX-105 | 85 |
| Sloan Ranger — GX-104 | 70 |
| South Moulton — LL-103 | 30 |
| Speed Week — LL-112 | 30 |
| St. Catherines Point — GB-121 | 250 |
| Take Off — GK-114 | 85 |
| Tickertape — GB-713 | 125 |
| Tiger Moth — GX-701 | 85 |
| Tintarella — GK-108 | 100 |
| Touch Down — GB-409 | 100 |
| White Knight — GW-110 | 50 |
| White Lady—LW-119 | 30 |
| White Window — GB-711 | 100 |
| Disque Rouge—LK-114 | 30 |

## 1989

| Name & Model # — Description | New + Box |
|---|---|
| Aqua Club—LL-105 (sold in USA only ) | $75 |
| Bar Oriental — GR-104 | 200 |
| Bar Oriental — GR-104, (Variant) | 300 |
| Beaujolais — LR-109 | 75 |
| Boca Verde — GX-402 | 95 |
| Bondi Diver—GK-115 | 75 |
| Blue Jet — GS-701 | 75 |
| Blue Jet — GS-104 ( NO DAY DATE ) | 100 |
| Blue Leaves — GN-104 | 200 |
| Bright Lights — GX-706 | 60 |
| Casbah Rock — LN-105 | 60 |
| Chic-on — GX-111 | 75 |
| Coldsteel — GY-104=lg., 105=small | 100 |
| Color Window — GB-715 | 85 |
| Croque Monsieur — GX-112 | 75 |
| Day Off — GY-400=lg., 401=small | 150 |
| Eclipses — GB-128 | 175 |
| Figueiras — GB-125 | 75 |
| Geoglo — GW-403 (also no date only=GW-112 ) | 70 |
| Glowing Arrow — GX-109 | 100 |
| Golden Bond — GP-101=lg., 102=small | 150 |
| Greenie — GX-110 | 65 |
| Greenroom — GN-103 | 65 |
| Hang Twelve — GJ-102 | 100 |
| Harajuku — GB-124 | 175 |
| High Flyer — GX-704 | 100 |
| Iron Man—GY-116=lg., 117=small | 175 |
| Kailua Diver — GB-712 | 100 |
| Lucretia — GB-126 | 125 |
| MBA — GX-403 | 75 |
| Medici's — GB-127 | 350 |
| Metalsphere — GY-102 =lg., 103=small | 150 |
| Metropolis — GX-405 | 75 |
| Moonquake — GX-404 | 95 |
| Petrodollar — GG-402 | 85 |
| Petrodollar — GG-106 ( NO DATE ) | 125 |
| Pink Betty—LK-118 | 55 |
| Pink Champagne—LP-100 (sold in USA only ) | 55 |
| Pinkdrip—LP-107 | 55 |
| Pink Hurrycane—LN-106 | 65 |
| Rosehip — GP-100 | 100 |
| Rush For Heaven — GN-105 | 175 |
| Sandy Mountains — GG-105 | 150 |
| Shibuya — GG-104 | 160 |
| St. Germain — GB-123 | 175 |
| Steeltech — GY-100=lg., 101=small | 100 |
| Stormy Weather — GV-100 | 100 |
| Tango Azul — GX-401 | 85 |
| Taxi Stop — GB-410 | 140 |
| Wipeout — GB-714 | 200 |

**The Swatches below all =$30.00 to $50.00  New + Box**
Alpine–GW-113, Big City–LB-124, Croque Moiselle–LN-107, Frost–LW-125, Greengo–LW-124, Grey Line–GB-411, Icebreaker–GX-113, Lemon Iceberg–GK-116, Lobro–LB-123, Mint Icicle–LG-105, Noblesse Oblige–LX-100, Peak Season–LJ-100, Pluto–LX-101, Silver Thread–LB-121, Sun Lady–LB-125

## 1990

| Name & Model # — Description | New + Box |
|---|---|
| African-Can—GK-120 | $75 |
| Computrip—GN-108 | 55 |
| Copper Dusk—GK-121=lg./128=small | 100 |
| Cosmesis—GM-103 | 75 |
| Country - Side—GX-114 | 65 |
| Gilda's Love—GB-133 | 70 |
| Good Shape—GN-704 (with date) | 55 |
| Good Shape—GN-113 (no date) | 75 |
| Hopscotch—GN-106 | 60 |
| Johnny Guitar—GX-116 | 55 |
| Knight of the Night—GB-716 | 55 |
| Knight of the Night—GB-140 | 100 |
| Louis Louis—GB-106 | 85 |
| Mango Dream—GB-105 | 75 |
| Metroscape—GN-109 | 75 |
| Passion Flower—GN-703 | 65 |
| Ravenna—GB-107 | 80 |
| Real Stuff—GX-115 | 75 |
| Red Line—GB-118/119 | 100 |
| Robin—GJ-103 | 70 |
| Short Leave—GW-701 (with date) | 55 |
| Short Leave—GW-114 (no date) | 75 |
| Silver Rivet—GG-107=lg./108=small | 150 |
| Sogno—GV-101 | 80 |
| Steel Feathers—GX-406 | 65 |
| Stop Fight—GY-402/403 | 100 |
| Stucchi—GN-107 | 150 |
| Tender Too—GB-131 | 100 |
| The Burglar—GB-717 (with date) | 55 |
| The Burglar—GB-134 (no date) | 125 |
| Top Sail—GB-132 | 90 |
| Tristan—GB-135 | 65 |

**The Swatches below all =$30.00 to $50.00  New + Box**
Audry–LL-106, Ascot–GX-117, Betty Lou–LN-111, Black Night –LB-127, Blade Runner–LK-121, Blue Neptun–GB-718, Blue Tone–GX-119, BMX–GP-103, Bongo–LN-110, Bookey's Bet–GX-118, Broadcast–BG-720, Brode D'OR–LA-102, Byzanthium–LG-106, English Breakfast–GX-707, Coral Beach–LN-112, Darjeling –LK-103, Fitless–LJ-102, Forsail–LI-100, Freeway–LY-100, Frutti–LW-126, Gym Session –LI-101,Hacker's Reward–GK-122, Honor Ride–GJ-104, Isolde–LK-120, Lady Glance –LB-126, Neutrino–LJ-103, Papaya Swing–LN-113, Pink Mermaid–LN-109, Pink Podium–LK-119, Port-o-call–LW-127, Saturniac–LL-107, Scoob-A-Doo–GV-102, Signorina–LN-108, Stirling Rush–GX-407, Traffic Jam–GB-412, Tough Turf–LX-104, True West–LF-104, Turbine–GK-117, Tutti–GW-700, World Record–GB-721,

## 1991

| Name & Model # — Description | New + Box |
|---|---|
| Ameris —GK-132 | $75 |
| Asetra —GK137=lg./ 138=small | 150 |
| Be Bop —GX-120 | 50 |
| Beau —GX-408 | 50 |
| Bermudas —GK-133 | 75 |
| Bikini —GJ-105 | 65 |
| Blue Flamingo —GN-114 | 60 |
| Bold Face —GN-112 | 50 |
| Boutique —LX-108 | 30 |
| Champ —GJ-106 | 50 |
| Compass —LV-100 | 30 |
| Crash !!! —GG-111 (USA version Pink Avis GY-105 ) | 65 |
| Cubistic Rap —GR-110 (USA version Hot RapGR-113 ) | 65 |
| Cupydus —GG-112 | 70 |
| Dahlia —LL-109 | 30 |
| Debutante —LM-106 | 30 |
| Engineer —GB-139 | 75 |
| Exotica —LR-110 | 30 |
| Fixing —GB-413 | 30 |
| Fortnum —GB-136 | 30 |
| Franco —GG-110 | 75 |
| Galleria —GG-114 | 75 |
| Genji —GB-723 | 50 |
| Giro —GX-700 | 30 |
| Gold Inlay —GB-141 (USA version Black Inlay GB-145 ). | 60 |
| Golden Bride —LK-123 | 30 |
| Gulp!!! —GK-139 | 55 |
| Hice-speed —LL-110 | 30 |
| High Beam —GM-107 | 30 |
| Hula —LL-108 | 30 |
| Ibiskus —GL-101 | 85 |
| Investment —LB-129 | 30 |
| Julia —LB-128 | 30 |
| Karaburun —GK-135=lg./ GK-136=small | 125 |
| Lutece —LX-106 | 30 |
| Mark —GM-106 | 85 |
| Mason —LN-114 | 30 |
| Montebello —LK-126 | 30 |
| Nero —GB-722 | 30 |
| Noseweelie —GN-115 | 30 |
| Obelisque —GM-104 | 30 |
| One Step —GX-708 | 55 |
| Pink Nugget—LP-110 | 65 |
| Plaza —GX-121 | 30 |
| Polka —LP-109 | 30 |
| R.S.V.P. —GK-129 | 30 |
| Rara Avis —GV-103 | 60 |
| Rave —GK-134 | 50 |
| Reflector —GK-130 | 30 |
| Saphire Shade —GN-110=lg./ 111=small | 100 |
| Sappho —LV-101 | 30 |
| Sevruga —LL-111 | 55 |
| Skychart —GN-705 | 30 |
| Spot Flash —GB-414 | 30 |
| Stalefish —GG-113 | 55 |
| Stiffy —LK-127 | 30 |
| Strawberry Fields —LK-122 | 30 |
| The Boss —GR-109 | 50 |
| The Globe —GB-137 | 75 |
| Tip Tap —GB-138 | 50 |
| Tour —GL-102 | 50 |
| Typesetter —GK-131 | 50 |
| Vincis Twist —LK-124 | 30 |

## 1992

| Name & Model # — Description | New + Box |
|---|---|
| Alexander —GX-123 | $50 |
| Back Stage —GN-120 | 50 |
| Baiser D'antan —GB-148 | 50 |
| Blue Anchorage —GK-140 | 50 |
| Blue Segment —GK-148=lg./GK-149=small | 65 |
| Blu-Lui —GK-400 | 50 |
| C.E.O. —GX-709 | 50 |
| Chicchirichi —GR-112 (egg carton packing for Mothers day) | 60 |
| Coupon —LK-129 (USA version World Order —LK-136 ) | 30 |
| Curling —GB-117 | 50 |
| Diaquiri —GK-144 | 50 |
| Delave —GK-145 | 50 |
| Discobolus —GK-141 | 50 |
| Ean Code —GB-143 (USA version Global Relief —GB-146 ) | 60 |
| Essaouira —LP-111 (USA version Minaret —LP-112 ) | 30 |
| Hookipa —GN-118 | 50 |
| Frische Fische —GG-116 | 60 |
| George —GX-409 | 50 |
| Glance —GB-149 | 50 |
| Gold Smile —GN-123=lg./GN-124=small | 100 |
| Golden Waltz —GK-142=lg./GK-143=small | 75 |
| Gruau —GK-147 | 50 |
| Gruene-Lui —GK-401 | 50 |
| Gutenburg —GB-703 | 50 |
| Mazzolino —GG-115 | 50 |
| Mogador —GL-103 (USA version Kasbah-GL-104 ) | 60 |
| Nuni —GM-108 | 60 |
| Nuni —GM-108 (variation W/misspelled fuor ) | 150 |
| Orly —GM-110 | 50 |
| Palco —GX-119 | 50 |
| P.D.G. —GX-122 | 50 |
| Perlage —LK-133 | 55 |
| Perroquet —GN-119 | 60 |
| Photoshooting —GN-122 | 55 |
| Piccolo —LK-132 | 50 |
| Steel Lite —GG-403=lg./GG-404=small | 75 |
| Tailleur —GM-109 | 50 |
| Tedophorus —GR-111 | 50 |
| Tuba —GV-104 | 65 |
| Yuri —GG-118 | 60 |

## 1992 ( continued )

**The Swatches below all =$30.00 to $50.00  New + Box**
After Dark —GB-144, Artic Star —GJ-108, Barajas —GB-416, Batticuore —GB-724, Black Line —GK-402, Classic Three —GB-725, Classic For —GB-726, High Pressure —GK-701, Jefferson —GK-704, North Pole —GN-121, Open Windows —GK-702, Schnell —GN-117, Stream —GK-146, Tweed —GB-147, Wave Rebel —GJ-107.

## 1992 ( continued )

**The Swatches below all =$30.00 to $50.00  New + Box**
Barbarella —LK-137, Bleached —LK-139, Classic Three —LB-130, High Heel —LN-116,Fleur De Lyss —LV-102, Gin Rosa —LN-115, Malpensa —LX-109, Piastrella—LK-131, Polar Ice —LJ-104, Raissa —LB-131, Red Cloud —LK1-34, Red Knot —LK-130,Rising Star —LK-135, Rote-Lei —LK-128, Ski Slope —LN-117, Snow Collage —LK-138.

## 1993

| Name & Model # — Description | New + Box |
|---|---|
| Algarve—GN-128 | $50 |
| Bachelor —GX-410 / GX-127= no day date | 50 |
| Beach Volley—GK-153 | 50 |
| Big Enuff—GB-151 | 75 |
| Black Jade—GK-158= large / GK-159= small | 60 |
| Cancun—GN-126 | 50 |
| Cappuccino—GG-121 | 50 |
| Chaise Longue—GJ-109 | 50 |
| Classic Cinque—GB-727 | 50 |
| Clubs—GM-402 | 50 |
| Collage Dore—GR-116 | 50 |
| Cool Fred—GK-150 | 50 |
| Crazy Eight—GN-125 | 50 |
| Cuzco—GK-154 | 50 |
| Delhi—GX-125 | 50 |
| Diamonds—GN-706 / GN-133=no day date | 50 |
| Dotchair—GR-115 | 55 |
| Drop—GK-708=large / GK-709=small | 55 |
| Ellypting—GB-152 (24 HOUR DIAL) | 60 |
| Flake—GK-165=large / GK-166=small | 55 |
| Fluo Seal—GV-700 / GV-106=no dat date | 50 |
| Fritto Misto—GR-114 | 50 |
| Geenset—GG-704 / GG-124=no day date | 50 |
| Il Poeta—GP-107 | 50 |
| La Chate Botte —GG-123 | 50 |
| Loden—GK-167 | 50 |
| Masquerade,—GP-105 | 50 |
| Master—GN-130 | 50 |
| Neige—GM-116 | 50 |
| Ombrellone—GO-100 | 50 |
| Paella—GN-129 | 50 |
| People—GZ-124 | 85 |
| Perspective—GK-169 | 50 |
| Postcard—GN-127 | 50 |
| Rocking—GM-137 (24 HOUR DIAL) | 65 |
| Sari—GM-111 | 50 |
| Screw Driver—GM-114=large / GM-115=small | 50 |
| Silver Patch—GN-132 | 50 |
| Silver Planet—GM-112 | 50 |
| Sixy Three Lui—GM-703 | 50 |
| Sketch—GP-106 | 50 |
| Skin Print—GP-103 | 50 |
| Sol—GK-151 | 50 |
| Soleil—GL-105 | 50 |
| Space People—GN-134 | 50 |
| Space Tracing—GK-163 | 50 |
| Spades—GK-152 | 50 |
| Sport Section—GK-164 | 50 |
| Sugarless—GM-113 | 50 |
| Tarot—GN-131 | 50 |
| Tin Toy—GK-155 | 65 |
| Tisane—GK-162 | 50 |
| Top Class GK-707 / GK-176=no day date | 50 |
| Voie Humaine—GX-126 | 50 |
| Voie Lactee—GG-122 | 50 |
| White Onyx—GK-160=large / GK-161=small | 60 |

**The Swatches below all =$30.00 to $50.00  New + Box**
Chesa Veglia—LK-144, Classic Cinque—LB-133, Classi-fied—LL-112, Dawn—LP-113, Ete—LV-103, Ginger Elle—LK-140, Hearts—LX-110, Hielo—LK-146, Infusion—LK-143, La Belle Au Bois Dormant—LP-114, Mariana—LN-118, Pelota—LG-107, Petit Four—LM-108, Saturing—LG-108, Sixy Five Lei—LM-107, Summer—LK-141, Sophomore—LX-111, Tee—GB-728, GB-153=no dat-date, TGV—LB-134, Tourmaline—LK-142, Tournevis—LK-145

## 1994  &  1995

The 1994 regular Swatches all about =$30 to $50 New + Box
Chronos—$80to$90, Scuba=$50 to $55, Automatic=$70 to $80
MusiCall=$50 to $55, Aque Chrono=$90 to $100

Prototype, Dummy, one of a kind hybrids & test models. This type swatches were made in very limited amounts and were never made in production and never sold at the retail stores. The prices vary greatly from **$400.00** to **$8,000**.

Note: VARIANT & factory errors are not protype. Variant watches may have smaller or larger hands, different colors may be found in the hands, different colors may be found in the cases, and date or calendar variations or other errors.

**BEWARE of Fakes Forgeries & Refurbished Watches.**

**Hocus Pocus**--GZ122, Ca.1991, (special), extra high dome shaped crystal.

**Hollywood Dreams**--GZ-116, Ca.1990, (special)diamond style bezel.

**Lady Limelight**--LB-110, black case & band, rhinestones on dial for the hours markers.

**Mille Pattes**--GZ-103, Ca.1986, (ART), blue green case smoke colored band.

**Modele Aves Personnages**--GZ-100, Ca. 1986, ( Art ), yellow case, red band.

**Mimmo Paladino**--GZ-113, Ca.1989 (Art), black case & band.

**Rorrim 5**--GZ-107, Ca.1987, (ART), "5" Million Swatches sold.

**Velvet Underground**--GZ-999, Ca.1985, (special)

## SPECIAL EDITIONS

| Name & Model # — Description | New + Box |
|---|---|
| Bergstrussli — GZ-105, 1987, TP.9,999 | $1,200 |
| Bonaparte — GX-106, 1988 | 400 |
| Breakdance — GO-001, 1985, TP.9,999 | 1,500 |
| Baby Breakdance —LO-001, TP.9,999 | 900 |
| Chandelier —GZ-125, 1992 | 135 |
| Chronometers' — GP-104, BMX, TP.1,500, 1990 | 900 |
| Chronometers' — GK-124, Jelly Fish, TP.2,000 | 700 |
| Chronometers' — GB-719, Knight of the Night, & TP.1,500, 1990 | 800 |
| Chronometers' — GK-125, Turbine,TP.1,500, 1990. Fachhandel Logo —SEE 1983 pricing | 900 |
| Eggdream—GZ-128, 1994 (Easter) TP.33,333 | 85 |
| Hocus Pocus — GZ-122, TP.14,999, 1991 | 475 |
| Hollywood Dream — GZ-116, 1990, TP.9,999 | 1,350 |
| Sir Limelight — any style | 150 |
| Lady Limelight — any style | 200 |
| Limelight II —any style | 400 |
| Lady Limelight II — any style | 175 |
| Mozart — GZ-114, TP.7,500 | 600 |
| Olympia — GZ-400 & Olympia II=402 | 600 |
| Olympia — LZ-100 & Olympia II=102 | 500 |
| Olympia III—GZ-404 (1993) | 95 |
| Original Jelly Fish — TP.200 | 7,000 |
| Pompadour — GX-107 | 350 |
| PUFFS' — any style, 1988, (5 different models & 20 made of each, Total=120) | 10,000 |
| Roi Soleil—GZ-127 (1993) | 175 |
| Tresor Magique—SAZ—101, Platinum & Automatic.. | 900 |
| Velvet Underground —GZ-999 BLACK TP.500 | 4,000 |
| Velvet Underground —GZ-999 WHITE TP.500 | 4,500 |
| Xmam by Xian Lax—GZ-139/140, 1994 Tp.22,222. | 250 |

## ART

| Name & Model # — Description | New + Box |
|---|---|
| Folon — GZ-109, NO.1, TP.5,000 | $450 |
| Folon — GZ-106, NO.2, TP.5,000 | 550 |
| Folon — GZ-108, NO.3, TP.5,000 | 450 |
| Kiki Picasso —1985, TP.140 (two piece dial equal a perfect match every 217 days) | 10,000 |
| Keith Haring — GZ-104, Blanc Sur Noir, TP.9,999, 1986 | 1,000 |
| Keith Haring — GZ-103, Mille Pattes, TP.9,999, 1986 | 1,100 |
| Keith Haring — GZ-100, Modele Avec Personnages, TP.9,999 | 1,000 |
| Keith Haring — GZ-102, Serpent, TP.9,999, 1986 | 1,200 |
| Pierre Alechinsky — GZ-401, TP.5,000, 1988 | 600 |
| Pol Bury — GZ-110, TP.5,000, 1988 | 600 |
| Valerio Adami — GZ-111, TP.5,000, 1988 | 600 |
| Mimmo Rotella, Marylin-GZ-133 & Bengala–GZ-132, 1994 set (22,222) | 180 |
| Mimmo Paladino — GZ-113, Arabic with serial # on back =1 to 100. | 10,000 |
| Rorrim 5 — GZ-107, 1987, TP.5,000 | 1,600 |
| Sam Francis —GZ-123 —TP=49,999 | 300 |
| Rosso BLACKOUT —GZ-119 | 65 |
| FLACK—GZ-117 | 80 |
| TEST—GZ-118 | 90 |
| WHEEL ANIMAL—GZ-120 | 55 |

## COLLECTOR ONLY

| Name & Model # — Description | New + Box |
|---|---|
| Golden Jelly — GZ-115, 1990/91 | $210 |
| Lots of Dots —GZ-121, 1991/92 | 150 |
| Scribble —GZ-124, 1993 | 90 |
| Crystal Surprise—GZ-129, 1994 | 75 |
| Point Of View—GZ-146, 1995 | 75 |

## AQUA CHRONOGRAPH

| Name & Model # — Description | New + Box |
|---|---|
| Bagnino—SBK-102/103 | $80 |
| Big Blue—SBN-101 | 80 |
| Black Rudder—SBB-100 | 80 |
| Blue Sky—SBN-100 | 80 |
| Lillibeth—SBK-104 | 80 |
| Red Harbour—SBG-100 | 80 |
| Seppia—SBM-102 | 80 |
| Silver Moon—SBK-100 | 80 |
| Sirena—SBK-101 | 80 |
| Waterpower—SBM-100/101 | 80 |

## CHRONOGRAPH

| Name & Model # — Description | New + Box |
|---|---|
| Black Friday — SCB-100, 1990 | $200 |
| Sand Storm — SCB-104, 1990 | 325 |
| Signal Flag — SCN-101, 1990 | 300 |
| Skate Bike — SCB-105,1990 | 300 |
| Skipper —SCN-100, 1990 | 200 |
| White Horses — SCN-100, 1990 | 500 |
| Chronograph — SETS, 1990 | 1,900 |
| Flash Arrow — SCL-100, 1991 | 100 |
| Goldfinger — SCM-100, 1991 | 175 |
| Navy Berry — SCR-100, 1991 | 125 |
| Neo Wave — SCJ-100, 1991 | 120 |
| Rollerball — SCB-107, 1991/92 | 125 |
| Silver Star — SCN-102, 1991 | 80 |
| Wall Street — SCB-106, 1991/92 | 115 |
| Award — SCB-108, 1992 | 80 |
| Grand Prix — SCJ-101, 1992 | 80 |
| J F K — SCN-103, 1992 | 80 |
| Sirio — SCM-101, 1992 | 80 |
| Colossal —SCB-109, 1992-93 | 80 |
| Timeless Zone —SCN-104, 1992-93 | 80 |
| Alabama—SCN-105 /106, 1993 | 80 |
| Blue Chip—SCK-101, 1993 | 70 |
| Golden Globe—SCG-100/ 101, 1993 | 80 |
| Greentic—SCV-100, 1993 | 70 |
| Honeytree—SCN-107, 1993 | 70 |
| Jelly Stag—SCK-104, 1993 | 70 |
| Jet Lag—SCM-102, 1993 | 70 |
| Lodge—SCB-111, 1993 | 70 |
| Moon Shadow—SCB-110, 1993 | 70 |
| Pinksprings—SCL-103, 1993 | 70 |
| Riding Star—SCK-102, 1993 | 70 |
| Sound—SCL-102, 1993 | 70 |
| Wild Card—SCK-100, 1993 | 70 |
| Windmill—SCK-103, 1993 | 70 |
| Croccante—SCK-401 | 80 |
| Echodeco—SCN-112 | 70 |
| Fumo Di Londra—SCK-105 | 70 |
| Fury—SCN-109 | 70 |
| Hitch Hiker—SCG-104 | 70 |
| Inspyal—SCG-102/103 | 70 |
| Lemon Breeze—SCK-106 | 70 |
| Miobiao—SCB-112 | 70 |
| Ocean Breeze—SCK-107 | 70 |
| Performance—SCN-108 | 70 |
| Pleasure Dome—SCM-106/107 | 70 |
| Pearl Frame—SCN-401 | 80 |
| Power Steel—SCN-110/111 | 70 |
| Tyrone—SCG-105 | 70 |
| Whipped Cream—SCK-400 | 80 |

## SCUBA

| Name & Model # — Description | New + Box |
|---|---|
| Barrier Reef — SDN-100, 1990/91 | $75 |
| Bora Bora — SDN-400, 1990/91 | 250 |
| Deep Blue — SDN-100, 1990/91 | 135 |
| Merou — SDK-101, 1990/91 | 250 |
| Blue Moon—SDN-100, 1991/92 | 75 |
| Happy Fish—SDN-101, 1991/92 | 135 |
| Hyppocampus—SDK-103, 1991/92 | 70 |
| Medusa—SDK-102, 1991/92 | 75 |
| Captain Nemo — SDB-101, 1992 | 60 |
| Coming Tide — SDJ-100, 1992 | 60 |
| Jelly Bubbles — SDK-104, 1992 | 60 |
| Sea Grapes — SDK-105, 1992 | 65 |
| Black Wave or Shamu — SDB-102, 1992- | 60 |
| Divine —SDN-102, 1992-93 | 50 |
| Red Island — SDK-106, 1992/93. | 50 |
| Spray-up —SDN-103, 1992/93 | 50 |
| Bay-Breeze —SDJ-101, 1993 | 50 |
| Bermuda Trangle—SDM-106, 1993 | 50 |
| Blue Ice—SDK-107, 1993 | 50 |
| Bombola—SDB-103, 1993 | 50 |
| Cherry Drops SDG-102 / 103, 1993 | 50 |
| Golden Island—SDK-112, 1993 | 50 |
| Mint Drops—SDK-108 / 109, 1993 | 50 |
| Over The Wave—SDN-105, 1993 | 50 |
| Rowing —SDN-104, 1993 | 50 |
| Sailor's Joy—SDG-100, 1993 | 50 |
| Silver Trace—SDT-100, 1993 | 50 |
| Swordfish—SDG-101, 1993 | 50 |
| Tech Diving—SDK-110, 1993 | 50 |
| Tipping Compass—SDK-111, 1993 | 50 |
| Beach Virgin—SDG-104, 1994 | 50 |
| Black Gondola—SDM100/101, 1994 | 50 |
| Color Wheel—SDV-101, 1994 | 50 |
| Decompression—SDN-112/113, 1994 | 50 |
| En Vague—SDN-109, 1994 | 50 |
| Lunaire—SDK-113, 1994 | 50 |
| Mind the Shark"Day"—SDK-902, 1994 | 50 |
| Mind the Shark "Night"—SDK-902, 1994, (illuminated) | 50 |
| Morgan—SDM-102, 1994 | 50 |
| Pacific Beach—SDN-110, 1994 | 50 |
| Pearsheel—SDK-118, 1994 | 50 |
| Red Marine—SDK-114/115, 1994 | 50 |
| Seaclip—SDO-100, 1994 | 50 |
| Sea Floor—SDN-108, 1994. | 50 |
| Seahorse—SDK-119, 1994 | 50 |
| Ship of Glory—SDG-105, 1994 | 50 |
| Spark Vessel—SDK-116/117, 1994 | 50 |
| Starflash—SDM-103, 1994 | 50 |
| Underpressure—SDN-114/115, 1994 | 50 |

# AUTOMATIC

| Name & Model # — Description | New + Box |
|---|---|
| Black Motion— SAB-100, 1991 | $80 |
| Blue Matic— SAN-100, 1991 | 80 |
| Rubin— SAM-100, 1991 | 80 |
| 5th Avenue — SAB-101, 1992 | 80 |
| Francois 1ER — SAK-100, 1992 | 80 |
| Red Ahead — SAK-101, 1992 | 80 |
| Time to Move (Earth Summit) —SAK-102, 1992 | 80 |
| | |
| Baru—SAN-102, 1993 | $65 |
| Black Circles—SAB-102, 1993 | 65 |
| Brick-Ett—SAN-400, 1993 | 65 |
| Copper Rush—SAK-107 / 108, 1993 | 65 |
| Gran Via—SAG-100, 1993, 1993 | 65 |
| Graue Hutte—SAK-400, 1993 | 65 |
| Happy Wheels—SAK-109, 1993 | 65 |
| Mappamondo—SAN-101, 1993 | 65 |
| Montenapoleone—SAK-103, 1993 | 65 |
| Nachtigall—SAK-104, 1993 | 65 |
| Roppongi—SAM-400, 1993 | 65 |
| St. Peter's Gate—SAK-106, 1993 | 65 |
| | |
| Abendrot—SAN-103, 1994 | $60 |
| Arcimboldo—SAO-100, 1994 | 60 |
| Avenida—SAG-400, 1994 | 60 |
| Bresse—SAN-104, 1994 | 60 |
| Charms—SAM-401/402, 1994 | 60 |
| Classic Cheddar—SAM-103, 1994 | 60 |
| Eismeer—SAK-112, 1994 | 60 |
| Girasole—SAP-100, 1994 | 60 |
| Grin—SAG-101, 1994 | 60 |
| Marechal—SAM-101/102, 1994 | 60 |
| Ramarro—SAK-111, 1994 | 60 |
| Round—SAK-401, 1994 | 60 |
| Ruisseau—SAK-110, 1994 | 60 |
| Time & Stripes—SAN-105, 1994 | 60 |
| Serti Misterieux—SAK113/114, 1994 | 60 |
| Silver Baron—SAM-104, 1994 | 60 |

# STOP WATCH

| Name & Model # — Description | New + Box |
|---|---|
| Andale—SSK-105, 1993 | $50 |
| Black Deco—SSM-101, 1993 | 45 |
| Coffeebreak—SSK-100, 1992 | 75 |
| Jess' Rush—SSB-100, 1992 | 80 |
| Metal Flash—SSK-104, 1993 | 50 |
| Movimento—SSK-102, 1993 | 50 |
| Nightshift—SSB-101, 1993 | 50 |
| Orologio—SSK-101, 1993 | 50 |
| | |
| Double Run—SSN-104/105, 1994 | $50 |
| Esperydes—SSN-103, 1994 | 50 |
| Green Speed—SSK-110/111, 1994 | 50 |
| Rusher—SSK-108/109, 1994 | 50 |
| Time Cup—SSN-101, 1994 | 50 |
| Tres Vite—SSN-102, 1994 | 50 |
| Vitesse—SSK-106/107, 1994 | 50 |
| Yellow Star—SSM-102, 1994 | 50 |

# MUSICALL

| Name & Model # — Description | New + Box |
|---|---|
| Europe In Concert—SLB-101,1993 | $50 |
| Spartito—SLM-101,1993 | 60 |
| Tone In Blue—SLK-100,1993 | 60 |
| | |
| Boogie Mood—SLK-104,1994 | $50 |
| Brown Piano—SLF-100,1994 | 50 |
| Double Rythm—SLK-103,1994 | 50 |
| Fagotto—SLJ-101,1994 | 50 |
| Frandango—SLR-100,1994 | 50 |
| Martingala—SLG-100/101,1994 | 50 |
| Sax—SLM-102,1994 | 50 |
| Tambour—SLJ-100,1994 | 50 |
| Variation—SLN-100/101,1994 | 50 |

# OLYMPIC

| Name & Model # — Description | New + Box |
|---|---|
| Olympic Games Collection, set of nine Olympic swatches + the box with history and poster, 1994 | $525 |
| 1.) Atlanta, S watch Gent—GZ-136 | 45 |
| 2.) London, Chronograph—SCZ-102 | 85 |
| 3.) Los Angeles, Stop Watch—SSZ-100 | 55 |
| 4.) Moscow, Lady Swatch—LZ-103 | 40 |
| 5.) Roma, Pop Swatch—PMZ-101 | 45 |
| 6.) Seoul, Scuba—SDZ-100 | 50 |
| 7.) Stockholm, Automatic—SAZ-103 | 65 |
| 8.) St. Moritz, Swatch Gent—GZ-134 | 45 |
| 9.) Tokyo, Musicall—SLZ-100 | 45 |

IOC 100—SCZ-101, 1994 Chronograph ( not part of set) (commemoring 100th year ) ... 125

# IRONY

| Name & Model # — Description | New + Box |
|---|---|
| Backward—YGS-401, 1994 | $80 |
| Crown Head—YGS-402, 1994 | 80 |
| Greengammon—YSL-100, 1994 | 80 |
| Handsome Prince—YGG-400, 1994 | 80 |
| Happy Joe—YGS-400, 1994 | 80 |
| Ocean Storm—YGS-103, 1994 | 80 |
| Odalisque—YLS-102 | 80 |
| Red Amazon—YLS-103, 1994 | 80 |
| Red Jack—YGS-100, 1994 | 80 |
| Renverse—YGG-100, 1994 | 80 |
| Sleeping Beauty—YLG-101, 1994 | 80 |
| Spieglein—YLS-101, 1994 | 80 |

# POP SWATCH

| Name & Model # — Description | New + Box |
|---|---|
| Aqua Pink — BK-120, 1989 | $250 |
| Burning Sun — BY-001, 1986/87 | 350 |
| Chromolux — PWBB-123, 1989 | 350 |
| Roses Are Forever — BC-101, 1988 | 50 |
| Sputnik — PWR-106, 1990 | 50 |
| Snowflake — BW-001, 1986/87 | 350 |
| POP SWATCH (most styles) 1986/87 | 300 |
| POP SWATCH (most styles)1988 | 200 |
| POP SWATCH (most styles)1989 | 125 |
| POP SWATCH (most styles)1990 & **1991** | 50 |
| POP SWATCH (most styles)1992 & **1993** | 50 |

# POP SPECIAL

| Name & Model # — Description | New + Box |
|---|---|
| Bottone — PWK-153, 1991, TP.14,999 | $135 |
| Haute Couture –white=pwbw-104 & black=pwbb-142, 1989 | 200 |
| Pop Diva — BB-106, TP.9,999, 1988 | 500 |
| Encantador — PWB-151, 1990, TP.9,999 | 200 |
| Veruschka —PWZ-103, (Mothers day ), 1992 | 75 |
| ORB—PWZ-104, designed by Vivienne Westwood. | 150 |

# POP ART

| Name & Model # — Description | New + Box |
|---|---|
| POP ART — (Vegi SET), one more time by Alfred Hofkunt | $575 |
| Gu(h)rke – PWZ-100, cucumber,TP.9,999, 1991 | 150 |
| Bonju(h)r — PWZ-101, bacon & eggs,TP.9,999,1991 | 150 |
| Verdu(h)ra — PWZ-102, red pepper,TP.9,999, 1991 . | 200 |

**Big Enuff**—GB-151, note dial has a cut out grill metal effect, multi-colored band, Ca. 1993.

Accutron — AC-kew-tron
Agassiz — A-guh-see
Antiquarian — an-tih-KWAIR-ee-un
Art Nouveau — art noo-VOE
Astrolabe — AS-trow-labe
Audemars, Piguet — aw-dee-MAR, PEE-gay
Automaton — aw-TAW-muh-tahn
Baguette — bah-get
Bannatyne — BAN-uh-tyne
Basse-Taille — boss-tie
Basscine — bah-seen
Basel — BAH-zuhl
Baume & Mercier — bome-MAY & mair-cyay
Beaucourt—buh-sahn-son
Benrus — BEN-rus
Bergeon — BEAR-juhn
Berne — bairn
Berthoud — bair-TWO
Besancon — beh-sah-cone
Bezel — BEZ-EL
Biel — beel
Bienne — by-en
Blancpain — blahnk-PAn
Blois — blu-wah
Bombe' — boom-bay
Bovet — boe-vay
Breguet et Fils — bruh-GAY ay fee
Breitling — BRITE-ling
Brevet — bree-VET (or) bree-VTAY
Bucherer — boo-shay-er
Calibre — KAL-ih-breh
Capt — kapt
Carillon — KARE-il-lahn
Cartier — kar-t-yay
Cartouche — kar-toosh
Champleve — shamp-leh-VAY
Chatelaine — SHATT-e-lane
Chaton — sha-tawn
Chopard — show-par
Chronograph — Kronn-oh-graff
Chronometer — kroe-NOM-meh-tur
Cie — see
Cloisonne' — kloy-zoe-NAY
Cooksey —Cook-see
Cortebert — coh-teh-ber
Corum — Kore-um
Craze — krayze (or) crazing — krayze-ing
Cuvette — koo-vet
Cyma Travannes — SY-ma  TA-VA
Damaskeen — dam-us-KEEN
  * damaskeen = A special terminology or American idiom
Detent — dee-TENT
Ditisheim — DI-tish-heim
Doxa — docks-uh
Droz — droze
Dauphine — doug-feen
Ebauche — AY-boesh
Ebel — AY-ble
Elinvar — EL-in-var
Ermeto — air-MET-oh
Escapement — es-cape-ment
Escutcheon — es-KUHCH-un
ETA — EE-ta
Fahys — fah-z
Fasoldt — fa-sole-dt
Favre Leuba — fahv-ruh  lew-buh
Fecit — FEE-sit =(made by)
Fleur de lis — flur duh lee
Foliot — FOE-lee-ut
Fontainemelon — fone-ten-meh-loh
Francillon — fran-see-yoh
Freid — freed
Frodsham — FRAHD-shum
Fusee — few-ZEE
Gadroon—ga-drewn
Gallet — gah-lay
Girrard Perregaux — jir-ard  per-ay-go
Glashutte — GLASS-hew-tay
Glycine — gly-seen
Gouache — goo-wash
Grande sonnnerie — grahnd  shon-uh-ree
Grenchen — GREN-chun
Gublin — goo-blin
Guilloche — gill-LOWSH
Guinand — gwee-nahnd
Hampden — HAM-dun
Hebdomas — heb-DOM-us
Helical — HEL-ih-kul
Helvetia — hel-VEE-shuh
Henlein — HEN-line
Heuer — HEW-er
Horology — haw-rahl-uh-gee
Huyghens — hi-guhnz
Illinois—ill-ih-NOY

Ingraham — ing-gram
Invar — in-VAR
Isochronism — eye-SOCK-roe-nism
Jacot— zha-koe
Jaeger — YAY-gur
Japy — zja-pee
Jaquet Droz — zha-KAY  droze
Jours — goo-or
Jurgensen — JUR-gun-sun
Karrusel — kare-us-sell
Kessels — KESS-ulz
La Chaux de Fonds — lah show  duh Fawn
A. Lange & Sohne — A. lahng un  zoo-nah
Landeron — lan-der-on
Lapis LAZULI — lay-pis  laz-you-lye
Lavaliere — la-vahl-yare
Le Coultre — luh-kool-tray
Le Locle — luh  LOKEl
Lemania — leh-mahn-yuh
Leonidas — lee-OH-ih-dus
Le Phare — luh-fahr
Le'pine — lay-peen
Le Roy — luh  roy
Leschot—leh-show
Ligne — line
Longines — LAWNG-jeen
Loupe—loop
Lucien Piccard (Arnex) — lew-see-en  pee-kar (ar-nex)
Lyon — lee-OHn
Mathey — ma-tay
Mido — me-DOE
Mollineaux — MOLE-ih-noe
Moser, Henri & Cie—awn-ree  mow-say  eh  see
Movado — moe-VAH-doe
Mozart — MOE-tsart
Nardin — nar din
Nashua — NASH-U-uh
Neuchatel — noo-sha-TELL
Nicole — nee-kol
Niello — nye-el-oh
Oignon — ohn-yoh
Omega — oh-me-guh
Osaka—oh-sah-kah
Otay — oh-tay
Oudin — oo-dan as in (soon)
Paillard — pay-lar
Pallet — PAL-let
Parachute — PAR-ah-shoot
Patek, Philippe — Pa-tek  fee-leep
Patina—pah-teen-ah
Pave' — pah-vay
Piaget — pee-uh-jaay
Piguet — pee-gay
Pique — pee-kay
Quare — kwair
Rado — rah-doe
Remontoire— rem-on-twor
Repousse' — reh-poo-say
Rococo — roe-ko-ko
Roskopf — ROSS-cawf
Sangamo — san-guh-moe
Schaffausen — shaf-HOW-zun
Schild — sheild
Shugart — sugar with a T, or Shug-gart
Sonneire — shon-uh-ree
Sonnerie — SUTH-ee-bee
Sotheby — SUTH-ee-bee
Souscription — sue-skrip-tshown
Stackfreed — stack-freed
St. Imier — sahnt  imm-yay
Tavannes — ta-va
Tempus Fugit — TEM-pus  FYOO-jit = (time flies)
Tissot — tee-SOh
Tobias — toe-bye-us
Tonneau — tun-noe
Touchon — too-shahn
Tourbillon — toour-bee-yohn
Vacheron & Constantin — VASH-er-on , CON-stan-teen
Valjoux — val-goo
Verge — vurj
Veritas — VAIR-ih-tas
Vermeil — vair-may
Vertu — ver-too
Virgule — VIR-gool
Wittnauer — Wit-nower
Woerd — verd

# European Terminology — U. S. A. Terminology

AIGUILLES............................................Hour Hand
ANCHOR or ANCRE ......................Lever Escapement
BAGUETTE.......................................Long & Narrow
BALANCIER.................................................Balance
BOITE-DOUBLE........................................ Pair-case
BOMBE...........................................Convex or Bulges
BREVET............................................................ Patented
CALIBRE ........................................................... Model
CHASED.....................................................Embossing
CHATON................................................. Jewel Setting
CHRONOMETRE....................................Chronometer
CIE...................................................................... Company
COMPENSE...........................................Compensating
CUVETTE or DOME.......... Inside Hinged Dust Cover
DEPOSE ......................................Register  Trademark
DOG  SCREW.............................................Case Screw
DOME................................. Inside Hinged Dust Cover
EBAUCHE............................... Raw Blank Movement
EMPIERRE........................................................Jewelled
ECHAPPEMENT A' ANCRE..........Lever escapement
FAUSSE  COTES...................................Damaskeening
FLUTED .......................................................Grooved
GENEVE  STRIPES.............................Damaskeening
GUILLOCHE........................................Engine Turned
HOOK...................................... Pin Lever Escapement
INVENIT  ET  FECIT.............................. Made By
JACQUE-MART.................... Figures That Strike Bells
JOURS ............................................ Days As In 8 Days
LE  PINE .......................................................Open Face
LIGNE........................................................................ Size
MONTRE A' TACT............................ Watch by touch
MARQUE  DEPOSE (M.D.)..........Register  Trademark
OIGNON or TURNIP ..... Large Bulbous French Watch
PARACHUTE .......................................shock resisting
PAVE............................................................... Cover
PIQUE........................................... Pin Work Decoration
PERPETUELLE ...................................... Self-Winding
POLYCHROME.....................................................Color
POUSSETTE ................................................ Push Piece
REPOUSSE .................................................. Embossing
RATTRAPANTE ...................................... Split seconds
REFERENCE # ....................................Case # & Style
REMONTOIRE.................Constant Force Escapement
RESSORT DE CROCHEMENT ........... All-or-nothing
RESSORT  SPIRAL.....................................Hairspring
RUBIS.................................................... Ruby Jewel
SAVONETTE................................................. Hunting Case
SHAGREEN............................ Shark or Ray Fish Skins
SPIRAL  BREGUET...................... Overcoil hairspring
TANGENT  SCREW............................. Endless Screw
TONNEAU ......................................Barrel Shaped
TOUT-OU-RIEN.................................. All-or-nothing

ADJUSTED-Adjusted to compensate for temperature, positions, and isochronism.

ALARM WATCH-A watch that will give an audible sound at a pre-set time.

ALL or NOTHING PIECE-A repeating watch mechanism which ensures that ALL the hour & minutes are struck or sounded or nothing is heard.

ANALOGUE-A term used to denote a watch dial with hands rather than digital display.

ANNEALING-Heating and cooling a metal slowly to relieve internal stress.

ANTI-MAGNETIC-Not affected by magnetic field.

ANTIQUARIAN-Of antiques or dealing in, also the study of old and out-of-date items.

Arbor

ARBOR-The mechanical axle of a moving part; on the balance it is called the staff, on the lever it is called the arbor.

ASSAY-Analyzing a metal for its gold or silver content.

AUTOMATON-Automatic working figures moving in conjunction with the movement mechanism. Striking *Jacquemarts* or jacks which are figures (may be humans provided with hammers) striking bells to supply the sound for the hour & quarter hours these hammers take the place of the bells clapper. *Automata* plural of **automaton**.

AUXILIARY COMPENSATION-For middle temperature errors found on marine chronometers.

BAGUETTE-A French term for oblong shape. A watch having it's length at least 3 times it's width. A long narrow diamond.

Balance Cock

BALANCE COCK-The bridge that holds the upper jewels and the balance and secured at one end only.

Balance Spring

BALANCE SPRING-Also called the hairspring; the spring governing the balance.

Balance Staff

BALANCE STAFF -The shaft of the balance wheel.

Balance Wheel

BALANCE WHEEL-A device shaped like a wheel that does for a watch what a pendulum does for a clock.

Banking Pins

BANKING PINS-The two pins which limit the angular motion of the pallet.

Bar Movement

BAR MOVEMENT-A type of movement employing about six bridges to hold the train. In use by 1840.

Barrel

BARREL-Drum-shaped container that houses the mainspring.

BEAT-Refers to the tick or sound of a watch; about 1/5 of a second. The sound is produced by the escape wheel striking the pallets.

Beetle Hand

BEETLE HAND-Hour hand resembling a stag beetle; usually associated with the poker-type minute hand.

BELL METAL-Four parts copper and one part tin used for metal laps to get a high polish on steel.

O S. Htg. Bezel,

BEZEL-The rim that covers the dial (face) and retains the crystal.

Balance Wheel

BRASS — STEEL

EFFECT OF HEAT — EFFECT OF COLD

MEAN TIME SCREWS

BI-METALLIC BALANCE-A balance composed of brass and steel designed to compensate for temperature changes in the hairspring.

BLIND MAN'S WATCH- A Braille watch; also known as a tact watch.

BLUING or BLUEING-By heating steel to 540 degrees, the color will change to blue.

BOMBE'- Convex on one side.

Bow

BOW-The ring that is looped at the pendant to which a chain or fob is attached

BOX CHRONOMETER-A marine or other type chronometer in gimbals so the movement remains level at sea.

BOX JOINTED CASE-A heavy hinged decorative case with a simulated joint at the top under the pendant. ( BOX CASE )

BREGUET KEY-A ratcheting watch key permitting winding in only one direction.

**Overcoil Hairspring**

BREGUET SPRING-A type of hairspring that improves time keeping also called overcoil hairspring.

BRIDGE-A metal bar which bear the pivot of wheels and is supported at both ends .(see cock.)

BUBBLE BACK-A Rolex wrist watch which were water proof (Oyster) and auto wind (Perpetual) Ca. 1930 to 1950's.

BULL'S EYE CRYSTAL-Used on old type watches; the center of the crystal was polished which achieved a bull's eye effect.

CALENDAR WATCH-A watch that shows the date, month and day.

CALIBRE or CALIBER-**Size** of a watch movement also to describe the model, style or shape of a watch movement.

CAP JEWEL-Also called the end stone, the flat jewel on which the staff rests.

CASE SCREW-A screw with part of th head cut away.

1 PER HOUR
7-1/2 PER HOUR
60 PER HOUR
600 PER HOUR
CENTER WHEEL
AND PINION
THIRD WHEEL
AND PINION
FOURTH WHEEL
AND PINION
ESCAPE WHEEL
AND PINION

CENTER WHEEL-The second wheel; the arbor for the minute hand; this wheel makes one revolution per hour.

CHAIN (Fusee)-Looks like a miniature bicycle chain connecting the barrel and fusee.

—Chamfer—

CHAMFER-Sloping or beveled. Removing a sharp edge or edges of holes.

CHAMPLEVE-An area hollowed out and filled with enamel and then baked on.

CHAPTER-The hour, minute & seconds numbers on a dial. The chapter ring is the zone or circle that confines the numbers.

CHRONOGRAPH-A movement that can be started and stopped to measure short time intervals and return to zero. A stopwatch does not keep the time of day.

CHRONOMETER ESCAPEMENT - A detent escapement used in marine chronometers.

CLICK-A pawl that ratchets and permits the winding wheel to move in one direction; a clicking sound can be heard as the watch is wound.

CLOCK WATCH-A watch that strikes the hour but not on demand.

CLOISONNE-Enamel set between strips of metal and baked onto the dial

CLUB TOOTH-Some escape wheels have a special design which increases the impulse plane; located at the tip of the tooth of the escape wheel.

COARSE TRAIN-16,000 beats per hour.

COCK -The metal bar which carries the bearing for the balance's upper pivot and is supported at one end.

COMPENSATION BALANCE-A balance wheel designed to correct for temperature.

COMPLICATED WATCH-A watch with complicated works;other than just telling time, it may have a perpetual calendar, moon phases, up and down dial, repeater, musical chimes or alarm.

CONTRATE WHEEL-A wheel with its teeth at a right angle to plane of the wheel.

CONVERTIBLE- Movement made by Elgin & other companies; a means of converting from a hunting case to a open-face watch or vice-versa.

CRAZE(crazing)-A minute crack in the glaze of enamel watch dials.

Railroad Style

Round Style    Antique Style
CROWN-A winding button.

Crown Wheel

CROWN WHEEL-The escape wheel of a verge escapement; looks like a crown. Also the lower illustration shows a crown wheel used in a stem winding pocket watch.

Curb Pin

CURB PINS-The two pins that change the rate of a watch; the two pins,in effect,change the length of the hairspring.

CUVETTE

CUVETTE-The inter dust cover of a pocket watch.

CYLINDER ESCAPEMENT-A type of escapement used on some watches.

DIAL-The face of a watch. Some are made of enamel.

DAMASKEENING-The art of producing a design, pattern, or wavy appearance on a metal. American idiom or accepted expression of the watch term for damascene.

DISCHARGE PALLET JEWEL-The left jewel.

Double Roller

DOUBLE ROLLER-A watch with one impulse roller table and a safety roller, thus two rollers.

DRAW-The angular position of the pallet jewels in the pallet frame which causes those jewels to be drawn deeper into the escape wheel under pressure of the escape wheel's tooth on the locking surface.

DROP-The space between a tooth of the escape wheel and the pallet from which it has just escaped.

DUMB –REPEATER-A repeating watch with hammers that strikes a block instead of a bells or gongs.

DEMI-HUNTER-A hunting case with the center designed to allow the position of the hands to be seen without opening the case.

DETENT ESCAPEMENT-A detached escapement . The balance is impulsed in one direction; used on watches to provide greater accuracy. Detent a locking device.

DUPLEX ESCAPEMENT-An escape wheel with two sets of teeth, one for locking and one for impulse.

EBAUCHE(ay-boesh)-A movement not completely finished or in the rough; not detailed; a raw movement; a movement made up of two plates ,train, barrel & did not include a dial, case, or escapement.

ECCENTRIC-Not exactly circular, *Nonconcentric*. A cam with a lobe or egg shape.

ENGINE TURNING-Engraving a watch case with a repetitive design by a machine.

ELECTRONIC WATCH-Newer type watch using quartz and electronics to produce a high degree of accuracy.

ELINVAR-A hairspring composed of a special alloy of nickel, steel, chromium, manganese and tungsten that does not vary at different temperatures.

END SHAKE-The up and down play of an arbor between the plates and bridge or between the jewels.

END STONE-The jewel or cap at the end o the staff.

EPHEMEROUS TIME-The time calculate for the Earth to orbit around the sun.

ESCAPE WHEEL-The last wheel in a goin train; works with the fork or lever and es capes one pulse at a time.

Fork

FORK-The part of the pallet lever that engages with the roller jewel.

FREE SPRUNG-A balance spring free from the influence of a regulator.

FULL PLATE -A plate (or disc) that covers the works and supports the wheels pivots. There is a top plate, a bottom plate, half, and 3/4 plate. The top plate has the balance resting on it.

ESCAPEMENT-The device in a watch by which the motion of the train is checked and the energy of the mainspring communicated to the balance. The escapement includes the escape wheel, lever, and balance complete with hairspring.

FARMER'S WATCH(OIGNON)-A large pocket watch with a verge escapement and a farm scene on the dial.

FECIT-A Latin word meaning"made by ".

FIVE-MINUTE REPEATER-A watch that denotes the time every five minutes, and on the hour and half hour, by operating a push piece.

FLINQUE-Enameling over hand engraving.

FLY BACK-The hand returns back to zero on a timer.

FOB-A decorative short strap or chain.

FUSEE-A spiral grooved, truncated cone used in some watches to equalize the power of the mainspring.

GRANDE SONNERIE-(**Grand strike**) a watch or clock that strikes the hour, 1/4 hours and minutes if minute repeater, a Petite Sonnerie strikes hour only.

Foliot

FOLIOT-A straight-armed balance with weights on each end used for regulation; found on the earliest clocks and watches.

GENEVA STOP WORK-A system used to stop the works preventing the barrel from being over wound.

GILT (or GILD)-To coat or plating with gold leaf or a gold color.

GOING BARREL-The barrel houses the mainspring; as the spring uncoils, the barrel turns, and the teeth on the outside of the barrel turn the train of gears as opposed to toothless fusee barrel.

GOLD-FILLED-Sandwich-type metal; a layer of gold, a layer of base metal in the middle, another layer of gold-then the layers of metals are soldered to each other to form a sandwich.

GOLD JEWEL SETTINGS-In high-grade watches the jewels were mounted in gold settings.

GREAT WHEEL-The main wheel of a fusee type watch.

HACK-WATCH-A watch with a balance that can be stopped to allow synchronization with another timepiece.

HAIRSPRING-The spring which vibrates the balance.

HAIRSPRING STUD-A hairspring stud is used to connect the hairsprind to the balance cock.

HALLMARK-The silver or gold or platinum markings of many countries.

HEART CAM-PIECE-A heart-shaped cam which causes the hand on a chronograph to fly back to zero.

HELICAL HAIRSPRING-A cylindrical spring used in chronometers.

HOROLOGY (haw-rahl-uh-jee)-The study of time keeping.

HUNTER CASE-A pocket watch case with a covered face that must be opened to see the watch dial.

IMPULSE-The force transmitted by the escape wheel to the pallet by gliding over the angular or impulse face of the pallet jewel.

IMPULSE PIN(Ruby pin)(roller pin)-A pin on the balance which keeps the balance going .

INCABLOC-A patented shock absorbing device which permits the end stone of the balance to give when the watch is subjected to an impact or jolt. 1st. used in 1933.

INDEX-Another term for the racquet-shaped regulator which lengthens or shortens the effective length of the hairspring.

INDEPENDENT SECONDS-A seconds hand driven by a independently by a separate train but controlled by the time train.

ISOCHRONISM-"Isos" means equal; chronos means time-occurring at equal intervals of time. The balance and hairspring adjusted will allow the watch to run at the same rate regardless whether the watch is fully wound or almost run down.

JEWEL-A bearing made of a ruby or other type jewel; the four types of jewels include; cap jewel, hole jewel, roller jewel or ruby pin, pallet jewel or stone.

KARRUSEL-An invention of Bonniksen in 1894 which allows the entire escapement to revolve within the watch once in 52 1/2 minutes (in most karrusels), this unit is supported at one end only as opposed to the tourbillon which is supported at both ends and which most often revolves once a minute.

KEY SET-Older watch that had to be set with a key.
LEAVES-The teeth of the pinion gears.

Le PINE' CALIBRE-Introduced by J.A. LePine' about 1770. Swiss for **open face.**

LEVER ESCAPEMENT-Invented by Thomas Mudge in 1760.

Lever

LEVER SETTING-The lever used to set railroad watches.

LOCKING-Arresting the advance of the escape wheel during the balance's free excursion.

LUGS-The metal extensions of a wrist watch case which the bracelet or band are attached usually with a spring bar.

MAIN SPRING-A flat spring coiled or wound to supply power to the watch. The non-magnetic mainspring was introduced in 1947

MAIN WHEEL-The first driving wheel, part of the barrel.

MALTESE CROSS-The part of the stop works preventing the barrel from being over wound.

MARINE CHRONOMETER- An accurate timepiece; may have a detent escapement and set in a box with gimbals which keep it in a right position.

MEAN TIME- Also equal hours; average mean solar time; the time shown by watches.

Meantime Screw

MEANTIME SCREWS-Balance screws used for timing,usually longer than other balance screws; when turned away from or toward the balance pin, they cause the balance vibrations to become faster or slower.

MICROMETRIC REGULATOR-A regulator used on railroad grade watches to adjust for gain or loss in a very precise way.

MICRO-SECOND-A millionth of a second.

MINUTE REPEATER -A watch that strikes or sounds the hours , and minutes on demand.

MOVEMENT-The works of a mechanical watch without the case or dial. (quartz watches have modules)

MUSICAL WATCH-A watch that plays a tune on demand or on the hour.

MULTI-GOLD-Different colors of gold-red, green, white, blue, pink, yellow and purple.

NANOSECOND-One billionth of a second.

**N.A.W.C.C.** - National Association of Watch and Clock Collectors address is P.O. Box 33, Columbia, Pa. 17512. TEL. 1- 717- 684- 8261

NURENBURG EGG-Nickname for a German watch that was oval-shaped.

OVERCOIL-The raised up portion of the balance hairspring, not flat. Also called Breguet hairspring.

PATINA-Oxidation of any surface & change due to age. A natural staining or discoloration due to aging.

PAIR-CASE WATCH-An extra case around a watch-two cases,hence, a pair of cases. The outer case kept out the dust. The inner case could not be dustproof because it provided the access to the winding and setting keyholes in the watch case.

PALLADIUM-One of six platinum metal used watches in place of platinum because it is harder, lighter and cheaper.

OIGNON-Large older (1700s) style watch in the the shape of a onion or *in the shape of a bulb.*

OIL SINK-A small well around a pivot which retains oil.

PALLET-The part of the lever that works with the escape wheel-jeweled pallet jewels, entry and exit pallets.

Parachute

OVERBANKED-A lever escapement error; the roller jewel passes to the wrong side of the lever notch, causing one side of the pallet to rest against the banking pin and the roller jewel to rest against the other side, thus locking the escapement and stopping the motion of the balance.

PARACHUTE-An early shock proofing system designed to fit as a spring on the end stone of balance.

PAVE'- A number of jewels or stone set close together. Paved in diamonds.

Pendant

Stem UP — Stem Down

Stem Left — Stem Right

Dial Up — Dial Down

PENDANT-The neck of the watch; attached to it is the bow (swing ring) and the crown.

PILLARS-The rods that hold the plates apart. In older watches they were fancy.

PINCHBECK-A metal similar in appearance to gold. Named after the inventor. Alloy of 4 parts copper &3 parts zinc.

POSITION-As adjusted to five positions; a watch may differ in its time keeping accuracy as it lays in different positions . Due to the lack of poise, changes in the center of gravity, a watch can be adjusted to six positions: dial up, dial down, stem up, stem down, stem left, and stem right.

QUICK TRAIN-A watch with five beats or more per second or 18,000 per hour.

PINION-The larger gear is called a wheel. The small solid gear is a pinion. The pinion is made of steel in some watches.

RACK & PINION LEVER ESCAPEMENT-Developed by Abbe de Huteville in 1722 and by Peter Litherhead in 1791; does not use a roller table, but a pinion.

PLATE-A watch has a front and a back plate or top and bottom plate. The works are in between.

POISE-A term meaning in balance to equalize the weight around the balance.

PONTILLAGE(bull's eye crystal)-The grinding of the center of a crystal to form a concave or so called bull's eye crystal.

Receiving Pallet

RECEIVING PALLET-Also called left or entrance jewel, the first of two pallet jewels with which a tooth of the escape wheel comes into engagement.

ROLLED GOLD- Thin layer of gold soldered to a base metal.

ROLLER JEWEL-The jewel seated in the roller table, which receives the impulse from the pallet fork.

ROLLER TABLE-The part of the balance in which the roller jewel is seated.

REPEATER WATCH-A complicated watch that repeats the time on demand with a sounding device.

ROTOR-Oscillating weight for self-wind watches.

SAFETY PINION -A pinion in the center wheel designed to unscrew if the mainspring breaks; this protects the train from being stripped by the great force of the mainspring.

SAFETY ROLLER-The smaller of the two rollers in a double roller escapement.

SAPPHIRE CRYSTAL - Scratch resistant glass with a hardness of 9. Mineral glass has a hardness of 5.

SHAGREEN-The skin of a horse, shark, ray fish & other animal usually dyed *GREEN* or a *BLUE GREEN*. Then used as a ornamental covers for older watch cases.

SIDEREAL TIME-The time of rotation of the Earth as measured from the stars.

SIDE-WINDER-A mismatched case and movement.; a term used for a hunting movement that has been placed in an open face case and winds at 3 o'clock position. Open face winds at 12 o'clock.

REPOUSSE'-A watch with hammered, raised decoration on the case.

RIGHT ANGLE ESCAPEMENT-Also called English escapement.

SILVEROID-A type of case composed of alloys to simulate the appearance of silver.

SINGLE ROLLER-The safety roller and the roller jewel are one single table.

SIZE-System used to determine the size of the movement to the case.

SKELETON WATCH-A watch made so the viewer can see the works. Plates are pierced and very decorative.

SKULL WATCH-A antique pendant watch that that is hinged at jaw to reveal a watch.

SLOW TRAIN-A watch with four beats per second or 14,000 per hour.

SNAIL-A cam shaped much like a snail. The snail determines the # of blows to be struck by a repeater.(A count wheel)

SNAILING-Ornamentation of the surface of metals by means of a circle design; also called damaskeening.

SOLAR YEAR-365 days, 5 hours, 48 minutes, 49.7 seconds.

SOUSCRIPTION- The cheapest Breguet watch which he made with high quality made in batches or group lots in advance to lower the cost.(ebauches)

SPOTTING-Decoration used on a watch movement and barrel of movements.

SPRING BAR-The metal keeper that attaches the band to the lugs of a wrist watch & is spring loaded.

SPRING RING-A circular tube housing a coiled type spring.

STACKFREED-Curved spring and cam to equalize the uneven pull of the mainspring on 16th century German movements.

STAFF-Name for the axle of the balance.

SUN DIAL-A device using a gnomon or style that cast a shadow over a graduated dial as the sun progresses, giving solar time.

SWIVEL-A hinged spring catch with a loop of metal that may be opened to insert a watch bow.

TANK WATCH-A wrist watch case design which the shape looks like the track & body of the military tank.

TOP PLATE-The metal plate that usually contains the name and serial #.

TORSION-A twisting force.

TOURBILLON-A watch with the escapement mounted on a platform pivoted at both ends which revolves most often once a minute. This is designed to eliminate position errors.

TRAIN-A series of gears that form the works of a watch. The train is used for other functions such as chiming. The time train carries the power to the escapement.

TRIPLE CASE WATCH-18th and 19th century verge escapement, fusee watches made for the Turkish market. A fourth case sometimes added in Turkey.

UP AND DOWN DIAL OR INDICATOR-A dial that shows how much of the mainspring is spent and how far up or down the mainspring is.

Pallet
Verge
Pallet
Crown
Contrate Wheel

VERGE ESCAPEMENT-Early type of escapement with wheel that is shaped like a crown.

VERMEIL-Gold plated over silver.

VIRGULE ESCAPEMENT-Early escapement introduced in the mid 1700s.

WIND INDICATOR-A watch that indicates how much of the mainspring is spent. The **illustration** shows a modified Geneva stop works. (see up and down dial)

WATCH GLASS PROTECTOR- A snap on metal grill that covers the crystal.

WATCH PAPER-A disc of paper with the name of the watchmaker or repairman printed on it; used as a form of advertising and found in pair-cased watches.

WOLF TEETH-A winding wheel's teeth so named because of their shape.

## Am. Waltham W. Co.

| Date | Serial # |
|---|---|
| 1852 | 50 |
| 1853 | 400 |
| 1854 | 1,000 |
| 1855 | 2,500 |
| 1856 | 4,000 |
| 1857 | 6,000 |
| 1858 | 10,000 |
| 1859 | 15,000 |
| 1860 | 20,000 |
| 1861 | 30,000 |
| 1862 | 45,000 |
| 1863 | 65,000 |
| 1864 | 110,000 |
| 1865 | 180,000 |
| 1866 | 260,000 |
| 1867 | 330,000 |
| 1868 | 410,000 |
| 1869 | 460,000 |
| 1870 | 500,000 |
| 1871 | 540,000 |
| 1872 | 590,000 |
| 1873 | 680,000 |
| 1874 | 730,000 |
| 1875 | 810,000 |
| 1876 | 910,000 |
| 1877 | 1,000,000 |
| 1878 | 1,150,000 |
| 1879 | 1,350,000 |
| 1880 | 1,500,000 |
| 1881 | 1,670,000 |
| 1882 | 1,835,000 |
| 1883 | 2,000,000 |
| 1884 | 2,350,000 |
| 1885 | 2,650,000 |
| 1886 | 3,000,000 |
| 1887 | 3,400,000 |
| 1888 | 3,800,000 |
| 1889 | 4,200,000 |
| 1890 | 4,700,000 |
| 1891 | 5,200,000 |
| 1892 | 5,800,000 |
| 1893 | 6,300,000 |
| 1894 | 6,700,000 |
| 1895 | 7,100,000 |
| 1896 | 7,450,000 |
| 1897 | 8,100,000 |
| 1898 | 8,400,000 |
| 1899 | 9,000,000 |
| 1900 | 9,500,000 |
| 1901 | 10,200,000 |
| 1902 | 11,100,000 |
| 1903 | 12,100,000 |
| 1904 | 13,500,000 |
| 1905 | 14,300,000 |
| 1906 | 14,700,000 |
| 1907 | 15,500,000 |
| 1908 | 16,400,000 |
| 1909 | 17,600,000 |
| 1910 | 17,900,000 |
| 1911 | 18,100,000 |
| 1912 | 18,200,000 |
| 1913 | 18,900,000 |
| 1914 | 19,500,000 |
| 1915 | 20,500,000 |
| 1916 | 20,500,000 |
| 1917 | 20,900,000 |
| 1918 | 21,800,000 |
| 1919 | 22,500,000 |
| 1920 | 23,400,000 |
| 1921 | 23,900,000 |
| 1922 | 24,100,000 |
| 1923 | 24,300,000 |
| 1924 | 24,350,000 |
| 1925 | 24,800,000 |
| 1926 | 25,200,000 |
| 1927 | 26,100,000 |
| 1928 | 26,400,000 |
| 1929 | 26,900,000 |
| 1930 | 27,100,000 |
| 1931 | 27,300,000 |
| 1932 | 27,550,000 |
| 1933 | 27,750,000 |
| 1934 | 28,100,000 |
| 1935 | 28,600,000 |
| 1936 | 29,100,000 |
| 1937 | 29,400,000 |
| 1938 | 29,750,000 |
| 1939 | 30,050,000 |
| 1940 | 30,250,000 |
| 1941 | 30,550,000 |
| 1942 | 31,050,000 |
| 1943 | 31,400,000 |
| 1944 | 31,700,000 |
| 1945 | 32,100,000 |
| 1946 | 32,350,000 |
| 1947 | 32,750,000 |
| 1948 | 33,100,000 |
| 1949 | 33,500,000 |
| 1950 | 33,560,000 |
| 1951 | 33,600,000 |
| 1952 | 33,700,000 |
| 1953 | 33,800,000 |
| 1954 | 34,100,000 |
| 1955 | 34,450,000 |
| 1956 | 34,700,000 |
| 1957 | 35,000,000 |

## AURORA W. CO.

| Date | Serial # |
|---|---|
| 1884 | 10,001 |
| 1885 | 60,000 |
| 1886 | 100,000 |
| 1887 | 160,000 |
| 1888 | 200,000 |
| 1889 | 215,000 |
| 1891 | 230,901 |

## COLUMBUS W. CO.

| Date | Serial # |
|---|---|
| 1875 | 1,000 |
| 1876 | 3,000 |
| 1877 | 6,000 |
| 1878 | 9,000 |
| 1879 | 12,000 |
| 1880 | 15,000 |
| 1881 | 18,000 |
| 1882 | 21,000 |
| 1883 | 25,000 |
| 1884 | 30,000 |
| 1885 | 40,000 |
| 1886 | 53,000 |
| 1887 | 75,000 |
| 1888 | 97,000 |
| 1889 | 119,000 |
| 1890 | 141,000 |
| 1891 | 163,000 |
| 1892 | 185,000 |
| 1893 | 207,000 |
| 1894 | 231,000 |
| 1895 | 251,000 |
| 1896 | 273,000 |
| 1897 | 295,000 |
| 1898 | 317,000 |
| 1899 | 339,000 |
| 1900 | 361,000 |
| 1901 | 383,000 |

### SPECIAL BLOCK OF SERIAL NOS.

| Date | Serial # |
|---|---|
| 1894 | 500,001 |
| 1896 | 501,500 |
| 1898 | 503,000 |
| 1900 | 504,500 |
| 1902 | 506,000 |

## ELGIN WATCH CO.

| Date | Serial # |
|---|---|
| 1867 | 10,000 |
| 1868 | 30,000 |
| 1869 | 60,000 |
| 1870 | 100,000 |
| 1871 | 150,000 |
| 1872 | 200,000 |
| 1873 | 250,000 |
| 1874 | 300,000 |
| 1875 | 400,000 |
| 1876 | 450,000 |
| 1877 | 500,000 |
| 1878 | 550,000 |
| 1879 | 600,000 |
| 1880 | 750,000 |
| 1881 | 900,000 |
| 1882 | 1,000,000 March, 9th |
| 1883 | 1,250,000 |
| 1884 | 1,500,000 |
| 1885 | 1,750,000 |
| 1886 | 2,000,000 Aug 4th |
| 1887 | 2,500,000 |
| 1888 | 3,000,000 June 20th |
| 1889 | 3,500,000 |
| 1890 | 4,000,000 Aug 16th |
| 1891 | 4,300,000 |
| 1892 | 4,600,000 |
| 1893 | 5,000,000 July 1st |
| 1894 | 5,500,000 |
| 1895 | 6,000,000 Nov 26th |
| 1896 | 6,500,000 |
| 1897 | 7,000,000 Oct. 28th |
| 1898 | 7,500,000 |
| 1899 | 8,000,000 Jan 18th |
| 1900 | 9,000,000 Nov 14th |
| 1901 | 9,300,000 |
| 1902 | 9,600,000 |
| 1903 | 10,000,000 May 15th |
| 1904 | 11,000,000 April 4th |
| 1905 | 12,000,000 Oct.6th |
| 1906 | 12,500,000 |
| 1907 | 13,000,000 April 4th |
| 1908 | 13,500,000 |
| 1909 | 14,000,000 Feb 9th |
| 1910 | 15,000,000 April 2nd |
| 1911 | 16,000,000 July 11th |
| 1912 | 17,000,000 Nov.6th |
| 1913 | 17,500,000 |
| 1914 | 18,000,000 |
| 1915 | 18,500,000 |
| 1916 | 19,000,000 |
| 1917 | 20,000,000 |
| 1918 | 21,000,000 |
| 1919 | 22,000,000 |
| 1920 | 23,000,000 |
| 1921 | 24,000,000 |
| 1922 | 25,100,000 |
| 1923 | 26,050,000 |
| 1924 | 27,000,000 |
| 1925 | 28,000,000 |
| 1926 | 29,100,000 |
| 1927 | 30,050,000 |
| 1928 | 31,500,000 |
| 1929 | 32,000,000 |
| 1930 | 32,500,000 |
| 1931 | 33,000,000 |
| 1932 | 33,700,000 |
| 1933 | 34,200,000 |
| 1934 | 35,000,000 |
| 1935 | 35,650,000 |
| 1936 | 36,200,000 |
| 1937 | 37,100,000 |
| 1938 | 37,900,000 |
| 1939 | 38,200,000 |
| 1940 | 39,100,000 |
| 1941 | 40,200,000 |
| 1942 | 41,100,000 |
| 1943 | 42,200,000 |
| 1944 | 42,600,000 |
| 1945 | 43,200,000 |
| 1946 | 44,000,000 |
| 1947 | 45,000,000 |
| 1948 | 46,000,000 |
| 1949 | 47,000,000 |
| 1950 | 48,000,000 |
| 1951 | 49,500,000 |
| 1952 | 52,500,000 |
| 1953 | 53,500,000 |
| 1954 | 54,000,000 |
| 1955 | 54,500,000 |
| 1956 | 55,000,000 |

## HAMILTON WATCH CO.

| Date | Serial No. |
|---|---|
| 1893 | 1-2,000 |
| 1894 | 5,000 |
| 1895 | 11,500 |
| 1896 | 16,000 |
| 1897 | 27,000 |
| 1898 | 50,000 |
| 1899 | 74,000 |
| 1900 | 104,000 |
| 1901 | 143,000 |
| 1902 | 196,000 |
| 1903 | 260,000 |
| 1904 | 340,000 |
| 1905 | 425,000 |
| 1906 | 590,000 |
| 1907 | 756,000 |
| 1908 | 921,000 |
| 1909 | 1,087,000 |
| 1910 | 1,150,500 |
| 1911 | 1,290,500 |
| 1912 | 1,331,000 |
| 1913 | 1,370,000 |
| 1914 | 1,410,500 |
| 1915 | 1,450,500 |
| 1916 | 1,517,000 |
| 1917 | 1,580,000 |
| 1918 | 1,650,000 |
| 1919 | 1,700,000 |
| 1920 | 1,790,000 |
| 1921 | 1,860,000 |
| 1922 | 1,900,000 |
| 1923 | 1,950,000 |
| 1924 | 2,000,000 |
| 1925 | 2,100,000 |
| 1926 | 2,200,000 |
| 1927 | 2,250,000 |
| 1928 | 2,300,000 |
| 1929 | 2,350,000 |
| 1930 | 2,400,000 |
| 1931 | 2,450,000 |
| 1932 | 2,500,000 |
| 1933 | 2,600,000 |
| 1934 | 2,700,000 |
| 1935 | 2,900,000 |
| 1936 | 2,900,000 |
| 1937 | 3,000,000 |
| 1938 | 3,200,000 |
| 1939 | 3,400,000 |
| 1940 | 3,600,000 |
| 1941 | 3,800,000 |
| 1942 | 4,025,000 |

DATE LETTERS
B on 950B=1942-50
C on 992B=1942-50
S on 950B=1950-55
OTHER DATE
LETTERS =
1930s to 1950s

## HAMPDEN W. CO.

| Date | Serial # |
|---|---|
| 1877 | 60,000 |
| 1878 | 91,000 |
| 1879 | 122,000 |
| 1880 | 153,000 |
| 1881 | 184,000 |
| 1882 | 215,000 |
| 1883 | 250,000 |
| 1884 | 300,000 |
| 1885 | 350,000 |
| 1886 | 400,000 |
| 1887 | 450,000 |
| 1888 | 500,000 |
| 1889 | 555,500 |
| 1890 | 611,900 |
| 1891 | 666,500 |
| 1892 | 722,000 |
| 1893 | 775,000 |
| 1894 | 833,000 |
| 1895 | 888,500 |
| 1896 | 944,000 |
| 1897 | 1,000,000 |
| 1898 | 1,128,000 |
| 1899 | 1,256,000 |
| 1900 | 1,384,000 |
| 1901 | 1,512,000 |
| 1902 | 1,642,000 |
| 1903 | 1,768,000 |
| 1904 | 1,896,000 |
| 1905 | 2,024,000 |
| 1906 | 2,152,000 |
| 1907 | 2,280,000 |
| 1908 | 2,408,000 |
| 1909 | 2,536,000 |
| 1910 | 2,664,000 |
| 1911 | 2,792,000 |
| 1912 | 2,920,000 |
| 1913 | 3,048,000 |
| 1914 | 3,176,000 |
| 1915 | 3,304,000 |
| 1916 | 3,432,000 |
| 1917 | 3,560,000 |
| 1918 | 3,680,000 |
| 1919 | 3,816,000 |
| 1920 | 3,944,000 |
| 1921 | 4,072,000 |
| 1922 | 4,200,000 |
| 1923 | 4,400,000 |
| 1924 | 4,600,000 |

## E. HOWARD & CO.

| Date | Serial # |
|---|---|
| 1858-60) | 131-1,900 |
| 1860-61) | 1,901-3,000 |
| 1861) | 3,001-3,100 |
| 1861) | 3,101-3,250 |
| 1861) | 3,401-3,500 |
| 1861-71) | 3,501-28,000 |
| 1868-83) | 30,001-50,000 |
| 1869-90) | 50,001-71,000 |
| 1869-90) | 100,001-105,000 |
| 1880-90) | 200,001-227,000 |
| 1895) | 228,001-231,000 |
| 1884-99) | 300,001-309,000 |
| 1895) | 309,001-310,000 |
| 1890-95) | 400,001-405,000 |
| 1890-99) | 500,001-501,500 |
| 1896-1903) | 600,001-601,500 |
| 1896-1903) | 700,001-701,500 |

## HOWARD WATCH CO. (KEYSTONE)

| Date | Serial # |
|---|---|
| 1902 | 850,000 |
| 1903 | 900,000 |
| 1909 | 980,000 |
| 1912 | 1,100,000 |
| 1915 | 1,285,000 |
| 1917 | 1,340,000 |
| 1921 | 1,400,000 |
| 1930 | 1,500,000 |

## ILLINOIS WATCH CO.

| Date | Serial # |
|---|---|
| 1872 | 5,000 |
| 1873 | 20,000 |
| 1874 | 50,000 |
| 1875 | 75,000 |
| 1876 | 100,000 |
| 1877 | 145,000 |
| 1878 | 230,000 |
| 1879 | 250,000 |
| 1880 | 300,000 |
| 1881 | 350,000 |
| 1882 | 400,000 |
| 1883 | 450,000 |
| 1884 | 500,000 |
| 1885 | 550,000 |
| 1886 | 600,000 |
| 1887 | 700,000 |
| 1888 | 800,000 |
| 1889 | 900,000 |
| 1890 | 1,000,000 |
| 1891 | 1,040,000 |
| 1892 | 1,040,000 |
| 1893 | 1,160,000 |
| 1894 | 1,160,000 |
| 1895 | 1,220,000 |
| 1896 | 1,250,000 |
| 1897 | 1,330,000 |
| 1898 | 1,330,000 |
| 1899 | 1,370,000 |
| 1900 | 1,410,000 |
| 1901 | 1,450,000 |
| 1902 | 1,500,000 |
| 1903 | 1,650,000 |
| 1904 | 1,700,000 |
| 1905 | 1,800,000 |
| 1906 | 1,840,000 |
| 1907 | 1,900,000 |
| 1908 | 2,100,000 |
| 1909 | 2,150,000 |
| 1910 | 2,200,000 |
| 1911 | 2,300,000 |
| 1912 | 2,400,000 |
| 1913 | 2,500,000 |
| 1914 | 2,600,000 |
| 1915 | 2,700,000 |
| 1916 | 2,800,000 |
| 1917 | 3,000,000 |
| 1918 | 3,200,000 |
| 1919 | 3,400,000 |
| 1920 | 3,600,000 |
| 1921 | 3,750,000 |
| 1922 | 3,900,000 |
| 1923 | 4,000,000 |
| 1924 | 4,500,000 |
| 1925 | 4,700,000 |
| 1926 | 4,800,000 |
| 1927 | 5,000,000 |

(Sold to Hamilton)

| Date | Serial # |
|---|---|
| 1928 | 5,200,000 |
| 1929 | 5,350,000 |
| 1930 | 5,400,000 |
| 1931 | 5,500,000 |
| 1932 | 5,600,000 |

## ROCKFORD W.Co.

| Date | Serial # |
|---|---|
| 1874 | 22,200 |
| 1875 | 42,600 |
| 1876 | 63,000 |
| 1877 | 83,000 |
| 1878 | 103,000 |
| 1879 | 124,000 |
| 1880 | 144,000 |
| 1881 | 165,000 |
| 1882 | 185,000 |
| 1883 | 206,000 |
| 1884 | 226,000 |
| 1885 | 247,000 |
| 1886 | 267,000 |
| 1887 | 287,500 |
| 1888 | 308,000 |
| 1889 | 328,500 |
| 1890 | 349,000 |
| 1891 | 369,500 |
| 1892 | 390,000 |
| 1893 | 410,000 |
| 1894 | 430,000 |
| 1895 | 450,000 |
| 1896 | 470,000 |
| 1897 | 490,000 |
| 1898 | 510,000 |
| 1899 | 530,000 |
| 1900 | 550,000 |
| 1901 | 570,000 |
| 1902 | 590,000 |
| 1903 | 610,000 |
| 1904 | 630,000 |
| 1905 | 650,000 |
| 1906 | 670,000 |
| 1907 | 690,000 |
| 1908 | 734,000 |
| 1909 | 790,000 |
| 1910 | 824,000 |
| 1911 | 880,000 |
| 1912 | 936,000 |
| 1913 | 958,000 |
| 1914 | 980,000 |
| 1915 | 1,000,000 |

## SOUTH BEND W. CO.

| Date | Serial # |
|---|---|
| 1903 | 380,501 |
| 1904 | 410,000 |
| 1905 | 445,000 |
| 1906 | 480,000 |
| 1907 | 515,000 |
| 1908 | 550,000 |
| 1909 | 585,000 |
| 1910 | 620,000 |
| 1911 | 635,000 |
| 1912 | 690,000 |
| 1913 | 725,000 |
| 1914 | 760,000 |
| 1915 | 795,000 |
| 1916 | 825,000 |
| 1917 | 865,000 |
| 1918 | 900,000 |
| 1919 | 935,000 |
| 1920 | 970,000 |
| 1921 | 1,005,000 |
| 1922 | 1,040,000 |
| 1923 | 1,075,000 |
| 1924 | 1,110,000 |
| 1925 | 1,145,000 |
| 1926 | 1,180,000 |
| 1927 | 1,215,000 |
| 1928 | 1,250,000 |
| 1929 | 1,275,000 |

## SETH THOMAS W. Co.

| Date | Serial # |
|---|---|
| 1885 | 5,000 |
| 1886 | 20,000 |
| 1887 | 40,000 |
| 1888 | 80,000 |
| 1889 | 150,000 |
| 1890 | 235,000 |
| 1891 | 330,000 |
| 1892 | 420,000 |
| 1893 | 510,000 |
| 1894 | 600,000 |
| 1895 | 690,000 |
| 1896 | 780,000 |
| 1897 | 870,000 |
| 1898 | 960,000 |
| 1899 | 1,050,000 |
| 1900 | 1,140,000 |
| 1901 | 1,230,000 |
| 1902 | 1,320,000 |
| 1903 | 1,410,000 |
| 1904 | 1,500,000 |
| 1905 | 1,700,000 |
| 1906 | 1,900,000 |
| 1907 | 2,100,000 |
| 1908 | 2,300,000 |
| 1909 | 2,500,000 |
| 1910 | 2,725,000 |
| 1911 | 2,950,000 |
| 1912 | 3,175,000 |
| 1913 | 3,490,000 |
| 1914 | 3,600,000 |

## BALL WATCH CO. (Hamilton)

| Date | Serial # |
|---|---|
| 1895 | 13,000 |
| 1897 | 20,500 |
| 1900 | 42,000 |
| 1902 | 170,000 |
| 1902 | 462,000 |
| 1910 | 600,000 |
| 1915 | 603,000 |
| 1920 | 623,000 |
| 1925 | 620,000 |
| 1930 | 637,000 |
| 1935 | 641,000 |
| 1938 | 647,000 |
| 1939 | 650,000 |
| 1940 | 651,000 |
| 1941 | 652,000 |
| 1942 | 654,000 |

(Waltham)

| Date | Serial # |
|---|---|
| 1900 | 060,700 |
| 1905 | 202,000 |
| 1910 | 216,000 |
| 1915 | 250,000 |
| 1920 | 260,000 |
| 1925 | 290,000 |

(Illinois)

| Date | Serial # |
|---|---|
| 1929 | 800,000 |
| 1930 | 801,000 |
| 1931 | 803,000 |
| 1932 | 804,000 |

(Elgin)
1904-1906
S # range
11,853,000-12,282,000

(E. Howard & CO.)
1893-1895
S # range
226,000-308,000

(Hampden)
1890-1892
8 # range
626,750-657,960-759,720

## Audemars Piguet

| Date | Serial # |
|---|---|
| 1882 | 2,000 |
| 1890 | 4,000 |
| 1895 | 5,350 |
| 1900 | 6,500 |
| 1905 | 9,500 |
| 1910 | 13,000 |
| 1915 | 17,000 |
| 1920 | 25,000 |
| 1925 | 33,000 |
| 1930 | 42,000 |
| 1935 | 42,000 |
| 1940 | 44,000 |
| 1945 | 48,000 |
| 1950 | 55,000 |
| 1955 | 65,000 |
| 1960 | 75,000 |
| 1965 | 90,000 |
| 1970 | 115,000 |
| 1975 | 160,000 |
| 1980 | 225,000 |

## International W.Co. (Schaffhausen)

| Date | Serial # |
|---|---|
| 1875 | 4,000 |
| 1885 | 10,000 |
| 1900 | 150,000 |
| 1905 | 300,000 |
| 1910 | 500,000 |
| 1915 | 600,000 |
| 1920 | 700,000 |
| 1925 | 750,000 |
| 1930 | 800,000 |
| 1935 | 850,000 |
| 1940 | 900,000 |
| 1945 | 955,000 |
| 1950 | 1,000,000 |
| 1955 | 1,200,000 |
| 1960 | 1,500,000 |

## A. Lange & Sohne

| Date | Serial # |
|---|---|
| 1870 | 5,000 |
| 1875 | 10,000 |
| 1880 | 20,000 |
| 1885 | 25,000 |
| 1890 | 30,000 |
| 1895 | 35,000 |
| 1900 | 40,000 |
| 1905 | 50,000 |
| 1910 | 60,000 |
| 1915 | 70,000 |
| 1920 | 75,000 |
| 1925 | 80,000 |
| 1930 | 85,000 |
| 1935 | 90,000 |
| 1940 | 100,000 |

## LONGINES

| Date | Serial # |
|---|---|
| 1867 | 1 |
| 1870 | 20,000 |
| 1875 | 100,000 |
| 1882 | 250,000 |
| 1888 | 500,000 |
| 1893 | 750,000 |
| 1899 | 1,000,000 |
| 1901 | 1,250,000 |
| 1904 | 1,500,000 |
| 1905 | 1,750,000 |
| 1907 | 2,000,000 |
| 1909 | 2,250,000 |
| 1911 | 2,500,000 |
| 1912 | 2,750,000 |
| 1914 | 3,000,000 |
| 1915 | 3,250,000 |
| 1917 | 3,500,000 |
| 1919 | 3,750,000 |
| 1922 | 4,000,000 |
| 1925 | 4,250,000 |
| 1926 | 4,500,000 |
| 1928 | 4,750,000 |
| 1929 | 5,000,000 |
| 1934 | 5,250,000 |
| 1937 | 5,500,000 |
| 1938 | 5,750,000 |
| 1940 | 6,000,000 |
| 1945 | 7,000,000 |
| 1950 | 8,000,000 |
| 1953 | 9,000,000 |
| 1956 | 10,000,000 |
| 1959 | 11,000,000 |
| 1962 | 12,000,000 |
| 1965 | 13,000,000 |
| 1967 | 14,000,000 |
| 1969 | 15,000,000 |

## OMEGA

| Date | Serial # |
|---|---|
| 1895 | 50,000 |
| 1900 | 500,000 |
| 1905 | 1,000,000 |
| 1910 | 2,500,000 |
| 1915 | 4,500,000 |
| 1920 | 6,000,000 |
| 1925 | 7,000,000 |
| 1930 | 9,500,000 |
| 1935 | 11,000,000 |
| 1940 | 14,500,000 |
| 1945 | 14,500,000 |
| 1950 | 15,500,000 |
| 1955 | 16,500,000 |
| 1960 | 18,000,000 |
| 1965 | 23,000,000 |
| 1970 | 28,000,000 |
| 1975 | 35,000,000 |

## PATEK PHILIPPE & CO.

| Date | Serial # |
|---|---|
| 1840 | 100 |
| 1845 | 1,200 |
| 1850 | 3,000 |
| 1855 | 8,000 |
| 1860 | 15,000 |
| 1865 | 22,000 |
| 1870 | 35,000 |
| 1875 | 45,000 |
| 1880 | 55,000 |
| 1885 | 70,000 |
| 1890 | 85,000 |
| 1895 | 100,000 |
| 1900 | 110,000 |
| 1905 | 125,000 |
| 1910 | 150,000 |
| 1915 | 175,000 |
| 1920 | 190,000 |
| 1925 | 200,000 |
| 1930 | 700,000 |
| 1935 | 725,000 |
| 1940 | 750,000 |
| 1945 | 800,000 |
| 1950 | 805,900 |
| 1955 | 820,000 |
| 1960 | 824,000 |
| 1965 | 850,000 |
| 1970 | 860,000 |
| 1975 | 870,000 |
| 1980 | 880,000 |
| 1985 | 890,000 |
| 1970 | 895,000 |
| 1940 | 900,000 |
| 1945 | 915,000 |
| 1950 | 930,000 |
| 1955 | 940,000 |
| 1960 | 960,000 |
| 1965 | 975,000 |
| 1970 | 995,000 |
| 1975 | 1,000,000 |
| 1960 | 1,100,000 |
| 1965 | 1,130,000 |
| 1970 | 1,250,000 |
| 1975 | 1,350,000 |
| 1980 | 1,450,000 |
| 1985 | 1,600,000 |
| 1990 | 1,850,000 |

## ROLEX (Case S #)

| Date | Serial # |
|---|---|
| 1925 | 25,000 |
| 1926 | 27,500 |
| 1927 | 30,500 |
| 1928 | 33,000 |
| 1929 | 35,500 |
| 1930 | 38,000 |
| 1931 | 40,000 |
| 1932 | 43,000 |
| 1933 | 49,000 |
| 1934 | 55,000 |
| 1935 | 62,000 |
| 1936 | 92,000 |
| 1937 | 98,000 |
| 1938 | 118,000 |
| 1939 | 136,000 |
| 1940 | 165,000 |
| 1941 | 194,000 |
| 1942 | 224,000 |
| 1943 | 253,000 |
| 1944 | 284,000 |
| 1945 | 348,000 |
| 1946 | 413,000 |
| 1947 | 478,000 |
| 1948 | 548,000 |
| 1949 | 608,000 |
| 1950 | 673,500 |
| 1951 | 735,500 |
| 1952 | 804,000 |
| 1953 | 869,000 |
| 1954 | 935,000 |
| 1955 | 1,010,000 |
| 1956 | 1,095,000 |
| 1957 | 1,167,000 |
| 1958 | 1,249,000 |
| 1959 | 1,323,000 |
| 1960 | 1,401,000 |
| 1961 | 1,489,000 |
| 1962 | 1,557,000 |
| 1963 | 1,635,000 |
| 1964 | 1,713,000 |
| 1965 | 1,791,000 |
| 1966 | 1,870,000 |
| 1967 | 2,164,000 |
| 1968 | 2,426,000 |
| 1969 | 2,689,000 |
| 1970 | 2,952,000 |
| 1971 | 3,215,000 |
| 1972 | 3,478,000 |
| 1973 | 3,741,000 |
| 1974 | 4,260,000 |
| 1975 | 4,530,000 |
| 1976 | 5,000,000 |
| 1977 | 5,000,000 |
| 1978 | 3,480,000 |
| 1979 | 5,960,000 |
| 1980 | 6,430,000 |
| 1981 | 6,910,000 |
| 1982 | 7,380,000 |
| 1983 | 7,860,000 |
| 1984 | 8,340,000 |
| 1985 | 8,810,000 |
| 1986 | 9,300,000 |
| 1987 | 9,760,000 |
| 1987 1/2 | 9,999,999 |
| 1987 3/4 | R000,001 |
| 1988 | R399,999 |
| 1989 | L000,001 |
| 1990 | L999,999 |
| 1990 1/2 | E000,001 |
| 1991 1/4 | X999,999 |
| 1991 1/2 | X000,001 |

## VACHERON

| Date | Serial # |
|---|---|
| 1830 | 30,000 |
| 1835 | 40,000 |
| 1840 | 50,000 |
| 1845 | 60,000 |
| 1850 | 75,000 |
| 1855 | 95,000 |
| 1860 | 105,000 |
| 1865 | 125,000 |
| 1870 | 140,000 |
| 1875 | 155,000 |
| 1880 | 170,000 |
| 1885 | 180,000 |
| 1890 | 196,000 |
| 1895 | 223,000 |
| 1900 | 256,000 |
| 1905 | 289,000 |
| 1910 | 322,000 |
| 1915 | 355,000 |
| 1920 | 385,000 |
| 1925 | 400,000 |
| 1930 | 410,000 |
| 1935 | 420,000 |
| 1940 | 440,000 |
| 1945 | 464,000 |
| 1950 | 488,000 |
| 1955 | 512,000 |
| 1960 | 536,000 |
| 1965 | 560,000 |
| 1970 | 585,000 |

The above list is provided for determining the **approximate** age of your watch. Match serial number with date. Watches were not necessarily sold in the exact order of manufactured date.

# ADVERTISE IN THE GUIDE

**ATTENTION DEALERS:** This book will receive world-wide <u>BOOKSTORE</u> distribution, reaching thousands of people buying & selling watches. It will also be sold directly to THE WATCH COLLECTOR'S MARKET as well. We will be offering limited advertising space in our next edition. Consider advertising in the Guide, as it is an annual publication, your ad will pull all year long or longer. Unlike monthly or quarterly publications, your ad will stay active for years at a *cost savings* to YOU.

### PRINTED SIZES
**FULL PAGE** — 7 1/2 " LONG X 4 3/4" WIDE
**HALF PAGE** — 3 1/2" LONG X 4 3/4" WIDE
**FOURTH PAGE** — 1 7/8" LONG X 4 3/4" WIDE

<u>AD RATES</u> ARE SET IN THE LATE SUMMER PRIOR TO EACH EDITION'S RELEASE. CONTACT US FOR AD RATES BETWEEN **(AUGUST & SEPTEMBER )**.

NOTE: Submit your ad on white paper in a version of the actual printed size. We must ask that all ads be neatly & professionally finished, *camera ready.* **FULL PAYMENT** must be sent with all ads. Your ad will be run as received.

|← 4 3/4 →|
| 1/2 | 3 1/2 |
| 7 1/2 | |
| 1/4 th | 1 7/8 |
| 1/4 th | 1 7/8 |

## AD DEAD LINE NEXT EDITION IS - OCTOBER 15

This "GUIDE" is the PROFESSIONAL STANDARD and used by collector's and dealer's throughout the world. <u>Do not miss this opportunity to advertise in the guide.</u>

SEND YOUR AD TO:
### COOKSEY SHUGART PUBLICATIONS
P. O. BOX 3147
CLEVELAND, TN. 37320-3147
Office: (423) 479-4813 — Fax: (423) 479-4813

# JOIN THE NAWCC

The National Association of Watch & Clock Collectors, Inc.
invites you to become an active member of the
world's largest horological association.

## BENEFITS OF MEMBERSHIP

Subscription to the BULLETIN
Subscription to the MART
Participation in National Conventions
Participation in Regional Conventions
Participation in local Chapter activities
Advance notice of National Seminars
FREE Research services of the NAWCC Library & Museum
FREE Admission to the Watch & Clock Museum
Use of the NAWCC Lending Library

Establish friendships with others who share a fascination
for watches and clocks. Time is wasting! **JOIN TODAY !!**
Annual NAWCC membership dues are only **$40.00 (US)**
or **$50.00 (Non-US)**. Payment must be in US funds
drawn on a US bank or International money order.

------------------------------------------------------------------------

## MEMBERSHIP APPLICATION

To enjoy the benefits of membership, please complete this form and
send it, with your check or money order to:
**NAWCC, 514 Poplar St, Columbia PA 17512-2130**
(717) 684-8261

**Name** _____

**Street** _____

**City** _____ **State** _____ **Zip**_____

**Phone (** ) _____ **Amt Enclosed $40 [** ] **$50 [** ]

Were you previously an NAWCC member? **Yes [** ] **No [** ]

What was your previous Member Number? _____

If recommended by an NAWCC member, please give name and number:

**COOKSEY SHUGART NAWCC # 23843**

At the end of the 18th Century developed the art of erotic watches. The complicated automatic watches by **I G J** with automatism can give bright revival of the most extraordinary miracle of horology: the automatism.
La MONTRE EROTIQUE are available in **18K − Yellow Gold** and in **Stainless Steel**. Movement ETA Mecaline 2824 - 2, 25 jewels.

**Want to buy the above please Call, Fax or Write**
**R. Attou, Unterdorf 8558 Raperswilen TG Switzerland**
**Tel: 0041-54633959 Fax: 0041-54633916**